Dictionary of Literary Biography

1 *The American Renaissance in New England,* edited by Joel Myerson (1978)

2 *American Novelists Since World War II,* edited by Jeffrey Helterman and Richard Layman (1978)

3 *Antebellum Writers in New York and the South,* edited by Joel Myerson (1979)

4 *American Writers in Paris, 1920-1939,* edited by Karen Lane Rood (1980)

5 *American Poets Since World War II,* 2 parts, edited by Donald J. Greiner (1980)

6 *American Novelists Since World War II, Second Series,* edited by James E. Kibler Jr. (1980)

7 *Twentieth-Century American Dramatists,* 2 parts, edited by John MacNicholas (1981)

8 *Twentieth-Century American Science-Fiction Writers,* 2 parts, edited by David Cowart and Thomas L. Wymer (1981)

9 *American Novelists, 1910-1945,* 3 parts, edited by James J. Martine (1981)

10 *Modern British Dramatists, 1900-1945,* 2 parts, edited by Stanley Weintraub (1982)

11 *American Humorists, 1800-1950,* 2 parts, edited by Stanley Trachtenberg (1982)

12 *American Realists and Naturalists,* edited by Donald Pizer and Earl N. Harbert (1982)

13 *British Dramatists Since World War II,* 2 parts, edited by Stanley Weintraub (1982)

14 *British Novelists Since 1960,* 2 parts, edited by Jay L. Halio (1983)

15 *British Novelists, 1930-1959,* 2 parts, edited by Bernard Oldsey (1983)

16 *The Beats: Literary Bohemians in Postwar America,* 2 parts, edited by Ann Charters (1983)

17 *Twentieth-Century American Historians,* edited by Clyde N. Wilson (1983)

18 *Victorian Novelists After 1885,* edited by Ira B. Nadel and William E. Fredeman (1983)

19 *British Poets, 1880-1914,* edited by Donald E. Stanford (1983)

20 *British Poets, 1914-1945,* edited by Donald E. Stanford (1983)

21 *Victorian Novelists Before 1885,* edited by Ira B. Nadel and William E. Fredeman (1983)

22 *American Writers for Children, 1900-1960,* edited by John Cech (1983)

23 *American Newspaper Journalists, 1873-1900,* edited by Perry J. Ashley (1983)

24 *American Colonial Writers, 1606-1734,* edited by Emory Elliott (1984)

25 *American Newspaper Journalists, 1901-1925,* edited by Perry J. Ashley (1984)

26 *American Screenwriters,* edited by Robert E. Morsberger, Stephen O. Lesser, and Randall Clark (1984)

27 *Poets of Great Britain and Ireland, 1945-1960,* edited by Vincent B. Sherry Jr. (1984)

28 *Twentieth-Century American-Jewish Fiction Writers,* edited by Daniel Walden (1984)

29 *American Newspaper Journalists, 1926-1950,* edited by Perry J. Ashley (1984)

30 *American Historians, 1607-1865,* edited by Clyde N. Wilson (1984)

31 *American Colonial Writers, 1735-1781,* edited by Emory Elliott (1984)

32 *Victorian Poets Before 1850,* edited by William E. Fredeman and Ira B. Nadel (1984)

33 *Afro-American Fiction Writers After 1955,* edited by Thadious M. Davis and Trudier Harris (1984)

34 *British Novelists, 1890-1929: Traditionalists,* edited by Thomas F. Staley (1985)

35 *Victorian Poets After 1850,* edited by William E. Fredeman and Ira B. Nadel (1985)

36 *British Novelists, 1890-1929: Modernists,* edited by Thomas F. Staley (1985)

37 *American Writers of the Early Republic,* edited by Emory Elliott (1985)

38 *Afro-American Writers After 1955: Dramatists and Prose Writers,* edited by Thadious M. Davis and Trudier Harris (1985)

39 *British Novelists, 1660-1800,* 2 parts, edited by Martin C. Battestin (1985)

40 *Poets of Great Britain and Ireland Since 1960,* 2 parts, edited by Vincent B. Sherry Jr. (1985)

41 *Afro-American Poets Since 1955,* edited by Trudier Harris and Thadious M. Davis (1985)

42 *American Writers for Children Before 1900,* edited by Glenn E. Estes (1985)

43 *American Newspaper Journalists, 1690-1872,* edited by Perry J. Ashley (1986)

44 *American Screenwriters, Second Series,* edited by Randall Clark, Robert E. Morsberger, and Stephen O. Lesser (1986)

45 *American Poets, 1880-1945, First Series,* edited by Peter Quartermain (1986)

46 *American Literary Publishing Houses, 1900-1980: Trade and Paperback,* edited by Peter Dzwonkoski (1986)

47 *American Historians, 1866-1912,* edited by Clyde N. Wilson (1986)

48 *American Poets, 1880-1945, Second Series,* edited by Peter Quartermain (1986)

49 *American Literary Publishing Houses, 1638-1899,* 2 parts, edited by Peter Dzwonkoski (1986)

50 *Afro-American Writers Before the Harlem Renaissance,* edited by Trudier Harris (1986)

51 *Afro-American Writers from the Harlem Renaissance to 1940,* edited by Trudier Harris (1987)

52 *American Writers for Children Since 1960: Fiction,* edited by Glenn E. Estes (1986)

53 *Canadian Writers Since 1960, First Series,* edited by W. H. New (1986)

54 *American Poets, 1880-1945, Third Series,* 2 parts, edited by Peter Quartermain (1987)

55 *Victorian Prose Writers Before 1867,* edited by William B. Thesing (1987)

56 *German Fiction Writers, 1914-1945,* edited by James Hardin (1987)

57 *Victorian Prose Writers After 1867,* edited by William B. Thesing (1987)

58 *Jacobean and Caroline Dramatists,* edited by Fredson Bowers (1987)

59 *American Literary Critics and Scholars, 1800-1850,* edited by John W. Rathbun and Monica M. Grecu (1987)

60 *Canadian Writers Since 1960, Second Series,* edited by W. H. New (1987)

61 *American Writers for Children Since 1960: Poets, Illustrators, and Nonfiction Authors,* edited by Glenn E. Estes (1987)

62 *Elizabethan Dramatists,* edited by Fredson Bowers (1987)

63 *Modern American Critics, 1920-1955,* edited by Gregory S. Jay (1988)

64 *American Literary Critics and Scholars, 1850-1880,* edited by John W. Rathbun and Monica M. Grecu (1988)

65 *French Novelists, 1900-1930,* edited by Catharine Savage Brosman (1988)

66 *German Fiction Writers, 1885-1913,* 2 parts, edited by James Hardin (1988)

67 *Modern American Critics Since 1955,* edited by Gregory S. Jay (1988)

68 *Canadian Writers, 1920-1959, First Series,* edited by W. H. New (1988)

69 *Contemporary German Fiction Writers, First Series,* edited by Wolfgang D. Elfe and James Hardin (1988)

70 *British Mystery Writers, 1860-1919,* edited by Bernard Benstock and Thomas F. Staley (1988)

71 *American Literary Critics and Scholars, 1880-1900,* edited by John W. Rathbun and Monica M. Grecu (1988)

72 *French Novelists, 1930-1960,* edited by Catharine Savage Brosman (1988)

73 *American Magazine Journalists, 1741-1850,* edited by Sam G. Riley (1988)

74 *American Short-Story Writers Before 1880,* edited by Bobby Ellen Kimbel, with the assistance of William E. Grant (1988)

75 *Contemporary German Fiction Writers, Second Series,* edited by Wolfgang D. Elfe and James Hardin (1988)

76 *Afro-American Writers, 1940-1955,* edited by Trudier Harris (1988)

77 *British Mystery Writers, 1920-1939,* edited by Bernard Benstock and Thomas F. Staley (1988)

78 *American Short-Story Writers, 1880-1910,* edited by Bobby Ellen Kimbel, with the assistance of William E. Grant (1988)

79 *American Magazine Journalists, 1850-1900,* edited by Sam G. Riley (1988)

80 *Restoration and Eighteenth-Century Dramatists, First Series,* edited by Paula R. Backscheider (1989)

81 *Austrian Fiction Writers, 1875-1913,* edited by James Hardin and Donald G. Daviau (1989)

82 *Chicano Writers, First Series,* edited by Francisco A. Lomelí and Carl R. Shirley (1989)

83 *French Novelists Since 1960,* edited by Catharine Savage Brosman (1989)

84 *Restoration and Eighteenth-Century Dramatists, Second Series,* edited by Paula R. Backscheider (1989)

85 *Austrian Fiction Writers After 1914,* edited by James Hardin and Donald G. Daviau (1989)

86 *American Short-Story Writers, 1910-1945, First Series,* edited by Bobby Ellen Kimbel (1989)

87 *British Mystery and Thriller Writers Since 1940, First Series,* edited by Bernard Benstock and Thomas F. Staley (1989)

88 *Canadian Writers, 1920-1959, Second Series,* edited by W. H. New (1989)

89 *Restoration and Eighteenth-Century Dramatists, Third Series,* edited by Paula R. Backscheider (1989)

90 *German Writers in the Age of Goethe, 1789-1832,* edited by James Hardin and Christoph E. Schweitzer (1989)

91 *American Magazine Journalists, 1900-1960, First Series,* edited by Sam G. Riley (1990)

92 *Canadian Writers, 1890-1920,* edited by W. H. New (1990)

93 *British Romantic Poets, 1789-1832, First Series,* edited by John R. Greenfield (1990)

94 *German Writers in the Age of Goethe: Sturm und Drang to Classicism,* edited by James Hardin and Christoph E. Schweitzer (1990)

95 *Eighteenth-Century British Poets, First Series,* edited by John Sitter (1990)

96 *British Romantic Poets, 1789-1832, Second Series,* edited by John R. Greenfield (1990)

97 *German Writers from the Enlightenment to Sturm und Drang, 1720-1764,* edited by James Hardin and Christoph E. Schweitzer (1990)

98 *Modern British Essayists, First Series,* edited by Robert Beum (1990)

99 *Canadian Writers Before 1890,* edited by W. H. New (1990)

100 *Modern British Essayists, Second Series,* edited by Robert Beum (1990)

101 *British Prose Writers, 1660-1800, First Series,* edited by Donald T. Siebert (1991)

102 *American Short-Story Writers, 1910-1945, Second Series,* edited by Bobby Ellen Kimbel (1991)

103 *American Literary Biographers, First Series,* edited by Steven Serafin (1991)

104 *British Prose Writers, 1660-1800, Second Series,* edited by Donald T. Siebert (1991)

105 *American Poets Since World War II, Second Series,* edited by R. S. Gwynn (1991)

106 *British Literary Publishing Houses, 1820-1880,* edited by Patricia J. Anderson and Jonathan Rose (1991)

107 *British Romantic Prose Writers, 1789-1832, First Series,* edited by John R. Greenfield (1991)

108 *Twentieth-Century Spanish Poets, First Series,* edited by Michael L. Perna (1991)

109 *Eighteenth-Century British Poets, Second Series,* edited by John Sitter (1991)

110 *British Romantic Prose Writers, 1789-1832, Second Series,* edited by John R. Greenfield (1991)

111 *American Literary Biographers, Second Series,* edited by Steven Serafin (1991)

112 *British Literary Publishing Houses, 1881-1965,* edited by Jonathan Rose and Patricia J. Anderson (1991)

113 *Modern Latin-American Fiction Writers, First Series,* edited by William Luis (1992)

114 *Twentieth-Century Italian Poets, First Series,* edited by Giovanna Wedel De Stasio, Glauco Cambon, and Antonio Illiano (1992)

115 *Medieval Philosophers,* edited by Jeremiah Hackett (1992)

116 *British Romantic Novelists, 1789-1832,* edited by Bradford K. Mudge (1992)

117 *Twentieth-Century Caribbean and Black African Writers, First Series,* edited by Bernth Lindfors and Reinhard Sander (1992)

118 *Twentieth-Century German Dramatists, 1889-1918,* edited by Wolfgang D. Elfe and James Hardin (1992)

119 *Nineteenth-Century French Fiction Writers: Romanticism and Realism, 1800-1860,* edited by Catharine Savage Brosman (1992)

120 *American Poets Since World War II, Third Series,* edited by R. S. Gwynn (1992)

121 *Seventeenth-Century British Nondramatic Poets, First Series,* edited by M. Thomas Hester (1992)

122 *Chicano Writers, Second Series,* edited by Francisco A. Lomelí and Carl R. Shirley (1992)

123 *Nineteenth-Century French Fiction Writers: Naturalism and Beyond, 1860-1900,* edited by Catharine Savage Brosman (1992)

124 *Twentieth-Century German Dramatists, 1919-1992,* edited by Wolfgang D. Elfe and James Hardin (1992)

125 *Twentieth-Century Caribbean and Black African Writers, Second Series,* edited by Bernth Lindfors and Reinhard Sander (1993)

126 *Seventeenth-Century British Nondramatic Poets, Second Series,* edited by M. Thomas Hester (1993)

127 *American Newspaper Publishers, 1950-1990,* edited by Perry J. Ashley (1993)

128 *Twentieth-Century Italian Poets, Second Series,* edited by Giovanna Wedel De Stasio, Glauco Cambon, and Antonio Illiano (1993)

129 *Nineteenth-Century German Writers, 1841-1900,* edited by James Hardin and Siegfried Mews (1993)

130 *American Short-Story Writers Since World War II,* edited by Patrick Meanor (1993)

131 *Seventeenth-Century British Nondramatic Poets, Third Series,* edited by M. Thomas Hester (1993)

132 *Sixteenth-Century British Nondramatic Writers, First Series,* edited by David A. Richardson (1993)

133 *Nineteenth-Century German Writers to 1840,* edited by James Hardin and Siegfried Mews (1993)

134 *Twentieth-Century Spanish Poets, Second Series,* edited by Jerry Phillips Winfield (1994)

135 *British Short-Fiction Writers, 1880-1914: The Realist Tradition,* edited by William B. Thesing (1994)

136 *Sixteenth-Century British Nondramatic Writers, Second Series,* edited by David A. Richardson (1994)

137 *American Magazine Journalists, 1900-1960, Second Series,* edited by Sam G. Riley (1994)

138 *German Writers and Works of the High Middle Ages: 1170-1280,* edited by James Hardin and Will Hasty (1994)

139 *British Short-Fiction Writers, 1945-1980,* edited by Dean Baldwin (1994)

140 *American Book-Collectors and Bibliographers, First Series,* edited by Joseph Rosenblum (1994)

141 *British Children's Writers, 1880-1914,* edited by Laura M. Zaidman (1994)

142 *Eighteenth-Century British Literary Biographers,* edited by Steven Serafin (1994)

143 *American Novelists Since World War II, Third Series,* edited by James R. Giles and Wanda H. Giles (1994)

144 *Nineteenth-Century British Literary Biographers,* edited by Steven Serafin (1994)

145 *Modern Latin-American Fiction Writers, Second Series,* edited by William Luis and Ann González (1994)

146 *Old and Middle English Literature,* edited by Jeffrey Helterman and Jerome Mitchell (1994)

147 *South Slavic Writers Before World War II,* edited by Vasa D. Mihailovich (1994)

148 *German Writers and Works of the Early Middle Ages: 800-1170,* edited by Will Hasty and James Hardin (1994)

149 *Late Nineteenth- and Early Twentieth-Century British Literary Biographers,* edited by Steven Serafin (1995)

150 *Early Modern Russian Writers, Late Seventeenth and Eighteenth Centuries,* edited by Marcus C. Levitt (1995)

151 *British Prose Writers of the Early Seventeenth Century,* edited by Clayton D. Lein (1995)

152 *American Novelists Since World War II, Fourth Series,* edited by James R. Giles and Wanda H. Giles (1995)

153 *Late-Victorian and Edwardian British Novelists, First Series,* edited by George M. Johnson (1995)

154 *The British Literary Book Trade, 1700-1820,* edited by James K. Bracken and Joel Silver (1995)

155 *Twentieth-Century British Literary Biographers*, edited by Steven Serafin (1995)

156 *British Short-Fiction Writers, 1880-1914: The Romantic Tradition*, edited by William F. Naufftus (1995)

157 *Twentieth-Century Caribbean and Black African Writers, Third Series*, edited by Bernth Lindfors and Reinhard Sander (1995)

158 *British Reform Writers, 1789-1832*, edited by Gary Kelly and Edd Applegate (1995)

159 *British Short-Fiction Writers, 1800-1880*, edited by John R. Greenfield (1996)

160 *British Children's Writers, 1914-1960*, edited by Donald R. Hettinga and Gary D. Schmidt (1996)

161 *British Children's Writers Since 1960, First Series*, edited by Caroline Hunt (1996)

162 *British Short-Fiction Writers, 1915-1945*, edited by John H. Rogers (1996)

163 *British Children's Writers, 1800-1880*, edited by Meena Khorana (1996)

164 *German Baroque Writers, 1580-1660*, edited by James Hardin (1996)

165 *American Poets Since World War II, Fourth Series*, edited by Joseph Conte (1996)

166 *British Travel Writers, 1837-1875*, edited by Barbara Brothers and Julia Gergits (1996)

167 *Sixteenth-Century British Nondramatic Writers, Third Series*, edited by David A. Richardson (1996)

168 *German Baroque Writers, 1661-1730*, edited by James Hardin (1996)

169 *American Poets Since World War II, Fifth Series*, edited by Joseph Conte (1996)

170 *The British Literary Book Trade, 1475-1700*, edited by James K. Bracken and Joel Silver (1996)

171 *Twentieth-Century American Sportswriters*, edited by Richard Orodenker (1996)

172 *Sixteenth-Century British Nondramatic Writers, Fourth Series*, edited by David A. Richardson (1996)

173 *American Novelists Since World War II, Fifth Series*, edited by James R. Giles and Wanda H. Giles (1996)

174 *British Travel Writers, 1876-1909*, edited by Barbara Brothers and Julia Gergits (1997)

175 *Native American Writers of the United States*, edited by Kenneth M. Roemer (1997)

176 *Ancient Greek Authors*, edited by Ward W. Briggs (1997)

177 *Italian Novelists Since World War II, 1945-1965*, edited by Augustus Pallotta (1997)

178 *British Fantasy and Science-Fiction Writers Before World War I*, edited by Darren Harris-Fain (1997)

179 *German Writers of the Renaissance and Reformation, 1280-1580*, edited by James Hardin and Max Reinhart (1997)

180 *Japanese Fiction Writers, 1868-1945*, edited by Van C. Gessel (1997)

181 *South Slavic Writers Since World War II*, edited by Vasa D. Mihailovich (1997)

182 *Japanese Fiction Writers Since World War II*, edited by Van C. Gessel (1997)

183 *American Travel Writers, 1776-1864*, edited by James J. Schramer and Donald Ross (1997)

184 *Nineteenth-Century British Book-Collectors and Bibliographers*, edited by William Baker and Kenneth Womack (1997)

185 *American Literary Journalists, 1945-1995, First Series*, edited by Arthur J. Kaul (1998)

186 *Nineteenth-Century American Western Writers*, edited by Robert L. Gale (1998)

187 *American Book Collectors and Bibliographers, Second Series*, edited by Joseph Rosenblum (1998)

188 *American Book and Magazine Illustrators to 1920*, edited by Steven E. Smith, Catherine A. Hastedt, and Donald H. Dyal (1998)

189 *American Travel Writers, 1850-1915*, edited by Donald Ross and James J. Schramer (1998)

190 *British Reform Writers, 1832-1914*, edited by Gary Kelly and Edd Applegate (1998)

191 *British Novelists Between the Wars*, edited by George M. Johnson (1998)

192 *French Dramatists, 1789-1914*, edited by Barbara T. Cooper (1998)

193 *American Poets Since World War II, Sixth Series*, edited by Joseph Conte (1998)

194 *British Novelists Since 1960, Second Series*, edited by Merritt Moseley (1998)

195 *British Travel Writers, 1910-1939*, edited by Barbara Brothers and Julia Gergits (1998)

196 *Italian Novelists Since World War II, 1965-1995*, edited by Augustus Pallotta (1999)

197 *Late-Victorian and Edwardian British Novelists, Second Series*, edited by George M. Johnson (1999)

198 *Russian Literature in the Age of Pushkin and Gogol: Prose*, edited by Christine A. Rydel (1999)

199 *Victorian Women Poets*, edited by William B. Thesing (1999)

200 *American Women Prose Writers to 1820*, edited by Carla J. Mulford, with Angela Vietto and Amy E. Winans (1999)

201 *Twentieth-Century British Book Collectors and Bibliographers*, edited by William Baker and Kenneth Womack (1999)

202 *Nineteenth-Century American Fiction Writers*, edited by Kent P. Ljungquist (1999)

203 *Medieval Japanese Writers*, edited by Steven D. Carter (1999)

204 *British Travel Writers, 1940-1997*, edited by Barbara Brothers and Julia M. Gergits (1999)

205 *Russian Literature in the Age of Pushkin and Gogol: Poetry and Drama*, edited by Christine A. Rydel (1999)

206 *Twentieth-Century American Western Writers, First Series*, edited by Richard H. Cracroft (1999)

207 *British Novelists Since 1960, Third Series*, edited by Merritt Moseley (1999)

208 *Literature of the French and Occitan Middle Ages: Eleventh to Fifteenth Centuries*, edited by Deborah Sinnreich-Levi and Ian S. Laurie (1999)

209 *Chicano Writers, Third Series*, edited by Francisco A. Lomelí and Carl R. Shirley (1999)

210 *Ernest Hemingway: A Documentary Volume*, edited by Robert W. Trogdon (1999)

211 *Ancient Roman Writers*, edited by Ward W. Briggs (1999)

212 *Twentieth-Century American Western Writers, Second Series*, edited by Richard H. Cracroft (1999)

213 *Pre-Nineteenth-Century British Book Collectors and Bibliographers*, edited by William Baker and Kenneth Womack (1999)

214 *Twentieth-Century Danish Writers*, edited by Marianne Stecher-Hansen (1999)

215 *Twentieth-Century Eastern European Writers, First Series*, edited by Steven Serafin (1999)

216 *British Poets of the Great War: Brooke, Rosenberg, Thomas. A Documentary Volume*, edited by Patrick Quinn (2000)

217 *Nineteenth-Century French Poets*, edited by Robert Beum (2000)

218 *American Short-Story Writers Since World War II, Second Series*, edited by Patrick Meanor and Gwen Crane (2000)

219 *F. Scott Fitzgerald's The Great Gatsby: A Documentary Volume*, edited by Matthew J. Bruccoli (2000)

220 *Twentieth-Century Eastern European Writers, Second Series*, edited by Steven Serafin (2000)

221 *American Women Prose Writers, 1870-1920*, edited by Sharon M. Harris, with the assistance of Heidi L. M. Jacobs and Jennifer Putzi (2000)

222 *H. L. Mencken: A Documentary Volume*, edited by Richard J. Schrader (2000)

223 *The American Renaissance in New England, Second Series*, edited by Wesley T. Mott (2000)

224 *Walt Whitman: A Documentary Volume*, edited by Joel Myerson (2000)

225 *South African Writers*, edited by Paul A. Scanlon (2000)

226 *American Hard-Boiled Crime Writers*, edited by George Parker Anderson and Julie B. Anderson (2000)

Documentary Series

1 *Sherwood Anderson, Willa Cather, John Dos Passos, Theodore Dreiser, F. Scott Fitzgerald, Ernest Hemingway, Sinclair Lewis*, edited by Margaret A. Van Antwerp (1982)

2 *James Gould Cozzens, James T. Farrell, William Faulkner, John O'Hara, John Steinbeck,*

Thomas Wolfe, Richard Wright, edited by Margaret A. Van Antwerp (1982)

3 *Saul Bellow, Jack Kerouac, Norman Mailer, Vladimir Nabokov, John Updike, Kurt Vonnegut,* edited by Mary Bruccoli (1983)

4 *Tennessee Williams,* edited by Margaret A. Van Antwerp and Sally Johns (1984)

5 *American Transcendentalists,* edited by Joel Myerson (1988)

6 *Hardboiled Mystery Writers: Raymond Chandler, Dashiell Hammett, Ross Macdonald,* edited by Matthew J. Bruccoli and Richard Layman (1989)

7 *Modern American Poets: James Dickey, Robert Frost, Marianne Moore,* edited by Karen L. Rood (1989)

8 *The Black Aesthetic Movement,* edited by Jeffrey Louis Decker (1991)

9 *American Writers of the Vietnam War: W. D. Ehrhart, Larry Heinemann, Tim O'Brien, Walter McDonald, John M. Del Vecchio,* edited by Ronald Baughman (1991)

10 *The Bloomsbury Group,* edited by Edward L. Bishop (1992)

11 *American Proletarian Culture: The Twenties and The Thirties,* edited by Jon Christian Suggs (1993)

12 *Southern Women Writers: Flannery O'Connor, Katherine Anne Porter, Eudora Welty,* edited by Mary Ann Wimsatt and Karen L. Rood (1994)

13 *The House of Scribner, 1846-1904,* edited by John Delaney (1996)

14 *Four Women Writers for Children, 1868-1918,* edited by Caroline C. Hunt (1996)

15 *American Expatriate Writers: Paris in the Twenties,* edited by Matthew J. Bruccoli and Robert W. Trogdon (1997)

16 *The House of Scribner, 1905-1930,* edited by John Delaney (1997)

17 *The House of Scribner, 1931-1984,* edited by John Delaney (1998)

18 *British Poets of The Great War: Sassoon, Graves, Owen,* edited by Patrick Quinn (1999)

19 *James Dickey,* edited by Judith S. Baughman (1999)

See also DLB 210, 216, 219, 222, 224

Yearbooks

1980 edited by Karen L. Rood, Jean W. Ross, and Richard Ziegfeld (1981)

1981 edited by Karen L. Rood, Jean W. Ross, and Richard Ziegfeld (1982)

1982 edited by Richard Ziegfeld; associate editors: Jean W. Ross and Lynne C. Zeigler (1983)

1983 edited by Mary Bruccoli and Jean W. Ross; associate editor Richard Ziegfeld (1984)

1984 edited by Jean W. Ross (1985)

1985 edited by Jean W. Ross (1986)

1986 edited by J. M. Brook (1987)

1987 edited by J. M. Brook (1988)

1988 edited by J. M. Brook (1989)

1989 edited by J. M. Brook (1990)

1990 edited by James W. Hipp (1991)

1991 edited by James W. Hipp (1992)

1992 edited by James W. Hipp (1993)

1993 edited by James W. Hipp, contributing editor George Garrett (1994)

1994 edited by James W. Hipp, contributing editor George Garrett (1995)

1995 edited by James W. Hipp, contributing editor George Garrett (1996)

1996 edited by Samuel W. Bruce and L. Kay Webster, contributing editor George Garrett (1997)

1997 edited by Matthew J. Bruccoli and George Garrett, with the assistance of L. Kay Webster (1998)

1998 edited by Matthew J. Bruccoli, contributing editor George Garrett, with the assistance of D. W. Thomas (1999)

1999 edited by Matthew J. Bruccoli, contributing editor George Garrett, with the assistance of D. W. Thomas (2000)

Concise Series

Concise Dictionary of American Literary Biography, 7 volumes (1988-1999): *The New Consciousness, 1941-1968; Colonization to the American Renaissance, 1640-1865; Realism, Naturalism, and Local Color, 1865-1917; The Twenties, 1917-1929; The Age of Maturity, 1929-1941; Broadening Views, 1968-1988; Supplement: Modern Writers, 1900-1998.*

Concise Dictionary of British Literary Biography, 8 volumes (1991-1992): *Writers of the Middle Ages and Renaissance Before 1660; Writers of the Restoration and Eighteenth Century, 1660-1789; Writers of the Romantic Period, 1789-1832; Victorian Writers, 1832-1890; Late-Victorian and Edwardian Writers, 1890-1914; Modern Writers, 1914-1945; Writers After World War II, 1945-1960; Contemporary Writers, 1960 to Present.*

Concise Dictionary of World Literary Biography, 20 volumes projected (1999-   ): *Ancient Greek and Roman Writers; German Writers; African, Carribbean, and Latin-American Writers.*

American Hard-Boiled Crime Writers

American Hard-Boiled Crime Writers

Edited by
George Parker Anderson
University of South Carolina
and
Julie B. Anderson
Midlands Technical College

A Bruccoli Clark Layman Book
The Gale Group
Detroit • San Francisco • London • Boston • Woodbridge, Conn.

Printed in the United States of America

The paper used in this publication meets the minimum requirements
of American National Standard for Information Sciences–Permanence
Paper for Printed Library Materials, ANSI Z39.48-1984.♾™

Library of Congress Cataloging-in-Publication Data

American hard-boiled crime writers / edited by George Parker Anderson and Julie B. Anderson.
    p. cm.–(Dictionary of literary biography: v. 226)
"A Bruccoli Clark Layman book."
Includes bibliographical references and index.
ISBN 0-7876-3135-3 (alk. paper)
1. Detective and mystery stories, American–Bio-bibliography–Dictionaries. 2. American fiction–20th
century–Bio-bibliography–Dictionaries. 3. Novelists, American–20th century–Biography–Dictionaries.
4. Detective and mystery stories, American–Dictionaries. 5. American fiction–20th century–Dictionaries.
6. Crime in literature–Dictionaries. I. Anderson, George Parker, 1957– . II. Anderson, Julie B.,
1959– . III. Series.

PS374.D4 A45 2000
813'.087209'003–dc21   00–028761
                                                                                          CIP

10 9 8 7 6 5 4 3 2 1

For Cynthia

Contents

Plan of the Series xii

Introduction xiv

Lawrence Block (1938–   ) .3
   John L. Cobbs

Howard Browne (1908–1999) 11
   Marcia B. Dinneen

James Lee Burke (1936–   ) 19
   Dean G. Hall

W. R. Burnett (1899–1982) 31
   Katherine Harper

James M. Cain (1892–1977) 48
   Bobbie Robinson

Raymond Chandler (1888–1959) 70
   Robert F. Moss

James Crumley (1939–   ) 92
   Martin Kich

Carroll John Daly (1889–1958) 100
   Chuck Etheridge

Thomas B. Dewey (1915–1981) 106
   Marvin S. Lachman

Davis Dresser (Brett Halliday) (1904–1977) 112
   Anita G. Gorman

James Ellroy (1948–   ) 120
   Katherine M. Restaino

Loren D. Estleman (1952–   ) 131
   Katherine Harper

Steve Fisher (1913–1980) 140
   Katherine M. Restaino

William Campbell Gault (1910–1995) 149
   Marvin S. Lachman

David Goodis (1917–1967) 157
   David Schmid

Joe Gores (1931–   ) .166
   Peter Kenney

Sue Grafton (1940–   ) 175
   Carol McGinnis Kay

Dashiell Hammett (1894–1961) 188
   Charles Brower

Joseph Hansen (1923–   ) 209
   Karl L. Stenger

Chester Himes (1909–1984) 216
   Jeff Siegel

Ed Lacy (Len Zinberg) (1911–1968) 226
   Jennifer Hynes

Elmore Leonard (1925–   ) 233
   Frederick William Zackel

Kenneth Millar (Ross Macdonald) (1915–1983) . . . 247
   Frederick William Zackel

Marcia Muller (1944–   ) 267
   Rebecca E. Martin

Frederick Nebel (1903–1967) 283
   Katherine Harper

Bill Pronzini (1943–   ) 289
   Marvin S. Lachman

Mickey Spillane (1918–   ) 301
   Sue Laslie Kimball and George Parker Anderson

Jim Thompson (1906–1977) 310
   Tim Dayton

Raoul Whitfield (1898–1945) 329
   Douglas Ivison

Charles Willeford (1919–1988) 336
   Douglas Levin

Cornell Woolrich (1903–1968) 349
   David Schmid

Checklist of Further Reading 365

Contributors 369

Cumulative Index 373

Plan of the Series

The advisory board, the editors, and the publisher of the *Dictionary of Literary Biography* are joined in endorsing Mark Twain's declaration. The literature of a nation provides an inexhaustible resource of permanent worth. We intend to make literature and its creators better understood and more accessible to students and the reading public, while satisfying the standards of teachers and scholars.

To meet these requirements, *literary biography* has been construed in terms of the author's achievement. The most important thing about a writer is his writing. Accordingly, the entries in *DLB* are career biographies, tracing the development of the author's canon and the evolution of his reputation.

The purpose of *DLB* is not only to provide reliable information in a convenient format but also to place the figures in the larger perspective of literary history and to offer appraisals of their accomplishments by qualified scholars.

The publication plan for *DLB* resulted from two years of preparation. The project was proposed to Bruccoli Clark by Frederick G. Ruffner, president of the Gale Research Company, in November 1975. After specimen entries were prepared and typeset, an advisory board was formed to refine the entry format and develop the series rationale. In meetings held during 1976, the publisher, series editors, and advisory board approved the scheme for a comprehensive biographical dictionary of persons who contributed to North American literature. Editorial work on the first volume began in January 1977, and it was published in 1978. In order to make *DLB* more than a reference tool and to compile volumes that individually have claim to status as literary history, it was decided to organize volumes by

topic, period, or genre. Each of these freestanding volumes provides a biographical-bibliographical guide and overview for a particular area of literature. We are convinced that this organization—as opposed to a single alphabet method—constitutes a valuable innovation in the presentation of reference material. The volume plan necessarily requires many decisions for the placement and treatment of authors who might properly be included in two or three volumes. In some instances a major figure will be included in separate volumes, but with different entries emphasizing the aspect of his career appropriate to each volume. Ernest Hemingway, for example, is represented in *American Writers in Paris, 1920–1939* by an entry focusing on his expatriate apprenticeship; he is also in *American Novelists, 1910–1945* with an entry surveying his entire career, as well as in *American Short-Story Writers, 1910–1945, Second Series* with an entry concentrating on his short stories. Each volume includes a cumulative index of the subject authors and articles. Comprehensive indexes to the entire series are planned.

Since 1981 the series has been further augmented by the *DLB Yearbooks,* which update published entries and add new entries to keep the *DLB* current with contemporary activity. There have also been *DLB Documentary Series* volumes which provide biographical and critical source materials for figures whose work is judged to have particular interest for students. One of these companion volumes is devoted entirely to Tennessee Williams.

We define literature as the *intellectual commerce of a nation:* not merely as belles lettres but as that ample and complex process by which ideas are generated, shaped, and transmitted. *DLB* entries are not limited to "creative writers" but extend to other figures who in their time and in their way influenced the mind of a people. Thus the series encompasses historians, journalists, publishers, book collectors, and screenwriters. By this means readers of *DLB* may be aided to perceive literature not as cult scripture in the keeping of intellectual high priests but firmly positioned at the center of a nation's life.

DLB includes the major writers appropriate to each volume and those standing in the ranks behind them. Scholarly and critical counsel has been sought in deciding which minor figures to include and how full their entries should be. Wherever possible, useful references are made to figures who do not warrant separate entries.

Each *DLB* volume has an expert volume editor responsible for planning the volume, selecting the figures for inclusion, and assigning the entries. Volume editors are also responsible for preparing, where appropriate, appendices surveying the major periodicals and literary and intellectual movements for their volumes, as well as lists of further readings. Work on the series as a whole is coordinated at the Bruccoli Clark Layman editorial center in Columbia, South Carolina, where the editorial staff is responsible for accuracy and utility of the published volumes.

One feature that distinguishes *DLB* is the illustration policy–its concern with the iconography of literature. Just as an author is influenced by his surroundings, so is the reader's understanding of the author enhanced by a knowledge of his environment. Therefore *DLB* volumes include not only drawings, paintings, and photographs of authors, often depicting them at various stages in their careers, but also illustrations of their families and places where they lived. Title pages are regularly reproduced in facsimile along with dust jackets for modern authors. The dust jackets are a special feature of *DLB* because they often document better than anything else the way in which an author's work was perceived in its own time. Specimens of the writers' manuscripts and letters are included when feasible.

Samuel Johnson rightly decreed that "The chief glory of every people arises from its authors." The purpose of the *Dictionary of Literary Biography* is to compile literary history in the surest way available to us–by accurate and comprehensive treatment of the lives and work of those who contributed to it.

The *DLB* Advisory Board

Introduction

Dictionary of Literary Biography 226: American Hard-Boiled Crime Writers presents entries on thirty-one writers whose lives and careers span the history of hard-boiled writing, from its birth in the American pulp magazines of the 1920s to the beginning of the twenty-first century. The writers included in the volume are intended to represent the nature and development of a type and style of writing that has cultural as well as literary roots and that in its evolution has been extraordinarily affected by market forces. In his biography *Ross Macdonald* (1984) Matthew J. Bruccoli provides a working definition of hard-boiled literature: "realistic fiction with some or all of the following characteristics–objective viewpoint, impersonal tone, violent action, colloquial speech, tough characters, and understated style; usually, but not limited to, detective or crime fiction."

Despite being a recognized tradition in American letters, hard-boiled writing did not begin or evolve as a school or movement. It is more accurate to characterize the genre as a collection of individual responses to a rapidly changing and often violent America. Beyond any set of characteristics that can be offered to define it as a style, hard-boiled writing can be defined in terms of cause and effect: it begins in the writer's imagination of a world where crime and the threat of violence are endemic and any just or harmonious resolution is temporary; it ends by evoking in readers an awareness that such a world is their own and is never wholly safe or secure. The readers of hard-boiled fiction learn to be wary of the facile promises of the American dream.

Critics have linked the hard-boiled tradition to classic nineteenth-century American literature–especially the archetypal American hero, Natty Bumppo of the Leatherstocking tales, whom D. H. Lawrence in his *Studies in Classic American Literature* (1923) described as "hard, isolate, stoic, and a killer." In "Murder and the Mean Streets: The Hard-Boiled Detective Novel" (1970) George Grella compares the hard-boiled detective heroes of Dashiell Hammett, Raymond Chandler, and Ross Macdonald (Kenneth Millar)–the writers he believes best represent the tradition–to Bumppo, or Hawkeye as he is also called:

The American detective hero has his archetype's pronounced physical ability, dealing out and absorbing great quantities of punishment. Like Hawkeye, he is proficient with his gun and seldom goes anywhere without it. Like the lonely man of the forests, he moves outside the established social code, preferring his own instinctive justice to the often tarnished justice of civilization. The private detective always finds the police incompetent, brutal, or corrupt, and therefore works alone. . . . Finding the social contract vicious and debilitating, he generally isolates himself from normal human relationships. His characteristic toughness and his redeeming moral strength conflict with the values of his civilization and cause him, like Natty Bumppo or Huckleberry Finn, to flee the society which menaces his personal integrity and spiritual freedom.

In American history and legend, hardy individualists undaunted by a lawless frontier–from Daniel Boone and Kit Carson to the mythical Paul Bunyan–are celebrated. Precursors for the anti-authoritarian, individualistic code of the hard-boiled hero are also found in work of the vernacular humorists as well as in dime novels that proliferated in the last decades of the nineteenth century.

By the 1920s the lawless frontier had disappeared, replaced in the popular imagination by an urban society that was even more menacing. The writers of the 1920s had only to open their newspapers to find immediate inspiration for writing about crime. With the passage of the Eighteenth Amendment to the Constitution, which forbade the manufacture, sale, and transportation of liquor, the country overnight had become a nation of scofflaws. As alcohol consumption continued during the decade, gangs organized to create and maintain an underground network for the distribution of illegal drink. The apparent influence of criminals, who were often able to corrupt the police and public officials, created an atmosphere of perceived anarchy. The public fascination with crime created the environment for hard-boiled fiction to emerge and flourish. "Hardboiled style," as Leroy L. Panek observes in "The Naked Truth" (*Armchair Detective,* Fall 1988), "grew from its writers' attempts to realistically depict the world of criminals and police officers, to portray their heroes' participation in this world, and to write arresting, occasionally flamboyant, prose."

As the hard-boiled detective hero was conceived by Carroll John Daly—the writer credited with the creation of the type—he was clearly a wish-fulfillment figure, a slang-talking tough guy who could cope with an anarchic world with his fists and his guns. Daly's most famous protagonist, private investigator Race Williams, initially appeared in a story in the 1 June 1923 issue of *Black Mask*. Although Daly's work—with its crudely drawn characters, unrealistic action, and overwrought prose—was not held in high esteem by *Black Mask* editors, it was commercially successful. During the next dozen years, Daly had some fifty more Race Williams stories published in the magazine, and in 1930 he was voted the favorite author by its readers. The private investigator as a type clearly had strong appeal.

Black Mask and retired army captain Joseph T. "Cap" Shaw, its editor from 1926 to 1936, were crucial to the development of hard-boiled fiction. *Black Mask* was one of many pulps—cheap magazines that were printed on rough wood-pulp paper—that thrived in the first half of the century. In 1920 H. L. Mencken and George Jean Nathan, neither of whom cared for detective fiction, founded *The Black Mask* and sold it after six months as a means of subsidizing their literary magazine, *The Smart Set*. When Shaw took over as editor, he "meditated on the possiblility of creating a new type of detective story," as he recalled in his introduction to *The Hard-Boiled Omnibus* (1946). Shaw disliked the British type of detective story, which he termed "the deductive type, the cross-word puzzle sort, lacking—deliberately—all other human emotional values." Believing that "the creation of a new pattern was a writer's rather than an editor's job," he searched the magazine "for a writer with the requisite spark and originality." He found Dashiell Hammett.

Hammett, who had published his first Continental Op story in *Black Mask* four months after the first Race Williams story had appeared, was as interested as Shaw in remaking the detective story, as Shaw relates in his introduction:

> It was apparent that Mr. Hammett shared our hope for a medium in which he could achieve his aim while developing his talent into a highly skillful instrument. We pointed out that this particular medium—the magazine mystery story—was both constrained and restrained. We felt obliged to stipulate our boundaries. We wanted simplicity for the sake of clarity, plausibility, and belief. We wanted action, but we held that action is meaningless unless it involves regonizable human character in three-dimensional form.
>
> Dashiell Hammett had his own way of phrasing this: If you kill a symbol, no crime is committed and no effect is produced. To constitute a murder, the victim must be a

Joseph T. Shaw, editor of Black Mask *magazine from 1926 to 1936*

real human being of flesh and blood.

> Simple, logical, almost inevitable. Yet, amazingly, this principle had been completely ignored by crime writers—and still is, in the deductive type of mystery story.

Shaw maintained that "character conflict is the main theme; the ensuing crime, or its threat, is incidental." With *Red Harvest* (1929), *The Dain Curse* (1929), *The*

Maltese Falcon (1930), and *The Glass Key* (1931)–all of which were serialized in *Black Mask* before being published as books–Hammett set the standard for hard-boiled fiction.

By encouraging this "new pattern" in *Black Mask*, Shaw was also promoting a new style: "*Such distinctive treatment comprises a hard, brittle style–which Raymond Chandler, one of its most brilliant exponents, declares belongs to everybody and to no one–a full employment of the functions of dialogue, and authenticity in characterization and action. To this may be added a very fast tempo, attained in part by typical economy of expression.*" The style that emerged in *Black Mask*, Shaw writes, "*was rather extravagantly tagged as the 'hardboiled' school.*" Writers who contributed to the hard-boiled style of the magazine include Frederick Nebel and Raoul Whitfield, as well as such writers as George Harmon Coxe, Roger Torrey, Forrest Rosaire, Paul Cain, and Lester Dent. The medium provided by *Black Mask* as guided by Cap Shaw focused and sharpened the efforts of writers who were seeking to write realistically and entertainingly about their violent culture. Some pulp writers were able to achieve book publication, which greatly increased their fame and influence. Chandler brought hard-boiled fiction to a new level of critical respect with novels featuring Philip Marlowe, including *The Big Sleep* (1939), *Farewell, My Lovely* (1940), and *The Long Good-Bye* (1953).

As the term *hard-boiled* became current, it was used so ubiquitously and indiscriminately as to verge on becoming meaningless. James M. Cain, who was seen by many as the epitome of the hard-boiled school when his first novel, *The Postman Always Rings Twice*, was published in 1934, always resisted the label. Cain achieved his success as a novelist after being a journalist and had his own set of personal influences that included Mencken, not Shaw and *Black Mask*. In the preface to *The Butterfly* (1947) he is emphatic: "I belong to no school, hard-boiled or otherwise, and I believe these so-called schools exist mainly in the imagination of critics, and have little correspondence in reality anywhere else."

The success of *Black Mask* inspired many imitations and contributed to a healthy pulp market for mystery fiction. Steve Fisher, for example, beginning in the mid 1930s sold more than five hundred stories to the pulps, not only to *Black Mask* but also to magazines such as *Sure-Fire Detective Magazine*, *Spicy Mystery Stories*, *Thrilling Detective*, *True Gang Life*, *The Shadow*, *Detective Fiction Weekly*, *New Mystery Adventures*, *Underground Detective*, *Phantom Detective*, *Ace Detective*, *Detective Tales*, *Headquarters Detective*, *Hardboiled*, *Federal Agent*, *Popular Detective*, *Pocket Detective*, *Crime Busters*, *Detective Romances*, and *Detective Story Magazine*. Woolrich, who published six mainstream novels between 1926 and 1932, found his true métier in the mystery pulps, placing stories in magazines such as *Ace-High Detective*, *Black Mask*, *Detective Fiction Weekly*, *Dime Detective*, *Double Detective*, and *Street & Smith's Detective Story* between 1934 and 1940 before writing his first crime novel, *The Bride Wore Black* (1940). Yet, of course, while the pulp market provided the venue for writers to develop, much of what was regarded as hard-boiled fiction was of poor quality. As Chandler writes in "The Simple Art of Murder" (1950), "The realistic style is easy to abuse: from haste, from lack of awareness, from inability to bridge the chasm that lies between what a writer would like to be able to say and what he actually knows how to say. It is easy to fake; brutality is not strength, flipness is not wit, edge-of-the-chair-writing can be as boring as flat writing. . . . There has been so much of this sort of thing that if a character in a detective story says 'Yeah,' the author is automatically a Hammett imitator."

Several authors represented in *DLB 226* initiated detective novel series in the years surrounding World War II. In 1939 Davis Dresser, writing under his best-known pseudonym Brett Halliday, published *Dividend on Death,* the first of fifty novels featuring detective Mike Shayne. The Shayne character was so popular that in 1956 Dresser and Leo Margulies founded *Mike Shayne Mystery Magazine,* which continued to publish ghost-written Mike Shayne stories until 1985, eight years after Dresser's death. Thomas B. Dewey began his series of novels featuring Mac, a detective with no surname, with *Draw the Curtain Close* (1947). Chandler directly inspired Howard Browne, whose first novel about detective Paul Pine was *Halo in Blood* (1946). William Campbell Gault's most famous PI was Brock "The Rock" Callahan, who initially appeared in *Ring Around Rosa* (1955).

The two most important hard-boiled detectives to premiere following the war were undoubtedly Mickey Spillane's Mike Hammer and Ross Macdonald's Lew Archer. With his first six Hammer novels–*I, The Jury* (1947), *My Gun Is Quick* (1950), *Vengeance Is Mine!* (1950), *The Big Kill* (1951), *One Lonely Night* (1951) and *Kiss Me, Deadly* (1952)–Spillane enjoyed unprecedented commercial success and at the same time became the whipping boy for critics who, like Grella in "Murder and the Mean Streets," regarded him as "the man who represents the perversion of the American detective novel":

In Spillane the wisecrack, the wit, the repartee, the rapid action and pace, the inevitable urgency of event, as well as the stylistic grace and gusto of a Chandler or Macdonald, are absent. What remains of the essence of the American thriller is the toughness, the sexuality, the

A 1936 dinner in Los Angeles for Black Mask *writers: (standing) R. J. Moffat (a guest), Raymond Chandler, Herbert Sinson, Dwight Babcock, Eric Taylor, Dashiell Hammett; (seated) Arthur Barnes, John K. Butler, W. T. Ballard, Horace McCoy, and Norbert Davis*

violence and a distorted version of its themes, motifs and values. The detective's solipsistic belief in himself, his unerring rightness, his intensely lonely virtue, all become a vivid argument for a totalitarian moral policeman whose code, no matter how vicious, must be forced upon every man.

Macdonald, whose first Archer novel, *The Moving Target,* was published in 1949, was intent on taking the hard-boiled novel in a different direction, as is written in a 28 August 1952 letter to his publisher, Alfred A. Knopf: "The old-line hard-boiled novel with its many guns and fornications and fisticuffs has been ruined by its practition-ers, including the later Chandler. Spillane pulled the plug. I have no intention of plunging after it down the drain." Beginning with *The Galton Case* (1959) and continuing through his last novel, *The Blue Hammer* (1976), Millar, in the estimation of critics, achieved his aspiration, "to write 'popular' novels which will not be inferior to 'serious' novels." He never approached Spillane's popularity, though. By the time his total sales exceeded 5 million in 1971, more than 100 million copies of Spillane's books had been sold.

In the 1950s, with the decline of the pulps and the rise of the paperback original, the market for hard-boiled fiction profoundly changed. As Bill Pronzini and Jack Adrian explain in the introduction to *Hard-Boiled: An Anthology of American Crime Stories* (1995), Fawcett Gold

Medal led a group of publishers, including Avon, Dell, Popular Library, and Lion, into the practice of "paying royalty advances on the number of copies printed, rather than on the number of copies sold; thus writers received handsome initial payments, up to four times as much as hardcover publishers were paying":

> Instead of a bulky magazine full of short stories, Fawcett published brand-new, easy-to-read novels in a convenient pocket-size format. . . . Instead of printing hundreds of thousands of copies of a small number of titles, Fawcett printed hundreds of thousands of copies of many titles in order to reach every possible outlet and buyer. As a result, many Gold Medal novels, particularly in the early 1950s, sold more than a million copies each.

During the decade writers such as Jim Thompson, David Goodis, and Charles Willeford—none of whom wrote about a private eye—were drawn to the new market, in which the preferred length for a novel was a short fifty thousand words. Ed Lacy, whose black private detective Toussaint Marcus Moore first appeared in *Room to Swing* (1957), and Chester Himes, whose violent tales of Harlem police detectives Grave Digger Jones and Coffin Ed Johnson began with *For Love of Imabelle* (1957), also pub-lished paperback originals.

DLB 226 features eleven hard-boiled authors who began writing about modern crime in or since the 1960s.

Elmore Leonard, who began his career writing Westerns, turned to modern settings in the late 1960s and became a best-selling crime novelist in the 1980s. Leonard in his novels seems to capture the authentic voices of cops and criminals. James Ellroy, another modern hard-boiled writer who does not focus on a private detective, has written a social history of Los Angeles through the crime novel in his LA Quartet—*The Black Dahlia* (1987), *The Big Nowhere* (1988), *L.A. Confidential* (1990), and *White Jazz* (1993).

In the 1970s and 1980s there was a resurgence of interest in the hard-boiled private detective as many distinguished series had their start. Represented in *DLB 226* are Joseph Hansen's insurance investigator Dave Brandstetter, the first gay hard-boiled hero, whose first case is recorded in *Fadeout* (1970); Bill Pronzini's Nameless detective, in *The Snatch* (1971); Joe Gores's series featuring the detectives of the Daniel Kearny Associates agency, in *Dead Skip* (1972); James Crumley's Milo Milodragovitch, in *The Wrong Case* (1975), and his C. W. Sughrue, in *The Last Good Kiss* (1978); Lawrence Block's Matthew Scudder, in *Sins of the Father* (1976); Loren D. Estleman's Amos Walker, in *Motor City Blue* (1980); and James Lee Burke's Dave Robicheaux, in *Neon Rain* (1987). Both Block's and Burke's detectives are alcoholics, whose twelve-step programs are incorporated into their personal codes. The reading public for hard-boiled fiction has broadened considerably as women have become avid readers, being particularly drawn to female detectives such as Marcia Muller's Sharon McCone, who first appeared in *Edwin of the Iron Shoes* (1977) and Sue Grafton's Kinsey Millhone, in *"A" Is for Alibi* (1982). All of these series, with the exception of Hansen's Brandstetter, who apparently died of a heart attack at the end of *A Country of Old Men: The Last Dave Brandstetter Mystery* (1991), continued. The tradition of hard-boiled fiction shows no signs of weakening as the twenty-first century begins.

—*George Parker Anderson*

Acknowledgments

This book was produced by Bruccoli Clark Layman, Inc. Karen L. Rood is senior editor. George Parker Anderson was the in-house editor.

Production manager is Philip B. Dematteis.

Administrative support was provided by Ann M. Cheschi, Dawnca T. Williams, and Mary A. Womble.

Accountant is Kathy Weston. Accounting assistant is Amber L. Coker.

Copyediting supervisor is Phyllis A. Avant. Senior copyeditor is Thom Harman. The copyediting staff includes Brenda Carol Blanton, James Denton, Melissa D. Hinton, William Tobias Mathes, Jennifer S. Reid, and Nancy Smith. Freelance copyeditor is Rebecca Mayo.

Editorial associates are Margo Dowling and Richard K. Galloway.

Layout and graphics supervisor is Janet E. Hill. The graphics staff includes Karla Corley Brown and Zoe R. Cook.

Office manager is Kathy Lawler Merlette.

Photography editors are Charles Mims, Scott Nemzek, and Paul Talbot.

Digital photography supervisor is Joseph M. Bruccoli. Digital photographic copy work was performed by Zoe R. Cook and Abraham R. Layman.

SGML supervisor is Cory McNair. The SGML staff includes Tim Bedford, Linda Drake, Frank Graham, and Alex Snead.

Systems manager is Marie L. Parker.

Typesetting supervisor is Kathleen M. Flanagan. The typesetting staff includes Kimberly Kelly Brantley, Mark J. McEwan, Patricia Flanagan Salisbury, and Alison Smith. Freelance typesetters are Wanda Adams and Delores Plastow.

Walter W. Ross did library research. He was assisted by Steven Gross and the following librarians at the Thomas Cooper Library of the University of South Carolina: circulation department head Tucker Taylor; reference department head Virginia W. Weathers; Brette Barclay, Marilee Birchfield, Paul Cammarata, Gary Geer, Michael Macan, Tom Marcil, Rose Marshall, Sharon Verba; interlibrary loan department head John Brunswick; and Robert Arndt, Jo Cottingham, Hayden Battle, Barry Bull, Marna Hostetler, Nelson Rivera, Marieum McClary, and Erika Peake, interlibrary loan staff.

Dictionary of Literary Biography® • Volume Two Hundred Twenty-Six

American Hard-Boiled
Crime Writers

Dictionary of Literary Biography

Lawrence Block

(24 June 1938 –)

John L. Cobbs
Kutztown University

BOOKS: *Death Pulls a Doublecross* (New York: Fawcett, 1961); republished as *Coward's Kiss* (New York: Countryman, 1987);

Markham: The Case of the Pornographic Photos (New York: Belmont Books, 1961; London: Consul Press, 1965); republished as *You Could Call It Murder* (New York: Countryman, 1987);

Mona (New York: Fawcett, 1961; London: Muller, 1963); republished as *Sweet Slow Death* (New York: Berkley, 1986);

The Girl with the Long Green Heart (New York: Fawcett, 1965; London: Muller, 1967);

Swiss Shooting Talers and Medals, by Block and Delbert Ray Krause (Racine, Wis.: Whitman, 1965);

The Thief Who Couldn't Sleep (New York: Fawcett, 1966; Harpenden, U.K.: No Exit, 1996);

The Canceled Czech (New York: Fawcett, 1966; Harpenden, U.K.: No Exit, 1996);

Tanner's Twelve Swingers (New York: Fawcett, 1967; London: Coronet, 1968);

Two for Tanner (New York: Fawcett, 1967; Harpenden, U.K.: No Exit, 1997);

Deadly Honeymoon (New York: Macmillan, 1967; London: Hale, 1981);

Here Comes a Hero (New York: Fawcett, 1968);

Tanner's Tiger (New York: Fawcett, 1968; Harpenden, U.K.: No Exit, 1997);

After the First Death (New York: Macmillan, 1969; London: Hale, 1981);

The Specialists (New York: Fawcett, 1969; London: Hale, 1980);

Such Men Are Dangerous: A Novel of Violence, as Paul Kavanagh (New York: Macmillan, 1969; London: Hodder & Stoughton, 1971); republished, as Block (New York: Jove, 1985);

Lawrence Block at the time of publication of his 1998 novel Hit Man *(photograph by Sigrid Estrada)*

Me Tanner, You Jane (New York: Macmillan, 1970);

No Score, as Chip Harrison (New York: Fawcett, 1970);

Chip Harrison Scores Again, as Harrison (New York: Fawcett, 1971);

Ronald Rabbit Is a Dirty Old Man (New York: Geis, 1971);

Not Comin' Home to You, as Kavanagh (New York: Putnam, 1971; London: Hodder & Stoughton, 1976);

republished, as Block (New York: Countryman, 1986);

The Triumph of Evil, as Kavanagh (Cleveland: World, 1971; London: Hodder & Stoughton, 1972); republished, as Block (New York: Countryman, 1986);

Make Out with Murder, as Harrison (New York: Fawcett, 1974); republished as *Five Little Rich Girls,* as Block (London: Allison & Busby, 1984);

The Topless Tulip Caper, as Harrison (New York: Fawcett, 1975); republished, as Block (London: Allison & Busby, 1984);

The Sins of the Fathers (New York: Dell, 1976; London: Hale, 1979);

In the Midst of Death (New York: Dell, 1976; London: Hale, 1979);

Time to Murder and Create (New York: Dell, 1977; London: Hale, 1979);

Burglars Can't Be Choosers (New York: Random House, 1977; London: Hale, 1979);

The Burglar in the Closet (New York: Random House, 1979; London: Hale, 1980);

The Burglar Who Liked to Quote Kipling (New York: Random House, 1979; London: Hale, 1981);

Writing the Novel from Plot to Print (Cincinnati: Writer's Digest Books, 1979; London: Poplar Press, 1986);

Ariel (New York: Arbor House, 1980; London: Hale, 1981);

The Burglar Who Studied Spinoza (New York: Random House, 1981; London: Hale, 1982);

A Stab in the Dark (New York: Arbor House, 1981; London: Hale, 1982);

Real Food Places: A Guide to Restaurants That Serve Fresh, Wholesome Food, by Block and Cheryl Morrison (Emmaus, Pa.: Rodale, 1981);

Telling Lies for Fun and Profit: A Manual for Fiction Writers (New York: Arbor House, 1981);

Code of Arms, by Block and Harold King (New York: R. Marek, 1981);

Eight Million Ways to Die (New York: Arbor House, 1982; London: Hale, 1983);

The Burglar Who Painted Like Mondrian (New York: Arbor House, 1983; London: Gollancz, 1984);

Sometimes They Bite (New York, Arbor House, 1983);

Like a Lamb to Slaughter (New York: Arbor House, 1984);

When the Sacred Ginmill Closes (New York: Arbor House, 1986; London: Macmillan, 1987);

Write for Your Life (New York: Write for Your Life Seminars, 1986);

Into the Night, by Block and Cornell Woolrich (New York: Mysterious Press, 1987; London: Simon & Schuster, 1988);

Random Walk (New York: Tor, 1988);

Spider, Spin Me a Web: Lawrence Block on Writing Fiction (Cincinnati: Writer's Digest Books, 1988);

Out on the Cutting Edge (New York: Morrow, 1989; London: Orion, 1993);

A Ticket to the Boneyard (New York: Morrow, 1990; London: Orion, 1994);

A Dance at the Slaughterhouse (New York: Morrow, 1991; London: Orion, 1994);

The Perfect Murder: Five Great Mystery Writers Create the Perfect Crime, by Block and others, edited by Jack Hitt (New York: HarperCollins, 1991);

A Walk Among the Tombstones (New York: Morrow, 1992; London: Orion, 1993);

The Devil Knows You're Dead (New York: Morrow, 1993; London: Orion, 1994);

Some Days You Get the Bear (New York: Morrow, 1993);

A Long Line of Dead Men (New York: Morrow, 1994; London: Orion, 1995);

The Burglar Who Traded Ted Williams (New York: Dutton, 1994; Harpenden, U.K.: No Exit, 1994);

The Burglar Who Thought He Was Bogart (New York: Dutton, 1995; Harpenden, U.K.: No Exit, 1995);

The Burglar in the Library (New York: Dutton, 1997; Harpenden, U.K.: No Exit, 1997);

Even the Wicked (New York: Morrow, 1997; London: Orion, 1996);

Tanner on Ice (New York: Dutton, 1998; Harpenden, U.K.: No Exit, 1998);

Hit Man (New York: Morrow, 1998; London: Orion, 1998);

Everybody Dies (New York: Morrow, 1998; London: Orion, 1998);

Keller's Greatest Hits: Adventures in the Murder Trade (New York: Morrow, 1998);

The Collected Mystery Stories (London: Orion, 1999);

The Burglar in the Rye (New York: Dutton, 1999).

OTHER: "Keller's Choice," in *Murder on the Run* (New York: Berkley Prime Crime, 1998).

Lawrence Block is certainly one of the most—if not the most—prolific writers of detective fiction in the United States. He has published more than fifty novels, in addition to dozens of short stories, a detailed bimonthly newsletter on his life and writing, and extensive nonfiction articles, many of them on the craft of writing, including a widely read column for more than twenty years in *Writer's Digest.* Whereas most mystery writers would be grateful to have created a single enormously successful sleuth, Block is the originator of two best-selling series: the fourteen Matt Scudder novels have established his reputation in the hard-bitten, hard-drinking tradition of Dashiell Hammett and Raymond Chandler, while his nine novels of the "Burglar" series, featuring the whimsical "detective thief" Bernie Rhodenbarr in cat-and-mouse investigations among the rich, have overtones of the British tea-cozy school of polite detection. A third series of thriller novels, about hero Evan Tanner, who capitalizes on his bizarre inability to sleep to survive exotic adventures and overcome fearsome villains, has been less successful only by comparison.

Born to Jewish parents on 24 June 1938 in Buffalo, New York, Lawrence Block lived what he described in an unpublished August 1998 interview as a "normal childhood." He later wrote that he was unaware of "anything specifically Jewish" about his fiction. He attended prestigious Antioch College in Yellow Springs, Ohio, but left after a couple of years to work for a literary agency and pursue his interest in writing. He married Loretta Ann Kallett in 1960; they had two children, Amy Jo and Jill Diana.

Block recalls that his first story, written anonymously because of the censorship of the times, was about a college girl in New York who is trying to discover whether or not she is a lesbian. Before he was twenty, he had already begun cranking out "soft-core sex novels" for less than $1,000 apiece. He remembers the period fondly:

> With my first books, I was doing a novel a month for this paperback publisher, I suppose you would call it soft core porn now. They didn't give me any specifications or tell me what to write or anything. I just wrote. This was in the early 1960s, and it was a great training ground, because you could write virtually any kind of novel as long as it was erotic. I don't think any kind of training like that exists now because there is no more soft core porn. It's all hard core and there's no room for writing in hard core. These were just novels, essentially, with some pretty tame sex scenes scattered through them, and it was a very forgiving form. You could learn a lot. The first crime novel that I sold actually started out to be my monthly soft core book, but a couple of chapters in, I decided to write it as a suspense novel. I liked the feel of it.

Block wrote his potboilers under pen names such as Andrew Shaw, Sheldon Lord, and Jill Emerson, but no bibliography has been compiled of the dozens of paperbacks that he produced during his early years. He is adamant about not identifying his early hack writing: "I don't think the world missed any great literature for my having spent a couple of years writing crap. I wasn't really capable of writing anything very good." His first "serious" novel, *Mona* (1961), bears a strong resemblance to his pseudonymous work.

From 1961 through the early 1970s, Block mainly wrote formula fiction—mostly thrillers such as *Death Pulls a Doublecross* (1961), *Deadly Honeymoon* (1967), and

Dust jacket for Block's 1986 novel, the first to depict his detective character, Matt Scudder, as a recovering alcoholic

After the First Death (1969). Some of Block's novels in this period—notably those written under the pen name of Paul Kavanagh—rank with his later mysteries; two of the best are *The Specialists* (1969) and *Such Men Are Dangerous: A Novel of Violence* (1969), both of which anticipate in tone and style the Matt Scudder novels.

In 1966 Block published *The Thief Who Couldn't Sleep,* which he calls "the first book that was uniquely my own." It initiated a series of novels about Evan Tanner, a Korean War veteran whose brain injury makes it impossible for him to sleep. Hyperactive and glib to the point of aberration and fluent in virtually every major language of the world, Tanner is involved in a series of dramatic foreign intrigues. Within the context of the times in which they were written, the Tanner novels served as something of a parody of the enormously popular James Bond novels of Ian Fleming. Block described Tanner as a "border-jumping action-adventure hero" and moved him around the world more than Fleming did Bond.

Setting the tone for the series, *The Thief Who Couldn't Sleep,* in which Tanner must locate more than five hundred pounds of gold hidden during the Greek/Turkish War of 1922, features a gorgeous, buxom blond as well as an intelligence organization so secret that it is unnamed. *The Canceled Czech* (1966), perhaps the best of the Tanner books, is quite similar to the first. Again, Tanner is charged with a bizarre mission–he must kidnap a dying man in eastern Europe–during which he encounters a secret agency with a nameless chief and the obligatory blond. At one point he is roped into impersonating a rabble-rousing speaker at a neo-Nazi rally. Block published what was apparently the last of the Tanner novels, *Me Tanner, You Jane,* in 1970 before moving on to more serious detective fiction. Although he wrote twenty years later in his personal newsletter that "I would hate to have to write a book about Tanner now. I've grown since then," he returned to the character in *Tanner on Ice* (1998), a reprise that coincided with the republication of the earlier novels in the series by Signet.

In the early 1970s Block wrote several light, somewhat erotic, caper novels about "perennial adolescent" Chip Harrison, "coming of age." Block "liked the voice" he created in the novels, but he realized "there was no way to have him come of age forever." In the later books, which Block describes as "a sort of Nero Wolfe pastiche," Chip works for a private detective.

Block was struggling with new forms, new personae–and himself. It was a difficult time in his life. In a candid entry he wrote for the *Contemporary Authors Autobiography,* he remarked, "I suppose what I was doing then was falling apart." His marriage ended in divorce in 1973, and he was having serious trouble writing for the first time in his career: "most of what I began ended abruptly fifty or sixty pages in when I found it impossible to think of a reason why any of the characters should go on, or anything for them to do if they did." He left New York and lived for a time in a hotel in Los Angeles; he then traveled peripatetically back across the country before finally settling in Greenwich Village in New York at the end of 1976.

Before he left New York in 1973, Block had written the first three novels of the series that was to win him acclaim as one of the masters of American hard-boiled mystery fiction–*The Sins of the Fathers* (1976), *In the Midst of Death* (1976), and *Time to Murder and Create* (1977). Although Block was a well-established writer, his publisher delayed bringing out the books because of market conditions. Although his personal problems had no effect on his craftsmanship, Block may have used the feelings of bitterness, cynicism, and disillusionment he experienced in the early 1970s in creating his detective. Matt Scudder, an alcoholic and a dropout from the

New York police, "does favors" for friends that take him to the seamiest and most depraved corners of New York City. His own morals are hardly pristine, for he indulges in casual affairs and shows a willingness to bribe and lie to crack a case. He has no qualms about taking the law into his own shaky hands.

Of all the detectives in modern American mystery writing, Scudder is among the most hard-boiled and the most damaged. His fundamental decency combined with his knowledge of the seamiest side of life give him a flexible tolerance of, and ability to deal with, all but the most depraved characters. In the early novels Scudder is barely functional; working out of his fleabag hotel room he shuffles from moral cesspool to moral cesspool and from bar to bar, often in the company of prostitutes and gangsters. His best friend is a hit man and his girlfriend, Elaine, is a sympathetic but convincing prostitute still turning tricks for "respectable" clients. All of the novels in the series take their tone from Scudder's narrative persona, and his lean first-person narration is reminiscent of the dark broodings of Chandler's Philip Marlowe. "For clean close-to-the-bone prose," claims Martin Cruz Smith, "the line goes from Dashiell Hammett to James M. Cain to Lawrence Block. He's that good."

In the first chapter of *The Sins of the Father* Scudder is shown as chronically drunk, jobless, and living in a cheap hotel. He does not have an official detective license and appears to have little future of any kind. He says that he has "lost the faith. . . . What it amounted to is that I found out that I didn't want to be a cop anymore. Or a husband, or a father. Or a productive member of society." Scudder's grim rejection of social "goods" is a consequence of his having accidentally killed a little girl in a barroom shootout when he was a cop. Although he was in no way responsible, the cloud of his bitter guilt hangs over all the books of the series, and he sees the world as a theater of brutal and random violence from which God, if not dead, has completely decamped.

The Sins of the Fathers established the theme of moral ambiguity for the series. The father of a murdered prostitute, an old friend of Scudder's, persuades him to reopen the investigation of his daughter's death. When the detective does, he unveils a sordid morass of hypocritical religion and parental betrayal. Ultimately, Scudder effectively passes a judgment upon a perverse minister who has committed murder and attempted to pin the crime on his own son. He deliberately forces the man to commit suicide rather than turn him over to the police; Scudder personally hands him the lethal pills. Like all the Scudder novels to follow, *The Sins of the Fathers* depicts a world where conventional morality is often inverted–a world in which whores and grifters and gangsters may not be as bad as they seem, nor priests and politicians and doctors as good.

The other Scudder novels published in the 1970s maintained the detective's character and psychology, if anything intensifying the grim vision of a lost man, decent but flawed, in a plodding struggle with a corrupt world. In the second novel in the series, *In the Midst of Death,* Scudder is involved in a case in which an honest cop is framed for a murder rap because he collaborates in a special prosecutor's investigation of dishonesty within the New York Police Department. In *Time to Murder and Create,* Scudder probes the ugly murder of a petty thief and blackmailer. He discovers that the sordid trail leads to much more "respectable" people—among them a prominent candidate for the governorship of New York, who turns out to be a pederast and an accomplice to murder.

The year 1977 was a watershed for Block, for not only did he begin to put his personal life back together but also his career began to take its mature form as he initiated the Bernie Rhodenbarr series, which serves as a wry literary counterpoint to his hard-boiled novels. Although Block is reticent to discuss the details of his personal life, he evidently had to deal with his own battle with alcohol, as he asserts that "In early April of 1977 something monumental happened. I stopped drinking." A similar act of will later became central to his development of the Matt Scudder character, who after moving toward irrevocable alcoholism, eventually hits bottom and then finds a rough salvation in the rooms of Alcoholics Anonymous (AA). Block, however, put the Scudder series on hold for a time as he began the "Burglar" novels, publishing *Burglars Can't Be Choosers* (1977), *The Burglar in the Closet* (1979), *The Burglar Who Liked to Quote Kipling* (1979), and *The Burglar Who Studied Spinoza* (1981) before his fourth Scudder novel.

A hero detective who is also a criminal, Rhodenbarr is a deliberate contradiction in terms—the focus of a series that is comic where the Scudder series is serious, delicate rather than brutal, and clever rather than profound. The effete Rhodenbarr trades in rare books, and keeps company with an even more effete lesbian groomer of poodles, Carolyn Kaiser, who is intrigued by Bernie's lockpicking and housebreaking background and becomes his partner in crime. There is no implication that there might be a sexual relationship between them; in fact, there is little development of sexuality in the "Burglar" novels at all. Where Scudder slogs through the slums, Rhodenbarr hobnobs with the social and intellectual elite, whom he may protect or from whom he may steal, depending on his whims and circumstances.

Dust jacket for Block's 1991 novel, in which Scudder's investigation leads him to the pornographic-movie industry in New York City

In the same year that Block published *The Burglar Who Studied Spinoza,* a novel involving rare books and arcane knowledge, he brought out the brutal Scudder novel *A Stab in the Dark* (1981). Hired to investigate the nine-year-old ice-pick murder of a pregnant woman, Scudder uncovers a series of similar killings. In this novel Block shows his detective beginning to recognize the dangerous morass of his alcoholism. Paired with Elaine, a woman who also loves to drink, Scudder sees the possibility of sobriety in AA but still cannot commit himself to the program.

In 1982 Block published the fifth Scudder novel, *Eight Million Ways to Die,* in which the detective solves the murder of a prostitute. Block considered the novel to be "more effectively executed than anything I'd written previously." *Eight Million Ways to Die* is distinguished by brilliant sketches of Hell's Kitchen and other seedy areas of New York City, as well as a pervasive sense of violence. While some of the violence in the novel is directly related to Scudder's immediate case, much of it is peripheral to the plot, presented as detail in a graphic portrait of a brutal world subject to savagery, often without apparent causality. Every few pages Scudder describes some horrible happening that characterizes life in the city: an old man salvages a discarded television set that blows up and kills his wife when he plugs it in; a team of father-and-son pornographers precipitate a shoot-out in which a young mother's head is blown off; a man kills his neighbor to protest a dog lifting its leg on his property. It is, as Landon C. Burns notes in his 1996 essay, "a world of random violence, but it is also one of ambiguity and uncertainty as well." In addition to the story of Scudder's investigation, Block also focuses on the detective's struggle with his alcoholism. The novel ends with Scudder making a fateful declaration at an AA meeting, "I'm Matt, and I'm an alcoholic." *Eight Million Ways to Die* won an Edgar Award from the Mystery Writers of America and a Shamus Award from the Private Eye Writers of America.

For all of the first five novels of the series, from *The Sins of the Fathers* to *Eight Million Ways to Die,* Scudder's alcoholism was a central theme. Heavy drinking has often been characteristic of hard-boiled detectives in American fiction, and there have been several who bordered on outright dipsomania, at least in terms of the amount they seemed to drink in their novels. With Sam Spade, Philip Marlowe, and most of the rest, though, heavy drinking has been mainly used to illustrate the detective's toughness and to indicate his identification with the brutal underworld through which he moves. Often, the sleuth's ability to outdrink his enemies—and his friends—is a talent that enables him to survive a tough world. Scudder's drinking, however, is both a disability and a reflection of his damaged psychology—part of the "dropping out" by which he has abandoned his family and his job and accepted a life on the fringes of a rotten society.

So important is Scudder's alcoholism, in fact, that it constitutes the major leitmotif binding the early novels together. As Block remarks, "In a sense, all five books constituted one big novel which was resolved . . . when Scudder came to terms with his drinking problem. With that ghost laid, what could drive him? His catharsis behind him, the man's fictional d'etre had no raison." The author considered ending the series with *Eight Million Ways to Die* and publically declared in 1982 that he had written his last Matt Scudder novel. Four eventful years passed before Block returned to the Scudder character in a novel. In 1983 Block married a second time, to Lynne Wood, and published his fifth Bernie Rhodenbarr novel, *The Burglar Who Painted Like Mondrian.* Block then published two short story collections, *Sometimes They Bite* (1983) and *Like a Lamb to Slaughter* (1984), which include some Scudder stories.

Once he again started to write Scudder novels, Block reconceived his detective as a recovering alcoholic.

Block's ongoing use of AA meetings in the novels following *Eight Million Ways to Die* is a key to understanding the thematic dynamics of the later books—and, retrospectively, the first five as well. Beyond having Scudder frequently drop in to AA meetings—often, apparently on a daily basis—Block does little to "preach" or even overtly to present the philosophy of Alcoholics Anonymous, which demands personal commitment to the AA program and to the 12-step recovery program by which addicts are led from initial acknowledgment of their addiction, through steps promoting psychological, social, and spiritual regeneration, to "carrying the AA message" to the still-suffering alcoholic and the world at large. There is, however, some limited discussion of the philosophy of the program that occurs naturally when Scudder meets characters through AA.

Although Block does not emphasize Scudder's by-the-numbers adherence to the 12-step process, the detective's progress through the various stages of recovery is recognizable in the novels following *Eight Million Ways to Die.* In keeping with the AA slogans stressing acceptance ("Life on life's terms") and "letting go," Scudder gradually moves beyond the despair and cynicism of his past. Respecting the stress on anonymity in AA—the recovering alcoholic's participation is a private process, shared only with fellow program members—Block tells the reader almost nothing of what actually happens in the meetings at which Scudder spends so much time in the later novels.

The first of the "recovery" Scudder novels is *When the Sacred Ginmill Closes* (1986), a book which, ironically, is "just soaked in booze," as one critic put it. The narrative voice is that of Scudder a decade after his last drink. Throughout the novel he remembers the sad world of his drinking days and the depths of his drunkenness. There is nothing romantic about the way Block paints the barroom world through which Scudder plods in this novel to solve a series of bar-related crimes—a robbery, blackmail, and the murder of the wife of a barfly friend. The sights and smells of the dirty, smoky rooms and the sordid lives men lead there come right off the page. After *Eight Million Ways to Die* Block was getting even more positive critical acclaim, and the reviewer in *The New York Times* called *When the Sacred Ginmill Closes* a masterpiece: "what is most impressive here, as usual in this series, is how far the plot can stray from suspensefulness without losing the reader's interest. . . . [The novel] absorbs New York city bar life so atmospheric that you can almost smell the beer in the woodwork."

Following the pattern established in *When the Sacred Ginmill Closes,* Block in subsequent novels shows

Scudder, recovering from alcoholism and still attending AA meetings, investigating ugly murders with roots in the past. Plodding through the mean streets of New York he digs out the criminals, usually men with a psychotic bent and vicious sadism in their character. *Out on the Cutting Edge* (1989) traces Scudder's search for a missing young Indiana girl, who came to New York to be a star, among the drug addicts of the slums of Hell's Kitchen. In *A Ticket to the Boneyard* (1990) Scudder is nearly killed by a crazed, vengeful criminal he apprehended years before, who has sworn to murder not only Scudder but also his friends. *A Dance at the Slaughterhouse* (1991) is the story of Scudder's odyssey through the pornography and sex houses of New York, where "snuff" films (pornographic films in which the characters are actually killed for the perverse pleasure of the viewers) are made, to find a rapist who has killed an heiress. Widely critically acclaimed, this book won the Edgar Award for the best mystery novel of the year.

Scudder's personal sense of justice and morality is a theme Block explores throughout the series. In *A Walk Among the Tombstones* (1992)—a novel the reviewer for *The Washington Times* called "Well-written, well-plotted, and very nasty"—Scudder is hired by criminals, a heroin trafficker and a counterfeiter, to hunt the murderers of women they care about. Preying on those who out of fear have no recourse to the legal system, the culprits are a vicious pair who kill for fun—torturing and violating women physically in a variety of hideous ways before killing them. At the end of the novel, Scudder turns the killer over to the man whose wife he tortured, raped, and killed, knowing that the vengeful husband is likely to reciprocate in kind, as he does. In *The Devil Knows You're Dead* (1993) Scudder tries to vindicate a mentally handicapped vet accused of murder. Despite his deepening commitment to his friend Elaine, he has an affair with the murdered man's widow.

Block continued to switch his attentions between the Rhodenbarr and Scudder series. In 1994, the same year he published *The Burglar Who Traded Ted Williams,* one of the cleverest novels of that series, Block also brought out *A Long Line of Dead Men*—a juxtaposition that vividly shows the light and the dark sides of Block's writing. In *A Long Line of Dead Men,* one of Block's most tightly woven plots, a club of randomly selected men hire Scudder to find out why so many of them are dying young. Block published *The Burglar Who Thought He Was Bogart* (1995) and *The Burglar in the Library* (1997) before returning to his hard-boiled series. In *Even the Wicked* (1997) Scudder matches wits with a serial killer who advertises his murders before he commits them. In the fourteenth novel of the series, *Everybody Dies*

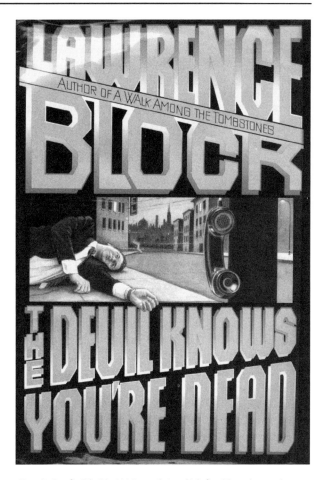

Dust jacket for Block's 1993 novel, in which Scudder takes on the case of a mentally handicapped veteran accused of murder

(1998), Scudder is married and on the verge of respectability when his old thug friend Mick Ballou asks for his help in finding out who killed a couple of his henchmen.

It is not, of course, just Block's effective handling of Scudder's alcoholism and recovery that makes these novels worthwhile. Aside from his dipsomania, Scudder is a fascinating character. Despite his rough edges, there is a decency in his ongoing battle with the New York underworld that belies his occasional brutality and the apparently callous cynicism with which he defends himself from the atrocities he encounters. In the course of the series, Scudder slowly forgives himself for the killing of the little girl years before and shows flashes of redeeming virtue. One of the most idiosyncratic and singular characteristics of his behavior is his habit of occasionally walking into a randomly selected church and stuffing a chunk of his earnings into the poor box—an enigmatic offering from a man who has no ties to any church or religion.

The supporting characters in the Scudder series are also notable. Under Scudder's influence, Elaine moves out of the life she knew as a prostitute and eventually opens a small business; she and Scudder move awkwardly but firmly toward commitment and eventually marriage. It is representative of the realism of the books that he accepts her as she is and was, without muddying their relationship with romantic expectations. Another important local color character is Mick Ballou, a hulking, brutal Irish former gangster still on the shady side of the law. Originally a drinking buddy of Scudder's in all-night binges, as each matched the other shot-for-shot, in the later novels Ballou drinks whiskey till dawn while Scudder drinks seltzer; however, they still reminisce about old times and go to the "Butcher's Mass" for night workers at the local Catholic church as the sun rises.

Another character who enlivens most of the books in the series is T. J., whom Scudder met in his police days. A hustler and a jive-talking, street-wise black hipster, T. J. can drop his "rap" and put on his "Brooks Brothers voice" to con targets on the phone. His specialty is picking up "evil" information on "The Deuce"—West Forty-second Street—one of the sleaziest sections of the city but a rich information resource for an observant and clever young man who can change personae like a chameleon. As critics have noted, the city of New York is also virtually a character in these novels, and Hell's Kitchen, the Bowery, West Forty-second Street, and the Upper East Side come alive through Scudder's eyes. Block combines sharp dialogue with vivid, sometimes lyrical, descriptive passages of New York in all its diversity.

Whether Lawrence Block will write any more Matt Scudder novels remains to be seen, but the series as it now stands is certainly one of the significant exempla of the hard-boiled genre. No other hard-boiled writer has more thoroughly delineated a gritty urban degeneracy than has Block in his clear-eyed depiction of the underside of New York that is Scudder's milieu. In his 1981 book *Telling Lies for Fun and Profit*, one of several on the craft of writing, Block includes "A Writer's Prayer," in which he asserts "that a major element of writing honestly lies in respecting the reader. Please, Lord, don't ever let me hold my audience in contempt." No serious critic of the Matthew Scudder books would suggest that he ever has.

Interviews:

Lawrence Block and Ernie Bulow, *After Hours: Conversations with Lawrence Block* (Albuquerque: University of New Mexico Press, 1995);

Edward J. McFadden, *Pirate Writings: Tales of Fantasy, Mystery and Science Fiction*, no. 7 (Summer 1995);

Adam Meyer, "Still Out on the Cutting Edge: An Interview with the Mystery Man: Lawrence Block," *Pirate Writings: Tales of Fantasy, Mystery and Science Fiction*, no. 7 (Summer 1995);

Clair E. White, "Talking Mystery with Lawrence Block," *Writers Write: The Internet Writing Journal* (October 1999).

References:

Landon C. Burns, "Matthew Scudder's Moral Ambiguity," *Clues: A Journal of Detection,* 17 (Fall/Winter 1996): 19–32;

Donna Casella, "The Matt Scudder Series: The Saga of an Alcoholic Hardboiled Detective," *Clues: A Journal of Detection,* 14 (Fall/Winter 1993): 31–50;

Jerome Charyn, *The New Mystery* (New York: Dutton, 1993);

Stephen King, "No Cats: An Appreciation of Lawrence Block and Matt Scudder," in *The Sins of the Fathers,* by Block (Arlington Heights, Ill.: Dark Harvest, 1992).

Papers:

Lawrence Block's papers are at the University of Oregon in Eugene.

Howard Browne
(15 April 1908 – 28 October 1999)

Marcia B. Dinneen
Bridgewater State College

BOOKS: *Warrior of the Dawn; the Adventures of Tharn* (Chicago: Reilly & Lee, 1943);

Halo in Blood, as John Evans (Indianapolis: Bobbs-Merrill, 1946; Harpenden, U.K.: No Exit Press, 1988);

If You Have Tears, as Evans (New York: Mystery House, 1947); republished as *Lona* (New York: Lion, 1952);

Halo for Satan, as Evans (Indianapolis: Bobbs-Merrill, 1948; London: Boardman, 1949);

Halo in Brass, as Evans (Indianapolis: Bobbs-Merrill, 1949; London: Foulsham, 1951);

Thin Air (New York: Simon & Schuster, 1954; London: Gollancz, 1955);

Return of Tharn (Providence: Grandon, 1956);

The Taste of Ashes (New York: Simon & Schuster, 1957; London: Gollancz, 1958);

The Paper Gun (Missoula, Mont.: Dennis McMillan, 1985);

Pork City (New York: St. Martin's Press, 1988; London: W. H. Allen, 1988);

Scotch on the Rocks (New York: St. Martin's Press, 1991);

Incredible Ink (Tucson: Dennis McMillan, 1997).

PRODUCED SCRIPTS:
MOTION PICTURES
Portrait of a Mobster, based on the novel by Harry Grey, Warner Bros., 1961;

The St. Valentine's Day Massacre, TCF/Los Altos (Corman), 1967;

Bootleggers, Howco Productions, 1974;

Capone, TCF/Santa Fe (Corman), 1975.

TELEVISION
Cheyenne, ABC, 1956–1963;

"Seven Against the Wall," *Playhouse 90,* CBS, 1956;

Colt .45, ABC, 1957–1959;

77 Sunset Strip, ABC, 1958–1964;

Asphalt Jungle, ABC, 1961;

The Virginian, NBC, 1962–1970;

Destry, ABC, 1964;

Howard Browne

Mission Impossible, CBS, 1966–1973–episodes written by Browne include "Cat's Paw" (1970), "Stone Pillow" (1971), and "Leona" and "Boomerang" (1972);

Mannix, CBS, 1967–1968;

The Bold Ones, NBC, 1969–1972;

Alias Smith and Jones, ABC, 1971–1973;

Longstreet, script consultant, ABC, 1971–1972;

Banacek, NBC, 1972–1974–including "No Sign of the Cross," script by Browne and Robert Presnell Jr., 1972.

SELECTED PERIODICAL PUBLICATIONS–
UNCOLLECTED: "Hard Guy," as H. B. Carleton, *Amazing Stories* (November 1942);

"Planet of No Return," as Wilbur S. Peacock, *Planet Stories* (Winter 1942);

"They Gave Him Rope," as Carleton, *Fantastic Adventures* (March 1943);

"Star Sheppard," as William Brengle, *Fantastic Adventures* (August 1943);

"Halo Round My Dead," as John Evans, *Mammoth Detective* (February 1945);

"The Man from Yesterday," as Lee Francis, *Fantastic Adventures* (August 1948);

"The Seventh Bottle," as Ivar Jorgensen, *Fantastic Stories* (August 1954);

"A Night on Hell Street," *Rogue for Men* (June 1956);

"A Profit Without Honor," *Amazing Science Fiction Stories*, 58 (May 1984): 71–81;

"Adventures in Hollywood, or Life on the Cutting Room Floor," *Mystery Scene*, 3 (1987).

Howard Browne, who also wrote under several pen names, is principally known for his hard-boiled mystery novels featuring private investigator Paul Pine. Pine is typical of the hard-boiled hero with his terse wisecracks, cynical attitude, and tough guy, man-of-action demeanor. Browne also wrote an enormous amount of pulp fiction, superhero novels, and screenplays for motion pictures and television.

Howard Carleton Browne was born in Omaha, Nebraska, on 15 April 1908, the only child of George Browne, a bakery owner who died before his son was born, and Rose Carlton Browne, a schoolteacher. He grew up in Arapahoe and Lincoln. Browne told Bill Pronzini in *Twentieth Century Crime and Mystery Writers* (1991) that while his high-school teachers were "extolling the virtues and values of reading the classics," he was "out behind the barn," reading *Flynn's Detective Weekly.*

In his 1978 interview with Caleb A. Lewis, Browne said that at age seventeen he "realized that formal schooling was interfering with my education" and dropped out of school. He hitchhiked to Chicago to spend a weekend seeing Babe Ruth and the Yankees play the White Sox and stayed in the city for the next twenty-four years. Recalling his attraction to Chicago, Browne told critic David A. Bowman, "I fell in love with that town the way you fall in love with a woman." Browne held several jobs, including waiting on tables in a tuberculosis sanatorium, laboring in a steel mill, and putting eggs into cartons at a produce company. In 1929 he settled into a job as credit manager for a chain of furniture stores and in 1931 married Esther Levy. They had two children: Allen Myles, born 1932, and Sue Ann, born 1939.

Browne hated his job as a manager. As he recalled in the autobiographical "A Profit Without Honor," published in the May 1984 issue of *Amazing Stories,* he turned to writing fiction after "five years of repossessing beds from under sick women." In 1933 Browne wrote four short stories and sold them to the *Chicago Daily News* for $15 apiece. All that Browne remembered about these stories is the name of one, "Hotel Service." The editor suggested that he write short fiction for the pulps; instead, Browne decided to write a novel. As a child, Browne had loved Tarzan books; his first novel was *Warrior of the Dawn; the Adventures of Tharn* (1943), a prehistory adventure story in the manner of Edgar Rice Burroughs. The continuing adventures of Tharn were originally published in three parts in *Amazing Stories,* beginning with the October 1948 issue. These stories were republished as the book *Return of Tharn* (1956).

While Browne attempted to get his novel published, he tried writing some short detective stories in the style made popular by *Black Mask* magazine. In 1941 he sent two stories to *Mammoth Detective,* a new magazine published by Ziff-Davis that was then located in Chicago. The publisher Bernard Davis invited Browne to his office, commended his writing, and offered him a job editing *Mammoth Detective.* Browne accepted immediately. From 1941 through 1956, with a break of a few years, Browne edited several other magazines for Ziff-Davis including: *Amazing Stories, Fantastic Adventures, Mammoth Mystery, Mammoth Western,* and *South Sea Stories.* After work, Browne wrote his own pulp stories under various pseudonyms and on a variety of subjects. Of particular interest, in view of his later work, were a series of four detective stories, written as William Brengle, about a character named Lafayette Muldoon. Muldoon is more a businessman than a detective, and his character lacks development. Like many other writers, Browne used his work for the pulps to hone his craft; lessons learned through Muldoon were applied to the realization of Paul Pine. The first Muldoon story is "Tavern in the Town," published in the August 1943 issue of *Mammoth Detective.* This story and the other three are included in Browne's collection of short stories, *Incredible Ink* (1997).

Browne's entire concept of what constitutes good detective writing changed after he read Raymond Chandler's *Farewell My Lovely* (1940). Browne told Bowman that Chandler wrote "like I had been trying to write and didn't know how." Browne created his own "Philip Marlowe" in Paul Pine, who first appeared in "Halo in Blood" in the May 1946 issue of *Mammoth Detective.* He expanded what was a shorter version of the novel into *Halo in Blood* (1946). Because the novel was to be published by Bobbs-Merrill, a rival publishing company, Browne used one of his pen names, John Evans. Coincidentally, years later Browne came across an obscure pulp story by Chandler, "No Crime in the

Mountains" (1941), which featured a private-eye hero named John Evans.

Halo in Blood introduced Browne's Chicago-based private detective Paul Pine, modeled after a wisecracking skip tracer Browne knew from his credit-manager days named Paul Prye. In talking to Bowman in 1986, Browne voiced his displeasure with the work, describing his first detective novel as "pure imitation Chandler" with its "forced wisecracks and an ersatz toughness." Browne also said the novel suffered from "overplotting" with its three major plotlines, one stretching over a twenty-five-year period. Nevertheless, readers responded enthusiastically to the hard-nosed Pine, a thirty-one-year-old former investigator with the state attorney's office with a dent in his nose, a chip on his shoulder, and a ready wit.

Similarities to Chandler's Marlowe are readily apparent. Like Marlowe, Pine has a shabby office, a penchant for using his fists, and a cynical attitude toward the "law"—not the concept of justice but the individuals in the legal system who too often lose sight of truth. Pine and Marlowe are essentially lonely men; both invariably come to the aid of ladies in distress, but love relationships do not work out. Like Chandler, Browne uses the first-person-narrative voice of his detective to comment on the world; both writers report the decay of their respective cities, Los Angeles and Chicago, and the demoralization of the citizens. In the course of Browne's series Chicago and its people become ever more corrupt.

Browne in *Halo in Blood* sets the standard for subsequent Paul Pine novels with his crisp writing and quirky descriptions. He often creates effective similes, as when Pine describes a Packard as a car with "eighty-five-hundred dollar's worth of custom-built metal and plush and plate glass. Calling it a car would be the same as calling Buckingham Palace a home." The *Dictionary of American Slang* (1967) includes eighty-six quotes from Browne's first three Pine novels, *Halo in Blood, Halo for Satan* (1948), and *Halo in Brass* (1949). Examples include Pine's designation of the twelve ministers in *Halo in Blood* as "harp polishers" and the funeral as a "cold-meat party." In *Halo for Satan* license plates are referred to as "pads" in the sentence "The job [automobile] was wearing California pads," and "plaster" stands for a tail or shadow: "I went after him. He probably knew he had a plaster by this time." *Halo in Brass* includes references to narcotics as a "deck of nose candy" and to a bar as a "grog-mill."

The first Pine novel includes two physical descriptions of the detective. In giving his qualifications to his new client John Sandmark, Pine states:

Dust jacket for Browne's 1988 novel, based on the murder of Chicago Tribune *reporter Jake Lingle during the Prohibition era*

I'm thirty-one, five feet eleven, one hundred and seventy pounds. The dent in the bridge of my nose came from high-school football. I was an investigator in the State's Attorney's office until a change in administration gave me a new boss. He had a nephew who needed a job. I went into business for myself about a year ago.

Another view of Pine comes through the eyes of femme fatale Leona Sandmark, his client's stepdaughter, who sees more of the inner man and in essence defines a hard-boiled dectective:

You've got a hard finish. . . . But I don't believe you are quite so hard underneath it. Perhaps that finish is there because you've seen too much of the wrong side of people. You go in for crisp speech and a complete lack of emotion. In a way you're playing a part . . . and it's not always an attractive part. Yet there's plenty of strength to you, and a kind of hard-bitten code of ethics. A woman could find a lot of things in you that no other man would give her . . . Besides, you're rather good- looking in the lean, battered sort of way that all sensible women find so attractive in a man.

As in subsequent Paul Pine novels, *Halo in Blood* combines various seemingly unrelated plotlines into a tightly knit whole. The story begins with Pine trying to avoid getting a speeding ticket. Attempting to hide himself in a funeral procession, Pine becomes an uninvited mourner at a funeral for a John Doe that, strangely, has twelve clergymen officiating. The casket is described in Pine's typically understated, terse style as "one of these cheap pine black boxes that run about fifty bucks and aren't worth more than ten." Although it seems that the funeral has no connection to Pine's current job–John Sandmark hired him to prevent the marriage of Leona to the shady Jerry Marlin–the identity of John Doe becomes central to the plot. Another plotline concerns another case Pine is working on that supposedly involves a kidnapping. Pine is to deliver the ransom and later discovers that he has been set up and has risked his life for $25,000 in counterfeit bills. The conclusion of the novel ties the different strands of the plot together: John Doe is identified; Leona Sandmark commits suicide; and Pine exposes a cop who murdered a man twenty-five years ago.

In *Halo in Blood,* as in the subsequent novels, Pine is a poor judge of women; he gets "sapped" on the head at least once; and he has to contend with several dead bodies. In this first Pine novel, although still hung up on an unidentified lost love, Pine falls for the beautiful socialite Leona. He does not, however, let his feelings for her interfere with his decision to turn her in to the police for murder. Pine uses his fists, but he does not resort to violence except in self-defense–he is not a killer. Although the novels have a heavy body count, the murders are not portrayed graphically. Details are minimal; the "whodunit" aspect of the crime is more important than how it was done. In *Halo in Blood* there are six murders, including that of a watchman shot in San Diego twenty-five years previous to the action of the novel; John Doe and Kenneth Clyne are beaten to death with a blackjack; Jerry Marlin is shot, as are C. L. Baird and John Sandmark. A final violent death is the suicide of Leona Sandmark.

The endings of each novel are reminiscent of English drawing-room mysteries, with all the suspects gathered together to hear Pine reveal the killer. Once the main mystery is solved, there is a double twist in the final chapter, exposing an additional murderer or a secret identity. In *Halo in Blood* Pine discovers that Leona has used C. L. Baird to murder Marlin and Clyne and then shot him. In *Halo for Satan* it is revealed that Bishop McManus, who hired Pine, is a murderer and an imposter. Also characteristic of Pine novels is the setting in Chicago, complete with wind, traffic, and gangsters, some of whom are fictional while others are thinly disguised portraits of actual Chicago "hoods."

In his 26 May 1946 review in *The New York Times* Isaac Anderson described *Halo in Blood* as "a tough yarn about a tough detective." In the *The Saturday Review* of 25 May 1946 it was labeled a "super-toughie." The reviewer for the 25 May issue of the *Springfield Republican* stated, "If you like a funeral with 12 ministers for a starter . . . this one is for you."

If You Have Tears is not a Pine novel, nor is it set in Chicago. Bowman describes its genesis: before *Halo in Blood* was published, a fan walked into Browne's office at Ziff-Davis and said, "I just read a short story in *Mammoth Detective* called 'Halo Round My Dead' by John Evans. I want Evans to turn it into a book." Browne told the fan that he was Evans and said the story was as long as it needed to be. However, when the fan handed Browne a check for $1,000 and asked, "Can you get it to sixty thousand words?," Browne replied, "I certainly can." The expanded story became *If You Have Tears* (1947), Browne's third novel.

The book is about California banker Larry Sungail, who has worked his way up from delivering mail to being considered for promotion to branch manager. It is also about the making of a killer. When Sungail becomes involved with his beautiful secretary Lona Kennedy, the straitlaced banker turns first to embezzling money from the bank and then to the callous murder of his wife for her life insurance, which he needs to cover up the missing funds.

The planning and execution of the crime appears ingenious as Sungail takes advantage of the presence in his neighborhood of a harmless vagrant, commonly known at St. Peter. Although Sungail seems to have thought of everything, he did not consider the possibility that while he assumed the disguise of St. Peter, complete with Bible, the real St. Peter would be jailed in another county for vagrancy. Sungail is arrested, breaks out of jail, and goes to Lona; he murders Lona when she informs him that she never loved him, only his money. The novel concludes with a final irony: As part of his disguise, Sungail had used a small case to look like the Bible St. Peter always carried. If he had looked inside the case, which he had found alongside the road, he would have discovered cash from a bank robbery, more than enough to cover up his embezzlement.

Once *Halo in Blood* was published, Browne was so pleased with the critical and popular reception that he "developed delusions of grandeur" and took a two-year sabbatical from his job as magazine editor to work freelance and, as he wrote in the foreword to *Halo in Brass,* "damned near starved to death." The publisher offered Browne a contract and a $1,000 advance on his next book, but only if he completed it in time for their spring 1948 list. Looking for a change of scene to write the novel, Browne moved to Burbank, California, with his family. By the time the move was complete, he had only five weeks to write the novel.

Starting from scratch, without the faintest idea of a plot, Browne searched his memory for a starting point. As he told Bowman, he remembered an evening spent in a Chicago restaurant with a group of friends when someone asked, "What would be the most valuable thing you could hold in one hand?" Browne's answer was a manuscript written by Jesus Christ, which became the focus of his fourth novel. *Halo for Satan* was completed within the deadline, but Browne said in the foreword to *Halo in Brass* that the experience "came close to ending my marriage" and resulted in a bad case of writer's block that took months to break. One positive result of this pressure of the deadline was Browne's development of a "gimmick" for the ending where the killer is, seemingly, someone impossible to suspect. Neither Pine nor the reader has the slightest suspicion that Bishop McManus, the client, is an imposter and a murderer.

In *Halo for Satan* Pine is called in by Bishop McManus to negotiate the purchase of an Aramaic manuscript, allegedly written by Christ. The price is $25 million. From the beginning the language of the novel reflects Pine's insight into people and Browne's effective descriptive writing: the secretary at the rectory "worked up a smile that was bankrupt before it was born," and the bishop's desk has "a bronze ashtray big enough to bathe a camel in."

In the search for Raymond Wirtz, the paleographer who found the manuscript, Pine encounters the first of the females he suspects of having stolen the manuscript, "a girl lovely enough to make you gnaw your nails," and a murder victim who has ties to the mob. Another person looking for Wirtz and the manuscript is mob boss Antuni, modeled on Al Capone, who hopes to donate it to the Vatican in exchange for absolution for his sins. Much like Dashiell Hammett's *The Maltese Falcon* (1930), the plot involves murder (though Browne has six to Hammett's two), double crosses, and the desperate competition of opposing factions, struggling to get their hands on the manuscript. Added to the mix is a mysterious international thief. Pine compares the situation to a novel written by "Eric Ambler with a hangover." Although Pine unveils a murderer whom it seemed impossible to suspect, he does plant clues of the bishop's true identity.

In *Halo for Satan* the character of Pine continues to grow into a three-dimensional character with his flippant humor, his self-deprecation, his sense of fair play, and his weaknesses for scotch and the wrong women. He also shows a compassionate side. In describing the mob boss Antuni, Pine looks beyond his crime-filled past and sees a desperately ill human being: "He seemed to be having trouble keeping his eyes open and his head off his chest. He was old and tired and suffering, and his story was told. So much talking had emptied all the limited strength out of him." Such compassion was not characteristic of the Paul Pine of *Halo in Blood*. As a novel *Halo for Satan* shows Browne's development: the writing is sharper, and the plot is tight.

After Browne finished this novel, he wrote a series called *Mike Mysteries* for radio. In each show a murder is committed, the police arrive, the lieutenant comes in and says, "it was a perfect crime, Mr. Jones, but you overlooked one little detail." Then the radio station had three minutes of commercials, after which the "one little detail" was revealed. Browne wrote ten radio scripts a week. He remarked to Bowman that "There are still dents in the office paneling where I'd pound my head trying to find ideas."

In *Halo in Brass,* the third Paul Pine book and the last of his "Halo" novels, Browne touches on lesbianism, an unusual subject for the times. Going back to his roots, Browne begins the novel in Lincoln, Nebraska, where Pine meets a friend's parents who want him to find their missing daughter. Accurately assessing the Fremont's economic position, Pine charges them only $5 per day instead of his usual $30. When Pine discovers that their missing daughter is a murdering transvestite, he offers them a lie, that Laura died in a fire, a kindness seemingly at odds with his hard-nosed demeanor.

As in the previous novels, Browne's brief characterizations are effective. Describing Mrs. Fremont, Pine notes that "She was one of those small birdlike females who are active in church socials and the local chapter of the Eastern Star [a division of the Masons] and who work up quite a reputation for strawberry preserves. She would go into her eighties and die with patient resignation, knowing in advance that the wings would fit and the harp would be in tune." The book has five murders, one of which occurs before the action of the novel; another missing girl; gangsters; the murdering transvestite; and an unusual collage of women, ranging from the church-oriented Mrs. Fremont to the imperious Cornellia Van Cleve to the reformed prostitute Eva Griswold.

After its beginning in Nebraska, the novel shifts back to Pine's Chicago territory. Critic Bowman states that the "whole feel of the book—from settings and characters to the plot itself—is as stylized as a Hollywood *film noir*." The scenes appear as if they belonged in a black-and-white movie with the camera set at oblique angles, providing a disturbing viewpoint on an unpleasant world. The wholesomeness of the initial scene in Nebraska with the Fremonts quickly shifts into a murder scene once Pine takes the case. It is a book, as described by Bowman, filled with a "real moral darkness," portraying a world where the only truly innocent character is murdered and the most sympathetic is a former whore; it is a world where women do not need men, and the key to the mystery is based on lesbianism. Critics Bowman, Pronzini, and Jim Sandoe describe the novel as Browne's best to that time. As Sandoe states, "It has an assurance and an ease that the earlier books lack."

In 1948 Bernard Davis, Browne's former boss at Ziff-Davis, flew to California to ask him, as Browne recalled to Bowman, to "cut out this book writing nonsense" and return to Chicago. Browne packed up his family and moved, and when Ray Palmer left Ziff-Davis in 1949, Browne became editor in chief of the fiction group. In 1950 when the company relocated to New York, the family moved to Larchmont, New York.

Browne's next novel *Thin Air* (1954) almost disappeared into thin air itself when he left the only copy of the manuscript on a commuter train. After hours of telephoning, he located it at the White Plains station and slept with it under his pillow that night. Because Ziff-Davis had recently eliminated its book-publishing division, Browne could finally abandon the John Evans pseudonym for good and write this novel under his own name.

The genesis of the novel was a call to Browne's agent from *The Saturday Evening Post,* looking for Browne to write a suspense novel but without a private detective. Since the magazine was an important one and paid well, Browne jumped at the chance. He developed a story line about a man, Ames Coryell, who drives to Maine to bring his wife and young daughter home from a summer vacation. When they arrive home, his wife promptly disappears, but, strangely, the three-year-old daughter says, "Mommy didn't come home with us." The plot develops with Coryell, an advertising executive, using the resources of his agency to do what the police did not: find his wife. Although the editor of *The Saturday Evening Post,* Ben Hibbs, rejected the story as highly implausible, Kay Bourne, the editor of *Cosmopolitan,* bought it the next day. A short story with the title "Thin Air" appeared in the October 1953 issue of the magazine.

This second non-Pine novel is more successful than the first, perhaps because Coryell, unlike Sungail, is a likeable character who is out to discover the truth and find his wife, not murder her. Of necessity, in his search for her he takes on the aspect of a hard-boiled detective. The influence of James Cain, Bowman comments, can be detected in this novel as Coryell is transformed into a tough guy who "almost makes Paul Pine look soft." *Thin Air* was Browne's most profitable book.

It was sold to television for an *Armstrong Circle Theatre* production and as a CBS *Movie of the Week.* The story also was used in an episode of *The Rockford Files.*

Bantam had reprinted the "Halo" books, which were selling so well that Browne's editor at Simon and Schuster urged him to write another Paul Pine novel. Browne wanted to continue the "Halo" titles with "Halo for Hire," but Lee Wright, his editor, felt that people would think that they had already read it. The book became *The Taste of Ashes* and begins with Pine talking to a child. He has been called to Olympic Heights, a wealthy Chicago suburb, by Selen Delastone, a matriarch who wants Pine to kill someone who is blackmailing her. Murder is, of course, against Pine's creed, and he refuses the job, but he becomes involved anyway when a friend, the previous detective on the case, is found murdered (one of five murders in the book). Local police cover up the crime by calling it a suicide, which does not sit well with Pine. It turns out the police and the entire town are owned by the wealthy Delastone family, which has a rather nasty skeleton in the closet. Bowman notes that the novel is "filled with a sense of real pain and moral darkness." Political corruption disguises murder, and family "honor" hides incest.

Despite the hard-boiled nature of *The Taste of Ashes,* Browne futher humanizes his detective. At one point Pine reflects on life as a private eye: "Private dicks had no business being married. Private dicks should live with nothing except a few books and a bottle or two on the pantry shelf and a small but select list of phone numbers for ready reference when the glands start acting up. Private dicks should be proud and lonely men who can say no when the hour is late and their feet hurt." Marriage is not in Pine's future, but he reflects on the married life because of the death of his friend and fellow P.I. Sam Jellco. In this novel Pine discovers that a private investigator, such as Jellco, can also have a family. Pine himself, unlike the Pine in the first "Halo" novel, is not just a wise-talking, hard-drinking "gumshoe"; he is a man who takes the time to enjoy the company of a child.

In 1956, while Browne was still working on *The Taste of Ashes,* he received a call from a friend, Roy Huggins, a television producer for Warner Bros., who asked Browne to come to California and write for his Western series *Cheyenne.* Browne had never seen a television script but flew to Hollywood, wrote the script, and returned to New York. Three weeks later he received a seven-year contract that more than doubled his current earnings. According to Browne, as quoted by Bowman, "I signed the contract, divorced my wife, and came to California."

Browne married Doris Ellen Kaye in 1959; they adopted a baby girl, Melissa, and he began his career as a television writer. On occasion he also wrote for the screen; three movies were about gangsters: *Portrait of a Mobster* (1961), starring Vic Morrow as Dutch Schultz; *The St. Valentine's Day Massacre* (1967), with George Segal and Jason Robards; and *Capone* (1975), with Ben Gazzara in the title role. A fourth movie, *Bootleggers* (1974), starring Slim Pickens and Jaclyn Smith, was a comedy. He worked on television shows such as *77 Sunset Strip, Maverick, Mannix,* and *Mission Impossible.* He also worked as story editor for *Perry Mason* and *Longstreet.* Browne told Bowman that working on *Mission Impossible* was "the most fun I ever had writing for television." In the early 1970s Browne retired from Hollywood. During his years there he had been employed by virtually every major studio and had written more than one hundred television scripts. Browne then started teaching writing courses at the University of California in San Diego.

Browne, however, was not through with Paul Pine, and, after a hiatus of twenty-five years, Pine reappeared in *The Paper Gun* (1985), in a limited edition of only 350 copies, that includes the title novella and the short story "So Dark for April." Browne's only short story to feature Paul Pine, "So Dark for April," was originally published in *Manhunt* in 1953. Browne's plan in *The Paper Gun* was to make observations, using Pine's unique style, on what had happened to Chicago, as a city, during the past twenty years, focusing on the inner city and its air of decay and abandonment. Browne remarked in an interview with Lewis, "By comparison, Chandler's 'mean streets' were sylvan glades." The story centers around the murder of a teenage girl that triggers three other violent killings within twenty-four hours. The story, though, has a tacked-on, unsatisfactory conclusion. Browne explains, as quoted in Pronzini, that it is "not that I ran into a dead end or a terminal case of writer's block; it's simply that . . . I lost interest in the private eye genre." Browne later said to John Dinan, regarding the "glamour-loaded life" of a P.I., "For sheer excitement it ranks one notch behind applying for food stamps."

Browne's novel *Pork City* (1988) is a departure from his previous work in that it is based on an actual event: the murder on 10 June 1930 at high noon in downtown Chicago of the *Chicago Tribune* reporter Jake Lingle. The novel includes both fictional characters and real people, including crime bosses "Bugsy" Malone and Al Capone. Set during Prohibition, the plot concerns the search to find the killer. The owner of the *Tribune* does not trust the local police, known to be hand-in-hand with the

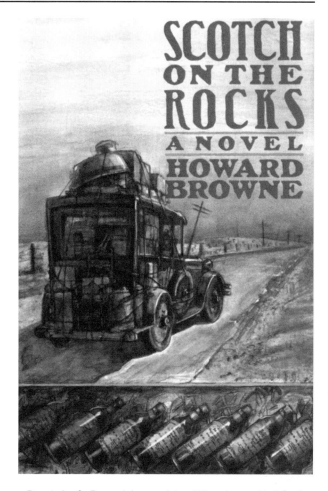

Dust jacket for Browne's last novel, in which an impoverished family comes into possession of a truck loaded with bootleg scotch

crime lords, and forms his own group to investigate the murder. He also offers a $25,000 reward. Part of the strategy of the investigation is to cause trouble for the crime bosses with raids of their "businesses." When Capone's loss of revenue amounts to $6 million in one month, he decides to find the killer and/ or provide someone to take the fall to satisfy those investigating the murder. In a way, law works with crime, resulting in an unusual type of justice.

The pace of the novel is fast; the dialogue is snappy. Drawing on his years in Hollywood, Browne uses cinematic quick-cutting to push the plot along. Unlike earlier novels, this one is short on murders—only two—but the twists in the plot and the confrontations between characters keep the suspense high.

Browne's last novel, *Scotch on the Rocks* (1991), is also set during Prohibition and includes three story lines, which are woven together to form a novel that is more an adventure story with humor than a hard-boiled mystery. The Dawson family, who have just lost their farm and possessions at auction, are forced to move in with distant relatives, but en route they discover an abandoned truck, loaded with illegal scotch. The second story line concerns Lee Vance, a gambler and con man, who has been run out of town for dealing from the bottom of the deck at poker. Vance encounters the Dawson family and convinces them that he knows someone who will buy the scotch for $60,000. A third story line focuses on the criminal "owners" of the stolen scotch. The main part of the action is the journey from Texas to Kansas City, where the scotch is finally sold, and the adventures along the way. The story has a quick pace, because of Browne's technique of cutting between characters in alternate scenes within a parallel time frame.

Browne, who in 1985 won the Life Achievement Award from the Private Eye Writers of America, lived in Carlsbad, California, until his death on 28 October 1999. His principle contributions to hard-boiled mystery are the novels centering on Paul Pine. Although Browne's debt to Chandler's Philip Marlowe is profound—Browne in fact told interviewer Lewis, "Had there been no Philip Marlowe, there would've been no Paul Pine"—his detective became something more than a "smugged copy" of Marlowe. Pine has his own style and identity and became one of the best "tough guy" heroes of his era. The novels increasingly showed a complexity and character all their own. Except for his first Paul Pine effort, each of the three following novels was selected by critics as among the ten best mysteries of the year.

Interview:

Caleb A. Lewis, "Interview with Howard Browne," *Armchair Detective,* 11 (1978): 172–176.

References:

Robert A. Baker and Michael T. Nietzel, "Paul Pine–John Evans (Howard Browne)," in *Private Eyes: One Hundred and One Knights; A Survey of American Detective Fiction 1922–1984* (Bowling Green, Ohio: Bowling Green State University Popular Press, 1985), pp. 83–85;

David A. Bowman, "Halo for Hire: The Novels of Howard Browne," *Armchair Detective,* 19 (Spring 1986): 147–156;

John A. Dinan, *Chicago Ain't No Sissy Town: The Regional Detective Fiction of Howard Browne* (San Bernardino, Cal.: Brownstone, 1995);

David Geherin, "Paul Pine," in his *The American Private Eye: The Image in Fiction* (New York: Ungar, 1985), pp. 95–103;

Caleb A. Lewis, "The Return of Paul Pine," *Armchair Detective,* 11 (1978): 79–85;

James Sandoe, "The Reviewer at Work," *Armchair Detective,* 11 (1978): 84–85.

Papers:

Howard Browne's manuscript collections are held at the University of Wyoming in Laramie and the Mugar Library at Boston University.

James Lee Burke

(5 December 1936 –   )

Dean G. Hall
Kansas State University

BOOKS: *Half of Paradise* (Boston: Houghton Mifflin, 1965; London: Phoenix, 1997);

To the Bright and Shining Sun (New York: Scribners, 1970);

Lay Down My Sword and Shield (New York: Crowell, 1971);

Two for Texas (New York: Pocket Books, 1982; London: Phoenix, 1999); republished as *Sabine Spring* (Wichita: Watermark, 1989);

The Convict: Stories (Baton Rouge: Louisiana State University Press, 1985); republished as *The Convict and Other Stories* (Boston: Little, Brown, 1990; London: Orion, 1995);

The Lost Get-Back Boogie (Baton Rouge: Louisiana State University Press, 1986);

The Neon Rain (New York: Holt, 1987; London: Mysterious Press, 1991);

Heaven's Prisoners (New York: Holt, 1988; London: Vintage, 1990);

Black Cherry Blues (Boston: Little, Brown, 1989; London: Century, 1990);

A Morning for Flamingoes (Boston: Little, Brown, 1989; London: Century, 1992);

A Stained White Radiance (New York: Hyperion Press, 1992; Arrow, 1993);

In the Electric Mist with Confederate Dead (New York: Hyperion Press, 1993; London: Orion, 1993);

Dixie City Jam (New York: Hyperion Press, 1994; London: Orion, 1994);

Burning Angel (New York: Hyperion Press, 1995; London: Orion, 1995);

Cadillac Jukebox (New York: Hyperion Press, 1996; London: Orion, 1996);

Cimarron Rose (New York: Hyperion Press, 1997; London: Orion, 1997);

Sunset Limited (New York: Doubleday, 1998; London: Orion, 1998);

Heartwood (New York: Doubleday, 1998; London: Orion, 1999);

Purple Cane Road (New York: Doubleday, 2000).

James Lee Burke (photograph by Pearl Burke; from the dust jacket for Black Cherry Blues, *1989)*

SELECTED PERIODICAL PUBLICATION–UNCOLLECTED: "Lessons in Race, Dialogue, and Profanity," *The Southern Review,* 29 (Winter 1993): 51–57.

James Lee Burke's reputation as a writer of hard-boiled detective fiction was solidified when *Black Cherry Blues* (1989), his third novel about retired New Orleans police officer Dave Robicheaux, won an Edgar Award as the best crime novel of 1989. Even though Burke had been writing and publishing novels for more than twenty years before he created Robicheaux, he did not view his entry into the field of hard-boiled fiction as a departure. Looking back on his career, in a 1995 interview with Rick Schultz, Burke maintained, "I've always written about people who have no voice. That's never changed in my writing." In a 1996 interview with Steven Womack, Burke commented, "I never thought of my books as essentially changing directions. The themes have always remained the same. I've always written about the same people, the same situations. . . . The series and the earlier works are one story." Burke, though, has also stretched the hard-boiled genre through his characterization of Robicheaux, who in some novels in the series sees and talks to the dead.

Evocation of place is a hallmark in Burke's detective series, and his descriptions of nature set the novels apart from other hard-boiled fiction. Robicheaux's experiences of the sights, sounds, and smells of the bayou as well as New Orleans nightlife do more than create the mood of individual scenes. His complex appreciation of the physical world operates at two levels. He has a streak of romanticism that is evident as he communes with nature, soothing his soul by walking in the woods or floating through the bayou and lazily fishing. At the same time, however, he is aware that the undersurface of the bayou is alive with needlenose gars ripping apart something dead and that in the seemingly peaceful woods, birds of prey are carrying screaming animals away for lunch. As Burke told Schultz, "I was influenced a great deal by the early naturalists. The naturalists believed that environment is character. Hence, the author describes the physical world as a player in these stories."

The locale for most of the novels in the series is small-town Cajun Louisiana, but Robicheaux often takes jaunts into larger cities, especially New Orleans, which he refers to as "the Big Sleazy." At the end of the first novel in the series, *The Neon Rain* (1987), Robicheaux quits his work as a detective on a New Orleans police force that is rife with cops on the take or otherwise disinclined to stand up for the victims of the dangerous undertow just below the surface of the genteel South of honor, decorum, and tradition. Over the course of the novels, the detective tries to return to a life where he can practice the simple values handed down to him by his parents. He eventually becomes a deputy in a small town in the parish of New Iberia and tries to remove himself even further from urban evil as he spends more and more of his time running a bait and boat rental shop. Robicheaux attempts to create for himself an Eden, a place where he can work for himself, generally control his own time, spend time with his acquired family, and escape from the negative forces that always seem to end up seeking him out and threatening everything he holds dear, including his own sense of right and wrong. He finds, however, that he cannot escape his past, whether it be his own nightmares of time served in Vietnam, the reappearance of various felons, or his longing for an idyllic probably-never-existing vision of the South now under attack from selfish politicians, greedy and polluting land developers, and the general drift away from codes of personal integrity.

James Lee Burke, an only child, was born on 5 December 1936 in Houston and graduated, in the bottom quarter of his class of two hundred, from Lamar High School in 1955. He had already begun his lifelong battle with alcohol and blames his low performance and low self-image on his early drinking. His father, James Lee Burke Sr., was an engineer for natural gas companies and his mother, Frances, was a secretary. Burke knew early that he wanted to be a writer, for he recalls in an interview with Duley Brainard, "In the fourth grade my cousin Lynn and I started writing stories for *The Saturday Evening Post* in Big Chief notebooks." He attended the University of Southwestern Louisiana from 1955 to 1957 and credits an English professor there, Lyle Williams, for improving his writing and changing his life; Burke then moved on to the University of Missouri, where he obtained a B.A. in 1959 and an M.A. in 1960.

While in graduate school Burke met and courted Pearl Chu Pai, a Peking-born expatriate who escaped from China by boat in 1949. Burke and Pearl were married in 1960 and have four children: James, Andree, Pamela, and Alafair. Burke had a varied career before finally establishing himself enough to take up writing full time: he worked as an English teacher at several colleges (including the University of Southwestern Louisiana, the University of Montana, Miami-Dade Community College, and Wichita State University) and at a variety of jobs, including as a surveyor and pipe fitter for a Texas oil company, a social worker in Los Angeles, and a Job Corps teacher in Kentucky. Burke was able to turn full time to writing after he won a Guggenheim Fellowship in 1989. He now lives in Missoula, Montana, and New Iberia, Louisiana.

Bits and pieces of all Burke's work experiences turn up in his novels, but the most obvious connection between his fictional hard-boiled narrator, Robicheaux, and his own life was the ongoing battle not to let alcoholism destroy his life. In his own estimation, he "hit bottom in 1977" and was only able to keep sober for the next five years with the help of therapists and priests. In the *Publishers Weekly* interview, Burke reveals, "I used to think that alcohol somehow enhanced a person's writing. It took me years for me to realize that I had written in spite of alcohol, not because of it. . . . One way or another it's on every page. The 12-step fellowship gave me back my life, literally. Then I began to write about it in *The Neon Rain*. Dave and the 12-step recovery program came together." The seductions of alcohol, its frightening hold and its resultant nightmares, are constants in the Robicheaux series.

In his first novel, *Half of Paradise* (1965), set in Louisiana, Burke intertwines the fates of three men, each of whom succumbs to his own demons; each of the three men's stories begins in desperate circumstances and, after some hopeful developments, ends in failure. Writing in *The New York Times Book Review* of 14 March 1965, Wirt Williams commented that Burke's novel "was a solid debut for a writer to be taken seriously." In his second novel, *To the Bright and Shining Sun* (1970), Burke's main character and narrator is the naive and idealistic Perry Woodson Hatfield James, a Kentucky teenager who tries to escape the brutal mines but learns harsh lessons when his father is murdered in a mine explosion purposely set by antiunion forces. It too was positively reviewed: Martin Levin, in *The New York Times Book Review* of 9 August 1970, commented that the story was "authentic as moonshine," and the reviewer for *Publishers Weekly* (1 June 1970) concluded that the novel was "a powerful and cruel picture of the Appalachia many Americans would like to forget."

In his mid thirties, with two well-received novels to his credit, Burke changed agents and signed with the William Morris Agency, fully confident that his third novel, *Lay Down My Sword and Shield* (1971), would be equally welcomed. However, the story of Hack Holland, a Korean war veteran with a Baylor law degree who runs afoul of the Texas conservative political power structure when he seeks a congressional seat as a Democrat, did not receive the same positive reviews. Though he stayed with William Morris, he was upset with the current publisher, Crowell, about the way the new novel had been advertised and elected to seek a new publisher for his *The Lost Get-Back Boogie,* a novel he eventually revised and published in 1986. Burke recalled for Dulcy Brainard in *Publishers Weekly* the difficult quest for its publication in the 1970s: "It was under submission for nine years and drew about 100 rejections many of which were condemning. That book wasn't just rejected, it was flung back at me with a catapult." As Burke reported in a 1993 *Writer's Digest* interview with W. C. Stroby, William Morris "returned all my material, cut me loose, and suddenly it was ground zero again."

Eleven years passed before Burke managed to publish his fourth novel, the paperback original *Two for Texas* (1982), which shows his burgeoning interest in Texas history as well as signaling his interest in exploring the fortunes of a particular family through time. In *Two for Texas,* Son Holland, the grandfather of Hack Holland of *Lay Down My Sword and Shield,* escapes from a penal camp along the Mississippi River to eventually join Sam Houston and partici-

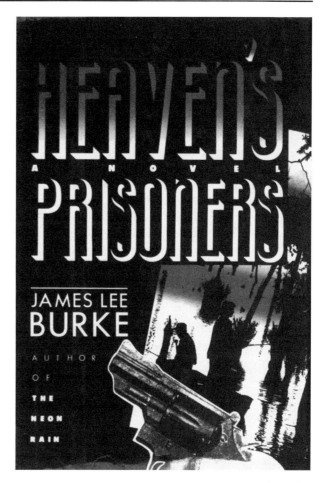

Dust jacket for Burke's 1988 novel, in which Dave Robicheaux's unwillingness to drop a case leads to the murder of his wife

pate in the defeat of Santa Anna shortly after the destruction of the Alamo. Burke carries the Holland family series forward in *Cimarron Rose* (1997), in which the great-grandson of Son Holland, Billy Bob Holland, defense attorney and former Texas Ranger living in Deaf Smith, Texas, exercises many of the detective skills of Robicheaux to defend his illegitimate son against a murder charge. Billy Bob is also featured in *Heartwood* (1999).

Burke's settings feature geographies from his family's deep roots in Cajun Louisiana and southern Texas. Burke's progenitors lived for more than 150 years in New Iberia, the Louisiana parish setting for many of the Robicheaux novels. Moreover, his Texas connections are obvious and seep into his fiction. As he told Schultz in 1995, "My great great grandfather fought under Sam Houston in 1835 and then became a sugar farmer in New Iberia in 1836 and my family has been there ever since." In *Y'All Come: Texas Monthly On Line* Nelson D. Ross quotes Burke, "In *Two for Texas* and *Lay Down My Sword and Shield* I made use of my great grandfather's diary–his name was Sam Morgan Holland, that's the drover we meet in the novel. He was a preacher later in life but he lived a violent life. He fought other men; he fought whiskey; eventually he found peace. It is his story; the search for redemption and atonement for the men that he killed." Much of Burke's popularity is doubtless attributable to the sense of place and of history he creates in his novels.

In the nearly fifteen years from 1971 to 1985 during which he published only one book, Burke kept writing and supported himself primarily as a teacher. In 1985 the Louisiana State University Press published *The Convict: Stories* and the next year brought out a revised version of *The Lost Get-Back Boogie*. During his lean publication years Burke maintained faith in his abilities, telling Brainard, "I thought that my talent was there for a reason and honestly believed these guys were all wet. . . . To me those editors were just dumbheads." He said to Scroby, "I owe those people at LSU Press a lot. . . . They resurrected my whole career. Suddenly I was back in business."

When finally published, *The Lost Get-Back Boogie* was nominated for a Pulitzer Prize. Its main character clearly anticipates the Robicheaux character, for like the detective, Iry Paret is born in the same Cajun South, gets drunk regularly, and has two Purple Hearts, though his are from the Korean conflict rather than from the Vietnam War à la Robicheaux. Also like Robicheaux, Paret has a violent streak, defends the unpopular and victimized–in this case the Riordan family whose grandsire is opposing a polluting pulp mill–and lives by his own code. Moreover, descriptions of Montana in this novel clearly echo those Burke later uses in *Black Cherry Blues,* and the descriptions of the Paret homestead and family home are quite close to the homestead and home of the detective.

From the first Dave Robicheaux novel, *The Neon Rain,* readers could tell that a new player had pushed into the hard-boiled detective genre; Robicheaux has been hardened by his experiences in Vietnam, where he says he learned several lessons, chief of which was "Never trust authority," and fourteen years on the job as a street cop and detective in New Orleans. In this first novel differentiating the good guys from the bad guys is difficult. Robicheaux drinks on the job and threatens witnesses. While suspended from the force, he shoots a man with a sawed-off shotgun, attacks bodyguards by swinging a sack filled with nuts and bolts, shoots a man in the face who is trying to scramble from his car after being pulled over, handcuffs a couple of other cops to a car bumper, and punches an internal affairs col-

league. His partner, Cletus (Clete) Purcell, also drinks while on the clock. Purcell provokes responses from criminals to justify his use of force, seems to be on the take, and admits to Robicheaux that for ten grand he shot one of the "sleazeballs" in the head and left him in a hog lot to be eaten by pigs. At the end of *The Neon Rain,* Clete abandons his wife and runs off to be a soldier of fortune in Honduras and to escape a possible murder rap.

Clearly, if these two are the "heroes" of the novel, then the lines separating right from wrong are twisted in peculiar ways. In a passage that suggests his affinity with the criminal sociopaths he pursues, Robicheaux admits that "anyone who has ever fired a weapon at another human being knows the terrible adrenalin-fed sense of omnipotence and arrogance that you feel at the moment and the secret pleasure you take in the opportunity being provided you." Such candid insights demark the series and engage the reader; Robicheaux does, indeed, have a code he lives by, and the gradual revealing of that code throughout the series fosters a more sympathetic reading of both Robicheaux and Clete.

The Neon Rain begins with Robicheaux's visit to Angola penitentiary in the last hours before Johnny Massina is to be executed; as part of Massina's attempt to expiate his guilt, he tells Robicheaux that there is a hit out on him. Since Robicheaux had previously taken Johnny to a couple of AA meetings, Johnny compares this confession to "step five" in the AA recovery program–a recurring source of Robicheaux's own code. Robicheaux eventually finds out that he has incurred the wrath of the mob by pressing for an autopsy on a black girl he had discovered floating in the bayou while fishing. Common practice in southern policing, at least in Robicheaux's world, is to exert as little effort as legally possible when dealing with blacks, redbones (individuals with some Native American blood), and white "trash." Perhaps because Robicheaux grew up surrounded by these people in poverty conditions (both he and his brother have white streaks in their jet black hair as a result of vitamin deficiency associated with malnutrition as they were growing up), his internal law book reads that disenfranchised victims deserve to have the crimes committed against them fully investigated and that perpetrators "take the fall" either under the law or payback by other means.

The plot entails Robicheaux's solving the black girl's murder as well as uncovering the reasons his interest in her triggered such a heavy response from the mob, and thickens as threads connecting federal agencies, undercover snitches, and drugs and gunrunning in support of South American guerrillas bind tighter and tighter on the detective. Playing on his history of alcoholism, the bad guys set up Robicheaux to make it appear he has fallen off the wagon; he is stripped of his badge, his gun, his self-respect, and his energy—as he says, when he wakes up in the drunk tank, "It was the lowest day of my life, except perhaps for the day my wife left me for the Houston oilman." Throughout the series Robicheaux's fight for sobriety and dealing with the long-term effects of his years of drinking give birth to themes of human frailty, temptation, and forgiveness of self and others; here, as Robicheaux struggles against unquenchable desires for alcohol and to put his life and career back in order, he prays, "Dear God, my higher power, even though I've abandoned You, don't abandon me."

His prayers are answered in part in the form of Annie, a young woman from Kansas. A classical musician and a social worker who deals with the civilized surface of the "other" New Orleans, Annie reveals both courage and naiveté when she tells Robicheaux that the hoodlums who have broken into her house "are weak people or they wouldn't have guns." Her actions later save both their lives, and, once drawn into Robicheaux's world, she becomes his sounding board for expressing his convoluted feelings and values. For example, when Annie feels sullied because one of the men had touched her, Robicheaux gives her advice he continually has trouble following himself about letting the bad guys touch the soul: "What happens outside of us doesn't count. . . . It's what we do with it, the way we react to it that's important." He then shares one of his Vietnam experiences in which he showed himself, to his lights, to be less brave than she.

Confessing his own history to Annie in an effort to comfort her moves their intimacy beyond the physical and sets up their long-term relationship; eventually he shares one of his most keen self-reflexive insights with her: "I don't like the world the way it is, and I miss the past. It's a foolish way to be." He understands that he is a throwback to a past that never really was, and he recognizes his knight-errantry as foolishly out of fashion in the cesspool world of the nether side of New Orleans. Yet, though his personal code is battered and bent beyond the squeaky clean, it is not broken, and Robicheaux continually gets up off the mat to swing once again at the villains and fiends who inhabit the nightmare world of the hard-boiled.

The first Robicheaux novel ended with Robicheaux's retiring from the New Orleans police force, with both Annie and his houseboat in tow, to a boat rental and baitshop business in New Iberia, a

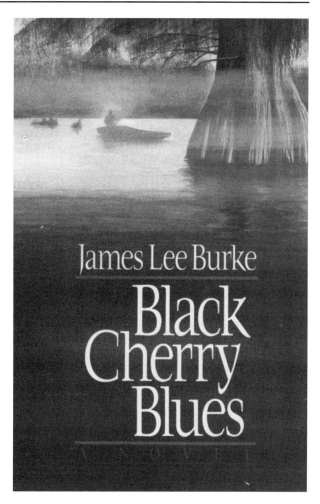

Dust jacket for Burke's third Robicheaux novel, in which the detective has visions of his dead wife and father

lazy laid-back small town up the Bayou Teche. If one were to rely on the ending of the *The Neon Rain*, one would expect that Robicheaux has escaped into his idealized past: "It was the Louisiana I had grown up in, a place that never seemed to change, where it was never a treason to go with the cycle of things and let the season have its way."

Just a few pages into the second novel in the series, *Heaven's Prisoners* (1988), Robicheaux's rescue of a young Salvadoran girl, Alafair, from a plane that crashes near his fishing boat initiates events that rip asunder his idyllic planned retirement from policing. Robicheaux keeps secret from Immigration and Naturalization the existence of Alafair, and she appears as his adopted daughter in later novels. When Robicheaux finds that one man killed in the crash has disappeared in official reports of the incident, he pulls at that loose thread using his old contacts in New Orleans to help identify the missing victim and discovers that a friend from his youth, Bubba Rocque, now a hoodlum, is somehow involved. At that point Robicheaux concludes, "I needed to disengage. I wasn't a cop anymore, and my obligations were elsewhere"; he understands that his new life and his old life need to be kept separate. As to be expected, however, even the initial inquiry has consequences which come in the forms of a Drug Enforcement Administration (DEA) officer telling him to butt out and two hoods beating him and warning him not to stick his nose into other people's business.

Robicheaux knows himself fairly well, however: "I had quit the New Orleans police department, the bourbon-scented knight-errant who said he couldn't abide any longer the political hypocrisy and the addictive, brutal ugliness of metropolitan law enforcement, but the truth was that I enjoyed it, that I got high on my knowledge of man's iniquity, that I disdained the boredom and predictability of the normal world as much as my strange alcoholic metabolism loved the adrenaline rush of danger and my feeling of power over an evil world that in many ways was mirrored in my own soul." Robicheaux is addicted to digging into the bowels of humanity's sinfulness. His continued pursuit of evil eventually adds more guilt to his already tortured soul when the bad guys break into his house and murder Annie in their bedroom.

Burke deepens Robicheaux's character as he articulates more of his moral boundaries. As he quotes the lines of a psalm, he seems to come to terms with his grief as he realizes that his instinct is to come to the aid of helpless victims: "I have no theological insight, my religious ethos is a battered one, but those lines seem to suggest an answer that my reason cannot, namely, that the innocent who suffer for the rest of us become anointed and loved by God in a special way; the votive candle of their lives had made them heaven's prisoners."

Burke's own continuing battle against alcoholism, his crediting of a twelve-step program for providing him with coping mechanisms, are transformed into Robicheaux's code; at one point in this novel Robicheaux could "bring down" Bubba by teasing him into assaulting his wife, Claudette, but chooses not to do so: "But I couldn't take them down by provoking a sociopath into assaulting his wife. This may sound noble; it's not. The alcoholic recovery program I practiced did not allow me to lie, manipulate, or impose design or control over other people, particularly when its intention was obviously a destructive one. If I did, I would regress, I would start to screw up my own life and the lives of those closest to me, and eventually I would become the same drunk I had been years ago." So Robicheaux's

apparent "nobility" (Clete many times in the series greets Robicheaux, "Hello, noble mon") actually is protection of himself and grows out of specific understandings that his own selfhood is at risk if he blurs any further the distinctions between himself and the bad guys. Robicheaux's hard-boiled philosophy, then, is a convoluted amalgam of the recovery steps of AA and piecemeal Christianity; he is fond of quoting St. Augustine "who admonished we should never use the truth to injure." The truth is not an absolute piety, but controlling others for destructive purposes is an absolute crime.

Recognizing that he needs the clout and fear that a badge creates to avenge Annie's death, Robicheaux joins the New Iberia police force as a detective, thus setting up his on-again, off-again relationship with the local cops that becomes a staple in later novels. Robicheaux does, indeed, even the score, and the connections between the plane that brought Alafair into his life and his boyhood friend are eventually untangled. Left alone with Alafair and faced with raising her as a single parent at the end of the novel, Robicheaux is back on the wagon but contemplates that he and Bubba Rocque may have "been more alike than I cared to admit." He recognizes that the differences between himself and the criminal class he so despises may be the result of a few critical life choices that at the time seemed insignificant and were casually made; like his fears of slipping again into alcoholism, his knowledge of how easy it is to slip over to the other side haunts him personally and the entire series thematically.

In addition to his usual Cajun landscape, Burke sets much of the action of *Black Cherry Blues* in Montana, where Robicheaux has to go to track down a killer who has framed him with a murder indictment. His real antagonist, though, is an oil company working with the mob. Through neglect of safety regulations, the company is responsible for the death of Robicheaux's father; it also pollutes and destroys the land and forever changes the values of the communities into which it intrudes. For Robicheaux, the company epitomizes the values of the present, an attitude that fits well with his feeling that the past is better than the present and that almost everything—the environment, government, the character of people—is in decline.

Robicheaux's belief in a past that provides a benchmark of both personal and cultural stability and strength is a pervasive theme in the series. In *Black Cherry Blues,* Robicheaux views the past as a key to his own identity: "I wanted to go into yesterday. And I don't think that's always bad. Sometimes you simply need to walk through a door in your mind and lose thirty or forty years in order to remember who you are." He contends that "We are the sum total of what we have done and where we have been, and I sincerely believe that in many ways the world in which I grew up was better than the one in which we live today."

Black Cherry Blues begins with Robicheaux's recurring horrific dream of Annie's murder and the nightmarish echo of her calling his name; the dream scene combines two themes that resonate not only in this novel but in the other Robicheaux novels: his guilt for living a life that drags his family into association with violent criminals and the importance of dreams as conduits into the past, the present, and even the future. Robicheaux is not only haunted by dreams of his service in Vietnam and of myriad other violent episodes in his long career as a cop but also by the delirium tremens of the recovering alcoholic. His nightmares cause him to wake up in the middle of the night screaming and dripping sweat.

More important, Burke also allows Robicheaux to make preternatural contacts with his dead wife and father through dreamlike visions. In the course of the novel Annie appears to him several times with "clues" and advice on how to proceed in uncovering the evidence he needs to save himself from a frame-up. She also provides words of encouragement when his spirits are flagging. At the end of the novel Robicheaux has expiated his guilt and achieved a sort of peace. Annie and his father appear to him a last time early in the morning when he is deep in the marsh. "It's good-bye for real this time, Dave. It's been special," she says as she wades into the water; his father winks and gives him a thumbs-up and also simply walks away into the marsh. Readers of the Robicheaux series come to expect that the hard-as-nails detective will live in and rely upon his dreams to find his way when he feels confused and worn down; this distinctly otherworldly, quasi-romantic element is one of the character traits that make Robicheaux unusual in the hard-boiled genre.

Robicheaux's former partner, Cletus, resurfaces in *Black Cherry Blues;* when last together in *The Neon Rain,* Robicheaux had been disgusted with Clete's behavior and had told him "never call me partner, again." That antipathy deepens when Robicheaux discovers that Clete is now working for the mob in Montana, and some of the more interesting aspects of this novel are their arguments about right and wrong, law and lawlessness. Robicheaux's overzealous condemnations of Clete's actions and moral baseness ring ever more hollow as Clete saves Robicheaux's life from a hit man and "disappears" him into the woods, apparently following the lead of

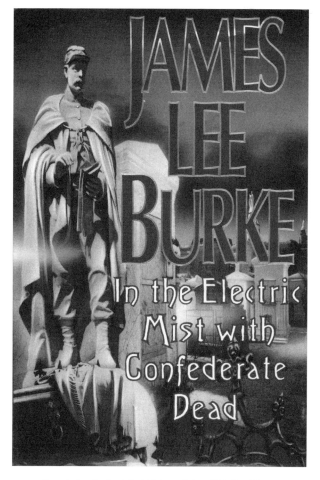

Dust jacket for Burke's 1993 novel, in which Confederate soldiers seem to interact with Robicheaux and others

the mob that had previously dealt with some local Indians protesting the oil company by making them permanently disappear. Robicheaux's visions of right and wrong are tested as the clock runs down toward his trial and he must pressure the bad guys into overreacting. Finally, after a Native American woman Clete has been intimate with is murdered by the mob, Clete inflicts his own personal vengeance by sabotaging the mobsters' plane, which crashes with four of them aboard.

Rob Carney in "Clete Purcel to the Rampaging Rescue: Looking for the Hard-Boiled Tradition in James Lee Burke's *Dixie City Jam*" sees Burke's portrait of Robicheaux in *Black Cherry Blues* and in other novels as nearly disqualifying the series from "the hard-boiled school" and credits the character of Clete as the needed antidote to the overly prissy Robicheaux. The countervailing attitudes of the two characters, however, are certainly a large part of what makes the series compelling. Through Robicheaux's interaction with Clete, Burke complicates his examination of the moral consequences of skating the line between legality and illegality. The series is not about a cardboard hard-boiled hero but about a man who pursues his own vision of justice in a violent world. Robicheaux's psychological torments and the intrusiveness of his dreams and memories are an important part of Burke's contribution to the hard-boiled genre.

The fourth novel in the Robicheaux series, *A Morning for Flamingoes* (1989), takes place mostly in New Orleans, the locale and history Robicheaux thought he had left behind when he moved to a small town and opened his bait shop. Trying to make ends meet, Robicheaux becomes a deputy for the New Iberia police force, assuming that small town policing would not involve him in the moral dilemmas he so often encountered in the Big Easy. A routine prisoner transfer goes wrong, however, when Robicheaux's temporary partner simply ignores too many standard safety procedures: the prisoner, Jimmie Lee Boggs, shoots Robicheaux and kills the other policeman. As the wounded Robicheaux stumbles backward and down an embankment toward a coulee, his mind transports him back to Vietnam. Rather than hearing what is going on around him during this assault he hears only the voice of the medic of his unit yelling about a chest wound. Boggs forces Tee Beau, a fellow prisoner wanted for murder, to follow Robicheaux down the embankment to finish the kill. Tee Beau, however, shoots into the ground near Robicheaux's head, sparing his life, thereby putting himself at odds with Boggs and creating a debt that Robicheaux feels has to be repaid.

After a few months Robicheaux recovers physically from his wound but is still wounded emotionally; he cannot escape recurring dreams of being hunted. Moreover, Tee Beau's grandmother, swearing that her grandson is innocent of the murder charge against him, has made a personal plea to Robicheaux. His twin motives push the plot of the novel: Robicheaux needs to take Boggs "off the board" to rid himself of nagging dreams and needs to investigate Tee Beau's murder charge not only to placate the grandmother but also to settle his perceived debt to the man who refused to kill him.

As Robicheaux begins to unravel the Tee Beau situation, he becomes involved with Gros Mama, a *traiteur,* who is purported to have special powers; her abilities to foresee the future, read people's "auras," and cast spells over her enemies are rooted in the voodoo tradition still nurtured by some African Americans whose ancestors were brought to enslavement from some of the Caribbean islands. She is "the juju woman who could blow the fire out of a burn; stop bleeding by pressing her palm against a wound; charm worms out of a child's stomach; cause a witch to invade the marriage bed, straddle the husband, and fornicate with him until his eyes crossed and he would remain forever discontent with his wife." She can also supposedly sense the circumstances under which others are going to die ("Gros Mama say they both got the gris-gris, they carry it in them just like a worm").

Such talk would normally be dismissed as nonsense by a hard-boiled investigator, but Robicheaux has had too many mystical experiences himself not to be influenced by Gros Mama's words. Her ability is in some measure confirmed by her insight into Robicheaux's haunted condition: "You wake up tired in the morning, cain't open and close your hands on the side of the bed. You dragging a big chain all day long. Food don't taste no good, womens is just something for other mens. You can tell the whole round world I lying, but me and you knows better." Typical of the situations Burke creates, much of what Gros Mama knows and predicts can reasonably be explained away as coming from ordinary sources, but in Burke's fictional world the extraordinary is given its due and her vision is not dismissed as hocum. Robicheaux's own experience of becoming unstuck in time—sometimes the present, memory, the past before he was even born, and the future seem to him to be happening simultaneously—also undermines the assumptions of a purely rational world.

The locale of the novel moves to New Orleans when Robicheaux accepts an undercover assignment for the DEA to pursue Boggs. Robicheaux agrees to let himself be known as a cop turned dirty because his desire to take revenge on Boggs outweighs his deep distaste for becoming part of the criminal class that repulsed him so much when he had been a cop in New Orleans. Robicheaux becomes reacquainted with Bootsie Mouton, his first love in his teenage years. Their relationship, to both of them, was the real thing, and Bootsie hurts still from his dumping her so many years before; Robicheaux feels guilty for abandoning her and is yet unable to explain to himself, to her, or to anyone else what caused him to leave her. All he knows is that his bouts with depression set in about then: "I began to experience bone-grinding periods of depression and guilt that seemed to have no cause or origin." He began to feel himself to be intrinsically bad and that anyone who loved him must also be bad; as he looks back upon the breakup with Bootsie, he recognizes "that I had just made the initial departure on a long alcoholic odyssey."

In the twenty years that have passed, Bootsie has married twice, the second time into the local mob fam-

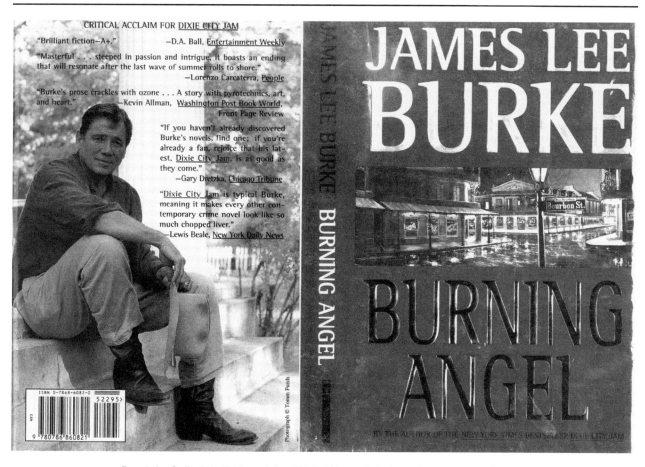

CRITICAL ACCLAIM FOR DIXIE CITY JAM

"Brilliant fiction—A+."　　　　—D.A. Ball, Entertainment Weekly

"Masterful . . . steeped in passion and intrigue, it boasts an ending that will resonate after the last wave of summer rolls to shore."
　　　　—Lorenzo Carcaterra, People

"Burke's prose crackles with ozone . . . A story with pyrotechnics, art, and heart."　　—Kevin Allman, Washington Post Book World, Front Page Review

"If you haven't already discovered Burke's novels, find one; if you're already a fan, rejoice that his latest, Dixie City Jam, is as good as they come."
　　　　—Gary Dretzka, Chicago Tribune

"Dixie City Jam is typical Burke, meaning it makes every other contemporary crime novel look like so much chopped liver."
　　　　—Lewis Beale, New York Daily News

JAMES LEE BURKE
BURNING ANGEL
BY THE AUTHOR OF THE NEW YORK TIMES BESTSELLER DIXIE CITY JAM

*Dust jacket for Burke's 1995 novel, in which Robicheaux finds that in "a careless wink of the eye"
one can find oneself "in step with the great armies of the dead"*

ily, the Giaconos. She is still connected financially to that family even though her husband is now dead; thus, when Robicheaux reestablishes contact with her in the present, she is part of the crowd he has gone undercover to bust. Some of the more interesting exchanges in the novel are between the two old loves, who knew each other's character so well in the past, feeling around in each other's emotional and moral fields to see if any foundation of their previous affection still exists. Both are yearning yet suspicious. By the end of the novel the void in Robicheaux's life caused by Annie's murder begins to be filled by Bootsie, who becomes his wife and is an important character in the subsequent novels in the series.

In *A Morning for Flamingoes*, as in his other novels, Burke muddies the distinctions between the good guys and the bad. His depiction of the mob family of Tony Cardo that Robicheaux infiltrates defies the usual stereotypes, and the motives and interests of the DEA are not wholly honorable. Cardo is somewhat sympathetically characterized and seems likable despite his involvement with drug dealing. He exhibits some integrity, suffers under the abuse from his harridan wife, and, most touching to Robicheaux, is gentle and loving to his young son who is doomed to living in a wheelchair. Moreover, Tony and Robicheaux share memories of their stints in Vietnam. As the plot progresses, the plan to entrap and jail Cardo becomes less and less important to Robicheaux, who differentiates between those who make their money through criminal means and those who are inherently evil. All of the loose ends of the plot are tied up at the end, but the knots are those of Robicheaux's devising and reflect his values of right and wrong, justice and injustice.

A Stained White Radiance (1992) begins with the wife of the Weldon Sonnier, the eldest brother in a family Robicheaux knows from his childhood, reporting a bullet fired through a window in their home. Robicheaux's investigation leads not only to a run-in with the mob when a local cop is murdered while investigating a break-in at Weldon Sonnier's home but also to disturbing knowledge of the Sonnier family's past. He learns that all the children–Drew, whom he had dated before he went to off to war; Lyle, who was under his command in Vietnam; and Weldon, who has become involved with criminals such as Joey Gouza—were abused and involved sexually with each other as kids. Robicheaux again is aided by Clete Purcell, who has set up his own private detective business: "I had marked Clete off as a turncoat, a pitiful facsimile of the friend I'd once had, but I came to learn that his loyalty and courage went far deeper into his character than his personal problems."

The ugliness of the world Robicheaux must deal with even affects the solace he sometimes seeks in the natural world. He knows well that mood can determine what the eye chooses to notice: "I should have felt good about the day; it wasn't hot, like yesterday, the trees were loud with birds, the wind smelled of watermelons, the roses in my garden were as big as fists. But my eye registered all the wrong things: a fire burning in the middle of the marsh, where there should have been none; buzzards humped over a dead rabbit in the field, their beaks hooked and yellow and busy with their work; a little boy with an air rifle on the bank of the bayou, taking careful aim at a robin in an oak tree."

When the mob drops off a $2,000 bribe and the head and finger of the cop killer in an effort to redirect Robicheaux's energies away from them, they present him with a dilemma as well. Robicheaux has reasoned in terms close to these himself, and here he examines his reasons for including in his official police report the bribery attempt but not the gruesome body parts: "Was my report dishonest? No, it was worse. It concealed the commission of a homicide. But some situations involve a trade-off. In this case the fulfillment of a professional obligation would require that my home and my family become the center of a morbid story that would live in the community for decades, and Joey Gouza would succeed in inflicting a level of psychological damage on my daughter, in particular, that might never be undone." Such decisions are never easy for Robicheaux, who is seldom satisfied with by-the-book solutions.

In Burke's sixth Robicheaux novel, *In the Electric Mist with Confederate Dead* (1993), a Hollywood moviemaking enterprise shooting a Civil War film on location intrudes upon the calm of New Iberia. Problems emerge because the funding for the film comes from a friend of Robicheaux's teenage years now turned hoodlum. Although the local movers and shakers only see the economic advantages to their small town, Robicheaux and some other citizens understand that big crime money brings with it big crime personalities and values.

Burke in this novel creates a series of moral dilemmas, both public and private. For the town, the choices are between the money the movie company

represents and the ethical costs to the town as it has to be hospitable, even respectful, to criminals transplanted from New Orleans. Robicheaux's assigned temporary partner from the FBI, Rosie, must choose between respecting and ignoring procedure as she grapples not only with her own frustrations with the system but also with the temptation to use her official position to revenge her experiences as a victim. When Robicheaux violates several laws in his quest for a kidnapper, she tells him, "I think I'm beyond all my parameters now, Dave." In the climactic scene Rosie empties her service revolver into a man she mistakenly believes is armed and then asks herself why she kept firing rounds well beyond what she knew was necessary to bring the situation under control. When Robicheaux secretly drops a gun beside the bad guy she has killed to protect her from a future haunted by guilt and self-doubt, the supposedly clear lines of what is legal and what is just become blurred—another version of a common theme in Burke's series.

Robicheaux must balance his personal and professional integrity and honor against his determination to prevent the criminals from escaping to ravage again. The tradition of honor is represented and articulated by a Confederate general who appears in Robicheaux's visions. The general's ideal of honorable conduct is shown by his refusal to call down cannon fire on northern troops at a latrine because they were not then on the field of battle. He tells Robicheaux, "'No matter what occurs in your life, no matter how bad the circumstances seem to be, you must never consider a dishonorable act as a viable alternative.'" For Robicheaux, however, special situations change the rules. He tells his partner, "The army taught me what a free-fire zone is, Rosie. It's a place where the winners make up the rules after the battle's over. Anyone who believes otherwise has never been there." The dilemma—the evident necessity of ruthlessness and the consequent betrayal of one's own sense of right behavior—is always with Robicheaux. When Robicheaux's daughter Alafair is kidnapped, the general tries one last time to counsel him against violating the criminals' civil rights: "Don't use those whom you love to justify a dishonorable cause." Robicheaux's refusal of such counsel apparently leads the general to repudiate him: "Then you will do it on your own, suh, and without me." At that moment, it seems, Robicheaux separates himself from the long-treasured tradition of southern honor or, perhaps, it separates itself from him.

Burke's use of the Confederate general brings an element of magical realism to the hard-boiled genre. In previous novels Robicheaux has nightmares, daydreams, hallucinations, and dry drunks that intrude into the narrative of police procedure and detection and serve as rich layering of his personality and past, but his visions are always personal to him. At first his encounters with the Confederate dead seem to fit into this established pattern, for, as Bootsie explains to Robicheaux when he begins to see and then to carry on long conversations with long-dead soldiers, the Civil War movie, with its period costumes and re-creation of military fighting, may be triggering his visions. But Burke goes further, for Robicheaux is not the only person who sees and talks to the Confederate dead: one of the actors sees them, as do Robicheaux's daughter Alafair and one of her young playmates. Moreover, even though the general says he will not accompany Robicheaux in the last confrontation, a crutch, similar to the one the general is seen leaning on throughout the novel, trips up the fleeing felon. Even more difficult to explain at a literal level is a photograph Alafair finds in a book about the Civil War: the general with whom Robicheaux has been interacting throughout the novel is shown with seven of his aides and enlisted men. In the back row, not explained, is the likeness of the modern Dave Robicheaux.

Although *Dixie City Jam* (1994) is based on the unlikely premise that a wrecked World War II Nazi submarine is floating around in the Gulf of Mexico, the novel is less surreal than its predecessor. Burke once again delves into the seamy underlife of New Orleans, concentrating on the uneasy relations between the Irish and Italians, Jews and anti-Semites, blacks and whites, and good cops and bad cops. Robicheaux is at the nexus of these tensions because he has twice found the German submarine, which is swept around the Gulf by tides and storms. The sub is a moving target, necessitating that the concerned parties, with their various reasons for raising the sub, all focus on Robicheaux as the person capable of locating it again.

Robicheaux's main adversary is Will Buchalter, a neo-Nazi who not only exhibits unsual physical cruelty—at one point, for example, he administers electric shocks to Robicheaux's genitals—but also is a master of psychological manipulation. Robicheaux discovers that Buchalter had previously driven a police officer to suicide by undermining his credibility, sanity, and professionalism. Buchalter enjoys the terror and fear he creates as much as physical attacks. For example, part of his psychological warfare involves sneaking into Robicheaux's home and simply allowing them to discover that he had stood in their bedroom watching them sleep.

Bootsie takes up alcohol in an effort to cope with the fear and stress Buchalter is causing in her life, so Robicheaux must counsel her about the demon that he barely keeps at bay himself even as he contends with a maniac who seems to have almost mystical powers.

With *Burning Angel* (1995), Burke arguably pushes the hard-boiled genre even further into new territory than he did in *In the Electric Mist with the Confederate Dead*. The title refers to Sonny Boy Marsallus, a local hood who has a connection to an old plantation and who literally haunts the novel. After Robicheaux has to identify Sonny's mangled, decomposing body, he feels guilt for having let Sonny out of jail, where he might have been safe. This circumstance perhaps can explain Sonny's appearance in Robicheaux's nightmares, but when Bootsie receives a phone call from the positively dead Sonny warning her that Robicheaux is in danger, a clear line is overstepped. Robicheaux's explanation of the intrusion of the dead upon the living is metaphysical: "I've always subscribed to the notion that perhaps history is not sequential; that all people, from all of history, live out their lives simultaneously, in different dimensions perhaps, occupying the same pieces of geography, unseen by one another, as if we are all part of one spiritual conception."

Burke explored the effects the past has upon the present in previous novels, but in *Burning Angel* the means he chooses are as radical as he has ever attempted. Burke is interested in the same asynchronous intermingling of the past and present South that William Faulkner explored in "The Bear," but whereas Faulkner kept the narrative lines of past and present realistically separated, Burke cares less for the constraints of realism and more for the mystical ways the past and the dead might intrude into the present. Robicheaux at times seems less the hardboiled realist than he does a thoroughgoing mystic, as when he asserts, "if you should ever doubt the proximity of the past . . . you only had to look over your shoulder . . . and you can see and hear with the clarity of a dream . . . yes, just a careless wink of the eye, just that quick, and you're among them, wending your way with liege lord and serf and angel, in step with the great armies of the dead."

Burke continues to explore the effect of the past on the present in *Cadillac Jukebox* (1996) and *Sunset Limited* (1998). The plot of *Cadillac Jukebox* hinges on the murder of a civil-rights leader nearly thirty years before the real action of the novel begins. Robicheaux takes up the cause of Aaron Crown, the supposed assassin, whom he finds personally reprehensible and about whose innocence he is not certain. There seems to be no logical reason for Robicheaux to defend Crown, an admitted racist, who is the subject of a book by Buford LaRose, a gubernatorial candidate who is touted as the best and brightest of the new South. Robicheaux, though, is sensitive enough to see something of himself in Crown, as he explains to his adopted daughter Alafair: "The guy loved his daughter, which means he has emotions and affections like the rest of us. That's something we don't like to think about when we assign a person the role of assassin and community geek." In the course of his investigation Robicheaux is pitted against the intertwined forces of the politically, economically, and socially respectable —"The LaRoses are what other people wanted to be"—and the mentally deranged who do the dirty work that oils the political machinery of kickbacks, illegal campaign contributions, and other crimes necessary to gain and keep power in Louisiana.

Burke's *Sunset Limited* features the return to New Iberia of Pulitzer Prize–winning photojournalist Megan Flynn and her movie brother, Cisco, the children of a labor organizer who was the victim of an unsolved murder forty years in the past. A casual remark Megan makes to Robicheaux begins the most convoluted plot of any of Burke's fiction so far. The action of the novel jumps back and forth in time as Robicheaux picks through layers of crimes and their cover-ups. Through the structure and content of his novel, Burke suggests why the South is so slow to change: everybody hides something, everybody has demons, and things cannot improve until the past is brought to light.

James Lee Burke has proved himself a skilled craftsman in the hard-boiled genre of detection. His plots and subplots are intricately woven, and his sharp dialogue etches characters into the readers' minds. While recognizable in the lineage of hard-boiled heroes in attitude and action, Dave

Robicheaux is also a complex, fully human character who Burke has used to explore the fluid borders of right and wrong, justice and injustice, integrity and corruption. In a statement he gave to the *Twentieth Century Crime and Mystery Writers,* Burke maintains that "the artist must tell the truth about the period in which he lives and expose those who would exploit their fellow men and make the earth an intolerable place. . . . I hope my work will be remembered because it details the lives of people who possess both courage and compassion."

Interviews:

Carter Dale, "Trouble in the Big Easy: An Interview with James Lee Burke," *Armchair Detective,* 25, no. 1 (1992): 40–50;

Dulcy Brainard, *Publishers Weekly* (20 April 1992);

W. C. Stroby, "Hanging Tough with James Lee Burke, *Writer's Digest* (January 1993): 38–40;

Rick Schultz, "The Mr. Showbiz Interview Archive: James Lee Burke," *People On Line* (8 September 1995);

Steven Womack, "A Talk with James Lee Burke," *Armchair Detective,* 29 (Spring 1996): 138–143.

References:

Rob Carney, "Clete Purcel to the Rampaging Rescue: Looking for the Hard-Boiled in James Lee Burke's *Dixie City Jam," Southern-Quarterly: A Journal of the Arts in the South,* 34 (Summer 1996): 121–130;

Samuel Coale, "The Dark Domain of James Lee Burke: Mysteries," *Clues: A Journal of Detective Fiction,* 18 (Spring–Summer 1997): 113–135;

Anneke Leenhouts, "Local Noir: Putting Southern Louisiana on the Map in the Crime Fiction of James Lee Burke," in *'Writing' Nation and 'Writing' Region in America* (Amsterdam, Netherlands: VU UP, 1996), pp. 217–225.

W. R. Burnett

(25 November 1899 – 25 April 1982)

Katherine Harper
Bowling Green State University

See also the Burnett entry in *DLB 9: American Novelists, 1910–1945.*

BOOKS: *Little Caesar* (New York: MacVeagh/Dial, 1929; London: Cape, 1929);

Iron Man (New York: MacVeagh/Dial, 1930; London: Heinemann, 1930);

Saint Johnson (New York: MacVeagh/Dial, 1930; London: Heinemann, 1931);

The Silver Eagle: A Chicago Novel (New York: MacVeagh/ Dial, 1931; London: Heinemann, 1932);

The Giant Swing (New York & London: Harper, 1932; London: Heinemann, 1933);

Dark Hazard (New York: Harper, 1933; London: Heinemann, 1934);

Goodbye to the Past: Scenes from the Life of William Meadows (New York & London: Harper, 1934; London: Heinemann, 1935);

The Goodhues of Sinking Creek (New York & London: Harper, 1934);

King Cole (New York & London: Harper, 1936); republished as *Six Days' Grace* (London: Heinemann, 1937);

The Dark Command: A Kansas Iliad (New York & London: Knopf, 1938; London: Heinemann, 1938);

High Sierra (New York & London: Knopf, 1940; London: Heinemann, 1940);

The Quick Brown Fox (New York: Knopf, 1942; London: Heinemann, 1943);

Nobody Lives Forever (New York: Knopf, 1943; London: Heinemann, 1944);

Tomorrow's Another Day (New York: Knopf, 1945; London: Heinemann, 1946);

Romelle (New York: Knopf, 1946; London: Heinemann, 1947);

The Asphalt Jungle (New York: Knopf, 1949; London: Macdonald, 1950);

Stretch Dawson (Greenwich, Conn.: Fawcett Gold Medal, 1950; London: Muller, 1960);

W. R. Burnett at the time of Captain Lightfoot *(1954; photograph by Carl Levy)*

Little Men, Big World (New York: Knopf, 1951; London: Macdonald, 1952);

Vanity Row (New York: Knopf, 1952; London: Macdonald, 1953);

Adobe Walls: A Novel of the Last Apache Rising (New York: Knopf, 1953; London: Macdonald, 1954);

Big Stan, as John Monahan (Greenwich, Conn.: Fawcett Gold Medal, 1953);

31

Captain Lightfoot (New York: Knopf, 1954; London: Macdonald, 1955);

It's Always Four O'Clock, as James Updyke (New York: Random House, 1956);

Pale Moon (New York: Knopf, 1956; London: Macdonald, 1957);

Underdog (New York: Knopf, 1957; London: Macdonald, 1957);

Bitter Ground (New York: Knopf, 1958; London: Macdonald, 1958);

Mi Amigo: A Novel of the Southwest (New York: Knopf, 1959; London: Macdonald, 1960);

Conant (New York: Popular Library, 1961);

Round the Clock at Volari's (Greenwich, Conn.: Fawcett Gold Medal, 1961);

The Goldseekers (Garden City, N.Y.: Doubleday, 1962; London: Macdonald, 1963);

Sergeants 3 (New York: Pocket Books, 1962);

The Widow Barony (London: Macdonald, 1962);

The Abilene Samson (New York: Pocket Books, 1963);

The Roar of the Crowd: Conversations With an Ex-Big Leaguer (New York: C. N. Potter, 1964);

The Winning of Mickey Free (New York: Bantam Pathfinder, 1965);

The Cool Man (Greenwich, Conn.: Fawcett Gold Medal, 1968);

Good-bye, Chicago: 1928, End of an Era (New York: St. Martin's Press, 1981; London: Hale, 1982).

PRODUCED SCRIPTS:

MOTION PICTURES

The Finger Points, screenplay by Burnett and John Monk Saunders, First National, 1931;

Law and Order, based on Burnett's novel *Saint Johnson,* screenplay by Burnett (uncredited), John Huston, and Tom Reed, Universal, 1932;

The Beast of the City, based on Burnett's novel *Saint Johnson,* screen story by Burnett, M-G-M, 1932;

Scarface: Shame of a Nation, based on novel by Armitage Trail, screenplay by Burnett, Ben Hecht, John Lee Mahin, and Seton I. Miller, United Artists, 1932;

The Whole Town's Talking, based on Burnett's serial "Jail Breaker," screenplay by Burnett (uncredited), Robert Riskin, and Jo Swerling, Columbia, 1935;

Some Blondes Are Dangerous, based on Burnett's novel *Iron Man,* screenplay by Burnett and Lester Cole, Universal, 1937;

The Westerner, screenplay by Burnett (uncredited), Niven Busch, Swerling, and others, United Artists, 1940;

The Get-Away, screenplay by Burnett, Wells Root, and J. Walter Ruben, M-G-M, 1941;

High Sierra, based on Burnett's novel, screenplay by Burnett and Huston, Warner Bros., 1941;

This Gun for Hire, screenplay by Burnett and Albert Maltz, Paramount, 1942;

Wake Island, screenplay by Burnett and Frank Butler, Paramount, 1942;

Action in the North Atlantic, additional dialogue by Burnett, Warner Bros., 1943;

Background to Danger, screenplay by Burnett, Warner Bros., 1943;

Crash Dive, screenplay by Burnett and Swerling, 20th Century-Fox, 1943;

San Antonio, screenplay by Burnett and Alan LeMay, Warner Bros., 1945;

The Man I Love, screenplay by Burnett (uncredited), Jo Pagano, and Catherine Turney, Warner Bros., 1946;

Nobody Lives Forever, screenplay by Burnett from his novel, Warner Bros., 1946;

Belle Starr's Daughter, screenplay by Burnett, 20th Century-Fox, 1948;

The Walls of Jericho, screenplay by Burnett (uncredited) and Lamar Trotti, 20th Century-Fox, 1948;

Yellow Sky, based on Burnett's *Stretch Dawson,* screenplay by Burnett and Trotti, 20th Century-Fox, 1948;

Night People, a.k.a. *The Last Man on Earth,* Burnett (uncredited), 20th Century-Fox, 1948;

The Asphalt Jungle, based on Burnett's novel, screenplay by Burnett (uncredited), Ben Maddow, and Huston, M-G-M, 1950;

Vendetta, screenplay by Burnett and Peter O'Crotty, RKO, 1950;

The Racket, screenplay by Burnett and William Wister Haines, RKO, 1951;

Dangerous Mission, screenplay by Burnett, Horace McCoy, and Charles Bennett, RKO, 1954;

Captain Lightfoot, based on Burnett's novel, screenplay by Burnett and Oscar Brodney, Universal, 1955;

I Died a Thousand Times, based on Burnett's *High Sierra,* screenplay by Burnett, Warner Bros., 1955;

Illegal, screenplay by Burnett, James R. Webb, and Frank Collins, Warner Bros., 1955;

Accused of Murder, based on Burnett's *Vanity Row,* screenplay by Burnett and Robert C. Williams, Republic, 1956;

The Hangman, screenplay by Burnett (uncredited) and Dudley Nichols, Paramount, 1959;

September Storm, screenplay by Burnett and Steve Fisher, 20th Century-Fox, 1960;

The Lawbreakers, screenplay by Burnett and Paul Monash, M-G-M, 1961;

Sergeants 3, screenplay by Burnett, United Artists, 1962;

Burnett (center) with actor Edward G. Robinson and director Mervyn LeRoy on the set of the 1930 movie version of Burnett's first novel, Little Caesar *(1929)*

4 for Texas, screenplay by Burnett (uncredited), Robert Aldrich, and Teddi Sherman, Warner Bros., 1963;

The Great Escape, screenplay by James Clavell and Burnett, United Artists, 1963;

Ice Station Zebra, screenplay by Burnett (uncredited) and Douglas Heyes, M-G-M, 1968;

Stiletto, screenplay by Burnett (uncredited), Harold Robbins, and A. J. Russell, Avco Embassy, 1969.

TELEVISION

"The Big Squeeze," based on story by Burnett, teleplay by Burnett and Robert C. Dennis, *The Untouchables,* ABC, 18 February 1960;

"Debt of Honor," teleplay by Burnett, *The Naked City,* ABC, 23 November 1960.

OTHER: "Dressing Up," *Great American Short Stories: O. Henry Memorial Prize Winning Stories, 1919–1932* (Garden City, N.Y.: Doubleday, Page, 1933);

"The Ivory Tower," in *The Best American Short Stories 1946,* edited by Martin Foley (Boston: Houghton Mifflin, 1946);

"Round Trip," in *Hard-Boiled,* edited by Bill Pronzini and Jack Adrian (New York: Oxford University Press, 1995), pp. 55–64.

SELECTED PERIODICAL PUBLICATIONS–UNCOLLECTED: "Along the Tracks," *Scribner's Magazine* (April 1930): 367–373;

"For Charity's Sake," *Esquire* (June 1934): 29+.

An author of Westerns and a successful screenwriter, W. R. Burnett is best known for his hard-boiled crime fiction. With the popular and critical success of the novels *Little Caesar* (1929) and *The Asphalt Jungle* (1949), he all but created two popular subgenres: the gangster novel and the criminal "caper" story. These novels, along with a third, *High Sierra* (1940), inspired movies that became classics of film noir.

For the first twenty years of his life, William Riley Burnett led a sheltered existence. He was born in Springfield, Ohio, on 25 November 1899, scion of a family that had long been prominent in state politics. His grandfather had served as the mayor of

Columbus, while his father, Theodore Addison Burnett, was a chief aide to Governor James Cox. His mother was the former Emily Upson Colwell Morgan. Growing up, young Bill Burnett enjoyed all the privileges and pleasures of a wealthy Midwestern household, including a postsecondary education at the Miami Military Institute in Germantown. Shortly before the end of World War I, he attempted to enlist in the U.S. Army Balloon Corps but was turned down. Disappointed, he enrolled instead in the journalism program at Ohio State University. He did not, however, find it stimulating enough, even when supplemented by football. Restless and dissatisfied, he dropped out after a single semester.

For the next year, Burnett drifted from one short-term job to another. He tried his hand at boxing, in vaudeville, as an insurance salesman, and as a factory worker. In 1920 he married Marjorie Louise Bartow; faced with the need to provide for two, he took a desk job at the Ohio Bureau of Labor Statistics. It was tedious work, and he hated it. Whenever he had free time, he immersed himself in a book or in writing stories of his own. His tastes at the time ran to ancient history and to European naturalism, whose practitioners—Emile Zola, Giovanni Verga, Prosper Merrimée—recalled Greek tragedy in their focus on long, slow slides triggered by human weakness. By 1927 Burnett had written dozens of imitative short stories, at least one play, and draft versions of five novels, but he was unable to sell a word.

Burnett's father knew that his son was miserable in his civil service job. In 1927 he was able to offer Burnett a position as a desk clerk at a hotel on Chicago's North Side. Burnett jumped at the opportunity to move to Chicago. Two premier little magazines—*Poetry* and *The Little Review*—were published in the city, which had inspired writers such as Theodore Dreiser, Ben Hecht, and Carl Sandburg.

Burnett was ill prepared for the culture shock he experienced in moving to the big city. "The city of Chicago appalled me," he told interviewers Ken Mate and Pat McGilligan more than fifty years later. "The contrast between Columbus, Ohio, for God's sake, and Chicago—why, you could be run over by a bus in Chicago and nobody would even look at you. It was a great thing for a writer, because it hit me with such impact." Chicagoans, or at least the ones he met, regarded newcomers with suspicion. The Northmere Hotel, his new workplace, was a seedy, third-rate place frequented by prostitutes, vagrants, and low-echelon gangsters. Burnett took every opportunity to lose himself in a good book or to scribble a few lines of a short story.

Burnett's literary interests soon made him a contact who helped to shape the course of his career. "Barber," a minor member of the Terry Druggan bootlegging gang, found the desk clerk's obsession with books fascinating. What kind of a man, he wondered aloud, wanted to read about things that had never happened, let alone write about them? Burnett responded that he was just as curious about the sort of a man who would join a gang. Barber offered to introduce him to the underworld, and the two men visited mob hangouts, speakeasies, and prizefights, a tour that culminated in the gangster's drunkenly firing a pistol from a rooftop just for fun.

Burnett mulled over his experiences for almost a year, allowing a plot to develop in his mind. He consulted a textbook for a sociological point of view. Then he sat down and began to write. At the end of seven weeks, he had a novel. He called it "The Furies," in reference to the winged goddesses of mythology who swooped down to exact justice on unpunished murderers. With all the brash confidence of the beginning writer, he mailed the typescript to the top editor in the country, Maxwell Perkins of Charles Scribner's Sons. Perkins read and liked it, but Burnett balked when the editor requested extensive rewrites before he would accept it for publication. Withdrawing "The Furies" from Scribners, he submitted it to the smaller Dial Press, which accepted it as written, requesting only that Burnett come up with a less obscure title. The book rolled off the presses in June 1929 as *Little Caesar*.

The action begins in a back room at Chicago's Club Palermo. The owner, Sam Vettori, outlines a plan for his gang to rob the Casa Alvorado nightclub at midnight on New Year's Eve. An accomplice in the floor show will signal them in and later misdirect the police. Cesare "Rico" Bandello, leader of the robbery crew, is a small, slim young man with dreams of wealth and power. When Rico shoots an off-duty police official during the holdup, his reputation as tough guy is established. He returns to the Club Palermo and challenges Vettori in front of the others, and the gang smoothly changes hands with no further bloodshed. Rico's utter ruthlessness is shown when he kills his young getaway driver, who had gone to confess his sin to a priest, leaving him to die on the cathedral steps.

For the next year the gangster's power steadily increases. He conducts bold territorial raids and displays open contempt for the lawmen who shadow him. Soon, kingpin Diamond Pete Montana bows to Rico's power. Even the racketeer-politician known as the Big Boy expresses admiration. His fall begins when the Casa Alvorado inside man, after days of relentless questioning by detectives, cracks and names Rico as the triggerman in the New Year's Eve robbery. Rico's friend

Burnett in a publicity photograph for the Little Caesar *movie (courtesy of the* Baltimore News-American *collection, University of Maryland at College Park)*

Otero dies at the hands of pursuing lawmen while rushing his chief out of town. The "big man" himself escapes, first to Hammond, Indiana, then to a gang hideout in Toledo, where he assumes a false identity.

Rico's fatal flaw is his arrogance. He bristles at the patronizing manner of the Ohio hoods, who know him only by an alias and think him old-fashioned. One night, unable to bear their taunts any longer, he draws himself up and snarls, "I'm Rico!" Within days, one of the men drunkenly passes the news on to a Chicagoan, and Rico must again run for his life. As he dashes up an alley, a police officer shouts for him to surrender. Instead, Rico whirls, a pistol in his hand. The officer fires. Fatally wounded, the gangster can only utter a desperate cry as he finally realizes his own mortality: "Mother of God, is this the end of Rico?"

Gangsters were a familiar subject by 1929. They were denounced on the front page of big-city newspa-

pers, portrayed on the motion picture screen, and fictionalized in popular novels, plays, even poetry. Rico Bandello, however, was something altogether new. He was not a stock villain, a comic figure, or a straw-man set up for the purpose of psychoanalysis, as was the title character of Frank Packard's *The Big Shot* (1929). Instead, Rico was a sharply drawn antihero who just happened to be a gangster.

Many critics lauded Burnett's originality and power in this first of the mainstream gangster novels. Herbert Asbury enthused in the 2 June 1929 *New York Herald Tribune* that "Mr. Burnett has written not only the most exciting book of the year but the most important novel of the post-war underworld that has ever been published; and in his principal character . . . he has created as true and accurate a figure as can be found anywhere in American fiction. A better story of this type may appear at some time in the future, and a more accurate portrait of a gang chieftain may be drawn, but it is a matter of very grave doubt." In *Time* (1 July 1929) the magazine's book critic concurred, writing that "Author Burnett, impersonal, powerful, may prove to be the novelist which Ernest Hemingway once promised to be but is not yet. *Little Caesar* is masterly writing as well as great reporting." In *Bookman* (June 1929) T. S. Mathews, who became one of Burnett's most ardent supporters, praised the book's "hard American English" and its unemotional, reportorial style. He guessed, correctly, that it was Burnett's first published novel but not the first that he had written. "If he can go on to other and less lurid stories of American life and handle them as dispassionately and as intensely as he has handled this one," Mathews predicted, "his name should become a household word." Before the public release of the novel, the Literary Guild chose it as a main selection, a move that exposed it to an audience that might otherwise have passed it by. The Dial Press advertised their new success as "A breathless story of Chicago's underworld told with the brilliance of a French classic."

Burnett's first novel has characteristic traits that become constants in his future work. The hallmark of any Burnett novel is tight, terse, almost staccato prose. Nonessential words are excised. Sentences and paragraphs are short, and speech is rendered realistically:

> Rico got on a street-car.
> "Well, how's things?" he said to the conductor.
> "All right," said the conductor; "getting cooler, ain't it? Reckon we'll have winter before we know it."
> "Yeah," said Rico.

Conversations and text alike are peppered with slang. The British publishers of *Little Caesar* were so baffled by the language that they included a three-page glossary with the first edition, some of the terms laughably mistranslated: "yegg," for example, which means a safe-robber, was given the genteel definition "a fellow."

Burnett's heroes are invariably lower-middle-class men who long for a better life and will do whatever it takes to attain it. Their success, however, depends upon Fate. They may fall victim to their own hubris, or to the treachery of an associate, or to blind chance—or even, as in Rico's case, to a combination of all three. For Burnett, though, failure does not necessarily mean a violent end. As the writer makes clear in later books, he considers humiliation a worse punishment than death.

Burnett often uses names to indicate character traits, particularly in his first novel. Rico Bandello—a pidgin-Italian translation of "rich gangster"—personifies the typical gunman's greed and arrogance. Sam Vettori's name suggests victory, an irony considering that the character loses in rapid succession his dignity, his business, his physique, and his life, as he is ultimately hanged for planning the nightclub robbery. The third man in the line of succession is Sam's nephew Ottavio, who plays a boorish Octavius to Rico's Caesar. Even the minor characters are appropriately named: a former boxer turned gunman, for example, is called Sansone, the Italian form of *Samson*. The German name of a gang-unit detective, Rieger, literally means "squad member," while a cunning member of the opposition mob is dubbed Liska, Czech for "fox."

Little Caesar was quickly bought as a motion picture property. Studio head Jack L. Warner later claimed that he discovered it when a friend handed him a copy to while away a long train trip. Director Mervyn LeRoy told a different story: Warner handed him a set of galley proofs to look over, saying that he had no time to read them himself. In his autobiography, *Mervyn LeRoy: Take One* (1974), the director remembers he "read straight through the night, my excitement heightening with every page." He rushed back to the studio and convinced Warner to purchase the rights. However the deal came about, the picture was made in 1930, starring Edward G. Robinson in a star-making role. To avoid trouble with local censorship boards, Rico's last line was altered to "Mother of Mercy" in most prints. *Little Caesar* is deservedly considered one of the finest and most exciting movies to emerge from the early talkie period.

Offered a contract with Warner Bros., Burnett brought Marjorie to Hollywood in early 1930. His crime stories had begun to appear in mainstream magazines. In "Round Trip," which was published in *Harper's Monthly Magazine* (August 1929), Burnett depicts a confidently tough Chicagoan in no-nonsense Ohio. "Dressing Up," which appeared also in *Harper's* (November 1929) is the gritty tale of Blue, a simple-minded gunman who struts through South Chicago in a new outfit, which he brags was bought with his bonus for shooting a member of a rival gang. Before long, he realizes that he is being shadowed. He is initially unworried because he feels nothing bad could happen to a man wearing brand-new silk underwear. As he works his way little by little toward home, however, his enemies close in. As his building comes into view and Blue sighs with relief that death "ain't in the cards," a window opens and machine-gun fire cuts him down. "Dressing Up" was selected as a co-recipient of the O. Henry Memorial Award for Best Short Story of 1929. It has been anthologized more that a dozen times and remains the best known of Burnett's short works.

Burnett's second novel was published in January 1930, while *Little Caesar* was still fresh in readers' minds. *Iron Man* tells the story of Coke Mason, a none-too-bright

Ann Dvorak as Cesca Camonte and Paul Muni as her brother, gangster Tony Camonte, in a still from the 1932 movie Scarface: Shame of a Nation, *written by Burnett, Ben Hecht, and others (Caddo/United Artists)*

boxer who dreams of winning the middleweight championship. Though physically tough, he is at heart an innocent. His only armor against the realities of the fight game is his manager and best friend, Regan. Thanks to a merciless training regimen, Coke is prepared when offered a match with the champion. He wins a long, bloody battle and becomes the top man in his division, achieving the dream he and Regan have shared. Then, just as life is looking its brightest, Coke's gold-digging former wife reappears, ready to cash in on his success. A modern Delilah, Rose in a few months saps the strong man's vitality by encouraging him to live "the good life." When Coke obeys her demand that he fire Regan, the manager immediately approaches another boxer to take away the championship. The final paragraphs of *Iron Man* trace the beaten Coke's confused impressions as his handlers bring him back to consciousness and haul him from the ring.

Like its predecessor, *Iron Man* is told in abrupt, rat-a-tat phrasing that captures the essence of Coke and Regan's hard-boiled world. Critics singled out the fight

scenes for special praise—"magnificently described, if unavoidably a bit repetitious," said Theodore Purdy in *Saturday Review of Literature* (8 February 1930)—as they did the character of Regan. Still puzzled over Burnett's unconventional style, some tried to force him into the standard highbrow-lowbrow spectrum. "*Iron Man* . . . is not literature, but it is something," hemmed Herbert Gorman in *The New York Herald Tribune* (5 January 1930): "Mr. Burnett is not a great writer, but there is a barometric quality about him that tells the state of the psychological weather today. He is not a mere exploiter of the 'goddam' school of fiction, but an honest and intense fellow who knows (or is sure he knows, which is much the same thing) what he is writing about and who pursues his pathway to its logically appointed end."

Far from suffering the usual second-novel slump, *Iron Man* proved nearly as popular as *Little Caesar*. The Book-of-the-Month Club chose it as a main selection, making Burnett the first author ever to have his first two novels selected. Humorist Corey Ford, writing as "John Riddell," devised a *Vanity Fair* parody, "Iron Man of Manhattan" (May 1930), which combined the plot of the hard-boiled novel with that of a Katharine Brush romance released the same week. Universal Pictures produced a movie version of the novel within the year, with Lew Ayres as Coke, Robert Armstrong as Regan, and Jean Harlow as Rose. The novel was made into a movie a second time in 1937 as *Some Blondes Are Dangerous* and again under its original title in 1951.

Burnett's third book was inspired by a newspaper article about history buffs who reenacted Wild West events. He traveled to Tombstone, Arizona, checked into a deserted hotel, and wrote furiously for three weeks. The result, *Saint Johnson* (1930), is less interesting for the student of hard-boiled fiction than is its movie treatment. After a faithful adaptation of the novel was released in 1932 by Universal as *Law and Order*, M-G-M hired Burnett to rewrite the story, with the villainous Clanton brothers replaced by thinly veiled portraits of mobsters Al Capone and "Machine Gun" Jack McGurn. *The Beast of the City* (1932), starring Walter Huston, who had played much the same role in the Universal movie, was the most graphically violent American picture to date, with on-screen shootings galore, police manhandling, and even the mass hanging of one gang by another (the victims of which are identified by a bored reporter munching on a sandwich). At the climax, Huston and a squad of policemen march across a nightclub toward a line of mobsters, each side riddling the other with bullets. The McGurn character falls to his knees, blood running from his mouth. The dying "Capone" half-rolls out of camera range, still clutching the edges of an overturned table. Fully two minutes into the battle, the deafening explosions slow and then stop. The room is silent—because every man in it is dead.

When he moved to Chicago in 1927, Burnett had written and abandoned five full-length novels. By 1931, with three successes to his name, he began to revise these early efforts. *The Silver Eagle: A Chicago Novel* (1931), originally begun five years before, tells the story of Harworth, a shady Chicagoan who amasses a fortune and wants desperately to join the social elite. The group of young people he hopefully approaches are a shallow lot who are amused by his attempts to acquire "class." In the end the would-be clubman proves unable to escape his past; after he severs what he thinks are the last of his gang ties, his old associates reward his defection with a drive-by shooting.

Burnett's revision of his early novel was unsuccessful. Instead of reconceiving the book as a whole, he took the earlier draft, a straight account of class and generational conflict influenced by the plays of Noel

Coward, and spiked it with the underworld characters his readers had come to expect. The seams are evident: Harworth sounds less like a Midwestern racketeer than a socially ambitious English tradesman. Edward Weeks in the December 1931 issue of *The Atlantic Monthly* obviously wanted to like the book but could not bring himself to be completely positive:

> Harworth, with his big shoulders, his love of money, and his silly monocle, is sometimes a little too theatrical, but in his affection for his manager, Stein (a fine figure!), and in his dealings with Molina (Capone?) we see him plain and alive. It is a good story, swift in action and weak only in this particular—society and gangsters don't mix any better here than in actuality. When Mr. Burnett writes of hard guys, they are hard and no mistake; when he writes of artists or society folk, they are—well, stuffed shirts.

Burnett's negotiations to sell *The Silver Eagle* to Paramount Pictures ended when the Hays Office, guardian of the moviegoing public's morals, objected to the work on the grounds that, even though Harworth dies in the end, he is portrayed as having profited from crime.

That *Scarface: Shame of a Nation* (1932) made it past the Hays Office at all is a surprise; that it escaped with only a few cuts of exceptionally violent or suggestive scenes and an alternate ending for more censorial states is astonishing. By the time Burnett was brought into the project, chief writer Hecht had all but discarded Armitage Trail's 1930 novel in favor of an original plot that cast an Al Capone figure, Tony Camonte, as a Chicago Cesare Borgia. Hecht's strengths were in overall plotting and man-woman dialogues, which he concentrated on, while Burnett and two others worked to dramatize well-known gangland events. The murder of Dion O'Banion, the owner of a flower shop, is implied in typical, terse Burnett style. When Little Boy meets Camonte on the street, Camonte bends to sniff a rose in his friend's lapel. "Nice. Did you pick one up for me?" he inquires. "Didn't have time," murmurs Little Boy. The men nod knowingly at each other, and the screen fades to black.

The Giant Swing (1932) is Burnett's most ambitious novel. Its basic plot is as old as *The Odyssey*: a character of humble origins—in this case, an Ohio dance-hall piano player—decides to try his luck in another place, triumphs, and returns to his hometown years later to see how it and its residents have changed. The language of this novel is more poetic, more literary, than that of Burnett's earlier books. Though a few of its characters are swaggeringly tough, its hero avoids conflict, even to the point of giving up the woman he loves without a struggle. Burnett told interviewers at the time that he had written the initial draft in just four weeks but neglected to mention that this had been in the early 1920s; as he later admitted, *The Giant Swing* was really a ten-year effort, involving two drastic rewrites and the cutting of twenty thousand words.

Some critics swooned over Burnett's first attempt at Art. Focusing more on the man than on his creation, Lisle Bell in *New York Herald Tribune* of 11 September 1932 acknowledged Burnett's talent for creating low-brow characters, saying that he "understands their idiom as well as their appetite, and when occasion requires, he can speak their language with a crisp and exact intonation. But he is too wise a craftsman to depend upon that source of inspiration alone. He uses it for what it is worth, as flavor and as stimulant, but he doesn't make the mistake of believing that novels with a tough crust need no filling." Readers, however, largely ignored *The Giant Swing*.

Burnett added a bit more grit to his next effort, *Dark Hazard* (1933). Protagonist Jim Turner, the night clerk at a Chicago hotel, must battle his fear of a tenant who makes a game of taunting him almost to the breaking point. He eventually earns this man's respect and then his help in handicapping greyhound races. Turner becomes obsessed by a jet black dog called Dark Hazard, so much so that his wife tells him to choose between it and her. The weak-willed clerk cannot decide and spends the rest of the book seesawing between affection for the two most precious things in his world.

The writer made no secret of the fact that he had based Jim Turner on himself and Marg Turner on his own wife, Marjorie. Readers could note similarities between the description of the main character in the second paragraph of the novel and the dust jacket photo of Burnett:

> The night clerk did not look like a night clerk. He was a big, light-haired man of thirty-four, with powerful, broad shoulders, a strong neck which widened out at the base, and a large face with pronounced masculine features; there were marked bony ridges above his gray eyes, and his forehead, of medium height, was very wide. He had tried to plaster his coarse blond hair into conventional smoothness, but it stuck up behind. He was dressed like a night clerk should be dressed, smartly, unobtrusively, but muscles bulged under his hand-me-down coat and his necktie was crooked. One thing kept him from being a very formidable-looking man—an air of sleepy good nature, somewhat like a tame bear.

Burnett posed for publicity shots alongside his own greyhounds, one of which had set a California speed record in 1932. Like his creator, Turner is a gambling addict, and is in a long-term, loving marriage that is beginning to crack under the strain. *Dark Hazard* was filmed twice by Warner Bros., first in 1934 with Edward G. Robinson in the lead, then as *Wine, Women, and Horses* (1937) starring Barton MacLane.

Burnett's next two book-length works were historical novels based on events in his own family. In the boldly experimental *Goodbye to the Past: Scenes from the Life of William Meadows* (1934), the title character dies at the end of the first chapter. The following chapter presents a flashback to a few years before, and each succeeding one to a still earlier time, until, in the final pages, Meadows is an infant. Many critics were dubious about this technique, and one suggested that readers start with the last chapter and work their way forward. Fred T. Marsh of *The New York Times* was a great fan of Burnett's, and it grieved him to see the writer turn out what he called "a bad novel [but] a good book." He devoted the whole of his 9 September 1934 column to scolding the author for not trying harder to write the Great American Novel. In the process he gave Burnett some of the highest praise of his career:

> Most of W.R. Burnett's tales are so good, so filled with action and the vernacular, that the quality of his prose and the subtle touches which grace his celebrations of a man's world have been more or less overlooked. No one in his field writes so well as Burnett. He has no mannerisms, no affectations. He has not borrowed from Hemingway the theatrical device of consistent and reiterated understatement. But he gets out of the language all he has to say, all he wants to reveal, about his people. That, after all, is what makes his stories so effective.

Ignoring Marsh's advice to concentrate on more important topics, Burnett next turned to a rewrite of his novelette "Hard Wood," which four years before had made the finals of a competition sponsored by *Scribner's Magazine*. Maxwell Perkins's correspondence, now held by Princeton University, documents the editor's struggle to convince the stubborn young author of the need for rewrites. At first, still feeling the sting of Perkins's criticism of *Little Caesar*, Burnett resisted; then he suddenly realized that Perkins had seen a side of his characters that he had not and obediently made every change, including a complete new ending. The revised version, *The Goodhues of Sinking Creek*, was published in 1934 and, like its predecessor, sold poorly.

By the mid 1930s, America was slowly becoming aware of the specter of European fascism. To an antiextremist such as Burnett, things were nearly as frightening at home, where Father Charles Coughlin spouted hate-filled "sermons" on coast-to-coast radio and populist governor Huey Long ruled Louisiana like a baron of old. *King Cole* (1936), published shortly after Long's assassination, was a response to what the author saw as an alarming rightward shift in American politics. Its protagonist, Governor Read Cole, is advised by his reelection staff to blame "foreigners and radicals" for the economic woes of his state. Soon, right- and left-wing mobs are battling in the streets, and Cole must declare martial law to keep the peace. His speeches turn into huge anti-Red rallies staffed by jackbooted troops; at one of these, a radical takes a shot at him and instead hits the governor's only friend. By the end of the novel, Cole's family and mistress have abandoned him, the friend has died, and Cole has once again been chosen governor. He staggers away from his victory party, seeing nothing ahead but another two years in office—and then, perhaps, the presidency of the United States. *The Dark Command: A Kansas Iliad,* published two years later, applies a similar formula to historical events, as a charismatic villain based on William Quantrill all but takes over Civil War–era Kansas with a band of armed, uniformed raiders.

The second of Burnett's best-remembered crime novels is *High Sierra* (1940). Its hero, Roy Earle, is the last living member of the Dillinger gang, a tired old man at age thirty-eight. Released from prison, he heads west to direct the robbery of a resort hotel. En route, he befriends an Ohio family traveling west whose youngest member—a pretty, fresh-looking girl with a clubfoot—reminds him of his childhood sweetheart. Roy is appalled to find that his fellow bandits—Red, Babe, and Marie—are barely out of their teens and have never progressed beyond gas-station holdups. In this and several subsequent novels, Burnett includes a group of three misfits to serve as foils to his protagonist.

After spending a few days getting to know the Goodhues, Roy pays a gang doctor to operate on Velma's foot. She soon learns to walk normally and even to dance. Just before the robbery, however, this "innocent" abruptly tells Roy that she loves a man in Ohio and plans to marry him. After that, everything goes wrong. First, Roy takes out his hurt and anger on a hotel security guard. Then the inside man panics and jumps into the getaway car, which skids off a mountain road, killing Babe and Red. Roy and Marie find their backer dead of a heart attack, and when a detective tries to blackmail them, Roy kills him. Ignoring Marie's pleas, he forces all his money on her and puts her on a bus. Then he flees into the mountains, pursued by lawmen who think him a "mad-dog" killer. Taunting the officers who call for him to surrender, Roy does not see a police sniper aiming at him with a deer rifle. His final thought is an image from his childhood—combined with the happy realization that he loves Marie.

High Sierra was a turning point in Burnett's writing. While he had previously given readers enough of a glimpse into his characters' minds to see what made

them tick, this novel was the first in which he revealed deep emotion. Neither a minimalist figure like Rico Bandello nor a realistic but dull-witted character like Coke Mason, Roy is a thinking, feeling man, capable of frustration, nostalgia, curiosity, and love. Unlike Burnett's earlier creations, Earle realizes that Fate is against him, and he thumbs his nose at it by allowing a little dog said to be a jinx follow him around. Only when he realizes that he is dragging Marie into the unknown with him does he snap back to his senses and send her away to face her own destiny. Burnett delves into the thoughts of other characters as well—Marie, Doc Parker, Louis Mendoza, and all of Roy's peers. The "good" characters, who in this case are the outsiders, are shown only on the surface. The only exception may have been meant as a sly editorial comment: the final pages reveal the ignoble thoughts of a newspaperman.

For all its originality as a novel, *High Sierra* bears an unsettling resemblance to a Broadway success of five years before, Robert Sherwood's *The Petrified Forest.* Both works are set in out-of-the-way places and revolve around a robbery foiled by an informer. Both feature desperadoes with noble names: Sherwood's is called Duke Mantee, though Burnett tops that with the double "Roy Earle." (Humphrey Bogart played both characters in the movie versions.) Gabby in the stage play and Marie in the novel have jealous boyfriends who push them around, and both dream aloud of escape to a place or situation they cannot define. Both Pa Goodhue and Sherwood's Gramp Maple ramble on at length about changing values in America and speak of Duke/Roy as—like themselves—representative of a bygone day. Burnett had alluded to dozens of other authors in his earlier novels without copying their work, so it seems likeliest that these similarities are either an homage to *The Petrified Forest* or mere coincidence. Certainly, Sherwood never complained.

It is interesting to read the pleased, if flustered reaction of a female critic in the 2 August 1940 *Spectator,* who has obviously never read anything like *High Sierra:*

> Mr. Burnett's earlier work is unknown to me, but the wrapper describes him as 'the masterly reporter of the underworld,' and he certainly does appear to know his gangster stuff. Better than that, he knows how to hold it together and make it march in decent narrative form. He sees it as legitimate material, in fact, and does not have to bone and pulp it, removing all predicates, &c., before offering it home to our business and bosoms. In fact, this author is not primarily moved by the all-but-unmanageable sensibility of the gangster, which has hitherto broken the hearts and prose styles of too many American writers; rather he views him detachedly as a man of natural appetites and rational processes, who takes the wrong turning for likely and unremarkable reasons, as you or I might. . . . Justice is

done, but the pang of regret which the author wrings from us is more justifiable, or at least more excusable, than usual. Roy Earle is a live character, normal and natural; his story has pace and warmth as well as form; and the slang is lovely.

By the end of the war this same critic had become enough of an expert to say with authority that Burnett's latest product was readable but not nearly as tough as she had come to expect.

High Sierra was filmed three times: under its original title in 1941, starring Bogart; as the 1949 Western *Colorado Territory;* and in 1955 as *I Died a Thousand Times,* with Jack Palance and Shelley Winters working from a Burnett script. After completing the 1941 picture, Bogart recorded an audio-drama version that was broadcast to American troops over Armed Forces Radio.

Having set fascism aside for the space of one book, Burnett returned to the subject in his 1942 novel, *The Quick Brown Fox.* In this variation on *King Cole* Burnett attacks what he saw as Americans' blind acceptance of celebrity. When reporter Ray Benedict learns that his girlfriend's cousin has been rescued at sea after having saved the lives of fourteen sailors, he, like the rest of Nyland, Ohio, eagerly awaits the man's return. The newspaper owner is so taken with Brant Harding that he suggests the handsome, well-spoken young man run for office. Benedict, though, after interviewing Harding and his friends—an American adventurer and a massive Samoan—begins to realize that his subject is less than heroic. There are cracks in the trio's rescue story, and when pressed they cheerfully admit it is a fake. Given enough money or power, Harding brags in private, he will undertake any task for anyone—including his current European client. By the time Benedict convinces his employer of Harding's designs, it is too late: the hero is on the Congressional ballot and has eloped with the publisher's daughter to ensure positive coverage. Ohioans mass behind him, too dazzled by his star status to notice that his speeches are thinly veiled Nazi rhetoric. Harding quickly forms an elite military-political unit to crush opponents. Only when Benedict and a few brave friends use their freedom of the press—and quietly remind the Samoan that Harding had murdered his beloved cousin—are they able to defeat him.

The Quick Brown Fox is an early example of what the French dubbed the *serie noir* (black series). There are no happy endings. Benedict and his friends win the day but are uneasy victors, for the voters, still blissfully unaware of Harding's plans for them, are equally open to the next personable extremist to come along. In fact, this seems likely to happen, as the candidate's army of faceless strongarm men have now slipped back into their respectable places in the community. Milton Hin-

Humphrey Bogart as Roy Earle in a still from the 1941 movie version of Burnett's novel High Sierra *(1940), for which Burnett and John Huston wrote the screenplay (Warner Bros.)*

dus of the *New York Herald Tribune* commented in his review of 1 February 1942: "Little Caesar has grown into a monstrosity looking strangely like certain well-known European and Asiatic gentlemen." Fred T. Marsh wrote at length in *The New York Times* (8 February 1942) about the author's talent in general, adding that the current novel

remains straight Burnett, slanted his own way, and is one of his best, if not his best—although it lacks, it seemed to me, completion. He is an economical story writer, which is all to the good; but perhaps too much so here. At any rate, the tale itself is a rattler. Hear the men talk in these pages—and I don't mean his quotations from St. Adolf, as he sneeringly calls the master himself. He is really good; he puts the finger on a dozen absurdities, hypocrisies, stupidities and sillinesses of this democracy. After you have finished the story, look it over for plan, balance, skill in contrivance and play of ideas. It's even better than you thought.

In the majority of Burnett's writing, the plot twists and multiple characters make third-person narration a necessity. *The Quick Brown Fox* depends upon hidden thoughts and motives; it is one of only two novels that takes the viewpoint of a single character.

Burnett had dedicated nearly all of his books, including this one, to his wife, Marjorie, and told interviewers again and again how grateful he was for her support. Nevertheless, the marriage ended in divorce about the time *The Quick Brown Fox* was published. In 1943 he married Whitney Forbes Johnstone, a union that lasted until his death. The couple had two sons, William Riley III (the "Butch" of Burnett's later dedications) and James Addison.

Nobody Lives Forever was originally a 1943 *Collier's* serial about a trio of confidence men who know of a rich widow ripe for the picking. They are not young or handsome enough to attract her attention, so their leader, a drug addict named Doc Ganson, hires attractive "master con" Jim Farrar to woo her, with the understanding that he will pass along a generous finder's fee from the proceeds. Instead of fleecing Gladys Halvorsen and leaving town, however, Farrar falls in love with and marries her. Warner Bros. optioned the story, intending to star John Garfield in a Burnett-scripted adaptation. Garfield, however, surprised everyone by enlisting in the military. Rather than recast the picture, the studio chose to keep renewing its option until the war was over. In the meantime, Burnett fleshed out his characters and turned the serial into a full-length novel. The film version, with Garfield, Geraldine Fitzgerald, and Walter Brennan, eventually reached theaters in 1946.

While it does not match the quality of some of the earlier novels, *Tomorrow's Another Day* (1945) is still a minor gem. Lonnie Drew, a devil-may-care young gambler, wins a restaurant in a card game and discovers, to his surprise, that he can be happy holding down a real job. He falls in love with a beautiful customer, Mary O'Donnell, but his interest earns him the enmity of her escort, Jack Pool, another gambler who is jealous of the younger man's success. When Lonnie and Mary marry, he decides to give up gambling, after just one more high-stakes wager to set them up for life. He unwisely agrees to use his impeccable credit to lay off a $100,000 horse-race bet for Pool. However, minutes after he has signed a receipt for his enemy's money, two masked gunmen burst in and take it away. Only then does a smiling Pool reveal that the cash belongs not to him, but to a murderous Chicago mobster, Gus Borgia. It is up to the newlyweds to use what little time they have to raise the necessary cash and preserve not only Lonnie's life but his reputation.

A recurring minor character in Burnett's novels is the figure of a nerve-wrecked writer—at least partially based on Burnett—who comments on but does not affect the action. Burnett's surrogate in *Tomorrow's*

Another Day is Lonnie's accountant, Ray Cooper, a former sportswriter who considers himself cured of alcoholism because he now drinks only beer. Although he is nearly frantic over his friend's predicament, Ray finds himself longing to lock himself in his room, "put on his pajamas, get in bed, and lose himself as long as possible among the brutal intricacies of Roman history." Ray's character is one-third of the misfit trio in the book, the others being Pinky and Willy, a Mutt-and-Jeff pair of roughnecks whom Mary softens into an ideal cook and chauffeur. Perhaps consciously making a connection, Burnett reuses a character name from *Little Caesar*. In the 1929 book, Joe Pavlovsky is one of rival Little Arnie's men, who good-naturedly greets Rico while he is hiding in Hammond and forces him to flee even further east. In *Tomorrow's Another Day*, Joe is an up-and-coming young hoodlum—the elder Pavlovsky's son?—who comes to Lonnie's aid, partially to repay an old favor and partially to get in good with Borgia. (Similarly, Burnett assigned Willy's surname, Fiala, to a Mob-connected character in the 1961 *Round the Clock at Volari's,* perhaps recalling that the chauffeur's brother was a Chicago gangster.)

With a few notable exceptions—Gladys in *Nobody Lives Forever* and Doll in *The Asphalt Jungle* (1949)—Burnett had little success creating believable female characters. His difficulty is evident in *Romelle* (1946), his only novel to center on a heroine. In this variation on the Bluebeard legend, Romelle La Rue, a nightclub singer, marries Jules, a mysterious Frenchman, within days of meeting him. Almost immediately she suspects that there is a dark secret in his past, perhaps having to do with a locked trunk he has warned her not to touch. "Admirers of Mr. Burnett's fast-paced, tough stories will be grieved to learn that this one is neither fast nor particularly tough," remarked the reviewer in *The New Yorker* (14 September 1946). The next day in *The New York Times* James MacBride called the book "anemic" and complained of "too many telegraphed punches, and far too much supine writhing on the part of the heroine."

"When I have something to say and I can't say it in one book, I do a trilogy," Burnett told Mate and McGilligan in 1983. *The Asphalt Jungle* was the first installment of what has come to be called the writer's City Trilogy, a portrait of an unnamed Midwestern metropolis as it devolves from normalcy to imbalance to anarchy. It was also the first example of Burnett's second new subgenre, one that inspired endless imitation: the caper novel, which tracks a crime step-by-step from planning through completion and usually beyond.

The Asphalt Jungle is Burnett's longest, most complex book. As it opens, a mild-looking little German man knocks at the door of Cobby's horse parlor in the middle of the night. Criminal mastermind "Doc" Riemenscheider is only hours out of prison, but he has already managed to lose his police tail. He has purchased a burglary plan from a fellow convict and has come to ask for Cobby's help, and that of his financier, attorney Alonzo Emmerich. The job, as planned, requires three men. Cobby suggests loyal Gus Minisi to drive and, to blow the safe, a clever thief named Louis Bellini, who has been semiretired since starting a family. The third man is a more difficult choice: the gunman who will protect them until the jewels are fenced must be tough, drug free, and trustworthy. Doc insists on Dix Handley, a brutal Kentuckian he had overheard both threatening Cobby and stating a personal code of honor. Emmerich expresses such delight at the plan that a suspicious Doc investigates. The attorney, he finds, is on the brink of bankruptcy. Even so, he decides to proceed. The burglary is free of trouble until the last moment, when a security guard opens the door. Dix clubs him, and the man's pistol goes off, mortally wounding Louis.

Emmerich is waiting when Doc and Dix arrive with the jewels—as is a crooked private detective he has hired to rob them. Both strongarms pull their guns, and the detective is shot dead, while Dix is wounded. Sparing Emmerich to negotiate with the insurance company, Dix and Doc go into hiding. Meanwhile, the police step up the dragnet begun when Doc first eluded his tail. A sadistic detective who knows Cobby's fear of violence beats the little bookie into a confession. Officers arrest Gus, then barge into the Bellini flat, where they find Louis laid out in his coffin. Emmerich, told that he is in custody, steps away to call his wife, then kills himself. Now, only Dix and Doc remain. Doc hires a cabbie to take him to Cleveland, where he can catch a plane to Mexico and spend the rest of his life ogling young girls. The gunman and his lover, Doll, plan to drive to Dix's family farm. Dix's wound has become infected, however, and by the time they reach Kentucky, he is raving and nearly unconscious. The farm, Doll learns, was sold years before. She manages to get Dix to his mother's house, where he soon dies. Meanwhile, Doc waits in a café while the cabbie buys gas. As three teenagers are dancing to the jukebox, the old lecher urges them on, plying them with nickels. He does not notice the policemen standing beside him until it is too late. They have been watching him, they say, for two or three minutes—about the time it takes to play a phonograph record.

One of the keys to *The Asphalt Jungle* is the obsessive nature of its characters. Even sideline figures are driven by some inner desire. Cobby yearns for prestige and its accompanying security. He glories in his friendship with "big man" Emmerich and relishes his status

Dust jacket for the second novel (1951) in Burnett's City Trilogy, in which he traces the decline into anarchy of an unnamed Midwestern city

as "the biggest non-syndicate bookie in the city," neither of which protects him from Sergeant Dietrich's ready fists. Angela, Emmerich's mistress, is self-obsessed to the exclusion of everything else; by the end of the book, she has been protectively taken up by Detective Andrews, who views all women through chivalrous eyes. The reader learns almost at once that Lou Farbstein of the *World* is obsessed with finding an example of complete honesty. He finds his man in Commissioner Theo Hardy, whose own existence is driven by an old-fashioned work ethic. Through their identical desires, the author hints, Riemenschneider and Emmerich are essentially the same person: both are middle-aged and of German heritage, and both lust after wealth and much younger women. Only their professions separate them, and even this line is blurred when the attorney becomes a criminal and the thief a negotiator for Emmerich's life. Characteristically, Burnett gives the three misfits of the novel—crooked-backed Gus, socially handicapped Louis, and Dix, with his reputation for mental instability—the noble obsessions of friends, family, and home. After Louis's passing, a fourth outsider, Doll, steps in to replace him and to take over the yearning for family. Her lover dies, but not before looking from her to his unmarried brother and assuring him, "Her name's Dorothy Pelky, and she's all right." After a lifetime of hope and disappointments, Burnett suggests, this character may finally be able to achieve her dream.

Critical reaction to *The Asphalt Jungle* was almost unanimously positive. Bryan Forbes of *The Spectator* of 11 August 1950 classed it with Graham Greene's entertainments and termed it "a book well worth reading." Both Elizabeth Bullock of *The New York Times* and Victor P. Hass of the *Saturday Review of Literature* (who rated it, respectively, as the best and second best book of Burnett's career) noted guiltily that they had rooted for the criminals, while aware that they should be on the side of the police. "Such dillydallying on the part of the reader is, of course, ridiculous," continued Hass in his 15 October 1949 review, "and the heartless Mr. Burnett, having tied the reader into knots, unravels him and slaps him good for sneaking around in the dark corners of the jungle and enjoying himself." Nearly forty years after the initial release of the novel, H. R. F. Keating listed it as one of the one hundred best mystery and crime books ever written.

The book's first, best-known Hollywood adaptation was directed by John Huston for M-G-M in 1950, with Sterling Hayden as Dix, Jean Hagen as Doll, Sam Jaffe as Doc Riemenschneider, Louis Calhern as Emmerich, and, in the small role of Angela, Marilyn Monroe. "It's a dirty, nasty picture about dirty, nasty people, and I wouldn't cross the street to see it," studio head Louis B. Mayer is reputed to have said, but *The Asphalt Jungle* was a box office smash and remains a top-quality example of 1950s film noir. Other adaptations were not nearly so successful: M-G-M Westernized the premise eight years later as the Alan Ladd vehicle *The Badlanders,* and a third version, *Cairo* (1965), transplants the caper from the Midwest to the Middle East. In the fourth version, *Cool Breeze* (1972), even the thieves' motive is changed: they commit the robbery not for personal gain, but to raise money for the Black Power movement. A television series "suggested by" the novel ran for five months on ABC in 1961.

In *Little Men, Big World* (1951), the second book of the trilogy, the Big Midwestern City is beginning to slip. Its more dangerous sections—confined in *The Asphalt Jungle* to Camden Square—have grown in size and political clout. Corruption is more overt. Police Commissioner Stark has control of his territory, but not the absolute authority wielded by predecessor Hardy. The rackets are directed by a faceless power broker, called the Mover, via manager Orval "Arky"

Wanty—like Dix Handley, a Southern-born racketeer "too countrified for the city, too citified for the country." After years of urban living, Arky has grown hard and shrewd, but when his common-law wife's teenaged cousin abandons a baby with them, he slowly begins to regain his humanity. Then a territory war breaks out. An attempt by the rival mob to assassinate Arky accidentally kills his wife, and he returns to his old, murderous ways.

Arky is dealt a second blow when the opposition guns down a respected district judge who, years before, had shown him compassion and found him a job. The killing is all the more significant because, as Arky alone knows and the murder investigators are finding out, this man was the Mover. Learning that the commissioner plans to smear the dead man's reputation in the newspapers, the newly humanized Arky humbly offers himself as a sacrifice in his friend's stead. In the end the racketeer not only redeems himself, but buys the Big Midwestern City a few more years of civilization.

Reviewers, disappointed that *Little Men, Big World* was not a second *Asphalt Jungle,* described it variously as "weary," "sober," and "squalid." It was never made into a motion picture, but television's *Studio One* picked it up as a one-hour teleplay in 1952, starring Jack Palance as Arky and Sheppard Strudwick as the Mover.

As *Vanity Row* (1952) opens, Burnett's Midwestern city is in total collapse. Urban blight has enveloped the entire metropolis, save the single city block of the title. Political corruption is rampant. The most noticeable change, however, is in people. Characters in *The Asphalt Jungle* are innately noble: Dix's code of honor, Hardy's and Farbstein's determination to do right, and Doll's and Gus's devotion lift them above their environment. Reporter Ben Reisman of the second book is a good man eaten up with longing for an honest world. *Vanity Row,* by comparison, includes not a single "good" character. Its newspaperman, Perc Wesson, not only notes the corruption around him but also revels in it. High-minded Hardy and realist Stark have been succeeded by Commissioner Prell, a puppet in the hands of the Big Boys. Even the supposed hero operates on purely selfish motives. There is no glimpse of countryside, no chivalrous Southerner to play Damon to the Pythian city. The plot—in which a detective follows orders to frame a supposedly innocent woman for a political murder—is incidental.

With the exception of the British *Spectator,* reviews of *Vanity Row* were uniformly negative. James Kelly in the 17 August 1952 *New York Times* complained that it was "too overdrawn, too much an opéra bouffe of big city corruption," and advised its author to, in future novels, "let the reader work up a little sympathy for *somebody,* even a cop." Burnett coscripted the film adaptation, *Accused of Murder,* but by the time this reached the screen, Republic Pictures had tacked on a traditional Hollywood ending.

Perhaps wary of further savaging, Burnett used the pseudonym John Monahan on his next hard-boiled book, a paperback original he called "The Outer Darkness"–an appropriately noirish name for this tale of loneliness and romantic temptation, set against the backdrop of a serial murder investigation. The publishers, however, chose to retitle it *Big Stan* (1953), the nickname of the main character. Anthony Boucher, a Burnett fan who seems not to have known Monahan's identity, in the 31 January 1954 issue of *The New York Times* called it "a first-rate study, rare in any type of fiction, of two mature people who succeed in *not* committing adultery. Evenly poised between the straight novel and the whodunit, it's a satisfactory book either way." After a foray into Irish folk history in *Captain Lightfoot* (1954), Burnett tried a change of pace with the jazz novel *It's Always Four O'Clock* (1956), published under the pseudonym James Updyke. It is a tough but nonviolent book–"cool" in the Beat sense of the word–but, its hipster lingo is enough to make even a dedicated fan lay it aside. Much better is *Underdog* (1957), the writer's last major crime novel, which compares the thoughts and actions of an old-school criminal with those of a much younger counterpart. "Nobody writes this kind of thing better, and it's still a pretty exciting kind of thing," said Christopher Pym in the 13 December 1957 issue of *The Spectator.*

Burnett published two paperback "quickies" within a three-month period in 1961. The first, *Conant,* is an urban retelling of his 1953 Western *Pale Moon.* In the earlier book, a drifter is recruited by a powerful Arizona family to run for mayor on their behalf; he marries their headstrong daughter and instigates a three-way struggle for control of the town. *Conant* updates the ranchers to racketeers and the Old West to modern-day Chicago. Boucher in the 9 July 1961 issue of *The New York Times* thought highly enough of it–or its author–to announce, "The material is familiar enough, but Burnett–the only authentic Old Master of toughness left now that Hammett and Chandler are dead–combines vigor and restraint in a manner that few of his successors have troubled to learn. There's a genuine pro at work here."

It is sometimes erroneously reported that science-fiction writer Robert Silverberg authored *Round the Clock at Volari's* (1961) using Burnett's name. In a 1981 letter to his bibliographer, Thomas D. Clareson, Silverberg explained, "What I did is better described as editing, though probably I did some writing." Whether all or only partially Burnett's, the book bears his unmistakable stamp. It reads like a

Burnett with his second wife, Whitney Forbes Johnstone Burnett, at the time of publication of Little Men, Big World
(photograph by Charles Bell)

sequel to *Vanity Row,* or a substitute in which municipal corruption has not been permitted to take root. Instead, a reformist administration has stripped its crooked predecessors of their power and chased the few it did not jail into exile. The old regime's posh "headquarters," Volari's Restaurant, has been all but abandoned. A gang of robbers learns that Volari's is still owned by the brother of a former power and that there is $200,000 in the safe. They break in, spiriting away two employees to make it look like an inside job. Jim Chase, a disgraced prosecutor, sees a chance to redeem himself and sets out on their trail. Like Arky in *Little Men, Big World,* Chase is ashamed of his past. Unlike him, he feels no loyalty toward his former employers: after dispatching the thieves, he turns his back on a crooked official who has asked his help to sneak back into town. One of the only reviewers to bother with *Round the Clock at Volari's* was Boucher, who reported with obvious disappointment on 17 September 1961 in *The New York Times* that it was "well told, of course, and with a good

Burnett in Los Angeles, 1981

theft-and-murder subplot, but minor by Burnett's standards."

Between 1962 and 1967 Burnett turned out mainly adventure books of minor importance, with the exception of *The Abilene Samson* (1963), which may well be his best Western. Among his movie work of the period is his adaptation, with James Clavell, of Paul Brickhill's *The Great Escape,* the true story of a mass exodus by British airmen from a German POW camp. The tense, often funny screenplay, produced by United Artists in 1963, was nominated for an Academy Award. By 1968 Burnett had become disenchanted with the writing business. He contributed just one more hard-boiled paperback original, *The Cool Man* (1968), and then stopped submitting manuscripts for more than a decade.

The 1970s were not kind to Burnett. Age caught up with the once-hearty sportsman, and his health began to decline. By the time Mate and McGilligan

interviewed him, he was nearly blind, walked with a cane, and, in their words, seemed "a near-Joycean figure: wielding his putter against would-be muggers as he walked his dog." Midway through the decade, a major Hollywood studio released an unauthorized Western adaptation of *Captain Lightfoot,* a film for which the writer was neither credited nor paid. He was vocally bitter about this injustice for the rest of his life. Worst of all, the Burnetts lost their house in the Los Angeles suburb of Bel Air to a fire, along with the writer's manuscripts and working papers. After that, the couple moved to a smaller residence in Marina del Rey, south of Santa Monica.

Despite all this bad fortune Burnett had occasional reason to celebrate. In 1980 his peers in the Mystery Writers of America honored him with the group's highest honor, the Grand Master Award. At about the same time, scholars outside the United States began to take a closer look at popular culture, and discussions of Burnett's novels began to appear in German, French, and Mexican literary journals. The French hard-boiled detective magazine *Polar* devoted its entire November 1980 issue to articles on the writer and reprints of his toughest short stories.

Burnett's final novel, *Good-bye, Chicago: 1928, End of an Era* (1981), was written years before its publication. He originally called it "Chicago '28"; then "Chicago" (which he changed because of potential conflict with the Broadway musical); and then "The Loop," under which title it was first announced for publication in 1977. A motion picture director optioned the manuscript at that time, but the proposed movie was never produced. In the opening paragraph of the novel, a woman is found drowned in the Chicago River. The detective assigned to the case learns that she is the runaway wife of a colleague, a man he is not at all certain he wants to work for or with. From this promising beginning, the book branches out erratically, following the thoughts and actions of so many characters that a reader needs a checklist to keep track of them all. The writer's final book is far beneath his earlier efforts.

Critics who had anticipated the old Burnett magic were quick to register disappointment. "*Good-bye, Chicago* is his 34th book. He should have quit when he was ahead," said Francis DeAndrea in the June 1981 issue of the trade publication *Best Sellers.* "It's not that [it] is poorly written. In fact, it is well written. The trouble is that Burnett has managed to tell a story about gangland Chicago during the Roaring '20s that lacks any zip or excitement. . . . Everything considered, I'm at a loss for a reason why this book was ever published." The critic in the 15 February *Kirkus Reviews* also scolded the publisher: "Someone has done a disservice to the reputation of influential crime-writer Burnett . . . by publishing this oddly prissy and even-more-oddly amateurish tale of cops and gangsters. . . . Suspense readers—especially admirers of Burnett's earlier work—will want to pretend that this book never happened."

William Riley Burnett published nothing more in his lifetime. He died at his California home on 25 April 1982 at the age of eighty-two. According to Mate and McGilligan, he had written more than twenty new short stories by that time and was simultaneously working on drafts of five novels.

Interest in the writer and his works has since grown. Crime and detective fiction anthologists who had previously looked only to the pulps discovered Burnett's early "slick" pieces. Most recently, "Round Up" appeared in the 1995 collection *Hard-Boiled,* edited by Bill Pronzini and Jack Adrian. The writer has been made the subject of dissertations and academic articles, seriously discussed in college literature classes, and celebrated on the World Wide Web. Cable television pipes a steady stream of his movies into American homes. The highest-profile titles among his writings have been in print somewhere in America or Europe almost continuously since their first release. In 1984 London's Zomba Books released a one-volume collection of four Burnett novels as part of its popular Black Box Thrillers series. Fourteen years after that, The Mysterious Press brought out a facsimile of the first edition of *Little Caesar.* Death may have been "the end of Rico," but, happily, it was not the end of W. R. Burnett.

Interview:

Ken Mate and Pat McGilligan, "Burnett," *Film Comment* (January–February 1983): 59–68; republished with additional material as "W. R. Burnett: The Outsider," in *Backstory: Interviews with Screenwriters of Hollywood's Golden Age,* edited by McGilligan (Berkeley: University of California Press, 1986), pp. 49–84.

References:

Stanley J. Kunitz, "William Riley Burnett," in *Authors To-day and Yesterday* (New York: Wilson, 1933), pp. 225–226;

Michael J. Larsen, "W. R. Burnett," in *Critical Survey of Mystery and Detective Fiction,* edited by Frank N. Magill (Pasadena: Salem, 1988), pp. 242–248;

Douglas A. Noverr, "Chicago as Setting and Force in William Riley Burnett's *Little Caesar," Midwestern Miscellany,* 14 (1986): 25–33.

Papers:

Most of W. R. Burnett's papers were lost in the Bel Air fire. Records of his tenure with the Harold Ober Associates agency are available at the Firestone Library, Princeton University. Smaller collections of letters and other papers are at the Harry Ransom Humanities Research Center, University of Texas at Austin, and at Columbia University. The publication records for *The Goldseekers* are in the Doubleday collection at the Library of Congress.

James M. Cain
(1 July 1892 – 27 October 1977)

Bobbie Robinson
Abraham Baldwin College

BOOKS: *Our Government* (New York: Knopf, 1930; London: Allen & Unwin, 1930);

The Postman Always Rings Twice (New York: Knopf, 1934; London: Cape, 1934);

Serenade (New York: Knopf, 1937; London: Cape, 1938);

Mildred Pierce (New York: Knopf, 1941; London: Hale, 1943);

Love's Lovely Counterfeit (New York: Knopf, 1942);

Career in C Major and Other Stories (New York: Avon, 1943);

Three of a Kind: Career in C Major, The Embezzler, Double Indemnity, preface by Cain (New York: Knopf, 1943; London Hale, 1956);

Past All Dishonor (New York: Knopf, 1946);

The Butterfly (New York: Knopf, 1947);

Sinful Woman (New York: Avon, 1947);

The Moth (New York: Knopf, 1948; London: Hale, 1950);

Jealous Woman (New York: Avon, 1950);

The Root of His Evil (New York: Avon, 1951; London: Hale, 1954); republished as *Shameless* (New York: Avon, 1958);

Galatea (New York: Knopf, 1953; London: Hale, 1954);

Mignon (New York: Dial, 1962; London: Hale, 1963);

The Magician's Wife (New York: Dial, 1965; London: Hale, 1966);

Rainbow's End (New York: Mason-Charter, 1975; London: Magnum, 1975);

The Institute (New York: Mason-Charter, 1976; London: Magnum, 1977);

The Baby in the Icebox and Other Short Fiction, edited by Roy Hoopes (New York: Holt, Rinehart & Winston, 1981; London: Hale, 1982);

Cloud Nine (New York: Mysterious Press, 1984; London: Hale, 1985);

The Enchanted Isle (New York: Mysterious Press, 1985);

60 Years of Journalism, edited by Hoopes (Bowling Green, Ohio: Bowling Green University Popular Press, 1985).

James M. Cain

Collections: *Everybody Does It* (New York: New American Library, 1949)–comprises *Career in C Major* and *The Embezzler;*

Three of Hearts, preface by Cain (London: Hale, 1949)–comprises *Love's Lovely Counterfeit, Past all Dishonor,* and *The Butterfly;*

Jealous Woman, Sinful Woman (London: Hale, 1954);

Cain X 3, preface by Tom Wolfe (New York: Knopf, 1969)–comprises *The Postman Always Rings Twice, Mildred Pierce,* and *Double Indemnity;*

Hard Cain, preface by Harlan Ellison (Boston: G. K. Hall, 1980)–comprises *Sinful Woman, Jealous Woman,* and *The Root of His Evil.*

PLAY PRODUCTIONS: *Crashing the Gates,* Stamford, Conn., February 1926;

The Postman Always Rings Twice, New York, Lyceum Theater, 26 February 1936;

7–11, Cohasset, Mass., 1938.

PRODUCED SCRIPTS: *Algiers,* motion picture, script by Cain and John Howard Lawson, United Artists, 1938;

Stand Up and Fight, motion picture, script by Cain, Harvey Fergusson, and Jane Murfin, M-G-M, 1939;

Gypsy Wildcat, motion picture, script by Cain, James Hogan, Gene Lewis, and others, Universal Pictures, 1944.

SELECTED PERIODICAL PUBLICATIONS–
UNCOLLECTED: "Comeback," *Redbook,* (June 1934): 40–43, 65–66;

"Hip, Hip, the Hippo," *Redbook,* March 1936;

"The Birthday Party," *Ladies' Home Journal,* May 1936;

"Everything but the Truth," *Liberty,* 17 July 1937;

"Vincent Sargent Lawrence," *Screen Writer* (January 1947): 11–15;

"Cigarette Girl," *Manhunt,* May 1953;

"Two O'Clock Blonde," *Manhunt,* August 1953;

"Death on the Beach," *Jack London's Adventure Magazine,* October 1958;

"The Visitor," *Esquire,* September 1961.

OTHER: "The Girl in the Storm," in *For Men Only: A Collection of Short Stories,* edited by Cain (Cleveland: World, 1944).

"I, so far as I can sense the pattern of my mind, write of the wish that comes true, for some reason a terrifying concept, at least to my imagination. . . . I think my stories have some quality of the opening of a forbidden box, and that it is this, rather than violence, sex, or any of the things usually cited by way of explanation, that gives them the drive so often noted." James M. Cain offered this explanation of his writing in the preface to *The Butterfly* in 1947, when his most important fiction was behind him. With publication of his first novel, *The Postman Always Rings Twice,* in 1934 Cain immediately became a best-selling author, and critics at once pigeonholed him in the hard-boiled school. In 1941 Edmund Wilson identified Cain as the best of "the poets of the tabloid murder" in his seminal work on the California novelists of the 1930s, *The Boys in the Back Room.* Throughout his career Cain resisted the label, arguing in *The Butterfly* preface that he belonged "to no school, hard-boiled or otherwise." But the reputation has stuck.

The leisure and privilege James Mallahan Cain enjoyed as a child and his intellectual pursuits as a young man seem antithetical to the passions and violence of his work. His characters, whose attitudes and outlooks are at odds with middle-class sensibilities, come from the underbelly of society. However, suggests Paul Skenazy in his 1989 study, "Cain's writings develop from his failed ambitions, his unacknowledged insecurities, and a life-long sense of exclusion into a curious mixture of recounted experiences, the recasting of unsatisfied desires, and the creation of alternative male personalities." Cain's life prepared him for the tough-guy persona of his fiction.

All four of Cain's grandparents emigrated from Ireland in 1850 and settled in New Haven, Connecticut, where his parents grew up. His father, James W. "Jim" Cain, was born in 1860. When Jim was sixteen, his mother, Mary Kelly Cain, died. Jim's father, P. W. Cain, remarried three years later, but Jim was unable to accept his new stepmother and gradually began to spend more and more time in town with the Mallahans, family friends whose youngest daughter, Rose, captivated his attentions.

Jim Cain entered Yale University in 1880. Though an undistinguished student, he was handsome, bright, well spoken, and athletic. In 1890 he became head of the preparatory school of St. John's College in Annapolis, Maryland, and that same year married Rose Mallahan.

Rose Mallahan Cain was an attractive woman with a beautiful voice. As a young woman she spent seven years studying voice and began an opera career in New Haven. In his unpublished memoirs, quoted in Roy Hoopes's *Cain: The Biography of James M. Cain* (1987), her son wrote that she lacked "An obsessive desire to be a singer. What she wanted was to be a wife to a good-looking Yale man she knew and have five children by him." Two years after her marriage, on 1 July 1892, she bore her first son, whom she called Jamie, named for his father and her family. Eventually another son and three daughters were born, all in Annapolis.

One of Cain's earliest memories is of an event that occurred when he was about three years old. Cain's mother remembered Jamie's boasting that he could beat his father in a footrace, so she instigated a downhill run. Jamie started immediately, but instead of running his father walked with long strides, grinning the whole while, not even bothering to put out his cigarette. Cain was humiliated and dissolved into tears. All his life he believed that his father ought to have held back and given him the illusion of victory. The incident returned to Cain often after he became a writer and figures in the fabric of his fiction. In a memo to David Madden (He wrote nearly one hundred pages of auto-

Cain's parents, James W. Cain and Rose Mallahan Cain

biographical material to aid Madden as he was working on his 1970 Twayne study.) Cain said he always put his reader in the place of that small child and never forgot that he wants to win: "This, rather than any penchant for violence as such, is the reason . . . for plunging the action along at the bull's eye without any flinching, for giving the reader what he came for."

Cain's childhood in Annapolis was for the most part uneventful, though being advanced two years beyond his age in school had a profound effect on him. Cain was a bright and creative student when he persuaded his father, who was president of the school board, to arrange to move him to fifth grade to be with one of his friends. Cain regretted all his life that his father did not have the good sense to refuse his request. Immediately, he was overwhelmed at being the smallest and least mature boy in the class. He suffered the humiliation of being pushed around by the bigger boys and frightened by the blossoming young girls. In his autobiographical notes for Madden, Cain said he

quickly realized "I was a midget among giants, and this fact, more than anything else, I think meant that my schooling, especially my college years, meant nothing whatever to me."

In 1903 Jim Cain was named president of Washington College, and the family moved to Chestertown, Maryland. Ike Newton, a bricklayer hired to build a brick walkway through the campus, provided another influence on the young Cain that proved fundamental to his writing. Newton worked steadily and talked incessantly. In his notes for Madden, Cain said he was Ike's constant companion and avid audience: "It was pure enchantment. I was simply enthralled–not so much by his stories or his ideas as such, as by the language he couched them in. It was pure bucolic vulgate, but so rich, so expressive, so full of color that I couldn't hear enough of him. I can't say Ike taught me how to write dialogue, but I owe this man a great debt for stirring in me a respect for his lingo and all that went with it, for exciting in me a feeling for simple speech, for the way people actually talk, for the country idiom as distinguished from the citified. . . . [I]f a writer owes a debt to what his ears pick up, mine would be to Ike." Cain's mother also greatly affected his sense of language and style. Her speech was terse and clear, her written language colorful, concise, sprinkled with few adjectives. Cain later recalled in a private memo, "If I have any talent to write, I got it from her."

Cain entered Washington College in 1907 at fifteen. Though bright, he was an erratic student who directed his energies toward only those courses that piqued his interests. Speech and Greek were not his forte, but he excelled in German and French and was a talented math student. Cain also apparently used his college years to affront his father by remaining indifferent to campus life. He avoided any athletic involvement, engaged in few extracurricular activities, and refused to edit the college's literary magazine. In 1910 he took a B.A. without distinction.

Cain was totally unprepared for going to work when he graduated from college; it had never occurred to him that people were expected to make a living. "Never once, in our house," Cain told Madden, "was there so much as a hint that life was hard, that work was the lot of all. We lived in grand style, with the grubby aspects of life concealed from the children." In those first three or four years after graduation, he lived in Baltimore and searched for work that would interest him. Cain held several jobs from 1910 to 1913; he was a clerk for a gas and electric company, an inspector of construction for state roads, and principal of a high school in Vienna, Virginia. During this time he heard a great deal of serious music and suddenly decided to become an opera singer. He left his job at the school and moved to Washington, D.C., in 1913 to enroll in singing classes. Cain tried to support himself by selling insurance, but he failed miserably. His singing career foundered also; he hated the endless hours of practice at the piano and discovered what his mother and his friends, all of whom had opposed his decision to pursue opera, had known all along–he had no real talent for professional singing.

Discouraged and broke, Cain took a job in September 1914 at Kann's, a department store in Washington, but quit when he did not get the raise to $25 a week he wanted. Cain recounts in his unpublished memoirs that, aggravated and depressed, he left the store and wandered up Pennsylvania Avenue and sat on a bench across from the White House in Lafayette Park. With no clue how he was going to make a living and knowing he was no farther along than the day he finished college, Cain suddenly heard his own voice say, "You're going to be a writer!"

In his notes for Madden, Cain wrote, "I've thought about it a thousand times, trying to figure out why that voice said what it did–without success. There must have been something that had been gnawing at me from the inside. . . . Nor did I have any realization that the decision I'd made wasn't mine to make. . . . [It] would not be settled by me, but by God." For the first time Cain felt assured that he had a calling. The decision came to him at his lowest point, when he had just realized he would never be a singer. On 29 June 1940 he wrote to Edmund Wilson, "the decision was no clarion call. Writing to me was distinctly a consolation prize." Nevertheless, the experience in Lafayette Park shaped the rest of Cain's life.

Having suffered some indignities when his mother refused to support his decision to become an opera singer, Cain hesitantly went home to reveal his new plans. In his notes for Madden, Cain recalled that to his great surprise his mother was fully supportive of his new ambition, telling him writing was "what you were born for." Even his father was enthusiastic, offering him advice to pepper his writing with "a good stock of quotations."

Cain's experiences in southern Maryland, Baltimore, and Washington from 1910 to 1913, which seemed aimless and pointless at the time, eventually crept into his fiction: his distressing work at the insurance company appeared in *Double Indemnity* (1936); his job as an inspector of roads played a part in *The Moth* (1948), *Mignon* (1962), and *Past All Dishonor* (1946); and his brief, futile attempt at a music career informed his understanding of singers and their profession in *Serenade* (1937), *Career in C Major* (1943), and *Mildred Pierce* (1941). He transferred some of his experiences in Baltimore whorehouses to Virginia City, Nevada, for *Past All Dishonor*. His knowledge of the environs and people of southern Maryland provided the backdrop to *Galatea* (1953) and *The Magician's Wife* (1965). When Cain finally made the decision to become a writer, he had at his disposal much of his necessary material.

Cain's writing career had a shaky beginning. Having received his parents' approval for his career choice, he settled down in Chestertown in 1914 and wrote short stories and brief sketches, but got none of this early work published. About this same time a math and English professor in the preparatory school became sick, and his father asked Cain to assume responsibility for the classes. Cain accepted and by all accounts was a good teacher.

He made the rule in his math class that only two grades were possible, perfect and zero. His students accepted this dictum. According to his notes for Madden, Cain told his students, "There's no such thing in math, as being pretty nearly right. It's all right or it's all

Front page of the final issue of the army newspaper Cain co-edited during his World War I service

wrong." He was equally dogmatic in his English classes, though eventually he came to the conclusion that writing could not be taught. What he could teach, however, were grammar, syntactical integrity, rhetorical principles, and, threading all these, punctuation. He told his students, "When you learn how to punctuate, you'll be free to be yourselves. Instead of being in a straitjacket of what can be put between commas with a period at the end, you can write as freely as you talk, and know that you can set it up so it reads." All this terseness in design and execution and his mania for mathematical exactness had a profound effect on his writing. Cain viewed the plotting in his best work as a matter of mathematical logic, his "getting the algebra right."

Though Cain enjoyed his teaching career and in 1917 took an M.A. in English drama and the American short story from Washington College, he knew he had not yet found his niche and decided to leave the school and move to Baltimore. In the summer of 1917 he took a job as a weightmaster in the meat cold-storage room at Swift and Company making $25 a week. After a week of reporting to work at 3:00 A.M., however, he looked for other work. His short tenure in meatpacking was, as usual, not wasted effort. Decades later he translated that experience into fiction in *Galatea* and *The Magician's Wife.*

Cain had little problem finding another job. Wandering through the streets of downtown Baltimore, he passed the *Baltimore American* building and impulsively went into the city room and persuaded the editor to give him a job as a reporter covering a police district. He worked at the *Baltimore American* until the end of 1917, when he moved to *The Baltimore Sun* for more money. In 1918 at twenty-five Cain had at last found a satisfying job that allowed him to write. For the next fourteen years he was employed primarily as a journalist, and for the rest of his life thought of himself as a newspaperman.

The United States had declared war on Germany in April 1917, and Cain immediately registered for the draft. Unconvinced that America's participation in the war was essential, he knew he would have to serve some time in the military to clarify his feelings. Initially, he was turned down for service because of a weak lung; but when his case was reviewed again, Cain persuaded a doctor to pass him. At Camp Meade, Maryland, Cain acted with bravado and convinced his captain that he could do all sorts of things well that he really knew little about. During his first afternoon on duty he met Gilbert Malcolm, a graduate of Dickinson Law School (in the 1950s, president of the college) who also had misrepresented his abilities. Malcolm, too, had worked a short time for a newspaper, and the two men soon became friends.

Cain sailed with his troop for France on 7 July 1918. Though he later said he was a combat newspaperman during the war, he saw little real action. After the Armistice, Cain and Malcolm edited and redesigned *The Lorraine Cross,* the division headquarters newspaper that had been initiated 6 February 1919; they stayed with the paper until 5 June 1919, their last day in the army. The paper quickly became a huge hit with the troops, and Cain enjoyed a position of privilege and authority. The war apparently left no scars on Cain; he seldom made any reference to it later in his novels or interviews.

When he sailed for France in 1918 Cain was "pledged" to Mary Rebekah Clough, whom he had known as a classmate at Washington College. On 17 January 1920 she became the first of his four wives. Mary was beautiful, refined, and part of the Eastern Shore establishment; her incompatibility with Cain's rough exterior, salty talk (which he had acquired in the army), and taste for liquor quickly surfaced. They separated in 1923 and finally divorced in 1927.

Cain returned to *The Baltimore Sun* after the war as a financial writer. In the early 1920s he became interested in political and industrial problems and the postwar labor movement. Conflicts in the mining fields of West Virginia also intrigued him. Cain persuaded *The Baltimore Sun* to send him to cover the treason trial of William Blizzard, an official of the United Mine Workers who had been indicted for his role with an armed march in West Virginia. In the fall of 1922 Cain actually worked underground in the mines at Ward, West Virginia, and became a card-carrying member of the United Mine Workers. His first magazine piece came from his experiences at the trial. "The Battleground of Coal" was published in the October 1922 issue of *The Atlantic Monthly.* Cain realized that to appear in such a quality magazine one had to have something to say and the ability to say it well. That knowledge gave him confidence and courage, and he turned an important corner in his writing career.

As Cain collected voluminous notes for early articles on the coal disputes, he became convinced that he was gathering enough background for the novel he had long put off attempting. He knew that if he were to break out of journalism he must write a novel, and he believed he had one in him. Accordingly, shortly after publication of *The Atlantic Monthly* article Cain took three months off from *The Baltimore Sun* to make the effort. When the winter was over, however, he had written and discarded three novels and was convinced he could not write at all. Depressed and chagrined, Cain returned to his job at *The Baltimore Sun.* Later, in the preface to *Three of a Kind,* Cain summed up his failure: "The last [draft] I wouldn't have written at all if I hadn't squirmed at the idea of facing my friends with the news that my great American novel was a pipe dream." He identified his problem as his inability to construct a convincing plot that advanced the story line. He had concentrated on background and "didn't seem to have the slightest idea where I was going, . . . even which paragraph should follow which."

Those skills for which Cain later became famous—pacing, dialogue, economy, and narrative drive—were the essential elements still missing from his writing. His unconvincing characters were "homely . . . and spoke a gnarled and grotesque jargon that didn't seem quite adapted to long fiction; it seemed to me that after fifty pages of ain't, brungs, and fittens, the reader would want to throw the book at me." He was so overwhelmed with facts that he could not wring from them a convincing fictional narrative, a problem Cain would face again when he wrote historical fiction. He did not return to writing fiction for ten years, but like all of Cain's experience his time wrestling with the problems of West Virginia and the miners was not wasted. Later he transposed his experience in the mines into *Past All Dishonor,* and his familiarity with the mountaineers as well as the mines reemerged in *The Butterfly* (1947).

A growing influence on Cain was the writing of H. L. Mencken. By 1920 Cain's fever for language and writing was high, and his reading of Mencken's "The Clowns March In" column during the early part of the year mesmerized him. Immediately, Cain began to read *The Smart Set* and bought several of Mencken's books. After steeping himself in Mencken's work, Cain knew his own writing was forever altered. He began to send articles to *The Smart Set* in 1920; they were all rejected, but Mencken took note of Cain's work, and the two men began a relationship that lasted until Mencken's death. Though they never became close friends, Cain was a lifelong admirer.

By 1923 Cain was ready to leave Baltimore. His marriage to Mary was deteriorating, and a growing dissatisfaction with management of the newspaper and his assignments led him to accept a job teaching journalism at St. John's College in Annapolis, his home as a young boy, where he remained for a year. In January 1924 Mencken launched a new magazine, *The American Mercury,* and encouraged Cain to submit an essay for the first issue. Cain was excited by Mencken's request, knowing that first issues became collectors' items, and suggested an article on the labor leaders he had encountered in recent years. The first issue did not contain his piece, however, and that lapse remained one of the great disappointments of his life. Cain recalled in his memoirs that he knew Mencken appreciated the article and planned it for the first issue; but, Mencken told him later, union printers refused to set it because the portrait

of a labor leader was not sufficiently flattering. Cain's essay did not appear in the magazine until 1924.

Most of Cain's nonfiction ultimately appeared in *The American Mercury.* From 1922 to 1948 he wrote for *The American Mercury, The Nation, The Saturday Evening Post, The Atlantic Monthly, Esquire, Vanity Fair, The Screen Writer,* and *Saturday Review of Literature.* Most often in these magazine pieces Cain is a debunker. His targets included editorial writers, college professors, and female politicians. Though he generally shows more impartiality toward his subjects than does Mencken, his tough persona in the essays offers perspective on Cain the fiction writer. Eight of the most ferocious essays were published in *The American Mercury* and collected in *Our Government* by Knopf in 1930.

Early in 1924 Cain contracted tuberculosis, an event that brought on an important turn in his career: "Until then," he wrote to Madden, "I had had this driving compulsion to avoid being a 'failure in life,' to be a credit to my father. But with the T.B. I was relieved of that—after all, who can hold a lunger to a high ambition? I began doing what I wanted to do, having so little time to live, it seemed, and that was how I made the big writing try again." While Cain was in this frame of mind, Mencken encouraged him to leave Baltimore and move to New York City.

Cain had met Elina Tyszecka, a Finnish immigrant, on one of his trips to New York in September 1923, and when he moved to the city, they lived together. They married in 1927; the marriage lasted until 1942. Elina spoke no English and had two children, to whom Cain evidently was a devoted father.

In later years Cain listed Walter Lippmann in the same breath with Mencken, producer Philip Goodman, and screenwriter Vincent Lawrence as the men who most profoundly influenced his life. He met Lippmann when he moved to New York and talked himself into a job with the respected, conservative *New York World,* which Lippmann edited. Cain admired Lippman tremendously as a man and a writer, but his regard for him as a stylist approached hero worship. Like Cain, Lippmann had a passionate love for the English language. Even more important, Cain wrote to Madden, Lippman did not "laugh or sneer at me, or look down on me for writing my editorials, some of which went through the chopper a dozen times, something the newspaper business scorns. . . . That he would respect my style, and the pains I took to achieve it, was a big thing in my life."

Soon after beginning work at the *New York World* Cain met theatrical producer Philip Goodman through Mencken and began the last real detour from writing novels he would take before making the life-changing move to Hollywood. Goodman was to become by far

The editorial page staff of the New York World *in the mid 1920s: (standing, left to right) William O. Scroggs, Cain, Allan Nevins, Rollin Kirby, and L. R. E. Paulin; (seated) Charles Merz, Walter Lippmann, and John L. Heaton*

the closest friend Cain ever had. During his years in New York under the influence of Goodman, many of the best plays Cain saw portrayed a "tough" attitude, among them Eugene O'Neill's *The Hairy Ape* (1922) and Laurence Stallings and Maxwell Anderson's *What Price Glory* (1924). The central characters were outsiders, and the plays took a stark view of society. Goodman had read some of Cain's dramatic dialogues in *The American Mercury* and urged Cain to write a play for him.

Cain's idea grew out of his West Virginia experience; he wanted to write about a widely held belief in the area that the Second Coming was near. In 1926 *Crashing the Gates* was staged on the road in New England. The play failed badly, but as usual Cain learned something from the writing, mainly, he wrote to Madden, that "you should never jeopardize a big design by insistence on small imperfections," in this case the instances of profanity Cain sprinkled liberally through-

out the dialogue. He did not realize that his audience would object to profanity in a play about a "minefield Jesus." Though Cain had used conversational profanity in his writing before, he immediately dropped it. Goodman brought in screenwriter Vincent Lawrence to rework the play. Cain and Lawrence became good friends and worked for more than a year, but the play never got off the ground. Goodman did not reproduce it, and Cain finally let it go.

During his seven years at the *New York World,* from 1924 to 1931, Cain wrote both political and social editorials and became aware of how the tabloid newspapers capitalized on the public's interest in violence and sex. His best work was a series of satiric articles about the American scene on colorful, offbeat topics from motherhood to hog calls that engaged active imaginations and won Cain a wide following. These articles instigated some overblown controversies and established Cain as a clever, sophisticated newspaperman. In 1931 the *New York World* was sold, but Cain quickly became managing editor of *The New Yorker,* a position he held for only nine months because of his strained relationship with Harold Ross, the founder of the magazine. With the help of his agent he then secured a contract with a movie studio in Hollywood.

Leaving New York was difficult, but Cain knew he needed the change professionally. In his memoirs Cain says: "I'd been gradually coming to the conclusion that if I was to write anything of the kind I'd been dreaming about for so long it could not be based in New York." He thought he could find his literary footing in the West.

Cain arrived in Hollywood in November 1931 with a six-month contract to Paramount for $400 a week, twice his newspaper salary. His first job was an unsuccessful attempt to write a remake of *The Ten Commandments* (1923). He worked on many scripts with equal lack of success and began a long odyssey of moving among the major studios. In his seventeen years in Hollywood he worked off and on for Paramount, Columbia, M-G-M, Universal, Warner Bros., United Artists, and RKO. His tenure often lasted a few weeks, occasionally up to six months. The movies Cain received credits for include *Duchess of Delmonico* (1934), *Money and the Woman* (1940), and *The Bridge of San Luis Rey* (1943).

During the early days with the studios Cain continued to write articles for the New York magazines and published "The Baby in the Icebox" in the January 1933 issue of *American Mercury,* a short story that helped to jumpstart his career as a fiction writer. Mencken thought it one of Cain's finest pieces and showed a prepublication copy of the story to Alfred A. Knopf, who had published *Our Government* and still had an option on Cain's next two books. Knopf praised the story and encouraged Cain to try a novel. On 4 December 1932 Cain wrote Knopf that he had started a novel the month before but lost heart to continue; Knopf's note was the boost he needed to try it again.

The idea for a novel had grown from a murder story Cain had mulled over for a couple of years, trying to give it some direction. One of Cain's favorite pastimes when he first moved to California was to go for long drives through the canyons and valleys and over to the beaches of Southern California. In an unpublished interview quoted by Hoopes, Cain recalled that on these drives he often stopped at a gas station where "always this bosomy-looking thing comes out—commonplace, but sexy, the kind you have ideas about." One day he read in the paper that a woman who ran a filling station had killed her husband. She was his station attendant. Having lost a second studio job, this

time with Columbia, Cain decided in February 1932 to write his story. In the preface to *Three of a Kind* (1943) he says he also made the critical decision to cast his fiction in a new voice. Rather than using the rural language of the eastern roughneck, which he had preferred when writing in the first person, he used the language of the western roughneck, "the boy who is just as elemental inside as his eastern colleague, but who has been to high school, completes his sentences, and uses reasonably good grammar." He believed he had the speech imprinted firmly in his mind and could tell a long story in the first person.

Also instrumental to the birth of the first novel was a conversation Cain had with Lawrence. Cain had always thought truth was the most important element to a story, but Lawrence convinced him that truth had its narrative limits. The writer's greatest task was to convince the audience or reader to care about the people at the center, which Lawrence believed always led to a love story. In the preface to *Three of a Kind* Cain devoted three pages to discussion of Lawrence's ideas about crafting tough-guy-as-story. He wrote in the January 1947 issue of *The Screen Writer* that "the core of his thinking is also the core of my novels; if ever a man had an intellectual parent . . . I must acknowledge such a relationship with Lawrence."

In early conversations about story construction Lawrence explained to Cain his conception of "the love rack," that poetic point in the story when the lovers fall in love. Cain recalled in the preface to *Three of a Kind* that he never totally understood precisely what Lawrence meant about the love rack, but the idea niggled at him nonetheless. Once when Lawrence discussed the concept, Cain asked why the whole story could not be the love rack. He did not think it necessary to pay so much attention only to the episode in which the lovers fall in love; Cain thought every episode in the narrative could be written with a view of its effect on the love story, an idea that intrigued Lawrence.

Cain and Lawrence discussed a murder case that dominated the news media in 1927. It was another story of a woman who conspired with a lover to murder her husband. Lawrence had heard that when the woman sent her lover away while she committed the murder, she gave him a bottle of wine. Though he desperately wanted the wine on the train, he had no corkscrew and was afraid to request one for fear of giving someone a reason to remember him later. After the murder the police found that the bottle contained enough arsenic to kill many men. Cain immediately realized he had the mortar to hold his story together. In an 11 March 1959 letter Cain described his central characters as "a couple of jerks who discover that a murder, though dreadful

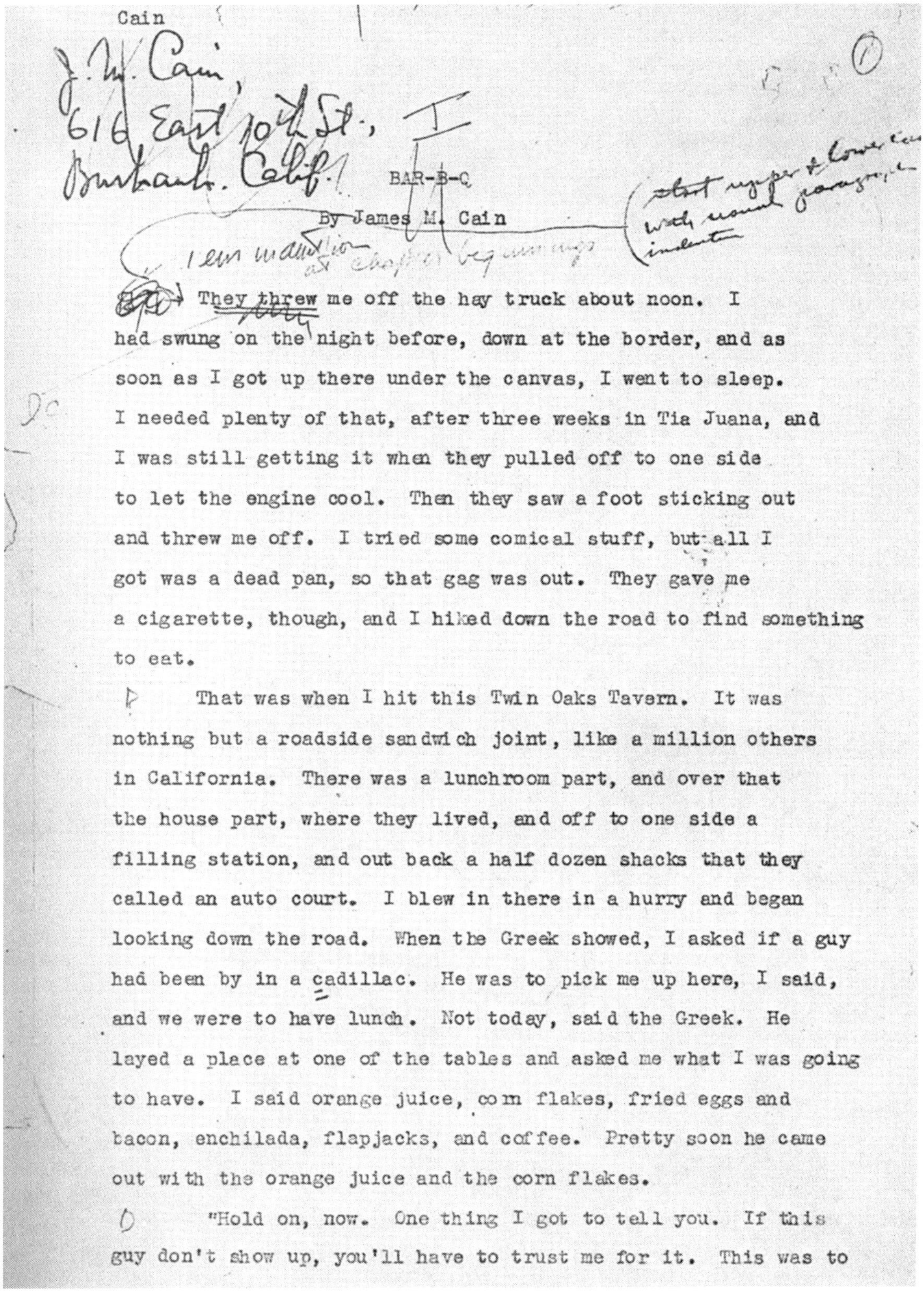

Cain

J. M. Cain,
616 East 10th St.,
Burbank. Calif.   I

BAR-B-Q

By James M. Cain

(start upper & lower case
with usual paragraph
indent)

1 em indention at chapter beginnings

They threw me off the hay truck about noon. I
had swung on the night before, down at the border, and as
soon as I got up there under the canvas, I went to sleep.
I needed plenty of that, after three weeks in Tia Juana, and
I was still getting it when they pulled off to one side
to let the engine cool. Then they saw a foot sticking out
and threw me off. I tried some comical stuff, but all I
got was a dead pan, so that gag was out. They gave me
a cigarette, though, and I hiked down the road to find something
to eat.

That was when I hit this Twin Oaks Tavern. It was
nothing but a roadside sandwich joint, like a million others
in California. There was a lunchroom part, and over that
the house part, where they lived, and off to one side a
filling station, and out back a half dozen shacks that they
called an auto court. I blew in there in a hurry and began
looking down the road. When the Greek showed, I asked if a guy
had been by in a cadillac. He was to pick me up here, I said,
and we were to have lunch. Not today, said the Greek. He
layed a place at one of the tables and asked me what I was going
to have. I said orange juice, corn flakes, fried eggs and
bacon, enchilada, flapjacks, and coffee. Pretty soon he came
out with the orange juice and the corn flakes.

"Hold on, now. One thing I got to tell you. If this
guy don't show up, you'll have to trust me for it. This was to

First page of the typescript draft for the novel that was published in 1934 as The Postman Always Rings Twice
(The Manuscript Division, Library of Congress)

enough morally, can be a love story too, but then wake up to discover that once they've pulled the thing off, no two people can share this terrible secret and live on the same earth. They turn against each other." Lawrence found the idea startling, but he was encouraging. Shortly, Cain wrote his most famous opening sentence: "They threw me off the hay truck about noon."

Frank Chambers in *The Postman Always Rings Twice* (1934) is the signature Cain hero, and he became the tough character against whom all hard-boiled heroes are measured. Frank is a bum, a drifter who is in California because everybody has to be somewhere. When he comes to the Twin Oaks Tavern, a "roadside sandwich joint, like a million others in California," he takes a job as a handyman and mechanic with Nick Papadakis, the Greek owner, even though he has little experience or expertise. Frank meets Nick's wife, Cora, and immediately thinks, "Except for the shape, she really wasn't any raving beauty, but she had a sulky look to her, and her lips stuck out in a way that made me want to mash them in for her." Frank quickly makes advances to Cora, which she returns, and the next day they make love.

Frank and Cora plan to murder Nick in the tub by knocking him out from behind and holding him underwater until he drowns and then pass the death off as an accident. The murder is unsuccessful and Nick survives, but Frank and Cora stage an automobile wreck that kills him. A district attorney who knows the truth has them arrested and tricks them into turning on each other. In the first draft Cora spends a long period in prison while she suffers through a lengthy trial. Eventually she gets off by telling a desperate lie, but the love story goes nowhere. Lawrence advised Cain to break the story open by getting Cora out of jail so the story could move. The fix was a struggle for Cain, but he eventually created a foxy lawyer who manipulates the prosecutor into an untenable squeeze among three insurance companies; two of them will lose big if Cora is convicted. Cora gets off when the lawyer exposes the misconduct of the insurance companies and forces them to say she is not guilty. Frank and Cora get away with the murder, but their reunion becomes the love rack Lawrence saw as the crux of every good story. They patch up their relationship, but Cora dies in an automobile accident and Frank is wrongly convicted for her murder and sentenced to die in the electric chair. He lives only long enough to write his story and give it to a priest who promises to "find somebody to print it."

Frank and Cora are drifters through Depression-era America, emotional cripples willing to prostitute themselves to fulfill their desires. A creature of the road, Frank is an aimless loner whose ambitions extend only to satisfying his various appetites. He assesses people as winners and losers, victims and victimizers. Frank has no social or economic ambitions; "itchy feet" keep him perpetually on the move. Cora wants "to be something," which for her is being proprietress of the Twin Oaks. The location of the restaurant on the highway places it beyond the community and constraints of the town. In Cain's world the road symbolizes the wilderness where the rules of society do not operate and where characters are free to set their own social and ethical codes. The road and the wilderness represent a power, freedom, and animality that society inhibits. When Frank and Cora succumb to the lure of the wilderness, the result is the typical fate for tough characters: devastation and violence that follow from the wish-come-true trappings of new beginnings and resurrections.

Always the reporter, Cain researched thoroughly the possibilities of calculated maneuvering among insurance companies before he made the textual changes. When he was convinced that not only was the plan plausible but the practice widespread, he knew he had made a breakthrough in his novel. Use of that device cut eighty thousand words from the original text. Cain also made another fundamental shift in narrative technique that would become a stylistic trademark and leave an indelible impact on American literature. He discovered that by telling his story in the first person he was limited in the way he could introduce or close quotation in the dialogue. He could include "I said" or "he says," but could not allow for any rhetorical or literary editorializing on mood or attitude of the characters. He realized that such monotony was as bad as the *fittens* and *brungs* he disparaged in his early attempts at fiction. Cain decided to depend on the reader to figure out who was speaking from the context. Such writing made reading easier, moved the action faster, and made for a more direct visual presentation on the printed page.

Cain spent six months working on the novel that he originally called "Bar-B-Que." He was concerned that he had pared his story so that it was now too short to be taken as a novel, but he sent the 159-page manuscript to Knopf. Though Knopf said he liked the manuscript, he thought it needed significant work. He did not like the insurance deal, thought the end was too "soppy," and the story simply too short at 35,000 words to rate as a novel. He also did not like the title. After much wrangling, during which time Walter Lippmann wanted to offer the book to Macmillan and both Mencken and Blanche Knopf supported it enthusiastically, Knopf finally agreed to take the manuscript without revision. He paid Cain a $500 advance and provided a standard contract. Cain would receive royalties on the retail sales: 10 percent up to 2,500 copies sold, 12 percent up to 5,000, and 15 percent for sales exceeding 5,000. Additionally, Knopf held the options for Cain's next two books.

Cain had two more tasks before the novel was launched. On 18 August 1933 he wrote to Knopf and dedicated the book to Lawrence. A few days later Lawrence helped him overcome the problematic title. Cain recalled in the preface to *Three of a Kind* that while they were discussing the agony of waiting out publication responses, Lawrence told him about sending his first play to a producer and then watching every day for the postman. When he could stand the suspense no longer, he would go into the backyard, but he kept listening for the postman's ring. "And no fooling about that ring. The son of a bitch always rang twice, so you'd know it was the postman." Cain knew immediately he had his title; the postman certainly rang twice for Frank Chambers and Cora Papadakis.

When *The Postman Always Rings Twice* hit the stands in 1934 Cain was instantly famous. According to biographer Hoopes *The Postman Always Rings Twice* was "probably the first of the commercial books in American publishing, the first novel to hit . . . the grand slam of the book trade: a hard-cover best seller, paperback best seller, syndication, play *and* movie." In a review titled "Six Minute Egg" in the 18 February 1934 issue of *The New York Times Book Review,* Harold Strauss praised Cain's crafting of the hard-boiled style as the perfect mode of narration. His concluding statement captures the essence of the novel and Cain's achievement: "Cain is an old newspaper man who learned his reporting so well that he makes Hemingway look like a lexicographer. . . . He can get down to the primary impulses of greed and sex in fewer words than any writer we know of. We . . . defy anyone who has broached that remarkable first sentence to put his book down." The review that perhaps most helped to secure the reputation of the novel was written by Franklin P. Adams in the *New York Herald Tribune* and published that same day. The review was glowing, and Adams supplied a comment that followed Cain throughout his career from one dust jacket to another: "Mr. Cain has written the most engrossing, unlaydownable book that I have any memory of."

Virtually every publication in the country that reviewed books dealt with *The Postman Always Rings Twice;* most of them raved. Even reviewers with negative reactions admired its power. Lewis Gannett in his 1 February 1934 column for the *New York Herald Tribune* wrote, "I hate the book! Ever since I read it two weeks ago, it has been sticking in the back of my mind and I can't stop talking about it." Novelist Gertrude Atherton in the January 1935 issue of *New York American* found many of the scenes "disgusting" and the characters "scum" but argued that the book was a work of art; so

"beautifully is it built, so superb is its economy of word and incident, so authentic its characters and so exquisite the irony of its finish, it is a joy to any writer who respects his art." British reaction to the book was equally intense; it was a huge success abroad.

Within a month of publication Cain had a movie deal on the book, which was climbing to the top of the best-seller list. He had achieved the pinnacle for any professional writer, a commercial best-seller and a critically successful literary piece. Critics concentrated most on Cain's terse, economical, sparse narrative style, as they would for years afterward.

Despite early enthusiasm the movie version of *The Postman Always Rings Twice* was slow in coming; M-G-M had difficulty coming up with a script that would pass muster with the Hays Office. Rather than alter the plot to make it acceptable to the censors, the studio decided to launch a stage version. Cain agreed with some reluctance to write the play and spent the summer on the project. He also began writing furiously for the magazines again and continued a newspaper column he was writing for the Hearst Corporation. Additionally he kept up a running correspondence chastising Knopf for advertising him as a tough writer. He wrote Knopf on 3 August 1934, "I protested to the New York critics about their labeling me as hard-boiled, for being tough or hard-boiled is the last thing in the world that I think about, and it is not doing me any good to have such a thing stamped on me." Knopf stopped the advertising but predicted rightly in his response, dated three days later, that "every review of every other hard-boiled book" for the next several years would somehow work Cain and *The Postman Always Rings Twice* into its discussion. For the rest of his career Cain tried to discourage the hard-boiled label, but he could never dislodge it.

In the fall of 1934 Cain and his family moved from Burbank to Beverly Hills. Their new home gave the Cains a place to entertain Hollywood society and provided easier access to the studios, where he still wanted to find regular work. Hollywood was expensive, so Cain worked diligently to find ideas for a serial that would bring quick money and help to ease the financial hardship.

In a 21 August 1944 letter to Knopf, Cain recalled a conversation he had with Arthur Krock one day when they were working for the *New York World*. Krock told him about an incident when he worked for another newspaper in which a dreadful typo appeared in an ad for ladies' underwear. The ad was supposed to read "IF THESE SIZES ARE TOO BIG, TAKE A TUCK IN THEM." But when the paper was printed, the *T* in *TUCK* had been changed to an *F*. When Krock bullied the printer into an explanation, the man told him, "Mr. Krock, you do nothing your whole life but watch for something like that happening, so as to head it off, *and then*, Mr. Krock, you catch yourself watching for chances to do it." Cain mulled over Krock's story and realized the powerful potential of the printer's compulsion.

Remembering the tales of intrigue within and between insurance companies that he learned of while writing *The Postman Always Rings Twice*, Cain wondered what would happen if an insurance agent who had spent his life trying to keep people from defrauding his company decided to pull off a scam himself. He also wondered what would prompt a man who had been basically decent and honest his whole life to engage in such a deed. The answer came quickly to him–a woman. Murder would again be his love rack. Cain knew he could capitalize on the success of the first novel, so in November 1934 he began the serial *Double Indemnity.*

Walter Huff, an insurance agent, devises a complicated scheme that will allow Phyllis Nirdlinger to collect $25,000 on a "double indemnity" clause when her husband dies in an accident. Huff tricks the husband into signing the policy, murders him, impersonates him on a train, and fakes an accidental death. Cain threads another narrative into the story that explores a growing love relationship between Huff and Lola Nirdlinger, Phyllis's stepdaughter. Lola confides to Huff her suspicions that years before Phyllis contributed to her mother's death, and Huff realizes that Phyllis has used him to get rid of her husband. They turn on each other like vipers. Huff confesses the murder to his employers, but they prevent the case from coming to trial because the details of the insurance policy and the crime would be bad for business. They give Huff a boat ticket and plan for him to disappear. When he gets on the boat, Huff discovers that the insurance company made the same offer to Phyllis. Hating each other, they commit suicide by jumping overboard.

Like *The Postman Always Rings Twice, Double Indemnity* is a story of adultery and murder, but the locus changes from the marginal rural world of drifters and itinerants to that of suburban malcontents. Cain's vision is no rosier, however. Though the sadistic appetites and animalistic behaviors of the earlier novel are somewhat ameliorated, the baseness of the characters leads to equal violence and destruction. Huff represents Frank Chambers's rejection of social authority in a more "civilized" light, but the results are identical. Huff's momentary passion for Phyllis and his greedy desire to collect insurance money from the company that has provided his paycheck and lifestyle are a correlative to Frank Chambers's rejection of and rebellion against a moral code society sanctions. In Cain's world, characters resort to crime without conscience to alter their natural destiny, but punishment always results when affection and ambition are perverted to achieve base desires. Cain heroes try to re-create themselves in what appear to be better circumstances, but the regeneration never materializes.

Along with *The Postman Always Rings Twice, Double Indemnity* molded the classic Cain narrative in which love leads to betrayal and violence, and greed for money or sex or both results in adultery, murder, and then death for the lovers. In *Public Journal: Marginal Notes on Wartime America* (1945) Max Lerner finds in Cain's work "love and death coiled up with each other like fatal serpents. It is love-in-death and death-and-rebirth-in-love." Passion in Cain is always fatal, drawing lovers inexorably to crime by a set of circumstances that predict fulfillment, but fate intervenes and denies the promise. In this dark, bleak world every potential positive is turned upside down; pain, nightmare, and destruction become the payoff.

Cain finished *Double Indemnity* by the end of summer 1935, but when *Redbook* refused it, he was immediately discouraged. He wrote to Edith Haggard, his New York agent, on 15 July that it was "a piece of tripe and will never go between covers while I live. The penalty, I suppose, for doing something like this is that you don't even sell it to magazines." Cain also received word that the Hays Office was up in arms about the story. From then on he never reversed his opinion that it was lousy. He wrote it fast to make money and believed it had all the earmarks of haste. Also he knew he had underestimated the potential for a tale of murder and murderers; it was worthy of his best effort. In the preface to *Three of a Kind* he says he realized the author has a "mandate . . . to discover, if he can, what forces of destiny brought these particular people to this dreadful spot, at this particular time on this particular day." In this frame of mind Cain might well have rewritten *Double Indemnity,* but *Liberty* suddenly bought it for $5,000 and scheduled it as an eight-part serial beginning in early 1936.

The serial created a huge stir with the reading public. As the weekly installments appeared, readers were standing in lines at newsstands demanding the next issue. *Liberty* and other magazines clamored for Cain to write another serial. At the same time he was pressured for another novel by Knopf, who had recently returned from Europe where he discovered a huge following for some American novelists–especially John O'Hara, Dorothy Parker, Thomas Wolfe, Ernest Hemingway, William Faulkner, and James M. Cain.

Cain was suffering from overwork and financial troubles. He was spreading himself too thin, trying to write everything and failing to focus on one task to do well. He had been writing serials, novels, short stories, screenplays, stage plays, and an occasional newspaper

Cain in his Hollywood office in the mid 1940s

article. In addition, his health was deteriorating. He had an operation to correct gall bladder trouble, but he suffered from an undiagnosed ulcer that continued to plague him for years. At the same time, his second marriage was failing.

For a couple of years Cain had been ruminating on a story that he wanted to write, but about which he lacked his usual bravado. He had played with the idea for the story at least since 1915, when he had talked with a professor at Washington College about a plot that involved a famous singer who would commit a crime, get away with it, and then realize he could never sing again without betraying his identity. After some thought, Cain decided someone else–probably a woman–would commit the crime for the singer. During the 1920s when Cain lived in New York and attended

operas and concerts regularly, he formulated another dimension to the story; he began to see a relationship between the singer's sexual identity and the quality of the voice. Cain wrote to Knopf on 17 April 1935 that when he heard a singer was homosexual, he often decided the voice was "very disagreeable and of a peculiar kind."

Cain began to devote more and more attention to the timbre and quality of a man's voice. The more he pondered voice quality, the more accurate he believed his theory about the relationship between homosexuality and voice. He discussed his theory with male and female singers whom he met; nothing they told him dissuaded his incentive. During this period the Cains hosted musical evenings every Friday night for friends from the movie community. Cain wrote in an undated letter to actress Constance Cummings that one evening at a dinner party he told Dr. Samuel Hirshfeld about the story he was working on. When Hirshfeld asked why he had doubts about the plot, Cain said he did not want to write a novel a doctor would laugh at. "Well, I'm not laughing," said Hirshfeld, "I'm hanging on the edge of my seat." When he finally began the novel, Cain maintained the basic plot sequence that he had developed a couple of years earlier.

Cain finished *Serenade* (1937), his most problematic novel for modern readers, in early July 1937. As in other Cain novels artistry provides a metaphor for sexual power and creativity. John Howard Sharp loses his voice when the advances of a homosexual conductor challenge his sexuality. He becomes sexually and artistically impotent, regaining his voice only after he violently assaults Juana, a Mexican whore, one night in a church during a horrific storm. The correspondence of artistic ability and sexual power is set at odds in the dramatic scene in which Juana pretends to be a matador and kills Stephen Hawes, the conductor. Hawes, disguised and caricatured, is murdered by the greater drive of normal sexual prowess, symbolized by the "natural" Juana as the matador.

The usual themes of love, betrayal, murder, and retribution ground the narrative. A new and sinister motif is evident, however, when Sharp's artistic power becomes his destruction. His distinctive singing voice leads to their identification, and the Mexican police shoot Juana in the street. Thus, Sharp destroys Juana with the voice she had restored. His confession in a final scene does not ameliorate the horror of the tale, though. *Serenade* is Cain's bleakest statement on man's elemental and instinctual experiences. The racial stereotyping of the Mexicans and the homophobia pervading the book mirror Cain's own and the nation's mentality in the 1930s.

At the time Cain believed he was on the leading edge of psychology with his specious observations about homosexuality and its relationship to the human voice. Sharp's homosexuality is a sometime thing, and Cain covers his bases by saying that "every man has got five percent of that in him, if he meets the one person that'll bring it out." Cain, though, was aware the premise might not be entirely solid, and he wrote to Mencken on 8 December 1937 for affirmation. Mencken assured Cain he was not bothered by the implications of the book. Although bothered by the coincidences in the plot, Mencken responded in a 10 December letter, "the main thing is that the story tells itself magnificently. I defy any person under the rank of archbishop to read ten pages and then fail to go to the end."

The reviews were mixed from the beginning. Many said the novel was just what one would expect from the man who wrote *The Postman Always Rings Twice*. Some maintained that Cain went too far in his choice of theme and thought he was after sensational shock effect. Lewis Gannett in the *New York Herald Tribune* of 30 November 1937 said that although "the bare outlines of Mr. Cain's plot are consistently revolting, he manages to invest his most sordid details with glimpses of the human subconscious which give them much dignity." Several reviews were in line with the reviewer for the 5 December issue of the *Pittsburgh Post Gazette,* who did not like the content but praised the artistry, narrative control, and economy, aguing that "the sensationalism of its subject matter was more than matched by the brilliance of its execution" and that it was "literature of the high order." Though the book proved highly controversial in many circles—it was denounced by the Catholic Church, for example—the medical community did not lift an eyebrow. In fact, one Los Angeles psychiatrist wrote to Cain that it was required reading in most psychiatry courses in the country. On the personal level, the novel caused Cain some problems as his theme led a few men to assume he was a homosexual.

The book did not sell as well initially as Cain had hoped, and Knopf wanted to launch an advertising campaign that would manipulate the controversy. Cain refused, but he became concerned that many readers might be stopped by the homosexual theme when sales suddenly dropped off after 25,000 copies sold. More worrisome was the general consensus among some screenwriter friends that the story lagged after Juana and Sharp returned to Mexico. Cain was doubly depressed over the poor sales because he had lived with the story for twenty years. The novel produced something of a sensation, however, and Cain was again a hot property, courted by studios to do scriptwriting and pursued by New York agents for manuscripts.

Mildred Pierce (1941) is the last of Cain's 1930s novels, and in it Cain departed from his successful formula. Mildred and her daughter, Veda, surpass Cora Papadakis and Phyliss Nirdlinger to become the classic bitches in Cain's fiction. Mildred is Cain's version of the ordinary, mousy woman who uses men to achieve her ends. A victim of the Great Depression, Mildred exploits her skills as a waitress to become a successful restauranteur. Determined to shelter and promote the daughter she idolizes, Mildred sacrifices every scruple. Veda, in turn, uses her mother—and the men Mildred has used—to advance her own ambitions for professional opera and to satisfy her sexual appetites. Ultimately, Mildred loses everything trying to support the lifestyle Veda requires. When Mildred discovers her current husband and Veda in bed together, she

Illustration for Cain's Double Indemnity *when it was serialized in* Liberty *(1936)*

renounces them both and ends up exactly where she began, with her disaffected first husband—the father of her children—and flat broke.

Mildred Pierce is a departure in other ways for Cain. He shifts from the fast-paced first-person to third-person narration. Cain himself thought this point of view left his hand "palsied," and critics have viewed the novel as overlong and shapeless. Because of this narrative mode, though, Cain gives his fullest treatment of the day-to-day details of the life of his characters. As in his previous work, the novel revolves around love, money, and sex, but though success is perverse and wish fulfillment destructive, there is no murder.

The year 1941 was personally disastrous for Cain, as his suffering from ulcer and gallstone pains led to the removal of half his stomach, leaving him unemployed and in debt. Moreover, the year marked a turning point in his career. *Mildred Pierce* is the last of his critically acclaimed novels. Cain was aware that the literary winds had begun to shift and that the public mood was changing as World War II approached.

Attuned to the somberness of the war mood hanging over the country, he suspected there was truth in the claim, made in the 26 September 1941 issue of *The New York Times,* that the nation had outgrown the world of James M. Cain and James T. Farrell. Deeply affected by the war though he was, the infirm, forty-nine-year-old Cain had no hope of entering the service.

A week before the bombing of Pearl Harbor, Cain finished a novel he had started earlier in the year while recuperating from stomach surgery. Intended solely for the magazines and the movies, *Love's Lovely Counterfeit* (1942) was the only novel Cain ever wrote with the movie version specifically in mind. It involved a series of double crosses among a politician, his chauffeur, and a former mistress and was originally conceived as an exploration of the sinister side of Los Angeles politics. With the beginning of the war, however, Cain decided that to attack specifically any American city was in bad taste, so he changed the locale to a fictitious midwestern city. The change failed to help the sale of the novel, which Cain could not peddle to the magazines or a studio. Finally Knopf stepped in and paid a $1,500 advance to publish it as a book.

Cain had difficulty finding suitable material for stories or novels during the war, though he made a great deal of money from the sale of his books to the studios. In seventeen years in Hollywood he made $380,000. He wrote a serial that he called "Galloping Dominoes," a thinly disguised revision of a play he had written in 1938, *7-11,* which was produced in Maine but never made Broadway. The serial never sold, and Cain was experiencing despair he blamed on the war. He wrote in a 23 May 1942 letter to Knopf that it had "swept into discard every idea I had cooking." By late 1942 Cain was drinking and eating to excess and was $4,000 in debt. His rocky marriage to Elina had finally dissolved, and he faced a costly settlement. The breakup of his marriage may well have profoundly affected Cain's career, for his best work had been written under Elina's steadying influence. Hoopes asserts that his "inability to match these stories in his later books can be traced to their separation." Cain's financial situation, at least, soon brightened, though, as he was offered a job making $1,000 a week to write a script for the Signal Corps. The movie never got off the ground, but Cain was $34,000 richer when he was released from the project.

Publication of *Three of a Kind* in 1943 revived Cain's career. The anthology included a preface by Cain and collected *Double Indemnity* along with two other serials: *Career in C Major* (originally published as "Two Can Sing") and *The Embezzler* (originally published as "Money and the Woman"). These works cemented Cain's reputation as the stylist of brief, first-person, confessional narratives in which the hero acknowledges his sins and grants a voyeuristic glance into his immoral life. The collection was both a commercial and literary success. In the 9 May 1943 issue of *Book Week* A. C. Spectorsky wrote that "Cain's style—grit, gore and gutsy lustiness—is as timely as war news, his plots are almost as exciting."

Cain had always believed the best way for an author to get attention from Hollywood was to write a novel that hit big with the print media in New York. *Three of a Kind* proved his point. The success of the anthology brought *Double Indemnity* to the attention of Billy Wilder, who immediately set about purchasing the rights. Determined to maintain the original as closely as possible, Wilder rejected all attempts to alter the basic plot to get past the censors. The movie, shot in forty days, was a huge national success.

Cain jumped from project to project during most of 1943. In the fall of that year he edited an anthology of short stories directed toward the millions of men serving in the armed forces. *For Men Only* (1944)

included works by Ernest Hemingway, Damon Runyon, Ring Lardner, John Steinbeck, John O'Hara, and Farrell. Cain's contribution was "The Girl in the Storm." In his introduction for the volume Cain concluded, "The world's great literature is peopled with thoroughgoing heels, and in this book you will find a beautiful bevy of them, with scarcely a character among them you would let in the front door. I hope you like them. I think they are swell." Cain's characters were at home in such a collection.

By the end of 1943 Cain's relationship with actress Kate Cummings, with whom he had had an affair since before his breakup with Elina, was unpleasantly over. He married actress Aileen Pringle in July 1944. Cain and his third wife, however, quickly proved immensely incompatible; they separated in 1946 and divorced in 1947.

Cain had toyed with the idea of an historical novel for years and in 1942 had begun research for a story about a young man from Annapolis who falls in love with a California prostitute. Roger Duval, a soldier on a mission for the Confederacy, meets the whore Morina, follows her to Virginia City, and quits the Southern army. Ultimately, he kills a rich miner who intends to marry Morina and set her up as the madam of her own house. The pair run away together, begin robbing trains, and then head for Mexico to hide in the hills. One morning, thinking they are being followed, Duval goes to investigate and accidentally kills Morina when he hears a twig snap behind him. "The end of this story," Cain recalled in his memoirs, "which compressed the whole relationship in one blazing moment, I am very proud of."

Cain titled the book *Past All Dishonor* (1946). Though he was able to draw in part on his own experiences, the rest he researched with his usual meticulous attention. Cain thought this novel was his most solid treatment of the theme that overlay his best work, the wish that comes true and the horrific results for the principle characters: "If you give people everything they want and nothing they ought to have, that'll wind them up in hell, too," he wrote in the novel. Cain was convinced the public and the reviewers would think this novel was his best. At the time, he too believed it was.

While waiting for the manuscript to be typed and edited, Cain decided to return to "The Butterfly," a novel about incest he had worked on sporadically for several years. Before he learns the truth of Kady's parentage, Jess is tormented by the incestuous relationship he believes he is having with Kady. Jess Tyler, a Kentucky mountaineer, kills Moke Blue, the man who broke up his marriage and, unknown to Jess, had fathered Kady, who Jess believes is his own daughter. The psychologically complex novel exploits Cain's major

Fred MacMurray as Walter Neff and Barbara Stanwyck as Phyllis Dietrichson in a still from the 1944 movie version of
Double Indemnity *(Paramount Pictures)*

themes of passion and betrayal, adultery, and death. Cain uses first-person narration to its maximum potential in Jess's self-doubt and delusion. His knowledge of truth is painfully limited, and the reader comes to realize that Jess clearly is not trustworthy to tell his own story.

Cain had trouble beginning the story and told Hoopes that he wrote the beginning at least fifty times, but with the novel finished for the time being (later he would rewrite it) and *Past All Dishonor* safely deposited with Knopf, Cain was comfortably at the height of his fame. When reviews of *Past All Dishonor* came in, Cain and Knopf were elated. Most reviews were glowing; the critics for the *Boston Herald* of 13 May 1946 and the *Louisville Courier-Journal* of 24 June said it was "Cain at his best," and many others agreed. Reviews were collectively the most positive since *The Postman Always Rings Twice*. Nonetheless, a few naysayers emerged; Cain was most distressed by the reviewers who questioned the depth and validity of his research and implied that he had written the novel with the movies in mind. Malcolm Cowley in the 24 June 1946 issue of *The New Republic* said that Cain "used to be a writer before he got so tethered in celluloid." Edmund Wilson in the 25 May 1946 issue of *The*

New Yorker hit on both scores: "The characters talk straight post-Hemingway, full of phrases unknown in 1861, with occasional ladlings-in of the language of *Huckleberry Finn* when the author remembers this period. . . . Cain has been eaten alive by the movies."

Cain was furious with Cowley and Wilson, feeling they questioned his artistic integrity without reason. He purposefully had made Morina a prostitute rather than the niece of a madam to give the story more truth and impact; he also knew that doing so would cause him grief with the studios because of Hays Office censorship. His premonitions were sound; the novel was turned down by virtually every well-known director and producer in Hollywood. Cain, however, did receive some encouragement in his penchant for historical fiction. Many critics focused on the realism of his period writing, and the success of Margaret Mitchell's *Gone With the Wind* (1936) as a novel and a movie prompted him to continue with a series of Civil War novels.

In 1946 Cain engaged in one of the few public projects of his career. Partially in response to his own troubles in managing his literary financial affairs and partially in an attempt to protect fellow artists, he proposed the creation of the American Authors' Authority within the Screen Writer's Guild. Cain had 1.5 million books in print, many reprinted by several different houses. Often he was confused about how much money should be coming to him in royalties and suspicious that he did not get his fair share. In addition, if a studio owned dramatic rights to his work, he had to fight to produce a play version of his own novel; he had suffered a huge fight with M-G-M over *The Postman Always Rings Twice*. He knew that he did not make nearly the money on his own work that the publishers and the studios earned. Cain proposed that the American Authors' Authority should own the rights to all work by its members and act as the business agent among the publisher, studios, magazines, and radio.

The plan had merit, but Cain was not a good political organizer. He kept up the argument during 1946 in a series of newspaper and journal articles. The governing board of the Screen Writer's Guild immediately supported Cain's project, but many of the most active and well-heeled members fought the proposal. Ultimately, the plan was defeated, but not before some opponents tried to tie it to communism. The growing mood in Hollywood was conservative, and Joseph McCarthy–era blacklisting was already rumbling. Cain had always jokingly referred to himself as a "registered Democrat," but he was naive politically. He paid little attention to the arrests of his friends and never seems to have taken the McCarthy movement seriously.

With *Past All Dishonor* in 1946 and *The Butterfly* in 1947 Cain reached the height of his reputation as a novelist whose specialty was shock and sensationalism. By this time the critics were beginning to tire of hard-boiled literature, of which Cain was the acknowledged master, despite his assiduous attempts to relinquish the tough-guy label. While many reviewers praised the novels individually, they also echoed Robert Gorham Davis, who in the 9 February 1947 issue of *The New York Times* wrote that "Hard-boiled literature makes entertainment out of suffering by de-humanizing it. The important question is whether it can succeed in this without de-humanizing its audience." Suspicion was growing that hard-boiled literature desensitized readers to the horrors of violence and perversion and, indeed, provoked them to take pleasure in both.

In July 1946 Cain had met Florence Macbeth, a Chicago opera star whom he had idolized since his days of study to become an opera singer. The two were married a year later, 19 September 1947, when his divorce from Aileen Pringle became final. Cain remained with Florence until her death on 5 May 1966. Soon after the marriage ceremony, Florence, who did not like Hollywood, persuaded Cain to return to the East Coast. With the shifting critical landscape Cain approached

the move with a vow to amount to something; he told Florence he intended to shift from a newspaperman and movie scriptwriter who was a sometimes novelist to "a plain, professional 100 per cent novelist." The move to Hyattsville, Maryland, proved the death knell for Cain masterpieces.

Cain began working out the plot of *The Moth* in the early 1930s when he saw the spectacle of hoboes night after night riding freight cars, staring without hope or expectation into the middle distance. His purpose was to write the story of a young boy who, as Cain says in an unpublished article quoted by Hoopes, was growing up in Baltimore "letting the Depression happen to him." The novel is overlong, highly episodic, and unlike anything Cain had written before. Jack Dillon, secretly in love with an adolescent, is forced by gossipmongering to leave home and take to the rails. After several years and a series of adventures and misadventures, Dillon returns home to his dying father and reunites with a now much older Helen Legg, whom he plans to marry. *The Moth* was not a critical success. Reviewers and critics were despairing of the hardboiled novel, but a softer, mellower Cain had little appeal either. Though Cain had been interested in broadening his palette, he was beginning to have second thoughts.

After publication of *The Moth* Cain began another Civil War novel. Following his usual methods of intense research, he set up to write in the Library of Congress. During late 1948 and into 1949 Cain went to the library almost daily, but his research did not go smoothly. He bogged down in a minutia of historical detail that became almost paralyzing. He was also drinking a great deal again and his weight soared to 250 pounds. When he realized his drinking was affecting his work, he made a final push to stop. After two years of complete sobriety he lost sixty pounds.

Cain's first few years after returning to Hyattsville were consumed by his research on the new novel, his health concerns, and a couple of lawsuits. One suit charged that *Serenade* was obscene; the other claimed that Cain had stolen the basic plot for *Mildred Pierce* from an unpublished short story a woman had sent to him. The lawsuits caused Cain considerable time and stress, but finally both went in his favor. The timing was miserable; Cain's writing was already not going well, and his finances were again in disarray. Fortunately, the paperback sales of his novels continued to surge. Because he was strapped for money, Cain wrote three books that never appeared in hardcover. Avon published *Sinful Woman* in 1947, *Jealous Woman* in 1950, and *The Root of His Evil* in 1951 as original paperbacks. Cain was never proud of these novels, but he believed the only book that ever hurt a writer was no book. He

Covers for two of Cain's novels that were first published in paperback editions

maintained from the early days of his career that anything written for magazines or newspapers did not count; since most paperbacks were never reviewed and went quickly from newsstand to oblivion, he regarded them as of no more significance than magazine features.

In 1952 Cain quickly wrote a novel about an idea he had first had in California, but which did not come together until his experience with losing weight. *Galatea* is about a young man, Duke, who specializes in training fighters for the ring. In order to pay off a debt for $86 Duke stole, a judge orders him to work for a restauranteur who has a wife so fat she must use two bathroom scales to weigh herself. Duke believes the husband indulges Holly's appetite because he wants her to eat herself to death so he can inherit her family wealth and social position. Duke puts Holly in weight training, monitors her weight loss, and falls in love with his creation. In the final scene, however, Duke impulsively kills her.

When Cain finished the novel, he sent it somewhat sheepishly to Knopf. Though Cain liked the story, he feared it might be rejected. Knopf surprised Cain by saying that though not up to his best work, it

certainly had merit; Blanche Knopf also thought it was a good story. Both, however, expressed concern for the ending. Cain was initially distressed by their response, but reconsidered the conclusion. With a little alteration, he made a happy ending, but the final scenes are confusing. The predominant Cain theme is still there–the wish that comes true: "We all get what we pray for," Holly says at the end. "The trouble is we get it all." In this novel, though, the wish has lost its frightening edge.

By this time Cain was beginning to think his career was over. He suffered from periodic bouts of writer's block; his finances were perpetually problematic and his spirits lagging. He began to grant more on-air interviews with television and radio stations and agreed to an occasional lecture. He also tried to revive his short-story writing but had little success. When *Galatea* came out in the summer of 1953, the reviews were not good, further unsettling Cain. The reviewer for the 5 September 1953 issue of *The Nation* said Cain "is running down." Though Cain had high hopes for the book, hardcover sales lagged at fewer than 12,000 copies.

In early 1954 Cain was ready to return to his Civil War novel. He was intrigued by the Red River campaign of 1863 and decided to focus on the love affair between a Union soldier and the daughter of a Southern businessman, Mignon Fournet, and their trials in selling thousands of dollars' worth of cotton that both the North and the South claim. He labored over the novel off and on for the next three years but became increasingly bogged down in the plot and in re-creating an historical period. He finally sent the manuscript to Knopf in early 1957, but the publisher was neither enthusiastic nor encouraging, saying that the story was too complicated for the brevity of the manuscript. Cain had no new version ready for another three years.

When Knopf rejected "Mignon" in 1957, Cain was sixty-six years old and had worked on the novel sporadically for ten years. He spent most of 1959 and 1960 buried in the revision, but Knopf rejected it again. This time Cain did not agree with Knopf's suggestions for a rewrite and told his agent to look for a new publisher. While the agent shopped the manuscript around, Cain tinkered with the story, changed the ending, and cut out some historical intricacies. Dial finally published the novel in 1962. Though it sold 15,000 copies, it did not live up to the high expectation Cain had set for himself—to produce a commercial success equal to *Gone With the Wind*. Cain had twelve years invested in it, and it was his only major work since he left Hollywood.

Because *Past All Dishonor* had enjoyed the highest sales of any of his hardcover books, Cain had been teased into thinking he was a writer of historical fiction. However, his first historical novel had followed on the heels of his best work and came at the height of his Hollywood fame with the release of three blockbuster movies made from his novels. *Mignon* had no such crest to ride. Disheartened and discouraged, Cain told Luther Nichols in a 13 May 1963 *New York Times* interview, "All that reading and labor, and a kind of mouse is born." After what he regarded as the failure of *Mignon*, Cain never again had a period of feeling on top of his form.

In his later years Cain resisted all requests to write an autobiography, believing that he had no story to tell. His attitude is puzzling because he had always thought of biography as "the mother of history," as he wrote in an 11 May 1943 letter to Edmund Wilson. He did, however, begin to write his memoirs, maintaining that he was capable of reminiscing in an interesting and readable way. When he was approached by biographer David Madden, Cain agreed to write a series of autobiographical notes. Interestingly, he wrote all of these notes in the third person. Madden was the first critic to identify Cain in a formal way as a tough-guy writer. Cain still adamantly rejected the label, though he finally conceded Madden's point that the label did not negate other qualities of his work.

In 1969 the publication of *Cain X 3*, containing *The Postman Always Rings Twice, Double Indemnity,* and *Mildred Pierce,* created a minirevival of Cain's celebrity. In addition, the publication of Madden's *James M. Cain* (1970), a volume in the Twayne authors series, convinced Cain he should be more accessible to interviewers and scholars. He also kept busy with new work, publishing two more novels, *Rainbow's End* in 1975 and *The Institute* in 1976. Neither sold well. Cain died of natural causes on 27 October 1977.

Cain always considered writing a good way to make a living and never pretended that he did not write for money. Also, he never believed the critics understood him. In the preface to *Three of a Kind,* he wrote: "I am probably the most misread, misreviewed and misunderstood novelist now writing." Throughout his career critics tried to force him into boxes where he simply would not fit. Though many reviewers attributed his style, pacing, and momentum to his experience as a newspaperman, Cain was a master stylist and an authority on the English language. He was obsessed with the simplicity and brevity of good language use. He was most distressed by critics who said his writing was ruined by the influence of the movies.

Cain's vision is cynical and pessimistic, and his work presents a hard-boiled view of life that is its own justification. His best work lacks sentimentality, tenderness, and romance; the tone is stark and blunt. Madden notes that Cain is accused "of presenting violence without context, sadism without motive, death without dignity, sex without love, money without comfort, murder without malice." Critics who chastise Cain for not making his work socially significant fail to acknowledge that his work presents a particular slice of life—albeit low-life—of the 1920s, 1930s, and even the 1940s. His central characters often are average, all-American kids turned tough guys who become violent in an absurd world, but he refuses to judge their behavior. He is most interested in how his characters act rather than in why they behave as they do.

On 11 November 1977 University of Maryland professor Carl Bode spoke at Cain's memorial service and identified the critical confusion that still surrounds Cain: "The critics do their damnedest to put writers in pigeonholes, but James M. Cain wouldn't pigeonhole. He was not a tough-guy writer. He was not a detective-story writer or a writer of hard-nosed mystery as exemplified in the works of Raymond Chandler and Dashiell Hammett. And he was not a Hemingway. He was his own person. There has never been any writer quite like him, and the kind of work he did will be with us for a long while." Interest in Cain has undergone a revival in recent years, brought on by remakes of several movies from his novels in the 1980s. Hoopes's full-scale biography published in 1982 and studies by Madden in 1985 and Skenazy in 1989 have further established Cain's place in the history of American fiction writing. His work continues to be studied in university classes as examples of spare, precise prose.

Biography:

Roy Hoopes, *Cain: The Biography of James M. Cain* (New York: Holt, Rinehart & Winston, 1982; revised edition, Carbondale: Southern Illinois University Press, 1987).

References:

Harlan Ellison, "Introduction," *Hard Cain: Sinful Woman, Jealous Woman, The Root of His Evil* (Boston: Gregg Press, 1980);

Richard Fine, *James M. Cain and the American Authors' Authority* (Austin: University of Texas Press, 1992);

W. M. Frohock, *The Novel of Violence in America,* second edition (Dallas: Southern Methodist University Press, 1957);

David Madden, *Cain's Craft* (Metuchen, N.J.: Scarecrow Press, 1985);

Madden, *James M. Cain* (New York: Twayne, 1970);

William Marling, *The American Roman Noir: Hammett, Cain, and Chandler* (Athens & London: University of Georgia Press, 1995);

Joyce Carol Oates, "Man Under Sentence of Death: The Novels of James M. Cain," in *Tough Guy Writers of the Thirties,* edited by Madden (Carbondale & Edwardsville: Southern Illinois University Press, 1968), pp. 110–128;

Paul Skenazy, *James M. Cain* (New York: Continuum, 1989);

Edmund Wilson, *The Boys in the Back Room: Notes on California Novelists* (San Francisco: Colt, 1941).

Papers:

Most of James M. Cain's voluminous correspondence is housed in the Library of Congress. Other holdings can be found in the Alfred A. Knopf files in New York, the New York Public Library, and the Harold Ober Associates file in Princeton Library. His unpublished memoirs are owned by Alice Piper, a neighbor and close friend from his last years and the executor of Cain's estate.

Raymond Chandler

(23 July 1888 – 26 March 1959)

Robert F. Moss
University of South Carolina

See also the Chandler entry in *DS 6: Hardboiled Mystery Writers.*

BOOKS: *The Big Sleep* (New York: Knopf, 1939; London: Hamilton, 1939);

Farewell, My Lovely (New York: Knopf, 1940; London: Hamilton, 1940);

The High Window (New York: Knopf, 1942; London: Hamilton, 1943);

The Lady in the Lake (New York: Knopf, 1943; London: Hamilton, 1944);

Five Murderers (New York: Avon, 1944);

Five Sinister Characters (New York: Avon, 1945);

The Finger Man and Other Stories (New York: Avon, 1947);

The Little Sister (London: Hamilton, 1949; Boston: Houghton Mifflin, 1949);

The Simple Art of Murder (Boston: Houghton Mifflin, 1950; London: Hamilton, 1950);

The Long Good-Bye (London: Hamilton, 1953; Boston: Houghton Mifflin, 1954);

Playback (London: Hamilton, 1958; Boston: Houghton Mifflin, 1958);

Raymond Chandler Speaking, edited by Dorothy Gardiner and Kathrine Sorley Walker (London: Hamilton, 1962; New York: Houghton Mifflin, 1962);

Killer in the Rain (London: Hamilton, 1964; Boston: Houghton Mifflin, 1964);

Chandler Before Marlowe, edited by Matthew J. Bruccoli (Columbia: University of South Carolina Press, 1973);

The Blue Dahlia: A Screenplay, edited by Bruccoli (Carbondale and Edwardsville: Southern Illinois University Press, 1976; London: Elm Tree Books, 1976);

The Notebooks of Raymond Chandler & English Summer, edited by Frank MacShane (New York: Ecco, 1976; London: Weidenfeld & Nicolson, 1977);

Raymond Chandler's Unknown Thriller: The Screenplay of Playback (New York: Mysterious Press, 1985; London: Harrap, 1985);

Poodle Springs, by Chandler and Robert B. Parker (New York: Putnam, 1989; London: Macdonald, 1990).

PRODUCED SCRIPTS: *Double Indemnity,* motion picture, script by Chandler and Billy Wilder, Paramount, 1944;

And Now Tomorrow, motion picture, script by Chandler, Frank Partos, and Frank Patton, Paramount, 1944;

The Unseen, motion picture, script by Chandler and Hager Wilde, Paramount, 1945;

The Blue Dahlia, motion picture, Paramount, 1946;

The Lady in the Lake, motion picture, script by Chandler (uncredited) and Steve Fisher, M-G-M, 1947;

Strangers on a Train, motion picture, script by Chandler and Czenzi Ormonde, Warner Bros., 1951.

Upon the publication of his first novel, *The Big Sleep* (1939), Raymond Chandler was hailed as one of the leading practitioners of the American hard-boiled detective novel, but he received virtually no recognition as a writer of serious literature. During the course of his career his reputation slowly grew, first in England and then in the United States. He did not begin to receive academic attention until after his death, but today his books are studied in classrooms not only as premier examples of the detective novel but also as important works of twentieth-century American literature.

Few of Chandler's critics have connected his work with that of modernist writers such as Ernest Hemingway, F. Scott Fitzgerald, E. E. Cummings, and Ezra Pound, perhaps because Chandler did not publish his first novel until 1939, long after the modernist movement had crested. He was, nevertheless, of the same generation as most of the Paris expatriates and other experimental writers of the 1920s. He shared the same upbringing in a culture of strict Victorian morality, witnessed trench warfare firsthand, and was greatly disillusioned after World War I was over. His writing explores some of the same themes as his fellow modern-

Raymond Chandler in 1945, working on the script for The Blue Dahlia *(1946)*

ists: the corruption of society, a search for moral standards and codes of conduct, and the need to find order amid chaos.

Raymond Thornton Chandler was born in Chicago on 23 July 1888. His father, Maurice Benjamin Chandler, worked as a civil engineer for a western railway company. His mother, Florence Thornton Chandler, was Anglo-Irish and had moved to the United States in the 1880s. Their marriage was rocky, in part because of Maurice Chandler's alcoholism, and ended in divorce when Raymond was seven years old. Left with no support, Florence Chandler and her only son moved to England in 1895 to live with her mother and an unmarried sister in South London.

As a child Chandler spent summer holidays in Waterford, Ireland, where he stayed with his uncle Ernest Thornton, an Irish Protestant who headed a solicitor's office. There, in the Anglo-Irish class system, he got his first glimpse of social stratification. Though he chafed against his family's snobbery, Chandler was nevertheless influenced by the class prejudices around

him, developing in particular a strong contempt for Irish Catholics. This class-consciousness was intensified after 1900 when he enrolled as a day student at Dulwich College preparatory school, one of the better English public schools. His course of study included mathematics, the classics, and modern languages. Chandler's years at Dulwich also immersed him in the public school code, which emphasized gentlemanly behavior and the value of honor, self-sacrifice, and public service.

In 1905, at the age of seventeen, Chandler left Dulwich to study modern languages on the Continent. He spent six months in Paris, taking classes in commercial French at a business college, then moved on to Munich, Germany, where he worked with a private tutor. When he returned to England in 1907, he became a naturalized British subject, passed the civil service examination, and took a clerkship in the supply and accounting departments of the Admiralty. Chandler had literary ambitions, and he hoped the easy hours in the civil service would allow him time to write on the side. He detested the bureaucratic atmosphere, though, and resigned after six months.

For the next three years Chandler tried unsuccessfully to make a career as a London man of letters. He worked briefly as a reporter for the *Daily Express,* from which he was fired, then wrote as a freelancer for the *Westminster Gazette,* contributing poems, satirical sketches, and short articles on European affairs. The low pay—about £3 a week—was hardly enough to support him. In 1911 he began contributing essays and reviews to *The Academy,* a London literary weekly. Twenty-seven poems and eight essays from this period have been located. Chandler's critics agree that these works have little literary merit, calling them abstract, derivative, and overly sentimental. Some commentators, though, such as Jacques Barzun and Frank MacShane, have argued that the poetry and essays show early indications of the romantic sensibility that would emerge in Chandler's detective fiction. Many of these works project a speaker who is at odds with an oppressive, materialistic world and longs for escape to a distant land of chivalry and art. The desire for romance and escape remained a strong part of Chandler's artistic temperament, but he had not yet learned to integrate it with concrete, objective realism.

In 1912 Chandler decided he had no future as a London writer. He borrowed £500 from his uncle and sailed to the United States. He stayed briefly in St. Louis and Omaha before moving to Los Angeles, where he lived in furnished rooms and worked odd jobs, including stringing tennis rackets and picking apricots. In 1913 he enrolled in a night-school bookkeeping course and got a job as an accountant with the Los Angeles Creamery. Chandler's mother soon came over from England to join him, and the two lived together until her death in 1924.

When the United States declared war on Germany in 1917, Chandler enlisted—though with the Canadian, not the U.S., army. He was sent to France and assigned to the Seventh Battalion of the Canadian Expeditionary Force, a battalion that had seen some of the most brutal trench fighting on the Western front. Chandler remained on the front lines for only a few months before being transferred to the Royal Air Force (RAF) for training as a pilot. He remained in England for the rest of the war, and the Armistice came before he completed flight school. Little more is known about Chandler's war experiences. His letters make only passing references to his military service; his only attempt to write about combat is a brief unpublished sketch titled "Trench Raid."

Following his discharge in 1919, Chandler spent some time in the Pacific Northwest, where he made another abortive attempt at a writing career. He worked briefly for a British bank in San Francisco and then returned to Los Angeles. He became involved in an affair with Cissy Pascal, the wife of a friend, and by July she had filed for a divorce from her husband. She was forty-eight; Chandler was thirty-one. He continued to live with his mother, who did not approve of his relationship with Cissy. In the early 1920s Chandler took a job as a bookkeeper for the Dabney Oil Syndicate, which was thriving in the midst of the Los Angeles oil boom. He did well with the company, being promoted to auditor and then vice president. A month after the death of his mother from cancer in January 1924, Chandler married Cissy. He continued in his business career, earning $1,000 a month—the equivalent of a modern salary of more than $100,000 a year. He also began drinking heavily, behaving erratically, and having affairs with the younger women who worked in his office. In 1932, after receiving warnings and reprimands, he was fired from his job.

Chandler turned to fiction writing to earn a living, choosing the detective pulp market, in part because he could get paid while learning his craft and in part because he thought the form had potential for forceful and honest writing. His first short story, "Blackmailers Don't Shoot," was published by *Black Mask,* the most prestigious of the pulps, for $180—a penny a word. He spent the next six years writing for *Black Mask* and other detective magazines. During his career, Chandler published twenty-four stories and novellas in periodicals: "Blackmailers Don't Shoot" (December 1933), "Smart-Aleck Kill" (*Black Mask,* July 1934), "Finger Man" (*Black Mask,* October 1934), "Killer in the Rain" (*Black Mask,* January 1935), "Nevada Gas" (*Black Mask,* June 1935), "Spanish Blood" (*Black Mask,* November 1935), "Guns at Cyrano's" (*Black Mask,* January 1936), "The Man Who Liked Dogs" (*Black Mask,* March 1936), "Noon Street Nemesis" (*Detective Fiction Weekly,* May 1936), "Goldfish" (*Black Mask,* June 1936), "The Curtain" (*Black Mask,* September 1936), "Try the Girl" (*Black Mask,* January 1937), "Mandarin's Jade" (*Dime Detective,* November 1937), "Red Wind" (*Dime Detective,* January 1938), "The King in Yellow" (*Dime Detective,* March 1938), "Bay City Blues" (*Dime Detective,* June 1938), "The Lady in the Lake" (*Dime Detective,* January 1939), "Pearls Are a Nuisance" (*Dime Detective,* April 1939), "Trouble Is My Business" (*Dime Detective,* August 1939), "The Bronze Door" (*Unknown,* November 1939), "I'll Be Waiting" (*Saturday Evening Post,* December 1939), "No Crime in the Mountains" (*Detective Story,* September 1941), "Professor Bingo's Snuff" (*Park East,* June–August 1951), and "Marlowe Takes on the Syndicate" (*London Daily Mail,* 6–10 April 1959). Only three of these stories were written after 1939, the year Chandler published his first novel. His pulp magazine career was his literary apprenticeship, where he learned the detective form and developed the style that would make him famous as a novelist.

Chandler admitted that he had no natural talent for the detective story and that he had to teach himself how to write in the conventions of the genre. He studied the work of F. Austin Freeman, Erle Stanley Gardner, and fellow *Black Mask* authors. His greatest influence was Dashiell Hammett, the best of the early hard-boiled detective writers. Chandler felt Hammett was working in the same vein as Theodore Dreiser, Ring Lardner, Sherwood Anderson, and Ernest Hemingway, advancing, as he phrased it in his 1944 essay "The Simple Art of Murder," "a rather revolutionary debunking of both the language and material of fiction." The traditional English mystery novel was set in a detached world of wealth and gentility, involved unrealistic and clichéd characters, and was built around ratiocination–the step-by-step solution of a murder through deduction from trifling clues. Hammett made his crimes more realistic, setting his stories in urban environments and creating characters drawn more closely from everyday life. "Hammett took murder out of the Venetian vase and dropped it into the alley," Chandler wrote in "The Simple Art of Murder." "Hammett gave murder back to the kind of people that commit it for reasons, not just to provide a corpse."

Chandler picked up the hard-boiled detective story where his predecessor left off, adopting Hammett's objective style, attention to physical detail, and use of the American vernacular. Chandler's early stories, though better than the average *Black Mask* fare, indicate that he had yet to find his own voice and technique. The style is marred by awkwardness and overwriting, particularly in descriptive passages. Hammett's influence on Chandler is readily apparent, as the plots move quickly and contain hard-edged, almost random violence–as many as seven murders in a single story. In the denouements Chandler relies on long conversations, offering two or three possible explanations for the events in the case and taxing the reader's ability to make sense of what has happened.

The most notable difference between Chandler's early stories and his mature fiction is the character of his detectives. The protagonist of the early stories, Mallory, has much in common with Hammett's Continental Op and Sam Spade. Though fundamentally honest, Mallory's moral stance is often ambiguous. For the first half of "Blackmailers Don't Shoot" he seems to be blackmailing a Hollywood actress. Mallory turns out to be a private detective trying to foil an extortion plot, but his employer is an underworld gambler. His primary motivations are money and occupational pride: he is hired to complete a job, and he is determined to

Chandler as a student at Dulwich College preparatory school in England

collect. Mallory's violent methods echo those of the Continental Op in *Red Harvest.* In both "Blackmailers Don't Shoot" and "Smart-Aleck Kill," Mallory gets caught in the middle of blackmail plots and plays off one criminal against another, allowing them to eliminate each other. These techniques worked well for Hammett's characters, but such stories were a pose for Chandler.

As Chandler's writing matured, his heroes began evolving closer to the character of Philip Marlowe. His later detectives tend to be poor and are often seen sitting idle in their offices, waiting for work. Despite their poverty, they are not motivated by money. They work instead because of friendship, sympathy for people (usually women) in trouble, and personal pride and curiosity. In many stories they receive no payment at all. The detectives take more beatings than they dish out, often ending up unconscious from being sapped or drugged; repeatedly they turn to wisecracking and alcohol to buoy themselves. In his later pulp stories, Chandler's "shop-worn Galahad" reached full development—a battered, reflective man who pursues justice despite poor odds and poorer recompense.

Behind this world-weariness of the detective hero is a growing sense of moral compromise. The detective has his code, but it fails to function in a corrupt world. Sam Delaguerra, the policeman protagonist of "Spanish Blood," is stripped of his badge but continues investigating on his own to solve the murder of an old friend. Delaguerra learns that his friend's wife is the murderer, but he covers it up out of loyalty to his dead friend. He gets his police badge back in the end, but "it's not as clean as it was." Similarly, Ted Malvern, the hero of "Guns at Cyrano's" is drawn into an extortion case when he comes to the aid of Jean Adrian, whom he finds unconscious in the hallway of his apartment building. The chivalric damsel-in-distress motif becomes more complicated when Malvern learns that Adrian is involved in blackmailing a corrupt senator. In the end he covers up for her because she has a partially noble motive for her crimes: she wants to revenge an old friend, the senator's abandoned illegitimate daughter. These types of compromises also occur in "The Curtain," "Try the Girl," "Mandarin's Jade," "Red Wind," and "The Lady in the Lake." Chandler's detectives can no longer bash their way through a case and trust that justice will be served in the end. Instead, they have to make difficult ethical decisions and, ultimately, compromise their standards of honor and integrity.

With this advance in character came maturation in technique. The pace of the stories slowed somewhat, allowing the narrator to reflect on the world around him and heightening the mood and atmosphere of the stories. In a May 1948 letter to Frederick Lewis Allen, the editor of *Harper's Magazine,* Chandler looked back on his pulp stories and commented, "My theory was that readers just *thought* they cared about nothing but the action . . . . The things they really cared about, and that I cared about, were the creation of emotion through dialogue and description." Chandler began incorporating more descriptive passages—particularly of setting—into his writing, giving the stories a stronger sense of place. Although gamblers, gangsters, and civic corruption were still essential material, Chandler began taking his detectives into Beverly Hills and the insulated world of apparently respectable wealth. Hangers-on and those catering to the vices of the wealthy—pornographers, dope doctors, nightclub operators,

bogus spiritualists—play increasingly larger roles. The detectives begin ranging farther from the city, into the mountains at Puma Point (Big Bear Lake) and the beaches at Bay City (Santa Monica), giving a broader picture of life in the Los Angeles area. Chandler's stories were moving from blood-and-guts adventure toward perceptive social realism.

Chandler was also developing a distinctive style by merging the hard-edged vernacular of the genre with the literary sophistication gleaned from his classical education. The result is a blending of terse, slangy prose with lyrical passages and formal diction. In Chandler's later pulp stories, he incorporated more wit and irony into his writing. The effect can be seen by comparing the openings of "Killer in the Rain," published at the beginning of 1935, and "Bay City Blues," published more than three years later. The earlier story begins tersely and objectively: "We were sitting in a room at the Berglund. I was on one side of the bed, and Dravec was in the easy chair. It was my room." The later story uses humor to soften the objectivity and to immediately establish the wry, self-aware voice of the narrator: "It must have been Friday because the fish smell from the Mansion House coffee-shop next door was strong enough to build a garage on. Apart from that it was a nice warm day in spring, the tail of an afternoon, and there hadn't been any business in a week." The narrative style reflects the character of Chandler's mature narrators: world-weary, clever, and sarcastic.

Chandler's narrators use wit to shield themselves against excessive emotion and sentimentality, responding with a wisecrack rather than revealing how they genuinely feel. Much of the heroes' toughness, furthermore, is a product not of physical action but of dialogue. They engage in sarcastic banter with criminals and cops, using humor to show resolve or to refuse to divulge important information. Chandler's detectives are self-aware, realizing that their hard-boiled exterior is merely a pose—a carryover from the author's own self-awareness: Chandler knew that his stories walked a fine line between believability and cliché. He had a tendency to burlesque the hard-boiled conventions even while conforming to them, and this tension—between the tough-guy persona and ironic self-awareness—forms the foundation of his mature style.

Although by the late 1930s Chandler was one of the leading pulp-magazine writers, he earned little from his stories. To make a good living from pulp writing, an author had to be able to produce rapidly, and Chandler never published more than five stories in a single year. In 1938, the earliest year for which payment records survive, Chandler earned only $1,275. He and Cissy kept their furniture in storage, lived in furnished rooms, and moved as often as three times a year. The pulp jungle had provided him with his apprenticeship, but he was ready to move on to more lucrative markets.

In the spring of 1938 Chandler began working on his first novel, *The Big Sleep*. The story is drawn from two of his *Black Mask* novelettes, "Killer in the Rain" and "The Curtain," along with a small portion of "Finger Man"–a process he called "cannibalization." Chandler did not cut and paste passages but rather rewrote entire scenes, in the process tightening his prose and enriching his descriptions. The novel took only three months to complete, and it was published by Alfred A. Knopf in February 1939.

The Big Sleep begins with Marlowe's being hired to quash a blackmail attempt, but he soon uncovers a complex web of pornography, gambling, extortion, and murder. By the end of the novel he is investigating the disappearance of a former bootlegger, which puts him at odds with both gangsters and the Los Angeles police. Despite this complicated and often confusing plot, the heart of *The Big Sleep* is not the solution of the murders–the whodunit–but rather the world the story depicts and the movement of Marlowe within that world. Chandler's characters repeatedly comment on the corruption of Los Angeles and the modern world in general. The novel depicts a city in which pornographers and gamblers operate under the protection of crooked policemen, young women use their sexuality to ruin men, and wealth can buy immunity from damaging publicity and legal prosecution. It is a fallen world where glamorous appearances mask sordid deeds and everyone is a grifter.

This mood is further advanced through Chandler's skillful description of setting. His evocative details of sordid locations are particularly vivid, from Marlowe's shabby office–with "venerable magazines" and "net curtains that needed laundering"–to a downtown building's vacant rooms–with "a tarnished and well-missed spittoon on a gnawed rubber mat." In sharp contrast to these low places is the elegant Sternwood mansion high in the Hollywood foothills, where the family "could no longer smell the stale sump water or the oil, but they could still look out their front windows and see what had made them rich. If they wanted to." Consistent throughout the setting of the novel is the sense of a once-grand place now gone to seed, as in Eddie Mars's Cypress Club, a "rambling frame mansion" that was once a rich man's home, became a hotel, then ended up an illegal casino. The club has about it "a general air of nostalgic decay"; the ballroom is "still a beautiful room," but there is "roulette in it instead of measured, old fashioned dancing."

It is within this corrupt, fallen world that Marlowe must operate. Philip Durham, who wrote the first book-length critical study of Chandler's novels, *Down*

These Mean Streets a Man Must Go: Raymond Chandler's Knight (1963), advanced the influential interpretation that Marlowe's character is a questing knight in the modern world. This interpretation is based largely on *The Big Sleep,* in which Marlowe's code of conduct is articulated and tested. Key to this code is professional pride: honestly performing the job for which he has been hired. In this case, Marlowe is hired by General Sternwood, a wealthy Los Angeles oil man, to protect his daughters from blackmail and other threats. After he saves one of the Sternwood daughters from a robbery attempt outside a gambling club, she offers herself to him. Marlowe kisses her but refuses to go further. "Kissing you is nice," he tells her, "but your father didn't hire me to sleep with you. . . . The first time we met I told you I was a detective. Get it through your lovely head. I work at it, lady, I don't play at it." He offers a similar explanation to the other Sternwood daughter when she, too, tries to seduce him: "It's a question of professional pride. . . . I'm working for your father. He's a sick man, very frail, very helpless. He sort of trusts me not to pull any stunts." This professional ethic causes Marlowe to pursue his employer's interests even against that employer's specific instructions: investigating the disappearance of Rusty Regan, the former bootlegger who married General Sternwood's daughter Vivian and became friends with the old man.

As Durham argues, the basis of Marlowe's professional pride has less to do with a commercial or work ethic than it does with an older, chivalric code. The connection between Marlowe and a knight is made on the first page of the novel, when he stands in the hallway of the Sternwood mansion and looks up at a stained-glass picture of a knight attempting to rescue an imprisoned lady. The knight is not getting anywhere, and Marlowe speculates that if he lived in the house, "I would sooner or later have to climb up there and help him." Throughout the novel Marlowe plays the role of knight errant to General Sternwood, questing for justice in loyal service to his lord despite sexual and financial temptation and threats of physical harm. Durham sums up the character of Chandler's detective as follows:

> In his knightly role Marlowe rescued ladies who did not deserve it, protected an old man sick and helpless . . . saw to it that some of the criminal element received its due–always moving through a lonely world with dignity and integrity, never deviating from his code in a febrile society that made unreasonable demands on any honest man.

Durham sees Marlowe as an urban extension of the literary hero developed in the frontier tales of James Fenimore Cooper and the westerns of Owen Wister and

Chandler in the 1920s

Zane Grey: courageous, virtuous, physically strong, and committed to imposing justice on an unjust world.

More recent critics such as Peter J. Rabinowitz have accepted Durham's Marlowe-as-knight interpretation, but they argue that in the end this chivalric code fails. In his 1980 essay "Rats Behind the Wainscoting: Politics, Convention, and Chandler's *The Big Sleep*," Rabinowitz directly disputes Durham's thesis:

> *The Big Sleep* does not depict the triumph of justice and fair play; to the contrary, it traces Marlowe's descent from moderately optimistic knighthood to a despairing recognition of his own impotence. . . . He may be able to perform a few good acts, such as protecting General Sternwood from heartbreak and avenging [small-time hood] Harry Jones's death. But this is a far cry from the administration of justice, which Marlowe comes to realize is no longer possible for an individual in our urban society.

Rabinowitz points out that midway through *The Big Sleep* Marlowe recognizes the failure of knighthood. He looks down at a chessboard where he has been working a problem and realizes that his last move—with a knight—is wrong: "Knights had no meaning in this game. It wasn't a game for knights." Despite this recognition, he continues trying to act according to his code.

He has already compromised his standards by participating in the cover-up of three murders, but he goes on working for General Sternwood and begins looking for Rusty Regan.

In the end Marlowe realizes that in trying to follow his code he has only helped further deception. "I do all this," he tells Vivian Regan, "for twenty-five bucks a day—and maybe just a little to protect what little pride a broken and sick old man has left in his blood, in the thought that his blood is not poison, and that although his two little girls are a trifle wild, as many girls are these days, they are not perverts or killers." Carmen Sternwood, though, is a pervert and a killer, as the denouement shows. She murdered Rusty Regan, her brother-in-law, when he rejected her sexual advances. When he learns the truth, Marlowe sacrifices his own honor and sense of justice to protect General Sternwood's pride. He covers up the murder, rationalizing that death cannot bother Regan now: "You just slept the big sleep, not caring about the nastiness of how you died or where you fell. Me, I was part of the nastiness now. Far more a part of it than Rusty Regan was. But the old man didn't have to be." In a way *The Big Sleep* functions as a bildungsroman: Marlowe learns about the moral illness of the modern world and his own inability to function within it. He begins the story with his knightly code; it is tested and it fails. His final statements are bitter, the struggles of a man who has lost his sense of moral order and is reaching out for a source of support.

Considering the limitations of the detective genre, *The Big Sleep* was a commercial success, selling ten thousand copies in a market where few mystery novels sold more than five thousand. In its publicity material for the novel, Knopf linked Chandler with James M. Cain and Dashiell Hammett and tried to promote him as the next major talent in the hard-boiled field. The book was widely reviewed, but it was segregated to columns dedicated to mystery fiction, and the reviews focused not on the literary merits of the novel but rather on the toughness of its tone and material. Isaac Anderson of *The New York Times* (12 February 1939) noted, "Most of the characters in this story are tough, many of them are nasty and some of them are both. . . . As a study in depravity, the story is excellent, with Marlowe standing out as almost the only fundamentally decent person in it." The anonymous mystery critic for *Time* (6 March 1939) reviewed the entire novel in a single sentence: "Detective Marlowe is plunged into a mess of murderers, thugs and psychopaths who make the characters of Dashiell Hammett and James Cain look like something out of Godey's Lady's Book."

Reviewers in Britain, where Chandler first gained respect as a literary writer, were equally dismissive. Nicholas Blake of *The Spectator* (31 March 1939) wrote that *The Big Sleep* "is American and very, very tough after the *Thin Man* fashion. Almost everyone in the book is wonderfully decadent, and the author spares us no blushes to point out just how decadent they are." These notices are less indicative of the reaction to Chandler than they are of the reviewers' attitudes toward detective fiction, which was considered an escapist form not worthy of serious critical attention. It would be another decade before Chandler began receiving recognition as a writer of serious literature, but he had graduated from the pulp-magazine market and launched a career as a mystery novelist.

In March 1939, a month after *The Big Sleep* was published, Chandler wrote out a plan for future work. He intended to write three more detective novels by the spring of 1941–a rate of a book every eight months–then, if he could earn enough money from them, move to England and abandon detective fiction in favor of genteel novels and fantastic short stories. This plan proved difficult to achieve, primarily because he could not produce at the rate he anticipated. During 1939 and 1940 he alternated working on drafts of three separate detective novels, discarded much of the material he wrote, and was distracted by illness and worries over the developing war in Europe. As with *The Big Sleep,*

Chandler was again "cannibalizing" earlier pulp stories, but the integrating process was moving much slower than it had for his first novel.

Chandler and his wife continued to move frequently during the early years of his novel-writing career. In May 1939 they left Riverside, California, and rented a cabin in the San Bernardino Mountains near Big Bear Lake, a resort town that provided relief from the summer heat in Los Angeles. They spent the next winter in La Jolla, north of San Diego, then moved back to Arcadia outside Los Angeles in 1940. Through all these moves, Chandler continued work on his second novel. He had completed a rough draft of "The Second Murderer," the working title of *Farewell, My Lovely,* while still at Big Bear Lake, but he decided to rewrite the entire story before submitting it to Knopf. He completed this rewrite in May 1940, and the novel was published in October.

Farewell, My Lovely draws upon the stories "Try the Girl" and "Mandarin's Jade" and maintains two separate plotlines. In the first, Marlowe is investigating the murder of a black nightclub owner by a gigantic former convict named Moose Malloy. In the other, he is hired to recover stolen jewelry, but his client is murdered during the ransom delivery. The two plots eventually converge around the character of Helen Grayle, a former nightclub singer who married a wealthy man and changed her identity. Her attempt to keep her past from being uncovered is the driving force behind the murders.

Chandler had some difficulty manipulating the two plots, and the novel has often been criticized for being poorly constructed. Peter Wolfe, in his critical study *Something More Than Night: The Case of Raymond Chandler* (1985), concludes that the construction of *Farewell, My Lovely* "distracts more than it enriches. Running downhill after its fine opening on Central Avenue, it ends as a hodgepodge of false starts, loose ends and melodramatic gleams."

In his 1981 study Jerry Speir offers a contrasting view, arguing that the seeming disorganization and narrative loose ends help advance the overall thematic purpose of the novel and show the development of Marlowe's character. *The Big Sleep* ends with Marlowe's recognition that corruption is inescapable. *Farewell, My Lovely* moves onward from that point, exploring the causes of corruption. As Marlowe investigates the murders, he realizes the connection between the two cases and begins to suspect a wide-ranging conspiracy to silence him. His initial theory is that he has stumbled upon a well-organized jewel theft ring, with a gigolo as finger man, the Bay City Police Department providing protection, and a crooked sanatorium serving as a place to imprison people who get in the way. The apparent

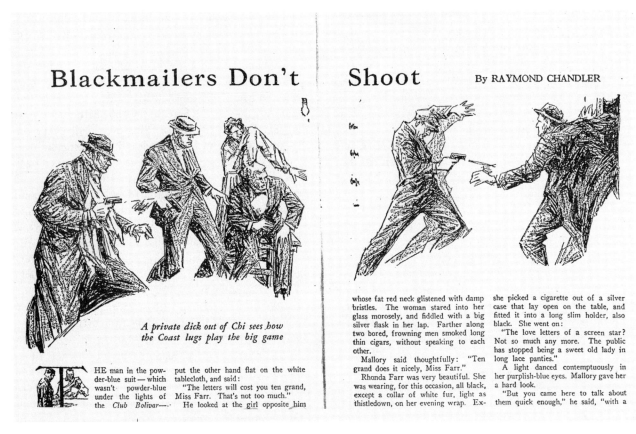

Opening pages of Chandler's first detective story, published in the December 1933 issue of Black Mask

mastermind of the crime ring is Laird Brunette, a racketeer rumored to control the entire town of Bay City. Marlowe does not know how Helen Grayle and Moose Malloy figure in, but he moves forward, looking for an explanation that will tie all the loose pieces into a coherent whole.

By the end of the novel, the idea of a sweeping conspiracy is punctured. "The crime pervading society," Speir argues, "is not the result of general collusion, but is instead simply a compilation of individual rackets and petty people protecting his or her own picayunish scheme"–a phony psychic who preys on wealthy women, a crooked dope doctor selling "needle-cures" to alcoholics, an illegal gambling-ship operator who wants only to protect his profits. Marlowe learns that corruption is more widespread than he initially thought, that it does not flow from a criminal mastermind but is entrenched in the very structure of society. Sergeant Galbraith, a policeman who considers himself an honest man even though he participates in protection rackets, tells Marlowe, "A guy can't stay honest if he wants to. . . . You gotta play the game dirty or you don't eat. A lot of bastards think all we need is ninety thousand FBI men in clean collars and brief cases. Nuts. The per-

centage would get them just the way it does the rest of us." Red Norgaard, a former cop who befriends Marlowe, also rejects the simplistic view of corruption. "These racketeers are a new type," he says. "Above all they're business men. What they do is for money. Just like other business men." *Farewell, My Lovely* suggests that the line between the right and wrong sides of the law is blurry at best. Chandler stops short of blaming the societal malaise on the general immorality of individuals, but it is an allegation he is moving toward.

Speir also argues that in the course of *Farewell, My Lovely* Marlowe begins to see himself as a figure of futility, making great efforts for no reason and with no one caring about his struggles. He exposes Mrs. Grayle's identity, but he is unable to prevent any of the murders from happening. In fact, his investigations prompt at least two of the murders. Because Marlowe starts digging into her past, Mrs. Grayle concocts the stolen-jewelry ruse that gets his client killed. By orchestrating a meeting of Moose Malloy and Mrs. Grayle at his apartment, Marlowe sets up Malloy's murder at the end of the novel. When Marlowe calls the police to report the shooting, their response is to chastise him for his efforts: "so you had to play clever." In *Farewell, My*

Lovely, Marlowe's understanding of his role as a detective is becoming increasingly cynical and uncertain.

Farewell, My Lovely received positive reviews, though again strictly as a genre book. The reviewers' comments were essentially the same as they had been for *The Big Sleep,* highlighting the toughness of Chandler's characters and sordidness of his material. The sales were disappointing—less than 7,500 copies—but Knopf blamed the war and the detective market, not the book itself. Chandler was discouraged by the response, but he continued writing, alternating between two different novels and making only slow progress. The Chandlers spent the summer of 1940 at Big Bear Lake again, and they moved four more times during the next two years—to Santa Monica, Pacific Palisades, Brentwood, and Idyllwild. They occasionally visited other pulp-detective writers such as W. T. Ballard and Cleve Adams, and Chandler corresponded regularly with Erle Stanley Gardner, the creator of Perry Mason. The Chandlers' social life during this time, however, was hindered by Cissy's recurring illnesses and their frequent moves.

It took Chandler almost two years to finish *The High Window,* a book that had an original plot rather than being adapted from earlier pulp stories. He finished the final draft in March 1942, and the book was published by Knopf in August. The story follows a line similar to that of *The Big Sleep.* Marlowe is hired by a wealthy Pasadena widow to investigate a small crime: the theft of a rare gold coin. His investigation, though, quickly involves him in more serious crimes: gambling, blackmail, and murder. Chandler's descriptions of the Belfont Building and the Bunker Hill neighborhood, where several of the murders take place, emphasize shabbiness and decay, conveying the impression of old grandeur lost. Standing in sharp contrast are the descriptions of his client's house in Pasadena and a posh illegal gambling club in Idle Valley, a thinly disguised version of Malibu Lake. In these settings Chandler focuses on the detachment of the rich, whose money allows them to wall themselves off from unpleasantness.

Marlowe operates within both of these worlds—Bunker Hill and Idle Valley—and his movement between them sets up much of the thematic content of the book. He is bitter, doubting, and weary with his profession. He repeatedly comments on how tired and lonely he is, and he characterizes himself as "about as much use as a hummingbird's spare egg" and as looking "like a two-time loser sneaking home from a reefer party." Along with this weariness comes both a heightening of Marlowe's hard-boiled pose—particularly his wisecracking—and an increased awareness of the artificiality of that pose. The other characters in the book frequently comment on his manner, telling him, "your

tough guy act stinks" and "I wouldn't carry that tough-guy manner too far." Marlowe knows his hard talk is stale, but he explains why he still uses it: "the meaningless talk had a sort of cold bracing effect on me, making a mood with a hard gritty edge." As his outlook darkens and his self-confidence wanes, Marlowe increasingly falls back on his hard-boiled pose as a means of support.

The futility Marlowe felt in *Farewell, My Lovely* is intensified in *The High Window* and shows the extent to which he has changed since Chandler's first novel. In *The Big Sleep* he identifies himself with the heroic figure of a knight in stained glass; in *The High Window* he associates himself with a caricatured lawn jockey that sits outside his client's house, patting it on the head and calling it "brother." The story—as Chandler indicated in his 1939 plan for future work—was conceived as a burlesque of the detective genre. A strong element of that burlesque remains in the completed novel, but "the joke," as Marlowe says about the lawn jockey toward the end of the novel, "seemed to have worn thin."

Most of Chandler's critics agree that *The High Window* is a transitional novel in which Chandler was moving from the chivalrous themes of *The Big Sleep* to the darker, more sentimental mood of his later novels. Chandler recognized that his detective was becoming increasingly cynical and ineffective. When he delivered the novel for publication in March 1942, he warned Blanche Knopf in a letter, "I'm afraid the book is not going to be any good to you. No action, no likable characters, no nothing. The detective does nothing."

Marlowe's disengagement derives in part from the loss of his feeling of loyalty that had anchored his moral code in the first novel. General Sternwood in *The Big Sleep* and Mrs. Murdock in *The High Window* play similar roles: they both hire Marlowe to do their dirty work for them, and Marlowe steadfastly performs his duties in their service, going so far as to cover up crimes. There is an essential difference, however, for though Marlowe respects General Sternwood and makes sacrifices to protect the old man's pride, no such bond exists in *The High Window.* Mrs. Murdock is selfish, manipulative, and rude, and Marlowe dislikes her from their first meeting. He risks his life, lies to the police, and covers up murders for her, but he has no real justification for his actions. In *The Big Sleep* Marlowe repeatedly cites a work ethic as his motivation, but beneath runs a deeper reason: a chivalric dedication to a noble individual. In *The High Window* he again explains his actions by citing professional ethics, but he shows no sense of personal loyalty. When he agrees to let the cover-up of a murder stand, Marlowe tells Mrs. Murdock's son: "I've been working for your mother

Dust jacket for Chandler's first novel (1939), the first appearance in book form of his detective hero Philip Marlowe

and whatever right to my silence that gives her, she can have." But, he adds, "I don't like her. I don't like you. I don't like this house. I didn't particularly like your wife."

As in the previous two novels, Marlowe again fails to see that justice is done. At the end of the story, he has uncovered a rare-coin counterfeiting racket, a blackmailing scheme, and four different murders. The most important of his discoveries is that his own client, Mrs. Murdock, murdered her husband eight years earlier by pushing him out of a high office window. Despite this knowledge, Marlowe removes himself from the case completely, allowing the police to untangle it on their own. His only action is to take his client's young secretary, the one person in the story whom he likes, back to her parents in Wichita, Kansas. It is a retreat away from the corrupt city to a more innocent place. While he is gone, the cops crack the counterfeiting ring, but they never tie in the Murdock family. Mrs. Murdock and her son, both murderers, get away with their crimes because they have wealth and power. Speir sums up Marlowe's predicament by saying, "His striving is for order, predictability, understanding . . . but he keeps discovering chaos, ambiguity, stupidity. He is capable of recognizing his own irrational romantic idealism, but continues to long for 'the justice we dream of but don't find.'"

Chandler followed *The High Window* with *The Lady in the Lake,* a novel on which he had been work-

ing intermittently since 1939. He finished the final draft in April 1943, and it was published by Knopf in November. The plot is drawn from two of Chandler's *Dime Detective* stories, "Bay City Blues" and "The Lady in the Lake," and he incorporated descriptive details from "No Crime in the Mountains." Much of the novel was written during the first two years of World War II, and the war provides a backdrop for the action, from the opening scene–where rubber blocks are being dug out of the street to be recycled for the war effort–to the closing–where soldiers guarding a dam shoot a fleeing murderer.

The story begins when Marlowe is hired by Derace Kingsley, an executive for an upscale cosmetics company, to find his wife, who supposedly has run off to Mexico with a young playboy. Marlowe traces Mrs. Kingsley's movements to a lake cabin in the resort village of Puma Point, where he discovers the drowned body of a woman named Muriel Chess. The case becomes more complicated when Mrs. Kingsley's lover turns up murdered, and Marlowe begins to suspect a connection between Mrs. Kingsley's disappearance and the suspicious suicide of a doctor's wife. Marlowe's key discovery is that the body in the lake is actually that of Mrs. Kingsley, not Muriel Chess. The crimes in the book are ultimately linked by illicit romance. Muriel Chess, a former nurse, was having an affair with the doctor who employed her. She killed the doctor's wife, then–with the help of a corrupt Bay City cop–committed the other murders in an attempt to cover up the original crime and make a new life for herself.

Of Chandler's seven novels, *The Lady in the Lake* is the most tightly and effectively plotted. The story turns on an old detective-story trick, mistaken identity, but Chandler handles the device smoothly. The plot works in the opposite direction of *Farewell, My Lovely.* In that novel, Marlowe begins to piece together the case bit by bit; just as he is about to figure it all out, the structure dissolves into a series of random episodes. In *The Lady in the Lake,* seemingly random coincidences mount as the story progresses, and only at the end does Marlowe tie everything together into an understandable whole. It is the closest Chandler came to writing the type of deductive mystery story he derided in his letters and essays, though he is aware of the coincidental nature of the plot and has Marlowe comment upon it periodically.

The book is a departure from Chandler's first three novels in other ways as well. He focuses not on figures of wealth and power–the Sternwoods, the Grayles, the Murdocks–but rather on middle-class characters. The wealthiest person in the book is Derace Kingsley, who has a good income and is a member of the Los Angeles Athletic Club, but he is merely an executive in his company, fears losing his job if his reputation is tarnished, and does not have the kind of money needed to buy immunity from law and scandal. The story also requires no compromise on Marlowe's part: he does not cover up any murders; the two killers—Muriel Chess and Lieutenant Degarmo—are not arrested, but only because they are killed.

The atypical nature of the novel seems largely due to the setting. Much of the action takes place in Puma Point, away from the urban corruption of Los Angeles and its suburbs. Most commentators have noted the Edenic qualities in Chandler's portrait of the mountains. In *Something More Than Night,* for instance, Wolfe comments, "Chandler's novel pulsates with moving descriptions of natural landscapes. The rich, detailed scene painting of flora and fauna in *Lady* takes Chandler's artistry beyond the mean streets, cheap lodgings, and low dives of today's city. The freshness and the ringing brightness marking his descriptions of the manless banks of Little Fawn Lake send out vibrations found only in the best nature writing." The town of Puma Point functions as an escape, a retreat away from the futile moral chaos of the city.

All is not well in the mountains, of course. They have become a resort area for Los Angelenos. Tourists crowd the small town, and the quiet of the woods is broken by "the cheerful din of auto horns, children screaming, bowls rattling, skeeballs clunking, .22s snapping merrily in the shooting galleries, juke boxes playing like crazy." Marlowe quickly learns that murder has invaded Puma Point, but crime—like the tourists—has come in from Los Angeles. Crystal Kingsley and Muriel Chess are both hiding out from their problems in the city. The other murderer, Lieutenant Degarmo, comes up from Los Angeles as well.

Unlike in the city, however, justice functions in Puma Point. The community is close-knit and looks out for its residents. The locals Marlowe meets—particularly beautician and reporter Birdie Keppel and Constable Jim Patton—are unsophisticated, honest, and competent. Outwardly slow and rustic, Patton is more able than he appears. He has a sharp eye for evidence, is a good judge of character, and does not try to bully or intimidate his way through a case. In Bay City, Marlowe is harassed, threatened, and even framed by crooked policemen; in Puma Point, he and Patton establish a partnership based on trust and cooperation, and together they solve the case. When the accused murderer, Degarmo, draws a gun in Kingsley's cabin, Patton, in classic western fashion, outdraws him with his .45-caliber frontier Colt and shoots the pistol from Degarmo's hand. Marlowe has been searching for a place where honesty, loyalty, and justice can function; he seems to have found it in Puma Point.

The Lady in the Lake sold better than any of Chandler's previous novels—six thousand copies in the first printing, followed by two additional printings—but it was hardly enough to make him a financial success. He had established himself as one of the leading American detective novelists, but the 1940s mystery market was commercially limited. Detective writers depended primarily upon hardback sales for their income, and sales of a mystery novel seldom topped ten thousand copies. The paperback industry was still in its infancy, and it would not become an important market until after the war ended. Avon published two 25¢ editions of *The Big Sleep* in 1942 and 1943, and Pocket published an edition of *Farewell, My Lovely* in 1943. The total royalties from these printings amounted to less than $1,000. At age fifty-five, Chandler had been writing professionally for ten years and was at the top of his form, yet his income was only a few thousand dollars a year.

As did many other novelists during the 1930s and 1940s—including F. Scott Fitzgerald and William Faulkner—Chandler turned to Hollywood screenwriting to earn the income his books could not produce. In mid 1943 he signed a contract to collaborate with Billy Wilder on the screen version of James M. Cain's *Double Indemnity.* He received $9,750 for thirteen weeks of work, almost as much as he had earned from the combined sales of his first four novels. With the money, Chandler and his wife rented a modest house south of Hollywood—their first substantial residence since he lost his job in the oil industry. The film was a success, and it immediately established Chandler's reputation as a screenwriter. He initially intended to write only the one movie then return to his novels, but Paramount offered a three-year, $1,000-a-week contract that was too lucrative for him to refuse.

Chandler's career as a screenwriter was a mixture of success and frustration. In 1944 he worked on two screenplays, *And Now Tomorrow* and *The Unseen.* He received a screen credit for both films, but his work was essentially limited to polishing dialogue. Chandler was friendly with other screenwriters such as Robert Presnell Jr. and H. Allen Smith, but he and Cissy did not mix in Hollywood social circles. Chandler recognized the artistic potential of movies and applied himself to learning the craft, but he chafed against the structure of the studio system and the superficiality of movie people. He despised actors, agents, and money men and considered many of the industry's business practices to be dishonest and corrupt. Most of all, he disliked the limits on his independence as a writer. Chandler desired freedom from deadlines and a chance to work with the few directors and producers whom he respected. He was unable to attain such conditions.

Dust jacket for Chandler's second novel (1940), in which Marlowe works on two separate investigations that ultimately intersect

During these years Chandler resumed drinking heavily. He was becoming increasingly aware of his own aging–his wife was now in her seventies–and reacted with periods of melancholy and womanizing. He scored his biggest Hollywood success with *The Blue Dahlia* (1946), an original screenplay that he completed in only a few weeks and while on the bottle. The script won an Edgar Award from the Mystery Writers of America and an Oscar nomination for best screenplay. Chandler, nevertheless, was becoming increasingly unhappy in Los Angeles.

In 1946 Chandler and his wife moved to La Jolla. Their life there was quiet, almost reclusive; they had few friends and seldom made social engagements. Chandler had discovered dictation machines while working in the Hollywood studios, and he used them in La Jolla to dictate an extensive correspondence with his publishers, agents, and other literary contacts. In the spring of 1947 he signed a contract with Universal to write an original screenplay at $4,000 a week. He worked on *Playback* mostly at his home in La Jolla, and the writing moved slowly. After receiving two extensions, he finally finished the script in early 1948, but the film was never produced. His career as a screenwriter was nearing its end.

Chandler's break from Hollywood was made possible in part by the development of the American paperback publishing industry, which was flourishing in the postwar book market. Although Chandler published no new fiction during his screenwriting years, his first four novels were all widely reprinted in paperback editions in both England and the United States. Chandler began earning additional royalties on past work when Avon brought out three paperback collections of his pulp stories: *Five Murderers* (1944), *Five Sinister Characters* (1945), and *The Finger Man and Other Stories* (1947). On 8 March 1947 he wrote to his friend, mystery critic James Sandoe, "I am a damn fool not to be writing novels. I'm still getting $15,000 a year out of those I did write. If I turned out a really good one in the near future, I'd probably get a lot out of it."

Chandler had been working on a fifth Marlowe novel for several years, but he had difficulty completing it. His contract with Paramount had called for only twenty-six weeks of work a year, and he had intended to spend the remaining time on the novel. Screen writing, however, drained him mentally and physically; he spent most of his time off relaxing and trying to recover his creative energy. After finishing the *Playback* project, Chandler resumed work on the novel in earnest. He also took steps to ensure that he would be able to earn a living from novel-writing alone and would no longer be dependent on Hollywood for income. In May 1948 he signed with Brandt and Brandt, a leading New York literary agency whose clients included Stephen Vincent Benét, E. E. Cummings, John Dos Passos, John P. Marquand, and James Gould Cozzens.

One of the first issues Chandler took up with his new agents was whether he should leave Alfred A. Knopf and seek a new publisher for his upcoming novel. Under the contracts for Chandler's first four novels, Knopf received half of the royalties from his paperback sales. Because of this arrangement, Knopf was making far more money from Chandler's paperback editions than they had paid him for the original hardbound editions, a situation Chandler found infuriating. He also believed that Knopf had failed to promote his novels properly. Bernice Baumgarten, the agent at Brandt and Brandt who handled Chandler's account, agreed that Knopf was unsuitable. She recommended that he find a new American publisher that did not maintain a regular list of mystery novels, which would increase the chance of his new book being promoted and received as serious fiction. Chandler's work on the novel still progressed slowly, but he completed a first draft by July of 1948 and then spent two months revising before submitting it to his agent. Because he was still seeking a firm to replace Knopf, *The Little Sister* was published first in England in June 1949. Chandler finally settled on Houghton Mifflin as his new American publisher, and they released the first American edition of the novel in September.

The plot of *The Little Sister* revolves around three members of the Quest family, who have come to Los Angeles from Manhattan, Kansas. The little sister of the title, Orfamay Quest, hires Marlowe to find her missing brother Orrin. Marlowe soon discovers that Orfamay has a sister named Mavis Weld, who is a rising movie star, and that Orrin Quest is involved in a scheme to blackmail Mavis and her boyfriend, a gangster named Steelgrave. The scheme collapses into a series of ice-pick murders, and Marlowe is left to decide who is responsible.

The Little Sister is not as strong as Chandler's previous novels. He recognized that the plot was awkward, and in October 1949 he wrote to Sandoe, "it's the only book of mine I have actively disliked. It was written in a bad mood and I think that comes through." The frustration of his Hollywood years and an increasing dissatisfaction with his own writing resulted in an increased tendency to spoof himself and in long, bitter diatribes that interrupt the flow of the story. The whole of chapter 13 is an extended condemnation of corrupt Los Angeles, taking place in Marlowe's thoughts as he drives around the city and punctuated by the refrain, "You're not human tonight, Marlowe." Chandler was writing his own frustrations with the city into his novel.

Despite its flaws, *The Little Sister* has been praised by critics for its detailed portrait of Hollywood. Spier argues that "The book's analysis of Hollywood extends to the moguls at the top as well as nobodies being absorbed from the bottom. . . . Clearly both ends of the Hollywood spectrum are seen to operate from morally bankrupt, socially decadent postures; for everyone from baron to would-be starlet, all morality goes by the boards in pursuit of fame and fortune." At the root of this moral bankruptcy is debased and exploited sexuality: "Too much sex," producer Jules Oppenheimer tells Marlowe while explaining the flaws of Hollywood, "All right in its proper time and place. But we get it in carload lots. Stand up to our necks in it. Gets to be like flypaper." This criticism of the failings of Los Angeles—money corruption, superficiality, pretension, diseased sexuality—underlies Chandler's first four novels; in *The Little Sister* it is brought to the forefront and is bitter and didactic.

Marlowe's mood is similarly dark. As in the previous novels, he again abandons hope of being able to resolve the crimes and of restoring justice; instead, he resigns himself merely to protecting a decent person from further trouble. Mavis Weld, who in her own words is "far from being young and innocent anymore," has fought her way up the movie ladder, associates with racketeers, and uses her sexuality to control men. Marlowe, nevertheless, sees something admirable in her: loyalty and self-sacrifice. Mavis tries to protect her brother and sister, even though they are blackmailers and murderers and show no loyalty to her. Marlowe could crack the case and explain everything to the cops, but doing so would ruin Mavis Weld's career. So, he does nothing.

Underlying *The Little Sister* are dark conclusions about human behavior and the nature of evil. Several commentators have pointed out that Chandler frequently depicts immigrants from the Midwest coming to Los Angeles and falling prey to the corrupt life in the city. *The Little Sister* at first seems to advance the same theme: Orrin Quest has come from Kansas to work in the aircraft industry and is drawn into criminal behavior. The denouement, however, reverses the pattern: the Midwestern morals of the Quest family are flawed from the start. Behind their screen of Protestant self-righteousness, Orrin and Orfamay think nothing of blackmailing their sister; their mother back home in Kansas is apparently complicit in the scheme. Orfamay, furthermore, sells out her brother for $1,000 in "blood money." These acts are not a result of the formerly innocent Quests being corrupted by the city, William Marling argues in his *Raymond Chandler* (1986). Rather, "The immorality that overtakes them is the product of a fatal mix of flaws: once land-hungry pioneers, disciplined by family and church, they conceive themselves anew in a land without strictures, where exotic, even rapacious, behavior is rewarded. Their flaws stem from pioneer materialism and a failure to understand that human obligations persevere in the urban world." In *The Lady in the Lake,* Marlowe escaped to the mountains and found rural people who were uncorrupted. *The Little Sister* shows no such faith. Coldhearted greed is a fundamental human force, not merely the product of a debased urban society.

Critics also frequently note that Chandler makes his most bitter comment on a second cause of human corruption, female sexuality, through the character Dolores Gonzales, a Hollywood starlet who is a friend of Mavis Weld. All of Chandler's previous novels feature women as killers: Carmen Sternwood in *The Big Sleep,* Mrs. Grayle in *Farewell, My Lovely,* Mrs. Murdock in *The High Window,* and Muriel Chess in *The Lady in the Lake.* All four use their sexuality to control and destroy men—to "make saps out of every one of them." The pattern is amplified and even caricatured in Dolores. Everything she does oozes sexuality and flirtation. Like Chandler's other temptresses, she has the power to turn men to jelly and when she is crossed she turns murderous. She gets Orrin Quest "clean knocked out of his mind," entices him into committing blackmail, and then murders him when he becomes a liability. The entire plot of the book is driven by her desire for revenge against Steelgrave, an old lover, and

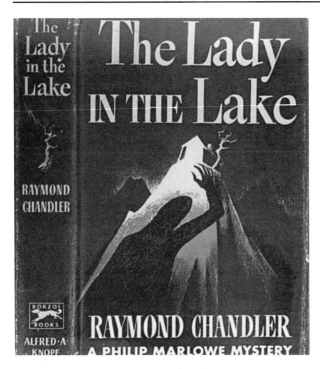

Dust jacket for Chandler's fourth novel (1943), in which Marlowe finds that the corruption of Los Angeles has spread to the countryside

she coldheartedly murders strangers just to frame him. She is "slim, dark, and lovely and smiling. Reeking with sex. Utterly beyond the moral laws of this or any world I could imagine."

Chandler's female characters, such as Dolores Gonzales, have caused many critics to accuse him of misogyny and chauvinism. Joyce Carol Oates, for example, assessed Chandler's career in a 1995 *New York Review of Books* article and commented, "Like the Los Angeles smog of which he speaks so knowingly, Marlowe's misogyny permeates the novels; yet, it is with a supreme lack of self-consciousness that he informs us repeatedly of his aversion for the female. . . . The noir tradition, or cliche, has it that women are evil and disgusting if they are sexual beings; if they are not sexual beings, they scarcely exist." Wolfe in *Something More Than Night* sums up *The Little Sister* as "a further installment in Chandler's extended poison pen letter to women." Chandler's defenders, such as Tom Hiney in *Raymond Chandler: A Biography* (1997), argue that the misogyny charges result from critics' misunderstanding Marlowe's character. "For every deceitful and sinful woman in Chandler's fiction," Hiney writes, "there are a dozen deceitful and sinful men. Marlowe has no ranking system for his prejudices: he hates 'sham and pettiness' wherever he finds it, and has seen far too much hypocrisy among LA's power brokers to be much impressed by the concept of a male, white utopia."

Hiney is correct that Chandler was not a believer in a male utopia, but characters such as Dolores make clear that, in the world of Chandler's novels, female sexuality is a deadly, destructive force.

The Little Sister sold better than any of Chandler's previous books—sixteen thousand copies in the United States and twenty-six thousand in England. His earnings from hardback sales totaled $10,000, and he received an additional $10,000 for a pre-publication abridgment of the novel that appeared in *Cosmopolitan* magazine. When combined with the continuing paperback royalties for his previous novels, these sales were enough to allow Chandler to live solely on the income from his fiction. In 1950, however, he accepted an offer to work on a screenplay for Alfred Hitchcock, a director he had long admired. The movie was an adaptation of Patricia Highsmith's thriller *Strangers on a Train* (1950). Chandler finished the script that year, but Hitchcock was dissatisfied and hired Czenzi Ormonde to rework it. Chandler was outraged by the arrangement and considered refusing the screen credit. It was a frustrating experience and his last movie project. From then on he was determined to work only as a novelist.

Because of his growing commercial success, Chandler found himself devoting more and more time to business matters—keeping tax records, negotiating the sale of translation or reprint rights, arranging for a Philip Marlowe radio and television series—and was often distracted from his writing. Because he was not financially dependent on producing another novel quickly, he spent time working on other projects, such as a series of fantastic stories, only one of which, "Professor Bingo's Snuff," was published. "From now on," he wrote to Carl Brandt, the head of the Brandt and Brandt Agency, in December 1950, "I am going to write what I want to write as I want to write it." This determination is reflected in his sixth novel, *The Long Good-Bye* (1953).

Chandler began working on the book not long after *The Little Sister* was published, but he was distracted by his wife's chronic illnesses and his own ailments, including bronchitis, shingles, and a skin allergy that caused his fingers to split and forced him to wear gloves while reading and typing. He finished the first draft in May 1952 and sent it to Brandt and Brandt, along with a note explaining his intentions: "I wrote this as I wanted to because I can do that now. . . . You write in a style that has been imitated, even plagiarized, to the point where you begin to look as if you were imitating your imitators. So you have to go where they can't follow you." His agents liked the book as a whole, but Baumgarten criticized Marlowe for being too Christlike and sentimental and suggested revision. The comments outraged Chandler and ultimately led to his

Covers for collections of Chandler's stories that were published as paperback originals in 1945 and 1947, respectively

terminating his contract with Brandt and Brandt. He began revising the novel, however, and–after taking a long-desired trip with Cissy to England–submitted a reworked version to his publishers. *The Long Good-Bye* was published in England in November 1953 and in the United States in March 1954.

The Long Good-Bye is Chandler's most ambitious novel. It is longer than his previous books and moves at a much slower pace. In the earlier novels the main action takes place in the course of only three to five days. *The Long Good-Bye* begins in November and does not end until August of the following year; episodes are frequently separated by a week or more. Chandler's standard characters are all there–dope doctors, tough cops, hard-boiled racketeers, gambling clubs, untouchable wealthy families, murderous blondes, corrupt politicians–and the framing and scope of the story allow him to dwell on and develop his motifs more fully. The novel contains digressions and didactic commentary on the condition of modern society; such passages are intrusive, but they are not as clumsy as those in *The Lit-*

tle Sister, in part because of the slower pace of the book and in part because many of the speeches are made by characters other than Marlowe.

The novel opens with Marlowe recalling his initial meeting with the man who later betrays him: "The first time I laid eyes on Terry Lennox he was drunk in a Rolls-Royce Silver Wraith outside the terrace of The Dancers." In the first part of the novel, Marlowe befriends Lennox, a playboy who was severely wounded in World War II, and helps him escape to Mexico after he is accused of beating his wealthy wife to death. Lennox's apparent suicide in a small Mexican village then seems to end the matter. In the second part of the novel, Marlowe is hired to take care of Roger Wade, an alcoholic novelist, and Wade ends up dead, too, another apparent suicide. The two plotlines are, of course, connected, and Marlowe must investigate the past and risk his life to uncover the truth.

The structure of the story allows Chandler to address new material, much of it reflecting his reactions to his changing life as he grew older. Natasha Spender, who was a friend of Chandler's during the 1950s, has identified both Terry Lennox and Roger Wade as partial self-portraits. In her essay "His Own Long Goodbye," included in *The World of Raymond Chandler* (1977), she notes, "He wrote *The Long Goodbye* as Cissy lay dying. . . . It may well reflect the interior dialogues between facets of his own personality as he looked back on their long life together." By making Roger Wade a best-selling genre author–though of historical romances rather than detective stories–Chandler is able to vent his own suspicions that he had wasted his talent in a subliterary field. Chandler uses Wade's drinking to treat the issue of alcoholism and its effects on a writer, a problem he had been struggling with increasingly since his tenure in Hollywood. As an American who was raised in England and wounded during World War II, Lennox shares many biographical features with his creator. Chandler's critics have followed Spender's lead and largely agree that *The Long Good-Bye* is the most personal of Chandler's books.

The dominant chords of the story are the same as they have been throughout Chandler's novels: wealth and the nature of money, the corruption attendant upon wealth, and the functioning of a code of loyalty and honor within a fallen world. While Marlowe has long recognized that money buys its possessors immunity from the laws of society and a degree of protection from the nastiness of the world, he comes to learn in the course of the novel that this privilege is not as strong as it appears to be. Harlan Potter–Terry Lennox's father-in-law–is a powerful multimillionaire, and his wealth can keep his family's troubles out of the papers and free from prosecution, but it cannot remedy their more basic ills.

Chandler's scorn of the wealthy is most apparent in the character of Harlan Potter. With a net worth of over $100 million, Potter is by far the wealthiest man in any of the Marlowe novels. He owns several newspapers, contributes heavily to politicians' campaigns, and can easily silence any publicity about his family and protect them from prosecution. Potter lectures Marlowe bitterly on the ills of modern society: politics dominated by party machines, the venality of journalism, an economy based on built-in obsolescence, and the elevation of appearance over quality. He does not consider his actions corrupt, explaining that "all I and people of my kind expect is to be allowed to live our lives in decent privacy." This expectation fails. As Marlowe tells Potter, "You don't like the way the world is going so you use what power you have to close off a private corner to live in as near as possible to the way you remember people lived fifty years ago before the age of mass production. You've got a hundred million dollars and all it has bought you is a pain in the neck."

Part of the problem with money is that although society clearly distinguishes between legitimate and illegitimate wealth, the actual line is quite fuzzy. "That's the difference between crime and business," a detective tells Marlowe. "For business you gotta have capital. Sometimes I think it's the only difference." Marlowe's friend Bernie Ohls makes a similar statement: "There ain't no clean way to make a hundred million dollars. . . . Maybe the head man thinks his hands are clean but somewhere along the line guys got pushed to the wall, nice little businesses got the ground cut from under them and had to sell out for nickels, decent people lost their jobs. . . ."

Harlan Potter does not think of himself as a criminal: he does not buy off cops and politicians, does not employ goons and hitmen, does not use his control of newspapers to smear his enemies. But, "there's a peculiar thing about money," to use Potter's own words, "In large quantities it tends to have a life of its own, even a conscience of its own. The power of money becomes difficult to control." Potter would never pay to have Marlowe roughed up, but his Reno estate sits next to that of Chris Mady, a racketeer who virtually runs Nevada. "Could be they say hello once in a while," a reporter tells Marlowe. "Could be some character that is on Mady's payroll hears from another buzzing too loud about things that are not any of his business. Could be that this passing remark gets passed on and a guy with large muscles gets a hint to go out and exercise himself and two or three of his friends." The wealthy try to deny their culpability and hide behind a veil of privacy and politeness; money and crime, however, are inextricably linked.

The power of money is stronger in *The Long Good-Bye* than in any previous novel, but Marlowe for the first time is able to defeat it. He discovers that Eileen Wade, Roger's wife, murdered both her husband and Terry Lennox's wife. Harlan Potter's power hushes up Sylvia Lennox's death, and Eileen Wade's social status ensures that her husband's murder is ruled a suicide. Marlowe does not go to the police with the truth; rather, he rigs justice on his own and allows Eileen Wade to go free. In the night after Marlowe confronts her she writes out a detailed confession and kills herself with an overdose of morphine. Marlowe's actions trouble his conscience, but he makes his motives clear: he wants the truth to come out and he wants to clear the name of his friend, Terry Lennox. Merely rigging the case so that Eileen confesses and commits suicide is not enough. The district attorney, afraid of stirring up trouble, refuses to release the confession. Marlowe, with the complicity of a couple of honest cops, steals a photostat of the confession and, after considerable effort and personal risk, manages to get it published in the Los Ange-

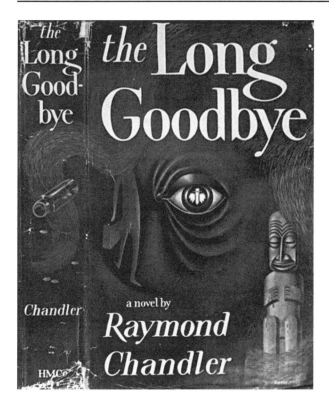 

Dust jackets for the British (1953) and American (1954) editions of Chandler's last major novel

les *Journal,* an independent paper. For the first time in a Chandler novel, the full truth is made public.

Despite this victory, *The Long Good-Bye* does not end on a note of triumph. The truth comes out but, as Marlowe puts it, "I didn't think it would do [District Attorney] Springer any harm." Corruption, in Chandler's view, is not the result of structures or institutions. The problems of the modern world are rooted in individual moral failings. "We don't have mobs and crime syndicates and goon squads," Ohls tells Marlowe, "because we have crooked politicians and their stooges in City Hall and the legislatures. Crime isn't a disease, it's a symptom. . . . We're a big rough rich wild people and crime is the price we pay for it, and organized crime is the price we pay for organization. We'll have it with us a long time. Organized crime is just the dirty side of the sharp dollar." These sentiments go against the grain of the dime novel and detective story tradition, in which the lone hero purges corruption and returns a community to moral stability. Marlowe can expose injustice and make the facts of a particular case known, but doing so does not help remedy the larger moral disease.

In May 1952, as he was finishing the first draft of *The Long Good-Bye,* Chandler had written to Carl Brandt and explained his intentions for the novel: "I didn't care

whether the mystery was fairly obvious, but I cared about the people, about this strange corrupt world we live in, and how any man who tried to be honest looks in the end either sentimental or plain foolish." Marlowe appears just this way at the end of the novel. His efforts to resolve the murders fall short not only because of the nature of crime and corruption but also because the core value upon which his code is founded—loyalty—no longer functions. At first, Marlowe likes Terry Lennox because of his politeness and manners. He has "an honourable wound" from World War II and, like Marlowe, appears to behave according to a personal code of conduct. After Lennox's apparent suicide, Marlowe remembers him through rituals such as pouring an extra cup of coffee and having a gimlet at the bar they used to frequent. His detective work throughout the story is undertaken out of loyalty to his lost friend.

This effort is sentimental, as Marlowe and other characters repeatedly point out, and the denouement proves it foolish as well. Lennox did not kill his wife, Marlowe learns, but he faked his own suicide so that the case would be brought to a quick close. Lennox's deception—his bogus suicide, his familiarity with gangsters, his willingness to be "a kept poodle" to the Potter wealth—amounts to a betrayal of trust to Marlowe. When Lennox returns to Los Angeles disguised as a

Mexican gentleman, he asks Marlowe to go to have a drink—a symbolic renewal of friendship. Marlowe rejects him. "You had nice ways," he tells Lennox, "and nice qualities but there was something wrong. You had standards and lived up to them, but they were personal. They had no relation to any kind of ethics or scruples. You were a nice guy because you had a nice nature. But you were just as happy with mugs or hoodlums as with honest men. . . . You're a moral defeatist." What Marlowe has been seeking, more than anything else, is friendship—a bond with someone who shares his ethical convictions, an ally in a morally debased world. The search ends in failure. At the close of the novel, Marlowe is left alone. "I never saw any of them again," he says. "Except the cops. No way has yet been invented to say goodbye to them."

The British response to *The Long Good-Bye* was even more enthusiastic than to his previous books and showed that Chandler had developed a considerable literary reputation in England. J. Maclaren Ross of the *London Sunday Times* (29 November 1983) commented, "Mr. Raymond Chandler, whose early work belonged superficially to the *genre* popularised by Dashiell Hammett, has become, during recent years, the object of an ecstatic cult among intellectuals in both hemispheres. From the basic pattern of the American crime story outlined by his predecessors he has evolved a highly personal vision of a jungle world ruled by racketeers and rich megalomaniacs." The anonymous reviewer for *The Times Literary Supplement* (1 January 1984) praised the novel for its characterizations and social criticism: "Marlowe is a connoisseur of men and women, a serious and involved student of moral fibre, in his own laconic and elliptical fashion, and there are one or two studies of weakness in the present book which should command respect." Starting in the mid 1940s, some influential British journalists and intellectuals, including Leonard Russell, Elizabeth Bowen, W. H. Auden, Alistair Cooke, and J. B. Priestley, had discovered Chandler's novels and began arguing for his literary value. By the mid 1950s, their arguments were widely accepted in England, and Chandler was being read and discussed not as a detective writer but as an important literary novelist.

The American reception of *The Long Good-Bye* was less warm. Though it was awarded an Edgar Award from the Mystery Writers of America, the novel did not sell as well as *The Little Sister,* and the reviews of the novel were mixed. Anthony Boucher of *The New York Times Book Review* (25 April 1954) praised the story, writing, "Perhaps the longest private-eye novel ever written (over 125,000 words!), it is also one of the best—and may well attract readers who normally shun even the leaders in the field." The reviewer for *The New Yorker* (27 March 1954) found fault, arguing that "Mr. Chandler has practically abandoned anything resembling a coherent plot to devote himself to an exhaustive study of manners and mores in California . . . the story, which has to do with nymphomania in exalted circles as much as anything else, hardly seems worth all the bother." Chandler was disappointed with the American response to the novel, and his awareness of his growing reputation in England caused him increasingly to consider returning to the country where he had spent his childhood.

Soon after the publication of *The Long Good-Bye,* Cissy Chandler's health worsened. She had been ill with heart and respiratory trouble for some time and spent much of the summer of 1954 in the hospital, where she was diagnosed with fibrosis of the lungs and confined to an oxygen tent. She died on 12 December. Chandler was devastated by her death. He began drinking heavily, and in February 1955 attempted suicide. He was put in the county hospital initially and then spent six days in a private sanatorium. After his release, Chandler decided to leave California. He sold his house in La Jolla, went briefly to New York, and then sailed for England.

During the last four years of his life Chandler divided his time between England and the United States. In London he was treated as a celebrity and established a circle of acquaintances that included writers, artists, and critics. He also suffered from depression and continued his excessive drinking, which on several occasions resulted in his being hospitalized. He was working periodically on a novel version of his screenplay *Playback,* but his drinking and depression hindered his production. In London he met Helga Greene, who eventually became his agent, and under her care and encouragement he completed the novel in December 1957. It was published the following July.

Playback is a short novel—only 205 pages—and bears little resemblance to the screenplay from which it was drawn. Philip Marlowe is hired by a secretive lawyer for what seems a simple case: follow a woman on a train until she stops traveling, then report her location. Marlowe soon realizes that this woman, Betty Mayfield, is being blackmailed by a man named Larry Mitchell, and the case takes a murderous turn when Mitchell's body first turns up dead on Betty's hotel balcony and then disappears. In the end it is revealed that Betty Mayfield was wrongly indicted for murder in the past, and Mitchell's death forces her to relive the nightmare of being falsely accused. This repeating of the past is the source of the title.

Playback is Chandler's weakest novel. The plot is slight and lacks tension and danger. Because the reader does not learn of Betty Mayfield's earlier murder indict-

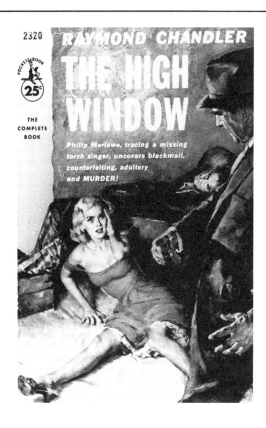

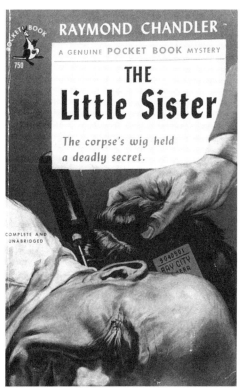

Paperback editions of four of Chandler's novels

ment until the end of the book, the concept of "play-back" does not play an active role in the story. Chandler's decision to set the novel in a town called Esmeralda–a thinly disguised version of La Jolla–allows him to treat new material, including satirical portraits of the town's wealthy retirees, but the setting lacks the vividness and symbolic resonance of his depiction of Los Angeles. Chandler's difficulties in writing the novel are reflected both in dialogue and characterization. The tension between Marlowe and his lawyer client is overplayed and unnecessary. Marlowe's wisecracking repartee with Betty Mayfield and his client's secretary seems almost a burlesque of the hard-boiled style that Chandler had perfected two decades before.

The greatest difference between *Playback* and Chandler's earlier novels is in the character of Philip Marlowe. Marlowe repeatedly emphasizes that he is getting old and tired. Rather than being cagey, he is much more up front in his investigations. When he follows Betty Mayfield to a motel, he comes right out and asks the desk clerk for a room next to hers. "This was a new one for me," he comments. "In no city hotel in the world would it work. It might work here. Mostly because I didn't give a damn." He takes a similarly straightforward approach to the Esmeralda police. After discovering the body of a murdered man, Marlowe goes directly to the police station and reports the crime. In return he receives cooperation. Captain Alessandro and his officers are polite, competent civil servants and are not under the thumbs of wealth. This change in the depiction of the police is in part a result of Chandler's research: during a visit to the San Diego jail he was impressed by the manners and efficiency of the cops he met. The effect on the novel, though, is a weakening of the overall sense of a corrupt, irredeemable world.

Marlowe's code of conduct shows a similar slippage. His policy toward money–not to accept payment for an incomplete job or dishonest behavior–is still strict, but it takes on the element of parody. He and Betty Mayfield repeatedly swap $5,000 in signed traveler's checks. At one point he improbably produces a receipt book from his jacket and carefully phrases a statement that the money is merely being put in his care, not paid to him. More serious lapses occur in his code of sexual propriety. In all of his first six novels, Marlowe sleeps with only one woman: Linda Loring in *The Long Good-Bye*. In *Playback* alone he sleeps with two: his client's secretary and Betty Mayfield. The latter affair is particularly questionable because he is in her employ at the time. Marlowe, in fact, tells her just before their tryst, "When I want your beautiful white body, it won't be while you're my client." Then he

sleeps with her anyway. What was once an iron-bound rule has become an empty phrase.

Both these romantic episodes are set up with awkward, unbelievable dialogue, and the women's motivation is implausible. When Marlowe first meets Helen Vermilyea, his client's secretary, they trade a series of hard-boiled barbs, then immediately set a date for that evening. She is the widow of a jet airplane pilot who was killed in a crash, and she writes off her sexuality by saying, "A woman's body is not so sacred that it can't be used–especially when she has already failed at love." Betty Mayfield's attraction to Marlowe seems similarly superficial. After he berates her for not coming clean about Larry Mitchell's death, she falls sobbing into Marlowe's arms. "Women have so few defenses," he comments, "but they certainly perform wonders with those they have." In previous novels Marlowe resisted such temptations and seemed disgusted by any efforts to use sexuality as a tool or defense. In *Playback*, he has become susceptible.

Behind Marlowe's sexual behavior lies a romantic sense of loss. There was no indication in *The Long Good-Bye* that Marlowe's relationship with Linda Loring was anything more than a passing fling; in *Playback*, she appears to be his lost true love. Marlowe refuses to sleep with Helen Vermilyea in his own house, explaining, "I had a dream here once, a year and a half ago. There's still a shred of it left. I'd like it to stay in charge." Similarly, before they sleep together, Betty Mayfield asks Marlowe if he has another woman. "There was once," he says, "for a brief moment. But that's a long time ago now." In the face of this lost love, Marlowe's flings seem to be meaningless, desperate acts. "It was a cry in the night," Marlowe tells Betty Mayfield in the morning. "Let's not try to make it more than it was." Chandler was struggling with alcohol and depression after Cissy died, and in London he became infatuated with younger women, who generally rejected him. Marlowe's new behavior, more than anything, seems to reflect Chandler's own feelings of loss and romantic despair.

At the end of the novel Marlowe regains the dream. Linda Loring telephones from Paris and asks him to marry her. Marlowe accepts, and even the crass demands of his client cannot disturb his reverie. "I hardly heard it," he says. "The air was full of music." In a 21 July 1958 interview with *Newsweek*, Chandler explained the denouement by saying, "I thought it was time Marlowe was given something worth having, some love of his own. You see, there's a lot of him in me, his loneliness." The ending seems a wish-fulfillment on Chandler's part. He tried to make *Playback* upbeat and hopeful, but the story is at odds with Marlowe's character and temperament.

During the last year of his life Chandler struggled with alcoholism and poor health, spending a large amount of time in hospitals and clinics. He started working on another novel, tentatively titled "Poodle Springs," in which Marlowe and Linda Loring were newlyweds, but he completed only the first three chapters. (The novel was later completed by Robert B. Parker and published in 1989.) Chandler became involved in the personal affairs of his Australian-born secretary, who was in the process of divorcing her husband; the situation sapped his money and his spirits. The matter led to conflicts with several of his friends, including his agent Helga Greene, and a dispute over who would be named the beneficiary of his will. In February 1959 Chandler was hospitalized in La Jolla, and while recuperating proposed marriage to Helga Greene. She accepted. They planned to move back to London, but Chandler's health did not permit it. He made a brief trip to New York to accept the presidency of the Mystery Writers of America—an honorary post—then returned to La Jolla and became ill with pneumonia. He died in the Scripps Clinic on 26 March 1959.

Raymond Chandler's seven Philip Marlowe novels, taken as a whole, place him at the forefront of American detective novelists. Dashiell Hammett began the hard-boiled tradition, providing its distinctive material and legitimizing the use of the American vernacular. Chandler took up the tradition from his predecessor and carried it further, adding a distinctive style, a biting wit, and a concern for descriptive detail. As a social realist, he documented three decades of American life, capturing on paper how it looked and felt to live in Los Angeles in the 1930s, 1940s, and 1950s. Above all, Chandler was a moralist and a social critic who wrestled with the issues of corruption, moral decay, and personal responsibility. His novels are about the struggles of an individual to make sense of and function within a changing modern world. As such, Chandler's writing transcends the formulaic constraints of the detective genre and leaves a lasting legacy to American literature.

Letters:

Raymond Chandler Speaking, edited by Dorothy Gardiner and Kathrine Sorley Walker (Boston: Houghton Mifflin, 1962);

Letters: Raymond Chandler and James M. Fox, edited by James Pepper (Santa Barbara, Cal.: Neville & Yellin, 1978);

Selected Letters of Raymond Chandler, edited by Frank Mac-Shane (New York: Columbia University Press, 1981);

The Australian Love Letters of Raymond Chandler (Ringwood, Australia: McPhee Gribble, 1995).

Bibliographies:

Matthew J. Bruccoli, *Raymond Chandler: A Checklist* (Kent, Ohio: Kent State University Press, 1968);

Bruccoli, *Raymond Chandler: A Descriptive Bibliography* (Pittsburgh: University of Pittsburgh Press, 1979).

Biographies:

Frank MacShane, *The Life of Raymond Chandler* (New York: Dutton, 1976);

Tom Hiney, *Raymond Chandler: A Biography* (New York: Atlantic Monthly Press, 1997).

References:

Al Clark, *Raymond Chandler in Hollywood* (New York: Proteus, 1982);

Philip Durham, *Down These Mean Streets a Man Must Go: Raymond Chandler's Knight* (Chapel Hill: University of North Carolina Press, 1963);

George Grella, "Murder and the Mean Streets," *Contempora,* 1 (March 1970): 6–15; republished in *Armchair Detective,* 5 (1971): 1–10;

Miriam Gross, ed., *The World of Raymond Chandler* (London: Weidenfeld & Nicolson, 1977);

William Luhr, *Raymond Chandler and Film* (New York: Ungar, 1982);

William Marling, *Raymond Chandler* (Boston: Twayne, 1986);

Joyce Carol Oates, "The Simple Art of Murder," *New York Review of Books,* 42 (21 December 1995);

Robert B. Parker, *Perchance to Dream: Robert B. Parker's Sequel to Raymond Chandler's The Big Sleep* (New York: Putnam, 1991);

Peter J. Rabinowitz, "Rats Behind the Wainscoting: Politics, Convention, and Chandler's *The Big Sleep,*" *Texas Studies in Literature and Language,* 22 (1980): 224–245;

Jerry Speir, *Raymond Chandler* (New York : Ungar, 1981);

J. K. Van Dover, ed., *The Critical Responses to Raymond Chandler* (Westport, Conn.: Greenwood Press, 1995);

Peter Wolfe, *Something More Than Night: The Case of Raymond Chandler* (Bowling Green, Ohio: Bowling Green University Popular Press, 1985).

Papers:

The two major collections of Raymond Chandler's papers are held by the University of California, Los Angeles Library and the Bodleian Library, Oxford.

James Crumley

(12 October 1939 –   )

Martin Kich
Wright State University

See also the Crumley entry in *DLB Yearbook: 1984.*

BOOKS: *One to Count Cadence* (New York: Random House, 1969);

The Wrong Case (New York: Random House, 1975; London: Hart-Davis, MacGibbon, 1976);

The Last Good Kiss (New York: Random House, 1978; London: Panther, 1978);

Dancing Bear (New York: Random House, 1983; London: Penguin, 1987);

The Muddy Fork and Other Things: Short Fiction and Nonfiction (Northridge, Cal.: Lord John Press, 1984); rearranged and republished as *Whores: Short Fiction and Nonfiction* (Missoula, Mont.: Dennis McMillan, 1988); enlarged as *The Muddy Fork and Other Stories* (Livingston, Mont.: Clark City Press, 1991);

The Mexican Tree Duck (New York: Mysterious Press, 1993);

Bordersnakes (New York: Mysterious Press, 1996).

James Crumley deserves to be regarded as a serious novelist who has chosen to write in the detective genre. Like his protagonists, he seems driven to seek complete answers where only partial or superficial answers can be found; in this sense, the detective mystery as a form has become an extended metaphor for Crumley's search for self-expression as a novelist. Also like his protagonists, Crumley has wandered between the geographic and climatic—and the cultural and spiritual—extremes of northern Montana and southern Texas. What one of his detectives says to the other in *Bordersnakes* (1996) might be a rhetorical question posed by Crumley to himself: "You ever realize that you and me, we've always lived close enough to the border to run if we have to?" Since the 1969 publication of his first novel, *One to Count Cadence,* Crumley has published five novels and a collection of shorter pieces. Although he has not been prolific, the stylistic intensity evident in each of his novels is indicative of Crumley's empathy for his tormented characters and his intimate knowledge of the hard milieus in which they operate.

James Crumley (photograph by Michael Gallacher; from the dust jacket for The Mexican Tree Duck, *1993)*

On 12 October 1939, James Crumley was born in Three Rivers, Texas, a town located in Live Oak County, about halfway between San Antonio and the Gulf port of Corpus Christi. At the time of Crumley's birth, Three Rivers had about 1,350 residents. His father, Arthur Roland Crumley, worked as an oil-field laborer before acquiring a supervisory position with a small drilling outfit, and his mother, Ruby Criswell Crumley, was employed as a waitress, a cashier, and a bookkeeper. During World War II his family lived in

New Mexico, but, when he was in the second grade, they returned to Texas.

For the rest of Crumley's childhood, his family lived on five thousand acres of oil-company land outside of Santa Cruz, Texas–south of Three Rivers in adjacent San Patricio County. More than half the residents of Santa Cruz were Mexican Americans, but it was a strictly segregated community. Because Santa Cruz did not have a school, Crumley attended the one in nearby Mathis, a town of about two thousand residents in which the major industry was onion-packing and the main diversion of the youngsters was fights in which they threw onions at each other like snowballs. Crumley's classmates sometimes bullied him because he was an outsider and smarter than most of them–maintaining a straight-A average in his high-school courses. Eventually he gained enough size and toughness to hold his own. Growing to 5' 10" and nearly two hundred pounds, he established himself athletically and socially by playing high-school football.

After high school, Crumley entered Georgia Tech on a Navy ROTC scholarship. He did not like the class-consciousness that was common among the naval officers he encountered, and, on his first training cruise, he discovered that he was prone to seasickness. He soon left Georgia Tech, and in 1958 he enlisted in the U.S. Army. He was assigned to a communications security unit in the Philippines. Although he enjoyed the comradeship of his fellow soldiers, his obvious intelligence caused him some problems with officers.

Following his discharge, Crumley attended Texas A & I University, initially on a football scholarship. He was, however, too restless to enjoy the life of a student athlete, and during the next few years, he left school several times, taking work as a laborer in the oil fields and as a bartender. He completed his B.A. in 1964 and was accepted into the prestigious creative writing program at Iowa State University, where he studied under the novelists R.V. Cassell and Richard Yates.

After completing his M.F.A. in 1966, Crumley began teaching in the English department at the University of Montana at Missoula, a position he left after the publication of *One to Count Cadence*. He has since held a series of visiting professorships at the University of Arkansas at Fayetteville (1969–1970), at Colorado State University (1971–1974), at Reed College in Portland, Oregon (1976–1977), at Carnegie-Mellon University (1979–1980), and at the University of Texas at El Paso (1981–1984). From 1974 to 1976, he worked full time as a freelance writer. Since 1984 he has devoted himself to his writing career and has worked intermittently as a screenwriter. He collaborated with Tim Hunter on a screenplay of his novel *Dancing Bear* (1983), which was unproduced. He has also written magazine pieces and

book reviews for regional and national publications. Crumley has been married twice–to Judith Anne Ramsey in 1975 and to Bronwyn Pughe in 1979–and twice divorced. He has five children and five grandchildren. Since the mid 1980s, he has made Missoula, Montana, his home base–as close to a permanent home as he has had in his adult life.

In its unsparing depiction of the habits of soldiers in peacetime and of their behavior in battle, *One to Count Cadence* was inevitably and rightly compared to James Jones's *From Here to Eternity* (1951). Still, as the product of a much different era, Crumley's novel is much more pointedly political than Jones's work. The novel is narrated by Jacob Slagstead "Slag" Krummel. Most of it is told in flashback, as excerpts from a journal that Krummel compiles as he recovers in an army hospital in the Philippines from a battle wound suffered in Vietnam. He recounts how in 1962 he was given command of a unit in the Operations Section of the 721st Communications Security Detachment at Clark Air Force Base in the Philippines.

At the center of the story are Krummel's ambivalent feelings concerning Joe Morning, a soldier in his unit. Although Krummel appears to be a thoroughly upright individual, in actuality his conformity masks a certain expediency, for he is determined to meet his superiors' expectations of him as a soldier, regardless of what those expectations might be. In contrast, Morning is a habitual nonconformist and regards any behavior that undermines military authority to be morally justified. Yet, underneath this seemingly automatic rebelliousness, Morning has a sense of conscience that he consistently follows even when it is not in his best interests. Krummel admires Morning's imagination and audacity but is often compelled to discipline him.

When the unit is sent to Vietnam on an intelligence mission and is attacked by the Vietcong, Krummel is surprised by Morning's enthusiasm for combat, and, in the novel's most ambiguous moment, Krummel shoots Morning. Readers are never sure–and Krummel himself never seems sure–whether he has shot Morning intentionally or accidentally. In any case, Krummel is also wounded, and he and Morning are both shipped back to the Philippines to recover.

Crumley might have ended his novel at this point, but instead he extends it and complicates the issues even more. Morning deserts the army and joins a guerrilla insurrection in the Philippines. He has decided to choose his cause. In contrast, Krummel remains in the army and is recruited to serve with the CIA. He is wounded again while on a secret mission in Laos, and while recuperating from this second wound, he finally comes to terms with himself. Morning sends Krummel a letter in which he anticipates the failure of the insur-

Dust jacket for Crumley's third novel (1978), which introduces his second series character, C. W. Sughrue

rection and his own death. He is trying to explain himself to Krummel, to achieve some sort of closure, but his feelings remain conflicted. Krummel recognizes that, though his sense of purpose and of self are less defined than Morning's, he is sustained by what he does as a soldier. For him, this level of self-recognition seems finally to be enough.

Though published at the height of the Vietnam War, *One to Count Cadence* provides much more than a politicized view of that war and, indeed, of war in general. As most reviewers recognized, Crumley explores in a complex way how the war in Vietnam divided even those fighting it and how, paradoxically, the war experience bound those men together. Several reviewers, most notably Sarah Blackburn in the 2 November 1969 issue of *Book World,* complained that Crumley is too drawn to the conventional notion of combat as a male rite of passage. A more common complaint was that the descriptions of the soldiers' vices were more detailed than necessary or unnecessarily repetitive.

Regardless of what flaws it may have as a first novel, *One to Count Cadence* is central to Crumley's later development. In his hard-boiled detective novels, Crumley explores an American experience that recalls the terrors of the war in Vietnam. Violence intrudes suddenly and catastrophically on individuals conditioned by boredom and accustomed to brutality. The enemy is often indistinguishable from both confederates and regular civilians. Those in authority cannot be trusted to act with good judgment or with a proper sense of justice. Neither victory nor defeat is final; survival amounts to recurring firefights. Drug and alcohol abuse slows the damage to the spirit, but it also garishly distorts the perception of situations so raw that they would be difficult to comprehend even with a clear eye and head. In the 28 June 1993 issue of *Publishers Weekly* Dulcy Brainard reviewed *The Mexican Tree Duck* (1993) in terms that can be applied to all of Crumley's detective novels: "the novel's heart beats in wartime Vietnam. There . . . most of Crumley's memorable cast spent their formative years, learning about arms, reconnaissance, and dope, and forging the relationships that hold them together or, in this tale that turns on betrayals, tears them apart as effectively as an AK-47."

Following the publication of *One to Count Cadence,* Crumley's first marriage ended, and he remarried. He also came to recognize that he lacked the enthusiasm for teaching that might sustain a long university career and that he did not know how he should proceed as a novelist, given that in *One to Count Cadence* he had drawn extensively on his formative experiences in the army. His rereading of Raymond Chandler's novels led him to try his hand at a detective novel–without having any sense at the time that this decision would shape his career as a novelist.

In *Twentieth-Century Crime and Mystery Writers* (1985) Crumley describes himself as "a bastard child of Raymond Chandler"–asserting even that "without his books, my books would be completely different." Crumley has paid homage to Chandler by recycling elements of his story lines and by echoing the wryly lyrical, figurative style of Marlowe's observations. Moreover, reviewers have noted similar connections between Crumley's novels and Ross Macdonald's. However, as marked as these influences are, Crumley's detective novels need to be viewed in a larger literary context to appreciate his achievement. In his remarks in *Twentieth-Century Crime and Mystery Writers,* Crumley ultimately separates himself from detective novelists working strictly in the Chandler–Macdonald tradition: "my vision of justice is less clear-cut, perhaps more complex, more confused, closer perhaps to Robert Stone and Harry Crews, than to detective fiction."

Crumley, who like Crews and Stone is difficult to categorize, owes much to three groups of peculiarly American writers. First, the masculine energy that drives Crumley's protagonists and leaves them one wrong choice away from permanent madness can be traced to the novels of James Jones, Vance Bourjaily, and James Drought. Because this persona is associated with the two decades following World War II, the traits and attitudes of Crumley's protagonists seem in some ways anachronistic—equally chauvinistic and romantic. Second, a balancing influence is the hippie sensibility evident more whimsically in the antinovels of Richard Brautigan and more dementedly in the "journalism" of Hunter Thompson. While the characters of Jones, Bourjaily, and Drought cannot find a social context in which their unfocused energy is not destructive, the hippies are passive wanderers, descendants of the Beats too mindblown to remember any spiritual aims. Instead of tearing up the landscape, the hippies simply clutter it. And third, Crumley adds to his mix a slick, if ultimately self-conscious cynicism—a half-tired, wry attitude toward the evolution of the popular culture that seems straight out of the novellas of Nathanael West and the early work of John O'Hara. This perspective makes images stand out from their backgrounds so clearly and compellingly that one is left thinking that almost anything might be symbolic and that probably next to nothing actually is. Little wonder, given this odd combination of influences, that Crumley's novels leave his readers as wrung out as his characters are strung out.

All of Crumley's detective novels are set at least in part in Montana, and his descriptions of the landscapes of both Texas and Montana reflect his personal experience of their vastness, harshness, and fragility. Milton "Milo" Milodragovitch, the protagonist of *The Wrong Case* (1975) and *Dancing Bear,* is the grandson of a Russian immigrant who with a stone killed a self-promoting but inconsequential Western outlaw named Dalton Kimbrough. Afterward he parlayed his resulting fame into a career as a lawman, into considerable political influence, and into a sizable fortune from his unimpeded operation of gambling parlors, opium dens, and brothels.

Milo's father, who never held a job in his life, was a heavy drinker and a womanizer, and he committed suicide with his shotgun. His mother, who was also an alcoholic and later hanged herself with her nylons at a fat farm, had a will drawn up stipulating that Milo cannot inherit most of the family fortune until he is fifty-three—an age at which he will have presumably outgrown the vices of youth. She also donated all of her husband's clothes to the Salvation Army, and for a long while Milo was preoccupied with buying them back from the transients who were wearing them.

Milo's personal assets include three thousand acres of timber in the foothills of the Diablo Range, which he inherited directly from his grandfather, and part ownership of a bar. He says of himself in *The Wrong Case,* "Age and sorrow, those were my only assets, my largest liabilities." Somewhat later, a woman asks rhetorically, "You're rather a profane and unhappy man, aren't you?"

A Korean War veteran, Milo served as a deputy sheriff for about ten years before becoming too disillusioned with the job to continue in it. Twice divorced when first introduced to readers in *The Wrong Case,* he operated as a private investigator specializing in divorce cases, until no-fault divorce made his occupation obsolete. He has an uneasy relationship with the police department in his hometown of Meriwether, in particular with a Lieutenant Jamison, who is married to one of his former wives and is a stepfather to his only son. Further complicating matters, Milo and Jamison were friends growing up and even served together in Korea. In many ways the relationship between Milo and Jamison echoes the relationship between Krummel and Morning in *One to Count Cadence,* but there are as many contrasts as parallels. Also, Milo's level of dissipation—his alcoholism and cocaine use—exceeds even the debaucheries of the soldiers in the Philippines.

At the beginning of *The Wrong Case,* a pretty English professor named Helen Duffy asks Milo to find her brother. He protests truthfully that he has no investigative expertise beyond tailing adulterers. Nevertheless, he takes the case, partly because he has nothing else to do, but primarily because he has an almost immediate attraction to Helen Duffy's vulnerability and a determination to prove himself worthy of her affection.

As the title suggests, however, everything about this case is wrong. The supposedly studious brother turns out to be a promiscuous homosexual with a fondness for pistol tricks and a heroin habit. His death by overdose turns out to have been a murder, not the accident it is initially called, and as Milo begins to find the connections to a rapid expansion of the drug trafficking in Meriwether, the bodies start to pile up. The death of an alcoholic former lawyer named Simon is particularly painful to Milo. It turns out that the source of all the trouble is an ineffectual bar owner known for his unkept promises to buy the next round and for his generally poor business sense. He dies of a heart attack when Milo starts to confront him. Milo himself has been severely beaten. Then, after he has finally "solved" the case, Helen Duffy's imperious mother arrives to reveal to him that Helen is a chronic liar, that her "brother" was actually her illegitimate son, and that she has been cheating on Milo with his regular handball

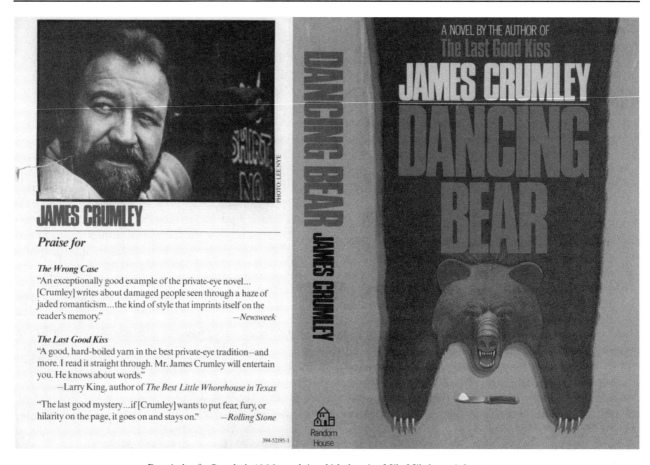

Dust jacket for Crumley's 1983 novel, in which detective Milo Milodragovitch exposes a multinational waste-disposal corporation that is involved in drug trafficking

opponent. The novel closes on this short paragraph: "As I stood there, the blunt shadow of the western ridge advanced darkly to the verge of the creek. I sat down, heard the sound of a car driving away, I drank my beer, and forgave her."

The reviews of *The Wrong Case* were generally positive. Most reviewers suggested that for the plot and mood of the novel Crumley owed a debt to Ross Macdonald. In the 14 April 1975 issue of *Publishers Weekly,* the reviewer opens: "*The Wrong Case,* purposefully fashioned after Ross Macdonald's California mysteries, even starts with a Lew Archer epigraph. The derivation weakens the book's opening and closing, but it is in the major, center section where Crumley rivals his model by creating startlingly real characters."

Most reviewers agreed that there was an unusual energy in Crumley's style and that in the tawdriness and sordidness of Milo's existence, the hard-boiled attitudes of Sam Spade, Philip Marlowe, and Lew Archer had found a disturbing new framework. Specifically, in the 23 June 1975 issue of *Newsweek,* P. S. Prescott asserts: "Properly deferring to hallowed conventions, Crumley writes about damaged people seen through a

haze of jaded romanticism, but he asserts his own tone of voice. . . . Crumley is a vivid writer. He makes Milo much more vulnerable, much more involved in this sordid case than Hammett or Chandler would have done. . . . this kind of style imprints itself on a reader's memory as the nicely tangled plot never can." In the 14 September 1975 issue of *The New York Times Book Review,* however, Newgate Callendar complained that Crumley's originality was undermined by his use of many of the conventions and clichés of the detective novel: "Crumley is not exactly a trailblazer. He also is rather self-indulgent and stretches out things rather uncomfortably. . . . Crumley has the general idea, but his technique needs refining; and while he can handle the situations well enough, a cliche is still a cliche."

While Milo is a native Westerner gone to seed, Crumley's other detective, C. W. (Chauncey Wayne) Sughrue (pronounced as if it begins with a *Sh*), is the author's take on the Western transient. In *The Last Good Kiss* (1978), the novel that introduces the character, Sughrue describes himself as "a second-rate hired gun or a first-rate saddle tramp." In a foreshadowing of his later, unconventional life, Sughrue was delivered by his father, not by an obstetrician, and he then saw little of his father afterward. His father's military service in World War II had left him restless, and Sughrue's occasional stays with him were marked by his father's attempts to engage him in Native American rituals intended to reveal a mystical relationship with the land. A native of Moody County in South Texas, Sughrue has spent as much of his life there as he has spent anywhere else—which is to say little time at all.

Sughrue did three hitches in Vietnam. During his third tour, he became briefly infamous for dropping a grenade into the hole where the elderly members, women, and children of a Vietnamese family were hiding. A platoon leader by this time, Sughrue had spent most of a month in the bush without sleeping. Dishonorably discharged, he avoided a prison term by agreeing to serve as a domestic spy for the army, enrolling in Western universities and infiltrating radical student organizations. After earning an M.A. in English from Colorado State University, he tried journalism with a small newspaper in Omaha but soon discovered that he could earn more money doing repossessions for a finance company. When the flower children crowded into San Francisco, he moved there and made a good living locating missing children.

After the San Francisco scene became too brutally sordid, Sughrue drifted to Meriwether, Montana, where he works as a private investigator out of an office in a double-wide trailer that he shares with a marriage counselor and two real-estate salesmen. He owns five acres out in the woods, on which there is an unfinished cabin; like Milo, he is also a silent partner in a bar. He drives an El Camino, and he has been engaged, by his count, to more than three dozen women, but is unmarried when he is introduced. He has earned his reputation as a "mean" man.

The Last Good Kiss may be Crumley's best novel. Sughrue is hired to find Abraham Trahearne, a renowned novelist with a Hemingwayesque disposition, who is reminiscent of Roger Wade in Chandler's *The Long Goodbye* (1953). A hero of the Pacific theater of World War II, Trahearne periodically goes off on a binge, escaping the family estate in Montana where he lives with his new wife, Melinda, and where his mother shares another house with his former wife, Catherine, who has hired Sughrue. Sughrue trails him to San Francisco, where coincidentally a woman saloon keeper hires him to find a daughter, named Betty Sue Flowers, who mysteriously disappeared a decade before. Trahearne asks to accompany Sughrue on what seems to be a hopeless quest.

In this marvelously paced story, peopled with eccentric but credibly realized characters, Sughrue discovers that Betty Sue Flowers had gone from orgies in hippie communes to prostitution and pornographic films. In the process the pretty teenager became an unkempt woman seemingly contented with her own grossness. Sughrue follows her trail to a sort of private halfway house, where he realizes that Betty Sue Flowers is really Melinda Trahearne and that Trahearne has contrived the whole situation in order to learn about and wallow in the unsavory details of his wife's untilthen mysterious past.

Unfortunately, Betty Sue Flowers had doublecrossed mob-connected pimps and porn producers, and Sughrue's investigation has led them directly to her. During a dramatic paramilitary-like rescue, Trahearne shows himself to be a bumbling, self-indulgent blowhard, and although Melinda returns with him to Montana, he clearly cannot cope with what he has learned about her past. On the night that she decides to leave him, someone shoots her dead—perhaps Catherine Trahearne or someone hired by her or perhaps the mobsters making an example of her. In any case, Sughrue blames Trahearne, and when the novelist unselfconsciously shows up in the bar where the novel began, Sughrue cannot conceal his contempt and his rage: "'You're dead,' I said. 'Go home before you start to stink.'"

The reviews of the novel were generally positive, with a good deal of praise for the complexity of its characterizations, for the vividness of its Western landscapes, for the shifting rhythms of its dialogue, for its manic energy and its humor, and for its knowing depiction of the transient subculture of contemporary America. In the 28 August 1978 issue of *Publishers Weekly,* the reviewer opens by asserting, "Marvelously constructed and jolting with surprises, Crumley's third novel should solidify his distinguished reputation." Several reviewers argued that the novel clearly transcends its genre and even its origins in the work of Chandler and Macdonald. In the 20 October 1978 issue of *The Wall Street Journal,* Bruce Cook observed: "Crumley's books should resolve any of the lingering doubts that even sniffy academics might have that it is possible to write well and seriously using a form that had its origins in the disreputable pulp paper detective magazines of the Twenties and Thirties." In a 23 March 1978 *Rolling Stone* review, Greil Marcus made one of the more interesting comparisons, judging Crumley's novel at least the equal of Robert Stone's *Dog Soldiers* (1974). It should also be noted that reviewers of Crumley's subsequent novels have sometimes commented on the gradual increase in the stature of *The Last Good Kiss* as readers discover or rediscover it through the other novels.

The Last Good Kiss remains Crumley's best work because in his three subsequent novels the scenes that parallel the raid to rescue Betty Sue Flowers/Melinda

Dust jacket for Crumley's 1996 novel, in which Milodragovitch and Sughrue team up to work on a case

involved in drug trafficking. In the second Sughrue novel, *The Mexican Tree Duck,* the detective is hired to find a prominent woman who has supposedly been kidnapped. At the climax, he recruits his old army buddies to raid a compound south of the border, and, not surprisingly—since Sughrue has taken on some powerful businessmen and government officials—the young woman with whom he has fallen in love ends up a casualty. In *Bordersnakes* Milo and Sughrue formally join forces for the first time. Each has previously appeared briefly in the other's novels, and Crumley has laid the groundwork for their deepening friendship. Each relates his progress in alternating chapters as they separately rampage across the Southwest in search of whoever has put out a contract on Sughrue's life and the banker who has run off with Milo's long-withheld inheritance. By the time the novel reaches its climax, the two quests have merged conveniently into one violent confrontation, and in the whole process, the two detectives have taken enough punishment—self-inflicted and not—to have killed them several times over.

Reviewers of *Dancing Bear, The Mexican Tree Duck,* and *Bordersnakes* have tended to voice two related concerns: first, that the plots of the novels have become progressively more convoluted, thus subordinating the element of detection; and, second, that the excesses in the characterization of Milo and Sughrue have become too outsized. In the July 1993 *Booklist,* Bill Ott concludes his boxed review of *The Mexican Tree Duck* with these ambivalent observations:

> Crumley exposes the still-raw nerve ends of his Vietnam vets as vividly as anyone, and he makes us feel his characters' adrenalin pump as they prepare to attack the bad guys. Yet this has become awfully familiar terrain, and Crumley's take on the attraction/repulsion of violence doesn't seem quite as fresh as it did in 1978. Still, that's only to say that the next good kiss rarely feels quite as good as the last one. What really matters is this: Crumley can still write a sentence so tight the spaces between the words seem filled with meaning.

Along much the same lines, the reviewer of *Bordersnakes* in the 30 September 1996 *Publishers Weekly* describes the novel as "lit by flashes of brutal lyricism but bordering on incoherence" and closes: "Crumley's harsh realism is vitiated here by James Bondish gadgetry and gunplay. While the plot reads at times like an overbudget Western directed by an LSD-addled Raymond Chandler, the far-flung cast . . . is drawn with panache."

Although flawed, Crumley's last three novels do contain some brilliantly conceived incidents and some startling prose. Twice in *Dancing Bear,* Milo describes in great detail his surveillance skills, only to have them

Trahearne have become more elaborately conceived, more expansively narrated, and a good deal less credible. The violence in *The Wrong Case* and *The Last Good Kiss* may not be believable in a real-world context, but Crumley makes it credible within his fictive world because the protagonists and antagonists are drawn on the same scale. In his next three novels, however, as the criminal schemes have become greater conspiracies involving rogue corporations and government agencies, Milo and Sughrue's personalities and habits have necessarily been amplified, even to the point of self-caricature, in order to strike a narrative balance between them and their antagonists.

In the second Milodragovitch novel, *Dancing Bear,* an old woman who had once been one of his father's mistresses initially hires Milo to identify a couple that she has observed meeting illicitly. It turns out, however, that she, her niece, and a wealthy freelance journalist have conspired to force Milo, in effect, to expose a multinational waste-disposal corporation that not only is illegally polluting wilderness areas but also is heavily shown up as less foolproof or less expert than he thinks they are. In the first instance, his cover is blown when he parks his van, with its bogus sign advertising television repair, outside the home of a cantankerous old man who has been having extended difficulties getting his television fixed. The old man creates such a scene about the poor service he has received that Milo has to agree to look at the television. In the second instance, Milo trails a man across the desolate night landscape of Montana's interstates without being spotted. The next morning, however, the man's car blows up when he starts it, and Milo finds his own vehicle booby-trapped with a hand grenade. He has been so concerned with not being identified as a tail that he has not noticed the men tailing him. In such instances, Crumley is, of course, parodying some of the conventions of the hard-boiled detective novel—one of which is that the detective is a consummate professional and often is more skilled in his investigative techniques than the police are in theirs. On a deeper level, however, Crumley is extending the conventions of the genre by giving them a postmodern, absurdist edginess. In the environments in which Crumley's detectives operate, there is more hard irony than sophisticated wit, more deadpan observations than clever wisecracks.

In *The Mexican Tree Duck* Sughrue is initially hired by two hugely fat but soft-spoken and tidy twins who own a pet store and want a tank full of their tropical fish repossessed. At first they seem like hopeless cases, but it turns out that they have a warehouse of weaponry, including a Sherman tank. Their trip with Sughrue out to a biker gang's fortress to get the fish is the kind of set piece that Crumley does well. The violence crackles like heat lightning—makes everyone blink but does no permanent harm—and the mismatched characters mix with all sorts of unexpected, ironic, and quietly hilarious turns.

Crumley is equally adept at expository passages. At one point in *Bordersnakes,* Sughrue reflects wryly on the eccentricities of old people—specifically his mother-in-law: "Wynona [his wife] had told me enough about her mother so I knew she was about a thousand ants short of a picnic, and often mean as a sow with a shoat stuck under the bottom rail, but as far as Lester [his adopted son] and I were concerned she was as sweet as strawberry honey." The similes are neither pointedly coherent nor clearly mixed. Instead, the oddly disjointed figurative language vividly reflects the uneasiness that the woman precipitates. A simi-

lar effect is achieved, again in *Bordersnakes,* in the description of Carver D, an effete, obese newspaper publisher who is the first "Texas Communist" Milo has ever met:

> His bloated face floated over a body that seemed to be a large pile of mashed potatoes covered by a once-expensive and once-elegant white suit that could have covered a small truck and might have been retrieved from a vegetable dump. His deep, rumbling voice had been hoarsened by cheap bourbon from the brown paper sack at his knee and by years of the same Gitane smoke that turned his fat fingers into small yellow tubers harvested from a graveyard. His large brown eyes, as melancholy as prunes in Cream of Wheat, shone with secret knowledge and sparkling wit, and when he smiled, you wanted to laugh.

Here the food-related similes pile up and slop over each other on the page like the food that must mix and back up in the huge man's digestive tract.

Early on in *The Wrong Case,* Milo tells Helen Duffy, "This is the great American west. Where men came to get away from laws. Almost everything in this state is legal. And a lot of things that are illegal are done in spite of the law." As his own and Sughrue's subsequent adventures show, many illegal things are also done in the service of justice in this strange West in which each possibility is a disappointment and each disappointment is an occasion for greater optimism and another reason to continue on. At the end of *Bordersnakes,* Milo and Sughrue pack up and head back to Montana, where further adventures may be waiting.

Interview:

Charles L. P. Silet, "Drugs, Cash, and Automatic Weapons: An Interview with James Crumley," *Armchair Detective,* 27, no. 1 (1994): 8–15.

References:

Keith Newlin, "C.W. Sughrue's Whiskey Visions," *Modern Fiction Studies,* 29 (Autumn 1983): 545–555;

Daniel L. Wilson, "Looking for Natty Bump: The Confluence of the Frontier Hero and the Private Eye in the Montana Novels of James Crumley," M.A. thesis, University of Florida, 1992.

Carroll John Daly

(14 September 1889 – 16 January 1958)

Chuck Etheridge
McMurry University

BOOKS: *The White Circle* (New York: E. J. Clode, 1926; London: Hutchinson, 1927);

The Snarl of the Beast (New York: E. J. Clode, 1927; London: Hutchinson, 1928);

The Man in the Shadows (New York: E. J. Clode, 1928; London: Hutchinson, 1929);

The Hidden Hand (New York: E. J. Clode, 1929; London: Hutchinson, 1930);

The Tag Murders (New York: E. J. Clode, 1930; London: Hutchinson, 1931);

Tainted Power: A Race Williams Detective Story (New York: E. J. Clode, 1931; London: Hutchinson, 1931);

The Third Murderer (New York: Farrar & Rinehart, 1931; London: Hutchinson, 1932);

Murder Won't Wait (New York: I. Washburn, 1933; London: Hutchinson, 1934);

The Amateur Murderer (New York: I. Washburn, 1933; London: Hutchinson, 1933);

Murder from the East (New York: E. J. Clode, 1935; London: Hutchinson, 1935);

Death's Juggler (London: Hutchinson, 1935); republished as *The Mystery of the Smoking Gun* (New York: Frederick A. Stokes, 1936);

Mr. Strang (New York: Frederick A. Stokes, 1936; London: Hale, 1937);

Emperor of Evil (London: Hutchinson, 1936; New York: Frederick A. Stokes, 1937);

Better Corpses (London: Hale, 1940);

The Legion of the Living Dead (Toronto & London: Popular Publications, 1947);

Murder at our House (London: Museum Press, 1950);

Ready to Burn (London: Museum Press, 1951);

The Adventures of Race Williams: A Dime Detective Book (New York: Mysterious Press, 1988);

The Adventures of Satan Hall: A Dime Detective Book (New York: Mysterious Press, 1988).

Editions: *Murder from the East: A Race Williams Story* (New York: International Polygonics, 1978);

The Snarl of the Beast, introduction by Charles Shibuk (Boston: Gregg Press, 1981);

The Snarl of the Beast (New York: HarperPerennial, 1992);

The Hidden Hand (New York: HarperPerennial, 1992).

OTHER: "The False Burton Combs," in *The Hard-Boiled Detective: Stories From Black Mask Magazine 1920–51,* edited by Herbert Ruhm (New York: Vintage, 1977), pp. 3–30;

"The Knights of the Open Palm," in *The Great American Detective: 15 Stories Starring America's Most Celebrated Private Detectives,* edited by William Kittredge and Steven M. Kreutzer (New York: Mentor, 1978), pp. 18–38;

"Three Gun Terry," in *The Black Mask Boys: Masters in the Hard-Boiled School of Detective Fiction,* edited by William P. Nolan (New York: Morrow, 1985), pp. 43–72.

Although he is credited with the creation of the genre of hard-boiled detective fiction, Carroll John Daly is a largely forgotten writer. During his prime, however, the news that a particular pulp magazine carried one of Daly's works could boost its circulation by as much as 20 percent. While Daly created other series heroes, Race Williams is his best known and most successful invention, a tough private eye, the literary father of Dashiell Hammett's Sam Spade and Raymond Chandler's Phillip Marlow and the grandfather of contemporary hard-boiled literary detectives such as Robert B. Parker's Spenser and Sara Paretsky's V. I. Warshawski.

Many who have written about Daly's work are often dismissive of it. "Crude" and "sloppy" are two terms that most often appear in appraisals of his fiction. Others argue, however, that his work has been more influential than that of more accepted authors such as Hammett. In a fan letter written in the 1950s, Mickey Spillane credits Daly as being his sole influence: "Yours was the first and only style of writing that ever influenced me in any way. Race was the model for Mike [Hammer]; and I can't say more in this case than imitation being the most sincere form of flattery." Daly's Williams is the archetypal private

Dust jacket for Carroll John Daly's 1927 novel. It is the first of his seven books that feature Race Williams, the prototype of the hard-boiled detective (courtesy of Special Collections, Thomas Cooper Library, University of South Carolina).

investigator—tough, wisecracking, resourceful, occasionally violent, occasionally compassionate, and always governed by a strong internal code. Critic Dale H. Ross writes that Williams's code can be boiled down to one simple maxim: "Never kill anybody who does not deserve it." Such an appraisal, though, is too narrow, for Race is available to those in need (even those who cannot afford to pay him), protective of those weaker than himself, and relentlessly courageous.

Although Daly is no stylist, his works are more sophisticated than he is given credit for. His novels contain allusions to authors such as William Shakespeare, Samuel Pepys, and Nathaniel Hawthorne. His prose style is rhythmic, and he shows a strong command of American vernacular at a time when most detective fiction was still being written using stilted, formal diction. More impor-

tant, Daly could flat-out tell a story, an ability that literary critics consistently undervalue. Finally, the invention of a literary genre is not an insignificant literary achievement—he may in fact have coined the term *hard-boiled,* a term several of his characters apply to themselves. Daly, of course, was a man of his time, and his work contains descriptions that are offensive to many—women are "dames," Asians are "yellow"—but no more so than many other writers of the modern period whose literary stature is far greater.

The biographical material available on Daly is sketchy. He was an intensely private person, perhaps a recluse. It is known that Daly was born on 14 September 1889 in Yonkers, New York, and that after finishing high school he was for a time a student at the De La Salle Institute as well as at The American Academy of Dramatic Arts. After leaving school he unsuccessfully tried careers in sales, in law, in stenography, and in the theater. He later became part owner of what is believed to have been the first movie theater in Atlantic City, New Jersey. Eventually, he owned a small chain of movie houses.

On 11 December 1913 Daly and Margaret G. Blakely were wed. The couple had one child, John, who is better known as the actor Jack Daly. After Daly began his writing career in 1922, the family moved to a row house on Concord Avenue in suburban White Plains, New York, where Daly lived for the greater part of his life, isolating himself for months at a time. Despite the fact that most of Daly's major fiction is set in New York City, he rarely went there. As his close friend Erle Stanley Gardner wrote in *The Atlantic Monthly* in 1965, Daly "wanted no part of the rough and tumble." He once bought a .45 for research purposes and was arrested on the way home on concealed-weapons charges.

With the support of a well-off uncle, Daly turned to writing in the early 1920s. He sold his first story, "Dolly," to *The Black Mask* in 1922. In December of that year, *The Black Mask* published "The False Burton Combs," generally acknowledged to be the first hard-boiled detective story. In this early story, the unnamed narrator is approached by the troubled son of the influential and wealthy John B. Combs. The narrator, who describes himself as an "adventurer" who "takes risks" for a living, agrees to protect young Burton Combs, who has become embroiled with a group of rum-runners. While posing as Combs at a vacation resort, he becomes involved with the lovely young Marion. When he is kidnapped by the rum-runners, the detective faces certain death until he finds a gun (slipped to him by Marion, who, he does not realize until much later, has concealed herself in the car along with him). Bullets fly; the good guys win; and the detective gets the girl. The story contains several classic Daly elements, most notably the figure of the tough and humorous detective, though the protagonist here does not yet espouse the fully developed moral code that later becomes a feature of the author's work. Other elements—the lovely young woman who is more than she seems, the hidden weapon, the violent conclusion—become recurring motifs in Daly's fiction and later in hard-boiled detective fiction as a whole.

In writing "The False Burton Combs" Daly was responding to the society and the times in which he lived. The Prohibition Era gave rise to organized crime and to increasing lawlessness as gangsters scrambled to meet the demand for alcohol, which did not go away when the legal supply did. Organized crime meant spreading corruption as the various gangs infiltrated police departments or bribed police officials on active duty. The influence of organized crime spread to elected officials as well, and gangs sometimes sponsored their own candidates for political office. Caught in the midst of this ram-

pant lawlessness and seeming anarchy, the average individual felt unsafe and powerless. The idea that one individual with honor, physical vigor, and the courage of his convictions could combat these negative forces—could impose order—was enormously appealing, and it was in the world of rum-running and vendetta killing that the hard-boiled detective arose.

In "The False Burton Combs" the innocent are ultimately protected and the criminals—in this case, bootleggers—are served cool, hard justice, as dispensed by a pistol. Although Daly wrote several generations after the cowboy gunslinger first rode into America's mythic consciousness, the desire for a hero to impose some sort of law in a lawless land is as relevant to Prohibition Era New York as it was to those in frontier towns in the American West. In the fictional world that Daly developed, the forces of evil and dark are always strong and Race Williams is virtually alone in his fight for right. Victory is only temporary, and order is not restored because it never really existed.

In 1923 Daly wrote two important stories that helped to establish the hard-boiled genre. The first, "Three Gun Terry," was published in the 15 May issue of *The Black Mask*. The title character, Terry Mack, is regarded as the first tough-guy private investigator. Terry is more obviously "tough" than is the narrator of "The False Burton Combs"—he keeps not one but three guns on him at all times, whereas his predecessor was caught without a firearm in his climactic conflict. Terry, like Race Williams, is more forceful than thoughtful, whereas the narrator of "The False Burton Combs" triumphs by a combination of deception and physical courage. Daly continued to publish regularly in *The Black Mask*, and the 1 June number featured "The Knights of the Open Palm," marking the first appearance of Race Williams, who would grace the pages of the famous pulp for more than a decade, leaving in his wake a trail of bloody corpses.

Daly's most significant and successful hero, Race is Daly's alter ego. The author according to William P. Nolan in *The Black Mask Boys* (1985), once said he was "Carroll John Daly in the daytime and Race Williams at night." The character may well have been a wish fulfillment for Daly, who, Nolan asserts, wore large spectacles, was "mousy looking," and had a "fear of dentists." In contrast, Race Williams stands six feet tall and weighs 180 pounds—a large man by the standards of the time. He describes himself as one who occasionally does a little "honest shooting" and informs the reader that "I never bumped off a guy what didn't need it."

In "The Knights of the Open Palm" Race is approached by Earnest Thompson, whose seventeen-year-old son, Willie, has disappeared right before he was to testify at the trial of several members of the Ku Klux Klan. Williams heads to "Clinton," a fictitious town "in the West." He discovers that most of the population of this little hamlet is either in the Klan or is so fearful that they will not help Race find Thompson. With the help of one fearless family Race manages to save the boy and foil the Klan, along the way using his .44 to reduce its membership. Daly's use of the Klan as the bad guys is interesting, especially since one might expect him to reflect dominant cultural attitudes toward African Americans, just as he does in the case of Asians and women. Evidently, Daly regarded the Klan as thugs–like any other organized group that existed outside the law–and, in a setting that was far removed from the author's familiar New York, he thought it more plausible to use Klansmen as villains than to use urban-style criminals.

Although Daly's association with *The Black Mask* was a boon to both the author and the magazine, his relationships with its editors was sometimes strained. The editorship changed four times during the course of Daly's career. Not only did the October 1922 issue contain Daly's first story, it was also the first number published under the editorship of George W. Sutton. Sutton had an unclear sense of purpose for the pulp–he promised that the magazine would carry "Western yarns" as well as "weird, creepy mystery tales" and "ghost stories"–yet he did "discover" Daly and Hammett. Sutton also recognized the importance of recurring heroes to build readership and therefore insure the continued success of the magazine. It was actually Sutton's assistant, Harry North, who was Daly's advocate at *The Black Mask,* however; according to Ron Goulart in *The Dime Detectives* (1988), Sutton once told Daly point-blank that he did not like his work, but, according to Daly, said "You can make money with this boy Williams, every one seems to like him but me." Philip C. Cody succeeded Sutton and encouraged Daly to create more Race Williams tales while highlighting Hammett's work.

Joseph Thompson Shaw, or "Cap," as he was called, took over the editorial reins of *The Black Mask* in late 1926. Often described as a legend, Cap Shaw is credited with the development and refinement of the hard-boiled genre. He nurtured Raymond Chandler and fostered the evolution of his celebrated prose style. Shaw's relationship with Daly, however, was problematic. Although he serialized the stories that became *The Snarl of the Beast* (1927), the editor was not fond of Daly's fiction and would not have published any of it if Williams had not been so enormously popular. Shaw shortened the title of the magazine to *Black Mask* and added the subtitle "The He-Man's Magazine." According to Nolan, he wanted to publish authors who were "six footers," but he made an exception to his rule for the 5' 9" creator of Race Williams. Relations between the two were difficult, and Daly left *Black Mask* in 1934; he returned to the magazine after Shaw left and ultimately outlasted the editor at *Black Mask* by nearly a decade.

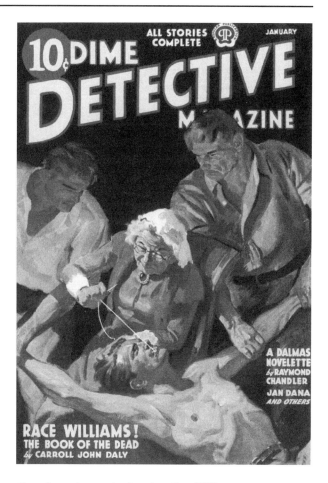

Cover for a pulp magazine featuring a Race Williams story. Daly moved to Dime Detective *when his relations with* Black Mask *soured.*

Although the distinction of being the first hard-boiled detective novel goes to Daly's earlier book, *The White Circle* (1926), the first Race Williams novel, *The Snarl of the Beast,* is regarded as his best work and is often cited as originating the genre. In the opening line of *The Snarl of the Beast* Race notes, "It's the point of view in life that counts. For an ordinary man to get a bullet through his hat as he walked home at night would be something to talk about for years. Now with me; just the price of a new hat–nothing more." Race goes on to define himself in a blustery passage that introduces the existential situation explored by scores of hard-boiled progeny:

> Under the laws I'm labeled on the books and licensed as a private detective. Not that I'm proud of that license but I need it, and I've had considerable trouble hanging onto it. My position is not exactly a healthy one. The police don't like me. The crooks don't like me. I'm just a halfway house between the law and crime; sort of working both ends against the middle. Right and wrong are not written on the statutes for me, nor do I find my code of morals in the essays of long-winded professors. My ethics are my own. I'm not

saying they're good and I'm not admitting they're bad, and what's more I'm not interested in the opinions of others on that subject. When the time comes for some quick-drawing gunman to jump me over the hurdles I'll ride to the Pearly Gates on my own ticket. It won't be a pass written on the back of another man's thoughts. I stand on my own legs and I'll shoot it out with any gun in the city–any time, any place. Thirty-fourth street and Broadway, in the five o'clock rush hour, isn't barred either. Race Williams–Private Investigator–tells the whole story. Right! Let's go.

Race must find his way as an individual within a violent, chaotic world. He does have a strong sense of right and wrong, but he distinguishes between that which is morally right and that which is legal and always follows the course that enables him to do the former. Although Daly is no political philosopher, Race's code seems almost Emersonian in its insistence on and adherence to a higher law than that written by humanity.

Race is waylaid by The Beast, a large, powerful man who seems impervious to harm–even to the detective's .44s. During Race's pursuit of The Beast a policeman is killed, and, for a brief while, suspicion falls on Williams. Race agrees to help the police apprehend the criminal, and, in a seemingly unrelated case, is hired to protect a broken-down young man named Daniel Davidson from his evil stepfather, who wants his stepson dead so that he can inherit his late wife's estate. Unable to handle the pressures of his life, Davidson has become a cocaine addict–a "snowbird," in the vernacular of the time. The young man is being protected by Milly, a self-confessed "thief" and "bad woman" who nonetheless seems to genuinely have Daniel's best interests at heart.

After a series of car chases and gun battles, Race discovers that The Beast and Daniel Davidson's stepfather are the same person, and, of course, the evil Beast is no match for the hard-boiled hero. When examining The Beast's body, Race discovers that the criminal wore a shirt of chain mail underneath his clothing, and it is only because the detective aimed at his adversary's head that he was able to triumph. By this time Daniel has become so ill he will not survive; however, Race insists that Milly take the money–she is Davidson's heir–and begin a new life in Europe, away from the evil influences that nearly brought her down before. He pronounces her "a good Kid," which constitutes a ringing endorsement in the Race Williams lexicon.

Although Daly's purpose is always to entertain, he does confront social problems in his work, including the lawlessness of the Prohibition Era and the corruption of government officials. He also directly confronts more specific social concerns, such as the rise of the Ku Klux Klan in "The Knights of the Open Palm" and that of the dangers of drug abuse in *The Snarl of the Beast.*

Daly was a hard-working and prolific writer, often sleeping all day and writing all night. During the 1920s and into the 1930s, Daly remained enormously popular and continued to sell his work not only to *Black Mask* but to the other leading pulps, including *Dime Detective* and *Detective Fiction Weekly.* He was so prolific that he often had more than one story appear in the same issue of a pulp magazine, necessitating the use of a pseudonym–usually "John D. Carroll." Although Shaw at *Black Mask* actively encouraged his authors to write novels and published them in serial format, thinking correctly that such a practice would boost sales, Daly's other markets were not as open to serializing long works. Daly got around this policy by writing series of closely related but self-contained short stories that could be read independently.

Daly generally wrote about different detectives in different publications. In *Dime Detective* he wrote mainly about Vee Brown, a much different hero than Race; Brown is from a wealthy background and composes popular songs, à la Detective Boldt in the Ridley Pearson thrillers. Brown appears in book form in *Murder Won't Wait* (1933) and *Emperor of Evil* (1936). For *Detective Fiction Weekly* Daly created Satan Hall, a prototype of the modern Dirty Harry rogue-cop, who ignores procedures, takes the law into his own hands, and ultimately makes sure justice is served. He appears in the books *Death's Juggler* (1935) and *The Adventures of Satan Hall: A Dime Detective Book,* published by The Mysterious Press in 1988. Daly, however, did not practice literary segregation, and one detective would occasionally appear in the pages of a magazine other than his usual one, as was the case when Race Williams appeared in the pages of *Dime Detective* after his creator had left *Black Mask,* the literary equivalent of the detective's hometown.

The second most highly regarded novel in the Daly canon is *Murder from the East* (1935), the seventh and last Race Williams book published in Daly's lifetime. In it, Race is engaged by a powerful but mysterious government figure called "The General," who asks the detective to help him solve "The Torture Murders." Representatives of a mythical Asian country called Astran are kidnapping the children of government employees and ransoming them for government secrets. Intimately involved in the plot is Mark Yarrow, an Astranian businessman. Although The General never says anything about his own personal plight, Race discovers that the government official's own daughter has been kidnapped and that he is being blackmailed.

Race is stunned when he confronts Yarrow and discovers the businessman is married to The Flame, also known as Florence Drummond, a beautiful red-headed woman whom Race has encountered before. The Flame is the prototypical woman in Daly's fiction–tough, resourceful, a bad but not too bad girl, not content to be "a shop girl," who has become enticed into criminal activity by the allure of the trappings of wealth. Williams's own feelings are mixed. He is attracted to her and may even love her; he has tried to help her "go straight" several times, yet he has resisted becoming fully involved with her because "to love The Flame" is to die. In his dealings with Florence as well as with other women, Race's relationship is remarkably chaste; as far as his love life goes, he is a gun-wielding priest. Florence herself is a combination of the virtuous Marion of "The False Burton Combs" and Milly, described as a "Girl of the Night" in *The Snarl of the Beast.* At one point, when Race is facing certain death, The Flame slips him a gun and he fights his way out, just as Marion did for the false Burton Combs in the 1922 story.

Ultimately, Race uses his .44s to save the kidnapped girl, vanquish the threat to the United States, and kill Mark Yarrow—a man who, in the Williams Code of Ethics, needs killing. The Flame leaves him. Despite its apparently racist assumptions—the mixed-race Yarrow's name may be a clumsy bastardization of the stereotypical Asian pronunciation of the word "yellow"—the novel does have some interesting features. In it, the Flame is at her most ambiguous; she seems to be, alternately, both wholly good and wholly bad; this situation is one of the few Race finds himself in that a woman must extricate him from. And, although the novel was written in 1935, Daly is perhaps prophetic in his concern that the biggest threats to the United States may come from other countries rather than from crime and internal corruption. Race changes with the times; in later tales he moves from his native New York to California, where he confronts the criminal element associated with Hollywood. Some of these stories have been collected in *The Adventures of Race Williams: A Dime Detective Book* (1988).

Daly continued to write and publish into the 1950s. His last novel was published in 1951, and he "retired" in that decade, moving to California in 1953 to be near his son, who was then working regularly in television and movies. In reality, Daly never retired and continued to write as long as his health permitted, publishing his last story in 1958. He died at the Los Angeles Community Hospital on 16 January 1958.

Daly's legacy is worth remembering. In addition to the creation of the hard-boiled genre of detective fiction, he leaves behind a body of eminently readable novels and memorable characters. Whenever a modern reader encounters a tough, wise-cracking, literary-allusion-spouting detective, that reader is encountering one of the literary offspring of Race Williams—and of Carroll John Daly.

Cover for the 15 December 1934 issue of a pulp featuring Daly's police detective Satan Hall, who ensures that justice will be served even when the legal system stands in the way

References:

Ron Goulart, *The Dime Detectives* (New York: Mysterious Press, 1988);

William Kittredge and Steven M. Krauser, introduction to *The Great American Detective: 15 Stories Starring America's Most Celebrated Private Eyes,* edited by Kittredge and Krauser (New York: Mentor, 1978);

Stephen Metz, "In Defense of Carroll John Daly," *Mystery FANcier,* 2 (May 1978): 19–22;

William F. Nolan, "Behind the Mask: Carroll John Daly," in *The Black Mask Boys: Masters in the Hard-Boiled School of Detective Fiction,* edited by Nolan (New York: Morrow, 1985), pp. 35–43;

Dale H. Ross, "Carroll John Daly," in *Critical Survey of Mystery and Detective Fiction,* edited by Frank N. McGill (Pasadena, Cal.: Salem Press, 1988), pp. 445–449;

Herbert Ruhm, introduction to *The Hard Boiled Detective: Stories from Black Mask Magazine 1920–1951,* edited by Ruhm (New York: Vintage, 1977).

Thomas B. Dewey

(6 March 1915 – 22 April 1981)

Marvin S. Lachman

BOOKS: *Hue and Cry* (New York: Jefferson House, 1944); republished as *Room for Murder* (New York: New American Library, 1950); republished as *The Murder of Marion Mason* (London: Dakers, 1951);

As Good As Dead (New York: Jefferson House, 1946; London: Dakers, 1952);

Draw the Curtain Close (New York: Jefferson House, 1947; London: Dakers, 1951); republished as *Dame in Danger* (New York: New American Library, 1958);

Mourning After (New York: Mill & Morrow, 1950; London: Dakers, 1953);

Handle with Fear (New York: Mill & Morrow, 1951; London: Dakers, 1955);

Every Bet's a Sure Thing (New York: Simon & Schuster, 1953; London: Dakers, 1953);

Mountain Girl, as Cord Wainer (New York: Fawcett, 1953);

Kiss Me Hard, as Tom Brandt (New York: Popular Library, 1953);

Run, Brother, Run!, as Brandt (New York: Popular Library, 1954; London: Consul Press, 1961);

Prey for Me (New York: Simon & Schuster, 1954; London: Boardman, 1954); republished as *The Case of the Murdered Model* (New York: Avon, 1955);

The Mean Streets (New York: Simon & Schuster, 1955; London: Boardman, 1955);

The Brave, Bad Girls (New York: Simon & Schuster, 1956; London: Boardman, 1957);

My Love Is Violent (New York: Popular Library, 1956; London: Consul Press, 1961);

And Where She Stops (New York: Popular Library, 1957); republished as *I.O.U. Murder* (London: Boardman, 1958);

You've Got Him Cold (New York: Simon & Schuster, 1958; London: Boardman, 1959);

What Women Want to Know, by Dewey and Harold M. Imerman (New York: Crown, 1958; London: Hammond, 1960);

Thomas B. Dewey

The Case of the Chased and the Unchaste (New York: Random House, 1959; London: Boardman, 1960);

Go to Sleep, Jeannie (New York: Popular Library, 1959; London: Boardman, 1960);

The Girl Who Wasn't There (New York: Simon & Schuster, 1960; London: Boardman, 1960); republished as *The Girl Who Never Was* (New York: Mayflower, 1962);

Too Hot for Hawaii (New York: Popular Library, 1960; London: Boardman, 1963);

The Golden Hooligan (New York: Dell, 1961); republished as *Mexican Slayride* (London: Boardman, 1961);

Hunter at Large (New York: Simon & Schuster, 1961; London: Boardman, 1962);

Go, Honeylou (New York: Dell, 1962; London: Boardman, 1962);

How Hard to Kill (New York: Simon & Schuster, 1962; London: Boardman, 1963);

The Girl with the Sweet Plump Knees (New York: Dell, 1963; London: Boardman, 1963);

A Sad Song Singing (New York: Simon & Schuster, 1963; London: Boardman, 1964);

Don't Cry for Long (New York: Simon & Schuster, 1964; London: Boardman, 1965);

Only on Tuesdays (New York: Dell, 1964; London: Boardman, 1964);

The Girl in the Punchbowl (New York: Dell, 1964; London: Boardman, 1965);

Nude in Nevada (New York: Dell, 1965; London: Boardman, 1966);

Can a Mermaid Kill? (New York: Tower, 1965);

Portrait of a Dead Heiress (New York: Simon & Schuster, 1965; London: Boardman, 1966);

Deadline (New York: Simon & Schuster, 1966; London: Boardman, 1967);

A Season for Violence (Greenwich, Conn.: Fawcett, 1966);

Death and Taxes (New York: Putnam, 1967; London: Hale, 1969);

The King Killers (New York: Putnam, 1968); republished as *Death Turns Right* (London: Hale, 1969);

The Love-Death Thing (New York: Simon & Schuster, 1969);

The Taurus Trip (New York: Simon & Schuster, 1970; London: Hale, 1972).

OTHER: *A Pride of Felons,* edited by Dewey, Gordon and Mildred Gordon (The Gordons), and Jean Leslie (New York: Macmillan, 1963);

Sleuths and Consequences, edited by Dewey (New York: Simon & Schuster, 1966);

"The Big Job," in *The Best Detective Stories of the Year,* edited by Anthony Boucher (New York: Dutton, 1966; London: Boardman, 1966), pp. 109–128.

SELECTED PERIODICAL PUBLICATIONS–
UNCOLLECTED: "Never Send to Know," *Ellery Queen's Mystery Magazine,* 45 (January 1965): 29–32;

"The Prevalence of Monsters," *Ellery Queen's Mystery Magazine,* 45 (April 1965): 82–85;

"Lucien's Nose," *Ellery Queen's Mystery Magazine,* 48 (July 1966): 89–92.

Though clearly in the Dashiell Hammett–Raymond Chandler tradition, Thomas B. Dewey was also a forerunner of the more sensitive school of hard-boiled private-detective fiction that took hold in the 1970s. Yet, Mac, Dewey's best series character, is also as hard-edged and tough as his fictional colleagues. Dewey wrote when most of his contemporaries were either staunchly right-wing, as were Mickey Spillane, Cleve F. Adams, and Richard S. Prather, or apolitical. He was an exception, creating a private detective aware of what was happening in the world, yet unashamedly liberal and compassionate. Dewey consistently addressed the political and social issues of his day but never resorted to polemics.

Thomas Blanchard Dewey was born in Elkhart, Indiana, on 6 March 1915, a distant relative of Admiral George Dewey of Spanish-American War fame. His father taught English at the college level; his mother was a homemaker. Dewey graduated from Kansas State Teachers College at Emporia in 1936 and then did postgraduate work at the University of Iowa before moving to Los Angeles, where he was an editor at the Storycraft Correspondence School from 1938 to 1942. During World War II he worked for the U. S. State Department in Washington, D.C., as an administrative and editorial assistant. Because of a lung condition, he did not serve in the military service. Then, before becoming a full-time writer in 1952, Dewey worked for a Los Angeles advertising agency, starting in 1945. He married three times, with two children, Thomas B. Jr. and Deborah, resulting from his first marriage. His first two marriages ended in divorce.

Writing during his spare time in Washington, he published his first book, *Hue and Cry,* creating Singer Batts, an amateur detective who was the protagonist in four of Dewey's first five books: *Hue and Cry* (1944), *As Good As Dead* (1946), *Mourning After* (1950), and *Handle with Fear* (1951). A Shakespearean scholar and bibliophile, Batts resembles Rex Stout's Nero Wolfe in his erudition and his lack of interest in ordinary social amenities. Though Batts is the owner of a hotel in Preston, Ohio, he has little interest in business. The stories are narrated by Batts's assistant, Joe Spinder, who is similar to Stout's Archie Goodwin. Yet, in many respects, Batts is the opposite of Wolfe. He has no interest in food and must be reminded to eat. He is thin and a sloppy dresser. His drink of choice is whiskey, not beer.

The Batts novels are perceptive in their observations of small-town behavior, especially its gossip. Batts largely avoids involvement with residents and views solving a crime as an intellectual exercise. Because they recognize his intelligence, his fellow townspeople, though at first suspicious of him,

Dust jacket for Dewey's 1958 novel, in which his principal detective character—a Chicago private eye known only as Mac—becomes involved in the politics of the McCarthy era

terization and formal deduction of Rex Stout or the sensational sex-cum-sadism peddled by Mickey Spillane."

Dewey soon resolved any conflicts that existed. After publishing one more Batts book, *Handle with Fear,* another blend of puzzle and action, he returned to Mac, the private detective he had created in *Draw the Curtain Close* (1947), in *Every Bet's a Sure Thing* (1953). Dewey chronicled Mac's adventures in seventeen novels.

Though he published a new Mac novel almost every year from 1953 to 1970, Dewey did not have any of his books sold to the movies and apparently did not feel financially secure in writing only one series. Sometimes using pseudonyms, Dewey in 1953 also began writing paperback originals, which replaced the pulp magazines as a market for hard-boiled fiction. As "Cord Wainer" he published *Mountain Girl* (1953), a nonmystery resembling some of the rural books of Erskine Caldwell. Writing as "Tom Brandt," Dewey published two thrillers, *Kiss Me Hard* (1953) and *Run, Brother, Run!* (1954). Using his own name, he published *My Love Is Violent* in 1956 and *And Where She Stops,* the following year, introducing Pete Schofield, Dewey's third and final series character.

Schofield eventually appeared in nine lighthearted private-detective novels: *And Where She Stops* (1957), *Go to Sleep, Jeannie* (1959), *Too Hot for Hawaii* (1960), *The Golden Hooligan* (1961), *Go, Honeylou* (1962), *The Girl with the Sweet Plump Knees* (1963), *The Girl in the Punchbowl* (1964), *Only on Tuesdays* (1964), and *Nude in Nevada* (1965). Dewey made Schofield one of the rare married private eyes, and a continuing plot device is the jealousy of his wife, Jeannie, when Pete's work places him in contact with beautiful women. The books were advertised as "sizzlers," though their sexual content is relatively tame. Little is risqué, except for clients, unexpected corpses, and criminals constantly interrupting the sex life of the Schofields.

It is because of the more serious Mac series that Dewey will be remembered. Much has been made of the absence of a last name for Mac; except for two occasions when Mac gives last names (both different and probably neither real), Dewey was consistent in making his detective Everyman. When he gives his name as "Mac" in *Draw the Curtain Close,* he is told, "That's anybody's name." Mac's response is: "That's who I am."

Dewey's characterization of Mac makes him memorable, though he is as faceless as he is nameless. He is the first-person narrator of the series, so readers never objectively "see" him. He is thirty-eight in the first book and about forty in the second. Thereafter, his age is not specified, though in later books, he admits to feeling "old," especially after beatings. Still, Mac is physically tough, a former boxer, and as indestructible

regarding him as "a guy who doesn't work, who just thinks," are eager to consult him.

The Batts series is quite different from Dewey's Mac books. Batts, in the tradition of the genius-detective complete with a "Watson" as narrator, contrasts with fellow Midwesterner Mac, who tells his own stories and is always emotionally involved with his clients. Urban problems, mainly in Chicago and Los Angeles, often form the background for the Mac series. Yet, there are elements in the Batts books that presage the Mac novels.

Hue and Cry has a great deal of action and shows the effect of juvenile delinquency on a small Midwestern town. A Chicago gangster appears in Preston in *As Good As Dead,* a mystery about a beautiful woman who disappeared from there twenty years before. Reviewing the third book about Batts in the 30 July 1950 *The New York Times Book Review,* Anthony Boucher said that in *Mourning After,* Dewey apparently cannot decide "whether he is being influenced by the eccentric characas most private detectives, continuing to investigate even after he is beaten, knifed, or shot. As he says in *Draw the Curtain Close,* "I'm hard to hurt."

In the first book of the series, readers learn that, like so many other private detectives, Mac was an honest cop who quit the police force because of a corrupt administration. He retains one police friend, the veteran homicide detective Donovan, who kids Mac about his idealism, calling him "dreamer," but respects him for his principles. Besides the protagonist, Donovan is the lone recurring character in the series. Other aspects of Mac's code are revealed in the first book, namely that he derives no pleasure from hitting people and will not shoot an unarmed person.

Mac is often hired as a bodyguard, as in *Draw the Curtain Close.* Consistent with his code of not accepting dishonestly made money, he at first refuses a large fee because it is offered by a hoodlum. He eventually does the same work for another client for much less money. As in many of his bodyguard cases, murder forces him to find a killer. The book is nearly as violent as Hammett's *Red Harvest* (1929) as there are twelve deaths, mostly due to a war among gangsters. There is also a much sought after original Gutenberg Bible, reminiscent of the statue Sam Spade hunts in Hammett's *Maltese Falcon* (1930).

In much of his second appearance, *Every Bet's a Sure Thing,* Mac is on a train from Chicago to Los Angeles, trailing a woman and two children and trying to prevent kidnapping, the first of many times he protects children. He ignores personal danger when $75,000 worth of heroin is planted on him. Both Boucher and James Sandoe, the leading mystery critics of the era, commended *Every Bet's a Sure Thing.* Boucher called it "warm and human" in *The New York Times Book Review* and Sandoe thought it the best of Dewey's six books to that time. Though Mac often visits Los Angeles, where Dewey was living, his creator made Chicago his home base. Los Angeles, following the success of Chandler's Philip Marlowe, then had a surfeit of private detectives, while there were few in the Midwest.

Though he grew up in poverty, Mac cares little for money, living in a modest apartment that is part of his office. A novel that shows Mac's typical lack of concern about money is *Prey for Me* (1954), in which he works on a case with little likelihood of remuneration because he feels an obligation to a murdered woman. Although he did not know her, she had his phone number with her when she was killed. In *The Girl Who Wasn't There* (1960), Mac is taken to a hospital emergency room after a beating and has to tell the nurse that he cannot afford treatment because he has no health insurance. *The Girl Who Wasn't There* also contains a good example of Mac's self-deprecation. Although he

asserts "heroism is for heroes" and makes no claim to being a hero, his actions prove otherwise.

In *The Mean Streets* (1955)—the title is taken from a famous phrase in Chandler's essay "The Simple Art of Murder"—Dewey offers a harsh, yet sympathetic picture of teenagers at risk. While working undercover as a high-school teacher and baseball coach, Mac tries to turn around the lives of the young people he meets. Typically, for Dewey it is adults who are responsible for the young being led into lives of crime. Dorothy B. Hughes in the *Albuquerque Tribune* considered it the best account of juvenile delinquency to appear in a mystery. In his review, Boucher said Dewey was the heir to Hammett and Chandler. In the *San Francisco Chronicle* Lenore Glen Offord wrote that Dewey in Mac "combines toughness with integrity as well as it's ever been done."

Dewey did not shun political or social controversy. He showed Mac to be concerned about wiretaps and the possibility of a police state in *The Brave, Bad Girls* (1956) and opposed to McCarthyism in *You've Got Him Cold* (1958) as the detective detests the practice of law enforcement officials trying to turn people into informers. Mac is called "a white knight" in *How Hard to Kill* (1962), a book that clearly shows how his work reflects his philosophy. Dewey's idealistic hero believes that a murder must not go unsolved because it would affect "the structure of civilization."

Most critics consider *A Sad Song Singing* (1963), a book Sandoe classified as "a softboiled-hardboiled" in the 1 September 1963 *Library Journal,* to be Dewey's strongest. Mac's client is a seventeen-year-old girl whose folksinger boyfriend is missing. In this poignant combination of detective story and coming-of-age novel, Dewey takes Mac out of his urban environment and places him in a hostile, rural Midwestern setting. Despite the attractiveness of his naive client, Mac does not become romantically involved and develops what amounts to a father-daughter relationship with her. Consistently throughout the series, Mac follows the code Chandler gave Marlowe of not taking advantage of vulnerable women, especially virgins. *A Sad Song Singing* is another of the books in which Mac's—and Dewey's—political and philosophical beliefs show. Although he is threatened with the loss of his license, Mac tries to protect young beatniks against police brutality. He also stands up for freedom riders and peace marchers.

Most critics, including Boucher, were enthusiastic in their praise of *A Sad Song Singing.* Dorothy B. Hughes called it "a little gem." In *1001 Midnights* (1986) Bill Pronzini calls it Dewey's "masterwork . . . one of the ten best private-eye novels ever written."

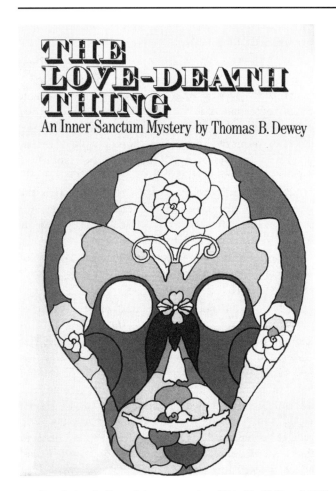

Dust jackets for Dewey's last two novels, published in 1969 and 1970, in which Mac shifts his base of operations from Chicago to Los Angeles

Dewey often was ahead of his time in the themes he explored. Well before the 1980s, when child abuse and incest became common themes in private-detective novels, Dewey had Mac show concern for the young. *Don't Cry for Long* (1964) describes Mac's recurring nightmare of his helplessness as atrocities are committed against children. In practice he does act, in this case trying to prevent the kidnapping of a congressman's teenage daughter. Dewey's sympathy for the young is also present in *Deadline* (1966), which has a downstate Illinois setting and demonstrates there can be as much cruelty in a small town as in Chicago. It is a book of rapidly mounting suspense in which Mac is brought into a case only four days before a scheduled execution. It begins, "Peter Davidian was twenty-two years old. That's young to die." Police homophobia against a gay artist is important to the plot of *Portrait of a Dead Heiress* (1965). Not only is Mac tolerant of homosexuals in this book, but also he seems to favor a woman having the freedom to choose to have an abortion, an illegal act at the time. The gynecologist who performed the opera-

tion is pursued by a dishonest policeman. Almost thirty years before the bombing in Oklahoma City gave militias prominence, Dewey had Mac battle a right-wing extremist group, one with its own military training camp, in *The King Killers* (1968).

Dewey wrote few short stories. He did not publish any in the pulp magazines and wrote only a handful for digest-sized magazines, too few for a collection. However, his only Mac short story, "The Big Job," originally published in the December 1965 issue of *The Saint Magazine,* was chosen by Boucher for inclusion in *The Best Detective Stories of the Year* (1966). Dewey also edited two Mystery Writers of America anthologies of short stories during the 1960s: *A Pride of Felons* (1963) and *Sleuths and Consequences* (1966).

The last of Dewey's nonseries paperback original books, *A Season for Violence* (1966), was published by Fawcett Gold Medal, the quintessential publisher of hard-boiled books. Dewey's sexiest book, it is set during a steamy summer in a fictional Midwestern city. The trial of the son of one of the town's wealthiest families for rape leads to extortion and murder. Dewey reveals the immorality of the town's leaders, including their drug use and extramarital affairs, in the manner of the 1957 movie *Peyton Place*.

The last two Mac books bring the detective to Los Angeles. He is hired to find a runaway teenage girl in *The Love-Death Thing* (1969), one of many private-detective novels of the time about missing "flower children." Dewey is sympathetic toward them and also perceptive regarding the convergence of two distinct cultures in that city's Fairfax Avenue district, where elderly Jews coexist with the newly arrived hippies. Mac moves to Los Angeles permanently in *The Taurus Trip* (1970), Dewey's last book and one with such expected components of the Southern California scene as movie stars, an astrologer, and gangsters.

When Dewey's longtime publisher, Simon and Schuster, declined to publish the last mystery he wrote, he decided to turn to his father's profession of teaching. He became assistant professor of English at Arizona State University in Tempe in 1971. In 1973 he obtained a Ph.D. from the University of California at Los Angeles. Dewey taught at Tempe until he retired in 1977. He died on 22 April 1981.

Despite good reviews and though most of his hardcover books eventually were reprinted in paperback, Dewey never achieved great renown or financial success. His books have been out of print since 1985, which seems consistent with Robin Winks in *Detective Fiction* (1988) having listed him with writers who won "ephemeral success but were destined to be forgotten."

Yet, other knowledgeable critics believe that Dewey deserves greater acclaim. Major 1985 works about private-detective fiction, *The American Private Eye: The Image in Fiction* by David Geherin and *Private Eyes: 101 Knights: A Survey of American Dectective Fiction 1922–1984* by Robert A. Baker and Michael T. Nietzel, devote considerable space to Dewey and Mac, stressing the detective's professionalism, humanity, and believability. Pronzini readily acknowledges Dewey's influence in the creation of his own nameless detective and considers Mac the best fictional private detective of them all. In his *Encyclopedia Mysterioso* (1994), William L. De Andrea called Dewey "one of the more mystifyingly underrated writers in the mystery genre." In his *A Reader's Guide to the Private Eye Novel* (1993), Gary Warren Niebuhr selected three Dewey books on his list of "One Hundred Classics and Highly Recommended Titles."

References:

Robert A. Baker and Michael T. Nietzel, "Mac Robinson–Thomas B. Dewey," in their *Private Eyes: 101 Knights: A Survey of American Detective Fiction 1922–1984* (Bowling Green, Ohio: Bowling Green University Popular Press, 1985), pp. 80–83;

David Geherin, "Mac," in his *The American Private Eye: The Image in Fiction* (New York: Ungar, 1985), pp. 140–147.

Papers:

Thomas B. Dewey's manuscripts are in the Mugar Memorial Library, Boston University.

Davis Dresser
(Brett Halliday)
(31 July 1904 – 4 February 1977)

Anita G. Gorman
Slippery Rock University

BOOKS: *Mardi Gras Madness,* as Anthony Scott (New York: Godwin, 1934);

Test of Virtue, as Scott (New York: Godwin, 1934);

Writing The Sex Novel 1934–35 Model, pamphlet, as Eliot Storm and Anthony Scott (N.p.: Privately printed, 1934);

Love Is a Masquerade, as Kathryn Culver (New York: Phoenix, 1935);

Ten Toes Up, as Scott (New York: Godwin, 1935);

Virgin's Holiday, as Scott (New York: Godwin, 1935);

The Feminine Touch, as Culver (New York: Phoenix, 1936);

Ladies of Chance, as Scott (New York: Godwin, 1936);

Satan Rules the Night, as Scott (New York: Godwin, 1936);

Stolen Sins, as Scott (New York: Godwin, 1936);

Let's Laugh at Love, as Davis Dresser (New York: Hillman-Curl, 1937);

Million Dollar Madness, as Culver (New York: Hillman-Curl, 1937);

Too Smart for Love, as Culver (New York: Hillman-Curl, 1937);

Green Path to the Moon, as Culver (New York: Hillman-Curl, 1938);

One Reckless Night, as Peter Shelley (New York: Godwin, 1938);

Mum's the Word for Murder, as Asa Baker (New York: Stokes, 1938; London: Gollancz, 1939);

Once to Every Woman, as Culver (New York: Godwin, 1938);

Romance for Julie, as Dresser (New York: Hillman-Curl, 1938);

Temptation, as Scott (New York: Godwin, 1938);

Too Many Finances, as Culver (New York: Hillman-Curl, 1938);

Dividend on Death, as Brett Halliday (New York: Holt, 1939; London: Jarrolds, 1941);

Girl Alone, as Culver (New York: Gramercy, 1939);

The Kissed Corpse, as Baker (New York: Carlyle, 1939);

Death on Treasure Trail, as Don Davis (London: Hutchinson, 1940; New York: Morrow, 1941);

Davis Dresser at the time of Shoot to Kill *(1964)*

Death Rides the Pecos, as Dresser, edited, with an introduction, by Erle Stanley Gardner (New York: Morrow, 1940; London: Ward, Lock, 1940);

The Hangmen of Sleepy Valley, as Dresser (New York: Morrow, 1940); republished as *The Masked Riders of Sleepy Valley* (London: Ward, Lock, 1941);

The Private Practice of Michael Shayne, as Halliday (New York: Holt, 1940; London: Jarrolds, 1941);

Return of the Rio Kid, as Davis (New York: Morrow, 1940; London: Ward, Lock, 1940);

The Uncomplaining Corpses, as Halliday (New York: Holt, 1940; London: Jarrolds, 1942);

Bodies Are Where You Find Them, as Halliday (New York: Holt, 1941);

Guns from Powder Valley, as Peter Field (New York: Morrow, 1941);

Gun Smoke on the Mesa, as Dresser (New York: Carlton, 1941; London: Ward, Lock, 1941);

Lynch-Rope Law, as Dresser (New York: Morrow, 1941; London: Ward, Lock, 1942);

Rio Kid Justice, as Davis (New York: Morrow, 1941);

Tickets for Death, as Halliday (New York: Holt, 1941; London: Jarrolds, 1942);

Two-Gun Rio Kid, as Davis (New York: Morrow, 1941);

The Corpse Came Calling, as Halliday (New York: Dodd, Mead, 1942); abridged as *The Case of the Walking Corpse* (New York: Quinn, 1943);

Fight for Powder Valley, as Field (New York: Morrow, 1942); republished as *The Land Grabber* (New York: Bantam, 1949);

Law Man of Powder Valley, as Field (New York: Morrow, 1942);

Trail South from Powder Valley, as Field (New York: Morrow, 1942);

Blood on the Black Market, as Halliday (New York: Dodd, Mead, 1943); republished as *Heads You Lose,* foreword by Halliday (New York: Dodd, Mead, 1956);

Murder Wears a Mummer's Mask, as Halliday (New York: Dodd, Mead, 1943); republished as *In a Deadly Vein* (New York: Dell, 1956; London: Mayflower, 1964);

Powder Valley Vengeance, as Field (New York: Morrow, 1943);

Sheriff on the Spot, as Field (New York: Morrow, 1943);

Death Rides the Night, as Field (New York: Jefferson House, 1944);

Michael Shayne's Long Chance, as Halliday (New York: Dell, 1944; London: Jarrolds, 1945);

Midnight Round-up, as Field (New York: Jefferson House, 1944);

Murder and the Married Virgin, as Halliday (New York: Dodd, Mead, 1944; London: Jarrolds, 1946);

The Smoking Iron, as Field (New York: Morrow, 1944);

Dead Man's Diary and Dinner at Dupre's, as Halliday (New York: Dell, 1945);

The End of the Trail, as Field (New York: Jefferson House, 1945);

Marked for Murder, as Halliday (New York: Dodd, Mead, 1945; London: Jarrolds, 1950);

Murder Is My Business, as Halliday (New York: Dodd, Mead, 1945; London: Jarrolds, 1945);

The Road to Laramie, as Field (New York: Jefferson House, 1945);

Blood on Biscayne Bay, as Halliday (Chicago: Ziff-Davis, 1946; London: Jarrolds, 1950);

Powder Valley Showdown, as Field (New York: Jefferson House, 1946);

Counterfeit Wife, as Halliday (Chicago: Ziff-Davis, 1947; London: Jarrolds, 1950);

Blood on the Stars, as Halliday (New York: Dodd, Mead, 1948); republished as *Murder is a Habit* (London: Jarrolds, 1951);

Before I Wake, by Dresser and Kathleen Rollins, as Hal Debrett (New York: Dodd, Mead, 1949; London: Jarrolds, 1953);

Call for Michael Shayne, as Halliday (New York: Dodd, Mead, 1949; London: Jarrolds, 1951);

A Taste for Violence, as Halliday (New York: Dodd, Mead, 1949; London: Jarrolds, 1952);

A Lonely Way to Die, by Dresser and Rollins, as Debrett (New York: Dodd, Mead, 1950);

This Is It, Michael Shayne, as Halliday (New York: Dodd, Mead, 1950; London: Jarrolds, 1952);

Framed in Blood, as Halliday (New York: Dodd, Mead, 1951; London: Jarrolds, 1953);

When Dorinda Dances, as Halliday (New York: Dodd, Mead, 1951; London: Jarrolds, 1953);

The Avenger, by Dresser and Ryerson Johnson, as Matthew Blood (New York: Fawcett, 1952);

Charlie Dell, as Anderson Wayne (New York: Coward-McCann, 1952; London: Hale, 1953); republished as *A Time to Remember* (New York: Popular Library, 1959);

What Really Happened, as Halliday (New York: Dodd, Mead, 1952; London: Jarrolds, 1953);

Murder on the Mesa, as Dresser (London: Ward, Lock, 1953);

One Night With Nora, as Halliday (New York: Dodd, Mead, 1953; London: Mayflower, 1968); republished as *The Lady Came by Night* (London: Jarrolds, 1954);

Death Is a Lovely Dame, by Dresser and Johnson, as Blood (New York: Fawcett, 1954);

She Woke to Darkness, as Halliday (New York: Torquil, 1954; London: Jarrolds, 1955);

Death Has Three Lives, as Halliday (New York: Torquil, 1955; London: Jarrolds, 1955);

Stranger in Town, as Halliday (New York: Torquil, 1955; London: Jarrolds, 1956);

The Blonde Cried Murder, as Halliday (New York: Torquil, 1956; London: Jarrolds, 1957);

Shoot the Works, as Halliday (New York: Torquil, 1957; London: John Long, 1958);

Weep for a Blonde, as Halliday (New York: Torquil, 1957; London: John Long, 1958);

Murder and the Wanton Bride, as Halliday (New York: Torquil, 1958; London: John Long, 1959);

Date With a Dead Man, as Halliday (New York: Torquil, 1958; London: John Long, 1960);

Fit to Kill, as Halliday (New York: Torquil, 1958);

Die Like a Dog, as Halliday (New York: Torquil, 1959; London: John Long, 1961);

Target: Mike Shayne, as Halliday (New York: Torquil, 1959; London: John Long, 1960);

Dolls Are Deadly, as Halliday (New York: Torquil, 1960);

The Homicidal Virgin, as Halliday (New York: Torquil, 1960; London: Mayflower, 1963);

Murder Takes No Holiday, as Halliday (New York: Torquil, 1960);

The Careless Corpse, as Halliday (New York: Torquil, 1961);

Killer From the Keys, as Halliday (New York: Torquil, 1961);

Murder in Haste, as Halliday (New York: Torquil, 1961; London: Mayflower, 1963);

Murder by Proxy, as Halliday (New York: Torquil, 1962; London: Mayflower, 1968);

Never Kill a Client, as Halliday (New York: Torquil, 1962);

Pay-Off in Blood, as Halliday (New York: Torquil, 1962);

Too Friendly, Too Dead, as Halliday (New York: Torquil, 1963; London: Mayflower, 1964);

The Body Came Back, by Halliday (New York: Torquil, 1963);

The Corpse That Never Was, by Halliday (New York: Torquil, 1963);

A Redhead for Mike Shayne, as Halliday (New York: Torquil, 1964);

Shoot to Kill, as Halliday (New York: Torquil, 1964);

Michael Shayne's 50th Case, as Halliday (New York: Torquil, 1964).

Collections: *Michael Shayne Takes Over,* as Halliday (New York: Holt, 1941; London: Jarrolds, 1944)—comprises *Dividend on Death, The Private Practice of Michael Shayne, The Uncomplaining Corpses,* and *Bodies Are Where You Find Them;*

Michael Shayne Investigates, as Halliday (London: Jarrolds, 1943)—comprises *Bodies Are Where You Find Them* and *The Corpse Came Calling;*

Michael Shayne Takes a Hand, as Halliday (London: Jarrolds, 1944)—comprises *Murder Wears a Mummer's Mask* and *Blood on the Black Market;*

Michael Shayne's Triple Mystery, as Halliday (Chicago: Ziff-Davis, 1948)—comprises *Dead Man's Diary, A Taste for Cognac,* and *Dinner at Dupre's.*

OTHER: "The Million-dollar Motive," as Halliday, in *Murder Cavalcade,* edited by Ken Crossen (New York: Duell, 1946; London: Hammond, 1953), pp. 289–305;

"1910—Murder at the Brown Palace," as Halliday, in *Denver Murders,* edited by Lee Casey (New York: Duell, Sloan & Pearce, 1946);

"Human Interest Stuff," as Halliday, in *Ellery Queen's Murder by Experts* (Chicago: Ziff-Davis, 1947; London: Sampson, Low, 1950), pp. 17–29;

"Extradition," as Halliday, in *The Queen's Awards, 1948: The Winners of the Third Annual Detective Short-Story Contest Sponsored by Ellery Queen's Mystery Magazine,* edited by Ellery Queen (Boston: Little, Brown, 1948; London: Gollancz, 1950), pp. 162–178;

"Michael Shayne As I Know Him," in *Four & Twenty Bloodhounds,* edited by Anthony Boucher (New York: Simon & Schuster, 1950), pp. 321–327;

"You Killed Elizabeth," as Halliday, in *20 Great Tales of Murder By Experts of the Mystery Writers of America,* edited by Halliday and Helen McCloy (New York: Random House, 1951; London: Hammond, 1952), pp. 79–97;

Dangerous Dames, edited by Halliday (New York: Dell, 1955);

"Dead Man's Code," as Halliday, in *Crime for Two,* edited by Frances and Richard Lockridge (Philadelphia: Lippincott, 1955), pp. 125–136;

Big Time Mysteries, edited by Halliday (New York: Dodd, Mead, 1958);

The Second Book of Crime-Craft: A Selection from 20 Great Tales of Murder, edited by Halliday and McCloy (London: Transworld, 1958);

Murder in Miami, edited by Halliday (New York: Dodd, Mead, 1959);

"Death Goes to the Post," as Halliday, in *Dames, Danger, Death,* edited by Leo Margulies (New York: Pyramid, 1960), pp. 64–91;

Murder, Murder, Murder, edited by Dresser and McCloy (New York: Hillman-Curl, 1961);

Best Detective Stories of the Year: 16th [and 17th] *Annual Collection,* edited by Halliday, 2 volumes (New York: Dutton, 1961–1962);

"Pieces of Silver," as Halliday, in *Alfred Hitchcock Presents Stories for Late at Night,* edited by Hitchcock (New York: Random House, 1961), pp. 141–153;

"I'm Tough," as Dresser, in *Best Detective Stories of the Year,* edited by Halliday (New York: Dutton, 1962), pp. 115–118;

"Michael Shayne," as Halliday, in *The Great Detectives: A Host of the World's Most Celebrated Sleuths Are Unmasked by Their Authors,* edited by Otto Penzler (Boston: Little, Brown, 1978), pp. 217–225.

SELECTED PERIODICAL PUBLICATIONS—
UNCOLLECTED: "Big Shot," as Dresser, *Argosy* 285 (1938): 61–69; republished, as Halliday, *Ellery Queen's Mystery Magazine,* 10 (August 1947): 36–47;

"Murder Before Midnight," as Halliday, *Popular Detective*,
38 (March 1950): 11–36;

"Women Are Poison," as Halliday, *The Saint* (November
1954);

"The Reluctant Client," as Halliday, *Manhunt*, 3 (June
1955): 1–10;

"Not Tonight Danger," *Ellery Queen's Mystery Magazine* (September 1957);

"Second Honeymoon," *Ellery Queen's Mystery Magazine*, 34
(July 1959): 11–25;

"Florida's Case of Judge Chillingworth," as Halliday, *Official Detective Stories* (January 1961): 8–11.

A prolific author, Davis Dresser wrote more than
seventy romance, western, and mystery novels and dozens
of short stories under his own name as well as under the
pseudonyms Brett Halliday, Anthony Scott, Kathryn Culver, Asa Baker, Don Davis, Matthew Blood, Peter Shelley,
Sylvia Carson, Anderson Wayne, Peter Field, Eliot Storm,
Jerome Shard, Christopher Shayne, and Hal Debrett (a
joint pseudonym with his first wife, Kathleen Rollins).
Under his best-known pen name, Brett Halliday, Dresser
wrote nearly fifty novels and created Mike Shayne, one of
the most popular fictional dectectives, who debuted in the
1939 novel *Dividend on Death*. Although Dresser stopped
writing Mike Shayne mysteries in the 1960s, stories and
novels continued to be written by other authors using the
Halliday name. The rough and likable Shayne is Dresser's
most important contribution to hard-boiled fiction.

Davis Dresser was born in Chicago on 31 July
1904 to William Justus Dresser, an accountant, and his
wife, the former Mary Davis, a homemaker. When
Dresser was five years old, the family moved to a ranch
in the vicinity of Monahans, in west Texas. Here Dresser
learned to ride horses and gained the knowledge and
interest that provided him with the background for the
westerns he later wrote. Here, too, Dresser suffered a
serious injury when a horse threw him onto a barbed
wire fence; for the rest of his life, his eyesight in one eye
virtually gone, he had to wear a patch to prevent persistent headaches caused by sunlight.

At the age of fourteen and before he donned the eye
patch, Dresser joined the U.S. Army; as the story is usually told, he served as a member of the cavalry at Fort Bliss
in El Paso, riding with General John Joseph Pershing in
pursuit of Pancho Villa; however, Dresser's widow, Mary
Dresser, asserts that he actually served in the border patrol
along the Rio Grande, a stint he later described as boring.
Two years later, his age having been discovered, Dresser
was discharged from the army. After finishing high school,
he set out in search of adventure, working as a mule skinner in construction camps, digging graves, and laboring in
the oil fields of the southwestern United States and Mexico. On 2 October 1923 Dresser entered Tri-State College

(now University) in Angola, Indiana, to study civil engineering, attending the school until 1925. According to university records, he did not graduate, although most
references state that he earned a certificate of civil engineering. He then traveled and worked as a surveyor and
engineer, settling in Miami because of its climate. He
began his writing career in 1927 but did not have much
success for several years.

Dresser's first published novel was *Mardi Gras Madness* (1934), which he wrote as Anthony Scott, one of several pseudonyms he used during the 1930s. As Kathryn
Culver, Dresser wrote eight romances, all aimed at a
female audience, including *Million Dollar Madness* (1937), in
which the hero, Rodney Burton, learns that he will inherit
one million dollars if he reaches his twenty-fifth birthday
"without having committed the tragic folly of entering into
the state of matrimony before that date." Burton at first
believes that his marriage, which occurs on his twenty-fifth
birthday, disqualifies him from the inheritance, but he later
realizes that because of the difference in time zones, he can
still claim the money. Dresser himself was married for the
first time in 1934, to writer Kathleen Rollins.

Dresser tried his hand at detective fiction during the
1930s and entered the Dodd, Mead Red Badge mystery
writing contest; although he did not win, he finally found
a publisher for *Mum's the Word for Murder* (1938), which was
published under the name Asa Baker, a name he also used
for the 1939 novel, *The Kissed Corpse*. In both stories, Asa
Baker begins his first-person narration with a reference to
writer's block, a condition soon relieved by Baker's
encounter with detective Jerry Burke. In *Mum's the Word for
Murder* would-be killers plot "that each do the job for one
of the others . . . each proposing to commit an *unmotivated
murder* as the price of having his victim done in." A variation of this plot was used by Patricia Highsmith for her
1950 novel, *Strangers on a Train,* the basis for Alfred Hitchcock's 1951 movie.

Although he wrote *Dividend on Death* in 1935, it took
Dresser four years to get it published; the book was
rejected by at least twenty publishers who regarded
hard-boiled detectives as passé. As a tribute to Henry Holt
editor Brett Stokes, who thought the novel promising,
Dresser adopted "Brett" as the first name of his pseudonym, Brett Halliday, which he used for the first time
when the novel was finally published. The origin of the
surname is unknown. In the late 1930s Dresser wrote
some crime stories as Halliday that were about construction crews laboring along the Mexican border. These stories, dubbed Dresser's "engineering stories" by Ellery
Queen, have become collectors' items. Included in this
group are the often anthologized "Human Interest Stuff,"
originally published in the September 1938 issue of *Adventure,* and "Extradition," which won second prize in a contest sponsored by *Ellery Queen's Mystery Magazine*.

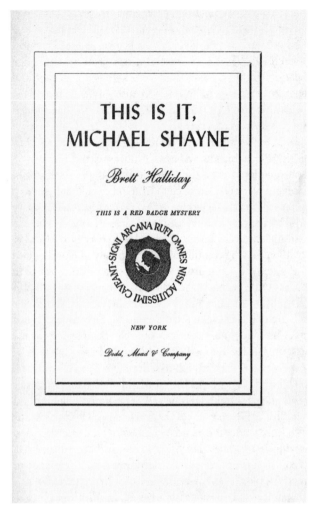

*Title page for a 1950 novel about Dresser's most popular
character, written under his best-known pseudonym*

Dividend on Death introduces Michael Shayne, a likable, virile, smart private investigator who drinks cognac at any hour of the day and uses his head and sometimes his fists more than his gun. Though essentially moral, Shayne flirts with illegality in order to determine guilt and apprehend criminals. Dresser's protagonist, who tugs at his earlobe when he is deep in thought, is physically distinctive:

> He had a tall angular body that concealed a lot of solid weight, and his freckled cheeks were thin to gauntness. His rumpled hair was violently red, giving him a little-boy look curiously in contrast with the harshness of his features. When he smiled, the harshness went out of his face and he didn't look at all like a hard-boiled private detective who had come to the top the tough way.

Dividend on Death also introduces characters who reappear in subsequent novels: Will Gentry, "a stolid, persevering

man who ran the Miami detective bureau as it had been run for thirty years"; Peter Painter, the recently appointed chief of the Miami Beach detective bureau, whose fancy Palm Beach suit, Panama hat, and "narrow line of a beautifully trimmed and exceedingly black mustache" mark him as an adversary of the rough-and-tumble Shayne; and the beautiful Phyllis Brighton, who initiates the plot by telling Shayne that she fears she will kill her own mother.

Dividend on Death presents a complicated story of murder, impersonation, art forgery, and theft, with Freudian theory served up by the malevolent Dr. Joel Pedique, who says of his patient Phyllis Brighton that she "'is subject to certain . . . ah . . . hallucinations, I may call them in non-technical terms, stimulated by a violent sexual oestrus and marked by unmistakable symptoms of an Electra complex.'" Shayne solves the crime via his wits, his brawn, his courage, and his attractiveness to women. At the end of the novel, Shayne, having solved multiple related crimes, kisses Phyllis Brighton good-bye, and the novel ends on a melancholy note: "Something new had come into his life . . . and gone out of it." As he reads the list of his cash receipts, the "muted beat of evening traffic drifted up from the street below and into the room through an open window. The sound was not unlike the rumble of a distant drum, but Shayne's mind was occupied with other things and he paid no heed to it."

Commenting on the first Halliday novel, Wolfgang Saxon, the writer of Dresser's obituary in *The New York Times* of 6 February 1977, asserted that the "fast-paced world of violence, intrigues, complex twists and voluptuous women assured the author of a wide readership for many years." Saxon's retrospective remarks contrast somewhat with contemporary reviewer Kay Irvin, who faulted the disjointed structure of the lively story in *The New York Times* of 1 October 1939: "Since Michael Shane [*sic*] manages to be a not wholly unlikable figure, it seems possible that Brett Halliday may become popular with readers whose first demand is for nonchalant rough stuff. But he is an inexpert story-teller. His plot breaks in two."

The second Shayne novel, *The Private Practice of Michael Shayne* (1940), also featuring the nasty Peter Painter and the affable Will Gentry, introduces Shayne's friend, newspaper reporter Tim Rourke. The first Shayne book to achieve some popularity with the reading public, *The Private Practice of Michael Shayne* focuses on greed and includes prominent Miami citizens who demonstrate the seaminess of urban life, a city councilman who runs a crooked gambling hall, and a killer who has fixed a horse race; Shayne's actions, in contrast, show his essential loyalty and integrity, despite his creative tampering with evidence. Isaac Anderson in *The New York Times* of 11 February 1940 wrote that "the story here recorded is packed with thrills, quick thinking and quicker action"; the reviewer for *The Saturday Review of Literature* (10 February 1940) considered it "vividly depicted." Certainly, Dresser's second Shayne novel shows a greater command of plot, coherence, and style. In this suspenseful tale, Shayne continues to be suspected by the hapless Peter Painter and continues to court Phyllis Brighton, who returns as the detective's wife in the third Shayne novel, *The Uncomplaining Corpses* (1940), a story that elicited a negative comment in *The New York Times* (25 August 1940): "Michael Shayne gets results, but he is no shining example to hold up to the youth of our land. Perhaps we are old-fashioned, but we do admit to a preference for detectives who play the game according to the rules."

Other Shayne books followed regularly, with *Bodies Are Where You Find Them* (1941), *Tickets for Death* (1941), *The Corpse Came Calling* (1942), *Blood on the Black Market* (1943), *Murder Wears a Mummer's Mask* (1943), *Michael Shayne's Long Chance* (1944), and *Murder and the Married Virgin* (1944) rounding out the first ten books of the series. In *Blood on the Black Market,* Phyllis is dead; not until three years later in *Blood on Biscayne Bay* does Dresser reveal that she died in childbirth along with their baby. According to the novelist, he killed off Phyllis because 20th Century-Fox did not care for a married detective. The role of romantic interest was later assumed by Shayne's secretary, Lucy Hamilton, a woman first encountered in *Michael Shayne's Long Chance.* As he was developing the Mike Shayne series, Dresser was also under contract with Morrow to write further novels in the Peter Field series of Powder Valley Westerns, written previously by Harry Sinclair Drago; after 1946, he focused primarily on the Shayne novels, which were becoming increasingly popular.

The Shayne novels usually take place in Miami, where Dresser lived until 1939, when he moved to Colorado. *Murder Wears a Mummer's Mask* (1943) takes place in Central City, Colorado, during its frontier festival. He also used other locales, including New Orleans, the setting for such books as *Mike Shayne's Long Chance* (1944), *Murder and the Married Virgin* (1944), and *Murder Is My Business* (1945). Perhaps the idealism and heroism promoted during the war years influenced Dresser's treatment of his gruff, profit-seeking detective. In *Blood on the Black Market,* Dresser appeals to the patriotism of wartime readers as Mike Shayne exposes the bootlegging of rationed gasoline. In *Murder Is My Business* (1945), which deals with drug trafficking and AWOL soldiers crossing into Mexico, Mike Shayne agrees to look into the death of a soldier even though his mother is too poor to pay for the investigation. *A Taste for Violence* (1949) shows Shayne taking on police corruption and unfair labor practices in a Kentucky mining town.

The popularity of the Michael Shayne character led to his turning up in twelve "B" movies and in a radio serial in the 1940s. Seven movies were produced by 20th Century-Fox, all starring Lloyd Nolan: *Michael Shayne, Private*

Detective (1940), *Sleepers West* (1941), *Dressed to Kill* (1941), *Blue, White, and Perfect* (1941), *The Man Who Wouldn't Die* (1942), *Just Off Broadway* (1942), and *Time to Kill* (1942). Only the first was based on a Halliday novel. *Time to Kill,* in fact, was based on Raymond Chandler's *The High Window* (1942). Hugh Beaumont starred as Mike Shayne in five films in the latter half of the 1940s: *Murder Is My Business* (1946), *Larceny in Her Heart* (1946), *Blonde for a Day* (1946), *Three on a Ticket* (1947), and *Too Many Winners* (1947). Of the Beaumont movies, only the last was based on a Halliday novel (*Tickets for Death*). A Michael Shayne radio series debuted in October 1944 via the Don Lee Network. Starting in 1946, Shayne stories were broadcast on the Mutual Network; the series was later syndicated by the Don Sharpe organization. The radio series, which ended in 1952, starred Wally Maher, Robert Sterling, and Jeff Chandler. Dresser did not participate directly in the writing of any of these projects.

In "Michael Shayne As I Know Him," an essay he wrote as Brett Halliday for Anthony Boucher's *Four and Twenty Bloodhounds* (1950), Dresser asserts that the hero was based on a man he met while employed on an oil tanker in Mexico. As the story goes, Dresser went ashore at Tampico, stopping at a bar filled with knife-wielding Mexicans hostile to American sailors. The only other American in the bar, a large red-haired man drinking tequila, helped Dresser escape, and the novelist never forgot his rescuer. Some time later Dresser saw the same man drinking cognac in a New Orleans tavern. The man admitted he was a private investigator and then abruptly told Dresser to leave; two thugs entered, and Dresser saw the detective depart with them. That same evening, Dresser decided to write a novel featuring a redheaded private investigator named Michael Shayne.

In his essay Dresser reveals that after he told this story on a Denver radio program, the "real" Mike Shayne "turned up one day" in a cabin near Dresser's on the Gunnison River in western Colorado. He supposedly became Dresser's friend from then on. Dresser writes, "From small things he has let slip out since then, I believe he had heard about the radio broadcast and, being in the neighborhood, had taken the trouble to look me up out of curiosity." Dresser recounts his subsequent friendship with Shayne, Shayne's marriage (with Dresser acting as best man), his wife's death, and Shayne's later relationship with his secretary. Dresser alludes to the "subtle change in Mike's inner character" after his wife's death: "the hard outer shell of assumed cynicism was cracked, and for the first time in his life he wasn't afraid to let traces of gentleness and pity shine through." Dresser praises Shayne's determination, his "logical mind which refuses to be sidetracked," his "lack of personal concern." Whether any of these biographical details is

Dust jackets for two of Dresser's Shayne novels, published in 1959 and 1964, respectively

based on truth cannot be determined, and much of the story of Dresser's encounter with the detective seems an entertaining fabrication designed by the author to heighten interest in his detective hero.

Dresser wrote the Shayne novels in a straightforward style, using third-person narration, with realistic dialogue and concise, concrete descriptions. The opening of *This Is It, Michael Shayne* (1950), one of seventeen Shayne novels Dresser wrote in the 1950s, provides a good example:

> Michael Shayne stepped from the deep-sea fishing boat onto the wharf and walked toward his parked car with a rolling motion of his rangy body. Since early morning he had ridden the ocean swells under a clear sky, and now his face tingled with the cool night breeze on sunburned skin, and his eyes were drowsy from strain and the glare of bright sunlight on the water. He felt stretchy and yawny, luxuriously relaxed after a day of good-fellowship combined with moderate amounts of aged liquor, and a fair day's catch.

In *Twentieth Century Crime and Mystery Writers* (1991) Dennis Lynds, who wrote more than eighty Shayne novellas under the Halliday pseudonym for the *Mike Shayne Mystery Magazine* in the 1960s, asserts that Dresser "knew that his audience did not want literary style, or unique plot, or dazzling psychology–they wanted to see their hero in action." In an unpublished essay the writer Helen McCloy, Dresser's second wife, to whom he was married from 1946 until 1961, reveals that her husband usually spent one or two months working out a story in his mind, "making only a few notes on any handy scrap of paper, usually an old envelope." With two fingers he typed out a chapter a day, never employing a typist, never revising, and never missing a deadline.

In one of the more unusual novels in the series, *She Woke to Darkness* (1954), Dresser makes author Brett Halliday the suspect for the murder of a young woman encountered at the annual dinner of the Mystery Writers of America (MWA) in New York City. Halliday, of course, asks for and gets Mike Shayne's help in solving the mystery. The device of using actual MWA members as characters in detective fiction was first used, according to Bill Pronzini in *Gun in Check: A Study of Alternative Crime Fiction* (1982), three years before the Halliday endeavor, in Carl H. Hodges's *Naked Villainy* (1951). *She Woke to Darkness* was the first novel published by the Torquil Publishing Company, which Dresser owned. After his divorce from McCloy in 1961, he married another writer, Mary Savage, that same year.

The popularity of the Shayne character continued through the 1950s and 1960s. In 1956 Dresser and Leo Margulies founded the *Michael Shayne Mystery Magazine* (the name was later changed to *Mike Shayne Mystery Magazine*), which started appearing on newsstands in September of that year. Dresser served as the first editor of the publication, which ran until August 1985, eight years after Dresser's death. Although each magazine contained a Mike Shayne story, it is impossible to determine the authorship of all the stories, and it is likely that Dresser did not write many of them. In 1960–1961, a television series starring Richard Denning as Mike Shayne was broadcast and later syndicated by the Don Sharpe organization; thirty-two hour-long shows were made. Unhappy with the series, Dresser vociferously called it a travesty of his work, and his opposition was an important factor in its termination.

Dresser wrote most of the Michael Shayne novels until 1965, occcasionally purchasing plots from other writers. According to Jacques Barzun and Wendell Hertig Taylor in *A Catalogue of Crime* (1989), Dresser's plots were "complicated but often adroitly worked out." Anthony Boucher credits Dresser with providing adequate clues for the astute reader. Bernard Drew in his 1980 essay "The Mike Shayne Caper" quotes Halliday ghostwriter Robert Terrall, who declares that there are two types of heroes, the "strong, valiant Achilles and the wily, crafty Odysseus," and believes that Mike Shayne embodies both types.

After Dresser stopped writing Shayne novels, the writers who continued to use the Mike Shayne character and the Brett Halliday byline carefully constructed a character consistent with the detective of the earlier novels written by Dresser. A "Mike Shayne Bible," a typescript from Charles E. Fritch, editor of *Mike Shayne Mystery Magazine,* provided writers with data about Shayne, for example, his "coarse, stubby, unruly red hair," the scar on his left shoulder, personal characteristics ("a simple, logical guy" who tells the truth), and idiosyncratic behavior (he likes "rubbing the lobe of his left ear" and "scraping his thumbnail along the harsh reddish stubble on his jawline"). After November 1982, the Mike Shayne stories that began each issue of *Mike Shayne Mystery Magazine* were written by two English professors at Eastern Kentucky University, Hal Blythe and Charlie Sweet, who together have used the

pseudonym Hal Charles but who use the name Brett Halliday when writing Mike Shayne stories and novels. Although some earlier ghostwriters erred on occasion, the later team of Sweet and Blythe were meticulous in their reincarnation of the Shayne character.

Davis Dresser died of cancer on 4 February 1977 at his home in Montecito, California, near Santa Barbara, where he moved in 1961. He was survived by his wife, Mary; a son, Halliday (by his third wife); and a daughter, Chloe Dresser Peck (by his second wife). "Michael Shayne," a second essay by Dresser that treats the detective as a real person, appears under the Halliday name in Otto Penzler's *The Great Detectives* (1978); here Dresser sums up much of the appeal of the redheaded sleuth: "He has no special or esoteric knowledges [*sic*] to help him solve his cases. A reader can identify with him because he is an ordinary guy like the reader himself. He solves his cases by using plain common sense and a lot of perseverance, and absolute fearlessness."

References:

Robert A. Baker and Michael T. Nietzel, "The Prolific Knight: Michael Shayne–Brett Halliday (Davis Dresser)," in their *Private Eyes: One Hundred and One Knights: A Survey of American Detective Fiction, 1922–1984* (Bowling Green, Ohio: Bowling Green State University Popular Press, 1985), pp. 94–98;

Bernard A. Drew, "The Mike Shayne Caper," *Paperback Quarterly,* 3, no. 1 (1980): 51–56;

William K. Everson, "The Private Eyes: 2. Marlowe to Klute," in his *The Detective in Film* (Secaucus, N.Y.: Citadel, 1972), pp. 221–222;

David Geherin, "Mike Shayne," in his *The American Private Eye: The Image in Fiction* (New York: Ungar, 1985), pp. 84–92;

Michael R. Pitts, "Michael Shayne," in his *Famous Movie Detectives,* volume 1 (Metuchen, N.J.: Scarecrow Press, 1979), pp. 183–194;

Bonnie Plummer, "Writing Under a House Name: Brett Halliday," *Clues: A Journal of Detection,* 7 (Fall–Winter 1986): 39–47;

William Ruehlmann, "The Far Side of the Brave New World," in his *Saint With A Gun: The Unlawful American Private Eye* (New York: New York University Press, 1984), pp. 105–131;

John Tuska, "Detective Series in the Forties," in his *The Detective in Hollywood* (Garden City, N.Y.: Doubleday, 1978), pp. 255–264;

Tuska, "Michael Shayne," in his *In Manors and Alleys: A Casebook on the American Detective Film* (New York: Greenwood Press, 1988), pp. 318–332.

Papers:

Davis Dresser's papers are at Boston University.

James Ellroy
(4 March 1948 –)

Katherine M. Restaino
Fairleigh Dickinson University

BOOKS: *Brown's Requiem* (New York: Avon, 1981; London: Allison & Busby, 1984);

Clandestine (New York: Avon, 1982; London: Allison & Busby, 1984);

Blood on the Moon (New York: Mysterious Press, 1984; London: Allison & Busby, 1985);

Because the Night (New York: Mysterious Press, 1985; London: Century Hutchinson, 1987);

Suicide Hill (New York: Mysterious Press, 1986);

Silent Terror (New York: Avon, 1986); republished as *Killer on the Road* (New York: Avon, 1990);

The Black Dahlia (New York: Mysterious Press, 1987; London: Century Hutchinson, 1988);

The Big Nowhere (New York: Mysterious Press, 1988; London: Mysterious Press, 1989);

L.A. Confidential (New York & London: Mysterious Press, 1990);

White Jazz (New York: Knopf, 1992; London: Century, 1993);

Hollywood Nocturnes (New York: Otto Penzler Books, 1994); republished as *Dick Contino's Blues and Other Stories* (London: Arrow, 1994);

American Tabloid (New York: Knopf, 1995; London: Century, 1995);

My Dark Places: An L.A. Crime Memoir (New York: Knopf, 1996; London: Century, 1996);

Crime Wave: Reportage and Fiction from the Underside of L.A. (New York: Vintage, 1999; London: Century, 1999).

Collection: *L.A. Noir: The Lloyd Hopkins Novels* (London: Arrow, 1997; New York: Mysterious Press, 1998)—comprises *Blood on the Moon*, *Because the Night*, and *Suicide Hill*.

OTHER: "Ellroy on Ellroy . . . and Hopkins," *Mysterious News*, 1 (February 1986): 8–9;

"High Darktown," *New Black Mask 5*, edited by Matthew J. Bruccoli and Richard Layman (New York: Harcourt Brace Jovanovich, 1986);

James Ellroy at the time of My Dark Places: An L.A. Crime Memoir *(1996; photograph by Marion Ettlinger)*

"Dial Axminister 6-400," *New Black Mask 8*, edited by Bruccoli and Layman (New York: Harcourt Brace Jovanovich, 1987);

"Since I Don't Have You," *A Matter of Crime 4*, edited by Bruccoli and Layman (New York: Harcourt Brace Jovanovich, 1988);

"Torch Number," in *Justice for Hire*, edited by Robert Randisi (New York: Mysterious Press, 1990);

Murder and Mayhem: An A–Z of the World's Most Notorious Killers, introduction by Ellroy (London: Arrow, 1992);

"Dick Contino's Blues," *Granta* (1994);

"Hollywood Shakedown," *GQ*, 67 (November 1997): 424–433, 474–477;

"Hush-Hush," *GQ*, 68 (September 1998): 256–268;

"Tiajuana, Mon Amour," *GQ*, 69 (February 1999): 150–157, 190;

"The Trouble I Cause," *GQ*, 70 (March 2000): 232, 237–243, 354.

James Ellroy–whose haunting experiences, in particular the shocking murder of his mother, formed him as a child, shaped his young adult years, and led him later to combine lyricism and violence in his novels–might be called the James Joyce of American hard-boiled fiction. As did Joyce, Ellroy draws on family and social history as inspiration in his fiction, loves words for sound as well as meaning, relies on stream of consciousness as a major storytelling technique, and at times is so experimental in his prose that he makes extraordinary demands upon the reader. From *Brown's Requiem* (1981), his first novel, through and beyond his poignant memoir, *My Dark Places: An L.A. Crime Memoir* (1996), Ellroy's work seethes with violence, rage, and poetry. The tender, lyric quality of his writing, in sharp contrast to the violent images he often evokes, is apparent in the prologue of *My Dark Places,* as he writes to his murdered mother nearly forty years after her death: "I failed you as a talisman–so now I stand as your witness. Your death defines my life. I want to find the love we never had and explicate it in your name. I want to take your secrets public. I want to burn down the distance between us. I want to give you breath."

Lee Earle Ellroy, who would later call himself James Ellroy, was born 4 March 1948 in Los Angeles, the only child of Armand and Geneva Hilliker Ellroy. In *My Dark Places* Ellroy describes his parents as a couple "who excelled at appearances. They were a great looking and cheap couple, along the lines of Robert Mitchum and Jane Russell in *Macao*. They stayed together for fifteen years. It had to be sex." Ellroy's father worked in a variety of business capacities and served as accountant and business manager for Rita Hayworth in the late 1940s and early 1950s. Geneva, called Jean, was a registered nurse. Jean and her son later moved to El Monte, fourteen miles east of downtown Los Angeles, where she worked as a nurse at the Packard Bell Electronics plant. Ellroy visited his father on weekends. Armand Ellroy passed on to his son many of the habits and traits that were to form him as a person and a writer, including a love of reading as well as a predilection in his early years for shiftlessness.

On Sunday, 22 June 1958, the body of Jean Ellroy was found by the side of the road next to Arroyo High School. She had been strangled; her stocking and a sash cord were tied tightly around her neck. Ellroy learned what had happened to his mother when he arrived at his mother's home after having spent the weekend with his father. He was ten. The murder of his mother became an obsession for Ellroy that doubtless will be with him always.

Beyond the emotional impact of murder on the victim's family, Jean Ellroy's death was to make real for her son the murder of Elizabeth Short, the Black Dahlia, whose mutilated body was discovered on 15 January 1947 in a vacant lot at the corner of Thirty-ninth Street and Norton Avenue in Central Los Angeles. Known for always wearing black, Short aspired to an acting career but is thought to have worked as a prostitute. Her body, drained of blood, washed, and cut in half, was discovered by a young mother who was walking by the lot with her child. The body showed evidence of torture–cigarette burns on her breasts and stab wounds; her mouth was grotesquely disfigured and her throat was slashed from ear to ear. The Black Dahlia's hair had been washed, given a henna rinse, and set. To this day the murder that is featured so prominently in Ellroy's fiction remains unsolved.

Ellroy became aware of the Black Dahlia murder about six months after his mother's death when his father gave him a copy of Jack Webb's *The Badge* (1958), an account of the Los Angeles Police Department (LAPD) that included a description of the case. Ellroy grew up entranced by the Black Dahlia, connecting her fate to his mother's murder, which bore a faint resemblance to the famous case. As a youngster Ellroy believed that his mother, like Elizabeth Short, was a loose woman who drank with men and had sex with them on the weekends, beliefs his father reinforced. Ellroy spent his teenage years harboring this distorted view of his mother–a view that he did not change until he made a search for her killer in 1994–1995. As recorded in *My Dark Places,* the search for the killer, though unsuccessful, allowed Ellroy to recover a truer memory of his mother. The woman he then came to know anew cared about her son, made him go to church even though he did not want to, worked hard, and restricted her partying to weekends when Ellroy was visiting his father though she did on occasion entertain men when her son was present.

Ellroy and his father resided in a small apartment on Beverly Boulevard in a neighborhood between Hancock Park and Hollywood. Each week his father gave him two books, but because Ellroy could not get enough to read, he started to shoplift at Chevalier's, the local bookstore. He graduated from reading Ken Holt and the Hardy Boys to reading

 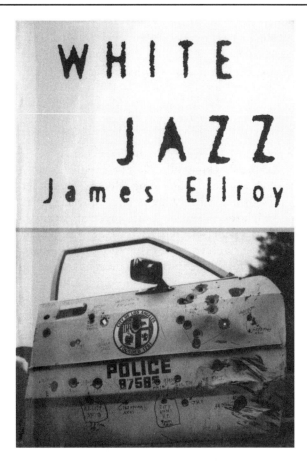

Dust jackets for the first (1987) and last (1992) novels in Ellroy's L. A. Quartet

Dashiell Hammett, Raymond Chandler, and Mickey Spillane. During this period of his life Ellroy often returned to *The Badge,* which contained accounts of the Club Mecca firebombing, Mickey Cohen's activities, and the Brenda Allen call-girl scandal–all of which Ellroy has used in his books. It is also possible that the staccato, telegraphic quality of *The Badge* and Webb's *Dragnet,* which began as a radio show in 1949 and as a television series in 1952, influenced the development of Ellroy's writing style.

Ellroy's teenage years were deeply troubled. He drank, preached the concepts of American nazism, and hassled weaker boys. His father, who had a stroke on 1 November 1963 and whose health continued to deteriorate, could do little to control his son. Ellroy cut classes, failed the eleventh grade because of truancy, and stole most of the food he ate. In 1965 he joined the army but soon came to detest its structured life; by using the excuse of his father's poor health and also faking psychiatric problems, he was able to obtain an honorable discharge just before his father's death on 4 June 1965.

With his return to civilian life, Ellroy began a career as a petty thief to support his alcohol and drug

habits. He was first arrested in 1965 for shoplifting a steak, but because of his age he was sent to a juvenile facility. After his release he continued to steal because he needed food, drugs, drink, and clothing. He spied on former female classmates through bedroom windows and sometimes broke into their homes to steal their underwear. The brief stints of time he spent in the Los Angeles County Jail taught him much about low-life types and temporarily restored his health since he had no access to drugs and liquor. Over a twelve-year period his record includes approximately thirty arrests, twelve convictions, and eight months of jail time. Ellroy decided to change his ways in 1977 when he almost died from pneumonia. He began to control his alcoholism and was able to work as a caddy at the Bel-Air and Hillcrest country clubs. He uses these experiences in his novels, particularly the first one, *Brown's Requiem.*

When Ellroy wrote *Brown's Requiem* (1981), he was working as a caddy in Los Angeles. *Brown's Requiem* is the story of Fritz Brown, an alcoholic former vice cop from the Los Angeles Police Department who becomes a sleazy private eye working as a "repo" man–hired to repossess the cars of people who are in arrears on their monthly payments.

Brown works a case involving some low-life types: Freddy "Fat Dog" Baker, a caddy and arsonist; Richard "Hot Rod" Ralston, who runs a welfare scam focusing on caddies who work off the books while collecting government checks; Captain Hayward Cathcart, a bad cop on the take; and Sol Kupferman, a furrier, bookie, and rackets man whose two children, Jane Baker, a cellist, and "Fat Dog" Baker, do not know their parentage. In the complicated, almost convoluted plot many of Ellroy's formative influences are evident—his love of classical music, particularly Anton Bruckner; his knowledge of and fascination with Los Angeles; the ethos of the country club and the stratification of the caddies' society. The descriptions of Los Angeles are both realistic and poetic, and the scenery is real, not imagined: the seedy Gold Cup Coffee Shop on Hollywood Boulevard, the country clubs, Silver Lake, and the fleabag hotels—all are places Ellroy knew intimately. Indeed, the hotels described in the novel are quite similar to the Westwood, where Ellroy lived for $25 a week.

Important themes and motifs found in Ellroy's subsequent fiction were born in *Brown's Requiem,* his only novel to feature a private eye. The corruption of the LAPD was to become a major theme in novels such as *The Big Nowhere* (1988) and *L.A. Confidential* (1990), and from the first Ellroy's fascination with the Black Dahlia case is evident: as Fritz Brown and his boyhood friend Walter unwind by taking their favorite ride, the "Topanga Run," Walter asks him who he thinks "really killed the Black Dahlia," which he then refers to as "a mutual obsession from our boyhood days." The similarity of the description of the Topanga Canyon Run—which leads north and east from the Pacific Coast Highway to the San Fernando Valley—to Raymond Chandler's description of Philip Marlowe's famous drive from the Pacific Coast Highway to downtown Los Angeles in *The Little Sister* (1949) has led critics to cite the passage as evidence of Chandler's influence on Ellroy. Although *Brown's Requiem* was nominated for the Shamus Award by the Private Eye Writers of America, it was not reviewed in major newspapers. In a winter 1991 review in *The Armchair Detective* on the occasion of its republication, critic Marvin Lachman commended the novel for its "sheer readability" but thought some readers might find "the plot scarcely believable and the violence excessive."

Because he was not yet able to support himself as a writer, Ellroy was still working as a caddy when he wrote *Clandestine* (1982), which tells the story of Freddy Underhill, a college-educated cop who likes golf and one-night stands. While Underhill has a tough-guy, no-nonsense approach to life and crime,

he possesses a poetic streak that enables him at the beginning of the novel "to contemplate . . . nightfall and neon and what I could do about it in what I would later know to be the last season of my youth." Determined to become a top cop, Underhill is already a hero because he has killed two robbers who mortally wounded his partner, Wacky Walker, with whom he worked out of the Wilshire district. He inherits Night Train, Wacky's ferocious Labrador retriever, who provides the only humor found in this dark tale of obsession and corruption.

When Margaret Cadwallader, one of Underhill's one-night stands, is found murdered in her Hollywood apartment, he decides to investigate the case on his own, even though it is not in his jurisdiction. Through some illegal maneuvers, he mistakenly identifies Eddie Engels, a homosexual, as the murderer. Underhill then manages to become part of the investigative team, headed by Lieutenant Dudley Smith, an officer who figures prominently in Ellroy's later novels.

Haunted by his inability to solve the Black Dahlia case, Smith believes Engels is a rapist-murderer and is determined to have him confess. In a prolonged, violent episode, Smith, Underhill, and two other cops take Engels to a deserted motel, where they beat a confession out of him—introducing the reader to a setting that reemerges as the Victory Motel, a major site of activity in *L.A. Confidential*. The motel as an interrogation site is not imagined: the LAPD actually owned a motel that it used for such purposes in the 1950s.

Clandestine is Ellroy's first extensive portrayal of police corruption as a major theme in hard-boiled crime fiction. As he told Ray Greene in an interview that appeared in *Boxoffice* in September 1997: "hard-boiled crime fiction is the story of bad white men doing bad things in the name of authority." In his second novel Ellroy shows that these "bad things" include the use of extreme violence to obtain information and confessions, bribery and other unethical behavior, and even participation in criminal activity. Underhill's involvement with Lorna Weinberg, a crippled assistant district attorney, results in the couple's realization that they have been undercut by Smith, who announces to the press that Engels is a multiple killer. Smith makes them both accomplices in a miscarriage of justice because they realize too late that Engels has a legitimate alibi for the night of the murder. After Engels commits suicide before he can be released, Lorna and Underhill leave law enforcement and marry.

Parallels to Ellroy's personal history are evident in the wrap-up of his novel. After four years

First page from the manuscript for Ellroy's 1990 novel, L. A. Confidential *(Collection of Richard Layman)*

pass, the murder of Marcella De Vries Harris, whose body is found by the side of the road near the high school in El Monte, leads Underhill to make a chance connection with the killing of Margaret Cadwallader. Through a complicated turn of events and a trip to Tunnel City, Wisconsin (the birthplace of Jean Ellroy), Underhill is able to establish links in the histories of the two women that supply the motive for the murders and explain the history of a lonely little boy who actually lost two mothers. A good writer deals with what he knows, and Ellroy here clearly intertwines the circumstances of his mother's murder into his plot. In *My Dark Places* he called the novel "a thinly veiled, chronologically altered account of my mother's killing." *Clandestine* was nominated for an Edgar Award for best original paperback by the Mystery Writers of America.

Ellroy's style in his early novels was descriptive and smooth-flowing. A good example of his style is illustrated by his description of a recurring figure in the L.A. Quartet: "Dudley Smith was a lieutenant in the homicide bureau, a fearsome personage and legendary cop who had killed five men in the line of duty. Irish-born and Los Angeles-raised, he still clung tenaciously to his high-pitched, musical brogue, which was as finely tuned as a Stradivarius.''

Blood on the Moon (1984), *Because the Night* (1985), and *Suicide Hill* (1986) feature Sergeant Lloyd Hopkins of the Robbery and Homicide Division, a dedicated but tormented cop who engages in mind games with psychotic criminals. Hopkins is profoundly affected by his job in a city torn by violence, crime, corruption, and the Watts riots. As originally written, *Blood on the Moon* was rejected as too violent by seventeen publishers. Nat Sobel, Ellroy's literary agent, convinced him to revise the book and placed it with Mysterious Press. *Blood on the Moon* is the only Ellroy novel before *L.A. Confidential* to be made into a movie, *Cop* (1987), in which Hopkins was played by James Woods.

As Hopkins pursues criminals with a no-holds-barred mentality in *Blood on the Moon,* his family life deteriorates. His wife, Janice, can no longer tolerate his telling their daughters bedtime stories about the good cop who destroys the scumbags of the city. Because Penny experiences vicarious pleasure from her father's adventures, an alarmed Janice decides to move to San Francisco with the girls. After Janice's departure, Hopkins becomes more obsessed with hunting killers, even if it means resorting to illegal tactics. *Blood on the Moon* becomes a psychological novel in which Hopkins and a homicidal sexual deviant, Teddy Verplanck, engage in a long, slow dance of catch-me-if-you-can. As Verplanck stalks his vic-

tims, he becomes more daring in his challenges to his pursuer. Hopkins becomes romantically involved with Kathleen McCarthy, one of Verplanck's high-school classmates and a potential victim, using her to draw the killer into the open. Although Hopkins manages to save her, Kathleen cannot forgive him for what he has done. In a farewell letter at the end of the novel she writes: "I love you and I need your shelter, but the mortar that binds us is blood, and if we stay together it will own us and we will never have a chance to be sane. . . . But I hurt for your future most of all. You have chosen to stalk ugliness and try to replace it with a numbing kind of love, and that is a painful road to follow."

In *Because the Night* Ellroy tells the story of Hopkins and his mentor, Captain Arthur "Dutch" Peltz, who is now the only stabilizing force in his life. The action of the novel is woven around three separate strands: the disappearance of Jacob Herzog, a legendary cop who had worked Metro and Vice and was dubbed "The Alchemist" because "he could fake anything"; the cold-blooded killings of three people in a liquor-store robbery; and a series of other murders instigated by a brilliant psychotic psychiatrist, Dr. John Havilland, who calls himself the Night Tripper after a 1960s rock-and-roll legend. Havilland uses drugs to lure patients with sexual hang-ups into his sick world, "beyond the green door."

Hopkins investigates the liquor-store murders and tries to discover Herzog's whereabouts. He discovers that Thomas Goff, Havilland's goon who locates human research subjects for the psychiatrist, is responsible for the liquor-store caper; later, when Hopkins searches Herzog's apartment, he finds evidence linking Goff, Havilland, and Herzog. Hopkins persuades Linda Wilhite, a prostitute and a patient of Havilland, to help him get information about the doctor, who he discovers has Hopkins's name on a list of policemen he is researching. *Because the Night* is an engrossing story of two clever men playing a nerve-racking exchange of roles as the hunter and the hunted.

The last book in the trilogy Ellroy refers to as "Hopkins in Jeopardy" is *Suicide Hill,* which opens with a psychiatrist's report describing Hopkins as a sociopath stressed out by his nineteen years on the force. Because of his methods and previous exploits, Hopkins is feared by corrupt cops as much as he is by criminals, and an effort is made to force him to retire. The case that is the focus of the novel involves a series of bank robberies in which the girlfriends of bank managers are kidnapped and held until the managers agree to cooperate with the thieves. If a manager should refuse to obey orders, his wife is

Dust jacket for Ellroy's 1990 novel, in which three police officers with conflicting motives investigate
the links between a mass murder and a pornography ring

informed of his infidelities and his girlfriend is killed. In his review of *Suicide Hill* in the 6 July 1986 *New York Times Book Review*, Newgate Callender characterized it as being overwritten "with the author's manipulative hand too much in evidence," much the same view he expressed about *Blood on the Moon* in his 22 July 1984 review.

Although Ellroy in a February 1986 article for *Mysterious News* said that "Hopkins has two more adventures to endure before I let him off the hook," he decided against continuing the series. There was little more he could do with his vigilante knight-cop: his character as conceived could not gain in knowledge, depth, or understanding. Looking back on the books in the 1993 video documentary *James Ellroy: Demon Dog of American Crime Fiction*, the novelist admits to being slightly embarrassed by Hopkins.

In Ellroy's next novel, *Silent Terror* (1986), which was republished in 1990 as *Killer on the Road*, the search for serial killer Martin Michael Plunkett becomes a cross-country pursuit. Plunkett, known as the Shroud Shifter, kills people from Los Angeles to Westchester County, New York, over a dozen or so years. Sometimes after he murders couples, he

arranges their corpses in erotic poses. Developing a new technique in his fiction, Ellroy creates newspaper headlines and articles to summarize parts of the action, almost making readers believe that they are reading true crime, not crime fiction. The mind games played between Thomas D. Dusenberry, head for the Federal Bureau of Investigation's (FBI) Serial Killer Task Force, and Plunkett are similar to those played by Hopkins and Havilland in *Because the Night*, but Dusenberry, in many ways a more stable personality than Hopkins, is too decent to survive. He sells the story of his hunt for the Shroud Shifter and then kills himself. Two checks, made out to his children, are found on his body. *Silent Terror* is one of the few instances in which Los Angeles is not the focal point of an Ellroy book. Although the novel shows Ellroy developing a plot within a broader milieu, the story lacks the decadent urban atmosphere so identified with his work.

The Black Dahlia (1987), based on the famous murder case, is dedicated to Ellroy's mother: "Mother: Twenty-nine Years Later / This Valediction in Blood." Ellroy is factual in his description of the crime—the victim's prolonged, torturous death; the evisceration and dismemberment of her body; and the arrangement of the corpse at the location where it was discovered—and objective in his presentation of the murder victim and her family background. He, of course, goes beyond the facts of the case in devising a solution that focuses on the fictional Spragues, an extremely dysfunctional family beset by insanity, sexual promiscuity, and incest. The investigators Ellroy creates, Bucky Bleichert and Lee Blanchard, are members of the LAPD and former professional boxers. Like Hopkins, they are obsessed with justice, obtained at any cost; they are violent and harbor no guilt for killing the "scum" they deem as undeserving of life.

Ellroy began a major phase of his literary career with the publication of *The Black Dahlia*, the first novel in his L.A. Quartet. *The Big Nowhere* (1988), *L.A. Confidential* (1990), and *White Jazz* (1992) complete his compelling social history of Los Angeles from the 1940s through the 1950s. The four novels are connected by Ellroy's desire to render the social milieu of Los Angeles through these pivotal years. His emphasis throughout is on horrific murders, the corruption evident in police and political circles, and the racism manifest in the city. Ellroy mixes fact with fiction, frequently alluding to the actual mobsters (Mickey Cohen, Johnny Stompanato, and Bugsy Siegel) and the various divisions of the LAPD as well as the cases investigated (the Black Dahlia, serial killings) that fascinated him originally when he read *The Badge*. Despite his use of factual markers, Ellroy in a July 1996 *Writer's Digest* interview told Steve Boisson that "the L.A. Quartet is 95% imagined."

Ellroy uses the communist scare in Hollywood in the 1950s as the impetus for the action in *The Big Nowhere*. The action turns around Danny Upshaw, a young homicide detective; Mal Considine, a detective with the district attorney's bureau; and Buzz Meeks, a crooked former cop who serves as a pimp for Howard Hughes. (The reclusive Hughes is a recurring character in later Ellroy fiction including *American Tabloid* and "Since I Don't Have You," a short story included in the 1994 collection *Hollywood Nocturnes*). Against a background of violence, drugs, and sex—heterosexual, homosexual, and bisexual—Ellroy's characters are caught up in the ugliness of the blacklist that destroyed many careers in the film industry, with the dirty tricks used by the unions to try to gain power in Hollywood, and with the corruption and physical threats posed by such gangsters as Johnny Stompanato, Lana Turner's lover, who was killed by her daughter, Cheryl Crane.

The action of *L.A. Confidential*, covering the years from 1950 to 1958 in Los Angeles, is driven by three cops with conflicting agendas: "Trashcan" Jack Vincennes, a cop in the narcotics division who sets up Hollywood celebrities for sensational exposés in the scandal sheet *Hush-Hush* and who also serves as a technical adviser to a television program, "Badge of Honor," the counterpart of Jack Webb's "Dragnet"; Bud White, who as a child saw his father murder his mother, and who likes to shoot first and then sort everything out; and Ed Exley, whose greatest concern is his quest for political advancement.

The focal crime of the novel is the Nite Owl Massacre, named after a Hollywood Boulevard coffee shop in which three patrons—including a man identified as the gangster Duke Cathcart and a Rita Hayworth lookalike, Susan Nancy Lefferts—and three employees were killed during late evening hours on 14 April 1953. As a result of the incident, described as a robbery gone bad, three young black men are accused of the crime and shot while resisting arrest. The case is reopened a few years later when Otis John Shortell, a convict, links the Nite Owl murders to a pornography ring. The intended victim was actually Duke Cathcart, who was trying to take over Pierce Patchett's prostitution, pornography, and drug businesses. Patchett's "Fleur-de-Lis" operation features prostitutes who look like movie stars. It is a lucrative business because men pay well for the experience of such a glamorous illusion. In addition, a hidden camera was often set up so that pictures could be taken for blackmail purposes.

Ed Exley, Jack Vincennes, and Bud White each become involved in the case for different reasons. Ed Exley was on duty the night the murders took place; Bud White becomes involved with Lynn Bracken, one of the movie-star call girls who looks like Veronica Lake; Jack Vincennes is working out of Vice and is investigating Patchett's Fleur-de-Lis operations, with special attention given to the call girl and pornography operations.

Exley is credited with solving the reopened case and is promoted to chief of detectives because the department needs a hero to keep attention away from its internal scandal. Uproar over the case could lead to public revelations about Exley's father, Preston, a legendary figure in the LAPD, and Ray Dieterling, the father of animation. Because the men, now partners in the development of an amusement park similar to Disneyland, face possible prosecution and cannot afford to be subject to ridicule, they commit suicide. The resolution of the case also leads to the resignation of Ellis Loew, the corrupt district attorney. Ellroy ends this part of the L.A. Quartet on an ironic note: "Very simply, these two men symbolized the fulfillment of a vision—Los Angeles as a place of enchantment and high quality everyday life. More

Dust jacket for the nonfiction work in which Ellroy deals with the 1958 murder of his mother

than anyone else, Raymond Dieterling and Preston Exley personified the grand and good dreams that have built this city."

Although the Nite Owl Murders are an invention, the social background surrounding the case is realistically portrayed. Ellroy used a researcher to verify historical facts, and much of what occurs in *L.A. Confidential* is accurate. There are references to the 1951 "Bloody Christmas" scandal, in which two policemen scuffled with six Mexicans in a rough Los Angeles neighborhood. The two cops were injured. When word got back to the precinct about the policemen's injuries, which were exaggerated, the police on duty in the stationhouse beat the prisoners in the holding cell, seriously injuring some of them. A call-girl ring offering prostitutes who looked like movie stars actually existed. So seamless is Ellroy's mix of fact and fiction that it is often difficult to know where the one leaves off and the other begins.

White Jazz, the final piece in the quartet, is set within the milieu of the race riots in the Watts section of Los Angeles in 1958. Lieutenant Dave "the Enforcer" Klein, the narrator, depicts the corruption, bias, and unmitigated violence of the LAPD as seen in the earlier

novels. The corrupt Captain Dudley Smith, first introduced in *Clandestine,* and Ed Exley are key players along with mobster Mickey Cohen and Pete Bondurant, former L.A. County deputy sheriff, private eye, and investigator/bodyguard for Howard Hughes, who later emerges as a major figure in *American Tabloid* (1995).

White Jazz focuses on the LAPD at the time when the city was the scene of major narcotics traffic, police corruption, and cover-ups regarding drug and vice cases, a particularly vicious series of murders, and overt racism toward all minorities. Dudley Smith, involved in a cover-up, money laundering, and other criminal activities, is critically wounded in a shoot-out with a robber, is paralyzed, has lost an eye, and suffers brain damage. He will never recover; Exley declares him a hero and grants a special pension so that he can spend his days in a nursing home.

Much of the story is told through sections of Klein's rambling stream of consciousness, which are then followed by fuller newspaper accounts of the action. This technique allows Ellroy to summarize the events of the plot and also reinforces the idea that history as experienced is both personal and official. Klein, caught in the crossfire between corruption and testifying about the collusion between the LAPD, especially Dudley Smith and the mob headed by Mickey Cohen, has no other choice but to disappear.

There are significant stylistic differences between Ellroy's early novels, from *Brown's Requiem* through the Hopkins trilogy, and the L.A. Quartet. Ellroy moved from a traditional third-person narrative and a reliance on figurative language to a stream-of-consciousness, telegraphic style in the L.A. Quartet. But even within the L.A. Quartet, there are noticeable stylistic differences. More so than in *The Black Dahlia* and *The Big Nowhere,* Ellroy employs newspaper headlines and articles in *L.A. Confidential* and *White Jazz,* serving not only to emphasize their gritty realism but also to provide needed clarification for a prose style that becomes more experimental in the third novel of the quartet.

Ellroy's development of a terser, less figurative style in *L.A. Confidential* was evidently spurred by concerns about the length of the novel. Ellroy related in his interview with Boisson that when his agent told him that his draft of eight hundred manuscript pages was too long, he realized he "needed to go back and just cut words. That's when I started to develop that telegraphic style." He found he was able to reduce the manuscript to 682 pages, but by taking so much out and often relying on fragments of sentences Ellroy understood that he was placing extraordinary demands on his reader. Commenting on *White Jazz,* Wendy Lesser in *The New York Times Book Review* notes that "we can't really begin to care about characters who never even get to inhabit a complete sentence," and she cites as an illustration:

"Shotgun roar–full auto–one long blast. Spatter spray/random pistol shots/screams–muzzle flash lit up Steve Wenzel, faceless.
"Screams.
"I ripped through them out the window."

While he maintained that he had achieved "the perfect voice" for the novel, Ellroy continued, "I'll never use it again. There were still people who found the book unreadable."

In 1994 Ellroy published *Hollywood Nocturnes,* a collection of hard-boiled short stories that had previously appeared in magazines. Ellroy was fascinated by accordian player Dick Contino. Ellroy went to Las Vegas to meet Contino, who was working there as a lounge singer in the early 1990s. Other stories in *Hollywood Nocturnes* bring back familiar characters from Ellroy's novels, incuding Buzz Meeks, Mickey Cohen, Howard Hughes, and Lee Blanchard.

In *American Tabloid* Ellroy moves from the largely personal stories of rogue cops to a tale of political intrigue leading up to the assasination of President John F. Kennedy. Originally inspired by Don DeLillo's novel about the assassination, *Libra* (1988), Ellroy at first thought he could not write a novel on the same subject, but he told Paul Gray in a 1995 interview that he knew he could "write an epic in which the assassination is only one crime in a long series of crimes. I can write a novel about the unsung leg breakers of history. I can do a tabloid sewer crawl through the private nightmare of public policy." The story of the Kennedy political dynasty, the rumors of the family's connections with the Mafia, the battle between Robert Kennedy and Jimmy Hoffa, the loss of the casinos in Havana once Castro gained power, and the Bay of Pigs invasion are major plot points for Ellroy's story of intrigue, spying, counterspying, and corruption. Pete Bondurant, Special Agent Kemper Boyd, and Ward J. Littell, an FBI man who specializes in surveillance work, are featured in a scenario that involves J. Edgar Hoover, Howard Hughes, and Sam Giancana. The novel takes the reader up to the brink of the assassination, its action ending at 12:15 P.M. on 23 November 1963.

In his 10 April 1995 review of *American Tabloid* in *Time,* Gray characterized Ellroy's approach to history and the violent nature of his books: "*American Tabloid* is history as Hellzapoppin, a long slapstick routine careening around a manic premise: What if the fabled American innocence is all shuck and jive? To underscore his thesis, Ellroy uses spurts of unimaginable violence the way other writers deploy commas and periods. 'Sal burned a man to death with a blow torch. The man's wife came home unexpectedly. Sal shoved a gasoline-soaked rag in her mouth and ignited it. He said she died shooting flames like a dragon.'" Ellroy has spoken of *American Tabloid* as the first book in a projected trilogy he refers to as Underworld U.S.A. He envisions the second novel beginning fifteen minutes after action in *American Tabloid* ends and covering through 1968 and the third, focusing on Vietnam, continuing his social history into 1973.

In an interview that aired on 26 January 1997 on CBS's *Sunday Morning,* Ellroy told correspondent Anthony Mason why he wrote *My Dark Places:* "I wanted to know how I was derived from my mother. The capture of her was more important than the capture of her killer." The search for Jean Ellroy's murderer decades after the act offers the reader insight into the author's psyche and the experiences that drive him to explore the violent underbelly of society in his fiction. It is not surprising that Ellroy's successful foray into writing true crime led to *Crime Wave: Reportage and Fiction from the Underside of L.A.* (1999), dedicated to Curtis Hanson, director and co-screenwriter of the movie version of *L.A. Confidential* (1998), whom Ellroy credits with capturing the essence of the story and the times. *Crime Wave* is an anthology of nonfictional pieces and short stories Ellroy wrote for the magazine *GQ.* In his 15 March 1999 review in *Booklist,* Bill Ott found the collection less compelling than Ellroy's novels: "most readers will miss Ellroy's narrative voice: edgy, profane, verging on the outrageous. The self-styled Demon Dog of American literature puts himself on a bit of a leash here, but there's enough wolfing to please hardcore fans."

Although his métier is the description of a violent, chaotic world, James Ellroy is anything but a wild man when it comes to his art. A conscious, painstaking craftsman, he carefully outlines his works—his outline for *American Tabloid,* for example, was 250 pages, about half the size of the published book—and his departures from his outlines as he writes usually concern characterization rather than plot. In the documentary *James Ellroy: Demon Dog of American Crime Fiction* the author remarks that he has nothing more to write about Los Angeles, but it is all but certain that, whether he changes his mind and returns to the Los Angeles setting or goes back to his plan for an Underworld U.S.A. trilogy or embarks on some new project, Ellroy will continue his hardboiled critique of American social history.

Interviews:

Duane Tucker, "An Interview with James Ellroy," *Armchair Detective,* 17 (Spring 1984): 150–155;

Fleming Meeks, "James Ellroy: Purging the Demons of His Youth," *Publishers Weekly,* 237 (15 June 1990): 53–54;

Paul Gray, "The Real Pulp Fiction," *Time,* 145 (10 April 1995): 75–76;

Charles Silet, "Mad Dog and Glory: A Conversation with James Ellroy," *Armchair Detective,* 28 (Summer 1995): 236–244.

References:

Steve Boisson, "James Ellroy: Crossing the Dividing Line," *Writer's Digest,* 76 (July 1996): 26–31;

Kateri Butler, "Novelist James Ellroy's Search for His Mother's Killer," *L.A. Weekly* (17 February 1995): 21–25;

Josh Cohen, "James Ellroy: Los Angeles and the Spectacular Crisis of Masculinity," *Women: A Cultural Review,* 7 (Spring 1996): 1–15;

William Frieburger, "James Ellroy, Walter Mosley and the Politics of the Los Angeles Crime Novel," *Clues,* 17 (Fall–Winter 1996): 87–104;

Lee Horsley, "Founding Fathers: Genealogies of Violence in James Ellroy's L.A. Quartet," *Clues,* 19 (Spring–Summer 1998): 131–161;

James Ellroy: Demon Dog of American Crime Fiction, video, First Run Features, 1993.

Loren D. Estleman

(15 September 1952 –)

Katherine Harper
Bowling Green State University

BOOKS: *The Oklahoma Punk* (Canoga Park, Cal.: Major, 1976); republished as *Red Highway* (New York: PaperJacks, 1988);

The Hider (Garden City, N.Y.: Doubleday, 1978);

Sherlock Holmes vs. Dracula: or, The Adventure of the Sanguinary Count (Garden City, N.Y.: Doubleday, 1978; London: New English Library, 1978);

Dr. Jekyll and Mr. Holmes (Garden City, N.Y.: Doubleday, 1979; Harmondsworth, U.K.: Penguin, 1981);

The High Rocks (Garden City, N.Y.: Doubleday, 1979; London: Hale, 1983);

Motor City Blue (Boston: Houghton Mifflin, 1980; London: Hale, 1982);

Stamping Ground (Garden City, N.Y.: Doubleday, 1980);

Aces and Eights (Garden City, N.Y.: Doubleday, 1981; London: Hale, 1982);

Angel Eyes (Boston: Houghton Mifflin, 1981; London: Hale, 1982);

The Wolfer (New York: Pocket Books, 1981; London: Hale, 1983);

The Midnight Man (Boston: Houghton Mifflin, 1982; London: Hale, 1983);

Murdock's Law (Garden City, N.Y.: Doubleday, 1982; London: Hale, 1983);

The Glass Highway (Boston: Houghton Mifflin, 1983; London: Hale, 1984);

Mister St. John (Garden City, N.Y.: Doubleday, 1983; London: Hale, 1985);

Kill Zone (New York: Mysterious Press, 1984; London: Mysterious Press, 1987);

The Stranglers (Garden City, N.Y.: Doubleday, 1984; London: Hale, 1988);

Sugartown (Boston: Houghton Mifflin, 1984; London: Macmillan, 1986);

This Old Bill (Garden City, N.Y.: Doubleday, 1984);

Gun Man (Garden City, N.Y.: Doubleday, 1985);

Roses Are Dead (New York: Mysterious Press, 1985; London: Century, 1987);

Any Man's Death (New York: Mysterious Press, 1986; London: Mysterious Press, 1989);

Loren D. Estleman (photograph by Deborah Morgan; courtesy of Loren D. Estleman)

Every Brilliant Eye (Boston: Houghton Mifflin, 1986; London: Macmillan, 1986);

Lady Yesterday (Boston: Houghton Mifflin, 1987; London: Macmillan, 1987);

The Wister Trace: Classic Novels of the American Frontier (Ottawa, Ill.: Jameson, 1987);

Bloody Season (New York: Bantam, 1988);

Downriver (Boston: Houghton Mifflin, 1988; London: Macmillan, 1988);

General Murders: Ten Amos Walker Mysteries (Boston: Houghton Mifflin, 1988; London: Macmillan, 1989);

The Best Western Stories of Loren D. Estleman, edited by Bill Pronzini and Martin H. Greenberg (Athens: Swallow Press/Ohio University Press, 1989; Bath, U.K.: Chivers Press, 1990);

The Black Moon, by Estleman, Robert Randisi, W. R. Philbrick, Ed Gorman, and L. J. Washburn (New York: Lynx, 1989);

Peeper (New York: Bantam, 1989; Bath, U.K.: Chivers Press, 1991);

Silent Thunder (Boston: Houghton Mifflin, 1989; London: Pan/Macmillan, 1989);

Western Story (New York: Doubleday, 1989);

Sweet Women Lie (Boston: Houghton Mifflin, 1990; London: Macmillan, 1990);

Whiskey River (New York: Bantam, 1990; London: Scribners, 1991);

Eight Mile and Dequindre (Eugene, Oreg.: Mystery Scene Press, 1991);

Motown (New York: Bantam, 1991);

Sudden Country (New York: Doubleday, 1991);

King of the Corner (New York: Bantam, 1992);

People Who Kill (Eugene, Oreg.: Mystery Scene Press, 1993);

City of Widows (New York: Forge, 1994; Bath, U.K.: Chivers Press, 1994);

Edsel: A Novel of Detroit (New York: Mysterious Press, 1995);

Stress (New York: Mysterious Press, 1996);

Billy Gashade (New York: Forge, 1997);

Never Street (New York: Mysterious Press, 1997);

Jitterbug: A Novel of Detroit (New York: Forge, 1998);

The Witchfinder (New York: Mysterious Press, 1998; London: Hale, 1999);

Journey of the Dead (New York: Forge, 1998);

The Rocky Mountain Moving Picture Association (New York: Forge, 1999);

The Hours of the Virgin (New York: Mysterious Press, 1999);

Thunder City: A Novel of Detroit (New York: Forge, 1999).

OTHER: Sir Arthur Conan Doyle, *Sherlock Holmes: The Complete Novels and Stories,* introduction by Estleman (New York: Bantam, 1986);

"The Crooked Way," in *P.I. Files,* edited by Estleman and Martin H. Greenberg (New York: Ballantine, 1990), pp. 86–102;

"Snow Angels," in *Invitation to Murder: All New Stories of Mystery and Suspense,* edited by Ed Gorman and Greenberg (Arlington Heights, Ill.: Dark Harvest, 1991), pp. 277–292;

"The Hack," in *Deals With the Devil,* edited by Estleman, Mike Resnick, and Greenberg (New York: Daw, 1994), pp. 348–355;

"Pickups and Shotguns," in *Homicide Host Presents: A Collection of Original Mysteries,* compiled by Helen Esper Olmsted (Aurora, Colo.: Write Way, 1996), pp. 216–227.

Many of Loren D. Estleman's readers know him best as a Pulitzer Prize–nominated author of Western nonfiction and novels; others admire what the reviewer in *The New York Times* of 19 March 1995 termed his "nifty series about the Motor City in its hot-wheels heyday." A legion of readers in yet another area—the hard-boiled mystery—revere him as a novelist in the true Dashiell Hammett–Raymond Chandler tradition. To date, he has written or cowritten a total of fifty books. The thirty-one mystery and crime titles among them prove him an intricate plotter, an adept with the English language, and a man with a soft spot for his adopted hometown—for, in this author's world, the city of Detroit is as important as any of his human characters.

Estleman, who jokes that his middle initial stands for "Danger, or possibly Dagwood," was born in Ann Arbor, Michigan, in 1952, the son of a truck driver and a postal worker. He attended Eastern Michigan University and graduated with a degree in English literature and journalism in 1974. Two years later, while working as editor in chief of a weekly community newspaper, he wrote *The Oklahoma Punk,* a sensationalistic gangster novel loosely based on the life of Wilbur Underhill, an early public enemy. The book was published only in paperback and was not a commercial success. The four books that followed, however—a pair of Westerns, *The Hider* (1978) and *The High Rocks* (1979), and the speculative horror novels *Sherlock Holmes vs. Dracula* (1978) and *Dr. Jekyll and Mr. Holmes* (1979)—established the young writer's reputation in the publishing industry. The Holmes pastiches have been continuously in print since their first release.

Estleman's first hard-boiled mystery was *Motor City Blue* (1980). He decided to try his hand at the genre because, as he explained seventeen years later in an interview conducted for this profile, "It's the most vibrant fiction being written today, a medium that can be made to say anything. It's the new mainstream." To prepare himself to write he first immersed himself in Detroit history, from its founding as a British fort through the modern day. He took walks through the city's seamier sections and set down what he found in merciless prose. Early in the novel, Estleman's private detective, Amos Walker, gives the reader a cinematic impression of a neighborhood in decay:

> Dry, grainy snow—the kind that usually falls in the city—heaped the sills of unused doorways and lined the

"Martha Burns," he reflected, as if I'd just mentioned the name. "I'm not sure I--"

"Beryl Garnet said you offered to record her," I said.

A sly look came over his features. His expressive face must have been something to see when they had him in court on the payola charge. "She's marrying money, I bet," he said. "He's paying you to look up her past. I bet there's big dough in it."

"Wrong twice. Her father's looking for her and I'm getting my usual fee. Which is probably less than what you'd slip a deejay to turn a bomb into a hit."

"Hell. The way she carried on I thought she had William Clay Ford on the hook at least."

"She was here, then. When?"

"What's it worth?"

"Depends on what you've got to sell."

"I got expenses to meet. Rent. Utilities. It's gonna be a long winter. I'm gonna burn a lot of gas."

"Not as much as you're burning right now, brother."

"I need some guarantee I'll get paid for what I give."

"Sorry."

He thought about it a minute. The minister had stopped playing in the next room and was scratching something on his sheet music. Zacharias stepped over and pulled shut the

Page from the typescript for Estleman's 1980 novel Motor City Blue *(Collection of Loren D. Estleman)*

gutters in narrow ribbons, where the wind caught and swept it winding like white snakes across the pavement, picking up crumples of muddy newspaper and old election campaign leaflets and empty condom wrappers and broken Styrofoam cups as it went, rattling them against the pitted sides of abandoned cars shunted up to the curb; weathering the corners off ancient buildings advertising various hetero- and homosexual entertainments; banging loose boards nailed over the windows of gutted stores defiled with skulls and crossbones and spray-painted graffiti identifying them as street-gang hangouts, Keep Out; buckling a billboard atop a brownstone two blocks south upon which a gaggle of grinning citizens gathered at the base of the Renaissance Center, near where its first suicide landed, urged me to Take Another Look at Detroit.

Motor City Blue opens as Walker witnesses a kidnapping, and recognizes the victim as his old army commander. For the next week, he alternates between looking into the abduction and aiding a paying client, a "retired" gang boss who fears that his ward has become involved with the pornographic picture trade. Little by little, the detective discovers links between the two cases, and from both to a third, more high-profile crime—and realizes that the kidnappers are as aware of him as he is of them.

Though critics showed great enthusiasm for later books in this series, many were ambivalent about the initial entry. The reviewer for the *Kirkus Reviews* of 1 July 1980 dismissed it as "moderately engaging" and "painless." The remarks by Newgate Callendar in *The New York Times* for 26 October were lukewarm: the novel "moves nicely along, makes its points and stops. It is conventional, but it is also expertly written." By December, however, the newspaper had named *Motor City Blue* to its list of the Most Notable Books of the Year.

Amos Walker, the protagonist of *Motor City Blue* and twelve other mysteries to date, is his creator's most popular character, a former police cadet turned private investigator who works Detroit from high-toned Grosse Pointe to the inner-city neighborhoods gutted during the race riots of the 1960s. It is no coincidence that the character bears a strong physical resemblance to the author—solemn-looking, medium build, dark hair and mustache, and a cleft chin: the writer admitted in a 1991 *Armchair Detective* interview that Walker is "a compendium of every police officer I have ever known and part of myself, or what I would like to be." In the first book of the series, the detective is thirty-two years old; since then, he has gradually aged to and remains in his mid-forties. Like his creator, Walker grew up in a small town west of the city, is divorced (Estleman, however, has remarried), and enjoys old movies and jazz music.

Estleman's detective served as a military policeman in Vietnam and attended the Detroit police acad-

emy, from which he was expelled for breaking the nose of a fellow cadet who made advances on him. He lives in blue-collar Hamtramck and works out of a "third-floor wheeze-up" downtown, getting from place to place in a succession of nondescript American cars equipped with heavy-duty engines that "can hit sixty-five while you're still closing the door on the passenger side." His closest friends, if he can be said to have any, are Lieutenant (later Captain and Inspector) John Alderdyce of the Detroit police; Iris, former heroin addict and prostitute; and investigative reporter Barry Stackpole, who escaped minus one leg and half a hand from a mob car-bombing and has since lived out of a suitcase, always ready to move to a safer port. In the post-1980s books, a relationship of sorts has sprung up between Walker and Lieutenant Mary Ann Thaler, a police detective who is following in Alderdyce's wake through the hierarchy of the department.

Among his literary influences Estleman lists Jack London, champion of the two-fisted loner, and Edgar Allan Poe, whose sway is more apparent in the two Sherlock Holmes novels than in the Walker series. In his novels he makes references to authors as disparate as Miguel de Cervantes, Edward Arlington Robinson, and Richard Connell. Although Estleman claims that he "didn't discover Chandler until I was well established as a professional writer of mystery fiction," allusions to the world the earlier writer created are frequent in the series, even in the earliest books. The emphysemic, wheelchair-bound old mobster who hungrily watches Walker smoke cigarettes in the first novel is reminiscent of General Sternwood in Chandler's *The Big Sleep* (1939), who takes vicarious enjoyment in Philip Marlowe's brandy-drinking. Walker enjoys—if that is the word—the same brusquely cordial relationship with Alderdyce that Marlowe has with Bernie Ohls, and his hatred of crooked Inspector Proust echoes Marlowe's feelings toward the lawmen of Bay City. Like his predecessor, Walker keeps a whiskey bottle in his bottom desk drawer; a poster on his office wall of Marlowe's most famous portrayer, Humphrey Bogart, accentuates the similarity still further.

Estleman also has stylistic similarities to Chandler. Like Marlowe, who in *Farewell, My Lovely* (1940) observes that the gaudily dressed Moose Malloy "looked about as inconspicuous as a tarantula on a slice of angel food," Amos Walker has a penchant for absurd similes. In *The Midnight Man* (1982), for example, he remarks, "The corrugated steel trailer was easy to overlook, like a brontosaurus on a whole wheat roll." In his descriptions, Estleman achieves passages that in their rhythm and tone bear comparison to Chandler's best work. In the celebrated opening of his

1938 story "Red Wind," Chandler describes a portentous evening:

> There was a desert wind blowing that night. It was one of those hot dry Santa Anas that come down through the mountain passes and curl your hair and make your nerves jump and your skin itch. On nights like that every booze party ends in a fight. Meek little wives feel the edge of the carving knife and study their husbands' necks. Anything can happen. You can even get a full glass of beer at a cocktail lounge.

In *The Midnight Man* Estleman vividly evokes a sweltering summer day that has much the same edge:

> It was one of those gummy mornings we get all through July and August, when the warm wet towel on your face is the air you're breathing, and the headache you wake up with is the same one you took to bed the night before. Milk turns in the refrigerator. Doors swell. Flies clog the screens gasping for oxygen. Everything you touch sticks, including the receiver you pick up just to stop the bell from jangling loose your tender brain.

In his later work it is clear that Estleman writes consciously within the Chandler tradition. His 1987 story "Bodyguards Shoot Second," included in the collection *General Murders: Ten Amos Walker Mysteries* (1988), is an homage to the classic Chandler short story "Trouble Is My Business."

Estleman is able to smoothly detail even the filthiest setting or the most vicious fistfight. As Robert A. Baker and Michael T. Nietzel assert in their study *Private Eyes: One Hundred and One Knights* (1985), Estleman "writes like Torme sings and vintage Desmond played. You can feel what's coming but the notes always tumble together just a little better than you ever anticipated." His narrative is polished to the point where no excess words can be trimmed, as in the poetic opening of *The Midnight Man*:

> Look for us on starless nights when the moon is new. Look closely, because we're hard to see. We don't run in packs like wolves or feral dogs; we fear each other as much as we fear the light. The shadows are our home, and we know them as you know the staircase to your bedroom, the light switch on your bathroom wall. Look for us, but keep your distance. We're the Midnight Men, and the prey we're stalking could be you.

Estleman's twenty-year career has inextricably linked his name to the city of Detroit, though it is unlikely the chamber of commerce approves of the author's frequent remarks about filthy streets, drug abuse, graffiti, racial conflicts, and vice. He is often able to characterize large areas in a single descriptive state-

Dust jacket for Estleman's first novel to feature private investigator Amos Walker

ment, such as "Erskine Street, where they took down the red lights a long time ago for the same reason a church needs no sign to tell you it's a house of God." Even the Renaissance Center, the glittering towers intended to represent a revitalized Detroit, is described in various books as being "lit up like a whorehouse on Saturday night" and having "all the sinister beauty of a stiletto with a jeweled handle." As a reviewer noted in *The New York Times* of 20 April 1986, "There is a kind of poetry in his snapshots of the underside of a city with which he so clearly has a love-hate relationship." Asked in the late 1990s about his true feelings toward Detroit, Estleman replied, "Places aren't evil; people are, or they aren't. Jam enough humanity into one relatively small area and their prevailing characteristics increase a thousandfold. Detroit is equal parts exalting and frightening, but the greatest danger is to ignore its dark side, to pretend it doesn't exist." No one who has read an Estleman mystery can claim ignorance of this dark side—or, for that matter, of the city's possibilities once improvements are made.

The city as Estleman describes it is thoroughly up-to-date, but Walker himself could easily be a product of *Black Mask,* the pulp magazine that gave birth to the hard-boiled detective in the 1920s. He smokes one cigarette after another—longing to, but unable to snap a match off his thumbnail for effect—and drinks in the manner of Hammett's Continental Op, which is to say continuously, while seldom losing his reason. He wears a battered fedora that is often the subject of comment by other characters. Like his creator, Walker is a technophobe who shies away from any invention more complicated than a microfiche reader. Estleman calls the character an anachronism, even more so today than at the time he created him. "When you can find your long-lost biological parents at the click of a key or run a credit check on a stranger without getting up from your ergonomically designed swivel, what's more obsolete than a private detective?" he wonders, adding, "Walker's saving grace is that through a combination of courage and judgment—two things not programmed into any hard drive—he makes himself indispensable." Estleman also refers to his detective as a knight-errant, an apt description, for Walker's attitude toward women is chivalrous without being patronizing. Indeed, much of the danger he faces results from his delving further than necessary into a case on behalf of a female client or suspect, not all of whom are as innocent as he wishes them to be.

Sometimes, against his better judgment, Walker admires the criminals with whom he is forced to associate. He admits respect for a clever African American henchman in *Motor City Blue,* and a red-haired gunman in *Lady Yesterday* (1987) impresses him with his loyalty, his bravery under fire, even the way he walks, "like a snow tiger rolling the stiffness out of its muscles." Even so, Walker never gives in to the temptations of a criminal lifestyle: however blemished his reputation may become in the course of a case, it is always restored by the conclusion. Estleman remains true to the Chandler prescription articulated in "The Simple Art of Murder," for his detective is a man "who is not himself mean, who is neither tarnished nor afraid."

Estleman's style and his characters noticeably mature over the course of the first half-dozen Amos Walker books, which he turned out one per year, in alternation with Westerns. *Angel Eyes* (1981) concerns the detective's search for a woman who had put him on retainer to find her if and when she disappeared. In *The Midnight Man,* Walker acts for the first time from purely noble motives: when a police sergeant who once did him a favor is paralyzed by a black militant's bullet, Walker repays him by tracking down the shooter at no

charge. He is dogged at every step by a bounty hunter who travels in a bulletproof mobile home equipped with a cache of semiautomatic weapons and a built-in cell. In the fourth book, *The Glass Highway* (1983), Walker is hired by a Detroit newscaster to track down his son, who has been lured into Grosse Pointe's pill-popping youth culture. He succeeds, only to find himself inextricably tangled in a drug case involving Central American gangsters and the government's witness protection program. *Sugartown* (1984) has one of the quieter but more memorable openings of the series, as an elderly Polish woman with work-roughened hands walks with queenlike dignity into Walker's office and hands him her life savings to find her grandson, whom she has not seen for nineteen years. Kathleen Maio of the *Wilson Library Bulletin* singled out this scene as representative of the author's ability to write "of the threadworn respectability of working people stranded on the edge of an urban wasteland." The novel won the Private Eye Writers of America Shamus Award and is considered by many critics to be the best in the series.

In 1984 Estleman created a second continuing character, Walker's polar opposite. Peter Macklin is a weary, middle-aged man with an alcoholic wife and a sullen, drug-addicted son. He owns a large house in the suburbs, but spends little time there, as he is usually on the road with his job as an "efficiency expert"—mob jargon for a contract assassin. Estleman explained in 1997 that in creating Macklin, he wanted to explore the life and thought processes of a professional killer "without passing judgment or making him heroic. Too often in fiction, hit men are presented as psychos, as if to say that normal people don't harbor dark thoughts about . . . pulling off the perfect murder. . . . My observation is that most killers for hire are depressingly ordinary, treat their work as just another job, and never talk about it at home. Perhaps this is the ultimate evil: the reduction of murder to mundane routine." Macklin's ordinariness, combined with his quick mind and his utter lack of concern for human life, make him the best in his field—and a hazard to mobsters who hope to challenge the status quo.

The character appears in three books to date: *Kill Zone* (1984), *Roses Are Dead* (1985), and *Any Man's Death* (1986). In the first, Macklin is used as a bargaining tool by his imprisoned employer, who will receive prison "good time" if the assassin can save a boatload of hostages from a terrorist group. Macklin does his job, picking off the villains one by one in creative fashion. In the second book, Macklin must contend with a new problem: his cocky son, Roger, newly weaned off heroin, wants to follow in his father's footsteps. The junior and senior Macklins face off in *Any Man's Death,* at which point Estleman

Loren D. Estleman is a veteran journalist of police-court news and a graduate of Eastern Michigan University. He has written twelve earlier books, including three Amos Walker mysteries, and several westerns, and books pitting Sherlock Holmes against Dracula and Jekyll and Hyde. His *Aces and Eights* won the 1982 Golden Spur Award of the Western Writers of America. He lives in Whitmore Lake, Michigan.

Dust jacket for Estleman's fourth Amos Walker mystery (1983), in which the detective's search for a newscaster's son leads to his involvement with gangsters from Central America

let the series lapse. He gives three reasons for his decision: his workload at the time was just too heavy to continue; he "wanted to prevent the possibility of the series degenerating into an Executioner-type monthly bloodfest, with numbers on the covers to help readers avoid buying the same book twice"; and the series as written had already evolved into an ideal trilogy. Estleman, however, leaves open the possiblilty of reviving the character for at least one more book.

One of the most intriguing Amos Walker novels, *Every Brilliant Eye* (1986), continues the theme of the ordinary man as killer. The detective sets out to find reporter Barry Stackpole, whom he has not seen since weeks before, when they escaped from a police raid on an after-hours bar. On searching the reporter's latest short-term residence, he finds a half-completed typescript describing a murder committed while Barry was a correspondent in Vietnam; the first-person account is so full of detail that he finds himself wondering whether his friend has blood on his hands. As he searches, Walker must keep up his guard against two predators: an editor who has set her sights on the manuscript, and an unknown person who is systematically murdering homeless men and women. By the

time Walker completes his investigation–and realizes his many errors–it is too late: because he has allowed himself to imagine Barry in the role of killer, their relationship can never be the same again.

The reviewer for *Time* praised the next in the series, *Lady Yesterday*, proclaiming that the author "ranks behind Elmore Leonard in fame but not in quality as Detroit's other macho laureate." The book describes a double investigation on behalf of Walker's friend Iris, who begins receiving death threats soon after hiring him to find the father she has never met. The client in *Downriver* (1988) is not searching for the usual missing relative or friend. Richie De Vries has just finished a prison term for torching an abandoned building during the 1967 riots; he was charged not with arson, but with abetting a gang that hijacked an armored car while the police were busy with De Vries. He hires Walker to contact the robbers and demand their $200,000 proceeds as compensation for the twenty years he has lost. In the process, the detective discovers the sometimes ironic paths taken by a group of young radicals between their late-1960s heyday and the Yuppie Decade.

In addition to his detective novels Estleman has published two collections of crime stories. The first *General Murders: Ten Amos Walker Mysteries,* contains tales originally printed in magazines and anthologies during the previous six years. One of these, "Fast Burn," pushed Estleman into the headlines in early 1994, when a Maine man was discovered to have changed a few place names and republished it under his own name. The nine-story collection *People Who Kill* (1993), containing stories that appeared in magazines between 1977 and 1990, was released as the eighth in the Author's Choice series from the Mystery Scene Press: unlike the big-budget *General Murders,* the paperback was neither widely distributed nor reviewed.

Estleman devoted one of his three 1989 crime novels to a character who might be called the anti-Walker. Ralph Poteet, the narrator of *Peeper,* has been demoted to the mail room of his employer's agency–the aptly named Lovechild Confidential Inquiries–for taking and selling keyhole snapshots of prominent adulterers. He is a foul-mouthed, sexist homophobe, who sees no harm in taking advantage of a monsignor's indiscretion or bedding down an eighteen-year-old suspect. In an in-joke for readers of the Amos Walker series, Poteet describes himself as the "best private star in town. Well, except for this one-man show over on West Grand River, but he's a Boy Scout." To date, *Peeper* is Poteet's only appearance in print. The same year, at the request of his friend Robert Randisi, Estleman worked with four other mystery writers to create a collaborative detective novel, *The Black Moon.*

In *Silent Thunder,* Estleman's third crime novel of 1989, Walker is contracted by a larger agency to represent a wealthy woman accused of murdering her husband, a weapons collector. The victim, Walker soon discovers, was involved with mercenaries who sought something even more powerful than firearms: plutonium. The next, and the last mystery in the Amos Walker series until 1997, was *Sweet Women Lie* (1990). The two title characters are Gail Hope, a star of 1960s beach movies, and a character who has been mentioned in earlier books but never seen: Walker's former wife, Catherine. One of the pair wants to help a renegade government agent escape assassination by his employers. The other is married to him.

After the publication of *Sweet Women Lie,* Estleman temporarily shelved Walker and concentrated on what he then called the Detroit Trilogy, a series that tracks the (d)evolution of the city from the Prohibition era through the pre-riot 1960s and forward to the present. *Whiskey River* (1990), the author's own favorite among his works, describes the uneasy friendship between a newspaper columnist and an up-and-coming young gangster. In the second book, *Motown* (1991), set in the months just prior to the devastating riots, Estleman has two foci: a potential war between Sicilian and African American gangs and the infiltration of a Nader's Raiders-like consumer group by a representative of the Ford Motor Corporation. In *King of the Corner* (1992), set in the early 1990s, former Tigers pitching sensation "Doc" Miller finishes a prison term for manslaughter and returns to Detroit, where he becomes involved in the lives of his brother's family and a quasi-religious militant group that has gained legitimacy with church and civic leaders. For these books Estleman draws not only on the substantial underworld history of Detroit but also that of other major cities, blending fact and fiction into a seamless whole.

With the completion of the trilogy, Estleman spent the last half of the 1990s filling in his account of Detroit in the twentieth century with the Henry Ford–era adventure *Thunder City* (1999); *Jitterbug* (1998), about the search by 1940s detectives for a patriotic serial killer; *Edsel* (1995), set in the years just before the debut of the title auto; and *Stress* (1996), which tracks a young African American patrolman's reactions to the racial tensions of the early 1970s. (The Stop the Robberies, Enjoy Safer Streets unit–STRESS–was the antigang shock troop of the Detroit Police Department.) Estleman's historical books were highly praised. A typical view was expressed by the reviewer of *Stress* in *Publisher Weekly:* "It's difficult to believe that Detroit will ever find a more eloquent poet than Estleman, who . . . celebrates the gristle and sinew of the city as well as its aching heart."

The books of Estleman's Detroit series are longer than his mysteries and are even more descriptive. Like the Walker novels, they are intricately plotted; multiple character connections link each story to all the others. Tabloid columnist Connie Minor narrates the first and fourth books published and is interviewed by the protagonist in the second. In *Motown* the infant sons of two characters in *Whiskey River* are grown to manhood and carrying on where their gangster fathers–one tortured to death on the other's orders–had left off. A toddler in *Edsel* who is raised by relatives while his father finishes a prison term escapes the bleak future Minor predicts for him and grows up to handle murder investigations in *Stress* and *King of the Corner.* The connections among the seven novels are so many and subtle that the series repays multiple readings.

The publication in 1997 of *Never Street* marked the return of Amos Walker after a seven-year absence–"just in time," noted Marilyn Stasio in *The New York Times* of 27 April, "to smack a little sense into a genre that's getting dumber by the minute." She devoted more than half her biweekly column to praise of "Amos

Walker, who is on my short list of hard-boiled private eyes with staying power." The novel deals with Walker's search for an obsessive film noir fan, who once told his psychiatrist that he fantasized getting up from his chair and walking onto the screen. The man's wife reports that she briefly left the room as he was watching the Dick Powell classic *Pitfall.* When she returned, he had vanished. Praising the premise for the work, the critic for the 1 March *Library Journal* asserted, "Estleman ingeniously interweaves the real-life noir imitations with scenes from the movies themselves, producing a novel that is part parody, part tribute." The reviewer for the 10 February *Publisher Weekly* agreed, calling the book "a welcome shot of retrograde private-eye cool." The cast of characters—an oily, Porter Hall–like business partner, a smooth-talking shrink and his hulking assistant, and the "woman in the case," a femme fatale named Vesta Mannering—are familiar film noir types but, as with the genre the novel celebrates, people and things are not necessarily what they seem. *Never Street* is divided into four "reels," each named after a cinematic technique; the last, "Smash Cut," ends with a confrontation in a darkened theater that is the equal of any denouement in the film noir. Estleman has continued the Walker series with *The Witchfinder* (1998) and *The Hours of the Virgin* (1999).

Estleman's readers are often surprised to hear that he is not and never has been a resident of Detroit or its suburbs. Instead, he, his second wife—a former managing editor who writes under the name Deborah Morgan—and her two grown children live in the small Michigan town of Whitmore Lake, about sixty miles distant. He writes for up to six hours a day, every day, using an old Underwood manual typewriter, and can complete a novel in as little as three months. "I don't write fast, but I do write steadily," he points out, "and when you do that and refuse to mire yourself down in lame excuses like The Block, you will tend to produce." He has amassed an impressive collection of reference materials for use at home and supplements these resources with exhaustive library research and location work.

Over the course of his career Estleman has established himself as one of the top writers in his field: *Time* magazine has said that "For urban edge and macho color . . . nobody tops Loren D. Estleman." *Publisher Weekly* has dubbed him "the reigning king of the traditional, tough-yet-tender style of crime novel"; and *The New York Times* of 23 October 1983 called him both "a hard worker in a field mined with exploding talent" and one of "the top echelon of American private-eye specialists." Estleman was nominated for a Pulitzer Prize for *This Old Bill,* a biographical novel about Buffalo Bill Cody, in 1984, and has received four Golden Spur Awards from the Western Writers of America. *Whiskey River* was nominated for an Edgar by the Mystery Writers of America for Best Novel of 1991. The Private Eye Writers of America has given Estleman the annual Shamus Award three times and also honored him with a lifetime achievement award in 1999. An author still in his prime, the diligent Estleman likely has years of writing ahead of him to build on an already impressive career.

Interviews:

Jean Ross, "Loren D. Estleman: *CA* Interview," *Contemporary Authors,* New Revision Series, volume 27 (Detroit: Gale, 1988), pp. 155–158;

Keith Kroll, "The Man from Motor City," *The Armchair Detective,* 24, no. 1 (1991): 4–11.

References:

Robert A. Baker and Michael T. Nietzel, *Private Eyes: One Hundred and One Knights* (Bowling Green, Ohio: Bowling Green State University Popular Press, 1985);

Joseph Hynes, "Looking for Endings: The Fiction of Loren D. Estleman," *Journal of Popular Culture,* 29, no. 3 (1995): 121–127.

Papers:

Loren D. Estleman's papers are held at the main library of Eastern Michigan University, special collections division.

Steve Fisher

(29 August 1913 – 27 March 1980)

Katherine M. Restaino
Fairleigh Dickinson University

BOOKS: *Spend the Night,* as Grant Lane (New York: Phoenix Press, 1935);

Satan's Angel (New York: Macaulay, 1935);

Murder of the Admiral, as Stephen Gould (New York: Macaulay, 1936);

Forever Glory (New York: Macaulay, 1936);

Murder of the Pigboat Skipper, as Gould (New York: Hillman-Curl, 1937);

The Night Before Murder (New York: Hillman-Curl, 1939);

Homicide Johnny, as Gould (New York: Mystery House, 1940; London: S. Pemberton, 1946);

I Wake Up Screaming (New York: Dodd, Mead, 1941; London: Hale, 1943; revised edition, New York: Bantam, 1960; revised again, New York: Vintage, 1991);

Destroyer (New York & London: Appleton, Century, 1941);

Destination Tokyo (New York & London: Appleton, Century, 1943);

Winter Kill (New York: Dodd, Mead, 1946);

The Sheltering Night (New York: Fawcett, 1952);

Giveaway (New York: Random House, 1954);

Take All You Can Get (New York: Random House, 1955);

Susan Slept Here; A Comedy in Two Acts, by Fisher and Alex Gottlieb (New York: S. French, 1956);

No House Limit: A Novel of Las Vegas (New York: Dutton, 1958);

Image of Hell (New York: Dutton, 1961);

Saxon's Ghost (Los Angeles: Sherbourne, 1969);

The Big Dream (Garden City, N.Y.: Doubleday, 1970);

The Hell-Black Night (Los Angeles: Sherbourne, 1970).

PLAY PRODUCTION: *Susan Slept Here,* by Fisher and Alex Gottlieb, New York, Forty-first Street Theater, 12 July 1961.

PRODUCED SCRIPTS:

MOTION PICTURES

Typhoon, screen story by Fisher, script by Allen Rivkin and Leonard Lee, Paramount, 1940;

Steve Fisher (photograph by Michael Fisher; from the dust jacket for The Big Dream, *1970)*

To the Shores of Tripoli, script by Fisher and Lamar Trotti, 20th Century-Fox, 1942;

Berlin Correspondent, script by Fisher and Jack Andrews, 20th Century-Fox, 1942;

Johnny Angel, RKO Radio, 1945;

Lady in the Lake, based on novel by Raymond Chandler, script by Fisher and Chandler (uncredited), M-G-M, 1946;

Dead Reckoning, script by Fisher and Oliver H. P. Garrett, Columbia, 1947;

That's My Man, script by Fisher and Bradley King, Republic, 1947;

Song of the Thin Man, script by Fisher and Nat Perrin, M-G-M, 1947;

The Hunted, based on Fisher's short story "You'll Always Remember Me," Allied Artists, 1947;

I Wouldn't Be in Your Shoes, based on novel by Cornell Woolrich, Monogram, 1948;

Tokyo Joe, screen story by Fisher, script by Cyril Hume and Bertram Millhauser, Santana-Columbia, 1949;

A Lady Without Passport, screen treatment by Fisher and others, script by Hume, M-G-M, 1950;

Roadblock, script by Fisher and George Bricker, RKO Radio, 1951;

Whispering Smith vs. Scotland Yard, Royal-Exclusive-RKO, 1952;

Battle Zone, Allied Artists, 1952;

Flat Top, Monogram, 1952;

The Big Frame, script by Fisher and John Gilling, Royal-RKO Radio, 1952;

San Antone, Republic, 1953;

The Woman They Almost Lynched, Republic, 1953;

City That Never Sleeps, Republic, 1953;

The Man from the Alamo, script by Fisher and D. D. Beauchamp, Universal-International, 1953;

Sea of Lost Ships, Republic, 1953;

Terror Street, Exclusive-Lippert, 1954;

Hell's Half Acre, Republic, 1954;

The Shanghai Story, script by Fisher and Seton I. Miller, Republic, 1954;

The Big Tip-Off, Allied Artists, 1955;

Las Vegas Shakedown, Allied Artists, 1955;

Betrayed Women, Allied Artists, 1955;

Night Freight, Allied Artists, 1955;

Silent Fear, NAC-Gilbralter, 1955;

The Toughest Man Alive, Allied Artists, 1955;

Top Gun, script by Fisher and Richard Schayer, Fame–United Artists, 1955;

The Restless Breed, Alperson–20th Century-Fox, 1957;

Courage of Black Beauty, Alperson–20th Century-Fox, 1957;

I, Mobster, Alperson–20th Century-Fox, 1958;

September Storm, screen story by Fisher, script by W. R. Burnett, Alperson–20th Century-Fox, 1960;

Law of the Lawless, Lyles-Paramount, 1964;

Black Spurs, Lyles-Paramount, 1964;

Young Fury, screen story by Fisher and A. C. Lyles, script by Fisher, Lyles-Paramount, 1965;

Johnny Reno, screen story by Fisher and Andrew Craddock, script by Fisher, Lyles-Paramount, 1966;

Waco, Lyles-Paramount, 1966;

Red Tomahawk, screen story by Fisher and Craddock, script by Fisher, Lyles-Paramount, 1966;

Fort Utah, screen story by Fisher and Craddock, script by Fisher, Lyles-Paramount, 1967;

Hostile Guns, script by Fisher and Sloan Nibley, Lyles-Paramount, 1967;

Arizona Bushwhackers, Lyles-Paramount, 1968;

Rogue's Gallery, Lyles-Paramount, 1968;

The Great Gundown, Sun Productions, 1977.

TELEVISION

The George Sanders Mystery Theatre, NBC, 1957;

"Man on a Raft" (pilot), *Michael Shayne, Detective*, NBC, 28 September 1958;

Bringing Up Buddy, CBS, 1960–1961;

The Dick Powell Show, NBC, 1961–1963;

Luke and the Tenderfoot (pilot), CBS, 6 and 13 August 1965;

The Wild, Wild West, CBS, 1965–1970;

Cannon, CBS, 1971–1976;

McMillan and Wife, NBC, 1971–1976;

Barnaby Jones, CBS, 1973–1980;

S.W.A.T., ABC, 1975–1977;

Switch, CBS, 1975–1978;

Starsky and Hutch, ABC, 1975–1979;

On Our Own, CBS, 1977–1978;

Fantasy Island, ABC, 1978–1980.

OTHER: "Cornell Woolrich: 'I Had Nobody,'" *Armchair Detective*, 3 (April 1970): 164–165;

"Pulp Literature: A Sub-Culture Revolution in the Late 1930s," *Armchair Detective*, 5 (1971/1972): 91–92, 95.

Steve Fisher earned a living in the pulp-magazine market through his ability to develop simple, fast-moving plots devoid of embellishments but invested with real emotion. Although many of his hard-boiled stories featured the unsentimental private eye, Fisher made a niche for himself among genre writers by revealing a more human side of his private eyes, cops, and adventurers. In his essay "Pulp Literature: A Sub-Culture Revolution in the Late 1930s" in *The Armchair Detective*, Fisher claimed that a story he originally published in May 1938 contributed significantly to a tonal change in the genre: "One of my *Black Mask* stories was 'Wait for Me,' about a white Russian whore in Shanghai trying to escape the country, a U.S. sailor tagging after her everywhere, calling out 'Wait for me,' but she didn't, and in her devious manipulations to obtain a phony passport, was murdered in an upstairs room while the sailor waited for her below. All he wanted to say was that he would marry her, and that way she could have a legitimate passport. Well, that one broke the old style and even plot taboos, and other stories like it followed by me, Gruber and Woolrich . . . and since *Black Mask* was still regarded as the beacon light of pulp fiction, other magazines began to take notice of this not so very subtle style change . . . the subjective tough-tender school."

Born on 29 August 1913 in Marine City, Michigan, Stephen Gould Fisher grew up in the Los Angeles area. Because his mother, an actress, was away from home fre-

to the center of the floor
lay the sprawled figure of
a man

HOTEL MURDER

By STEVE FISHER

*A room locked from the inside, a corpse shot in the back,
and three suspects—that's the problem Mike Hanlon faces!*

FOOTSTEPS padded quickly along the corridors of the Hotel Wellinglex. Crystal over-head lights shafted white beams on the red plush carpets. A room door slammed.

A shot!

The bell captain, in the hall on the twentieth floor, turned suddenly. He rushed to the door of the room from which the explosion had sounded. He tried the knob, reached for his keys; then remembering his instructions, hesitated. He waited impatiently until there was someone else in the hall.

"Get the police—quickly!"

The man in the hall ran to the bell captain.

"But—"

"I've got to stay here," the hotel employee said. "I heard a shot. Unless it's suicide, there's a killer in that room. Hurry now! Get someone!"

Mike Hanlon, of the Homicide Division, got off the elevator and came swinging up the hall. The red-faced Irish dick had a ragged cigar jammed in his mouth. His black eyes were glittering.

The bell captain was in a nervous

158

First page of a Fisher story in Thrilling Detective *magazine in the 1930s* quently, she enrolled Fisher in Oneonta Military Academy; at the age of sixteen, he ran away from the school and enlisted in the navy, where he spent four years on a submarine. During his navy stint Fisher wrote more than two hundred stories about navy and submarine life, many of which were published in the ship's newspaper and other navy magazines.

After his discharge from the navy, Fisher returned to California and tried to become a full-time writer, but he was not selling any stories. Frustrated by his lack of success as well as by the absence of a writers' community, Fisher decided to hitchhike to New York City in 1934. In his first months Fisher fit the stereotype of the struggling author living in Greenwich Village: he was evicted from his apartment for not paying the rent, was forced to pawn his typewriter on several occasions, and was even pushed to the extreme of making tomato soup by pouring a bottle of ketchup stolen from a drugstore lunch counter into hot water. He became so desperate for money that he went from the offices of one pulp magazine to another in an attempt to collect his unsold stories so that he could try to market them to other magazines. He was given $60 at the first magazine for a story; $125 at another stop; and upon returning to his room, Fisher found a check for $250 from a third magazine. By the end of the week, Fisher's rounds to collect his stories had earned him $600.

Fisher was also able to connect with other writers. The friends he made during his years in Greenwich Village and other New York neighborhoods included his close friend Frank Gruber, who in *The Pulp Jungle* (1967) provides details of Fisher's life, as well as Roger Torrey, Cornell Woolrich, Carroll John Daly (the creator of Race Williams, the first hard-boiled private eye), and other writers who belonged to the American Fiction Guild, a society for pulp writers. He also befriended Edythe (Edie) Syme, an editor at *Dime Detective* who became his first wife in 1935.

Gradually Fisher's stories began to appear in print, beginning with "Hell's Scoop" in the March 1934 issue of *Sure-Fire Detective Magazine*. His stories appeared in pulps such as *Spicy Mystery Stories, Thrilling Detective, True Gang Life, The Shadow, Detective Fiction Weekly, New Mystery Adventures, Underground Detective, The Mysterious Fu Wang, Phantom Detective, Ace Detective, Saucy Romantic Adventures, Mystery Adventure, Detective Tales, The Whisperer, Headquarters Detective, Hardboiled, Doc Savage, Black Mask, Feds, Federal Agent, Popular Detective, Pocket Detective, Clues, Detective Romances, Crime Busters,* and *Detective Story Magazine*. During his career he published more than five hundred stories in the pulps and created several series characters, including Kip Muldane, a Hawaiian private eye operating in Hawaii for *Black Mask,* the Kid and Sheridan Doome for *The Shadow* and *Shadow Magazine,* and Mr. Death for *Dare-Devil Aces*.

Most of Fisher's work appeared in the pulps under the name of Steve Fisher, but he used the pen names of Stephen Gould and Grant Lane under certain circumstances. If he had more than one story in a particular issue of a pulp, one would carry the Fisher byline and the other either Lane or Gould. The Kid stories, chronicling the adventures of Danny Garrett, the shoeshine kid detective, appeared on a regular basis in *The Shadow*. They were first published under Fisher's name from 1937 through 1939 and were usually featured as the cover story once a month. After Fisher began to sell more stories to other magazines, he wrote the remaining twenty-nine Kid stories as Grant Lane, the last of which, "Clue for the Kid," appeared in the September 1943 issue of *The Shadow*.

Some of Fisher's early stories reflected his experiences with the sea, as may be seen from such titles as "Murder in the Navy" in the November 1934 *Thrilling Detective,* "The Navy Spirit" in the February 1935 *True Gang Life,* and "The Tattooed Skipper" in the 1 May 1935 *The Shadow*. As Stephen Gould, Fisher joined his knowledge of sea life with his penchant for private-eye stories and created the character of Sheridan Doome, a naval intelligence officer whose face was badly mutilated in an explosion that shattered his nerve endings, thereby depriving him of the ability to show facial expressions. He had a slit for a mouth and blotches for eyes and his body was held upright by steel braces, but his brain functioned brilliantly. In every story he was called on to solve a murder; he engaged in a gunfight, defied death, and tricked the murderer into confessing. The stories that appeared in *The Shadow* between 15 November 1937 and 15 January 1938 were later sent by Fisher to H. N. Swanson, his Hollywood agent, for possible sale to the movies. Swanson rejected the stories because he did not think a horrible-looking detective would have audience appeal.

Fisher's big break in the pulps came when his friend Gruber convinced Fanny Ellsworth, the newly appointed editor of *Black Mask,* to buy Fisher's story "Murder at Eight." Under the editorship of Joseph "Cap" Shaw, *Black Mask* had become the premier pulp of its type and had done much to establish the image of the tough-talking, gun-toting, violence-prone private eye. In 1937 Shaw, who had rejected Fisher's stories, was replaced by Ellsworth, formerly the editor of *Ranch Romances,* who was pleased by the author's "tough-tender" style. In all, Fisher published nine stories in *Black Mask:* "Murder at Eight" (August 1937), "No Gentleman Strangles his Wife" (February 1938), "Death of a Dummy" (February 1938), "You'll Always Remember Me" (March 1938), "Wait for Me" (May 1938), "Hollywood Party" (June 1938), "Jake and Jill" (January 1939), "Flight to Paris" (February 1939), and "Latitude Unknown" (April 1939).

At the time that Fisher was writing stories for the pulps, he was also writing novels, the first of which, *Spend*

Dust jacket for Fisher's 1941 novel, in which a homicide detective frames a screenwriter for the murder of an actress

and *American Magazine,* through the 1940s Fisher's main market was the pulps.

Fisher may have written even more stories for the pulps than those found under his known pseudonyms. In *Danger Is My Business* (1993), Lee Server explains that *Spicy Mystery Stories* offered its writers three cents more per word for stories with "hot spots," or sexually provocative situations, and paid authors immediately—an attractive combination for a pulp writer. Fisher's only acknowledged story for that pulp is "Shanghai Sue," which appeared in the July 1934 issue, but he wrote similar stories under his own name for *Saucy Romantic Adventures:* "G is for Girl" (May 1936), "White Sails Against the Sun" (July 1936), and "Aloha Oe" (August 1936). It is possible, according to Server, that Fisher wrote many more "saucy" and "spicy" stories under another pseudonym he never revealed. Whether or not he wrote more than five hundred stories with which he is credited, Fisher's output was not only prodigious but also professional. He would work through the night to meet deadlines and often had no idea of a story line when he sat down at his typewriter on Sunday night to create a story due for *The Shadow* on Monday morning.

Fisher's stories were direct and simple in plot, and the characters, while well defined, were neither complex nor stereotypical. In short, the plots and the people were believable because Fisher had the gift, evident in all of his writing, of focusing on what he knew. In his short stories he usually drew on either his navy years or the excitement and ambience of New York City in the 1930s and 1940s. Later, after he moved back to Los Angeles, he captured the feel of that city in the post–World War II years in his stories, novels, and screenplays.

A representative Fisher story is "Goodbye Hannah," which originally appeared in the December 1938 issue of *Double Detective.* The story has been anthologized several times, most recently in *My Favorite Mysteries* (1989) by Elliott Roosevelt, who selected it because "neither Fisher nor anybody else has ever been in much better form than in this oddly romantic tough story." "Goodbye Hannah" tells the tale of Hannah Stevens, a young woman who attempts to save Ronald Watt, her playboy fiancé, from Nicki Spioni, a mobster threatening Watt's life because of his gambling debts. Spioni falls in love with Hannah, who then disappears and is thought to be dead. The narrator, New York City homicide detective Johnny Smith, stays on the case and eventually finds Hannah in an apartment on the Upper West Side where she is working as a prostitute, her face badly scarred from a knife wound she received during a scuffle with Spioni. Smith decides that Hannah's mother should remember her daughter as a beautiful woman taken in the prime of her life, so he identifies a Jane Doe with a battered skull as Hannah. Fisher uses motifs associated with many other

the *Night* (1935), appeared under the name Grant Lane; it was followed by *Satan's Angel* later in that same year. The books were not successful and neither was reviewed for any major newspaper or magazine. Fisher wrote two of his next three novels as Gould—*Murder of the Admiral* (1936) and *Murder of the Pigboat Skipper* (1937)—both featuring Sheridan Doome. Although the works and the character were considered unbelievable, the reviewer for the 30 May 1936 *Saturday Review* commented favorably on the author's knowledge of the navy.

Not able to rely on his novels as a major source of income, Fisher continued to write stories under all three names for all types of pulps: romances, science fiction, mystery and detective stories, adventure tales, and army and navy stories. He clearly was adept at writing for the market, which paid writers by the word. Fisher also managed to sell stories to the "slicks," large-circulation magazines printed on slick paper that paid much more for stories than did the pulps. His first such story was "About Bread on Water," which appeared in the 5 June 1937 *Liberty.* Although he published other stories and novellas in *Liberty* as well as some of the other slicks, including *Collier's, The Saturday Evening Post, Cosmopolitan,* hard-boiled stories—Smith is a drinker who looks "as if he had been hit in the face with a ton of wet towels"—but the poignancy of the ending is memorable. Smith's obsession for Hannah—he makes a shrine of her pictures on his dresser—anticipates Ed Cornell's shrine to Vicky Lynn in Fisher's best-known novel, *I Wake Up Screaming* (1941).

In September 1937 Gruber convinced Swanson, a former pulp writer turned successful Hollywood agent, to represent Fisher, who wanted to write for the movies and was interested in returning to Los Angeles where his mother still lived. By this time Fisher had two infant sons and needed a contract with a studio that would pay more money than he could earn writing stories for the pulps and the slicks, for he realized that once he had committed himself to a studio as a writer he would no longer have time to write many magazine stories. Swanson convinced Fisher that he should remain in the East, at least for a while, because it would be difficult to meet his salary demands. At Swanson's urging, Fisher entered into an agreement with the Harold Ober Literary Agency in New York City to act on his behalf in selling stories and ideas for magazine serials to the slicks.

Despite Swanson's reservations, Fisher decided to move to Paris in 1939 and follow the lead of other expatriates who went abroad to live cheaply and develop their talents. During his six months abroad, Fisher had his first Hollywood break. Swanson sold Fisher's short story "If You Break My Heart," which was published in *Liberty* of 13 November 1937, to Universal Pictures. The story became the movie *Nurse from Brooklyn* (1938). Another short story, "Shore Leave," was sold to Monogram and made into *Navy Secrets* (1939), starring Fay Wray of *King Kong* fame. Swanson then sold Paramount Pictures another Fisher story that became the movie *Typhoon* (1940), featuring Dorothy Lamour and Robert Preston. The sale of these stories made it possible for Fisher to return to the United States.

Fisher then went to Hollywood in the latter part of 1939 to work as a writer at Paramount, but his option was dropped and he returned to New York where he wrote *Homicide Johnny* (1940), a novella that Swanson sold to 20th Century-Fox. Fisher had featured his protagonist, Johnny West, a member of the police force in Mamaroneck, New York, in some of his pulp stories and had published another West novel, *The Night Before Murder* (1939), prior to *Homicide Johnny*. The Mamaroneck setting was authentic because Fisher and his family were actually renting a home in the town, a suburb to the north of New York City, at the time that he was writing the stories. In both novels Johnny West is romantically involved with Penny Lane, the local librarian, who functions as an amateur detective.

The Night Before Murder deals with a murder that takes place in the summer home of Rhea Davis, a Broad-way actress who wishes to serve as a mentor to young people hoping for careers in the theater. Davis invites several theater folk to her home for the summer, but most of them decline the invitation after they receive phone calls warning them that they will die if they go. Dorothy Noel, a young actress, and Clifton Dell, an aspiring playwright, do go to Mamaroneck and become involved in a series of events based on a secret in Dorothy's past. Several people die before the mystery is solved. The climax is not satisfactory as Fisher does not do the necessary groundwork in order to establish the motivation for the murder.

Homicide Johnny opens with West's resignation from the police force. Although he is planning to relocate in San Francisco and work as a private eye, he decides to stay in Mamaroneck when Harry Waters, editor of *The Mamaroneck Star*, is murdered. Not well liked by people in the community, Waters had caused problems for many, including Dr. Jim Hale, owner of a local sanitarium, who had developed a drug for the treatment of cancer patients. A series of murders related to Hale and Waters's death ensues. *Homicide Johnny* showed Fisher's ability to play off the methods of the professional cop and the amateur detective as well as his sense of humor. "Sometimes," Johnny West comments, "I think murder brings out the best in people."

Fisher's next and most famous novel, *I Wake Up Screaming*, was bought by Darryl Zanuck for 20th Century-Fox and turned into the film noir thriller of the same title starring Betty Grable, Carol Landis, Victor Mature, and Laird Cregar. *I Wake Up Screaming*, both as a novel and a movie, shows Fisher's trademark tough-and-tender approach. Background and atmosphere are important in this novel of Hollywood in the 1940s, where five men—a screenwriter who is also the narrator of the story, a publicity agent, a director, a producer, and a juvenile lead who is outgrowing his career—decide to pool their resources to promote Vicky Lynn, formerly a secretary in the writers' building of their studio, as a budding starlet. When Lynn is found murdered in the apartment she shares with her sister Jill, all of her promoters are considered suspects. Ed Cornell, a moody, tubercular homicide detective, knows that the true killer is Harry Williams, the switchboard operator in the sisters' Hollywood apartment building. He, however, helps to hide Williams and frames the screenwriter for the murder because he believes the screenwriter should be punished for having had a relationship with Lynn.

The psychological ramifications and the atmosphere are more significant than the plot itself. Ed Cornell maintains a shrine of pictures, lighted candles, and one of Lynn's lace handkerchiefs in his apartment, and the discovery of this shrine is a revelation to readers of the novel and viewers of the film. Cornell is Fisher's portrait of Cornell Woolrich. Like the writer, he is a tall, skinny redhead who wears a derby and speaks with a nasal twang. More-

Humphrey Bogart as Warren "Rip" Murdock and Lizabeth Scott as Coral Chandler in a still from the movie Dead Reckoning *(1947), for which Fisher and Oliver H. P. Garrett wrote the script (Columbia Pictures)*

over, Cornell, described at one point as the "crepes of wrath," is clearly fashioned after the brooding, introspective, psychologically impaired characters that appear in many Woolrich short stories and novels. The intensity of Cornell's obsession with the murdered girl and his relentless efforts to frame the wrong man for the murder, even to the point of Cornell's willingness to find a sanctuary for the real murderer, show Fisher's ability to understand and capture the repressed sexual sensibilities of both Woolrich and his fictional counterparts.

Woolrich did not appear to have any hard feelings about being the source of Fisher's portrayal of Ed Cornell. Years later when he was writing a screenplay for Monogram Pictures based on Woolrich's *I Wouldn't Be in Your Shoes* (1948), Fisher did not know how to end the script because he found the conclusion of the original story murky. As Fisher recalled in his 1970 essay "Cornell Woolrich: 'I Had Nobody'" in *The Armchair Detective,* Woolrich seldom rewrote or edited any of his work, which resulted in discrepancies in the plot and endings that were not clearly explained. Fisher called Woolrich for clarification about the story's ending, and Woolrich advised Fisher to use the denouement of *I Wake Up Scream-*

ing. Fisher's only subsequent contact with Woolrich occurred in April 1968 when he received a response to a letter he had written to Woolrich, who was then recovering from the amputation of one of his legs: "You've been in my thoughts so many times over the years. Still young, still dashing, the way we like to stay in our memories of each other. The Steve that wrote *I Wake Up Screaming* and *The Shores of Tripoli.*"

Fisher and his family moved permanently to Los Angeles in 1941. Swanson was able to negotiate contracts for him over the next ten years with Paramount, Warner Bros., 20th Century-Fox, M-G-M, and Columbia. Fisher's salary increased from $400 to $1,500 a week as he established himself as a competent writer of original screen stories and screenplays. Usually his contracts contained a provision for a twelve-week layoff from the studio to enable him to write novels and plays. He was able to sell "The Hunted," a story about a young woman hounded by a cop that first appeared in the August 1939 issue of *Clues Detective Stories,* to Monogram Pictures for $2,000. He was given another $2,000 to write the script, $500 for rewrites and additional dialogue, and 10 percent of the producer's profits. One of Fisher's more unusual deals was with Republic Studios in 1949 for a then untitled story and screenplay: $5,000 payable upon the signing of the contract, $5,000 upon the studio's receipt of the first draft, and $5,000 upon delivery of the final screenplay. If more time was needed to work on the script, Fisher was to receive an additional $1,250 per week, and he was to retain radio and publication rights. If the picture earned Academy Award nominations for acting, directing, best screenplay, best picture, or best supporting actor or actress, Fisher was to be given a thoroughbred racehorse to be selected by him, but not to exceed $5,000 in price.

Even though Fisher was doing well financially in Hollywood, he never felt he was earning enough money and continued writing for the pulps and the slicks. His stories in the pulps were usually attributed to Lane and Gould and appeared only occasionally under the Fisher byline; the stories in the slicks continued to carry Fisher's name. As early as 1938 Swanson had urged Fisher to stop writing for the pulps and to sell only to the better magazines such as *Collier's* and *The Saturday Evening Post*. In a letter dated 5 March 1938 Swanson warned Fisher that the pulp market would dry up.

Fisher's prolific output of short stories was eventually supplanted by his writing for the movie studios and television and his concentration on novels. Fisher wrote original screen stories and/or screenplays for both A and B movies. His original scripts included *Berlin Correspondent* (1942), *Battle Zone* (1952), *Flat Top* (1952), and *City That Never Sleeps* (1953). The hard-boiled, tough-tender, noir qualities of his best-known novel were duplicated in such movies as *Johnny Angel* (1945), *Lady in the Lake* (1946), *Dead Reckoning* (1947), *The Hunted* (1947), and *I Wouldn't Be in Your Shoes* (1948). He wrote a whole series of crime dramas or cinematic pulps for Allied Artists in 1955, including *The Big Tip-Off, Las Vegas Shakedown,* and *Betrayed Women*. Despite his success writing for the movies, Fisher's finances suffered with the collapse of the pulp market, which Swanson had predicted. In a letter to Swanson dated 1 November 1952, Fisher informed his agent that he could no longer retain him because he had not earned any money in the last year. "In a way," he continued, "ten years in pictures, was how to make money without working, how to get to know beautiful women, and how to forget to be a writer." By this time Fisher had moved from a beautiful home in Beverly Hills to a rundown apartment in Hollywood. From the mid to the late 1960s Fisher wrote screenplays for Westerns produced by A. C. Lyles at Paramount. These films, most of which were based on screen treatments developed by Fisher with other collaborators, reflect Fisher's dependability as a writer and the work habits he had established in his years as a writer for the pulps.

Although for most of his career Fisher earned his living as a writer of short stories, screenplays, and tele-

Dust jacket for Fisher's 1970 novel, which mixes murder with movie-studio intrigue in Hollywood

vision scripts, he spent a lot of time writing novels. Fisher's 1941 novel *Destroyer* describes a situation in which the United States must defend its coastlines against attacks by Germany, Italy, and Japan, with major scenes set at sea and in the Canal Zone. The novel was well reviewed by the critics who noted the fast-paced action and realistic details known only to an experienced seaman. Drake de Kay in his review in *The New York Times* of 7 September 1941 described the novel as a "thrilling yarn by a well-known short story writer, cut to the pattern of slick-paper magazines." Another war novel, *Destination Tokyo* (1943), was made into a film with the same title, scripted by Delmar Daves and Albert Maltz.

With the exception of *Destroyer* and *Destination Tokyo*, Fisher's novels written after *I Wake Up Screaming* take on darker, more morbid tones. His next novel, *Winter Kill* (1946), set in an office in a depressing building on lower Fifth Avenue in the garment center of New York City, tells the story of five people who share a one-room office with five desks and one telephone for a rent of ten dollars per desk per week. Fisher unfolds vignettes for each of the principals, including Johnny Ryan, a private eye; Mousy Loomis, a shyster who sells protection to hotels; and Tom Sales, a literary agent who reads manuscripts for one dollar apiece. Each character has a sad tale, and each office-mate, with the exception of Loomis, tries to help the others. Loomis's murder of a cop and his attempted frame of Ryan leads to his death by the detective's hand. Ryan then uses Loomis's protection money to help each of his office-mates find his own office. *Winter Kill* is a sentimental story, almost like O. Henry in its plotlines, but it does have realistic detail. Fisher actually spent some time in a similar office, and the character of literary agent Sales was based on Ed Bodin, a "seedy pulp agent" who marketed stories for one dollar a story and shared an office with a private eye, a button broker, and a repo man.

In *The Sheltering Night* (1952) Fisher describes the plight of Ronnie, a young woman who runs away to Greenwich Village in order to escape her domineering mother in Los Angeles, leaving both her husband and young child behind. Once in New York, Ronnie, whose face is badly scarred from being hit as a child by her mother, becomes a highly paid model, her scar giving her a mysterious look. The novel is a psychological study of a young woman in deep distress because of her love-hate relationship with her mother and her inability to reclaim her daughter, who is being raised by Ronnie's grandmother.

After *Giveaway* (1954), a novel about contestants on television game shows, and *Take All You Can Get* (1955), which focuses on used-car hucksterism in Southern California, Fisher returned to the subject of crime in *No House Limit: A Novel of Las Vegas* (1958) and *The Big Dream* (1970). In *No House Limit*—a story of blackmail, frame-ups, the mafioso, and revenge—Fisher was able to rely on his own experience and love of gambling. He creates a fast-paced narrative that captures the flavor of Las Vegas while also instructing the reader on how to play craps. *The Big Dream* is both a Hollywood novel and a murder mystery in which Fisher portrays studio intrigue and the growing tension in the 1950s between the movies and television. At one point in the story Nemo Jones, a scriptwriter, seems to speak for Fisher when he asks: "What's wrong with a good, hard, fast, suspense story, a murder mystery, a jungle adventure that'll have your hair standing on end? Is that old-fashioned in your book?"

Both *Saxon's Ghost* (1969) and *The Hell-Black Night* (1970) move into the realm of suspense. *Saxon's Ghost* tells the story of Joe Saxon, the last of the old-time magicians, who refers to himself as the "psychic detective" or "ghost

breaker." When his assistant Ellen Hayes, a former topless dancer, disappears during his act, Saxon attempts to find her through psychic means as well as old-fashioned detecting. Fisher's final novel, *The Hell-Black Night,* is the story of Kelly Saunders, a hard woman who uses men to get money and security. About to be evicted from her apartment in San Francisco because her former live-in lover is no longer paying the rent, Kelly, down to her last $37.53, tries to contact every man she knows for help, including her former husband, who is shot when he tries to kill her. Fisher increases the tension by confining the action of the novel to a single night of torrential rains. The novel has less dialogue than Fisher's other books, but the suspense generated by the plot, the atmosphere of psychic and psychological terror, and the amorality of the protagonist make *The Hell-Black Night* a haunting book.

The popularity of television, which in the early and mid 1950s had precipitated Fisher's period of financial and artistic depression, eventually provided him with a market to make a good living as a writer again. In the late 1950s Fisher started to write scripts for *The George Sanders Mystery Theatre* and *Michael Shayne, Detective.* His career in television was at its height during the 1970s when Fisher wrote for many different types of shows, including detective and mystery series. He died on 27 March 1980 in Canoga Park, where he had bought a house. Fisher in the last decade or so of his life had come full circle. His television work, like his work for the pulp market in the 1930s, demonstrated his ability to produce stories of a realistic or romantic nature, with strong plots and engaging dialogue.

References:

Frank Gruber, *The Pulp Jungle* (Los Angeles: Sherbourne, 1967), pp. 27–35, 55, 143–148;

Francis Nevins Jr., *Cornell Woolrich: First You Dream, Then You Die* (New York: Mysterious Press, 1988), pp. 228–229, 336–337;

William F. Nolan, "History of a Pulp: The Life and Times of *Black Mask*," in *The Black Mask Boys,* edited by Nolan (New York: Morrow, 1985), pp. 19–34;

John F. Ryder, "Portrait of a Successful Writer," *Hollywood Diary* (15 May 1961): 10–11;

Jon Tuska, "Interlude: Film Noir," in *The Detective in Hollywood* (Garden City, N.Y.: Doubleday, 1978), pp. 339–361.

Papers:

Steve Fisher's correspondence with H. N. Swanson is housed in the Margaret Herrick Library of the Center for Motion Picture Study, Beverly Hills, California.

William Campbell Gault

(9 March 1910 – 27 December 1995)

Marvin S. Lachman

BOOKS: *Don't Cry for Me* (New York: Dutton, 1952; London: Boardman, 1952);

The Bloody Bokhara (New York: Dutton, 1952); republished as *The Bloodstained Bokhara* (London: Boardman, 1953);

Thunder Road (New York: Dutton, 1952);

The Canvas Coffin (New York: Dutton, 1953; London: Boardman, 1953);

Mr. Fullback (New York: Dutton, 1953);

Shakedown, as Roney Scott (New York: Ace, 1953);

Blood on the Boards (New York: Dutton, 1953; London: Boardman, 1954);

Run, Killer, Run (New York: Dutton, 1954; London: Boardman, 1955);

Gallant Colt (New York: Dutton, 1954);

Ring Around Rosa (New York: Dutton, 1955; London: Boardman, 1955); republished as *Murder in the Raw,* as Bill Gault (New York: Dell, 1956);

Mr. Quarterback (New York: Dutton, 1955);

Speedway Challenge (New York: Dutton, 1956);

Square in the Middle (New York: Random House, 1956; London: Boardman, 1957);

Day of the Ram (New York: Random House, 1956; London: Boardman, 1958);

Fair Prey, as Will Duke (Hasbrouck Heights, N. J.: Graphic, 1956; London: Boardman, 1958);

Bruce Benedict, Halfback (New York: Dutton, 1957);

The Convertible Hearse (New York: Random House, 1957; London: Boardman, 1958; republished, as Bill Gault, New York: Bantam, 1959);

End of a Call Girl (New York: Fawcett, 1958; republished as *Don't Call Tonight* (London: Boardman, 1960);

Night Lady (New York: Fawcett, 1958; London: Boardman, 1960);

Dim Thunder (New York: Dutton, 1958);

Rough Road to Glory (New York: Dutton, 1958);

Death Out of Focus (New York: Random House, 1959; London: Boardman, 1959);

The Wayward Widow (New York: Fawcett, 1959; London: Boardman, 1960);

William Campbell Gault (photograph by Tim Putz; from the dust jacket for The Big Stick, *1975)*

Sweet Wild Wench (New York: Fawcett, 1959; London: Boardman, 1961);

Come Die with Me (New York: Random House, 1959; London: Boardman, 1961);

The Sweet Blond Trap (New York: Zenith, 1959);

Drag Strip (New York: Dutton, 1959);

Million Dollar Tramp (New York: Fawcett, 1960; London: Boardman, 1962);

The Hundred-Dollar Girl (New York: Dutton, 1961; London: Boardman, 1963);

Dirt Track Summer (New York: Dutton, 1961);

Through the Line (New York: Dutton, 1961);

Vein of Violence (New York: Simon & Schuster, 1961; London: Boardman, 1962);

County Kill (New York: Simon & Schuster, 1962; London: Boardman, 1963);

Road-Race Rookie (New York: Dutton, 1962);

Two-Wheeled Thunder (New York: Dutton, 1962);

Dead Hero (New York: Dutton, 1963; London: Boardman, 1964);

Little Big Foot (New York: Dutton, 1963);

Wheels of Fortune: Four Racing Stories (New York: Dutton, 1963);

The Checkered Flag (New York: Dutton, 1964);

The Karters (New York: Dutton, 1965);

The Long Green (New York: Dutton, 1965);

Sunday's Dust (New York: Dutton, 1966);

Backfield Challenge (New York: Dutton, 1967);

The Lonely Mound (New York: Dutton, 1967);

The Oval Playground (New York: Dutton, 1968);

Stubborn Sam (New York: Dutton, 1969);

Quarterback Gamble (New York: Dutton, 1970);

The Last Lap (New York: Dutton, 1972);

Trouble at Second (New York: Dutton, 1973);

Gasoline Cowboy (New York: Dutton, 1974);

Wild Willie, Wide Receiver (New York: Dutton, 1974);

The Big Stick (New York: Dutton, 1975);

Underground Skipper (New York: Dutton, 1975);

Showboat in the Backcourt (New York: Dutton, 1976);

Cut-Rate Quarterback (New York: Dutton, 1977);

Thin Ice (New York: Dutton, 1978);

The Sunday Cycles (New York: Dodd, Mead, 1979);

Super Bowl Bound (New York: Dodd, Mead, 1980);

The Bad Samaritan (Don Mills, Ont.: Worldwide Library, 1982);

The Cana Diversion (Don Mills, Ont.: Worldwide Library, 1982);

Death in Donegal Bay (New York: Walker, 1984; London: Hale, 1987);

The Dead Seed (New York: Walker, 1985; London: Hale, 1987);

The Chicano War (New York: Walker, 1986);

Cat and Mouse (New York: St. Martin's Press, 1988);

Dead Pigeon (New York: Carroll & Graf, 1992);

Man Alone (Brooklyn: Gryphon Books, 1995).

SELECTED PERIODICAL PUBLICATIONS–
UNCOLLECTED: "Picture of Doom," *10 Detective Aces,* 40 (December 1940): 61–67;

"The Revolt of Widow Murphy," *Detective Fiction Weekly,* 145 (24 May 1941): 24–28;

"Three Men in a Hearse," *Flynn's Detective Magazine,* 150 (September 1942): 43–48;

"They Die by Night," *Detective Tales,* 22 (September 1942): 100–114;

"Shadows in the Night," *Street and Smith's Detective Story Magazine,* 171 (December 1945): 5–24;

"They'd Die for Linda," *Street and Smith's Detective Story Magazine,* 172 (September 1946): 83–101;

"Hot-House Homicide," *Black Mask,* 29 (September 1946): 10–34, 98;

"The Bloody Bokhara," *Black Mask,* 32 (November 1948): 36–66, 127;

"Keeper of the Cat-Bride," *15 Mystery Stories,* 39 (April 1950): 10–30;

"Dead-End for Delia," *Black Mask,* 35 (November 1950): 50–59, 127;

"Blood on the Rocks," *Popular Detective,* 40 (March 1951): 9–29;

"Sweet Rolls and Murder," *The Saint Detective Magazine,* 1 (October–November 1953): 67–83;

"But the Prophet Died," *Dell Mystery Novels,* no. 1 (January–March 1955): 46–101;

"The Unholy Three," *Manhunt,* 4 (May 1956): 36–50;

"I'll Be Waiting," *Mike Shayne's Mystery Magazine,* 1 (January 1957): 98–117;

"Don't Crowd Your Luck," *Ellery Queen's Mystery Magazine,* 29 (May 1957): 103–124;

"Stolen Star," *Manhunt,* 5 (November 1957): 53–61.

William Campbell Gault, who Bill Pronzini called in his introduction to Gault's *Dead Pigeon* (1992) "a legend in his own time," had four distinct literary careers. In the 1930s and 1940s he wrote about three hundred short stories, mostly for pulp magazines, and then in the 1950s he made a successful transition to mystery novels, mostly about hard-boiled private detectives. In an interview with David Wilson in the 6 June 1982 *Los Angeles Times,* Gault explained the appeal of the hard-boiled detective: "It's the individual man . . . It's a revolt against the corporate and the conglomerate man, just one dirty guy doing a seedy job in a miserable world." In the early 1960s through the late 1970s he left mystery writing to concentrate on young-adult sports books but then, after a hiatus of almost twenty years, he returned with *The Bad Samaritan* (1982) for another decade of mystery writing.

William Campbell Gault was born in Milwaukee, Wisconsin, on 9 March 1910. He went to high school in suburban Wauwatosa and in 1929 attended the University of Wisconsin at Madison for a year. During the 1930s he held varied jobs, including working as a sole cutter in a shoe factory. He left the factory to become manager of Milwaukee's Blatz Hotel. Writing in his spare time, he published his first story when he won a fiction contest sponsored by the *Milwaukee Journal* in 1936. He continued selling fiction to newspapers and then began selling to pulp magazines.

Gault became one of the most prolific and reliable writers for pulp magazines in their last decade, writing every type of fiction, though specializing in detective and sports stories. His early pulp stories, using simple plots and told at top speed, were enormously readable, but they give little hint that he would write some of the best private detective novels of the 1950s. Although readers may be put off by coincidences and sentimentality in "The Revolt of Widow Murphy," a story that appeared in the 24 May 1941 issue of *Detective Fiction Weekly* about a woman trying to prove her son innocent of a murder charge while she searches for the gangster who killed her policeman husband, they are pulled along by the rapid development. There are many gangsters in Gault stories, and they often try to fix prize fights; boxers were favorite Gault characters. Other frequently used protagonists include former convicts battling their past criminal associations to go "straight." In an early World War II story, "They Die by Night," published in the September 1942 number of *Detective Tales,* former convict Jordan, now an expert mechanic at a factory, has his patriotism tested but chooses to protect the design of a new fighter plane from spies.

Gault was wed twice, marrying his second wife, Virginia Kaprelian, in 1942. They had a daughter and a son. In 1943 Gault went into the U.S. Army, serving two years in the infantry, including service in Hawaii, where he trained Japanese American troops. He resumed writing late in 1945 after his army discharge. The Gaults moved to Southern California, living in the Pacific Palisades section of Los Angeles before settling permanently in Santa Barbara.

Gault's postwar stories often combine crime and veterans overcoming problems of adjustment. Another frequent Gault character was the man suspected of murder who has to prove his innocence while avoiding the police. After the war the success of Raymond Chandler's Philip Marlowe inspired Gault and many other writers to write stories with the private detective as hero. Gault created Mortimer Jones, who appeared in five of the nine stories he published between 1946 and 1950 in *Black Mask,* the most prestigious pulp magazine of all. A former police detective, Jones is a mix of the hard-boiled and the old-fashioned, eccentric sleuth. Jones even drives an ancient Dusenberg, Ellery Queen's car of choice, which he admits is too conspicuous for trailing people. Writing before the success of Mickey Spillane's ultra-hard-boiled Mike Hammer, Gault permitted Jones in his debut story, "Hot-House Homicide," published in the September 1946 issue of *Black Mask,* to effect a scholarly look to impress clients. A potentially trite plot, in which Jones is hired to follow the young wife of an elderly man, is rescued by the clever observations of

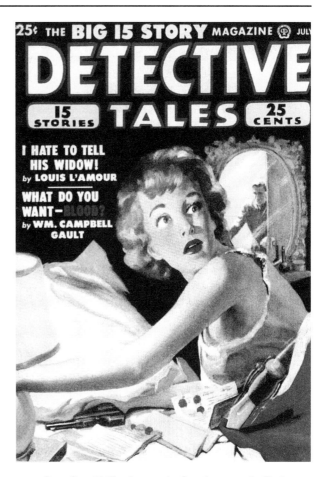

Cover for a 1949 pulp magazine featuring a story by Gault

the first-person narrator—for example, Jones describes a gangster as having "more rackets than a Davis Cup player"—and the tightness of the storytelling.

With improved postwar economic conditions and the competition of television, the pulp market began to tighten as magazines ceased publication. Only the skill and popularity of writers such as Gault, John D. MacDonald, and Fredric Brown kept the market alive until the early 1950s. When pulps were no longer a viable market, Gault turned to novels. Since his writing was not bringing in sufficient money for his family, he was forced to work full time, first at a Douglas aircraft plant and then for the post office, and to write at night.

Gault achieved success in 1952 with his first novel, *Don't Cry for Me,* one of three non-series mysteries he wrote before publishing his first private detective novel. Much of the interest in *Don't Cry for Me* centers on why protagonist Pete Worden, a wealthy former college-football star, seems bent on destroying his life by drinking and associating with crooks. When a murdered gangster is found in his apartment,

Worden must find the killer while avoiding a revenge-seeking mob. It is a book that perfectly captures its locale: Los Angeles during the Christmas season. Gault adroitly uses a National Football League championship game and the Korean War to place his novel in a specific time: December 1950. An interesting supporting character is Worden's friend Tommy Lister, a pulp writer based on Fredric Brown.

Gault credited Brown, a longtime friend from a Milwaukee writing group called Allied Authors, for getting his first book published. Brown recommended Gault's book highly to his publisher, Dutton, predicting it would win an Edgar. In a dust-jacket blurb for the book, Brown said Gault "can write like an angel." Anthony Boucher, in *The New York Times Book Review* of 14 September 1952, called Gault "Saroyan-with-discipline" and praised the book as a "nearly full-scale serious novel." *Don't Cry for Me* proved the accuracy of Brown's prediction, being honored by Mystery Writers of America with its Edgar for best first novel. Gault was able to quit the post office and return to full-time writing.

Gault's second mystery of 1952, *The Bloody Bokhara,* is his only novel not set in California. Instead, he uses his native Milwaukee and the Armenian community there that he knew from his second marriage. Praising Gault's use of the Oriental rug business as unusual background, Boucher selected it as one of ten books on his best of the year list in *The New York Times Book Review* of 7 December 1952, calling it an "Oddly likable fusion of tough melodrama with Saroyanesque warmth."

In 1952 Gault also published the first (and most popular) of his sports novels for boys, *Thunder Road,* a book about auto racing that remained in print for three decades. In his young-adult novels, he was one of the first writers to include minorities. In *Mr. Quarterback* (1955) the protagonist is a boy of Polish American origins going to an Ivy League school. His hero in *Drag Strip* (1959) is Juan Arragon, a Hispanic from the slums. Gault received the Boys Clubs of America Junior Book Award in 1957.

Publishing one of his sports novels along with three other books in 1953, Gault established himself as a writer capable of both prolificacy and variety. *The Canvas Coffin* features a champion prizefighter as a most unusual amateur detective. Suffering temporary amnesia due to the blows to his head he received during a bout, Luke Pilgrim is not sure he even was with Brenda Vane the night she was murdered, let alone whether he killed her. In addition to preparing to defend his middleweight title, he must prove his innocence. The book's climax, a brutal prizefight, is followed by the solution to the murder.

Imagining what the average person might do upon inheriting a great deal of money was a favorite theme of Gault's. He returned to it in *Million Dollar Tramp* (1960) and *The Bad Samaritan* (1982), but he first explored it in *Blood on the Boards* (1953). Sergeant Joe Burke quits the Los Angeles Police Department and indulges himself at first by buying a house and new furniture. Then, bored and lonely, he joins a Los Angeles amateur theater group, an unusual setting for a tough book. Gault's protagonist is unsentimental, and the writer's ironic style punctures overlarge egos in the theater and elsewhere in Southern California. In one of the inside jokes Gault liked to use, he named one of the writers in this book Roney Scott, a pseudonym he had used for pulp stories and later used for a novel.

In *Shakedown* (1953), writing as Scott, Gault created Joe Puma, a tough Los Angeles private eye who claims, perhaps jokingly, to read Mickey Spillane. Basically honest, Puma sometimes accepts clients who are not engaged in legal enterprises. *Shakedown* was Gault's first book published as a paperback original, a form then becoming increasingly popular with the former readers of pulps. Several paperback publishers reprinted some of his hardcover books at about that time as by "Bill Gault," a variation on his name Gault did not especially like. They assumed that the shortened version of his name was more appropriate for a writer they were promoting as "hardboiled." Unlike some of his contemporaries, Gault avoided gratuitous violence and sex, but his lack of illusions regarding a world of gangsters and dishonest politicians and his direct writing style stamp him as hard-boiled as any.

In 1953 a popular digest-sized magazine using new stories, *Manhunt,* was launched, temporarily revitalizing the market for short hard-boiled fiction. Also, *Ellery Queen's Mystery Magazine* bought the right to include the name of the now defunct *Black Mask* on its title page. Gault wrote for both *Manhunt* and *Ellery Queen's Mystery Magazine,* using Puma as his hero. A Puma story, "Don't Crowd Your Luck," won a prize in a 1957 contest held by *Ellery Queen's Mystery Magazine.* Gault also wrote short stories for the other major digest-sized magazines, while continuing to produce full-length novels.

Run, Killer, Run (1954) was another book in which Gault features his archetypal protagonist. In this case Tom Spears is the innocent man on the run. Suspected of killing his estranged wife, he needs to find the real killer. Offering to help him is another of Gault's favorite characters of the 1950s, the bar girl who appears to have a heart of gold, but Spears wonders whether he can trust anyone.

In *Ring Around Rosa* (1955) Gault created his most famous series character, Brock "The Rock" Callahan, a former star football player for the Los Angeles Rams who becomes a Beverly Hills private detective. He appears in fourteen books. Because Callahan is a stubborn man, albeit one of integrity, the depictions of his relationships with clients, the police, and criminals are always interesting and one of the strengths of the series. He is often choosy about his clients and asserts that he is for rent, not for sale. Boxing, the sport Gault so often wrote about in his pulp stories, was also a subject he used often in books, and his first client in *Ring Around Rosa* is a Filipino boxer whose fiancée is missing. The dialogue in the opening conversation between two proud and prickly men, detective and prospective client, effectively delineates them. Sensitive because Callahan's questions imply a lack of morality on the part of the woman, the boxer rails, "To hell with you. . . . You don't need Filipino money. Big, Beverly Hills bastard, Brock Callahan." Eventually, the two men, each respecting the other's athletic ability, come to an agreement.

Also in *Ring Around Rosa* Callahan meets and falls in love with Jan Bonnet, a Beverly Hills interior decorator who appears in most books in the series. She asks him to quit his job and go into a line of work that is less dangerous and more remunerative. He refuses, setting up a conflict that continues throughout the series. Their relationship is one of the more memorable in private eye fiction because both are portrayed as strong-willed individuals.

Callahan returns in *Day of the Ram* (1956) to investigate the murder of his client, a Los Angeles Ram quarterback. The quarterback originally hired the detective to discover whether an unsigned note offering money was a bribery attempt and may have been murdered because he initiated the investigation. The novel is notable for Gault's evocation of the sports atmosphere in Los Angeles in the mid 1950s, especially with regard to the Rams' popularity and their rivalry with the Chicago Bears. Gault emphasizes the vulnerability of underpaid professional football players to those wanting to fix games. *Day of the Ram* is generally considered the best football mystery ever written. In his 1965 introduction to *Vein of Violence* (1961) Boucher called it "a football classic."

The Convertible Hearse (1957), the next and arguably the best novel featuring Callahan, captures Southern California culture, especially the importance of the automobile, more fully than any other Gault book. He creates "Loony Leo," a character apparently based on "Madman Muntz," a television salesman of the time, to show how used cars were sold. The novel moreover concerns stolen cars and gangs in the 1950s, when gangsters were grown-up hoodlums, not the teenage drug dealers who became a staple of the mystery, even

Dust jacket for Gault's 1963 novel, one of fourteen in which his Beverly Hills private detective Brock "The Rock" Callahan appears

in the works of Gault, by the 1980s. Gault manages to provide a satisfying solution to the plot while exploring Callahan's psyche, including his reaction to being forced to kill a man. Brock's relationship with Jan also becomes more complex in *The Convertible Corpse* when he is tempted by another woman.

Though he was writing juvenile books along with his hardcover mysteries, most of which were reprinted in paperback, Gault felt the economic need to start another series and brought back Joe Puma as the major character in six books published between 1958 and 1961: *End of a Call Girl* (1958), *Night Lady* (1958), *Sweet Wild Wench* (1959), *The Wayward Widow* (1959), *Million Dollar Tramp* (1960), and *The Hundred-Dollar Girl* (1961). He also has an important minor role in *The Cana Diversion* (1982). Puma is as tough as Callahan, but Gault made him less of an observer of the California scene, perhaps because he appeared in books that were shorter than Callahan's, usually only 144 pages.

Both Callahan and Puma have working-class sensibilities and are only marginally successful financially. Callahan, however, is able to mingle with the affluent of Los Angeles because of his football fame and his relationship with Jan Bonnet, a successful professional. Gault often allows Callahan and Bonnet to comment on what they perceive as the phoniness of the powerful and wealthy. In *Death Out of Focus* (1959) and *Vein of Violence* (1961) the movie industry is Callahan's target. Puma, always more insecure than Callahan, deals reluctantly with the wealthy and their snobbery in "San Valdesto"—Gault's fictionalization of his own Santa Barbara—in *The Wayward Widow* and *Million Dollar Tramp.*

Gault uses both detectives to comment on the world of sports. In the Puma novel *Night Lady* Gault explores professional wrestling, which he did not consider a true "sport" and often derided in his books. Puma, though, ruminates on the show-business images wrestlers project and protects the reputation of his wrestling client, whose career would likely be ruined if his homosexuality is revealed. The Callahan novel *Come Die with Me* (1959) is about horse racing, another sport Gault considered dishonest. During his investigation of the murder of a jockey, Callahan is critical of the Santa Monica police, whom he distrusts, continuing a tradition in hard-boiled fiction that began with Chandler, who wrote of corruption there, though he called it "Bay City." The last novel to feature Puma, *The Hundred-Dollar Girl,* is about boxing and corruption and includes the inevitable fixed fight. Gault handled the multifaceted subject of professional sports so well that Boucher said in *The New York Times Book Review* of 2 April 1961, "Gault deals with sports better than any mystery writer I know."

Robert A. Baker and Michael T. Nietzel write of Gault's Callahan and Puma in their section on "compassionate" private eyes in *Private Eyes: 101 Knights: A Survey of American Detective Fiction 1922–1984* (1985). Recurring evidence of their compassion is a willingness to help children without fee. In his May 1956 *Manhunt* story, "The Unholy Three," Puma helps an eleven-year-old boy who is worried about his older sister going with someone he thinks is evil. In *County Kill* (1962) Callahan is "consulted" by a twelve-year-old football fan whose father is charged with murder in San Valdesto.

In *Dead Hero* (1963), one of the best Callahan books, a former teammate thinks his wife may be unfaithful and asks Callahan to follow her, which he does only as a personal favor, disliking anything resembling divorce work. There is more detection here than in most private-eye books and even a dying message clue. Callahan's teammate is murdered, but before he died he took a copy of *The World in the Evening* by Christopher Isherwood from the shelf as a possible clue to his killer. Callahan is suspected of the murder and, on the run, has to prove his innocence. Separated from his car, he is forced to take a bus to get off the streets, observing, "*nobody* (except a servant) walks in the residential areas of Beverly Hills; anyone on foot is automatically suspect." There are other trenchant comments about Southern California. Non-mystery literature, a great

interest of Gault's, is frequently mentioned in this and other books. Gault claimed that even the best mystery writers could not compare to the best mainstream writers. In a December 1986 letter to *Mystery and Detective Monthly,* Gault disparages the genre, asserting that no mystery story could ever be considered a classic.

After he completed *Dead Hero* in 1962, Gault decided to give up writing mysteries. He was having trouble marketing his work; *Dead Hero* was rejected twice before being accepted. Believing his financial prospects from mysteries were limited, he decided to concentrate on writing sports fiction for boys because these books stayed in print far longer than his crime fiction.

Despite the additional time available, Gault did not increase his output of juvenile fiction. He published fifteen books for juveniles in the twelve years from 1952 through 1963 and twenty in the seventeen years from 1964 through 1980. Moreover, by the late 1970s he was having difficulty marketing his juvenile works. Three of five juvenile novels he submitted were rejected.

In 1980 his agent was able to sell two previously written Callahan novels to a new publisher of paperback originals, Worldwide Library's Raven House Books, a mystery branch of the enormously successful Harlequin books. In 1981 Gault was invited back to his hometown, Milwaukee, to be honored at the annual World Mystery Convention (Bouchercon). He was pleasantly surprised to find that fans not only remembered him but also had missed his work. The warm way he was greeted, as well as a resurgence of American interest in crime fiction, encouraged him to resume writing private detective novels. Gault had retained a considerable international following, especially in France, where many of his books were translated. In 1982, though he had not published a mystery in almost two decades, the French magazine *Hard-Boiled Dicks* devoted an entire issue to him.

Gault's Callahan had often complained of the life and the smog in Los Angeles. In a soliloquy in *Vein of Violence,* for example, Callahan wonders why he still resides in Los Angeles, which he detests, and decides it is because that is where the troubled people who are his clients live. However, in the first of his Raven House books, *The Bad Samaritan,* Gault allows his character to move to San Valdesto by making him the beneficiary of a considerable inheritance from a rich relative. The novel begins with Callahan married to Jan Bonnet and retired in the fictional city modeled on Santa Barbara. Callahan is soon bored by inactivity, though, and during the rest of the series seeks ways to keep busy and satisfy his social conscience. In *The Bad Samaritan* he battles pornographic moviemakers who exploit children.

In *The Cana Diversion* Callahan reluctantly becomes involved in the anti-nuclear movement when Jan, protesting the building of a power plant, is arrested. Gault, for the first and only time, brought his major detectives together. Joe Puma also moved to San Valdesto, and, typically, is having trouble making ends meet. He may have been involved in shady business, but when Puma is murdered, Callahan, using motivation similar to that of Sam Spade in *The Maltese Falcon,* feels something must be done, even if they were not partners.

The Cana Diversion was picked by the Private Eye Writers of America (PWA) as the Best Paperback Original of 1982. The following year, Gault received "The Eye," the PWA's award for lifetime achievement. He negotiated contracts to have his new books published in hardcover, and some of his early books were reprinted in paperback, after being out of print for more than twenty years. He also became a frequent attendee at Bouchercons and a correspondent to *Mystery and Detective Monthly.* His curmudgeonly and irreverent comments, in person and print, made him enormously popular.

In his 1980s hardcovers *Death in Donegal Bay* (1984) and *The Dead Seed* (1985), Gault failed to make the Callahan books as vigorous as they once had been. Francis M. Nevins commented in the May–June 1984 issue of *The Mystery Fancier* on the "thin plot . . . writing plain and flavorless" of *Death in Donegal Bay* and said Callahan was now "tamed and domesticated." In *The Armchair Detective* (Winter 1985) Allen J. Hubin characterized it as "a tepid tale." Gault seemed to be running out of devices to overcome Brock's boredom, and a wealthy Callahan seemed a less interesting character. In *The Mystery Fancier* for September–October 1987, reviewer Marvin S. Lachman found *The Dead Seed* "slow" and thought that some of the dialogue of Callahan and Jan sounded like a bad imitation of Dashiell Hammett's Nick and Nora Charles. In *The Dead Seed* Gault resurrects that staple of Southern California crime fiction, the religious cult, here called "The New Awareness." Unlike the cults created by Boucher, Ross Macdonald, and Richard S. Prather, it is strangely lifeless.

Gault had always been a socially aware writer, though in his earlier detective stories Callahan commented only briefly on dishonesty, inequities in American society, and materialism. *The Chicano War* (1986) was his first major attempt in adult fiction to write of racial tensions, and it proved to be a compelling book. Though Callahan believes that "The harsh truth is that some kids, thanks to us, are beyond redemption," he has been funding The Tomorrow Club, a group trying to help "the underprivileged kids in mostly over-privi-

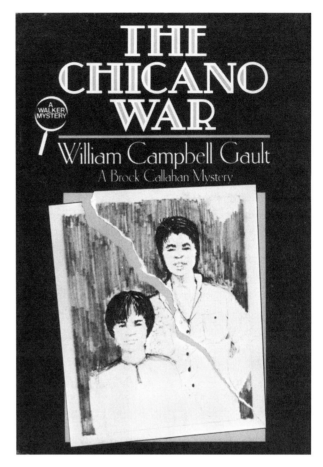

Dust jacket for Gault's 1986 novel, in which Callahan searches for the missing brother of his young Hispanic client

leged San Valdesto." An eleven-year-old Hispanic boy "hires" Callahan because his brother has disappeared and may be a victim of an attempt by older mobsters to foment warfare among Chicano youth gangs in order to secure control of the drug market. The Tomorrow Club is run by a black former football player and convict, one of the few African Americans in Gault's mysteries, and much of the dialogue is about race.

"Pleasant" is how Hubin characterized *Cat and Mouse* (1988), the last Callahan novel to appear in hardcover. In contrast to the racial issues raised in his previous novel, Callahan is involved with more pedestrian neighborhood concerns, beginning with a dead cat on his lawn. Thereafter, Gault was no longer published in hardcover; his last mystery, *Dead Pigeon* (1992), was a paperback original. The plot involves the murder of another old Callahan teammate and brings the detective back to the Los Angeles area, where he is now on friendlier terms with the Santa Monica police, and includes another religious cult, "Inner Peace."

Shortly before his death on 27 December 1995, Gault published his last book, *Man Alone* (1995), a nonmystery he wrote in 1957 and put aside when his hard-back publisher thought it too grim and different from his usual detective and sports writing. One of the best books about a professional writer in Hollywood, the novel follows the career of John Calvin, who writes for *Dime Detective* and other pulps before he publishes a successful mainstream novel. With work as a screenwriter comes money, but Calvin also finds he must make compromises to hold on to the success he has achieved. He must finally decide whether he will succumb to Hollywood and become a hack or retain his integrity.

An author whose best work, mainly written in the 1950s, deserves a wider audience, William Campbell Gault never lost the compulsion to write. In the 1980s he continued to send unpaid letters to *Mystery and Detection Monthly,* saying there in July 1986, "I have to write; that is the nature of this critter." With a certain pride, he said in his column in *Mystery Scene* for August 1986, "When people ask me what I do. . . . I tell them I am an old pulp writer."

Interviews:

"William Campbell Gault," *Paperback Quarterly,* 2 (Summer 1979): 8–13;

"*Entretien avec William Campbell Gault,*" *Hard-Boiled Dicks,* no. 3 (June 1982): 8–17;

"Interview: William Campbell Gault," *Ellery Queen's Mystery Magazine,* 80 (November 1982): 87–88.

Bibliography:

"*Bibliographie chronologique,*" *Hard-Boiled Dicks,* no. 3 (June 1982): 21–33.

References:

Robert A. Baker and Michael T. Nietzel, "The Rock-Like Knight: Brock Callahan," in their *Private Eyes: 101 Knights: A Survey of American Detective Fiction 1922–1984* (Bowling Green, Ohio: Bowling Green Univeresity Popular Press, 1985), pp. 89–94;

Anthony Boucher, introduction, *Vein of Violence* (New York: Award Books, 1965);

Charles Cooper, "Brock, the Rock Callahan," *Armchair Detective,* 25 (Spring 1992): 226–229;

David Geherin, "Brock Callahan," in his *The American Private Eye: The Image in Fiction* (New York: Ungar, 1985), pp. 147–155;

Hard-boiled Dicks, special Gault issue, edited by Roger Martin, no. 3 (June 1982).

Papers:

William Campbell Gault's manuscripts are held in the library at the University of Oregon in Eugene.

David Goodis

(2 March 1917 – 7 January 1967)

David Schmid
State University of New York at Buffalo

BOOKS: *Retreat from Oblivion* (New York: Dutton, 1939);

Dark Passage (New York: Messner, 1946; London: Heinemann, 1947);

Nightfall (New York: Messner, 1947; London: Heinemann, 1948); republished as *The Dark Chase* (New York: Lion, 1953);

Behold This Woman (New York: Appleton, 1947);

Of Missing Persons (New York: Morrow, 1950);

Cassidy's Girl (New York: Fawcett, 1951; London: Miller, 1958);

Of Tender Sin (New York: Fawcett, 1952);

Street of the Lost (New York: Fawcett, 1952; London: Fawcett, 1959);

The Burglar (New York: Lion, 1953);

The Moon in the Gutter (New York: Fawcett, 1953);

Black Friday (New York: Lion, 1954);

The Blonde on the Street Corner (New York: Lion, 1954);

Street of No Return (New York: Fawcett, 1954; London: Miller, 1958);

The Wounded and the Slain (New York: Fawcett, 1955; London: Miller, 1959);

Down There (Greenwich, Conn.: Fawcett, 1956; London: Fawcett, 1958); republished as *Shoot the Piano Player* (New York: Grove, 1962);

Fire in the Flesh (Greenwich, Conn.: Fawcett, 1957; London: Fawcett, 1958);

Night Squad (Greenwich, Conn.: Fawcett, 1961; London: Muller, 1962);

Somebody's Done For (New York: Banner, 1967).

Collection: *Nightfall, Down There, Dark Passage, The Moon in the Gutter* (London: Zomba, 1983).

PRODUCED SCRIPTS: *The Unfaithful,* motion picture, script by Goodis and James Gunn, Warner Bros., 1947;

The Burglar, motion picture, Columbia Pictures, 1957;

"An Out For Oscar," television, based on novel by Henry Kane, *The Alfred Hitchcock Hour,* 5 April 1963.

SELECTED PERIODICAL PUBLICATIONS–UNCOLLECTED: "Death's Behind That Door," *Double-Action Detective,* 1 (February 1940);

"Bullets for Nazis," *Captain Combat,* 1 (June 1940);

"Things to Worry About," *Detective Fiction Weekly,* 138 (20 July 1940);

"Death Flies the Coffins of Hitler!" *Battle Birds,* 2 (November 1940);

"All Bolixed Up," *Detective Yarns,* 2 (April 1941);

"Hot Lead for Heinkels," *Air War,* 1 (Winter 1941);

"Three Guesses," *Hooded Detective,* 3 (January 1942);

"A Smile and a Nod," *Crack Detective,* 3 (September 1942);

"The Last Dogfight," *Dare-Devil Aces,* 33 (February 1946);

"It's a Wise Cadaver," *New Detective Magazine,* 8 (July 1946);

"The Cop on the Corner," *Popular Detective,* 33 (September 1947);

"Black Pudding," *Manhunt* (December 1953).

Unlike Dashiell Hammett and Raymond Chandler, David Goodis is not a household name. Even among aficionados of hard-boiled crime fiction, Goodis is less well known than James M. Cain and Cornell Woolrich. Nevertheless, during the course of a career spanning nearly thirty years, Goodis produced an important and enduring body of work. Although sharing with other writers in the genre certain themes, such as urban angst, paranoia, and alienation, Goodis made a distinctive contribution to American hard-boiled crime fiction. In a marked contrast with Hammett's Sam Spade or Chandler's Philip Marlowe, who move purposefully in a corrupt world, the archetypal Goodis hero is more acted upon, a man trapped by both a haunted past and a sordid present. No other writer in the genre matches Goodis's empathetic obsession with the lives of losers, victims, drop-outs, and has-beens. Although the hero tries to cheat his fate, his attempt to live a decent life is doomed to failure, and Goodis lovingly examines the destruction of hopes and dreams that defines his hard-boiled universe.

David Goodis (center) with Humphrey Bogart and Lauren Bacall, the stars of the movie Dark Passage *(1947), based on Goodis's 1946 novel of the same title*

David Loeb Goodis was born in Philadelphia, Pennsylvania, on 2 March 1917, into a solid middle-class Jewish family, the eldest son of William and Mollie (Halpern) Goodis. His brother, Jerome, was born in 1919, but died at the age of three of meningitis. His other brother, Herbert, was born mentally retarded in 1923. After graduating from Simon Gratz High School in Philadelphia, Goodis attended Indiana University at Bloomington. He then transferred to Temple University in Philadelphia, and graduated with a B.Sc. in journalism in 1938. Upon leaving college, Goodis found a job writing copy for an advertising agency in Philadelphia.

While working for the agency, Goodis wrote and published his first novel, *Retreat from Oblivion* (1939), a Hemingwayesque study of the infidelities of two couples set against the background of wars in Spain and China. Although some critics liked the book, Lisle Bell in *Books* (30 July 1939) reviewed the novel in devastating terms: "The opening sentence in 'Retreat from Oblivion' is as follows: 'After a while it gets so bad that you want to stop the whole business.' It refers to Herb's state of mind, but it's not an inaccurate summary of what one is inclined to say about David Goodis's novel." Responses such as this one

apparently persuaded Goodis that his dreams of being a "serious" writer were unrealistic. In a 16 August 1966 letter to William David Sherman quoted by Sherman in a note for *Sight & Sound,* Goodis wrote of this stage of his career: "At first I wanted to write very solemnly and handle only the important issues. But I quickly found out that the most important issue was putting food in one's belly."

With the exception of his first novel, Goodis's writing career can be divided into three periods. His early period is as a pulp fiction writer in New York; he then moved on to publishing hardback novels during his Hollywood years; finally, he produced a string of paperback original novels while living in Philadelphia. The first of these three periods began for Goodis in 1939, when he moved to New York City. In the next few years, while working for a variety of public relations firms, Goodis started writing for the pulps. Sometimes putting out as much as ten thousand words a day, he published his work in dozens of pulp magazines, including *Horror Stories, Terror Tales, Western Tales,* and *Dime Mystery Magazine.* According to Mike Wallington in his introduction to a 1983 collection of the author's novels, Goodis once boasted of having written five million words over a five-year period. Although such a figure may be something of an exaggeration, Goodis published at least fifty stories between 1939 and 1944, including whole issues of aviation-war magazines such as *Battle Birds* and *Fighting Aces.* Goodis's apprenticeship in the pulps gave him crucial training in expressing his thoughts clearly and simply, with a minimum of literary embroidery.

Goodis's first trip to Hollywood came in 1942, when he was invited by Universal Pictures to write a treatment for a project named *Destination Unknown.* Although the studio did not use the treatment, the trip was still important for Goodis, because he met and married a young woman named Elaine (last name unknown). The couple separated almost as soon as Goodis returned to New York, but the figure of Elaine casts a long shadow in Goodis's work. His books are full of sadistic, bullying women who dominate their weak male partners, and by all accounts this pattern accurately reflects Elaine and Goodis's relationship.

Goodis was not noticed by Hollywood again until 1946, when he broke away from the pulps and published his first hard-boiled crime novel, *Dark Passage* (1946). Originally serialized in *The Saturday Evening Post,* which paid Goodis $25,000 for the rights, *Dark Passage* was adapted by writer-director Delmer Daves into a film starring Humphrey Bogart and Lauren Bacall before being published as a hardback. It is one of Goodis's best-known novels, and it is the novel in which Goodis starts to develop his characteristic constellation of themes and literary techniques. Goodis's hero, Vincent Parry, begins the novel in prison, having been wrongly convicted of the murder of his wife.

After he escapes from prison, the rest of the novel is divided between his efforts to find a safe place to stay and his attempts to discover his wife's real murderer and thus clear his name.

The most immediately noticeable characteristic of the novel is its paranoia. Given Parry's situation, such paranoia is understandable, but Goodis sees paranoia as a more generally appropriate reaction to an unstable and dangerous world. Goodis believes Parry's fear of constant betrayal to be a sensible attitude, but this view is complicated by the fact that Parry also desperately wants and needs to trust and love someone. *Dark Passage* thus presents an archetypal Goodis hero who is torn between the desire for self-preservation and the desire for human contact. As is typical in his work, by the conclusion of the novel neither of these desires is unambiguously fulfilled—the open-ended conclusion is another Goodis trademark. Goodis is less interested in the eventual fate of his characters than he is in analyzing their emotional isolation and their efforts to overcome that isolation.

Dark Passage is not only a representative Goodis hard-boiled novel in terms of its themes but also in terms of its style. The novel contains several stylistic features that became closely associated with Goodis. For example, there is the use of the striking image that draws attention to itself by its excess. When Parry is trying to figure out a way to break out of jail, Goodis writes, "Like a snake gliding into a pool a thought glided into his mind." The image grabs the reader's attention simply because it is so unnecessarily vivid. Another stylistic oddity appears in Goodis's work for the first time in *Dark Passage,* the silent conversation. When Parry finds the murdered body of his friend George Fellsinger, Goodis inserts an imagined conversation between Parry and his dead friend:

> Without sound, Parry said, "Hello, George." Without sound, Fellsinger said, "Hello, Vince." "Are you dead, George?" "Yes, I'm dead." "Why are you dead, George?" "I can't tell you, Vince. I wish I could tell you but I can't." "Who did it, George?" "I can't tell you, Vince. Look at me. Look what happened to me. Isn't it awful?"

The silent conversation, whether between two different characters or as an internal monologue or as an exchange between a character and an object, appears frequently in Goodis's novels, serving as a convenient way to advance the plot or explore the emotional states of the characters.

Dark Passage was generally well received, with an especially enthusiastic response coming from the influential critic Anthony Boucher in the *San Francisco Chronicle* of 20 October 1946: "Here is the most notable writing talent to emerge in the field in a long time. Mr. Goodis has an originality of naturalism, a precise feeling for petty lives, a creatively compelling vividness of detail that you might

perhaps match if you could combine top Woolrich with early Odets. This is the goods."

With the success of *Dark Passage,* Goodis signed a lucrative renewable contract with Warner Bros. that allowed him six months of working on his own novels each year and the other six months writing screenplays. Initially, things went well for Goodis in Hollywood. His first screenplay, *The Unfaithful* (1947), starring Ann Sheridan and directed by Vincent Sherman, was a big success, as was the film version of *Dark Passage.* In addition, movie rights to his next two novels, *Nightfall* (1947) and *Behold This Woman* (1947), were sold immediately. As described by James Sallis, there is much anecdotal evidence concerning Goodis's bizarre behavior while living in Hollywood. Although he earned $750 a week, Goodis slept on a sofa that he rented in a friend's house for $4 a month. According to the author's friends, one of his most enduring habits was frequenting ghetto bars and nightclubs in both Los Angeles and, later, in Philadelphia. His friend Allan Norkin told biographer Philippe Garnier that Goodis referred to this predilection as "going to the Congo," and he reportedly searched out obese black women whom he paid to abuse him verbally and perhaps physically.

Although black women do not play a significant role in Goodis's novels, abusive women are a prominent feature of his work. For example, in *Behold This Woman,* Clara Ervin bullies everyone in order to get her way. Goodis describes her eventual death under the wheels of her lover's car with great attention to detail, lingering on her facial expressions as she dies, but he reserves his greatest enthusiasm for his vivid descriptions of Clara's casual brutality toward her husband, George, and stepdaughter, Evelyn. This brutality usually takes the form of emotional or verbal abuse, but if circumstances demand it, Clara is more than willing to use physical violence, as when she beats George:

> He parted his lips to say something, and Clara's open palm cracked hard across his mouth. His legs began to give way, and as Clara observed his weakness, she began to beat his face with her open hand. As she struck him, she was saying slowly and distinctly, "I'm—only doing—this—and this—and this—to help you, George."

Goodis's sadistic female protagonist appears with monotonous regularity in his oeuvre, but at this stage of his career, Goodis balances working out his own masochistic obsessions with examining more complex concerns.

In *Nightfall* Goodis returns to the theme of paranoia. The book begins with Goodis's hero, Donald Vanning, hiding in New York City and living under an assumed identity. While on his way to a new job in Chicago, Vanning has the bad luck of running into a gang of bank robbers who force Vanning to help them.

After Vanning escapes with the gang's money, killing a member of the gang in self-defense in the process, he is hunted by both the police and the gang, hence the need for anonymity and subterfuge.

The internal dynamics of criminal gangs is a subject that Goodis returns to in later novels, but in *Nightfall,* the emphasis is squarely on how Vanning's situation produces an extremely paranoid view of the world. Despite Vanning's participation in a crime, he is not really a criminal type, just as Parry is innocent of the crimes he is accused of in *Dark Passage*. Goodis's heroes can usually survive in the dangerous situations they find themselves in, but such situations are not their natural milieu. In Vanning's case, he is unable to maintain the disguise he started off with when he went on the run, and his loneliness leads him to crave human contact. Vanning gives in to his need when he strikes up a conversation in a bar with a woman named Martha, even though he knows it is a foolish thing to do. Indeed, Vanning's decision turns out to be incredibly unfortunate, because Martha is connected with the gang, and through his association with her, Vanning falls into their hands. Her betrayal shows the extent to which, for Goodis, women are the personification of treachery and a fertile source of paranoia in their own right.

After the publication of *Behold This Woman* and *Nightfall,* Goodis's situation in Hollywood became more difficult. Goodis was aggravated when he was required by Warner Bros. to write eleven treatments of a screenplay titled "Of Missing Persons" in April and May 1948. In June, Goodis wrote a novel based on the screenplay material, and the story of Paul Ballard–the head of the Missing Persons Bureau in a large city who is unhealthily obsessed with and nearly destroyed by his job–might be read as a fictionalized version of Goodis's own frustrations with his situation. Although the novel *Of Missing Persons* (1950) was well reviewed, with the critic for the *Chicago Sunday Tribune* of 9 July describing it as a "magnificent yarn of scrupulous police work" with "dramatic realism and tense impact," the screenplay was never produced. Goodis's time in Hollywood was coming to an end.

In July, Goodis's agent asked Warner Bros. to renew his contract, but they did not pick up the option, and Goodis received his last check from the company in August. Goodis hung on in Hollywood until 1950, when, prompted partly by his own sense of failure and partly by his affection for his family, he returned to 6305 North 11th Street, Philadelphia, to live with his parents and to help with the care of his brother, Herbert. From this point on, Goodis's public appearances were few and far between, and to all intents and purposes he lived the life of a recluse until his death in 1967.

Goodis's move to Philadelphia signals the start of the most prolific stage of his career, the production of paperback original novels, most of them written for Fawcett Gold Medal for about $1,500 each. Wallington notes the similarities of Goodis's concerns in his paperback originals: "there are not a dozen books here: rather, with remarkable imagination and depth, and not a little madness, he has written and rewritten his one book a dozen or so times." Certainly, the novels that Goodis published after 1950 show a remarkable continuity of theme, setting, and character.

The third stage of his career got off to a spectacular start with the publication of *Cassidy's Girl* (1951), easily the most commercially successful of Goodis's novels, reportedly selling over one million copies. Critics such as Sallis and Garnier have called this book a new departure for Goodis, but it is more accurate to describe it as a continuation of earlier themes in that it focuses on the attempt of the hero to gain control over his life by ridding himself of the ghosts of the past and the monsters of the present. In another sense, however, *Cassidy's Girl* is an unusual book for Goodis in that, although the book is undoubtedly noir in terms of its sensibilities and setting, crime does not figure in the plot. Rather, most of the story concerns James Cassidy's attempt to break away from his sadistic and seductive wife, Mildred, and to start a new life with Doris, a young alcoholic.

Like so many of Goodis's heroes, Cassidy is on the run from his past. He is a former airline pilot whose life fell apart when the plane he was piloting crashed through no fault of his own, killing most of the passengers. Driving a bus for a living gives him some feeling of control in his life, but his security is thoroughly undermined by Mildred, who is a fantasy figure for Cassidy. Mildred knows that Cassidy is obsessed with her voluptuous body, and she uses her physical charms to keep reasserting her control over him. In trying to break away, Cassidy chooses someone who is the complete opposite of Mildred. Where Mildred is dominating, Doris is passive; and where Mildred is almost impossibly voluptuous, Doris is skinny and anemic. The opposition between the sexually aggressive woman and the shrinking waif appears again and again in Goodis's fiction. Although the hero is attracted to the waif, he normally ends up with the sexual aggressor, and indeed, Cassidy eventually returns to Mildred.

There is more at stake here, however, than Cassidy's choice of a particular type of woman. Goodis uses his character to dramatize one of his most fundamental beliefs–that people who want more out of life and who believe that they can assert some control over the direction of their life are usually doomed to fail. For Goodis, true "happiness" lies in accepting the hand that fate has dealt. Although Cassidy believes that he and

Doris can build a new life together, when Cassidy's bus crashes, again through no fault of his own, he realizes that Doris needs whiskey more than she needs him. Cassidy then decides to follow his friend Shealy's advice to "Just slide down and enjoy the trip."

Yet, no matter how sensible the advice to surrender to fate appears, Goodis's heroes rarely follow it willingly. They instead put themselves through mental and physical torture in order to exorcise the past rather than simply acquiesce. In *Of Tender Sin* (1952), Alvin Darby eventually resurrects his troubled marriage but only at the cost of having to remember his incestuous childhood relationship with his sister and having to plunge himself into the sordid and dangerous milieu of skid row. Similarly, in *Street of the Lost* (1952), Chester Lawrence decides to help a Chinese woman being victimized by the local crime boss, Matthew Hagen, even though he knows his action will make him Hagen's target. In this sense, Goodis's protagonists are idealists who are faced with a choice between involvement and noninvolvement. Even though it is easier and safer to stay uninvolved, they consistently choose to do the right thing, to get involved, in spite of the costs to themselves.

In his next novel, *The Burglar* (1953), Goodis explores the tension between involvement and noninvolvement and combines that theme with an exploration of the internal dynamics of a criminal "family." In Nat Harbin's case, he wants to become uninvolved. Initially, Harbin is the leader of a gang of burglars. After he meets and falls in love with the mysterious Della, Harbin leaves the gang and thus breaks up this criminal family. Theoretically, the breakup gives Harbin the freedom to live his life in a new way, but in practice, everything that makes life worth living for Harbin is destroyed.

Although Harbin, unlike Goodis's previous protagonists, is a professional criminal, he has many similarities with Vanning, Parry, and Cassidy. Like them, Harbin is desperate to assert some control over the direction of his life but finds it extremely difficult to do so. In Harbin's case, there are two factors keeping him tied down. The first is his loyalty to the other members of the gang, to Gladden, who is the daughter of Harbin's criminal mentor, Gerald Gladden, in particular. When Gerald died, Harbin informally adopted Gladden (a name given to her by Harbin), promising the father that he would look after her. Their relationship is complicated further by Harbin and Gladden's mutual attraction, a fact that neither can admit to the other. The other members of the gang, Baylock and Rizzio, are the second factor keeping Harbin from breaking away, because they are convinced that for reasons of safety, the gang must stay together.

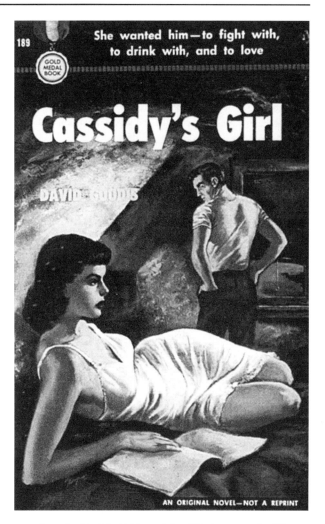

Cover for Goodis's 1951 novel, in which the protagonist fails to break away from his sadistic wife

Eventually, however, Harbin accomplishes his purpose, and because, like other Goodis heroes, he is both a cynic and a hopeless romantic, the means of escape comes through a woman. When Della and Harbin meet, they fall in love as couples in Goodis novels always fall in love, completely and utterly: "The liquid of her lips poured into his veins. There was a bursting in his brain as everything went out of his brain and Della came in, filling his brain so that his brain was crammed with Della." Unfortunately, as happens so often in Goodis's fiction, Harbin makes a serious mistake in trusting a woman: Della is working in league with a crooked cop who is after the emeralds the gang stole on a recent job. Although it ultimately turns out that Della really does fall in love with Harbin, by then it is too late and the damage is done. The book ends with multiple deaths and with Gladden and Harbin drowning together, redeemed by finally confessing their love for one another.

For Harbin, the environment of the criminal gang dictates the failure of his attempt to break away and make a better life for himself, and one might speculate that Goodis had gleaned a similar message from his own trajectory in life, for after apparently making it on his own for a time he found himself back where he started, in Philadelphia. Regardless, in his next novel, *The Moon in the Gutter* (1953), Goodis writes another story of a doomed attempt to break out of one's accustomed life, and this time it is the city that is blamed.

Bill Kerrigan, the hero of the novel, lives in the dockland slums of Philadelphia, but he yearns to get out, partly because his environment is so closely identified in his mind with the tragic death of his sister, who committed suicide after being raped. Working against this desire to get away is the fact that the slums are the only world that Kerrigan has ever known, and so he has a multitude of psychic and emotional ties to the place. Typically, Kerrigan's dilemma is expressed in a conflict between two women, who both desire Kerrigan. On the one hand, there is his girlfriend, Bella, a voluptuous and fiery-tempered woman who eventually hires men to kill Kerrigan when she thinks she is going to lose him. On the other hand, there is Loretta Channing, a cool and sophisticated upper-class woman who offers Kerrigan a way out of the slums.

Despite being tempted by Loretta and even being briefly married to her, Kerrigan eventually chooses to stay where he is. In one sense, this is a positive choice, based on his perception that Loretta was only using him for her own amusement, but Kerrigan's decision also reflects a fatalistic belief that there is no escape and that the same streets that killed his sister also make it impossible for him to leave: "They'd learn the hard way that Vernon Street was no place for delicate bodies or timid souls. They were prey, that was all, they were destined for the maw of the ever hungry eater, the Vernon gutter."

Kerrigan is an exemplary Goodis protagonist because he has no room to maneuver, only a choice between equally unpromising alternatives. The same could be said of Hart, the hero of Goodis's next novel, *Black Friday* (1954). Wanted by the police for the murder of his brother, Hart stumbles into the clutches of a criminal gang. Like Chester Lawrence in *Of Tender Sin,* Hart makes the mistake of becoming involved; when he sees a dying man laying in the street, he agrees to take and hide the man's wallet, thus making him a target of the gang. Like all of Goodis's heroes, however, Hart is extremely adaptable. Although he is held prisoner in the house, he manages to ingratiate himself with the leader of the gang, Charley, and eventually becomes a member. Unfortunately, the situation eventually spins out of control, and once again, women are the cause.

Charley's lover, Frieda, is the sexually aggressive woman of this particular book, as Goodis's description of her suggests: "Frieda was a big woman. She was one-sixty if she was an ounce, more solid than soft, packed into five feet five inches, and molded majestically." Frieda falls for Hart, a circumstance that precipitates Hart's break with Charley. To complicate matters further, Myrna, who next to Frieda is a waif, is also in love with Hart, and Hart falls for her. Just as in *The Burglar,* Goodis shows in great detail the overheated emotional atmosphere of a criminal family, and inevitably, the situation explodes in violence, with Myrna being killed by a bullet from Charley's gun that was intended for Hart. At the end of the book Hart is back where he began, back on the streets, alone. Goodis shows his characters the possibility of love and happiness for a moment and then snatches it away again, as a way of emphasizing the degree of their loneliness and isolation. Boucher, writing in *The New York Times* of 21 November 1984 called *Black Friday* "as deliberately fruitless as an Existentialist novel," but also acknowledged that "it's written with striking economy, skill and conviction."

Even when Goodis's heroes do succeed in acquiring their love interest, as Ralph Creel seems to do in *The Blonde on the Street Corner* (1954), it does not bring them happiness. In choosing the lush and hypersexual Lenore, Ralph realizes that he is giving up on the decent but sexually unenticing Edna Daly as well as giving up any chance of improving his own life. At the end of the novel Ralph has settled into a state of entropy. His choice of Lenore is motivated more by lack of energy than by love.

In one of the best of his later novels, *Street of No Return* (1954), Goodis offers an unusually political subtext as he explores his characteristic themes against a backdrop of a series of race riots between whites and Puerto Ricans. Whitey, whose real name is Eugene Lindell, is an alcoholic, who at the beginning of the novel seems resigned to his existence. The reader learns that in his previous life Whitey was a successful singer but then became involved with a girl named Celia, who was dating Sharkey, the leader of a criminal gang. When Whitey refused to stop seeing Celia, Sharkey had him beaten nearly to death by fellow gang members Chop and Bertha, thus ruining his singing career and precipitating his decline into alcoholism.

Like Cassidy, Whitey has learned to enjoy his decline and feel comfortable with it, but this all changes when he sees Chop one night, walking down the other side of the street. Whitey is now faced with a choice—to stay where he is, amid the security of the bottle and his fellow lushes, or to follow Chop and risk not only further beatings but also having to reopen the psychic wounds of the past. Whitey follows Chop, and thus both relives his painful past and becomes embroiled in a complicated scheme of police corruption and simmering racial tension. At the end of it all, the bruised and battered Whitey has seen Celia again but that is all—he does not even get to speak with her. Like the circularity that characterizes

Hart's fate in *Black Friday*, Whitey finishes the book in the same place he began–sitting in a doorway with his friends, drinking. Goodis does not suggest that Whitey is any the wiser for his decision to follow Chop but clearly he does want his reader to admire Whitey's indomitability, no matter how foolish it seems. Once again, Goodis sneers at love while at the same time understanding its power as a motivating force.

Apart from his description of Whitey's obsessiveness, Goodis's sensitive portrayal of the plight of the Puerto Rican community as a colorful background in *Street of No Return* is one of the strengths of the novel. Reflecting on how some of the Puerto Ricans tried to get him out of a dangerous situation, Whitey says to himself

> People call them Puerto Ricans and right away they're branded like with an iron and given a low road to travel, the lousiest places to live, like where you saw them jam-packed sleeping on a cold floor. But you saw some damn fine quality in that house. That Chávez. He was really something, that Chávez. And Luis, too. Luis almost got himself slashed bloody going to bat for you.

The efforts of Chávez and Luis were to no avail, however, which illustrates Goodis's belief that racial tension is not easily alleviated. Like Whitey's failed attempt to alter his fate, the attempts to combat racism also seem doomed.

Goodis's interest in racism carried over into his next novel, *The Wounded and the Slain* (1955), which relates the story of James Bevan's vacation in Jamaica, his murder of a robber, and his attempts to clear a Jamaican man wrongly accused of the murder. It was apparently inspired by a trip Goodis took to Jamaica and Haiti in 1955, where he was reportedly shocked by the squalid living conditions endured by the native population. There is anecdotal evidence to suggest that, despite Goodis's problematic obsession with obese black women, he was genuinely and deeply disturbed by racism. Biographer Garnier records Goodis's friend Dick Levy remembering Goodis once saying that he could not understand a world that tolerated racism.

Whatever his motivations for writing *The Wounded and the Slain*, Goodis's engagement with the issue of racism soon passed, and in his next and last major novel, *Down There* (1956), Goodis returned to his characteristic themes. The story of the nightclub piano player, Eddie, has very strong resemblances to that of Whitey in *Street of No Return*. Eddie, whose real name is Edward Webster Lynn, is a former concert pianist who walked away from his career after his wife committed suicide. Racked with guilt over his wife's death and scared by the anger he feels for the man he holds responsible for her death, Eddie has tried to escape from his past and take refuge in a sordid and bland present. Just as Whitey was confronted with a figure from his past, Eddie is confronted by his brother, Turley, who is in trouble and needs Eddie's help. Eddie undoubtedly realizes what will happen if he allows Turley to disrupt his placid new life: "Don't look, Eddie said to himself. You take one look and that'll do it, that'll pull you into it."

Almost against his own will, Eddie does of course become involved. His decision to help Turley unleashes a tragic chain of circumstances, including Eddie's murder of another man in self-defense, his wrenching revisiting of his past, and the death of a woman whom he was beginning to love. Having lost everything, without evident gain, Eddie finds himself back in the bar at the end of the novel, playing the piano, trying to find refuge again. Goodis thus sends a mixed message in this book and his previous ones–his characters are almost invariably punished when they break their isolation and try to connect with the world, and yet Goodis suggests that they have no choice. It seems that in Goodis's world, pain and destruction are an unavoidable accompaniment of what it means to be alive, and there is simply no getting away from that fact.

By this point of his career, Goodis had published fifteen novels, ten of them in the six years he had been living in Philadelphia. By all accounts, his life had now settled into a predictable pattern. Each day, Goodis worked in his room in the morning, until he broke for lunch and a nap, and then he resumed work until late in the afternoon. His mother, who prepared all of his meals, guarded Goodis's time, telling all callers that her son was working and was not to be disturbed. Apart from seeing a few close friends, Goodis was not often seen in public.

On two notable occasions, Goodis broke out of his established routine. In 1957 an old friend of Goodis's from Hollywood, Paul Wendkos, was given the job of directing the film adaptation of *The Burglar*. Wendkos persuaded Columbia Pictures to let him shoot the film in Goodis's stamping grounds of Philadelphia and Atlantic City, and in addition he persuaded Goodis to write the screenplay, resulting in the only film adaptation Goodis ever did of his own work. The project turned out to be Goodis's last and happiest experience of working on movies, and as a result *The Burglar* is his best screenplay. Goodis's other notable public appearance in the last part of his life came in 1962, with the New York premiere of Francois Truffaut's film adaptation of *Down There*, *Tirez Sur La Pianiste* (Shoot the Piano Player). Although Goodis was reportedly flattered at the attention–it was the last film to be based on one of his novels during his lifetime–he was also puzzled by the emphasis being placed on existentialism, angst, and art in his work. According to Nick Kimberley in *David Goodis/Pulps Pictured: For Goodis' Sake!* (1989), when asked about such things, Goodis responded, "I just tried to tell a story, that's all."

After 1956, the pace of Goodis's literary production slowed dramatically: he published just two more books

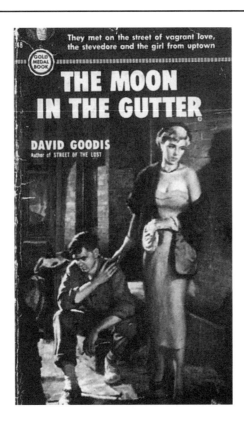

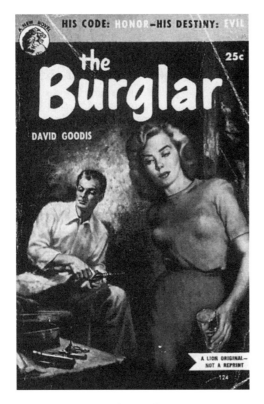
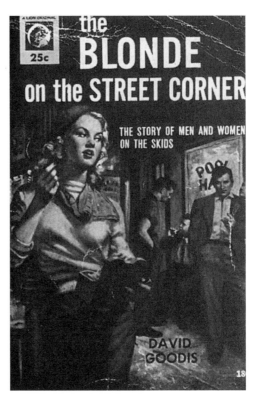

Covers for four of Goodis's novels that were published as paperback originals in the 1950s

before his death in 1967. *Fire in the Flesh* (1957) is the story of "Blazer," a petty arsonist who is suspected of setting a major fire in which five people die. Although Blazer feels he is innocent, he cannot be sure, because he blacked out while drinking on the night of the fire. The book revolves around Blazer's attempts to clear himself and find who really did set the fire. The dilemma of a wrongly accused man who could be betrayed or caught at any moment is a quintessential Goodis situation, but Goodis does not handle it as adroitly as he does in earlier books such as *Dark Passage* and *Nightfall*. Unlike Parry and Vanning, Blazer is not given any depth as a character, and the book relies more on gruesome descriptions of violence than it does on evocations of paranoia. Most suspiciously, the book is full of happy endings, with Blazer finally understanding and thus transcending the causes of his pyromania, and other characters finding true love. Such a neat resolution suggests a waning of Goodis's talents, for among the greatest strengths of Goodis's earlier novels had been the suggestive ambiguity of their endings. Goodis now shied away from that ambiguity, preferring cleaner and less interesting conclusions.

Goodis's decline is clear in his next book, *Night Squad* (1961). The story centers around Corey Bradford and his divided loyalties. Bradford is a former cop who has been fired for corruption; he is hired by Walter Grogan, the local crime boss, to find out who is trying to kill him. On the same night, Bradford is also hired by the leader of an elite police unit, the Night Squad, to try and infiltrate the crime boss's organization. The tension is generated by Bradford's attempts to keep each employer from finding out about his relationship with the other employer, but the story quickly degenerates into a series of gun battles and violent confrontations, with little suspense or complexity. Like *Fire in the Flesh,* the book again ends positively, with Bradford choosing to remain on the side of law and order, thus honoring the memory of his dead policeman father. The open-endedness and ambiguity of Goodis's earlier books has been replaced by a restrictive degree of moral certainty.

It is ironic that Goodis's characters began to exert more control over their fates at the time that Goodis began to lose control over his. Although Goodis was apparently happy living with his parents, it was obviously an arrangement that could not last. The disintegration began in 1963, with the death of Goodis's father, and with his mother's death three years later Goodis's last safe haven fell apart. Goodis apparently seldom worked in the last few years of his life. In 1965 he became obsessed with the belief that the producers of the television series *The Fugitive* had stolen the idea from *Dark Passage* and brought legal action. The suit was eventually settled for the derisory sum of $12,000 after Goodis's death, and he went to his grave haunted by a sense of injustice.

In 1966 Goodis admitted himself into a psychiatric hospital, and on 7 January 1967 at Albert Einstein Medical Center, David Goodis died at the age of forty-nine. According to James Sallis, his death was due to a combination of heart trouble, years of smoking unfiltered cigarettes, and the aftereffects of a severe beating suffered when he refused to give up his wallet to muggers. A single posthumous novel, *Somebody's Done For* (1967), followed, but it does nothing to change the impression that Goodis's talents were at a low ebb in his final years.

Goodis always had a low opinion of his own work. In the 16 August 1966 letter to William Sherman, Goodis said of his first novel, "It was nothing, and the same applies to most of the sixteen others since then." The underwhelming response to Goodis's death seemed to confirm the accuracy of Goodis's words. Only the *Philadelphia Inquirer* printed more than a cursory obituary, and even that was full of errors. Indeed, after his death, Goodis and his work fell into obscurity for twenty years, with none of his novels being reprinted until Black Lizard republished novels such as *Black Friday* and *Nightfall,* starting in 1987. Since then, a new generation of readers actively interested in resurrecting the pulp fiction of the 1940s and 1950s has become familiar with Goodis's work. As a result, his reputation has steadily improved, and he is currently regarded as among the most important and inventive American hard-boiled crime fiction writers. Wallington quotes Goodis as saying, "In practically all my work, pulp and serious fiction, I've been concerned with the way people handle their problems." The author's doom-laden and emotional explorations of human survival may well garner an enduring audience.

Biography:
Philippe Garnier, *Goodis: La Vie En Noir Et Blanc* (Paris: Editions de l'Olivier, 1998).

References:
Meredith Brody, "Missing Persons: David Goodis," *Film Comment,* 20 (September–October 1984): 42–43;

James Sallis, "David Goodis: Life in Black and White," in his *Difficult Lives: Jim Thompson, David Goodis, Chester Himes* (Brooklyn, N.Y.: Gryphon Books, 1993), pp. 47–71;

William David Sherman, "David Goodis/Dark Passage," *Sight & Sound,* 38 (Winter 1968/1969): 41;

Mike Wallington, introduction, *David Goodis: Nightfall, Down There, Dark Passage, The Moon in the Gutter* (London: Zomba Books, 1983);

Adrian Wootton and Paul Taylor, eds., *David Goodis/Pulps Pictured: For Goodis' Sake!* (London: British Film Institute, 1989).

Joe Gores

(25 December 1931 –   )

Peter Kenney

BOOKS: *A Time of Predators* (New York: Random House, 1969; London: W. H. Allen, 1970);

Marine Salvage: The Unforgiving Business of No Cure, No Pay (Garden City, N.Y.: Doubleday, 1971);

Dead Skip (New York: Random House, 1972; London: Gollancz, 1973);

Final Notice (New York: Random House, 1973; London: Gollancz, 1974);

Interface (New York: M. Evans, 1974; London: Futura, 1977);

Hammett: A Novel (New York: Putnam, 1975; London: Macdonald, 1976);

Gone No Forwarding (New York: Random House, 1978; London: Gollancz, 1979);

Come Morning (New York: Mysterious Press, 1986; London: Century, 1988);

Wolf Time (New York: Putnam, 1989);

32 Cadillacs (New York: Mysterious Press, 1992);

Mostly Murder (Eugene, Ore.: Mystery Scene Press, 1992);

Dead Man (New York: Mysterious Press, 1993);

Menaced Assassin (New York: Mysterious Press, 1994);

Contract Null and Void (New York: Mysterious Press, 1996);

Cases (New York: Mysterious Press, 1999);

Speak of the Devil: 14 Tales of Crimes and Their Punishments (New York: Mysterious Press, 1999).

PRODUCED SCRIPTS: "No Immunity for Murder," "Bad Dude," "Sad Sunday," "Was It Worth It, Lady?," and "Case Without a File," television, *Kojak,* CBS, 1975–1977;

"In The Finest Tradition," television, *Eischied,* NBC, 1979;

"Love on Instant Replay," television, *Kate Loves a Mystery Series,* NBC, 1979;

"On His Last Legs" and "This, My Firstborn Son," television, *The Gangster Chronicles,* NBC, 1981;

"Fallen Angel," *Strike Force,* 1982;

Joe Gores (photograph by Dori Gores)

Hammett, motion picture, based on novel by Gores, script by Gores, Denis O'Flaherty, Thomas Pope, and Ross Thomas, Zoetrope Studios, 1982;

"Pretty Good Dancing Chicken," television, *Magnum P.I.,* CBS, 1983–1984;

"Seven Dead Eyes," television, *Mickey Spillane's Mike Hammer,* CBS, 1983–1986;

"To Steele a Plot," television, *Remington Steele,* NBC, 1985;

"Death Trip," television, *T. J. Hooker,* ABC, 1985;

"Blind Chess," television, *B. L. Stryker,* ABC, 1989.

OTHER: "Writing the Mystery Short Story," *The Writer,* 84 (August 1971): 13–16, 46;

Honolulu, Port of Call: A Selection of South Sea Tales, edited by Gores (New York: Ballantine, 1974);

"Goodbye Pops," in *Every Crime in the Book,* edited by Robert L. Fish (New York: Putnam, 1975), pp. 208–214;

Tricks and Treats, edited by Gores and Bill Pronzini (Garden City, N.Y.: Doubleday, 1976); republished as *Mystery Writers' Choice* (London: Gollancz, 1977);

"Hammett the Writer," *Xenophile 12* (1978).

Joe Gores has acquired a well-deserved reputation as one of the most skilled and versatile American crime novelists. He has won the Edgar Allan Poe Award from the Mystery Writers of America in three separate categories—for best first mystery novel, best mystery short story in an American magazine, and best episode in a television dramatic series. For *Hammett* (1975), a fictionalized account of Dashiell Hammett's work as a private investigator, Gores received the Falcon Award for best detective novel from the Maltese Falcon Society of Japan. His prolific and varied writing has led to his recognition as one of the foremost current writers of the hard-boiled detective novel. As Philip French noted in the 10 October 1975 issue of *TLS: The Times Literary Supplement,* "Mr. Gores's style is hard-boiled to the point of being petrified."

Joseph Nicholas Gores was born in Rochester, Minnesota, on 25 December 1931, to Joseph Mathias Gores, an accountant, and Mildred Dorothy (Duncanson) Gores. He received a B.A. from the University of Notre Dame in 1953. Gores wrote his first story in the eighth grade, and by the time he left Notre Dame, his desire to write had been strengthened, in part because of the advice he received from one of his favorite instructors, which he recounted in the August 1988 issue of *Writer's Digest:* "Go to a big city and find a small room that has a bed and a table and a chair in it. Put your typewriter on the table and your backside on the chair and start typing. When you stand up ten years later, you'll be a writer." After he graduated, Gores for two years worked as an instructor at Floyd Page's Gymnasium in Palo Alto, California, and in his free time began to pursue his writing career. He collected some three hundred printed rejection slips annually before selling a story, "Chain Gang," to *Manhunt* for $65 in 1957.

During the years of trying to establish himself as a writer, Gores held a variety of jobs. He served in the U.S. Army from 1958 to 1959 and worked at various times as a laborer, logger, truck driver, and carnival worker. By far his most important work for his development as a hard-boiled writer, though, was his own career as a private investigator. Gores was introduced to the detective profession by Gene Mathews of the L.A. Walker Company, whom he met at a Palo Alto gym. Moving to San Francisco, Gores took a job with L.A. Walker in which his main duty was to repossess cars. He later worked in a similar capacity for David Kikkert and Associates, clearly the model for his series of novels detailing the exploits of the Daniel Kearny Associates (DKA) agency. Although his work as a private detective was interrupted for periods of time, it was Gores's main occupation from 1955 through 1967. The work was valuable not only for providing experiences he could draw upon in his stories but also for the development of his writing style. Gores in his *Writer's Digest* interview relates that as a private detective he had to write thousands of field reports and it was in answering the who, what, where, when, and why questions that he learned the "essentials of good storytelling."

Before he wrote his first novel in 1968, Gores concentrated solely on short stories, publishing more than a hundred in a variety of magazines, including *Negro Digest, Ellery Queen's Mystery Magazine,* and *Argosy.* He also found time to continue his formal education, receiving his M.A. in English literature from Stanford University in 1961. Gores remembered in the *Writer's Digest* interview that initially he had been denied entrance to the graduate program in creative writing at Stanford because the twenty short stories he had submitted as samples were considered to "read as if they had been written to be sold." In his development as a writer Gores was influenced by the works of Dashiell Hammett, Ross Macdonald, and Raymond Chandler.

In 1963–1964 Gores taught English at Kakamega Boys Secondary School in Kenya. In his comments to *Contemporary Authors,* Gores reflects on his growing self-awareness as a writer: "While living in Africa I read Robert Ardrey's *African Genesis,* and a few years later Joseph Campbell's *The Hero with a Thousand Faces.* From these I came to understand what my basic fictional theme was: A hero who has been stripped of society's defenses must overcome danger and death armed only with the genetic survival skills inherited from his prehuman ancestors." In 1964 Gores married Susan Hall. From 1968 to 1976 Gores worked as manager and auctioneer at Automobile Auction Company, a position that allowed him the flexibility to devote more of his time to writing.

Joe Gores   DLB 226

Gores in the summer of 1953 (photograph by Al Eilers; from the dust jacket for Cases, *1999)*

Gores began his first novel, *A Time of Predators* (1969), as a result of an encouraging letter he received from Lee Wright of Random House. In the novel Paula Halstead takes her own life after being raped by a gang of teenaged hoodlums whom she had earlier witnessed committing a crime. Her husband, Professor Curtis Halstead, discovers the body and a suicide note. From that moment on, Halstead begins to revert to the person he had been as a young commando in combat. Obsessed with vengeance, Halstead methodically tracks down the four boys responsible for his wife's death. He kills two of them; the others kill themselves through fear and stupidity. Halstead goes free because of lack of evidence. *A Time of Predators* was praised by Allen Hubin as "A thoughtful novel this, and exceedingly well done" in the 24 August 1969 issue of *The New York Times Book Review*. It received an Edgar Allan Poe Award for best first mystery novel in 1969. That same year Gores also received another Edgar for his short story "Goodbye Pops," which originally appeared in the December 1969 issue of *Ellery Queen's Mystery Magazine*.

After publishing a work of nonfiction, *Marine Salvage: The Unforgiving Business of No Cure, No Pay* (1971), Gores returned to fiction with *Dead Skip* (1972), the first book in a remarkable series of private-eye procedurals. One of the great strengths of the series is its authenticity, and Gores's dedication of the novel—"This one is for/ Dave Kikkert,/ who lives it every day,/ and for/

Tony Boucher and Fred Dannay"—alludes to his long experience in the business of repossessing cars. The hero of the novel is not so much one man as it is the whole of the Daniel Kearny Associates agency. Dan Kearny himself is a stocky man with a massive jaw and flat nose and a limitless supply of determination. He is a hard-driving boss and mentor whose crew of mostly young agents mature noticeably throughout the series.

In the first chapter of *Dead Skip* the reader follows Bart Heslip, a black DKA agent, on a routine repossession of a 1972 Mercury Montego. After collecting the car from a deadbeat bigot, Heslip returns to the agency:

> Heslip unlocked the chain-link storage lot under the concrete abutments of the skyway adjacent to the DKA office, unhooked the Mercury, and ran it in, then swiftly made out a condition report on a printed snap-out multiple form. This covered mileage, mechanical condition, lights, glass, body, rubber, power extras such as steering, seats, windows, brakes. He also checked the glove box, trunk, under the seats, on the back ledge, and behind the visors for personal property. Each item was meticulously noted, down to a box of Kleenex.
>
> His thoroughness was professional and habitual, and owed nothing at all to Willets' threats. Threats were cheap in Heslip's business. He had started as a field agent with Daniel Kearny Associates three years before, when he had realized he wasn't going to be middleweight champ of the world after all; it was the only profession he knew which could give him the same one-on-one excitement he'd found in the ring.

Gores's assurance in such descriptions draws the reader into the novel.

The main action of the novel begins when Heslip is found unconscious in a wrecked Jaguar that had previously been repossessed. Bart's close friend Larry Ballard does not believe Bart was driving the car and suspects he was assaulted before being placed in the car and pushed off Twin Peaks. Kearny gives Ballard seventy-two hours to find the person who assaulted Bart, who is in a deep coma at Trinity Hospital and cannot provide any information. Working from a list of Bart's car repossession cases, Ballard reduces the suspects to six people and then to one, Charles N. Griffin, a *dead skip,* a term used to describe a subject who has "skipped out" of the area covered by the field agent and for whom all obvious leads have been exhausted. At this point, Kearny also starts to concentrate on the case.

Critics showed an early appreciation for the DKA series in reviewing *Dead Skip*. Writing in the 12 November 1972 "Newgate Callendar" column for *The New York Times Book Review*, the reviewer praised Gores for his realistic descriptions of detective work and for his "unsentimental prose and earthy dialogue." In *The Sat-*

168

urday Review of 25 November 1972, O. J. Bailey found the story "superb in its swift, to-the-point plotting and on-the-mark dialogue."

Gores followed up with his second DKA novel, *Final Notice,* in 1973. In this book the reader knows who the villains are early in the story. Trouble starts when Larry Ballard repossesses a car owned by an aging dancer, Chandra, and finds $500 inside a comic book on the front seat. Later, agent Ed Dorsey is assaulted by two men outside the DKA office. Kearny learns the assailants are enforcers for the New York mob and begins to investigate the possible link between the $500 and the attack on Dorsey. The leads soon widen to include Phil Fazzino, a man who ascends to leadership of the mob in Northern California after the former boss dies in an apparent accident, and his girlfriend, Wendy Austin. DKA agents start following the suspects and investigating all clues, asking hundreds of personal, business, and social questions, both by phone and in person. After an exhaustive investigation, Kearny knows that Fazzino is a murderer but does not have enough evidence to get a conviction in court. Kearny then ensures a hard-boiled version of swift justice by tipping off the mob that Fazzino had arranged the assassination of the previous boss.

With *Dead Skip* and *Final Notice* Gores set a standard for realism in private detective procedurals, due as much to his powers of observation as to his experience. In his *Writer's Digest* interview Gores stresses the importance of daily observation to becoming a good writer:

> Next in importance to reading and writing is observation. John D. MacDonald remarked somewhere that he went to parties to stand in a corner and watch the people. If you are the center of attention—leather patches on your elbows, a swirl of rich pipe smoke around your head, drawling, "Yes, I'm well into my next book"—you aren't going to learn very much, except about yourself. And you probably know that all too well already. A little pocket or handbag notebook is not a bad idea—jot down bits of dialogue, a line of description, a character who is intriguing, ideas. I have carried one my whole professional life.

Gores has also found similarities between writing and detecting. In an interview with Wayne Warga in the *Los Angeles Times* of 13 March 1981 he draws a comparison between a detective who "digs around in the garbage of people's lives" and a novelist who "invents people and then digs around in their garbage."

The idea for Gores's fifth novel, *Hammett,* arose during a casual conversation with his agent, Henry Morrison. Gores works within the framework of Hammett's life in San Francisco in 1928. The thirty-four-year-old Hammett was then separated from his wife

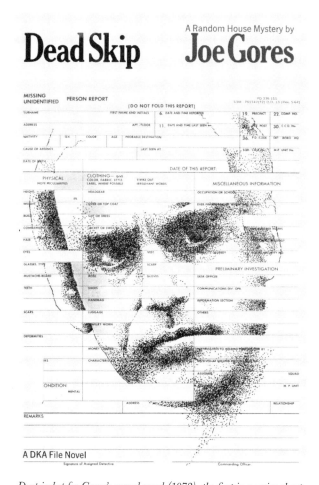

Dust jacket for Gores's second novel (1972), the first in a series about the Daniel Kearny Associates (DKA) detective agency

and writing full time, in the process of getting *Red Harvest* (1929) ready for publication. Gores imagines that an old associate of Hammett's from his days as a Pinkerton operative shows up and unsuccessfully tries to enlist him as a worker for a citizens reform committee that is attempting to clean up the city. When Hammett later learns that his friend has been murdered, he goes to the crime scene and inevitably becomes involved. Hammett sets out to solve the murder of his friend for much the same reason that Sam Spade begins to work on the murder of Miles Archer in *The Maltese Falcon* (1930)—a man is supposed to do something about it when his partner is killed.

In *The New York Times Book Review* of 9 November 1975 the reviewer praised Gores for his "evocative picture of San Francisco in 1928—with its beauty, its venality, its dirty cops and politicians." Not every critic was so enthusiastic, however. A reviewer in *Newsweek* (8 September 1975) gave the book a mixed critique: "Gores's professionalism shows: booze and slaughter, white slavery and miscellaneous mayhem, grotesque characters

Dust jacket for Gores's fifth novel (1975), in which the protagonist is the writer Dashiell Hammett

and accurate geography, affectionate attention to period details and references to historical figures are all sure buffers against boredom. But the portrait of Hammett (which is the novel's claim on our attention) is inadequate, and the story crudely written. Gores has two doubtful theories to advance: first, that Hammett the writer resisted perceiving evil that Hammett the old manhunter would instinctively have sensed; second, that Hammett perceived that his art was insufficient to portray one of the truly evil people in this story—a handicap that apparently does not apply to Gores."

Gores's life took important turns in the mid 1970s. In 1976 he co-edited with Bill Pronzini the mystery anthology *Tricks and Treats* and also began to write for television. His success in television was immediate as he received his third Edgar Allan Poe Award in 1975 for "No Immunity for Murder," the first episode he wrote for *Kojak*. The following year, his first marriage having ended in divorce, Gores married Dori Jane Corfitzen on 16 May 1976. His wife has been an important influence on the course of his life and career. The cou-

ple have raised two children, Timothy and Gillian, and are world travelers. As Gores related in his *Writer's Digest* interview, "We love to deliberately remove ourselves from all our usual props of living—our own hearth, our dog, our usual food, our friends, even our own language—and thus keep our survival instinct strong and functional." In his note introducing his 1999 novel *Cases,* Gores writes that his wife works with him on all his novels.

Gores returned to the DKA series in *Gone No Forwarding* (1978), a novel that begins with the understated description of the brutal murder of Adán Espinosa, the alias of the mob boss Fazzino who Kearny had informed upon at the end of *Final Notice:*

> Espinosa, lying on the bed in his shorts with a drink balanced on his bare chest and the TV turned to the Channel 4 news, yelled at her without turning his head, "Use your goddam key!"
> More gentle kicks. Jesus. Women. She could have had the cab driver carry her packages to the door for her. He swung his bare feet to the rug and set his drink on top of the bureau.
> He swung the door open, saying, "Wendy, why in the hell—"
> "Goodbye, Phil."
> The bulky, swarthy man in the heavy topcoat pulled both triggers at once from three feet away. Assorted bits of Espinosa were blown against the side of the dresser by the sawed-off 12-gauge shotgun.
> The killer stepped unhurriedly across the threshold to roll the eviscerated corpse over onto its face. He jerked down the boxer-style shorts and shoved a shiny new penny up between the buttocks with a quick jabbing motion. The body had voided in death, so he wiped his middle finger on the shorts before crossing the room to pick up the leather satchel.

At the precise moment of the killing, DKA office manager Kathy Onoda is receiving a delinquent auto payment from Kasimir Pivarski at the DKA office. Some months later Onoda dies from a massive blood clot, and then days later Kearny is served a notice of complaint by the state licensing board regarding DKA's handling of the Pivarski payment. Without Onoda, Kearny has no readily available witness to the transaction and must send his agents scurrying to find former employees who may have witnessed the transaction in order to save his license. He ultimately realizes that mob lawyer Wayne Hawley is behind the license problem and has used it to create an alibi for his hit man. The critic for the Newgate Callendar column in *The New York Times Book Review* of 14 May 1978 had high praise for the book, which he saw as being "in the best tradition of the West Coast private-eye novel." Gores, the critic asserted, had "never a wasted word" in his writing and had "a fine feeling for characterization."

During much of the 1980s Gores was occupied with writing for television and movies. In 1982 Gores's *Hammett* was made into a movie after being in production for several years and with much of it supposedly reshot by executive producer Francis Ford Coppola. It was the first American movie for German director Wim Wenders. The movie actually helped to move Gores's career toward scriptwriting. Besides his work on *Kojak,* he also wrote scripts for shows such as *Magnum P.I.* and *Mickey Spillane's Mike Hammer.* Gores believes that he has benefited as a novelist from his scriptwriting, which has taught him a sense of pace, as he remarked in his *Writer's Digest* interview: "There's a clock, a second-counter, down in the corner on film rushes. Those tenths of a second going off, and nothing happening, are devastating. So you become very aware of pace and timing. I think this goes back into the novels just as the visual sense goes from the novels into the screen work."

Eight years passed between the publication of *Gone, No Forwarding* and the appearance of his next novel, *Come Morning,* in 1986. In *Come Morning,* Runyan, a former convict, is pitted against an insurance investigator who wants to recover the diamonds Runyan had stolen eight years earlier and then hidden before going to prison. Other people are also out for the stones: a gangster willing to kill for the diamonds, Runyan's partner in the theft who recently escaped from prison, and the temptress Louise Graham, who pretends to be interested in writing a book about Runyan. The critic in the 30 March 1986 issue of *The New York Times Book Review* gave the novel a mixed review, pointing out that "nothing much gets past Runyan, the former prisoner. He is smart, a survivor, always one step ahead of the opposition. One can work up a lot of respect for this man. But Mr. Gores ends up all but canonizing him, and that is a bit too much. After a while it is hard to figure out if Runyan is an angel of death or an angel of mercy." Mystery novelist Lawrence Block in his *Washington Post Book World* review of 2 March 1986 was more positive: "*Come Morning* is a pure pleasure to read. . . . Within the mystery field, Gores has won awards and fans. He deserves a wider audience, and this book should get it for him."

After *Wolf Time* (1989), a mystery that centers on corruption and presidential politics, Gores in 1992 published the fourth and funniest installment of the DKA series, *32 Cadillacs.* When the wife of gypsy king Staley Zlachi sends out word that the king is dying in a small town in Iowa, a struggle immediately begins for the coveted throne and titular leadership of the two million gypsies from four nations and sixty tribes who live in the United States. Since it is known that Zlachi wishes

to be buried in a pink Cadillac convertible and since tradition calls for the dying king to choose his successor and dictates that the new king should be the biggest and most successful thief among the gypsies, the two leading candidates vying for the throne indulge in competitive chicanery that results in the hiring of Daniel Kearny Associates to repossess the Caddies. Although the book is full of humor and heroes on all sides as DKA agents and gypsies strive to outwit each other, it also shows the DKA operatives relentlessly pursuing their foes. As Gores noted in the Spring 1994 issue of *The Armchair Detective,* "the subject of your investigation is the enemy—that's how real private eyes think."

Gores's *32 Cadillacs* was widely praised. Marilyn Stasio admired Gores's originality in *The New York Times Book Review* of 20 December 1992 and called the novel "a fall-down-funny account of how the gypsies and the repo men lock wits and bump fenders over that fleet of hot cars." Wes Lukowsky in *Booklist* (15 October 1992) lamented the fourteen-year delay between DKA novels but praised Gores's portrayal of Kearny and his operatives as "carefully drawn, substantial characters with lives outside their profession," comparing his technique to that used by Ed McBain in his 87th Precinct novels. A reviewer in *Kirkus Reviews* (15 September 1992) was equally enthusiastic, calling *32 Cadillacs* the "crown of a distinguished career." Max Boot summarized his review with this remark in the 5 March 1993 issue of *Christian Science Monitor:* "This is what detection fiction ought to be."

In *Dead Man* (1993) Gores tells the story of Eddie Dain, a young computer whiz in northern California whose on-line private investigations bring two hit men to his door. After his wife and child are killed and he is left for dead, Dain undergoes extensive rehabilitation and is bent on avenging his family. Wes Lukowsky in the *Booklist* of 1 October 1993 praised Gores's style and dialogue and noted that Dain evolves as a character "through three stages: the nerd, the avenging angel, and, finally, the complete human being." A reviewer in *Publishers Weekly* (11 October 1993) saw the lighthearted side of *Dead Man,* calling it a "comic detective story with a hero both hard-boiled and sensitive, who finally recovers his soul." In *The New York Times Book Review* (26 December 1993) Marilyn Stasio remarked that "Mr. Gores writes some of the hardest, smoothest, most lucid prose in the field" and added that "he works some elaborately brutal variations on the basic hunt-and-prey plot."

In *Menaced Assassin* (1994) Gores shows again that civilization has done little to change man's basic brutal nature, as a mysterious killer, calling himself Raptor, duels Lieutenant Dante Stagnaro of the Organized Crime Task Force. A highlight of the novel is the scene

JOE GORES   102   THE ROAD TO ROME

The glorious city of San Francisco   X

HERE ———→   "Until we go," we must work, ~~this~~ city for all it is worth ①

As *has pointed out*

but <u>carefully</u>. We are in Kalderasha territory here."

was about to break

~~Now Lulu broke out the wine and beer for those who wished~~

but

~~to stay and gossip. But~~ Sonia Lovari was on her feet again.

we cannot leave this city until the soul of

"Baro Rom, ~~there is a topic we have not touched upon."~~ ~~She~~

has been consoled.

~~paused for effect.~~ "Your dead brother, Ephrem Poteet — What are

we going to do about his wife, Yana Poteet -- the woman who

murdered him? I spit upon her shadow, I would curse her progeny

except the syphlitic whore will never be able to bear children."

Everyone knew that Sonia had hated Yana since Yana had told

gadjo

a ~~gadje~~ repossessor where to find the Cadillac Sonia was driving.

The repo man had taken it away from her; she had never forgotten. *Rudolph*

Rudolph believed that it might also have something to do with him.

~~It was Lulu~~ who rose to answer, ~~speaking in council for the~~ → *Reverse*

~~I supposed Staley by rising to leaping to~~ ~~him~~ ~~The council~~

~~first time that evening.~~

"~~Yes,~~ Yana Poteet is a disgrace to the <u>Rom</u> and no longer a

member of this <u>kumpania</u>. ~~But what further is there for us to~~

~~do?" She raised her shoulders in a most expressive shrug.~~ "We

have already in solemn <u>kris</u> declared her <u>marime</u>. ~~Should we try~~

But we must remember   *was born a cowleover her*

~~to lay some further Rom curse upon her,~~ remember that she has ~~stood~~①

many powers -- <u>and</u> the second sight. Leave her to the <u>gadje</u>'s

justice. Murder is a blasphemy that breaks even their teeth." *and they will*

There was a murmur of

~~Others called~~ ~~in agreement, and Sonia sat down again, if~~

~~not satisfied in her hatred,~~ ~~at least temporarily silenced.~~

Staley bent his head slightly rose to his feet. He spread his

~~Staley was again erect,~~ arms wide as if in benediction,   *Reverse*

every inch a King.   *2.*

and

"~~Now~~ go, my children, ~~to~~ bring glory upon this tribe!"

avenge Ephrem our old son.

Revised typescript pages for Gores's work in progress. The sixth novel in the DKA series, it has the working title "The Road to Rome"
(Collection of Joe Gores).

1. But it wouldn't do for Sonia to initiate a witch-hunt for Yana, when he and Staley were looking for her themselves. Lulu surprised him by leaping to the rescue.

2. Lulu was about to break out wine + beer for those who wished to stay and gossip. But Staley shook his head slightly and rose to his feet. He noticed that Ramon Ristik's bright eyes were brighter than usual. Yana was his sister, of course. Yet he had scrupulously observed the ban on her as Lulu had ascertained by keeping her eye on Ristik

Staley spread his arms wide as if in benediction, every inch a king.

"Go my children, and bring glory upon this tribe —

TO "Yana Poteet is a disgrace etc.
REVERSE

in which Raptor stalks Professor Will Dalton during his lecture on paleontology. The reviewer in the 15 August 1994 issue of *Kirkus Reviews* saw the book as an ambitious failure: "The interplay between killer and cop has been done much better before, and the mystery fizzles like a damp firecracker, but the interweaving of the story with excerpts from Will's lecture and Raptor's confession shows just how magnificently ambitious this failure is." A reviewer for *Publishers Weekly* (22 August 1994) was more impressed with Gores's achievement: "Drawing on a variety of conventions and styles, from the procedural to the gothic, Gores wedges a passionate lecture on evolution into a taut investigation and waxes ornate in the Raptor's chilling and vivid reveries. A professional killer from New Jersey is the likely suspect for a few of the hits, but the real criminal mind is extremely well hidden, right to the end, when few of the hoods are still standing. In his latest, Gores demonstrates masterful narrative sleight-of-hand."

Gores returns to a lighter mood with *Contract Null and Void* (1996), the fifth book in the DKA series. The central theme concerns union corruption, and the main action begins with the murder of a notorious union leader, but Gores skillfully weaves several plotlines together. A reviewer in the 13 May 1996 issue of *Publishers Weekly* had high praise for the latest DKA entry: "Gores loads his tale to the bursting point, keeping it all together with bouts of scabrous humor, odd moments of tenderness and virtuoso narrative juggling. After allowing his trusting readers to meander through a series of minor movements, Gores jerks in the reins and dashes for the finish, a crafty collision of weird people that brings the main gambit into crystalline focus." The book received similar praise from a critic writing in *The New York Times Book Review* (7 July 1996): "Master of a surreal comedic style, Mr. Gores keeps finding outlandish assignments for his repo

men. But in the inspired ending, aptly called 'walpurgisnacht,' the plot lines converge and all the insanity, believe it or not, makes perfect sense."

Gores's novel *Cases* (1999) is in its particulars his most autobiographical, for the protagonist, Pierce Duncan, as Gores comments in his prefatory note, "stole my grandfather's name and much of my early life." Although the incidents of the novel are often based on Gores's notebooks of his early cases with L.A. Walker, he is careful to claim that the novel is a conglomeration:

> In *Cases* I have tried to mix fact and fiction so thoroughly that nobody—not even myself—can now untangle them. I have also tried to honestly re-create the language, raw prejudices, hopes, dreams, despairs, sentimentality, violence, and social and marital attitudes of America's early fifties as seen through the eyes of a somewhat naive twenty-one-year-old man.

As he has throughout his career, Gores attempts to write a suspense novel that is true to the world he has experienced. In the *Writer's Digest* interview Gores considers "suspense novels to be as serious as anything else and a very abiding form of literature. A good suspense novel is better than all but the very, very best of the 'straight novel' variety. The suspense novel has just as much humanity, just as many insights, in the hands of a good writer. It's the quality of the writer that counts."

Interview:
James McKimmey, "Joe Gores," *Writer's Digest,* 68 (August 1988): 31–35.

Reference:
Peter Kenney, "Specialists in Skip-Tracing and Repossessions," *Mystery Readers Journal,* 11 (Summer 1995): 8–9.

Sue Grafton
(24 April 1940 –)

Carol McGinnis Kay
University of South Carolina

BOOKS: *Keziah Dane* (New York: Macmillan, 1967;
London: Peter Owen, 1968);
The Lolly-Madonna War (London: Peter Owen, 1969);
"A" Is for Alibi (New York: Holt, Rinehart & Winston,
1982; London: Macmillan, 1986);
"B" Is for Burglar (New York: Holt, Rinehart & Winston,
1985; London: Macmillan, 1986);
"C" Is for Corpse (New York: Holt, 1986; London: Mac-
millan, 1987);
"D" Is for Deadbeat (New York: Holt, 1987; London:
Macmillan, 1987);
"E" Is for Evidence (New York: Holt, 1988; London:
Macmillan, 1988);
"F" Is for Fugitive (New York: Holt, 1989; London: Mac-
millan, 1989);
"G" Is for Gumshoe (New York: Holt, 1990; London:
Macmillan, 1990);
"H" Is for Homicide (New York: Holt, 1991; London:
Macmillan, 1991);
"I" Is for Innocent (New York: Holt, 1992; London: Mac-
millan, 1992);
Kinsey and Me, edited by Steve Humphrey, introductions
by Grafton (Santa Barbara: Bench Press, 1992);
"J" Is for Judgment (New York: Holt, 1993; London:
Macmillan, 1993);
"K" Is for Killer (New York: Holt, 1994; London: Mac-
millan, 1994);
"L" Is for Lawless (New York: Holt, 1995; London: Mac-
millan, 1996);
"M" Is for Malice (New York: Holt, 1996; London: Mac-
millan, 1997);
"N" Is for Noose (New York: Holt, 1998; London: Mac-
millan, 1998);
"O" Is for Outlaw (New York: Holt, 1999; London: Mac-
millan, 1999).

PRODUCED SCRIPTS: *Lolly-Madonna XXX,* motion
picture, based on the novel by Grafton, screenplay
by Grafton and Rodney Carr-Smith, M-G-M,
1973;

*Sue Grafton at the time of her 1996 novel, "M" Is for Malice
(photograph by Michael Goldman)*

"With Friends Like These," television, *Rhoda,* CBS,
April 1975;
Walking Through the Fire, television, based on the novel
by Laurel Lee, CBS, April 1979;
Sex and the Single Parent, television, based on the novel by
Jane Adams, CBS, September 1979;
Nurse, television, based on the novel by Peggy Ander-
son, CBS, April 1980;

175

Mark, I Love You, television, based on the novel by Hal Painter, CBS, December 1980;

Seven Brides for Seven Brothers, television, pilot, script by Grafton and Steven Humphrey, CBS, October 1982;

"I Love You, Molly McGraw" and "A House Divided," television, *Seven Brides for Seven Brothers,* CBS, 1982–1983;

Svengali, television, story by Grafton, script by Frank Cucci, CBS, March 1983;

A Caribbean Mystery, television, based on the novel by Agatha Christie, script by Grafton and Humphrey, CBS, October 1983;

A Killer in the Family, television, script by Grafton, Humphrey, and Robert Aller, ABC, October 1983;

Sparkling Cyanide, television, based on the novel by Christie, script by Grafton, Humphrey, and Robert Malcolm Young, CBS, November 1983;

Love on the Run, television, script by Grafton and Humphrey, NBC, October 1985;

Tonight's the Night, television, script by Grafton and Humphrey, ABC, February 1987.

OTHER: *Writing Mysteries: A Handbook by the Mystery Writers of America,* edited by Grafton (Cincinnati: Writer's Digest Books, 1992);

"An Eye for an I: Justice, Morality, The Nature of the Hard-boiled Private Detective, and All That Existential Stuff," in *Crown Crime Companion,* edited by Otto Penzler (New York: Random House/Crown Trade Paperbacks, 1995) pp. 92–102;

"The Use of the Journal in the Writing of a Private Eye Novel," in *Writing the Private Eye Novel: A Handbook by the Private Eye Writers of America,* edited by Robert J. Randisi (Cincinnati: Writer's Digest Books, 1997).

SELECTED PERIODICAL PUBLICATIONS– UNCOLLECTED: "Breaking and Entering," *Writer,* 96 (January 1983): 16–18, 28;

"How To Find Time To Write When You Don't Have Time To Write," *Writer,* 99 (December 1986): 7–10;

"What I'm Reading: Sue Grafton," *Entertainment Weekly* (16 September 1994): 105.

Sue Grafton, along with Marcia Muller and Sara Paretsky, are credited with introducing the woman hard-boiled detective. Her popular detective, Kinsey Millhone, appeared initially in 1982 in *"A" Is for Alibi,* the beginning of a highly successful series titled alphabetically. With Grafton more than halfway through the alphabet at this point and with more than forty-two million copies of *"A"* through *"O"* sold in this country alone, Grafton holds a secure place as a popularizer and reshaper of the genre.

Like her prototypical predecessors, Dashiell Hammett's Continental Op or Raymond Chandler's Philip Marlowe, Kinsey Millhone is a professional private investigator who narrates the novels. She is a tough loner with few possessions and a wisecracking cynic who plays along the edges of legality in her investigations, willingly picking a lock, stealing mail, and telling lies; yet, there is an inviolate core of morality unique to the detective for which she, like Marlowe and the Op, will unhesitatingly risk bodily harm. What Grafton expands and revises from the early version of the hard-boiled detective is a rich exploration of the psychology that lies behind the detective's actions, as well as the actions of other figures in the novels. In his article, "The Simple Art of Murder," in *The Atlantic Monthly* of December 1944, Chandler said he did not "care much about [the] private life" of his protagonist. In contrast, Grafton cares deeply about the private life and thoughts of Kinsey Millhone.

Grafton is more interested in learning why someone would kill than she is in devising new and more spectacular methods of blood and mayhem. The body count is not high in a Grafton novel. Focusing more on internal conflicts and less on the violence, then, Grafton has taken some cues from Ross Macdonald and modified the genre from an exercise in male mythmaking into serious, albeit often sardonic, commentary on major contemporary social concerns. Her fifteen novels repeatedly explore issues of class divisions; corruption in the systems intended to permit society to function, such as the judiciary or health care; and divisive attitudes, such as ageism and homophobia. Coming even closer to home, the theme receiving the most consistent and biting attention is what a character in *"D" Is for Deadbeat* calls the "harm families do." As Natalie Hevener Kaufman and Carol McGinnis Kay point out in *"G" Is for Grafton: The World of Kinsey Millhone* (1997), every novel in the series is a study in the myriad ways families can fail their members: from *"A" Is for Alibi* and a wife who kills her unsavory husband to *"O" Is for Outlaw* and its several spousal betrayals, Grafton examines how family members lie to, cheat, demean, abuse, neglect, and just plain hurt each other. The predominance of Grafton's theme of family pain and her abiding interest in the dark side of human motivations are not unexpected if one considers the author's own life, especially her childhood, which she discussed candidly during three 1996 interviews granted during the preparation of *"G" Is for Grafton* and in subsequent interviews in 1998.

Sue Taylor Grafton was born in Louisville, Kentucky, on 24 April 1940 to Cornelius Warren Grafton and Vivian Harnsberger Grafton. She was the second of two children, three years younger than her sister, Ann. At first glance Grafton's childhood might seem idyllic. Her father, C.W., or "Chip," was a successful municipal-bond attorney and her mother was a former high-school chemistry teacher; both parents were devoted lovers of literature, and the house was full of a wide variety of books, which the girls were encouraged to read. In addition, Chip wrote and published four novels, three of which were critically well-received mysteries: *The Rat Began to Gnaw the Rope* (1943), *The Rope Began to Hang the Butcher* (1944), and *Beyond a Reasonable Doubt* (1951). From her parents, Grafton has said, she learned a love of the written word and the pleasure of exploring ideas. Grafton also credits her father with teaching her—by example—to learn to focus on a goal and to be persistent.

From her parents, however, Grafton also learned more painful lessons about human nature and personal relationships. Both parents were alcoholics. Grafton's earliest memories are of living quite happily with her mother and sister during World War II, while her father served as a major in the army. During that period Vivian maintained enough control over her drinking to function diligently, but when Chip returned, Grafton's mother apparently felt she could relinquish responsibility to her husband. In one of the many parallels that can be drawn between Grafton's experience and that of her protagonist, this major family shift occurred when Grafton was five years old—the same age at which Kinsey's parents died in a car accident. From then until her death fifteen years later, Vivian sank into a non-functioning state, with only periodic bouts of recovery.

Chip's alcoholism seems not to have prevented him from functioning effectively, and he was clearly the dominant figure in the household. He drank a couple of jiggers of whiskey in the morning and headed out to work, leaving his daughters to fend for themselves—and increasingly for their mother as well. Her father praised the girls for being strong and regretted that their mother was so weak that they all had to focus on helping her. As a child, Grafton was flattered by her father's confidence in her, but when he offered the same argument years later to justify leaving most of his estate to her stepmother, Grafton says she finally realized that "he had co-opted me to agree to my own abandonment." Little wonder that Grafton's detective fears abandonment above all else in life.

Grafton is able to look back on this difficult childhood, with its imposition of adult responsibilities onto two young children, with objectivity and even generosity. In her 1994 interview with Rosemary Herbert, she focuses on what she gained from the experience: "It was the perfect training for a writer. It was the great gift of my life that I was raised not only with intellectuals

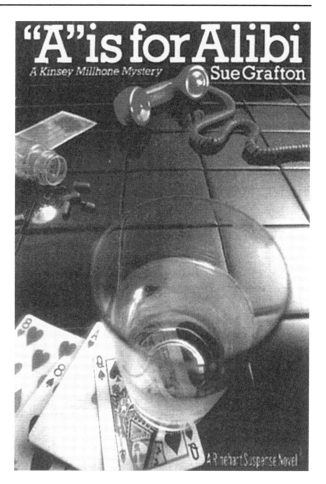

Dust jacket for the 1982 novel that introduces Grafton's private detective, Kinsey Millhone

and with people who valued the language and the written word, but with people who were somehow incapable of parenting me very well, so that I was left to my own devices." Like Kinsey, she learned to parent herself. Without adult guidance, Grafton did pretty much whatever she wanted to. She played with a group of neighborhood children whenever she chose, used the bus or her feet to wander from one end of Louisville to the other, went to the movies both days of the weekend, plus, of course, she read everything in the house. As she grew up, she also increasingly wrote short stories, both as a way to understand her daily life and as a way to escape from it, thus establishing a lifelong pattern of using her writing to ground herself.

Grafton explains in an introduction to one of her autobiographical stories in *Kinsey and Me* (1992) that by the time she was eighteen she knew two things: she wanted to become a writer and she wanted "to get out of that house." In 1957 she attended the University of Louisville, where she majored in English. Grafton loved being an English major. She did what she had always enjoyed doing–she read literature and then talked and thought about it with other interested readers.

Grafton's sophomore and junior years were spent at Western Kentucky State Teachers College before returning to the University of Louisville for her senior year and graduation. On 14 February 1959, shortly before her nineteenth birthday, Grafton married a college classmate, James L. Flood, whom she met after she transferred schools. She says little about Flood or this first marriage, a reticence echoed by Kinsey Millhone regarding her first husband prior to *"O" Is for Outlaw*. Grafton simply says she was ill prepared for marriage because of the obvious gaps in the functioning of her birth family. Their first child, Leslie, was born on 5 January 1960, but the marriage was already beginning to break apart and Grafton prepared to return to the University of Louisville.

The years 1960 and 1961 marked an emotionally draining period for Grafton. Less than four months after Leslie's birth, Grafton's mother, stricken with cancer, committed suicide on Grafton's twentieth birthday. Again, Grafton's mapping of her own experience on to Kinsey's psyche is obvious, not only in the fear of abandonment but also in having Kinsey's parents' deaths close to her birthday. (The detective often notes when someone has a birthday, and pivotal events often occur on or near someone's birthday.) Barely a year later, her father remarried. Grafton's second child, Jay, was born on 29 April 1961, and shortly thereafter she divorced her husband, who successfully insisted on maintaining custody of their daughter.

As a single mother with a four-month-old baby, Grafton began graduate studies in English in fall 1961 at the University of Cincinnati, full of expectations for solace from the one reliable part of her life–literature. Graduate school, however, proved to be just one more painful experience. Grafton found the faculty's approach to the material and the careerist focus of graduate school different from the world of the undergraduate English major, in which good writing had been celebrated. In contrast, she found graduate school a study in literary demolition. She "hated" the intellectualizing and critical posturing that she saw leeching the lifeblood out of a piece of literature. "This is not the way real writers work," she insisted. Rejecting an approach she considers "bogus" and antithetical to creativity, she was so "absolutely incensed" that she refused to take her final exams that semester. She simply left the program, more determined than ever to become a writer and to do it her own way.

In the year that followed, Grafton worked a variety of jobs to pay the rent while she wrote short stories and novels at night. For a short time she worked in an employment agency, but she was uncomfortable with the sense that everyone in the system was being short-changed by the cheap, temporary jobs offered to clients. After she married Al Schmidt on 22 April 1962, she, Schmidt, and Jay moved to San Francisco as a result of his position with Connecticut General Life Insurance, and she worked briefly as a file clerk for the Kern County Land Company.

When Schmidt went to work for Human Factors Research, the family moved to Santa Monica, where Grafton obtained a job as an admissions clerk in St. John's Hospital. She sought this job, in part, she says, because she liked the television doctor Ben Casey and the hospital shows at the time. A more significant reason may have been the great respect, even affection, she already had for hospitals–they were the safe haven to which her family had taken her mother during her worst crises and they "would make her well" for a time. Later Grafton worked as a cashier and then as a medical secretary in a clinic for the indigent at St. John's Hospital. In these jobs, Grafton learned a great deal about the daily functioning of hospitals, knowledge that is reflected in the many hospital visits made by Kinsey Millhone throughout the series, particularly in *"C" Is for Corpse, "H" Is for Homicide, "K" Is for Killer,* and *"O" Is for Outlaw*.

When Schmidt's job with Human Factors Research moved the family to Santa Barbara in 1964, Grafton began work as a medical secretary/receptionist–in white uniform–for Joe L. Atchison, a general practitioner, for whom she developed great respect. She worked for him for several years, and he delivered her third child, Jamie, on 5 March 1966. The real challenge of the job for Grafton lay in overcoming her innate squeamishness. Her other medical jobs had been removed from the sight of one of Grafton's personal phobias, her fear of injections–another characteristic shared by her protagonist. In this position, however, she watched and listened to the world of hands-on medicine, became faint, and went on with her work anyway, showing the same kind of personal determination that is a hallmark of Kinsey Millhone.

During this period of family life and medical work in the 1960s, Grafton continued to write at night and on the weekends. Five of the seven novels written during this period and her subsequent years in Hollywood are still in closets in Grafton's house, but the fourth and fifth ones were published: *Keziah Dane* in 1967 and *The Lolly-Madonna War* in 1969. *Keziah Dane* was entered for the Anglo-American Book Award; while it did not win, the competition did gain an English publisher for the novel, Peter Owen, which also published *The Lolly-Madonna War* after American publishers considered it "too savage." Following the advice of a mentor, Eustice Cockrell, whom she describes as "an old-time screenwriter," Grafton used her advance from Peter Owen to obtain an American agent. She had come to know Cockrell because he was the father of one of her close friends, and he gave her invaluable guidance during her early years in California, not about writing itself, but about finding her way through the Hollywood maze. Grafton's continuing gratitude is unmistakable: Cockrell is the inspiration for the appealing character Henry Pitts, Kinsey's closest friend in the series.

In 1972 M-G-M bought the movie rights to *The Lolly-Madonna War* for $25,000, the largest single amount Grafton had yet received for her writing, enough to suggest that she could make a living as a writer. In contrast, her personal life was going less well as her second marriage was crumbling. Selling the movie rights to *The Lolly-Madonna War* gave her enough financial security to leave Schmidt, taking Jay and Jamie with her. Knowing her income from the movie rights would not last indefinitely, however, she worked for a few months at Upjohn, a Santa Barbara agency offering temporary domestic help. She worked short stints as a maid, cook, server at cocktail parties, or whatever the employer needed. This experience is reflected throughout the novels in such scenes as Kinsey's visit to the wealthy Callahans' home in *"C" Is for Corpse,* her disguise as a hotel maid in *"L" Is for Lawless,* and many other instances in the series in which Kinsey is empathetic to the humanity of the domestic worker, who is often an invisible part of the furniture to the employer and the persons being served.

Grafton soon moved in with Rodney Carr-Smith, a British motion-picture producer whom she had met during negotiations for *The Lolly-Madonna War.* The next year, 1973, was a chaotic nadir similar to 1960–1961. She and Schmidt went through a bitter divorce, during which, she says, neither of them behaved well. She and Carr-Smith went through an equally painful relationship as they tried to collaborate on screenplays (including *Lolly-Madonna XXX*) and to develop a life together in an apartment in West Los Angeles. Resentful of Carr-Smith's efforts to persuade her that she could not write—or live—without him and determined to write her own way, Grafton severed the brief relationship, and Carr-Smith moved out of the apartment.

In 1974 Grafton met fellow tenant Steven Humphrey. She was initially resistant to becoming involved since she had been burned several times and was just beginning to be confident she could support herself and her children by writing screenplays and teleplays. Fortunately, however, she realized they were a good match. In 1975 Humphrey went to Ohio State University to begin the doctoral program in philosophy, and the following year Grafton joined him there, continuing to

Dust jacket for Grafton's 1985 novel, in which Kinsey is beaten and shot by the villains

write screenplays and teleplays while living in Columbus. They were married on 1 October 1978 and have had a mutually supportive, strong, and secure relationship for more than twenty years.

In this same period of growing personal stability in the late 1970s, Grafton also came to some major decisions about her writing career. She was comfortably successful as a screenwriter and thought she could continue to earn money in this way, but, as everything about her life suggests, she needed to be able to write her own way. She freely admits she is not, by temperament, a team player, and she did not like working in the "groupthink" world of movies and television, where nonwriters often tell the writer what to write. She recalls being told virtually every word to include in the script for a 1975 episode of *Rhoda* for CBS. By the time the show aired, Grafton recalled, no more than five lines were her own. Then, the producers complained that the show lacked her usual fresh touch.

Grafton fully understood that producers paid the money and could therefore have what they wanted, but having done what they asked for years, she came to feel such disenchantment about the system and about herself for cooperating in her own corruption that she decided she must get out. Around 1977 she decided she must focus on her solo writing, and although she continued to write teleplays—a few of them with her husband—she increasingly shifted her primary attention to her own fiction as Humphrey was finishing his doctorate. After he received his degree in 1981, they moved to Santa Barbara, where Grafton completed the first novel in the Millhone series.

Turning to her father's genre of detective fiction, a genre she had loved reading since she was a teenager, Grafton began to play with the idea of creating a female version of the Philip Marlowe/Sam Spade hardboiled private eye. Five years of thinking, writing, and rewriting led Grafton to reconceive the genre. She had moved from considering the genre a form of escapist literature, with an emphasis on the tough persona of the detective as a figure of fantasy, to a belief, as she asserts in the January 1983 issue of *The Writer,* that the detective novel allows for "a serious examination of contemporary social issues." This seriousness of purpose does not preclude a sense of playfulness: the alphabetical titles were the result of Grafton's reading Edward Gorey's *The Gashlycrumb Tinies* (1963), a collection of poems about Victorian children who meet grizzly demises ("A is for Alice who fell down the stairs, B is for Basil assaulted by bears," and so forth.). Most of the novels also match locales and prominent family names to the novels' titles: for example, in *"B" is for Burglar,* Kinsey's case involves Elaine Boldt and she takes a trip to Boca Raton.

Grafton's first hard-boiled novel, *"A" Is for Alibi,* was published in 1982, with a first-edition run of six thousand copies. She dedicated the novel to her father, who died in March, just prior to its publication. It won the second Mysterious Stranger Award from the Cloak and Clue Society in Milwaukee. Since Tony Hillerman had won the first award and because this was her first such recognition, Grafton still keeps the award—a personable witch—perched on her computer as she writes.

Marian Wood, the editor at Holt who accepted Grafton's manuscript of *"A" Is for Alibi,* says she wanted to publish the novel because it was a good piece of writing, not particularly because it broke any new ground in detective fiction. Wood considered it a well-crafted mainstream novel, rich in sensory details and complex characters. Like subsequent readers, Wood especially responded to the resilience and the humor of Kinsey Millhone, a thirty-two-year-old private investigator in fictitious Santa Teresa, California—a tribute to Ross Macdonald, who used this name for Santa Barbara in his Lew Archer novels. Grafton is unusual among writers in openly considering her central character her alter-

ego, and she writes in *Kinsey and Me* that she sees Kinsey as "a stripped-down version of my 'self' . . . a celebration of my own freedom, independence and courage." Like Grafton, Millhone is a gutsy, self-created, independent person who reveals personal insecurities and great compassion. Also like her creator, Millhone has a survivor's off-beat sense of humor.

In *"A" Is for Alibi* the reader learns a great deal about Kinsey Millhone and her background. Left an orphan at the age of five when her parents were killed in an automobile accident, Kinsey was reared by her Aunt Virginia, whose ideas about child care were somewhat eccentric and contrary to feminine stereotypes— she taught Kinsey to shoot at the age of eight, and she steadfastly refused to teach her to cook. By the time the series opens, her aunt has also died, ten years earlier when Kinsey was twenty-two. Kinsey has been married and divorced twice, and she now lives alone in a small garage apartment owned by Henry Pitts, eighty-one, who becomes her closest friend during the series. A former police officer, she has been a licensed private investigator for five years when the series opens (both Grafton and Kinsey went solo in their professions in 1977). Fiercely independent and with a low-maintenance style of living—she drives an old VW bug—Kinsey deals with the world her way, cracking a joke, cursing, punching someone in the nose, or crying— whatever she thinks appropriate in response to the behavior of people around her.

In this first novel, Kinsey is hired by Nikki Fife to find the killer of her husband, Lawrence. Nikki has finished serving an eight-year jail sentence for the murder, but she swears she is innocent, and now that she is free, she has the opportunity and the money to pursue the case. In the course of the investigation, Kinsey solves two additional related murders, as well as the case for which she was hired.

Grafton's lifetime of reading detective fiction and her experiences as a screenwriter served her well in *"A" Is for Alibi.* The setup for the investigation is conventional and credible as a lean, striking woman appears unannounced at the private eye's shabby office and hires the private investigator to find the real killer of her husband. Kinsey's narrative voice is laconic yet packed with startling images that echo Raymond Chandler's figurative language. She describes palm trees as "Spanish exclamation points" and an apartment complex as having "salmon-pink stucco eroding around the edges as though animals had crept up in the night to gnaw the corners away." Kinsey even finds herself sexually tempted by a male version of the femme fatale in the character of Charlie Scorsoni, who dupes her into bed and turns out to be a killer. Despite Grafton's distaste for Hollywood, her skills as a screenwriter are evident:

the plot twists are fast paced and satisfying, and the dialogue has both realism and snap. Grafton credits her screenwriting experience for teaching her how to structure a story, develop tension, handle dialogue, get into and out of a scene, and write action.

For readers and reviewers alike, though, the major appeal of the novel lies in the irrepressible central character: Kinsey Millhone's dry wit, her combination of bravery and vulnerability, and her gritty determination to solve the case are extremely engaging. She is funny about other people (the waiter at an elegant restaurant "stands at your table and recites the menu like a narrative poem") and about herself ("I even shaved my legs just to show I had some class"). Also, the other characters are also often amusing; for example, a woman in her sixties tells Kinsey, "The only cleavage I got left, I sit on."

The conclusion of the novel, however, came in for some negative commentary from reviewers. There are two final confrontation scenes because there are two killers, acting separately and with different motivations for a total of three murders, not just the one for which Kinsey was hired. One conclusion happens easily and incredibly: Kinsey figures out that Lawrence's first wife, Gwen, must have killed him; when Kinsey confronts her—over lunch—she almost immediately confesses and rushes away. Shortly thereafter, Gwen is killed in a hit-and-run "accident." The second and much more powerful confrontation comes when Kinsey figures out that Charlie Scorsoni, Lawrence's law partner, must have killed three women, including Gwen Fife, in a futile effort to cover up an initial crime of embezzlement. In the final scene, he pursues Kinsey across a deserted beach at night until he finally catches her hiding in a garbage bin. He lifts the lid, and she sees the glint of a butcher knife in his hand. The last line of the novel is classic hard-boiled understatement: "I blew him away."

Grafton has said on many occasions that the specific impetus for the plot of *"A" Is for Alibi* came out of her frustrations and anger over the custody fights she was still engaged in with her second husband at the time. Three court battles over custody and many sleepless nights had left her contemplating the morality of murder. The law-abiding Grafton knew that she would not actually commit murder—her joking that she would not look good in a prison dress is a typical Millhone/Grafton wisecrack—but she had all the satisfaction of a former wife doing the deed through the actions of Gwen Fife in the novel.

Stung by a few of the reviews, Grafton took three years to produce the second novel in the series. *"B" Is for Burglar* appeared in 1985, after which a Millhone novel has appeared annually through *"M" Is for Malice*, published in 1996. Beginning with *"N" Is for*

Dust jacket for Grafton's 1986 novel, in which Kinsey is chased through a morgue

Noose (1998), Grafton began to slow the pace to every eighteen months in order to ensure that she could maintain the quality of the work. Each early novel had a larger first-edition print run than the previous one: *"B" Is for Burglar*, 8,500; *"C" Is for Corpse*, 10,500; *"D" Is for Deadbeat*, 12,500; *"E" Is for Evidence*, 24,000. Then the first big jump in numbers came with a first run of more than 60,000 for *"F" Is for Fugitive*, followed by *"G" Is for Gumshoe* with more than 100,000; *"H" Is for Homicide*, more than 150,000; *"I" Is for Innocent*, more than 300,000; *"J" Is for Judgment*, more than 450,000; *"K" Is for Killer*, 600,000; and *"L" Is for Lawless*, 750,000. *"M" Is for Malice* was her first novel to have a first print run of one million copies, as have *"N" Is for Noose* and *"O" Is for Outlaw*. In addition, her novels have been translated into twenty-six languages and are sold in twenty-eight countries.

From *"G" Is for Gumshoe* forward, each novel has hit the best-seller lists during the first week after publication. Part of the explanation for the major spurt in sales beginning with *"F" Is for Fugitive* lies in the aggressive marketing undertaken by Grafton and her publisher, with Grafton doing an unusually large twenty-seven-city book tour for that novel. An equal, or more important, explanation lies in Grafton's continuing development as a writer. This series is one of the few to get stronger as it has unfolded.

In *"B" Is for Burglar* (1985) Kinsey is hired to look for a missing woman who turns out to have been murdered. Grafton maintains the strengths of the first novel and solves the problem of the conclusion in fine style: Kinsey identifies the murderers and confronts them when they catch her trying to collect a piece of incriminating evidence in the basement of their house. The single confrontation scene is suspenseful and scary, and Kinsey is impressive in both her mental and physical prowess as she fights with the killers and sustains a broken arm, a gunshot in the same arm, and a broken nose.

The ending of *"B" Is for Burglar* is the second instance of what proves to be a pattern in the final scenes of Grafton's novels: she deliberately places Kinsey in a physically threatening final situation—traditional hard-boiled fare—but, as is demonstrated in *"G" Is for Grafton,* the nature of the threat is such that the greatest challenge to Kinsey is psychological as much as, or more than, physical. In *"A" Is for Alibi* Kinsey had told another character about her first homicide case—a mother who killed her children by tying them up and stuffing them into garbage cans. Still haunted by the photographs of the children's bodies in the garbage cans, Kinsey is nonetheless forced by her pursuer in the final scene to hide in the only available spot—a garbage bin. Her physical safety is thus bought at a high emotional cost. In *"B" Is for Burglar* the internal challenge may not seem as traumatic, but it is challenging for Kinsey: the confrontation takes place in a dark basement infested with spiders, one of her bêtes noires from the natural world.

By the time of *"C" Is for Corpse* (1986), Kinsey faces a more obvious personal challenge as the killer chases her through a morgue. Part of her effort to play off the image of male hard-boiled detective, Grafton says, was her determination to give Kinsey some real flaws, a whole cadre of human vulnerabilities. One of those frailties is the shared Grafton-Kinsey fear of being given injections, a fear so deep that the detective almost passes out when she even considers the prospect. A deeper fear for independent, autonomous Kinsey is loss of self-control. In *"C" Is for Corpse,* then, the killer chasing her through the morgue carrying a syringe full of a tranquilizer is one of her worst nightmares come to life.

Neither Grafton nor Kinsey says much in an overt way about male hard-boiled predecessors, nor are there any suggestions that the job is harder because

Kinsey is female. On the contrary, Kinsey says in the first novel, "Most of my days are the same: checking and cross-checking, filling in blanks, detail work that was absolutely essential to the job but scarcely dramatic stuff. The basic characteristics of any good investigator are a plodding nature and infinite patience. Society has inadvertently been grooming women to this end for years." In fact, the only time Kinsey expresses regret for being female on the job also occurs in *"A" Is for Alibi,* when she has to do an extended stakeout. She hates such work, and she recalls that a mentor once told her "men are the only suitable candidates for surveillance work because they can sit in a parked car and pee discreetly into a tennis-ball can, thus avoiding unnecessary absences." Once in a rare while Kinsey complains that someone will ask her to do something she suspects a male detective would never be asked to do, as when she is asked to calm down a distraught elderly woman.

Grafton's references in the novels to her male predecessors are infrequent, and the few that exist are comic in tone. In *"A" Is for Alibi* one of the dogs being clipped in a pet grooming parlor is an elegant poodle named "Dashiell," and he steps in a pile of dog excrement. The more violent end of the hard-boiled spectrum is reduced to the status of a joke in *"B" Is for Burglar,* when elderly, feisty Julia Oshner becomes so interested in Kinsey's career that she half-teasingly offers to become Kinsey's partner when this case is over. But she is afraid she does not know enough bad words to do the job right, she says, so to get ready, she has started reading Mickey Spillane. Being diminished to the possessor of bad language and an ability to pee into a tennis-ball can do not exactly make the male detective a heroic figure, so by and large Kinsey remains silent about her male counterparts and simply does her own job.

Kinsey, however, does greatly admire some men. *"C" Is for Corpse* offers another hallmark of Grafton's work in the appealing character of Bobby Callahan, a young man who hires Kinsey to find out the identity of the person who tried to run him off the road. The consequent wreck, which others consider an accident, left Bobby with severe injuries and partial amnesia, but he is convinced that he must have known something dangerous to someone. The characterization of Bobby is a celebration of Grafton's appreciation for personal courage. For Grafton, bravery does not consist exclusively of the surge of adrenaline that comes with standing up to the threat of physical pain. Bravery is evident in any act through which the actor maintains personal autonomy. Bobby survived a terrible car wreck, but to Kinsey the most impressive demonstration of his bravery is his determination to regain his physical strength by working out at the gym, to ignore the pitying stares of others,

Dust jacket for Grafton's 1990 novel, in which Kinsey is stalked by a hit man as she searches for a missing elderly woman

and to find out the truth of what happened to him. His emotional strength is what attracts Kinsey to him.

The series is full of such psychologically strong characters, who refuse to let catastrophes of all kinds, including betrayal by family, friends, or their own bodies (in the form of injuries or disease) stop them from finding a way to live independently and responsibly. They personify Grafton's belief, as she told Rosemary Herbert, that "One always rescues oneself in this world!" For example, Francesca Voigt in *"I" Is for Innocent* tells Kinsey how she started her successful business of making turbans for cancer patients: she was receiving chemotherapy herself, and "One morning in the shower, all my hair fell out in clumps. I had a lunch date in an hour and there I was, bald as an egg. I improvised one of these from a scarf I had on hand. . . . The idea for the business got me through the rest of the chemo and out the other side. Funny how that works. Tragedy can turn your life around if you're open to it." Grafton, though, does not show that such reversals are automatic. Her wounded characters renew their lives only when they are "open" to the possibility and have great determination.

Part of Grafton's strength as a writer is her insistence on trying new things. Kinsey has only a few friends who appear throughout the series: Henry Pitts, Kinsey's octogenarian landlord and closest friend; Rosie, imperious owner of Rosie's Tavern and a kind of Brothers Grimm wicked-stepmother figure; and Jonah Robb, a policeman who is briefly her lover and always a good source of information. Other characters are important for brief periods: for example, Vera Lipton is identified as a close friend in the early novels, but may be disappearing from the series as she has not been mentioned since *"L" Is for Lawless.* In addition, Robert Dietz, fellow private investigator who is a voice on the phone in *"A" Is for Alibi,* becomes her bodyguard and lover in *"G" Is for Gumshoe,* reappears in *"M" Is for Malice,* and is referred to in *"N" Is for Noose* and *"O" Is for Outlaw.* Although these several characters reoccur throughout the series, new characters appear in every novel and, more important, the situations, plotlines, and tone vary greatly from book to book.

The world of each novel is unique. *"D" Is for Deadbeat* (1987) is a dark, troubling world in which the murder victim is an alcoholic whose drunk driving killed five members of a family, leaving the remaining members emotionally destroyed. His killer turns out to be a teenager in the family whose action, Kinsey speculates, may have actually balanced the scales of justice. The moral ambiguities are disturbing to both Kinsey and the reader. In contrast, the moral questions are easy in the next novel, which focuses much more on Kinsey herself. *"E" Is for Evidence* (1988) presents the first time the detective becomes her own client as she is framed for arson; in addition, complicating the case as a personal imbroglio is the brief return of her second husband, Daniel Wade, who turns out to be a spy for the person who framed her.

"F" Is for Fugitive (1989) is the first novel in which Kinsey is away from Santa Teresa for the entire book: while her apartment is being rebuilt after being bombed at the end of *"E" Is for Evidence,* she works in Floral Beach, California (based on Avila Beach), and stays with her clients, the Fowlers, one of the most dysfunctional—and aptly named—families in all of fiction. In *"G" Is for Gumshoe* (1990) Kinsey is on the road again briefly, this time to the Mojave Desert—with lyric descriptions along the way—to look for a missing elderly woman. For the first time she is the target for a contract killer, and she hires a bodyguard, Robert Dietz, with whom she falls in love. *"H" Is for Homicide* (1991) offers the only time Kinsey works undercover; the novel is a kind of "kidnap" novel in which Kinsey is kept a virtual prisoner in a Los Angeles apartment by a crook running an automobile accident scam. None of Kinsey's usual resources in people and setting appear in this gritty novel.

Returning to the Santa Teresa setting in *"I" Is for Innocent* (1992), Grafton uses Kinsey to explore the ugly world of domestic violence as she investigates the bizarre shooting of a woman through the peephole in her front door. The structure of this novel is the closest Grafton comes to courtroom drama as Kinsey must investigate a case that has been tried in criminal court; therefore, the transcripts from the trial are a major source of information for her. Also, because she is working for a lawyer, she constantly thinks about what he needs to make his case in civil court.

"J" Is for Judgment (1993), arguably her best novel and Grafton's own favorite, is a powerful study of the impact of the past on the present. Kinsey is hired to find Wendell Jaffe, who allegedly committed suicide five years earlier but who has recently been spotted in Mexico. During the search, the detective discovers that living in Lompoc she has an entire family—aunts, cousins, and a grandmother—who knew of her existence yet never made any effort to contact her. The interweaving of the case with Kinsey's personal

history results in one of the most complex and compelling novels in the series.

While the ending of *"J" Is for Judgment* is satisfying in terms of the theme of the burden of the past, it is unconventional in terms of the detective genre. At first the conclusion seems conventional as Kinsey confronts the murderer, who confesses and gives her reasons for killing Jaffe. She then jumps off the marina breakwater and swims out into the ocean in an apparent suicide attempt. Kinsey swims after her, but becomes too exhausted to save her. Only months later, when no body turns up, does Kinsey begin to question the reality of the suicide. She wonders whether the confession was too easily given and considers a string of suspicious facts: the missing millions have never turned up; all the killer's bank accounts had been stripped and her house mortgaged to the hilt; the woman was an excellent swimmer; and she owned a boat that was never found. The formula of detective fiction leads readers to expect some sense of restored order, even if limited in scope or duration, and throughout the series Kinsey calls for a settling of accounts for wrongdoers. Neither Kinsey nor the reader can be certain whether any degree of order has been restored this time. In the epilogue Kinsey says, "I've never believed the perfect crime was possible. Now I'm not so sure."

Widely considered to be the other contender for the title of "best novel in the series." *"K" Is for Killer* (1994) is Kinsey's brooding descent into an underworld of darkness and ambiguity. The case forces Kinsey, a morning person, to do most of her investigating during the night as she questions nurses on the night shift at a hospital, prostitutes, and all-night disc jockeys. Kinsey enters more personally into a figurative underworld when, frustrated by the refusal of the police to arrest the person she knows is the murderer, she calls the Mafia and tips them off, knowing they will kill the murderer. Kinsey thus becomes the killer in the title of this book, a radical departure from anything Grafton had previously done. Reviewers quickly embraced this novel. Tom Nolan in *The Wall Street Journal* of 2 May 1994 praised *"K" Is for Killer* for taking a "fine series to a new level of seriousness and accomplishment." Typical is Joann Gutin's description of the novel as "darkly brilliant" in the 17 September 1995 *San Jose Mercury News.*

A real change of pace, *"L" Is for Lawless* (1995) is almost lighthearted, involving a cross-country chase for stolen money that does not even have a murder until the final confrontation scene in a cemetery in Louisville. The killer gets away, leaving Kinsey with a concussion and a lot of explaining to do. For some readers and reviewers, this novel is not as satisfying as others and interrupted the succession of rich and complex novels that began with *"G" Is for Gumshoe.* Emily

Melton wrote for many in the 19 July 1995 *Booklist:* "This time the plot sounds slightly contrived, the writing is a little tired, and Kinsey's spunky earthiness is sometimes grating." Critics were more positive about *"M" Is for Malice* (1996), which proved to be vintage Grafton again. While the murder does not occur until well into the novel and the final confrontation scene lacks serious physical threat for Kinsey, much of what readers have come to expect from Grafton is here: the depiction of a richly nuanced world of upper-class greed, venomous family relationships, and new insights into Kinsey's psyche.

Kinsey continues to be highly introspective in *"N" Is for Noose* (1998) and *"O" Is for Outlaw"* (1999). In *"N" Is for Noose,* the physical cold she endures as she investigates a case in Nota Lake, a shabby ski area near the Nevada line, is matched by an emotional chill as she erroneously begins to suspect that the police, whom she normally defends, are corrupt. Her suspicions about the police lead her to ponder the complex reasons for some of her own behavior: she realizes that she entered the police academy and joined the Santa Teresa Police Department at twenty-one (for a two-year stint) in part because of the ambivalence she felt about the police who rescued her from the wrecked car in which her parents died when she was five years old. She had been both relieved and terrified by the sight of the big, armed, serious men in uniform, and she always associated their image with the "jeopardy and pain" of the experience. In high school she became rather wild and knew the police had the power to jail her, for example, for using marijuana. "In retrospect," Kinsey says, "I can see that I'd applied to the police academy, in part, to ally myself with the very folks I feared. Being on the side of the law was, no doubt, my attempt to cope with that old anxiety."

Even more self-analysis is required from Kinsey in *"O" Is for Outlaw* as she confronts her relationship with her first husband, Mickey Magruder, a fellow police officer, about whom nothing has been revealed prior to this novel, except that Kinsey left him and considers him a "bum." Not even his name has been given. In one of the biggest surprises in the series, Grafton forces Kinsey to reevaluate leaving Mickey: she had walked out in 1972 when he asked her to give him an alibi for a night when he was accused of beating a suspect to death. In the opening of this novel, she discovers a letter written to her from a woman who claimed to be with Mickey that night, thus triggering Kinsey's need to learn the truth. If Mickey was an adulterer but not a murderer, Kinsey may have contributed to his spiral downward as he quit the police, drank too much, and lived and worked in ever shabbier circumstances. She who fears abandonment above everything else may

have abandoned someone else. Admirably, her persistent drive to balance the scales includes herself; if she was wrong about Mickey, she must seek his forgiveness and try to make it right.

Grafton says each book is the most difficult she has ever written. The cruel fact is that critics and readers alike wonder how long any writer can sustain a series of novels featuring the same central figure at a high level of excellence. When someone is routinely called one of the best writers of detective-fiction writing, reviewers start circling for signs of decay. If the author changes the central character who attracted the readers in the first place, some readers will cry "Foul," but if the author does not change the character, both the author and readers are likely to become bored with the predictability of it all.

Grafton has been able to sustain her series by continuing to find new situations to put Kinsey into and new questions about human behavior for her to explore and by letting her evolve as a character. The praise Grafton received for *"O" Is for Outlaw,* the fifteenth in the series, attests to her impressive achievement. The reviewer in *Kirkus Reviews* (1 July 1999) calls *"O" Is for Outlaw* one of the best novels from a literary "magician." Melton in her review in *Booklist* (1 June 1999) welcomes it as a reversal of the leveling off she saw beginning with *"L" Is for Lawless;* she calls *"O" Is for Outlaw* "a novel of depth and substance that is, in every way," the best of the series. The 30 August 1999 review in *Publishers Weekly* concludes: "Kinsey's examination of her youthful self-righteousness and naivete initiates a provocative contemplation of guilt, morals and loyalty that graces one of the very best entries in a long-lived and much-loved series."

Kinsey began as Grafton's variation on the male hard-boiled detective: she drank only jug wine and was a tough, hard-punching, smart-mouthed private investigator who wore no makeup and dressed almost exclusively in jeans and turtlenecks. In the three most recent novels, however, Kinsey no longer carries a gun with her on a daily basis; she talks about "the vanilla finish" to a sip of wine; she wears an occasional skirt; and she even indulges in eyeliner. More significant, she is increasingly reflective rather than reactive. She focuses more and more of her attention on understanding herself and her place in the world around her. Several reviewers have observed that Grafton's original jaded eye is clearly mellowing. In an 8 May 1994 review in the *Los Angeles Times* Charles Champlin noted that "Millhone doesn't age much but she grows wiser, quieter, more feeling." Kinsey is still in her thirties in *"O" Is for Outlaw,* since each novel follows the previous one by only a few weeks or months in fictional time, but Kinsey is beginning to sound like a person of maturity evaluating her life. Robert Moyer puts it more succinctly in the

Hmmm. Debating about the nature of this book. My concern is
that it isn't set in Santa Teresa. I went 'out of town' for 'N'
and I'm wondering if I should come back for 'O.'
I love the title 'Outlaw' and I can't think how to make that work
if we're talking old fashioned murder mystery.
On one hand I know readers will protest.
On the other hand, I'm the boss and I get to do what I want.
Maybe Henry gets snatched & the two of them end up having an ad-
venture together somewhere.
Seems a bit gimmicky, but maybe there's a way to make that work.
I kind of like the idea of Henry being threatened.
Kinsey would certainly be vulnerable if his life were at stake.
That would explain why she doesn't go to the cops.

Another misgiving that surfaces is that I don't want to stray too
far into Superwoman territory. Kinsey as avenger. Kinsey as
rescuer. Kinsey vs the Mob.
I don't want the Fate of the Free World to hang in the balance.
On the other hand, she's allowed to be heroic, slightly larger
than life as long as she doesn't take herself too seriously.
She's allowed to go up against the bad guys in a high stakes con-
test.
What happens to the outlaw of Outlaw.
Is that Kinsey or some guy?

Are there any other 'O' words of interest?
Let me check my Websters for candidates.
Oath
Obit
Outcast
Outlaw...

Outcast isn't a crime. Obit is not easily translated to other
languages. Oath isn't very interesting.
So Outlaw it is.

What if there's a clock ticking.
This is about a crime in progress.
Somebody wants out and the criminals have to find him because
they're worried about betrayal.
A heist.
What would these people want to steal?
A Brink's truck...
A payroll...
A victim...
It would have to be something big enough to justify all the
trouble they're going to go to in the end.

Page from Grafton's notes for her 1999 novel (Collection of Sue Grafton)

Winston-Salem Journal of 15 December 1996: "Kinsey is growing up."

Grafton's skills as a creator of appealing, introspective characters and fast-paced, quip-filled explorations of the dark side of human behavior have garnered an increasing number of awards for the novels. *"B" Is for Burglar* won the Shamus Award from the Private Eye Writers of America and an Anthony Award from Bouchercon; *"C" Is for Corpse* won an Anthony; *"E" Is for Evidence* won the Doubleday Mystery Guild Award, as did *"F" Is for Fugitive,* which also won The Falcon Award from the Maltese Falcon Society of Japan. *"G" Is for Gumshoe* received three awards: Doubleday Mystery Guild, an Anthony, and the Shamus. Doubleday Mystery Guild awards went to *"H" Is for Homicide, "I" Is for Innocent, "J" Is for Judgment, "K" Is for Killer,* and *"M" Is for Malice. "H" Is for Homicide* also won an American Mystery Award. *"O" Is for Outlaw* has received the 2000 Ridley Award from the Partners in Crime and Boise Chapter of Sisters in Crime and the Readers' Choice Award from the Friends of Libraries and Ameritech.

Grafton's next novel, *"P" Is for . . . ,* is scheduled for publication in 2001, and Grafton has said she will finish the alphabet with *"Z" Is for Zero* if she thinks she can continue to generate new ideas and sustain quality. The risk for her, like every other writer of a successful series, is that the novels can sink under the weight of their own strengths—the character of Kinsey is what many readers and reviewers have found so appealing about the novels, but some worry that the mellowing process may cause the series to lose its sharp edge, biting humor, and occasional violence. For scores of other readers and critics, though, Grafton's deft hand with setting a scene and exploring her characters' psyches is such that they will follow Kinsey wherever she takes them, even into new, perhaps softer, certainly more mature, incarnations of the hard-boiled genre.

Interviews:

Bruce Taylor, "G is for (Sue) Grafton: An Interview with the Creator of the Kinsey Millhone Private Eye Series Who Delights Mystery Fans as She Writes Her Way Through the Alphabet," *Armchair Detective,* 22, no. 1 (1989): 4–13;

Kevin Nance, "Fear Drives Author," *Columbia* (S.C.) *State,* 12 June 1994, pp. F1–F2;

Rosemary Herbert, "Sue Grafton," in her *The Fatal Art of Entertainment: Interviews with Mystery Writers* (New York: G. K. Hall, 1994), pp. 29–53;

Susan Goodman, "Sue Grafton and Tony Hillerman," *Modern Maturity* (July–August 1995): 74–82.

References:

Robert A. Baker and Michael T. Nietzel, "Kinsey Millhone–Sue Grafton," in their *Private Eyes: 101 Knights: A Survey of American Detective Fiction 1922–1984* (Bowling Green, Ohio: Bowling Green State University Popular Press, 1985), pp. 309–310;

Scott Christianson, "Talkin' Trash and Kickin' Butt: Sue Grafton's Hard-Boiled Feminism," in *Feminism in Women's Detective Fiction,* edited by Glenwood Irons (Toronto: University of Toronto Press, 1995), pp. 127–148;

Barbara H. Franklin, "'W' Is for Writer," *University of Louisville Alumni Magazine* (Fall 1995): 11–12;

Catherine Elizabeth Hoyser, "Sue Grafton," in *Great Women Mystery Writers: Classic to Contemporary,* edited by Kathleen Gregory Klein (Westport, Conn.: Greenwood Press, 1994), pp. 134–137;

Glenwood Irons, "New Women Detectives: 'G' is for Gender-Bending," in his *Gender, Language, and Myth: Essays on Popular Narrative* (Toronto: University of Toronto Press, 1992), pp. 127–141;

Natalie Hevener Kaufman and Carol McGinnis Kay, *"G" Is for Grafton: The World of Kinsey Millhone* (New York: Holt, 1997; revised and enlarged, 2000);

Kathleen Gregory Klein, *The Woman Detective: Gender and Genre* (Urbana: University of Illinois Press, 1988);

Peter J. Rabinowitz, "'Reader, I Blew Him Away': Convention and Transgression in Sue Grafton," in *Famous Last Words: Changes in Gender and Narrative Closure,* edited by Alison Booth (Charlottesville: University of Virginia Press, 1993), pp. 326–346;

Maureen T. Reddy, "The Feminist Counter Tradition in Crime: Cross, Grafton, Paretsky, and Wilson," in *The Cunning Craft: Original Essays on Detective Fiction and Contemporary Literary Theory,* edited by Ronald G. Walker and June M. Frazer (Macomb: Western Illinois University Press, 1990), pp. 174–187;

Reddy, *Sisters in Crime: Feminism and the Crime Novel* (New York: Continuum, 1988);

B. Ruby Rich, "The Lady Dicks: Gender Benders Take the Case," *Village Voice Literary Supplement,* June 1989, pp. 24–26;

Rachel Schaffer, "Grafton's Black Humor," *Armchair Detective,* 30 (Summer 1997): 316–322;

Priscilla L. Walton, "'E' Is for En/Gendering Readings: Sue Grafton's Kinsey Millhone," in *Women Times Three: Writers, Detectives, Readers,* edited by Kathleen Gregory Klein (Bowling Green, Ohio: Bowling Green State University Popular Press, 1995), pp. 101–115;

Ann Wilson, "The Female Dick and The Crisis of Heterosexuality," in *Feminism in Women's Detective Fiction,* edited by Irons (Toronto: University of Toronto Press, 1995), pp. 148–156.

Dashiell Hammett

(27 May 1894 – 10 January 1961)

Charles Brower

See also the Hammett entries in *DS 6: Hardboiled Mystery Writers: Raymond Chandler, Dashiell Hammett, Ross Macdonald* and *DLB Yearbook: 1991.*

BOOKS: *Red Harvest* (New York & London: Knopf, 1929);

The Dain Curse (New York: Knopf, 1929; New York & London: Knopf, 1930);

The Maltese Falcon (New York & London: Knopf, 1930; London & New York: Knopf, 1930);

The Glass Key (London: Knopf, 1931; New York: Knopf, 1931);

The Thin Man (New York: Knopf, 1934; London: Barker, 1934);

Secret Agent X-9, books 1 and 2 (Philadelphia: McKay, 1934);

$106,000 Blood Money (New York: Spivak, 1943);

The Battle of the Aleutians, by Hammett and Robert Colodny (Adak, Alaska: U.S. Army Intelligence Section, Field Force Headquarters, Adak, 1944);

The Adventures of Sam Spade (New York: Spivak, 1944); republished as *They Can Only Hang You Once* (New York: The American Mercury/Spivak, 1949);

The Continental Op (New York: Spivak, 1945);

The Return of the Continental Op (New York: Spivak, 1945);

Hammett Homicides, edited by Ellery Queen (New York: Spivak, 1946);

Dead Yellow Women, edited by Queen (New York: Spivak, 1947);

Nightmare Town, edited by Queen (New York: Spivak, 1948);

The Creeping Siamese, edited by Queen (New York: Spivak, 1950);

Woman in the Dark, edited by Queen (New York: Spivak, 1951);

A Man Named Thin, edited by Queen (New York: Ferman, 1962);

The Big Knockover, edited by Lillian Hellman (New York: Random House, 1966); republished as *The*

Dashiell Hammett

Dashiell Hammett Story Omnibus (London: Cassell, 1966);

The Continental Op, edited by Steven Marcus (New York: Random House, 1974);

Woman in the Dark (New York: Knopf, 1988);

Nightmare Town, edited by Kirby McCauley, Martin H. Greenberg, and Ed Gorman (New York: Knopf, 1999).

Collection: *Complete Novels* (New York: Library of America, 1999).

PRODUCED SCRIPTS:

City Streets, motion picture, original screen story, Paramount, 1931;

Mister Dynamite, motion picture, original screen story, Universal, 1935;

After the Thin Man, motion picture, original screen story, M-G-M, 1936;

Another Thin Man, motion picture, original screen story, M-G-M, 1939;

Watch on the Rhine, motion picture, screenplay, Warner Bros., 1943.

OTHER: *Creeps by Night,* edited by Hammett (New York: Day, 1931; London: Gollancz, 1932);

After the Thin Man, in *Black Mask 5* and Black Mask *6,* edited by Matthew J. Bruccoli and Richard Layman (San Diego, New York & London: Harvest, 1986).

Dashiell Hammett is generally credited with bringing a new degree of authenticity as well as artistry to the crime fiction that flourished in the pulp magazines of the first decades of the twentieth century. Hammett created several of the most famous American detectives: the anonymous, world-weary Continental Op; Sam Spade, the cynical protagonist of *The Maltese Falcon* (1930); and Nick and Nora Charles, the husband-and-wife detectives introduced in *The Thin Man* (1934). He based the characters of Nick and Nora on his own relationship with playwright Lillian Hellman. At the time of the publication of *The Thin Man* Hammett was at the height of his fame; however, his literary output ended with that novel because of a variety of factors, including his alcoholism and ill health and to some extent his stormy relationship with Hellman.

At the time of his death in 1961, Hammett's literary achievement had been overshadowed by his unpopular political affiliations. Hellman strove to rectify the situation, in part by idealizing Hammett and their relationship, and the author's continued fame has relied almost as much on a romanticized persona as on his fictional works. Hammett's artistic legacy is a vision of a violent, morally rudderless society in which his characters try to navigate with only their own ethical codes to guide them. His prose—brutal, ironic, and slangy—quickly and permanently came to be considered the epitome of the hard-boiled style.

Samuel Dashiell Hammett was born on 27 May 1894 on his grandfather's farm, Hopewell and Aim, near Baltimore, Maryland, to Richard and Annie Bond Hammett. His education was limited: in 1908 he left the Baltimore Polytechnic Institute after being enrolled in the high school for less than a semester. Hammett contributed to the family's failing finances with a series of office jobs. In 1915 he began working for the Baltimore office of the Pinkerton's National Detective Agency, an organization that provided a variety of services from insurance investigations to strikebreaking. He traveled throughout the western United States on assignment for the agency for two years, and his experiences as a Pinkerton operative provided much of the material for his subsequent career as a writer. Hammett found that the life of a detective satisfied his desire for travel and adventure, although some of the activities of Pinkerton agents troubled him: during the sometimes violent labor disputes of the time, operatives were often hired to disrupt protests, with force if necessary. The brutality of his fellow agents helped to crystallize Hammett's leftist sympathies.

Beginning with his induction in June 1918, Hammett served during World War I with the U.S. Army Motor Ambulance Corps at Camp Mead, Maryland. He contracted Spanish influenza, which later progressed to tuberculosis, and received a medical discharge from the army in May 1919. The next year, having relocated to the West Coast and briefly returned to work for Pinkerton, he was admitted to Cushman Hospital in Tacoma, Washington. Hammett was hospitalized at Cushman and another Public Health Service hospital in San Diego from November 1920 until May 1921. During that time he commenced a relationship with one of his nurses at Cushman, Josephine Dolan, whom he married in July 1921 when she was six months pregnant with their first child. The Hammetts eventually had two daughters, Mary, born in 1921, and Josephine, born in 1926.

Hammett continued to work as a Pinkerton operative for as long as his health permitted. In 1921 he participated in two of the most famous criminal investigations of the day, involving the murder charge against movie comedian Fatty Arbuckle and the theft of $125,000 in gold specie from the ocean freighter *Sonoma*. In 1922 he entered Munson's Business College with the intention of training to be a journalist. Hammett supported his family primarily with a disability stipend from the military, over which he was constantly having to wrangle with the U.S. Veterans Bureau.

Hammett turned his serious attention to writing and published his first story, "The Parthian Shot," in H. L. Mencken and George Jean Nathan's magazine *The Smart Set* in October 1922. Over the next several years

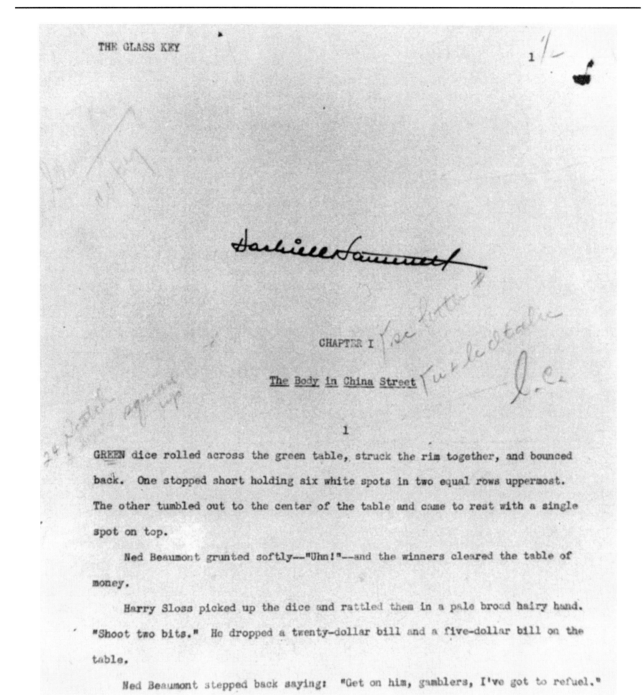

THE GLASS KEY

CHAPTER I

The Body in China Street

1

GREEN dice rolled across the green table, struck the rim together, and bounced back. One stopped short holding six white spots in two equal rows uppermost. The other tumbled out to the center of the table and came to rest with a single spot on top.

Ned Beaumont grunted softly—"Uhn!"—and the winners cleared the table of money.

Harry Sloss picked up the dice and rattled them in a pale broad hairy hand. "Shoot two bits." He dropped a twenty-dollar bill and a five-dollar bill on the table.

Ned Beaumont stepped back saying: "Get on him, gamblers, I've got to refuel." He crossed the billiard-room to the door. There he met Walter Ivans coming in. He said: "'Lo, Walt," and would have gone on, but Ivans caught his elbow as he passed, and turned to face him.

First page from the typescript for Hammett's fourth novel (Christie's London auction catalogue, 27 March 1985) he wrote prodigiously, publishing in a variety of genres from light verse and comic sketches to articles for professional journals, but he had his most promising success when he utilized his experience as a detective. In one of his earliest published works, "From the Memoirs of a Private Detective," which appeared in *The Smart Set* in March 1923, Hammett offers twenty-nine brief—some only a sentence long—anecdotes and insights from his Pinkerton years. This article already demonstrates two of the most notable characteristics of Hammett's writing: a dry sense of humor and a cynical view that criminality is a basic human quality. The final entry, in fact, comments on the commonness of lawbreaking and the relative ineffectiveness of investigators: "29. That the lawbreaker is invariably sooner or later apprehended is probably the least challenged of extant myths. And yet the files of every detective bureau bulge with the records of unsolved mysteries and uncaught criminals."

Hammett found his greatest success in another magazine founded by Mencken and Nathan, *Black Mask,* a pulp devoted to stories of crime and adventure. In October 1923 he published "Arson Plus," his first *Black Mask* story featuring a nameless operative for the Continental Detective Agency. *Black Mask* readers took to the character immediately, and Hammett published almost exclusively in the pulp for the next three years, featuring the Continental Op, as he is conventionally known, in twenty-six stories.

The Op has few of the exaggerated qualities possessed by the heroes usually featured in pulp fiction. He is short and thick with middle age. He has years of experience and a native toughness and resourcefulness: as he puts it in "The Whosis Kid" (March 1925), "Most of those who meet sudden ends *get themselves* killed. I've had twenty years of experience at dodging that. I can count on being one of the survivors of whatever blow-up there is." He is more tenacious than cerebral, although he demonstrates formidable deductive skills as well. He is not above ruthlessness if a situation warrants. In "The Gutting of Couffignal" (December 1925), for example, the Op, assigned to guard the presents at a lavish wedding, rallies an island community against a criminal gang of Russian expatriates. At the end of the story, hobbled by a twisted ankle, he shoots the beautiful Princess Zhukovski in the leg as she tries to flee, despite her confidence that he will not:

> I had never shot a woman before. I felt queer about it.
>
> "You ought to have known I'd do it!" My voice sounded harsh and savage and like a stranger's in my ears. "Didn't I steal a crutch from a cripple?"

The Op is above all a professional. Hammett does not give him much of a past or any significant relationships outside of his job. Each Op story begins with his investigation of a case and ends when that investigation is resolved. In most stories he offers insights into the profession gained from his twenty-odd years of experience. In "Zigzags of Treachery" (1 March 1924) he gives the four rules for following a subject: "Keep behind your subject as much as possible; never try to hide from him; act in a natural manner no matter what happens; and never meet his eye. Obey them, and, except in unusual circumstances, shadowing is the easiest thing a sleuth has to do." In the story he also gives advice on interrogating a suspect and the most effective way to shoot a man. In "The Girl with the Silver Eyes" (June 1924) the Op ruminates on the unsavory professional necessity of dealing with informants: "But detecting is a hard business, and you use whatever tools come to hand. This Porky was an effective tool if handled right, which meant keeping your hand on his throat all the time and checking up every piece of information brought in."

Beginning in 1924 Hammett used some of his stories to rehearse the themes, situations, and characterizations that he later used in his novels. In "The House in Turk Street" (15 April 1924), for example, Hammett places the Op among an exotic assortment of criminals similar to Caspar Gutman and his associates in *The Maltese Falcon.* He soon began to tire of the character, however, and the worst Op stories show that Hammett was not immune to lazy, indifferent writing. After *Black Mask* editor Phil Cody rejected two of his stories, he perhaps disingenuously admitted in a letter—which Cody published in the magazine in August 1924—that "the trouble is that this sleuth of mine has degenerated into a meal-ticket."

Nevertheless, Hammett continued to publish new Op adventures nearly every month. The Op stories of 1925, such as "The Gutting of Couffignal," escalate the level of violence in accordance with *Black Mask* readers' bloodthirsty tastes. "The Scorched Face" (May 1925) has similarities to *The Dain Curse* (1929) in its depiction of a religious cult that fronts for a blackmail ring. "Corkscrew" (September 1925), in which the Op travels to an Arizona border town and pits crooks against each other to stop the smuggling of illegal aliens, clearly anticipates *Red Harvest* (1929). In "Dead Yellow Women" (November 1925), a sordid tale of tong wars and smugglers, the Op matches wits with an Oriental villain, Chang li Cheng; the story expresses Hammett's penchant for exoticism, which also informs *The Dain Curse* and *The Maltese Falcon.*

Most important to these early stories is Hammett's developing literary voice. An essential element of

Hammett's style is his knack for concise, evocative detail. The Op's eye for detail is one marker of his professional competence: his success at his job—and possibly his life—depends on his ability to discern telling characteristics.

Hammett became adept at using flat understatement, which he put to a variety of purposes. In "The Scorched Face" he uses it to convey effectively the horror of discovering a body in the woods: "At the base of the tree, on her side, her knees drawn up close to her body, a girl was dead. She wasn't nice to see. Birds had been at her." The Op understates for comic effect as well, as in his description from the same story of an interview subject: "a sleek-haired young man whose very nice manners and clothes completely hid anything else—brains for instance—he might have had. He was very willing to help me, and he knew nothing. It took him a long time to tell me so. A nice boy." Mostly, though, the Op's penchant for understatement tends to emphasize how tough he is, despite his frequent protests to the contrary. In "The Whosis Kid," for example, he coolly considers strategy in a fight with a larger opponent: "I've always had a reasonable amount of pride in my ability to sock. It was disappointing to have this big heaver take the best I could give him without a grunt. But I wasn't discouraged. He couldn't stand it forever. I settled down to make a steady job of it."

In one of his more impressive early efforts, "The Tenth Clew" (January 1924), Hammett uses a subdued irony reminiscent of Stephen Crane's "The Open Boat" (1898). The Op is knocked off a ferry into the fogbound San Francisco Bay; although he initially keeps his cool in this desperate situation, exhaustion begins to set in: "But for the moaning horns I would have ceased all effort. They had become the only disagreeable part of my situation—the water was pleasant, fatigue was pleasant. But the horns tormented me. I cursed them petulantly and decided to swim until I could no longer hear them, and then, in the quiet of the friendly fog, go to sleep. . . ." Finally, a passing boat rouses his failing will: "Life—the hunger of life—all at once surged into my being."

At other times Hammett employs an impressionistic style, relying on little more than a series of disjointed sensory details to suggest chaotic action. In "The Scorched Face" a deadly fight is conveyed through staccato images:

> A body came out of nowhere, hit my back, flattened me to the landing.
> The feel of silk was on my cheek. A brawny hand was fumbling at my throat.
> I bent my wrist until my gun, upside down, lay against my cheek. Praying for my ear, I squeezed.
> My cheek took fire. My head was a roaring thing, about to burst.

> The silk slid away.
> Pat hauled me upright.
> We started down the stairs.
> Swish!
> A thing came past my face, stirring my bared hair.
> A thousand pieces of glass, china, plaster, exploded upward at my left.

Hammett took a hiatus of nearly a year from writing fiction beginning in 1926, spurred by a conflict with the *Black Mask* management over payment as well as by the necessity to find more secure employment after the birth of his second daughter. In March 1926 he began writing advertising copy for the Albert S. Samuels Jewelry Company. He developed a close personal bond with the owner of the company, Albert Samuels, who served as something of a patron to the aspiring writer, encouraging his ambitions and accommodating his frequent infirmity. Hammett dedicated *The Dain Curse* to Samuels and named several of its characters after his Samuels Jewelry coworkers.

Hammett's chronic health problems worsened, however, necessitating that he give up working full time for Samuels and live essentially separately from his family after July 1926. Despite his condition, he drank heavily and pursued a series of sexual affairs. Hammett's *The Glass Key* (1931) is dedicated to one of his lovers, Nell Martin, who dedicated her novel *Lovers Should Marry* (1933) to him. He also returned to writing fiction, at the invitation of former infantry captain Joseph T. Shaw, the new editor of *Black Mask,* who considered Hammett the exemplar of the direction in which he intended to take the pulp. In January 1927, the same month that *Black Mask* announced his return, Hammett began a stint of nearly three years reviewing mystery novels for *The Saturday Review of Literature,* a position he probably gained with Shaw's help.

Hammett revived the Op with his longest works to that point, a pair of connected stories that together came to about thirty-five thousand words. In "The Big Knockover," which appeared in February 1927, the Op gets a tip that an army of criminals are in San Francisco to pull a big bank heist. The heist, which involves robbing two banks simultaneously in broad daylight, is carried off with the efficiency of a military campaign. Afterward the mastermind begins to kill off his cohorts for their share of the take. The Op follows the grisly trail, finding a series of corpses that, as he observes, comprises a "*Who's Who in Crookdom*." Only at the end of the story does he learn that the mastermind is a little old Greek man he had unwittingly allowed to get away. In the sequel, "$106,000 Blood Money," published in the May 1927 issue of *Black Mask,* the Op is still on the trail of Papadopoulos, whom he eventually locates with the help of the brother of one of the crooks the old man double-crossed. Hammett also provides a foil character for the dogged Op in Jack Counihan, a feckless rookie Continental operative who sells his loyalties to Papadopoulos.

"The Big Knockover" and "$106,000 Blood Money" demonstrate Hammett's growing command of his craft. In keeping with the *Black Mask* template, both stories feature terrific levels of violence: "The Big Knockover" includes more than a score of dead bodies, and both end with shootouts inside the villains' lair. They also showcase Hammett's encyclopedic command of underworld lore, as exemplified by his précis of the heist conspirators:

> There was Dis-and-Dat Kid, who had crushed out of Leavenworth only two months before; Sheeny Holmes Snobomish Shitey, supposed to have died a hero in France in 1919; L. A. Slim, from Denver, sockless and underwearless as usual, with a thousand-dollar bill sewed in each shoulder of his coat; Spider Girrucci wearing a steel-mesh vest under his shirt and a scar from crown to chin where his brother had carved him years ago; Old Pete Best, once a congressman; Nigger Vojan, who once won $175,000 in a Chicago crap-game–*Abracadabra* tattooed on him in three places; Alphabet Shorty McCoy; Tom Brooks, Alphabet Shorty's brother-in-law, who invented the Richmond razzle-dazzle and bought three hotels with the profits; Red Cudahy, who stuck up a Union Pacific train in 1924; Denny Burke; Bull McGonickle, still pale from fifteen years in Joliet; Toby the Lugs, Bull's running-mate, who used to brag about picking President Wilson's pocket in a Washington vaudeville theatre; and Paddy the Mex.

The main female characters in the stories, Big Flora and Nancy Regan, anticipate women that appear in the novels. Big Flora, one of the heist ringleaders, whom the Op assists in removing a bullet from a fellow crook, is as formidable as Dinah Brand of *Red Harvest* and Hammett's other amoral gang molls. At one point the Op remarks about Big Flora: "If I live to be a million I'll never forget the picture this handsome brutal woman made coming down those unplaned cellar stairs. She was a beautiful fight-bred animal going to a fight." Nancy, a socialite with an attraction for the underworld, represents a type that also includes Opal Madvig in *The Glass Key* and Dorothy Wynant in *The Thin Man*.

The stories also show that Hammett was thinking more seriously about the implications of the hard-boiled code embodied by the Op. Several times in the stories the Op voices the weary cynicism that finds its fullest expression in *Red Harvest*. Young Counihan, portrayed initially as a well-intentioned idiot, betrays not only the Op's growing affection for

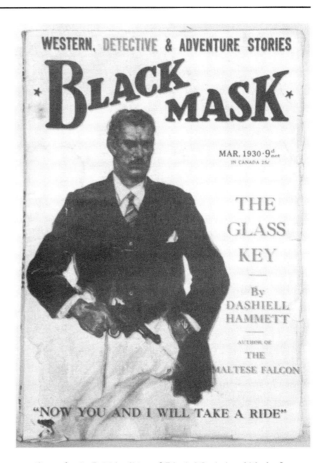

Cover for the British edition of Black Mask *in which the first installment of Hammett's novel appeared*

him but also his professional ethic and, ultimately, himself, as the Op tells him:

> The money Papadopoulos showed you didn't buy you. You met the girl and were too soft to turn her in. But your vanity–your pride in looking at yourself as a cold proposition–wouldn't let you admit it even to yourself. You had to have a hard-boiled front. So you were meat to Papadopoulos' grinder. He gave you a part you could play to yourself–a super-gentleman-crook, a mastermind, a desperate suave villain, and all that kind of romantic garbage. That's the way you went, my son. You went as far as possible beyond what was needed to save the girl from the hoosegow–just to show the world, but chiefly yourself, that you were not acting through sentimentality, but according to your own reckless desires. There you are. Look at yourself.

The Op's speech shows that Hammett was already considering the issues of loyalty and betrayal that dominate his best novels. Most famously, the climax of *The Maltese Falcon* turns on Spade's wrestling with the same issues that Counihan faces, although with much more compelling complexity.

Hammett explores further the implications of the Op's professional code in "The Main Death" (June 1927), one of the last stories he published before concentrating on novel writing. The Op's client is an unsavory old man, Bruno Gungen, whose assistant, Main, has been murdered and robbed of $20,000 of Gungen's money; Gungen is more concerned, however, with evidence that seems to point to adultery between his young wife and Main. The Op plays loose with the law and his professional obligations: he establishes that the Main death was a suicide, which his wife tried to cover up for the sake of the life insurance; he steals back the stolen money from the thieves and lies about evidence in order to protect Mrs. Gungen's privacy from her repulsive husband. "The Main Death" is a good illustration of Hammett's ethical vision as described by Donald T. Bazelon in "Dashiell Hammett's Private Eye: No Loyalty Beyond the Job": "The question of doing or not doing a job competently seems to have replaced the whole larger question of good and evil."

Hammett's first novel, *Red Harvest,* was published by Knopf in February 1929. It originally appeared in *Black Mask* from November 1927 to February 1928 as four interrelated stories: "The Cleansing of Poisonville," "Crime Wanted–Male or Female," "Dynamite," and "19th Murder." Hammett reworked the four parts into a cohesive narrative and submitted the whole to Knopf, who recommended further, more substantial revisions. Despite the revisions, *Red Harvest* is still the most episodic of his novels. The Continental Op comes to the mining town of Personville at the behest of the town's crusading newspaper editor, who is murdered the night the Op arrives. He finds a town that its inhabitants call "Poisonville," run completely by bootleggers, racketeers, and corrupt policemen. Although *Red Harvest* is not explicitly a political novel, it is informed by the labor unrest Hammett had witnessed during his years as a Pinkerton op. Responsibility for the corrupt state of Personville is laid squarely at the feet of its leading capitalist, Elihu Willsson, who brought the gangsters to town to break a mining strike ten years earlier. Willsson, father of the murdered newspaper editor, grudgingly hires the Continental Agency to clean up Personville in any manner the Op sees fit.

The Op proceeds to pit the leading crooks of Personville–Whisper Thaler, Pete the Finn, Lew Yard, and the crooked police chief, Noonan–against each other. After he establishes that Don Willsson was murdered by a romantic rival, the elder Willsson wants to call off their arrangement and let Personville's criminals return to business as usual. The Op takes malicious pleasure in telling him that he intends to honor their contract: "I've got ten thousand dollars of your money to play with. I'm going to use it opening up Personville from

Adam's apple to ankles. I'll see you get my reports regularly as possible. I hope you enjoy them."

Red Harvest is the most elaborately plotted of Hammett's novels. Almost everyone in the large cast of characters practices some manner of subterfuge, usually either to protect himself or implicate someone else. The French novelist André Gide, in the 7 February 1944 *New Republic,* praised Hammett's dialogue, "in which every character is trying to deceive all the others and in which the truth slowly becomes visible through a fog of deception." There are several possible suspects in each of the key murders in the novel. Complicating matters further is the Op's self-confessed "very un-nice part," as he purposefully withholds information at times in order to stoke the animosity among the criminal factions. He allows Noonan to think that Thaler killed Noonan's brother, for example, even though the Op knows that the real killer is one of the chief's former deputies.

The Op forms a partnership of sorts with Dinah Brand, a carelessly alluring seductress who is intimate with Personville's underworld. He describes her with characteristic irony:

> She was an inch or two taller than I, which made her about five feet eight. She had a broad-shouldered, full-breasted, round-hipped body and big muscular legs. The hand she gave me was soft, warm, strong. Her face was the face of a girl of twenty-five already showing signs of wear. Little lines crossed the corners of her big ripe mouth. Fainter lines were beginning to make nets around her thick-lashed eyes. They were large eyes, blue and a bit blood-shot.
> Her coarse hair–brown–needed trimming and was parted crookedly. One side of her upper lip had been rouged higher than the other. Her dress was of a particularly unbecoming wine color, and it gaped here and there around one side, where she had neglected to snap the fasteners or they had popped open. There was a run down the front of her left stocking.
> This was the Dinah Brand who took her pick of Poisonville's men, according to what I had been told.

The Op seems to admire most Dinah's mannish qualities: her physical strength and proficiency with a gun, her tough talk, and her ability to hold her liquor. She readily cooperates with him, giving him the information–not necessarily reliable–that he uses to pit the rival gangsters of Personville against each other.

The Op's machinations culminate in a peace conference at the home of Elihu Willsson, ostensibly to resolve the simmering conflicts "without turning Personville into a slaughterhouse." Actually, the Op intends for the conference to have precisely that effect. He lies to the assembled group, telling them that Noonan knew all along that Thaler was not his brother's killer, thus assuring the corrupt chief's doom at the hands of the vengeful Whisper. After the meeting he confesses to Dinah that he's afraid he's gone "blood-simple," arranging murders out of sheer sadistic pleasure: "I looked at Noonan and knew he hadn't a chance in a thousand of living another day because of what I'd done to him, and I laughed, and felt warm and happy inside." To calm him Dinah gives him laudanum, a liquid form of opium; when he wakes up after a night of hallucinatory dreams, he finds himself holding Dinah's icepick, with its point plunged into her breast.

The Op relies on Reno Starkey, one of Personville's gangsters, to provide him an alibi but nonetheless soon finds himself under suspicion of murdering not only Dinah but also a lawyer who was intending to extort him. Meanwhile, the "red harvest" continues, leaving all of Poisonville's original gangleaders dead or dying. The Op returns to old Willsson and blackmails him into having the national guard brought in to restore order to the town. Lastly, he exonerates himself of Dinah's murder, extracting a confession from the mortally wounded Starkey. The Op spends a week on his reports after leaving Personville, but his efforts to put his activities in a positive light are futile: "They didn't fool the Old Man. He gave me merry hell."

Response to *Red Harvest* was enthusiastic, with most reviewers seemingly thrilled by its sensational aspects. Herbert Asbury, writing in the March 1929 *Bookman,* called it "the liveliest detective story that has been published in a decade" and referred to the murder of Dinah Brand as an "excellent crime" and "one of the high points" of the novel. Asbury compared Hammett favorably to Ernest Hemingway, a subject to which reviewers and scholars have often returned. The stylistic similarities between the two authors are readily apparent: both favor unadorned—at times opaque—descriptions and characterization. Less superficially, critics recognized that Hammett had imbued the crime genre with a world-weariness and existential anxiety similar to Hemingway's modernism. It is a quality Gide refers to in his journals as Hammett's "implacable cynicism."

The extent of the Op's ethical crisis in *Red Harvest* was unprecedented in American crime fiction. He not only arranges murders and stirs the boiling hatreds of Personville—and in the process goes "blood-simple"—but also for the last several chapters is unconvinced of his own innocence in Dinah's murder. When Reno Starkey asks him "How the hell did you figure you didn't croak her?," he responds, "I had to take it out in hoping I hadn't, till just now." Although he is relieved of direct guilt in that crime, by his own admission he bears responsibility for at least a dozen deaths. Moreover, he acknowledges that his efforts are probably of transient value: in the middle of the night he presents

Personville back to Willsson, "all nice and clean and ready to go to the dogs again." The Op's recognition of his existential plight differentiates him, as John Cawelti notes in *Adventure, Mystery, and Romance: Formula Stories as Art and Popular Culture* (1976), "from a bloodthirsty manhunter like Mickey Spillane's Mike Hammer," whose similar ruminations border on self-parody.

Hammett's triumph in *Red Harvest* was to combine the moral questioning usually associated with serious literature with bloody action and terse, often hilarious dialogue. Lines such as "I haven't laughed so much since the hogs ate my kid brother" place him in a warped tradition of American humor descended from Mark Twain, another writer who lived in San Francisco for a time. The similarities between Hammett and Twain were expounded upon by Frederick Gardner in the 31 October 1966 *Nation:* Hammett "did for slang . . . what Twain had previously done for the American vernacular: used it on the level of art. . . . He selected the witty, colorful elements of the jargon and used them naturally, knowledgeably, without dazzling or digressing for the sake of innovation but always to progress the story." In addition to their mutual virtuosity with the language, Gardner observes, the two writers share a moral vision "torn between fondness for human beings and disgust over their depravity." The opening of the novel has been frequently celebrated by critics for its brilliant evocation of hard-boiled speech, as well as the efficiency with which it sets the tone for the action to come:

> I first heard Personville called Poisonville by a red-haired mucker named Hickey Dewey in the Big Ship in Butte. He also called his shirt a shoit. I didn't think anything of what he had done to the city's name. Later I heard men who could manage their r's give it the same pronunciation. I still didn't see anything in it but the meaningless sort of humor that used to make richardsnary the thieves' word for dictionary. A few years later I went to Personville and learned better.

Hammett began his second novel, *The Dain Curse,* immediately upon completing *Red Harvest.* It also first appeared serially in *Black Mask,* from November 1928 to February 1929. With its generational curse, incest, drug use and brainwashing, religious cultism, and diabolical mastermind for a villain, the plot of *The Dain Curse* is Hammett's most exotic. In fact, the novel is filled with the sort of fantastic detail that Hammett tended to laugh at as a book reviewer; in a 1932 interview with Elizabeth Sanderson for *The Bookman,* he referred to the novel as "a silly story." Despite his deserved reputation for realism, Hammett also at times made use of the lurid conventions of the pulp genre.

Dust jackets for Hammett's first four novels

Like *Red Harvest*, *The Dain Curse* was clearly written with serial publication in mind. The novel is sustained by the relationship at its center, between the Continental Op and Gabrielle Leggett, a deeply troubled young woman who believes herself to be the latest bearer of a curse passed down through her mother's family, the Dains. The Op meets her while investigating the disappearance of some not particularly valuable, flawed diamonds that were in the possession of Gabrielle's father, Edgar Leggett, a scientist. He quickly senses some dark aspect to the Leggett family, not necessarily connected to the theft of the diamonds.

The disappearance of the diamonds is soon overshadowed by Edgar Leggett's apparent suicide. In the long letter of confession he leaves behind, Leggett reveals a past identity and admits to killing his first wife, Gabrielle's mother, out of love for his sister-in-law, the current Mrs. Leggett; he had since lived as a fugitive, twice killing men—including most recently a private detective whom he had framed for stealing the diamonds—who threatened to expose him. The Op recognizes immediately that Leggett's confession is a fraud and that he was actually murdered. Alice Leggett reveals her true madness, asserting that she used Gabrielle, then five years old, to murder the girl's mother, training her to play a game in which she held a gun to the woman's head as she slept.

The twisted secrets of the Dain-Leggett family are only the first of many plot convolutions in the novel. Gabrielle does indeed seem to be at the center of a considerable amount of misfortune, usually involving fatal violence. Each time the Op comes to be involved: he rescues her from the Temple of the Holy Grail, a religious cult—"the fashionable one just now," as one character calls it—in the process killing its insane leader, Joseph Haldorn, who suffers from delusions of godhood; and he is called to Quesada, California, after Gabrielle elopes, only to find her new husband dead and her kidnapped. The Op comes to suspect that the source of Gabrielle's calamities is not a family curse but rather the devious activities of one person.

Ultimately, novelist Owen Fitzstephan, a friend of the Leggett family whom the Op knows from a previous investigation, is revealed to be the most thoroughly besotted with Gabrielle of all, the éminence grise that has been manipulating her life; he murdered her father, aunt, doctor, and husband. He reveals that he himself is a Dain, cousin to Gabrielle's mother. The Op infuriates Fitzstephan, who barely survives his own accomplice's attempt to kill him with explosives, by accepting his courtroom insanity plea at face value: "As a sane man who, by pretending to be a lunatic, had done as he pleased and escaped punishment, he had a joke—if you wanted to call it that—on the world. But if he was a lunatic who, ignorant of his craziness, thought he was pretending to be a lunatic, then the joke—if you wanted to call it that—was on him."

More satisfactory than the exposing of Fitzstephan is the Op's curing Gabrielle of her addiction to morphine. The detective's evolving feelings for the young woman, from initial scorn to compassion and implied deeper affection, perhaps represent Hammett's effort to redeem him after the "very un-nice doings" of *Red Harvest*. Her strange features—she has "a pointed chin and extremely white, smooth skin"; large eyes that change colors between green and brown; "remarkably small" forehead, mouth, and teeth; and ears that have "no lobes, and were queerly pointed at the top"—seem to be part of her allure, although to her they represent the physical expression of her cursed nature. Her faith that the Op will dispel the curse is touchingly portrayed. Hammett leaves understated the detective's motives for helping Gabrielle through the anguish of withdrawal: "I'm damned if I'll make a chump of myself by telling you why I did it, why it was neither revolting or disgusting, why I'd do it again and be glad of the chance."

The Dain Curse received positive reviews when it was published in July 1929. Bruce Rae, in the 18 August 1929 *New York Times Book Review*, found the resolution "a bit illogical" but praised the "racy narrative style of the author's detective mouthpiece." Will Cuppy, in the *New York Herald Tribune* of 11 August 1929, recommended the novel "for its weird characters and really astonishing speed." Critics have tended to affirm Hammett's assessment of *The Dain Curse*, however; the novel suffers from implausibility and uneven pacing, with the action broken up by extended confessions and revelatory speeches. Even Hammett's wit seems to fail him somewhat: after the Op kills Joseph Haldorn he quips, "Thank God he wasn't really God."

In *The Dain Curse* the Op resembles conventional detective heroes more than in his previous adventures, primarily because of his tendency to conclude each episode of the novel by expounding, sometimes at length, on the solution to one of a series of mysteries. When he exposes Alice Leggett as her husband's killer in a drawing room full of people—a stock situation of melodramatic thrillers—he cannot resist making fun of himself: "I filled my lungs and went on, not exactly bellowing, but getting plenty of noise out. . . . I didn't give her a chance to answer any of these questions, but sailed ahead, turning my voice loose. . . . 'You,' I thundered, my voice in fine form now. . . ." Because of the ostensibly respectable milieu in which the novel operates, as opposed to the rougher setting of *Red Harvest*, Hammett has less opportunity to demonstrate his knowledge of underworld argot. The judgment of contemporary reviewers notwithstanding, the dialogue and the Op's narration are considerably less lively than in *Red Harvest* and the best short stories.

Respectability is a thin disguise for intellectual licentiousness and worse in Hammett's portrayal of the Leggetts and their social circle. Early in the novel, Fitzstephan–who could just as easily be talking about himself–refers to Leggett as "mentally, or spiritually, sensual . . . to the point of decadence" and suggests that he has an "abnormal appetite for the fantastic." Fitzstephan is erudite but mostly a fraud: the Op teases him by asking "How's the literary grift go?" By the end of the novel he is completely grotesque, his shattered physical condition manifesting his twisted obsessions. Such depictions of the privileged, whose eccentric affectations are nearly always symptomatic of a more fundamental moral corruption, became a convention of the hard-boiled school.

Similarly, the Temple of the Holy Grail allows Hammett to portray the faddish spirituality typically associated with California culture. The headquarters of the cult, a "six story yellow brick apartment building" on Pacific Avenue in San Francisco, is the setting for the most memorable scenes of the novel. Even the sensible Op is not immune to the phantasmagoric effects of the Temple: while spending the night there he grapples with a glowing, semi-corporeal attacker, a trick of light and a narcotic gas the Haldorns pump into the rooms of the temple. These eccentric situations and characters, mostly at odds with the Op's more realistic milieu, perhaps demonstrate Hammett's dissatisfaction with the constraints of a genre he had helped create. With *The Dain Curse* Hammett seems finally to have exhausted his interest in the Continental Op: he featured the character in three more *Black Mask* stories before retiring him for good.

Most critics agree that with his next novel, *The Maltese Falcon,* Hammett made good on the ambition he expressed in a 20 March 1928 letter to Blanche Knopf, to raise the detective story to the level of literary art. *The Maltese Falcon* appeared in five installments in *Black Mask* beginning in September 1929 and was published by Knopf the following February. The most significant difference between the protagonist, San Francisco detective Sam Spade, and the Continental Op is that Spade is self-employed, and therefore acting primarily in his own interest. The ambiguity of Spade's motives–whether he is led by personal loyalty, professional integrity, or greed–is more the focus of the novel than the search for the identity of his partner's killer or the whereabouts of the Maltese falcon. Hammett emphasizes this duplicity in the description of Spade that opens the novel: "He looked rather pleasantly like a blond satan."

Compared to the sensationalistic violence of Hammett's first two novels, *The Maltese Falcon* is restrained. Spade's partner, Miles Archer, and the man Archer was supposed to be following, Floyd Thursby, are killed offstage in quick succession. The police consider Spade a suspect in Thursby's murder, and Archer's wife, with whom Spade has been having an affair, thinks that Spade killed her husband. As he had with the Op in *Red Harvest,* Hammett for a time leaves Spade's guilt a possibility: the police catch Spade in a lie about his whereabouts at the time of Thursby's murder, and the objective narration provides no confirmation of Spade's alibi. Further, Spade is apparently unmoved by his partner's death–he tells his secretary the morning after the murder to have the name on the office door changed from *Spade & Archer* to *Samuel Spade*.

Spade locates Miss Wonderly, the woman who hired him and Archer to follow Thursby, and so begins to penetrate layers of deception surrounding the search for a priceless artifact, a gold statue of a falcon that dates back to the Knights of Malta, or Knights Templar. Wonderly, whose real name is Brigid O'Shaughnessy, is only one of the people searching for the falcon: she arrived in San Francisco days before Joel Cairo, an effeminate "Levantine"; the obese, ostentatious Caspar Gutman; and Gutman's "gunsel," the young psychotic Wilmer. Spade allies himself with Brigid, even though he knows he cannot trust her, mockingly resisting her efforts to manipulate him. He maintains a grinning, ironic posture with the entire group, in fact, proving himself more than their equal in terms of deviousness. Spade receives the falcon from a dying Captain Jacobi, whose boat, *La Paloma,* brought the statue into the country; he offers to sell it to Gutman for $10,000 and his cooperation in framing Wilmer for the murders of Thursby and Jacobi.

The statue turns out to be a fake, and Cairo and Gutman plan to leave town in search of the real article, although Spade calls the police down on them. He then extracts from Brigid the truth, that she killed Miles Archer. He had known all along that the killer was not Thursby, as she had maintained: "Miles hadn't many brains but Christ! he had too many years' experience as a detective to be caught like that by the man he was shadowing." In a climactic speech Spade justifies giving Brigid to the police with no less than eight reasons, but ultimately he rejects her pleas that they run off together as a matter of male pride: "If that doesn't mean anything to you forget it and we'll make it this: I won't because all of me wants to–wants to say to hell with the consequences and do it–and because . . . you've counted on that with me the same as you counted on that with the others." He allows, though, that things might have been different if the falcon had been real: "Well, a lot of money would have been at least one more item on the other side of the scales." From the police comes the news that Gutman has been shot dead by Wilmer—death continues to haunt the search for the falcon. The novel ends on an ambiguous note, with Spade being rebuked by his loyal secretary, Effie Perine.

The Maltese Falcon was an immediate critical and popular success, reprinted seven times in its first year. The novel was widely proclaimed to have reinvented the mystery genre. Spade's character, particularly, seemed unprecedented to the reviewers: Donald Douglas, in the 9 April 1930 *New Republic,* characterized Hammett's detective as "a scoundrel without pity or remorse, taking his whiffs of drink and his casual amours between catching crooks, treating the police with a cynical contempt, always getting his crook by foul and fearless means, above the law like a satyr." Gilbert Seldes in the *New York Graphic* observed that "the romance of the story is blown to bits by bitter realism." Again there were comparisons to Hemingway, although Spade's and Brigid's exploitation of each other outstrips any of Hemingway's male-female relationships in terms of cynicism. Spade is a huge cad—he avails himself of Brigid sexually, afterward sneaking out to search her hotel room at the Coronet, and later forces her to submit to a strip search to confirm that she did not palm a missing thousand-dollar bill—but at the same time Brigid is hardly deserving of gallantry.

Spade exemplifies a certain species of American ideal, as Hammett asserted in his introduction to the 1934 Modern Library edition of the novel:

> He is a dream man in the sense that he is what most of the private detectives I worked with would like to have been and what quite a few of them in their cockier moments thought they approached. For your private detective does not—or did not ten years ago when he was my close colleague—want to be an erudite solver of riddles in the Sherlock Holmes manner; he wants to be a hard and shifty fellow, able to take care of himself in any situation, able to get the best of anybody he comes in contact with, whether criminal, innocent by-stander or client.

Nevertheless, Spade is a serious-minded professional as, for example, his careful, thorough search of Brigid's room demonstrates. At the same time, he completely—and proudly—lacks the traditional literary detective hero's high-mindedness, as evidenced by his response to Brigid's appeal for his help: "'I'm not Christ,' he said irritably. 'I can't work miracles out of thin air.'" He can, however, play Gutman, Brigid, Cairo, and Wilmer as effectively as the Op manipulates the racketeers of Personville. But like the Op at the end of *Red Harvest,* he derives no satisfaction from his part in the affair—in

Hammett in New York in 1930 (by permission of the Harry Ransom Humanities Research Center, University of Texas at Austin)

Spade's case, he has only the promise of "some rotten nights" to come.

Critics have debated whether or not Spade can be considered a heroic character, or if he fails to meet even his own professed ethical standards, such as they are. Leo Gurko argues in *Heroes, Highbrows, and the Popular Mind* (1953) that Spade acts "simply to save his own skin" and that *The Maltese Falcon* is emblematic of "Darwinism carried to its ferociously logical extreme." Irving Malin (1968), by contrast, sees the novel as a classical romance in which Spade "shares the archetypal qualities of such mythic heroes as Odysseus, Samuel, and Jesus in a peculiarly contemporary way." Hammett's choice of a third-person, objective narration denies readers the same access to Spade's thoughts as they have to the Op's. The consequent "lasting ambiguity of the character," as Julian Symons puts it, is at the heart of the greatness of the novel.

The Maltese Falcon is famous for its objective, as opposed to omniscient, point of view; the reader follows Spade throughout but is not privy to his motives. Hammett perfects his technique of isolating salient details to reveal inner states. Nowhere is this device better illustrated than in the climax of the novel, when Spade finally attempts to justify how he has behaved to that point. Spade's sardonic pose is transformed by inner turmoil: "Blood streaked Spade's eyeballs now and his long-held smile had become a frightful grimace." The ending of the novel maintains this tone, somberly echoing the opening. For Spade another week begins, although his normally casual facade still shows signs of strain: "His face was pasty in color, but its lines were strong and cheerful and his eyes, though still somewhat red-veined, were clear." The final exchange between Spade and Effie leaves much understated, to considerable effect:

> Her voice was queer as the expression on her face. "You did that, Sam, to her?"
> He nodded. "Your Sam's a detective." He looked sharply at her, put his arm around her waist, his hand on her hip. "She did kill Miles, angel," he said gently, "offhand, like that." He snapped the fingers of his other hand.
> She escaped from his arm as if it had hurt her. "Don't, please, don't touch me," she said brokenly. "I know—I know you're right. You're right. But don't touch me now—not now."
> Spade's face became as pale as his collar.

Hammett also makes effective use of the San Francisco setting of *The Maltese Falcon*, with frequent references to specific streets and much of the action taking place in renamed but recognizable versions of actual locations. Moreover, the story gains plausibility by virtue of the historic reputation of the city for lawlessness and exoticism. The novel takes place in a nighttime world, shrouded in "night-fog, thin, clammy, and penetrant." As Gurko's argument implies, Hammett depicts San Francisco as an urban jungle, a vision reminiscent of another, similarly brutal novel set in the city: Frank Norris's *McTeague* (1899).

The Maltese Falcon has been adapted for the screen three times, most notably in a 1940 Warner Bros. production directed by John Huston and starring Humphrey Bogart as Spade. Although physically the opposite of Spade as described in the novel, Bogart defines the character in the popular imagination. Endlessly referenced and parodied in popular culture, Sam Spade and *The Maltese Falcon* have achieved an iconic status.

Hammett went to Hollywood in the summer of 1930; the motion-picture industry, which had recently made the transition to sound, welcomed writers of good dialogue. With his wit and style, he immediately fell in with a coterie of writers who had their initial success in New York, including Ben Hecht, S. J. Perelman, and Nunnally Johnson. Hammett's first screenplay, for the 1931 Paramount movie *City Streets*, was a success at the time. More important for Hammett was his meeting Lillian Hellman, a script reader for M-G-M, in November 1930. She was significantly younger than Hammett and, like him, married, but the two began an affair. The relationship was the most important and sustained of Hammett's life, and it has had considerable influence on how he has been remembered. Although the attraction between them was immediate, their romance was not entirely blissful. Hammett clearly had no intention of giving up sexual affairs with other women, and Hellman reciprocated with her own series of liaisons.

Hammett had already completed his fourth novel, *The Glass Key*, before *The Maltese Falcon* was published. Wary of the book-buying market in the first years of the Depression, Knopf decided to withhold the book until the year after its predecessor was published. The novel appeared in installments in *Black Mask* beginning in March 1930 but was not published in book form until January 1931. Considered by many—including the author himself—to be his best novel, *The Glass Key* is Hammett's further attempt to break with the conventions of detective fiction. The protagonist of the novel, Ned Beaumont, is not a detective—is, in fact, a criminal. Arguably, his most admirable quality is resiliency, embodied in his credo: "I can stand anything I've got to stand." Hammett refers to him as "Ned Beaumont" throughout the novel, as if to discourage familiarity. A self-described "gambler and a politician's hanger-on," Beaumont is lieutenant to Paul Madvig, the chief power broker in an unnamed city based on the Baltimore of Hammett's youth.

Madvig's current preoccupation is to win the heart of Senator Henry's daughter, Janet, which he hopes to do by enabling the senator to retain his office in the upcoming election. Those efforts are complicated, however, when the senator's son, Taylor, is found dead in the street. Beaumont is deputized into the investigation of Taylor's death, but only so he can track down Taylor's bookie, Bernie Despain, who also owes Beaumont a bundle from a horse race the night before. Beaumont's cynical modus operandi in acquiring his money—he goes to New York to extort Despain by framing him for Taylor's murder—epitomizes the tone of the entire novel: characters are motivated almost exclusively by self-interest, for political gain or personal validation.

Beaumont's activities begin to have consequences for his boss when poison-pen letters appear around town, implying that Madvig is obstructing the investigation of Henry's death. The fact that Madvig might be accused of the killing is an indication of his waning political power. Another telling indication is the ascendancy of Madvig's rival, Shad O'Rory, who takes advantage of Madvig's electioneering to make inroads into his control over the city. When Madvig responds by shutting down O'Rory's nightclubs, the rivalry between the two factions erupts into open conflict. Disagreements over Madvig's commitment to the Henrys and his handling of O'Rory drive a wedge between him and Beaumont. Beaumont plans to leave town, but he is drawn back into the gang war, as a hostage of O'Rory's. With a seemingly suicidal obstinance, he endures several days of brutal beatings at the hands of O'Rory's henchman, the animalistic Jeff Gardner.

Although Beaumont and Madvig reunite while Beaumont recovers in the hospital, he continues to mock his friend's folly in courting the Henry family, even in front of Janet Henry. Treachery surrounds Madvig: his own daughter, Opal, sides with O'Rory to see her father punished for killing Taylor, her lover, and seems to be the author of the poison-pen letters, and Janet makes overtures of friendship to Beaumont primarily, as it turns out, to gain his help in hanging Madvig. The suspense of the novel ultimately turns on the nature and extent of Beaumont's loyalty to his boss and friend.

Beaumont's interest in Janet seems to grow even as his worst suspicions of her are confirmed. She has been leading Madvig on, allowing him to romance her even as she loathes him for killing her brother; in fact, she is the one sending the accusatory letters. She also contributes to the final break between Beaumont and Madvig, who tells Beaumont that he killed Taylor in a struggle after the boy witnessed him kiss his sister and that he then foolishly tried to hide the truth to preserve his chances with Janet. In response Beaumont brutally tells Madvig of Janet's true feelings: "She's always thought you killed her brother. She hates you. She's been trying to play you into the electric chair. . . . She was in my rooms this morning telling me this, trying to turn me."

To the end Beaumont continues to pursue his ambiguous agenda. He agrees to help Janet build her case against Madvig, even giving a sworn statement of his confession to the district attorney. At the same time he dispenses with Madvig's enemies, provoking the sadistic Jeff Gardner to kill his boss, O'Rory. Ultimately, he establishes the truth about Taylor's death: that Senator Henry killed his own son and, having learned that Paul has confessed, intends to kill him and thus forever hide what really happened. He had gone after his son the night of his death out of political necessity: "I did not care to lose Paul's friendship through my son's hot-headedness." In keeping with his thoroughgoing selfishness, Henry asks Beaumont to let him kill himself and avoid a scandal, but Beaumont refuses: "You'll take what's coming to you."

Janet is well aware that Beaumont thinks she prostituted herself. He denies any intention of judging her,

Photograph by Hammett, showing his reflection and that of the playwright Lillian Hellman, whose relationship with Hammett lasted from November 1930 until his death

although he proceeds to do so anyway, disapproving of her and her father's naked opportunism:

> You're all right, only you're not all right for Paul. Neither of you were anything but poison for him. I tried to tell him that. I tried to tell him you both considered him a lower form of animal life and fair game for any kind of treatment. I tried to tell him your father was a man all his life used to winning without much trouble and that in a hole he'd either lose his head or turn wolf.

Still, Beaumont's existential view of the world leads him not to judge her too harshly. "Whatever you've done you've paid for and been paid for and that goes for all of us." Surprisingly, despite Beaumont's estimation of her and father, Janet wants to leave town with him and he is willing to have her along.

With his rivals neutralized, Madvig is free to begin rebuilding his organization, and he pleads with Beaumont to stay and help. The novel closes not with their reconciliation, however, but with Madvig's devastated reaction to the news that Beaumont and Janet are leaving together. "Madvig's lips parted. He looked dumbly at Ned Beaumont and as he looked the blood went out of his face again. When his face was quite bloodless he mumbled something of which only the word 'luck' could be understood, turned clumsily around, went to the door, opened it, and went out, leaving it open behind him." As in *The Maltese Falcon,* in *The Glass Key* Hammett skillfully portrays intense emotion through evocative objective detail.

The Glass Key garnered Hammett's usual positive reviews, although perhaps inevitably it was judged to miss the high standard established by *The Maltese Falcon.* Bruce Rae asserted in *The New York Times Book Review* on 3 May 1931 that "Mr. Hammett's new book is bound to find favor, although probably not as much as was accorded . . . *The Maltese Falcon,*" and Dorothy Parker—an acquaintance in whose opinion Hammett was particularly interested—praised the novel in *The New Yorker* of 25 April 1931 but observed that it "seems to me nowhere to touch its predecessor." An exception was Will Cuppy, writing in the 26 April 1931 *New York Herald Tribune,* who thought that *The Glass Key* was "about twice as good as *The Maltese Falcon.*"

In *The Glass Key* Hammett's cynicism finds it fullest expression. In the unnamed urban setting, loyalties are precarious, and what loyalty characters do demonstrate is generally misplaced. Madvig, the crime boss, is the most forthright character in terms of his relationships with others, but he is depicted as a fool, blinded by love for a woman who despises him and still living by the rules of his boyhood days "running errands for Packy Flood in the old Fifth." The Henrys, superficially the symbols of respectability, are revealed to be the most treacherous characters in the novel. The senator is willing to pimp his daughter and kill his son to further his political ambitions; yet, Janet and her brother are also shown to be untrustworthy and manipulative. They are reminiscent of Hammett's other morally bankrupt characters of privilege, the Leggetts in *The Dain Curse* and Elihu Willsson in *Red Harvest.* Beaumont's decision to take Janet with him is clearly received by Madvig as the greatest treachery of all, but, as usual, Hammett leaves Beaumont's motives understated.

As he had in *The Maltese Falcon,* Hammett in *The Glass Key* uses an objective narration that follows the protagonist closely but scrupulously refrains from revealing his motives. Hammett is at his most concise in this novel, his subtle, complex plot borne along almost entirely by dialogue and nuance. Thematically, the novel is most akin to *Red Harvest,* which also presents a whole class of people operating, most unsuc-

cessfully, in a corrupting urban environment. Extended through the large cast of characters, ambiguity of motive takes on the status of a social condition; *The Glass Key* can thus be seen as the fullest realization of Hammett's existential vision.

Beaumont is the most laconic of Hammett's protagonists, at no point justifying himself as Spade does in the climax of *The Maltese Falcon.* Consequently, his character has been the source of critical debate. In *Dashiell Hammett: A Life* (1983) Diane Johnson implies that Beaumont is an autobiographical portrait, Hammett's "most plausible and fallible hero," while William F. Nolan, in "Setting the Record Straight on *Dashiell Hammett: A Life*" (*Armchair Detective,* winter 1984) contends that "Hammett is not creating a hero; he's drawing a portrait of moral failure." The only character in the novel who seems to understand him is O'Rory's henchman Jeff, who calls him a "massacrist." Beaumont does seem driven to act self-destructively, finding grim satisfaction in suffering his way through a losing streak at gambling or Jeff's brutal beatings. In New York after Despain, he recklessly confronts the bookie in one of his hangouts and is sucker punched by Despain's crony. The next morning—sick, shaky, and still drunk from the night before—Beaumont insists on going up against Despain again. Whether motivated by masochism or fatalism, Beaumont's penchant for suffering finds its ultimate expression in his willingness to leave town with a woman he has consistently described as poisonous.

Critics have also debated the significance of the title of the novel. It refers directly to a dream of Janet Henry's, in which she and Beaumont are lost in the woods and hungry. They come upon a house filled with food but also with poisonous snakes. When Janet tells Beaumont that they managed to outmaneuver the snakes and claim the food, Beaumont accuses her of lying: "It starts out to be a nightmare and winds up something else and all the dreams I ever had about food ended before I got a chance to do any actual eating." Later, as they are leaving, Janet confesses the true ending to the dream: the glass key they used to unlock the door shattered, and they were overwhelmed by the snakes. In *Hammett: A Life at the Edge* (1983) Nolan argues that "Ned Beaumont himself is the key of glass, fragile in character and, at the end, broken." Richard Layman in *Shadow Man: The Life of Dashiell Hammett* (1981) suggests that the key functions as a more general comment on the events of the narrative, symbolizing the irrevocable consequences of knowledge: "Once a door is opened and you learn what is on the other side, you must live with all that is found there, not simply the best of it, and what is found there can never be unlearned." Whatever Hammett's specific symbolic intent, the title completes the theme of irreparableness that dominates *The Glass Key*.

After writing four novels in less than three years, Hammett took another three years to complete his fifth and last novel, *The Thin Man*. He made a start on it as early as 1930, originally focusing on a detective, Guild, who became the policeman Nick Charles assists in the published version of the novel, and an eccentric inventor, Claude Wynant, whom Hammett retained as the elusive title character. When he resumed the work on the novel in 1933, Hammett was clearly influenced by his relationship with Hellman and his nights spent in bars and at cocktail parties. Finally completed during a period of concentrated effort in May 1933, the novel was published in expurgated form in *Redbook* in December. Knopf's hardcover edition, with the racy passages restored, appeared the following month, in January 1934. *The Thin Man* rivaled *The Maltese Falcon* as Hammett's greatest popular success, although it has subsequently been judged his weakest novel by most critics.

The great success of the novel was due to Hammett's charming creations, Nick and Nora Charles. Nick, a retired private detective, is content to spend his days drinking and managing the profits from his young wife's inherited family business. The Charleses are in New York for the holidays, and the novel consequently has a superficially lighter tone than Hammett's other works. Nick is reluctantly persuaded to help investigate the disappearance of inventor Claude Wynant and the murder of his assistant and lover, for which Wynant is the most likely suspect. The mystery involves the couple with another of Hammett's neurotic families, Wynant's former wife and his two children, as well as various lowlifes associated with the murdered girl, who was apparently using Wynant.

Nick tells the story with a fixed bemusement, presumably the product of the innumerable drinks he fixes for himself at all hours. Despite Hammett's return to the use of first-person narration, Nick is a different sort of narrator than the Op; although no less observant, he is far less inclined to self-reflection. He is, in fact, even more circumspect than Spade and Ned Beaumont. This change in characterization has led most critics to conclude that the novel lacks moral seriousness. Nick never faces the challenges to his sense of integrity or identity that are essential to Hammett's hard-boiled novels, and consequently *The Thin Man* has nearly always been found to be less compelling than its predecessors.

The novel also suffers from a lackluster plot. Like other literary detectives, as Layman observes, Nick "withholds clues from the police as well as the reader–a defect Hammett objected to loudly when he found it in the work of others. Unlike Hammett's pre-

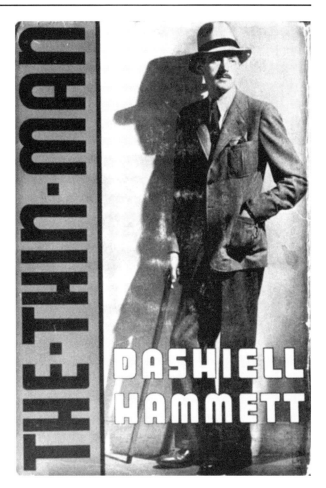

Dust jacket, with Hammett's picture, for his 1934 novel that introduced the husband-and-wife detectives Nick and Nora Charles

vious novels in which the detectives went hunting for evidence, in *The Thin Man* the evidence comes to Nick Charles." So much of the action takes place in the Charleses' hotel room that Nick quips, "We might just as well be living in the lobby." Hammett gives Nick a history with the Wynants–including the suggestion of a past sexual liaison between him and Mimi Jorgensen, Wynant's former wife–but ultimately fails to make a convincing case that Nick and Nora's involvement with the investigation is anything more than arbitrary. Further, the villain of the novel is the Wynant family lawyer, Herbert Macaulay, by most critics' estimation the least interesting character. The central revelation of the novel, that the elusive thin man, Wynant, has been dead for months, seems of little consequence to any of the characters.

Nonetheless, Nick is an engaging narrator. When confronted by a hopped-up gunman in their hotel room, he exhibits obvious admiration for Nora as well as Hammett's characteristically dry, absurd wit:

Hammett speaking at an anti-Nazi rally at Madison Square Garden in the late 1930s

"I got to talk to you," the man with the gun said. "That's all, but I got to do that." His voice was low, rasping.

I had blinked myself awake by then. I looked at Nora. She was excited, but apparently not frightened: she might have been watching a horse she had bet on coming down the stretch with a nose lead.

I said: "All right, talk, but do you mind putting the gun away? My wife doesn't care, but I'm pregnant and I don't want the child to be born with–"

He smiled with his lower lip. "You don't have to tell me you're tough. I heard about you." He put the pistol in his overcoat pocket. "I'm Shep Morelli."

"I never heard about you," I said.

In the comic highlights of the novel, Nick and Nora go to the Pigiron Club, a speakeasy owned by Studsy Burke, an underworld acquaintance of Nick's. There they drink with Shep Morelli, despite the fact that he threatened them and wounded Nick slightly. Hammett takes these opportunities to return to the same shady milieu he had previously explored in *Red Harvest* and *The Glass Key* but with a lighter touch. The visits to the Pigiron Club climax with an unexpected explosion of violence–one of the few incidents of action in the novel–when a belligerent man with a "thin, tremulous, effeminate voice" comes over to the party's table:

Morelli hit the fat man in his fat belly, as hard as he could without getting up. Studsy, suddenly on his feet, leaned over Morelli and smashed a big fist into the fat man's face. I noticed, foolishly, that he still led with his right. Hunchbacked Pete came up behind the fat man and banged his empty tray down with full force on the fat man's head. The fat man fell back, upsetting three people and a table. Both bar-tenders were with us by then. One of them hit the fat man with a blackjack as he tried to get up, knocking him forward on hands and knees, the other put a hand down inside the fat man's collar in back, twisting the collar to choke him. With Morelli's help they got the fat man to his feet and hustled him out.

Pete looked after them and sucked a tooth. "That God-damned Sparrow," he explained to me, "you can't take no chances on him when he's drinking."

In a taxicab afterward, Nora remarks, "They oughtn't've hit that fat man like that, though it must've been funny in a cruel way"–a statement that could serve as a fitting assessment of Hammett's comic vision.

Hammett emphasizes the happiness of the Charleses' marriage by surrounding them with examples of failed unions: Mimi Jorgensen, former wife of Claude Wynant, has married an unfaithful fraud; Nick's broker, Harrison Quinn, is willing to leave his wife for Dorothy Wynant, who has barely disguised contempt for him. Nick and Nora, while perhaps not the most conventional couple, are clearly devoted to each other and are completely open with each other in all matters, including their harmless flirtations. In that regard, Nora at one point asks a racy question of Nick—"Tell me the truth: when you were wrestling with Mimi, didn't you have an erection?"—that was referenced by Knopf in an advertisement in order to titillate reader interest. Nick and Nora have "one of the few marriages in modern literature where the man and the woman like each other and have a fine time together," Hellman proudly observed in *An Unfinished Woman: A Memoir* (1969), although she recalled that Hammett told her she also inspired the manipulative ingenue Dorothy and her devious mother.

Nevertheless, in Hammett's depiction of Nora, *The Thin Man* is clearly something of a love letter to Hellman. Nick is regularly moved to comment on his wife's attractiveness. She is the only one of Hammett's significant female characters without any tendency toward treachery or sadism. She is an ideal companion, spunky and adventurous, cultured (her holiday reading is the memoirs of Russian opera bass Feodor Chaliapin), gracious, and good-hearted. Like Hammett's tough gang molls, she is "a woman with hair on her chest," as a policeman says admiringly at one point. Nora seems immediately to captivate almost everyone she meets, particularly detective Guild and Dorothy. In return, she regards Dorothy with an almost maternal affection, even though she is not much older than the girl.

Nora has the last words of *The Thin Man*—"it's all pretty unsatisfactory"—which might be used to describe the tone for the critical response to the novel. Although reviewers welcomed Hammett's return, T. S. Matthews suggested in the 24 January 1934 *New Republic* that the author was "coasting," that "though his New York setting is authentic, and contains some very lifelike policemen, speakeasy proprietors, and 'rats,' the crime and the criminal are in the orthodox tradition." The reviewer for the *Times Literary Supplement* (14 June 1934) faulted the novel for its static quality, observing that "there is little movement in it, if we deduct what goes to the getting of drinks or the making of telephone calls."

Defenders of the novel have made the case that underneath its comic tone *The Thin Man* offers a vision of society fully as corrosive as that in Hammett's earlier work, if not more so. The most historically precise of Hammett's novels, its literary failings are offset somewhat by what A. Alvarez sees as the acuity of "its view of New York just after the crash, with its nervy, slanderous parties, sporadically violent speakeasies, disintegrating boozing, and permanent hangover." Sinda

Gregory observes in *Private Investigations: The Novels of Dashiell Hammett* (1985): "The book works successfully on a lighter level, and we can be amused by the eccentricities of the Wynant family and the social lives of the wealthy, yet if we step back we see something else at work that is not amusing and not so light. The first of these perspectives exists exclusive of the second—Hammett never insists that the reader must look beyond the obvious meaning of his novels. But the second perspective—not only is the world neither charming nor gay, it is painful, destructive, and personally divisive—depends upon the first, for the reverberations between the outward cheerfulness and the inner chill give an unexpected edge to the entire novel."

Hammett's literary career effectively ended with the publication of *The Thin Man*. In March 1934 he published his last original story, "This Little Pig," in *Collier's* magazine. He was for the rest of his life plagued by a profound sense of writer's block. During the early part of the 1930s, however, he was perhaps at the height of his fame, a circumstance that made his lack of productivity particularly galling for him. At one point he expressed the intention to leave behind mystery fiction for play writing, but he apparently sublimated that desire into supporting Hellman's literary ambitions. Her first, extremely successful work for the stage, *The Children's Hour* (1934), was based on a premise suggested by Hammett and benefited greatly from his careful editing and directions for revision. Over the years of their relationship, as Hammett's celebrity waned and Hellman became more prominent, he continued to serve as mentor to her, a role he approached with generosity and conscientiousness.

In 1934 he collaborated briefly on a comic strip for the Hearst newspaper syndicate, *Secret Agent X-9*, with *Flash Gordon* creator Alex Raymond. He also found more work in Hollywood, planning sequels for *The Thin Man* and adapting his story "On the Make" for the Universal movie *Mister Dynamite* (1935). Hammett made a lot of money in Hollywood during the first half of the decade, ultimately selling the rights to his *Thin Man* characters to M-G-M for $40,000 in 1937. His profligacy outstripped his capacity to earn, however, and by the latter half of the decade his career as a screenwriter had been fatally undermined by his reputation for unreliability.

During his time in Hollywood, Hammett also devoted himself to a variety of leftist political organizations, often serving in relatively high-profile positions as an executive officer or celebrity spokesman. He was involved in the activities of the Screen Writers Guild, which since its formation in 1933 had been engaged in rancorous labor negotiations with studio executives, and became a member of the Communist Party in 1936

*Hammett (in rear, holding sheet of paper) in Adak, Alaska, during World War II
with the staff of* The Adakian, *the military newspaper he founded and edited*

or 1937. In 1938 he was elected chairman of the Motion Picture Artists Committee, which, like most other communist front organizations of the time, raised money for antifascist efforts in Europe and Asia. Hammett also gave talks on matters literary and political under the auspices of the League of American Writers. His most intense political activity coincided with a fourteen-month period of sobriety, but he resumed drinking and suffered a physical and mental collapse, for which he was hospitalized for several months in 1938.

In the turbulent political climate of the early 1940s, Hammett was a vocal antifascist and opponent of the war in Europe, serving as president of the League of American Writers beginning in 1941. The League officially stood behind the U.S. entry into World War II in 1941, however, and Hammett, anxious to contribute more directly to the war effort, volunteered for military service but was rejected because of his age and ill health. During this period he adapted Hellman's antifascist play *Watch on the Rhine* for the screen and taught writing courses in propaganda techniques. In September 1942 Hammett was accepted into the army, at the age of forty-seven, and assigned to Fort Monmouth, New Jersey. A year later Corporal Hammett was in Fort Randall in Alaska's Aleutian Islands. Hammett felt fulfilled by his military service, and

he devoted himself to his duties as founding editor of *The Adakian,* a newspaper that circulated among the fifty thousand troops of the Aleutian force.

Discharged as a sergeant in September 1945, Hammett returned uneasily to civilian life. He was still a literary celebrity, with paperback editions of his magazine fiction–including *The Continental Op* (1945), *Hammett Homicides* (1946), and *Nightmare Town* (1948)–introducing his stories to a new readership, although Hammett was receiving little money from them. There were also radio series based on the Op, Nick and Nora, and Sam Spade, the last of which was found to infringe on Warner Bros. and Hammett's ownership of the character. He was also garnering the first appreciative assessments of his contributions to American fiction, notably from British authors Robert Graves and Alan Hodge in their *The Long Week-end: A Social History of Great Britain 1918–1939* (1940) and from fellow mystery writer Raymond Chandler in his 1944 essay "The Simple Art of Murder," in which he famously proclaimed that Hammett "took murder out of the Venetian vase and dropped it into the alley" and that he "gave murder back to the kind of people that commit it for reasons, not just to provide a corpse; and with the means at hand, not hand-wrought dueling pistols, curare and tropical fish."

Hammett was again drinking heavily, however, with a potentially fatal abandon. As Hellman recalled in *An Unfinished Woman,* "the years after the war, from 1945 to 1948, were not good years. The drinking grew wilder and there was a lost, thoughtless quality I had never seen before." Told by doctors he was drinking himself to death, Hammett was finally able to give up alcohol for good by the end of 1948. He rededicated himself to his political commitments, although American leftists were increasingly at odds because of fractious debates over their allegiances. Hammett's activities, along with those of many others, came under government scrutiny as Communist and un-American. In June 1949 he became the chairman of the Conference for Civil and Human Rights, and as a trustee for bail fund of the Civil Rights Congress was called to testify in federal court in July 1951. Hammett was eventually found in contempt of court because he would not divulge–and by some accounts did not know–the whereabouts of Communist leaders who had fled bail and the names of other contributors of the bail fund. He served time in prison from July to December 1951.

Because of the dominant anti-Communist sentiment of the time, Hammett was subject to general disapprobation, from which his literary reputation did not recover in his lifetime. Periodicals around the country denounced him in the most extreme terms: a commentator in *Hollywood Life* (13 July 1951) asserted that he was "without any question one of the red masterminds of the nation," and Oliver Pilat in the *New York Post* (23–27 July 1951) wrote an uncharitable five-part assessment of Hammett's career that concluded, "So far as the record shows, Hammett possesses no more of a social or political philosophy now than he did in his Pinkerton days. He is still concerned entirely with doing a job, no longer as an operative for a detective agency, but as an operative for the Communist Party."

Hammett's prison term was not the end of the legal troubles he faced because of his Communist associations. In March 1953 he testified before the Senate Committee on Government Operations, chaired by Senator Joseph McCarthy, concerning the purchase by the State Department of books by known Communists; the questioning by the senators was acrimonious, and accusations were made that Hammett's invoking the Fifth Amendment against self-incrimination was a "voluntary act of self-incrimination before the bar of public opinion." Hammett's books were pulled from State Department libraries around the world, although President Dwight Eisenhower had them replaced when he learned of the action. In February 1955 Hammett was called to testify before the New York State Joint Legislative Committee, again because of his association with the Civil Rights Congress.

In the latter part of the 1950s Hammett was plagued by health and financial problems. His books were out of print; the royalties from his creations had long run out;

Hammett testifying in March 1953 before Senator Joseph McCarthy's Committee on Government Operations about the purchase by the State Department of books by Communist writers

and from 1951 until his death he was subject to a federal judgment for tax evasion. He did work on an autobiographical novel during this period, "Tulip," which he abandoned sometime around 1953; the extant fragment of it was published in *The Big Knockover* (1966), edited by Hellman. He lived in a gatehouse in Katonah, New York, on property owned by friends until near the end of his life, when he moved to New York with Hellman. He died of lung cancer on 10 January 1961. As a veteran of two wars, Hammett was buried in Arlington National Cemetery, over the objections of commentators in the press who recalled his Communist activities.

Hammett's reputation, in eclipse at the time of his death, subsequently proved to outlast the vicissitudes of political partisanship. His importance to the detective genre is undisputed, and his best novels, *Red Harvest, The Maltese Falcon,* and *The Glass Key,* have attained the status of classics of American literature. He has been the subject of four biographies, more than a dozen book-length critical studies, and scores of articles in both scholarly journals and popular magazines.

Hammett has exerted a continued fascination as a personage, as well. His colorful personal history and great charisma were always part of his success during his lifetime, and after his death Hellman sought to salvage his reputation with new editions of his fiction and idealized biographical accounts of him in her memoirs. In 1975 mystery writer Joe Gores paid homage to Hammett by making him the hero of a novel set in 1928 San Francisco, and in 1978 Jason Robards won an Academy Award for best supporting actor for playing Hammett in *Julia,* based on portions of Hellman's autobiographies. He has been portrayed on television, as well, by Sam Shepard in *Dash and Lilly,* a 1999 Arts and Entertainment Network dramatization that drew heavily on Joan Mellen's biography, *Hellman and Hammett: The Legendary Passion of Lillian Hellman and Dashiell Hammett* (1996).

At the end of the twentieth century, Hammett's literary reputation seems secure. New printings of his works continue to appear, and in 1999 the Library of America edition of his complete novels was published. His lean, ironic prose and understated, sometimes mean, sometimes romantic view of human nature has continued to exert an influence, particularly on detective fiction, but also on literature and popular culture more generally, including motion pictures and television.

Bibliography:

Richard Layman, *Dashiell Hammett: A Descriptive Bibliography* (Pittsburgh: University of Pittsburgh Press, 1979).

Biographies:

Richard Layman, *Shadow Man: The Life of Dashiell Hammett* (New York: Harcourt Brace Jovanovich, 1981);

Diane Johnson, *Dashiell Hammett: A Life* (New York: Random House, 1983);

William Nolan, *Dashiell Hammett: A Life at the Edge* (New York: Congdon & Weed, 1983);

Joan Mellen, *Hellman and Hammett: The Legendary Passion of Lillian Hellman and Dashiell Hammett* (New York: HarperCollins, 1996).

References:

A. Alvarez, "The Thin Man," *Spectator* (11 February 1966): 169–170;

Donald T. Bazelon, "Dashiell Hammett's Private Eye: No Loyalty Beyond the Job," *Commentary,* 7 (1949): 467–472;

Christopher Bentley, "Radical Anger: Dashiell Hammett's *Red Harvest,*" in *American Crime Fiction: Studies in the Genre,* edited by Brian Docherty (New York: St. Martin's Press, 1988), pp. 54–70;

John Cawelti, *Adventure, Mystery, and Romance: Formula Stories as Art and Popular Culture* (Chicago: University of Chicago Press, 1976);

Raymond Chandler, "The Simple Art of Murder," *Atlantic Monthly* (December 1944): 53–59;

Dennis Dooley, *Dashiell Hammett* (New York: Ungar, 1984);

Robert I. Edenbaum, "The Poetics of the Private Eye: The Novels of Dashiell Hammett," in *Tough Guy Writers of the Thirties,* edited by David Madden (Carbondale: Southern Illinois University Press, 1968), pp. 80–103;

Frederick Gardner, "The Return of the Continental Op," *Nation* (31 October 1966): 454–456;

Sinda Gregory, *Private Investigations: The Novels of Dashiell Hammett* (Carbondale: Southern Illinois University Press, 1985);

Leo Gurko, *Heroes, Highbrows, and the Popular Mind* (Indianapolis: Bobbs-Merrill, 1953);

Lillian Hellman, introduction to *The Big Knockover and Other Stories,* by Dashiell Hammett (New York: Random House, 1966);

Richard Layman, *Literary Masters: Dashiell Hammett,* Gale Study Guides to Great Literature, volume 3 (Detroit: Gale/Manly, 1999);

Layman, *Literary Masterpieces: The Maltese Falcon,* Gale Study Guides to Great Literature, volume 3 (Detroit: Gale/Manly, 1999);

Irving Malin, "Focus on *The Maltese Falcon:* The Metaphysical Falcon," in *Tough Guy Writers of the Thirties,* edited by David Madden (Carbondale: Southern Illinois University Press, 1968), pp. 104–109;

Edward Margolies, *Which Way Did He Go?: The Private Eye in Dashiell Hammett, Raymond Chandler, Chester Himes, and Ross Macdonald* (New York: Holmes & Meier, 1982), pp. 17–31;

Christopher Metress, *The Critical Response to Dashiell Hammett* (Westport, Conn.: Greenwood Press, 1994);

Metress, "Dashiell Hammett and the Challenge of New Individualism: Rereading *Red Harvest* and *The Maltese Falcon,*" *Essays in Literature,* 17 (1990): 242–260;

William F. Nolan, *Dashiell Hammett: A Casebook* (Santa Barbara: McNally & Loftin, 1969);

Robert Schulman, "Dashiell Hammett's Social Vision," *Centennial Review,* 29 (Fall 1985): 400–419;

Julian Symons, *Dashiell Hammett* (San Diego: Harcourt Brace Jovanovich, 1985);

John S. Whitley, "Stirring Things Up: Dashiell Hammett's Continental Op," *Journal of American Studies,* 14 (1980): 443–455;

Peter Wolfe, *Beams Falling: The Art of Dashiell Hammett* (Bowling Green: Bowling Green University Popular Press, 1980).

Papers:

The papers of Dashiell Hammett are at the Harry Ransom Humanities Research Center, University of Texas at Austin.

Joseph Hansen

(19 July 1923 –   )

Karl L. Stenger
University of South Carolina, Aiken

BOOKS: *Lost on Twilight Road,* as James Colton (Fresno, Cal.: National Library, 1964);

Strange Marriage, as Colton (Los Angeles: Argyle Books, 1965);

The Corrupter and Other Stories, as Colton (San Diego: Greenleaf Classics, 1968);

Known Homosexual, as Colton (Los Angeles: Brandon House, 1968); revised as *Stranger to Himself,* as Hansen (Los Angeles: Major Books, 1978); revised edition republished as *Pretty Boy Dead* (San Francisco: Gay Sunshine, 1984);

Cocksure, as Colton (San Diego: Greenleaf Classics, 1969);

Gard, as Colton (New York: Award Books, 1969);

Hang-Up, as Colton (Los Angeles: Brandon House, 1969);

Fadeout (New York: Harper & Row, 1970; London: Harrap, 1972);

The Outward Side, as Colton (New York: Olympia, 1971);

Todd, as Colton (New York: Olympia, 1971);

Tarn House, as Rose Brock (New York: Avon, 1971; London: Harrap, 1975);

Death Claims: A Dave Brandstetter Mystery (New York: Harper & Row, 1973; London: Harrap, 1973);

Longleaf, as Brock (New York: Harper & Row, 1974; London: Harrap, 1974);

Troublemaker: A Dave Brandstetter Mystery (New York: Harper & Row, 1975); republished as *Trouble Maker* (London: Harrap, 1975);

One Foot in the Boat (Los Angeles: Momentum, 1977);

The Man Everybody Was Afraid Of: A Dave Brandstetter Mystery (New York: Holt, Rinehart & Winston, 1978; London: Faber, 1978);

Skinflick: A Dave Brandstetter Mystery (New York: Holt, Rinehart & Winston, 1979; London: Faber, 1980);

The Dog and Other Stories (Los Angeles: Momentum, 1979);

A Smile in His Lifetime (New York: Holt, Rinehart & Winston, 1981; London: Owen, 1982);

Joseph Hansen

Gravedigger: A Dave Brandstetter Mystery (New York: Holt, Rinehart & Winston, 1982; London: Owen, 1982);

Backtrack (Woodstock, Vt.: Countryman, 1982; London: Gay Men's Press, 1987);

Job's Year (New York: Holt, Rinehart & Winston, 1983; London: Arlington, 1988);

209

Nightwork: A Dave Brandstetter Mystery (New York: Holt, Rinehart & Winston, 1984; London: Owen, 1984);

Brandstetter and Others: Five Fictions (Woodstock, Vt.: Countryman, 1984);

Steps Going Down (Woodstock, Vt.: Countryman, 1985; London: Arlington, 1986);

The Little Dog Laughed: A Dave Brandstetter Mystery (New York: Holt, 1986);

Early Graves: A Dave Brandstetter Mystery (New York: Mysterious Press, 1987);

Obedience: A Dave Brandstetter Mystery (New York: Mysterious Press, 1988);

Bohannon's Book: Five Mysteries (Woodstock, Vt.: Countryman, 1988);

The Boy Who Was Buried This Morning: A Dave Brandstetter Mystery (New York: Viking, 1990);

A Country of Old Men: The Last Dave Brandstetter Mystery (New York: Viking, 1991; Harpenden, U.K.: No Exit, 1993);

Living Upstairs (New York: Dutton, 1993);

Bohannon's Country: Mystery Stories (New York: Viking, 1993);

Jack of Hearts (New York: Dutton, 1995);

A Few Doors West of Hope: The Life and Times of Dauntless Don Slater (Universal City, Cal.: Homosexual Information Center, 1998).

OTHER: "The Mystery Novel as Serious Business," *Armchair Detective: A Quarterly Journal Devoted to the Appreciation of Mystery, Detective, and Suspense Fiction,* 17 (Summer 1984): 250–254;

"Homosexuals. Universal Scapegoats," in *Murder Ink,* edited by Dilys Winn (New York: Workman Publishing, 1984), pp. 131–133;

"Matters Grave and Gay," in *Colloquium on Crime. Eleven Renowned Mystery Writers Discuss Their Work,* edited by Robin W. Winks (New York: Scribners, 1986), pp. 111–126;

"Autobiography, 1992," in *The Gay & Lesbian Literary Companion,* edited by Sharon Malinowski and Christa Brelin (Detroit, Washington, D.C. & London: Visible Ink Press, 1995), pp. 231–252.

Joseph Hansen is the father of the gay mystery novel. While the typical hero of the hard-boiled mystery novel before Hansen was tough, macho, and unquestionably heterosexual, Hansen expanded the genre by introducing Dave Brandstetter, tough, macho, and unabashedly homosexual. The mainstream reading public gradually embraced this unconventional detective and, even though Hansen had not planned to write about Brandstetter beyond the first novel, his daring creation unexpectedly became, as he put it in a 1991 interview with Peter Burton, his

"bread and butter" as well as his claim to fame and was featured eventually in twelve novels and two short stories. Hansen's expressed goal was to turn gay stereotypes and clichés on their heads: "I wanted to correct as many misapprehensions ordinary mortals have about homosexuals and the way they live as I could in the space of fifty thousand words."

While admiring Dashiell Hammett, Raymond Chandler, and Ross Macdonald, Hansen felt that "there was room in the form to say important things about men and women and how they cope with life." Asked by Burton to characterize his writing, Hansen responded: "I am a homosexual, and I write largely about homosexuals because I believe I am able to do this with some accuracy, and can throw some light on a segment of our society that is poorly understood and badly treated." By combining suspenseful storytelling with an enlightening view of gay life, he extended the boundaries of the hard-boiled detective story, opening the door for such mystery writers as Nathan Aldyne, Steve Johnson, Grant Michaels, Michael Nava, Richard Stevenson, John Morgan Wilson, Mark Richard Zubro, R. D. Zimmerman, Katherine V. Forrest, Ellen Hart, and Sandra Scoppettone.

Joseph Hansen was born on 19 July 1923 in Aberdeen, South Dakota, as the youngest of three children of Henry Harold Hansen, the owner of a shoe store, and Alma Rosebrock Hansen. Hansen discovered his love for the written word at an early age. When he was seven years old, he was forced to stay in bed for eight months because of a strep infection, and he devoured Carl Sandburg's *Abraham Lincoln: The Prairie Years* (1926). In 1932 the Hansen family felt the impact of the Great Depression and scattered for a while: Joseph's oldest sibling, Louise, moved to California while his brother, Bob, accompanied his father to Minneapolis. Nine-year-old Joseph stayed behind in Aberdeen with his mother and coped with dismal circumstances by writing "Philosophy from a Boy to Older Folks," an unpublished essay offering his ideas on how to improve the plight of the country.

In 1933 Hansen and his mother joined his father and brother in Minneapolis, where he immersed himself in sports. After three years the Hansen family pulled up roots yet again and joined Louise and her new husband, Joe Hubbard, in Altadena, California. Living in a one-room cabin soon caused friction, and Hansen, his parents, and brother moved to Pasadena, where he discovered his love for classical music and became involved in the boys' choir of an Episcopal church. Hansen also appeared in school plays, won awards for public speaking, and wrote articles for the John Marshall Junior High School paper, eventually serving as its editor. In "Autobiography, 1992," his autobiographical sketch included in *The Gay & Lesbian Literary Companion* (1995), Hansen explains that in an attempt to squelch his budding homosexuality and to escape "a whole new set of impulses I didn't want and couldn't handle," he entered an intensely religious phase and, reaching "a peak of hysteria," even considered becoming a minister.

Hansen's religious phase came to an end when he left high school for Pasadena Junior College. He developed a new circle of sophisticated friends who opened his eyes and ears to the works of William Shakespeare, Edgar Allan Poe, Henry David Thoreau, Ralph Waldo Emerson, James Joyce, Jean Cocteau, Arthur Rimbaud, Charles Baudelaire, Erik Satie, and Igor Stravinsky. Hansen was startled and delighted by Walt Whitman's frank treatment of homosexuality. Feeling more free to be himself, he soon entered into an intimate relationship with Robert Ben Ali, a local playwright and director of plays who, he remarks in his autobiographical sketch, "saw to it that I got an education in theater." When Hansen was drafted to serve in World War II, he avoided conscription by declaring his homosexuality, an event he later described in his first Brandstetter mystery, *Fadeout* (1970), as well as in the autobiographical novel *Job's Year* (1983).

In the early 1940s Hansen wrote plays and poems while drifting from one job to the next. Having worked for a radio station, a newspaper, an art gallery, and a library, Hansen found a more stable job in 1943 as a clerk in the Pickwick Bookshop on Hollywood Boulevard, which enabled him to move into his own apartment. His relationship with Ben Ali came to an end when Hansen met Jane Bancroft, an aircraft plant worker, at the bookstore. In his autobiographical sketch he describes his first impression of his future wife: "Slender, narrow-hipped, tall for a girl, she wore bell-bottom jeans and cut her hair short like a boy's. I found her a treat to look at. . . . Here was a bright new friend to learn from." They shared interests in philosophy, literature, music, and painting and soon discovered their love for each other; they were married on 4 August 1943 and their daughter, Barbara, was born in July 1944. When Houghton Mifflin optioned a novel Hansen was writing and paid him a $500 advance, his dream of seeing his work in print seemed to become a reality, only to be dashed when the publisher decided against publication of the finished product.

In order to support his family, Hansen started to work as a clerk/typist in the shipping department of a film-processing plant in Hollywood, a job he held for the next ten years. Finding it more and more difficult to believe in his future as a writer, he started composing folk songs, put together a weekly radio program featuring folk music, and released a couple of record

Dust jacket for Hansen's 1970 novel, which introduced the gay insurance investigator Dave Brandstetter

albums of his songs in the early 1950s. In 1955 he wrote the scripts for two episodes of the popular television series "Lassie," but the working conditions disillusioned him to such a degree that he decided never to write for television again. In 1956 Hansen's luck changed when several of his poems about his childhood in South Dakota were published in periodicals, including *The Saturday Review* and *The New Yorker*. Encouraged by these publications, Hansen devoted himself increasingly to his writing. He quit his job at the film-processing plant and took a four-hour-a-night job at a bookstore in Los Angeles.

In the early 1960s Hansen was introduced by his friend and lover, Wayne Placek, to Don Slater, a gay activist who edited *ONE*, a small groundbreaking magazine for homosexuals. When Slater published several of Hansen's short stories, he did so under the pseudonym "James Colton," a precautionary measure designed to protect the writer and the magazine from prosecution.

As Hansen remarks in his autobiographical sketch, "Though by today's standards as chaste as a Sunday school paper, yet simply because of its subject matter, *ONE* sometimes ran into trouble with authorities, postal and other." Hansen kept this nom de plume when he submitted his first novel, "Valley Boy," to several publishers. As this novel did not follow the "tacitly agreed-upon formula of earlier homosexual novels—sin, suffering, and suicide," it was rejected by publishers. Eventually it was published as *Lost on Twilight Road* (1964) by a small California publishing company, National Library, specializing in pulp pornography.

Having finally found an outlet for his writing, even if it was less than reputable, Hansen published seven additional erotic pulp novels and a collection of short stories that had originally appeared in *ONE*. While his publishers insisted on including some graphic sex scenes, Hansen made sure that his homosexual characters were portrayed in a positive light and without the formulaic tragic ending. One of these novels, *Known Homosexual* (1968), was his first attempt at the mystery genre. Hansen considered this book, which featured a gay murder victim as well as several gay characters, to be of a better quality than his other pulp novels and republished it without the obligatory sex scenes under his own name as *Stranger to Himself* in 1978 and as *Pretty Boy Dead* in 1984. While this mystery novel does not feature a detective, it revolves around the love affair between the African American protagonist, Steve Archer, and the white murder victim, Coy Randol, foreshadowing Brandstetter's interracial relationship with television reporter Cecil Harris.

In 1965 Hansen was named editor of *ONE,* and he decided to change the direction of the magazine; his opinion that it was time to educate the straight public caused a rift with Don Slater, and Hansen launched *Tangents.* For the next five years he wrote editorials, articles, book reviews, and stories directed, above all, at a homosexual audience while his wife contributed an advice column as well as worked on the design of the magazine. As other publications entered the gay marketplace, the subscription base for *Tangents* eroded, and the magazine ceased to exist in 1970.

In the same year that Hansen's magazine folded, Joan Kahn, the courageous mystery editor at Harper and Row, accepted *Fadeout* for publication, launching Hansen's Brandstetter series and his mainstream literary career. Hansen at first could not believe his luck and feared that this publication by a major publishing house was a fluke. He wrote two more sexually graphic pulp novels under his pen name James Colton for Olympia Press, *The Outward Side* and *Todd,* both published in 1971. Hansen, however, should not have worried because the reviewers treated *Fadeout* kindly and

embraced its openly gay protagonist, the insurance investigator Dave Brandstetter.

Hansen told Jean W. Ross in 1986 that his goal was "to write a truly orthodox mystery novel this time and make the detective—more or less in the tough-guy mold of the detectives of Ross Macdonald, Raymond Chandler, and Dashiell Hammett—a homosexual; because it was, as far as public opinion is concerned, the least likely sort of profession that could be given to a homosexual." Brandstetter's approach to investigating the mysterious disappearance of Fox Olson, a closeted writer and musician, is analytical and detached. Even though in the midst of a deep personal crisis—the death of his longtime lover—the insurance investigator keeps a cool head and pursues the truth with dogged determination. He ignores homophobic slurs and turns to physical violence only as a last resort.

"The whole novel," Hansen told Ross, is "a headstand." When Fox Olson is found shot to death, his lover, Doug Sawyer, is suspected of killing him during a quarrel. Brandstetter's investigation, however, reveals that Fox's brother-in-law has embezzled funds from his employer and has shot Fox in cold blood for the insurance money. Whereas the heterosexual characters commit adultery, blackmail, bribery, embezzlement, and murder, the gay lovers appear as decent, kind, and faithful—a deliberate reversal of conventional "clichés and popular misconceptions." Even though the book sold poorly initially and even though Hansen had not conceived Brandstetter as a recurring character, the positive critical reception of the novel encouraged him to bring the detective back in *Death Claims* (1973) and *Troublemaker* (1975).

In order to supplement the meager royalties his mysteries yielded, Hansen published two historical gothic novels—*Tarn House* (1971) and *Longleaf* (1974)—as "Rose Brock," his mother's maiden name. In 1974 Hansen was thrilled when he received a grant from the National Endowment for the Arts for an extended stay in London, where he reveled in the cultural life of the city and made many friends. He planned to write a large, serious novel, but his writing faltered. Upon his return to Los Angeles he put the unfinished manuscript in a drawer and regained his confidence by returning to Brandstetter. To Hansen's consternation Joan Kahn as well as fourteen publishing houses rejected the fourth Brandstetter mystery before Henry Holt acquired *The Man Everybody Was Afraid Of* (1978) for publication. In addition to his writing, Hansen taught classes in writing, first at the Beyond Baroque Foundation in Hollywood and later at the University of California, Irvine; at UCLA; and at the writers conference of Wesleyan University in Connecticut.

In 1980 Hansen's new publisher began to republish the earlier Brandstetter mysteries as paperbacks, winning the gay investigator new readers. Increasing book sales indicated that Hansen had tapped a rich vein, and he published Brandstetter mysteries at regular intervals until 1991: *Skinflick* (1979), *Gravedigger* (1982), *Nightwork* (1984), *The Little Dog Laughed* (1986), *Early Graves* (1987), *Obedience* (1988), *The Boy Who Was Buried This Morning* (1990), and *A Country of Old Men: The Last Dave Brandstetter Mystery* (1991). During these years he also wrote autobiographical novels, *A Smile in His Lifetime* (1981) and *Job's Year* (1983), as well as non-Brandstetter mysteries, *Backtrack* (1982) and *Bohannon's Book* (1988).

Commentators such as Robert A. Baker and David Geherin have stressed the unity of the Brandstetter series and have suggested that the mysteries should be read as one continuing novel since in their totality they provide a multifaceted picture of the gay existence in post-Stonewall America. Brandstetter's character develops and matures over a span of twenty years and is shaped by the societal and cultural changes of the 1970s and 1980s. When the reader first meets him in *Fadeout,* the forty-five-year-old Brandstetter has lost his lover of twenty years, Rod Fleming, to cancer and has given up the will to live. His job as a death-claims investigator at Medallion Life, the insurance company owned by his father, however, forces Brandstetter to rejoin the living. His long-term commitment to a single partner stands in marked contrast to his father's nine marriages to younger and younger women, undermining the common notion that gay men lead more promiscuous lives than heterosexuals.

As *Death Claims* opens, Brandstetter has entered into a rocky relationship with Doug Sawyer, the murder suspect he had cleared in *Fadeout.* Doug is mourning the death of his previous lover as well, a French race-car driver who was killed at LeMans, and the ghosts of the dead lovers haunt the new relationship. In *Skinflick* Brandstetter not only has to deal with the breakup of their three-year-old relationship but also with the death of his father and consequently the loss of his job at Medallion Life Insurance because of homophobia. He begins to freelance for Sequoia Life and in *Gravedigger* enters into a long-term relationship with Cecil Harris, a twenty-one-year-old African American television reporter, whom he had first met eighteen months earlier in *The Man Everybody Was Afraid Of* but whom he had rejected then because of his age. Cecil is Brandstetter's life partner for the remaining six mysteries, at times serving as his sidekick and assisting him with his investigations. At the beginning of *Obedience,* Brandstetter is ready to notify those insurance companies he has been freelancing

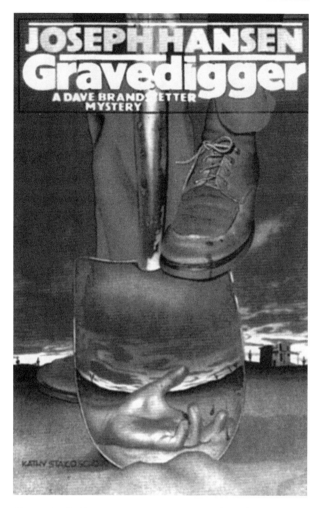

Dust jacket for Hansen's sixth Brandstetter novel (1982), in which the investigator begins a long-term relationship with Cecil Harris, an African American television reporter

for that he plans to give up his sleuthing, but he is eventually coaxed out of retirement for two final cases. At the end of *A Country of Old Men: The Last Dave Brandstetter Mystery,* age catches up with the detective and he apparently succumbs to a heart attack: "he couldn't breathe, and the pain was fierce, and it was morning, so it wasn't supposed to be dark, but it was dark as night."

While the sympathetic portrayal of the well-adjusted Brandstetter serves Hansen's goal to convince his readers that gay men and women are no different from other people, the author acknowledges the inevitable diversity within the gay community by including several unappealing gay characters. James Levin in *The Gay Novel in America* (1991) criticizes Hansen for his sometimes unflattering portrayals, for the novels include promiscuous, effeminate, as well as closeted gay men; fanatic gay activists; hustlers; and

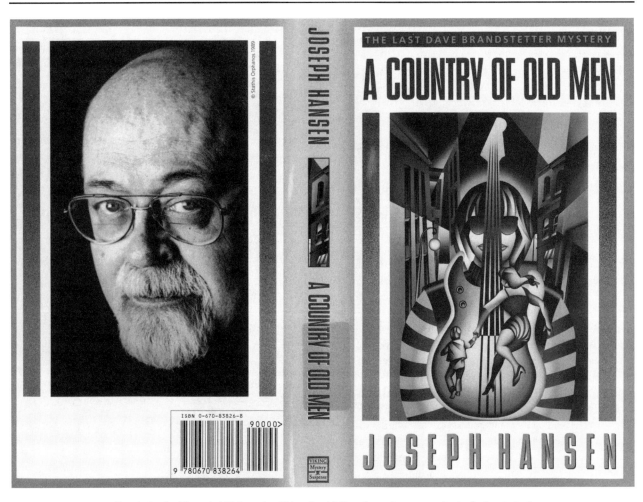

Dust jacket for Hansen's 1991 novel, which ends with Brandstetter's apparent death of a heart attack

transvestites. Two of his homosexual characters even commit murder. Commentators such as Jim Kepner and Ted-Larry Pebworth, however, have praised his courage. The early Brandstetter mysteries derive much of their suspense from the gradual uncovering of hidden homosexual relationships that have come back to haunt closeted characters. Starting in *The Man Everybody Was Afraid Of,* Hansen broadens his subject matter by including such topical hot-button issues as the smuggling of pre-Columbian pottery, religious fanaticism (*Skinflick* and *Gravedigger*), the porn industry (*Skinflick*), the illegal dumping of toxic waste (*Nightwork*), right-wing paramilitary groups (*The Little Dog Laughed* and *The Boy Who Was Killed This Morning*), AIDS (*Early Graves*), drug dealing and addiction (*Obedience, Death Claims,* and *A Country of Old Men*), Asian organized crime (*Obedience*), and child neglect (*A Country of Old Men*).

Hansen's writing is characterized by a subtle sense of irony, and his lean, terse prose as well as his atmospheric evocations of the Southern California landscape have been widely praised. *Fadeout,* for example, opens with a spare yet evocative description:

> Fog shrouded the canyon, a box canyon above a California ranch town called Pima. It rained. Not hard but steady and gray and dismal. Shaggy pines loomed through the mist like threats. Sycamores made white, twisted gestures above the arroyo. Down the arroyo water pounded, ugly, angry and deep. The road shouldered the arroyo. It was a bad road. The rains had chewed its edges. There were holes. Mud and rock half buried it in places. It was steep and winding and there were no guard rails.

Hansen's use of the third-person narrator in all Brandstetter mysteries ensures a detached perspective. In Robert A. Baker and Michael T. Nietzel's *Private Eyes: One Hundred and One Knights* (1985), Hansen encapsulated the objective technique he has observed in his series: "Let your characters live and move and have their beings. Never explain. Let what happens next do the explaining."

Since the apparent demise of Dave Brandstetter, Hansen has published *Bohannon's Country: Mystery Stories* (1993), featuring the rugged, heterosexual former deputy sheriff Hack Bohannon, who was introduced in *Bohannon's Book*. When he is not caring for the horses he keeps in a canyon on the California central coast, Bohannon solves crimes with the help of former rodeo rider George Stubba and the young student priest Manuel Rivera. Hansen's main focus, however, has been a series of novels he plans to write about Nathan Reed, a gay man whose experiences in Southern California are based on Hansen's own life. He has written two books in the series, *Living Upstairs* (1993) and *Jack of Hearts* (1995), which he plans to total twelve novels, covering Reed's life from age seventeen to seventy.

Hansen, like the fictional mystery writer Jack Helmers in *A Country of Old Men,* evidently yearns to write the great American novel instead of mysteries. Many Brandstetter devotees, however, will surely agree with the sentiment of the fan who writes to Helmer, "I love your [mystery] books, and do not want them to stop." Even if Hansen has made his final contribution to the hard-boiled genre, though, his importance is clear, for he not only expanded the field but also has made his own distinctive mark.

Interviews:

Jean W. Ross, interview with Joseph Hansen, in *Contemporary Authors. New Revision Series,* 16 (Detroit: Gale, 1986), pp. 155–158;

Peter Burton, "Joseph Hansen," in *Talking To . . .* (Exeter, U.K.: Third House Publishers, 1991), pp. 34–41.

References:

Robert A. Baker and Michael T. Nietzel, *Private Eyes: One Hundred and One Knights: A Survey of American Detective Fiction* (Bowling Green: Bowling Green University Popular Press, 1985), pp. 219–226;

Ernest Fontana, "Joseph Hansen's Anti-Pastoral Crime Fiction," *Clues: A Journal of Detection,* 7 (Spring–Summer 1986): 89–97;

David Geherin, *The American Private Eye: The Image in Fiction* (New York: Ungar, 1985), pp. 176–183;

James W. Jones, "Joseph Hansen," in *Contemporary Gay American Novelists. A Bio-Bibliographical Critical Sourcebook,* edited by Emmanuel S. Nelson (Westport, Conn.: Greenwood Press, 1993), pp. 189–196;

Jim Kepner, "Joseph Hansen," in *Gay and Lesbian Literature,* edited by Sharon Malinowski (Detroit & London: St. James Press, 1994), pp. 177–180;

Kepner, "Joseph Hansen," in *The Gay & Lesbian Literary Companion,* edited by Malinowski and Christa Brelin (Detroit, Washington, D.C., & London: Visible Ink Press, 1995), pp. 227–231;

James Levin, *The Gay Novel in America* (New York: Garland, 1991);

John R. Milton, "Literary or Not," *South Dakota Review,* 26 (Summer 1988): 3–5;

Ted-Larry Pebworth, *The Gay and Lesbian Literary Heritage,* edited by Claude J. Summers (New York: Holt, 1995), pp. 357–358, 500–504;

B. A. Pike, "Joseph Hansen," in *Detective Fiction,* edited by John Cooper and Pike (Somerset, U.K.: Barn Owl Books, 1988), pp. 90–92.

Chester Himes

(29 July 1909 – 12 November 1984)

Jeff Siegel

See also the Himes entries in *DLB 2: American Novelists Since World War II, First Series; DLB 76: Afro-American Writers, 1940–1955;* and *DLB 143: American Novelists Since World War II, Third Series.*

BOOKS: *If He Hollers, Let Him Go* (Garden City, N.Y.: Doubleday, Doran, 1945; London: Grey Walls Press, 1946);

Lonely Crusade (New York: Knopf, 1947; London: Falcon Press, 1950);

Cast the First Stone (New York: Coward-McCann, 1952); unexpurgated edition published as *Yesterday Will Make You Cry* (New York: Norton, 1998);

The Third Generation (Cleveland: World, 1954);

The Primitive (expurgated edition, New York: New American Library, 1956); unexpurgated edition published as *The End of a Primitive* (New York: Norton, 1997);

For Love of Imabelle (Greenwich, Conn.: Fawcett, 1957); republished as *A Rage in Harlem* (New York: Avon, 1965; London: Panther, 1969);

Il pleut des coups durs, translated by C. Wourgaft (Paris: Gallimard, 1958); original English version published as *The Real Cool Killers* (New York: Avon, 1959; London: Panther, 1969);

Couché dans le pain, translated by Janine Hérisson and Henri Robillot (Paris: Gallimard, 1959); original English version published as *The Crazy Kill* (New York: Avon, 1959; London: Panther, 1968);

Dare-dare, translated by Pierre Verrier (Paris: Gallimard, 1959); original English version published as *Run Man, Run* (New York: Putnam, 1966; London: Muller, 1967);

Tout pour plaire, translated by Yves Malartic (Paris: Gallimard, 1959); original English version published as *The Big Gold Dream* (New York: Avon, 1960; London: Panther, 1968);

Imbroglio nego, translated by Fillion (Paris: Gallimard, 1960); original English version published as *All Shot Up* (New York: Avon, 1960; London: Panther, 1969);

Chester Himes (Collection of Joseph S. Himes Jr.)

Ne nous énervons pas! translated by Fillion (Paris: Gallimard, 1961); original English version published as *The Heat's On* (New York: Putnam, 1966; London: Muller, 1966); republished as *Come Back, Charleston Blue* (New York: Dell, 1967; Harmondsworth, U.K.: Penguin, 1974);

Pinktoes (Paris: Olympia, 1961; expurgated edition, New York: Putnam/Stein & Day, 1965; London: Barker, 1965);

Une affaire de viol, translated by André Mathieu (Paris: Editions Les Yeux Ouverts, 1963); original English version published as *A Case of Rape* (New York: Targ, 1980);

Retour en Afrique, translated by Pierre Sergent (Paris: Plon, 1964); original English edition published as *Cotton Comes to Harlem* (New York: Putnam, 1965; London: Muller, 1966);

Blind Man with a Pistol (New York: Morrow, 1969; London: Hodder & Stoughton, 1969); republished as *Hot Day, Hot Night* (New York: Dell, 1970);

The Quality of Hurt: The Autobiography of Chester Himes (Garden City, N.Y.: Doubleday, 1972; London: Joseph, 1973);

Black on Black: Baby Sister and Selected Writings (Garden City, N.Y.: Doubleday, 1973; London: Joseph, 1975);

My Life of Absurdity: The Autobiography of Chester Himes (Garden City, N.Y.: Doubleday, 1977);

Plan B, translated by Hélène Devaux-Minié (Paris: Lieu Commun, 1983); original English version published as *Plan B: A Novel,* edited, with an introduction, by Michel Fabre and Robert E. Skinner (Jackson: University Press of Mississippi, 1993);

Un Joli coup de lune, translated by Devaux-Minié (Paris: Lieu Commun, 1988);

The Collected Stories of Chester Himes (New York: Thunder's Mouth, 1990).

In 1957 Chester Himes was so down and out in Paris that he was ready to write almost anything to make a buck—even a detective novel. Himes was at that point a "serious" novelist who had never written what the French called a *roman policier.* Instead, he had written five post–World War II protest novels in the style of Richard Wright that had earned him a reputation as a talented, alienated, and bitter young man. But these books, which included *If He Hollers, Let Him Go* (1945) and *Lonely Crusade* (1947), had not earned Himes any money. Their commercial failure had increased his bitterness and alienation and was one of the reasons he had left the United States and became an expatriate in 1953. When Marcel Duhamel, the editor of Gallimard's prestigious La Serie Noire (Black Series), told Himes he would buy a thriller in the tradition of Dashiell Hammett and Raymond Chandler, he started writing.

Himes wrote the first seven chapters, as he recalls in the first volume of his autobiography, *The Quality of Hurt* (1972), quickly and easily. He based the action on a classic con game that he heard about from another black expatriate in Paris. Always, he kept in mind Duhamel's advice: first, keep yourself out of it; second, always give the action in detail, like a movie; and third, avoid stream of consciousness—the reader does not care who is thinking what. Himes took the first eighty pages and brought them to Duhamel, who was pleased with the beginning but pointed out that Himes had not included any detectives—a necessary ingredient for the

genre. Himes then went back to his typewriter and created Grave Digger Jones and Coffin Ed Johnson, the two toughest cops in the history of American literature.

Grave Digger and Coffin Ed can trust no one but each other—not their colleagues, who hate them because they are black, and not Harlem, which fears them because they enforce the white man's law. This fundamental relationship between the detectives and their world is the basis of what Himes called his seven Harlem domestic novels. Himes's approach to the genre makes him more than just another overlooked mystery writer or an African American author who never got his due because of his color. It makes him an important American writer whose work revolves around the touchstone of postmodern American life—race relations in the United States.

During the course of his career Himes was taken to task by many black critics for his unflattering portraits of Harlem life—his pimps and grifters and con artists as well as the high yellow women who provide their deadly motivation. Many white critics dismissed Himes as a genre writer, not noticing that his work rarely includes a traditional puzzle and that Coffin Ed and Grave Digger rarely use traditional genre methods to solve the crime. In their efforts to enforce their respective literary laws, the critics often did not see what Himes really wrote about—whether it was possible for black and white to live together in the United States. His Harlem domestic novels are protest books that have been stripped of their affectations; they are genre works that have been infused with a greater sense of purpose. As critic James Sallis suggests in *Difficult Lives: Jim Thompson, David Goodis, Chester Himes* (1993), Himes's Harlem books are almost a literary form unto themselves.

Himes, who died in 1984, would not be surprised that critics have been slow to recognize the serious purpose infusing his detective novels, for while he was alive he always felt his work was misunderstood and underappreciated. This attitude is so characteristic of Himes that it is one of the few established truths about him. Getting a handle on the facts of his life is difficult, made so not only by his poverty and his incessant wanderings throughout the United States and Europe but also by Himes's perverse interpretation of what was important. He wrote two volumes of autobiography—*The Quality of Hurt* and *My Life of Absurdity* (1977)—but they are more notable for what they do not include than for what they do. Although he details his womanizing, his drinking, and his criminal youth with an unapologetic forthrightness that verges on exaggeration, Himes spends little time discussing the creative process. He provides few insights into why he started writing, into the creation of the Harlem domestic novels, and even fewer into his

Himes (lower right) with his parents, Joseph and Estelle, and his brothers, Joseph Jr. (left) and Edward

most famous creations, Grave Digger and Coffin Ed. Instead, and especially in *My Life of Absurdity,* there are long passages about meals, pets, an especially recalcitrant Jaguar he bought with his movie money, and his search for a house.

What is known is that Chester Bomar Himes was born on 29 July 1909 in Jefferson City, Missouri, the youngest of three sons. His parents–Joseph Sandy Himes and Estelle Bomar Himes–did not care much for each other, a fact that colored Himes's private and professional persona for the rest of his life. His father was a darkly colored black man, while his mother was so light she could have passed for white at a time when that was an appealing option for many blacks tired of segregation and Jim Crow. She claimed she could trace her lineage back to the white family that had owned her grandparents, and this difference–which was tied up in the social structure of middle-class black America before the Civil Rights movement–meant that Estelle thought she was entitled to think she was better than Joseph.

It was an advantage she used at every opportunity. When Chester was a young boy and Joseph taught

history and metal trades at African American colleges in the South, Estelle's contempt for her husband, his work, and anyone associated with his nonwhite institution helped to make the Himeses' stay a short one. When Chester was in high school and poverty forced the Himeses to live with Joseph's family in Cleveland, Estelle threw her husband's failure in his face in front of his family. Not only was he not good enough as a teacher, she said, but he certainly was not good enough as a menial laborer. Their two-odd decades together were a vicious dance that spared no one, certainly not their youngest son. Himes often watched as his parents hit each other and tried to break up their fights when he was old enough to do so. Eddie, the oldest, was ten years his brother's senior and left home as soon as he could. Joseph, only a year older than Chester and his close friend, was blinded in a school accident when the brothers were teenagers, and his blindness seems to have spared him much of his parents' violence. Their home life did not derail the Himes children's ambition. Eddie became a leader in a waiters' union and put his brother up when he visited New York after World War II. Joseph became an important sociologist, so respected that he was even allowed to speak at white colleges in the South in the 1950s.

Himes blamed himself for Joseph's blindness, which occurred as a result of a science experiment gone awry. Chester, who was being punished by his mother, was not allowed to participate, forcing Joseph to complete the experiment without his brother's help. Himes was convinced, he later wrote, that if he had been there to assist his brother the accident would not have happened. This pattern–accepting both the responsibility and the almost paralyzing guilt for an action–not only haunted Himes for the rest of his life but also is integral to the characters he created.

Himes and his family, after an almost nomadic existence in the South, arrived in Cleveland in the mid 1920s. In 1926 Himes graduated from Glenville High School and got a job as a busboy at Wade Park Manor Hotel. Hotel employees during Prohibition, as Richard Wright detailed in *Black Boy* (1945), provided a host of services that were not part of their official duties. They procured liquor and prostitutes for guests, directed them to speakeasies and gambling houses, and were available for running errands and providing small favors. In most cases they were well paid for their efforts, and Himes was no exception. He was making more money than his father, spending little time at home, and frequenting the illegal saloons and dice parlors that dotted Cleveland's black ghetto, especially the Bucket of Blood section around Scovill Avenue. He writes in *The Quality of Hurt* that he acquired a nickname, Little Katzi, and became a feared and respected man who had a reputation for violence and was considered capable of murder–an anecdote that, like many others in Himes's autobiographies, may or may not be true. More important, Himes acted as if it were true.

Two incidents interrupted Himes's burgeoning career as a teenaged gangster. The first occurred in 1926, when he fell down an elevator shaft at the hotel while working and suffered serious back injuries. He had to wear a brace for almost a year, and his back bothered him the rest of his life. Because the hotel was at fault in the accident, he received a pension from the state that enabled him to quit his job that fall and enroll in Ohio State University in Columbus.

Himes broadened his horizons at Ohio State but not in the classroom. Again, he was angered and confused by the system of northern segregation that allowed him to attend the school but not to live on campus in the university dormitories. Forced to live off-campus in the African American ghetto of Columbus, he soon started associating with the same sort of people that he had in Cleveland. He tells several stories about luring women classmates to after-hours bars and speakeasies and shocking these more proper and mid-

dle-class students. Although he had done reasonably well in African American schools in the South and in Cleveland, he failed all of his courses in the first quarter and dropped out of school in the second quarter because of several disciplinary matters, including the incidents with the female students.

When Himes returned to Cleveland, he fell back into the same life he had before he left. He became involved with people who took drugs, sold bootleg whiskey, and pimped. He had been arrested for passing bad checks with phony student identification in Columbus, and a lenient judge had paroled him into his father's custody–a decision that did not turn out to be the advantage it seemed. His parents had finally divorced, but Himes was forced to live with his father because of the judge's ruling. The sight of his father, broken and bitter, erased what little self-restraint he had left. Himes wrote that he would do "anything to keep away from that room that stank of my father's fear and defeat."

Although Himes had committed a few minor thefts before, including stealing five pistols from a national guard armory, he had not been involved in a serious crime before returning to live with his father. In one of his haunts in Cleveland, Himes overheard a black chauffeur discussing the amount of money and jewels that his employer, a man named Samuel Miller, kept in the house. This boasting, wrote Himes, was not unusual. Black domestics often bragged about their employers' wealth in order to impress other blacks. Himes made a note of the employer's name, cased the house, and picked a snowy night in November to rob it. He tells the tale of his crime in *The Quality of Hurt* in a deadpan, matter-of-fact style. He surprised the Millers, forced them to open their safe, took some cash and a reported $10,000 in jewels, and then stole the Miller's Cadillac and drove away through the snow.

Himes was arrested in Chicago two days later. He had tried to pawn one of the jewels, and a suspicious shop owner had called police. Himes is not clear on what he was doing in Chicago. He had driven the Cadillac to a Cleveland train station, where he bought a ticket to Chicago with an ill-formed plan of fencing the jewels and then fleeing to Mexico. On a deeper level, Himes must have known he could not carry out his plan, writing in his autobiography, "But I couldn't run; I could never run. I have always been afraid that that one stupid mental block is going to get me killed."

The Chicago police arrested Himes not for his crime in Cleveland but for an unsolved burglary in Chicago. They tried to beat a confession out of him, wrote Himes, and kept beating him when he would only confess to the Cleveland crime. Eventually, he was returned to Cleveland to be sentenced. The twenty-year term the judge pronounced was harsh but not surprisingly so. He was a black man convicted of robbing a white couple; he had a record; and he was already on probation. Yet, Himes was puzzled and angered by the jail sentence: "He had hurt me in a way that I would never get over, I thought."

Paradoxically, prison gave Himes the freedom to write. He was free of his parents and their constant fighting, free of the streets and his hoodlum pals, and free of self-doubt. The Ohio state penitentiary at the beginning of the depression was a brutal and violent place, and it forced Himes to create a new identity for himself in order to survive. He never discusses specifically why he started writing, although he says that the other prisoners did not harass cons who wrote. Himes's high-school diploma and six months of college put him far above most of his illiterate and uneducated colleagues.

Himes served seven and a half years of hard time, of menial labor, overcrowding, and endless days of the stupid, petty, violent grievances of prison life. His descriptions of that existence in his short stories and in the novel *Cast the First Stone* (1952) usually come back to the idea of time and the inmates' attempts to kill it. For many of the prisoners, too much time translated into trouble, into knife fights and brawls in the prison yard. "The only effect [prison] had on me," Himes wrote, "was to convince me that people will do anything—white people, black people, all people." Between 1932 and his release in 1936, he sold eight stories and probably worked on a half-dozen more. That pace almost certainly kept him at a desk writing, away from the other cons and their ability to turn an everyday argument into a fatal stabbing.

The centerpiece of Himes's prison writing is the short story "To What Red Hell," published in *Esquire* in October 1934. It was his second story in the magazine, a home for top-rate fiction. He had sold his first story, "His Last Day," an account of a man about to die in the electric chair, to *Abbott's Monthly* in November 1932, and *Abbott's* and other African American magazines and newspapers were regularly publishing his work. Most of the pieces he wrote were prison sketches, but he also wrote an occasional romance and shifted toward crime stories as he became more confident in his ability.

"To What Red Hell" is a fictionalized account of the fire in the Ohio penitentiary on Easter Monday in 1930. The fire killed 317 inmates in their cells in less than an hour, and it touched off nine days of rioting in response to the conditions that made so many deaths possible. In Himes's hands, the fire is not only terrifying but also symbolic of the purgatory people live in on earth. Jimmy, the protagonist, is a former war hero and championship boxer who is paralyzed by the crisis,

unable to do any more than wander the yard as men die around him. The story marks one of the first times that Himes addresses the theme that is central to all of his subsequent writing: how racism incapacitates the black man. Jimmy should be able to help and has helped in the past, but now he cannot. All of of Himes's characters, especially Grave Digger and Coffin Ed, eventually face circumstances in which they must will themselves to act. The system, in which a man is judged solely by the color of his skin, has broken Jimmy because he is the wrong color and by breaking him has made him incapable of action. The irony—for there is always irony in Himes's work—is that the system now needs Jimmy.

Himes was paroled in 1936 and bounced around the country for the next two decades before leaving for his self-imposed exile in France. The record of his personal and professional lives is clouded in a haze of myth and contradiction. He wrote; he drank; and he had affairs with women who were almost always white and matched him neurosis for neurosis. That he was married in 1937 to a black woman named Jean Lucinda Johnson was never more than a minor inconvenience. Himes supported himself in the Los Angeles shipyards during World War II, and he lived in tenements and flop houses in Harlem, working as a janitor and caretaker. He spent a few months in 1948 at Yaddo Writer's Colony in Saratoga Springs, accepted favors from people such as Louis Bromfield and Blanche Knopf, and endured a hellish summer in the southern California desert living in a shack without running water. Most importantly, he seethed against a system that seemed to conspire against him. Himes was not an easy man to get along with, and he made enemies who bore him lifelong grudges.

Himes published his first novel, *If He Hollers, Let Him Go,* in 1945 and his second, *Lonely Crusade,* two years later. Each expanded on the theme first broached in "To What Red Hell"—that racism was not just absurd but that it was the single most important problem facing American society. Significantly, Himes advanced his thesis without suggesting that there was any way to solve the problems posed by racism. He rejected every possible political solution, including capitalism, communism, liberalism, and trade unionism.

In *If He Hollers, Let Him Go* Bob Jones, who supervises other black workers at a Los Angeles shipyard, seems to embody everything for which the African American middle class can hope. His life falls apart, however, when he is accused of raping a white employee at the shipyard, who may or may not have been raped and who has previously attempted to seduce Jones. Nothing that anyone does—Jones, his influential friends in the African American community,

Himes, with the French writer Fred Kassak, receiving the Grand Prix de la Litterature Policiere in 1958. Himes was the first American to win the prestigious award for detective fiction published in France (© Universal Photo 23039 Edimedia).

or the white liberals who hear about his case—can save him from what seems to be a preordained fate. Lee Gordon, the trade-union organizer in *Lonely Crusade,* seems just as trapped, but he walks into his undoing more or less willingly, making him more of a martyr and less of a victim than Jones. Gordon organizes the black workers at an aircraft plant, where his opposition includes not only the company but also the white members of the union and the Communist Party, the last personified by another of Himes's sexually perverse white women. Gordon knows he will almost certainly fail, but he makes the attempt anyway—for Himes, an upbeat ending.

Both novels produced passionate responses, pro and con, but Himes was especially conscious of the savage criticism he received. He recalled the reception of his second book in *The Quality of Hurt:* "The left hated it, the right hated it, Jews hated it, blacks hated it. I think that what the great body of Americans most disliked was the fact that I came too close to the truth." The vitriolic criticism reached its height in the 9 September 1947 issue of *New Masses.* Lloyd W. Brown accused Himes of "pandering to every depraved element of white chauvinism" and in the course of his review likened him to the racist Mississippi senator Theodore Bilbo as well as to Uncle Tom and "the nameless

wretched slave who betrayed Nat Turner and his people." The U.S. Communist Party, still influential with the Left, actually called for a boycott of *Lonely Crusade.* Himes, always ready to believe the worst, was even convinced that his publishers—Doubleday for *If He Hollers, Let Him Go* and Knopf for *Lonely Crusade*—had made conscious efforts to sabotage the books.

In the summer of 1948 Himes appeared at the University of Chicago, then one of the great bastions of American liberalism, to discuss the role of the black writer in American society. Himes told the audience that African American writers in the United States faced three conflicts. The first conflict, he argued, is that if the writer is honest, the truth about his oppression will be self-degrading. American racism, he maintained, cannot be rationalized as a human problem or as an African problem because it exists only in America. The black writer "will realize in the end that he possesses this heritage of slavery; he is a product of this American culture; his thoughts and emotions and reactions have been fashioned by his American environment." Second, he argued that the American marketplace for all its openness places constraints on the writer's honesty and on writing truly about race. Publishers are reluctant to buy honest books because they do not want to offend readers, and editors, no matter how well-meaning, are so ignorant about the obstacles facing the black writer that they assume the honest writer is psychotic. Finally, the black writer who does manage to be heard will be reviled by black and white alike for telling a truth the audience does not want to hear. Black readers, especially, will not appreciate the honesty. "The American Negro, we must remember," Himes told the audience, "is an American. The face may be the face of Africa, but the heart has the beat of Wall Street." More than one critic has noted that Himes left his audience stunned and shell-shocked.

Himes continued his pattern of drinking and philandering and permanently separated from his wife in spring 1952 (divorced 1978). He never wrote the protest novel he owed Knopf after *Lonely Crusade,* and what he finally published—*Cast the First Stone* in 1952 and *The Third Generation* in 1954—were more works of autobiography than protest, the first an account of prison life featuring a white protagonist and the second a chronicle of a black family with three sons, a strong mother, and a weak father. In 1953, with the money from the European sale of *Lonely Crusade* and the advance for *Third Generation,* Himes left the United States for France. For all practical purposes, he never returned, though he did keep his American citizenship.

Once in France, Himes began an affair almost immediately with a white woman (he called her Alva in his autobiography, though that was not her name) and quickly wrote *The Primitive* (1956), his final and most compelling protest novel, in which he pays back everyone he ever thought slighted him: New York publishers, Jews, homosexuals, white women, and the black middle class. The publisher, New American Library, changed the title from Himes's original "The End of a Primitive" and edited the work extensively, but the editing did not diminish the power of the novel. Kriss Cummings and Jesse Robinson once spent a weekend together, which leads them to spend another week together in Manhattan in the middle of the 1950s. Kriss is lonely, bored, and a drunk; Jesse—a writer with more than a passing resemblance to Himes—is lonely, angry, and a drunk. Himes turns the two inside out, ripping away the scab of polite camaraderie that passes for race relations between them, and then turns up the heat. The violent denouement is sad and pathetic, but eminently logical.

In 1957 Himes took up Marcel Duhamel's offer to publish a *roman policier.* In *The Primitive* Himes evidently had exorcised the demon that insisted that white women play a crucial role in his work. White women are missing from the Harlem novels, and the books are better for it, though Himes got little credit from his detractors for eliminating one of their most serious objections. Sex and women, however, do play a key role in the Harlem novels. Rather than rely on the stereotyp-

ical femme fatale, Himes's handling of sex and women fits neatly into his vision of an America divided by race and by its inability to heal this division. In Himes's view, the only relationship between the sexes is sex.

In the early Harlem books, Himes backs off a little from the racial abyss of his protest novels, finding a new way to explore his theme. These books—starting with *For Love of Imabelle* (1957) and more or less including *The Real Cool Killers* (1959; originally published as *Il pleut des coups durs,* 1958), *The Crazy Kill* (1959; originally published as *Couché dans le pain,* 1959), *The Big Gold Dream* (1960; originally published as *Tout pour plaire,* 1959), and *All Shot Up* (1960; originally published as *Imbroglio nego,* 1960)—are not utopian visions of race relations nor even white liberal versions of race relations, which is what Himes's critics demanded he write. Himes spares no one: not the African American elite, who mouth support for integration and yet have a substantial financial stake in segregation; not the white establishment, which will integrate only on its own, heavily discounted, terms; and hardly anyone else in between. In Himes's eyes, everyone is complicit in the sickness of the society; everyone is guilty. His rogue preachers, crooked cops, bureaucratic social workers, two-bit hustlers, cheap grifters, and high yellow women—especially his high yellow women—are too busy scamming and conning to worry about integration and race relations.

The only characters in the Harlem novels concerned with the issue of racial justice are Grave Digger and Coffin Ed, who strive mightily and violently—the bodies often pile up with a Spillane-like frequency—to maintain order and keep the peace and to protect the downtrodden. Of course, achieving racial harmony through violence is self-defeating, a fact Himes begins to suggest in his later work, beginning with *Cotton Comes to Harlem* (1965; originally published as *Retour en Afrique,* 1964). In *Blind Man with a Pistol* (1969), considered to be Himes's most sophisticated Harlem book, the detectives are reduced to shooting at rats as a race riot goes on around them. At the end of *Blind Man with a Pistol,* the final complete Harlem novel, they are no longer the larger-than-life figures who stood in front of the Savoy Hotel in *For Love of Imabelle* but garbage men, and the goals they worked for in the first couple of books seem as silly and pathetic as the blind man with a pistol who starts the riot by shooting up an elevated train. Himes was continuing to escalate his portrayal of a disintegrating society in the unfinished Harlem novel, *Plan B: A Novel* (1993; originally published in French as *Plan B,* 1983), in which America is engulfed in a race war that forces Grave Digger and Coffin Ed to take opposite sides.

By their appearance Grave Digger and Coffin Ed do not seem to be the kind of men who can solve America's race problems. Himes never made it clear how much he may have based the characters on real-life models. In 1933 he had written a short story, "He Knew," featuring a pair of black cops, one of whom was named Jones. He claimed in a 1972 interview with Michael Mok that the duo were based on a pair of Watts policemen he had known during the war. Regardless, Grave Digger and Coffin Ed are tall, loose-jointed, sloppily dressed, ordinary-looking dark brown men who wear shabby gray overcoats and misshapen snap-brim hats. Himes is fond of writing that they look like two farmers in town for the day to attend the county fair. There are, though, depths to each character—violent, unseen, and impenetrable depths. "You've got to be tough to be a colored cop up in Harlem," says Lieutenant Anderson, a white cop who commands the night shift at the duo's Harlem precinct, but not even Anderson knows how tough tough can be. In *For Love of Imabelle,* the reader soon learns of the reputation Grave Digger and Coffin Ed have established:

> Grave Digger stood on the right side of the front end of the line, at the entrance to the Savoy. Coffin Ed stood on the left side of the line, at the rear end. Grave Digger had his pistol aimed south, in a straight line down the sidewalk. On the other side, Coffin Ed had his pistol aimed north, in a straight line. There was space enough between the two imaginary lines for two persons to stand side by side. Whenever anyone moved out of line, Grave Digger would shout, "Straighten up!" and Coffin Ed would echo "Count off!" If the offender didn't straighten up immediately, one of the detectives would shoot into the air. The couples in the queue would close together as though pressed between two concrete walls. Folks in Harlem believed that Grave Digger Jones and Coffin Ed Johnson would shoot a man stone dead for not standing straight in line.

In *For Love of Imabelle* a hoodlum throws acid in Coffin Ed's face, and Grave Digger must untangle the mess alone—which includes two men dressed as nuns, a phony gold scam, and a classic con for bilking naive people out of $10 bills. He is not happy about it, especially when he discovers that Imabelle, the high yellow woman who is the key to the case, is at the precinct on a minor charge while Ed is in a hospital room fighting for his life:

> He slapped her with such savage violence it spun her out of the chair to land in a grotesque splay-legged posture on her belly on the floor, the red dress hiked so high it showed the black nylon panties she wore. . . . He was wearing Coffin Ed's pistol along with his own. He had it in his hand without knowing he had drawn it. He had his finger on the hair-trigger, and it was all he

Cover for Himes's final complete novel about the Harlem police detectives Grave Digger Jones and Coffin Ed Johnson (1969)

could do to keep from blowing off some chunks of her fancy yellow prat.

In the seventh novel in the series, *The Heat's On* (1966; originally published as *Ne nous énervons pas!,* 1961), Ed returns the favor. Grave Digger is shot, and Coffin Ed must find an albino and $3 million worth of heroin by himself—even though he has been suspended for brutality and his white bosses would just as soon never hear from him again. Ed spends most of the book with a nervous tic, a trophy from his acid bath, and an itchy trigger finger:

> One whole side of Coffin Ed's face convulsed in a muscular spasm as his right hand flashed toward his hip. Red Johnny moved out of animal reflex; his head jerked about, eyes following the movement of Coffin Ed's hand; his left foot braced against the floor; his left arm flew up instinctively to ward off the blow. He didn't see the motion of Coffin Ed's left hand at all as it came from the front with Grave Digger's pistol and smashed the barrel in a back-handed swing straight across his loose-lipped mouth.

Himes (seated) in 1973 with his future wife, Lesley, and the writers Clarence Major, Ishmael Reed, Joe Johnson, and Quincy Troupe

The almost mythic struggle of Grave Digger and Coffin Ed is defined best in *Cotton Comes to Harlem*. It is not only Himes's best-known book, thanks to the 1970 movie version starring Godfrey Cambridge and Raymond St. Jacques, but also the best written. The line the two must walk is as narrow as it will ever be, and the challenge facing them will never be more immense.

In *Cotton Comes to Harlem* a black con man named Deke O'Malley poses as a preacher and uses a Back to Africa rally to cheat Harlem's poor out of $87,000. The rally, though, is hijacked by white gunmen, and the money—which ends up in a bale of cotton—bounces around Harlem, physically and metaphorically. O'Malley wants it, as does a white hustler calling himself Colonel Robert Calhoun, whose gimmick is a Back to the Southland movement ("$1,000 Bonus for Each Family of Five Able-Bodied Persons"). Himes does not leave African Americans with much of a choice. The O'Malleys of the world will cheat them if they try to leave the United States, and the Colonel Calhouns of the world will ship them back to the plantation if they stay in the United States. The scene in which O'Malley seduces the wife of one of the men killed at the rally, only hours after he has been riddled by a machine gun, speaks volumes about Himes's disgust with the African American elite. The woman—"good-looking with the defensive conceit with which they convinced them-

selves they were more beautiful than all white women"—is just as much to blame as O'Malley for the seduction, and she blesses him at the moment of climax: "Oh-oh! I think you're wonderful."

For the first time in the series Grave Digger and Coffin Ed are evidently overwhelmed by the corruption of their world. Midway through the novel, they frankly admit they are baffled. They have hauled in O'Malley, beaten him, acquired perjured testimony against him, and gotten nowhere. When Calhoun leads a march up Seventh Avenue deep into Harlem, their "straighten up/count off" routine does not work, and Grave Digger has to shoot Calhoun's hat off his head three times before the march breaks up. Even then Calhoun refuses to admit a black man has beaten him. The detectives fail to recover the money and must let Calhoun escape to Alabama in exchange for $87,000 to reimburse the people O'Malley had conned. The case makes as little sense at the end as it did in the beginning, and Grave Digger and Coffin Ed realize all they have done is to help maintain a corrupt status quo.

Himes insisted he never took the Harlem books seriously. Yet, he is most remembered not for the protest novels or *Pinktoes* (1961), a sexual satire on race relations, but for *Cotton Comes to Harlem* and *The Heat's On. For Love of Imabelle* won the French Grand Prix de la Litterature Policiere in 1958, and before the series ended, Himes was the most famous writer in France who did not speak French. The financial success of the books and the movies made from them gave him a security he had never known, and he and his second wife, a white British national named Lesley Packard whom he married in 1979, lived comfortably in Spain until he died on 12 November 1984.

Edward Margolies, a leading Himes scholar, has argued that high art subverts ordinary perceptions of reality and hints at alternate interpretations of experience, while pop culture tends to reinforce private fantasies and yet reconfirm social and moral attitudes. In the typical detective story, the fantasy of violence reinforces social order. However, in Himes's Harlem novels, violence ultimately does just the opposite. Excluded by a racist system, Grave Digger and Coffin Ed are trying to overthrow the social order. Despite his flaws as a writer, Chester Himes was an American original and deserves a place among the hard-boiled elite, for he was able to transcend the confines of genre writing to address the racial issues that are central to his native land.

Interviews:

Conversations with Chester Himes (Jackson: University Press of Mississippi, 1995).

Bibliography:

Michel Fabre, Robert E. Skinner, and Lester Sullivan, comps., *Chester Himes: An Annotated Primary and Secondary Bibliography* (Westport, Conn.: Greenwood Press, 1992).

Biography:

Edward Margolies and Michel Fabre, *The Several Lives of Chester Himes* (Jackson: University Press of Mississippi, 1997).

References:

Persephone Braham, "Violence and Patriotism: La Novela Negra from Chester Himes to Paco Ignacio Ta-bo II," *Journal of American Culture* (Summer 1997): 159–170;

David Cochran, "So Much Nonsense Must Make Sense: The Black Vision of Chester Himes," *Midwest Quarterly* (Autumn 1996): 11–31;

H. Bruce Franklin, *Prison Literature in America* (New York: Oxford University Press, 1978), pp. 181–237;

Peter Freese, *The Ethnic Detective: Chester Himes, Harry Kemelman, Tony Hillerman* (Essen: Verlag Die Blaue Eule, 1992);

Addison Gayle, *The Way of the New World* (Garden City, N.Y.: Doubleday, 1975), pp. 181–191;

A. Robert Lee, "Hurts, Absurdities, and Violence: The Contrary Dimensions of Chester Himes," *Journal of American Studies,* 12 (April 1978): 99–114;

James Lundquist, *Chester Himes* (New York: Ungar, 1976);

Edward Margolies, *Native Sons: A Critical Study of Twentieth-Century Negro Authors* (New York: Lippincott, 1968), pp. 87–101;

Margolies, "The Thrillers of Chester Himes," *Studies in Black Literature* (June 1970): 1–11;

Stephen F. Millikin, *Chester Himes: A Critical Appraisal* (Columbia: University of Missouri Press, 1976);

Gilbert H. Muller, *Chester Himes* (Boston: Twayne, 1989);

Raymond Nelson, "Domestic Harlem: The Detective Fiction of Chester Himes," *Virginia Quarterly Review* (Spring 1972): 260–276;

Ishmael Reed, "The Author and His Works, Chester Himes: Writer," *Black World,* 21 (March 1972): 24–38;

John Reilly, "Chester Himes's Harlem Tough Guys," *Journal of Popular Culture,* 9 (Spring 1976): 935–947;

James Sallis, *Difficult Lives: Jim Thompson, David Goodis, Chester Himes* (Brooklyn, N.Y.: Gryphon Books, 1993), pp. 72–98;

Charles L. P. Silet, ed., *The Critical Response to Chester Himes* (Westport, Conn.: Greenwood Press, 1999);

Robert Skinner, *Two Guns from Harlem: The Detective Fiction of Chester Himes* (Bowling Green, Ohio: Bowling Green State University Popular Press, 1989);

Skinner, "Streets of Fear: The Los Angeles Novels of Chester Himes," in *Los Angeles in Fiction,* edited by David Fine (Albuquerque University of New Mexico Press, 1995);

Robert P. Smith Jr., "Chester Himes in France and the Legacy of the Roman Policier," *CLA Journal,* 25 (September 1981): 18–27;

Richard Yarborough, "The Quest for the American Dream in Three Afro-American Novels," *MELUS,* 8 (Winter 1981): 33–59.

Papers:

Many of Chester Himes's papers are held at the Beinecke Rare Book and Manuscript Library, Yale University. Some materials are held in the archives of the Julius Rosenwald Fund, Fisk University, Nashville, Tennessee.

Ed Lacy
(Len Zinberg)
(1911 – 7 January 1968)

Jennifer Hynes

BOOKS: *Walk Hard–Talk Loud,* as Len Zinberg (Indiana-
  polis: Bobbs-Merrill, 1940);
What D'Ya Know for Sure? as Zinberg (New York: Double-
  day, 1947); republished as *Strange Desires* (New York:
  Avon, 1948);
Hold with the Hares, as Zinberg (New York: Doubleday,
  1948);
The Woman Aroused (New York: Avon, 1951; London:
  Hale, 1969);
Sin in Their Blood (New York: Eton Books, 1952); repub-
  lished as *Death in Passing* (London: Boardman,
  1959);
Strip for Violence (New York: Eton Books, 1953; London:
  Mayflower, 1969);
Route 13, as Steve April (New York: Funk & Wagnalls,
  1954);
Enter Without Desire (New York: Avon, 1954);
Go for the Body (New York: Avon, 1954; London: Board-
  man, 1959);
The Best That Ever Did It (New York: Harper, 1955; Lon-
  don: Hutchinson, 1957); republished as *Visa to Death*
  (New York: Permabooks, 1956);
The Men from the Boys (New York: Harper, 1956; London:
  Boardman, 1960);
Lead with Your Left (New York: Harper, 1957; London:
  Boardman, 1957);
Room to Swing (New York: Harper, 1957; London: Board-
  man, 1958);
Breathe No More, My Lady (New York: Avon, 1958);
Devil for the Witch (London: Boardman, 1958);
Shakedown for Murder (New York: Avon, 1958);
Be Careful How You Live (London: Boardman, 1958; New
  York: Harper, 1959); republished as *Dead End* (New
  York: Pyramid, 1960);
Blonde Bait (New York: Zenith, 1959);
The Big Fix (New York: Pyramid, 1960; London: Board-
  man, 1961);
A Deadly Affair (New York: Hillman, 1960);
Bugged for Murder (New York: Avon, 1961);

Ed Lacy at the time of The Hotel Dwellers *(1966)*

The Freeloaders (New York: Berkley, 1961; London: Board-
  man, 1962);
South Pacific Affair (New York: Belmont Books, 1961);
The Sex Castle (New York: Paperback Library, 1963; Lon-
  don: Brown, Watson, 1965); republished as *Shoot it
  Again* (New York: Paperback Library, 1969);
Two Hot to Handle (New York: Paperback Library, 1963;
  London: Brown, Watson, 1966);
Double Trouble (New York: Harper & Row, 1964; London:
  Boardman, 1965);

Moment of Untruth (New York: Lancer, 1964; London: Boardman, 1965);
Pity the Honest (London: Boardman, 1964; New York: McFadden, 1965);
Sleep in Thunder (New York: Grosset & Dunlap, 1964);
Harlem Underground (New York: Pyramid, 1965);
The Hotel Dwellers (New York: Harper & Row, 1966; London: Hale, 1968);
In Black & Whitey (New York: Lancer, 1967);
The Napalm Bugle (New York: Pyramid, 1968);
The Big Bust (New York: Pyramid, 1969; London: New English Library, 1970).

OTHER: "Five Minutes After I Left You . . . ," as Len Zinberg, in *The Best From Yank–the Army Weekly* (New York: Dutton, 1945), p. 209;
"Great Day," as Zinberg, in *The Best From Yank–the Army Weekly* (New York: Dutton, 1945), p. 95;
"Immigrant," as Zinberg, in *Cross Section 1945: A Collection of New American Writing,* 3 volumes, edited by Edwin Seaver (New York: Book Find Club, 1945), pp. 351–354;
"Up Queer Street," as Zinberg, in *Esquire's 2nd Sports Reader,* edited by Arnold Gingrich (New York: Barnes, 1946), pp. 136–143;
"The Right Thing," in *Best Short Stories by Afro-American Writers,* edited by Nick Aaron Ford and H. L. Faggett (Boston: Meador, 1950), pp. 184–188;
"Stickler for Details," in *A Pride of Felons: Twenty Stories by Members of the Mystery Writers of America,* edited by Hugh Pentacost (New York: Holt, 1962);
"Death by the Numbers," in *With Malice Toward All; An Anthology of Mystery Stories by the Mystery Writers of America,* edited by Robert L. Fish (New York: Putnam, 1968).

SELECTED PERIODICAL PUBLICATIONS–
UNCOLLECTED: "The Fighters," as Len Zinberg, *New Mexico Quarterly,* 7 (November 1937): 257–260;
"A Peaceful Death," as Zinberg, *Esquire* (January 1938): 64, 131;
"The Champ," as Zinberg, *Coronet* (April 1938): 8–10;
"Subway to Harlem," as Zinberg, *New Anvil,* 1 (March 1939): 21–22;
"Long Brown Letter," as Zinberg, *New Anvil,* 1 (June–July 1939): 19;
"The Flatfooted Angel," as Zinberg, *Esquire* (April 1940): 63, 141, 142;
"The Crazy Torpedo," as Zinberg, *Esquire* (February 1941): 23, 123;
"The Quiet Life," as Zinberg, *Matrix* (Winter 1942–1943): 18–21;
"Prodigal's Off Day," as Zinberg, *Decade of Short Stories,* 4 (Second Quarter 1943): 16–18;

"Home is Where . . . ?" as Zinberg, *New Republic,* 109 (25 October 1943): 570–571;
"A Little Girl Like Home," as Zinberg, *Matrix* (Fall 1943): 19–27;
"Come on, Baby," as Zinberg, *New Yorker,* 19 (15 January 1944): 61–62;
"Caramels," as Zinberg, *New Yorker,* 20 (1 July 1944): 53;
"The Critics," as Zinberg, *New Yorker,* 20 (19 August 1944): 18;
"Count Basie and Soft Italian," as Zinberg, *New Yorker,* 20 (28 October 1944): 64–67;
"162nd Street and Amsterdam," as Zinberg, *New Yorker,* 20 (16 December 1944): 56–57;
"The Temptation of St. Lucky Strike," as Zinberg, *New Yorker,* 21 (3 February 1945): 66–69;
"Embrace Me–at My Mother's Knee," as Zinberg, *New Yorker,* 21 (24 March 1945): 66–68;
"Death and Dick Tracy," as Zinberg, *New Yorker,* 21 (7 July 1945): 46–49;
"Feud," as Zinberg, *New Yorker,* 21 (4 August 1945): 54–57;
"A Guy Just Has to Learn," as Zinberg, *New Yorker,* 21 (6 October 1945): 52–54;
"Brushoff," as Zinberg, *New Yorker,* 22 (16 February 1946): 62–63;
"Ploestl Isn't in Long Island," as Zinberg, *New Yorker,* 22 (2 March 1946): 65;
"Something's Going to Happen," as Zinberg, *New Yorker,* 22 (22 June 1946): 81–83;
"What You Going For?" as Zinberg, *New Yorker,* 22 (19 October 1946): 122–123;
"Slam the Door," as Zinberg, *New Yorker,* 22 (9 November 1946): 108;
"On With the New," as Zinberg, *New Yorker,* 22 (28 December 1946): 57–58+;
"I'm a Little Man," as Zinberg, *Esquire* (January 1947): 141, 142, 144;
"Convert," as Zinberg, *New Yorker,* 22 (1 February 1947): 46;
"Guy Can Always Learn Something," as Zinberg, *New Yorker,* 23 (15 March 1947): 94;
"The Man Who Wouldn't Say Uncle," as Zinberg, *Esquire* (March 1949): 49;
"The *Real* Sugar," *Esquire* (April 1951): 85;
"The Paradise Package," *Esquire* (June 1951): 60, 120, 123, 124;
"World of the Pug," as Zinberg, *American Mercury,* 73 (November 1951): 71–79;
"Over the Transom," *American Writer* (October 1953): 13;
"Whodunit?–You?" *Writer,* 72 (February 1959): 14–16;
"I Did It for–Me," *The Saint* (September 1962);
"The Frozen Custard Caper," *Ellery Queen's Mystery Magazine* (January 1963);
"The Devil You Know," *The Saint* (April 1963);

Dust jacket for Lacy's 1955 novel, which features a detective who
works as an auto mechanic during the day
(Collection of Matthew J. Bruccoli)

"Have Typewriter, Should Travel," *Writer,* 77 (April 1964):
    16–17;
"The Square Root of Death," *The Saint* (October 1964);
"The Juicy Mango Caper," *Ellery Queen's Mystery Magazine*
    (February 1966);
"Sic Transit . . .," *The Saint* (March 1966);
"Break in the Routine," *Ellery Queen's Mystery Magazine* (June
    1966);
"The Eunuch," *The Saint* (August 1966);
"I Dunit," *P. S.* (August 1966): 8–15;
"Murder in Paradise," *Argosy* (July 1967): 1–128;
"More Than One Way to Skin a Cat," *Ellery Queen's Mystery
    Magazine* (July 1968).

The name Ed Lacy was the most successful pseudonym of writer Len Zinberg; his other pen name was
Steve April, which he used for one book. Zinberg began
his career as an aspiring writer of serious fiction and wrote
at first under his own name, but economic forces of the
twentieth-century publishing market channeled him into
the realm of the hard-boiled mystery, and as Ed Lacy he

wrote thirty novels. As Lacy, he won an Edgar Award for
best novel from the Mystery Writers of America for *Room
to Swing* (1957), a novel in which he pioneered the use of
an African American private detective. Critic Marvin
Lachman points out that Lacy, a white man married to a
black woman, was the only American mystery writer of
his time to consistently focus on problems of racial minorities. However, while Lacy made a tolerable living and
received encouraging reviews through writing both hardcovers and paperback originals, mostly in the suspense
genre, none of his books is currently in print.

Leonard S. Zinberg was born in New York City in
1911 and began his publishing career in the late 1930s by
publishing short stories in such little magazines as the *New
Mexico Quarterly, New Anvil,* and *Matrix.* Under the name
Len Zinberg he published his first three novels, *Walk
Hard–Talk Loud* (1940), *What D'Ya Know for Sure?* (1947),
and *Hold with the Hares* (1948). The first two deal, at least in
part, with aspiring prizefighters, while all three focus on
race relations; both themes were important in the later
Lacy novels. In 1944 *Walk Hard–Talk Loud* was adapted for
the Broadway stage; former champion Mickey Walker
played the lead role. Zinberg won a 20th Century-Fox
Film Corporation literary fellowship of $1,500 for "What
D'Ya Know For Sure?" in 1945, while he was serving in
the Army Air Force. He was one of five men in uniform to
receive the fellowship for unpublished works, which gave
the film company an option against the movie purchase of
his published work that it ultimately did not exercise. All
three of the Zinberg novels received favorable reviews
from such publications as *Library Journal, The New York
Times Book Review, The New Yorker,* and *New York Herald Tribune Weekly Book Review.* While early reviewers generally
praised his creativity and writing, some censured his
choice of street language–the same language that would
mark his hard-boiled writing as Ed Lacy.

During World War II Zinberg served in the Army
Air Force as a correspondent for *Yank* magazine, remaining overseas for twenty months. Between 1944 and 1947
he had several stories published in *The New Yorker,* most
with the byline "Private First Class Len Zinberg" or
"Corporal Len Zinberg." Most of these stories are war
pieces about young American servicemen in Italy or
Guadalcanal, and the decision to use Zinberg's army
rank in the byline was clearly intended to play upon the
patriotic interest of the reading audience. Zinberg eventually was promoted to the rank of sergeant. After leaving
the service Zinberg settled in New York City. He married
a black woman, Esther, and fathered a daughter, Carla.
When finances allowed, he took his family on extended
vacations to ocean resorts on the East Coast and in
Europe, in part to gather material for his writing.

Throughout the 1940s Zinberg published short
stories in several widely circulated periodicals, including

Esquire and *New Republic.* Unlike his earlier war stories in *The New Yorker,* Zinberg's pieces for *Esquire,* with their combination of violent men and shapely women, were moving in the direction of the detective fiction genre, and were aimed at a distinctly adult male audience. During this time Zinberg's writing also appeared in several short-story anthologies alongside respected authors. His short story "Immigrant" appeared with Richard Wright's "Three Days in Chicago" and three poems by Gwendolyn Brooks in *Cross Section 1945: A Collection of New American Writing.* Zinberg's short story "Up Queer Street" was reprinted along with Ernest Hemingway's "The Horns of the Bull" and F. Scott Fitzgerald's "Send Me In, Coach" in *Esquire's 2nd Sports Reader* (1946).

Although Zinberg continued to publish under his own name until late 1951, by 1950 his authorial persona had been almost completely subsumed by his alias: Ed Lacy. Under the name of Ed Lacy, thirty novels and some one hundred short stories appeared over the next thirty years. While his books written as Zinberg had been marketed as serious fiction, the Lacy books were published in two ways, sometimes as hardcover books from literary houses such as Harper and more often as 25¢ paperback originals from mass-market houses such as Avon, Eton, Zenith, Berkley, Lancer, Hillman, and Paperback Library. Most Lacy books fit into the subgenre of mystery known as the hard-boiled novel, characterized by Anthony Boucher, one-time president of the Mystery Writers of America and frequent reviewer of Lacy, as including racy language and descriptions and involving a whodunit solved by a vigorous physical hero who tends toward violence.

The writer who became known as Ed Lacy had powerful incentives to turn to the paperback market. As literary agent Paul Reynolds observes in "The Dollars and Cents of Mystery Writing," an article included in *The Mystery Writer's Handbook: A Handbook on the Writing of Detective, Suspense, Mystery and Crime Stories* (1956), between 1943 and 1953 the number of firms that published hardcover mysteries decreased by 25 percent while the paperback publication of hard-boiled mysteries enjoyed a 50 percent increase. Although a paperback original rarely was reviewed and had a short shelf life, there was money to be made in the market. Reynolds asserts that, while a typical "good" mystery writer without a well-known name might expect to earn about $2,800 from a hardcover book, with the income spread over a period of two years, the same writer might sell a novel to a paperback house for a $3,000 advance and probably earn another $250 in royalties.

Lacy, who had his wife and daughter to support, simply could not afford to ignore the paperback market. In a 1966 article on his career, "I Dunit," Lacy discusses his financial affairs in the 1950s and early 1960s. He claims that his income ranged between $5,000 and $10,000 a year–which he referred to as living in "modest comfort," that he traveled a great deal, and that his wife occasionally took a part-time job only so that she could escape from an apartment in which he worked every day. Lacy asserts that he took at least three months to finish a novel.

The Woman Aroused (1951) was Lacy's entrance into the hard-boiled fiction market. Although he had given this work a more sedate title, Lacy found that publishers such as Avon believed that certain words–such as "sin," "murder," and "death"–and seductive wordplay sold books. Thus, his title was changed so that the book fit with others in the Avon series, including *Kept Woman, The Hard-Boiled Virgin,* and *The Abortive Hussy. The Woman Aroused* focuses on George Jackson, a corporate writer and editor who fits one common characteristic of Lacy heroes: he has an unhappy marriage. Unlike Lacy's typical heroes, however, Jackson is not prone to violence, has no ties to boxing, and does not work–part-time or full-time–as a detective. In fact, Jackson is a mild-mannered conservative middle-aged public relations writer whose hobbies consist of tap dancing and placing small bets on horse racing. This novel also includes Lacy's early examination of ways societal problems can sometimes lead to crime. In it Jackson's former brother-in-law, a leftist character who kills a poor Puerto Rican hit man, feels guilty for the act; although he had acted in self-defense, he is troubled by issues of class and privilege. The title refers to the object of Jackson's midlife fling: a six-foot-tall temptress who nearly cheats Jackson out of his money, his home, and his sanity.

Following this first hard-boiled mystery, Lacy published four other paperbacks before switching to a hardcover novel. In *Sin in Their Blood* (1952) Lacy pioneers his use of major African American characters. In this book, blacks who pass as whites are blackmailed, while white police treat with scorn a sympathetic African American housekeeper. Recalling the early Zinberg books with their focus on prizefighting, the hero of *Sin in Their Blood,* private detective Matt Ranzino, is a former boxer. Lacy's next hard-boiled paperback, *Strip for Violence* (1953), also includes a main character who knows how to use his fists. Detective Hal Darling, who stands only 5' 1", must prove himself by the frequent use of his boxing and judo skills. *Enter Without Desire* (1954), which features a sculptor as a protagonist, and *Go for the Body* (1954), the first of two of mysteries that have boxing as a main theme, were Lacy's last paperback originals of this phase of his career.

In 1954 Lacy published one juvenile, *Route 13,* under the pseudonym Steve April. Recommended for boys ages fourteen to sixteen, the novel deals with subject matter common to the author's adult books: boxing and murder. Ten years later a second novel aimed particularly at young adults appeared under Lacy's name: *Sleep in Thunder* (1964). As did much of his other fiction, this novel focuses on racial discrimination–in this case

Dust jacket for the 1957 novel in which Lacy introduces Toussaint Marcus Moore, the first black private detective in American literature (Collection of Matthew J. Bruccoli)

toward the main character, a Puerto Rican youth, and his family. In the epigraph for the novel, Lacy writes, "I hope many real life Josés will read the book and think of themselves as the novel's hero."

Lacy entered the arena of the hardcover crime novel with *The Best That Ever Did It* (1955), which appeared in Harper's suspense series. This novel includes many of the typical features of Lacy's hard-boiled works. Barney Harris, who moonlights as a private detective from his day job as an auto mechanic to pick up extra cash, looks and acts like a tough guy. He claims to be 248 pounds of muscle, and in fact women are repeatedly impressed with his size and looks. During an interview with Cissy Lewis, former fiancée of the man whose murder Harris is investigating, she comments, "Gee, you sure look like a detective—so big and hard-boiled looking." When he first visits a recently widowed client, Betsy Turner, at her apartment, his comments on her appearance make his thoughts clear: "Frankly I didn't get the play—the carefully made-up face, those tight pants showing off her strong legs, the teasing outline of firm breasts whenever the coat touched them. Either Mrs. Turner was expecting somebody after I left, or

she wanted other kinds of work for her thirty a day." Such attention to sexual interplay marks Lacy's works in the hard-boiled genre. He published six more novels with Harper over the rest of his career, most in the suspense series: *The Men from the Boys* (1956), *Lead with Your Left* (1957), *Room to Swing, Be Careful How You Live* (1958), *Double Trouble* (1964), and *The Hotel Dwellers* (1966).

The Edgar-winning *Room to Swing* introduces African American private detective Toussaint Marcus Moore, who appeared again in a later Lacy paperback, *Moment of Untruth* (1964). Moore is recognized as the first black private detective in the American mystery genre. In *Room to Swing* Moore raises eyebrows as he drives a classic Jaguar, dates a beautiful light-skinned black woman, and mixes with a crowd of Madison Avenue whites. Although Lachman argues in "Ed Lacy: Paperback Writer of the Left" that at times Lacy's attention to race issues gets in the way of smooth plot development, such issues in *Room to Swing* are an integral part of the depiction of the main character. When Moore leaves New York City for southern Ohio to find a killer, he is repeatedly on the edge of brawling or being jailed when he stands up to bigots. Even among the Madison Avenue social crowd with whom Moore mingles he finds his skin color the center of cocktail party conversation and feels that he is invited only as a token African American. The title of the book refers to the desire of several black characters, including Moore's future wife, to live in Europe, where there is more "room to swing"—meaning less racial prejudice.

Lacy's interest in social and psychological issues is what sets much of his work above run-of-the-mill popular fiction. Even during the years that he was churning out stories for the paperback market, he still took great pride in his writing. In a 1959 article for *Writer,* "Whodunit?– You?," Lacy advised his reader, "don't look down your nose at the mystery novel" and went on to assert, "Frankly, I do not consider the mystery novel on any higher or lower literary level than any other commercial novel." His means of creating what he considered serious mystery fiction was to assign to his characters everyday worries about jobs, money, marital happiness, and, often, racial issues. In his article Lacy also explains his use of nonwhite characters: "[T]he simplest yarn is considerably changed, given new depth, if a character is a Mexican, a Puerto Rican, or a Negro. Whereas a white character drops into any restaurant for coffee without giving it a second thought, this simple act has to be considered (to some degree) by a person with a colored skin."

Lacy's career indeed is perhaps most notable for his creating a character such as Moore even before the Civil Rights movement was in full swing. His focus on African American and other minority characters evidently created confusion about the race of the nonexistent Ed Lacy. One of Lacy's earliest publications was the short story "The

Right Thing," which was first printed in the Baltimore newspaper *Afro-American* and later in a collection from that publication, *Best Short Stories By Afro-American Writers* (1950). Lacy's name also appears in *Black American Writers Past and Present: A Biographical and Bibliographical Dictionary* (1975).

Apart from race, the Marcus Moore novels also include some typical female Lacy characters. Because they were intended for an adult male reader, books in the hard-boiled genre tend to focus more on descriptions of the female body than on her psyche, and Lacy's works were no exception. In *Room to Swing,* during his first meeting with Kay Robbens, Moore focuses on her body at least as much as he focuses on his new lucrative job: "In the bucket seat her skirt fell away, showing thin thighs and sexy black garters. We both glanced at her legs for a split second. I told myself I'd have to make crystal certain she understood what I was being paid for." As an attractive, well-built black hired by a white woman, Moore is concerned with being stereotyped as a predator of white women or getting involved in what could only be a dead-end interracial relationship. While female characters often are given central positions in Lacy's books, their most important attributes seem to be their body parts and their habit of wearing revealing clothes.

Another of Lacy's memorable hardcover novels from the Harper series is *Lead with Your Left.* As in many of his works, Lacy focuses on a sympathetic character—in this case Dave Wintino, an Italian-Jewish police detective and former boxer—who must deal with prejudice. Wintino repeatedly defends his African American partner from insults from other cops, even while he defends himself against his wife's bigoted family and friends. While this aspect of the novel is an intriguing study of New York's race hierarchy, Lacy relies on some coincidences to tie together his plot—a characteristic of many of his novels. Although Wintino begins the book assigned to find out who murdered a former cop, he is pulled from the apparently dead-end case to protect a writer who has received threats. When he discovers the harassing thugs, they lead him to the murderer of the former cop, allowing Wintino to tie up both cases at once. *Lead with Your Left* nevertheless received fairly good reviews, with Boucher in *The New York Times Book Review* of 27 January 1957 calling its writing "as crisp and effective as [Wintino's] tastefully cool wardrobe."

Beginning with *Breathe No More, My Lady* (1958), Lacy turned back to the paperback market for some dozen novels published during the next ten years. In *Breathe No More, My Lady* he deals with one of his most frequent themes—the conflict between capitalism, portrayed as "the establishment," and the common man—as an advertising copywriter, Norm Connor, must make a career-changing decision: act according to his conscience or promote a book by a writer who has been accused of murder. In this novel Lacy includes a clever twist, having the writer

accused of murder, Matt Anthony, write a book about his trial while it is taking place. *Breathe No More, My Lady* also includes a boxing motif, as Connor becomes involved with Harry Brown, a college professor who is also a former prizefighter with dark memories of the sport, while he is investigating the murder to decide whether or not to publish the book.

The Big Fix (1960), Lacy's second boxing-centered mystery, focuses on Tommy Cork, whose career as a prizefighter is on the decline. When he is taken up by a wealthy backer, Arno Brewer, things seem too good to be true, and, indeed, they are: businessman Brewer is actually setting up a $50,000 insurance fraud with the boxer's life at stake. A police detective who is also a former fighter helps solve the case.

Toussaint Marcus Moore appears a second and last time in *Moment of Untruth* (1964). As the novel begins, Moore is employed as a postal worker, his wife having convinced him to quit his work as a private eye. His meager post-office salary, combined with the news that his wife is pregnant, spurs him to return to detective work when he is offered a lucrative case in Mexico City. As a tourist he experiences less racial prejudice than he finds at home. The title refers to the villain in Moore's case, a bullfighter who cheats to retain his position at the top of the sport; while the bull's death is referred to as the moment of truth, this bullfighter reverses the situation.

As in the first Moore novel and many of the other Lacy books, *Moment of Untruth* is replete with voluptuous women and sexual suggestion. His client is a beautiful widowed university professor, Grace Lupe-Varon, who is described as having the body and movements of a teenager. Grace, whose work involves reptile venom, is repeatedly shown handling snakes—an obvious sexual prop. The other woman Moore meets in Mexico is a burned-out prostitute—conveniently, the sometime girlfriend of the bullfighter he is shadowing. Moore turns down what might have been a fling with no consequences because he is in love with his pregnant wife. Again, Lacy undermines the stereotype of African American males lusting after white women.

Lacy created another African American hero in *Harlem Underground* (1965) and *In Black & Whitey* (1967), both of which focus on police detective Lee Hayes. In these novels Hayes often is involved in discussions about how to best address racial inequality in the United States. In *Harlem Underground* he goes undercover to infiltrate a black youth gang that is terrorizing the city. Once among the gang members, Hayes begins to understand their hopelessness and frustration; although he solves a murder and puts away the gang's leader, "Purple Eyes," Hayes has doubts about whose side he should be on. His position as an outsider within allows him a clearer picture of society and its problems. Lacy's *In Black & Whitey* pairs Hayes with

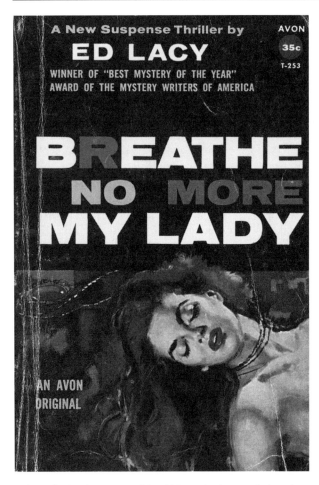

Cover for Lacy's 1958 novel in which a writer is accused of murder
(Collection of Matthew J. Bruccoli)

a Jewish partner as the two work to squelch an expected race riot in Harlem's Paradise Alley. Such a riot is anticipated because a white-supremacist group, WON ("Wipe Out Negroes"), is aggravating an already tense neighborhood. In this novel Hayes is an unambiguous hero, saving both the black residents from violence and the city from riots and arson. In his 1986 essay "Ed Lacy: Passage Through Darkness" Ray B. Browne argues that the Lee Hayes novels best depict Lacy's philosophy concerning the value of interracial compassion in society.

Lacy's last hardcover novel, *The Hotel Dwellers* (1966), was his first attempt in years to work outside of the mystery field. In fact, Harper was so accustomed to publishing Lacy in its suspense series that the endpapers of the book carried the "Harper Novel of Suspense" logo. In some of the books a slip was inserted with a disclaimer, stipulating that it was not a novel of suspense but an "adult novel." In his 1966 article Lacy writes that he would wait to see how *The Hotel Dwellers* sold before trying another straight novel, but he did not do so. He may have been experimenting with a work outside of his accustomed arena because of the poor market for mysteries; in the ten

years previous to *The Hotel Dwellers* Lacy had noticed a great oversupply in the genre. Indeed, the 1950s and 1960s have been described as the "Golden Age" of paperback originals, but the treasure had to be divided among an increasing number of writers.

Len Zinberg died of a heart attack in New York City on 7 January 1968. As Ed Lacy, though, he still had something to say, for his last two paperback originals were posthumously published: *The Napalm Bugle* (1968) and *The Big Bust* (1969). Both novels deal with writers, and both focus again on Cold War issues. *The Napalm Bugle* deals with a fictional attempt by the U.S. government to cover up the fact that a change in the rocket fuel supply will leave the nation defenseless for nearly two weeks. Korean War veteran Brad Armstrong, working for the antiwar newspaper *The Napalm Bugle,* becomes involved when the government loses track of a British journalist who has discovered the secret. In *The Big Bust* Long Island writer John O'Hara–who repeatedly informs acquaintances that he is not the famous novelist–is vacationing in Europe when he becomes involved in a clandestine attempt to locate some buried Nazi treasure.

Although a handful of scholars have written on his work, lamenting his near disappearance from the annals of the mystery, no full-length study of Ed Lacy has appeared. Lachman argues that much of Lacy's work, despite its flaws, is entertaining and historically interesting. Among the works he lists as worthy of rediscovery are *Sin in Their Blood, Strip for Violence, Go for the Body, The Best That Ever Did It,* and *Lead with Your Left.* Lacy's singular contributions to the hard-boiled genre, though, are clearly the four novels that feature his two main African American heroes, the occasional private eye Toussaint Marcus Moore and police detective Lee Hayes.

References:

Ray B. Browne, "Ed Lacy: Passage Through Darkness," in *Heroes and Humanities: Detective Fiction and Culture* (Bowling Green, Ohio: Bowling Green State University Popular Press, 1986), pp. 47–54;

Marvin Lachman, "Ed Lacy: Paperback Writer of the Left," in *Murder Off the Rack: Critical Studies of Ten Paperback Masters,* edited by Jon L. Breen and Martin Harry Greenberg (Metuchen, N.J. & London: Scarecrow Press, 1989), pp. 15–34;

Paul Reynolds, "The Dollars and Cents of Mystery Writing," in *The Mystery Writer's Handbook: A Handbook on the Writing of Detective, Suspense, Mystery and Crime Stories* (New York: Harper, 1956).

Papers:

The papers of Ed Lacy (Len Zinberg) are held at the Muger Memorial Library, Boston University.

Elmore Leonard

(11 October 1925 –)

Frederick William Zackel
Bowling Green State University

See also the Leonard entry in *DLB 173: American Novelists Since World War II, Fifth Series.*

BOOKS: *The Bounty Hunters* (Boston: Houghton Mifflin, 1953; London: Hale, 1956);

The Law at Randado (Boston: Houghton Mifflin, 1955; London: Hale, 1957);

Escape from Five Shadows (Boston: Houghton Mifflin, 1956; London: Hale, 1957);

Last Stand at Saber River (New York: Dell, 1959); republished as *Lawless River* (London: Hale, 1959); republished as *Stand on the Saber* (London: Corgi, 1960);

Hombre (New York: Ballantine, 1961; London: Hale, 1961);

The Big Bounce (New York: Fawcett, 1969; London: Hale, 1969);

The Moonshine War (Garden City, N.Y.: Doubleday, 1969; London: Hale, 1970);

Valdez Is Coming (London: Hale, 1969; New York: Fawcett, 1970);

Forty Lashes Less One (New York: Bantam, 1972);

Mr. Majestyk (New York: Dell, 1974; London: Penguin, 1986);

Fifty-Two Pickup (New York: Delacorte, 1974; London: Secker & Warburg, 1974);

Swag (New York: Delacorte, 1976; London: Penguin, 1985); republished as *Ryan's Rules* (New York: Dell, 1978);

The Hunted (New York: Delacorte, 1977; London: Secker & Warburg, 1978);

Unknown Man No. 89 (New York: Delacorte, 1977; London: Secker & Warburg, 1977);

The Switch (New York: Bantam, 1978; London: Secker & Warburg, 1979);

Gunsights (New York: Bantam, 1979);

Gold Coast (New York: Bantam, 1980; London: Allen, 1982);

City Primeval: High Noon in Detroit (New York: Arbor House, 1980; London: Viking, 1987);

Elmore Leonard at the time of the publication of Out of Sight
(photograph © 1996 by Linda R. Chen)

Split Images (New York: Arbor House, 1981; London: Allen, 1983);

Cat Chaser (New York: Arbor House, 1982; London: Viking, 1986);

Stick (New York: Arbor House, 1983; London: Lane, 1984);

LaBrava (New York: Arbor House, 1983; London: Viking, 1984);

Glitz (New York: Arbor House, 1985; London: Viking, 1985);

Bandits (New York: Arbor House, 1987; London: Viking, 1987);

Touch (New York: Arbor House, 1987; London: Viking, 1988);

Freaky Deaky (New York: Arbor House, 1988; London: Viking, 1988);

Killshot (New York: Arbor House, 1989; London: Viking, 1989);

Get Shorty (New York: Delacorte, 1990; London: Viking, 1990);

Maximum Bob (New York: Delacorte, 1991; London: Viking, 1991);

Notebooks (Northridge, Cal.: Lord John Press, 1991);

Rum Punch (New York: Delacorte, 1992; London: Viking, 1992);

Pronto (New York: Delacorte, 1993; London: Viking, 1993);

Riding The Rap (New York: Delacorte, 1995; London: Viking, 1995);

Out of Sight (New York: Delacorte, 1996; London: Viking, 1996);

Cuba Libre (New York: Delacorte, 1998; London: Viking, 1998);

Tonto Woman and Other Western Stories (New York: Delacorte, 1998; London: Viking, 1999);

Be Cool (New York: Delacorte, 1999; London: Viking, 1999);

Pagan Babies (New York: Delacorte, 2000; London: Viking, 2000).

Collections: *Elmore Leonard's Dutch Treat* (New York: Arbor House, 1985; London: Harmondsworth, U.K.: Viking, 1987)–comprises *The Hunted, Swag,* and *Mr. Majestyk;*

Elmore Leonard's Double Dutch Treat (New York: Arbor House, 1986)–comprises *City Primeval: High Noon in Detroit, The Moonshine War,* and *Gold Coast;*

Elmore Leonard: Three Complete Novels (New York: Wings Books, 1992)–comprises *LaBrava, Cat Chaser,* and *Split Images;*

Elmore Leonard's Western Roundup #1 (New York: Delta, 1998)–comprises *The Bounty Hunters, Forty Lashes Less One,* and *Gunsights;*

Elmore Leonard's Western Roundup #2 (New York: Delta, 1998)–comprises *Escape from Five Shadows, Last Stand at Saber River,* and *The Law at Randado;*

Elmore Leonard's Western Roundup #3 (New York: Delta, 1999)–comprises *Valdez Is Coming* and *Hombre.*

PRODUCED SCRIPTS: *The Moonshine War,* motion picture, M-G-M, 1970;

Joe Kidd, motion picture, Universal, 1972;

Mr. Majestyk, motion picture, United Artists, 1974;

High Noon, Part 2: The Return of Will Kane, television, CBS, 1980;

Stick, motion picture, script by Leonard and Joseph C. Stinson, Universal, 1985;

52 Pick-Up, motion picture, script by Leonard and John Steppling, Cannon, 1986;

The Rosary Murders, motion picture, script by Leonard and Fred Walton, New Line Cinema, 1987;

Desperado, television, NBC, 1988;

Cat Chaser, motion picture, script by Leonard and Joe Borrelli, Viacom, 1989.

OTHER: "The Odyssey," in *Naked Came the Manatee,* by Leonard, Carl Hiaasen, Dave Barry, and others (New York: Putnam, 1996), pp. 163–176.

Many critics consider Elmore Leonard to be the best living writer of crime fiction in the United States. Since the mid 1980s he has enjoyed enormous commercial success, and his style has influenced a generation of writers. Leonard began his career writing Westerns and adventure tales but because of changes in the market switched to writing fiction about contemporary crime in the 1970s. In his introduction to the omnibus collection *Elmore Leonard's Dutch Treat* (1985), George Will asserts that the effectiveness of Leonard's novels "derives from their realism. The realism is in the elusive path of the narrative. . . . He deals in small, telling details, not the Big Picture. However, he knows if you gather enough of the right details, you have, at the end of the day, a picture, and a true one." As Dick Lochte noted in the *Los Angeles Times* of 24 October 1993, "It's a mistake to categorize Leonard's novels as mysteries or thrillers. Murderers are not announced in their final chapters, secrets are not revealed, the fates of nations do not hang on their outcome. They are tales of heroes and villains engaged in mortal and moral struggle. What distinguishes them is Leonard's ability to create characters, conversations and situations that are as natural and convincing as they are unique."

Leonard writes realistically about the underworld in the tradition of James M. Cain and W. R. Burnett. His characters on the margins of society are often career criminals looking to get rich quick, hustling for a scam, or primed for the big heist. They may be con artists and they may be psychopathic killers. For most of his characters, survival is difficult enough, and success is impossibly elusive. In one of several unpublished interviews Leonard gave in the spring and summer of 1997, he asserted that his characters are "the kind of people who think they're hip, who are looking for a big score." He attempts to portray "the way they talk, the street parlance. People in crime and on the fringes of crime and people on the other side–they interest me. Nearly all the cops I've hung out with (since the 1980s) are on the investigative level–homicide, the state cops in Florida,

Leonard, posing in imitation of outlaw Bonnie Parker, with family members, 1934 (Collection of Elmore Leonard)

the FBI, probation officers—and they're interesting. Homicide cops all have this dry sense of humor; they're all funny guys, and not always are they trying to be."

Summarizing Leonard's career in *The New York Times* of 30 December 1984, Ben Yagoda wrote, "Where his westerns followed sturdy linear progressions, since he turned to contemporary stories his plots have gradually devolved into smoky improvisations grouped around a set of reliable elements." Forty years of writing have taught Leonard to trust in his own instincts, as he remarked in a 1997 interview: "I don't know what the book's about until I'm a hundred pages into it. I want to be surprised. I haven't done an outline in thirty years. I don't even start planning until the second act. And I don't worry about the opening or the closing." Leonard structures loosely: "I am conscious of my three acts. My books are 340 to 370 pages of manuscript. I figure a hundred, 110, 120 pages per act." Leonard likes this strategy because, he says, "I don't have to think about structure. I look at what I have, and think about the next 100 pages. Where does it look like I'm going with these people? What character is unimportant now that I can do something more with? What character am I not having any fun with?"

Leonard is a master at conveying the impression of authentic speech. Stephen King in a 10 February 1985 review in *The New York Times* is one of many who have praised Leonard's "almost eerily exact ear for the

tones and nuances of dialogue." Leonard, however, is careful to distinguish between actual speech and created dialogue: "When they talk about the realism of my dialogue—'the exact way these people talk'—how do they know?" What he writes, he maintains, "is the imitation of that speech. It's not a wiretap transcription, say, of a Mob social club. The dialogue has to have a purpose." In a 1998 interview published in *Film Comment,* Leonard responded to Patrick McGilligan's mentioning the abrupt twists in his plots: "If a plot twist is amazing, as you suggest, it must be at the same time believable. So I write each scene from a character's point of view, with the character's 'sound' proving the rhythm of the prose and the believability of what's taking place in the scene. The reader accepts it because the character is there. It might not be acceptable from my point of view, were I an omniscient author who thinks he knows everything. Their 'sound' is much more entertaining than mine, so I try to keep my nose out of it. I don't want the reader ever to be aware of me writing. And if the prose sounds like it was written, I rewrite it."

Elmore John Leonard Jr. was born in New Orleans, Louisiana, on 11 October 1925. His father, Elmore John Leonard, was a marketing executive with General Motors; his mother's maiden name was Flora Amelia Rivé. He was their second child; he had a sister six years older. The family moved from New Orleans to Dallas in 1928 and during the next four years lived for periods in Oklahoma City, Detroit, and Memphis, before finally settling in Detroit in October 1934. He has lived primarily in the Detroit area since his family's move there.

Leonard was eight years old and still living in Memphis when Bonnie Parker and Clyde Barrow were gunned down in Gibsland, Louisiana. He remembers that "after their deaths, their pictures were in every paper." Only in the early 1990s did Leonard realize how much of an impression the famous photograph–Bonnie Parker toting a pistol on her hip, her foot on the front bumper of the car–had made on him: "I gave *Life* magazine a photograph of me with my mother and my sister standing alongside the family car," a GM Oakland. "I have a wool cap on, I'm standing with one foot on the running boards, and I'm holding a cap pistol. I was imitating Bonnie." Surprising himself by readily recalling the 23 May 1934 date of the couple's death, Leonard commented on his memory of Depression-era criminals:

> I read somewhere that the most impressionable age for children is between five and ten. I was between five and ten when all those desperadoes were roaming the Midwest and holding up banks. They were kind of folk heroes. So many homes and farms had been repossessed, taken back by the banks, that when the banks were robbed, people cheered. And they could forgive the desperadoes for killing someone who occasionally got in the way. Those bank robbers of the 1930s truly influenced me. John Dillinger, Bonnie and Clyde, Pretty Boy Floyd–that's what I'm doing today.

Echoes of Bonnie and Clyde appear in several of his novels, most notably *Out of Sight* (1996), where bank robber and escaped convict Jack Foley holds Deputy U.S. Marshal Karen Sisco hostage. Early on, Foley tells Sisco, "Clyde Barrow–you ever see pictures of him, the way he wore his hat? You could tell he had that don't-give-a-shit air about him." Similar posing, role-playing, and posturing are important motifs in most of Leonard's novels.

Leonard credits his sister, who read to him when he was young, for his love for books. His mother not only read novels but also passed along to her son the urge to write: "She wrote only two short stories in thirty years, but her desire was to be a writer." By the time he was attending the University of Detroit High School, he was reading Book-of-the-Month Club selections. "I read all these contemporary novels in high school. One day I realized they just had too many words in them." From that day forward, Leonard was turned off by pages "full of type."

In high school Leonard was nicknamed "Dutch" after major-league baseball pitcher Emil "Dutch" Leonard. In 1942 his family moved when his father was transferred to Washington, D.C., but Leonard wanted to finish high school in Detroit: "I was playing football, quarterback my senior year, and I lived with the coach's family from early fall through spring, 1943, until my folks came back." In summer 1943, after graduation, Leonard drove across the United States to Hollywood with two friends.

Leonard, who had been rejected because of his poor eyesight when he tried to enlist in the U.S. Marines, was soon drafted and served in the U.S. Navy from 1943 to 1946. "I had a good time," Leonard recalls. "I was shipped to New Guinea, and all of us were parceled out to various groups from there." Sent to the Admiralty Islands, Leonard did not see combat but helped maintain airstrips that Australian and U.S. Navy fighter planes were using to bomb airstrips on Truk and Rabal. His unit was later transferred to Sangley Point in the Philippines. As is typical of Leonard, one of his fondest memories of the South Pacific was the speech patterns of one of his fellow sailors. "Eddie Mogck and I were walking through the New Guinea jungle, and he kept looking up at the trees. 'Look out for pythons,' he warned me. 'Don't want no parts of them fuckers!'"

After he returned to civilian life in 1946, now with his nickname "Dutch" tattooed on his left shoulder, Leonard enrolled in the University of Detroit, where he majored in English and philosophy. On 30 August 1949 he married Beverly Claire Cline, with whom he raised five children: Jane, Peter, Christopher, William, and Katherine, born between 1950 and 1966. During his senior year of college, Leonard began working as an office boy at Campbell-Ewald Advertising Agency. Within a year he was working in the Traffic and Production Department on the Chevrolet account. He graduated from the university with a bachelor of philosophy degree in 1950.

Leonard continued in the advertising business until 1966. For fifteen months during 1953–1954 he left Campbell-Ewald to join a smaller advertising agency "to learn about the business." He then went back to Campbell-Ewald and stayed to write Chevrolet car and truck ads, until 1961, when he left for good to write fiction full-time. During the next few years he wrote some educational scripts on history and geography for Encyclopedia Britannica Films. From this work, Leonard said, "I did learn something about film writing, though the narratives were almost entirely voice-overs."

Leonard started his writing career in 1950 during his first stint at Campbell-Ewald, waking early to write between 5 and 7 A.M. so he could spend his evenings with his growing family. His main reason for choosing Westerns as a place to begin was that there was a tremendous market for Western at that time, with at least a dozen pulp magazines still in business. Speaking of his early influences, Leonard asserted,

"My hero, when I was writing Westerns, was Hemingway. He made writing look easy." Leonard recalled often reading *For Whom the Bell Tolls* (1940) for inspiration, "seeing the book—set in the mountains of Spain with horses and guns—as a Western."

The first story Leonard sent out was titled "Tizwin," the Apache word for corn beer; it was published by *Dime Western* as "Red Hell Hits Diablo Canyon!" An editor at that magazine, Michael Tilden, encouraged the young writer "to use all my senses and not just my eyes and ears." The editor also advised Leonard not to quit his job to become a full-time writer of Westerns, warning him that "if you try to make a living in this market . . . you could become a hack." His sale of a twelve-thousand-word novella, "Trail of the Apache," to *Argosy* in 1951 not only brought him a much needed $1,000 but also helped him to acquire his first agent, Marguerite Harper, who represented such well-known Western writers as Luke Short and Peter Dawson. By the end of 1952 she had sold nine of his stories. During the decade Leonard wrote and sold more than thirty Western stories, publishing his work in *The Saturday Evening Post, Argosy, Dime Western,* and *Zane Grey's Western Magazine.*

Over time Leonard modified his opinion of Hemingway: "Once I realized I didn't share Hemingway's attitude about life in general—I certainly didn't take myself as seriously as he did—and that style, your voice, comes out of attitude, the kind of person you are and how you see things—then I looked for inspiration elsewhere and found Richard Bissell and Mark Harris." Leonard suggests that a careful reader can see the influence of Bissell on the Mississippi scenes he wrote for *Killshot* (1989).

Leonard easily made the transition from writing short stories to novels. The short stories he had published before beginning *The Bounty Hunters* (1953) gave him confidence: "I wasn't intimidated; I was just shooting for 60,000 words. I started putting it together, one scene at a time." The novel received a good notice from Hoffman Birney in his 11 April 1954 review for *The New York Times.* Leonard wrote and published three more Western novels before the end of the decade: *The Law at Randado* (1955), *Escape from Five Shadows* (1956), and *Last Stand at Saber River* (1959).

Although his Western stories were set in southern Arizona and New Mexico, Leonard did not visit the Southwest until 1959. At the time he was working on his fifth novel, *Hombre* (1961). He remembers rewriting the part of the book featuring the Santa Catalina Mountains because they "didn't look the same as I had written them." He received only $1,250 from Ballantine Books for the novel, which told the story of a white man who lived among the Apaches and was forced against his will

Dust jacket for Leonard's 1983 novel, the second featuring car thief Ernest Stickley Jr.

to enter white man's society. *Hombre* is the only Leonard novel that is not written in third person. A minor character tells the story, and the central character dies at the end, perhaps contributing to the reluctance of the publisher to buy the book. In 1977 *Hombre* was chosen as one of the twenty-five best Western novels of all time by the Western Writers of America.

Leonard wrote his last three Westerns before the end of the 1970s: *Valdez Is Coming* (1969), *Forty Lashes Less One* (1972), and *Gunsights* (1979). In his 1991 article on Leonard for *The Journal of Popular Culture,* Joseph Hynes notes that in the writer's career women and minorities have evolved "to heavier and more complex involvement in the action as well as to richer and more ambiguous characterization." He singles out *Forty Lashes Less One* as "perhaps the richest case of the minorities' acting outside the law to achieve justice." When Leonard's Western stories were later collected as *Tonto Woman and Other Western Stories* (1998), Wes Lukowsky in the July 1998 *Booklist* noted that "like Leonard's crime fiction, his Westerns are always character driven. Other similarities are apparent across genres: his contemporary women are always a half-step ahead of their men; it's no different in the heat of the desert sun."

In his first non-Western effort, *The Big Bounce* (1969), Leonard tells the story of a young drifter, Jack Ryan, who becomes caught up in a femme fatale's search for kicks; their goal is to steal a $50,000 payroll. When Leonard's agent Marguerite Harper became ill, she sent the manuscript on to H. N. "Swanie" Swanson, who had acted for clients such as Hemingway, F. Scott Fitzgerald, William Faulkner, and Raymond Chandler over the course of his career. Swanson, who had already sold *Hombre* and other Western stories to the movies for Leonard, then took over the author's career until the agent's death in 1990. Leonard remembers Swanson fondly: "He called me kiddo or boy. He was a tough old guy. His philosophy was get as much of the money up front and forget about the net; it never pays off for the writer." Swanson was "a terrific negotiator. He didn't give in. He'd be negotiating with publishers and say, 'If you don't want to pay the boy what we're asking, we'll go up the street—we're all friends,' meaning to other publishers."

Over the next three months the manuscript for *The Big Bounce* received eighty-four rejections. At that point, Leonard examined all the criticisms made by publishers and studio executives and made revisions. "What it needed was a stronger plot, but I didn't change any of the characters, whom the editors thought were unsympathetic. I'm glad I didn't change them. They're the same types of characters I'm dealing with today. Jack Ryan is a migrant worker. He was a burglar. A carpet cleaner. He wanted to play major league baseball, but he couldn't hit a curve ball. He was not your usual novel hero." Only after the movie rights were sold to Warner Bros. was the novel made into a paperback original for Fawcett.

Leonard set his next novel, *The Moonshine War* (1969), in Marlett, Kentucky, during Prohibition. Honoring his dead father, Son Martin must defend his "daddy's whiskey"—150 barrels of corn whiskey worth $125,000—not only from his one-time war buddy, Frank Long, a federal Prohibition agent, but also from a murderous gang of bootleggers armed with Thompson submachine guns. The war lasts one day shy of three weeks; it ends explosively. *The Moonshine War* was quickly sold to M-G-M, and Leonard was hired to write the screenplay, his first. He recalls that the studio sent him a copy of the script for *The Cincinnati Kid* (1965) to serve as a model.

Leonard's work on the script of *The Moonshine War* marked the beginning of a twenty-year period in which he often worked on movie or television projects even as he continued to write novels. In *Mr. Majestyk* (1974), the first original screenplay he sold to Hollywood, Vincent

Majestyk is, like many of Leonard's main characters, "a cool, quiet man," a former soldier turned melon farmer in a small town outside Phoenix, Arizona. Through circumstances not of his choosing, he comes into conflict with a small-time hood and a high-priced hit man who never recognizes Vincent's majesty; the hit man dies, still calling him "Farmboy." Leonard wrote the novelization of his screenplay after *Mr. Majestyk* was produced as a movie in 1974. He wrote and sold another original screenplay, *Joe Kidd,* in which the hero, played by Clint Eastwood in the 1972 movie, is hired by a land baron to hunt down Mexican-American outlaws. Much of Leonard's work in Hollywood, however, was turning his books into movies: *Fifty-Two Pickup* (1974) was adapted and produced in 1986, *Cat Chaser* (1982) in 1989, and *Stick* (1983) in 1985. Leonard has since given up writing scripts: "You put all your enthusiasm into writing the book; adapting it for the screen then is just work, especially after several rewrites. On top of that, there are so many people [in Hollywood] to please, who have little or no sense of story."

In 1974 Leonard and his wife, Beverly, separated after twenty-five years of marriage; they divorced in 1977. During this three-year period Leonard struggled with his alcoholism. In 1974 he joined Alcoholics Anonymous, but he continued to have trouble controlling his drinking. Leonard claims, "It took three years for the program to sink in. Finally on January 24, 1977, I quit cold and have not had a drink since."

In the mid 1970s Leonard began to write the contemporary crime fiction that has made his reputation. In *Fifty-Two Pickup,* his first novel, Harry Mitchell, a Detroit industrialist, has an affair and is blackmailed. Leonard's books in the latter half of the decade include *Swag* (1976), which introduces Ernest Stickley Jr., a car thief and armed robber who reappears in *Stick,* and *Unknown Man No. 89* (1977), in which process server Jack Ryan (an older and more likable character than in *The Big Bounce*) has to track down a missing stockholder, a murderer who unwittingly inherited $150,000 in stock. All three of these novels were praised in the "Newgate Callendar" column of *The New York Times.* The reviewer's praise of *Unknown Man No. 89* in the 22 May 1977 issue of the newspaper is indicative of Leonard's growing renown: "Leonard bows to no one in plot construction. Yet there is never the feeling of gimmickry in his plots; events follow a natural course. Above all, there is Leonard's style. He has a wonderful ear, and his dialogue never has a false note. He avoids artiness, writes clear expository prose and has the ability to create real people. . . . He can write circles around almost anybody active in the crime novel today." Leonard's last crime novel of the decade, *The Switch* (1978)—in which a kidnapped woman switches to the criminals' side after she learns that her philandering husband refuses to pay her ransom—was nominated for the award of best original paperback novel of 1978 by the Mystery Writers of America.

In 1978 Leonard "hung out" with the Detroit Police Homicide Section to write a nonfiction profile of its activities, and "Impressions of Murder" appeared in *The Detroit News* (12 November 1978): "I sat in the [homicide] squad room and listened to them talk. They trusted me and forgot I was there. They knew I admired them, liked them, and wanted to tell their story honestly." He later used these experiences in *City Primeval: High Noon in Detroit* (1980), his only police procedural. Leonard married for a second time on 15 September 1979 to Joan Leanne Lancaster Shepard. Recalling his wife, who died of lung cancer in 1993, Leonard remarks, "Joan was very close to me in my work. I'd read and she'd comment." Leonard met his third wife, Christine Kent, a few months after Joan's death; they were married on 19 August 1993.

Looking back on his career, Leonard believes he started to do his best work in the early 1980s. His first novel of the decade and his first set in Florida, *Gold Coast,* was published in 1980. Leonard had vacationed off and on in the state since the 1950s and had taken an interest in its changing culture. He marvels at the multicultural diversity of Florida "from Palm Beach and its super-rich to Little Havana in Miami. I was there during the Mariel boatlift, which accounted for an increase in crime in South Florida. Above Orlando it's completely different. Go west from Palm Beach and forty miles away you're in a completely different world. One of my characters who lived in that area had been north to prison but had never seen the ocean."

The main character of *Gold Coast,* Karen Hill Stohler DiCilia, is married briefly to a member of organized crime, widowed, and left not only $4,000,000 to live on but also the stipulation that as long as she lives "she's not to see anyone in a serious way that she might go to bed with." Leonard, who regrets that he did not give more of Karen's point of view in *Gold Coast,* says he has come to enjoy the challenge of using women as main characters in his novels. Also featured in the novel is Roland Crowe, Karen's mob-hired bodyguard who is actually after her inheritance. Roland's various relations—all backwoods criminal but with varying degrees of success at crime—appear in several of Leonard's subsequent novels, sometimes as comic relief and other times as vicious psychopaths.

In 1980 Leonard published *City Primeval: High Noon in Detroit,* his first novel with a police officer as hero. The protagonist is thirty-six-year-old Lieutenant Raymond Cruz, a classic "quiet" Leonard character, whose former wife accuses him of never showing emotion or telling her how he felt. Leonard plays with the motifs of the Wild

Dust jacket for Leonard's 1985 novel, in which a disabled police detective is stalked by a killer he helped send to prison

West in his depiction of his urban frontiersmen and the showdown between Cruz and the psychopath Clement Mansell, the "Oklahoma Wildman," who claims to have killed nine people, or as the detective explains, "four more than we know of and seven more than he'll ever be convicted for." Cruz is one of many Leonard characters whose self-image is in part fashioned on a pose he sometimes consciously assumes. His favorite pose is one in which "he could appear quietly unaffected, stand with hands in the pocket of his dark suit, expression solemn beneath the gunfighter moustache . . . his Dodge City pose: the daguerreotype peace officer, now packing a snub-nosed .38 Smith with rubber bands around the grip instead of a hogleg .44."

In 1981 Leonard hired Gregg Sutter, a longtime fan who had interviewed the author for the August 1980 issue of *Monthly Detroit* magazine, as a researcher to help him with the backgrounds of his novels. Sutter began working for Leonard as he was writing *Split Images* (1982). Leonard explains how Sutter aids his writing: "Maybe I'll tell him to find me a bailbondsman in Miami. Gregg will interview a half-dozen until he finds one who

Leonard at a book signing for his "breakout novel" (courtesy of Elmore Leonard and Vagabond Books)

understands what I need and is willing to cooperate. Gregg will do all the hard work; he'll interview the man, record and transcribe what he says. Then I'll visit the office, look around and see how it can fit in the book, and I'll ask specific questions." In 1986 Sutter wrote a two-part essay in *The Armchair Detective* describing his work as a researcher and how Leonard reformulates this raw research. As Sutter explains in "Part I," "What Dutch is looking for in research is a series of 'triggers' that inspire scenes or characters. . . . My job was to go after the bigger picture, in search of hidden triggers. Dutch would often shop the material very discriminately for a single fact, a gesture, or a backdrop; once he had it he'd be off and running again."

Leonard had a series of solid successes in the first half of the 1980s. In *Split Images* Leonard writes of Robbie Daniels, a millionaire who believes his wealth allows him the right to murder whomever he wants, and Bryan Hurd, the Detroit cop who brings him down. Leonard had originally planned to continue his characterization of Raymond Cruz from *City Primeval* in the novel, but Swanson "made me change the name, because United Artists had bought the rights to *City Primeval* and therefore owned the screen rights to the char-

acter. It meant I wouldn't be able to sell *Split Images* to any other studio." Leonard subsequently wrote *Cat Chaser, Stick,* and *LaBrava* (1983), which won the Edgar Allan Poe Award as the best novel of 1984 by the Mystery Writers of America.

Glitz (1985), Leonard's "breakout" novel, tells the story of Miami cop Vincent Mora, Atlantic City lounge singer Linda Moon, and Teddy Magyk, the psychopathic rapist-killer who wants Mora dead. Names are important to Leonard. Secondary characters in *Glitz* have names such as Ricky the Zit and Sal the Cat; the reader meets a homicide captain named Dixie Davies and a bodyguard born Moosleh Hajim Jababa who changed his name to DeLeon Johnson "so people would look at his name and know he was American." Leonard maintains that he has "to get the name right" before his characters will talk.

Leonard's fast-paced story, with its deadpan comic touches, opens with Mora being shot by a mugger:

> The night Vincent was shot he saw it coming. The guy approached out of the streetlight on the corner of Meridian and Sixteenth, South Beach, and reached Vincent as he was walking from his car to his apartment building. It was early, a few minutes past nine.

Vincent turned his head to look at the guy and there was a moment when he could have taken him and did consider it, hit the guy as hard as he could. But Vincent was carrying a sack of groceries. He wasn't going to drop a half gallon of Gallo Hearty Burgundy, a bottle of prune juice and a jar of Ragú spaghetti sauce on the sidewalk.

Vincent manages to shoot the mugger and survive but needs time to recuperate from his wounds. Recovering from his injuries, he visits Puerto Rico, unaware that a former convict just released from prison is stalking him.

Glitz has one of Leonard's most harrowing villains–Stephen King in his 10 February 1985 *Time* review calls him "one of popular fiction's really great crazies"–in Teddy Magyk, a mama's boy gone bad. In prison Teddy was another convict's "old lady"; out of prison, he lives with his aged mother in Marvin Gardens, a section of Atlantic City. For gas money, Teddy beats up and robs little old ladies; then he rapes and kills them. As he stalks Vincent Mora, the cop who sent him to prison, Teddy wants to shoot him in the streets in the dark of night, but he is worried about his mother's reaction: "what if the cop had a gun and had time to shoot back and hit his mom's car? How would he explain it?" DeLeon Johnson tells Vincent that Magyk cannot be scared off. "Police up there, police down here, they try all kinds of ways to nail his ass and they can't do it. Man must believe by now he's got fairy dust on him. Isn't nothing can touch him." In the climactic scene, the two men meet in a duel reminiscent of Leonard's earlier Westerns–the lawman against "the poor wimp who thought he was magic and couldn't be scared."

Leonard propels his story through action and dialogue. In the opening section of chapter 19, for example, Leonard uses only two expository sentences to set the scene that begins in the middle of a conversation:

"It's like you're in a hotel in *Star Trek*," Vincent said. "You know what I mean? It's so modern you don't know how to open anything or turn the lights on."
Dixie said, "They comped you to a suite? Come on."
"They like me," Vincent said. "Or they want to keep an eye on me."
He sat with the telephone in a corner of the gold sectional sofa, wrapped in a king-size gold towel. Dixie Davies was home in Brigantine, in the kitchen.

The sentences that definitely place Vincent in a luxury suite in Atlantic City and Captain Davies in his home in Miami are the last in the two-page section that are not direct conversation between the two men. Most published novels, Leonard asserts, have "too many

Leonard with his second wife, Joan Shepard Leonard (courtesy of Gregg Sutter)

words. I'm interested in moving the story forward through dialogue."

Leonard's art is the direct presentation of a scene. He explains that his novels are written in scenes and are always narrated from a character's point of view. "Once I know the purpose of the scene, I decide from whose point of view it will be seen and told most effectively. Point of view is all important. That decides the sound of the scene. I don't want the whole book to be with one sound, the main character's sound, or the bad guy's sound." Leonard's fascination and pleasure in creating different voices is certainly one of the main reasons he does not write traditional first-person narratives: "Then I'd be stuck writing 90,000 words from one person's point of view."

Leonard shifts points of view to create more suspenseful conflict and to keep his writing from becoming stale or predictable. Because the dominant character can be different in each new section or chapter, the reader not only is kept off balance but also is drawn more intimately into the action. During the writing of *Glitz*, Leonard recalls that his rewriting and altering the point of view in one scene changed the developing focus of the novel. In his original scheme, Leonard had intended Nancy Donovan, the co-owner of an Atlantic City casino, to be the main female character and Vincent

Mora's love interest. As he wrote about Donovan, though, Leonard found her a less compelling character than he had imagined. In contrast, he found writing about Linda Moon, the lounge singer from the casino, more interesting: "She was feisty, she wanted so much to make it so badly, she becomes the girl in the book."

Leonard so carefully modulates the sound and rhythm of his characters' voices that he warily monitors the work of copyeditors. Leonard remembers one copyeditor who "took a hundred-word sentence, broke it up with periods, and ruined the rhythm of the prose." Speech tags are also often a bone of contention with editors: "I always use 'said.' I'll only use one [variation on 'said'] per book. Sometimes there's a second 'said' in the same paragraph. I use it for a beat, a slight pause, not to identify the speaker. That rhythm [can be] destroyed by a copyeditor."

Leonard finds it "appropriate, but not always deliberate" that in most of the scenes he writes his characters tell stories or anecdotes to each another: "I want natural talk. Not necessarily talk about the plot. Most crime novels are set on the plot, and in real life we talk about all kinds of things. Movies, for instance. My purpose is to make the antagonists human and not simply bad guys. They want to be happy. They want to be rich. That most of all. How rich is not important. It could be two thousand dollars; that's all they need. But they're short-sighted, often not educated, and so they rob."

Glitz was Leonard's first book to reach *The New York Times* Best Sellers List, selling over 200,000 copies in hardcover alone. *Glitz* was another Book-of-the-Month Club selection for Leonard. The success of this book brought him national media attention, and Leonard was featured as a *Newsweek* cover story on 22 April 1985. There, Peter S. Prescott wrote that Elmore Leonard "is the best American writer of crime fiction alive, possibly the best we've ever had. . . . Take 'Glitz.' If it's not his best story, it's his most carefully textured novel; besides, the margin of difference between Leonard's better and lesser works would admit, with difficulty, a butterfly's wing. The plot isn't as strong as some that Leonard has conceived, but it's representational of the confrontational story that Leonard has often written." Stephen King wrote in his 10 February 1985 review of *Glitz* for *The New York Times* that "Mr. Leonard moves from low comedy to high action to a couple of surprisingly tender love scenes with a pro's unobtrusive ease and the impeccable rhythms of a born entertainer. He isn't out front, orating at the top of his lungs. . . . He's behind the scenes where he belongs, moving the props around and keeping the story on a constant roll."

Because of the success of *Glitz,* Leonard began earning big money. Leonard sold the movie rights to *Glitz* for $450,000 and the paperback rights for another $450,000. Arbor House paid $3 million for his next two novels. Earlier Leonard novels that had been out of print were republished. Since *Glitz,* all of Leonard's novels have been both commercial and critical successes. In 1985 Arbor House brought out *Elmore Leonard's Dutch Treat,* comprising *The Hunted, Swag,* and *Mr. Majestyk,* and the next year published a second Leonard trilogy as *Elmore Leonard's Double Dutch Treat* (1986), comprising *The Moonshine War, Gold Coast,* and *City Primeval.*

Leonard wrote his next novel, *Bandits* (1987), in reaction to President Ronald Reagan's policy in Nicaragua: "It was so ridiculous to call the Contras Freedom Fighters, with their death squads. I couldn't believe it. And when they were raising money in Louisiana with conservative oil men, I wondered how to rip them off." In the novel he creates a scenario in which a former convict, a former nun, and a former cop divert several million dollars headed for the Nicaraguan Contras. Although novelist Walker Percy in *The New York Times Book Review* of 4 January 1987 agreed that Leonard as a writer was "as good as the blurbs say," he believed that in this case his approach and subject were ill suited: "Nicaraguan politics, it turns out, may be a bit too heavy to be carried by the graceful pas de deux of Mr. Leonard's good guys and bad guys. For this reason, *Bandits* is not quite of a piece, like *Glitz.*" In the same year that *Bandits* was published, Arbor House also brought out *Touch,* in which a man with the stigmata, the manifestation of the crucifixion wounds of Christ, falls in love with a punk-rock record promoter.

Reflecting a more general willingness to dissect Leonard's writing, some reviewers were quite critical of his next crime novel, *Freaky Deaky,* in which police bomb disposal expert Chris Mankowski is pitted against two aging 1960s radicals, Skip Gibbs and Robin Abbott, who are out to rob the Ricks brothers, the two men they blame for their arrests. Cyra McFadden wrote in her 8 May 1988 review in *The New York Times Book Review:* "Leonard unleashes those five characters, along with assorted other petty criminals, in a story that seems largely driven by their sheer eccentricity. No one character emerges as the good guy who pulls events into focus—a departure for Leonard—and the plot becomes unnecessarily convoluted." Rhoda Koenig also expressed disappointment in her 2 May 1988 review for *New York* magazine: "For all the high-intensity emotions and action, *Freaky Deaky* is a rather weightless affair. Most of it is dialogue, easy to read but not too demanding of the reader's attention—your eye slides down the page unimpeded by any narration to create pacing and suspense. It is perfectly functional but in no way memorable, as all but one of the characters never rise above stereotypes or have any inner lives. . . . The weightlessness is emotional and moral, too. . . . Without any redeeming stylistic value, any hard-edged, glittering cynicism, this lack of distance between debauchee and victim collapses our reaction into a shrug and a 'So what?'" Despite these reactions, *Freaky Deaky* is Leonard's favorite book.

In his last novel of the 1980s, *Killshot,* ironworker Wayne Colson and his wife, Carmen, are pursued by two killers, the psychopath Richie Nix and a hit man known as Blackbird. Random chance plays a part in Leonard's novels, for not only does the plot hinge on the circumstance of Wayne being at the wrong place at the wrong time but also the teaming up of Nix and the Blackbird is coincidental: they meet when Nix tries to carjack the hit man. Sean French wrote in his 10 November 1986 *New Statesman* review of *Killshot,* "It's a book with the sort of themes that 'real' novels have, the vulnerability of innocence to evil and madness. The fumbling attempts of the forces of law to protect the couple are grippingly detailed and only in the story's perfunctory final shootout does Leonard seem to let the genre do his work for him."

Leonard is careful not to overwrite violent scenes. In *Killshot* he uses sound, not visual detail, in describing gunshots. At the outset of the novel, Blackbird "fired once. The sound filled the room and maybe it was heard on the other side of the wall in another room, or maybe not. It was sudden; if anyone heard it and said what was that and stopped to listen, there was nothing else to hear . . . . Only the shower running in the bathroom." Near the end of the novel, Blackbird is killed by Carmen. "She shot him. Fired his own gun at him and it was like the sound of it punched him in the belly, made him grunt and double over."

Leonard's string of successful novels continued into the 1990s with *Get Shorty* (1990), his first novel about Hollywood, and *Maximum Bob* (1991), which won the first annual International Association of Crime Writers North American Hammett Prize for the Best Crime Novel of 1991. The author describes the idea of *Get Shorty* in a single sentence: "A Miami loan shark goes to Hollywood and feels right at home." Along the way to his discovery of his knack for movie producing, Chili Palmer crosses paths with unsavory individuals from both organized crime and the movie business. The mob and Hollywood seem made for each other in this novel that affords Leonard free rein to examine role-playing. In her 29 July 1990 review for *The New York Times* Nora Ephron wrote that the novel was not as good as *LaBrava* but asserted, "even the not-great Elmore Leonards are redeemed by great, punchy, pitch-perfect Elmore Leonard dialogues and great Elmore Leonard sentences, long looping twisting strings of words that turn around and back up and go the other way, managing somehow (but how?) to avoid all the accouterments of punctuation like colons, semicolons and parentheses." *Maximum Bob* is

Dust jacket for Leonard's 1996 novel, about an escaped bank robber and a federal marshal who fall in love

a black comedy featuring circuit court judge Bob Gibbs, a colorful woman-chaser who routinely hands out the maximum sentences allowed by Florida law.

In 1991 Lord John Press of Northridge, California, brought out a limited edition titled *Notebooks* that combines notes Leonard made during a cross-country trip from Detroit to Los Angeles with the notebook he kept for his novel *Bandits.* Leonard's practice for each novel he writes is to use a spiral notebook with three sections, the first section for research notes, the second for notes about characters, and the third section for plot ideas. Once he begins writing the actual text, he uses special pads of 8 1/2" by 11" unlined yellow sheets he buys from a printer, the same as those he first used at Campbell-Ewald Advertising in the 1950s. Leonard writes in longhand, using a Mont Blanc pen with black ink. He typically writes one or two pages and then types his work, which he continues to revise and edit. For at least twenty years Leonard typed his work on an Olympia typewriter he had bought secondhand for $120. "I liked the sound," Leonard explains. He then switched to an IBM Wheelwriter 1000. At first he worried about this new technology: "it was so sensitive, and I tend to hit the keys hard."

The focus of *Rum Punch* (1992), Leonard's thirtieth novel, is a half-million-dollar payoff in illegal arms smuggling. The cast of characters includes the gun dealer Ordell Robbie and the former bank robber Louis Gara, who also appeared in *The Switch*. Leonard describes them in *Rum Punch* as "a light-skinned black guy and a dark-skinned white guy, both from Detroit originally where they met in a bar, started talking, and found out they'd both been to Southern Ohio Correctional and had some attitudes in common." Michael Dirda, writing for *The Washington Post Book World,* noted in his 19 July 1992 review that "Beneath its fast moving surface, *Rum Punch* is a novel about growing old, about the way that time changes us, about the old dream of starting over again and its cost." He compares Ordell and Louis in this book with how they appear in *The Switch* and decides, "There are no heroes in *Rum Punch,* only survivors." Dirda concludes, "Like many of Leonard's other books, this is not so much a whiz-bang boy's adventure as a hypnotic dance of death." In her 16 August 1992 review for *The New York Times Book Review,* Ann Arensberg wrote that "Leonard has compressed 'Rum Punch' into almost pure drama, as close to playwriting as novel writing can get (and get away with). Mr. Leonard never tells you; he shows you. . . . His style is the absence of style, stripped of fancy baggage (social philosophy, abnormal psychology, beautiful diction)—the absence, as far as it's possible, of an authorial ego. He puts his ego in the service of his characters and their stories, and by so doing strikes a blow for that most radical of notions: that no one human being is better than any other, that there is no 'other.'"

Pronto (1993) and *Riding The Rap* (1995) feature sixty-seven-year-old Harry Arno, a bookie who skimmed money from his mob bosses during a twenty-year period, and Raylan Givens, a U.S. marshal who protects him. In the first book the action shifts from Miami to Rapallo, Italy, then back to Miami as Arno is pursued by a mob hit man. In the second book a drug-addled Chip Ganz decides to kidnap Arno, believing that the bookie can pay his own ransom from the $3,000,000 he has stashed in the Bahamas. Ganz signs up two career criminals, Bobby Deo and Louis Lewis, to help him. After Harry disappears from his Miami hangouts, Givens comes to his rescue.

Riding The Rap is one of Leonard's funnier novels. Ganz's ludicrous plan for the kidnapping itself, for instance, is styled loosely on his own wacky interpretation of the Shi'ite Muslim hostage-taking in Lebanon during the 1980s; Ganz "visualizes" Harry as a hostage in "a damp basement full of spiders and roaches crawling around pipes dripping . . . huddled against the wall in

chains," but Louis asks, "Where we gonna find a basement in Florida?" Leonard likes to end a scene on a question. That way, he says, "the reader wants to know what's next." Leonard was influenced in this respect by George V. Higgins's *The Friends of Eddie Coyle* (1971).

In *Out of Sight* Leonard produced "a genuine love story," according to novelist Ed McBain in his review in the 29 December 1996 *Los Angeles Times.* Leonard found his inspiration for the novel in the newspapers. First he was struck by a photograph in a Detroit newspaper showing a female federal marshal in front of the Miami federal courthouse, the stock of a shotgun on her hip. That photograph triggered memories of the bank robbers of the Depression, and Leonard began to consider such a woman in conflict with an old professional bank robber. In January 1995 the coverage of a prison break in Palm Beach County suggested to Leonard the situation in which his two characters might meet. He saved all editions of three separate newspapers for three weeks and carefully studied all the stories, the photos, the diagrams of the escape route, and the biographies of the escapees. In the novel he contrived the situation of Jack Foley kidnapping deputy U.S. marshal Karen Sisco during his escape from prison.

As in Leonard's other later novels, posing, role-playing, and posturing are important motifs in *Out of Sight.* While nestled in the trunk of a car speeding down the freeway, Sisco remarks to Foley, "You must see yourself as some kind of desperado." Foley, surprised by her comment, replies thoughtfully, "I never actually thought of myself that way." He adds, "Unless I did without knowing it. Like some of those boys of yesterday." He then brings up Clyde Barrow and the careless way he wore his hat. They spend the next few minutes discussing the infamous shootout near Gibsland, Louisiana. Foley considers that "it wouldn't be a bad way to go, if you have to." Later in the novel Foley and his best friend and fellow bank robber Buddy stop at the Jewish Recycling Center to buy "new" clothes. Foley had hoped his new clothes would make him look like "a businessman, some kind of serious executive." Instead, "What he looked like was a guy who'd just been released from prison in a movie made about twenty years ago." Still, Foley poses in front of the store mirror: "He half turned and cocked his hip in a pose: a photo of Jack Foley taken shortly after his daring prison escape. His mind flicked to a picture of Clyde Barrow, hat cocked down on one eye."

In many of Leonard's novels, his characters deliberately, almost self-consciously, point out that their actions are not poses, not role-playing. In *Out of Sight,* Leonard contrives to bring Jack Foley and Karen Sisco together in a restaurant atop a Detroit hotel. While outside a snowstorm rages and cops are expected to be chas-

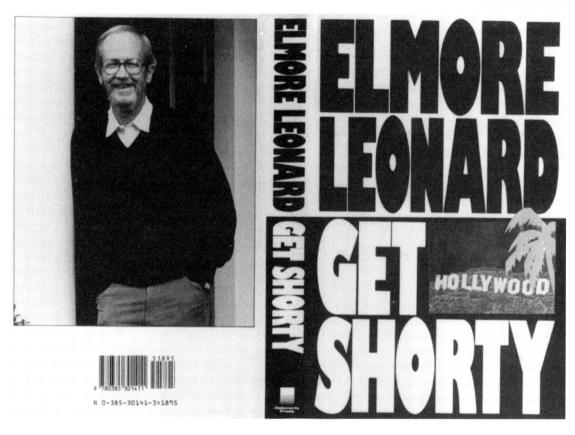

Dust jackets for Leonard's 1990 and 1999 novels, featuring loan shark turned Hollywood producer Chili Palmer

ing robbers, within the two are pretending to be "Gary" and "Celeste," lovers with no insuperable obstacles. Foley finds this masquerade difficult: "I don't think it works if we're somebody else. You know what I mean? Gary and Celeste. Jesus, what do they know about anything?" Sisco tells him, "If we're not someone else then we're ourselves. But don't ask me where we're going or how it ends, okay? Because I haven't a fucking clue. I've never played this before." When Foley answers her by saying, "It's not a game," she knew he meant it.

Not all critics were as convinced by the cop-and-robber-as-lovers premise of the novel as was McBain, who wrote that "whether their diametrically opposed occupations will stand in the way of true love becomes in Leonard's telling the stuff of high romance and taut suspense." Ralph Lombreglia in his 8 September 1996 review for *The New York Times* thought the main characters lacked credibility: "By the end, Karen Sisco and Jack Foley are bundles of contradictions impossible to resolve into believable human beings. They seem to be constantly going in and out of character. It would be nice to say that they are pulled out of their personalities by the profound influence of each other, but first you'd have to accept that a career outlaw and a federal officer would have such tenuous grasps of their own identities."

Leonard's next work was an historical novel, *Cuba Libre,* which was published on 15 February 1998, the centennial anniversary of the sinking of the U.S.S. *Maine.* The main characters are Ben Tyler, a gun smuggler; Virgil Webster, a marine from the ship; and Amelia Brown, the mistress of sugar planter Roland Boudreaux. The story begins three days after the destruction of the *Maine* with Tyler's arrival at Havana harbor, where he is to sell horses to American sugar planters and guns to the insurgents. When he sees the wreck and asks what it is, a harbor pilot informs him that it is the *Maine.* "The main what?" Tyler asks. Leonard took a full year, the most time for any of his novels, to complete *Cuba Libre.* Part of the reason for the long writing time was that he was continually researching the circumstances and the events leading up to the Spanish-American War: "I would open books all through that manuscript. Very few scenes could work with only what I knew."

Critics were generally more interested in *Cuba Libre* as a Leonard novel than for its historical setting. Brian Bethune, reviewing the novel in the 16 March 1998 *Maclean's,* noted "Leonard's characters may be far more inclined to action than to thought, but the page-turning excitement they generate does overcome the clumsy history lesson. In the end, their sheer unpredictability is *Cuba Libre*'s saving grace." In his 22 January 1998 review in *The New York Times* Christopher Lehmann-Haupt found that the novel fit easily into Leonard's oeuvre:

"Predictably, because this is a Leonard novel, the story that ultimately unfolds is yet another brilliant retelling of Chaucer's 'Pardoner's Tale,' with half a dozen or so different parties scheming to make off with a fortune in ransom money intended for the revolutionary cause. What Leonard does with his usual skill is modulate the reader's like and dislike of the various characters so that 'Cuba Libre' resolves itself in a satisfying finale of revenge."

Leonard published his thirty-fifth novel, *Be Cool,* a sequel to *Get Shorty,* in 1999. "This time," Leonard asserts, "Chili Palmer's in the music business. It's perfect for Chili Palmer. So many crooks with a history of Mob connections. It's right up his alley." Leonard shows no signs of slowing down and says he will never retire: "Not as long as I have the desire and the energy. At my age most writers have given up; they're tired or they're losing it. I don't feel that way. I will write as long as it's still fun." Leonard likes his own current writing habits: "One book a year isn't too much. Half the year off, and you start thinking again."

Interviews:

Joel M. Lyczak, "An Interview with Elmore Leonard," *Armchair Detective,* 16 (Summer 1983): 235–240;

Ben Yagoda, "Elmore Leonard's Rogues' Gallery," *New York Times,* 30 December 1984, p. 20;

Bill Kelley, "This Pen for Hire," *American Film,* 10 (December 1984): 52–56;

Jean W. Ross, Interview with Leonard, in *Contemporary Authors,* New Revision Series, volume 28 (Detroit: Gale Research, 1989), pp. 284–287;

Patrick McGilligan, "Get Dutch," *Film Comment,* 34 (March/April 1998): 43–52.

References:

David Geherin, *Elmore Leonard* (New York: Continuum, 1989);

Joseph Hynes, "'High Noon in Detroit': Elmore Leonard's Career," *Journal of Popular Culture,* 25 (Winter 1991): 183–184, 186;

Robert S. Prescott, "Making A Killing: With 'Glitz,' Leonard Finally Brings in the Gold," *Newsweek,* 105 (22 April 1985): 62–67;

Gregg Sutter, "Getting It Right: Researching Elmore Leonard's Novels, Part I," *Armchair Detective,* 19 (Winter 1986): 4–19;

Sutter, "Getting It Right: Researching Elmore Leonard's Novels, Part II," *Armchair Detective,* 19 (Spring 1987): 160–172.

Papers:

A collection of Elmore Leonard's papers prior to 1973 is at the University of Detroit Mercy Library.

Kenneth Millar
(Ross Macdonald)
(13 December 1915 – 11 July 1983)

Frederick William Zackel
Bowling Green State University

See also the Millar entries in *DLB 2: American Novelists Since World War II, First Series; DLB Yearbook: 1983;* and *DS 6: Hardboiled Mystery Writers: Raymond Chandler, Dashiell Hammett, Ross Macdonald.*

BOOKS: *The Dark Tunnel* (New York: Dodd, Mead, 1944); republished as *I Die Slowly* (New York: Lion, 1955);

Trouble Follows Me (New York: Dodd, Mead, 1946); republished as *Night Train* (London: Lion, 1955);

Blue City (New York: Knopf, 1947; London: Cassell, 1949);

The Three Roads (New York: Knopf, 1948; London: Cassell, 1950);

The Moving Target, as John Macdonald (New York: Knopf, 1949; London: Cassell, 1951); republished as *Harper* (New York: Pocket Books, 1966);

The Drowning Pool, as John Ross Macdonald (New York: Knopf, 1950); republished, as John Macdonald (London: Cassell, 1952);

The Way Some People Die, as John Ross Macdonald (New York: Knopf, 1951; London: Cassell, 1953);

The Ivory Grin, as John Ross Macdonald (New York: Knopf, 1952; London: Cassell, 1953); republished as *Marked For Murder* (New York: Pocket Books, 1953);

Meet Me at the Morgue, as John Ross Macdonald (New York: Knopf, 1953); republished as *Experience With Evil* (London: Cassell, 1954);

Find A Victim, as John Ross Macdonald (New York: Knopf, 1954; London: Cassell, 1955);

The Name Is Archer, as John Ross Macdonald (New York: Bantam, 1955); republished, as Ross Macdonald (London: Fontana, 1976)–comprises "Find the Woman," "Gone Girl," "The Bearded Lady," "The Suicide," "Guilt-Edged Blonde," "The Sinister Habit," and "Wild Goose Chase";

Kenneth Millar in 1961 (photograph by Ray Borges, Santa Barbara News-Press)

The Barbarous Coast, as Ross Macdonald (New York: Knopf, 1956); republished, as John Ross Macdonald (London: Cassell, 1957);

The Doomsters, as Ross Macdonald (New York: Knopf, 1958); republished, as John Ross Macdonald (London: Cassell, 1958);

The Galton Case, as Ross Macdonald (New York: Knopf, 1959); republished, as John Ross Macdonald (London: Cassell, 1960);

The Ferguson Affair, as Ross Macdonald (New York: Knopf, 1960; London: Collins, 1961);

The Wycherly Woman, as Ross Macdonald (New York: Knopf, 1961; London: Collins, 1962);

The Zebra-Striped Hearse, as Ross Macdonald (New York: Knopf, 1962; London: Collins, 1963);

The Chill, as Ross Macdonald (New York: Knopf, 1964; London: Collins, 1964);

The Far Side of the Dollar, as Ross Macdonald (New York: Knopf, 1965; London: Collins, 1965);

Black Money, as Ross Macdonald (New York: Knopf, 1966; London: Collins, 1966);

The Instant Enemy, as Ross Macdonald (New York: Knopf, 1968; London: Collins, 1968);

The Goodbye Look, as Ross Macdonald (New York: Knopf, 1969; London: Collins, 1969);

The Underground Man, as Ross Macdonald (New York: Knopf, 1971; London: Collins, 1971);

Sleeping Beauty, as Ross Macdonald (New York: Knopf, 1973; London: Collins, 1973);

On Crime Writing, as Ross Macdonald (Santa Barbara, Cal.: Capra, 1973)–comprises "The Writer as Detective" and "Writing *The Galton Case*";

The Blue Hammer, as Ross Macdonald (New York: Knopf, 1976; London: Collins, 1976);

Lew Archer, Private Investigator, as Ross Macdonald (New York: Mysterious Press, 1977)–comprises "Find the Woman," "Gone Girl," "The Bearded Lady," "The Suicide," "Guilt-Edged Blonde," "The Sinister Habit," "Wild Goose Chase," "Midnight Blue," and "The Sleeping Dog";

A Collection of Reviews, as Ross Macdonald (Northridge, Cal.: Lord John Press, 1979);

Self-Portrait: Ceaselessly Into The Past, as Ross Macdonald, edited by Ralph B. Sipper (Santa Barbara, Cal.: Capra, 1981);

Early Millar: The First Stories of Ross Macdonald and Margaret Millar (Santa Barbara, Cal.: Cordelia Editions, 1982).

Collections: *Archer in Hollywood,* as Ross Macdonald (New York: Knopf, 1967)–comprises *The Moving Target, The Way Some People Die,* and *The Barbarous Coast;*

Archer At Large, as Ross Macdonald (New York: Knopf, 1970)–comprises *The Galton Case, The Chill,* and *Black Money;*

Archer in Jeopardy, as Ross Macdonald (New York: Knopf, 1979)–comprises *The Doomsters, The Zebra-Striped Hearse,* and *The Instant Enemy.*

OTHER: *Great Stories of Suspense,* edited by Ross Macdonald (New York: Knopf, 1974).

Kenneth Millar, who wrote as Ross Macdonald, was the successor to Dashiell Hammett and Raymond Chandler in the development of the hard-boiled detective story into serious literature. Millar wrote two dozen novels between 1944 and 1976, eighteen of them featur-ing Lew Archer, the character for whom he is best known. Success, both commercial and critical, came gradually through the late 1950s and the early 1960s. Tom Nolan in *Ross Macdonald: A Biography* (1999) writes, "When he died in 1983, Ross Macdonald was the best-known and most highly regarded crime-fiction writer in America." Millar's work continues to have an impact not only on readers but also on authors. Mystery novel-ist Stephen Greenleaf in the December 1993 issue of *The Writer* notes that "my inspiration came from Dashiell Hammett and Raymond Chandler and, above all, Ross Macdonald, writers who wrestled the form out of the hands of the English masters and gave it an American voice and place and conscience. My inspirations were books that were driven not by plot or character or forensic verisimilitude, but by those that towered above the rest because of the strength and suitability of their style. Apocalyptic prose, I call it–words fit for the edges of experience, which is where these books take place."

While Millar is considered–and considered him-self–to be a disciple of Hammett and Chandler, ulti-mately he may have become a better novelist than either of his predecessors. In his 1 June 1969 review of Millar's *The Goodbye Look* (1969) in *The New York Times Book Review,* William Goldman called the Lew Archer books "the finest series of detective novels ever written by an American." John Leonard, editor of *The New York Times Book Review,* interviewed Millar for the same issue and wrote an accompanying article in which he declared: "Ten years ago, while nobody was looking–or rather, while everybody was looking in the wrong direction–a writer of detective stories turned into a major American novelist."

For his own part, Millar claimed he was bringing the detective novel "closer to the purpose and range of the mainstream novel." Nolan argues that the Archer novels rise above the hard-boiled genre because Millar used them to explore his own psyche: "In his novels, Millar resolved his contradictions: there he hid and revealed an aching loneliness, a melancholy humor, and a lifetime of anger, fear, and regret. These singular works changed their genre and changed the way read-ers saw the world. In these stories, ordinary families became the stuff of mystery; and there was always guilt enough to go around. We recognized ourselves as char-acters in Ross Macdonald's novels. And the most inter-esting Macdonald character of all was Kenneth Millar."

An only child, Millar was born in Los Gatos, Cal-ifornia, on 13 December 1915 to John Macdonald Millar and Annie Moyer Millar, both of whom were transplanted Canadians from the Northwest Territories. His father was a second-generation newspaper editor, and his mother was a trained nurse, the daughter of an Ontario farmer; both were forty years old at his birth.

*Millar with his wife, Margaret—also a mystery writer—and with their daughter, Linda Jane,
during the family's early years in Santa Barbara*

In 1919 the family moved to Vancouver, British Columbia, where his father took a job as a harbor pilot and the family lived in a waterfront hotel. When Millar was four years old, his parents separated. Later his father completely abandoned his semi-invalid wife and his five-year-old son. The abandonment was the defining event in Millar's life. In *Self-Portrait: Ceaselessly Into The Past* (1981) he writes, "Innumerable traces of my life run through my books. Most of them have to do with a broken family and a lost father."

Millar and his mother became charity cases. In "A Quiet Man," one of the writers' reflections collected in *Inward Journey: Ross Macdonald* (1984) by Ralph B. Sipper, Millar's friend Robert Easton writes, "Ken remembered begging for money and food on the streets at the age of six." At one point his mother was so desperate that she "took him as far as the gates of an orphanage, resolved to give him up, but changed her mind. Ken never forgot those gates." As Millar recalls in his fore-

word to *A Collection of Reviews* (1979), "My mother took me to her home territory in Ontario, and from then on I lived mostly with her and her people. But throughout my life I remained my father's son, even though I saw him infrequently, sometimes not for years at a time."

For the next fifteen years Millar was bounced from relative to relative. He writes in *Self-Portrait*, "My mother and I lived, when we were lucky, on the charity of her mother and her sister. They were good women . . . but in their puritanical household I felt both surrounded and displaced. I was my wandering father's son, after all, and my mother's female relatives could hardly help discerning on my brow the mark of the paternal curse." He claims he "must be the only American crime novelist who got his early ethical training in a Canadian Mennonite Sunday School." In Raymond A. Sokolov's 22 March 1971 *Newsweek* cover story on him, Millar remarked that "I felt uprooted from the time my parents separated. It was a good background for a novelist, but not for anything else I can think of." His second home was the public library: "I was a bookworm. Sometimes I would get up and read a whole book before breakfast."

In the late 1920s Millar attended St. John's School in Winnipeg, where he began to write fiction and verse. In high school he wrote for the school paper and was a wrestler for the school team. His circumstances, however, were seldom stable, and by the time he graduated from the Kitchener-Waterloo Collegiate & Vocational School in Kitchener, Ontario, in 1932, Millar calculated he had lived in fifty separate residences. In those fifty rooms, Millar writes in *Self-Portrait,* he "committed the sin of poverty."

Millar considers the effect of his childhood on his later choice to write crime fiction in *Self-Portrait:* "I had less choice than the reader may suppose. My one attempt to write a regular autobiographical novel about my unhappy childhood turned out so badly that I never showed it to my publisher." In a reference to Charles Dickens's childhood poverty, Millar quips, "I left the manuscript, I think, in an abandoned blacking factory. The deadly game of social Snakes and Ladders which occupied much of my youth had to be dealt with in another form, more impersonal and objective." Although his past permeates all of his work, Millar was always insistent that he wrote not about his past, but from it. In his foreword to *Archer in Hollywood* (1967) he suggests that writers cannot help but reveal something of their personal histories in their work: "We writers, as we work deeper into our craft, learn to drop more and more personal clues. Like burglars who secretly wish to be caught, we leave our fingerprints on the broken locks, our voiceprints in the bugged rooms, our footprints in the wet concrete and the blowing sand."

Millar was living in Kitchener when he discovered Hammett's *The Maltese Falcon* (1930), an experience he records in his essay "Down These Streets A Mean Man Must Go," which he collected in *Self-Portrait:* "Hammett's books were not in the thirties to be found on the open shelves of the Kitchener Public Library. . . . But one day in 1930 or 1931 I found *The Maltese Falcon* on the shelf of a lending library in a Kitchener tobacco shop, and I read a good part of it on the spot. It wasn't escape reading. As I stood there absorbing Hammett's novel, the slot machines at the back of the shop were clanking and whirring, and in the billiard room upstairs the perpetual poker game was being played. Like iron fillings magnetized by the book in my hands, the secret meanings of the city began to organize themselves around me like a second city." Millar summarizes the profound effect Hammett had on him: "For the first time that I can remember I was consciously experiencing in my own sensibility the direct meeting of art and contemporary actuality—an experience that popular art

at its best exists to provide—and beginning to find a language and a shape for that experience."

Hammett was the de facto leader of a revolution, particularly in language, that began in the 1920s at Captain Joseph T. Shaw's *Black Mask* magazine. Hammett and other *Black Mask* authors used language that was not upper class, not stilted and genteel, not gentlemanly, not even English. It was American as spoken at the bus station, at the racetrack, in the taxicab, and in the alleys. The best of the *Black Mask* authors and their successors transformed the hard-boiled crime story into serious literature. "The revolution was a real one," Millar writes in *On Crime Writing* (1973). "From it emerged a new kind of detective hero, the classless, restless man of American democracy, who spoke the language of the streets."

Millar saw *The Maltese Falcon* as a tragedy, as is clear from his statement on the novel made in a 29 May 1972 letter to Knopf editor Ashbel Green: "Hammett was the first American writer to use the detective story for the purposes of a major novelist, to present a vision, blazing if disenchanted, of our lives." As Millar wrote in *On Crime Writing* (1973), Sam Spade "possesses the virtues and follows the code of a frontier male. Thrust for his sins into the urban inferno, he pits his courage and cunning against its denizens, plays for the highest stakes available, love and money, and loses everything in the end."

His father's death in 1932 provided Millar with a small legacy; in *Self-Portrait* Millar writes that his father "ultimately bequeathed me his copy of *Walden* and a life insurance policy for two thousand dollars which in Canada, in the thirties, was exactly enough to see me through four years of University." In 1933 he entered the University of Western Ontario. Millar was deeply affected by the death of his mother, whom he found dead from a massive stroke on the bathroom floor in 1935. In the winter of 1936–1937 he dropped out of school and traveled by bicycle through England, Ireland, France, and Germany. Millar's experiences in Europe formed the backdrop to his first novel, *The Dark Tunnel* (1944).

In June 1938 Millar received his A.B. degree with honors from the University of Western Ontario. On the day after his graduation, Millar married Margaret Ellis Sturm, whom he had known in high school. They had both been members of their high-school debating team, and their first stories had appeared in the same issue of the Kitchener Collegiate Institute *Grumbler,* but they had not seen each other for several years following high school. Upon his return from his European tour Millar by chance had discovered her reading Thucydides in Greek at the public library. They saw each other every day thereafter.

In 1938 through 1939 Millar took graduate courses at Ontario College of Education and the University of Toronto for his high school teaching certification. In the spring of 1939 Margaret Millar was pregnant, and Millar had no job until the fall semester began. Using a typewriter he won on a radio quiz show, Millar began writing furiously. By selling a mix of children's stories, poems, and humorous articles, he managed to earn more than $100 for the summer. As Millar later explained in *Self-Portrait*, "Payment was just a cent a word, but the early joys of authorship were almost as sweet as sex." The Millars' only child, Linda Jane Millar, was born in June of 1939.

Millar taught history and English at Kitchener Collegiate Institute from 1939 to 1941. In 1941 his wife published her first mystery novel, *The Invisible Worm*, with Doubleday. It was the first of five novels she published in the next three years; over the course of her career Margaret Millar, an admired mystery writer in her own right, wrote more than two dozen novels. "Her books were humorous at first," Millar wrote in *Self-Portrait*, "then veered through the Gothic mode toward tragedy. Their success enabled me to leave high school teaching after two years and accept a full-time fellowship at the University of Michigan. Margaret's work was enabling me in another way. By going on ahead and breaking trail, she helped to make it possible for me to become a novelist, as perhaps her life with me had helped to make it possible for her." Millar worked as first reader and editor on his wife's novels, experience that later helped him to create his own works.

Millar returned to the United States with his wife and daughter in 1941 as a graduate student at the University of Michigan. The British poet W. H. Auden was a visiting professor that fall, and Millar enrolled in his undergraduate English course, Fate and the Individual in European Literature, which featured thirty-two required books. Through this course Millar was introduced to the works of Franz Kafka and Søren Kierkegaard. The two men became friends, and Auden visited the Millars' home. As quoted in Jerry Spier's *Ross Macdonald* (1978), Millar called Auden "the most important single influence on my life." Millar was awarded his M.A. in English in 1942. He was a teaching fellow and special assistant in English from 1941 to 1943, the year he completed the course work for his doctorate.

Millar wrote *The Dark Tunnel* in Ann Arbor in the fall of 1943. In *Self-Portrait* Millar notes that he "worked on it at night in one of the offices of the main classroom building, and the book preserves some of the atmosphere of that empty echoing pile." Completed within a single month, *The Dark Tunnel* was a spy novel, "suggested by my own experiences in Nazi Germany but showing the influence of John Buchan,"

set in a large midwestern university. His first novel included a macabre death that occurs as the result of a crime of passion as well as family intrigues and crises. It was published under his own name, as were his subsequent three novels.

By the time *The Dark Tunnel* was published in September 1944, Millar had enlisted in the U.S. Naval Reserve and was studying to be a communications officer at Harvard. He served the balance of World War II as an ensign and later as a lieutenant junior grade aboard the escort carrier *Shipley Bay* in the Pacific. He missed—and always regretted missing—witnessing combat off Okinawa, but his communications work kept him below deck for the entire action. When his duties relaxed, he found enough time to resume his writing. Millar's story "Find the Woman," written in two days in 1946, featured a Los Angeles private detective and thus was his first piece of detective fiction; it won a $400 prize and was published in *Ellery Queen's Mystery Magazine*. The suggestion to write it came from Millar's friend Anthony Boucher, whom he had met in San Francisco and who as a critic later played an important role in introducing Ross Macdonald and his Lew Archer novels to the world. While still aboard ship, Millar wrote his second novel, *Trouble Follows Me* (1946), which follows the adventures of a naval officer tracking down a Japanese secret agent–murderer.

Upon his discharge on 15 March 1946, Millar returned stateside and joined Margaret and their daughter, Linda, in Santa Barbara, California. The family settled in a four-room stucco house on Bath Street. Millar remembers the house and the time in his foreword to *Archer in Hollywood*: "It had orange trees in the back yard but no central heating. My wife and I used to sit and write in our overcoats. It was a lucky, slightly chill year and by the end of it I had written two books, *Blue City* and *The Three Roads*, which Alfred Knopf liked well enough to publish." *Blue City* was Millar's first novel published by Knopf, the manuscript having been declined by Dodd, Mead as too great a departure from his previous efforts.

Millar explains in *Self-Portrait* that *Blue City* (1947) was "about the underlife of an imaginary American city, abstracted from the several cities the war had taken me to." Johnny Weather, an angry, troubled young man, returns home after ten years to discover his father was the victim of an unsolved murder. After an arduous struggle with corrupt officials and police, Weather cleans up the town, uncovers his father's murder, and also discovers that his father played a part in the moral decline of the city. In *Blue City* Millar shows signs of Hammett's political cynicism as well as Chandler's distaste for overt sensuality. At the end the central character proclaims, "You couldn't build a City of God in the

Dust jacket for Millar's 1949 novel, written under an early pseudonym and the first to feature his detective Lew Archer

U.S.A. in 1946. But something better could be made than an organism with an appetite for human flesh. A city could be built for people to live in." Over the next twenty years Millar's concern with the psychology of crime came to supplant his concern for its sociology.

Blue City, as Matthew J. Bruccoli writes in his *Ross Macdonald* (1984), "might well have been dedicated to Hammett; it is Millar's first hard-boiled novel and shows the influence of Hammett's *Red Harvest. . . .* Functioning as a lone redresser—much like Hammett's Continental Op—John Weather solves the murder (with the help of a good whore whom he rehabilitates), cleans up the city, and reclaims his father's kingdom. *Blue City* introduces the theme of exile and return, which Millar would develop with increasing complexity." Bruccoli notes that Millar had not yet developed the point of view that distinguishes his mature work: "The story is told by the hero and thereby lacks the perspective or detachment that Millar would later achieve by means of Archer as narrator-observer." *Blue City* was condensed for *Esquire* and then was reprinted in paperback by Dell. It became Millar's first English publication when Cassell brought out a cloth edition in 1949.

Millar's next novel, *The Three Roads* (1948), was his only attempt at third-person narration. *The Three Roads,* Millar writes in *Self-Portrait,* "was my first California novel, written when I had spent no more than a few days on leave in Los Angeles. . . . That extraordinary city . . . seemed like the capital of an unknown civilization, barely remembered, or dimly foreseen." The title alludes to the crossroads where Oedipus unwittingly kills his father in *Oedipus Rex* and foreshadows Millar's lifelong obsession with the Oedipal quest, or as Millar puts it, "Exile and half-recovery and partial return." In

the novel Bret Taylor, a naval officer home from the war, searches for the murderer of his adulterous wife. Like Oedipus, the naval officer, who is consumed by justice, discovers he is the killer he is searching for. "He had to know the truth, and he had to see justice done. If he believed, as Paula [his fiancée] said she did, that there was no justice anywhere, he wouldn't be able to go on." A childhood trauma has blocked his recognition of his own guilt, and as Bruccoli points out, "Millar's favorite doubling device is employed: Taylor thinks he killed his unfaithful mother, and some twenty years later he does murder his unfaithful wife." In the course of his writing over the next ten years, Millar's priorities and those of his protagonists gradually shifted from the demand for justice to a desire for mercy.

The Three Roads was Millar's first major work set entirely in California, in what he calls "our instant society." In the foreword to *Archer in Jeopardy* (1979), he writes, "Most fiction is shaped by geography and permeated by autobiography, even when it is trying not to be. Both my father and his father were Scots-Canadian newspaper writers and editors. But I was born about five miles from San Jose, California." California as a setting was a critical element in the development of the hard-boiled genre. The state is sprawling, fluid, the Land of the Second Chance and the Big Gamble. In fast moving and socially mobile California anything can happen, even murder. As fabricated by Hammett, Chandler, and Millar, the California private investigator is a tough but humane man with eyes wide open. He understands the world and can accept its easy wickedness and pliant corruption.

Millar turned thirty-two years old in 1947, a year, he wrote in his foreword to *Archer in Hollywood,* that "wasn't so lucky." As he made an unsuccessful attempt to write a novel about his childhood, he began to doubt his vocation as a writer, and his mind "turned back toward the comparative safety of graduate school." Before he returned to Ann Arbor in 1947, however, Millar wrote his fifth novel, *The Moving Target* (1949), which was narrated by a private investigator. "I was in trouble," Millar recalled in his foreword, "and Lew Archer got me out of it. I resembled one of his clients in needing a character to front for me. Like many other writers–the most extreme is a man I knew who wrote fiction from the point of view of his pet turtle–I couldn't work directly with my own experiences and feelings. A narrator had to be interposed, like protective lead, between me and the radioactive material." In Archer, as Millar explains in *On Crime Writing,* he created a "welder's mask" that enabled him to handle "dangerously hot material." He asserts that "An author's heavy emotional investment in a narrator-hero can get in the way of the story and blur its meanings, as some of Chandler's books demonstrate. A less encumbered narrator permits greater flexibility, and fidelity to the intricate truths of life."

The private investigator Lew Archer is a vehicle Millar created to probe the unexamined lives of contemporary California. He is, as Millar notes in *Self Portrait,* "not so much a knight of romance as an observer, a socially mobile man who knows all the levels of southern California and takes a peculiar wry pleasure in exploring its secret passages." In *The Instant Enemy* (1968), the fourteenth novel in the series, Millar describes Archer standing transfixed before a Paul Klee painting, musing, "The man was in the maze; the maze was in the man." It is a tableau that evokes both the detective and the complexity of Millar's mature vision.

Although Millar apparently came up with the name Lew Archer without consciously thinking of Miles Archer, Sam Spade's murdered partner in *The Maltese Falcon,* the connection nonetheless indicates the detective's literary roots. As Millar developed the character, however, Archer became less a pastiche of Sam Spade and Philip Marlowe and took his own place in the hard-boiled canon. While Millar always recognized the debt he owed to Hammett and Chandler, he was also cognizant of his evolution away from them, as he affirms in *Self Portrait:* "Over the years I developed my own system of imagery, and I've kept pushing it into new colors, trying to be vivid in new ways. In plot terms, I've kept looking for new kinds of action."

Unlike Marlowe or Spade, who take center stage in the works in which they appear, Archer is not a traditional hero. Millar explains in *Self-Portrait* that "Archer is not a fantasy projection of myself and my personal needs. . . . Archer or a narrator like him is indispensable

to the kind of books I write. But he is not their emotional center. . . . While he is a man of action, his actions are largely directed to putting together the stories of other people's lives and discovering their significance. He is less a doer than a questioner, a consciousness in which the meanings of other lives emerge. This gradually developing conception of the detective hero as the mind of the novel is not wholly new, but it is probably my main contribution to this special branch of fiction."

In *Self-Portrait* Millar remarks that "I wasn't Archer, exactly, but Archer was me." In a July 1975 conversation Millar readily admitted that Archer was his alter ego, "a transitional figure between a world that is breaking up and one coming into being in which relationships and people will be important." Archer is not only the voice of the author but also a distancing agent. Millar explains that the detective is not the key element in his mysteries: "The most important person is the victim, for how his murder is resolved is the story in the book." Millar wrote the Archer novels in the first person and by design gives little or no physical description of the detective so that the reader is able to more easily identify with and become Archer. "We know Sherlock Holmes because Conan Doyle wrote eighty stories about him, yet in each story there is very little description about the detective. The detective describes and defines himself as he moves through the story." The reader follows Archer through the maze of the story, meeting and viewing other characters through Archer's eyes, but the detective is less important than the issues and themes his investigations uncover.

Knopf almost did not publish *The Moving Target.* On 2 September 1948 Alfred A. Knopf wrote to Millar criticizing the book the author had submitted under the initial title "The Snatch," which he called "a perfectly impossible title, of course, as I'm sure you will understand." Knopf asserted the book was "a big comedown for Kenneth Millar, not only from THE THREE ROADS but even from BLUE CITY." In particular he thought the ending was "unconvincing and thoroughly bad." Knopf suggested Millar shelve the book, but he also assured him that Knopf would still continue to be his publisher.

Knopf's letter arrived as Millar was packing to return to the University of Michigan for his doctoral studies. Over the next ten days Millar struggled with his options. In the end he agreed to change the title, to revise parts of the book (but not the ending), and to let it be published under the name John Macdonald, in memory of his father's first and middle names. Knopf agreed to publish it, provided the killer's motivation was more clearly explained. Millar received a $500 advance.

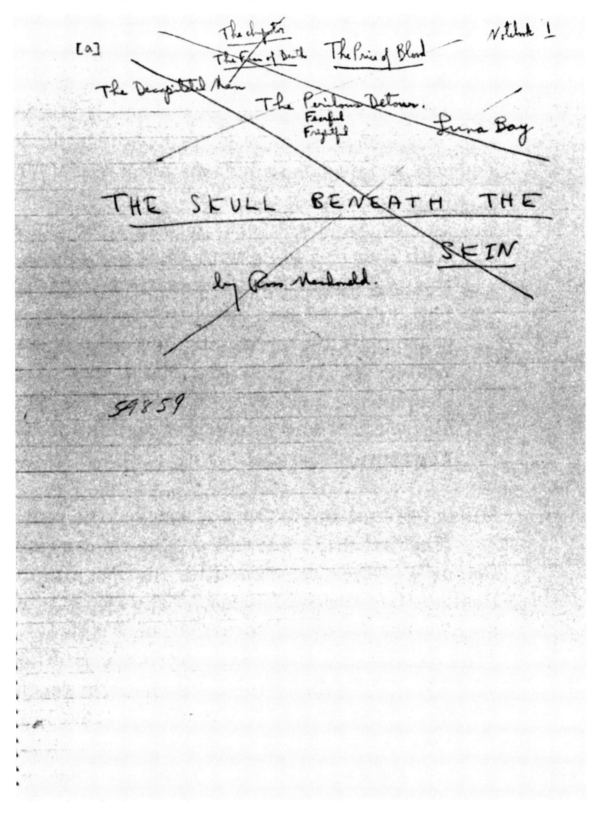

Trial titles and a page from the draft for the novel that was published in 1959 as The Galton Case
(Special Collections, University Library, University of California, Irvine)

You father is a disappointed man. He didn't have your advantages, I can tell you."

I was getting sick and tired of being reminded of my advantages. But I didn't say anything to her. I sat and ate my breakfast in silence. With the old man propped up opposite me, eyes closed and mouth open, it was a little like eating with a dead man at the table.

Something had broken in him long ago. He was a drunken bum. My father was a drunken bum. That was what I couldn't forgive him for. The old lady could forgive him, though. The lower he sank, the better she treated him. She cooked his meals and washed his clothes and worked an eight-hour day at the dairy to support him. She even gave him money for wine, and ~~sometimes~~ she let him beat her.

My aunts and uncles on her side of the family said that she was a saint, a foolish saint to put up with him all those years. I was beginning to wonder about that. I had a vague suspicion that maybe she had broken down, too. Maybe the two of them had broken down together, when she took the ball away from him and started running with it.

I think that morning was the closest I'd ever come to sympathizing with the old man. But I still had to get away from him. I had to get away from her, too.

She'd go on feeding me until I choked. She'd be pouring me cups of tea until I drowned in the stuff. She'd give me loving encouragement until I suffocated.

[Aug. 1967 - My story had begun to feed on its Oedipal roots.]

Save?

One reason why Millar so readily agreed to the use of a nom de plume was his wife's success as a mystery novelist. By the time *The Moving Target* was accepted for publication, Margaret Millar already had nine mysteries published. Partly in order to avoid confusion with his wife's career and partly to avoid looking as if he was trading on her better-known reputation, Millar wrote several novels over the next six years under the name of John Ross Macdonald, adding the "Ross" to avoid confusion with the writer John D. Mac-Donald. There was another reason for initiating the pen name: Millar at the time wanted to write "serious fiction," not detective fiction.

The revised *The Moving Target* was a modest success. Boucher, Millar's old friend, wrote in his 3 April 1949 assessment in *The New York Times Book Review* that although he found "nothing startlingly new about Mr. Macdonald's plot," the novel revealed a perceptive author: "The outstanding freshness of this novel comes instead from the fact that Macdonald as a writer, as a weaver of words and an observer of people, stands head and shoulders above most of his competitors." While Knopf brought out only one printing, the novel was picked up by the Mystery Guild, the first of ten Archer novels so chosen during the next quarter-century.

One reader who was not pleased with Millar's book was Chandler, who bitterly criticized his style in a letter to the mystery reviewer and critic James Sandoe on 14 April 1949:

> Have read *The Moving Target* by John Ross Macdonald and am a good deal impressed by it, in a peculiar way. In fact I could use it as a springboard for a sermon on How Not to be a Sophisticated Writer. . . .
>
> What strikes me about the book (and I guess I should not be writing about it if I didn't feel that the author had something) is first an effect that is rather repellent. There is nothing to hitch to; here is a man who wants the public for the mystery story in its primitive violence and also wants it to be clear that he, individually, is a highly literate and sophisticated character. A car is "acned with rust" not spotted. Scribblings on toilet walls are "graffiti" (we know Italian yet, it says); one refers to "podex osculation" (medical latin, too, ain't we hell?). "The seconds piled up precariously like a tower of poker chips," etc. The simile that does not quite come off because it doesn't understand what the purpose of the simile is.

With the publication of *Raymond Chandler Speaking* in 1962, Millar thirteen years after the fact learned of Chandler's criticism; for his own part, Millar never denied Chandler's influence upon him as a writer.

From the first, Lew Archer's private investigation practice was based in Hollywood, a location he shares with Chandler's Marlowe. "If California is a state of mind," Millar writes in the foreword to *Archer in Hollywood*, then "Hollywood is where you take its temperature. There is a peculiar sense in which this city existing mainly on film and tape is our national capital, alas, and not just the capital of California. It's the place where our children learn how and what to dream and where everything happens just before, or just after, it happens to us." Millar notes that the movies have affected his writing: "One thing that strikes me, over and above a recurrent fascination with Hollywood, is my use of film techniques. *The Moving Target* in particular is a story clearly aspiring to be a movie. It was no accident that when Warner Brothers made it into one . . . they were able to follow the story virtually scene by scene."

Three books featuring Archer followed in rapid succession: *The Drowning Pool* (1950), *The Way Some People Die* (1951), and *The Ivory Grin* (1952)—all written by Millar as John Ross Macdonald. In *The Drowning Pool*, which was dedicated to Boucher, Archer is involved in the affairs of the troubled Slocum family when he is hired to discover who sent a letter accusing Mrs. Slocum of adultery. The novel introduces, as Bruccoli notes, the theme of concealed parenthood and distressed children but lacks a quest for identity, a key theme for much of Millar's later works, because the daughter does not learn the truth of her paternity until the conclusion of the novel. *The Way Some People Die* features a woman murderer, the first of a series of homicidal women in Millar's work, which would lead some critics to brand Millar as a misogynist. As Bruccoli points out, "Most of his killers are women; they kill not for love, but for security. He has explained that women are frequently victims of society, and victims tend to victimize." After Anthony Boucher praised the novel in *The New York Times Book Review* (5 August 1951), Millar replied: "I am naturally grateful for your good opinion of *Way*. I sort of have a sneaking liking for it myself, feeling as I do that I broke loose out of my personal neuroses in it and embarked on pure narrative for the first time." In *The Ivory Grin* Archer is involved in a missing daughter case. The distinguished reviewer Julian Symons compared Millar's novel to Chandler's work in his review in *The Times Literary Supplement* on 20 November 1953: "Mr. John Ross Macdonald must be ranked high among American thriller writers. His evocations of scenes and people are as sharp as those of Mr. Raymond Chandler, and the speed of his writing is almost unmarred by either sentimentality or sadism."

Millar was growing in confidence as a writer, as he notes in the foreword to *Archer in Hollywood*: "The labor I'd put into forming a style had begun to pay off. Rummaging through old papers the other day, I found the opening paragraph of *Way* written out in a spiral notebook, for the first and final time, just as it was to be printed." That first paragraph instantly informs readers that they have entered Archer country:

> The house was in Santa Monica on a cross street between the boulevard, within earshot of the coast highway and rifleshot of the sea. The street was the kind that people had once been proud to live on, but in the last few years it had lost its claim to pride. The houses had too many stories, too few windows, not enough paint. Their history was easy to guess: they were one-family residences broken up into apartments and light-housekeeping rooms, or converted into tourist homes. Even the palms that lined the street looked as if they had seen their best days and were starting to lose their hair.

All the staples of Archer's California are present: the ever-present sounds of the freeway and the Pacific, the evocation of a world in transition, the sense of sadness and doubt from diminished expectations, and a subtle foreshadowing of violence.

While writing his mysteries, Millar also pursued postgraduate studies at the University of Michigan, where in February 1952 he earned a Ph.D. in English literature. His dissertation thesis was "The Inward Eye: A Study of Coleridge's Psychological Criticism." Bruccoli relates that Millar was gratified when he was told that his dissertation was the most distinguished ever submitted in English literature at the university, but he was disappointed that he was unable to find a publisher. After graduation he taught creative writing courses in the Adult Education Division of Santa Barbara City College during the 1950s and was instrumental in the creation of the Santa Barbara Writers Conference. Throughout his life he was a mentor to aspiring writers.

In *Meet Me at the Morgue* (1953) Millar chose as his protagonist a county probation officer, Howard Cross, who becomes involved in a kidnapping case of a four-year-old boy when one of his clients is accused of the crime. Millar wanted to use his own name for his non-Archer books and to use the Macdonald pseudonym for the Archer series, but Knopf rejected the idea and published the novel as written by John Ross Macdonald. When an editor complained about the lack in Millar's work of "the sharp contrast between good and evil, so noticeable in Chandler's books and so important to this kind of story," Millar wrote a five-page letter back to Knopf on 28 August 1952 to explain and defend his approach:

> Plot is important to me. I try to make my plots carry meaning, and this meaning such as it is determines and controls the meaning of the story. I know I have a tendency to subordinate individual scenes to the overall intention, to make the book the unit of effect. Perhaps this needs some correction, without going to the

opposite extreme. This opposite extreme is represented by Chandler, one of my masters with whose theory and practice I am in growing disagreement. For him any old plot will do. . . . I am interested in doing things in the mystery which Chandler didn't do, and probably couldn't.

Millar was sensitive to charges that he was merely imitating past masters. "I owe a lot to Chandler (and more to Hammett)," he wrote, "but it would be simple self-stultification for me to take him as the last word in the mystery. My literary range greatly exceeds his, and my approach to writing will not wear out so fast."

In his 1990 essay "Ross Macdonald: Revolutionary Author and Critic; or the Need for the Oath of Macdonald," Ray B. Browne describes Millar's maturing ambition: "Macdonald was one of the early crime fiction authors who saw the full ramifications of his kind of story. He felt that like all popular art, the crime story exists to be enjoyed, but that it reveals the shapes and meanings of life in all their subtlety and surprises, and that its real strength resides in its 'use for symbolic and psychological and social purposes.' Because of this appeal to a mass audience, Macdonald wanted to return mystery fiction to mainstream literature, 'where it began.'"

Millar wrote two more books as John Ross Macdonald. In his next novel, *Find A Victim* (1954), he returned to Lew Archer, who becomes involved in a case when he discovers a dying man, the victim of a shooting, on the side of the road while driving to Sacramento. The dust jacket for the novel revealed that John Ross Macdonald was Kenneth Millar. On 26 July 1954 the novel was reviewed in *Time* (a first for Millar), and the magazine proclaimed Millar as the successor to Hammett and Chandler. In 1955 Bantam Books brought out a collection of Millar's stories, *The Name Is Archer*. For the volume, which included "Find the Woman" and six other stories–"Gone Girl," "The Bearded Lady," "The Suicide," "Guilt-Edged Blonde," "The Sinister Habit," and "Wild Goose Chase"–Millar revised the stories and renamed the protagonists so that each featured Lew Archer.

Millar settled on the pseudonym Ross Macdonald with the publication of *The Barbarous Coast* (1956), in which Archer's search for a Toronto man's estranged wife leads him to a Hollywood studio crowd and the investigation of a murder. Millar turned forty while he was writing the novel. In the foreword to *Archer in Hollywood* Millar recalls his growing sense of confidence: "Though I've always been a slow developer, by that time I was getting myself and my form under more personal control. It was my largest book so far, in both social and moral complexity. In it I was

Dust jacket for Millar's eighth Lew Archer novel, in which he began to explore his personal history in fictional form

learning to get rid of the protective wall between my mind and the perilous stuff of my own life."

Events in Millar's family life soon contributed to Millar's further breaking down of his "protective wall." In February 1956 his seventeen-year-old daughter was charged in the vehicular homicide of a thirteen-year-old boy in Santa Barbara. That August she received eight years' probation and was ordered to undergo psychiatric treatments. As a direct consequence, the Millars for a year moved to Menlo Park in Northern California, where Millar himself underwent psychiatric treatment. Remembering this period in his life, Millar told Philip Oaks in the 24 October 1971 *Sunday Times* (London) that "I had reached the point where I could not see anything clearly ahead. I needed help, and I got it. What it did was take me deeper into life."

From 1958 to 1976 Millar wrote almost a book each year. In *Self-Portrait* Millar writes that *The Doomsters* (1958)—a novel that begins with a guilt-wracked man who seeks Archer's help and ends with his wife who has killed to secure her interest in her husband's fam-

ily fortune—marked "a fairly clean break with the Chandler tradition, which it had taken me some years to digest, and freed me to make my own approach to the crimes and sorrow of life." Archer, in *The Doomsters* and in subsequent novels, becomes less a crime fighter or social critic than an observer and psychologist. As Bernard A. Schopen states in his *Ross Macdonald* (1990), "In *The Doomsters* Macdonald demonstrated that Hammett and Chandler had not permanently fixed the boundaries of the American detective novel, that the form contained additional thematic and aesthetic possibilities."

Ten years after his first Lew Archer novel, Millar wrote what he considered his true breakthrough novel, *The Galton Case* (1959). In his foreword to *Archer at Large* (1970) Millar explains what he in that novel and thereafter began to explore: "My early years in Canada, for one thing. . . . It doesn't tell the naked truth, of course. It broke free of my actual life and my rather murky feelings, into the clearer and more ordered world where fiction lays out its concentrated, terrifying versions of the truth. Fiction, when it is working well, lifts out of the

The Millars with Alfred A. Knopf, whose firm published most of Kenneth Millar's books (photograph by Hal Boucher)

writer's life patterns which tend toward the legendary. But the patterns are disrupted and authenticated by bits and pieces of the original life-stuff—names and places, scraps of conversation, old feelings and forces like spawning salmon working their way back up the stream of time." Millar told Solokov that *The Galton Case* "marked the difference between my early and later books. There's no question that my work has deepened since then. Freud was one of the two or three greatest influences on me. He turned myth into psychiatry, and I've been trying to turn it back into myth again in my own small way."

The novel begins as Archer is hired by Gordon Sable, a lawyer representing the wealthy and ailing Mrs. Galton, who has had a change of heart and wants to find her son, missing for twenty years. The Galton estate is old California money; in the front of the family mansion is a lawn "the color of the ink they use to print the serial numbers on bank notes, and it stretched in unbroken smoothness for a couple of hundred yards." Twenty-two-year-old Anthony Galton and his pregnant, lower-class wife "dropped out of sight" in 1936 after he renounced

the family name and wealth to become John Brown, proletarian poet. Archer's identification of a decapitated skeleton in Northern California as the missing heir and his discovery of a young man, John Brown, claiming to be Frank Brown's son, however, is only the first stage of this intricate story of a murdered father and a lost son.

Archer is remarkably celibate for a hard-boiled private investigator. *The Galton Case,* the eighth novel in the series, is the first book in which Archer sleeps with a woman. In all eighteen novels, he sleeps with four, and not until the last novel in the series does he have a real love affair. Millar often joked that Archer was "so narrow that when he turns sideways he disappears." He was careful not to allow his detective to become the story. Archer is a catalyst; his presence is enough to generate reactions (often violent) in the behaviors of others. Despite the importance of *The Galton Case* to Millar, reviewers accepted it as a new mystery by a well-thought-of author and did not attach to it any special significance.

At the end of May 1959 the Millars were again profoundly troubled by the behavior of their daughter.

On 30 May nineteen-year-old Linda left her dormitory at the University of California, Davis, for a casino in Stateline, Nevada. Then she disappeared. Eleven days went by before she resurfaced in Reno, with no recollection of where she had been. According to her father, Linda was tormented by recurring guilt from her vehicular homicide. After the ordeal Millar was hospitalized and needed treatment for hypertension.

After *The Ferguson Affair* (1960), in which Millar featured a non-Archer protagonist (lawyer Bill Gunnarson) for the last time, Millar wrote *The Wycherly Woman* (1961), set mainly in Northern California. Archer is hired to find a missing daughter, who he discovers has been impersonating her murdered mother. The detective's weariness with the world is evident in the novel. When he stays at a cheap hotel, Archer notes that "Forty years as a bellhop hollows a man out into a kind of receptacle for tips. Twenty years as a detective works changes in a man, too." In the hotel lounge he picks up a drunk blonde, who passes out back in her room: "Her mouth was burned dry by neat whiskey, and her breath came harshly through it. I felt more deeply than ever that blend of pity and shame which kept me at my trade among the lost, battered souls who lived in hell, as she did." At the end of the novel a murderer reveals the emptiness of the modern idea of love: "Still we had something between us—something that was better than nothing. When we were together, at least we weren't alone." Spier argues that *The Wycherly Woman* is about "the endurance of human weaknesses. The proper response, then, to such situations is not fixing blame, but accepting responsibility for the human condition. Personal responsibility assumes a greater thematic importance in Macdonald's later works."

In Millar's world the haves and the have-nots are always in conflict, and the past always demands its due. Peter Wolfe in *Dreamers Who Live Through Their Dreams: The World of Ross Macdonald's Novels* (1976) points out that the five books from *The Wycherly Woman* to *Black Money* (1966) "deal with tragic sexual passion. Some of the tragedy is caused by money; money cuts across the passion in all the books." Dick Allen and David Chacko in their *Detective Fiction: Crime and Compromise* (1974) argue that "Macdonald's work might be called curiously Puritanical. One might live a lie for ten or fifteen years, but sooner or later he will be discovered; he will pay. In the meantime, his suffering will be enormous. The crime committed in the past will have informed his entire life."

Millar's next novel, *The Zebra-Striped Hearse* (1962), Spier asserts, "is one of Macdonald's cleverest and most involved excursions into the Freudian 'family fantasy.'" Wealthy Mark Blackwell hires Archer to investigate the man his daughter, Harriet, intends to marry. Archer discovers that the Blackwells have more to hide than the suitor, who suspects the Blackwells were involved in the murder of his wife. Spier writes, "In a very real sense, *The Zebra-Striped Hearse* is a chronicle of the end of a family—a symptom of evil in Macdonald's wasteland." The title refers to a vehicle driven by a group of beach bums who, a waitress angrily tells Archer, "got no respect for the living or the dead." According to Spier, "they are the natural products of a society out of touch with its own humanity."

The Crime Writers Association of London gave Millar its Silver Dagger for his novel *The Chill* (1964). In his foreword to *Archer At Large*, Millar writes that *The Chill*, "that basilisk of a book, was not easy to write. The opening two or three chapters took several months and went through seven or eight versions. I had my central idea, perhaps one of the stronger single plot lines that ever came to me. But I found that I had to imagine the whole development of the book before I could write an assured opening chapter." Hired to find a runaway bride, Archer follows her to a local college, where she is accused of murder. He encounters the dean of the college and his domineering mother, who are the nexus of three separate plotlines and murders. "Brilliantly conceived and beautifully written," writes Noble in his biography, "*The Chill* was a Macdonald masterwork."

Millar next wrote *The Far Side of the Dollar* (1965), in which the revelation that a father adopted his own son leads to murder. A late riser, he spent up to four hours a day in a battered leather chair in a spare bedroom writing his detective novels in spiral notebooks. A plank of wood across the arms of his chair was his writing table. He averaged a thousand words a day and worked Monday through Friday. He had a professional typist prepare his manuscripts for publication.

The reviews to *The Far Side of the Dollar* were some of his best yet. Anthony Boucher in *The New York Times Book Review* (20 January 1965) announced that in his view Millar was the greatest writer ever in the hard-boiled field:

Without abating in the least my admiration for Dashiell Hammett and Raymond Chandler, I should like to venture the heretical suggestion that Ross Macdonald is a better novelist than either of them. He owes an immeasurable debt to both in the matter of technique and style; but he has gone beyond their tutelage to develop the "hard-boiled," private-eye novel into a far more supple medium, in which he can study the common and uncommon man (and woman) as well as the criminal, in which he can write (often brilliantly and even profoundly) not only about violence and retribution but simply about "people with enough feeling to be hurt, and enough complexity to do wrong"—to quote from his latest.

First page of Millar's draft for The Underground Man *(Special Collections, University Library, University of California, Irvine)*

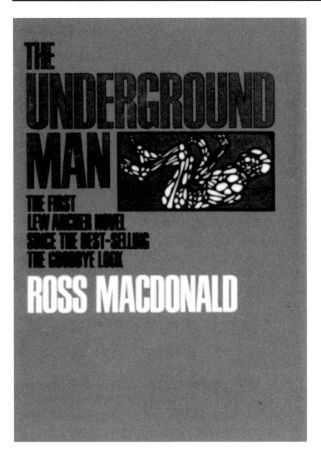

Dust jacket for Millar's 1971 novel, in which a fire, started to cover up a murder, threatens to destroy a city

Knopf published Boucher's review as an ad for the novel. The Crime Writers Association of London gave him its Golden Dagger for *The Far Side of the Dollar,* and in 1965 Millar was elected to the honorary position of president of the Mystery Writers of America.

In *Self-Portrait* Millar describes the long gestation of his nineteenth novel, *Black Money:* "I think I had the central idea for *Black Money* in my mind for close to twenty years. It took me all that time to figure out how I could write it and to decide where the central character came from, who he was and what the source of the black money was. Year after year I would return to these ideas, make more notes and a cross reference to a twenty-year-old notebook and put it away until I was ready to work on it." *Black Money* is centered on Frances Martel, a French aristocrat who marries a local girl, Ginny Fablon. Archer is hired to "find out who Martel is and where he came from and where his money came from."

Millar was influenced in writing the novel by F. Scott Fitzgerald's *The Great Gatsby* (1925)—a book, he writes in *Self-Portrait,* that "has obvious connections with American crime fiction and the revolution effected in the fiction during the twenties. The skeleton of Fitzgerald's

work, if not its nervous system, is that of a mystery novel." Like Fitzgerald's Jay Gatsby, Martel is a romantic who believes that money can buy the American Dream and thus has invented a past more suitable for his grandiose ambitions. Archer discovers that Martel is really Pedro Domingo, the son of a Panama bar girl, who has stolen money from a Nevada gambler to buy his golden girl, who, it turns out, is even less worthy of his devotion than Daisy was of Gatsby's.

In 1966 Millar's *The Moving Target* was made into the movie *Harper,* starring Paul Newman. The movie sale enabled the Millars to buy a modern, four-bedroom house. For the first time in their careers, the couple had room for themselves, their houseful of dogs, and their books. Because *Harper* was so successful, *The Drowning Pool* was made into a sequel in 1975, again starring Paul Newman. To capitalize on Millar's growing popularity and critical success, Knopf published *Archer in Hollywood,* an omnibus of Archer novels, in 1967. It was followed by *Archer At Large* in 1970 and by *Archer in Jeopardy* in 1979.

Millar published two more novels before the end of the 1960s. Spier writes that *The Instant Enemy* (1968) "is perhaps the bitterest of the Archer novels and no doubt reflects the violent times of war and student unrest in which it was written and published." *The Goodbye Look* (1969), Millar's twenty-first novel, was his first best-seller. The title comes from a situation where two men are face to face, ready to kill. The fiancée of Nick Chambers, the troubled young man at the heart of the novel, tells Archer, "They had a funny look on both their faces, as if they were both going to die. As if they really *wanted* to kill each other and be killed." Archer recognizes "that goodbye look. I had seen it in the war, and too many times since the war."

The Goodbye Look has many trademark Millar touches. When Archer asks Jean Swain, a woman searching for her lost father, "What's hurting, Jean?," she answers, "My whole life." Then she "spread both hands on her breasts as if the pain was overflowing her fingers." As Jean reminisces, Archer notes "her mind was being carried down the stream of memory, swept willy-nilly through subterranean passages toward roaring falls." Later, Archer attempts to explain his way of life to the wife of a psychiatrist: "I like to move into people's lives and then move out again. Living with one set of people in one place used to bore me." The woman counters, "That isn't your real motivation. I know your type. You have a secret passion for justice. Why don't you admit it?" Archer answers that he has "a secret passion for mercy. . . . But justice is what keeps happening to people."

The critical response to *The Goodbye Look* marked a turning point in Millar's career, as he was featured on the front page of *The New York Times Book Review* on 1 June

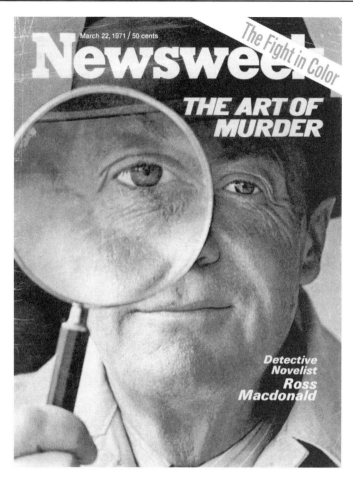

Newsmagazine cover featuring Millar under his best-known pseudonym

1969. Novelist William Goldman's praise of the writer in an essay titled "The finest detective novels ever written by an American" was used to advertise new editions of Millar's old works as well as his subsequent novels. Goldman maintained that "Ross Macdonald's work in the last decade has nothing remotely to do with hard-boiled detective novels. He is writing novels of character about people with ghosts. . . . All of his characters have them and so do all of us. We have each experienced those crazy moon-moments when we considered pitching everything and taking off with the rich divorcee down the hall. Macdonald's people do it, that's the only difference." In the same issue John Leonard concluded: "Macdonald's moral vision, his interest in psychology and sociology, his concern for the continuities of family life, his willingness to risk more of himself in his stories, his clean spare style ('beware the inflated rhetoric'), combined to move the detective novel–democratic, accessible to everyone, respecting unities of form, almost Elizabethan–into the mainstream of American letters." This new critical attention led to major (although mixed) reviews for Millar from *Newsweek, The New Yorker,* and *Time.*

The Millars were dealt a tremendous personal blow when their daughter, Linda Jane Millar Pagnusat, died in her sleep at the age of thirty-one in November 1970. She had suffered a slight stroke in 1968, and it and her death were attributed to a circulatory disorder. In a letter to a family friend at the time, Millar called his daughter "a valiant girl, one of the great moral forces in my life and after Margaret my dearest love. . . . there is some relief in the knowledge that Linda made a great effort and succeeded in it, though she died young."

In *The Underground Man* (1971) a small boy (modeled on Millar's grandson) that Archer has befriended is taken by his father, Stanley Broadhurst, and a mysterious young girl to his grandmother's mountainous lands above Santa Teresa. In the investigation of the cause of a forest fire that threatens the community, the father is found murdered and buried in a shallow grave; the fire was set by the killer to conceal his crime. Archer is hired by the boy's mother to retrieve her son, who was last seen with the young girl and a stranger. The detective encounters other murders in the course of his investigation, which eventually leads him back to the curious disappearance of the boy's grandfather fifteen years before.

The fire in the novel was a key in Millar's conception of the work. Millar told Sokolov in his *Newsweek* cover story that he "wanted a crime that threatened a whole city." In his novel Millar links the so-called Rattlesnake fire with the violence of war, imagery that suggests the consequences of uncontrolled passion. An example is Archer's description of the blaze and the efforts to control it: "under and through the smoke I caught glimpses of fire like the flashes of heavy guns too far away to be heard. The illusion of war was completed by an old two-engine bomber which flew in low over the mountain's shoulder. The plane was lost in the smoke for a long instant, then climbed out trailing a pastel red cloud of fire retardant." Later he sees flames "crashing through the thick chaparral like cavalry." At another time he "glanced up at the mountains, and was shocked by what I saw. The fire had grown and spread as if it fed on darkness. It hung around the city like the bivouacs of a besieging army."

As in all of Millar's later novels, forgiveness is essential, even if it alone is not enough. During his investigation Archer meets Ellen Strome, a Sausalito painter who is a link between the murder committed fifteen years before and the current rash of killings. When the young boy is rescued, Archer watches how Ellen "walked him out with her arm around his shoulders. . . . I knew it wasn't a solution. Ellen was far gone in solitude, and he was too old to need a mother, really. He had to live out his time of trouble, as she had. And there was no assurance that he would. He belonged to a generation whose elders had been poisoned, like the pelicans, with a kind of moral DDT that damaged the lives of their young."

The Underground Man was on the best-seller list of *The New York Times* for seventeen weeks, reaching number four. In his *Newsweek* story Sokolov asserts that in *The Underground Man* "Archer-Macdonald are working together at their peak, piecing together a most modern tragedy, making literature out of the thriller form, gazing more clearly than ever into the future as it rolls through the smog. Archer's leather-lined compassion for the small abducted boy is an implicit plea for human values in a society whose central message may be the freeway with its constant movement, noise, pollution, brutality and lack of human contact."

In his 14 March 1971 review for *The Los Angeles Times,* Robert Kirsch placed Millar "in a line of writers from Dostoyevsky to Raymond Chandler who have revealed the nether side of humanity and illuminated the worth of life in doing so." Kirsch asserted that Millar's major purpose in the Archer series was "to examine California as a microcosm of America. In so doing, he has touched universality. . . . Southern California is evoked effectively; no writer since Raymond Chandler has done

better in this regard. But I think Macdonald has more amplitude as an observer of life. Lew Archer is more developed as a protagonist, particularly in the later books. He is closer to Macdonald himself, to his concerns, his thoughtful and penetrating understanding of the California experience." He argued that Millar's novel "is, in the final analysis, a story of crime and punishment. But the crimes are shared and the punishment often built into life itself, in unhappy marriages, in the secret nightmare witnesses of children to violence and argument, in the endless pattern of private grudge, in love turned to hate; the victims are not only those who are the target of violence. Its fallout corrupts the innocent, exacts an exorbitant price in human suffering."

The New York Times Book Review (14 February 1971) allotted its entire front page and three additional pages to Eudora Welty's review of the novel:

> This is the medieval tale of romance and the faerie. It is exactly what Archer plunges into when he enters this case. Finding his way through their lies and fears, into other people's obsessions and dreams, he might as well be in a fairy tale with them. The mystery has handed him what amounts to a set of impossible tasks: Find the door that opens the past. Unravel the ever-tangling threads of time. Rescue the stolen child from fleeing creatures who appear to be under a spell and who forbid him to speak to them. Meet danger from the aroused elements of fire and water. And beware the tower. But Archer's own role in the fairy tale is clear to him; from the time he fed the blue jays with the small boy, he never had a choice. There is the maze of the past to be entered and come out of alive, bringing the innocent to safety. And in the maze there lives a monster; his name is Murder.

Millar's style, Welty wrote, "is one of delicacy and tension, very rightly made, with a spring in it. It doesn't allow a static sentence or one without pertinence. And the spare, controlled narrative, built for action and speed, conveys as well the world through which the action moves and gives it meaning, brings scene and character, however swiftly, before the eyes without a blur. It is an unbroken series of sparkling pictures."

Millar's next novel, *Sleeping Beauty* (1973), was inspired by the 1969 oil spill near Santa Barbara. Millar was an active conservationist and environmentalist; he helped form a group called Get Oil Out (GOO) following the disastrous spill. The opening of the novel reflects Millar's concern for the environment and is perhaps the most quoted passage of all of his work. Flying home from Mexico, Archer spots the oil spill that "lay on the blue water off Pacific Point in a free-form slick that seemed miles wide and many miles long. An offshore oil platform stood up out of its windward end like the metal handle of a dagger that

 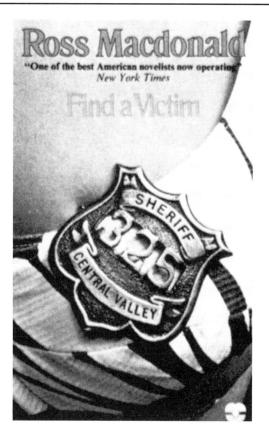

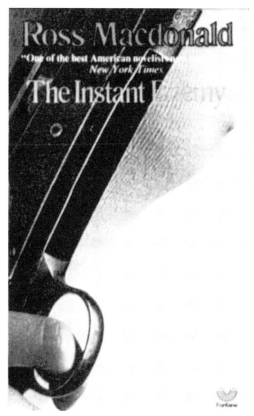 

Covers for British paperpack editions of Millar novels published in the early 1970s

had stabbed the world and made it spill black blood." In the novel Archer comes into conflict with three generations of the Lennox family, whose offshore drilling rig has caused the oil spill.

Although *Sleeping Beauty* received some negative reviews, it made the best-seller list for six weeks. Welty, to whom the novel is dedicated, wrote of it in her foreword to Millar's *Self-Portrait*:

> The spoils of the natural world are also the spoils of the innocent and vulnerable; his crime novels connect them in ways that reach far and far back. The 1969 oil spill is the explosive force of his fine novel *Sleeping Beauty*, where it is given the full strength of his tragic insight into its human motivation, its pattern of family connection. One speaks to him of the other: mistreatment of the natural world and the damage people do to their fellow human beings. Violence is all one language—or rather the same lack, deprivation, of any other language. One of the gentlest of men, Ken Millar (Ross Macdonald) has not found the basilisk face of evil to be inscrutable.

Two years after Millar was honored by the Mystery Writers of America with the Grand Master Award, his eighteenth and final Archer novel, *The Blue Hammer,* was published in 1976. The trigger for the novel is the theft of a valuable painting by the legendary Richard Chantry, who disappeared years before. What begins with Archer's investigation of artists and art dealers soon leads him to murder and revelations of secret familial relationships. Archer is portrayed as older—he admits to being fifty—and lonely: "I seemed to have entered another city, a convalescent city where the wars of love were over and I was merely one of the aging survivors." Nevertheless, he has his first real love affair, with a much younger journalist, Betty Jo Siddon. The title "The Blue Hammer" refers to the visible pulse of arterial blood in his lover's temple, "the beating of the silent hammer that meant she was alive." While there is no promise of an enduring relationship for Archer, the novel ends with an image that seems well suited as a summation of the Archer series as the detective accompanies the father of a multiple murderer on a visit to his son in jail. Flanked by armed guards, the father reaches out and touches his son's tears. *The Blue Hammer* received mixed reviews and was not a best-seller, although it did sell well.

Millar's writing career ended in 1980 due to the onset of Alzheimer's disease; he died on 11 July 1983 in Pinecrest Hospital in Santa Barbara. His body was cremated, and his ashes were scattered in the Pacific Ocean off the coastline of his adopted hometown.

Interviews:

John Leonard, "Ross Macdonald, His Lew Archer and Other Secret Selves," *New York Times Book Review,* 1 June 1969, pp. 2, 19;

Sam Grogg Jr., "Ross Macdonald at the Edge," *Journal of Popular Culture,* 7 (Summer 1973): 213–222;

Jerry Tutunjian, "A Conversation with Ross Macdonald," *Tamarack Review,* 62 (1974): 66–85;

Jane S. Bakerman, "A Slightly Stylized Conversation with Ross Macdonald," *Writers' Yearbook* (1981): 86, 88–89, 111.

Bibliography:

Matthew J. Bruccoli, *Kenneth Millar/Ross Macdonald* (Pittsburgh: University of Pittsburgh Press, 1983).

Biographies:

Matthew J. Bruccoli, *Ross Macdonald* (New York: Harcourt Brace Jovanovich, 1984);

Tom Nolan, *Ross Macdonald: A Biography* (New York: Scribner, 1999).

References:

Dick Allen and David Chacko, "The Detective" and "The Genre Extended," in their *Detective Fiction: Crime and Compromise* (New York: Harcourt Brace Jovanovich, 1974), pp. 77–78 and 291–293;

Harold Bloom, ed., " Ross Macdonald," in *Classic Crime and Suspense Writers* (New York: Chelsea House, 1994) pp. 144–157;

Ray B. Browne, "Ross Macdonald: Revolutionary Author and Critic; or the Need for the Oath of Macdonald," *Journal of Popular Culture,* 24 (Winter 1990): 101–111;

George Grella, "Evil Plots," *New Republic* (26 July 1975): 24–26;

Bernard A. Schopen, *Ross Macdonald* (Boston: Twayne Publishers, 1990);

Ralph B. Sipper, ed., *Inward Journey: Ross Macdonald* (Santa Barbara, Cal.: Cordelia Edition, 1984);

Robert E. Skinner, *The Hard-boiled Explicator: A Guide to the Study of Dashiell Hammett, Raymond Chandler, and Ross Macdonald* (Metuchen, N.J.: Scarecrow Press, 1985), pp. 17–24;

Raymond A. Solokov, "The Art of Murder," *Newsweek* (22 March 1971): 101–108;

Jerry Spier, *Ross Macdonald* (New York: Ungar, 1978);

Peter Wolfe, *Dreamers Who Live Their Dreams: The World of Ross Macdonald's Novels* (Bowling Green, Ohio: Bowling Green State University Popular Press, 1976).

Papers:

Kenneth Millar's papers are at the University of California Library at Irvine, which includes the Bruccoli Collection.

Marcia Muller

(28 September 1944 –   )

Rebecca E. Martin
Pace University

BOOKS: *Edwin of the Iron Shoes* (New York: McKay, 1977; London: Penguin, 1978);

Ask the Cards a Question (New York: St. Martin's Press, 1982; London: Hale, 1983);

The Cheshire Cat's Eye (New York: St. Martin's Press, 1983; London: Hale, 1983);

The Tree of Death (New York: Walker, 1983; London: Hale, 1986);

Double, by Muller and Bill Pronzini (New York: St. Martin's Press, 1984; London: Hale, 1986);

Games to Keep the Dark Away (New York: St. Martin's Press, 1984; London: Severn House, 1985);

Leave a Message for Willie (New York: St. Martin's Press, 1984; London: Women's Press, 1985);

The Legend of the Slain Soldiers (New York: Walker, 1985; London: Hale, 1985);

There's Nothing to Be Afraid Of (New York: St. Martin's Press, 1985);

Beyond the Grave, by Muller and Pronzini (New York: Walker, 1986);

The Cavalier in White (New York: St. Martin's Press, 1986);

The Lighthouse, by Muller and Pronzini (New York: St. Martin's Press, 1987; London: Hale, 1988);

Eye of the Storm (New York: Mysterious Press, 1988);

There Hangs the Knife (New York: St. Martin's Press, 1988);

Dark Star (New York: St. Martin's Press, 1989);

There's Something in a Sunday (New York: Mysterious Press, 1989; London: Women's Press, 1992);

The Shape of Dread (New York: Mysterious Press, 1989; London: Women's Press, 1992);

Trophies and Dead Things (New York: Mysterious Press, 1990; London: Women's Press, 1992);

Where Echoes Live (New York: Mysterious Press, 1991; London: Women's Press, 1992);

Pennies on a Dead Woman's Eyes (New York: Mysterious Press, 1992; London: Women's Press, 1993);

Wolf in the Shadows (New York: Mysterious Press, 1993; London: Women's Press, 1993);

Marcia Muller at the time of her 1991 novel Where Echoes Live
(photograph by Charles R. Lucke)

Till the Butchers Cut Him Down (New York: Mysterious Press, 1994; London: Women's Press, 1994);

The McCone Files (Norfolk, Va.: Crippen & Landru, 1995);

A Wild and Lonely Place (New York: Mysterious Press, 1995; London: Women's Press, 1995);

The Broken Promise Land (New York: Mysterious Press, 1996; London: Women's Press, 1996);

Both Ends of the Night (New York: Mysterious Press, 1997);

Detective Duos (New York: Oxford University Press, 1997);

While Other People Sleep (New York: Mysterious Press, 1998);

Duo (Unity, Maine: Five Star, 1998);

A Walk through the Fire (New York: Mysterious Press, 1999).

OTHER: "Merrill-Go-Round," in *The Arbor House Treasury of Mystery and Suspense,* edited by Bill Pronzini,

267

Barry N. Malzberg, and Martin H. Greenberg (New York: Arbor House, 1982), pp. 111–120;

"Cattails," in *The Web She Weaves,* edited by Muller and Pronzini (New York: Morrow, 1983), pp. 479–488;

The Web She Weaves: An Anthology of Mysteries and Suspicious Stories by Women, edited by Muller and Pronzini (New York: Morrow, 1983);

"Kindling Point," in *Witches' Brew: Horror and Supernatural Stories by Women,* edited by Muller and Pronzini (New York: Macmillan, 1984), pp. 282–299;

"Wild Mustard," in *The Eyes Have It,* edited by Robert J. Randisi (New York: Mysterious Press, 1984), pp. 201–211;

Child's Ploy, edited by Muller and Pronzini (New York: Macmillan, 1984);

"The Sanchez Sacraments," in *The Ethnic Detectives,* edited by Pronzini and Greenberg (New York: Dodd, Mead, 1985), pp. 283–305;

"The Broken Men," in *Women Sleuths,* edited by Pronzini and Greenberg (Chicago: Academy, 1985), pp. 163–221;

Dark Lessons: Crime and Detection on Campus, edited by Muller and Pronzini (New York: Macmillan, 1985);

She Won the West: An Anthology of Western and Frontier Stories by Women, edited by Muller and Pronzini (New York: Morrow, 1985);

Chapter and Hearse: Suspense Stories about the World of Books, edited by Muller and Pronzini (New York: Morrow, 1985);

Kill or Cure: Suspense Stories about the World of Medicine, edited by Muller and Pronzini (New York: Macmillan, 1985);

The Wickedest Show on Earth: A Carnival of Circus Suspense, edited by Muller and Pronzini (New York: Arbor House, 1985);

The Deadly Arts: A Collection of Artful Suspense, edited by Muller and Pronzini (New York: Arbor House, 1985);

1001 Midnights: The Aficionado's Guide to Mystery and Detective Fiction, edited by Muller and Pronzini (New York: Arbor House, 1986);

Hard-Boiled Dames: A Brass-Knuckled Anthology of the Toughest Women from the Classic Pulps, preface by Muller, edited by Bernard A. Drew (New York: St. Martin's Press, 1986);

"Deceptions," in *A Matter of Crime,* volume 1, edited by Matthew J. Bruccoli and Richard Layman (San Diego: Harcourt Brace Jovanovich, 1987), pp. 236–264;

"Cache and Carry," by Muller and Pronzini, in *Small Felonies,* edited by Pronzini (New York: St. Martin's Press, 1988), pp. 244–250;

Lady on the Case, edited by Muller, Pronzini, and Greenberg (New York: Bonanza, 1988);

"Silent Night," in *Mistletoe Mysteries,* edited by Charlotte MacLeod (New York: Mysterious Press, 1989), pp. 228–245;

"The Wall," in *Criminal Intent 1,* edited by Muller, Ed Gorman, and Pronzini (Arlington Heights, Ill.: Dark Harvest, 1993), pp. 7–70;

"Final Resting Place," in *The Eyes Still Have It,* edited by Randisi (New York: Dutton, 1995), pp. 165–184;

"All the Lonely People," in *Best of Sisters in Crime,* edited by Marilyn Wallace (New York: Berkley, 1997), pp. 15–30.

SELECTED PERIODICAL PUBLICATIONS–UNCOLLECTED: "Creating a Female Sleuth," *Writer,* 91 (October 1978): 20–22, 45;

"The Inner Suspense Story," *Writer,* 96 (December 1983): 23–25, 43;

"Should You Collaborate?" by Muller and Bill Pronzini, *Writer,* 98 (March 1985): 7–10, 45;

"Plotting the Realistic Detective Novel," *Writer,* 100 (June 1987): 12–15, 46;

"Free-Form Plotting in the Mystery," *Writer,* 102 (September 1989): 12–15;

"Deadly Fantasies," *Alfred Hitchcock's Mystery Magazine* (April 1989);

"Somewhere in the City," *Armchair Detective,* 23 (Winter 1990);

"The Reasons Why," *1996 Edgar Allan Poe Awards: Mystery Writers of America,* special supplement to *New York Times Magazine,* 21 April 1996.

With the publication of *Edwin of the Iron Shoes* in 1977 a new kind of hard-boiled detective arrived and changed the course of modern detective fiction. Sharon McCone, the private investigator featured in nineteen novels and more than a dozen short stories by Marcia Muller, is the widely acknowledged prototype for a spate of women detectives, including Sara Paretsky's V. I. Warshawski and Sue Grafton's Kinsey Millhone, both of whom first appeared in 1982. The longevity and popularity of the McCone series attest to the timeliness of McCone's appearance and to Muller's ability to create characters who can evolve with their times in a way that readers continue to care about.

While Muller is a pioneer, McCone is far from the first female detective. Both female and male authors have experimented with detective females since the 1860s. In the 1860s and 1870s in England and America, a few novels featuring female detectives or police investigators appeared. Seeley Regester's *Dead Letter: An American Romance* appeared in 1864 and is believed to feature the first female detective. In the twentieth century, Dorothy Sayers and Agatha Christie in England and Mary Roberts Rinehart and Mignon Eberhart in America did much to popularize both detective fiction and female amateur investigators.

Priscilla L. Walton and Manina Jones in *Detective Agency: Women Rewriting the Hard-Boiled Tradition* (1999) point out that the rising interest in female detectives in the 1970s was not produced by a self-conscious movement but by isolated women writers who "*independently* perceived a gap in what popular fiction had to offer and decided that the hard-boiled detective genre could uniquely accommodate their interests." P. D. James featured Cordelia Gray in two novels, the first in 1972 and again in 1982. Maxine O'Callaghan began her series of Delilah West novels with a short story published in 1974. Muller's McCone, however, is unique because she is a professional, not an amateur, and has chosen her profession, not come to it by chance, as does Cordelia Gray. She operates independently and is hard-boiled enough to fit into that all-American genre but humane and appealing enough to have exerted a discernible influence over the genre as a whole in the last twenty years.

Lawrence Block, author of the Matt Scudder series, remarked in a 28 April 1985 interview in *The New York Times Book Review* that women would have to modify the genre in order to succeed: "The hard-boiled private eye is a special figure in American mythology. . . . It seems to me that if they want to go into the profession seriously, women writers will have to change the myth itself, instead of trying to fit themselves into it." Muller has exerted just that kind of pressure, extending the boundaries of the hard-boiled novel not only to include women but also to embrace a wider range of humanity and behavior, to demonstrate that gunplay and choke holds are only one kind of violence, and to focus on social issues. Although Paretsky and Grafton have had more commercial success, they point without hesitation to Muller as their inspiration; she has led the way toward "redefining the mystery genre by applying different sensibilities and values to it," in the words of Marilyn Stasio, mystery reviewer for *The New York Times* (28 April 1985).

Marcia Muller was born on 28 September 1944 in Detroit, Michigan, the youngest child of Henry J. Muller, a marketing executive, and Kathryn Minke Muller. She has three siblings, a brother and two sisters. She attended public schools in Birmingham, Michigan. In a 28 July 1999 letter Muller recalled that as a child she was an avid reader of girls' mysteries, especially the Judy Bolton series by Margaret Sutton. She remarked, "I virtually learned to write from those books, and I see a lot of similarities between Judy and McCone." She always hoped to become a writer and

A Sharon McCone Mystery
Marcia Muller

GAMES TO KEEP THE DARK AWAY

Dust jacket for one of Muller's three 1984 novels featuring her detective character Sharon McCone

completed her first novel, a mystery about her dog, at the age of twelve.

Muller finished a B.A. in English at the University of Michigan in 1966. At the university, she told a *Publishers Weekly* interviewer in 1994, one professor memorably informed her she would never be a writer because she had "nothing to say." While admitting that at the age of nineteen this was true, Muller speaks of this blunt statement as "devastating." For three of her college years she was a member of the College Board of *Mademoiselle Magazine* observing life on her campus and reporting her impressions to the magazine. Despite the professor's discouraging words, she continued to write articles and essays and was a finalist in *Vogue* magazine's Prix de Paris competition in her senior year.

Muller married Frederick T. Gilson Jr., an officer in the U.S. Navy, in 1967. The navy posted her husband to California and Muller worked as a merchandising supervisor for *Sunset* magazine in Menlo Park from 1967 to 1969. Muller returned to Ann Arbor for an M.A. in journalism in 1971; she credits the program with instilling in her a sense of professionalism that has aided her in the practical business of deadlines, scheduling, and other professional obligations that confront the writer of fiction.

Moving back to California permanently, she worked from 1971 to 1973 as a field interviewer in San Francisco for the University of Michigan's Institute for Social Research, a job whose influence is evident in the attention she gives to the San Francisco milieu in her fiction. Muller told *Publishers Weekly* that the experience "required writing very detailed character sketches and descriptions of living conditions. It got me into parts of San Francisco and the Bay area where I never would have gone, and meeting people whom I never would have met." In a 1990 interview in *The Armchair Detective,* she goes further, saying "I've used a lot of settings and characters who were suggested to me by the people that I interviewed in depth."

Between 1973 and 1983, when she turned to fiction writing full time, Muller was a freelance writer and worked in a variety of part-time positions; in 1979 she became a partner in Invisible Ink, a firm that provided editorial services for writers. She began writing Sharon McCone stories in 1972 but not until 1977, after two other manuscripts were rejected, was *Edwin of the Iron Shoes* accepted at the publishing house David McKay. She was divorced from her first husband in 1981. Muller struggled for the next few years to place other manuscripts, but after the publication of *Ask the Cards a Question* (1982) and *The Cheshire Cat's Eye* (1983) she was finally able to write full-time. In 1991 she moved from San Francisco to Petaluma, California, and in 1992 she married longtime co-editor and co-author Bill Pronzini, creator of the Nameless Detective series, whom she credits as the strongest influence on her career.

Muller spoke of the early influences on her writing in a 26 November 1992 interview in the *Cleveland Plain Dealer:* "I came to mysteries first as a reader. . . . But it wasn't until I was in my 20s and someone gave me a Ross Macdonald novel that I became hooked. I used to ration his books. I never wanted to run out. That's when I fell in love with the genre." With this new enthusiasm, she devoured the novels of Raymond Chandler, Dashiell Hammett, and Dorothy Sayers and then started reading contemporary authors such as Agatha Christie, Ngaio Marsh, P. D. James, Dorothy Uhnak, and Lillian O'Donnell. She told *Publishers Weekly* that she was attracted to the depictions of "tough, very strong women characters. I had finally found the form I wanted to write."

Muller did not intend to start a revolution with her first Sharon McCone stories; she just wanted to make a living. She makes light of the credit she has received, claiming in a 1997 interview with *Mystery Review,* "I had little to do with other people entering the

field, particularly Sue Grafton and Sara Paretsky. A number of us were working in this same direction at the same time and I just happened to get there a few years earlier . . . mostly because both of them were employable and I wasn't so I had more time on my hands." She also points out the central role that Pronzini played in her development as a writer of crime fiction long before they married. As she struggled for acceptance following the publication of her first novel, he became interested in her work and introduced her to an editor who helped pave the way to publication.

Muller believes that changing social conditions in America were both the inspiration for the new women writers and the instigation for the interest that publishers began to evince in them during the late 1970s. "It was a case," she said to the *Cleveland Plain Dealer,* "of the publishing world catching up to reality. . . . We were all seeing real female private eyes and real prosecutors and real policewomen, but none in fiction because the idea was that only men read mysteries and men wouldn't be interested in reading about women in these roles. But then publishers began receiving enough manuscripts with women in them and they finally saw how things really were." Of herself and others such as Paretsky and Grafton, Muller told *Publishers Weekly,* "We wanted to write about people like us, like the women around us. The time was ripe."

In *Edwin of the Iron Shoes* (1977) Sharon McCone, the first-person narrator of the series, is the investigative arm of a San Francisco legal cooperative, All Souls, located in the Bernal Heights District and operating out of an old Victorian house that also serves as home to several of her colleagues. All Souls was founded to offer high quality, sliding scale services to clients who might not be able to afford traditional legal assistance. McCone is in her late twenties; she worked in department store security while completing a sociology degree at Berkeley, but when she was unable to find a job in her field, she took up private investigation full time, joining the legal coop started by friends from her university days. Neither celibate nor promiscuous, she has never married. She carries a gun, a .38, and will use it when pressed, though she is sensitive to the implications of going about armed and vulnerable to the emotional backlash from any killing into which she is forced. As an investigator, she is fallible and sometimes jumps to faulty conclusions because of her emotional involvement in a particular case.

In this first novel McCone has been investigating a series of arson and vandalism incidents in which one of the clients of the cooperative, antique dealer Joan Albritton, has been a victim. In the opening scene, the case becomes more serious as Albritton is murdered. In what will come to be a characteristic of Muller's novels, the plot revolves around a social issue, in this case real estate development and its influence on the urban environment. McCone's suspicion and that of the locals focuses on a group of real estate moguls who may have been trying to drive out the small antique and junk dealers from Salem Street, opening the way for pricey shops and condominiums.

Muller's intimate knowledge of Bay Area neighborhoods, their people and places, is evident in her careful delineation of characters and atmospheric depictions of settings. Her interest in social issues is apparent in her portrayal of the struggle for the soul of a neighborhood and the dangers of unrestrained growth. An author's interest in social issues can easily lead her to create caricatures who give speeches rather than speak, but Muller presents her characters with an admirable feel for the complexity of motivation and the unpredictable shaping influence of environment. The real estate plot is entangled with another mystery that puts a blot on the character of the murdered woman, who was involved in a criminal scheme to import stolen artworks.

The focal figure in the two plots is Cara Ingalls, a wealthy socialite and real estate broker and, coincidentally, the former lover of Homicide Lieutenant Greg Marcus. Although Ingalls, who is finally arrested for the murders of Albritton and Oliver van Osten, an art importer, is primarily presented as rapacious and unfeeling, Muller also reveals a sympathetic side of her that allows both the reader and McCone to understand, though not excuse or forgive, what she does. McCone comes to see some of herself in Ingalls: "She was my kind of woman, one who made her way on her own steam and refused to be held back." McCone's friend and boss, Hank Zahn, a continuing character throughout the series, notes that Lieutenant Marcus too may have seen a kinship between McCone and his former lover: "He sensed the same strength and independence in you, so he set out to put you in your place. Fortunately, you wouldn't stay put." At first Marcus considers both McCone and Ingalls as suspects, not so much because of motive and opportunity but because each is a strong and independent woman.

With *Edwin of the Iron Shoes,* which she foresaw as the start of a series, Muller faced the challenge not only of deciding the details of personality and appearance of her protagonist but also the difficulty of striking the proper balance between the appealing woman and the convincing private investigator. In "Creating a Female Sleuth," an article Muller wrote for the October 1978 issue of *The Writer,* she notes how her identification with her character came into play: "I constantly had to consider what I would do

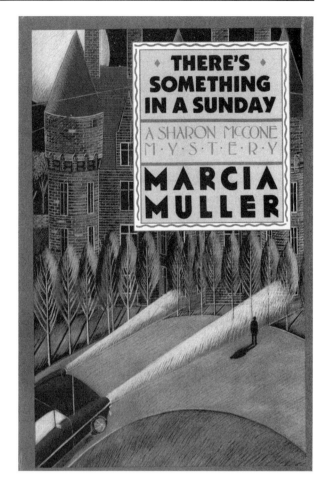

Dust jacket for Muller's 1989 novel in which McCone probes the secrets of a well-to-do social set

if I were a trained professional, how I would condition and curb my natural responses." Muller chose to give McCone a distinctive appearance–she is one-eighth Shoshone, but the Native American genes dominate the Scotch-Irish ancestry implied by her name. As for the more problematic part of the portrait, the first novel presents a McCone who is independent and assertive. She is a rudimentary feminist, alert to discrimination and aware of how cops view her.

Although she initially bristles at Marcus's smirks and put-downs, McCone eventually ends up in a relationship with him that lasts through several novels. She even accepts Marcus's calling her by the pet name "Papoose." As he first uses the word, "Yes, papoose, I can see you're learning a lot. It's a pity it hasn't improved your temper–or your appearance. . . . You look like you could use a bath," it is clearly an insult, not only racist, as McCone says, but sexist and ageist, as Marcus laughingly admits. As Marcus begins to show his less hard-edged side, his use of the word shifts to a term of endearment that McCone can tolerate, a

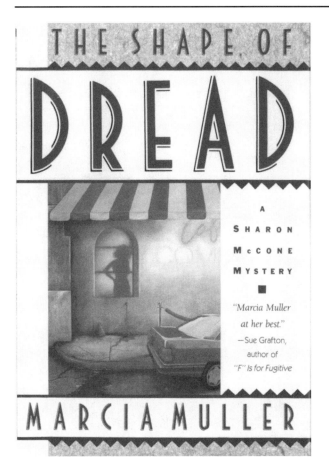

Dust jacket for Muller's 1989 novel in which McCone investigates the death of a comedienne

tolerance that the later, less naive and more cynical McCone would probably not muster.

In this first novel Muller uses McCone's relationship with Marcus to begin her examination of the balance of power between men and women, especially as this balance is affected by perceived gender and social roles. That she intends to work her way toward a middle ground on such issues is indicated in the remarks made by Marcus near the end of the novel, as he and McCone come closer together. In language that harkens back to his earlier insult, he says to McCone, "There are things you can teach me." To her response, "Such as?," he explains, "Things about a strong man and a strong woman. . . . About how two such people can be together without diminishing each other or tearing each other apart."

Edwin of the Iron Shoes achieved limited sales though it was widely and positively reviewed. Most reviewers seemed to realize that she was doing something new with the genre, praising both her characterizations and plotting. Not all reviewers were impressed, however. In a 27 November 1977 review in *The New York Times,*

pseudonymous reviewer Newgate Callendar asserted, "No new ground here." Muller's attempt to follow up with a second novel featuring McCone stalled for several years after her publisher dropped its mystery line.

When Muller was able to place *Ask the Cards a Question* (1982) with a new publisher, it too managed only limited sales. The sales of her early novels were restricted because they did not appear in paperback. Muller told *Publishers Weekly* she feels fortunate in the timing of her appearance in print, comparing her experience to that of new authors in the 1990s: "Back then, you could learn to write while making a living at it. It's not as easy for new writers now. It's such a tough market, and publishers aren't willing to bring people along slowly, the way I developed." Her early publisher, she says, "Allowed me to learn to write." By 1990 her popularity had grown to the point that the early novels were republished in paperback.

Muller's strategy in writing her novels has remained consistent through the years, though her approach has relaxed as she has gained confidence as a writer. *Edwin of the Iron Shoes,* she says, was a learning experience. In "Creating a Female Sleuth," Muller describes her "first unbreakable rule of plotting": "Knowing my solution was the real key to a plot that held together." However, the second rule is even more important: Be as flexible as possible. Finding that she was nearly at the end of *Edwin of the Iron Shoes*–but only had half the number of pages the project required– Muller realized that flexibility is the key to giving a mystery its interest and complexity, to keeping the story from taking the shortest route from one point to another. She developed a time chart to plot events and used character sketches to make sure characters acted consistently and did not hesitate to discard and rewrite when the plot required it. She details her method in "Free-Form Plotting in the Mystery," which was published in the September 1989 issue of *The Writer.*

In her remarks in her *Publishers Weekly* interview, Muller comments on the maturation of her approach to writing: "Now I start out with a situation, a subject or even a title. I have a vague idea of what happens and where it's going to end and just start writing," which, she notes, helps her to give the impression of "spontaneity and a sense of real life" to the characters' actions. She notes in a 1995 interview in *Mystery Scene,* "The early books I plotted a lot more tightly because I was really insecure."

McCone's politics are on the side of victims and the oppressed, but in the best hard-boiled tradition, she knows that no one, no matter how seemingly innocent, is incapable of crime. In *Ask the Cards a Question,* in which a second murder is committed to cover up the first, Muller involves four unlikely villains in a web of crime: a social service worker turned unscrupulous cynic, a "poor immigrant" Arab shopkeeper, a man blinded in an industrial accident, and a rather helpless and hapless gentleman widowed by the first murder. In what surely must be one of the most backhanded of compliments to the disabled, McCone's suspicions of the sightless murderer, Sebastian, were aroused when she recalled that Clemente, the social worker, had told her that "blind people can do almost anything sighted people can, given the proper training."

The ability Muller showed in *Edwin of the Iron Shoes* to create characters who are both sympathetic and criminal is again evident in *Ask the Cards a Question*. The portrait of Mr. Moe, the Arab owner of a small grocery store, is particularly striking because Muller makes a point of connecting his inhospitable demeanor to a series of family tragedies and to prejudice that he has experienced. Explaining his hostility toward the police, Moe says, "You have no idea what it is to be an Arab in this city. . . . Every year many of us are robbed, and some are killed. The robbers are never caught, the killers are never brought to justice. The police have no respect for us; they do not try to give protection. So we have contempt for the police—and fear."

Muller gives a fuller characterization of McCone in the novel through her relationship with Linnea Carraway, an old friend who, having left her husband and her children, spends her days drinking and sleeping in McCone's apartment. The stages of McCone's reaction to Linnea's depression—from sympathy to exasperation—reveals a more human side of the detective than she can easily show in her work. The reader sees McCone more as a person in this friendship that lacks the sexual tension of her relationship with Marcus, making the climax of the novel, in which McCone must shoot and kill Sebastian to save Linnea's life, all the more affecting. As the novel ends, her relationship with Marcus seems to have become increasingly tentative, though it continues through the third book in the series, *The Cheshire Cat's Eye*.

In *The Cheshire Cat's Eye*, as in her first novel, Muller combines a plot about antiques—in this case the practice of copying antiques, such as the Tiffany lamp dubbed "The Cheshire Cat's Eye," and passing them off as genuine—with social concerns. In the course of the novel she depicts the ongoing process of gentrification—the return of the predominantly white middle class from the suburbs to the urban neighborhoods of San Francisco—and its impact on racial tensions and the economics of city life. Muller was involved in a restoration project herself while she was writing the book, a circumstance that doubtless heightened not only her loving descriptions of the city's Victorian "painted ladies" but also her awareness of the effect of such

urban renewal upon a population, often poor and minority, that is displaced from its neighborhood as monied interests move in.

The novel is also interesting for Muller's handling of homosexual characters through McCone, whose reflection shows she is not entirely comfortable among gays: "Would the high-school cheerleader and navy brat from conservative San Diego have believed that, as an adult, she would not only tolerate what she then knew as 'homos,' but also include a few among her circle of friends? And yet even now, wasn't I, truthfully, uncomfortable when conversations with those friends turned to the details of gay life?" Muller portrays the lives of the homosexual characters with sympathy, but a gay man is eventually found to be guilty of three murders. By way of closure, McCone remarks, "I discovered I'd liked Paul Collins in spite of his murders. He was a gentle man, ill at ease with his nature, and ultimately the rough world had driven him too far. While knowing that did not excuse his crimes, it made them more understandable."

In a 1984 issue of *Clues: A Journal of Detection*, interviewer Frederick Isaac describes how important background is for Muller: "The quest for solid background is fundamental to Muller's working pattern. She chooses the subcultures of her stories first, and then develops her characters to fit into them." In Muller's hands, however, this method does not result in cardboard characters shaped to fit their environment, as both *Ask the Cards a Question* and *The Cheshire Cat's Eye* illustrate. Drawing interesting characters from a variety of San Francisco subcultures and creating tight, thought-provoking plots, Muller began to publish her novels on a regular basis.

Muller wrote fourteen more books in the 1980s, seven of which continue McCone's adventures: *Double,* a novel written collaboratively with Pronzini, *Games to Keep the Dark Away,* and *Leave a Message for Willie* were published in 1984; these were followed by *There's Nothing to Be Afraid Of* (1985), *Eye of the Storm* (1988), and *There's Something in a Sunday* and *The Shape of Dread,* both brought out in 1989. With each book, Muller gives McCone greater depth and a fuller personal history. She becomes part of a substitute family that revolves around All Souls. Her relationships with her colleagues and friends have an ongoing appeal, no doubt accounting in large part for the success of the series.

McCone discards the boyfriend who calls her "papoose," though they remain friendly rivals throughout the series, and she becomes involved in a more promising relationship with a disc jockey, Don DelBoccio, whom she meets in *Games to Keep the Dark Away*. She then, however, begins to feel the greatest strain in her personal life, a tension between the desire for stability

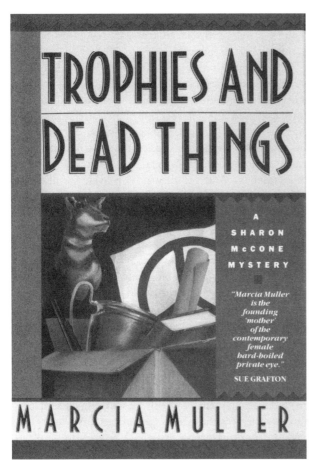

Dust jacket for Muller's 1990 novel, in which McCone is compelled to reevaluate her 1960s ideals

and her attraction to the excitement and danger of her job. The relationship with DelBoccio, which lasts through five novels, is finished by the time McCone meets George Kostakos, the Stanford professor whose daughter is missing in *The Shape of Dread*. The tentative nature of her relationship with Kostakos creates sadness and tension for McCone until the end of *Trophies and Dead Things* (1990), when they move into a new phase of their relationship.

She moves from her studio apartment in the increasingly dangerous Mission District into an "earth-quake cottage" in *Games to Keep the Dark Away*, devoting herself to its renovation over the next few books. New characters who overlap from novel to novel are introduced. They include Rae Kelleher, McCone's assistant, and Willie Whelan, a receiver of hot property in *Leave a Message for Willie*. Whelan becomes a purveyor of cut-rate jewelry and Rae's boyfriend in *Trophies and Dead Things*. Old characters such as Hank Zahn and his wife Anne-Marie Altman undergo changes and crises in their lives; Ted Smalley, long-time secretary to All Souls, declares his homosexual-

ity, and McCone and his other friends and colleagues deal with the grief that AIDS has brought to his life. These characters become more well rounded, with lives that take on depth and histories of their own.

As a departure from the hard-boiled McCone novels, in the 1980s Muller began two new series featuring women who are reluctantly drawn into detection. Muller introduces Chicana art historian and museum curator, Elena Oliverez, in *The Tree of Death* (1983). Set in Santa Barbara, the series is notable for the lively characterizations of Oliverez's mother and her boyfriend who live in a trailer park in Goleta as well as Muller's perceptive portrayal of tensions within the Hispanic community and her keen awareness of the tragic complexity of California history that is particularly apparent in the second Oliverez novel, *The Legend of the Slain Soldiers* (1985). The third novel in the series is *Beyond the Grave* (1986), which Muller wrote with Pronzini.

Muller found the Oliverez series challenging, especially using the character as a first-person narrator, as she reveals in her interview in *The Armchair Detective*: "After a while, it became difficult to relate to that character. You would think the problem would be due to the cultural differences, but that was not the case. It was because she was so young, not just in years but in attitude, and finally I found I just didn't share her concerns and problems. It was also a little restrictive coming up with convincing plot lines for an amateur detective working in a museum." Her statement points back to an important aspect in the success of the McCone series, "There is," says Muller, "a great deal of me in her."

Introduced in *The Cavalier in White* (1986), Joanna Stark is the director of a California company that provides security to museums and art galleries. She is about forty, more sophisticated and financially comfortable than McCone, who would never be found pursuing a suspect through the woods in high-heeled boots as Stark does in *Dark Star* (1989), the final work in this series. *Dark Star* was preceded by *There Hangs the Knife* (1988). In the series Muller shows solid knowledge of both the smiling and seamy sides of the art world and a good grasp of its arcane terminology; however, as she explained in *The Armchair Detective* interview, she found that the series ran its course sooner than she expected: "Joanna Stark was intended to be a long-running series until I wrote the first book and realized that what I was writing was a personal story that couldn't extend beyond three books." Muller found a certain relief in breaking from McCone to explore different voices, and the Stark novels, which are written as third-person accounts, allowed her a further distance from her main protagonist. In a 28 July 1999 letter, Muller maintained that the novels gave her a new perspective on McCone: "With Joanna Stark, I was able to portray a mature woman with something of a dark side and a checkered past. It deepened my abilities as a writer, and also allowed me to deepen McCone's character."

In *The Armchair Detective* interview, when pressed to identify an overarching theme in her work, Muller said she is not conscious of giving her books specific messages but "if the books have an underlying theme, it would be about how a past event can trigger a present explosion." While this might describe the situation in the mystery genre as a whole—after all, it is buried secrets from the past that nearly always create the violence of the present, whether in the eighteenth-century gothic novel, sensation fiction of the nineteenth century, or modern hard-boiled fiction—Muller has also indicated a more personal animus in her fiction. She told the *Cleveland Plain Dealer* that "I'm very opinionated, I get irritated about something, and it ends up in one of my books." She points out that she has not received much feedback from readers that would indicate they dislike the fairly overt political positions of her heroine and the novels as a whole. Indeed, it is likely that the combination of these two concerns, the power of the past and the political and social realities of the present, is one of Muller's greatest strengths, enabling her to write books in which the past is alive yet which are anchored in contemporary concerns.

In her works of 1989 and earlier, Muller takes on issues such as the problems of Vietnam veterans and paramilitary activities (*Leave a Message for Willie*), the travails of recent immigrants and refugees (*Ask the Cards a Question* and *There's Nothing to Be Afraid Of*), urban development and gentrification (*Edwin of the Iron Shoes* and *Cheshire Cat's Eye*), racism and the death penalty (*The Shape of Dread*), and homelessness and middle-class drug abuse (*There's Something in a Sunday*). Muller's incorporation of the topical issues of the 1980s in her novels clearly resonated with her readers.

Muller in her interview in *The Armchair Detective* points to *There's Something in a Sunday*, published in the last year of the decade, as a book marking a "transition . . . to a much harder-edged or darker book." *There's Something in a Sunday* is also a watershed book in terms of McCone's character development, for she becomes more self-aware as a result of her experiences. McCone is hired by Rudy Goldring, a custom shirtmaker, to find out why the mysterious Frank Wilkonson seems to be stalking Irene Lasser Johnstone, an old family friend. Her investigation deepens once Goldring is murdered, and she follows a trail that leads her to Wilkonson's unhappy wife, Jane; hypocritical, high-society activists Vicki and Jerry Cushman; and the world of the homeless. The woman

at the heart of the mystery, Irene Lasser Johnstone, is the wife of Wilkonson's employer, Harlan Johnstone, and a live-in babysitter for the Cushmans, a job arranged for her by Goldring. Her affair with Jerry Cushman and her having been raped by her stepson, Hal Johnstone, are secrets at the center of the plot. Violence and guilt touch every character in the novel.

Muller has McCone—uninvolved romantically and glad of it—observe several male-female relationships in crisis: Hank Zahn and his wife are having problems in their new marriage; Rae Kelleher and her husband separate by the end of the novel; Frank and Jane Wilkonson have a marriage characterized by frequent pregnancies and a husband who is otherwise inattentive; Vicki and Jerry Cushman's marriage is a nightmare of alcohol, drugs, and damaging secrets; and the problems in the marriage of Irene Lasser and Harlan Johnstone, once exposed, offer the key to the principal mystery. The author's powerful examination of relationships culminates in Jane Wilkonson's confession that she murdered her husband.

Just as in *The Cheshire Cat's Eye,* McCone finds herself sympathizing with a murderer, for she can only agree when Jane claims that all she "wanted was something of my own. Everybody's got to have something. Is it wrong to want that?" McCone's assurance that "it's not wrong at all" is further underscored in the final chapter as Rae announces that she has separated from her husband: "He wanted me to give up my dream for his, and that's totally unfair. I've got a right to a dream, too!" The experience of these particular horrors is the basis of McCone's new resolution, soon to be tested in *The Shape of Dread* and *Trophies and Dead Things,* to accept only relationships in which she can be herself without a struggle and pursue her own dreams.

The blacker mood that Muller points to in her next novels is not based on their plots or the nature of their murderous secrets, but on McCone's growing awareness and agonizing self-consciousness about her own cynicism, the violence within her, and her inability to be secure in any definition of what constitutes justice in the world of the 1990s. *The Shape of Dread* and *Trophies and Dead Things* close the door on two decades, the first on the self-interest-driven 1980s and the second on the 1960s, the decade whose idealism has been in the background of all the novels since the inception of the series. As these novels close those years, the tone of the series becomes more somber, even despairing, and the violence darker, but Muller finds ways to balance that tone and retain her protagonist's appeal.

In *The Shape of Dread* one of the All Souls attorneys asks McCone to undertake an investigation for his client, death row prisoner Bobby Foster. Foster was convicted of murdering a rising young comedienne, Tracy

Dust jacket for Muller's 1991 novel, in which McCone investigates crimes against the environment in Northern California

me, but no more so than tonight. I'd lost sympathy for almost everyone involved in my investigation. . . . What if it was indicative of something worse? What if I was also losing empathy . . . ? What if—worse yet—I was losing my enthusiasm for the work itself?" She contrasts her present state to the energy of her young assistant, Rae, who "hadn't spent year after year experiencing what amounted to living nightmares . . . hadn't spent over a decade uncovering secrets of people's lives that literally made one's flesh creep, hadn't repeatedly dealt with the havoc and destruction caused by human greed, carelessness, and stupidity." Significantly, at the end of the book, as she has one of the guilty figures cornered, she feels "nothing but rage—cold and steady" and has to talk herself out of executing him. "No sense," she thinks, "in letting this evil man live. No sense in going through the motions of arrest, trial, imprisonment, even execution, because it won't make any difference." Muller spins out a dramatic scene to a startling conclusion; McCone overcomes her dark impulse, but it will never wholly leave her.

While the 1980s take an emotional toll on McCone, the roots of her idealism in the 1960s come under attack in *Trophies and Dead Things*. Hank Zahn of All Souls—itself an outgrowth of the idealism of the 1960s and early 1970s—asks McCone to look into last-minute changes that a deceased client made in his will. Without consulting Hank, the client had disinherited his children and left his money to four unknowns. In the process of discovering the "who" of the case, McCone also learns the "why" and brings into the open the dark side of the 1960s: the violence, the drugs, the degeneration of idealists unrewarded or unwilling to accept compromise, and the darkness at both ends of the political spectrum.

Muller had just published *Trophies and Dead Things* when she identified in *The Armchair Detective* interview the power of the past to "trigger a present explosion" as a theme binding her works. The commentary that Muller offers on the 1960s and early 1970s in this novel is presented with an awareness of the good as well as the bad of those years. McCone thinks of her own feelings about the positive accomplishments of the antiwar movement and then thinks specifically about D. A. Taylor, "a pathetic and heroic figure" trapped by drug abuse and his "inability to let go of the past." He is, though, "heroic because of what that past had been. At least the man had once cared passionately about something besides himself, had stood for what he believed in. Perhaps I was allowing my view of him to be colored by the negative feelings I harbor toward much of what is currently going on in America: the lack of compassion, the fear of taking risks, the failure to embrace and hold tight to unselfish ideals."

Kostakos, but the body was never found, and there are rumors that she might still be alive. McCone's investigation takes her through the comedy club subculture and into the sad, bitter lives that are threaded through it. The young woman was murdered, but under far different circumstances than first believed, and she is discovered to be a person unlike the one her intensely suffering parents thought they knew. One of the most painful moments in the novel comes when Tracy's father, George Kostakos, with whom McCone feels a strong mutual attraction, thinks that his daughter may still be alive and may have planned her own kidnapping: "If she's not dead, she is someone I don't want to acknowledge as my own. . . . Please don't find Tracy alive. . . . And if you do, don't bring her back to me." The jealousy and greed of others and her own bloodless manipulation of people for personal ends are Tracy's undoing. The values of the characters coincide with the worst of those associated with the wheeling-and-dealing 1980s.

Although McCone saves an innocent man from a life in prison or worse, she is deeply disturbed by the case, as is evident in her reflection near the end of the novel: "The users of the world had always disgusted

McCone feels a strong sense of identification with this man "who had tried to make a difference–at whatever the personal cost." The personal cost for McCone is exemplified by her continuing awareness that the up close violence in her life, in this case her apprehension of a sniper, has a negative effect on her feelings about herself and on the way others view her. She begins to feel alienated from the people who have been like family to her, saying, "I doubt any of them would ever fully reconcile their prior conceptions of me with the near-murderous stranger they'd seen."

McCone's fears that she can no longer sympathize or empathize in her investigations is unfounded, but those feelings begin to have a different focus in subsequent books. *Where Echoes Live* (1991) is a turning point in the series. Plots begin to take her farther afield from her base of operations at All Souls, and she meets a man, Hy Ripinsky, who will later become what no other man has been to her, a soul mate. Her association with him through the newest works changes the focus of much of her concern and enlarges the world in which she does her job. In *Where Echoes Live,* McCone is asked by an environmental group to investigate events associated with a plan for large-scale commercial mining at an old mine site in Northern California. Muller uncovers not only greed and deception and the intent to do environmental harm in the Hong Kong company that purchased the land but also violent craziness of the homegrown variety. The opening of the novel evokes the eerie and ecologically fragile landscape in which much of the action occurs, and the working out of the plot allows Muller to give an in-depth description of the modern environmental movement.

Perhaps because Muller had decided to lessen McCone's connection to All Souls, in *Where Echoes Live* she introduces more involvement by McCone in issues affecting her real family. In the course of the story McCone drifts away from a relationship with George Kostakos and simultaneously becomes unmoored by her mother's announcement of the end of her own marriage. McCone's reactions are revealingly rueful as she is forced to recognize that her mother, to her surprise and consternation, is living the feminist principles that McCone has always espoused for herself and for those of her own generation. She is thrown off balance by the changes in her family, but this realistic development and her natural response to it–a situation with which many readers will identify–are occasions for the continuing development of her character.

In a series noted for the introspective quality of its protagonist, *Where Echoes Live* stands out for the personal crises she confronts and the new level of awareness that she reaches. Now approaching forty, McCone is forced to reexamine her relationship to her

family, her approach-avoidance response to her relationship with Ripinsky, and her deepening sense of certain fundamental qualities in herself that she regrets but realizes will not change. Much of her internal conflict is revealed in a conversation with her mother, who just keeps surprising her; as they are discussing McCone's undefined discomfort with Kostakos and unwillingness to completely commit to him and the secure and unruffled life he represents, her mother refers to the "circles" in which Kostakos fits different kinds of personalities. She continues, ". . . there's another side to you, something . . . wild that can't be contained. That side of you will never permit you to live a comfortable life in one of those circles–not even with a good man you love. But it *will* make you feel guilty and unhappy because you can't."

Muller also places McCone at odds with Rae Kelleher, an alter ego for her younger, more idealistic self. In the middle of the book, the tension between them comes to a climax. Rae, McCone finally realizes, having seen the barely controlled violence in her mentor, is having her own crisis about whether to continue in the profession. Using insights gathered from her discussion with her mother, McCone tells Rae that how a person reacts to her discoveries in the "cesspool" depends on the kind of person she is to begin with: "I've always claimed that the undesirable changes in me–cynicism, anger, whatever–have come about as a result of the things I've seen and done in the course of my work. But now I'm not so sure that's wholly true. Maybe as we get older our experiences don't change us so much as make us more who and what we really are." Much like the crisis in McCone's relationship with her mother that allows the daughter to see her mother as a real woman for the first time, McCone's conflict with Rae ushers in a new phase of their relationship, no longer circumscribed by the adopted roles of mentor and apprentice.

McCone has been a "touchstone" for Rae as Rae has developed from an amateur uncommitted to the profession into a licensed investigator, but until McCone meets Hy Ripinsky she has no touchstone against which to test her own actions, reactions, and values. "Touchstone" will become a key word in their relationship, but at the end of *Where Echoes Live* they have only come far enough for McCone to sense one of those guilty secrets about herself, that "danger . . . was the thing that brought me fully alive. Conquering it and my own fear was what gave me a reason for going on in the face of an increasing sense of futility. That was the real truth that I kept from George and the others, who would have found it a shameful addiction. And that was what Hy had intuited and accepted." Ripinsky accepts it because it is a quality they share. This understanding is

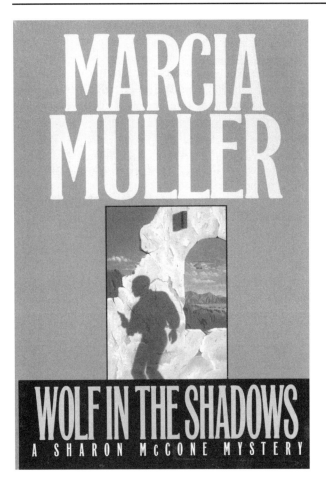

Dust jacket for Muller's 1993 novel, in which McCone becomes involved with international terrorists and Mexican immigrants

central to their relationship and allows for new areas of development in the series as McCone becomes involved with him, his complicated life and questionable past, and even more questionable associates.

In subsequent novels, Muller takes a risk by letting Ripinsky play such an important role in a series notable for the independence of its protagonist. In the 1990s critics such as Kathleen Gregory Klein, Sally R. Munt, and Walton and Jones have discussed the difficulties faced by authors who write about women detectives. In her *The Woman Detective: Gender and Genre* (1995) Klein argues that in their novels Muller and other women writers present female protagonists who are independent and have difficulty in relationships, but "for readers equally confused by society's changing views of women, the message of these novels seems remarkably clear: when women try to share men's freedom of choice in public and private, women lose."

Unlike hard-boiled male detectives who usually show little inclination for lasting relationships, McCone, while she speaks of her desire for independence, is

deeply involved with one man or another in almost every novel. With her conflicting desires for connection and independence, she often struggles to work out the issues raised in a relationship by her nontraditional profession. Klein points out that the tensions in McCone's relationship with Marcus are created not only by the lieutenant's derogatory attitude toward women but also because they are "professionally competitive." It was, as McCone says in *Games to Keep the Dark Away,* a relationship of "energy-sapping conflict." To write a successful novel about a woman detective, it is not enough to simply place the woman in the role traditionally assumed by a man. Making the woman more like a man, as Walton and Jones point out, "reveals the contradictions" between cultural expectations of male and female behavior. In the area of sexual behavior, for example, a casual attitude toward sex is more acceptable in a male detective than a female one. Readers, note Walton and Jones, are easily made uncomfortable by novels whose values are "*significantly* different from their own" and "are likely to choose to read a variant of the genre that does not challenge their preconceptions."

Authors such as Muller with their wide readerships are uniquely pressured to negotiate between readers' expectations about the genre and their expectations about women; as Walton and Jones assert, "Women's adaptation of the rules of hard-boiled fiction results in a necessarily ambivalent generic permutation: a 'woman's genre' that is defined by its status as a 'man's genre,' too." Since there is little agreement currently about how women are to balance professions, both traditional and nontraditional, with their personal lives and expected roles as wives and mothers, conflicted relationships are often present in detective novels that focus on women. Sally R. Munt in *Murder by the Book? Feminism and the Crime Novel* (1994) points out in discussing McCone and others that "for women 'identity' is still so bound up with relationships" that a woman detective's relations with a man is the area most likely to show tensions in a time of changing values. The risk that Muller takes in focusing McCone's attention on Ripinsky is that the independent and hard-boiled aspects of her protagonist's character will be overwhelmed by conventional romance as McCone fulfills a more traditional role, with a man at the center of her professional and personal life.

While *Where Echoes Live* brings Ripinsky and McCone together as kindred spirits, it also establishes him in a role in which he could become her mentor, creating a relationship that holds the negative possibilities that developed between McCone and Rae but perhaps exacerbated by the male-female tension. This role becomes apparent early on, when McCone confides her doubts to him, saying, "How can I go on doing what I do when I don't believe that anything can really be fixed?" When he does not answer the question, she gropes toward her own answer, speculating that "I guess you just go on. . . . Going through the motions. Because maybe *some* things can be fixed." It is important to note that Ripinsky does not answer the question but does provide the accepting atmosphere in which the doubts can be voiced.

Ripinsky is the person to whom McCone can talk about "almost bl[owing] two people away" and really *wanting* to do it. She can also tell him about the people she was once close to now without his looking at her as if she is an alien. Muller has had to work toward a careful balance in these novels, retaining on the one hand McCone's independent spirit, but making it believable—and acceptable to readers—that she is in an intense and close-knit relationship, one in which she and her partner frequently function as a unit. With each subsequent work, *Pennies on a Dead Woman's Eyes* (1992), *Wolf in the Shadows* (1993), *Till the Butchers Cut Him Down* (1994), *A Wild and Lonely Place* (1995), *The Broken Promise Land* (1996), *Both Ends of the Night* (1997), *While Other People Sleep* (1998), and *A Walk through the Fire* (1999), Muller has worked toward that balance, testing the relationship on the page and working out its kinks. On the negative side, Ripinsky has sometimes seemed too much the focus of the novels, either through McCone's constant thoughts and worries about him or because he is an important actor, even the catalyst, in the plot, as in *Wolf in the Shadows*.

Muller has tried to keep tension in the relationship by insisting in several works on Ripinsky's unpredictability and his mysterious, perhaps unsavory, past involving work he may have done for the CIA during and after the end of the war in southeast Asia or work he may have done for interests in the international drug trade. He will not speak of these years, so McCone is constantly looking for clues to his past, even to the extent of having a file on him and doubting his stability, ethics, reliability, and intentions. In an effort to project a professional distance and undercut sentimentality, she calls him "Ripinsky" and he calls her "McCone." Together they lack the appeal of Hammett's Nick and Nora Charles, but their relationship is such that each is allowed the freedom of independent action. As the novels progress, McCone establishes her own individual connection with the unsavory international security and antiterrorism outfit, RKI, with which Ripinsky has long-standing ties that loosen or strengthen from book to book.

Despite these reservations the association with Ripinsky undeniably has brought new life to the series, a point illustrated by *Wolf in the Shadows*. In this novel McCone's position at All Souls is thrown into crisis when the firm, which has become more successful but also more corporate and management-driven, offers her a promotion to a desk job. It is a "take it or leave it" proposition put forth by new partners who come out of 1980s, not a 1960s, background. During this upheaval, McCone finds that Ripinsky, who was doing a hostage negotiation job for RKI, is missing. RKI suspects that Ripinsky has run with the ransom money that was to be used to free Timothy Mourning, kidnapped owner of a pharmaceutical company. McCone goes into action, tracking Ripinsky through Southern California and into Mexico, trying to find him before RKI does because their stated mission is to kill him. Once she finds him the two team up to rescue Mourning and recover the money stolen from Ripinsky.

Continuing her concern with contemporary social issues, Muller gives a sympathetic treatment to Mexican immigrants, legal and illegal, and depicts in great detail the lengths to which impoverished people are willing to go to seek better lives. In setting much of her action in Mexico, Muller begins to expand her plots into the international arena, a change that can be convincingly handled because of McCone's involvement with Ripinsky and RKI. Their involvement also brings to prominence a theme that has existed in many of the novels: the role of ethical behavior in pursuit of justice. McCone has faced ethical dilemmas before, especially when she has been tempted to act outside the law to carry out a private vision of justice, but the shady background of the RKI partners and McCone's doubts about her increased involvement with them—involvement they wish to formalize with a job offer at the end of the novel—gives new relevance to the issue.

Muller highlights a change in her detective when McCone pulls the trigger on Marty Salazar, a bloodthirsty criminal who preys on those who cross the border and who is involved in the kidnapping of Mourning and the theft of the ransom money. She does not shoot to wound, and she does not shoot in self-defense. The FBI easily believes it was self-defense, but she knows it was nothing but murder and that "everything I believed in told me this was wrong. Everything I cared about told me this was right." In previous works McCone's idea of justice has encompassed not informing the police of details so that a more just arrangement could be achieved privately, but here, in a logical outgrowth of the investigator's developing character, justice equals murder. This development is made possible by her association with Ripinsky; now that McCone has a sympathetic sounding board for her actions in Ripin-

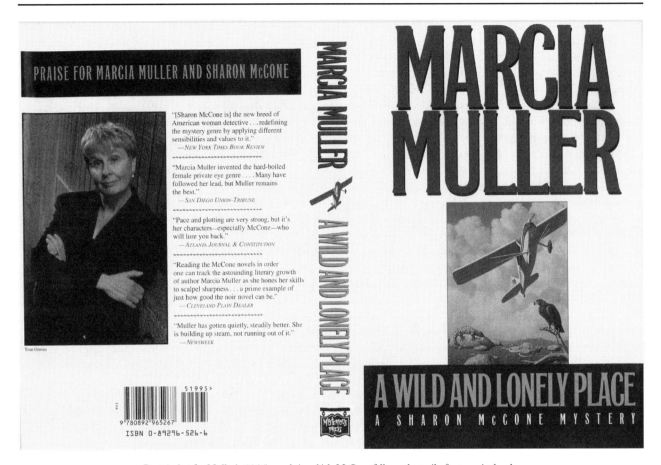

Dust jacket for Muller's 1995 novel, in which McCone follows the trail of a terrorist bomber

sky and now that readers have another character to compare her with so that her own actions will not seem horrific in an individualized way, her character can change, become more hard-boiled, but those new qualities are balanced by her warm emotional attachment to Ripinsky, her family and friends, and even her two cats.

Since *Wolf in the Shadows* began the trend to featuring far-flung settings in the novels, McCone has been involved in cases that have taken her across the United States and the western hemisphere: Nevada and Pennsylvania in *Till the Butchers Cut Him Down;* Florida, the Caribbean, and the Mojave Desert in the highly regarded *A Wild and Lonely Place;* and Arkansas, Florida, Washington, D.C., and the deep woods of northern Minnesota in *Both Ends of the Night.* Under the influence of Ripinsky, McCone takes up flying (as has Muller), and the colorful and dangerous world of aerobatic pilots forms the backdrop of *Both Ends of the Night.* The works continue to be characterized by carefully researched depictions of subcultures such as the country music industry in *Broken Promise Land* and the world of foreign diplomats in *A Wild and Lonely Place.*

After the all-or-nothing offer of a desk job from All Souls about which McCone agonizes throughout *Wolf in the Shadows,* she chooses to begin her own independent investigative agency, first under the roof of All Souls and then, in *Broken Promise Land,* in a suite of offices on the Embarcadero shared with Hank Zahn and Anne-Marie Altman, both longtime friends of McCone. Her most important connections to the past remain in place and her independence of action is maintained as she becomes a manager with her own staff, including her computer-savvy nephew Mick Savage, who is introduced in *Till the Butchers Cut Him Down,* Rae Kelleher, and Ted Smalley, the former secretary of All Souls.

Muller continues to focus attention on social and political issues and timely controversies. In *Till the Butchers Cut Him Down,* for example, she treats the issue of ruthless corporate downsizing and the work of "turn-around men," including McCone's friend "Suits" Gordon. He brings McCone her first job as an independent investigator, and the work takes her deep into the long-lasting and sometimes tragic effects on workers whose lives may be ruined when a company is "turned around."

The vexed issue of diplomatic immunity is explored in the most successful of the recent novels, *A Wild and Lonely Place,* which reviewers recognized as a departure for Muller. The story, which could be classified as both an international thriller and a mystery, involves McCone in international intrigue. Through her friend Adah Joslyn of the San Francisco Police Department McCone becomes involved in the mystery of the Diplo-Bomber, who claims responsibility for many bombings of embassies. Sensing that the bomber has a specific, undisclosed interest in the Azadi consulate, McCone's investigation takes her all the way to a tiny Caribbean island, barely more than a rock, to which Dawud Hamid, the elusive son of the consul, has taken his small daughter, Habiba. McCone's bonding with this helpless child provides the impetus for her search to the solution to the bombings, a solution that involves a one-man campaign against the abuses committed by diplomats and their associates, people who are, like Dawud Hamid, immune to prosecution. Habiba becomes a continuing presence in the series, as she is orphaned at the end of the novel and is later adopted by Zahn and Altman.

Plots that center on children leave themselves open to the charge of pandering to sentiment, a point that Marilyn Stasio makes in *The New York Times Book Review* of 8 October 1995. Stasio cites the appearance of Habiba in this novel, noting that "In their most transparent guise, children are the projection of their authors' own inner waifs." She quotes McCone's thoughts about Habiba: "From the moment she'd owned up to her loneliness I'd been solidly in her corner. I, too, had been a lonely child." Stasio notes, "As a rule, authors aren't this candid about why their sleuths get all choked up over the tykes in their stories." It is, though, this very straightforwardness that makes the device successful, because it is precisely the kind of personal reaction, reinforced by McCone's train of thought about her own family and her place in it, that is typical of this introspective character, who has had many opportunities to examine her personal development within the context of her unusual family. Muller successfully integrates the depiction of the child into her treatment of the theme of loneliness in the novel.

Children appear prominently in *Broken Promise Land* and *Both Ends of the Night,* but their presence is convincingly blended into the themes Muller develops in these novels. McCone's relationship with Habiba offsets the continued hardening of the detective's character, which is summarized in McCone's thoughts early in *A Wild and Lonely Place.* Thinking of her doubts about the ethics of RKI, McCone notes that her own ethics have developed a flexibility she

would not have guessed at in the past: "There was a time when I'd viewed everyone—both victims and perpetrator—through idealistic, compassionate eyes. No longer . . . last spring I'd cold-bloodedly shot another man and called it justice. I wasn't sure that I liked the woman I was becoming, but she was formed of life experiences I couldn't eradicate. You work with what you are, I often told myself on those dark, lonely nights when my misdeeds caught up with me." The McCone of old could look at her actions in the context of making society safer or better, but now the best she can do is work on one individual at a time and let society develop as it may.

Muller's focus in her later novels on the personal and professional relationship between McCone and Ripinsky suggests that McCone's career as a solo hard-boiled detective may be over. In *Both Ends of the Night,* for example, McCone and Ripinsky function more or less as a team, and the case is based on connections that McCone comes to through Ripinsky. The action of the novel is instigated when aerobatic flyer Matty Wildress, an old friend of Ripinsky and recently McCone's flight instructor, asks McCone's help in tracking down her missing lover. Wildress, McCone, and Ripinsky all become embroiled in a mystery that grows to encompass the federal Witness Protection Program and the financial finagling of a politically connected company that manufactures aircraft in Arkansas. Ripinsky takes part in the investigation; they speak of it constantly when they are together; and he is present and active in the climax of the novel in the Boundary Waters Canoe Wilderness. The acts that McCone once would have undertaken without a second thought are now slowed by her thoughts about what he is doing and whether he feels "excluded" by her decision to make the trip to Arkansas alone.

Throughout her career Muller has written in a variety of forms, publishing short fiction in the mystery and western genres, and writing extensively on the creative process and genre fiction. Despite the many difficulties of the collaborative form, which she explored in an article for *The Writer* in 1985, Muller has written three novels with her husband and has edited more than a dozen anthologies with him. Her standing in the mystery genre is indicated by her being given the Lifetime Achievement Award by the Private Eye Writers of America in 1993. Muller speculated in the *Mystery Review* interview that detective fiction is currently at peak popularity because "the more troubled the times the more people gravitate toward crime fiction because it examines the things that are frightening them and also because it provides a solution. The bad guys are caught, things are wrapped up and answers are provided . . . which they aren't in real life." However she chooses to continue the development of the McCone series, Muller is likely to keep giving readers the fiction that reassures them while also reflecting the problems of their times, just as she has for the last twenty years.

Interviews:

Frederick Isaac, "Situation, Motivation, Resolution: An Afternoon with Marcia Muller," *Clues: A Journal of Detection,* 5, no. 2 (1984): 20–34;

Bruce Taylor, "The Real McCone," *Armchair Detective,* 23 (Summer 1990): 260–269;

Michael Pettengell, "The First Lady of Female Detection: An Interview with Marcia Muller," *Mystery Scene,* no. 35 (1992): 35–38;

Nancy Pate, "It's no mystery where female PIs got started," *San Diego Union-Tribune,* 21 June 1993;

Dulcy Brainard, "Marcia Muller: 'The Time Was Ripe,'" *Publishers Weekly,* 8 August 1994, pp. 361–362;

Adrian Muller, "Marcia Muller," *Mystery Scene,* no. 50 (November–December 1995): 26, 28–29;

Barbara Davey, "Marcia Muller: On McCone & Other Matters," *Mystery Review,* 5 (Winter 1997): 34–37.

References:

Kathleen Gregory Klein, *The Woman Detective: Gender and Genre,* second edition (Urbana: University of Illinois Press, 1995), pp. 202, 206–209;

Sally R. Munt, *Murder by the Book? Feminism and the Crime Novel* (London & New York: Routledge, 1994), p. 49;

Bonnie C. Plummer, "Marcia Muller," in *Great Women Mystery Writers: Classic to Contemporary* (Westport, Conn.: Greenwood Press, 1994), pp. 244–247;

Priscilla L. Walton and Manina Jones, *Detective Agency: Women Rewriting the Hard-Boiled Tradition* (Berkeley: University of California, 1999), pp. 86–93.

Papers:

Marcia Muller's papers are at the Popular Culture Library of Bowling Green State University, Ohio. The holdings include manuscripts, drafts, foreign editions, monographs, correspondence, audio and video interviews, and other published and unpublished materials.

Frederick Nebel

(3 November 1903 – 2 May 1967)

Katherine Harper
Bowling Green State University

BOOKS: *Sleepers East* (Boston: Little, Brown, 1933; London: Collins, 1934);

But Not the End (Boston: Little, Brown, 1934);

Fifty Roads to Town (Boston: Little, Brown, 1936; London: Cape, 1936);

Six Deadly Dames (New York: Avon, 1950)—comprises "The Red Hots," "Get a Load of This," "Spare the Rod," "Pearls Are Tens," "Death's Not Enough," and "Save Your Tens";

The Adventures of Cardigan: A Dime Detective Novel (New York: Mysterious Press, 1988).

PRODUCED SCRIPTS: *The Isle of Lost Men,* motion picture, script by Nebel, Dudley Early, and George W. Pyper, Rayart, 1928;

Meet McBride, radio, CBS, 13 June 1936.

OTHER: "Try It My Way," in *Ellery Queen's Awards,* eleventh series (New York: Simon & Schuster, 1956), pp. 189–206;

"Winter Kill," in *The Hardboiled Dicks,* edited by Ron Goulart (Los Angeles: Sherbourne, 1965), pp. 101–146;

"Take It and Like It," in *The Hard-Boiled Detective,* edited by Herbert Ruhm (New York: Vintage, 1977), pp. 90–118;

"Rough Justice," in *The Black Mask Boys,* edited by William F. Nolan (New York: Morrow, 1985), pp. 157–174;

"Murder by Mail," in *Hard-Boiled Dames,* edited by Bernard A. Drew (New York: St. Martin's Press, 1986), pp. 91–116;

"Hell's Pay Check," in *Hard-Boiled Detectives,* edited by Stefan Dziemianowicz and Martin H. Greenberg (New York: Gramercy, 1992), pp. 1–24;

"Chain of Darkness," in *Tough Guys and Dangerous Dames,* edited by Robert Weinberg, Dziemianowicz, and Greenberg (New York: Barnes & Noble, 1993), pp. 95–122;

"Backwash," in *Hard-Boiled: An Anthology of American Crime Stories,* edited by Bill Pronzini and Jack

Frederick Nebel. The inscription is to the most influential editor of Black Mask *magazine (Special Collections, University Research Library, University of California, Los Angeles; from the Joseph T. Shaw Collection, No. 2050).*

Adrian (New York: Oxford University Press, 1995), pp. 83–108.

SELECTED PERIODICAL PUBLICATIONS–UNCOLLECTED: "The Kill," as Grimes Hill, *Black Mask* (March 1931);

"Murder & Co.," *Dime Detective* 8 (15 September 1933): 6–24;

"The Things You Say," *Saturday Evening Post* (3 February 1945): 16+;

"The Bribe," *Cosmopolitan* (September 1947): 26+.

Mystery writer Frederick Nebel made a career choice in 1936, one that he was sure would take him a step up in the world. At the time he was already a success, with three novels and more than two hundred short stories to his credit. Joseph "Cap" Shaw, the editor who molded *Black Mask* into the archetypal detective pulp, considered him one of the finest writers of hard-boiled prose, on par with Dashiell Hammett and Raymond Chandler. A major motion-picture studio had purchased the rights to Nebel's two most popular characters and planned to launch a movie series with a coast-to-coast radio broadcast. He was only thirty-three years old, and his future looked bright.

Unfortunately for connoisseurs of detective fiction, success in the low-status pulp magazines was not enough: Nebel longed for acceptance by a mainstream audience. In 1936, at the peak of his storytelling ability, he decided to taper off his hard-boiled mystery writing and take up with the more lucrative "slicks," nongenre magazines printed on smooth, high-quality paper. This gamble paid off monetarily but detracted from his fame: he died in 1967 in relative obscurity. Twenty years later, however, interest in Nebel revived. His three major series, featuring agency operatives Dick Donahue and Jack Cardigan and the unlikely team of reporter Kennedy and Police Captain MacBride, are considered by critics and fans alike as among the finest to emerge from the Golden Age of pulps.

To judge by the few biographical accounts available, Louis Frederick Nebel had a remarkable early life. He was born on 3 November 1903 near Grimes Hill in Staten Island, New York. At the age of fifteen he left school and spent the next two years working as a checker on the rough-and-tumble wharves. The slightly built youngster was surrounded by quick-tempered workers much older than he; brawls were common. Nevertheless, he stuck with the job and each night set down his observations in writing. His stepfather urged him to go back to school, but the boy refused. At seventeen he accepted a great-uncle's offer of work as a farmhand in northern Canada. He found his largely undeveloped new surroundings fascinating, and used them as background for further stories. A few years later, he returned to New York, to a more adventurous occupation as a railroad brakeman.

In 1926 the twenty-three-year-old Nebel signed on with a tramp steamer bound for the Caribbean. He spent months exploring Havana and other sultry West Indies ports that served as settings for his later fiction and then moved on to the colder climes of England and Scandinavia. In 1928 he arrived in Paris, where he met Dorothy Blank, the daughter of a merchandising manager. They were married in St. Louis, Missouri, on 12 May 1930. The newlyweds did not put down

roots at once: they lived for short periods in several cities before deciding to refurbish an old house in Ridgefield, Connecticut, where they settled for the next twenty-five years.

While working his way around the world and starting his family, Nebel spent every free moment at his typewriter. Between 1925 and 1930 he published approximately 120 short stories and articles in publications ranging from *Lariat* and *Five Novels Monthly* to the national magazine of the Elks Club. His Mountie series featuring Corporal Chet Tyson became a staple of the adventure pulp *Northwest Stories,* and *Air Stories* carried his series about a pair of happy-go-lucky flyers.

By far the most important magazine to carry Nebel's byline was *Black Mask*. He made his foray into hard-boiled detective fiction with a nonseries story, "The Breaks of the Game," published in March 1926. Encouraged by Cap Shaw to add detail to his characters over time, he became adept at the genre, which soon made up the bulk of his literary output. He published most stories under his own name and the variations "Louis Nebel" and "Eric Lewis," though on at least two occasions, when he had more than one piece in the same magazine, he used "Grimes Hill," the place of his birth.

The characters who were to become Nebel's most popular debuted in "Raw Law" (September 1928), the first of a *Black Mask* series subtitled "The Crimes of Richmond City." The metropolis of the title is similar to Hammett's Poisonville: dark, secretive, corrupt to the bone. Bootleg liquor is openly sold and the cop on the beat is slipped a weekly envelope. Packets of white powder pass from hand to hand in doorways. Every alley and canal is a potential body dump. Police Captain Steve MacBride, a tanned, wiry pipe-smoker, is one of the few dedicated lawmen in the city. He would like nothing better than to clean up his hometown but must approach the task cautiously for fear of retaliation against his wife and daughter. With the help of two trustworthy sergeants, Cohen and Moriarity, he sets to work to eliminate the criminal element.

MacBride's friend—and personal millstone—is John X. Kennedy, a reporter on the Richmond City *Free Press.* In "Winter Kill" (November 1935), Nebel describes the character as "slightly whimsical, sleepy-eyed, harmless-looking. His clothes were always haphazard, badly pressed; his yellow hair was rarely orderly and he always looked as if a stiff wind would blow him over." A shrewd, intelligent, and basically honest man, Kennedy has responded to the corruption around him not by giving in or ignoring it but by viewing it through a haze of alcohol. In all but the first few stories, he is constantly pickled: MacBride must haul him out of speakeasies or the backseats of parked cars in order to solicit his help. The reporter does not always remember basics, such as the need to eat regularly or to wear warm clothing in the winter. Nevertheless, when it comes to news, his mind and eye are sharp and his intuitions invariably prove correct.

Hard-boiled MacBride recognizes Kennedy as a genius fettered by addiction. While he often grinds his teeth over the reporter's antics, he also shows him an uncharacteristic level of compassion, making sure that he has food and a place to sleep and preventing his fellow officers from physically responding to Kennedy's vitriolic remarks. In one typical story, "Take It and Like It" (June 1934), a young woman is found beaten to death in the reporter's flat. Kennedy, inebriated as usual, happily admits to the crime; then he knocks the district attorney cold and walks away. MacBride, distraught at the thought of his friend as a murderer, races with the district attorney to track down the reporter and clear his name. His efforts prove unnecessary, for at the end of the story he finds Kennedy–and a Russian zither player he has picked up in a bar–literally sitting on the real killer. Listening to his friend coolly telephone in the details of the case, all a relieved MacBride can say is, "Thank God, Kennedy, old kid! Thank God!"

The Kennedy and MacBride stories, thirty-seven in all, ran for eight years in *Black Mask,* ending in August 1936 with the kidnap-murder tale "Deep Red." Though it was not the author's longest-running series, it was and remains his most popular. Robert Sampson is enthusiastic in his multivolume survey of pulp writing, *Yesterday's Faces:* "The series is brilliant. It contains the distilled essence of hardboiled writing, a curious mixture of complexity, savagery, and pathos. It is austere. It is understated to the point of grayness. It is coldly sentimental. It established at least one–perhaps two–characters who lived on the page and involved the reader with them in the quiet way of pure art." Sampson's reaction may be overstatement, but it is undeniable that Kennedy and MacBride's mutual affection, and the reporter's cutting one-liners, stay with the reader long after the story is over. Taken as a whole, "The Crimes of Richmond City" can be considered Frederick Nebel's magnum opus.

The writer's second hard-boiled series character, "Tough Dick" Donahue, was created at Cap Shaw's request to replace Hammett's Continental Op, and first appeared in the November 1930 issue of *Black Mask* in which the Op "retired." Nebel told historian Ron Goulart that he and Hammett "were not influenced by each other's work," but this seems unlikely when the two series are compared. While he had previously contented himself with stand-alone stories, once he created Donahue, Nebel began to compose short-term serials in true Hammett style. Both authors' characters work for branch offices of national investigation firms: Donahue in New York, the

Op in San Francisco. In *Red Harvest* (1929) the Op describes his superior at the Continental Detective Agency as "Pontius Pilate. . . . a gentle, polite, elderly person with no more warmth in him than a hangman's rope," while Donahue's boss, Asa Hinkle of the Inter-State Detective Agency, is "pontifical-looking," with a calm, cold voice and humorless gray eyes. Only the detectives' physical appearance is markedly different: the Op is short, paunchy, and middle-aged, while Donahue is six feet tall, tanned and well muscled, and marcels his black hair. Like his creator, he smokes a pipe. A dedicated bachelor, he eats most of his meals at Dominick's, which is described in "Get a Load of This" (February 1931) as "a quiet joint where you got good chili con carne and a Spanish sherry that wasn't cut but once."

The fifteen Donahue stories, which ran in *Black Mask* between 1930 and 1935, are noteworthy for their use of violence. As hard-boiled as Steve MacBride is, he relies for the most part on interviews, logic, and verbal traps to solve crimes. A Donahue story, more typical of the genre, is not complete without a third degree or vicious fistfight. "Rough Justice," the first in the series, contains both: interrogating a jewel thief, Donahue jerks the man's head back by the hair and snarls threats into his face. He later brawls with the thief and a crooked private eye, and knocks both unconscious at the cost of a facial cut that bloodies his clothing. Like other pulp heroes, Donahue frequently winds up at the wrong end of a blackjack, but he is more human than most in that he feels pain and must take time to recover before continuing his work.

Most Golden Age pulp writers demonstrated their characters' hard-boiled attitude strictly through dialogue. Nebel pays equal attention to the prose in between. Characters in his stories seldom "say" or "explain" anything: instead, they "clip," "huff," "grind," and even "chick," his term for the baby-talk of lovers. One female character is described as "tall and lean-hipped and look[ing] pliant in a pale blue peignoir." Most pulp writers' descriptions of pistol-whipping would emphasize the savagery of the act, but Nebel instead skillfully uses such an incident to further characterization: in the Donahue story "The Red-Hots" (December 1930) his hero steps in as a gangster beats a woman and "[strikes] Alfred playfully on the head with Alfred's gun." The adverb tells readers all they need to know about Donahue: violence is so much a part of him that it is automatic, offhanded. Few other writers pack so much into so few words.

In 1931 Nebel began another series for the new Popular Publications monthly *Dime Detective.* Cosmos Agency operative Jack Cardigan is similar to Donahue, but uses much more slang; he is seldom described in physical terms, except for his long arms and "shaggy mop of hair." Like all the fiction in *Dime Detective,* the Cardigan stories are half again as long as typical pulp stories and are

Cover for a pulp featuring a Nebel story about Cosmos Detective Agency operative Jack Cardigan

heavily padded; Nebel's ability to describe a situation in a few well-chosen words is not put into play. Their occasional tediousness is made up for by the presence of Cardigan's secretary and sidekick Pat Seaward, who dresses like a *Vogue* model and is equally quick with an icepack or a wisecrack. She is also handy with her fists, an asset since Cardigan is reluctant to manhandle female suspects. (He has no such compunction about their male counterparts.) The series ran for six years and forty-four stories and helped to keep Popular Publications afloat long enough to establish itself as a viable market.

Pulp-fiction scholars Sampson and Dave Lewis have noted in separate critiques that a police detective named Jack Cardigan plays a major role in the first Kennedy and MacBride story, "Raw Law." When Cardigan's partner is murdered and Captain MacBride finds himself helpless to investigate, the detective loyally quits the force and solves the case on his own. Lewis believes, however, that "[w]hile Nebel could not have been unaware of the names, it is unlikely that he ever considered them the same man," pointing out that the Cardigan who debuted in "Death Alley" in 1931 was named Steve and remained so for several stories before his perhaps accidental redubbing.

Nebel created other, less memorable detective characters over the years, most bearing a strong resemblance to his earlier successes: these include soldier of fortune Buck Jason for *Black Mask,* private dick Gallagher and "Poole of the *Telegram*" for *Detective Fiction Weekly,* and the team of Inspector Larsen and Sergeant Brinkhaus, who migrated between three magazines in as many years. Although the slightly more sober Kennedy-clone Poole never caught on with readers, Nebel permitted him to reveal what lies at the heart of every pulp-era detective. In "The Pinch" (17 September 1932), the reporter tells a sympathetic bartender, "I'm like a lot of you guys, Mac: hiding a real emotion under a wisecrack, afraid of being called soft, proud of being hard-boiled. Wise? Hell, under the skin we're a bunch of hicks!"

Dorothy Nebel has said that her husband had a wonderful sense of humor, a trait that is clear in his fiction. Pat Seaward, in particular, illustrates his comic touch, matching her boss Cardigan flip remark for flip remark. Kennedy's "jokes," by contrast, are lazily sarcastic observations that strip their subjects to the bone; in critic Paul Stuewe's words, they "often transcend mere wisecracking and approach the surreal zaniness of the

Marx Brothers' films." Nebel admitted to a personal fondness for pranks: Ron Goulart transcribed the writer's reminiscence of getting drunk with Hammett and walking around New York City on a clear night under an open umbrella. "The idea seemed to be (there was a small bet) that no one would pay any attention to us," Nebel explained. "No one did." The next morning, he woke to find that Hammett had left him a copy of *The Maltese Falcon* inscribed in memory of the event.

In 1933 Nebel published his first full-scale novel. *Sleepers East* must have come as a surprise to readers of his pulp stories, for though many of its characters are tough talkers and a gunshot rings out in its final pages, it is far from hard-boiled. Like Vicki Baum's *Grand Hotel* (1930), a best-seller the year before, the book brings together a disparate group of people in a confined space—in Nebel's case, a Pullman coach—and allows them to play out schemes and fantasies against each other. The publisher apparently expected critics to compare Nebel's novel to Baum's, for a blurb opposite the title page of *Sleepers East* warns, "This is the story of a thrilling game of hide-and-seek, played in the compartments of a speeding express train, with lives as forfeits. This is *not* a story of unrelated lives thrown together by accident." One by one, Nebel introduces a large cast, including a henpecked auto dealer, a tough female informant en route to trial, a coal heaver obsessed with his lover's fidelity, a celebrity-worshipping railroad secretary, and most important, the engineer Magowan, who has a mental breakdown and sends the train and its passengers rocketing through a night blizzard. An interesting minor character is the Pullman porter, who has patiently suffered years of racial abuse in order to see his son become a doctor and his daughter a successful stage actress.

Critics of the day found *Sleepers East* a pleasant surprise. The reveiwer for the 28 June 1933 *Boston Transcript* called it "a fascinating story. . . . splendidly done" and said that the "characters are all excellently drawn and humanly interesting." The critic for the 18 June *Books* deemed it "lively," adding that "Mr. Nebel's deduction is that brutal, blind, indiscriminate chance is the arbiter of life." The motion-picture adaptation of the novel was filmed by Fox Studios with Preston Foster and Wynne Gibson in 1934, and seven years later by successor 20th Century-Fox as a Mike Shayne mystery, *Sleepers West,* starring Lloyd Nolan.

Nebel's other two novels are even less in the hard-boiled tradition. *But Not the End* (1934) describes the attempts of a group of New York socialites to maintain their accustomed lifestyle during the Depression. The critic for *The New York Times* of 18 March gave the book a positive review, noting its "multitude of vivid, adeptly handled incidents [that] enliven . . . the story with an unabating interest." Two years later, *Fifty Roads to Town,* which again deals with people shut off from the world—in this

case, snowbound in a tiny Maine hotel—was even more enthusiastically received. William Rose Benét commented in the *Saturday Review of Literature* of 8 February 1936 that Nebel "writes with an economy of means, makes his own pattern of a story, keeps you guessing, can create characters (none too subtle, but real) and his dialogue is right." The critic for *The New York Times* of 2 February called the writing style "outstandingly masculine, not rough for its own sake but starkly objective, and unsoftened by feminine furbishings, sentimentality or frills."

Nebel had sold stories to and even written scenarios for motion pictures as early as 1928, but his best-known contribution to popular culture beyond the pulps began in 1936 with his radio dramatization of one of his pulp stories. *Meet McBride* was broadcast over CBS on 13 June of that year, as Warner Bros. was wrapping up production on the first of nine movies featuring Lieutenant Steve McBride and, not his alcoholic friend Kennedy, but wisecracking gal reporter Torchy Blane. The initial entry, *Smart Blonde,* starring Barton MacLane and Glenda Farrell, was the only one adapted directly from a Nebel story ("No Hard Feelings," *Black Mask,* February 1936); credits on subsequent motion pictures read, "Based on characters created by Frederick Nebel." The Torchy Blanes, as they came to be called, are romantic mysteries that bear little resemblance to the hard-bitten tales that supposedly inspired them. Their quality might have been better had Nebel agreed to move to Hollywood and write the scripts himself, but he had seen how life in the movie capital had demoralized his friend Hammett and refused all studio offers.

It was at this point in his career—and with son Christopher on the way—that Nebel made his move from the pulps to the slick magazines, effectively sabotaging his status as one of the great American hard-boiled writers. Stuewe asserts that "Nebel's novels are written in a polite, chatty, and often glibly superficial style," a description that applies equally well to the bulk of the author's post-1936 short fiction. His stories for such magazines as *Collier's, Liberty,* and *The Saturday Evening Post* are well written but ordinary. A few have mystery or suspense plots, but the majority—with titles such as "You Know How Women Are" and "Grampa and the Spirit of '76"—are mainstream tales or light romances, with little of the terseness or bite of his pulp fiction.

One noteworthy later story is "The Bribe," published in the September 1947 issue of *Cosmopolitan.* The opening sequence is reminiscent of Ernest Hemingway in its chilly treatment of a torrid setting: government investigator Rigby, relaxing in a Havana café, sees that he is being shadowed—not for the first time—by a seedy hustler. Brightman soon furtively slides into the next chair and begins to babble; his client, he says, needs information on

Rigby's black-market findings, and will pay $10,000 for even the smallest scrap. Rigby fusses with his pipe and the *Havana Post.* Then he puts on his hat, folds his newspaper, rises and strolls away, abandoning the hustler in midsentence. Much of the remaining story is standard romance, complicated by the investigator's struggle against the temptation of easy money, but it winds down on a fine hard-boiled note as he physically exorcises his demon:

> Rigby struck him. It was almost a reflexive action, as if done in self-defense, although Brightman had not moved and was astounded by the blow. Rigby felt like weeping. He struck again, backhand, his knuckles raking; and then forehand, the flat of his palm smacking. He groaned—bitter because Elizabeth would not be able now to lounge through long, assuaging weeks in Florida and later see the spring unfold in New England. And striking Brightman, hand-lashing him backward across the room, he knew he was flaying some potential evil in himself—the vague gray ghost that ranges somewhere far back in every man.

The publisher of *Cosmopolitan* saw possibilities in "The Bribe" and offered its author a flat $20,000 dollars in return for all rights. Surprised and pleased, Nebel agreed. In the long run, this decision turned out to be a mistake, for the publisher then offered the story to Metro-Goldwyn-Mayer, which snapped it up as a vehicle for Ava Gardner. The finished motion picture was one of the studio's biggest box-office draws of 1948. Thanks to the all-rights agreement, however, Nebel did not receive a penny in royalties.

When Shaw was assembling the stories that were to become *The Hard-Boiled Omnibus* in 1945, his first contacts were his favorite threesome: Hammett, Chandler, and Nebel. The first two agreed to give Shaw the use of their strongest pulp work, but Nebel wrote back an emphatic no. "The reason why I don't want to see my old *Black Mask* stuff between boards," he explained, "is because I think it served its purpose well when it was first published but I honestly cannot see what purpose it would serve now. . . . I can work up no enthusiasm." Despite Shaw's pleas to reconsider, Nebel refused to allow his stories to be reprinted. Whether out of hurt or because his friend requested it, Shaw did not even mention Nebel's name in the introduction to the volume. By 1950, however, the writer had finally realized the staying power of his pulp fiction and permitted Avon Books to publish half a dozen Donahue tales under the title *Six Deadly Dames.* He also authorized the televising of his magazine work on *Studio One* and other anthology shows.

Ellery Queen's Mystery Magazine and *The Saint* reprinted several of Nebel's early pieces between 1957 and 1961, and he wrote half a dozen new stories to supplement them. By that time, however, his health had begun to deteriorate. Eventually, he was in such discomfort that he and Dorothy gave up their Connecticut home and moved to the more hospitable climate of Laguna Beach, California. There, Nebel outlined a new novel and worked on it at intervals when his condition permitted. The book was never completed: he suffered a cerebral hemorrhage at the end of April 1967 and died on 2 May at the age of sixty-three.

In *The Pulp Jungle* (1967) Frank Gruber, a fellow pulp writer who admired Nebel's work, predicted that Nebel would be remembered for his contributions to *Black Mask,* not his later work. The truth of Gruber's prediction was proven by the subsequent interest in Nebel's work: *Six Deadly Dames* was republished in hardback in 1980; The Mysterious Press compiled a softback collection of six Cardigan stories in 1988; and a dozen other tales have appeared over the years in anthologies celebrating Golden Age pulps. All three major series are regularly discussed in scholarly studies of genre fiction. While Donahue, Cardigan, Kennedy, MacBride—the characters from whom for a time Nebel wished to distance himself—are celebrated by critics and may well attract future generations of readers, his mainstream fiction is viewed as only a footnote to his career.

References:

Ron Goulart, *The Dime Detectives* (New York: Mysterious Press, 1988);

E. R. Hagemann, "Cap Shaw and His 'Great and Regular Fellows': The Making of *The Hard-Boiled Omnibus,* 1945–1946," *Clues,* 2, no. 2 (1981): 143–152;

David Lewis, "The Backbone of *Black Mask,*" *Clues,* 2, no. 2 (1981): 116–127;

William F. Nolan, "Behind the Mask: Frederick Nebel," in his *The Black Mask Boys* (New York: Morrow, 1985), pp. 152–157;

Paul Stuewe, "Frederick Nebel," in *Critical Survey of Mystery and Detective Fiction,* edited by Frank N. Magill (Pasadena: Salem, 1988), pp. 1264–1268.

Papers:

The papers of Frederick Nebel are held at the library of the University of Oregon at Eugene. They include the manuscripts for Nebel's 3 novels, 97 short-story manuscripts, 275 published stories, the writer's early journals, and 950 letters between Nebel and his agent.

Bill Pronzini

(13 April 1943 –   )

Marvin S. Lachman

BOOKS: *The Stalker* (New York: Random House, 1971; London: Hale, 1974);

The Snatch (New York: Random House, 1971; London: Hale, 1974);

Panic! (New York: Random House, 1972; London: Hale, 1974);

The Jade Figurine, as Jack Foxx (Indianapolis: Bobbs-Merrill, 1972); as Pronzini (New York: Carroll & Graf, 1991);

A Run in Diamonds, as Alex Saxon (New York: Pocket Books, 1973); revised in *Carmody's Run,* as Pronzini (Arlington Heights, Ill.: Dark Harvest, 1992);

The Vanished (New York: Random House, 1973; London: Hale, 1974);

Undercurrent (New York: Random House, 1973; London: Hale, 1975);

Snowbound (New York: Putnam, 1974; London: Weidenfeld & Nicolson, 1975);

Dead Run, as Foxx (Indianapolis: Bobbs-Merrill, 1975); as Pronzini (New York: Carroll & Graf, 1992);

Games (New York: Putnam, 1976; London: Hamlyn, 1978);

The Running of Beasts, by Pronzini and Barry N. Malzberg (New York: Putnam, 1976);

Freebooty, as Foxx (Indianapolis: Bobbs-Merrill, 1976);

Blowback (New York: Random House, 1977; London: Hale, 1978);

Acts of Mercy, by Pronzini and Malzberg (New York: Putnam, 1977);

Wildfire, as Foxx (Indianapolis: Bobbs-Merrill, 1978); revised as *Firewind,* as Pronzini (New York: M. Evans, 1989);

Twospot, by Pronzini and Collin Wilcox (New York: Putnam, 1978);

Night Screams, by Pronzini and Malzberg (New York: Playboy Press, 1979);

Labyrinth (New York: St. Martin's Press, 1980; London: Hale, 1981);

A Killing in Xanadu (Richmond, Va.: Waves Press, 1980);

Bill Pronzini (courtesy of the author)

Prose Bowl, by Pronzini and Malzberg (New York: St. Martin's Press, 1980);

Hoodwink (New York: St. Martin's Press, 1981; London: Hale, 1981);

Masques (New York: Arbor House, 1981);

The Cambodia File, by Pronzini and Jack Anderson (Garden City, N.Y.: Doubleday, 1981; London: Sphere, 1983);

Duel at Gold Buttes, as William Jeffrey, by Pronzini and Jeffrey Wallmann (New York: Tower, 1981; London: Hale, 1982);

Scattershot (New York: St. Martin's Press, 1982; London: Hale, 1982);

Gun in Cheek: A Study of "Alternative" Crime Fiction (New York: Coward, McCann & Geoghegan, 1982);

Dragonfire (New York: St. Martin's Press, 1982; London: Hale, 1983);

Casefile: The Best of the "Nameless Detective" Stories (New York: St. Martin's Press, 1983);

Bindlestiff (New York: St. Martin's Press, 1983; London: Severn House, 1984);

Day of the Moon, as Jeffrey, by Pronzini and Wallmann (London: Hale, 1983);

Border Fever, as Jeffrey, by Pronzini and Wallmann (New York: Leisure, 1983; London: Hale, 1984);

The Gallows Land (New York: Walker, 1983; London: Hale, 1984);

Cat's-Paw (Richmond, Va.: Waves Press, 1983);

Starvation Camp (New York: Walker, 1983; London: Hale, 1984);

Quicksilver (New York: St. Martin's Press, 1984; London: Severn House, 1985);

The Eye, by Pronzini and John Lutz (New York: Mysterious Press, 1984);

Nightshades (New York: St. Martin's Press, 1984; London: Severn House, 1986);

Double, by Pronzini and Marcia Muller (New York: St. Martin's Press, 1984);

Bones (New York: St. Martin's Press, 1985);

Quincannon (New York: Walker, 1985);

Graveyard Plots: The Best Short Stories of Bill Pronzini (New York: St. Martin's Press, 1985);

Deadfall (New York: St. Martin's Press, 1986);

Beyond the Grave, by Pronzini and Muller (New York: Walker, 1986);

The Last Days of Horse-Shy Halloran (New York: M. Evans, 1987; London: Chivers, 1989);

Son of Gun in Cheek (New York: Mysterious Press, 1987);

The Lighthouse, by Pronzini and Muller (New York: St. Martin's Press, 1987; London: Hale, 1988);

Small Felonies: Fifty Mystery Short Shorts (New York: St. Martin's Press, 1988);

Shackles (New York: St. Martin's Press, 1988);

The Hangings (New York: Walker, 1989; London: Thorndike, 1990);

Jackpot (New York: Delacorte, 1990; London: Severn House, 1991);

The Best Western Stories of Bill Pronzini, edited by Martin H. Greenberg (Athens, Ohio: Swallow Press, 1990);

Breakdown (New York: Delacorte, 1991; London: Severn House, 1991);

Stacked Deck (Eugene, Oreg.: Pulphouse, 1991);

Quarry (New York: Delacorte, 1992);

Epitaphs (New York: Delacorte, 1992);

Carmody's Run (Arlington Heights, Ill.: Dark Harvest, 1992)—comprises a revision of *A Run in Diamonds* and three previously uncollected short stories, "Blood Money" (originally published as "Free-Lance Operation"), "The Desperate Ones," and "Death Warrant" (originally published as "The Web");

Demons (New York: Delacorte, 1993);

With an Extreme Burning (New York: Carroll & Graf, 1994);

Hardcase (New York: Delacorte, 1995);

Blue Lonesome (New York: Walker, 1995);

Sentinels (New York: Carroll & Graf, 1996);

Spadework (Norfolk, Va.: Crippen & Landru, 1996);

A Wasteland of Strangers (New York: Walker, 1997);

Illusions (New York: Carroll & Graf, 1997);

Six-Gun in Cheek: An Affectionate Guide to the "Worst" in Western Fiction (Minneapolis & San Francisco: Crossover Press, 1997);

Boobytrap (New York: Carroll & Graf, 1998);

Carpenter and Quincannon Professional Detective Services (Norfolk, Va.: Crippen & Landru, 1998);

Nothing But the Night (New York: Walker, 1999).

OTHER: *Tricks and Treats,* edited by Pronzini and Joe Gores (Garden City, N.Y.: Doubleday, 1976); republished as *Mystery Writers' Choice* (London: Gollancz, 1977);

Midnight Specials, edited by Pronzini (Indianapolis: Bobbs-Merrill, 1977; London: Souvenir, 1978);

Dark Sins, Dark Dreams, edited by Pronzini and Barry N. Malzberg (Garden City, N.Y.: Doubleday, 1978);

Werewolf! edited by Pronzini (New York: Arbor House, 1979);

Shared Tomorrows: Collaborations in Science Fiction, edited by Pronzini and Malzberg (New York: St. Martin's Press, 1979);

Bug-eyed Monsters, edited by Pronzini and Malzberg (New York: Harcourt Brace Jovanovich, 1980);

The Edgar Winners, edited by Pronzini (New York: Random House, 1980);

Voodoo! edited by Pronzini (New York: Arbor House, 1980);

Mummy! edited by Pronzini (New York: Arbor House, 1980);

Creature! edited by Pronzini (New York: Arbor House, 1981);

The Arbor House Necropolis: Voodoo!, Mummy!, Ghoul!, edited by Pronzini (New York: Arbor House, 1981); revised as *Tales of the Dead* (New York: Bonanza Books, 1982);

The Arbor House Treasury of Horror and the Supernatural, 2 volumes, edited by Pronzini, Malzberg, and Martin H. Greenberg (New York: Arbor House, 1981);

Specter! edited by Pronzini (New York: Arbor House, 1982);

The Arbor House Treasury of Great Western Stories, edited by Pronzini and Greenberg (New York: Arbor House, 1982);

The Arbor House Treasury of Detective and Mystery Stories from the Great Pulps, edited by Pronzini (New York: Arbor House, 1983);

The Web She Weaves: An Anthology of Mystery and Suspense Stories by Women, edited by Pronzini and Marcia Muller (New York: Morrow, 1983);

The Mystery Hall of Fame, edited by Pronzini, Charles G. Waugh, and Greenberg (New York: Morrow, 1984);

Child's Ploy, edited by Pronzini (New York: Macmillan, 1984);

Witches Brew: Horror and Supernatural Stories by Women, edited by Pronzini (New York: Macmillan, 1984);

The Western Hall of Fame, edited by Pronzini and Greenberg (New York: Morrow, 1984);

The Lawmen, edited by Pronzini and Greenberg (New York: Fawcett, 1984);

The Outlaws, edited by Pronzini and Greenberg (New York: Fawcett, 1984);

The Reel West, edited by Pronzini and Greenberg (Garden City, N.Y.: Doubleday, 1984);

The Best Western Stories of Steve Frazee, edited by Pronzini and Greenberg (Carbondale: Southern Illinois University Press, 1984);

The Best Western Stories of Wayne D. Overholser, edited by Pronzini and Greenberg (Carbondale: Southern Illinois University Press, 1984);

Baker's Dozen: 13 Short Mystery Novels, edited by Pronzini and Greenberg (New York: Greenwich House, 1984);

Chapter and Hearse, edited by Pronzini and Marcia Muller (New York: Morrow, 1985);

The Ethnic Detectives, edited by Pronzini and Greenberg (New York: Dodd, Mead, 1985);

Murder in the First Reel, edited by Pronzini, Waugh, and Greenberg (New York: Avon, 1985);

Baker's Dozen: 13 Short Espionage Novels, edited by Pronzini and Greenberg (New York: Bonanza Books, 1985);

Dark Lessons: Crime and Detection on Campus, edited by Pronzini and Muller (New York: Macmillan, 1985);

Kill or Cure, edited by Pronzini and Muller (New York: Macmillan, 1985);

Women Sleuths, edited by Pronzini and Greenberg (Chicago: Academy, 1985);

Police Procedurals, edited by Pronzini and Greenberg (Chicago: Academy, 1985);

The Wickedest Show on Earth: A Carnival of Circus Suspense, edited by Pronzini and Muller (New York: Morrow, 1985);

The Deadly Arts: A Collection of Artful Suspense, edited by Pronzini and Muller (New York: Arbor House, 1985);

She Won the West: An Anthology of Western and Frontier Stories by Women, edited by Pronzini and Muller (New York: Morrow, 1985);

The Cowboys, edited by Pronzini and Greenberg (New York: Fawcett, 1985);

The Warriors, edited by Pronzini and Greenberg (New York: Fawcett, 1985);

The Second Reel West, edited by Pronzini and Greenberg (Garden City, N.Y.: Doubleday, 1985);

A Treasury of Civil War Stories, edited by Pronzini and Greenberg (New York: Bonanza Books, 1985);

A Treasury of World War II Stories, edited by Pronzini and Greenberg (New York: Bonanza Books, 1985);

1001 Midnights: The Aficionado's Guide to Mystery and Detective Fiction, edited by Pronzini and Muller (New York: Arbor House, 1986);

Great Modern Police Stories, edited by Pronzini and Greenberg (New York: Walker, 1986; London: Severn House, 1987);

101 Mystery Stories, edited by Pronzini and Greenberg (New York: Avenel, 1986);

Locked Room Puzzles, edited by Pronzini and Greenberg (Chicago: Academy, 1986);

Mystery in the Mainstream: An Anthology of Literary Crimes, edited by Pronzini, Greenberg, and Malzberg (New York: Morrow, 1986);

The Railroaders, edited by Pronzini and Greenberg (New York: Fawcett, 1986);

The Third Reel West, edited by Pronzini and Greenberg (Garden City, N.Y.: Doubleday, 1986);

Wild Westerns: Stories from the Grand Old Pulps, edited by Pronzini (New York: Walker, 1986);

The Steamboaters, edited by Pronzini and Greenberg (New York: Fawcett, 1986);

The Cattlemen, edited by Pronzini and Greenberg (New York: Fawcett, 1987);

Prime Suspects, edited by Pronzini and Greenberg (New York: Ivy, 1987; London: Severn House, 1988);

Uncollected Crimes, edited by Pronzini and Greenberg (New York: Walker, 1987);

Suspicious Characters, edited by Pronzini and Greenberg (New York: Ivy, 1987; London: Severn House, 1988);

Manhattan Mysteries, edited by Pronzini, Carol-Lynn Rössel Waugh, and Greenberg (New York: Avenel, 1987);

The Horse Soldiers, edited by Pronzini and Greenberg (New York: Fawcett, 1987);

The Best Western Stories of Lewis B. Patten, edited by Pronzini and Greenberg (Carbondale: Southern Illinois University Press, 1987);

Baker's Dozen: 13 Short Detective Novels, edited by Pronzini and Greenberg (New York: Bonanza Books, 1987);

Criminal Elements, edited by Pronzini and Greenberg (New York: Ivy, 1988);

Cloak and Dagger, edited by Pronzini and Greenberg (New York: Avenel, 1988);

Lady on the Case, edited by Pronzini, Muller, and Greenberg (New York: Bonanza Books, 1988);

The Mammoth Book of Private Eye Stories, edited by Pronzini and Greenberg (New York: Carroll & Graf, 1988; London: Robinson, 1988);

The Gunfighters, edited by Pronzini and Greenberg (New York: Fawcett, 1988);

The Texans, edited by Pronzini and Greenberg (New York: Fawcett, 1988);

Homicidal Acts, edited by Pronzini and Greenberg (New York: Ivy, 1989);

Felonious Assaults, edited by Pronzini and Greenberg (New York: Ivy, 1989);

The Californians, edited by Pronzini and Greenberg (New York: Fawcett, 1989);

More Wild Westerns, edited by Pronzini (New York: Walker, 1989);

The Best Western Stories of Loren D. Estleman, edited by Pronzini and Greenberg (Athens: Swallow Press/ Ohio University Press, 1989);

The Arizonans, edited by Pronzini and Greenberg (New York: Fawcett, 1989);

The Best Western Stories of Frank Bonham, edited by Pronzini and Greenberg (Athens: Ohio University Press, 1989);

Christmas Out West, edited by Pronzini (New York: Doubleday, 1990);

New Frontiers, 2 volumes, edited by Pronzini and Greenberg (New York: Tor, 1990);

The Northerners, edited by Pronzini and Greenberg (New York: Fawcett, 1990);

The Northwesterners, edited by Pronzini and Greenberg (New York: Fawcett, 1990);

The Best Western Stories of Ryerson Johnson (Athens: Swallow Press/Ohio University Press, 1990);

The Montanans, edited by Pronzini (New York: Fawcett Gold Medal, 1991);

The Best Western Stories of John Jakes, edited by Pronzini (Athens: Ohio University Press, 1991);

The Best Western Stories of Les Savage, Jr., edited by Pronzini (Athens: Swallow Press/Ohio University Press, 1991);

Combat! edited by Pronzini (New York: Signet/Penguin, 1992);

The Best Western Stories of Ed Gorman, edited by Pronzini (Athens: Swallow Press/Ohio University Press, 1992);

William Campbell Gault, *Dead Pigeon,* introduction by Pronzini (New York: Carroll & Graf, 1992);

John Jakes, *In the Big Country,* edited by Pronzini (Thorndike, Maine: G. K. Hall, 1993);

Edward Gorman, *Gunslinger, and Nine Other Action-Packed Stories of the Wild West,* edited by Pronzini (New York: Barricade Books, 1995);

Frank Bonham, *One Ride Too Many and Twelve Other Action-Packed Stories of the Wild West,* edited by Pronzini (New York: Barricade Books, 1995);

Hard-Boiled: An Anthology of American Crime Stories, edited by Pronzini and Jack Adrian (New York & London: Oxford University Press, 1995);

William Campbell Gault, *Man Alone,* introduction by Pronzini (Brooklyn, N.Y.: Gryphon, 1995);

Ed Gorman and Martin H. Greenberg, eds., *The Fatal Frontier,* introduction by Pronzini (New York: Carroll & Graf, 1996);

H. A. DeRosso, *Under the Burning Sun,* edited by Pronzini (Unity, Maine: Five Star, 1997);

American Pulp, edited by Gorman, Pronzini, and Greenberg (New York: Carroll & Graf, 1997);

Detective Duos, edited by Muller and Pronzini (New York & Oxford: Oxford University Press, 1997);

Paul Gifford Cheshire, *Renegade River,* edited by Pronzini (Unity, Maine: Five Star, 1998).

SELECTED PERIODICAL PUBLICATIONS– UNCOLLECTED:

FICTION

"You Don't Know What It's Like," *Shell Scott Mystery Magazine,* 2 (November 1966): 102–116;

"Sacrifice," *Alfred Hitchcock's Mystery Magazine,* 18 (February 1973): 116–123;

"The Follower," *Alfred Hitchock's Mystery Magazine,* 18 (March 1973): 30–43;

"It's Not a Coffin," *Mike Shayne Mystery Magazine,* 35 (June 1974): 65–69;

"If You Play with Fire," *Mike Shayne Mystery Magazine,* 38 (February 1976): 123–128;

"Liar's Dice," *Ellery Queen's Mystery Magazine,* 100 (November 1992): 132–139;

"Shade Work," *Ellery Queen's Mystery Magazine,* 102 (November 1993): 122–127;

"A Taste of Paradise," *Ellery Queen's Mystery Magazine,* 103 (March 1994): 12–20;

"Out of the Depths," *Ellery Queen's Mystery Magazine,* 104 (September 1994): 140–155;

"Man on the Run," *Ellery Queen's Mystery Magazine,* 107 (February 1996): 60–69;

"The Monster," *Ellery Queen's Mystery Magazine,* 108 (November 1996): 80–83;

"The Horseshoe Nail," *Ellery Queen's Mystery Magazine,* 109 (February 1997): 132–154.

NONFICTION

"The 'Mystery' Career of Evan Hunter," *Armchair Detective,* 5 (April 1972): 129–132;

"The Saga of the Phoenix That Probably Should Never Have Arisen," *Armchair Detective,* 10 (April 1977): 106–111;

"It All Started with Hammett," *Mystery Writers Annual* (1978): 38–39;

"The Worst Mystery Novel of All Time," *Armchair Detective,* 13 (Spring 1980): 137–140;

"Forgotten Writers: Gil Brewer," in *The Big Book of Noir,* edited by Ed Gorman, Lee Server, and Martin H. Greenberg (New York: Carroll & Graf, 1998), pp. 191–200.

Bill Pronzini has distinguished himself as a prolific writer and as an anthologist with an encyclopedic knowledge of mystery and western fiction. He is especially adept at collaborating with others, having worked with at least seven writers on fiction and eight people as co-editors. Pronzini is perhaps best known as the creator of an enduring private detective who, despite being nameless, has a more complex personality than most of his fictional colleagues and is considered the detective embodiment of the ordinary American working man. Illustrating the dangers of categorization, Pronzini in an interview in the December 1998/January 1999 issue of *Mystery News* said, "I don't consider myself a hard-boiled writer," preferring to call what he writes "humanist crime fiction with an edge." Most critics and readers, however, think that Pronzini has created a character who fits the traditional Raymond Chandler hard-boiled mode: Although he is disgusted by sham, Nameless realizes he cannot essentially change an imperfect world. His concerns are those of the common man—work, money, health, and love.

William John Pronzini was born in Petaluma, California, on 13 April 1943. He was raised in Petaluma and has lived in northern California most of his life. His father, Joseph Pronzini (1908–1973), was a ranch worker and a shipyard steamfitter during World War II. His mother, Helene Guder Pronzini (1915–1995), was primarily a bookkeeper. He has a sister, Catherine, born in 1948.

Pronzini attended Santa Rosa Junior College for one and a half years, 1961–1962. His love of reading, especially pulp magazines, may have interfered with his formal education, for he quit college; however, it did

Dust jacket for the 1971 novel in which Pronzini introduces Nameless, a San Francisco private investigator who collects pulp magazines

not prevent his achieving his goal: a career in writing. He demonstrates the prolificacy associated with many of the pulp writers he read.

Pronzini has had three wives. He married Laura Patricia Adolphson in 1965 and Brunhilde Schier in 1972. His first two marriages ended in divorce. He married Marcia Muller on 27 May 1992. She is a leading mystery writer who is generally considered to have inaugurated the era of the female private detective. Pronzini has no children or stepchildren.

Pronzini held a variety of short-term jobs, including newstand clerk, sports reporter for the *Petaluma Argus Courier,* warehouseman, typist, salesman, and civilian guard with the U.S. Marshal's office, while writing in his spare time. "You Don't Know What It's Like" in the November 1966 issue of *Shell Scott Mystery Magazine* was his first published short story. Before his first novel appeared in 1971, he published about sixty more stories, mostly in various digest-sized magazines such as *Alfred Hitchcock's Mystery Magazine* and *Mike Shayne's Mystery Magazine.* Most of his stories were mysteries, including private detective, suspense, and humorous ones, but he also wrote science fiction and Westerns. By 1969 he was a full-time writer.

Dust jacket for Pronzini's first novel (1972) to appear under the Foxx pseudonym

In 1970 Pronzini went to Majorca with all expenses paid to write "erotic fiction" for an American publisher based there for tax purposes. In his introduction to *Carmody's Run* (1992) Pronzini said he used the money earned to finance his writing of "serious" crime fiction. He remained in Europe, spending some time in Germany, until 1973. He drew on his European experiences in various mysteries, including "Majorcan Assignment" in *Mike Shayne's Mystery Magazine* (October 1972).

Pronzini's first novel, *The Stalker* (1971), starts as a "big caper" novel: six men of the U.S. Air Force commit a successful payroll robbery in Illinois in 1959, shortly before they are discharged. Eleven years later, someone stalks the robbers, killing them at various locations in the United States, though most of the action takes place in the San Francisco area, near Pronzini's native Petaluma. There is considerable violence, beginning with the robbery and continuing as a revenge-minded killer implacably stalks his prey. For the most part tersely

written, despite what Pronzini acknowledged was overwriting, *The Stalker* was nominated for an Edgar, an award given by the Mystery Writers of America, as best first novel.

Later in 1971 Pronzini published his first Nameless detective novel, *The Snatch,* a book he expanded from a short story so titled in the May 1969 issue of *Alfred Hitchcock's Mystery Magazine.* The plot of the novel is a familiar one to readers of detective fiction, beginning with Nameless being hired by the father of a kidnapped boy to deliver a ransom. Pronzini's suspenseful storytelling and the characterization of his detective make the work memorable.

Pronzini did not originally call his character "Nameless." The sobriquet was the idea of Random House editor Lee Wright, after Pronzini had trouble thinking of a name. As Pronzini admits, his detective is in most ways his alter ego, though he is older in *The Snatch,* at forty-seven, than Pronzini, then twenty-eight. As the series evolved, Pronzini slowed the aging of Nameless so that he was still under sixty in the mid 1990s.

In *The Snatch* Pronzini gave his detective, who left the San Francisco Police after fifteen years, the characteristics of sympathy, bravery, and decency that persist throughout the series. The woman he is in love with in *The Snatch,* Erika Coates, tries to get him to give up detective work: "You're too honest and too sensitive and too ethical, too affected by real corruption and real human misery. . . ." Later, he shows these idealistic qualities as he asks the kidnapper who has become a killer, "What motivates you? . . . What do you use for a conscience, for a soul?" He also demonstrates courage, for though denying he is a hero, the apparently unarmed Nameless willingly faces the killer's gun.

Physically, Nameless is overweight and a heavy smoker. Reading and collecting pulp magazines are his passions, and he has a collection of about five thousand magazines. As his lover in *The Snatch* observes before breaking off their affair, he clearly wants to be a lone wolf detective in the tradition of pulp heroes. Pronzini cleverly uses the title of a 1931 pulp magazine that Nameless sees in a bookstore as a key to his detection. It triggers a word association in his mind that aides the investigation.

Throughout the series Pronzini makes many acute observations about northern California. On a chilly San Francisco day, for example, Nameless in *The Snatch* remarks "a cold wind coming in off the Bay. Fog in thick gray billows, like the smoke from a rubber fire, unfolded across the darkening sky." In *The Vanished* (1973), the second novel featuring Nameless, the detective is angered by the sex-oriented decadence of the Tenderloin district and the changes he observes in the

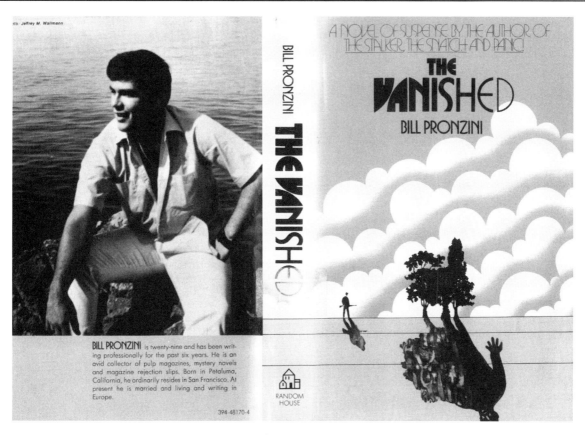

BILL PRONZINI is twenty-nine and has been writing professionally for the past six years. He is an avid collector of pulp magazines, mystery novels and magazine rejection slips. Born in Petaluma, California, he ordinarily resides in San Francisco. At present he is married and living and writing in Europe.

RANDOM HOUSE

394-48170-4

Dust jacket for Pronzini's second Nameless novel (1973), in which the overweight, chain-smoking detective seeks to overcome depression resulting from his concerns about injustice

architectural face of the city. "It seemed that every time I looked, another skyscraper was going up. . . . The old tired houses had been bought by speculators, skillfully cut up into apartments and rented as view property at inflated prices." In subsequent books Nameless travels widely in California, and through his eyes Pronzini evokes such places as San Jose, the Monterey peninsula, the Salinas farm country, the Napa/Sonoma wine regions, and the northern forests.

The Snatch received favorable reviews, and in *Catalogue of Crime* (1989) Jacques Barzun and Wendell Hertig Taylor praised it highly: "Pronzini has done a fine job of adding something new to the nearly worn-out kidnapping ploy. The twist at the end is masterly, and not unclued." Nevertheless, Pronzini published three nonseries thrillers before returning to Nameless in *The Vanished*. In the first of these thrillers, *Panic!* (1972), a man and woman are on the run in the desert, fleeing contract killers whose "hit" they witnessed. They are also fleeing their pasts. He had a failed marriage, and she feels condemned by society because of a lesbian experience. With this novel Pronzini became one of the first mystery writers to treat gay and lesbian characters with

dignity and sympathy. Fourteen years later in *Deadfall* (1986) Nameless has a gay client.

Like other prolific writers not yet established, Pronzini adopted pseudonyms because he wanted to sell more work than any publisher was willing to print under one name. In *Mike Shayne's Mystery Magazine* of April 1972, he and Jeffrey Wallman wrote the lead story in the issue, "Danger: Michael Shayne at Work," as Brett Halliday. Pronzini wrote his next two nonseries thrillers pseudonymously—*The Jade Figurine* (1972), as Jack Foxx, and *A Run in Diamonds* (1973), as Alex Saxon.

Pronzini used the Jack Foxx pseudonym for four novels in the 1970s, following *The Jade Figurine* with *Dead Run* (1975), *Freebooty* (1976), and *Wildfire* (1978). The first two Foxx novels, about freelance charter pilot Dan Connell, are stories that might have appeared in adventure pulps such as *Argosy,* though Connell is perhaps more psychologically complex than his pulp models as he struggles with guilt, blaming himself and his flying for the death of his partner in smuggling. *The Jade Figurine* invites comparison with Dashiell Hammett's *The Maltese Falcon* (1930) because of a plot involving a rare jade bird.

Writing as Saxon in *A Run in Diamonds,* Pronzini created Carmody, an American who operates out of Majorca, supplying illegal commodities, including identification papers. Pronzini uses Majorca as well as other European locales, such as Spain and Algiers, in which he had traveled in the early 1970s. Carmody did not return until 1992, when this novel and three short stories were revised and published as *Carmody's Run* under Pronzini's name.

In his second Nameless book, *The Vanished,* Pronzini further explores his detective's character. More introspective than most private detectives, Nameless broods when he is not on a case. Being hired to look for a missing soldier gives him purpose and helps overcome depression at thoughts of injustice in the world. In the first two Nameless books, the resolution depends on physical confrontation. Near the end of *The Vanished,* Nameless is attacked from behind by someone younger and more physically fit than he. "I was hurt all right, I was confused and the fear was there to feed the rage, and that wild anger was all I had left–that and self-preservation." It is a bloody fight, with Nameless delivering a brutal beating to his opponent.

In *Undercurrent* (1973) Pronzini combines violent action and colloquial speech with the plotting of the classic puzzle. Nameless again uses his knowledge of crime fiction when an old paperback mystery by fictional Russell Dancer (eventually a character in later books and a pseudonym Pronzini used once) provides a clue to the murder of the man he was hired to follow. Readers who enjoy solving the puzzle presented in mysteries should not read *Undercurrent* before *The Vanished,* for Pronzini gratuitously allows his detective to reveal the solution to his previous case. At times in *Undercurrent* Pronzini seems to be writing in haste, taking shortcuts such as likening characters to movie actors instead of describing them fully.

Following the Kennedy assassinations, Chappaquidick, and Nixon's resignation, fictional thrillers about politicians became popular and Pronzini capitalized on the trend with three novels. *Games* (1976) starts with a U.S. senator on an isolated Maine island with his mistress. Stalked by a madman, they flee into the wilderness to survive. Pronzini's Senator Jackman starts as a selfish character but begins to question his values during the ordeal. There is a paranoid U.S. president in *Acts of Mercy* (1977), in which Pronzini and Barry N. Malzberg write about murder in the White House and on the presidential train. For *The Cambodia File* (1981) Pronzini collaborated with the well-known Washington journalist Jack Anderson. Explaining his nonseries work, Pronzini said in a 1978 interview that he had encountered difficulty selling his private-eye series and

also wanted to remove himself from "category fiction" by using material he considered to have greater scope.

Four years passed between *Undercurrent* and the return of Nameless in *Blowback* (1977). In this fourth novel in the series, Nameless has a lesion on his lung and must spend a fretful weekend waiting to find whether it is malignant. Trying to distract himself, he anwers a friend's plea to help at a fishing camp in the Sierras where there is murderous jealousy in a party of six men and one woman. Most critics appreciated the insight the book provided into the protagonist's vulnerability, but Barzun and Taylor were not impressed: "Motivation rather weak. . . . Suspense tediously supplied by the hero's incessant fear about his lungs." The last Nameless novel of the 1970s was *Twospot* (1978), an experimental work Pronzini cowrote with fellow San Francisco area writer Collin Wilcox. The two authors successfully alternated the narrative between Nameless and Wilcox's police detective Frank Hastings. Nameless is hired by an Italian winemaking family in the Napa Valley, and Hastings enters the story when a connection to a political assassination plot is discovered.

Beginning in 1976 with *Tricks and Treats,* the annual anthology of the Mystery Writers of America (MWA) that he edited with Joe Gores, Pronzini has acted as editor or co-editor of more than seventy-five books, including many collections of western stories as well as some volumes of horror and science fiction. In 1980 he edited the first anthology of MWA award-winning short stories, *The Edgar Winners.* Pronzini has edited or co-edited collections of mystery stories of all types, including *The Arbor House Treasury of Detective and Mystery Stories from the Great Pulps* (1983), *The Web She Weaves: An Anthology of Mystery and Suspense Stories by Women* (1983), *Dark Lessons: Crime and Detection on Campus* (1985), *Women Sleuths* (1985), *Police Procedurals* (1985), *Locked Room Puzzles* (1986), *The Mammoth Book of Private Eye Stories* (1988), and *Hard-Boiled: An Anthology of American Crime Stories* (1995). Combining erudition with a sense of humor, he has brought together two collections of hilarious "alternative" mystery classics, Pronzini's name for bad but funny writing: *Gun in Cheek* (1982) and *Son of Gun in Cheek* (1987). With Muller he edited *1001 Midnights* (1986), one of the most comprehensive collections of essays about mystery fiction, with more than a thousand works evaluated. It was nominated for an Edgar in the Biographical/Critical Work category.

Interest in the private detective revived in the 1980s, and Pronzini published eleven Nameless novels in the decade. His use of crime fiction for clues and his frequent mention of mysteries was turning him into "The Mystery Fan's Detective." There are many references to pulp magazines and detective fiction in *Labyrinth* (1980), including in-jokes regarding Sam Spade and Philip Marlowe. Nameless reads an issue of *Black Mask* to pass time on surveillance. When his office is vandalized, he has nightmares about damage to his collection of pulp magazines, now numbering six thousand, at home. Mystery references also abound in *Hoodwink* (1981), winner of a Private Eye Writers of America Shamus Award for best novel. Nameless attends a pulp convention and combines pleasure and business, investigating an attempt to extort money from old writers by false allegations of plagiarism. In this novel Nameless meets Kerry Wade, the daughter of two pulp writers, who becomes his lover and later his wife. *Hoodwink* begins the strongest period in the Nameless series, with Pronzini combining the strengths of private eye fiction—action, suspense, and observation of place—with fair play detection. In *Hoodwink,* Nameless solves two locked room mysteries, one a shooting in a locked hotel room and the other an ax murder in a locked shed.

Nameless must deal with three seemingly impossible crimes in *Scattershot* (1982), including the disappearance of a client's husband from a locked automobile. Appropriately, in the course of the novel a newspaper columnist calls Nameless "Sam Spade and Sherlock Holmes all wrapped up in one package." The detective continues to face personal problems as his romance with Kerry Wade appears to be foundering and he faces a lawsuit that could cost him his license. Characteristically, he wonders whether he will have to sell his pulp collection to survive. Nameless's loneliness, vulnerability, and financial woes help to make him a character readers find likable and believable.

In the second Nameless book of 1982, *Dragonfire,* Pronzini successfully evokes San Francisco's Chinatown. He contrasts its attraction to tourists with the "real Chinatown," including the day-to-day life of its inhabitants, and captures local slang, such as "ABC" for American Born Chinese. It has an electrifying beginning as Chinese gunmen shoot Nameless and his policeman friend Eberhardt, a series character who first appears in *The Snatch.* The relationship between Nameless and Eberhardt is complex; their friendship is deep but is threatened with dissolution because of their differing personalities. Another ethnic mystery, *Quicksilver* (1984), is set in San Francisco's Japanese American community, the key to a present day mystery resting in the World War II internment of Nisei.

While he was making his name as a novelist, Pronzini continued to write short fiction, publishing about 250 stories to date. His fine collection of private eye stories *Casefile: The Best of the "Nameless Detective" Stories* (1983) was praised by Jon L. Breen in his *Ellery Queen's Mystery Magazine* review column for August 1983, and Douglas G. Greene included it while updat-

Dust jacket for the 1981 novel in which Nameless meets his future wife at a pulp-magazine collectors convention

ing "Queen's Quorum," a classic list of the best and most important short story collections in the November 1990 issue of *Crime and Detective Stories.* Especially strong is an expansion of a story that originally appeared in *Alfred Hitchcock's Mystery Magazine* of 30 January 1980, "Where Have You Gone, Sam Spade?" Pronzini combines impossible crime, fair play detection, bibliographic background, and insights into his detective's character. The 1996 collection of Nameless stories, *Spadework,* includes "Cat's-Paw," a 1983 story that won a Shamus, and "Incident in a Neighborhood Tavern," a 1988 story that was nominated for an Edgar.

Pronzini sometimes explores social issues in the Nameless series. In *Bindlestiff* (1983), for example, he explores homelessness as his story involves hoboes who ride freight trains. Nameless, though licensed to carry a gun, is loathe to do so, a circumstance that leads to a conclusion in which the detective must engage in a physical fight to bring a killer to justice. Pronzini's

Page 21

You understand?"

"Yes, ma'am, I understand."

"Now get off my property. And don't come back."

I didn't argue with her; it would have been an indefensible argument even if I'd had the inclination. All I did was nod and walk out into the sunlight and tree shadows. She followed me as far as the studio entrance. When I glanced back after a time she was still standing there, still hugging herself as if there was no more warmth in the day and little enough in her body.

As I came around the nearest of the big oaks into the parking circle, I saw that my car had a visitor. A slender little girl of nine or ten stood on its near side, peering at it the way you would at a giant and unfamiliar bug.

She turned her head when she heard me approaching, and her posture changed into a kind of poised wariness like a cat's when it sees a stranger -- not startled, not afraid, but ready to run if the situation called for it. I smiled and slowed my pace, but if that reassured her any, she didn't show it. Even though she was motionless, facing me as I came up, she still gave the impression of being on the verge of flight. No, not flight exactly. Up close, it seemed more like a readiness to retreat, to take refuge within herself. A defense mechanism of the shy, the vulnerable, the lonely.

"Hello," she said. She made eye contact all right and her voice was cordial, but she seemed uncomfortable, as if she wished one of us wasn't there. "Who are you?"

"Nobody special. Insurance man, I guess you could say."

Page from the typescript for "Crazybone," a Nameless novel scheduled to be published in August 2000 (Collection of Bill Pronzini) mixes murder with environmental issues in *Night-shades* (1984), which is concerned with a proposed development of a rural area near Shasta Lake, and *Jackpot* (1990), about pollution at Lake Tahoe.

In his third Nameless novel of 1984, *Double,* Pronzini collaborated with Marcia Muller, his future wife, as the writers placed Nameless and Muller's series protagonist, Sharon McCone, at a San Diego private detectives' convention. After Pronzini created John Quincannon, an 1890s San Francisco private investigator, in *Quincannon* (1985), he and Muller again collaborated in *Beyond the Grave* (1986), in which they cleverly have Muller's amateur detective Elena Oliverez, a museum director, use clues left by Quincannon to solve a present-day crime involving missing artifacts. Pronzini later wrote a series of short stories featuring Quincannon and his partner Sabina Carpenter, a former Pinkerton agent, that were collected as *Carpenter and Quincannon Professional Detective Services* (1998).

Pronzini's interest in the classical locked room mystery is evident in the Nameless series well into the 1980s. In his study of impossible crimes, *Locked Room Murders* (1979; revised, 1991), Robert Adey cites three novels and fifteen stories by Pronzini, more examples than from any other writer of private detective fiction. Adey calls *Bones* (1985) Pronzini's best Nameless book. Not only does the novel have a well worked out solution to a shooting in a locked study but also there is strong regional writing as Pronzini describes San Franciscans' dispassionate attitudes during an earthquake, likening them to Londoners in the Blitz during World War II.

In 1987 Pronzini, only forty-four years old, received The Eye, the lifetime achievement award from the Private Eye Writers of America. The following year he published *Shackles,* a novel that received more critical attention than any other book in the Nameless series and marked a turning point in Pronzini's characterization of his detective. In the novel Nameless is kidnapped and chained for three months in a cabin in the Sierras. The tension mounts as the reader, in addition to wondering about Nameless's fate, also is kept guessing as to the identity of his ski-masked kidnapper and his reason for choosing Nameless as his victim. In the winter 1989 issue of *The Mystery Fancier* Allen J. Hubin summed up the almost unanimously favorable reviews when he said, "Excellent suspense with a very convincing story line."

Increasingly in the post-*Shackles* books, the detection is less important than Nameless's emotional state, his relationship with Eberhardt, with whom he has quarrelled, and his love life, which is complicated by Wade's problems with her aging mother. Critics who agreed with David Geherin, who in *The American Private Eye* (1985) had wondered whether Pronzini's emphasis on ingenious solutions was not weakening the mood and atmosphere normally associated with private detective fiction, welcomed the change in the series.

In *Jackpot,* Pronzini's first book for Delacorte Press, Nameless suffers from post-traumatic stress syndrome in the aftermath of his experiences. *Breakdown* (1991) is set shortly after the October 1989 earthquake, and its effect on San Francisco is important, both physically and emotionally. Like his creator, who moved from the city to Sonoma County and since 1991 has lived in his native Petaluma, Nameless has become disenchanted with San Francisco, the city he once loved. In *Quarry* (1992) he is hired by a farmer to find his missing daughter. Neither the daughter nor the man with whom she apparently ran off, though, play a significant role in the novel, for the focus is on Nameless. He becomes the quarry of the killer, and the climax of the book is in a stone quarry.

The narrative drive of *Epitaphs* (1992), set largely among San Francisco's aging Italian community, makes it one of the best Nameless books of the 1990s. The effect of Nameless's mental status on his work grows more interesting, and the detective is more prone to violence. Regarding the murderer, he says, "If I'd had my gun right then I would have shot him dead. In cold blood, with no compunction at all." Because he has trouble controlling his temper, he even gets into a physical fight with Eberhardt, his friend of more than thirty years. Nameless is now willing to obtain evidence by breaking and entering, admitting he has lost patience and some of his scruples, but wondering if the change, while diminishing him as a person, has not made him a better detective. Another work that demonstrates the change in the series is *Demons* (1993), a novel that deals with sexual obsession, though Pronzini does not succeed in convincing the reader why Nedra Merchant should be the object of such strong desire on the part of men. Nameless's own obsession, collecting pulp magazines, is no longer even mentioned. His emotions are directed outwardly, and he expresses jealousy of Kerry Wade. There is legitimate detection in this book, but it is far less than in the 1980s.

Despite its strong fan base, the Nameless series has not achieved best-selling status—a failure that threatened its existence and led Pronzini to another change of publisher in the mid 1990s. While continuing the Nameless series with Carroll and Graff, Pronzini has also written nonseries books, including *Blue Lonesome* (1995), one of his most highly praised works, and *A Wasteland of Strangers* (1997), a story set in an isolated town that is told from the viewpoints of nine different residents. In *Hardcase* (1995), the last book for Delacorte, Nameless and Kerry are married in a wedding that has a great deal of slapstick due to extreme nervousness on his part. The book concludes on a more serious note, as Nameless contemplates a world in which "anybody can become a victim at any time." He counsels against giving in to fear. "You *have* to move on, hold the bad at bay with the good as long as you can. It's the only philosophy that makes any sense in this last screwed-up decade before the millenium."

Interviews:

Robert J. Randisi, "An Interview with Bill Pronzini," *Armchair Detective*, 11 (January 1978): 46–49;

Don Cole, "Conversation," *Poisoned Pen*, 1 (November 1978): 11–13;

Jean-Pierre Deloux, "*Entretien avec Bill Pronzini*," *Polar*, no. 20 (July 1981): 11–16;

Frederick Isaac, "Nameless and Friend," *Clues*, 4 (Spring/Summer 1983): 35–52;

Gary Warren Niebuhr, "Humanist Crime Fiction with an Edge: An Interview with Bill Pronzini," *Mystery News*, 16 (December 1998/January 1999): 6, 9.

Bibliographies:

Francis M. Nevins Jr. and Bill Pronzini, "Bill Pronzini: A Checklist," *Armchair Detective*, 13 (Fall 1980): 345–350;

Jacques Baudou, "*Bibliographie de Bill Pronzini*," *Polar*, no. 20 (July 1981): 17–19;

Douglas G. Greene, "A 'Nameless Detective' Checklist," in *Spadework*, by Pronzini (Norfolk, Va.: Crippen & Landru, 1996), pp. 189–191.

References:

Robert Adey, *Locked Room Murders*, revised edition (Minneapolis & San Francisco: Crossover Press, 1991), pp. 203–206;

Robert A. Baker and Michael T. Nietzel, "The Nameless Knight–Bill Pronzini," in their *Private Eyes 101 Knights: A Survey of American Detective Fiction 1922–1984* (Bowling Green, Ohio: Bowling Green University Popular Press, 1985), pp. 256–263;

David Geherin, "Nameless," in his *The American Private Eye: The Image in Fiction* (New York: Ungar, 1985), pp. 166–172;

George Kelley, "Bill Pronzini Revisited," *Mystery Fancier*, 2 (October 1978): 5–6;

Kelley, "The Suspense Novels of Bill Pronzini," *Mystery Fancier*, 1 (March 1977): 15–16;

Marvin Lachman, "The Mystery Fan's Detective," *Drood Review of Mystery*, 7 (February 1987): 1, 3–5; (April 1987): 4–6; (June 1987): 4–5; (September 1987): 4–5;

Polar, special Pronzini issue, no. 20 (July 1981).

Papers:

Bill Pronzini's manuscripts are in the Mugar Memorial Library, Boston University.

Mickey Spillane

(9 March 1918 –   )

Sue Laslie Kimball
Methodist College

and

George Parker Anderson
University of South Carolina

BOOKS: *I, the Jury* (New York: Dutton, 1947; London: Barker, 1952);

My Gun Is Quick (New York: Dutton, 1950; London: Barker, 1951);

Vengeance Is Mine! (New York: Dutton, 1950; London: Barker, 1951);

The Big Kill (New York: Dutton, 1951; London: Barker, 1952);

The Long Wait (New York: Dutton, 1951; London: Barker, 1953);

One Lonely Night (New York: Dutton, 1951; London: Barker, 1952);

Kiss Me, Deadly (New York: Dutton, 1952; London: Barker, 1953);

The Deep (New York: Dutton, 1961; London: Barker, 1961);

The Girl Hunters (New York: Dutton, 1962; London: Barker, 1962);

Me, Hood! (London: Corgi, 1963)–comprises "Me, Hood!," "Kick It Or Kill!," and "The Affair with the Dragon Lady";

Day of the Guns (New York: Dutton, 1964; London: Barker, 1965);

The Flier (London: Corgi, 1964)–comprises "The Flier" and "The Seven Year Kill";

The Return of the Hood (London: Corgi, 1964; New York: Dutton, 1964)–comprises "The Return of the Hood" and "The Bastard Bannerman";

The Snake (New York: Dutton, 1964; London: Barker, 1964);

Bloody Sunrise (New York: Dutton, 1965; London: Barker, 1965);

The Death Dealers (New York: Dutton, 1965; London: Barker, 1966);

Mickey Spillane

Killer Mine (London: Corgi, 1965; New York: New American Library, 1968)–comprises "Killer Mine" and "Man Alone";

The By-Pass Control (New York: Dutton, 1966; London: Barker, 1966);

The Twisted Thing (New York: Dutton, 1966; London: Barker, 1966); republished as *For Whom the Gods*

Would Destroy (New York: New American Library, 1971);

The Body Lovers (New York: Dutton, 1967; London: Barker, 1967);

The Delta Factor (New York: Dutton, 1967; London: Corgi, 1969);

Survival . . . Zero! (New York: Dutton, 1970; London: Corgi, 1970);

The Erection Set (New York: Dutton, 1972; London: W. H. Allen, 1972);

The Last Cop Out (New York: Dutton, 1973; London: W. H. Allen, 1973);

The Day the Sea Rolled Back (New York: Windmill, 1979; London: Eyre Methuen, 1980);

The Ship That Never Was (New York: Bantam, 1982);

Mike Hammer: The Comic Strip 1, edited by Max A. Collins and Ed Robbins (Park Forest, Ill.: K. Pierce, 1982);

Tomorrow I Die, introduced and edited by Collins (New York: Mysterious Press, 1984)—comprises "Tomorrow I Die," "The Girl Behind the Hedge," "Trouble . . . Come and Get It!," "Stand Up and Die!," "The Gold Fever Tapes," "Sex Is My Vengeance," "The Pickpocket," "The Screen Test of Mike Hammer," and "Everybody's Watching Me";

Mike Hammer: The Comic Strip 2, edited by Collins and Catherine Yronwode (Park Forest, Ill.: K. Pierce, 1985);

The Killing Man (New York: Dutton, 1989; London: Heinemann, 1990);

Black Alley (New York: Dutton, 1996; Bath, U.K.: Chives Press, 1996).

Editions & Collections: *Me, Hood!* (New York: New American Library, 1969)—comprises "Me, Hood!" and "The Return of the Hood";

The Tough Guys (New York: New American Library, 1969)—comprises "Kick It Or Kill!," "The Seven Year Kill," and "The Bastard Bannerman";

Vintage Spillane: A New Omnibus (London: W. H. Allen, 1974);

Mickey Spillane: Five Complete Mike Hammer Novels (New York: Avenel, 1989);

The Hammer Strikes Again: Five Complete Mike Hammer Novels (New York: Random House, 1989).

PRODUCED SCRIPTS: *Ring of Fear,* motion picture, script by Spillane (uncredited), Paul Fix, Phillip MacDonald, and James Edward Grant, Warner Bros., 1954;

The Girl Hunters, motion picture, based on Spillane's novel, script by Spillane, Robert Fellows, and Roy Rowland, Colorama/Fellane, 1963.

OTHER: *Murder is My Business,* edited by Mickey Spillane and Max A. Collins (New York: Dutton, 1994).

One of the most maligned writers of the twentieth century, Mickey Spillane has always been popular with readers. His name appears more than any other on lists of best-selling authors since World War II, yet his writing has been labeled "atrocious" by John G. Cawelti in his 1969 essay "The Spillane Phenomenon" in the *Journal of Popular Culture* and "nauseating" by Julian Symons in his *Mortal Consequences: A History from the Detective Story to the Crime Novel* (1972). A common complaint of critics, especially in his heyday in the early 1950s, is that Spillane uses gratuitous violence and sex to sell books, and undoubtedly these characteristics appeal to his vast audience. Beyond the contents of Spillane's novels, however, most readers respond positively to his style. In a quiz published on 23 July 1995 in *The New York Times Magazine,* Frank Gannon challenged readers to identify the author of ten quotations selected from the writings of Mickey Spillane and Ernest Hemingway. The readers taking the quiz, probably quite familiar with Hemingway if not with Spillane, scored only about 70 percent, suggesting that in many instances readers could not distinguish between the masculine style of the Nobel and Pulitzer Prize–winning Hemingway and that of Spillane.

Spillane writes in the tradition of Carroll John Daly, the popular writer for *Black Mask* who originated the hard-boiled detective in his character Race Williams. In a fan letter written to the older writer in the 1950s, Spillane remarked that though the character of Mike Hammer, Spillane's main hero, is "original, his personality certainly isn't." He asserts that "Hammer and the Race Williams of the middle thirties could be twins." Like Daly, Spillane gives the reader a compelling first-person narrator, fast-moving plots, and vivid descriptions of physical action.

Spillane told reporter Eve Oakley of the *Fayetteville Observer Times* (7 September 1980) that he was "a writer, not an author" and then explained the distinction: "An author can do one or two stories and he's finished. But a writer is like a good carpenter." Writers, Spillane maintains, write to entertain and make money. More than two hundred million copies of his books have sold over the course of his professional career. He is one of the five most-translated authors in the world and has rightly described himself on many occasions as the most widely read author in the history of mankind. Long ignored by the Mystery Writers of America, Spillane in 1995 was honored by the organization with the Grand Master Award for "longstanding and significant service to the mystery genre."

Frank Morrison Spillane was born on 9 March 1918 in Brooklyn, the only child of an Irish-Catholic bartender, John Joseph Spillane, and a Presbyterian mother, Catherine Anne Morrison. He claims to have been christened in both parental churches, but Spillane is quoted in *Current Biography* as saying, "Neither took." His father gave him the nickname Mickey while he was in grammar school. The family soon moved to Elizabeth, New Jersey, where Spillane was the only Irish boy in a tough Polish neighborhood. He later moved back to Brooklyn, where he attended Erasmus High School, working summers as a lifeguard at Breezy Point, Long Island. In 1939 he briefly attended Fort Hays State University in Kansas with the intention of becoming a lawyer. He was on the swimming and football teams and apparently attended more football practices than classes.

In 1940, while working as a part-time salesman for Gimbel's during the Christmas season, Spillane met Joe Gill, another employee of the company. Joe's brother Ray, an editor at Funnies, Inc., which produced comic books, hired Spillane as a scripter and assistant editor. While other writers required a week to turn out a Captain Marvel story, Spillane could produce one in a day. Much of Spillane's comic-book work of the time was unsigned and is now lost.

After the Japanese bombing of Pearl Harbor, Spillane enlisted in the Army Air Force, hoping for combat duty. Instead, he was assigned to teach fighter pilots in Florida and Mississippi. He met and married his first wife, Mary Ann Pearce, in Greenwood, Mississippi; during their seventeen-year marriage the couple raised four children, two boys and two girls. Discharged with the rank of captain, Spillane and the Gill brothers then established a comic-book factory in a rented store in Brooklyn. When he and his wife decided they wanted to buy four acres of land near Newburgh, New York, Spillane wrote *I, the Jury* (1947), his first novel, to earn the $1,000 he needed as a down payment on the land. A speedy writer, Spillane claims to have written *I, the Jury* in nine days. The novel that introduced Mike Hammer to the world sold more than eight million copies in its paperback edition alone.

Spillane had first conceived the story of *I, the Jury* as a comic book titled "Mike Danger" but had been unable to sell the idea in the slumping comic-book market of the time. In *Murder in the Millions: Erle Stanley Gardner, Mickey Spillane, Ian Fleming* (1984), J. Kenneth Van Dover suggests the importance of Spillane's comic-book training in his career as a novelist:

> His novels transpose into literary form several aspects of the art of the comic book. Spillane's characters are designed for immediate recognition. Their outlines are

Dust jacket for Spillane's 1952 novel, the sixth in the Mike Hammer series

simple; their colors are primary. His men are muscular; his women voluptuous. His landscapes—usually cityscapes—are generalized and are often rendered with ominous angles and dark shadows. Spillane's plots are far more complicated than those employed by the comics, but they progress in much the same manner: a Spillane novel consists of a set of discrete scenes—panels of action. Each panel is fixed against a certain background—an office, an apartment, a bar, a street—and usually contains only two characters—Hammer and an ally or an adversary. There are brief transitional panels in which Hammer drives from one confrontation to another, and there are thought panels in which the reader can almost see a cloud of ideas bubble from Hammer's head. And of course Spillane always gratifies the appetite for cartoon violence—Biff! Zowie! Smash!

Spillane, though, as Van Dover notes, did not maintain the distanced, omniscient point of view common to comic-strip art in his novels. Instead, like Daly in his Race Williams stories, he presented the action through the eyes of his protagonist: "Spillane's novels are intensely subjective. Nearly all are narrated in the first person, and the character of the narrator supplies the crucial tone of the action."

As Spillane told Julie Baumgold in an August 1995 article in *Esquire,* he was always conscious of his beginnings and endings in his writing, for the first sentence entices the reader to read on and the last sentence leads the reader to long for the next book. In the opening paragraph of *I, the Jury,* Spillane takes care to render the dominating presence of Mike Hammer:

> I shook the rain from my hat and walked into the room. Nobody said a word. They stepped back politely and I could feel their eyes on me. Pat Chambers was standing by the door to the bedroom trying to steady Myrna. The girl's body was racking with dry sobs. I walked over and put my arms around her.

When Hammer deduces from the crime scene that Jack Williams–a man who lost his right arm when he saved Mike from a Japanese bayonet in World War II–suffered horribly from a gunshot wound to the gut while the killer taunted him by keeping a chair with his pistol just out of reach, he vows vengeance to the corpse:

> I'm going to get the louse that killed you. He won't sit in the chair. He won't hang. He will die exactly as you died, with a .45 slug in the gut, just a little below the belly button. No matter who it is, Jack, I'll get this one. Remember, no matter who it is, I promise.

Hammer begins his investigation by questioning guests who attended Jack's recent party, among them Myrna, a former heroin addict, and the beautiful Charlotte Manning, a successful Park Avenue psychiatrist.

Pat Chambers, the police captain in homicide who remains Hammer's friend through all the novels, recognizes that Hammer's brand of justice–which in his first six adventures involved killing fifty-eight people–works more quickly and effectively than his own. When Pat says, "I'll be trying to beat you to the killer," Hammer replies, "I don't underrate the cops," adding, "But cops can't break a guy's arm to make him talk, and they can't shove his teeth in with the muzzle of a .45." He explains to Pat, who is already acquainted with Mike's ruthless methods, "A lot of guys tell me what I want to know because they know what I'll do to them if they don't." This conversation is the harbinger of all Mike Hammer novels to come, capturing the essence of the attitude and actions that for years incurred the wrath of critics.

In the concluding thirteenth chapter, Hammer has come to realize that Manning is responsible for Jack's death. As he lays out the circumstantial evidence that has led him to his conclusion, the woman slowly begins to undress before him, leading to one of the most memorable climactic scenes in hard-boiled fiction:

> "No, Charlotte, I'm the jury now, and the judge, and I have a promise to keep. Beautiful as you are, as much as I almost loved you, I sentence you to death."

> *Her thumbs hooked in the fragile silk of the panties and pulled them down. She stepped out of them as delicately as one coming from a bath-tub. She was completely naked now. A suntanned goddess giving herself to her lover. With arms outstretched she walked toward me. Lightly, her tongue ran over her lips, making them glisten with passion. The smell of her was like an exhilarating perfume. Slowly, a sigh escaped her, making the hemispheres of her breasts quiver. She leaned forward to kiss me, her arms going out to encircle my neck.*

> The roar of the .45 shook the room. Charlotte staggered back a step. Her eyes were a symphony of incredulity, an unbelieving witness to truth. Slowly, she looked down at the ugly swelling in her naked belly where the bullet went in. A thin trickle of blood welled out.

The only mitigation of this act of cold-blooded murder that Spillane allows his hero is his realization, after he has shot her, that Manning was coming toward him to reach a gun on a table behind him, its "safety catch off and the silencer still attached." When Manning gasps her final words, "How c-could you?," Hammer responds with the final line of the novel, "'It was easy,' I said." Hammer, however, is haunted by his execution of Manning in subsequent novels.

The success of *I, the Jury* set the stage for six more best-selling novels published in the next five years, five of which feature Mike Hammer: *My Gun Is Quick* (1950), *Vengance Is Mine!* (1950), *The Big Kill* (1951), *One Lonely Night* (1951), and *Kiss Me, Deadly* (1952). In the third novel in the Hammer series, *Vengance Is Mine!,* Spillane develops the character of his hero's secretary, Velda, who also appears in the first two novels. Velda shows that she is willing to sacrifice herself for Hammer and willing to wreak vengeance herself. As Max A. Collins and James L. Traylor write in their study *One Lonely Knight: Mickey Spillane's Mike Hammer* (1984), in the course of the series the "stereotypical secretary-in-love-with-her-boss" ultimately becomes "a woman the equal of Mike Hammer. . . . Velda does not play Effie Perrine to Hammer's Sam Spade; she is more Jane to his Tarzan."

The one non-Hammer novel of the period is *The Long Wait* (1951), in which Johnny McBride, alias George Wilson, is a tough guy suffering from amnesia who must search for his identity. Like Hammer, McBride and Spillane's later non-Hammer protagonists are virile, powerful, intelligent, and finally successful. In *One Lonely Knight,* Collins and Traylor

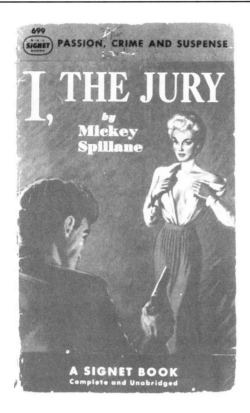

Covers for paperback editions of four of Spillane's best-selling Mike Hammer novels

attribute the writer's success to his combining "the excitement and action" of comic books with "a level of realism, where sex and particularly violence were concerned, that had not yet been seen in American popular fiction." They argue that Spillane instinctively understood his audience,

> a reading public that consisted largely of ex-servicemen, who had fought a tough, brutal war; who would expect the violence (and the sex) of even their fantasy to reflect the loss of innocence of that war; who were, to put it less pompously if more crudely, a bunch of horny ex-GIs looking for a hot read. The seven novels Spillane produced between 1947 and 1953 have a level of sex and particularly violence that seems to come out of nowhere; but it did come from somewhere: it came from World War II.

Spillane's heroes frequently set out alone to fight entire organizations—a big-city ring, the Mafia, or Communists. Hammer first opposes the Communists in *One Lonely Night,* a dark, surreal vision of the postwar urban jungle, in which the hero believes that God has chosen him to smite the evil ones. Early in the novel, Hammer meets a terrified woman on a bridge at night and kills her pursuer. She looks at the gun in his hand and jumps off the bridge herself because she is frightened by the look on Hammer's face, leading the detective to some soul searching: "Maybe I did have a taste for death. Maybe I liked it too much to taste anything else. Maybe I would be washed down the sewer with the rest of all of rottenness sometime." When a Communist ring kidnaps Velda, he goes to war and realizes his purpose on earth: "*I lived to kill so others could live. . . . I was the evil that opposed other evil, leaving the good and the meek in the middle to inherit the earth!*"

As the dimensions of the popular response to Spillane's novels became evident, the adverse critical reaction to Spillane's work began to build. In addition to such critics as Anthony Boucher, who in his reviews in *The New York Times* routinely deplored "the usual Spillane sex cum sadism," the attacks on Spillane took on a political edge as liberal critics saw Hammer as a cause or symptom of a sick society. In the *New Republic* of 11 February 1952 Malcolm Cowley concluded that Mike Hammer was "a homicidal paranoiac." Christopher La Farge in his article "Mickey Spillane and His Bloody Hammer," which originally appeared in the 6 November 1954 issue of *Saturday Review,* linked Spillane to Senator Joseph R. McCarthy: "Mike Hammer is the logical conclusion, almost a sort of brutal apotheosis, of McCarthyism: when things go wrong, let one man cure the wrong by whatever means he, as a privileged savior, chooses." In *Murder in the Millions* Van Dover makes a similar point without drawing a political comparison:

The mission of Mike Hammer is questioned only once, in *One Lonely Night,* and there, significantly, the debate takes place entirely within the mind of Hammer himself. He is a knight for whom loneliness is a necessity. It is his very alienation from any shared community values that enables him to justify his violent actions as ends in themselves. The ultimate criticism of the ethos of Spillane's fictional world must be that it is literally undebatable.

Nine years passed after *Kiss Me, Deadly* before Spillane published another novel. In 1952 he became a Jehovah's Witness after one of the members of the sect persuaded him that the theory of evolution is erroneous. In 1954 Spillane and his family established their permanent residence at Murrell's Inlet, South Carolina. Spillane continued to write during this period, however. Claiming he had tired of the long form of the novel, he experimented with shorter works during the years from 1953 to 1960, concentrating on heroes other than Mike Hammer. He wrote short stories for lower-rung publications such as *Male* and *Cavalier* and returned to his roots by writing for the Mike Hammer comic strip, which ran in newspapers from 1953 to 1954.

Several of the pieces Spillane wrote during this period were later collected by Collins in *Tomorrow I Die* (1984). Three of the narratives were originally published in *Manhunt,* the magazine many regard as the most important pulp magazine after *Black Mask.* The first installment of the novelette "Everybody's Watching Me" ran in the initial number of *Manhunt* in January 1953 and was featured prominently on the cover, helping to launch the magazine. Collins in his introduction suggests that the novelette is "a dry run of sorts for *The Deep* (1961), the novel that marked Spillane's return from short stories and men's magazines to the bookstores and bestseller lists." The story "Girl Behind the Hedge," which was first published in *Manhunt* in October 1953, though primarily told in first person, is notable because in it Spillane also employs third-person narration—a rarity for him. Another interesting *Manhunt* story is "The Pickpocket" (December 1954), in which the non-Hammer-like protagonist is a reformed pickpocket.

In January 1953 Spillane sold the movie rights of his novels for $250,000 to British producer Victor Saville, who subsequently produced four movies based on the books: *I, the Jury* (1953), starring Biff Eliot as Hammer; *The Long Wait* (1954); *Kiss Me, Deadly* (1955), starring Ralph Meeker; and *My Gun Is Quick* (1957), starring Robert Bray. Spillane was unhappy with the casting of Hammer in the movies and with the movies themselves. After he returned to writing Hammer novels with *The Girl Hunters* (1962)—in which the detective recovers from a seven-year bout with alcoholism to bat-

First page of cartoonist Walt Kelly's Mike Hammer parody in his Uncle Pogo So-So Stories *(1953)*

Spillane as Hammer and columnist Hy Gardner as himself in a still from the 1963 movie version of
Spillane's 1962 novel, The Girl Hunters *(Colorama/Fellane)*

tle a notorious Soviet assassin and rescue the missing Velda–Spillane not only wrote the script but also acted the part of Mike Hammer in the movie that was released in 1963. As most readers associated Hammer with the author, though the novelist is four inches shorter than his hero, the casting was successful. After playing Hammer in a movie adaptation of his work, Spillane declared, "I am Mike Hammer."

As Collins notes in his introduction to *Tomorrow I Die,* during the shooting of *The Girl Hunters* in Britain, Spillane agreed to allow his British publisher Corgi to collect some of his short works into paperbacks. Because he needed money "to keep the smoke coming out of the chimney," he told Baumgold in *Esquire,* he insisted on being paid in cash, and he remembers leaving the publisher's office "with his pockets stuffed." The British publications *Me, Hood!* (1963), *The Return of the Hood* (1964), *Killer Mine* (1965), and *The Flier* (1964) were the basis for books published in America by New American Library. Only *Killer Mine* is the same in both the British and American editions.

Impressed by the success of Ian Fleming's James Bond series, Spillane introduced a new series hero, Tiger Mann, in *Day of the Guns* (1964). A secret agent version of Mike Hammer, Mann appeared also in *Bloody Sunrise* (1965), *The Death Dealers* (1965), and *The By-Pass Control* (1966). Having divorced in 1962, Spillane married his second wife, Sherri Molinou, a model, singer, dancer, and actress, in November 1965, after she posed for the cover of *The By-Pass Control.* She was later the model for the cover of the paperback edition of *The Erection Set* (1972); the couple divorced in 1983. Spillane published a total of four Hammer novels in the 1960s: *The Girl Hunters, The Snake* (1964), *The Twisted Thing* (1966), and *The Body Lovers* (1967). In 1970 Spillane published the eleventh novel in the series, *Survival . . . Zero!,* in which a more mature, less obsessed Mike Hammer avenges a friend's murder and saves the world from foreign agents who possess a terrible biological weapon. Mike Hammer did not appear again in a novel for nearly twenty years.

In the 1970s and 1980s Spillane kept busy with television work, appearing in a series of Miller Lite Beer commercials and in 1974 appearing in an episode of *Columbo,* and continued to write. He published two adult novels, *The Erection Set* and *The Last Cop Out* (1973), and also wrote two books for children: *The Day the Sea Rolled Back* (1979), in which two boys discover treasure aboard a shipwreck that is exposed when the sea mysteriously recedes, and *The Ship That Never Was* (1982). Spillane's first book for children won a Junior Literary Guild Award. In 1983 he married his third wife, Jane Rodgers Johnson, who is twenty-eight years his junior. His twelfth and thirteenth books in the Hammer series are *The Killing Man* (1989), for which he was paid $1.5 million, and *Black Alley* (1996). In this latest novel there occurs a scene that would never have taken place in an early Hammer adventure: the detective takes Velda to dinner in a restaurant frequented by the killers, and he goes unarmed, relying on his notoriety: "Even thinking about what could have happened gave me the jumps. Either of those guys could have cleaned my plow if they had gotten past my reputation."

Although Spillane has remained a popular author throughout his career, he has not again attained the phenomenal sales he achieved with his first seven novels in the early 1950s. In these early novels, though, he established a formula that was attuned to–or in part created–the popular taste of an era. At mid century Mike Hammer's brutal code enthralled readers and alarmed cultural critics. In *One Lonely Knight,* Collins and Traylor rightly assert that Spillane must be considered in any history of twentieth-century popular fiction, but his significance within the hard-boiled tradition is less clear. Critics such as Collins and Traylor who argue that Spillane deserves to be recognized along with Dashiell Hammett and Raymond Chandler as one of the preeminent authors of the hard-boiled detective novel remain a distinct minority.

References:

Jeff R. Banks, "Anti-Professionalism in the Works of Mickey Spillane," *Notes on Contemporary Literature,* 3 (1973): 6–8;

Banks, "Spillane and the Critics," *Armchair Detective,* 12 (Fall 1979): 300–307;

Banks, "Spillane's Anti-Establishment Heroes," in *Dimensions of Detective Fiction,* edited by Larry N. Landrum, Pat Browne, and Ray B. Browne (Bowling Green, Ohio: Bowling Green University Popular Press, 1976), pp. 124–139;

Michael Barson, "Just a Writer Working for a Buck," *Armchair Detective,* 12 (Fall 1979): 292–299;

John G. Cawelti, "The Spillane Phenomenon," *Journal of Popular Culture,* 3 (Summer 1969): 9–22;

Max A. Collins and James L. Traylor, *One Lonely Knight: Mickey Spillane's Mike Hammer* (Bowling Green, Ohio: Bowling Green State University Popular Press, 1984);

Juddith Fetterley, "Beauty as the Beast: Fantasy and Fear in *I, the Jury,*" *Journal of Popular Culture,* 8 (1975): 775–782;

Richard W. Johnston, "Death's Fair-Haired Boy," *Life,* 32 (23 June 1952): 79–95;

Christopher La Farge, "Mickey Spillane and His Bloody Hammer," in *Mass Culture: the Popular Arts in America,* edited by Bernard Rosenberg (Glencoe, Ill.: Free Press, 1957), pp. 176–185;

Charles J. Rolo, "Simenon and Spillane: The Metaphysics of Murder for the Millions," in *Mass Culture: The Popular Arts in America,* edited by Bernard Rosenberg (Glencoe, Ill.: Free Press, 1957), pp. 165–175;

William Ruehlmann, *Saint with a Gun: The Unlawful American Private Eye* (New York: New York University Press, 1974);

J. Kenneth Van Dover, *Murder in the Millions: Erle Stanley Gardner, Mickey Spillane, Ian Fleming* (New York: Ungar, 1984);

Kay Weibel, "Mickey Spillane as a Fifties Phenomenon," in *Dimensions of Detective Fiction,* edited by Larry N. Landrum, Pat Browne, and Ray B. Browne (Bowling Green, Ohio: Bowling Green University Popular Press, 1976), pp. 114–123.

Jim Thompson

(27 September 1906 – 7 April 1977)

Tim Dayton
Kansas State University

BOOKS: *Now and On Earth* (New York: Modern Age, 1942);

Heed the Thunder (New York: Greenberg, 1946);

Nothing More Than Murder (New York: Harper, 1949);

The Killer Inside Me (New York: Lion Books, 1952; London: Sphere, 1973);

Cropper's Cabin (New York: Lion Books, 1952);

Recoil (New York: Lion Books, 1953; London: Corgi, 1988);

The Alcoholics (New York: Lion Books, 1953);

Bad Boy (New York: Lion Books, 1953);

Savage Night (New York: Lion Books, 1953; London: Corgi, 1988);

The Criminal (New York: Lion Books, 1953);

The Golden Gizmo (New York: Lion Books, 1954);

Roughneck (New York: Lion Books, 1954);

A Swell-Looking Babe (New York: Lion Books, 1954);

A Hell of a Woman (New York: Lion Books, 1954; London: Corgi, 1988);

The Nothing Man (New York: Dell, 1954);

After Dark, My Sweet (New York: Popular Library, 1955);

The Kill-Off (New York: Lion Library, 1957; London: Corgi, 1988);

Wild Town (New York: New American Library, 1957; London: Corgi, 1989);

The Getaway (New York: New American Library, 1959; London: W. H. Allen, 1972);

The Transgressors (New York: New American Library, 1961);

The Grifters (New York: Regency, 1963; London: Aomba, 1989);

Pop. 1280 (Greenwich, Conn.: Fawcett Gold Medal, 1964);

Texas By the Tail (Greenwich, Conn.: Fawcett Gold Medal, 1965; London: Xanadu, 1990);

South of Heaven (Greenwich, Conn.: Fawcett Gold Medal, 1967);

Ironside (New York: Popular Library, 1967);

The Undefeated (New York: Popular Library, 1969);

Nothing But a Man (New York: Popular Library, 1970);

Jim Thompson

Child of Rage (New York: Lancer Books, 1972);

King Blood (London: Sphere Books, 1973; New York: Otto Penzler Books, 1993);

More Hardcore: 3 Novels (New York: D. I. Fine, 1987)— comprises *The Ripoff, Roughneck,* and *The Golden Gizmo;*

Fireworks: The Lost Writings of Jim Thompson, edited by Robert Polito and Michael McCauley (New York: D. I. Fine, 1988).

Collection: *Hardcore: 3 Novels,* introduction by Roderick Thorp (New York: D. I. Fine, 1986)—comprises *The Kill-Off, The Nothing Man,* and *Bad Boy.*

PRODUCED SCRIPTS: *The Killing,* motion picture, script by Thompson and Stanley Kubrick, Harris-Kubrick Productions, 1956;

Paths of Glory, motion picture, script by Thompson, Kubrick, and Calder Willingham, United Artists, 1957;

"Indian Agent," "Death Patrol," "Joe Ironhat," and "Blood on the Rio," television, *Mackenzie's Raiders,* syndicated, Ziv Television, 1958–1959;

"Devil's Acres," television, *Man Without a Gun,* syndicated, Twentieth Century-Fox, 1960;

"Five for One," television, *Cain's Hundred,* NBC, 1961;

"My Name is Lisa and I'm Lost," television, *Dr. Kildare,* NBC, 1965;

"Adventure in the North Atlantic," television, *Convoy,* NBC, 1965.

OTHER: *This World, Then the Fireworks,* in *Jim Thompson: The Killers Inside Him,* edited by Max Allan Collins and Ed Gorman (Cedar Rapids, Iowa: Fedora Press, 1983), pp. 23–83.

Jim Thompson's importance in American crime fiction is based on works that undermine even as they depend upon their generic constraints. In his double relation to the genre, he is unlike other noteworthy paperback crime novelists of his era, such as Mickey Spillane or Gil Brewer, who typically produced competent and sometimes compelling work by executing their craft within the constraints of the genre. These writers succeed precisely because they skillfully combine the specific resources of crime fiction: suspense, violence, and sexual intrigue. In his best work, however, Thompson, while he too acknowledges the protocols of genre, does so in a way that turns the genre inside out. For example, the characteristic misogyny of the genre—epitomized in works such as Spillane's *I, the Jury* (1947) and Brewer's *13 French Street* (1951)—is also evident in Thompson's *A Hell of a Woman* (1954). In Thompson's book, however, the reader is to understand the misogyny of the main character, Robert "Dolly" Dillon, as a pathology, not as evidence of Dillon's incorruptibility and manliness.

In part, Thompson's double relation to genre emerges from a characteristic of his writing that Luc Sante identified in the early days of the Thompson revival of the mid 1980s and which was first glimpsed in the 1950s by Anthony Boucher in his reviews of the author's novels: the merging of mass-market and modernist literary sensibilities that are typically seen as

antagonistic. Influenced by modernist narrative techniques, Thompson was able to gain a distance from his narrators and his narratives that resulted in his making a personal mark on crime fiction. His innovations were not only formal and limited to narrative technique but also extended to his particular vision of the United States presented in his best work, a vision sometimes explicitly, sometimes implicitly, seriously at odds with the mainstream worldview of the Cold War era within which all of his major work was published.

James Myers Thompson was born on 27 September 1906 to Birdie Myers Thompson and James Sherman Thompson in the apartment above the Caddo County Jail, in Anadarko, Oklahoma, where Thompson's father was sheriff. As Robert Polito relates in his authoritative biography, *Savage Art: The Life of Jim Thompson* (1995), the Thompson side of the family originated from John Thompson, an ordained Presbyterian minister who emigrated from Scotland to the North American colonies in 1770; he started a family that moved westward through successive generations, arriving in Nebraska in 1879, fleeing the debts they accrued as farmers in the severe depression of the 1870s. The Myers side of the family were originally German Mennonites who had fled religious persecution to Holland early in the eighteenth century before immigrating to the United States in 1800. The Myers family arrived in Nebraska in 1889.

James Sherman Thompson worked as a high-school teacher and administrator in the 1890s and had known Birdie Myers as a student in the early years of that decade. They were reintroduced to one another in 1895 at a teachers' conference in Nebraska, but were not married until 1902. Married in Nebraska, they settled in Oklahoma, where Thompson's father had been working as a law officer since 1900. Jim Thompson was the second of three children and the only boy; his sisters, Maxine and Winifred ("Freddie"), were born in 1903 and 1916, respectively.

Thompson's father was an autodidact, a lawyer, a frontier lawman, and until 1907 a respected figure in the Oklahoma Republican Party. A large man, he enjoyed playing the hayseed before the unsuspecting and then shocking them with a burst of unusual erudition. When Thompson's father lost his position as sheriff in 1907 because he overcharged the county for services by about $5,000, he packed his family off to the Myers' family homestead in Burwell, Nebraska, and fled to Mexico. With his father absent for the next two years, Thompson grew close to his mother and sister, and while his father eventually returned to the family, relocating them to Oklahoma City in 1910 and then to Fort Worth, Texas, in 1919, a pattern developed early: a periodically absent father, a close and

Thompson and his wife, Alberta Hesse Thompson, in 1931

affectionate mother, and long stretches spent at the Myers' family home.

Thompson's background informs his writing in two primary ways. First, his family life, with its affections, disaffections, and disruptions, replays itself in various ways in his fiction. Many of Thompson's characters appear to be modeled on his relatives, most pointedly his father. The pleasure taken by Thompson's father in duping strangers with a slow-witted exterior reappears in later characters drawn by his son, most famously in the genial serial killer, Deputy Sheriff Lou Ford of *The Killer Inside Me* (1952). More generally, the tensions characteristic of the domestic world of Thompson's fictional characters were apparently drawn, in part, from his own domestic experiences, both as a young man and as an adult. Second, the geography of Thompson's boyhood and adolescence, passed in Nebraska, Oklahoma, and Texas, made him a writer of the southern Plains. The region provided him with both the language of his novels and the experience of an ostensibly healthy America which, as refracted through his fiction, becomes toxic.

Thompson underwent several formative experiences in Fort Worth, where he spent his adolescence, from 1919 to 1926. Here Thompson lived once again with his nuclear family, father included. After his ignoble departure from Anadarko, Thompson's father had

wandered and then found work as an accountant before setting up shop as an oil operator in Oklahoma. Thompson's father made a great sum of money during the oil boom of the late teens, but during the flush times of the early 1920s a series of bad breaks, bad deals, and bad judgments ruined him, dictating both that he would become that familiar American type, the man waiting for his next big break, and that his son would go to work early in life, around age fourteen. Both of these circumstances proved crucial to his son's writing career.

Thompson's father, as well no doubt as many other men Thompson met in Fort Worth and West Texas, provided the pattern for characters such as Dolly Dillon of *A Hell of a Woman* and Joe Wilmot of *Nothing More Than Murder* (1949), characters driven by the strength of their desire for a "good life" that always seems just beyond reach. More concretely, in his two most significant jobs in Fort Worth, Thompson became, in however small a way, an observer and a writer of the criminal underworld. Thompson worked first on the *Fort Worth Press,* primarily as an office boy, and then on an oil industry weekly, the *Western World,* where he "did a little of everything," as he recounts in *Bad Boy* (1953), the first of his two autobiographies. According to Thompson's older sister, Maxine, "a little of everything" included helping to write catchy advertising copy for dubious drilling ventures. More lucrative, and more explicitly criminal, was Thompson's full-time job as a bellboy at the Hotel Texas, in which he not only carried bags for the guests but also supplied them with illegal liquor, drugs, and prostitutes. After nearly two years at the hotel, Thompson suffered a physical breakdown, overcome by the demands of the night shift and the strain of attending high school. By the age of eighteen, Thompson had contracted tuberculosis and developed the alcoholism that would plague him sporadically throughout his life.

The job at the Hotel Texas affected Thompson profoundly: it prolonged to seven years a high-school career that ended in 1926 without a diploma, and it set up a duality in Thompson's life that stayed with him to the end. Thompson was both a hard-living, prematurely wised-up young man and a gentle son and brother who sacrificed his youth to support his family as his father became increasingly unable to do so. Yet, whatever damage the Hotel Texas experience did to Thompson, it also provided him with knowledge and material invaluable to a crime novelist, which he drew upon well into the 1960s.

The next key episode in Thompson's formation came in the oil fields of West Texas, where he drifted after giving up on high school. Taking on such work as he found, Thompson discovered the hobo "jungles" and temporary camps supporting drilling operations.

Living in this world put him in contact with members of the Industrial Workers of the World (I.W.W.), or Wobblies, as they were commonly known. The I.W.W. espoused a blend of Marxism and anarchism in iconoclastic and defiantly antielitist language. Labor historian Melvyn Dubofsky, in *Industrialism and the American Worker, 1865–1920* (1985) summarizes the achievements of the Wobblies in a way that speaks directly to the world of Thompson's novels: "Their actions revealed the gap between American ideals of equality and brotherhood and their practice, the distance between notions of a society based on law, not men, and one in which those with social and economic power abused or ignored the law in order to oppress the weak." In the oil fields Thompson was exposed to a reasonably coherent radical politics–contrasting sharply with his father's Republicanism–that pervades his fiction.

His encounter with the Wobblies also helped form Thompson into a writer in a more directly personal way, for he met Harry "Haywire Mac" McClintock, veteran organizer and songwriter for the I.W.W., who adopted the much younger man. McClintock inducted Thompson into the Wobblies, introduced him to the works of Karl Marx and other socialist writers, and ultimately persuaded him to give up the difficult life in the oil fields in favor of education and the pursuit of his ambition to write. The first writing that Thompson produced out of his oil field years, a series of six sketches published in two installments in *The Texas Monthly* in 1929, drew directly on his experiences there. A part of the tradition of "bottom dog" or hobo literature, Thompson's oil field sketches foreshadow his later development of chronically lonely male protagonists, some of whom, such as Joe Wilmot of *Nothing More Than Murder,* have a hobo past.

On the strength of McClintock's urging, Thompson left the oil fields in favor of the University of Nebraska at Lincoln; he was admitted in 1929 as a "special student" because he lacked a high-school diploma but was able to offer other evidence of fitness for college–probably his publications in *The Texas Monthly.* Under the tutelage of two faculty members, Russell True Prescott and Robert Crawford, Thompson developed significantly as a writer in his freshman year. Under Prescott he developed as a "literary" writer, developing a taut fictional style that marked an advance beyond his loose folkloric sketches for *The Texas Monthly.* Prescott was sufficiently impressed with Thompson to introduce him to Lowry C. Wimberly, editor of the prestigious *Prairie Schooner.* As a member of Wimberly's circle, Thompson became intimate with the bohemian literary scene of Lincoln and published a poem, a story, and three character sketches in the *Prai-*

rie Schooner between 1930 and 1931. Under Crawford, Thompson developed as a professional writer, learning how to produce publishable articles on a variety of subjects. Such training proved invaluable for one who would earn his living by his typewriter for much of his life.

While Thompson excelled as a student in English and journalism, his lack of interest in the agricultural curriculum at the university and a demanding grind of part-time work–undertaken to support his family more than himself–kept his grades low. Still, Thompson managed to find time to court, unsuccessfully and successfully. Thompson was first attracted to Lucille Boomer, the daughter of a professor, but his suit failed, in part at least because the difficult circumstances of his college life convinced Lucille and her mother that he would be an unsuitable husband. This rejection blighted much of the fall and winter of 1930–1931 and underscored Thompson's Wobbly scorn for the socially respectable. In February 1931, still reeling from his heartbreaking rejection, he went on a blind date with Alberta Hesse. Following a brief but intense courtship, they were married surreptitiously in the office of the Justice of the Peace in Marysville, Kansas, in September 1931. Their marriage produced three children–Patricia (born 1932), Sharon (1936), and Michael (1938)–and lasted until Thompson's death, surviving his recurrent struggles with alcoholism, financial difficulties, and the hostility of Thompson's sisters to Alberta.

The Great Depression provided the social and political background for Thompson's college career and early marriage. The Depression did not mark a significant change for the Thompson family insofar as their fortunes had gone into significant decline early in the 1920s, but Thompson was not insensitive to the general suffering engendered. Some of his employment at the time no doubt made him more familiar with it than he might have wished: as a door-to-door salesman for the Kay-Bee Clothing Company, Thompson had to collect on accounts from people who, had they any money to speak of, probably would not have bought from him in the first place. According to his wife, Thompson hated collecting on accounts, and the experience provided material for *A Hell of a Woman,* in which Dolly Dillon sells and collects on shoddy merchandise for the Pay-E-Zee Company. Despite his busy schedule, Thompson continued to publish. Besides the work in *Prairie Schooner,* he also published regional fiction in *Cornhusker Countryman,* and his first known crime fiction in *Nebraska Farmer.*

In fall 1931, with his previous employers fallen victim to the Depression or otherwise unable to provide work, Thompson dropped out of school after two years

Dust jacket for Thompson's second novel (1946), about murder and political corruption in Nebraska

of study. He spent much of 1932 and 1933 drifting through the southern Plains searching for work, before settling down in Oklahoma City with his father, who was separated from his wife and family again and subsisting on the kindness of friends and such relief work as the government provided. Oklahoma City had no regular job to offer, just stints of casual labor, but its relative stability provided Thompson the opportunity to restart his career as a professional writer. He wrote an unknowable amount of material for oil trade and regional farm magazines. He also drafted a novel, titled "The Unholy Grail," that would after sixteen years and much revision, be published as *Nothing More Than Murder*.

After moving back to Fort Worth in 1933, Thompson turned his hand to writing for the true crime magazines. Because he was working a punishing schedule at the posh Worth Hotel, Thompson wrote as part of a team, with his mother, his sister Freddie, and his wife collecting material that Thompson would then write up for publication. According to Freddie, Thompson was disturbed by the horrifying stories that were

reported to him or that he read in the paper. As Michael McCauley, Thompson's first biographer, observes in *Jim Thompson: Sleep With the Devil* (1991), the writer "seemed to have had almost no filter or distancing ability when it came to violence—he was always terribly affected by it." McCauley suggests that this characteristic accounts in part for the distinctiveness of Thompson's crime fiction: his novels are not "more violent" than those of his contemporaries in the sense of simply containing a greater number of violent scenes or piling up more dead bodies—the reverse is probably closer to the truth; the difference is that Thompson does not contrive to distance the reader from the violence he presents. Thompson's best work permits—forces—the reader to experience the horror depicted in a manner that approximates that of the murderer or that of the victim.

Thompson's apprenticeship in true crime not only put food on the table but also helped him establish habits and techniques that were useful to him after he moved seriously into crime fiction. Using excerpts from Thompson's true crime writing, Polito demonstrates how the writer manipulated point of view, shifting between first and third person, and adapted true crime's "trademark tone of incredulous horror." Polito points out that the market for true crime tended to be midwestern and southern in character, as opposed to the more urban, northern readership of the detective fiction magazines. This market differentiation coincided with Thompson's personal background and probably helped underpin the regional character of his later fictional world.

Thompson parlayed his success in true crime writing into a lucrative assignment to profile an Oklahoma police chief and returned with his family to Oklahoma City late in 1935. When the police chief was brought down by the disclosure of his involvement in an auto-theft ring, Thompson's manuscript—which he estimated at forty thousand words in his second autobiography, *Roughneck* (1954)—was worthless. Nevertheless, the move to Oklahoma City proved serendipitous. In April 1936 he was hired to bolster the staff of the Federal Writers' Project by his friend Bill Cunningham, whom Thompson knew as the author of *The Green Corn Rebellion* (1935), a novel dramatizing the attempted march on Washington in 1917 by socialist tenant farmers opposed to American involvement in World War I, and as a major figure in the Oklahoma Communist Party. The party, which Thompson joined in 1936, provided Thompson with an intellectual community that helped sustain him as a writer and solidified his radical political inclinations. Polito asserts that the effect of his involvement with the Left during this period was far reaching: "Nearly everything good that happened to

Jim Thompson as a writer–starting in 1936, and continuing deep into the next decade–came about as a result of his involvement with the radical left."

In the mid to late 1930s Thompson held steady employment, rising in the Federal Writers' Project from part-time to full-time, and eventually becoming the director of the project for the state of Oklahoma in March 1938. He enjoyed the active political and intellectual scene whose passing is mourned by the protagonist of his unfinished novel "The Concrete Pasture" in a passage quoted by Polito: "Nowadays . . . the way things were now . . . an eternity of active nothingness. Dostoyevsky's kind of eternity: a fly buzzing around an empty privy. But then, always so much . . . meetings . . . lectures . . . rallies." During this period Thompson was able to make further strides as a writer, as is evident in such stories as "The End of the Book," published in *American Stuff: An Anthology of Prose and Verse by Members of the Federal Writers' Project* (1937), and "Time Without End," published in *Economy of Scarcity: Some Human Footnotes* (1939). In these stories, both later collected in *Fireworks: The Lost Writings of Jim Thompson* (1988), as well as others, Thompson developed the technique of split narration, whereby the narrative focus shifts both between characters and between subjective and objective depictions of and reactions to reality. A technique Thompson likely learned from reading William Faulkner as well as from his true crime writing, split narration reappeared in his later crime fiction.

While Thompson appears to have been a highly competent writer and administrator for the Federal Writers' Project, the devolution of the project from federal to state control made him more vulnerable to attacks from the local newspapers and politicians, who had consistently been unhappy with "Communist infiltration" of the project. Thompson stepped down as director on 31 August 1939, as control of the project shifted to the state on 1 September. During Thompson's tenure as director a *Labor History of Oklahoma* (1939) was completed, and considerable work was done on the centerpiece of the project, *Oklahoma: A Guide to the Sooner State*. Although Angie Debo, who took over the project following Thompson's departure, is listed as the editor, Polito's examination of the extant drafts of the guide reveals that significant portions of the guide were written by the uncredited Thompson.

Thompson's departure from the Federal Writers' Project coincided with a red scare and witchhunt in Oklahoma City, in which several of Thompson's close friends and associates were convicted of belonging to the Communist Party and of distributing subversive literature. Thompson was not arrested–because as former director of the project for Oklahoma he was "too big a fish" for the local authorities to touch, as

Polito learned from Gordon Friesen, Thompson's friend and fellow party member. Thompson and Friesen were co-organizers of a committee to arrange for the legal defense of the jailed communists, but the community of politically radical activists and intellectuals was breaking up.

Arranging with the secretary of the Oklahoma Communist Party, Bob Wood, to deliver the party car to San Francisco, Thompson left Oklahoma City late in 1940, moving his wife, children, mother, sister Freddie, and a cousin to San Diego, though his sights were set ultimately on breaking into the movie industry in Hollywood. Thompson had destroyed the two writing projects he worked on most intensely during his five years in Oklahoma City–a documentary, "We Talked About Labor," for which he had received $1,800 from the Rockefeller Foundation, and a proletarian novel, "Always to Be Blessed"–after he could not find a publisher. His drinking grew worse, which reactivated his tuberculosis. Because no publisher showed interest in him or his work in California, Thompson settled for a job in an aircraft factory in San Diego to help support his extended family. His first year in California provides most of the material for his first published book, *Now and On Earth* (1942), a heavily autobiographical proletarian novel.

In *Roughneck,* Thompson mythologizes the circumstances of the composition of *Now and On Earth.* He asserts that he wrote the novel in ten lonely, whiskey-fueled days in a New York City hotel room paid for by his publisher, who lent him a typewriter and staked the small sum of money involved against Thompson's ability to produce a publishable novel. More arrestingly, he claims that he wrote the novel against a deadline. Thompson relates that on his way to New York he stopped in Oklahoma City to visit his father in the sanatorium to which the family had consigned him before they departed for California and promised to return soon to take him away. According to Thompson, his father, despairing of his return, committed suicide by choking himself to death with the stuffing from his mattress.

This self-mythologization has been cleared up by Polito, who reports that Thompson's father did not commit suicide, but rather, after years of suffering from mild dementia, worsened and died from "pneumonia, cardiovascular problems, and senility," according to his death certificate. Doubtless the tale Thompson constructed, however unfaithful to the facts, was faithful to his sense of responsibility for his father's death. As to the composition of the book, he did not arrive friendless in New York; many of his old Oklahoma friends had relocated there, and they introduced him to the left-wing literary and artistic scene, of which Thompson

Covers for Thompson's original paperbacks, 1952–1957

was briefly a part. In fact, Woody Guthrie, whom Thompson had met in Oklahoma, helped secure the contract for *Now and On Earth* with Modern Age Books. Modern Age gave him an advance on the novel, with which Thompson covered his expenses. He wrote the novel, not in ten days, but in a still impressive five weeks.

Publishing *Now and On Earth* did little or nothing to ease Thompson's financial straits, and he returned to San Diego and to work in the aircraft industry in 1942. This second stint in San Diego was no more pleasant than the first, and Thompson's drinking was worse. He returned in 1945 to New York, where through his old radical ties he was able to find a publisher willing to offer an advance on his second novel, *Heed the Thunder* (1946), also written in a five-week blitz.

Although *Heed the Thunder* is not a crime novel, it anticipates Thompson's work in the crime genre in important ways. Like his later work, it is a regional novel, set in rural Nebraska. Thompson admired writers who explored particular regions. He was a fan of the Nebraska writer Willa Cather, and his favorite novelist was William Faulkner, whose greatest works are firmly set in a small area of Mississippi. Also, crime does figure in the novel: Grant Fargo murders his cousin and lover Bella Barkley, and a young naif, Jeff Parker, uncomprehendingly becomes part of the world of political corruption when he begins his term in the state legislature. While Thompson later came to complain about the market for which he wrote, *Heed the Thunder* suggests that early on he inclined toward using crime in his fiction.

Following the publication of *Heed the Thunder,* Thompson returned to San Diego, where he wrote for the true crime magazines before taking a job with the *San Diego Journal* in 1947. At the *Journal* Thompson was valued for his writing ability, but his drinking made him an erratic employee. After he was berated by the publisher of the *Journal* for writing a piece critical of a local politician, Thompson departed for the *Los Angeles Mirror,* where he worked from early 1948 until early 1949, the year of publication of his next novel, *Nothing More Than Murder,* and his breakthrough into crime fiction.

According to Polito, Thompson nursed *Nothing More Than Murder* through "seventeen years and eight radical revisions." In the novel Joe Wilmot runs the Barclay movie theater, owned by his wife, Elizabeth Barclay Wilmot, daughter of a prominent local family. Wilmot becomes involved in a tortured triangle when he falls in love with Carol Farmer, a live-in maid and business college student. Joe and Elizabeth's marriage has deteriorated because of insuperable barriers, largely of class, while Joe is attracted to Carol precisely because

in her helplessness she reminds him of himself in his freight-hopping, hoboing days. Elizabeth and Joe devise a scheme whereby Joe will get Carol unencumbered by Elizabeth, while Elizabeth will get enough money to support herself comfortably. They plan an "accident" in the movie screening room built above their garage in which a woman, apparently Elizabeth, will be incinerated when the film catches fire. Joe will collect $25,000 in a fraudulent claim on the insurance company, to be forwarded to a fleeing Elizabeth, and there will be no obstacle to Carol and Joe's union. The only difficulty they face is arranging the death of an innocent woman.

Events, of course, do not go according to plan, and Thompson sardonically explores the evil consequences of Joe's attempt to live the good life. Joe half-glimpses the betrayal of his better self that his ambition has led to early in the novel, as he pauses from his murderous labors:

> I wasn't worried. Not too much. I guess I just had a touch of the blues. I had everything in the world to look forward to, and I had the blues. . . . Over in the yards a freight gave out with a highball. I took a drink and closed my eyes. I tried to imagine it was fifteen years ago, and I was on the freight, and I was looking at the city for the first time. And I thought, *Hell, if you had to be blue, why not then instead of now?*

By the end of the novel, Joe has tried to kill Carol in an unsuccessful attempt to cover up his own role in the murder. With his crimes discovered, he fully sees why he feels blue after he has become a success, not before, and the cost at which he had made something of himself: "*They can't hang me. I'm already dead. I've been dead a long, long time.*" The murder of innocence and compassion, usually by those who try hardest to fulfill the dictates of the American dream, becomes a central feature of Thompson's fiction.

Achieving sales of 750,000 in hardback and paper, *Nothing More Than Murder* received mixed reviews upon publication. The *San Francisco Chronicle* of 8 May 1949, the *Chicago Daily Sun Times* of 4 March 1949, the *New York Times Book Review* of 6 March 1949, and the *New York Herald Tribune Weekly Book Review* of 27 March 1949 ran negative reviews. More favorable were *The Saturday Review of Literature* of 26 February 1949, which called it "Grim—but very good," and *The New Republic* of 21 March 1949, in which the critic advised, "For those sure they can take it, I recommend *Nothing More Than Murder* . . . the grimmest tale in several seasons." *Nothing More Than Murder* has been accorded respectful attention from Polito, McCauley, and James Sallis. However, all three critics discuss the novel in terms of its prefiguration of Thompson's later

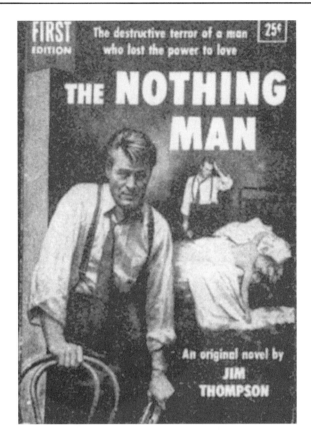
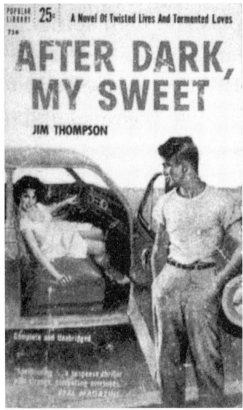

Covers for Thompson's original paperbacks, 1954-1957

work, rather than as an object of critical attention in its own right.

The publication of *Nothing More Than Murder* initiates the period, from 1949 to 1964, when Thompson was, however inconsistently, at the height of his powers as a writer. Three crucial features, all or some of which will characterize his later work, emerge here: (1) he successfully manipulates a "quasi-sympathetic" first-person narrative voice; (2) he works both within and against the conventions of the crime-fiction genre; and (3) innocence is embodied in characters eventually destroyed by the main character and is a residual characteristic of the main character himself. These features define Thompson's distinctive form of crime fiction.

Though completed in 1950, Thompson's next effort, *Recoil*, failed to find a publisher until 1953, after he had discovered and been discovered by Lion Books. The inability to find a publisher propelled Thompson to New York City, where he found a position on the editorial staff of *SAGA,* a "men's adventure magazine," supplementing his salary by authoring articles. In the anonymously published "An Alcoholic Looks at Himself" (collected in *Fireworks*), Thompson offers a self-portrait that is revealing as well as deceptive. As in his fiction, Thompson in the article creates a first-person persona who seems to betray a surprising candor. It is clear, however, that the persona is a construction for the occasion, a mix of fact and fiction. For example, the narrator of the article blames the loss of his job with the Federal Writers' Project on drink, rather than on a political purge. Thompson clearly chose to avoid the touchy politics of the situation because they would have distracted the reader from his thesis. The apparent true confession should be read as the product of a professional writer who is more concerned with using his experience than he is in honestly revealing it. Thompson left *SAGA* in the late summer of 1951 amidst differences with the publisher concerning unionization, working conditions, and the dismissal of the head editor. He then put in an unhappy eight-month stint with the sensationalist *Police Gazette* before meeting the editor of Lion Books, Arnold Hano.

Two weeks after an introductory meeting in which Hano had Thompson choose a synopsis—a brief outline of the principals and plot of a novel—from which to work up a sample of a completed novel, Thompson delivered to the editor nearly half of *The Killer Inside Me*. Thompson did more with the synopsis than Hano imagined possible, and after *The Killer Inside Me* and Thompson's second novel for Lion, *Cropper's Cabin* (1952), he never asked Thompson to work from a synopsis again, as he explained in an interview with Polito: "Very early on I realized that what Jim needed was encouragement more than anything else. . . . As far

as I was concerned, he was inventing a new genre for us. You unleash a guy like that, you simply don't try to direct him." Thompson moved in with his sister Maxine and her husband in Quantico, Virginia, to complete the manuscript.

Thompson's best-known novel, *The Killer Inside Me,* is told in the voice of the unforgettable Lou Ford, a deputy sheriff in desolate Central City, Texas. Ford presents an amiable, if mind-numbingly corny facade to a public that is generally only too willing to believe he is as stupid as he appears. Ford's act is not so much mock-humility as it is a means of torture, for he well knows that those he meets are pained by the relentless recitation of clichés he pretends to believe. Early in the novel he finds a likable man "too good to let go. Polite, intelligent: guys like that are my meat." Ford enjoys the strained smile on his victim's face after he reveals that "out of a clear sky" it came to him that "the boy is father to the man":

> I could hear his shoes creak as he squirmed. If there's anything worse than a bore, it's a corny bore. But how can you brush off a nice friendly fellow who'd give you his shirt if you asked for it?
>
> "I reckon I should have been a college professor or something like that," I said. "Even when I'm asleep I'm working out problems. Take that heat wave we had a few weeks ago; a lot of people think it's the heat that makes it so hot. But it's not like that, Max. It's not the heat, but the humidity. I'll bet you didn't know that, did you?"

Ford vents sadistic impulses through such verbal means until a violent sexual encounter with a prostitute, Joyce Lakeland, reawakens what he terms "*the sickness.*" Sexually abused as a child by the family housekeeper, Helene, who is also the former mistress of his father, Ford replayed his abuse in his adolescence, molesting a young girl. Ford's sense of guilt is compounded when his father frames Ford's adopted brother, Mike Dean, for the crime. Out of this mixture, Ford develops a split identity, in which his outward stupidity masks his inward intelligence and his outward normality hides his inward deviance. This split identity appears to shield Ford as he murders—or thinks he murders—Joyce Lakeland and a variety of others, both to vent his sadism and to cover up previous crimes, until the mask collapses upon him in a final conflagration.

In *The Killer Inside Me* Thompson repeats the concern with the loss of innocence that was notable in *Nothing More Than Murder*: Ford's terrifying violence results from an early violation compounded by his father's unwillingness to confront reality honestly. However, *The Killer Inside Me* differs in its extraordinarily explicit depiction of violence. Whereas the violence in *Nothing*

More Than Murder occurs largely offstage, in *The Killer Inside Me* violence takes center stage, appropriately enough, since Joe Wilmot is not a pathological sadist while Lou Ford is. Nevertheless, the precise quality of the violence in *The Killer Inside Me* distinguishes it from that in most hard-boiled crime fiction.

If one accepts Spillane's Mike Hammer novels as typical of the trend toward graphic depictions of violence in postwar hard-boiled writing, Thompson's depiction of violence appears decidedly atypical. Spillane's brand of violence functions through reader identification with the protagonist and with his morally sanctioned acts, but Thompson's violence positions the reader so that he or she sees the "logic," whether psychological or otherwise, behind the protagonist's acts—and to this degree sympathizes or identifies with him—but is not permitted any simple vicarious thrill. When Thompson has Lou Ford describe his fatal beating of his girlfriend Amy Stanton, the effect is deliberately unnerving, as the reader joins Ford in his detached observation of the scene:

> I hit her in the guts as hard as I could.
> My fist went back against her spine, and the flesh closed around it to the wrist. I jerked back on it, I had to jerk, and she flopped forward from the waist, like she was hinged.

Throughout this scene, an agonizing two pages long, Thompson both illustrates Ford's self-estrangement, whereby he and his acts seem nearly unrelated, and deromanticizes standard hard-boiled violence.

Although *The Killer Inside Me* became Thompson's best-known book, it—like the rest of Thompson's paperback originals—appears to have been largely ignored by reviewers. Upon its republication in 1965, Anthony Boucher called it "one of the half-dozen best paper-originals I've ever read" in *The New York Times Book Review* (4 April 1965). Despite the early lack of interest in it, *The Killer Inside Me* was the first of Thompson's works to receive serious critical attention. In "*The Killer Inside Me:* Fear, Purgation, and the Sophoclean Light" R. V. Cassill asserts that Thompson's novel ought to be read as a novel of ideas, centered on a rejection of the American consensus that through an inexorable process of progressive improvement evil may be eliminated from human experience. Whatever the merits of Cassill's essentially theological and profoundly conservative interpretation of Thompson, he argued convincingly for the seriousness of Thompson's fiction—though to little immediate effect. Yet, over the years *The Killer Inside Me* has come to be Thompson's signature work, the one that spearheaded his revival in the early 1980s.

The Killer Inside Me began a remarkable nineteen-month period in which Thompson provided Hano and Lion Books with so much material that some of it had to be published by other houses to avoid having too much Thompson product on the Lion racks. Thompson wrote three noncrime books for Lion: *The Alcoholics* (1953), a darkly comic day in the life of El Healtho, a spa specializing in the treatment—or mistreatment—of alcoholics; and two unreliable but interesting autobiographies, *Bad Boy,* which covers the years from his early childhood to 1929, and *Roughneck,* which covers 1929 to 1941.

The remainder of Thompson's output for Lion was crime fiction. *Savage Night* (1953) is a bizarrely bent mafia saga in which Charlie "Little" Bigger, a five-foot tall, tubercular, retired hit man is forced out of retirement to kill Jake Winroy, a racketeer turned witness for the state. In order to do the job, Charlie takes advantage of his youthful appearance, going undercover as a student at a nearby college and moving into the boarding-house where Winroy is staying. The house is populated by an eccentric group, one of whom Charlie suspects has been sent by "The Man" as a backup and to keep an eye on him. Charlie sympathizes with the luckless Winroy and fails to kill him, the job eventually falling to Ruthie Dorne, a poor college student who keeps house for the Winroys but also is an employee of The Man. After Ruthie kills Winroy, she and Charlie flee to an isolated farm in Vermont where Charlie's personal deficiencies magnify; he and Ruthie become estranged until Ruthie hacks away with an axe at Charlie's already diminished body.

Any summary of the events of *Savage Night* must impoverish it, since it is a novel deeply strange in both conception and execution. Thompson had originally told Hano that he wanted to restrict himself to a five-hundred-word vocabulary for *Savage Night,* and while he abandoned this limit, the intention indicates the obsession with diminishment in the novel. Charlie is not only short, he also wears contact lenses and dentures; Ruthie's left leg is normal down to the knee, where it becomes like that of a baby. The other principal characters are also in one way or another not whole. The tone of the novel, pervaded by Charlie's sense of his basic lack of a self and mired in his anxiety and exhaustion, contrasts with the robustness of the typical mob novel. In the expressionistic culmination, the tonal and thematic character of the work is replicated in its action and even in its physical presentation, as the chapters become shorter and shorter, until the last is but a single, four-word sentence.

While Boucher commented in *The New York Times* (7 September 1953) that *Savage Night* contained "the most experimental writing" in crime fiction in 1953, it

Thompson with his sisters, Maxine Thompson Kouba and Freddie Thompson Townsend, in the early 1960s

was not widely reviewed upon publication. *Savage Night* has fared better recently, hailed as one of Thompson's half-dozen best by Polito. McCauley calls it "Thompson's most inspired, most lyrical novel."

Also published by Lion and also a contender for the title of Thompson's best book is *A Hell of a Woman.* Here Thompson focuses on a concern pervasive in his work: the relationship between his male protagonist and the women who populate his world. Since *A Hell of a Woman* both undermines the misogyny common to much crime fiction and is formally experimental, it presents arguably Thompson's sharpest break from–and critique of–hard-boiled fiction conventions. *A Hell of a Woman* tells the story of Frank Dillon, a door-to-door salesman in the employ of the Pay-E-Zee Company who happens across a young woman in distress, Mona, who has access to $100,000, provided Dillon can liberate the money from its owner, Mona's aunt. The aunt, who deprives and abuses Mona, lives an impoverished life despite having a fortune stashed in the cellar. Joyce, Dillon's third or maybe fourth wife–they all blend together for him– walks out after a fight, the details of which go far to explain why Dillon's marriages are starting to add up.

Dillon's way is then clear to carry out his plan. He murders Pete Hendrickson, a day laborer, and the aunt, making it appear that they have killed each other during Hendrickson's burglary of her home.

Although Dillon's plan initially appears to have worked, it soon begins to unravel. Dillon is relieved of the money by his boss at Pay-E-Zee, who has caught him doctoring his accounts and pieced together his scheme. With the money lost to blackmail, Dillon's imagined happiness with Mona degenerates into the familiar vituperation. Later, Mona, all but abandoned by Dillon, kills herself. Dillon begins selling door-to-door again and comes across, as best one can gather from the fragmentary narrative, a rich widow who adopts him until he collapses under his own sense of defeat and in a drug-supplemented frenzy is either castrated by his companion or castrates himself before he ends his life.

Thompson's formal inventiveness as well as central thematic concerns are perhaps best seen in the autobiographies of Frank Dillon that begin chapters 12, 18, and 22. Presented as direct addresses to the reader, two of the autobiographies are titled "Through Thick and Thin: The True Story of a Man's Fight Against High

Odds and Low Women" while the third is titled "Upward and Onward," with the same subtitle. Dillon believes, despite the evidence of his life, that he can succeed in conventional terms, and that his marriages have failed because of his wives, who like the rest of the world are out to get him. Thus, Dillon is wedded to a self-contradictory individualism that tells him the rest of society is a jungle waiting to destroy him but that should he persevere, surely fortune and, in his words, "some little helpmeet to dwell with" will come his way. Thompson is, characteristically, sympathetic to as well as critical of his protagonist, who performs both the few actually decent gestures in the novel and the most horrifying acts.

A Hell of a Woman was greeted warmly by Boucher in *The New York Times* of 5 September 1954, who praised it as an example of Thompson's general excellence: "Once again the book exists beautifully on the two levels of simple narrative vigor and complex psychological depth." McCauley lists it as one of Thompson's "Best-crafted books—ingeniously plotted and structured, full of puns and ironies. . . . The first-person narration once again conveys and disguises an ingenious 'mystery' plot, in which the truth is concealed/revealed as a direct result of the narrator's delusions and observations." Polito maintains that while Thompson repeats many features of his other works in the novel, he also "ransacked so many other literary closets, both high and low, that *A Hell of a Woman* ranks as his wildest book." Tony Hilfer sees *A Hell of a Woman* as "the ultimate deconstruction of the femme fatale American style."

While *The Killer Inside Me, Savage Night,* and *A Hell of a Woman* are reckoned as Thompson's masterpieces for Lion, several others either published by Lion or written for Lion but published elsewhere are nearly as good: *Recoil* (1953), *The Criminal* (1953), *A Swell-Looking Babe* (1954), *The Nothing Man* (1954), *After Dark, My Sweet* (1955), and *The Kill-Off* (1957). Unusual, though not unique in Thompson's writing for Lion, *Recoil* features a single first-person narrator free of psychoses who survives to the end of the novel. It is the story of Pat Cosgrove, a former convict whose parole is secured by the scheming Doc Luther, a political lobbyist who intends to make Cosgrove the fall guy in an insurance fraud. The novel is noteworthy for Thompson's parodic depiction of ultrapatriotic 1950s America, featuring a "civic organization," the Phalange, whose name Thompson likely borrowed from the ultra-right-wing movement during the Spanish Civil War.

The main character of *A Swell-Looking Babe,* Bill "Dusty" Rhodes, shares some traits with Pat Cosgrove of *Recoil.* Both are young men uncertainly located in life, against whom the odds are stacked. But whereas in *Recoil* the contending forces play out in favor of the protagonist, the opposite is the case in *A Swell-Looking Babe.* Rhodes becomes entangled in a scheme to rob the wealthy bookies who room in the upscale hotel in which he is a bellboy, a job he has taken in order to support himself and his declining stepfather. Trapped by his quasi-Oedipal desire for a woman who resembles his dead stepmother, Rhodes manages to escape punishment for his role in the robbery but is implicated in the death of his stepfather, whom he did not kill but whose death he most certainly desired. Ironically, his lack of feeling for his stepfather, rather than making the woman of his desire available to him, as the Oedipal fantasy would have it, ultimately denies her to him.

Polito makes a sharp distinction between *Recoil* and *A Swell-Looking Babe,* both of which are third-person narratives. Whereas "Thompson steered the volatile contradictions of *Recoil* to a Hollywood finish, as though hoping for a movie deal," *A Swell-Looking Babe* "scavanged so deeply beneath Thompson family trauma that the bloody trench probably could be surveyed only by a distant third-person narration." He calls the novel "Thompson's ugliest dramatization of the guilt and revenge that haunts his 1950s fiction—and the most self-chastising."

Awareness of the contrast in resolutions between *Recoil* and *A Swell-Looking Babe* enriches one's reading of *The Nothing Man,* a novel fully as strange as *Savage Night.* The protagonist of *The Nothing Man* is Clinton Brown, a newsman whose penis was severed by the explosion of a mine during World War II. Brown narrates the novel, but his narrative is unreliable, as he comes to realize, because he is usually drunk. Brown's good looks and wit worsen the pain of his emasculation, and when he is pursued by women, he turns murderous. Or does he? Brown's emasculation may extend to his inability ultimately to act, to kill these women he believes he has killed, all of whom actually die by the hand of another. As does the contrast between *Recoil* and *A Swell-Looking Babe,* the absurdity of Brown's innocence makes a point basic to Thompson's world: the line between the guilty and the innocent, at least as these are commonly conceived, is thin indeed. Formally, *The Nothing Man* exploits Brown's unreliability as a narrator to create a highly unstable text; with its allusions to T. S. Eliot and Ernest Hemingway, *The Nothing Man* is Thompson's most obvious, if also perverse, flirtation with modernism.

Reviewing *The Nothing Man* upon its republication, Peter Prescott called it "typical of Thompson in good form" in the *Newsweek* of 17 November 1986. McCauley characterizes it as "Thompson's most radical take on the nature and reality of guilt. . . . That a man could be as close to murder as Brown and yet be 'inno-

Covers for Thompson's original paperbacks, 1957–1964

cent' points out not only the slippery, undefinable nature of guilt but the possibilities of redemption and innocence." Polito, discussing the adequacy of the conclusion of the novel, quotes a letter Thompson wrote to Boucher: "I spent more time arguing about *The Nothing Man* than I did writing it; and then, in order to make a sale, I had to botch up the ending." Polito finds the novel compromised only slightly by the tacked-on ending forced on him by his publisher, Dell, since one can see clearly that Thompson intended to end the novel ambiguously, with the protagonist unable to commit suicide, as he had planned, and unable to kill.

After Dark, My Sweet features a protagonist, William "Kid" Collins, a former boxer and escapee from a mental institution, whose combination of physical strength and mental weakness make him an appealing fall guy in a kidnapping plot engineered by the slippery Uncle Bud. Uncle Bud is a familiar type in Thompson's world, an amiable, smooth-talking, but dangerous and callous man. He convinces Collins and a young, hard-drinking widow, Fay Anderson, to abet him in a plot to kidnap the young son of a wealthy family. When the boy turns out to be diabetic and the kidnapping to be tantamount to murder, Collins and Fay want to restore the boy to his family. In an unusual Thompson ending, combining moral redemption and formal closure, Collins sets up a situation in which Uncle Bud is killed trying to collect the ransom money, while Fay, thinking Collins means to kill the boy, shoots her partner, clearing herself with the authorities and convincing herself that she is a person of some worth, willing as she is to defend the helpless. Collins sacrifices not only his life but also the perception that Fay has formed of him in order to make a decent life possible for her.

In *The Criminal* and *The Kill-Off,* both considerable technical accomplishments, Thompson employs multiple narrators to examine the nature and ambiguity of guilt. In *The Criminal* Thompson inverts the basic pattern of the detective story, in which the detective sifts through a multiplicity of potential clues and suspects to discover a limited pattern of significant clues and a single guilty party: the action of *The Criminal* moves outward from the singularity of the murder of Josephine Eddelman into multiplicity. Thompson begins the story by focusing on the young man accused of raping and killing the girl but concludes having subordinated the supposed central event to the depiction, via the multiple narrators, of "a hell of wretchedness and violence, bigotry, ignorance and class hatred." *The Kill-Off* features twelve narrators—one per chapter—each advancing the plot incrementally, each throwing a different light onto the murder of Luane Devore and onto the fundamental

dishonesty and decay that infest the small New England town of Manduwoc.

While Thompson enjoyed a great run writing for Lion and living in New York in the most secure and congenial circumstances he and his family had known since his time with the Federal Writers' Project, it proved brief. In 1954 Hano, Thompson's most sympathetic and perceptive editor, announced that he was leaving Lion. Shortly thereafter Lion Books was sold, finally closing up shop in 1957. Thompson, despite good sales figures and Boucher's advocacy in *The New York Times,* failed to find another publisher right away. One might well think Thompson a prize any paperback publisher would have coveted, and on the surface he would have been a perfect match for Fawcett Gold Medal, who had enlisted crime writers such as John D. MacDonald, David Goodis, Harry Whittington, Gil Brewer, and Peter Rabe. Perhaps Thompson was the odd man out in this cast because these other writers were distinguished by the ability to produce their work within the confines of the crime fiction genre, whereas Thompson often chose to challenge or invert the conventions of the genre. In any case, Thompson turned to more conventional crime stories, which he sold to the monthly crime fiction magazines, to his old standby, true crime writing, and for a few months to copyediting for the *New York Daily News* to support his family.

Thompson was saved from this drudgery by the young moviemaker Stanley Kubrick, who had read and was impressed by Thompson's fiction, and who needed a writer to provide scripts to match his visual brilliance. Thompson worked on the screenplays—scrupulously analyzed by Polito—for two excellent Kubrick films, *The Killing* (1956) and *Paths of Glory* (1957), moving to Hollywood in 1956. For the remainder of his life, Thompson divided his efforts between fiction, motion picture, and television writing.

While *Paths of Glory* was being shot in Europe, Thompson stayed in California and wrote *Wild Town* (1957), which features, in a subordinate role, the protagonist of *The Killer Inside Me,* Lou Ford, acting out a fate quite different from that depicted in the earlier novel. Ford works as a deputy sheriff in *Wild Town* because his father's premature death made it impossible for him to complete his medical education. He dons the mask of the clown to cover up his intelligence so that he might fit in, but in this novel no traumatic incident leads him to take a murderous turn. By creating two different versions of Lou Ford, Thompson implies that an accident of fate—the Lou Ford of *The Killer Inside Me* having been abused by his father's lover—differentiates the sick and the guilty from the healthy and the innocent. While *Wild Town* relies more heavily on plot than do Thompson's best novels, Boucher in *The New York*

J.T,   P. ~~120~~
                                                                                        /73

        I hesitated, thinkin' I should be able to come up with somethin'.
Because it was all so clear to me, Christ knew it was clear; love one
another and don't serew no one unless they're bendin' over, and forgive
us our trespasses because we may be a minority of one. For God's sake,
for God's sake -- why else had I been out here in Potts County, and why
else did I ~~break my back to~~ stay here? Why else, who else, what else but
Christ Almighty would put up with it?

        But I couldn't make him see that. He was as blind as the rest
of 'em.

        "Well, Nick? I ain't waiting much longer."

        "And you don't have to, Buck," I said. "You don't have to,
because I finally come to a decision. I've been a long time comin' to
it; it's been the product of thinkin' and thinkin' and thinkin', and
then some more thinkin'. And dependin' on how you look at it, it's the
god-dangest whingdingest decision ever made, or it's the skitty-assed
worst. Because it explains everything that goes on in the world -- it
answers everything and it answers nothing.

        "So here it is, Buck, here's my decision. I thought and I
thought and then I thought some more, and finally I came to a decision.
I decided I didn't no more know what to do than if I was just another
lousy human bein'!"

                        ### End ###
                        POP. 1280
                        a novel by
                        Jim Thompson

Final page of the revised typescript for Thompson's 1964 novel, Pop. 1280. *The crossed-out lines read: "I whirled around, drawing my gun.
We both fired at the same time" (from Michael J. McCauley,* Jim Thompson: Sleep with the Devil, *1991).*

Times (19 January 1958) called it "a first-rate exercise in a sort of post-Cain complex toughness," and it sold nearly a quarter of a million copies in little over a year for its publisher, New American Library.

Unfortunately, Thompson's relationship with New American Library was unhappy. Unlike those at Lion Books, the editors there were unwilling to permit him to follow his own lights as a writer and attempted to make him more conventional, even suggesting that he develop a series character. Thompson had to resist editorial meddling in order to make his next novel, *The Getaway* (1959), something other than a conventional caper and flight novel. Certainly much of the novel does conform to the demands of a caper and flight novel, if a rather gritty one. Former convict Carter "Doc" McCoy is a character much like Lou Ford and other Thompson protagonists in that he suffers from and cultivates a self-estrangement that renders it difficult for anyone to know what he really thinks or feels. He and his wife, Carol, pull off a bank heist, disposing along the way of their traitorous partner, Rudy. However, Rudy is not dead, and Doc and Carol have both the police and their former partner on their heels as they flee to Mexico.

In the final chapters of the novel Doc and Carol confront their true selves in supposed sanctuary, a comfortable hideaway for criminals. When they realize that their large but fixed supply of cash will eventually run out, the two are pitted against one another. Their fundamentally parasitic existence as criminals is thus revealed, driven home symbolically by the cannibalism that Doc discovers is practiced by those criminals whose money runs out. As one of the sanctuary employees tells Doc, politely but contemptuously, "Quite fitting, eh Señor? And such an easy transition. One need only live literally as he has done figuratively." Like the farm in *Savage Night,* the sanctuary in *The Getaway* exposes rather than conceals its denizens.

Once again Thompson found a champion for his work in Boucher, who in the 13 February 1959 *New York Times* said of *The Getaway:* "If any scholar is engaged in a thesis on Symbolism and Fantasy in the Modern Crime Novel, he is urged to make a study of Jim Thompson's *The Getaway.* . . . The story can be read simply as an unusually good thriller; but the ending casts new light on all the earlier excitement in a way that only Thompson could bring off." Among later critics, the novel is generally considered one of Thompson's best. Polito conjectures that "*The Getaway* may be Thompson's most subversive fiction because it so completely masks itself as a routine caper." McCauley asserts that "*The Getaway* is the best third-person crime novel Jim Thompson ever wrote." While Thompson was initially involved in the making of the movie ver-

sion of *The Getaway,* directed by Sam Peckinpah, he was eventually fired from the job because, Polito concludes, he was too committed to the dark insights of his novel.

The early 1960s were unkind to Thompson. His health was poor—he suffered a stroke in 1959 and bleeding ulcers in 1960—and some fast and loose dealings with New American Library had lost him his publisher. Despite the cautions of doctors, he continued to drink heavily, which made his family life difficult. He subsisted off of a little work for television and the sale of foreign rights to his works—in France, particularly, Thompson was highly regarded.

Despite hard times, Thompson gathered himself to write *The Grifters* (1963) whose main character, Roy Dillon, practices the short con, any of a variety of swindles that net him a relatively small amount of money, $20 or $100, but usually entail little risk. *The Grifters* focuses on a three-member cast: Dillon, his mother, Lilly, and his girlfriend, Moira. Dillon is just thirteen years younger than his mother, who had raised him with an indifference that has burdened him with one of the monumental Oedipal complexes in American literature. The novel, written in the third person, charts the conflict between Dillon, scarred by his tortured childhood, his mother, who has crossed her mob-boss employer, and Moira, who wants Dillon to quit the short con and take up the more lucrative big con. It is perhaps Thompson's most doom-ridden novel, since Dillon's fate appears determined—especially to him—from the opening of the novel. The sense of doom only intensifies as Dillon resists the efforts of others to offer him a way out of the cul-de-sac into which he hurtles.

The Grifters was favorably received by Boucher in *The New York Times* of 14 July 1963 but was not widely reviewed. Both McCauley and Polito place the novel below the top rank of Thompson's novels. McCauley finds its structure flawed, citing a major shift in tone toward the conclusion and finding unconvincing and hackneyed a subplot concerning Dillon's rejection of the otherwise appealing Carol Roberg because she is a survivor and victim of a Nazi concentration camp. Polito differs sharply in his assessment of the Carol Roberg episode, but finds Thompson's third-person narration awkward and at times obtrusive. Each of these objections may be countered: the Carol Roberg subplot is considerably more subtle and integral to the novel than McCauley allows; the structure of the book and its shift in tone accord with Lilly's abandonment of her attempt to steer Dillon off the path onto which she had, unwittingly, originally put him; and the third-person narration permits Thompson to comment on the character's consciousness and the limitations of this consciousness in a way that the first-person narration does not.

Pop. 1280 (1964), which is in many ways a black comic reprisal of *The Killer Inside Me,* is regarded as Thompson's last major novel. Sheriff Nick Corey of Potts County presides over a physical and moral squalor that he both abets and suffers. Like Lou Ford, he presents to the world–and initially to the reader–an affable face, posing as a country bumpkin since that is what the people of Pottsville want him to be. Corey is afflicted with a shrewish wife, pursued by two women, and burdened with maintaining order in a town that wants no order other than that of the decay it revels in. To keep his life going smoothly, Corey commits several murders, which he artfully arranges to appear to be the work of others. Attempting to understand the squalor of Potts County and his place in it, Corey arrives at the conclusion that he is Christ returned to Earth:

> It was all so clear to me, Christ knew it was clear: love one another and don't screw no one unless they're bending over, and forgive us our trespasses because we may be a minority of one. For God's sake, *for God's sake*–why else had I been put here in Potts County, and why else did I stay here? Why else, who else, what else but Christ Almighty would put up with it?

Pop. 1280 is both typical and atypical of Thompson's fiction: it relies on a powerfully executed first-person narrative voice and features a narrator who masks his intelligence so that he may be a part of the world in which he finds himself; but it also features a murderer-protagonist who constructs and is convinced by a full-blown delusional system, and it is written in a consistently comic mode.

While contemporary reviewers ignored *Pop. 1280,* later critics regard it highly. Tony Hilfer comments that "Nick Corey . . . may be the most unnerving first-person narrator in the crime novel genre. . . . Clearly, he is God's agent to enforce cosmic irony in Potts County." McCauley asserts, "More than any other novel, *Pop. 1280* proves that when Thompson was writing in top form about what he wanted to, he didn't write crime novels at all–he wrote subversive, sociopolitical novels anchored by philosophy." He qualifies this judgment elsewhere on the same page: "Jim Thompson found crime novel conventions particularly useful in conveying his vision of the world."

Thompson followed *Pop. 1280* with two lesser, though competent, efforts for Fawcett, *Texas by the Tail* (1965), a hotel caper novel, and *South of Heaven* (1967), a combination bildungsroman and crime thriller set in the 1920s West Texas oil fields Thompson knew so well. He then moved to Popular Library, for whom he wrote three novelizations, two based on movies and one based on a television series. An oddity, the "novelization" of *Ironside*–it bears little resemblance to the tele-

Thompson as Judge Grayle in a still from the 1975 movie version of Raymond Chandler's 1940 novel, Farewell, My Lovely *(EK/ITC)*

vision show of the same name–is worthy of more than a cursory mention. The opening sentences indicate both the distance of the novel from the show and the characteristic surplus of effort Thompson put into a book meant by its publisher to be a throwaway:

> It was the kind of place where if you didn't spit on the floor at home you could go down there and do it. The smell was thick enough to write your name on (if you were still using your own name)–the aroma of stale beer and cheap wine and cloying sweat, colored and given body by the gut-like strands of cigarette smoke.

Ironside falls into two basic parts: those focused on the Killer, as he is called, a criminal who sees himself as the scourge of the privileged and wicked, and those devoted to Chief Ironside and his investigative team. The passages devoted to the Killer and his world effectively sound the familiar Thompson waters; the passages devoted to Ironside and his team waver between throwaway description and dialogue and a competently executed detective story.

Thompson continued to write and publish until his health failed him. According to his family, when he became so crippled by strokes that he could no longer write or communicate in more than a few words, he simply gave up eating and permitted himself to waste away. He died in Hollywood on 7 April 1977.

Thompson was pulled back from nearly complete obscurity by his revival in the 1980s. The writer's popularity in France led to the release of the movies *Série Noire* (1979), based on *A Hell of a Woman*, and *Coup de Torchon* (1981), based on *Pop. 1280*, which no doubt helped fuel the revival of his work in the United States. Thompson's work was championed first by Geoffrey O'Brien in *The Village Voice Literary Supplement* in 1982. The next year Max Allan Collins and Ed Gorman brought out *Jim Thompson: The Killers Inside Him*, which included not only a previously unpublished novella, *This World, Then the Fireworks*, but also interviews with Albert Hano and Alberta Thompson. *The Killer Inside Me* was republished by William Morrow and Company in 1984; also, beginning in that year, many of Thompson's novels were republished by Bary Gifford at Creative Arts/Black Lizard Press. The timing of the revival suggests that it may in part have benefited from a reaction against the nostalgia for the 1950s then current in the country. While President Ronald Reagan was declaring that it was "morning again in America," some chose instead to celebrate the novels that Thompson wrote to explore the depths of the American night.

Precisely how Thompson's work will be valued in the future is uncertain. He no doubt will continue to be considered a master of his particular variant of crime fiction, but the more general question of how Thompson will be assessed as an American writer is more difficult to answer. As the literary canon is reevaluated and transformed, writers who worked in popular forms will doubtless have their promoters. The chances of Thompson being considered as something more than just a popular writer may well depend upon the nature and quality of the criticism that comes to be written about him. If so, then the direction is clear: since McCauley and, especially, Polito have lessened the temptation to speculate about autobiographical elements in Thompson's fiction, the way is now open for more rigorous critical methods to be applied. Thompson's reputation will only be enhanced by the application of sophisticated forms of narrative, ideological, and psychoanalytical analyses to his work.

Biographies:

Michael McCauley, *Jim Thompson: Sleep With the Devil* (New York: Mysterious Press, 1991);

Robert Polito, *Savage Art: The Life of Jim Thompson* (New York: Knopf, 1995).

References:

Gay Brewer, *Laughing like Hell: The Harrowing Satires of Jim Thompson* (San Bernardino, Cal.: Brownstone Books, 1996);

R. V. Cassill, "*The Killer Inside Me:* Fear, Purgation, and the Sophoclean Light," *Tough Guy Writers of the Thirties*, edited by David Madden (Carbondale: Southern Illinois University Press, 1968), pp. 230–238;

Arnold Hano, "Jim Thompson, 1906–1977," *Jim Thompson: The Killers Inside Him*, edited by Max Allan Collins and Ed Gorman (Cedar Rapids, Iowa: Fedora Press, 1983), pp. 17–22;

Tony Hilfer, *The Crime Novel: A Deviant Genre* (Austin: University of Texas Press, 1990), pp. 68–71, 137–150;

Geoffrey O'Brien, "Save These Books: Out of Print But Not Forgotten," *Village Voice Literary Supplement*, February 1982, p. 19;

James Sallis, *Difficult Lives: Jim Thompson, David Goodis, Chester Himes* (Brooklyn, N.Y.: Gryphon Books, 1993);

Sallis, "Strange Mirrors: The World of Jim Thompson," *North Dakota Quarterly*, 58 (Summer 1990): 128–148;

Luc Sante, "The Gentrification of Crime," *New York Review of Books*, 32 (28 March 1985): 18;

Domenic Stansberry, *Manifesto for the Dead* (Sag Harbor, N.Y.: Permanent Press, 2000);

David Thomson, "The Whole Hell Catalog," *New Republic*, 192 (15 April 1985): 37–41.

Papers:

Jim Thompson's papers are mostly in the possession of his family. See the notes to Polito's *Savage Art* for the most complete information on archival sources.

Raoul Whitfield

(22 November 1898 – 24 January 1945)

Douglas Ivison
Université de Montréal

BOOKS: *Green Ice* (New York & London: Knopf, 1930); republished as *The Green Ice Murders* (New York: Avon, 1947);

Silver Wings (New York: Knopf, 1930);

Wings of Gold (Philadelphia: Penn, 1930);

Danger Zone (New York: Knopf, 1931);

Death in a Bowl (New York & London: Knopf, 1931);

Five, as Temple Field (New York: Farrar & Rinehart, 1931);

The Virgin Kills (New York: Knopf, 1932; Harpenden, U.K.: No Exit, 1988);

Killer's Carnival, as Field (New York: Farrar & Rinehart, 1932);

Danger Circus (New York: Knopf, 1933).

Collection: *3 Star Omnibus* (New York: Knopf, 1936).

PRODUCED SCRIPT: *Private Detective 62,* motion picture, script by Whitfield and Rian James, Warner Bros., 1933.

OTHER: "Death in the Pasig," as Ramon Decolta, and "Inside Job," as Whitfield, in *The Hard-Boiled Omnibus: Early Stories from Black Mask,* edited by Joseph T. Shaw (New York: Simon & Schuster, 1946), pp. 97–111, 255–299;

"China Man," in *The Hardboiled Dicks,* edited by Ron Goulart (Los Angeles: Sherbourne, 1965; London: Boardman, 1967).

Raoul Whitfield

SELECTED PERIODICAL PUBLICATIONS–
UNCOLLECTED: "Scotty Troubles Trouble," *Black Mask,* 9 (March 1926): 82–90;

"Scotty Scouts Around," *Black Mask,* 9 (April 1926): 107–116;

"Jenny Meets the Boys," *Black Mask,* 9 (June 1926): 91–98;

"Black Air," *Black Mask,* 9 (July 1926): 74–91;

"Roaring Death," *Black Mask,* 9 (August 1926): 67–93;

"Flying Gold," *Black Mask,* 9 (September 1926): 110–120;

"Delivered Goods," *Black Mask,* 9 (November 1926): 68–73;

"Ten Hours," *Black Mask,* 9 (December 1926): 51–66;

"Uneasy Money," *Black Mask,* 9 (January 1927): 108–117;

"White Murder," *Black Mask,* 9 (February 1927): 98–107;

"Sky-High Odds," *Black Mask,* 10 (March 1927): 41–50;

"South of Savannah," *Black Mask,* 10 (May 1927): 120–128;

"Bottled Death," *Black Mask,* 10 (June 1927): 116–128;

"Live Men's Gold," *Black Mask,* 10 (August 1927): 26–36;

"Sixty Minutes," *Black Mask,* 10 (October 1927): 9–23;

"Red Pearls," *Black Mask,* 10 (November 1927): 86–93;

"The Sky's the Limit," *Black Mask,* 10 (January 1928): 119–128;

"Soft Goods," *Black Mask,* 10 (February 1928): 26–34;

"Little Guns," *Black Mask,* 11 (April 1928): 30–39;

"Black Murder," *Black Mask,* 11 (May 1928): 72–80;

"First Blood," *Black Mask,* 11 (June 1928): 5–22;

"Blue Murder," *Black Mask,* 11 (July 1928): 38–51;

"High Death," *Black Mask,* 11 (August 1928): 49–61;

"Red Wings," *Black Mask,* 11 (September 1928): 32–42;

"Ghost Guns," *Black Mask,* 11 (October 1928): 78–88;

"The Sky Trap," *Black Mask,* 11 (November 1928): 109–120;

"Outside," *Black Mask,* 11 (December 1929);

"West of Guam," as Ramon Decolta, *Black Mask,* 12 (February 1930): 50–57;

"Red Hemp," as Decolta, *Black Mask,* 13 (April 1930): 33–44;

"Signals of Storm," as Decolta, *Black Mask,* 13 (June 1930): 41–52;

"Enough Rope," as Decolta, *Black Mask,* 13 (July 1930): 25–36;

"Murder By Mistake," *Black Mask,* 13 (August 1930): 36–56;

"Nagasaki Bound," as Decolta, *Black Mask,* 13 (September 1930): 103–114;

"Nagasaki Knives," as Decolta, *Black Mask,* 13 (October 1930): 26–37;

"Murder in the Ring," *Black Mask,* 13 (December 1930): 7–32;

"The Caleso Murders," as Decolta, *Black Mask,* 13 (December 1930): 92–102;

"Silence House," as Decolta, *Black Mask,* 13 (January 1931): 33–44;

"Diamonds of Dread," as Decolta, *Black Mask,* 13 (February 1931): 80–91;

"About Kid Deth," *Black Mask,* 13 (February 1931): 92–115;

"The Man in White," as Decolta, *Black Mask,* 14 (March 1931): 111–122;

"Face Powder," *Black Mask,* 14 (April 1931): 6–32;

"The Blind Chinese," as Decolta, *Black Mask,* 14 (April 1931): 112–122;

"Soft City," *Black Mask,* 14 (May 1931): 6–34;

"Red Dawn," as Decolta, *Black Mask,* 14 (May 1931): 113–122;

"For Sale—Murder," *Black Mask,* 14 (June 1931): 78–107;

"Blue Glass," as Decolta, *Black Mask,* 14 (July 1931): 78–89;

"Diamonds of Death," as Decolta, *Black Mask,* 14 (August 1931): 46–54;

"Shooting Gallery," as Decolta, *Black Mask,* 14 (October 1931): 100–111;

"The Javanese Mask," as Decolta, *Black Mask,* 14 (December 1931): 49–60;

"Man Killer," *Black Mask,* 15 (April 1932): 6–28;

"The Siamese Cat," as Decolta, *Black Mask,* 15 (April 1932): 29–39;

"Walking Dynamite," *Black Mask,* 15 (May 1932): 6–26;

"The Black Sampan," as Decolta, *Black Mask,* 15 (June 1932): 95–105;

"Climbing Death," as Decolta, *Black Mask,* 15 (July 1932): 88–100;

"Blue Murder," *Black Mask,* 15 (September 1932): 6–22;

"Dead Men Tell Tales," *Black Mask,* 15 (November 1932): 8–26;

"The Magician Murder," as Decolta, *Black Mask,* 15 (November 1932): 88–96;

"Murder By Request," *Black Mask,* 15 (January 1933): 8–30;

"The Man from Shanghai," as Decolta, *Black Mask,* 16 (May 1933): 115–124;

"The Amber Fan," as Decolta, *Black Mask,* 16 (July 1933): 99–109;

"Dark Death," *Black Mask,* 16 (August 1933): 6–30;

"A Woman Can Kill," *Black Mask,* 16 (September 1933): 6–28;

"Money Talk," *Black Mask,* 16 (October 1933): 54–73;

"Not Tomorrow," *Black Mask,* 16 (November 1933): 60–76;

"Murder Again," *Black Mask,* 16 (December 1933): 60–80;

"High Murder," *Black Mask,* 16 (January 1934): 52–69;

"Death on Fifth Avenue," *Black Mask,* 16 (February 1934): 56–70;

"The Mystery of the Fan-Backed Chair," *Hearst's International-Cosmopolitan,* 98 (February 1935): 56–58, 169–172;

"The Great Black," *Hearst's International-Cosmopolitan,* 103 (August 1937): 62–64, 122–125.

One of the most popular and prolific contributors to the pulp magazines of the 1920s and early 1930s and a pioneer of the hard-boiled genre, Raoul Whitfield is now all but forgotten. In his brief writing career, using three names, Whitfield published more than 150 stories and 9 books of hard-boiled fiction and juvenile aviation adventures. Relentlessly violent and often oppressively bleak and cynical, his hard-boiled tales bear traces of his prewriting career as an actor, pilot, and reporter, as well as his travels as a child.

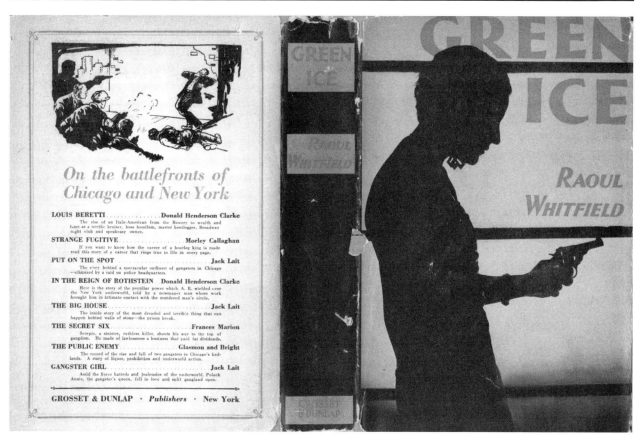

Dust jacket for Whitfield's first novel, published in 1930

A nephew of the steel magnate and philanthropist Andrew Carnegie, Raoul Fauconnier Whitfield was born, an only child, into a financially and socially privileged family on 22 November 1898 in New York City, where he spent most of his early childhood. While still a boy he moved to the Philippines with his father, who had accepted a position in the Territorial Government in Manila. During his teenage years he lived in the Philippines, also traveling to China and Japan. Whitfield later drew on these experiences in writing the twenty-six stories he published about Jo Gar, the Island Detective.

When he was eighteen, Whitfield became ill and returned to the United States. After regaining his health, he moved to California and used his photogenic good looks to become an actor in silent movies. Bored by acting and wanting to take part in World War I, Whitfield enlisted in the ambulance corps. Hoping to get into combat, he transferred to the air service. He received his flight training at Kelly Field in San Antonio, Texas, and, after winning his wings as a second lieutenant, was in France by the summer of 1918. Shortly before the war ended, Whitfield had

the opportunity to serve as a fighter pilot over the battlefields of France, an experience he was to use as the basis for the many extravagant aviation-adventure stories he later wrote.

Returning to the United States after the armistice, at his family's urging Whitfield moved to Pittsburgh to begin a career in the steel industry. He quickly switched careers, becoming a cub reporter with the *Pittsburgh Post* in 1919. As William F. Nolan reports in *The Black Mask Boys: Masters in the Hard-Boiled Fiction School of Detective Fiction* (1985), he believed that he had found his real career, as he "was born to be a writer." He worked at the *Pittsburgh Post* through the mid 1920s, during which time he married his first wife, Prudence Van Tine, a fellow employee of the newspaper. While working in the newspaper business, he developed the writing skills he later employed as a pulp writer and amassed some of the raw material for his hard-boiled stories. While still working as a journalist, Whitfield began writing adventure stories for pulp magazines. As he began to publish his stories, he quit the newspaper to become a full-time writer, and he and his wife moved to the west coast of Florida.

331

Whitfield quickly became a regular contributor to several pulps, publishing his first story in *Black Mask*, "Scotty Troubles Trouble," in March 1926. He would go on to appear in the pages of *Black Mask* more than ninety times in the next nine years; at his peak, he published one or two stories in each monthly issue. Although it is for this relationship and for the work that appeared in *Black Mask* that Whitfield is now remembered, he was at the same time a popular and prolific contributor of aviation-adventure fiction to pulps such as *Everybody's, War Stories,* and *Battle Stories;* in fact, he was so prolific that he was forced to adopt a pseudonym, Temple Field, for some of his stories in these magazines because editors did not want to be publishing too many stories by a single writer. Nolan cites a description of Whifield's writing process given by Fred Dannay: "[He] always wrote easily and quickly, with a minimum of correction. He had a particular talent for starting with a title and writing [a story] around it. . . . He would place neat stacks of chocolate bars to the right of his typewriter, and a picket fence of cigarettes to his left. He wrote and chain-smoked and ate, all in one unified operation."

While Whitfield's first publications in *Black Mask* were closer to the aviation-adventure stories he was publishing in other pulps than the hard-boiled fictions for which he was later to become known, he quickly adapted to the *Black Mask* style, modeled on the work of Dashiell Hammett, that its editor, Joseph T. Shaw, was promoting. Hammett was a key influence on Whitfield's developing style, which Shaw at first considered "hard and brittle and over-inclined to staccato." The editor, however, noted that Whitfield was "a hard, patient, determined worker," and the quality of his writing soon began to improve.

In the late 1920s Whitfield moved to Los Angeles and began publishing in *Adventure, Air Trails,* and *Triple-X*. In the December 1929 issue of *Black Mask* appeared the first of his "Crime Breeders" stories featuring Mal Ourney, which formed the basis of his first published novel, *Green Ice* (1930). During this time Whitfield began corresponding with Hammett, and they first met in San Francisco. They were to become longtime friends. After reading the Crime Breeders series, Hammett suggested that they be sent to his publisher, Knopf, for possible publication in book form. By the time *Green Ice* was published, Whitfield had moved to New York, where he and Hammett attended the theater and frequented bars, all the while discussing writing techniques. Prudence Whitfield, Nolan reports, later commented that her husband and Hammett "talked shop endlessly . . . debating whether a story should have seven murders or twenty-seven!"

Mal Ourney, the protagonist of *Green Ice,* walks out of prison, where he had served two years on a manslaughter charge (for a crime that he did not commit), and becomes involved in a series of vicious murders and a fight over some stolen emeralds, the green ice of the title. First, Dot Ellis, his former girlfriend for whom he had served the "bum rap," is shot to death while sitting in a taxi in the small prison town, just minutes after Ourney had refused to get into the cab with her. Fearing that he will be charged with her murder, Ourney takes a train to New York City to meet his friend Wirt Donner, with whom he had planned to go on a mission to eliminate "the breeders of crime." However, as he arrives at Donner's boardinghouse, Donner stumbles out the front door and dies, the victim of a gunshot to the stomach. The book moves from one brutal murder to another as it follows Ourney back to the prison town and then on to Duquesne, Pennsylvania, a steel town outside of Pittsburgh, and finally on to Pittsburgh, where the book concludes in a bloody shootout at a funeral.

While the narrative is tightly written and fast paced throughout, it comes most fully alive in the scenes set in Duquesne, a dirty steel town of "12,000 foreigners and 2,000 Americans," and in Pittsburgh. These sections of the novel clearly reflect Whitfield's experience as a reporter for the *Pittsburgh Post,* as Ourney poses as a reporter with the *Pittsburgh Post-Dispatch,* where he had previously worked, and enlists the help of the newspaper's editor. While the criminal underworld portrayed in *Green Ice* is a world in which nobody can be trusted and cynicism and self-interested greed are the rule, Ourney is an unambiguous hero, obsessively devoted to the elimination of evil.

Green Ice was generally well received, although some critics complained about its confusing plot and the quality of the writing, particularly its choppy and repetitive sentences. In a review in the *New York Evening Post,* Hammett dismissed these concerns: "What matters is that here are two hundred and eighty pages of naked action pounded into tough compactness by staccato, hammerlike writing." The mystery novelist S. S. Van Dine agreed, proclaiming *Green Ice* to be "a first-rate crook story—swift and exciting and colorful." Whitfield's most enduring novel, *Green Ice* has been regularly republished in various paperback editions over the years.

All the while, Whitfield continued to churn out aviation-adventure stories, largely addressed to a juvenile audience; he was described by the editor of *Battle Stories* as "America's foremost writer of aviation fight stories." His second book, *Silver Wings* (1930), was a collection of these stories (all but one of which had previously appeared in *Boy's Life*) and was lauded by the reviewer for the *Boston Globe* for presenting "stories that pulsate with the vitality and the glamour of the flying service." It was quickly followed by a similar collection titled *Wings of Gold* (1930).

In 1930 Whitfield began publishing one of his most important series of stories with the publication of "West of Guam" in the February 1930 issue of *Black Mask,* which introduced readers of the magazine to one of the more interesting private eyes of the period, Jo Gar, the Island Detective. Using the pseudonym Ramon Decolta, Whitfield published twenty-four Jo Gar stories in *Black Mask* over the next three years. From Manila in the Philippines, Jo Gar was "very brown," was constantly referred to as a half-breed, and spoke several languages, including English, Spanish, Tagalog, Chinese, Japanese, and Malay. The Jo Gar stories were obviously highly influenced by Whitfield's experience growing up in the Philippines. Interesting in their portrayal of a nonwhite private detective and for his travels throughout the Philippines and across the Pacific Rim, the Jo Gar stories have never been collected. Whitfield later published two Jo Gar stories under his own name in *Hearst's International-Cosmopolitan,* "The Mystery of the Fan-Backed Chair" (February 1935) and "The Great Black" (August 1937).

In late 1930 the Whitfields moved to Europe, living on the French Riviera for the next two years, and making trips to Italy, Sicily, and Tunisia. During this period, while continuing his prolific production of stories for the pulps, Whitfield published *Danger Zone* (1931), an autobiographical account of his wartime experience utilizing the conventions of juvenile adventure fiction, and, more significantly, *Death in a Bowl* (1931), first published in *Black Mask* as a three-part serial from September to November 1930.

In *Death in a Bowl* private detective Ben Jardinn must navigate the duplicity and intrigue of Hollywood in order to solve the murder of German conductor Hans Reiner, shot while conducting a concert at the Hollywood Bowl. Like Mal Ourney, Jardinn does not and cannot trust anyone—not his clients, all of whom could be involved in the murder; not Max Cohn, Jardinn's "best man"; not even Carol Torney, Jardinn's secretary and love interest. As Carolyn See observes in "The Hollywood Novel: The American Dream Cheat" (1968), Jardinn "is the only man here who is honorable, who has any idea, no matter how obscure, of what is really right." A sophisticated man who appreciates classical music, Jardinn is forced to adopt a pose of toughness and cynicism, which See argues is "an individual's defense against an intolerably meaningless world." His cynicism is validated when Cohn turns out to be the murderer.

Cover for the pulp-magazine issue that carried the first installment of Whitfield's novel about a murder at the Hollywood Bowl

Jardinn is an engaging hero, and the novel presents a vivid portrayal of a Hollywood that, as Woody Haut writes in *Pulp Culture: Hardboiled Fiction and the Cold War* (1995), "appears calm but underneath is seething with crime, corruption, violence, and possibility." Yet, despite some well-written and inventive set pieces, such as the murder of Hans Reiner, *Death in a Bowl* lacks the intensity of *Green Ice,* but W. C. Weber in *The Saturday Review of Literature* called it "a hard-boiled tale, capitally told." Jardinn was featured in two later stories published in *Black Mask:* "Murder By Request" (January 1933) and "Dark Death" (August 1933).

Five (1931) was the third book that Whitfield published in 1931, the first for which he used the pseudonym Temple Field. This novel, derived from the nine "Laughing Death" stories published in *Black Mask* from February to October 1929, is a straightforward story of revenge. When pilot Gary Greer's father, the prosecutor of Center City, is killed by gangsters, Greer goes on a quest to track down and kill the five men he holds responsible. In the process he fakes his own death

William Powell as detective Donald Free and Margaret Lindsay as Janet Reynolds in a still from the motion picture
Private Detective 62 *(1933), based on a story by Whitfield (Warner Bros.)*

in a plane crash and adopts several disguises, as the occasion arises, pretending to be a clergyman, a scrap merchant, an African American, and a carnival stunt pilot. The novel concludes in an air battle between Greer and the head gangster, a police detective. In winning this duel, Greer not only avenges his father but also cleans up Center City. *Five* is predictable, formulaic, and fast moving. While the reviewer for *Bookman* called it "easily one of the best thrillers of the season," modern readers would more likely agree with Bruce Rae, who wrote in *The New York Times Book Review* that *Five* "makes average reading."

The next year, 1932, was a year of change for Whitfield. He and his wife separated, to be divorced the following year, and he moved to California, having sold the movie rights to *Death in a Bowl* and been hired as a contract writer by Paramount Studios. He also published his final crime novel under his own name, *The Virgin Kills* (1932), the only one not based on material first published in *Black Mask*. The narrator, Al Connors, is a tough, cynical, sophisticated newspaper columnist, who, along with other celebrities, is invited to cruise up the Hudson River on the *Virgin*, a yacht owned by an unscrupulous financier and gambler, to watch the rowing regatta at Poughkeepsie. One of the rowers is killed during the race, and all those aboard the *Virgin* are suspects. While not a significant novel, *The Virgin Kills* is a highly readable story.

Killers' Carnival (1932), the second novel published using the Temple Field pseudonym, was based on "The Skyline Murders" series published in *Black Mask* from August 1931 to January 1932. Alan Van Cleve, a financially and socially privileged man-about-town and world traveler, becomes involved in the "steel arena" that is New York City, where he comes into conflict with Barney Ruys, a crooked lawyer who controls much of the crime in the city. Like many of Whitfield's heroes, Van Cleve moves easily between the worlds of the elite and the criminals; in fact, as the narrative progresses, the overlapping of the two worlds becomes increasingly evident. Van Cleve can trust no one, except for his girlfriend, as everyone is a potential betrayer of his trust, including the private detective he hired to help him. In the world of *Killers' Carnival*, as in Whitfield's other stories, loyalty is a commodity that can easily be bought and sold but never depended upon. Violent and fast moving, *Killers' Carnival* is always entertaining but rarely transcends the formulaic. As Isaac Anderson wrote in *The New York Times Book Review* of 21 August 1932, "you'll get your money's worth of murder in this book."

Whitfield's time in Hollywood resulted in the production of only one movie, *Private Detective 62* (1933), for which he and Rian James wrote the script. Directed by Michael Curtiz and starring William Powell as private detective Donald Free, the movie is a familiar blend of intrigue and betrayal, with more romance than in Whitfield's novels, ending in the marriage of the private detective and his client. It was enthusiastically reviewed in *The New York Times* but has been largely forgotten.

On 19 July 1933 Whitfield married his second wife, New York socialite Emily Davies Vanderbilt Thayer, who was described as "one of the leaders of New York's social intelligentsia" in *The New York Times*. After their wedding in New York, the Whitfields took their honeymoon in the southwestern United States, and then settled down on the Dead Horse Ranch in New Mexico, which had its own polo field and golf course. After marrying Emily, Whitfield produced little fiction, publishing his last story, "The Great Black," about Jo Gar, in 1937. His final book, *Danger Circus* (1933), was a circus-aviation adventure story written for the juvenile market.

The Whitfields' marriage quickly unraveled; they separated in February 1935, and he moved back to Hollywood, while Emily stayed at the ranch. A few months later she committed suicide by gunshot. Her body was discovered on 24 May 1935. Whitfield inherited Emily's estate, but by 1944 he had spent all her money and was hospitalized. Learning of Whitfield's situation, his old friend Hammett sent a check of $500 to cover Whitfield's medical expenses. Whitfield died of tuberculosis in a military hospital in Southern California on 24 January 1945.

Black Mask editor Shaw, as quoted by Nolan, remembered Whitfield as standing "shoulder to shoulder with the best" and, probably too charitably, declared that his early death foreclosed on what "might very well have been a brilliant future." While Whitfield never transcended the genres in which he wrote, he did make a significant contribution to hard-boiled fiction. His novels remain entertaining reading, and *Green Ice* in particular is an example of hard-boiled fiction at its most relentless. As well, Whitfield should be remembered for his Jo Gar stories, which also deserve increased attention. Nevertheless, despite the fact that some of his novels were reprinted in the 1980s, Whitfield remains only a footnote in discussions of better, and better-known, hard-boiled writers such as Hammett and Raymond Chandler.

Bibliography:
E. R. Hagemann, *A Comprehensive Index to Black Mask, 1920–1951* (Bowling Green, Ohio: Bowling Green State University Popular Press, 1982), pp. 84–86, 224–230.

References:
E. R. Hagemann, "Ramon Decolta, a.k.a. Raoul Whitfield, and His Diminutive Brown Man: Jo Gar, the Island Detective," *Armchair Detective*, 14 (Winter 1981): 3–8;

Woody Haut, *Pulp Culture: Hardboiled Fiction and the Cold War* (London: Serpent's Tail, 1995), pp. 67–68;

William F. Nolan, *The Black Mask Boys: Masters in the Hard-Boiled Fiction School of Detective Fiction* (New York: Morrow, 1985), pp. 129–151;

Carolyn See, "The Hollywood Novel: The American Dream Cheat," in *Tough Guy Writers of the Thirties*, edited by David Madden (Carbondale and Edwardsville: Southern Illinois University Press, 1968), pp. 199–217.

Charles Willeford

(2 January 1919 – 27 March 1988)

Douglas Levin

BOOKS: *Proletarian Laughter* (Yonkers, N.Y.: Alicat Bookshop Press, 1948);

High Priest of California (New York: Royal Books, 1953; London: Gollancz, 1990);

Pick-Up (New York: Beacon, 1955; London: Futura, 1992);

Wild Wives (New York: Beacon, 1956; London: Gollancz, 1990);

Honey Gal (New York: Beacon, 1958); republished as *The Black Mass of Brother Springer* (Berkeley, Cal.: Black Lizard, 1989);

Lust is a Woman (New York: Beacon, 1958);

The Woman Chaser (Chicago: Newsstand Library, 1960; London: Gollancz, 1991);

The Whip Hand, as W. Franklin Sanders, by Willeford and Sanders (Greenwich, Conn.: Fawcett, 1961);

Understudy for Love (Chicago: Newsstand Library, 1961);

No Experience Necessary (Chicago: Newsstand Library, 1962);

Cockfighter (Chicago: Chicago Paperback House, 1962; revised edition, New York: Crown, 1972);

The Machine in Ward Eleven (New York: Belmont Books, 1963; London: Consul Press, 1964);

Poontang and Other Poems (Crescent City, Fla.: New Athenaeum Press, 1967);

The Burnt Orange Heresy (New York: Crown, 1971);

The Hombre from Sonora, as Will Charles (New York: Lenox Hill, 1971; London: Hale, 1973); republished as *The Difference* (Tucson, Ariz.: Dennis McMillan, 1999);

A Guide for the Undehemorrhoided (Kendall, Fla.: Privately printed, 1977);

Off the Wall (Montclair, N.J.: Pegasus Rex, 1980);

Miami Blues (New York: St. Martin's Press, 1984; London: Macdonald, 1985);

New Hope for the Dead (New York: St. Martin's Press, 1985; London: Macdonald, 1986);

Something About a Soldier (New York: Random House, 1986);

Sideswipe (New York: St. Martin's Press, 1987; London: Gollancz, 1988);

Charles Willeford (photograph by David Poller; from the dust jacket for Everybody's Metamorphosis, *1988)*

New Forms of Ugly: The Immobilized Hero in Modern Fiction (Miami Beach, Fla.: Dennis McMillan, 1987);

Kiss Your Ass Good-Bye (Miami Beach, Fla.: Dennis McMillan, 1987; London: Gollancz, 1989);

The Way We Die Now (New York: Random House, 1988; London: Gollancz, 1989);

Everybody's Metamorphosis (Missoula, Mont.: Dennis McMillan, 1988);

I Was Looking for a Street (Woodstock, Vt.: Countryman, 1988; Edinburgh, U.K.: Polygon, 1991);

Cockfighter Journal: The Story of a Shooting (Santa Barbara, Cal.: Neville, 1989);

The Shark-Infested Custard (Novato, Cal: Underwood-Miller, 1993);

Writing and Other Blood Sports (Tucson, Ariz.: Dennis McMillan, 2000).

PLAY PRODUCTION: *High Priest of California: The Play,* New York, Sanford Meisner Theater, 7 October 1988.

PRODUCED SCRIPTS: *The Story of Mary Miller, Army Wife,* radio play episodes, Armed Forces Radio, 1948;
The Basic Approach, television, Canadian Broadcast Company, 1956;
Cockfighter, motion picture, New World Pictures, 1974.

OTHER: "Entrance to an Era," "In Time of This," "I Passed over the River," "Basement Pastoral," "The Apocalypse," in *The Outcast Poets,* edited by Oscar Baradinsky, The Outcast Poets Series of Chapbooks, no. 8 (Yonkers, N.Y.: Alicat Bookshop Press, 1947).

A writer of sharp, often sardonic prose coupled with dark wit, Charles Willeford belongs as much to the school of Nathanael West and Flannery O'Connor as among his hard-boiled crime-writing contemporaries. While his novels all inevitably contain crime and vice, it was only in the last years of his life that he achieved notoriety as a detective novelist with a series of four books that follow the personal and professional escapades of Miami police officer Hoke Moseley. The Moseley novels, published between 1984 and 1988, brought about a much deserved rediscovery of Willeford and resulted in the return to print of his strongest early works. This revival brought to a wider audience a writer of both depth and aspiration, who cared more for the literary merit of his work than for its commercial success.

Willeford concerned himself with issues relevant in the post–World War II era, including race and the banality of American materialism. In several of his best works, he reflects on questions of writing and art, invariably voicing a bleak outlook in regard to aesthetic value in America as it is affected by commercial forces and bad criticism. In his novels Willeford often creates portraits of artists or would-be artists, and these characters, sympathetic or not, generally meet bad ends.

Born on 2 January 1919 in Little Rock, Arkansas, Charles Ray Willeford III grew up as an only child in Los Angeles, where his family moved when he was a baby. Tubercular at the time of his son's birth, Charles Willeford II, a traveling sales manager for Whitman's chocolates, died when his son was two. In his second memoir, *I Was Looking for a Street* (1988), which recounts his youngest years, Willeford claims his father knew well that he was suffering from tuberculosis at the time of his marriage to Aileen Lowey Sawyers but did not inform her. Willeford goes on to bitterly speculate that

his father simply used his mother to perpetuate the family name before his early death.

Even with the death of his father, the young Willeford was surrounded by a doting family. In addition to his mother, he lived with his grandmother, Mattie Sawyers, his uncle, Roy Sawyers, and eventually his mother's second husband, Joe Cassidy, whom she married, probably in 1925. Before the Depression the family lived in a large house with enough income to afford a full-time cook. Willeford's mother, a music and voice teacher, also contracted tuberculosis, and she died when her son was eight. Shortly after her death, Joe Cassidy departed for New York, and Uncle Roy moved out as well, leaving Willeford to be raised by his grandmother.

In addition to attending St. Catherine's Military Academy in Anaheim, a Catholic boarding school where his stepfather placed him for a short time, Willeford also boarded from the ages of eight to ten at McKinley Industrial School for Boys in Van Nuys, near Los Angeles. During these years he developed his first strong taste for reading, going through the Horatio Alger and Tom Swift books at school and more racy titles from the lending library at the May Company, a department store where his grandmother worked as a milliner. The themes of inspirational and optimistic American writing, typified by this early encounter, later became the focus for Willeford's postwar assault on the emptiness of American dreams of prosperity and stable domesticity.

In 1929, better able to watch after himself at the age of ten, Willeford lived with his grandmother once again, this time in a two-room apartment. Two years later, as the Depression took hold, they were joined by additional family, an event that Willeford described as the "end of my idyllic life with Mattie." To make matters worse, Mattie Sawyers lost her job as times grew more difficult. Though his Uncle Roy helped out, young Willeford felt he was too much of a burden on his gradmother, and by 1933 he had become a freight-car rider, living along the rail lines of the Southwest in hobo jungles and relief camps, experiences that make up the majority of his memoir *I Was Looking for a Street.*

In 1935, having failed to complete even junior high school, sixteen-year-old Willeford lied about his age and joined first the National Guard and then the U.S. Army. After a brief period of serving as a truck driver at March Field, east of Los Angeles, Willeford spent two years, October 1936 through October 1938, in the Army Air Corps in the Philippines. He subsequently joined the cavalry upon reenlistment. In the autobiographical volume *Something About a Soldier* (1986), Willeford recounts his early military experiences, particularly his time in the Philippines. He notes

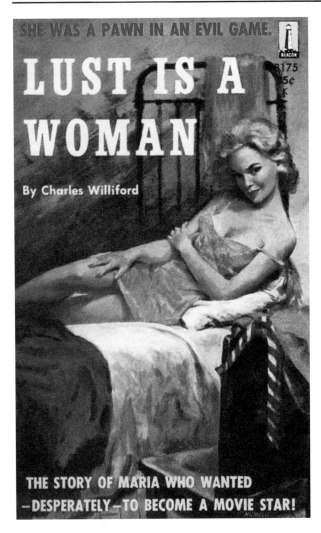

Cover—with his name misspelled—for one of the paperback melodramas
Willeford wrote in the late 1950s

that by the time of his enlistment he was already writing poetry and reading avidly.

In 1942 Willeford married Lora or Lara Bell Fridley in Azusa, California, near Los Angeles. Little is known about this woman, and the couple spent most of their marriage separated because of Willeford's military duty. She apparently traveled with him to Georgia, where he served as a training instructor at Fort Benning before being shipped to Europe. She filed for divorce when Willeford was assigned to Japan, and the divorce was granted on 19 May 1949.

During World War II, Willeford served as a tank commander in Europe with the 10th Armored Division of General George S. Patton's Third Army. He earned the Bronze Star, the Silver Star, the Purple Heart, and the Luxembourg Croix de Guerre. After recovering from wounds to the face and leg, Willeford studied art at Biarritz American University, France, between VE Day and November 1945, when he was shipped state-

side. He took up the study of art again in Lima, Peru, at Los Universitarias de Bellas Artes, from August to October 1949. When his school records caught up with him in Peru—he had no high school diploma—he had to leave the school. Willeford's interest in art is evident throughout his career, with a handful of novels that feature painters in leading or secondary roles.

Willeford's most brutal war experiences, otherwise almost entirely unmentioned in his autobiographical writing, inform his first published prose, which appears interspersed among verse in a chapbook titled *Proletarian Laughter* (1948). Dark, gruesome, and ironically celebratory about the American victory, the prose vignettes, called "schematics" by Willeford, recount episodes of wartime rape, murder, and the desecration of the dead. In one schematic the first-person narrator, presumably Willeford, explains to another soldier the significance of a line of eighty soldiers outside a house: "See that line. . . . There are two whores in that house. Nice girls who came up from Paris to pick up a piece of change. That's democracy." The cold, sharply observational, morbidly humorous pieces set the tone for much of Willeford's future writing.

After the war Willeford served in the Army of Occupation in Japan, where he had the opportunity to write a radio serial, *The Story of Mary Miller, Army Wife,* which was broadcast on Armed Forces Radio in 1948. Between hitches, he spent a short time in New York City, but eventually he reenlisted and found himself once more in California, stationed at Hamilton Air Force Base, near Novato, California (north of San Francisco), in 1950 after brief stays in Texas and Wyoming. During this period in California, he took classes at Marin College (though he earned no degree), acted in community theater, and made his first sustained effort to write novels. With W. Franklin Sanders, Willeford cowrote a hard-boiled novel about a kidnapping titled "Deliver Me From Dallas!," which was published with substantial changes in 1961 as *The Whip Hand* without Willeford's knowledge.

Willeford's first singly composed novel was *High Priest of California,* a paperback original, likely begun in 1950 while he was in Northern California, finished in Santa Barbara in 1952, and published in 1953. A short, focused novel set in San Francisco, it follows the vicious and witty used-car salesman Russell Haxby in his attempt to seduce Alyce Vitale, a married woman. Haxby's scheme includes spiriting off the woman's older and befuddled husband to his aunt's boarding-house and trying to get him to commit suicide by jumping out a window. When the husband refuses to cooperate, Haxby has him committed to a mental institution by trumping up the appearance of a suicide attempt. After Haxby finally sleeps with Alyce, he promptly abandons her, and the novel ends two pages later with Haxby getting a refreshing shave and a hot towel treatment.

Haxby is not, however, an ordinary rake. Smarter and funnier than everyone else in the book, he is the only figure with high aesthetic sensibility. He reads T. S. Eliot's "Burnt Norton" aloud with Béla Bartók's *Miraculous Mandarin* playing on his turntable. He also reads James Joyce and works at an ongoing project of retelling *Ulysses* (1922) in "simple terms" in order to bring "a great book to a simple-minded audience." He has the same intentions for *Finnegans Wake* (1939). Haxby may not appreciate the importance of style to Joyce's greatness, but he makes an effort after all—a rather strange effort for the protagonist of a pulp novel. In prototype, Haxby and *High Priest of California* embody one of Willeford's central strengths—the distinct mixture of violence and seaminess with artistic ideals, and Willeford presents the juxtaposition with few moral signposts. In Willeford's world the aesthetic sheds its promise of redemptive or compensatory power—a rejection of one aspect of Modernism, which Willeford studied extensively, first on his own and later as a student and professor.

In 1951, while he was stationed in Santa Barbara, Willeford married Mary Jo Hooker, née Norton, who had a son by her first marriage, John Stephen "Steve" Hooker (born 1945). At first Willeford maintained some distance from his stepson, but the relationship grew stronger as Steve grew into adulthood. Family life was marred by Willeford's desire to write and to live outside the constrictions of traditional American domesticity. Willeford's military assignments later separated him from his family, and at other times he left of his own accord, if only for a few weeks, when he became depressed by his domestic life.

One separation in 1953 was the result of a two-month hospitalization for depression, an experience that likely informs the hospital scenes in *Pick-Up* (1955), just as the whole of his depression infuses the spirit of the novel, which is his darkest work. Willeford had been hospitalized once before for depression, probably in 1949. His treatment for depression included electroshock therapy, an experience that figures prominently in the story "The Machine in Ward Eleven."

After the end of his hitch in 1953, the Willefords moved from California to Birmingham, Alabama, near Mary Jo's family. Willeford, though, was unable to support his family by writing, and feeling closed in by the proximity of his wife's relatives, he reenlisted in the Air Force and moved to West Palm Beach, Florida. In spite of—or because of—these challenges, Willeford continued to write, completing at the end of 1953 "Death Takes a Bride," which was published as *Wild Wives* (1956), and

a draft of what became the novel *Pick-Up*, which Willeford originally called "Until I Am Dead," a title also attributed to *Wild Wives*. At the publisher's request Willeford expanded *Pick-Up* by more than 50 percent.

Willeford's second published novel, *Pick-Up,* is one of his best, and it was selected in 1997 by the Library of America to represent the American noir tradition of the 1950s along with Jim Thompson's *The Killer Inside Me* (1952), Patricia Highsmith's *The Talented Mr. Ripley* (1955), David Goodis's *Down There* (1956), and Chester Himes's *The Real Cool Killers* (1959). Unlike nearly all of Willeford's other books, however, *Pick-Up* is almost without humor. It charts the downward spiraling relationship between two alcoholics, Harry Jordan, a failed painter turned fry cook, and Helen Meredith, a woman escaping from her mother's domination. Like *High Priest of California,* the novel is set in San Francisco. It depicts Helen and Harry's drinking binges, their hospitalization for alcoholism, a suicide pact, and Harry's eventual imprisonment. *Pick-Up* also introduces a concern that appears in several of Willeford's novels: race. The revelation in the penultimate sentence that Harry is black—contrasted with Helen's "very white" skin—recasts the entire story and deepens the pathos of the couple's mutual isolation.

Willeford's third published novel, incongruously titled *Wild Wives* by his publisher (only one wife figures in the book), is his only private investigator (PI) novel and the last set in San Francisco. In the tradition of the genre, down-on-his-luck PI Jake Blake takes a small job for Florence Weintraub, the femme fatale of the novel, and then finds himself accused of murdering her husband. Unlike most PIs in literature, however, Jake is not too smart and hardly a gentleman: he has sex with his client as they stand against the wall of a dinner club. The novel also contains a subplot involving a homosexual couple, whose quarrel provides another dead body that is the source of Jake's final undoing. Violent, graphic, offbeat, and droll, *Wild Wives* bends the genre and certainly fails to mete out justice.

In 1954 Willeford was assigned to Ernest Harmon Air Force Base in Newfoundland, and he was separated from his family for nearly two years. He served as base historian and also wrote speeches, reports, and articles for the base paper, receiving commendations and promotions for his hard work. He subsequently served in 1956 at Moody Air Force Base in Valdosta, Georgia, and frequently commuted to West Palm Beach on weekends. In August 1956 he was temporarily assigned to Mitchell Air Force Base, near New York City, so that he could appear on an NBC quiz show hosted by Mike Wallace called "The Big Surprise." Willeford answered questions about the modern novel and won $2,000. On 2 November 1956 he resigned

A. WATKINS, INC.
77 PARK AVENUE
NEW YORK 16, N. Y.

Approx 8,500 words

Charles Willeford
615 High Street
West Palm Beach, Fla.

$\bigtriangledown$

THE MACHINE IN WARD ELEVEN

By Charles Willeford

I like Ruben. He is a nice guy. He doesn't lock my door at night. He closes it, naturally, so that none of the doctors or any of the other nurses will notice that it isn't locked when they are just walking past, but he doesn't lock it. (An unlocked door gives me a delicately delightful sense of insecurity.) And this is the kind of thing a man appreciates in a place like this. A little thing here is a big thing. Ruben also lights my cigarettes, and he doesn't mind lighting them. The day nurse, Fred, always appears to be exasperated when I call out to him for a light. I don't blame Fred, of course; the day nurse has many things to do compared to Ruben's duties. Getting the hallway and latrines cleaned, the privileged patients off to O.T. And all of the meals are eaten during the day, too, and Fred is responsible for the cart, the collection of the trays and spoons afterwards, and so on. I have never had a chance to talk much to Fred, but at night, I talk to Ruben quite a little. Which means I listen, and that is what I need to do. There is a dark, liquid vacuum to fill. What Ruben tells me, I often remember. Like the cigarettes.

First Draft

First page of the typescript for Willeford's 1961 story about a psychopathic movie director (Collection of Betsy Willeford) from active duty and returned to West Palm Beach as a civilian, essentially settling in Florida for good. His final rank after a period in the inactive reserves was master sergeant. While he did pursue his education, attending Palm Beach Junior College and then the University of Miami, Willeford held no steady civilian employment until 1964, when he served briefly as an editor at *Alfred Hitchcock Mystery Magazine* and then began his teaching career. During these interim years he hoped to make a living with his writing—a hope he did not achieve until the last years of his life.

Willeford's first novel to reflect his new Florida milieu is *The Black Mass of Brother Springer.* The publisher insisted on a title change and eventually substituted the title under which it was originally published, *Honey Gal* (1958); a 1989 republication of the novel restored Willeford's title. In his diary Willeford notes that he wrote the book in six weeks, compares it favorably to the work of Albert Camus, and calls it "the best existentialist novel ever to be printed in English." Tempering this earlier evaluation in a letter to a friend in 1987, Willeford calls the book "weird" and says, "I was temporarily insane when I wrote it." Writing in the *Washington Post Book World* on 20 June 1993, writer and critic Barry Gifford, who republished four of Willeford's novels when he served as managing editor of Black Lizard Books, calls *The Black Mass of Brother Springer* Willeford's "masterpiece."

An outlandish story, *The Black Mass of Brother Springer* is narrated by Sam Springer, an accountant turned writer who has moved with his wife to the Miami area to write but finds his bank account depleted. Attracted by an advertisement for the sale of a monastery, Springer heads upstate in search of inspiration for an article. Instead of uncovering useful material, however, Springer, a white man, agrees to let Abbott Jack Dover, who is overseeing the sale of the monastery, ordain him as the Right Reverend Deuteronomy Springer and send him to Jacksonville as minister to an "all-Negro" church. Having abandoned his wife, Springer takes up his new position and leads a bus boycott after a black woman is arrested for refusing to give up her seat to a white man—a clear spoof of the Montgomery bus boycott of 1955–1956, with Springer playing the part of Martin Luther King Jr. Unlike King, however, Springer absconds with church funds and runs off to New York City with the wife of a church leader. Absurdist to the core, the novel ends with Springer acknowledging God by thanking Him "for nothing." Long after *Honey Gal* was published, Willeford claimed on many occasions that he had in fact anticipated Rosa Parks.

Like Springer, Willeford also looked for a way to find time to write without having to hold down a regular job. Not having employment, though, allowed him the freedom to take his family to the West Indies for a few months in 1958, where he originally intended to live and write for a year. Willeford's interest in the Caribbean Islands had begun in the mid 1950s when he visited Haiti, to which he returned many times over the next two decades. There he visited a painters' colony and began a lasting interest in Haitian art. The islands were also likely one source for Willeford's interest in cockfighting, out of which stemmed the novel *Cockfighter* (1962), which was made into a film in 1974. Though Willeford claims in *Cockfighter Journal: The Story of a Shooting* (1989), his diary of the making of the film, that he saw his first cockfight in Florida in the early 1960s, he had written an article about Caribbean cockfighting in 1958.

In the late 1950s and early 1960s, Willeford quickly wrote a few novels, including *Lust is a Woman* (1958) and *Understudy for Love* (1961), that he and critics considered weaker efforts. He later claimed that these works were hastily written to cover school expenses. However, among his quickly written efforts of this period is one of his strongest, if less recognized, books— *The Woman Chaser* (1960), which Willeford had titled "The Director." In a retrospective of Willeford's career in the March 1989 *Village Voice Literary Supplement,* critic Richard Gehr calls *The Woman Chaser* Willeford's best novel. In 1999 an independent moviemaking company adapted the novel for the screen; the movie *The Woman Chaser* premiered at the 1999 New York Film Festival.

The protagonist of *The Woman Chaser,* Richard Hudson, is a more fully developed version of Russell Haxby of *High Priest of California.* Like Haxby, Hudson is a successful used-car salesman, an aesthete, and a brute. Though he sleeps with several women, his sexual impulse is largely supplanted by the desire "To create something . . . One thing. That was all. One little thing. And then, maybe two things. But above all, ONE THING!" Hudson bends his artistic ambitions toward making the perfect movie. Though focused on art, Hudson manages to maintain a high level of sexual viciousness: he deflowers his seventeen-year-old stepsister and "helps" his impregnated secretary (whom he seduced and then sent back to the typing pool) by socking her in the stomach to induce a miscarriage. Like Haxby, Hudson is also insightful and witty and reads such high-brow writers as Joyce, Franz Kafka, Fyodor Dostoyevsky, Eliot, and Ezra Pound. He recognizes "artistic integrity" as "real integrity, . . . the only kind that means anything." The novel gains momentum and turns violent in the usual Willeford manner when Hudson's studio demands that he cut his movie—a dramatic exposé of bourgeois America—so that it can be broadcast on television, complete with commercial interrup-

Dust jacket for Willeford's 1971 novel, a dark satire of the art world

tions. By including film directions and dialogue within the text, Willeford knits the events together as if they too are part of a movie.

The links between *High Priest of California* and *The Woman Chaser* reveal another important aspect of Willeford's writing. An inveterate rewriter–and recycler–of earlier material, Willeford relied on the ephemeral nature of the paperback original to bring out books that used descriptions, character names, plot devices, and even dialogue of previously published works that he presumably assumed were forgotten. Two other works from this period–*No Experience Necessary* (1962) and *Cockfighter,* both of which were written in some form by 1958–saw new life when Willeford reworked them later. Several events and characters from *No Experience Necessary*–the old man's imprisonment, his friendship with a psychopath, the maimed girlfriend, the struggling painter, the grocery store heist–almost perfectly parallel one-half of *Sideswipe* (1987). It should be noted that *No Experience Necessary* is marred by the addition of two chapters–1 and 8–that are clearly not written by Willeford.

Cockfighter is Willeford's most tempered novel and, in spite of the subject matter, his most mainstream work.

The novel follows Frank Mansfield in his dogged pursuit of the Cockfighter of the Year award. So intent is Frank that he has taken a vow of silence and put his long-term relationship with Mary Elizabeth Gaylord on hold until he fulfills his goal. Willeford also shows his literary ambition by modeling the events of the novel loosely on *The Odyssey,* à la Joyce's *Ulysses.*

One of the greatest strengths of the novel lies in its documentation of the art of cockfighting, as many reviewers noted when the revised novel was published in hardback in 1972; it does for the blood sport of cockfighting what Hemingway did for bullfighting in *Death in the Afternoon* (1932). Willeford's detailed descriptions, while sometimes graphic and gory, also reveal Frank's dedication–verging on the sexual–to his cocks, such as Sandspur, whom he tries to revive during the bird's battle with Little David:

> I disentangled the gaff from Little David's wing and retreated to my starting line. I put Sandspur's head in my mouth and sucked the blood from his broken beak. I licked the feathers of his head back into place and spat as much saliva as I could into his open mouth. For the

remaining seconds I had left I sucked life into his clipped comb. The comb was much too pale. . . .

Willeford's greatest commercial breakthrough in the first half of his writing career came not from a book but from a story, "The Machine in Ward Eleven," which was originally published in *Playboy* magazine in 1961 and later anchored his collection of stories by the same title, published in 1963. A chilling story that is more macabre than hard-boiled, it follows the madness of Hollywood director Jake (J. C.) Blake (the same name as the detective in *Wild Wives,* but a different character) as he reflects on the events that landed him in a mental institution. Unable to maintain control on a location shoot for a television show, Blake had slugged his star and subsequently attempted suicide. The story reaches its climax when Blake desperately, and dangerously, tries to avoid his prescribed shock therapy by turning the tables on his tormenting psychiatrist.

Willeford later noted that the publication and response to "The Machine in Ward Eleven" was a pivotal event for him. He had been told that readers would not identify with a psychopath protagonist, but the *Playboy* publication belied that argument. An academic critic, William Bittner, who had written about Willeford earlier in *Nugget* magazine, wrote that the story collection *The Machine in Ward Eleven* would "probably mark a turning-point in Willeford's career." The Bittner essay was unpublished but provided to Willeford. A reviewer in *Science Fiction Quarterly* called the story "the weirdest tale that has been published in America since Edgar Allan Poe." The reception of the story confirmed for Willeford that madness as a theme as well as a criminally insane protagonist could strongly resonate with his audience.

Willeford received degrees in English—his B.A., magna cum laude, in 1962 and his M.A. in 1964—from the University of Miami, where he taught as an instructor of humanities from 1964 to 1967. Subsequently—from 1967 to 1980—he served as a professor of English and philosophy at Miami-Dade Junior College. Willeford downplayed his role as a college teacher, as he told Fred Shaw in a 19 December 1971 profile titled "Burnt Orange Heretic," published in *Tropic,* the *Miami Herald* magazine, "Teaching is fine. . . . The only problem is that, like a shooting war, it can play hell with a writer's time." However, while he was pressed to find the necessary time for longer projects, Willeford began writing incidental pieces and book reviews for the Miami papers that totaled well into the hundreds, if not more than a thousand, by the time of his death.

Fearful that he would never write another novel because of his duties as a community college teacher, Willeford turned to writing a Western at the rate of a

page a day as a form of daily discipline. The resulting work, *The Hombre from Sonora* (1971), which Willeford originally titled *The Difference* (published under this title in 1999), is a straightforward action-packed Western, almost wholly unmarked by Willeford's characteristic humor and eccentricities. The novel describes the coming-of-age story of Johnny Shaw, who fights to protect property his father has left him. The work contains some discussion of the banality of war—the Civil War in this case—which can be read as commentary on Willeford's own war experiences. The novel was published under the pseudonym Will Charles because Crown (of which Lenox Hill was an imprint) did not want to bring out two novels—the other was *The Burnt Orange Heresy* (1971)—by the same author in the same publishing season.

Willeford eventually was able to focus his attention on more ambitious writing, and his next book, *The Burnt Orange Heresy,* marked a turning point: it was his first book published in hardcover. In "Burnt Orange Heretic" Shaw suggests that this book would be a large breakthrough for the author, and it did receive positive reviews. Writing in *The New York Times* on 18 September 1971, Thomas Lask calls Willeford's characters "perfectly believable" and tells readers, "you will enjoy it." The reviewer for *The New Yorker* (6 November 1971) calls *The Burnt Orange Heresy* "a novel full of genuine fun, that also manages to make a level statement about the art world and its hermetic credulities." In spite of favorable reviews and a second printing, the book sold only moderately.

A dark satire on the pretensions of the art world, *The Burnt Orange Heresy* chronicles art critic James Figueras's pursuit of a big story. An expert on the Dadaesque French artist Jacques Debierue, who is best known for hanging an empty frame on a wall, Figueras has an opportunity to interview the reclusive artist and uncover the work that he has hidden from the world. Figueras's unveiling of the artist and his work comes at the price of an escalating series of crimes. Willeford again pits aesthetic questions against ambition and materialism, with art losing out in a vicious, darkly humorous way.

Willeford represents this conflict at the outset in a passage that also typifies the droll confidence, drive, and smugness of many Willeford protagonists; here Figueras reflects on his inclusion in a new art encyclopedia:

In my limited visionary world, the world of art criticism, where there are fewer than twenty-five men—and no women—earning their bread as full-time art critics (art reviewers for newspapers don't count), my name as an authority in this definitive encyclopedia means Suc-

Chapter Two

9

Hoke parked and locked his truck in the asphalt lot, dodged a kid on a ~~a~~ *forbidden* skateboard as he crossed the concrete walk, and climbed the ~~narrow~~ *steep* stairs to his apartment. He opened the jalousied windows, ~~watched~~ *checked* the length of the shaddows on *Ocean Boulevard,* ~~the beach,~~ *an admiring /* and took ~~a~~ look at the ocean. The water was *three black tankers skirted the Gulfstream on* snot-green and glassy; ~~this afternoon.~~ Thanks to daylight *the horizon.* savings time, the sun wouldn't set until almost eight o' clock, which gave Hoke ~~at least~~ *more than* two hours of sunlight for his afternoon swim and *daily run.* ~~exercise program.~~

Hoke removed his yellow jumpsuit, emtied the pockets, and washed it in the bathroom ~~when~~ *while* he took his shower. He put on his swimming trunks, ~~wrung~~ *twisted* his jumpsuit as dry as he could with his ~~twisting~~ *strong* hands, shook it out, and ~~then~~ hung the jumpsuit on a plastic hanger in the living room, where it would catch the ~~winds~~ *breeze* coming in from the sea through the ~~jalousied~~ windows. The jumpsuit would be dry by morning, and he could wear it to work again. Hoke had *reduced his wardrobe to* two yellow poplin jumpsuits, but he liked to wash the one he wore each day ~~each~~ *every* evening so he could wear ~~it~~ *the same one* again the next day. He felt that this daily chore simplified ~~things~~ *his life* even more, and he would ~~always~~ *also* have the other, fresher and newer, jumpsuit in reserve.

The apartment ~~also~~ had a living room, one bedroom, and one bath; ~~and~~ instead of a kitchen, there was a narrow galley and counter with two stools in the living room, ~~part of the apartment.~~ The rooms were large, however, having been built ~~back in 1946,~~ *during the Postwar construction boom,* and the ceilings were fourteen feet high. Hoke had ceiling fans in the living room and bedroom--installed by ~~some~~ *an* earlier tenant--*and left behind* and he ~~never used~~ *rarely turned on* the airconditioning.

Page from the typescript for New Hope for the Dead *(1985), Willeford's second novel featuring police detective Hoke Moseley*
(Collection of Betsy Willeford)

33.

Uncle Jake studdied the classified ads every day, and
after finding what he thought was a good investment, bought
a six-stool lunch counter on Santa Barbara Avenue, on
the western side of the Figueroa. Avenue. It was small
enough to run by himself, with a Negro dishwasher in the
tiny kitchen, and he served a daily special of beef stew,
with cole slaw and a roll, for thirty-five cents. He also
had a grill to make ten-cent hamburgers, and at night he
baked three or four apple pies. But Jake did not have
the right kind of personality to make a success out of a
place like this. Across the street, on the northwest corner, a large drive-in sandwich place was being constructed.
The construction workers at noon would cross the street
to eat lunch at Jake's place, but most of them brought
their own lunch, and would just order coffee. Others would
simply order a piece of pie. He would become furious with
those who just ordered pie.

"How can you work all day on pie?" he would ask. "Eat
the beef stew, something that'll stick to your ribs!"

He would glare at them with his good eye, and the tears
would streak down his face from his glass eye. He also
wore his suit and tie behind the counter, and never wore
an apron. The beef stew he made was short on meat and
heavy with potatoes, and the cole slaw was watery because
he cut the mayonnaise dressing with too much water. He
was also in competition with the drugstore lunch counter
on the corner, only fifty yards away, and the drugstore
served a well-balanced blue plate special, for only thirty-
five cents, which included a free cup of coffee.

Page from the typescript for I Was Looking for a Street, *Willeford's 1988 memoir of his early childhood (Collection of Betsy Willeford)* cess with an uppercase S. I thought about it for a moment. Only twenty-five full-time art critics in America, out of a population of more than two hundred million! This is a small number, indeed, of men who are able to look at art and understand it, and then interpret it in writing in such a way that those who care can share the aesthetic experience.

The 1970s began as a successful decade for Willeford. In addition to two new novels in 1971, he saw his revised version of *Cockfighter* published in 1972, and in 1974 he participated in the making of the movie of the novel, both as screenwriter and supporting actor. The movie, however, was a commercial failure, and Willeford's luck showed in the promotional poster: his name was misspelled.

In the mid 1970s Willeford hit a professional and personal wall. He had finished another novel, which was eventually published posthumously in 1993 as *The Shark-Infested Custard,* but was unable to find a publisher when the novel was shopped between 1974 and 1977. By 1975 he had also become disenchanted with his longtime literary agency, A. Watkins, and started to look for new representation. Jim Trupin began to serve as agent for Willeford in 1977 and continued in that role until the author's death. On the personal side, Willeford's marriage of twenty-five years ended in divorce in October 1976. Unable to see his finished work published and now alone, Willeford had hit one of his lowest points.

Capturing the decadence and amorality of the 1970s, *The Shark-Infested Custard* provides Willeford's trademark odd mixture of humor and bleakness. The novel follows the friendship of four swinging bachelors who live in a singles apartment building in Miami. On a bet, Hank Norton picks up a woman at a drive-in, who turns out to be a minor and dies of a drug overdose. In a quiet rage one of the four buddies, Don Luchessi, kills her pusher, and the friends have to dispose of two bodies. This episode only begins the four-part novel, which includes additional bouts of violence and crime, and circumstances eventually drive the four men to Chicago, where three are finally left with the task of disposing of another stiff, this time one of their own. Unlike many of Willeford's earlier works in which the central characters are, for instance, fry cooks or used-car salesmen, this novel has a more distinct white-collar sensibility. Nevertheless, while the main characters are professionals with money, they are equally caught up in the desolate, if tawdry, landscape that fills Willeford's writing.

Despondent about his inability to see *The Shark-Infested Custard* into print, Willeford began and abandoned several novel projects. One book, "The Battle of Maldon," was to depict racial conflict in a single twenty-four hour period on a military base in the 1950s. However, with the exception of a brief self-published memoir, *A Guide for the Undehemorrhoided* (1977), Willeford published no books for the remainder of the decade. Though his memoir primarily recounts Willeford's hemorrhoid surgery, it also provides the occasion for him to recount parts of his childhood and reflect on his lack of religious belief. The book also shows Willeford's willingness to turn his dark humor toward his own suffering.

Willeford's next effort, *Off the Wall* (1980), is a fictional telling of the Son of Sam serial murders. Willeford was given the project by the publisher, who paid in advance and provided Willeford with access to Craig Glassman, the volunteer deputy whose actions led to the arrest of David Berkowitz. Though *Off the Wall* is a respectable book—a compelling, well-written page-turner—Willeford's voice and outlook are largely muted. The project, however, allowed him to shake himself out of his doldrums and bend his creativity back in the direction of the oddball criminal—a direction that served him well for the remainder of his writing career. With his writing back on track, Willeford also had good fortune in his personal life: on 30 May 1981 he married Betsy Poller, née Liss, a writer for the now-defunct *Miami News* whom he had known for many years.

In the early 1980s Willeford attempted to publish another novel that he had begun a few years earlier titled "A Necklace of Hickeys." This crime novel is structurally experimental, and the narrative includes intrusions by a narrator named Willeford. Although the author could not find a publisher for the work, he recyled many of its events in a more conventional form in the second Hoke Moseley novel, *New Hope for the Dead* (1985). By 1983, however, Willeford was at work on a more straightforward crime novel, with its main focus on the character who became Freddy Frenger, the "blithe psychopath" of *Miami Blues* (1984).

In 1984, with the publication of *Miami Blues,* the first of the Hoke Moseley thrillers, the Charles Willeford renaissance began. When *Miami Blues* was published, virtually none of Willeford's books were in print. Within four years, at least a dozen books were in print. Willeford's reemergence as a formidable hardboiled writer was marked by both critical and popular interest.

The four Hoke Moseley books fall into a traditional genre—the police thriller. Unlike Willeford's other earlier attempt at strict genre fiction, *The Hombre from Sonora,* his distinct style, voice, outlook, and humor everywhere inform the Hoke Moseley novels. Though still violent and offbeat, the Hoke Moseley books have a more comforting and accessible moral system than many of Willeford's earlier works. While Willeford sometimes links detective Hoke Moseley to the criminals through shared traits and gestures, the moral economy of the books is clear: Hoke is the good guy and the killers are the bad guys, and some form of justice prevails in the end. This difference underscores the unconventionality of the earlier works and also suggests why he had trouble reaching a larger audience. While the Hoke Moseley books are anything but generic, they fit into a recognized category, which helped Willeford's agent to find a publisher. The success of these works broadened Willeford's audience and won him increasingly more lucrative book contracts.

The greatest strength of *Miami Blues* lies in its characterizations of Freddy Frenger, a psychopath who kills a charlatan Hare Krishna, who dies of shock after Frenger breaks his finger, and Hoke Moseley, a skilled but impoverished police detective. By sheer accident, or novelistic coincidence, Freddy takes up with Susan Waggoner, the Krishna's sister, and attempts to lead a normal domestic life, where he goes off to work everyday to rob pickpockets at a shopping mall. Both funny and poignant, the novel ends with Hoke strengthening his ties to his new female partner, Ellita Sanchez, a conclusion that seems to promise a second book in a series.

Miami Blues sold well, and the critical reception was even stronger. The review in *The New Yorker* on 23 April 1984 provided high praise: "it is a measure of [Willeford's] extraordinarily winning ways that we feel an almost equal sympathy for the monster, the not so stupid [Susan], . . . and the lonely, half-defeated Hoke. Mr. Willeford never puts a foot wrong, and this is truly an entertainment to relish." Writing in the *Village Voice* on 16 July 1985, Geoffrey O'Brien called *Miami Blues* "the best book on the mystery racks these days" and wrote that it had "a tempo so relentless words practically fly off the page." In 1986 the book was optioned by the actor Fred Ward, who eventually played Hoke in the movie of the novel, which was made after Willeford's death.

With newfound success and the promise to his publisher of another Hoke Moseley novel, Willeford got cold feet with the worry that commercial motivations would mar his art. Flying in the face of the detective series convention, Willeford wrote "Grimhaven," a Hoke Moseley novel that never saw print, though parts of it were reworked and incorporated into *Sideswipe*. A brutal and grim book, "Grimhaven" again reveals Willeford at odds with commercial expectations; the novel could never have satisfied the broader audience that Willeford had found with *Miami Blues*. In "Grimhaven" Hoke has left the police department and taken a job at his father's hardware store in an attempt to "simplify" his life. This plan is interrupted when his former wife places the care of their two daughters, Sue Ellen and Aileen, in his hands. Hoke strangles his daughters,

Dust jacket for a collection of stories published shortly after Willeford's death in 1988

robs his father, and chases after his former wife and her new beau. The novel ends with a happy Hoke Moseley: his arrest is imminent and the electric chair certain, but he will first enjoy several simple, quiet years on death row.

Willeford's agent convinced his client to discard "Grimhaven" and begin anew. In *New Hope for the Dead* Willeford pursued a new avenue by making Hoke's daughters strong and endearing characters who played important roles in the remainder of the series. *New Hope for the Dead* is the most episodic of the Hoke Moseley novels, with Hoke, Bill Henderson, and Ellita Sanchez solving a handful of cold cases. The main mystery focuses on the apparent suicide of a young junkie named Jerry Hickey, who is largely the victim of a broken and unloving family. Against the fabric of the crimes in the novel, Willeford adds depth to the story by juxtaposing the Hickey family with Hoke's and Ellita's. Willeford uses a similar technique in *Sideswipe*, in which he subtly compares Hoke's family to the makeshift criminal family assembled by Troy Louden.

Without his previous resistance, Willeford quickly launched into writing the next Hoke Moseley, *Sideswipe*, and the book came easily because it took parts from two previously written works, "Grimhaven" and *No Experience Necessary.* While Freddy of *Miami Blues* owes something to his prototype, Freddy Lenard of *No Experience Necessary,* Troy Louden and the criminal events of *Sideswipe* almost perfectly parallel the 1962 novel. Troy, a self-described "criminal psychopath," befriends an old man, Stanley Sinkiewicz, falsely accused of child molestation. After both men are released from jail, Stanley joins Troy in Miami, together with Troy's disfigured girlfriend, Dale Forrest, and a painter, James Frietas-Smith. The four eventually hold up a grocery store, with bloody results. Alternate chapters follow Hoke Moseley as he recovers from a breakdown and recuperates on Singer Island. Eventually the two stories meet when Ellita, in her ninth month of pregnancy, is shot trying to stop the heist, and Hoke returns to duty to wrap up the investigation and the novel.

As part of his hard and hearty lifestyle, Willeford smoked heavily, ate richly, and drank with relish, all of which doubtless played some part in his declining health. By 1986 he had had three heart attacks, but he continued to press on with his writing. Willeford completed a draft of the next Hoke Moseley book, *The Way We Die Now,* in early 1987, and in March, his agent negotiated a $225,000 advance. Willeford's reaction: "Holy shit! For that?" Willeford suffered from congestive heart disease, and his condition worsened in the next several months. Two of his earlier books, *High Priest* and *Wild Wives,* had been republished in 1987 by RE/Search Publications, and in the same year three other earlier titles–*Pick-Up, Cockfighter,* and *The Burnt Orange Heresy*–were brought out by Black Lizard Books, the series partly responsible for the American rediscovery of noir and hard-boiled writing. Willeford finally saw his audience and earnings grow, and recognition for his earlier works, but only at the end of his life. He continued to write until his death, from a heart attack, on 27 March 1988, just a few weeks after *The Way We Die Now* was published.

As in *New Hope,* several plots intertwine in *The Way We Die Now,* but the latter novel is more tightly woven and sharply paced. The main plot revolves around Hoke's investigating the disappearance of Haitian farm workers. In its focus on poverty and the exploitation of immigrant workers in the backwaters of Florida, *The Way We Die Now* contains the greatest social commentary of the series, without marring the action. The novel ends with Hoke promoted to lieutenant and the head of internal affairs, but time did not permit Willeford to continue his adventures.

Interest in Willeford continued to grow following his death. Dennis McMillan, a friend and publisher, published a collection of stories, *Everybody's Metamorphosis,* in 1988. *The Shark-Infested Custard* was published in 1993, and it together with the four Hoke Moseley novels were republished in paperback, with introductions by prominent crime writers such as Donald Westlake, Elmore Leonard, and Lawrence Block. Willeford's Black Lizard reprints also found a greater audience when that line was bought from Creative Arts Book Company by Vintage Books (a division of Random House), though the latter did not include *The Black Mass of Brother Springer* in its lineup. In 1997 a biography and appreciation of Willeford by Don Herron, Willeford's friend and fan, was also published by Dennis McMillan. Also in 1997, *Pick-Up* was published in the canon-setting Library of America's *Crime Novels: American Noir of the 1950s.* In 2000 McMillan published *Writing and Other Blood Sports,* which collects several essays by Willeford, including a version of his master's thesis that was initially published by McMillan in 1987 under the title *New Forms of Ugly: The Immobilized Hero in Modern Fiction.* Willeford's works have been published in Denmark, Finland, France, Germany, Italy, Japan, the Netherlands, Portugal, and Sweden.

Interview:

Sybil Steinberg, ed., "PW Interviews Charles Willeford," *Publishers Weekly,* 231 (6 February 1987): 78–79.

Biography:

Don Herron, *Willeford* (Tucson: Dennis McMillan, 1997).

References:

Julie Sloan Brannon, "The Rules are Different Here: South Florida Noir and the Grotesque," in *Crime Fiction and Film in the Sunshine State: Florida Noir,* edited by Steve Glassman and Maurice O'Sullivan (Bowling Green, Ohio: Bowling Green State University Popular Press, 1997), pp. 47–64;

Richard Gehr, "The Pope of Psychopulp: Charles Ray Willeford's Unholy Rites," *Village Voice Literary Supplement,* 72 (March 1989): 30–31;

Woody Haut, *Pulp Culture: Hardboiled Fiction and the Cold War* (New York & London: Serpent's Tail Books, 1995);

Fred Shaw, "The Burnt Orange Heretic," *Tropic* (magazine of the *Miami Herald*), 5 (19 December 1971): 30–34.

Papers:

Charles Willeford's papers are housed in the Special Collections of Boston University and in the Bienes Center for the Literary Arts, Broward County Library, Ft. Lauderdale, Florida.

Cornell Woolrich

(4 December 1903 – 25 September 1968)

David Schmid
State University of New York at Buffalo

BOOKS: *Cover Charge* (New York: Boni & Liveright, 1926);

Children of the Ritz (New York: Boni & Liveright, 1927);

Times Square (New York: Liveright, 1929);

A Young Man's Heart (New York: Mason, 1930);

The Time of Her Life (New York: Liveright, 1931);

Manhattan Love Song (New York: Godwin, 1932);

The Bride Wore Black (New York: Simon & Schuster, 1940; London: Hale, 1942); republished as *Beware the Lady* (New York: Pyramid, 1953);

The Black Curtain (New York: Simon & Schuster, 1941);

Black Alibi (New York: Simon & Schuster, 1942; London: Hale, 1951);

Phantom Lady, as William Irish (Philadelphia & New York: Lippincott, 1942; London: Hale, 1945);

The Black Angel (Garden City, N.Y.: Doubleday, 1943; London: Hale, 1949);

I Wouldn't Be in Your Shoes, as Irish (Philadelphia & New York: Lippincott, 1943; London: Hutchinson, 1946); republished as *And So To Death* (New York: Spivak, 1944); republished as *Nightmare* (New York: Reader's Choice, 1950);

Deadline at Dawn, as Irish (Philadelphia & New York: Lippincott, 1944; London: Hutchinson, 1947);

After-Dinner Story, as Irish (New York & Philadelphia: Lippincott, 1944; London: Hutchinson, 1947); republished as *Six Times Death* (New York: Popular Library, 1948);

The Black Path of Fear (Garden City, N.Y.: Doubleday, 1944);

If I Should Die Before I Wake, as Irish (New York: Avon, 1945);

Night Has a Thousand Eyes, as George Hopley (New York: Farrar & Rinehart, 1945; London: Penguin, 1949);

The Dancing Detective, as Irish (Philadelphia & New York: Lippincott, 1946; London: Hutchinson, 1948);

Borrowed Crimes, as Irish (New York: Avon, 1946);

Waltz into Darkness, as Irish (Philadelphia & New York: Lippincott, 1947; London: Hutchinson, 1948);

Dead Man Blues, as Irish (Philadelphia: Lippincott, 1947; London: Hutchinson, 1950);

Rendezvous in Black (New York: Rinehart, 1948; London: Hodder & Stoughton, 1950);

I Married a Dead Man, as Irish (Philadelphia: Lippincott, 1948; London: Hutchinson, 1950);

The Blue Ribbon, as Irish (Philadelphia: Lippincott, 1949; London: Hutchinson, 1951); republished as *Dilemma of the Dead Lady* (Hasbrouck Heights, N.J.: Graphic, 1950);

Fright, as Hopley (New York: Rinehart, 1950; London: Foulsham, 1952);

Savage Bride (New York: Fawcett Gold Medal, 1950);

Somebody on the Phone, as Irish (Philadelphia: Lippincott, 1950); republished as *The Night I Died* (London: Hutchinson, 1951); republished as *Deadly Night Call* (Hasbrouck Heights, N.J.: Graphic, 1951);

Six Nights of Mystery: Tales of Suspense and Intrigue, as Irish (New York: Popular Library, 1950);

You'll Never See Me Again, as Irish (New York: Dell, 1951);

Strangler's Serenade, as Irish (New York: Rinehart, 1951; London: Hale, 1952);

Eyes That Watch You, as Irish (New York: Rinehart, 1952);

Bluebeard's Seventh Wife, as Irish (New York: Popular Library, 1952);

Nightmare (New York: Dodd, Mead, 1956);

Violence (New York: Dodd, Mead, 1958);

Hotel Room (New York: Random House, 1958);

Death Is My Dancing Partner (New York: Pyramid, 1959);

Beyond the Night (New York: Avon, 1959);

The Doom Stone (New York: Avon, 1960);

The Ten Faces of Cornell Woolrich (New York: Simon & Schuster, 1965; London: Boardman, 1966);

The Dark Side of Love (New York: Walker, 1965);

Nightwebs: A Collection of Stories by Cornell Woolrich, edited by Francis M. Nevins Jr. (New York: Harper & Row, 1971; London: Gollancz, 1973);

Angels of Darkness (New York: Mysterious Press, 1978);

The Fantastic Stories of Cornell Woolrich (Carbondale: Southern Illinois University Press, 1981);

Cornell Woolrich

Rear Window and Four Short Novels (New York: Ballantine, 1984);
Darkness at Dawn: Early Suspense Classics (Carbondale: Southern Illinois University Press, 1985; London: Xanadu, 1989);
Vampire's Honeymoon (New York: Carroll & Graf, 1985);
Blind Date with Death (New York: Carroll & Graf, 1985);
Into the Night, by Woolrich and Lawrence Block (New York: Mysterious Press, 1987; London: Simon & Schuster, 1988);
Blues of a Lifetime (Bowling Green, Ohio: Bowling Green State University Popular Press, 1991).
Collection: *The Best of William Irish* (Philadelphia: Lippincott, 1960).

PRODUCED SCRIPTS: *Last Night,* based on Woolrich's "The Red Tide," radio, CBS, 15 June 1943;
The White Rose Murders, based on Woolrich's "The Death Rose," radio, CBS, 6 July 1943.

OTHER: "The Release," in *With Malice Toward All,* edited by Robert L. Fish (New York: Putnam, 1968), pp. 117–124.

Although his work is not as widely read as that of Dashiell Hammett and Raymond Chandler, Cornell Woolrich almost single-handedly invented the noir genre—creating a dark, psychologically menacing world—and producing some of the greatest works of pure suspense fiction ever written. Woolrich's work is hard-boiled in the sense that he rejects the tidy resolutions that characterize the deductive type of detective fiction. A Woolrich novel typically finishes with mystery and terror still actively present rather than conveniently dissolved. He also goes further than his better-known contemporaries in his evocation of the source, extent, and consequences of evil. Although the evil that Hammett's and Chandler's heroes fight has a specific manifestation that they can identify and, to some extent, neutralize, Woolrich's heroes, on the other hand, are victimized and damaged by forces of evil that are often abstract, nameless, and all-powerful. Woolrich's plots and techniques reflect a worldview far more bleak and pessimistic than that of most other hard-boiled writers, and his ability to evoke the dilemmas of those unfortunates caught in his world is his most signal contribution to the genre.

Cornell George Hopley-Woolrich was born in New York City on 4 December 1903, the son of Genaro Hopley-Woolrich, a civil engineer and Claire Attalie Tarler. After his parents divorced, Woolrich spent his early years with his father traveling through Mexico and Central America, before moving back to New York City at the age of twelve to live with his mother. He attended Columbia University intermittently between 1921 and 1926 but never graduated. During these years Woolrich developed the habits of chain-smoking and drinking that later undermined his heath. He also began to write, and he left Columbia to dedicate himself to writing full time when his first novel, *Cover Charge,* was published by Boni and Liveright in March 1926. Between 1926 and 1932 Woolrich published six novels, most of which can be classified as Jazz Age fiction in the manner of F. Scott Fitzgerald, who greatly influenced Woolrich.

Although Woolrich's second novel, *Children of the Ritz* (1927), was dismissed by many reviewers as a sellout, with the critic for *The New York Times* accusing him of "tempering the winds of his talent to the bleating lambs of public taste," it succeeded in attracting the attention of Hollywood. Under contract with First National to make a film version of *Children of the Ritz,* Woolrich moved to Los Angeles in 1928. (The movie was produced in 1929, but Woolrich did not receive a screen credit.) While in Hollywood, Woolrich met and married Violet Virginia (Gloria) Blackton, the daughter of a movie executive, in 1930. The couple separated after three months, and Woolrich subsequently moved back to New York. In 1932, after the family home was sold, Woolrich and his mother took an apartment together in Mahattan at the Hotel Marseilles, on Broadway at 103rd street, where he lived for the next twenty-five years, until his mother's death in 1957.

In his autobiography, *Blues of a Lifetime* (1991), Woolrich disparages all of his work written before the mid 1930s: "It would have been a lot better if everything I'd done until then had been written in invisible ink and the reagent had been thrown away." Certainly, there is little indication in his first novels of the master of suspense that Woolrich became, and there is a sharp break between the last novel of his early period, *Manhattan Love Song* (1932), and his first hard-boiled story, "Death Sits in the Dentist's Chair," published in *Detective Fiction Weekly* in August 1934 and later collected in *Somebody on the Phone* (1950).

In a letter to A. L. Furman, the editor of *The Third Mystery Companion* (1945), Woolrich described his move from romance to mystery fiction in terms of "killing them

dead now instead of marrying them off," but the reason for the switch was probably more profound, for there is little doubt that Woolrich was better suited temperamentally to the mystery genre. In *Blues of a Lifetime* Woolrich describes an epiphany he had as a young boy while living with his father in Mexico:

> one night when I was eleven and, huddling over my own knees, looked up at the low-hanging stars of the Valley of Anahuac, and knew I would surely die finally, or something worse. I had that trapped feeling, like some sort of poor insect that you've put inside a downturned glass, and it tries to climb up the sides, and it can't, and it can't, and it can't.

The realization of his inevitable death underlies everything most distinctive and powerful in Woolrich's hard-boiled fiction. The genre gave Woolrich the opportunity to explore the trapped feeling he mentions by creating an entire gallery of individuals who, in one way or another, feel themselves to be trapped or victimized by forces beyond their control. Rarely do Woolrich's characters find a way out of the trap, but perhaps through portraying their dilemmas, Woolrich found a way to cope with his own fear of death and the shadow that fear cast over his life.

"Death Sits in the Dentist's Chair" marked the beginning of a six-year apprenticeship Woolrich served in the pulp magazines before publishing his first crime novel in 1940. During this time he published more than one hundred stories of various types in dozens of pulps. These stories allowed Woolrich to develop the themes and methods that characterize the work of his mature period. "Death Sits in the Dentist's Chair" is typical of Woolrich's work in that he does not use a detective (Woolrich rarely uses a detective in his work), creates an unusual murder method (cyanide contained in a tooth filling), and brings his story to nail-biting suspenseful climax. The most characteristic feature of the story, though, is Woolrich's vivid evocation of Depression-era New York City. The Great Depression forms the backdrop to many Woolrich stories, but his interest in the Depression is not as social history. Rather, the Depression appeals to Woolrich because it demonstrates his pessimistic view of the universe, his belief that life victimizes people, leaving them with few or no options at all.

Of all the stories that Woolrich published between 1934 and 1940, perhaps the one that best demonstrates the directions that Woolrich's work took in his novels is "Three O'Clock," published in *Detective Fiction Weekly* in October 1938. (The story was included in three of his collections: *I Wouldn't Be in Your Shoes, Nightmare,* and *Rear Window and Four Short Novels.*) For Woolrich, the thought that one eventually has to die was terrifying enough, but the most acute form of this terror was to know in advance the exact moment and nature of one's death, a theme Woolrich fully explored in his 1945 novel *Night Has a Thousand Eyes*. In "Three O'Clock" Paul Stapp, the protagonist, has convinced himself that his wife is being unfaithful to him, and so he decides to blow both his wife and their house to bits by planting a bomb in the basement. Unfortunately for him, on the day he sets the bomb, his house is burgled, and the burglars leave Stapp tied up in the basement, unaware that they have left him next to the bomb that will explode in ninety minutes.

Woolrich takes the reader through Stapp's agonizing ninety-minute journey, analyzing in almost unbearable detail the torture Stapp goes through as he watches his life tick away:

> Then he'd hold out as long as he could with his eyes down, but when he couldn't stand it any more and would have to raise them to see if he was right, it had gained *two* minutes. Then he'd have a bad fit of hysterics, in which he called on God, and even on his long-dead mother, to help him, and couldn't see straight through the tears. Then he'd pull himself together again, in a measure, and start the self-deception over again. "It's only about thirty seconds now since I last looked . . . Now it's about a minute . . . " (But was it? But was it?) And so on, mounting slowly to another climax of terror and abysmal collapse.

"Three O'Clock" is distinguished from a run-of-the-mill suspense story by Woolrich's determination to make his reader feel sorry for Stapp, despite his being a thoroughly unlikeable man willing to murder his innocent wife on the flimsiest of evidence. He clearly believes that Stapp, no matter his culpability, deserves pity because of the terrible nature of his death. Woolrich's willingness to create less than sympathetic protagonists and then to insist on the reader's identification with those protagonists is one of the most original features of his work.

The reader's identification with a flawed protagonist is also a feature of Woolrich's first crime novel, *The Bride Wore Black* (1940), the first of six novels in what came to be called the Black series, because they all had the word *black* in their titles and reveal Woolrich's doom-laden view of the world. *The Bride Wore Black* begins with its protagonist, Julie Killeen, embarking on a mission. Julie systematically insinuates herself into the lives of several men and then kills them. For most of the book the reader is given no understanding of any rationale for Julie's behavior, and so to the suspense of wondering whether she will succeed in killing her next victim is added the suspense concerning her motivation. Eventually, the reader learns that Julie's

husband was killed on the steps of the church where they had just been married and that she has dedicated her life to tracking down and killing the drunk driver and his four friends whom she holds responsible for his death. The twist in the tale comes when Julie learns not only that her four victims were innocent but also that she had the opportunity to kill her husband's actual murderer without even knowing it.

Despite Julie's being a cold-blooded multiple murderer, Woolrich succeeds in making his reader feel sympathy for her. This approach demonstrates a common Woolrichian theme, namely that those who are inspired to commit terrible acts out of love are forgiven much. Readers are made to see how traumatic her husband's murder was for Julie, and although her actions cannot be condoned, they can be understood. That Julie Killeen exacts such extreme vengeance because of her love for her husband demonstrates the power that Woolrich attributes to love, and the terrible things human beings do for love is a theme Woolrich returned to regularly.

The Bride Wore Black was generally well received. The critic for the *Hartford Courant* described it as "the most exciting experience in crime fiction this reviewer has had in some considerable time." The *Baltimore Sun* reviewer added that "If it doesn't freeze your blood, then you are immune to literary chills." Perhaps the most perceptive review appeared in *The Saturday Review of Literature* of 7 December 1940, in which it was described as "An opus out of the ordinary, highly emotional and suspenseful, with a surprise finish that turns somersaults in amazingly agile, if implausible fashion. Odd."

Woolrich followed up his success with the publication of the second novel in the Black series, *The Black Curtain* (1941). In this novel Woolrich explores a situation that he had already used in his short fiction, in which the protagonist returns to consciousness after a blackout–caused by drugs, hypnosis, or amnesia– and gradually becomes convinced that he did something horrible he cannot remember. The novel begins with Frank Townsend being hit by a piece of a falling building while walking down a street. The blow restores his memory of his true identity, though he now has no memory of the previous three years. Townsend then begins the process of piecing his life back together. Townsend's recent past starts catching up with him when he is hunted down by unknown individuals. He decides he must find a way to lift the "black curtain" and go back into the life he had recently been living to find out what he did and how to clear his name. Although Woolrich never reveals what precipitated Townsend's original memory loss, he shows how Townsend both rediscovers and puts to rest his temporary identity so that his life can return to normal. Woolrich does a brilliant job of creating a genuinely paranoid atmosphere in the first part of the book, and readers are made to feel intensely Townsend's bewilderment at the disorienting return of his true identity and then his fear at being hunted for no apparent reason.

Although reviewers admired the suspenseful power of the book, some were less satisfied with its implausible resolution. For example, Kay Irvin in *The New York Times Book Review* of 15 June 1941 described the novel as "melodrama, unashamedly fantastic. It attempts no connection with probabilities. It never does completely bridge the gulf of those three years. But it is tense in mood and exciting in event. Once you start it, you'll want to follow all its thrills through to the end."

Throughout Woolrich's career praise for his achievements was accompanied by criticism of his sometimes outrageously sloppy plotting. Although his stories abound in incredible implausibilities, contradictions, and coincidences, it is possible to somewhat justify this sloppiness by noting how it contributes to the strength and persuasiveness of his pessimistic vision of the world. In his *Cornell Woolrich: First You Dream, Then You Die* (1988), biographer Francis M. Nevins Jr. uses the concept of "functional illogic" to refer to Woolrich's "ability, in his best work, to make coincidence and contradiction and implausibility functional to his black vision." A realist would not have had Julie Killeen pursue her quest for justice for years with no visible means of support, as though her rage were enough to feed her, but in this way Woolrich is able to communicate the ferocious power of the love that drives Killeen. Similarly, a careful writer would never ask a reader to believe that Frank Townsend had not a single scrap of identification on him either when his amnesia began or when it ended, but in this way Woolrich implicitly suggests that in a senseless universe senseless things happen and that tidy or plausible explanations are not always available. Again and again, throughout his career, he was willing to sacrifice every other aspect of his writing, including plausibility, to what he once called "the line of suspense."

The ostensible subject of Woolrich's next novel, *Black Alibi* (1942), is the mystery of who has been killing young women in the fictional South American city of Ciudad Real, but the development and resolution of this mystery is clearly secondary to the maintenance of suspense. Apart from the rather implausible plot, the book is essentially a collection of episodes describing young women being stalked—either by a killer jaguar or by a human killer masquerading as a jaguar—through lonely city streets, through a pitch-black city park, or through a cemetery closed for the night.

Woolrich in 1927

Each of these set pieces is a masterpiece of Woolrichian suspense, in which he gives the reader a vivid sense of the terror these young women feel:

> She was running along the winding graveled path now. She thought she'd never run so fast in her life before. A spray of gravel flew up, like sea foam, at the tiny prows of her plunging feet. Through the tunnel of trees. Down into the declivity of the meadow of the dead. Up again on the other side. Past the box hedge behind which her father and the great-aunts lay. A sob of helpless appeal winged back toward it as she darted by: *"Papacito!"* The whimper of a frightened thing, tossed over her shoulder as she fled head-long past the place. To someone who once could have protected her—but couldn't now any more.

Once these set pieces have been completed, the revelation of who was actually responsible for the murders is almost anticlimactic. *Black Alibi* demonstrates better than any other Woolrich novel how serious the author was about putting suspense first and everything else second.

All of Woolrich's crime novels up through *Black Alibi* had been edited by the most respected mystery fiction editor of the time, Lee Wright. The next work Woolrich showed Wright after *Black Alibi* was the story that was serialized under the title of "Phantom Alibi" and eventually published as the novel *Phantom Lady* (1942). Despite his success and the regard he had attained as a crime-fiction writer, Woolrich often had a low opinion of his own work and was hypersensitive about criticism. As Nevins records in his biography, when Wright suggested changing one paragraph in the *Phantom Lady* manuscript, Woolrich reacted by saying, "I knew you wouldn't like it, I knew it wasn't good enough for you!" and took the manuscript to another publisher. It was the last time Woolrich ever submitted any of his work to Wright. *Phantom Lady* is a significant book because it marked the first appearance of William Irish, a pseudonym that Woolrich used with increasing frequency in years to come. Opinions differ as to whether he started using the pseudonym because of his move to another publisher, or because he did not want to glut the market by releasing too many titles under his own name.

In *Phantom Lady,* easily his most popular book to that time, Woolrich again depicts the terror of knowing the exact moment and nature of one's death, but the main reason for the popularity of the novel was doubtless Woolrich's inventive use of the race-against-the-clock plotline. Although there had been dozens of books written about the race against time to save a man from the death penalty, Woolrich succeeded in giving this theme a particularly intense treatment. In the opening chapter, even though Woolrich's protagonist, Scott Henderson, has not yet been charged with any crime, the chapter title reads, "The Hundred and Fiftieth Day Before the Execution." By using this heading, Woolrich heightens the emotional intensity and suspense of the work by letting his reader know that the race against time and death has already begun. The forces of destruction are already arrayed against Henderson without his even being aware of them, an essential feature of Woolrich's fictional universe.

Once Henderson has been wrongly sentenced to death for the murder of his wife, his only hope is to find the woman he was with on the evening of his wife's murder. Obviously unable to pursue inquiries himself, Henderson is helped by his lover, Carol Richman, whose search for the "phantom lady" becomes the focus of suspense in the book, especially when none of the witnesses she initially questions can remember seeing Henderson with anyone on the night of the murder. As the day of the execution draws nearer, the suspense rises to a fever pitch until the climactic scene in which Carol narrowly avoids death at the hands of the real murderer. Although Henderson eventually escapes execution, the reader does not feel a profound sense of relief at the end of the novel because Woolrich refuses to draw a comforting moral from the events. The reader is left with the uneasy sense that Henderson's escape is only temporary and that all must submit to death sooner or later.

The character and plight of Carol Richman in *Phantom Lady* are suggestive of Woolrich's views of women as well as the justice system. Although Woolrich unquestionably has a dim view of some women–Henderson's wife, for example, is practically blamed for her own death because she leads her murderer on–and often makes his

female characters ridiculously forgiving of their imperfect husbands, many of Woolrich's women are portrayed as brave, intelligent, and resourceful. Although Carol shows a conventional feminine sense of loyalty and devotion to Henderson, she proves to be both courageous and cunning in getting information out of recalcitrant witnesses. That an ingenue such as Carol should have to go to such lengths in order to exonerate Henderson, however, is indicative of Woolrich's lack of faith in the institutions of justice, which in his work are generally presented as uncaring and punitive. While some cops can be persuaded to be sympathetic and helpful, there are just as many cops who can be brutally sadistic. Although Woolrich's female characters are often forced into their quests for justice by force of circumstance, they rarely rely for help on the conventionally defined forces of law and order, who are often completely absent from Woolrich's work.

Although justice is ultimately served in *Phantom Lady,* the search for and attainment of justice in Woolrich's work is often morally ambiguous, as is the case in his next novel, *The Black Angel* (1943). On the surface there are many similarities between *The Black Angel* and its predecessor. Like Carol Richman, Alberta Murray is involved in a race against time to free her husband, Kirk, who has been wrongly convicted of the murder of his lover, Mia Mercer. In order to exonerate Kirk, Alberta must acquaint herself with several possible suspects and somehow determine whether or not they killed Mercer. In the process Woolrich takes Alberta through more of the lowlife of the city than even Carol Richman experienced, and along the way Alberta is forced into some extraordinary situations, including working as a drug pusher and becoming a mobster's fiancée.

The differences between Alberta Murray's and Carol Richman's reactions to their predicaments, though, are significant, for Alberta's decisions are at times far more morally questionable than Carol's. At one point, for example, Alberta persuades a possible suspect, Marty, that she knows who killed Mia Mercer and where the murderer can be found. When the grieving Marty acts on Alberta's tip and is tricked into believing that he has killed Mercer's murderer, Alberta is convinced of his innocence and removes him from her list of suspects. Alberta subsequently feels no responsibility for Marty's death when he, believing his act of vengeance has left him nothing for which to live, commits suicide; in fact she convinces herself that she did him a favor by giving him something for which to die. The reader, however, may not be so easily convinced, and Woolrich clearly wants his audience to consider the methods sometimes used in the search for justice.

The sense of ambiguity in *The Black Angel* is heightened by a further point of contrast with *Phantom Lady.* Whereas Scott Henderson is fundamentally a decent person, Kirk, the motivation behind Alberta's search for justice, is obviously a heel and unworthy of his wife. When Alberta falls in love with Ladd Mason, a suspect who turns out to be the real murderer, it underlines the point that Kirk, even though technically innocent, lacks the qualities that attract Alberta to Mason. Although the book ostensibly finishes happily, with Kirk free and reunited with his loyal wife, Alberta now sees her husband's limitations. Moreover, Alberta is still in love with Mason, despite the fact that he killed Mercer. Once again, although Woolrich successfully generates and then releases suspense in *The Black Angel,* the appearance of justice that he creates at the end of the novel is much less harmonious and comforting than it appears at first glance. Woolrich's ambivalence about the possibility of achieving justice is a fundamental part of his pessimistic worldview.

By the mid 1940s Woolrich was at the top of his profession. He was regarded as the premier suspense writer in the country, and he was making good money both from his fiction and the sale of radio and movie rights. It appears, however, that Woolrich did not derive much enjoyment from his success or his reputation. In a letter he wrote for inclusion in *The Mystery Companion* (1943), Woolrich described his life in distinctly muted tones: "I have never had any other job or occupation than a writer . . . so you can see that very little has happened to me. This makes for a very uneventful life, with nothing to report. One day is exactly like another." Although Woolrich was naturally self-effacing to the point of being uncommunicative, his description of his life at this time is actually quite accurate. Woolrich and his mother had then been sharing an apartment in the Hotel Marseilles for eleven years, and the nature of their relationship is perhaps indirectly indicated by the dedication to *Phantom Lady:* "To Apartment 605, Hotel M——/ in unmitigated thankfulness / (at not being in it anymore)." In the last year of his life, Woolrich explained that this dedication referred to his attempt to break away from his mother in 1942, albeit only by moving to another room in the same hotel. Woolrich's attempt at independence lasted only three weeks, and then his mother persuaded him to come back. Woolrich later said he never regretted his decision to return. There is no doubt that Woolrich's mother jealously hoarded her son's attention, and made it difficult for him to form any other attachments during her lifetime. Whatever the peculiarities of his personal life, Woolrich continued to write and publish work at a phenomenal rate. In 1944 alone he published two new novels and a collection of short stories. *Deadline at Dawn* (1944), the second novel to appear under the name of Irish, is noteworthy for being the most optimistic of his major novels. It is also, along with *Phantom Lady,* Woolrich's best-known treatment of the "race against time" theme. All the events are compressed into just a few hours, and Woolrich emphasizes his theme by using clock

Cover for a 1938 pulp featuring a Woolrich story in which the shoes a man throws at a yowling cat link him to a murder

faces in the place of conventional chapter headings, so from the beginning the reader is focused on the relentless clock that the young protagonists—Bricky Coleman, a dancer for hire in a New York City dance hall, and Quinn Williams, one of her customers—are struggling against. Incredibly, both happen to be from the same small town in Iowa, a coincidence that changes a chance meeting of strangers into a friendship. Usually Woolrich's wild coincidences serve to destroy people, but here the coincidence is entirely benevolent.

Bricky and Quinn decide to help each other escape from the city, which Bricky consistently anthropomorphizes as evil: "I don't know fancy language; I only know there's an intelligence of its own hanging over this place, coming up from it. It's mean and bad and evil, and when you breathe too much of it, for too long, it gets under your skin, it gets into you—and you're sunk, the city's got you." In order to escape the influence of the city, they have to first undo the burglary that the desperate Quinn had committed earlier that night. When they go to return the money Quinn stole, however, they find the owner of the house shot dead. As Quinn had previously done some maintenance work in the house and had been seen outside the house earlier that night, he knows he will be a prime suspect. Bricky and Quinn now have to find the murderer in order to clear Quinn's name. Not only do they have no leads but also from the moment that they discover the body at 2 A.M., they have precisely four hours to find the murderer, because the bus for Iowa leaves at 6 A.M. Of course, they could catch the bus leaving the next day, but Woolrich brilliantly conveys how emotionally essential it is for this couple to catch this particular bus and none other.

Having set up the conditions for a suspenseful race against time, Woolrich sends his young protagonists out onto the streets of the quiet city to find a murderer. They not only succeed in tracking down the murderers, but they also set them up at the scene of the crime for the police to discover. With this feat accomplished, the lovers just manage to make the Iowa bus, and the result is one of the few authentically happy endings in the Woolrich canon: "Her eyes dropped blissfully closed. 'We're going home,' she thought drowsily. 'Me and the boy next door, we're going home at last.'" Although some reviewers objected to the excessive pathos and implausibility—the reviewer for *The New Yorker* of 26 February 1944 noted that "some staggering coincidences make a good deal of this hard to believe"—Elizabeth Bullock in the 12 March *Book Week* summed up the strengths of *Deadline at Dawn:* "These people are real, the mood of danger in the night is real and you will care very much what happens."

Woolrich's next book was *After-Dinner Story* (1944), a collection of previously published pulp short stories. This collection included what, thanks to Alfred Hitchcock's movie adaptation, would become Woolrich's most famous story, "Rear Window," a work originally published as "It Had to be Murder" in *Dime Detective* (February 1942). These soon followed the fifth entry in the Black series, *The Black Path of Fear* (1944), a novel in which Woolrich returns to his characteristic association of love with death, fear, and loss. Woolrich's protagonist, Scotty, begins the book in Havana with his lover, Eve Roman. They have just fled from Miami where Scotty worked as a driver for Eve's husband, Ed, a gangster and drug smuggler. On their first night in Havana, Eve is stabbed to death in a crowded bar, apparently with the same knife that Scotty had just bought in a tourist bazaar. Not surprisingly, the police arrest Scotty for the murder, and after Scotty escapes from the police, he must prove that he is innocent by finding the real murderer. The suspense of the situation is heightened by Scotty's unfamiliarity with the strange land, which makes his situation even more dangerous and difficult.

Woolrich effectively communicates Scotty's fear and paranoia as he skulks around Havana, anticipating arrest at any moment. To his paranoia is added the grief that Scotty feels at Eve's death. Even though Eve is murdered just a few pages into the book, Woolrich makes his reader feel how much the couple were in love, and how deeply the loss of Eve affects Scotty. Eventually, the situation is resolved but with Woolrichian ambivalence. Unable to prove that Ed ordered the killing, Scotty manages to escape to Miami and kills Ed and his henchman. Scotty then returns to Havana to give himself up, but the local police chief, secretly approving of what he has done, refuses to arrest him. Even though the book ends positively in the sense that Scotty avenges Eve's death, it is clear that Scotty has little left to live for without Eve.

Scotty in *The Black Path of Fear* is at least able to exercise some control over his own fate. For Woolrich, a far more terrifying situation is to know that one is a plaything in the hands of destiny, with absolutely no ability to determine the course of one's life. Of all his major novels, *Night Has a Thousand Eyes,* published in 1945 under the new pseudonym George Hopley, is the one most dominated by death and fate, and in it Woolrich returns to depict again the terror that is generated by knowing the exact moment and nature of one's death. The novel revolves around a prophecy made by a simple-minded recluse named Jeremiah Tompkins, who apparently has psychic powers. Tompkins predicts that millionaire Harlan Reid will die in the jaws of a lion at the stroke of midnight in three weeks. Despite the manifest absurdity of the prediction, a series of events seems to confirm Tompkins's other predictions, and the possibility is raised that Tompkins really is psychic.

Reid responds to this situation by torturing himself with the thought that he has no control over the outcome of his life, and Woolrich lovingly examines every bit of the gradually increasing emotional torment Reid undergoes as the moment of his death approaches. For example, Woolrich describes Reid watching the sun go down for the last time:

> It must have slipped through his grasp, little by little, escaping irretrievably downward; for they saw him convulsively expand and contract his hands several times, the way a clumsy person would fumble trying to hold onto a slippery ball that has just been thrown to him. Then they came together, palm to palm, over emptiness, and he let them drop, frustrated. "Good-bye," he sobbed softly. "Good-bye."

Reid's daughter, Jean, tries much harder than her father to maintain her belief in the existence of free will and the individual's ability to control one's life, but eventually she gives in to despair and tries to commit suicide. She is saved by policeman Tom Shawn.

Although Shawn and his colleagues eventually debunk many of Tompkins's "prophecies," Woolrich clearly does not want the reader to think of Tompkins as a fraud. The author comes up with an ingenious

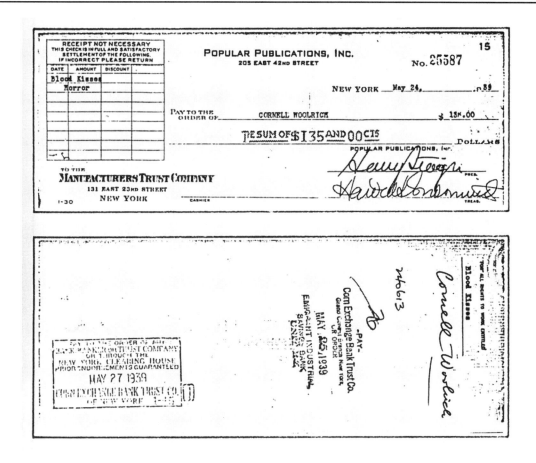

Front and back of a check for one of Woolrich's pulp stories (from Francis M. Nevins Jr., Cornell Woolrich: First You Dream, Then You Die, *1988)*

way of making Tompkins's prophecy about Reid's death come true, and so it remains possible that Tompkins really is psychic. At the same time, Woolrich wants his reader to consider the possibility that Reid's belief in the prophecy was just as responsible for his death as the prophecy itself. Despite the bleakness of the book, *Night Has a Thousand Eyes* actually ends quite positively. Shawn and Jean fall in love, and Shawn finds a way to make the dominance of fate work in his favor: "He felt as though there was no longer any need to worry about what happened to him, whether for good or ill; that was all taken care of from now on, that was all out of his hands." In spite of Shawn seeing the positive side of fate, Woolrich ultimately does not wholly dispel the sense of doom and fatalism that dominates the book.

Woolrich may have viewed *Night Has a Thousand Eyes* as an attempt to introduce himself to an audience other than mystery readers. *The New York Times,* instead of giving the book to regular mystery columnist Isaac Anderson, commissioned a separate review from novelist James MacBride, who wrote in the 2 December 1945 issue that "the author, a literary craftsman who is equally at home on several levels, tells his tale with a gusto Karloff might

envy: the pace never slackens, from the superb cinematic opening . . . to the gelid pay-off." MacBride concluded that "the present reader can only advise you to leave the night-light burning if you insist on finishing this one in bed." Despite such a positive review, *Night Has a Thousand Eyes* was not a commercial success.

In 1946, for the first time since 1940, Woolrich did not publish a new novel. Under the William Irish byline, he did publish two collections of previously published short stories, *The Dancing Detective* and *Borrowed Crimes.* Financially, the year proved to be the best of Woolrich's career. The combined proceeds from the sale of short fiction and novels and radio, television, and movie rights totaled $61,000, a healthy amount for the post–World War II period.

In 1947 Woolrich published his third novel as Irish, *Waltz into Darkness.* In some respects this novel marked a departure for Woolrich, and his publisher, Lippincott, billed it as his first mainstream novel. It was far more a love story than it was a crime story, and rather than use a contemporary setting, Woolrich set the novel in nineteenth-century New Orleans. In other respects, however, it was a typical Woolrichian study of the profound power of

TEL. ACADEMY 4-2100

ABSOLUTELY FIREPROOF

SUBWAY EXPRESS
STATION

Hotel Marseilles

LOCATED BETWEEN CENTRAL PARK & RIVERSIDE DRIVE

ON BROADWAY AT 103RD STREET

New York

Feb. 2nd, 1947

Dear Mr. Van Doren;

That was the kindest letter you sent me. I don't get very many, & at times it's like writing in a vacuum, you don't know if anyone likes it or not. (For that matter, you don't even know if anyone reads it or not.) So it did me a lot of good; made me want to write again for awhile.

However, I was foolish enough, because you had mentioned seeing The Black Angel picture, to go out & see it myself. I was so ashamed

Letter from Woolrich to Columbia University professor Mark Van Doren (from Francis M. Nevins Jr,
Cornell Woolrich: First You Dream, Then You Die, 1988)

when I came out of there. I was even
too ashamed to answer your letter immediately, it took me 2 or 3 days
to get over it. All I could keep
thinking of in the dark was: "Is
that what I wasted my whole life
at?" You see I'm going to be 40 next
Dec., & it sort of hits you cumul-
atively around then.

I don't like to look back at the
Columbia days for that reason; the
gap between expectation & accomplishment is too wide. Well, it's too late
now, so I'm stuck with it.

Thank you, anyway, very much.
I'm the one who's grateful to you.
You seem to please so easily.
                    Sincerely,
                    Cornell Woolrich

love, what evils it can endure, and how eventually it is overwhelmed by the terrible inevitability of death. The book begins with middle-aged bachelor Louis Durand about to meet his new bride for the first time, having previously only corresponded with her. The woman who gets off the steamboat and presents herself as Julia Russell is an impostor, Bonny Castle, who took Russell's place after she and an accomplice murdered Russell on the boat.

Woolrich presents a series of suspicious circumstances that make Durand wonder whether the woman he married really is Julia Russell, but his suspicions are not strong enough to stop Castle from looting all of his bank accounts and running away. Durand is shocked by the loss of life savings, but he is far more devastated by the betrayal of his love for Castle and his realization that her love for him was only a pretense. Determined to seek revenge, Durand and Russell's sister hire a private detective to find Castle. However, in one of those freak coincidences that occur frequently in Woolrich's work, Durand finds her first. Although he had intended to kill her, Castle is able to seduce Durand into changing his mind, because despite everything she has done, Durand still loves her. For Woolrich, Durand's largely unrequited love for Castle is to be admired, even though it is ruinous for both of them.

Durand and Castle start living and traveling together, and things go well until the private detective, Downs, catches up with them. To prevent Castle's arrest, Durand murders Downs, and from that point on in addition to being tortured by his desperate love for someone who does not care for him, Durand must live the life of a fugitive. Durand is shocked and disgusted by what he has done and even more so by Castle's casual reaction to the situation. As Durand's money runs out, Castle becomes increasingly frustrated, culminating in her poisoning of her husband. Even though Durand knows that Castle is responsible for his fast approaching death, he still professes his undying love for Castle—a declaration that finally makes Castle realize that she does indeed love Durand.

Most reviewers treated *Waltz into Darkness* as nothing more than a quirky variation on the mystery novel genre. The critic for *Kirkus Reviews* of 1 December 1946 called it "an ironical study of crime" while F. A. Boyl in the 1 February 1947 *Library Journal* compared it to the historical crime novels of Marie Belloc Lowndes. Will Cuppy of the *New York Herald-Tribune* dismissed it in a February 1947 review as a "whodunit thrown slightly out of gear in response to a popular trend and loaded with period color for good measure. It's still a characteristic Irish riddle." Such responses illustrate how difficult it was for Woolrich to break out of the mystery genre.

Woolrich was coming to the end of the most creative period in his career, and 1948 proved to be a watershed year. It began with the publication of *Rendezvous in Black*

(1948), the sixth and last entry in the Black series. In this novel Woolrich returns to the theme of the first book in the series, *The Bride Wore Black,* namely the avenging of a lover's death. Just as Julie Killeen spends years tracking down and killing the men she holds responsible for her husband's death, so Johnny Marr spends years punishing the men whom he holds responsible for the death of his fiancée, Dorothy. Woolrich, though, takes the well-worn theme of a lover's revenge one step further in *Rendezvous in Black,* for while Johnny, unlike Julie, has correctly identified the group of men responsible for the crime—one of the group did throw the bottle out of the plane that fell to the ground and killed Dorothy—he decides not to kill the men themselves but to murder the women attached to these men so that they can feel the same measure of loss and despair that he has experienced. Johnny's crimes are even more despicable than Julie's because he knows those he kills are innocent.

Woolrich wrings the maximum of suspense out of Johnny's systematic and implacable hunting of his victims, and in the end, as in *The Bride Wore Black,* he succeeds in making the reader feel sympathy for the murderer despite his horrible acts. For Woolrich, no matter what the crime, passionate love is a mitigating circumstance, and he clearly wants his reader to both understand and forgive Johnny, to some extent at least, because his crimes proceeded out of his profound love for Dorothy. As Johnny is finally hunted down and killed by the police, Woolrich unhesitatingly portrays him as a victim of the inevitably transitory and partial nature of love: "And what is love anyway but the unattainable, the reaching out toward an illusion? He died with her name on his lips."

Throughout his career, Woolrich was obsessed with analyzing both the power and the powerlessness of love. On the one hand, love was powerful in that it positively transformed lives and also inspired people to do terrible things. On the other hand, love was powerless in the face of blind chance and death. Woolrich's novels are full of characters whose happiness in love is destroyed by a freak accident or who are deeply in love but for whatever reason can derive no joy from the feeling. In his last major novel, *I Married a Dead Man* (1948), Woolrich crafts one of his most thought-provoking analyses of the duality of love and comes up with one of his most ingenious premises. The book begins with a young woman, Helen, traveling out to the West Coast by train. About to give birth, she has been abandoned by the father of the child and has little money and fewer prospects. On the train she meets and befriends Patrice Hazzard, a rich young woman who is also pregnant and about to meet the family of her husband, Hugh, for the first time. Just as Patrice lets Helen try on her wedding ring, the train crashes and Patrice and her husband are killed. Helen survives, and because she is wearing Patrice's wedding ring, Hugh Hazzard's family, never hav-

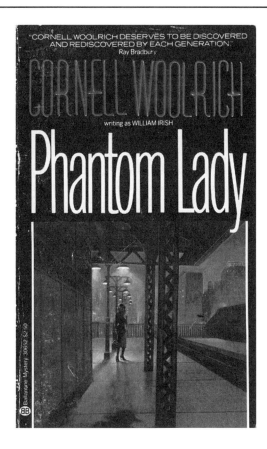

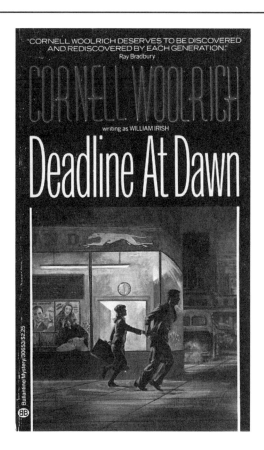

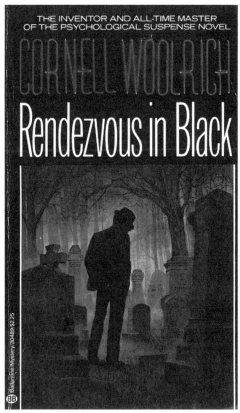

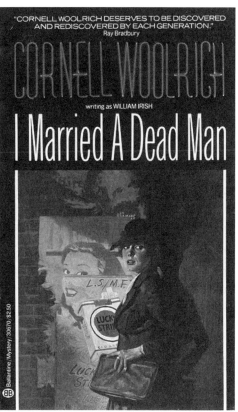

Covers for paperback reprints of four of Woolrich's novels

ing seen a photo of the real Patrice, assume that Helen is Patrice and welcome her into their family.

Helen is initially racked by guilt but persuades herself that she is only acting for her child. At first, things go well, although Woolrich has some brilliantly suspenseful scenes in which Helen nearly gives herself away by not knowing things that the real Patrice would know. When Hugh's brother, Bill, and Helen begin to fall in love, it seems as if Helen will have a blissfully happy and prosperous life. At this point of the story, of course, Woolrich begins to twist her fortune. Helen starts to receive a series of anonymous letters from someone who clearly knows about her deception. The author of the letters turns out to be Helen's former lover, Steve Georgesson, who blackmails Helen into marrying him so that he may one day inherit the Hazzard fortune.

When Helen, having decided that she must kill Georgesson, goes to his apartment, she finds him already shot dead. At this point, Helen is discovered by Bill, who immediately suspects her of having killed Georgesson; Helen in turn suspects Bill of having committed the murder. Even though both escape being charged with the crime, their eventual fate is in some sense worse than being punished for Georgesson's death: Helen and Bill each love and suspect the other, to the extent that they can never enjoy their love or their freedom. Never did Woolrich write a more powerful example of how even the strongest love is powerless in the face of the dark forces that rule his universe. Helen's despairing words at the end of the book are representative of the fate of many of Woolrich's most unforgettable characters: "We've lost. That's all I know. We've lost. And now the game is through."

I Married a Dead Man shows that Woolrich was still at the height of his powers fourteen years after his first crime story and eight years after his first crime novel. Although some continued to criticize him for his implausible plots, the critic for *The New York Times Book Review* (26 September 1948) gave the book a glowing notice: "Mr. Irish has given another happy demonstration, as in 'The Phantom Lady,' that a good, dramatic idea can exist for its own sake in a book, and not just as a come-on to the big movie money. This work of his is a fascinating experience." Woolrich's stature in the field is indicated by the Mystery Writers of America awarding him an Edgar for lifetime achievement in 1948. In retrospect, the presentation of the award on 19 April 1949 marks the end of the most active phase of Woolrich's career. Thereafter he produced little new work and was largely content to live off reprint and movie rights of his work. He augmented his income by passing off old stories as new by changing their titles repeatedly. What new work Woolrich did produce in the last stage of his career lacks the hard edge of his earlier fiction.

The one exception to this rule is *Fright* (1950), the second and last novel Woolrich published under the pseudonym Hopley, in which he explores how fear and paranoia destroy a man's life and the lives of those around him. Prescott Marshall, on the eve of his marriage to Marjorie, gets drunk and spends the night with a prostitute, Leona, who subsequently blackmails him. Driven to distraction by Leona's incessant demands for money, Marshall snaps and kills her. Desperate to get out of New York City, Marshall seizes the offer of a job in a small town in the Midwest. He cannot escape his guilt and paranoia, however, and Woolrich shows how these emotions drive Marshall to commit terrible acts. He compounds his original crime by killing a man whom he mistakenly believes to be spying on him, and he even forces the long-suffering Marjorie to have an abortion because he feels that a baby would inhibit his ability to leave town quickly. Eventually, Marjorie reaches her limit and returns to New York and her family.

Even though Marshall is thoroughly despicable, Woolrich once again succeeds in making readers empathize with him because of the hell in which he lives. Racked with terrifying imaginings about what Marjorie is telling everyone, Marshall follows her to New York City to try to persuade her to join him in San Francisco. He confesses all to Marjorie, who panics and tries to leave, precipitating Marshall's killing her and then himself. Woolrich paints a comprehensive picture of the carnage caused by guilt and fear, but he does not stop there. The twist in the tale is that Leona, the prostitute who was blackmailing Marshall, was not dead at all, but only unconscious. The fact that Marshall's paranoia and everything that sprang from it was completely unnecessary shows Woolrich's belief in the cruel jokes that fate can play on powerless mortals.

Strangler's Serenade (1951) is a more representative example of Woolrich's late work. The protagonist, "Champ" Prescott, is a New York City homicide detective, who visits a small Massachusetts island to recuperate from a gunshot wound. His arrival coincides with a series of murders that Prescott takes it on himself to solve. Despite containing a few episodes of genuine suspense, the majority of the book is a workaday mystery that is far more conventional and less interesting than Woolrich's major novels. *Strangler's Serenade* marks the start of a long fallow period for Woolrich. Between 1953 and 1958 Woolrich's total output of new work adds up to precisely one story, "The Black Bargain." However, thanks to reprint rights and television success, Woolrich's income remained fairly healthy. He also continued to produce work that was described as new—short-story collections such as *Nightmare* (1956) and *Violence* (1958) that in fact were made up of recycled versions of stories he had written for pulp magazines decades before.

The paucity of new work during this period can perhaps be attributed to developments in Woolrich's personal life. In spring 1956 his mother suffered a massive heart attack and from then on was unable to leave her room. Always emotionally shackled to his mother, Woolrich became even more of a prisoner in the Hotel Marseilles, where he drank more than he wrote. Claire Attalie Tarler died in October 1957 at the age of eighty-three, with Woolrich at her bedside.

At first, there were signs that Woolrich was going to assert his independence in the wake of his mother's death. He moved from the Hotel Marseilles to the Hotel Franconia, and although his aunt, Estelle Tarler Garcia, moved in with him and tried to take the place of his mother, he soon sent her packing. Woolrich also traveled, something he had never been able to do when his mother was alive, and his trip to Canada in 1961 was his first trip outside of New York City in thirty years. Moreover, he tried to explore new directions in his writing, for his most ambitious work of this period, *Hotel Room* (1958), was a collection of largely noncrime stories set in a New York City hotel at different periods of its history from its early fashionable years to its last days. In writing the book, which was dedicated to his mother, Woolrich drew upon his years of experience in hotel living. The collection, however, failed to win Woolrich a larger, nonmystery audience.

Woolrich became even more reclusive in his last years. After having cataract surgery in 1965, he moved into his last hotel, the upscale Sheraton-Russell, where he drank heavily, saw practically no one, and spent his evenings sitting in the hotel lobby, staring out at the life on the streets. The extent of his decline was vividly illustrated in January 1968 when, having failed to seek medical treatment for a gangrenous leg, he had to have it amputated. After a stroke rendered him unconscious, he died on 25 September 1968, less than two and a half months short of his sixty-fifth birthday. Like so many of his fictional characters, Woolrich died practically alone, with few friends or family to mourn him. He left his estate of some $850,000 to Columbia University to establish a scholarship fund for journalism in his mother's memory.

Cornell Woolrich is one of the major figures in the noir tradition of crime fiction. His best work is marked by the intense evocation of the lives of those who are victimized by the forces beyond their control and by his passionate belief that his readers should sympathize with those victims. On a scrap of paper found among his personal belongings after his death, Woolrich wrote, "I was only trying to cheat death. I was only trying to surmount for a little while the darkness that all my life I surely knew was going to come rolling in on me some day and obliterate me." Despite his pessimism about the inevitable triumph of death, Woolrich's enduring work has enabled him to cheat death in a way he perhaps never anticipated.

Bibliography:
Bjarne Nielsen, *Bibliography in Black: The Works of Cornell Woolrich* (Copenhagen: Antikvariat Pinkerton, 1988).

Biography:
Francis M. Nevins Jr., *Cornell Woolrich: First You Dream, Then You Die* (New York: Mysterious Press, 1988).

References:
Gary Indiana, "Man in the Shadows: The Strange Case of Cornell Woolrich," *Village Voice Literary Supplement,* 74 (May 1989): 26–27;

Francis Lacassin, "Cornell Woolrich: Psychologist, Poet, Painter, Moralist," *Clues: A Journal of Detection,* 8 (Fall–Winter 1987): 41–78;

A. Robert Lee, "The View from the Rear Window: The Fiction of Cornell Woolrich," in *Twentieth-Century Suspense: The Thriller Comes of Age,* edited by Clive Bloom (New York: St. Martin's Press, 1990), pp. 174–188;

Barry M. Malzberg and Don Yates, "The Last Days of Cornell Woolrich," in *The Big Book of Noir,* edited by Ed Gorman, Lee Server, and Martin H. Greenberg (New York: Carroll & Graff, 1998), pp. 163–164;

David Reid and Jayne L. Walker, "Strange Pursuit: Cornell Woolrich and the Abandoned City of the Forties," in *Shades of Noir: A Reader,* edited by Joan Copjec (London: Verso, 1993), pp. 57–96;

Stephen Soitos, "Some Psychological Themes in One of Cornell Woolrich's Novels," *Clues: A Journal of Detection,* 7 (Spring–Summer 1986): 75–87.

Checklist of Further Reading

Babener, Liahna K. "California Babylon," *Clues,* 1 (Fall 1980): 77–89.

Baker, Robert A., and Michael T. Nietzel. *Private Eyes: One Hundred and One Knights. A Survey of American Detective Fiction, 1922–1984.* Bowling Green, Ohio: Bowling Green State University Popular Press, 1985.

Bargainnier, Earl F., ed. *Comic Crime.* Bowling Green, Ohio: Bowling Green State University Popular Press, 1987.

Barzun, Jacques, and Wendell Hertig Taylor. *A Catalogue of Crime,* revised and enlarged edition. New York: Harper & Row, 1989.

Benstock, Bernard, ed. *Art in Crime Writing: Essays on Detective Fiction.* New York: St. Martin's Press, 1983.

Bloom, Harold, ed. *Classic Crime and Suspense Writers.* New York: Chelsea House, 1994.

Cawelti, John G. *Adventure, Mystery, and Romance: Formula Stories as Art and Popular Culture.* Chicago & London: University of Chicago Press, 1976.

Collins, Michael. "Expanding the *Roman Noir:* Ross Macdonald's Legacy to Mystery/Detective Authors," *South Dakota Review,* 24 (Spring 1986): 121–130.

Crowther, Bruce. *Film Noir: Reflections in a Dark Mirror.* New York: Ungar, 1989.

Docherty, Brian, ed. *American Crime Fiction: Studies in the Genre.* New York: St. Martin's Press, 1988.

Emck, Katy, "Feminist Detectives and the Challenges of Hardboiledness," *Canadian Review of Comparative Literature,* 21, no. 3 (1994): 383–398.

Geherin, David. *The American Private Eye: The Image in Fiction.* New York: Ungar, 1985.

Geherin. *Sons of Sam Spade: The Private-Eye Novel in the Seventies: Robert B. Parker, Roger L. Simon, Andrew Bergman.* New York: Ungar, 1982.

Goulart, Ron. *The Dime Detectives.* New York: Mysterious Press, 1988.

Gray, Piers. "On Linearity," *Critical Quarterly,* 38, no. 3 (1996): 122–133.

Gruber, Frank. *The Pulp Jungle.* Los Angeles: Sherbourne, 1967.

Guetti, James. "Aggressive Reading: Detective Fiction and Realistic Narrative," *Raritan,* 2 (Summer 1982): 128–138.

Gurko, Leo. *Heroes, Highbrows and the Popular Mind.* Indianapolis: Bobbs-Merrill, 1953.

Hagemann, E. R., ed. *A Comprehensive Index to Black Mask, 1920–1951.* Bowling Green, Ohio: Bowling Green State University Popular Press, 1982.

Hamilton, Cynthia S. *Western and Hard-Boiled Detective Fiction in America: From High Noon to Midnight.* Iowa City: University of Iowa Press, 1987.

Henderson, Leslie, ed. *Twentieth Century Crime and Mystery Writers,* third edition. Chicago: St. James, 1991.

Hoppenstand, Gary, ed. *The Dime Novel Detective.* Bowling Green, Ohio: Bowling Green University Popular Press, 1982.

Hubin, Allen J. *Crime Fiction, 1749–1980: A Comprehensive Bibliography.* New York: Garland, 1984.

Hubin. *1981–1985 Supplement to Crime Fiction, 1749–1980.* New York: Garland, 1988.

Irons, Glenwood. *Feminism in Women's Detective Fiction.* Toronto & Buffalo: University of Toronto Press, 1995.

Kittredge, William, and Steven M. Krauser. *The Great American Detective: 15 Stories Starring America's Most Celebrated Private Eyes.* New York: New American Library, 1978.

Klein, Kathleen Gregory. *The Woman Detective: Gender and Genre,* second edition. Urbana: University of Illinois Press, 1995.

Klein, ed. *Great Women Mystery Writers: Classic to Contemporary.* Westport, Conn.: Greenwood Press, 1994.

Klein, ed. *Women Times Three: Writers, Detectives, Readers.* Bowling Green, Ohio: Bowling Green State University Popular Press, 1995.

Klein, Marcus. *Easterns, Westerns, and Private Eyes: American Matters, 1870–1900.* Madison: University of Wisconsin Press, 1994.

Landrum, Larry N., Pat Browne, and Ray B. Browne, eds. *Dimensions of Detective Fiction.* Bowling Green, Ohio: Bowling Green State University Popular Press, 1976.

Madden, David, ed. *Tough Guy Writers of the Thirties.* Carbondale: Southern Illinois University Press, 1968.

Magill, Frank N., ed. *Critical Survey of Mystery and Detective Fiction: Authors.* Pasadena, Cal.: Salem Press, 1988.

Margolies, Edward. *Which Way Did He Go? The Private Eye in Dashiell Hammett, Raymond Chandler, Chester Himes and Ross Macdonald.* New York: Holmes & Meier, 1982.

Most, Glenn W., and William W. Stowe, eds. *The Poetics of Murder: Detective Fiction and Literary Theory.* New York: Harcourt Brace Jovanovich, 1983.

Munt, Sally R. *Murder by the Book? Feminism and the Crime Novel.* London & New York: Routledge, 1994.

Niebuhr, Gary Warren. *A Reader's Guide to the Private Eye Novel.* New York: G. K. Hall, 1993.

Nolan, William F. *The Black Mask Boys: Masters in the Hard-Boiled School of Detective Fiction.* New York: Morrow, 1985.

Nye, Russell B. *The Unembarrassed Muse: The Popular Arts in America.* New York: Dial, 1970.

Nyman, Jopi. *Hard-Boiled Fiction and Dark Romanticism.* New York: Peter Lang, 1998.

Panek, Leroy Lad. *Probable Cause: Crime Fiction in America.* Bowling Green, Ohio: Bowling Green State University Popular Press, 1990.

Porter, Dennis. *The Pursuit of Crime: Art and Ideology in Detective Fiction.* New Haven: Yale University Press, 1981.

Reddy, Maureen T. *Sisters in Crime: Feminism and the Crime Novel.* New York: Continuum, 1988.

Reilly, John M., ed. *Twentieth-Century Crime and Mystery Writers.* New York: St. Martin's Press, 1980.

Ruehlmann, William. *Saint with a Gun: The Unlawful American Private Eye.* New York: New York University Press, 1974.

Ruhm, Herbert, ed., *The Hard-Boiled Detective: Stories from* Black Mask *Magazine, 1920–1951.* New York: Vintage, 1977.

Shaw, Joseph T., ed. *The Hard-Boiled Omnibus: Early Stories from* Black Mask. New York: Simon & Shuster, 1949.

Silver, Alain, and Elizabeth Ward, eds. *Film Noir: An Encyclopedic Reference to the American Style,* third edition, revised and enlarged. Woodstock, N.Y.: Overlook Press, 1992.

Skinner, Robert E. *The Hard-Boiled Explicator: A Guide to the Study of Dashiell Hammett, Raymond Chandler and Ross Macdonald.* London: Scarecrow Press, 1985.

Skinner. *The New Hard-Boiled Dicks: Heroes for a New Urban Mythology,* second edition, revised and expanded. San Bernardino, Cal.: Brownstone Books, 1995.

Stephens, Michael L. *Film Noir: A Comprehensive, Illustrated Reference to Movies, Terms and Persons.* Jefferson, N.C.: McFarland, 1995.

Symons, Julian. *Mortal Consequences: A History: From the Detective Story to the Crime Novel.* New York: Harper & Row, 1972.

Van Dover, J. Kenneth. *Murder in the Millions: Erle Stanley Gardner, Mickey Spillane, Ian Fleming.* New York: Ungar, 1984.

Walker, Ronald G., and June M. Frazer, eds. *The Cunning Craft: Original Essays on Detective Fiction and Contemporary Literary Theory.* Macomb: Western Illinois University Press, 1990.

Walton, Priscilla L., and Manina Jones. *Detective Agency: Women Rewriting the Hard-Boiled Tradition.* Berkeley: University of California Press, 1999.

Wilt, David E. *Hardboiled in Hollywood.* Bowling Green, Ohio: Bowling Green State University Popular Press, 1991.

Winks, Robin W., and Maureen Corrigan, eds. *Mystery and Suspense Writers: The Literature of Crime, Detection, and Espionage,* 2 volumes. New York: Scribner, 1998.

Contributors

George Parker Anderson . . . . *University of South Carolina*

Charles Brower . . . . *Cayce, South Carolina*

John L. Cobbs . . . . *Kutztown University*

Tim Dayton . . . . *Kansas State University*

Marcia B. Dinneen . . . . *Bridgewater State College*

Chuck Etheridge . . . . *McMurry University*

Anita G. Gorman . . . . *Slippery Rock University*

Dean G. Hall . . . . *Kansas State University*

Katherine Harper . . . . *Bowling Green State University*

Jennifer Hynes . . . . *Beaumont, Texas*

Douglas Ivison . . . . *Université de Montréal*

Carol McGinnis Kay . . . . *University of South Carolina*

Peter Kenney . . . . *Birmingham, Alabama*

Martin Kich . . . . *Wright State University*

Sue Laslie Kimball . . . . *Methodist College*

Marvin S. Lachman . . . . *Santa Fe, New Mexico*

Douglas Levin . . . . *Portland, Oregon*

Rebecca E. Martin . . . . *Pace University*

Robert F. Moss . . . . *University of South Carolina*

Katherine M. Restaino . . . . *Fairleigh Dickinson University*

Bobbie Robinson . . . . *Abraham Baldwin College*

David Schmid . . . . *State University of New York at Buffalo*

Jeff Siegel . . . . *Dallas, Texas*

Karl L. Stenger . . . . *University of South Carolina, Aiken*

Frederick William Zackel . . . . *Bowling Green State University*

Cumulative Index

Dictionary of Literary Biography, Volumes 1-226
Dictionary of Literary Biography Yearbook, 1980-1999
Dictionary of Literary Biography Documentary Series, Volumes 1-19

Cumulative Index

DLB before number: *Dictionary of Literary Biography,* Volumes 1-226
Y before number: *Dictionary of Literary Biography Yearbook,* 1980-1999
DS before number: *Dictionary of Literary Biography Documentary Series,* Volumes 1-19

A

Aakjær, Jeppe 1866-1930 . . . . .DLB-214

Abbey, Edwin Austin 1852-1911 . . . . . . .DLB-188

Abbey, Maj. J. R. 1894-1969 . . . . .DLB-201

Abbey Press DLB-49

The Abbey Theatre and Irish Drama,
    1900-1945 . . . . .DLB-10

Abbot, Willis J. 1863-1934. . . . . .DLB-29

Abbott, Jacob 1803-1879 . . . . .DLB-1

Abbott, Lee K. 1947- DLB-130

Abbott, Lyman 1835-1922. . . . . .DLB-79

Abbott, Robert S. 1868-1940 . . . . . . .DLB-29, 91

Abe Kōbō 1924-1993. . . . . .DLB-182

Abelard, Peter circa 1079-1142?. DLB-115, 208

Abelard-Schuman. DLB-46

Abell, Arunah S. 1806-1888. . . . . .DLB-43

Abell, Kjeld 1901-1961. . . . . .DLB-214

Abercrombie, Lascelles 1881-1938. . . . . . .DLB-19

Aberdeen University Press Limited DLB-106

Abish, Walter 1931- DLB-130

Ablesimov, Aleksandr Onisimovich
    1742-1783. .DLB-150

Abraham à Sancta Clara 1644-1709. . . . . .DLB-168

Abrahams, Peter 1919- DLB-117, 225

Abrams, M. H. 1912- DLB-67

Abrogans circa 790-800 . . . . .DLB-148

Abschatz, Hans Aßmann von
    1646-1699 . . . . .DLB-168

Abse, Dannie 1923- DLB-27

Abutsu-ni 1221-1283 . . . . .DLB-203

Academy Chicago Publishers DLB-46

Accius circa 170 B.C.-circa 80 B.C. DLB-211

Accrocca, Elio Filippo 1923- DLB-128

Ace Books DLB-46

Achebe, Chinua 1930- DLB-117

Achtenberg, Herbert 1938- DLB-124

Ackerman, Diane 1948- DLB-120

Ackroyd, Peter 1949- DLB-155

Acorn, Milton 1923-1986. . . . . .DLB-53

Acosta, Oscar Zeta 1935?- DLB-82

Acosta Torres, José 1925- DLB-209

Actors Theatre of Louisville DLB-7

Adair, Gilbert 1944- DLB-194

Adair, James 1709?-1783?. DLB-30

Adam, Graeme Mercer 1839-1912 . . . . . .DLB-99

Adam, Robert Borthwick II 1863-1940 . . .DLB-187

Adame, Leonard 1947- DLB-82

Adamic, Louis 1898-1951 . . . . .DLB-9

Adams, Abigail 1744-1818 . . . . .DLB-200

Adams, Alice 1926-1999 . . . . Y-86

Adams, Brooks 1848-1927. . . . . .DLB-47

Adams, Charles Francis, Jr. 1835-1915 . . . .DLB-47

Adams, Douglas 1952-. Y-83

Adams, Franklin P. 1881-1960. . . . . .DLB-29

Adams, Hannah 1755-1832 . . . . .DLB-200

Adams, Henry 1838-1918 . . . . DLB-12, 47, 189

Adams, Herbert Baxter 1850-1901 . . . . . . .DLB-47

Adams, J. S. and C. [publishing house] DLB-49

Adams, James Truslow
    1878-1949 . . . . DLB-17; DS-17

Adams, John 1735-1826. . . . . .DLB-31, 183

Adams, John 1735-1826 and
    Adams, Abigail 1744-1818. . . . . .DLB-183

Adams, John Quincy 1767-1848. . . . . .DLB-37

Adams, Léonie 1899-1988 . . . . .DLB-48

Adams, Levi 1802-1832. . . . . .DLB-99

Adams, Samuel 1722-1803. . . . . .DLB-31, 43

Adams, Sarah Fuller Flower
    1805-1848 . . . . .DLB-199

Adams, Thomas 1582 or 1583-1652 . . . . .DLB-151

Adams, William Taylor 1822-1897 . . . . . . .DLB-42

Adamson, Sir John 1867-1950 . . . . .DLB-98

Adcock, Arthur St. John 1864-1930. . . . . .DLB-135

Adcock, Betty 1938- DLB-105

Adcock, Fleur 1934- DLB-40

Addison, Joseph 1672-1719 . . . . .DLB-101

Ade, George 1866-1944. . . . . .DLB-11, 25

Adeler, Max (see Clark, Charles Heber)

Adonias Filho 1915-1990. . . . . .DLB-145

Advance Publishing Company DLB-49

Ady, Endre 1877-1919 . . . . .DLB-215

AE 1867-1935. . . . . .DLB-19

Ælfric circa 955-circa 1010. . . . . .DLB-146

Aeschines circa 390 B.C.-circa 320 B.C.
    . . . . .DLB-176

Aeschylus
    525-524 B.C.-456-455 B.C. DLB-176

Aesthetic Poetry (1873), by Walter Pater. . .DLB-35

After Dinner Opera Company. Y-92

Afro-American Literary Critics:
    An Introduction DLB-33

Agassiz, Elizabeth Cary 1822-1907 . . . . . .DLB-189

Agassiz, Jean Louis Rodolphe
    1807-1873 . . . . .DLB-1

Agee, James 1909-1955 . . . . DLB-2, 26, 152

The Agee Legacy: A Conference at the University
    of Tennessee at Knoxville. Y-89

Aguilera Malta, Demetrio 1909-1981 . . . .DLB-145

Ai 1947- DLB-120

Aichinger, Ilse 1921- DLB-85

Aidoo, Ama Ata 1942- DLB-117

Aiken, Conrad 1889-1973 . . . . DLB-9, 45, 102

Aiken, Joan 1924- DLB-161

Aikin, Lucy 1781-1864. . . . . .DLB-144, 163

Ainsworth, William Harrison 1805-1882 ..DLB-21

Aistis, Jonas 1904-1973 . . . . .DLB-220

Aitken, George A. 1860-1917. . . . . .DLB-149

Aitken, Robert [publishing house] DLB-49

Akenside, Mark 1721-1770. . . . . .DLB-109

Akins, Zoë 1886-1958 . . . . .DLB-26

Aksahov, Sergei Timofeevich
    1791-1859 . . . . .DLB-198

Akutagawa, Ryūnsuke 1892-1927 . . . . . . .DLB-180

Alabaster, William 1568-1640 . . . . .DLB-132

Alain de Lille circa 1116-1202/1203. . . . . .DLB-208

Alain-Fournier 1886-1914 . . . . .DLB-65

Alanus de Insulis (see Alain de Lille)

Alarcón, Francisco X. 1954- DLB-122

Alarcón, Justo S. 1930- DLB-209

Alba, Nanina 1915-1968 . . . . .DLB-41

Albee, Edward 1928- DLB-7

Albert the Great circa 1200-1280. . . . . . . .DLB-115

Albert, Octavia 1853-ca. 1889 . . . . .DLB-221

Alberti, Rafael 1902-1999 . . . . .DLB-108

Albertinus, Aegidius circa 1560-1620. . . . .DLB-164

Alcaeus born circa 620 B.C. DLB-176

Alcott, Bronson 1799-1888. . . . . .DLB-1, 223

Alcott, Louisa May
    1832-1888 . . . . DLB-1, 42, 79, 223; DS-14

Alcott, William Andrus 1798-1859 . . . . .DLB-1

Alcuin circa 732-804 . . . . .DLB-148

Alden, Beardsley and Company DLB-49

Alden, Henry Mills 1836-1919 . . . . .DLB-79

Alden, Isabella 1841-1930 . . . . DLB-42

Alden, John B. [publishing house] DLB-49

Aldington, Richard
1892-1962 . . . . DLB-20, 36, 100, 149

Aldis, Dorothy 1896-1966 . . . . DLB-22

Aldis, H. G. 1863-1919 . . . . DLB-184

Aldiss, Brian W. 1925- DLB-14

Aldrich, Thomas Bailey
1836-1907 . . . . DLB-42, 71, 74, 79

Alegría, Ciro 1909-1967 . . . . DLB-113

Alegría, Claribel 1924- DLB-145

Aleixandre, Vicente 1898-1984 . . . . DLB-108

Aleksandravičius, Jonas (see Aistis, Jonas)

Aleksandrov, Aleksandr Andreevich (see Durova,
Nadezhda Andreevna)

Aleramo, Sibilla 1876-1960 . . . . DLB-114

Alexander, Cecil Frances 1818-1895 . . . . . DLB-199

Alexander, Charles 1868-1923 . . . . DLB-91

Alexander, Charles Wesley
[publishing house] DLB-49

Alexander, James 1691-1756 . . . . DLB-24

Alexander, Lloyd 1924- DLB-52

Alexander, Sir William, Earl of Stirling
1577?-1640 . . . . DLB-121

Alexie, Sherman 1966- DLB-175, 206

Alexis, Willibald 1798-1871 . . . . DLB-133

Alfred, King 849-899 . . . . DLB-146

Alger, Horatio, Jr. 1832-1899 . . . . DLB-42

Algonquin Books of Chapel Hill DLB-46

Algren, Nelson 1909-1981 . . . . . DLB-9; Y-81, Y-82

Allan, Andrew 1907-1974 . . . . DLB-88

Allan, Ted 1916- DLB-68

Allbeury, Ted 1917- DLB-87

Alldritt, Keith 1935- DLB-14

Allen, Ethan 1738-1789 . . . . DLB-31

Allen, Frederick Lewis 1890-1954 . . . . . . DLB-137

Allen, Gay Wilson 1903-1995 . . . . . DLB-103; Y-95

Allen, George 1808-1876 . . . . DLB-59

Allen, George [publishing house] DLB-106

Allen, George, and Unwin Limited DLB-112

Allen, Grant 1848-1899 . . . . DLB-70, 92, 178

Allen, Henry W. 1912- Y-85

Allen, Hervey 1889-1949 . . . . DLB-9, 45

Allen, James 1739-1808 . . . . DLB-31

Allen, James Lane 1849-1925 . . . . DLB-71

Allen, Jay Presson 1922- DLB-26

Allen, John, and Company DLB-49

Allen, Paula Gunn 1939- DLB-175

Allen, Samuel W. 1917- DLB-41

Allen, Woody 1935- DLB-44

Allende, Isabel 1942- DLB-145

Alline, Henry 1748-1784 . . . . DLB-99

Allingham, Margery 1904-1966 . . . . DLB-77

Allingham, William 1824-1889 . . . . DLB-35

Allison, W. L. [publishing house] DLB-49

The *Alliterative Morte Arthure and the Stanzaic
Morte Arthur* circa 1350-1400 . . . . DLB-146

Allott, Kenneth 1912-1973 . . . . DLB-20

Allston, Washington 1779-1843 . . . . DLB-1

Almon, John [publishing house] DLB-154

Alonzo, Dámaso 1898-1990 . . . . DLB-108

Alsop, George 1636-post 1673 . . . . DLB-24

Alsop, Richard 1761-1815 . . . . DLB-37

Altemus, Henry, and Company DLB-49

Altenberg, Peter 1885-1919 . . . . DLB-81

Altolaguirre, Manuel 1905-1959 . . . . DLB-108

Aluko, T. M. 1918- DLB-117

Alurista 1947- DLB-82

Alvarez, A. 1929- DLB-14, 40

Alver, Betti 1906-1989 . . . . DLB-220

Amadi, Elechi 1934- DLB-117

Amado, Jorge 1912- DLB-113

Ambler, Eric 1909-1998 . . . . DLB-77

America: or, a Poem on the Settlement of the British Colonies
(1780?), by Timothy Dwight DLB-37

American Conservatory Theatre DLB-7

American Fiction and the 1930s DLB-9

American Humor: A Historical Survey
East and Northeast
South and Southwest
Midwest
West DLB-11

The American Library in Paris Y-93

American News Company DLB-49

The American Poets' Corner: The First
Three Years (1983-1986) Y-86

American Proletarian Culture: The 1930s . . . DS-11

American Publishing Company DLB-49

American Stationers' Company DLB-49

American Sunday-School Union DLB-49

American Temperance Union DLB-49

American Tract Society DLB-49

The American Trust for the
British Library Y-96

The American Writers Congress
(9-12 October 1981) Y-81

The American Writers Congress: A Report
on Continuing Business Y-81

Ames, Fisher 1758-1808 . . . . DLB-37

Ames, Mary Clemmer 1831-1884 . . . . DLB-23

Amiel, Henri-Frédéric 1821-1881 . . . . DLB-217

Amini, Johari M. 1935- DLB-41

Amis, Kingsley
1922-1995 . . . . . . DLB-15, 27, 100, 139, Y-96

Amis, Martin 1949- DLB-194

Ammianus Marcellinus
circa A.D. 330-A.D. 395 . . . . DLB-211

Ammons, A. R. 1926- DLB-5, 165

Amory, Thomas 1691?-1788 . . . . DLB-39

Anania, Michael 1939- DLB-193

Anaya, Rudolfo A. 1937- DLB-82, 206

Ancrene Riwle circa 1200-1225 . . . . DLB-146

Andersch, Alfred 1914-1980 . . . . DLB-69

Andersen, Benny 1929- DLB-214

Anderson, Alexander 1775-1870 . . . . DLB-188

Anderson, Frederick Irving 1877-1947 . . . DLB-202

Anderson, Margaret 1886-1973 . . . . DLB-4, 91

Anderson, Maxwell 1888-1959 . . . . DLB-7

Anderson, Patrick 1915-1979 . . . . DLB-68

Anderson, Paul Y. 1893-1938 . . . . DLB-29

Anderson, Poul 1926- DLB-8

Anderson, Robert 1750-1830 . . . . DLB-142

Anderson, Robert 1917- DLB-7

Anderson, Sherwood
1876-1941 . . . . DLB-4, 9, 86; DS-1

Andreae, Johann Valentin 1586-1654 . . . . DLB-164

Andreas Capellanus
flourished circa 1185 . . . . DLB-208

Andreas-Salomé, Lou 1861-1937 . . . . DLB-66

Andres, Stefan 1906-1970 . . . . DLB-69

Andreu, Blanca 1959- DLB-134

Andrewes, Lancelot 1555-1626 . . . . . DLB-151, 172

Andrews, Charles M. 1863-1943 . . . . DLB-17

Andrews, Miles Peter ?-1814 . . . . DLB-89

Andrian, Leopold von 1875-1951 . . . . DLB-81

Andrić, Ivo 1892-1975 . . . . DLB-147

Andrieux, Louis (see Aragon, Louis)

Andrus, Silas, and Son DLB-49

Andrzejewski, Jerzy 1909-1983 . . . . DLB-215

Angell, James Burrill 1829-1916 . . . . DLB-64

Angell, Roger 1920- DLB-171, 185

Angelou, Maya 1928- DLB-38

Anger, Jane flourished 1589 . . . . DLB-136

Angers, Félicité (see Conan, Laure)

Anglo-Norman Literature in the Development
of Middle English Literature DLB-146

The Anglo-Saxon Chronicle
circa 890-1154 . . . . DLB-146

The "Angry Young Men" DLB-15

Angus and Robertson (UK) Limited DLB-112

Anhalt, Edward 1914- DLB-26

Anners, Henry F. [publishing house] DLB-49

Annolied between 1077 and 1081 . . . . DLB-148

Annual Awards for *Dictionary of Literary Biography*
Editors and Contributors Y-98, Y-99

Anselm of Canterbury 1033-1109 . . . . . . DLB-115

Anstey, F. 1856-1934 . . . . DLB-141, 178

Anthony, Michael 1932- DLB-125

Anthony, Piers 1934- DLB-8

Anthony, Susanna 1726-1791 . . . . DLB-200

The Anthony Burgess Archive at the Harry Ransom
Humanities Research Center Y-98

Anthony Burgess's 99 Novels:
An Opinion Poll Y-84

Antin, David 1932- DLB-169

Antin, Mary 1881-1949 . . . . DLB-221; Y-84

Anton Ulrich, Duke of Brunswick-Lüneburg
1633-1714 . . . . DLB-168

Antschel, Paul (see Celan, Paul)

Anyidoho, Kofi 1947- DLB-157

Anzaldúa, Gloria 1942- DLB-122

Anzengruber, Ludwig 1839-1889 . . . . . . .DLB-129

Apess, William 1798-1839 . . . . .DLB-175

Apodaca, Rudy S. 1939- DLB-82

Apollonius Rhodius third century B.C.
. . . . .DLB-176

Apple, Max 1941- DLB-130

Appleton, D., and Company DLB-49

Appleton-Century-Crofts. DLB-46

Applewhite, James 1935- DLB-105

Applewood Books DLB-46

Apuleius circa A.D. 125-post A.D. 164 . . .DLB-211

Aquin, Hubert 1929-1977 . . . . .DLB-53

Aquinas, Thomas 1224 or
1225-1274 . . . . .DLB-115

Aragon, Louis 1897-1982. . . . . .DLB-72

Aralica, Ivan 1930- DLB-181

Aratus of Soli circa 315 B.C.-circa 239 B.C.
. . . . .DLB-176

Arbasino, Alberto 1930- DLB-196

Arbor House Publishing Company DLB-46

Arbuthnot, John 1667-1735 . . . . .DLB-101

Arcadia House DLB-46

Arce, Julio G. (see Ulica, Jorge)

Archer, William 1856-1924 . . . . .DLB-10

Archilochhus mid seventh century B.C.E.
. . . . .DLB-176

The Archpoet circa 1130?-? DLB-148

Archpriest Avvakum (Petrovich)
1620?-1682 . . . . .DLB-150

Arden, John 1930- DLB-13

Arden of Faversham .DLB-62

Ardis Publishers Y-89

Ardizzone, Edward 1900-1979 . . . . .DLB-160

Arellano, Juan Estevan 1947- DLB-122

The Arena Publishing Company DLB-49

Arena Stage DLB-7

Arenas, Reinaldo 1943-1990 . . . . .DLB-145

Arensberg, Ann 1937- Y-82

Arghezi, Tudor 1880-1967. . . . . .DLB-220

Arguedas, José María 1911-1969 . . . . . . .DLB-113

Argueta, Manlio 1936- DLB-145

Arias, Ron 1941- DLB-82

Arishima, Takeo 1878-1923. . . . . .DLB-180

Aristophanes
circa 446 B.C.-circa 386 B.C. DLB-176

Aristotle 384 B.C.-322 B.C. DLB-176

Ariyoshi Sawako 1931-1984 . . . . .DLB-182

Arland, Marcel 1899-1986. . . . . .DLB-72

Arlen, Michael 1895-1956 . . . . . . DLB-36, 77, 162

Armah, Ayi Kwei 1939- DLB-117

Armantrout, Rae 1947- DLB-193

Der arme Hartmann ?-after 1150. . . . . . .DLB-148

Armed Services Editions DLB-46

Armstrong, Martin Donisthorpe
1882-1974 . . . . .DLB-197

Armstrong, Richard 1903- DLB-160

Arndt, Ernst Moritz 1769-1860 . . . . .DLB-90

Arnim, Achim von 1781-1831 . . . . .DLB-90

Arnim, Bettina von 1785-1859. . . . . .DLB-90

Arnim, Elizabeth von (Countess Mary Annette
Beauchamp Russell) 1866-1941 . . . . .DLB-197

Arno Press. DLB-46

Arnold, Edwin 1832-1904 . . . . .DLB-35

Arnold, Edwin L. 1857-1935 . . . . .DLB-178

Arnold, Matthew 1822-1888 . . . . DLB-32, 57

Arnold, Thomas 1795-1842. . . . . .DLB-55

Arnold, Edward [publishing house]. DLB-112

Arnow, Harriette Simpson 1908-1986. . . . . .DLB-6

Arp, Bill (see Smith, Charles Henry)

Arpino, Giovanni 1927-1987 . . . . .DLB-177

Arreola, Juan José 1918- DLB-113

Arrian circa 89-circa 155 . . . . .DLB-176

Arrowsmith, J. W. [publishing house] DLB-106

The Art and Mystery of Publishing:
Interviews Y-97

Arthur, Timothy Shay
1809-1885 . . . . DLB-3, 42, 79; DS-13

The Arthurian Tradition and Its European
Context DLB-138

Artmann, H. C. 1921- DLB-85

Arvin, Newton 1900-1963 . . . . .DLB-103

As I See It, by Carolyn Cassady DLB-16

Asch, Nathan 1902-1964 . . . . .DLB-4, 28

Ash, John 1948- DLB-40

Ashbery, John 1927- DLB-5, 165; Y-81

Ashbridge, Elizabeth 1713-1755 . . . . .DLB-200

Ashburnham, Bertram Lord
1797-1878 . . . . .DLB-184

Ashendene Press DLB-112

Asher, Sandy 1942- Y-83

Ashton, Winifred (see Dane, Clemence)

Asimov, Isaac 1920-1992. . . . . DLB-8; Y-92

Askew, Anne circa 1521-1546 . . . . .DLB-136

Aspazija 1865-1943 . . . . .DLB-220

Asselin, Olivar 1874-1937 . . . . .DLB-92

The Association of American Publishers Y-99

Asturias, Miguel Angel 1899-1974. . . . . . .DLB-113

At End of Day: The Last George V. Higgins
Novel. Y-99

Atheneum Publishers. DLB-46

Atherton, Gertrude 1857-1948 . . . . . DLB-9, 78, 186

Athlone Press. DLB-112

Atkins, Josiah circa 1755-1781 . . . . .DLB-31

Atkins, Russell 1926- DLB-41

The Atlantic Monthly Press. DLB-46

Attaway, William 1911-1986 . . . . .DLB-76

Atwood, Margaret 1939- DLB-53

Aubert, Alvin 1930- DLB-41

Aubert de Gaspé, Phillipe-Ignace-François
1814-1841 . . . . .DLB-99

Aubert de Gaspé, Phillipe-Joseph
1786-1871 . . . . .DLB-99

Aubin, Napoléon 1812-1890 . . . . .DLB-99

Aubin, Penelope 1685-circa 1731. . . . . . . .DLB-39

Aubrey-Fletcher, Henry Lancelot (see Wade, Henry)

Auchincloss, Louis 1917- DLB-2; Y-80

Auden, W. H. 1907-1973 . . . . .DLB-10, 20

Audio Art in America: A Personal Memoir. . . Y-85

Audubon, John Woodhouse
1812-1862 . . . . .DLB-183

Auerbach, Berthold 1812-1882 . . . . .DLB-133

Auernheimer, Raoul 1876-1948. . . . . .DLB-81

Augier, Emile 1820-1889 . . . . .DLB-192

Augustine 354-430. . . . . .DLB-115

Aulus Cellius
circa A.D. 125-circa A.D. 180? DLB-211

Austen, Jane 1775-1817 . . . . .DLB-116

Austin, Alfred 1835-1913. . . . . .DLB-35

Austin, Jane Goodwin 1831-1894 . . . . . . .DLB-202

Austin, Mary 1868-1934 . . . . . DLB-9, 78, 206, 221

Austin, William 1778-1841. . . . . .DLB-74

Author-Printers, 1476–1599. . . . . .DLB-167

Author Websites Y-97

The Author's Apology for His Book
(1684), by John Bunyan DLB-39

An Author's Response, by Ronald Sukenick. . Y-82

Authors and Newspapers Association DLB-46

Authors' Publishing Company DLB-49

Avallone, Michael 1924-1999. . . . . Y-99

Avalon Books. DLB-46

Avancini, Nicolaus 1611-1686 . . . . .DLB-164

Avendaño, Fausto 1941- DLB-82

Averroëö 1126-1198. . . . . .DLB-115

Avery, Gillian 1926- DLB-161

Avicenna 980-1037. . . . . .DLB-115

Avison, Margaret 1918- DLB-53

Avon Books DLB-46

Awdry, Wilbert Vere 1911-1997 . . . . .DLB-160

Avyžius, Jonas 1922-1999 . . . . .DLB-220

Awoonor, Kofi 1935- DLB-117

Ayckbourn, Alan 1939- DLB-13

Aymé, Marcel 1902-1967. . . . . .DLB-72

Aytoun, Sir Robert 1570-1638 . . . . .DLB-121

Aytoun, William Edmondstoune
1813-1865 . . . . .DLB-32, 159

B

B. V. (see Thomson, James)

Babbitt, Irving 1865-1933 . . . . .DLB-63

Babbitt, Natalie 1932- DLB-52

Babcock, John [publishing house] DLB-49

Babits, Mihály 1883-1941 . . . . .DLB-215

Babrius circa 150-200. . . . . .DLB-176

Baca, Jimmy Santiago 1952- DLB-122

Bache, Benjamin Franklin 1769-1798. . . . .DLB-43

Bacheller, Irving 1859-1950. . . . . .DLB-202

Bachmann, Ingeborg 1926-1973 . . . . .DLB-85

Bačinskaitė-Bučienė, Salomėja (see Nėris, Salomėja)

Bacon, Delia 1811-1859 . . . . DLB-1

Bacon, Francis 1561-1626. . . . . DLB-151

Bacon, Roger circa 1214/1220-1292 . . . . . DLB-115

Bacon, Sir Nicholas circa 1510-1579 . . . . . DLB-132

Bacon, Thomas circa 1700-1768 . . . . DLB-31

Bacovia, George 1881-1957 . . . . DLB-220

Badger, Richard G., and Company DLB-49

Bage, Robert 1728-1801 . . . . DLB-39

Bagehot, Walter 1826-1877. . . . . DLB-55

Bagley, Desmond 1923-1983 . . . . DLB-87

Bagnold, Enid 1889-1981 . . . . . . DLB-13, 160, 191

Bagryana, Elisaveta 1893-1991. . . . . DLB-147

Bahr, Hermann 1863-1934. . . . . DLB-81, 118

Bailey, Abigail Abbot 1746-1815. . . . . . . DLB-200

Bailey, Alfred Goldsworthy 1905- DLB-68

Bailey, Francis [publishing house]. DLB-49

Bailey, H. C. 1878-1961 . . . . DLB-77

Bailey, Jacob 1731-1808 . . . . DLB-99

Bailey, Paul 1937- DLB-14

Bailey, Philip James 1816-1902. . . . . DLB-32

Baillargeon, Pierre 1916-1967. . . . . DLB-88

Baillie, Hugh 1890-1966. . . . . DLB-29

Baillie, Joanna 1762-1851 . . . . DLB-93

Bailyn, Bernard 1922- DLB-17

Bainbridge, Beryl 1933- DLB-14

Baird, Irene 1901-1981 . . . . DLB-68

Baker, Augustine 1575-1641 . . . . DLB-151

Baker, Carlos 1909-1987 . . . . DLB-103

Baker, David 1954- DLB-120

Baker, Herschel C. 1914-1990 . . . . DLB-111

Baker, Houston A., Jr. 1943- DLB-67

Baker, Samuel White 1821-1893 . . . . DLB-166

Baker, Thomas 1656-1740 . . . . DLB-213

Baker, Walter H., Company
("Baker's Plays") DLB-49

The Baker and Taylor Company. DLB-49

Balaban, John 1943- DLB-120

Bald, Wambly 1902- DLB-4

Balde, Jacob 1604-1668. . . . . DLB-164

Balderston, John 1889-1954 . . . . DLB-26

Baldwin, James 1924-1987 . . . . . DLB-2, 7, 33; Y-87

Baldwin, Joseph Glover 1815-1864. . . . . DLB-3, 11

Baldwin, Richard and Anne
[publishing house] DLB-170

Baldwin, William circa 1515-1563 . . . . . . DLB-132

Bale, John 1495-1563 . . . . DLB-132

Balestrini, Nanni 1935- DLB-128, 196

Balfour, Sir Andrew 1630-1694 . . . . DLB-213

Balfour, Arthur James 1848-1930. . . . . . . DLB-190

Balfour, Sir James 1600-1657 . . . . DLB-213

Ballantine Books. DLB-46

Ballantyne, R. M. 1825-1894 . . . . DLB-163

Ballard, J. G. 1930- DLB-14, 207

Ballard, Martha Moore 1735-1812 . . . . . . DLB-200

Ballerini, Luigi 1940- DLB-128

Ballou, Maturin Murray
1820-1895 . . . . .DLB-79, 189

Ballou, Robert O. [publishing house] DLB-46

Balzac, Honoré de 1799-1855 . . . . DLB-119

Bambara, Toni Cade 1939- DLB-38, 218

Bamford, Samuel 1788-1872 . . . . DLB-190

Bancroft, A. L., and Company DLB-49

Bancroft, George 1800-1891. . . . . . DLB-1, 30, 59

Bancroft, Hubert Howe 1832-1918 . . .DLB-47, 140

Bandelier, Adolph F. 1840-1914 . . . . DLB-186

Bangs, John Kendrick 1862-1922 . . . . .DLB-11, 79

Banim, John 1798-1842. . . . . . . .DLB-116, 158, 159

Banim, Michael 1796-1874 . . . . DLB-158, 159

Banks, Iain 1954- DLB-194

Banks, John circa 1653-1706 . . . . DLB-80

Banks, Russell 1940- DLB-130

Bannerman, Helen 1862-1946 . . . . DLB-141

Bantam Books DLB-46

Banti, Anna 1895-1985. . . . . .DLB-177

Banville, John 1945- DLB-14

Banville, Théodore de 1823-1891. . . . . . . DLB-217

Baraka, Amiri 1934- DLB-5, 7, 16, 38; DS-8

Baratynsky, Evgenii Abramovich
1800-1844 . . . . DLB-205

Barbauld, Anna Laetitia
1743-1825. . . . . DLB-107, 109, 142, 158

Barbeau, Marius 1883-1969 . . . . DLB-92

Barber, John Warner 1798-1885. . . . . DLB-30

Bàrberi Squarotti, Giorgio 1929- DLB-128

Barbey d'Aurevilly, Jules-Amédée
1808-1889 . . . . DLB-119

Barbier, Auguste 1805-1882 . . . . DLB-217

Barbilian, Dan (see Barbu, Ion)

Barbour, John circa 1316-1395 . . . . DLB-146

Barbu, Ion 1895-1961. . . . . DLB-220

Barbour, Ralph Henry 1870-1944 . . . . DLB-22

Barbusse, Henri 1873-1935. . . . . DLB-65

Barclay, Alexander circa 1475-1552 . . . . . DLB-132

Barclay, E. E., and Company DLB-49

Bardeen, C. W. [publishing house]. DLB-49

Barham, Richard Harris 1788-1845 . . . . . DLB-159

Barich, Bill 1943- DLB-185

Baring, Maurice 1874-1945. . . . . DLB-34

Baring-Gould, Sabine
1834-1924 . . . . DLB-156, 190

Barker, A. L. 1918- DLB-14, 139

Barker, George 1913-1991 . . . . DLB-20

Barker, Harley Granville 1877-1946. . . . . . DLB-10

Barker, Howard 1946- DLB-13

Barker, James Nelson 1784-1858 . . . . DLB-37

Barker, Jane 1652-1727 . . . . DLB-39, 131

Barker, Lady Mary Anne 1831-1911 . . . . DLB-166

Barker, William
circa 1520-after 1576 . . . . DLB-132

Barker, Arthur, Limited DLB-112

Barkov, Ivan Semenovich
1732-1768. DLB-150

Barks, Coleman 1937- DLB-5

Barlach, Ernst 1870-1938 . . . . DLB-56, 118

Barlow, Joel 1754-1812. . . . . DLB-37

Barnard, John 1681-1770 . . . . DLB-24

Barne, Kitty (Mary Catherine Barne)
1883-1957 . . . . DLB-160

Barnes, Barnabe 1571-1609 . . . . DLB-132

Barnes, Djuna 1892-1982. . . . . DLB-4, 9, 45

Barnes, Jim 1933- DLB-175

Barnes, Julian 1946- DLB-194; Y-93

Barnes, Margaret Ayer 1886-1967 . . . . DLB-9

Barnes, Peter 1931- DLB-13

Barnes, William 1801-1886 . . . . DLB-32

Barnes, A. S., and Company DLB-49

Barnes and Noble Books DLB-46

Barnet, Miguel 1940- DLB-145

Barney, Natalie 1876-1972 . . . . DLB-4

Barnfield, Richard 1574-1627 . . . . .DLB-172

Baron, Richard W.,
Publishing Company DLB-46

Barr, Amelia Edith Huddleston
1831-1919 . . . . DLB-202, 221

Barr, Robert 1850-1912 . . . . .DLB-70, 92

Barral, Carlos 1928-1989 . . . . DLB-134

Barrax, Gerald William 1933- DLB-41, 120

Barrès, Maurice 1862-1923. . . . . DLB-123

Barrett, Eaton Stannard 1786-1820. . . . . . DLB-116

Barrie, J. M. 1860-1937. . . . . . . .DLB-10, 141, 156

Barrie and Jenkins DLB-112

Barrio, Raymond 1921- DLB-82

Barrios, Gregg 1945- DLB-122

Barry, Philip 1896-1949 . . . . DLB-7

Barry, Robertine (see Françoise)

Barse and Hopkins DLB-46

Barstow, Stan 1928- DLB-14, 139

Barth, John 1930- DLB-2

Barthelme, Donald
1931-1989 . . . . DLB-2; Y-80, Y-89

Barthelme, Frederick 1943- Y-85

Bartholomew, Frank 1898-1985 . . . . .DLB-127

Bartlett, John 1820-1905. . . . . DLB-1

Bartol, Cyrus Augustus 1813-1900. . . . . . . DLB-1

Barton, Bernard 1784-1849. . . . . DLB-96

Barton, Thomas Pennant 1803-1869 . . . . DLB-140

Bartram, John 1699-1777 . . . . DLB-31

Bartram, William 1739-1823 . . . . DLB-37

Basic Books DLB-46

Basille, Theodore (see Becon, Thomas)

Bass, Rick 1958- DLB-212

Bass, T. J. 1932- Y-81

Bassani, Giorgio 1916- DLB-128, 177

Basse, William circa 1583-1653 . . . . DLB-121

Bassett, John Spencer 1867-1928. . . . . . . .DLB-17

Bassler, Thomas Joseph (see Bass, T. J.)

Bate, Walter Jackson 1918-1999 . . . . . DLB-67, 103

Bateman, Christopher
[publishing house] DLB-170

Bateman, Stephen circa 1510-1584 . . . . . . DLB-136

Bates, H. E. 1905-1974. . . . . DLB-162, 191

Bates, Katharine Lee 1859-1929 . . . . DLB-71

Batiushkov, Konstantin Nikolaevich
1787-1855. . . . . .DLB-205

Batsford, B. T. [publishing house] DLB-106

Battiscombe, Georgina 1905- DLB-155

The Battle of Maldon circa 1000 . . . . .DLB-146

Baudelaire, Charles 1821-1867 . . . . .DLB-217

Bauer, Bruno 1809-1882 . . . . .DLB-133

Bauer, Wolfgang 1941- DLB-124

Baum, L. Frank 1856-1919 . . . . .DLB-22

Baum, Vicki 1888-1960 . . . . .DLB-85

Baumbach, Jonathan 1933- Y-80

Bausch, Richard 1945- DLB-130

Bausch, Robert 1945- DLB-218

Bawden, Nina 1925- DLB-14, 161, 207

Bax, Clifford 1886-1962 . . . . DLB-10, 100

Baxter, Charles 1947- DLB-130

Bayer, Eleanor (see Perry, Eleanor)

Bayer, Konrad 1932-1964 . . . . .DLB-85

Baynes, Pauline 1922- DLB-160

Bazin, Hervé 1911-1996. . . . . .DLB-83

Beach, Sylvia 1887-1962. . . . . .DLB-4; DS-15

Beacon Press DLB-49

Beadle and Adams DLB-49

Beagle, Peter S. 1939- Y-80

Beal, M. F. 1937- Y-81

Beale, Howard K. 1899-1959. . . . . .DLB-17

Beard, Charles A. 1874-1948 . . . . .DLB-17

A Beat Chronology: The First Twenty-five
Years, 1944-1969. . . . . .DLB-16

Beattie, Ann 1947- DLB-218; Y-82

Beattie, James 1735-1803 . . . . .DLB-109

Beatty, Chester 1875-1968 . . . . .DLB-201

Beauchemin, Nérée 1850-1931 . . . . .DLB-92

Beauchemin, Yves 1941- DLB-60

Beaugrand, Honoré 1848-1906 . . . . .DLB-99

Beaulieu, Victor-Lévy 1945- DLB-53

Beaumont, Francis circa 1584-1616
and Fletcher, John 1579-1625 . . . . . . .DLB-58

Beaumont, Sir John 1583?-1627. . . . . . . .DLB-121

Beaumont, Joseph 1616-1699. . . . . .DLB-126

Beauvoir, Simone de 1908-1986 . . . . DLB-72; Y-86

Becher, Ulrich 1910- DLB-69

Becker, Carl 1873-1945 . . . . .DLB-17

Becker, Jurek 1937-1997. . . . . .DLB-75

Becker, Jurgen 1932- DLB-75

Beckett, Samuel 1906-1989 . . . . . DLB-13, 15; Y-90

Beckford, William 1760-1844. . . . . .DLB-39

Beckham, Barry 1944- DLB-33

Becon, Thomas circa 1512-1567 . . . . . . .DLB-136

Becque, Henry 1837-1899 . . . . .DLB-192

Beùkoviù, Matija 1939- DLB-181

Beddoes, Thomas 1760-1808. . . . . .DLB-158

Beddoes, Thomas Lovell 1803-1849 . . . . .DLB-96

Bede circa 673-735. . . . . .DLB-146

Beecher, Catharine Esther 1800-1878 . . . . . .DLB-1

Beecher, Henry Ward 1813-1887 . . . . . .DLB-3, 43

Beer, George L. 1872-1920 . . . . .DLB-47

Beer, Johann 1655-1700 . . . . .DLB-168

Beer, Patricia 1919-1999 . . . . .DLB-40

Beerbohm, Max 1872-1956 . . . . DLB-34, 100

Beer-Hofmann, Richard 1866-1945. . . . . . .DLB-81

Beers, Henry A. 1847-1926 . . . . .DLB-71

Beeton, S. O. [publishing house] DLB-106

Bégon, Elisabeth 1696-1755 . . . . .DLB-99

Behan, Brendan 1923-1964 . . . . .DLB-13

Behn, Aphra 1640?-1689 . . . . DLB-39, 80, 131

Behn, Harry 1898-1973 . . . . .DLB-61

Behrman, S. N. 1893-1973 . . . . DLB-7, 44

Belaney, Archibald Stansfeld (see Grey Owl)

Belasco, David 1853-1931 . . . . .DLB-7

Belford, Clarke and Company. DLB-49

Belinksy, Vissarion Grigor'evich
1811-1848 . . . . .DLB-198

Belitt, Ben 1911- DLB-5

Belknap, Jeremy 1744-1798 . . . . DLB-30, 37

Bell, Adrian 1901-1980 . . . . .DLB-191

Bell, Clive 1881-1964. . . . . DS-10

Bell, George, and Sons. DLB-106

Bell, Gertrude Margaret Lowthian
1868-1926 . . . . DLB-174

Bell, James Madison 1826-1902. . . . . .DLB-50

Bell, Madison Smartt 1957- DLB-218

Bell, Marvin 1937- DLB-5

Bell, Millicent 1919- DLB-111

Bell, Quentin 1910-1996 . . . . .DLB-155

Bell, Robert [publishing house] DLB-49

Bell, Vanessa 1879-1961 . . . . DS-10

Bellamy, Edward 1850-1898 . . . . .DLB-12

Bellamy, John [publishing house]. DLB-170

Bellamy, Joseph 1719-1790. . . . . .DLB-31

Bellezza, Dario 1944-1996 . . . . .DLB-128

La Belle Assemblée 1806-1837 . . . . .DLB-110

Belloc, Hilaire 1870-1953 . . . . DLB-19, 100, 141, 174

Bellonci, Maria 1902-1986. . . . . .DLB-196

Bellow, Saul 1915- DLB-2, 28; Y-82; DS-3

Belmont Productions DLB-46

Bemelmans, Ludwig 1898-1962. . . . . .DLB-22

Bemis, Samuel Flagg 1891-1973. . . . . .DLB-17

Bemrose, William [publishing house] DLB-106

Ben no Naishi 1228?-1271? DLB-203

Benchley, Robert 1889-1945 . . . . .DLB-11

Bencúr, Matej (see Kukučin, Martin)

Benedetti, Mario 1920- DLB-113

Benedictus, David 1938- DLB-14

Benedikt, Michael 1935- DLB-5

Benediktov, Vladimir Grigor'evich
1807-1873 . . . . .DLB-205

Benét, Stephen Vincent
1898-1943 . . . . DLB-4, 48, 102

Benét, William Rose 1886-1950 . . . . .DLB-45

Benford, Gregory 1941- Y-82

Benjamin, Park 1809-1864. . . . . DLB-3, 59, 73

Benjamin, S. G. W. 1837-1914. . . . . .DLB-189

Benlowes, Edward 1602-1676 . . . . .DLB-126

Benn, Gottfried 1886-1956 . . . . .DLB-56

Benn Brothers Limited DLB-106

Bennett, Arnold 1867-1931 . . . DLB-10, 34, 98, 135

Bennett, Charles 1899-1995. . . . . .DLB-44

Bennett, Emerson 1822-1905. . . . . .DLB-202

Bennett, Gwendolyn 1902- DLB-51

Bennett, Hal 1930- DLB-33

Bennett, James Gordon 1795-1872. . . . . . .DLB-43

Bennett, James Gordon, Jr. 1841-1918. . . .DLB-23

Bennett, John 1865-1956 . . . . .DLB-42

Bennett, Louise 1919- DLB-117

Benni, Stefano 1947- DLB-196

Benoit, Jacques 1941- DLB-60

Benson, A. C. 1862-1925. . . . . .DLB-98

Benson, E. F. 1867-1940. . . . . .DLB-135, 153

Benson, Jackson J. 1930- DLB-111

Benson, Robert Hugh 1871-1914. . . . . . .DLB-153

Benson, Stella 1892-1933. . . . . DLB-36, 162

Bent, James Theodore 1852-1897 . . . . . . .DLB-174

Bent, Mabel Virginia Anna ?-? DLB-174

Bentham, Jeremy 1748-1832 . . . . DLB-107, 158

Bentley, E. C. 1875-1956 . . . . .DLB-70

Bentley, Phyllis 1894-1977. . . . . .DLB-191

Bentley, Richard [publishing house] DLB-106

Benton, Robert 1932- and Newman,
David 1937- DLB-44

Benziger Brothers DLB-49

Beowulf circa 900-1000 or 790-825 . . . . . . .DLB-146

Berent, Wacław 1873-1940 . . . . .DLB-215

Beresford, Anne 1929- DLB-40

Beresford, John Davys
1873-1947 . . . . DLB-162, 178, 197

Beresford-Howe, Constance 1922- DLB-88

Berford, R. G., Company DLB-49

Berg, Stephen 1934- DLB-5

Bergengruen, Werner 1892-1964 . . . . .DLB-56

Berger, John 1926- DLB-14, 207

Berger, Meyer 1898-1959 . . . . .DLB-29

Berger, Thomas 1924- DLB-2; Y-80

Berkeley, Anthony 1893-1971 . . . . .DLB-77

Berkeley, George 1685-1753 . . . . DLB-31, 101

The Berkley Publishing Corporation. DLB-46

Berlin, Lucia 1936- DLB-130

Bernal, Vicente J. 1888-1915 . . . . .DLB-82

Bernanos, Georges 1888-1948 . . . . .DLB-72

Bernard, Harry 1898-1979 . . . . DLB-92

Bernard, John 1756-1828 . . . . DLB-37

Bernard of Chartres circa 1060-1124? . . . DLB-115

Bernard of Clairvaux 1090-1153 . . . . DLB-208

Bernard Silvestris
  flourished circa 1130-1160 . . . . DLB-208

Bernari, Carlo 1909-1992 . . . . .DLB-177

Bernhard, Thomas 1931-1989 . . . . . . DLB-85, 124

Bernstein, Charles 1950- DLB-169

Berriault, Gina 1926-1999 . . . . DLB-130

Berrigan, Daniel 1921- DLB-5

Berrigan, Ted 1934-1983 . . . . DLB-5, 169

Berry, Wendell 1934- DLB-5, 6

Berryman, John 1914-1972 . . . . DLB-48

Bersianik, Louky 1930- DLB-60

Berthelet, Thomas [publishing house] DLB-170

Berto, Giuseppe 1914-1978 . . . . .DLB-177

Bertolucci, Attilio 1911- DLB-128

Bertrand, Louis "Aloysius"
  1807-1841 . . . . DLB-217

Berton, Pierre 1920- DLB-68

Besant, Sir Walter 1836-1901 . . . . . . DLB-135, 190

Bessette, Gerard 1920- DLB-53

Bessie, Alvah 1904-1985 . . . . DLB-26

Bester, Alfred 1913-1987 . . . . DLB-8

Besterman, Theodore 1904-1976 . . . . DLB-201

The Bestseller Lists: An Assessment Y-84

Bestuzhev, Aleksandr Aleksandrovich (Marlinsky)
  1797-1837 . . . . DLB-198

Bestuzhev, Nikolai Aleksandrovich
  1791-1855 . . . . DLB-198

Betham-Edwards, Matilda Barbara (see Edwards,
  Matilda Barbara Betham-)

Betjeman, John 1906-1984 . . . . DLB-20; Y-84

Betocchi, Carlo 1899-1986 . . . . DLB-128

Bettarini, Mariella 1942- DLB-128

Betts, Doris 1932- DLB-218; Y-82

Beveridge, Albert J. 1862-1927 . . . . DLB-17

Beverley, Robert circa 1673-1722 . . . . . DLB-24, 30

Bevilacqua, Alberto 1934- DLB-196

Bevington, Louisa Sarah 1845-1895 . . . . . DLB-199

Beyle, Marie-Henri (see Stendhal)

Bianco, Margery Williams 1881-1944 . . . DLB-160

Bibaud, Adèle 1854-1941 . . . . DLB-92

Bibaud, Michel 1782-1857 . . . . DLB-99

Bibliographical and Textual Scholarship
  Since World War II Y-89

The Bicentennial of James Fenimore Cooper:
  An International Celebration Y-89

Bichsel, Peter 1935- DLB-75

Bickerstaff, Isaac John 1733-circa 1808 . . . . DLB-89

Biddle, Drexel [publishing house] DLB-49

Bidermann, Jacob
  1577 or 1578-1639 . . . . DLB-164

Bidwell, Walter Hilliard 1798-1881 . . . . . . DLB-79

Bienek, Horst 1930- DLB-75

Bierbaum, Otto Julius 1865-1910 . . . . DLB-66

Bierce, Ambrose
  1842-1914? DLB-11, 12, 23, 71, 74, 186

Bigelow, William F. 1879-1966 . . . . DLB-91

Biggle, Lloyd, Jr. 1923- DLB-8

Bigiaretti, Libero 1905-1993 . . . . .DLB-177

Bigland, Eileen 1898-1970 . . . . DLB-195

Biglow, Hosea (see Lowell, James Russell)

Bigongiari, Piero 1914- DLB-128

Billinger, Richard 1890-1965 . . . . DLB-124

Billings, Hammatt 1818-1874 . . . . DLB-188

Billings, John Shaw 1898-1975 . . . . DLB-137

Billings, Josh (see Shaw, Henry Wheeler)

Binding, Rudolf G. 1867-1938 . . . . DLB-66

Bingham, Caleb 1757-1817 . . . . DLB-42

Bingham, George Barry 1906-1988 . . . . . DLB-127

Bingley, William [publishing house] DLB-154

Binyon, Laurence 1869-1943 . . . . DLB-19

Biographia Brittanica DLB-142

Biographical Documents I Y-84

Biographical Documents II Y-85

Bioren, John [publishing house] DLB-49

Bioy Casares, Adolfo 1914- DLB-113

Bird, Isabella Lucy 1831-1904 . . . . DLB-166

Bird, Robert Montgomery 1806-1854 . . . DLB-202

Bird, William 1888-1963 . . . . DLB-4; DS-15

Birken, Sigmund von 1626-1681 . . . . . . DLB-164

Birney, Earle 1904- DLB-88

Birrell, Augustine 1850-1933 . . . . DLB-98

Bisher, Furman 1918- DLB-171

Bishop, Elizabeth 1911-1979 . . . . DLB-5, 169

Bishop, John Peale 1892-1944 . . . . . DLB-4, 9, 45

Bismarck, Otto von 1815-1898 . . . . DLB-129

Bisset, Robert 1759-1805 . . . . DLB-142

Bissett, Bill 1939- DLB-53

Bitzius, Albert (see Gotthelf, Jeremias)

Bjørnvig, Thorkild 1918- DLB-214

Black, David (D. M.) 1941- DLB-40

Black, Winifred 1863-1936 . . . . DLB-25

Black, Walter J. [publishing house] DLB-46

The Black Aesthetic: Background DS-8

The Black Arts Movement, by
  Larry Neal DLB-38

Black Theaters and Theater Organizations in
  America, 1961-1982:
  A Research List DLB-38

Black Theatre: A Forum [excerpts] DLB-38

Blackamore, Arthur 1679-? DLB-24, 39

Blackburn, Alexander L. 1929- Y-85

Blackburn, Paul 1926-1971 . . . . .DLB-16; Y-81

Blackburn, Thomas 1916-1977 . . . . DLB-27

Blackmore, R. D. 1825-1900 . . . . DLB-18

Blackmore, Sir Richard 1654-1729 . . . . . . DLB-131

Blackmur, R. P. 1904-1965 . . . . DLB-63

Blackwell, Basil, Publisher DLB-106

Blackwood, Algernon Henry
  1869-1951 . . . . .DLB-153, 156, 178

Blackwood, Caroline 1931-1996 . . . . .DLB-14, 207

Blackwood, William, and Sons, Ltd. DLB-154

Blackwood's Edinburgh Magazine
  1817-1980 . . . . DLB-110

Blades, William 1824-1890 . . . . DLB-184

Blaga, Lucian 1895-1961 . . . . DLB-220

Blagden, Isabella 1817?-1873 . . . . DLB-199

Blair, Eric Arthur (see Orwell, George)

Blair, Francis Preston 1791-1876 . . . . DLB-43

Blair, James circa 1655-1743 . . . . DLB-24

Blair, John Durburrow 1759-1823 . . . . DLB-37

Blais, Marie-Claire 1939- DLB-53

Blaise, Clark 1940- DLB-53

Blake, George 1893-1961 . . . . DLB-191

Blake, Lillie Devereux 1833-1913 . . . DLB-202, 221

Blake, Nicholas 1904-1972 . . . . DLB-77
  (see Day Lewis, C.)

Blake, William 1757-1827 . . . . . . .DLB-93, 154, 163

The Blakiston Company DLB-49

Blanchot, Maurice 1907- DLB-72

Blanckenburg, Christian Friedrich von
  1744-1796 . . . . DLB-94

Blaser, Robin 1925- DLB-165

Blaumanis, Rudolfs 1863-1908 . . . . DLB-220

Bledsoe, Albert Taylor 1809-1877 . . . . .DLB-3, 79

Bleecker, Ann Eliza 1752-1783 . . . . DLB-200

Blelock and Company DLB-49

Blennerhassett, Margaret Agnew
  1773-1842 . . . . DLB-99

Bles, Geoffrey [publishing house] DLB-112

Blessington, Marguerite, Countess of
  1789-1849 . . . . DLB-166

The Blickling Homilies circa 971 . . . . DLB-146

Blind, Mathilde 1841-1896 . . . . DLB-199

Blish, James 1921-1975 . . . . DLB-8

Bliss, E., and E. White
  [publishing house] DLB-49

Bliven, Bruce 1889-1977 . . . . .DLB-137

Blixen, Karen 1885-1962 . . . . DLB-214

Bloch, Robert 1917-1994 . . . . DLB-44

Block, Lawrence 1938- DLB-226

Block, Rudolph (see Lessing, Bruno)

Blondal, Patricia 1926-1959 . . . . DLB-88

Bloom, Harold 1930- DLB-67

Bloomer, Amelia 1818-1894 . . . . DLB-79

Bloomfield, Robert 1766-1823 . . . . DLB-93

Bloomsbury Group DS-10

Blotner, Joseph 1923- DLB-111

Bloy, Léon 1846-1917 . . . . DLB-123

Blume, Judy 1938- DLB-52

Blunck, Hans Friedrich 1888-1961 . . . . DLB-66

Blunden, Edmund 1896-1974 . . . .DLB-20, 100, 155

Blunt, Lady Anne Isabella Noel
  1837-1917 . . . . .DLB-174

Blunt, Wilfrid Scawen 1840-1922 . . . . .DLB-19, 174

Bly, Nellie (see Cochrane, Elizabeth)

Bly, Robert 1926- DLB-5

Blyton, Enid 1897-1968 . . . . .DLB-160

Boaden, James 1762-1839 . . . . .DLB-89

Boas, Frederick S. 1862-1957 . . . . .DLB-149

The Bobbs-Merrill Archive at the
    Lilly Library, Indiana University Y-90

The Bobbs-Merrill Company. DLB-46

Bobrov, Semen Sergeevich
    1763?-1810. . . . . .DLB-150

Bobrowski, Johannes 1917-1965. . . . . .DLB-75

Bodenheim, Maxwell 1892-1954 . . . . . . .DLB-9, 45

Bodenstedt, Friedrich von 1819-1892 . . . .DLB-129

Bodini, Vittorio 1914-1970. . . . . .DLB-128

Bodkin, M. McDonnell 1850-1933 . . . . . . .DLB-70

Bodley, Sir Thomas 1545-1613 . . . . .DLB-213

Bodley Head DLB-112

Bodmer, Johann Jakob 1698-1783 . . . . . . .DLB-97

Bodmershof, Imma von 1895-1982 . . . . . . .DLB-85

Bodsworth, Fred 1918- DLB-68

Boehm, Sydney 1908- DLB-44

Boer, Charles 1939- DLB-5

Boethius circa 480-circa 524 . . . . .DLB-115

Boethius of Dacia circa 1240-? DLB-115

Bogan, Louise 1897-1970 . . . . .DLB-45, 169

Bogarde, Dirk 1921- DLB-14

Bogdanovich, Ippolit Fedorovich
    circa 1743-1803 . . . . .DLB-150

Bogue, David [publishing house] DLB-106

Böhme, Jakob 1575-1624 . . . . .DLB-164

Bohn, H. G. [publishing house] DLB-106

Bohse, August 1661-1742. . . . . .DLB-168

Boie, Heinrich Christian 1744-1806 . . . . . .DLB-94

Bok, Edward W. 1863-1930 . . . . . .DLB-91; DS-16

Boland, Eavan 1944- DLB-40

Bolingbroke, Henry St. John, Viscount
    1678-1751 . . . . .DLB-101

Böll, Heinrich 1917-1985 . . . . .DLB-69; Y-85

Bolling, Robert 1738-1775 . . . . .DLB-31

Bolotov, Andrei Timofeevich
    1738-1833 . . . . .DLB-150

Bolt, Carol 1941- DLB-60

Bolt, Robert 1924-1995 . . . . .DLB-13

Bolton, Herbert E. 1870-1953 . . . . .DLB-17

Bonaventura DLB-90

Bonaventure circa 1217-1274 . . . . .DLB-115

Bonaviri, Giuseppe 1924- DLB-177

Bond, Edward 1934- DLB-13

Bond, Michael 1926- DLB-161

Boni, Albert and Charles
    [publishing house] DLB-46

Boni and Liveright. DLB-46

Bonner, Paul Hyde 1893-1968. . . . . DS-17

Bonner, Sherwood 1849-1883 . . . . .DLB-202

Robert Bonner's Sons DLB-49

Bonnin, Gertrude Simmons (see Zitkala-Ša)

Bonsanti, Alessandro 1904-1984 . . . . DLB-177

Bontemps, Arna 1902-1973 . . . . .DLB-48, 51

The Book Arts Press at the University
    of Virginia. Y-96

The Book League of America DLB-46

Book Publishing Accounting: Some Basic
    Concepts Y-98

Book Reviewing in America: I. Y-87

Book Reviewing in America: II. Y-88

Book Reviewing in America: III Y-89

Book Reviewing in America: IV Y-90

Book Reviewing in America: V Y-91

Book Reviewing in America: VI Y-92

Book Reviewing in America: VII Y-93

Book Reviewing in America: VIII. Y-94

Book Reviewing in America and the
    Literary Scene Y-95

Book Reviewing and the
    Literary Scene Y-96, Y-97

Book Supply Company DLB-49

The Book Trade History Group Y-93

The Booker Prize. Y-96

The Booker Prize
    Address by Anthony Thwaite,
    Chairman of the Booker Prize Judges
    Comments from Former Booker
    Prize Winners Y-86

Boorde, Andrew circa 1490-1549 . . . . . . .DLB-136

Boorstin, Daniel J. 1914- DLB-17

Booth, Mary L. 1831-1889 . . . . .DLB-79

Booth, Franklin 1874-1948. . . . . .DLB-188

Booth, Philip 1925- Y-82

Booth, Wayne C. 1921- DLB-67

Booth, William 1829-1912. . . . . .DLB-190

Borchardt, Rudolf 1877-1945 . . . . .DLB-66

Borchert, Wolfgang 1921-1947 . . . . . .DLB-69, 124

Borel, Pétrus 1809-1859. . . . . .DLB-119

Borges, Jorge Luis 1899-1986 . . . . .DLB-113; Y-86

Börne, Ludwig 1786-1837 . . . . .DLB-90

Bornstein, Miriam 1950- DLB-209

Borowski, Tadeusz 1922-1951. . . . . .DLB-215

Borrow, George 1803-1881 . . . . . .DLB-21, 55, 166

Bosch, Juan 1909- DLB-145

Bosco, Henri 1888-1976. . . . . .DLB-72

Bosco, Monique 1927- DLB-53

Bosman, Herman Charles 1905-1951 . . . .DLB-225

Boston, Lucy M. 1892-1990 . . . . .DLB-161

Boswell, James 1740-1795. . . . . .DLB-104, 142

Botev, Khristo 1847-1876. . . . . .DLB-147

Bote, Hermann
    circa 1460-circa 1520. . . . . .DLB-179

Botta, Anne C. Lynch 1815-1891 . . . . .DLB-3

Botto, Ján (see Krasko, Ivan)

Bottome, Phyllis 1882-1963. . . . . .DLB-197

Bottomley, Gordon 1874-1948. . . . . .DLB-10

Bottoms, David 1949- DLB-120; Y-83

Bottrall, Ronald 1906- DLB-20

Bouchardy, Joseph 1810-1870 . . . . .DLB-192

Boucher, Anthony 1911-1968 . . . . .DLB-8

Boucher, Jonathan 1738-1804 . . . . .DLB-31

Boucher de Boucherville, George
    1814-1894 . . . . .DLB-99

Boudreau, Daniel (see Coste, Donat)

Bourassa, Napoléon 1827-1916 . . . . .DLB-99

Bourget, Paul 1852-1935 . . . . .DLB-123

Bourinot, John George 1837-1902 . . . . . . .DLB-99

Bourjaily, Vance 1922- DLB-2, 143

Bourne, Edward Gaylord
    1860-1908 . . . . .DLB-47

Bourne, Randolph 1886-1918 . . . . .DLB-63

Bousoño, Carlos 1923- DLB-108

Bousquet, Joë 1897-1950 . . . . .DLB-72

Bova, Ben 1932- Y-81

Bovard, Oliver K. 1872-1945. . . . . .DLB-25

Bove, Emmanuel 1898-1945 . . . . .DLB-72

Bowen, Elizabeth 1899-1973 . . . . . . .DLB-15, 162

Bowen, Francis 1811-1890. . . . . .DLB-1, 59

Bowen, John 1924- DLB-13

Bowen, Marjorie 1886-1952 . . . . .DLB-153

Bowen-Merrill Company. DLB-49

Bowering, George 1935- DLB-53

Bowers, Bathsheba 1671-1718 . . . . .DLB-200

Bowers, Claude G. 1878-1958 . . . . .DLB-17

Bowers, Edgar 1924- DLB-5

Bowers, Fredson Thayer
    1905-1991 . . . . .DLB-140; Y-91

Bowles, Paul 1910-1999 . . . . . .DLB-5, 6, 218; Y-99

Bowles, Samuel III 1826-1878 . . . . .DLB-43

Bowles, William Lisles 1762-1850 . . . . . . .DLB-93

Bowman, Louise Morey 1882-1944. . . . . . .DLB-68

Boyd, James 1888-1944 . . . . .DLB-9; DS-16

Boyd, John 1919- DLB-8

Boyd, Thomas 1898-1935 . . . . .DLB-9; DS-16

Boyesen, Hjalmar Hjorth
    1848-1895 . . . . .DLB-12, 71; DS-13

Boyle, Kay
    1902-1992 . . . . .DLB-4, 9, 48, 86; Y-93

Boyle, Roger, Earl of Orrery
    1621-1679 . . . . .DLB-80

Boyle, T. Coraghessan 1948- DLB-218; Y-86

Božić, Mirko 1919- DLB-181

Brackenbury, Alison 1953- DLB-40

Brackenridge, Hugh Henry
    1748-1816 . . . . .DLB-11, 37

Brackett, Charles 1892-1969 . . . . .DLB-26

Brackett, Leigh 1915-1978 . . . . .DLB-8, 26

Bradburn, John [publishing house] DLB-49

Bradbury, Malcolm 1932- DLB-14, 207

Bradbury, Ray 1920- DLB-2, 8

Bradbury and Evans DLB-106

Braddon, Mary Elizabeth
    1835-1915 . . . . .DLB-18, 70, 156

Bradford, Andrew 1686-1742 . . . . .DLB-43, 73

Bradford, Gamaliel 1863-1932. . . . . .DLB-17

Bradford, John 1749-1830 . . . . .DLB-43

Bradford, Roark 1896-1948 . . . . DLB-86

Bradford, William 1590-1657 . . . . DLB-24, 30

Bradford, William III 1719-1791 . . . . . DLB-43, 73

Bradlaugh, Charles 1833-1891 . . . . DLB-57

Bradley, David 1950- DLB-33

Bradley, Marion Zimmer 1930-1999 . . . . . DLB-8

Bradley, William Aspenwall
1878-1939 . . . . DLB-4

Bradley, Ira, and Company DLB-49

Bradley, J. W., and Company DLB-49

Bradshaw, Henry 1831-1886 . . . . DLB-184

Bradstreet, Anne
1612 or 1613-1672 . . . . DLB-24

Bradūnas, Kazys 1917- DLB-220

Bradwardine, Thomas circa
1295-1349 . . . . DLB-115

Brady, Frank 1924-1986 . . . . DLB-111

Brady, Frederic A. [publishing house] DLB-49

Bragg, Melvyn 1939- DLB-14

Brainard, Charles H. [publishing house] . . . DLB-49

Braine, John 1922-1986 . . . . .DLB-15; Y-86

Braithwait, Richard 1588-1673 . . . . DLB-151

Braithwaite, William Stanley
1878-1962 . . . . DLB-50, 54

Braker, Ulrich 1735-1798 . . . . DLB-94

Bramah, Ernest 1868-1942 . . . . DLB-70

Branagan, Thomas 1774-1843 . . . . DLB-37

Branch, William Blackwell 1927- DLB-76

Branden Press DLB-46

Branner, H.C. 1903-1966 . . . . DLB-214

Brant, Sebastian 1457-1521 . . . . .DLB-179

Brassey, Lady Annie (Allnutt)
1839-1887 . . . . DLB-166

Brathwaite, Edward Kamau
1930- DLB-125

Brault, Jacques 1933- DLB-53

Braun, Matt 1932- DLB-212

Braun, Volker 1939- DLB-75

Brautigan, Richard
1935-1984 . . . . .DLB-2, 5, 206; Y-80, Y-84

Braxton, Joanne M. 1950- DLB-41

Bray, Anne Eliza 1790-1883 . . . . DLB-116

Bray, Thomas 1656-1730 . . . . DLB-24

Brazdžionis, Bernardas 1907- DLB-220

Braziller, George [publishing house] DLB-46

The Bread Loaf Writers'
Conference 1983 . . . . Y-84

The Break-Up of the Novel (1922),
by John Middleton Murry DLB-36

Breasted, James Henry 1865-1935 . . . . . . DLB-47

Brecht, Bertolt 1898-1956 . . . . DLB-56, 124

Bredel, Willi 1901-1964 . . . . DLB-56

Bregendahl, Marie 1867-1940 . . . . DLB-214

Breitinger, Johann Jakob 1701-1776 . . . . . DLB-97

Bremser, Bonnie 1939- DLB-16

Bremser, Ray 1934- DLB-16

Brentano, Bernard von 1901-1964 . . . . . . DLB-56

Brentano, Clemens 1778-1842 . . . . DLB-90

Brentano's DLB-49

Brenton, Howard 1942- DLB-13

Breslin, Jimmy 1929-1996 . . . . DLB-185

Breton, André 1896-1966 . . . . DLB-65

Breton, Nicholas
circa 1555-circa 1626 . . . . DLB-136

The Breton Lays
1300-early fifteenth century DLB-146

Brewer, Luther A. 1858-1933 . . . . DLB-187

Brewer, Warren and Putnam DLB-46

Brewster, Elizabeth 1922- DLB-60

Breytenbach, Breyten 1939- DLB-225

Bridge, Ann (Lady Mary Dolling Sanders
O'Malley) 1889-1974 . . . . DLB-191

Bridge, Horatio 1806-1893 . . . . DLB-183

Bridgers, Sue Ellen 1942- DLB-52

Bridges, Robert 1844-1930 . . . . DLB-19, 98

The Bridgewater Library DLB-213

Bridie, James 1888-1951 . . . . DLB-10

Brieux, Eugene 1858-1932 . . . . DLB-192

Brigadere, Anna 1861-1933 . . . . DLB-220

Bright, Mary Chavelita Dunne (see Egerton, George)

Brimmer, B. J., Company DLB-46

Brines, Francisco 1932- DLB-134

Brink, André 1935- DLB-225

Brinley, George, Jr. 1817-1875 . . . . DLB-140

Brinnin, John Malcolm 1916-1998 . . . . . . DLB-48

Brisbane, Albert 1809-1890 . . . . DLB-3

Brisbane, Arthur 1864-1936 . . . . DLB-25

British Academy DLB-112

The British Critic 1793-1843 . . . . DLB-110

The British Library and the Regular
Readers' Group Y-91

British Literary Prizes Y-98

The British Review and London Critical
Journal 1811-1825 . . . . DLB-110

British Travel Writing, 1940-1997 . . . . . DLB-204

Brito, Aristeo 1942- DLB-122

Brittain, Vera 1893-1970 . . . . DLB-191

Brizeux, Auguste 1803-1858 . . . . DLB-217

Broadway Publishing Company DLB-46

Broch, Hermann 1886-1951 . . . . DLB-85, 124

Brochu, André 1942- DLB-53

Brock, Edwin 1927- DLB-40

Brockes, Barthold Heinrich
1680-1747 . . . . DLB-168

Brod, Max 1884-1968 . . . . DLB-81

Brodber, Erna 1940- DLB-157

Brodhead, John R. 1814-1873 . . . . DLB-30

Brodkey, Harold 1930-1996 . . . . DLB-130

Brodsky, Joseph 1940-1996 . . . . Y-87

Broeg, Bob 1918- DLB-171

Brøgger, Suzanne 1944- DLB-214

Brome, Richard circa 1590-1652 . . . . DLB-58

Brome, Vincent 1910- DLB-155

Bromfield, Louis 1896-1956 . . . . DLB-4, 9, 86

Bromige, David 1933- DLB-193

Broner, E. M. 1930- DLB-28

Bronk, William 1918-1999 . . . . DLB-165

Bronnen, Arnolt 1895-1959 . . . . DLB-124

Brontë, Anne 1820-1849 . . . . DLB-21, 199

Brontë, Charlotte 1816-1855 . . . .DLB-21, 159, 199

Brontë, Emily 1818-1848 . . . . DLB-21, 32, 199

Brook, Stephen 1947- DLB-204

Brook Farm 1841-1847 . . . . DLB-223

Brooke, Frances 1724-1789 . . . . DLB-39, 99

Brooke, Henry 1703?-1783 . . . . DLB-39

Brooke, L. Leslie 1862-1940 . . . . DLB-141

Brooke, Margaret, Ranee of Sarawak
1849-1936 .DLB-174

Brooke, Rupert 1887-1915 . . . . DLB-19, 216

Brooker, Bertram 1888-1955 . . . . DLB-88

Brooke-Rose, Christine 1926- DLB-14

Brookner, Anita 1928- DLB-194; Y-87

Brooks, Charles Timothy 1813-1883 . . . . . . DLB-1

Brooks, Cleanth 1906-1994 . . . . . . .DLB-63; Y-94

Brooks, Gwendolyn 1917- DLB-5, 76, 165

Brooks, Jeremy 1926- DLB-14

Brooks, Mel 1926- DLB-26

Brooks, Noah 1830-1903 . . . . DLB-42; DS-13

Brooks, Richard 1912-1992 . . . . DLB-44

Brooks, Van Wyck
1886-1963 . . . . .DLB-45, 63, 103

Brophy, Brigid 1929-1995 . . . . DLB-14

Brophy, John 1899-1965 . . . . DLB-191

Brossard, Chandler 1922-1993 . . . . DLB-16

Brossard, Nicole 1943- DLB-53

Broster, Dorothy Kathleen
1877-1950 . . . . DLB-160

Brother Antoninus (see Everson, William)

Brotherton, Lord 1856-1930 . . . . DLB-184

Brougham and Vaux, Henry Peter Brougham,
Baron 1778-1868 . . . . .DLB-110, 158

Brougham, John 1810-1880 . . . . DLB-11

Broughton, James 1913-1999 . . . . DLB-5

Broughton, Rhoda 1840-1920 . . . . DLB-18

Broun, Heywood 1888-1939 . . . . . . .DLB-29, 171

Brown, Alice 1856-1948 . . . . DLB-78

Brown, Bob 1886-1959 . . . . DLB-4, 45

Brown, Cecil 1943- DLB-33

Brown, Charles Brockden
1771-1810 . . . . .DLB-37, 59, 73

Brown, Christy 1932-1981 . . . . DLB-14

Brown, Dee 1908- Y-80

Brown, Frank London 1927-1962 . . . . DLB-76

Brown, Fredric 1906-1972 . . . . DLB-8

Brown, George Mackay
1921-1996 . . . . .DLB-14, 27, 139

Brown, Harry 1917-1986 . . . . DLB-26

Brown, Marcia 1918- DLB-61

Brown, Margaret Wise 1910-1952 . . . . . . DLB-22

Brown, Morna Doris (see Ferrars, Elizabeth)

Brown, Oliver Madox 1855-1874 . . . . . . .DLB-21

Brown, Sterling 1901-1989 . . . . . . .DLB-48, 51, 63

Brown, T. E. 1830-1897. . . . . .DLB-35

Brown, William Hill 1765-1793 . . . . .DLB-37

Brown, William Wells
1814-1884 . . . . .DLB-3, 50, 183

Browne, Charles Farrar 1834-1867 . . . . . . .DLB-11

Browne, Frances 1816-1879 . . . . .DLB-199

Browne, Francis Fisher 1843-1913. . . . . . . .DLB-79

Browne, Howard 1908-1999 . . . . .DLB-226

Browne, J. Ross 1821-1875 . . . . .DLB-202

Browne, Michael Dennis 1940- DLB-40

Browne, Sir Thomas 1605-1682 . . . . .DLB-151

Browne, William, of Tavistock
1590-1645 . . . . .DLB-121

Browne, Wynyard 1911-1964 . . . . .DLB-13

Browne and Nolan. DLB-106

Brownell, W. C. 1851-1928. . . . . .DLB-71

Browning, Elizabeth Barrett
1806-1861 . . . . .DLB-32, 199

Browning, Robert 1812-1889. . . . . . .DLB-32, 163

Brownjohn, Allan 1931- DLB-40

Brownson, Orestes Augustus
1803-1876 . . . . .DLB-1, 59, 73

Bruccoli, Matthew J. 1931- DLB-103

Bruce, Charles 1906-1971 . . . . .DLB-68

Bruce, Leo 1903-1979 . . . . .DLB-77

Bruce, Philip Alexander 1856-1933 . . . . . . .DLB-47

Bruce Humphries [publishing house] DLB-46

Bruce-Novoa, Juan 1944- DLB-82

Bruckman, Clyde 1894-1955. . . . . .DLB-26

Bruckner, Ferdinand 1891-1958 . . . . .DLB-118

Brundage, John Herbert (see Herbert, John)

Brutus, Dennis 1924- DLB-117, 225

Bryan, C. D. B. 1936- DLB-185

Bryant, Arthur 1899-1985 . . . . .DLB-149

Bryant, William Cullen
1794-1878. . . . . .DLB-3, 43, 59, 189

Bryce Echenique, Alfredo 1939- DLB-145

Bryce, James 1838-1922. . . . . .DLB-166, 190

Brydges, Sir Samuel Egerton
1762-1837 . . . . .DLB-107

Bryskett, Lodowick 1546?-1612. . . . . . . .DLB-167

Buchan, John 1875-1940 . . . . . . .DLB-34, 70, 156

Buchanan, George 1506-1582 . . . . .DLB-132

Buchanan, Robert 1841-1901 . . . . . . .DLB-18, 35

Buchman, Sidney 1902-1975 . . . . .DLB-26

Buchner, Augustus 1591-1661. . . . . .DLB-164

Büchner, Georg 1813-1837 . . . . .DLB-133

Bucholtz, Andreas Heinrich
1607-1671. .DLB-168

Buck, Pearl S. 1892-1973 . . . . .DLB-9, 102

Bucke, Charles 1781-1846 . . . . .DLB-110

Bucke, Richard Maurice
1837-1902 . . . . .DLB-99

Buckingham, Joseph Tinker 1779-1861 and
Buckingham, Edwin 1810-1833 . . . . . .DLB-73

Buckler, Ernest 1908-1984. . . . . .DLB-68

Buckley, William F., Jr.
1925- DLB-137; Y-80

Buckminster, Joseph Stevens
1784-1812 . . . . .DLB-37

Buckner, Robert 1906- DLB-26

Budd, Thomas ?-1698 . . . . .DLB-24

Budrys, A. J. 1931- DLB-8

Buechner, Frederick 1926- Y-80

Buell, John 1927- DLB-53

Bufalino, Gesualdo 1920-1996. . . . . .DLB-196

Buffum, Job [publishing house] DLB-49

Bugnet, Georges 1879-1981 . . . . .DLB-92

Buies, Arthur 1840-1901 . . . . .DLB-99

Building the New British Library
at St Pancras Y-94

Bukowski, Charles 1920-1994 . . . .DLB-5, 130, 169

Bulatović, Miodrag 1930-1991. . . . . .DLB-181

Bulgarin, Faddei Venediktovich
1789-1859 . . . . .DLB-198

Bulger, Bozeman 1877-1932. . . . . .DLB-171

Bullein, William
between 1520 and 1530-1576 . . . . . . .DLB-167

Bullins, Ed 1935- DLB-7, 38

Bulwer-Lytton, Edward (also Edward Bulwer)
1803-1873 . . . . .DLB-21

Bumpus, Jerry 1937- Y-81

Bunce and Brother. DLB-49

Bunner, H. C. 1855-1896 . . . . DLB-78, 79

Bunting, Basil 1900-1985 . . . . .DLB-20

Buntline, Ned (Edward Zane Carroll Judson)
1821-1886 . . . . .DLB-186

Bunyan, John 1628-1688 . . . . .DLB-39

Burch, Robert 1925- DLB-52

Burciaga, José Antonio 1940- DLB-82

Bürger, Gottfried August 1747-1794 . . . . . .DLB-94

Burgess, Anthony 1917-1993 . . . . . . .DLB-14, 194

Burgess, Gelett 1866-1951 . . . . .DLB-11

Burgess, John W. 1844-1931 . . . . .DLB-47

Burgess, Thornton W. 1874-1965 . . . . . . .DLB-22

Burgess, Stringer and Company DLB-49

Burick, Si 1909-1986 . . . . .DLB-171

Burk, John Daly circa 1772-1808 . . . . .DLB-37

Burk, Ronnie 1955- DLB-209

Burke, Edmund 1729?-1797 . . . . .DLB-104

Burke, James Lee 1936- DLB-226

Burke, Kenneth 1897-1993. . . . . .DLB-45, 63

Burke, Thomas 1886-1945 . . . . .DLB-197

Burlingame, Edward Livermore
1848-1922 . . . . .DLB-79

Burnet, Gilbert 1643-1715 . . . . .DLB-101

Burnett, Frances Hodgson
1849-1924 . . . . .DLB-42, 141; DS-13, 14

Burnett, W. R. 1899-1982 . . . . .DLB-9, 226

Burnett, Whit 1899-1973 and
Martha Foley 1897-1977 . . . . .DLB-137

Burney, Fanny 1752-1840 . . . . .DLB-39

Burns, Alan 1929- DLB-14, 194

Burns, John Horne 1916-1953. . . . . Y-85

Burns, Robert 1759-1796 . . . . .DLB-109

Burns and Oates DLB-106

Burnshaw, Stanley 1906- DLB-48

Burr, C. Chauncey 1815?-1883. . . . . .DLB-79

Burr, Esther Edwards 1732-1758 . . . . . . .DLB-200

Burroughs, Edgar Rice 1875-1950 . . . . .DLB-8

Burroughs, John 1837-1921 . . . . .DLB-64

Burroughs, Margaret T. G. 1917- DLB-41

Burroughs, William S., Jr.
1947-1981 . . . . .DLB-16

Burroughs, William Seward
1914-1997 . . . . . .DLB-2, 8, 16, 152; Y-81, Y-97

Burroway, Janet 1936- DLB-6

Burt, Maxwell Struthers
1882-1954 . . . . .DLB-86; DS-16

Burt, A. L., and Company. DLB-49

Burton, Hester 1913- DLB-161

Burton, Isabel Arundell 1831-1896 . . . . . .DLB-166

Burton, Miles (see Rhode, John)

Burton, Richard Francis
1821-1890 . . . . .DLB-55, 166, 184

Burton, Robert 1577-1640 . . . . .DLB-151

Burton, Virginia Lee 1909-1968 . . . . .DLB-22

Burton, William Evans 1804-1860. . . . . . .DLB-73

Burwell, Adam Hood 1790-1849 . . . . .DLB-99

Bury, Lady Charlotte 1775-1861 . . . . .DLB-116

Busch, Frederick 1941- DLB-6, 218

Busch, Niven 1903-1991 . . . . .DLB-44

Bushnell, Horace 1802-1876 . . . . DS-13

Bussieres, Arthur de 1877-1913 . . . . .DLB-92

Butler, Guy 1918- DLB-225

Butler, Josephine Elizabeth
1828-1906 . . . . .DLB-190

Butler, Juan 1942-1981 . . . . .DLB-53

Butler, Octavia E. 1947- DLB-33

Butler, Pierce 1884-1953 . . . . .DLB-187

Butler, Robert Olen 1945- DLB-173

Butler, Samuel 1613-1680 . . . . .DLB-101, 126

Butler, Samuel 1835-1902 . . . . .DLB-18, 57, 174

Butler, William Francis 1838-1910 . . . . . .DLB-166

Butler, E. H., and Company DLB-49

Butor, Michel 1926- DLB-83

Butter, Nathaniel [publishing house] DLB-170

Butterworth, Hezekiah 1839-1905. . . . . . .DLB-42

Buttitta, Ignazio 1899- DLB-114

Buzzati, Dino 1906-1972 . . . . .DLB-177

Byars, Betsy 1928- DLB-52

Byatt, A. S. 1936- DLB-14, 194

Byles, Mather 1707-1788. . . . . .DLB-24

Bynneman, Henry
[publishing house] DLB-170

Bynner, Witter 1881-1968. . . . . .DLB-54

Byrd, William circa 1543-1623 . . . . .DLB-172

Byrd, William II 1674-1744 . . . . DLB-24, 140

Byrne, John Keyes (see Leonard, Hugh)

Byron, George Gordon, Lord
1788-1824. . . . . DLB-96, 110

Byron, Robert 1905-1941 . . . . DLB-195

C

Caballero Bonald, José Manuel
1926- DLB-108

Cabañero, Eladio 1930- DLB-134

Cabell, James Branch 1879-1958. . . . . . DLB-9, 78

Cabeza de Baca, Manuel 1853-1915. . . . . DLB-122

Cabeza de Baca Gilbert, Fabiola
1898- DLB-122

Cable, George Washington
1844-1925 . . . . .DLB-12, 74; DS-13

Cable, Mildred 1878-1952 . . . . DLB-195

Cabrera, Lydia 1900-1991 . . . . DLB-145

Cabrera Infante, Guillermo 1929- DLB-113

Cadell [publishing house] DLB-154

Cady, Edwin H. 1917- DLB-103

Caedmon flourished 658-680 . . . . DLB-146

Caedmon School circa 660-899 . . . . DLB-146

Cafés, Brasseries, and Bistros DS-15

Cage, John 1912-1992. . . . . DLB-193

Cahan, Abraham 1860-1951. . . . . . . DLB-9, 25, 28

Cain, George 1943- DLB-33

Cain, James M. 1892-1977 . . . . DLB-226

Caird, Mona 1854-1932 . . . . DLB-197

Čaks, Aleksandrs 1901-1950. . . . . DLB-220

Caldecott, Randolph 1846-1886. . . . . . . DLB-163

Calder, John (Publishers), Limited DLB-112

Calderón de la Barca, Fanny
1804-1882 . . . . DLB-183

Caldwell, Ben 1937- DLB-38

Caldwell, Erskine 1903-1987 . . . . DLB-9, 86

Caldwell, H. M., Company DLB-49

Caldwell, Taylor 1900-1985. . . . . .DS-17

Calhoun, John C. 1782-1850 . . . . DLB-3

Călinescu, George 1899-1965. . . . . DLB-220

Calisher, Hortense 1911- DLB-2, 218

A Call to Letters and an Invitation
to the Electric Chair,
by Siegfried Mandel DLB-75

Callaghan, Mary Rose 1944- DLB-207

Callaghan, Morley 1903-1990 . . . . DLB-68

Callahan, S. Alice 1868-1894 . . . . . .DLB-175, 221

Callaloo Y-87

Callimachus circa 305 B.C.-240 B.C.
. . . . .DLB-176

Calmer, Edgar 1907- DLB-4

Calverley, C. S. 1831-1884 . . . . DLB-35

Calvert, George Henry 1803-1889 . . . . . DLB-1, 64

Calvino, Italo 1923-1985 . . . . DLB-196

Cambridge Press. DLB-49

Cambridge Songs (Carmina Cantabrigensia)
circa 1050. DLB-148

Cambridge University Press. DLB-170

Camden, William 1551-1623 . . . . .DLB-172

Camden House: An Interview with
James Hardin Y-92

Cameron, Eleanor 1912- DLB-52

Cameron, George Frederick
1854-1885 . . . . DLB-99

Cameron, Lucy Lyttelton 1781-1858 . . . . DLB-163

Cameron, William Bleasdell
1862-1951 . . . . DLB-99

Camm, John 1718-1778. . . . . DLB-31

Camon, Ferdinando 1935- DLB-196

Campana, Dino 1885-1932. . . . . DLB-114

Campbell, Gabrielle Margaret Vere
(see Shearing, Joseph, and Bowen, Marjorie)

Campbell, James Dykes 1838-1895 . . . . . DLB-144

Campbell, James Edwin 1867-1896. . . . . . DLB-50

Campbell, John 1653-1728 . . . . DLB-43

Campbell, John W., Jr. 1910-1971 . . . . DLB-8

Campbell, Roy 1901-1957 . . . . DLB-20, 225

Campbell, Thomas
1777-1844 . . . . DLB-93, 144

Campbell, William Wilfred
1858-1918 . . . . DLB-92

Campion, Edmund 1539-1581 . . . . DLB-167

Campion, Thomas
1567-1620. . . . . .DLB-58, 172

Camus, Albert 1913-1960. . . . . DLB-72

The Canadian Publishers' Records
Database. Y-96

Canby, Henry Seidel 1878-1961 . . . . DLB-91

Candelaria, Cordelia 1943- DLB-82

Candelaria, Nash 1928- DLB-82

Candour in English Fiction (1890),
by Thomas Hardy DLB-18

Canetti, Elias 1905-1994. . . . . DLB-85, 124

Canham, Erwin Dain 1904-1982 . . . . DLB-127

Canitz, Friedrich Rudolph Ludwig von
1654-1699 . . . . DLB-168

Cankar, Ivan 1876-1918 . . . . DLB-147

Cannan, Gilbert 1884-1955 . . . . .DLB-10, 197

Cannan, Joanna 1896-1961 . . . . DLB-191

Cannell, Kathleen 1891-1974 . . . . DLB-4

Cannell, Skipwith 1887-1957. . . . . DLB-45

Canning, George 1770-1827 . . . . DLB-158

Cannon, Jimmy 1910-1973 . . . . .DLB-171

Cano, Daniel 1947- DLB-209

Cantú, Norma Elia 1947- DLB-209

Cantwell, Robert 1908-1978 . . . . DLB-9

Cape, Jonathan, and Harrison Smith
[publishing house] DLB-46

Cape, Jonathan, Limited. DLB-112

Čapek, Karel 1890-1938 . . . . DLB-215

Capen, Joseph 1658-1725 . . . . DLB-24

Capes, Bernard 1854-1918 . . . . DLB-156

Capote, Truman
1924-1984 . . . . .DLB-2, 185; Y-80, Y-84

Caproni, Giorgio 1912-1990. . . . . DLB-128

Caragiale, Mateiu Ioan 1885-1936 . . . . . . DLB-220

Cardarelli, Vincenzo 1887-1959 . . . . DLB-114

Cárdenas, Reyes 1948- DLB-122

Cardinal, Marie 1929- DLB-83

Carew, Jan 1920- DLB-157

Carew, Thomas 1594 or 1595-1640 . . . . DLB-126

Carey, Henry
circa 1687-1689-1743 . . . . DLB-84

Carey, Mathew 1760-1839 . . . . .DLB-37, 73

Carey and Hart DLB-49

Carey, M., and Company DLB-49

Carlell, Lodowick 1602-1675 . . . . DLB-58

Carleton, William 1794-1869 . . . . DLB-159

Carleton, G. W. [publishing house] DLB-49

Carlile, Richard 1790-1843 . . . . .DLB-110, 158

Carlyle, Jane Welsh 1801-1866 . . . . DLB-55

Carlyle, Thomas 1795-1881 . . . . DLB-55, 144

Carman, Bliss 1861-1929 . . . . DLB-92

Carmina Burana circa 1230. . . . . DLB-138

Carnero, Guillermo 1947- DLB-108

Carossa, Hans 1878-1956 . . . . DLB-66

Carpenter, Humphrey 1946- DLB-155

Carpenter, Stephen Cullen ?-1820? DLB-73

Carpentier, Alejo 1904-1980. . . . . DLB-113

Carrier, Roch 1937- DLB-53

Carrillo, Adolfo 1855-1926. . . . . DLB-122

Carroll, Gladys Hasty 1904- DLB-9

Carroll, John 1735-1815 . . . . DLB-37

Carroll, John 1809-1884. . . . . DLB-99

Carroll, Lewis 1832-1898. . . . . . .DLB-18, 163, 178

Carroll, Paul 1927- DLB-16

Carroll, Paul Vincent 1900-1968 . . . . DLB-10

Carroll and Graf Publishers DLB-46

Carruth, Hayden 1921- DLB-5, 165

Carryl, Charles E. 1841-1920. . . . . DLB-42

Carson, Anne 1950- DLB-193

Carswell, Catherine 1879-1946. . . . . DLB-36

Carter, Angela 1940-1992 . . . . .DLB-14, 207

Carter, Elizabeth 1717-1806 . . . . DLB-109

Carter, Henry (see Leslie, Frank)

Carter, Hodding, Jr. 1907-1972 . . . . .DLB-127

Carter, John 1905-1975. . . . . DLB-201

Carter, Landon 1710-1778 . . . . DLB-31

Carter, Lin 1930- Y-81

Carter, Martin 1927-1997 . . . . .DLB-117

Carter and Hendee. DLB-49

Carter, Robert, and Brothers DLB-49

Cartwright, John 1740-1824 . . . . DLB-158

Cartwright, William circa 1611-1643 . . . . DLB-126

Caruthers, William Alexander
1802-1846 . . . . DLB-3

Carver, Jonathan 1710-1780 . . . . DLB-31

Carver, Raymond
1938-1988 . . . . DLB-130; Y-84, Y-88

Cary, Alice 1820-1871 . . . . DLB-202

Cary, Joyce 1888-1957 . . . . .DLB-15, 100

Cary, Patrick 1623?-1657 . . . . .DLB-131

Casey, Juanita 1925- DLB-14

Casey, Michael 1947- DLB-5

Cassady, Carolyn 1923- DLB-16

Cassady, Neal 1926-1968 . . . . .DLB-16

Cassell and Company DLB-106

Cassell Publishing Company DLB-49

Cassill, R. V. 1919- DLB-6, 218

Cassity, Turner 1929- DLB-105

Cassius Dio circa 155/164-post 229
. . . . .DLB-176

Cassola, Carlo 1917-1987 . . . . .DLB-177

The Castle of Perserverance
circa 1400-1425 . . . . .DLB-146

Castellano, Olivia 1944- DLB-122

Castellanos, Rosario 1925-1974 . . . . .DLB-113

Castillo, Ana 1953- DLB-122

Castillo, Rafael C. 1950- DLB-209

Castlemon, Harry (see Fosdick, Charles Austin)

Čašule, Kole 1921- DLB-181

Caswall, Edward 1814-1878 . . . . .DLB-32

Catacalos, Rosemary 1944- DLB-122

Cather, Willa 1873-1947 . . . . . DLB-9, 54, 78; DS-1

Catherine II (Ekaterina Alekseevna), "The Great,"
Empress of Russia 1729-1796 . . . . . . .DLB-150

Catherwood, Mary Hartwell
1847-1902 .DLB-78

Catledge, Turner 1901-1983 . . . . .DLB-127

Catlin, George 1796-1872 . . . . .DLB-186, 189

Cato the Elder 234 B.C.-149 B.C. DLB-211

Cattafi, Bartolo 1922-1979 . . . . .DLB-128

Catton, Bruce 1899-1978 . . . . .DLB-17

Catullus circa 84 B.C.-54 B.C. DLB-211

Causley, Charles 1917- DLB-27

Caute, David 1936- DLB-14

Cavendish, Duchess of Newcastle,
Margaret Lucas 1623-1673 . . . . .DLB-131

Cawein, Madison 1865-1914 . . . . .DLB-54

The Caxton Printers, Limited DLB-46

Caxton, William [publishing house] DLB-170

Cayrol, Jean 1911- DLB-83

Cecil, Lord David 1902-1986 . . . . .DLB-155

Cela, Camilo José 1916- Y-89

Celan, Paul 1920-1970 . . . . .DLB-69

Celati, Gianni 1937- DLB-196

Celaya, Gabriel 1911-1991 . . . . .DLB-108

A Celebration of Literary Biography Y-98

Céline, Louis-Ferdinand 1894-1961 . . . . . . .DLB-72

The Celtic Background to Medieval English
Literature DLB-146

Celtis, Conrad 1459-1508 . . . . .DLB-179

Center for Bibliographical Studies and
Research at the University of
California, Riverside Y-91

The Center for the Book in the Library
of Congress Y-93

Center for the Book Research Y-84

Centlivre, Susanna 1669?-1723 . . . . .DLB-84

The Century Company DLB-49

Cernuda, Luis 1902-1963 . . . . .DLB-134

"Certain Gifts," by Betty Adcock DLB-105

Cervantes, Lorna Dee 1954- DLB-82

Chaadaev, Petr Iakovlevich
1794-1856 .DLB-198

Chacel, Rosa 1898- DLB-134

Chacón, Eusebio 1869-1948 . . . . .DLB-82

Chacón, Felipe Maximiliano 1873-? DLB-82

Chadwyck-Healey's Full-Text Literary Databases:
Editing Commercial Databases of
Primary Literary Texts Y-95

Challans, Eileen Mary (see Renault, Mary)

Chalmers, George 1742-1825 . . . . .DLB-30

Chaloner, Sir Thomas 1520-1565 . . . . . . .DLB-167

Chamberlain, Samuel S. 1851-1916 . . . . . .DLB-25

Chamberland, Paul 1939- DLB-60

Chamberlin, William Henry
1897-1969 .DLB-29

Chambers, Charles Haddon
1860-1921 .DLB-10

Chambers, María Cristina (see Mena, María Cristina)

Chambers, Robert W. 1865-1933 . . . . . . .DLB-202

Chambers, W. and R.
[publishing house] DLB-106

Chamisso, Albert von 1781-1838 . . . . .DLB-90

Champfleury 1821-1889 . . . . .DLB-119

Chandler, Harry 1864-1944 . . . . .DLB-29

Chandler, Norman 1899-1973 . . . . .DLB-127

Chandler, Otis 1927- DLB-127

Chandler, Raymond 1888-1959 . . .DLB-226; DS-6

Channing, Edward 1856-1931 . . . . .DLB-17

Channing, Edward Tyrrell 1790-1856 . . .DLB-1, 59

Channing, William Ellery 1780-1842 . . . .DLB-1, 59

Channing, William Ellery II
1817-1901 . . . . .DLB-1, 223

Channing, William Henry
1810-1884 . . . . .DLB-1, 59

Chaplin, Charlie 1889-1977 . . . . .DLB-44

Chapman, George
1559 or 1560 - 1634 . . . . .DLB-62, 121

Chapman, John DLB-106

Chapman, Olive Murray 1892-1977 . . . . .DLB-195

Chapman, R. W. 1881-1960 . . . . .DLB-201

Chapman, William 1850-1917 . . . . .DLB-99

Chapman and Hall DLB-106

Chappell, Fred 1936- DLB-6, 105

Charbonneau, Jean 1875-1960 . . . . .DLB-92

Charbonneau, Robert 1911-1967 . . . . .DLB-68

Charles d'Orléans 1394-1465 . . . . .DLB-208

Charles, Gerda 1914- DLB-14

Charles, William [publishing house] DLB-49

The Charles Wood Affair:
A Playwright Revived Y-83

Charley (see Mann, Charles)

Charlotte Forten: Pages from her Diary . . .DLB-50

Charteris, Leslie 1907-1993 . . . . .DLB-77

Chartier, Alain circa 1385-1430 . . . . .DLB-208

Charyn, Jerome 1937- Y-83

Chase, Borden 1900-1971 . . . . .DLB-26

Chase, Edna Woolman 1877-1957 . . . . .DLB-91

Chase-Riboud, Barbara 1936- DLB-33

Chateaubriand, François-René de
1768-1848 .DLB-119

Chatterton, Thomas 1752-1770 . . . . .DLB-109

Chatto and Windus DLB-106

Chatwin, Bruce 1940-1989 . . . . . . .DLB-194, 204

Chaucer, Geoffrey 1340?-1400 . . . . .DLB-146

Chauncy, Charles 1705-1787 . . . . .DLB-24

Chauveau, Pierre-Joseph-Olivier
1820-1890 .DLB-99

Chávez, Denise 1948- DLB-122

Chávez, Fray Angélico 1910- DLB-82

Chayefsky, Paddy 1923-1981 . . . . DLB-7, 44; Y-81

Cheesman, Evelyn 1881-1969 . . . . .DLB-195

Cheever, Ezekiel 1615-1708 . . . . .DLB-24

Cheever, George Barrell 1807-1890 . . . . . .DLB-59

Cheever, John
1912-1982 . . . . DLB-2, 102; Y-80, Y-82

Cheever, Susan 1943- Y-82

Cheke, Sir John 1514-1557 . . . . .DLB-132

Chelsea House DLB-46

Chênedollé, Charles de 1769-1833 . . . . . .DLB-217

Cheney, Ednah Dow
1824-1904 . . . . .DLB-1, 223

Cheney, Harriet Vaughn 1796-1889 . . . . . .DLB-99

Chénier, Marie-Joseph 1764-1811 . . . . . . .DLB-192

Cherry, Kelly 1940- Y-83

Cherryh, C. J. 1942- Y-80

Chesebro', Caroline 1825-1873 . . . . .DLB-202

Chesnutt, Charles Waddell
1858-1932 . . . . DLB-12, 50, 78

Chesney, Sir George Tomkyns
1830-1895 .DLB-190

Chester, Alfred 1928-1971 . . . . .DLB-130

Chester, George Randolph 1869-1924 . . . .DLB-78

The Chester Plays circa 1505-1532;
revisions until 1575 . . . . .DLB-146

Chesterfield, Philip Dormer Stanhope,
Fourth Earl of 1694-1773 . . . . .DLB-104

Chesterton, G. K. 1874-1936
. . . . .DLB-10, 19, 34, 70, 98, 149, 178

Chettle, Henry
circa 1560-circa 1607 . . . . .DLB-136

Chew, Ada Nield 1870-1945 . . . . .DLB-135

Cheyney, Edward P. 1861-1947 . . . . .DLB-47

Chiara, Piero 1913-1986 . . . . .DLB-177

Chicano History DLB-82

Chicano Language DLB-82

Child, Francis James 1825-1896 . . . . . . .DLB-1, 64

Child, Lydia Maria 1802-1880 . . . . .DLB-1, 74

Child, Philip 1898-1978 . . . . .DLB-68

Childers, Erskine 1870-1922 . . . . DLB-70

Children's Book Awards and Prizes DLB-61

Children's Illustrators, 1800-1880 . . . . . . DLB-163

Childress, Alice 1920-1994 . . . . .DLB-7, 38

Childs, George W. 1829-1894 . . . . DLB-23

Chilton Book Company DLB-46

Chin, Frank 1940- DLB-206

Chinweizu 1943- DLB-157

Chitham, Edward 1932- DLB-155

Chittenden, Hiram Martin 1858-1917 . . . . DLB-47

Chivers, Thomas Holley 1809-1858. . . . . . DLB-3

Cholmondeley, Mary 1859-1925 . . . . DLB-197

Chopin, Kate 1850-1904. . . . . DLB-12, 78

Chopin, Rene 1885-1953 . . . . DLB-92

Choquette, Adrienne 1915-1973 . . . . DLB-68

Choquette, Robert 1905- DLB-68

Chrétien de Troyes
    circa 1140-circa 1190 . . . . DLB-208

Christensen, Inger 1935- DLB-214

The Christian Publishing Company DLB-49

Christie, Agatha 1890-1976. . . . . DLB-13, 77

Christine de Pizan
    circa 1365-circa 1431 . . . . DLB-208

The Christopher Isherwood Archive,
    The Huntington Library Y-99

Christus und die Samariterin circa 950 . . . . . . DLB-148

Christy, Howard Chandler
    1873-1952. DLB-188

Chulkov, Mikhail Dmitrievich
    1743?-1792 . . . . DLB-150

Church, Benjamin 1734-1778 . . . . DLB-31

Church, Francis Pharcellus 1839-1906 . . . . DLB-79

Church, Peggy Pond 1903-1986. . . . . DLB-212

Church, Richard 1893-1972 . . . . DLB-191

Church, William Conant 1836-1917 . . . . . DLB-79

Churchill, Caryl 1938- DLB-13

Churchill, Charles 1731-1764 . . . . DLB-109

Churchill, Winston 1871-1947 . . . . DLB-202

Churchill, Sir Winston
    1874-1965. . . . . DLB-100; DS-16

Churchyard, Thomas 1520?-1604 . . . . . . DLB-132

Churton, E., and Company DLB-106

Chute, Marchette 1909-1994 . . . . DLB-103

Ciardi, John 1916-1986. . . . . DLB-5; Y-86

Cibber, Colley 1671-1757 . . . . DLB-84

Cicero 106 B.C.-43 B.C.. . . . . DLB-211

Cima, Annalisa 1941- DLB-128

Čingo, Živko 1935-1987. . . . . DLB-181

Cioran, E. M. 1911-1995 . . . . DLB-220

Čipkus, Alfonsas (see Nyka-Niliūnas, Alfonsas)

Cirese, Eugenio 1884-1955. . . . . DLB-114

Cisneros, Sandra 1954- DLB-122, 152

City Lights Books. DLB-46

Cixous, Hélène 1937- DLB-83

Clampitt, Amy 1920-1994 . . . . DLB-105

Clapper, Raymond 1892-1944 . . . . DLB-29

Clare, John 1793-1864 . . . . DLB-55, 96

Clarendon, Edward Hyde, Earl of
    1609-1674. . . . . DLB-101

Clark, Alfred Alexander Gordon (see Hare, Cyril)

Clark, Ann Nolan 1896- DLB-52

Clark, C. E. Frazer Jr. 1925- DLB-187

Clark, C. M., Publishing Company DLB-46

Clark, Catherine Anthony 1892-1977. . . . . DLB-68

Clark, Charles Heber 1841-1915 . . . . DLB-11

Clark, Davis Wasgatt 1812-1871 . . . . DLB-79

Clark, Eleanor 1913- DLB-6

Clark, J. P. 1935- DLB-117

Clark, Lewis Gaylord 1808-1873 . . . DLB-3, 64, 73

Clark, Walter Van Tilburg
    1909-1971. . . . . DLB-9, 206

Clark, William (see Lewis, Meriwether)

Clark, William Andrews Jr.
    1877-1934. . . . . DLB-187

Clarke, Austin 1896-1974 . . . . DLB-10, 20

Clarke, Austin C. 1934- DLB-53, 125

Clarke, Gillian 1937- DLB-40

Clarke, James Freeman 1810-1888 . . . . . DLB-1, 59

Clarke, Pauline 1921- DLB-161

Clarke, Rebecca Sophia 1833-1906 . . . . . . DLB-42

Clarke, Robert, and Company DLB-49

Clarkson, Thomas 1760-1846. . . . . DLB-158

Claudel, Paul 1868-1955 . . . . DLB-192

Claudius, Matthias 1740-1815 . . . . DLB-97

Clausen, Andy 1943- DLB-16

Clawson, John L. 1865-1933 . . . . DLB-187

Claxton, Remsen and Haffelfinger DLB-49

Clay, Cassius Marcellus 1810-1903 . . . . . . DLB-43

Cleary, Beverly 1916- DLB-52

Cleary, Kate McPhelim 1863-1905. . . . . . DLB-221

Cleaver, Vera 1919- and
    Cleaver, Bill 1920-1981 . . . . DLB-52

Cleland, John 1710-1789 . . . . DLB-39

Clemens, Samuel Langhorne (Mark Twain)
    1835-1910 . . . DLB-11, 12, 23, 64, 74, 186, 189

Clement, Hal 1922- DLB-8

Clemo, Jack 1916- DLB-27

Clephane, Elizabeth Cecilia
    1830-1869 . . . . DLB-199

Cleveland, John 1613-1658. . . . . DLB-126

Cliff, Michelle 1946- DLB-157

Clifford, Lady Anne 1590-1676 . . . . DLB-151

Clifford, James L. 1901-1978 . . . . DLB-103

Clifford, Lucy 1853?-1929 . . . . .DLB-135, 141, 197

Clifton, Lucille 1936- DLB-5, 41

Clines, Francis X. 1938- DLB-185

Clive, Caroline (V) 1801-1873 . . . . DLB-199

Clode, Edward J. [publishing house] DLB-46

Clough, Arthur Hugh 1819-1861 . . . . DLB-32

Cloutier, Cécile 1930- DLB-60

Clouts, Sidney 1926-1982. . . . . DLB-225

Clutton-Brock, Arthur 1868-1924 . . . . . . DLB-98

Coates, Robert M. 1897-1973 . . . . . .DLB-4, 9, 102

Coatsworth, Elizabeth 1893- DLB-22

Cobb, Charles E., Jr. 1943- DLB-41

Cobb, Frank I. 1869-1923 . . . . DLB-25

Cobb, Irvin S. 1876-1944 . . . . DLB-11, 25, 86

Cobbe, Frances Power 1822-1904 . . . . . . DLB-190

Cobbett, William 1763-1835. . . . . .DLB-43, 107

Cobbledick, Gordon 1898-1969. . . . . . . .DLB-171

Cochran, Thomas C. 1902- DLB-17

Cochrane, Elizabeth 1867-1922 . . . . . DLB-25, 189

Cockerell, Sir Sydney 1867-1962 . . . . DLB-201

Cockerill, John A. 1845-1896. . . . . DLB-23

Cocteau, Jean 1889-1963 . . . . DLB-65

Coderre, Emile (see Jean Narrache)

Coetzee, J. M. 1940- DLB-225

Coffee, Lenore J. 1900?-1984 . . . . DLB-44

Coffin, Robert P. Tristram 1892-1955 . . . . DLB-45

Cogswell, Fred 1917- DLB-60

Cogswell, Mason Fitch 1761-1830 . . . . . . DLB-37

Cohen, Arthur A. 1928-1986 . . . . DLB-28

Cohen, Leonard 1934- DLB-53

Cohen, Matt 1942- DLB-53

Colbeck, Norman 1903-1987 . . . . DLB-201

Colden, Cadwallader 1688-1776. . . . . . DLB-24, 30

Colden, Jane 1724-1766 . . . . DLB-200

Cole, Barry 1936- DLB-14

Cole, George Watson 1850-1939 . . . . DLB-140

Colegate, Isabel 1931- DLB-14

Coleman, Emily Holmes 1899-1974 . . . . . . DLB-4

Coleman, Wanda 1946- DLB-130

Coleridge, Hartley 1796-1849. . . . . DLB-96

Coleridge, Mary 1861-1907 . . . . DLB-19, 98

Coleridge, Samuel Taylor
    1772-1834. . . . . .DLB-93, 107

Coleridge, Sara 1802-1852 . . . . DLB-199

Colet, John 1467-1519 . . . . DLB-132

Colette 1873-1954. . . . . DLB-65

Colette, Sidonie Gabrielle (see Colette)

Colinas, Antonio 1946- DLB-134

Coll, Joseph Clement 1881-1921 . . . . . . DLB-188

Collier, John 1901-1980 . . . . DLB-77

Collier, John Payne 1789-1883 . . . . DLB-184

Collier, Mary 1690-1762. . . . . DLB-95

Collier, Robert J. 1876-1918 . . . . DLB-91

Collier, P. F. [publishing house] DLB-49

Collin and Small. DLB-49

Collingwood, W. G. 1854-1932 . . . . DLB-149

Collins, An floruit circa 1653 . . . . DLB-131

Collins, Merle 1950- DLB-157

Collins, Mortimer 1827-1876 . . . . DLB-21, 35

Collins, Wilkie 1824-1889 . . . . . . .DLB-18, 70, 159

Collins, William 1721-1759. . . . . DLB-109

Collins, William, Sons and Company . . . DLB-154

Collins, Isaac [publishing house]. DLB-49

Collis, Maurice 1889-1973 . . . . .DLB-195

Collyer, Mary 1716?-1763? DLB-39

Colman, Benjamin 1673-1747 . . . . .DLB-24

Colman, George, the Elder 1732-1794 . . . . .DLB-89

Colman, George, the Younger
    1762-1836 . . . . .DLB-89

Colman, S. [publishing house] DLB-49

Colombo, John Robert 1936- DLB-53

Colquhoun, Patrick 1745-1820 . . . . .DLB-158

Colter, Cyrus 1910- DLB-33

Colum, Padraic 1881-1972. . . . . .DLB-19

Columella fl. first century A.D. DLB-211

Colvin, Sir Sidney 1845-1927 . . . . .DLB-149

Colwin, Laurie 1944-1992 . . . . DLB-218; Y-80

Comden, Betty 1919- and Green,
    Adolph 1918- DLB-44

Come to Papa Y-99

Comi, Girolamo 1890-1968 . . . . .DLB-114

The Comic Tradition Continued
    [in the British Novel] DLB-15

Commager, Henry Steele 1902-1998 . . . . . .DLB-17

The Commercialization of the Image of
    Revolt, by Kenneth Rexroth DLB-16

Community and Commentators: Black
    Theatre and Its Critics DLB-38

Commynes, Philippe de
    circa 1447-1511 . . . . .DLB-208

Compton-Burnett, Ivy 1884?-1969 . . . . . . .DLB-36

Conan, Laure 1845-1924 . . . . .DLB-99

Concord History and Life DLB-223

Concord Literary History of a Town DLB-223

Conde, Carmen 1901- DLB-108

Conference on Modern Biography Y-85

Congreve, William 1670-1729 . . . . . . .DLB-39, 84

Conkey, W. B., Company DLB-49

Connell, Evan S., Jr. 1924- DLB-2; Y-81

Connelly, Marc 1890-1980 . . . . DLB-7; Y-80

Connolly, Cyril 1903-1974. . . . . .DLB-98

Connolly, James B. 1868-1957 . . . . .DLB-78

Connor, Ralph 1860-1937 . . . . .DLB-92

Connor, Tony 1930- DLB-40

Conquest, Robert 1917- DLB-27

Conrad, Joseph 1857-1924 . . . . DLB-10, 34, 98, 156

Conrad, John, and Company DLB-49

Conroy, Jack 1899-1990 . . . . Y-81

Conroy, Pat 1945- DLB-6

The Consolidation of Opinion: Critical
    Responses to the Modernists. DLB-36

Consolo, Vincenzo 1933- DLB-196

Constable, Henry 1562-1613 . . . . .DLB-136

Constable and Company Limited DLB-112

Constable, Archibald, and Company. DLB-154

Constant, Benjamin 1767-1830 . . . . .DLB-119

Constant de Rebecque, Henri-Benjamin de
    (see Constant, Benjamin)

Constantine, David 1944- DLB-40

Constantin-Weyer, Maurice
    1881-1964 . . . . .DLB-92

Contempo Caravan: Kites in a
    Windstorm Y-85

A Contemporary Flourescence of Chicano
    Literature Y-84

"Contemporary Verse Story-telling,"
    by Jonathan Holden DLB-105

The Continental Publishing Company DLB-49

A Conversation with Chaim Potok Y-84

Conversations with Editors Y-95

Conversations with Publishers I: An Interview
    with Patrick O'Connor Y-84

Conversations with Publishers II: An Interview
    with Charles Scribner III Y-94

Conversations with Publishers III: An Interview
    with Donald Lamm. Y-95

Conversations with Publishers IV: An Interview
    with James Laughlin Y-96

Conversations with Rare Book Dealers I: An
    Interview with Glenn Horowitz Y-90

Conversations with Rare Book Dealers II: An
    Interview with Ralph Sipper Y-94

Conversations with Rare Book Dealers
    (Publishers) III: An Interview with
    Otto Penzler Y-96

The Conversion of an Unpolitical Man,
    by W. H. Bruford DLB-66

Conway, Moncure Daniel 1832-1907. .DLB-1, 223

Cook, Ebenezer circa 1667-circa 1732 . . . . .DLB-24

Cook, Edward Tyas 1857-1919 . . . . .DLB 149

Cook, Eliza 1818-1889. . . . . .DLB-199

Cook, Michael 1933- DLB-53

Cook, David C., Publishing Company DLB-49

Cooke, George Willis 1848-1923. . . . . .DLB-71

Cooke, Increase, and Company DLB-49

Cooke, John Esten 1830-1886 . . . . .DLB-3

Cooke, Philip Pendleton 1816-1850 . . . .DLB-3, 59

Cooke, Rose Terry 1827-1892 . . . . DLB-12, 74

Cook-Lynn, Elizabeth 1930- DLB-175

Coolbrith, Ina 1841-1928. . . . . .DLB-54, 186

Cooley, Peter 1940- DLB-105

Coolidge, Clark 1939- DLB-193

Coolidge, Susan (see Woolsey, Sarah Chauncy)

Coolidge, George [publishing house] DLB-49

Cooper, Anna Julia 1858-1964 . . . . .DLB-221

Cooper, Giles 1918-1966 . . . . .DLB-13

Cooper, J. California 19??- DLB-212

Cooper, James Fenimore 1789-1851. . . .DLB-3, 183

Cooper, Kent 1880-1965 . . . . .DLB-29

Cooper, Susan 1935- DLB-161

Cooper, William [publishing house] DLB-170

Coote, J. [publishing house] DLB-154

Coover, Robert 1932- DLB-2; Y-81

Copeland and Day. DLB-49

Ćopić, Branko 1915-1984 . . . . .DLB-181

Copland, Robert 1470?-1548 . . . . .DLB-136

Coppard, A. E. 1878-1957 . . . . .DLB-162

Coppée, François 1842-1908 . . . . .DLB-217

Coppel, Alfred 1921- Y-83

Coppola, Francis Ford 1939- DLB-44

Copway, George (Kah-ge-ga-gah-bowh)
    1818-1869 . . . . DLB-175, 183

Corazzini, Sergio 1886-1907 . . . . .DLB-114

Corbett, Richard 1582-1635 . . . . .DLB-121

Corbière, Tristan 1845-1875 . . . . .DLB-217

Corcoran, Barbara 1911- DLB-52

Cordelli, Franco 1943- DLB-196

Corelli, Marie 1855-1924. . . . . .DLB-34, 156

Corle, Edwin 1906-1956 . . . . Y-85

Corman, Cid 1924- DLB-5, 193

Cormier, Robert 1925- DLB-52

Corn, Alfred 1943- DLB-120; Y-80

Cornish, Sam 1935- DLB-41

Cornish, William
    circa 1465-circa 1524. . . . . .DLB-132

Cornwall, Barry (see Procter, Bryan Waller)

Cornwallis, Sir William, the Younger
    circa 1579-1614 . . . . .DLB-151

Cornwell, David John Moore (see le Carré, John)

Corpi, Lucha 1945- DLB-82

Corrington, John William 1932- DLB-6

Corrothers, James D. 1869-1917 . . . . .DLB-50

Corso, Gregory 1930- DLB-5, 16

Cortázar, Julio 1914-1984 . . . . .DLB-113

Cortéz, Carlos 1923- DLB-209

Cortez, Jayne 1936- DLB-41

Corvinus, Gottlieb Siegmund 1677-1746 . .DLB-168

Corvo, Baron (see Rolfe, Frederick William)

Cory, Annie Sophie (see Cross, Victoria)

Cory, William Johnson 1823-1892 . . . . . . .DLB-35

Coryate, Thomas 1577?-1617 . . . . . . DLB-151, 172

Ćosić, Dobrica 1921- DLB-181

Cosin, John 1595-1672. . . . . DLB-151, 213

Cosmopolitan Book Corporation DLB-46

Costain, Thomas B. 1885-1965 . . . . .DLB-9

Coste, Donat 1912-1957 . . . . .DLB-88

Costello, Louisa Stuart 1799-1870 . . . . . . .DLB-166

Cota-Cárdenas, Margarita 1941- DLB-122

Cotten, Bruce 1873-1954 . . . . .DLB-187

Cotter, Joseph Seamon, Sr. 1861-1949 . . . .DLB-50

Cotter, Joseph Seamon, Jr. 1895-1919 . . . . .DLB-50

Cottle, Joseph [publishing house]. DLB-154

Cotton, Charles 1630-1687 . . . . .DLB-131

Cotton, John 1584-1652 . . . . .DLB-24

Cotton, Sir Robert Bruce 1571-1631 . . . . .DLB-213

Coulter, John 1888-1980 . . . . .DLB-68

Cournos, John 1881-1966 . . . . .DLB-54

Courteline, Georges 1858-1929 . . . . .DLB-192

Cousins, Margaret 1905-1996 . . . . .DLB-137

Cousins, Norman 1915-1990 . . . . .DLB-137

Coventry, Francis 1725-1754 . . . . .DLB-39

Coverdale, Miles 1487 or 1488-1569 . . . . .DLB-167

Coverly, N. [publishing house] DLB-49

Covici-Friede DLB-46

Coward, Noel 1899-1973 . . . . DLB-10

Coward, McCann and Geoghegan DLB-46

Cowles, Gardner 1861-1946 . . . . DLB-29

Cowles, Gardner ("Mike"), Jr.
    1903-1985 . . . . DLB-127, 137

Cowley, Abraham 1618-1667 . . . . . DLB-131, 151

Cowley, Hannah 1743-1809 . . . . DLB-89

Cowley, Malcolm
    1898-1989 . . . . DLB-4, 48; Y-81, Y-89

Cowper, William 1731-1800 . . . . . . DLB-104, 109

Cox, A. B. (see Berkeley, Anthony)

Cox, James McMahon 1903-1974 . . . . DLB-127

Cox, James Middleton 1870-1957 . . . . DLB-127

Cox, Palmer 1840-1924 . . . . DLB-42

Coxe, Louis 1918-1993 . . . . DLB-5

Coxe, Tench 1755-1824 . . . . DLB-37

Cozzens, Frederick S. 1818-1869 . . . . DLB-202

Cozzens, James Gould
    1903-1978 . . . . DLB-9; Y-84; DS-2

Cozzens's *Michael Scarlett* Y-97

Crabbe, George 1754-1832 . . . . DLB-93

Crackanthorpe, Hubert 1870-1896 . . . . . . DLB-135

Craddock, Charles Egbert (see Murfree, Mary N.)

Cradock, Thomas 1718-1770 . . . . DLB-31

Craig, Daniel H. 1811-1895 . . . . DLB-43

Craik, Dinah Maria 1826-1887 . . . . . . DLB-35, 136

Cramer, Richard Ben 1950- DLB-185

Cranch, Christopher Pearse 1813-1892 . DLB-1, 42

Crane, Hart 1899-1932 . . . . DLB-4, 48

Crane, R. S. 1886-1967 . . . . DLB-63

Crane, Stephen 1871-1900 . . . . DLB-12, 54, 78

Crane, Walter 1845-1915 . . . . DLB-163

Cranmer, Thomas 1489-1556 . . . . . DLB-132, 213

Crapsey, Adelaide 1878-1914 . . . . DLB-54

Crashaw, Richard 1612 or 1613-1649 . . . DLB-126

Craven, Avery 1885-1980 . . . . DLB-17

Crawford, Charles 1752-circa 1815 . . . . . . DLB-31

Crawford, F. Marion 1854-1909 . . . . DLB-71

Crawford, Isabel Valancy 1850-1887 . . . . . DLB-92

Crawley, Alan 1887-1975 . . . . DLB-68

Crayon, Geoffrey (see Irving, Washington)

Creamer, Robert W. 1922- DLB-171

Creasey, John 1908-1973 . . . . DLB-77

Creative Age Press DLB-46

Creech, William [publishing house] DLB-154

Creede, Thomas [publishing house] DLB-170

Creel, George 1876-1953 . . . . DLB-25

Creeley, Robert 1926- DLB-5, 16, 169; DS-17

Creelman, James 1859-1915 . . . . DLB-23

Cregan, David 1931- DLB-13

Creighton, Donald Grant 1902-1979 . . . . . DLB-88

Cremazie, Octave 1827-1879 . . . . DLB-99

Crémer, Victoriano 1909?- DLB-108

Crescas, Hasdai circa 1340-1412? DLB-115

Crespo, Angel 1926- DLB-134

Cresset Press DLB-112

Cresswell, Helen 1934- DLB-161

Crèvecoeur, Michel Guillaume Jean de
    1735-1813 . . . . DLB-37

Crewe, Candida 1964- DLB-207

Crews, Harry 1935- DLB-6, 143, 185

Crichton, Michael 1942- Y-81

A Crisis of Culture: The Changing Role
    of Religion in the New Republic
    . . . . DLB-37

Crispin, Edmund 1921-1978 . . . . DLB-87

Cristofer, Michael 1946- DLB-7

"The Critic as Artist" (1891), by
    Oscar Wilde DLB-57

"Criticism In Relation To Novels" (1863),
    by G. H. Lewes DLB-21

Crnjanski, Miloš 1893-1977 . . . . DLB-147

Crocker, Hannah Mather 1752-1829 . . . . DLB-200

Crockett, David (Davy)
    1786-1836 . . . . DLB-3, 11, 183

Croft-Cooke, Rupert (see Bruce, Leo)

Crofts, Freeman Wills 1879-1957 . . . . DLB-77

Croker, John Wilson 1780-1857 . . . . DLB-110

Croly, George 1780-1860 . . . . DLB-159

Croly, Herbert 1869-1930 . . . . DLB-91

Croly, Jane Cunningham 1829-1901 . . . . . DLB-23

Crompton, Richmal 1890-1969 . . . . DLB-160

Cronin, A. J. 1896-1981 . . . . DLB-191

Cros, Charles 1842-1888 . . . . DLB-217

Crosby, Caresse 1892-1970 . . . . DLB-48

Crosby, Caresse 1892-1970 and Crosby,
    Harry 1898-1929 . . . . DLB-4; DS-15

Crosby, Harry 1898-1929 . . . . DLB-48

Cross, Gillian 1945- DLB-161

Cross, Victoria 1868-1952 . . . . .DLB-135, 197

Crossley-Holland, Kevin 1941- DLB-40, 161

Crothers, Rachel 1878-1958 . . . . DLB-7

Crowell, Thomas Y., Company DLB-49

Crowley, John 1942- Y-82

Crowley, Mart 1935- DLB-7

Crown Publishers DLB-46

Crowne, John 1641-1712 . . . . DLB-80

Crowninshield, Edward Augustus
    1817-1859 . . . . DLB-140

Crowninshield, Frank 1872-1947 . . . . DLB-91

Croy, Homer 1883-1965 . . . . DLB-4

Crumley, James 1939- DLB-226; Y-84

Cruz, Victor Hernández 1949- DLB-41

Csokor, Franz Theodor 1885-1969 . . . . . . DLB-81

Cuala Press DLB-112

Cullen, Countee 1903-1946 . . . . DLB-4, 48, 51

Culler, Jonathan D. 1944- DLB-67

The Cult of Biography
    Excerpts from the Second Folio Debate:
    "Biographies are generally a disease of
    English Literature" – Germaine Greer,

Victoria Glendinning, Auberon Waugh,
    and Richard Holmes Y-86

Cumberland, Richard 1732-1811 . . . . DLB-89

Cummings, Constance Gordon
    1837-1924 . . . . .DLB-174

Cummings, E. E. 1894-1962 . . . . DLB-4, 48

Cummings, Ray 1887-1957 . . . . DLB-8

Cummings and Hilliard DLB-49

Cummins, Maria Susanna 1827-1866 . . . . . DLB-42

Cumpián, Carlos 1953- DLB-209

Cundall, Joseph [publishing house] DLB-106

Cuney, Waring 1906-1976 . . . . DLB-51

Cuney-Hare, Maude 1874-1936 . . . . DLB-52

Cunningham, Allan 1784-1842 . . . . .DLB-116, 144

Cunningham, J. V. 1911- DLB-5

Cunningham, Peter F. [publishing house] . . DLB-49

Cunquiero, Alvaro 1911-1981 . . . . DLB-134

Cuomo, George 1929- Y-80

Cupples and Leon DLB-46

Cupples, Upham and Company DLB-49

Cuppy, Will 1884-1949 . . . . DLB-11

Curiel, Barbara Brinson 1956- DLB-209

Curll, Edmund [publishing house] DLB-154

Currie, James 1756-1805 . . . . DLB-142

Currie, Mary Montgomerie Lamb Singleton,
    Lady Currie (see Fane, Violet)

Cursor Mundi circa 1300 . . . . DLB-146

Curti, Merle E. 1897- DLB-17

Curtis, Anthony 1926- DLB-155

Curtis, Cyrus H. K. 1850-1933 . . . . DLB-91

Curtis, George William 1824-1892 DLB-1, 43, 223

Quintus Curtius Rufus fl. A.D. 35 . . . . . . DLB-211

Curzon, Robert 1810-1873 . . . . DLB-166

Curzon, Sarah Anne 1833-1898 . . . . DLB-99

Cushing, Harvey 1869-1939 . . . . .DLB-187

Cynewulf circa 770-840 . . . . DLB-146

Czepko, Daniel 1605-1660 . . . . DLB-164

D

D. M. Thomas: The Plagiarism
    Controversy Y-82

Dabit, Eugène 1898-1936 . . . . DLB-65

Daborne, Robert circa 1580-1628 . . . . DLB-58

Dacey, Philip 1939- DLB-105

Dach, Simon 1605-1659 . . . . DLB-164

Daggett, Rollin M. 1831-1901 . . . . DLB-79

D'Aguiar, Fred 1960- DLB-157

Dahl, Roald 1916-1990 . . . . DLB-139

Dahlberg, Edward 1900-1977 . . . . DLB-48

Dahn, Felix 1834-1912 . . . . DLB-129

Dal', Vladimir Ivanovich (Kazak Vladimir
    Lugansky) 1801-1872 . . . . DLB-198

Dale, Peter 1938- DLB-40

Daley, Arthur 1904-1974 . . . . .DLB-171

Dall, Caroline Wells (Healey)
    1822-1912 . . . . DLB-1

Dallas, E. S. 1828-1879. . . . . .DLB-55

The Dallas Theater Center DLB-7

D'Alton, Louis 1900-1951 . . . . .DLB-10

Daly, Carroll John 1889-1958 . . . . .DLB-226

Daly, T. A. 1871-1948 . . . . .DLB-11

Damon, S. Foster 1893-1971 . . . . .DLB-45

Damrell, William S. [publishing house] DLB-49

Dana, Charles A. 1819-1897 . . . . .DLB-3, 23

Dana, Richard Henry, Jr.
　1815-1882 .DLB-1, 183

Dandridge, Ray Garfield DLB-51

Dane, Clemence 1887-1965 . . . . .DLB-10, 197

Danforth, John 1660-1730 . . . . .DLB-24

Danforth, Samuel, I 1626-1674 . . . . .DLB-24

Danforth, Samuel, II 1666-1727 . . . . .DLB-24

Dangerous Years: London Theater,
　1939-1945 . . . . .DLB-10

Daniel, John M. 1825-1865 . . . . .DLB-43

Daniel, Samuel 1562 or 1563-1619 . . . . . . .DLB-62

Daniel Press. DLB-106

Daniells, Roy 1902-1979 . . . . .DLB-68

Daniels, Jim 1956- DLB-120

Daniels, Jonathan 1902-1981 . . . . .DLB-127

Daniels, Josephus 1862-1948 . . . . .DLB-29

Danis Rose and the Rendering of *Ulysses*. Y-97

Dannay, Frederic 1905-1982 and
　Manfred B. Lee 1905-1971 . . . . .DLB-137

Danner, Margaret Esse 1915- DLB-41

Danter, John [publishing house]. DLB-170

Dantin, Louis 1865-1945 . . . . .DLB-92

Danzig, Allison 1898-1987 . . . . .DLB-171

D'Arcy, Ella circa 1857-1937 . . . . .DLB-135

Darley, Felix Octavious Carr
　1822-1888 . . . . .DLB-188

Darley, George 1795-1846 . . . . .DLB-96

Darwin, Charles 1809-1882. . . . . DLB-57, 166

Darwin, Erasmus 1731-1802 . . . . .DLB-93

Daryush, Elizabeth 1887-1977 . . . . .DLB-20

Dashkova, Ekaterina Romanovna
　(née Vorontsova) 1743-1810 . . . . .DLB-150

Dashwood, Edmée Elizabeth Monica
　de la Pasture (see Delafield, E. M.)

Daudet, Alphonse 1840-1897. . . . . .DLB-123

d'Aulaire, Edgar Parin 1898-　and
　d'Aulaire, Ingri 1904- DLB-22

Davenant, Sir William 1606-1668 . . . .DLB-58, 126

Davenport, Guy 1927- DLB-130

Davenport, Marcia 1903-1996 . . . . DS-17

Davenport, Robert ?-? DLB-58

Daves, Delmer 1904-1977 . . . . .DLB-26

Davey, Frank 1940- DLB-53

Davidson, Avram 1923-1993 . . . . .DLB-8

Davidson, Donald 1893-1968 . . . . .DLB-45

Davidson, John 1857-1909 . . . . .DLB-19

Davidson, Lionel 1922- DLB-14

Davidson, Robyn 1950- DLB-204

Davidson, Sara 1943- DLB-185

Davie, Donald 1922- DLB-27

Davie, Elspeth 1919- DLB-139

Davies, Sir John 1569-1626 . . . . .DLB-172

Davies, John, of Hereford
　1565?-1618 . . . . .DLB-121

Davies, Rhys 1901-1978. . . . . .DLB-139, 191

Davies, Robertson 1913- DLB-68

Davies, Samuel 1723-1761 . . . . .DLB-31

Davies, Thomas 1712?-1785 . . . . . . .DLB-142, 154

Davies, W. H. 1871-1940. . . . . DLB-19, 174

Davies, Peter, Limited DLB-112

Daviot, Gordon 1896?-1952 . . . . .DLB-10
　(see also Tey, Josephine)

Davis, Charles A. 1795-1867 . . . . .DLB-11

Davis, Clyde Brion 1894-1962 . . . . .DLB-9

Davis, Dick 1945- DLB-40

Davis, Frank Marshall 1905-? DLB-51

Davis, H. L. 1894-1960 . . . . .DLB-9, 206

Davis, John 1774-1854 . . . . .DLB-37

Davis, Lydia 1947- DLB-130

Davis, Margaret Thomson 1926- DLB-14

Davis, Ossie 1917- DLB-7, 38

Davis, Paxton 1925-1994 . . . . Y-94

Davis, Rebecca Harding 1831-1910. . . . . .DLB-74

Davis, Richard Harding 1864-1916
　. . . . . DLB-12, 23, 78, 79, 189; DS-13

Davis, Samuel Cole 1764-1809 . . . . .DLB-37

Davis, Samuel Post 1850-1918. . . . . .DLB-202

Davison, Peter 1928- DLB-5

Davydov, Denis Vasil'evich
　1784-1839 . . . . .DLB-205

Davys, Mary 1674-1732 . . . . .DLB-39

DAW Books. DLB-46

Dawn Powell, Where Have You Been All
　Our lives? Y-97

Dawson, Ernest 1882-1947 . . . . .DLB-140

Dawson, Fielding 1930- DLB-130

Dawson, William 1704-1752 . . . . .DLB-31

Day, Angel flourished 1586. . . . . .DLB-167

Day, Benjamin Henry 1810-1889 . . . . .DLB-43

Day, Clarence 1874-1935. . . . . .DLB-11

Day, Dorothy 1897-1980 . . . . .DLB-29

Day, Frank Parker 1881-1950 . . . . .DLB-92

Day, John circa 1574-circa 1640. . . . . .DLB-62

Day, John [publishing house]. DLB-170

Day Lewis, C. 1904-1972. . . . . .DLB-15, 20
　(see also Blake, Nicholas)

Day, Thomas 1748-1789 . . . . .DLB-39

Day, The John, Company DLB-46

Day, Mahlon [publishing house] DLB-49

Dazai Osamu 1909-1948 . . . . .DLB-182

Dąbrowska, Maria 1889-1965 . . . . .DLB-215

Deacon, William Arthur 1890-1977. . . . . .DLB-68

Deal, Borden 1922-1985 . . . . .DLB-6

de Angeli, Marguerite 1889-1987. . . . . . . .DLB-22

De Angelis, Milo 1951- DLB-128

De Bow, James Dunwoody Brownson
　1820-1867 .DLB-3, 79

de Bruyn, Günter 1926- DLB-75

de Camp, L. Sprague 1907- DLB-8

De Carlo, Andrea 1952- DLB-196

De Casas, Celso A. 1944- DLB-209

The Decay of Lying (1889),
　by Oscar Wilde [excerpt] DLB-18

Dechert, Robert 1895-1975 . . . . .DLB-187

Dedication, *Ferdinand Count Fathom* (1753),
　by Tobias Smollett DLB-39

Dedication, *The History of Pompey the Little*
　(1751), by Francis Coventry DLB-39

Dedication, *Lasselia* (1723), by Eliza
　Haywood [excerpt] DLB-39

Dedication, *The Wanderer* (1814),
　by Fanny Burney DLB-39

Dee, John 1527-1608 or 1609. . . . . . .DLB-136, 213

Deeping, George Warwick 1877-1950 . . . .DLB 153

Defense of *Amelia* (1752), by
　Henry Fielding DLB-39

Defoe, Daniel 1660-1731 . . . . .DLB-39, 95, 101

de Fontaine, Felix Gregory 1834-1896. . . . .DLB-43

De Forest, John William
　1826-1906 . . . . .DLB-12, 189

DeFrees, Madeline 1919- DLB-105

DeGolyer, Everette Lee 1886-1956 . . . . . .DLB-187

de Graff, Robert 1895-1981. . . . . Y-81

de Graft, Joe 1924-1978 . . . . .DLB-117

De Heinrico circa 980?. DLB-148

Deighton, Len 1929- DLB-87

DeJong, Meindert 1906-1991. . . . . .DLB-52

Dekker, Thomas circa 1572-1632 . . . . DLB-62, 172

Delacorte, Jr., George T. 1894-1991 . . . . . .DLB-91

Delafield, E. M. 1890-1943 . . . . .DLB-34

Delahaye, Guy 1888-1969 . . . . .DLB-92

de la Mare, Walter
　1873-1956 . . . . DLB-19, 153, 162

Deland, Margaret 1857-1945 . . . . .DLB-78

Delaney, Shelagh 1939- DLB-13

Delano, Amasa 1763-1823 . . . . .DLB-183

Delany, Martin Robinson 1812-1885 . . . . .DLB-50

Delany, Samuel R. 1942- DLB-8, 33

de la Roche, Mazo 1879-1961 . . . . .DLB-68

Delavigne, Jean François Casimir
　1793-1843 . . . . .DLB-192

Delbanco, Nicholas 1942- DLB-6

Del Castillo, Ramón 1949- DLB-209

De León, Nephtal 1945- DLB-82

Delgado, Abelardo Barrientos 1931- DLB-82

Del Giudice, Daniele 1949- DLB-196

De Libero, Libero 1906-1981 . . . . .DLB-114

DeLillo, Don 1936- DLB-6, 173

de Lisser H. G. 1878-1944 . . . . .DLB-117

Dell, Floyd 1887-1969 . . . . .DLB-9

Dell Publishing Company DLB-46

delle Grazie, Marie Eugene 1864-1931.... DLB-81

Deloney, Thomas died 1600 .... DLB-167

Deloria, Ella C. 1889-1971 .... DLB-175

Deloria, Vine, Jr. 1933- DLB-175

del Rey, Lester 1915-1993 .... DLB-8

Del Vecchio, John M. 1947- DS-9

Del'vig, Anton Antonovich
1798-1831..................... DLB-205

de Man, Paul 1919-1983............... DLB-67

Demby, William 1922- DLB-33

DeMarinis, Rick 1934- DLB-218

Deming, Philander 1829-1915 .... DLB-74

Deml, Jakub 1878-1961................ DLB-215

Demorest, William Jennings
1822-1895 .... DLB-79

De Morgan, William 1839-1917........ DLB-153

Demosthenes 384 B.C.-322 B.C. DLB-176

Denham, Henry [publishing house] DLB-170

Denham, Sir John 1615-1669 .... DLB-58, 126

Denison, Merrill 1893-1975 .... DLB-92

Denison, T. S., and Company DLB-49

Dennery, Adolphe Philippe
1811-1899..................... DLB-192

Dennie, Joseph 1768-1812...... DLB-37, 43, 59, 73

Dennis, John 1658-1734 .... DLB-101

Dennis, Nigel 1912-1989 .... DLB-13, 15

Denslow, W. W. 1856-1915 .... DLB-188

Dent, Tom 1932-1998 .... DLB-38

Dent, J. M., and Sons DLB-112

Denton, Daniel circa 1626-1703 .... DLB-24

DePaola, Tomie 1934- DLB-61

Department of Library, Archives, and Institutional
Research, American Bible Society Y-97

De Quille, Dan 1829-1898 .... DLB-186

De Quincey, Thomas 1785-1859 ... DLB-110, 144

Derby, George Horatio 1823-1861....... DLB-11

Derby, J. C., and Company DLB-49

Derby and Miller DLB-49

De Ricci, Seymour 1881-1942 .... DLB-201

Derleth, August 1909-1971 .... DLB-9; DS-17

The Derrydale Press................. DLB-46

Derzhavin, Gavriil Romanovich
1743-1816..................... DLB-150

Desaulniers, Gonsalve 1863-1934....... DLB-92

Desbordes-Valmore, Marceline
1786-1859..................... DLB-217

Deschamps, Emile 1791-1871 .... DLB-217

Deschamps, Eustache 1340?-1404 ...... DLB-208

Desbiens, Jean-Paul 1927- DLB-53

des Forêts, Louis-Rene 1918- DLB-83

Desiato, Luca 1941- DLB-196

Desnica, Vladan 1905-1967 .... DLB-181

DesRochers, Alfred 1901-1978 .... DLB-68

Desrosiers, Léo-Paul 1896-1967 .... DLB-68

Dessì, Giuseppe 1909-1977 ....DLB-177

Destouches, Louis-Ferdinand
(see Céline, Louis-Ferdinand)

De Tabley, Lord 1835-1895 .... DLB-35

"A Detail in a Poem," by
Fred Chappell DLB-105

Deutsch, Babette 1895-1982 .... DLB-45

Deutsch, Niklaus Manuel (see Manuel, Niklaus)

Deutsch, André, Limited DLB-112

Deveaux, Alexis 1948- DLB-38

The Development of the Author's Copyright
in Britain DLB-154

The Development of Lighting in the Staging
of Drama, 1900-1945 .... DLB-10

The Development of Meiji Japan DLB-180

De Vere, Aubrey 1814-1902............ DLB-35

Devereux, second Earl of Essex, Robert
1565-1601 .... DLB-136

The Devin-Adair Company DLB-46

De Vinne, Theodore Low 1828-1914.... DLB-187

De Voto, Bernard 1897-1955 .... DLB-9

De Vries, Peter 1910-1993 ....DLB-6; Y-82

Dewdney, Christopher 1951- DLB-60

Dewdney, Selwyn 1909-1979 .... DLB-68

Dewey, Thomas B. 1915-1981 .... DLB-226

DeWitt, Robert M., Publisher DLB-49

DeWolfe, Fiske and Company DLB-49

Dexter, Colin 1930- DLB-87

de Young, M. H. 1849-1925............ DLB-25

Dhlomo, H. I. E. 1903-1956.......DLB-157, 225

Dhuoda circa 803-after 843 .... DLB-148

The Dial 1840-1844................. DLB-223

The Dial Press DLB-46

Diamond, I. A. L. 1920-1988 .... DLB-26

Dibble, L. Grace 1902-1998 .... DLB-204

Dibdin, Thomas Frognall
1776-1847 .... DLB-184

Di Cicco, Pier Giorgio 1949- DLB-60

Dick, Philip K. 1928-1982 .... DLB-8

Dick and Fitzgerald................. DLB-49

Dickens, Charles
1812-1870.........DLB-21, 55, 70, 159, 166

Dickinson, Peter 1927- DLB-161

Dickey, James 1923-1997
....DLB-5, 193; Y-82, Y-93, Y-96; DS-7, DS-19

Dickey, William 1928-1994 .... DLB-5

Dickinson, Emily 1830-1886 .... DLB-1

Dickinson, John 1732-1808............. DLB-31

Dickinson, Jonathan 1688-1747 .... DLB-24

Dickinson, Patric 1914- DLB-27

Dickinson, Peter 1927- DLB-87

Dicks, John [publishing house] DLB-106

Dickson, Gordon R. 1923- DLB-8

*Dictionary of Literary Biography
Yearbook* Awards........Y-92, Y-93, Y-97-Y-99

The Dictionary of National Biography
.... DLB-144

Didion, Joan 1934-
.... DLB-2, 173, 185; Y-81, Y-86

Di Donato, Pietro 1911- DLB-9

Die Fürstliche Bibliothek Corvey........... Y-96

Diego, Gerardo 1896-1987 .... DLB-134

Digges, Thomas circa 1546-1595 .... DLB-136

The Digital Millennium Copyright Act:
Expanding Copyright Protection in
Cyberspace and Beyond Y-98

Dillard, Annie 1945- Y-80

Dillard, R. H. W. 1937- DLB-5

Dillingham, Charles T., Company....... DLB-49

The Dillingham, G. W., Company DLB-49

Dilly, Edward and Charles
[publishing house] DLB-154

Dilthey, Wilhelm 1833-1911 .... DLB-129

Dimitrova, Blaga 1922- DLB-181

Dimov, Dimitr 1909-1966 .... DLB-181

Dimsdale, Thomas J. 1831?-1866....... DLB-186

Dinesen, Isak (see Blixen, Karen)

Dingelstedt, Franz von 1814-1881 ...... DLB-133

Dintenfass, Mark 1941- Y-84

Diogenes, Jr. (see Brougham, John)

Diogenes Laertius circa 200 ....DLB-176

DiPrima, Diane 1934- DLB-5, 16

Disch, Thomas M. 1940- DLB-8

Disney, Walt 1901-1966................ DLB-22

Disraeli, Benjamin 1804-1881........ DLB-21, 55

D'Israeli, Isaac 1766-1848.............DLB-107

Ditlevsen, Tove 1917-1976 .... DLB-214

Ditzen, Rudolf (see Fallada, Hans)

Dix, Dorothea Lynde 1802-1887 .... DLB-1

Dix, Dorothy (see Gilmer, Elizabeth Meriwether)

Dix, Edwards and Company DLB-49

Dix, Gertrude circa 1874-? DLB-197

Dixie, Florence Douglas 1857-1905 ......DLB-174

Dixon, Ella Hepworth 1855 or
1857-1932.....................DLB-197

Dixon, Paige (see Corcoran, Barbara)

Dixon, Richard Watson 1833-1900 ...... DLB-19

Dixon, Stephen 1936- DLB-130

Dmitriev, Ivan Ivanovich 1760-1837..... DLB-150

Dobell, Bertram 1842-1914 .... DLB-184

Dobell, Sydney 1824-1874 .... DLB-32

Dobie, J. Frank 1888-1964 .... DLB-212

Döblin, Alfred 1878-1957 .... DLB-66

Dobson, Austin 1840-1921......... DLB-35, 144

Doctorow, E. L. 1931- DLB-2, 28, 173; Y-80

Documents on Sixteenth-Century
Literature DLB-167, 172

Dodd, William E. 1869-1940 ....DLB-17

Dodd, Anne [publishing house] DLB-154

Dodd, Mead and Company DLB-49

Doderer, Heimito von 1896-1968 .... DLB-85

Dodge, Mary Abigail 1833-1896 .... DLB-221

Dodge, Mary Mapes
1831?-1905.............DLB-42, 79; DS-13

Dodge, B. W., and Company.......... DLB-46

Dodge Publishing Company DLB-49

Dodgson, Charles Lutwidge (see Carroll, Lewis)

Dodsley, Robert 1703-1764 . . . . .DLB-95

Dodsley, R. [publishing house] DLB-154

Dodson, Owen 1914-1983 . . . . .DLB-76

Dodwell, Christina 1951- DLB-204

Doesticks, Q. K. Philander, P. B. (see Thomson, Mortimer)

Doheny, Carrie Estelle 1875-1958 . . . . . . .DLB 140

Doherty, John 1798?-1854 . . . . .DLB-190

Doig, Ivan 1939- DLB-206

Domínguez, Sylvia Maida 1935- DLB-122

Donahoe, Patrick [publishing house] DLB-49

Donald, David H. 1920- DLB-17

Donaldson, Scott 1928- DLB-111

Doni, Rodolfo 1919- DLB-177

Donleavy, J. P. 1926- DLB-6, 173

Donnadieu, Marguerite (see Duras, Marguerite)

Donne, John 1572-1631 . . . . .DLB-121, 151

Donnelley, R. R., and Sons Company DLB-49

Donnelly, Ignatius 1831-1901 . . . . .DLB-12

Donohue and Henneberry DLB-49

Donoso, José 1924-1996 . . . . .DLB-113

Doolady, M. [publishing house] DLB-49

Dooley, Ebon (see Ebon)

Doolittle, Hilda 1886-1961 . . . . .DLB-4, 45

Doplicher, Fabio 1938- DLB-128

Dor, Milo 1923- DLB-85

Doran, George H., Company DLB-46

Dorgelès, Roland 1886-1973 . . . . .DLB-65

Dorn, Edward 1929-1999 . . . . .DLB-5

Dorr, Rheta Childe 1866-1948 . . . . .DLB-25

Dorris, Michael 1945-1997 . . . . .DLB-175

Dorset and Middlesex, Charles Sackville,
    Lord Buckhurst, Earl of 1643-1706 . . . .DLB-131

Dorst, Tankred 1925- DLB-75, 124

Dos Passos, John
    1896-1970 . . . . .DLB-4, 9; DS-1, DS-15

John Dos Passos: Artist Y-99

John Dos Passos: A Centennial
    Commemoration Y-96

Doubleday and Company DLB-49

Dougall, Lily 1858-1923 . . . . .DLB-92

Doughty, Charles M.
    1843-1926 . . . . DLB-19, 57, 174

Douglas, Gavin 1476-1522 . . . . .DLB-132

Douglas, Keith 1920-1944 . . . . .DLB-27

Douglas, Norman 1868-1952 . . . . . . .DLB-34, 195

Douglass, Frederick
    1817?-1895 . . . . DLB-1, 43, 50, 79

Douglass, William circa 1691-1752 . . . . . . .DLB-24

Dourado, Autran 1926- DLB-145

Dove, Arthur G. 1880-1946 . . . . .DLB-188

Dove, Rita 1952- DLB-120

Dover Publications DLB-46

Doves Press DLB-112

Dowden, Edward 1843-1913 . . . . . . .DLB-35, 149

Dowell, Coleman 1925-1985 . . . . .DLB-130

Dowland, John 1563-1626 . . . . .DLB-172

Downes, Gwladys 1915- DLB-88

Downing, J., Major (see Davis, Charles A.)

Downing, Major Jack (see Smith, Seba)

Dowriche, Anne
    before 1560-after 1613 . . . . .DLB-172

Dowson, Ernest 1867-1900 . . . . .DLB 19, 135

Doxey, William [publishing house] DLB-49

Doyle, Sir Arthur Conan
    1859-1930 . . . . DLB-18, 70, 156, 178

Doyle, Kirby 1932- DLB-16

Doyle, Roddy 1958- DLB-194

Drabble, Margaret 1939- DLB-14, 155

Drach, Albert 1902- DLB-85

Dragojević, Danijel 1934- DLB-181

Drake, Samuel Gardner 1798-1875 . . . . . .DLB-187

The Dramatic Publishing Company DLB-49

Dramatists Play Service DLB-46

Drant, Thomas early 1540s?-1578 . . . . . . .DLB-167

Draper, John W. 1811-1882 . . . . .DLB-30

Draper, Lyman C. 1815-1891 . . . . .DLB-30

Drayton, Michael 1563-1631 . . . . .DLB-121

Dreiser, Theodore
    1871-1945 . . . . DLB-9, 12, 102, 137; DS-1

Dresser, Davis 1904-1977 . . . . .DLB-226

Drewitz, Ingeborg 1923-1986 . . . . .DLB-75

Drieu La Rochelle, Pierre 1893-1945 . . . . . .DLB-72

Drinker, Elizabeth 1735-1807 . . . . .DLB-200

Drinkwater, John 1882-1937
    . . . . DLB-10, 19, 149

Droste-Hülshoff, Annette von
    1797-1848 .DLB-133

The Drue Heinz Literature Prize
    Excerpt from "Excerpts from a Report
    of the Commission," in David
    Bosworth's *The Death of Descartes*
    An Interview with David Bosworth . Y-82

Drummond, William Henry
    1854-1907 .DLB-92

Drummond, William, of Hawthornden
    1585-1649 . . . . DLB-121, 213

Dryden, Charles 1860?-1931 . . . . .DLB-171

Dryden, John 1631-1700 . . . . . . .DLB-80, 101, 131

Držić, Marin circa 1508-1567 . . . . .DLB-147

Duane, William 1760-1835 . . . . .DLB-43

Dubé, Marcel 1930- DLB-53

Dubé, Rodolphe (see Hertel, François)

Dubie, Norman 1945- DLB-120

Du Bois, W. E. B. 1868-1963 . . . . . DLB-47, 50, 91

Du Bois, William Pène 1916-1993 . . . . . . .DLB-61

Dubus, Andre 1936-1999 . . . . .DLB-130

Ducange, Victor 1783-1833 . . . . .DLB-192

Du Chaillu, Paul Belloni 1831?-1903 . . . . .DLB-189

Ducharme, Réjean 1941- DLB-60

Dučić, Jovan 1871-1943 . . . . .DLB-147

Duck, Stephen 1705?-1756 . . . . .DLB-95

Duckworth, Gerald, and Company
    Limited DLB-112

Dudek, Louis 1918- DLB-88

Duell, Sloan and Pearce DLB-46

Duerer, Albrecht 1471-1528 . . . . .DLB-179

Dufief, Nicholas Gouin 1776-1834 . . . . . . .DLB-187

Duff Gordon, Lucie 1821-1869 . . . . .DLB-166

Dufferin, Helen Lady, Countess of Gifford
    1807-1867 .DLB-199

Duffield and Green DLB-46

Duffy, Maureen 1933- DLB-14

Dugan, Alan 1923- DLB-5

Dugard, William [publishing house] DLB-170

Dugas, Marcel 1883-1947 . . . . .DLB-92

Dugdale, William [publishing house] DLB-106

Duhamel, Georges 1884-1966 . . . . .DLB-65

Dujardin, Edouard 1861-1949 . . . . .DLB-123

Dukes, Ashley 1885-1959 . . . . .DLB-10

du Maurier, Daphne 1907-1989 . . . . .DLB-191

Du Maurier, George 1834-1896 . . . . DLB-153, 178

Dumas, Alexandre *fils* 1824-1895 . . . . . . .DLB-192

Dumas, Alexandre *père* 1802-1870 . . . . .DLB-119, 192

Dumas, Henry 1934-1968 . . . . .DLB-41

Dunbar, Paul Laurence
    1872-1906 . . . . DLB-50, 54, 78

Dunbar, William circa 1460-circa 1522 . . . .DLB-132, 146

Duncan, Norman 1871-1916 . . . . .DLB-92

Duncan, Quince 1940- DLB-145

Duncan, Robert 1919-1988 . . . . . . .DLB-5, 16, 193

Duncan, Ronald 1914-1982 . . . . .DLB-13

Duncan, Sara Jeannette 1861-1922 . . . . . . .DLB-92

Dunigan, Edward, and Brother DLB-49

Dunlap, John 1747-1812 . . . . .DLB-43

Dunlap, William 1766-1839 . . . . DLB-30, 37, 59

Dunn, Douglas 1942- DLB-40

Dunn, Harvey Thomas 1884-1952 . . . . . . .DLB-188

Dunn, Stephen 1939- DLB-105

Dunne, Finley Peter 1867-1936 . . . . . . .DLB-11, 23

Dunne, John Gregory 1932- Y-80

Dunne, Philip 1908-1992 . . . . .DLB-26

Dunning, Ralph Cheever 1878-1930 . . . . . . .DLB-4

Dunning, William A. 1857-1922 . . . . .DLB-17

Duns Scotus, John circa 1266-1308 . . . . . .DLB-115

Dunsany, Lord (Edward John Moreton
    Drax Plunkett, Baron Dunsany)
    1878-1957 . . . . DLB-10, 77, 153, 156

Dunton, John [publishing house] DLB-170

Dunton, W. Herbert 1878-1936 . . . . .DLB-188

Dupin, Amantine-Aurore-Lucile (see Sand, George)

Durand, Lucile (see Bersianik, Louky)

Duranti, Francesca 1935- DLB-196

Duranty, Walter 1884-1957 . . . . .DLB-29

Duras, Marguerite 1914-1996 . . . . .DLB-83

Durfey, Thomas 1653-1723 . . . . .DLB-80

Durova, Nadezhda Andreevna (Aleksandr
    Andreevich Aleksandrov) 1783-1866 .DLB-198

Durrell, Lawrence 1912-1990 DLB-15, 27, 204; Y-90

Durrell, William [publishing house] DLB-49

Dürrenmatt, Friedrich
1921-1990 . . . . DLB-69, 124

Duston, Hannah 1657-1737. . . . . DLB-200

Dutton, E. P., and Company DLB-49

Duvoisin, Roger 1904-1980 . . . . DLB-61

Duyckinck, Evert Augustus
1816-1878. . . . . DLB-3, 64

Duyckinck, George L. 1823-1863. . . . . DLB-3

Duyckinck and Company. DLB-49

Dwight, John Sullivan 1813-1893 . . . . DLB-1

Dwight, Timothy 1752-1817 . . . . DLB-37

Dybek, Stuart 1942- DLB-130

Dyer, Charles 1928- DLB-13

Dyer, George 1755-1841 . . . . DLB-93

Dyer, John 1699-1757 . . . . DLB-95

Dyer, Sir Edward 1543-1607 . . . . DLB-136

Dyk, Viktor 1877-1931 . . . . DLB-215

Dylan, Bob 1941- DLB-16

The Dylan Thomas Celebration Y-99

E

Eager, Edward 1911-1964 . . . . DLB-22

Eames, Wilberforce 1855-1937. . . . . DLB-140

Earle, Alice Morse 1853-1911. . . . . DLB-221

Earle, James H., and Company DLB-49

Earle, John 1600 or 1601-1665 . . . . DLB-151

Early American Book Illustration,
by Sinclair Hamilton DLB-49

Eastlake, William 1917-1997 . . . . DLB-6, 206

Eastman, Carol ?- DLB-44

Eastman, Charles A. (Ohiyesa)
1858-1939 . . . . .DLB-175

Eastman, Max 1883-1969 . . . . DLB-91

Eaton, Daniel Isaac 1753-1814 . . . . DLB-158

Eaton, Edith Maude 1865-1914 . . . . DLB-221

Eaton, Winnifred 1875-1954. . . . . DLB-221

Eberhart, Richard 1904- DLB-48

Ebner, Jeannie 1918- DLB-85

Ebner-Eschenbach, Marie von
1830-1916. DLB-81

Ebon 1942- DLB-41

E-Books Turn the Corner. Y-98

Ecbasis Captivi circa 1045 . . . . DLB-148

Ecco Press. DLB-46

Eckhart, Meister
circa 1260-circa 1328 . . . . DLB-115

The Eclectic Review 1805-1868. . . . . DLB-110

Eco, Umberto 1932- DLB-196

Edel, Leon 1907-1997 . . . . DLB-103

Edes, Benjamin 1732-1803 . . . . DLB-43

Edgar, David 1948- DLB-13

Edgeworth, Maria
1768-1849 . . . . .DLB-116, 159, 163

The Edinburgh Review 1802-1929 . . . . DLB-110

Edinburgh University Press DLB-112

The Editor Publishing Company DLB-49

Editorial Statements DLB-137

Edmonds, Randolph 1900- DLB-51

Edmonds, Walter D. 1903-1998. . . . . DLB-9

Edschmid, Kasimir 1890-1966 . . . . DLB-56

Edwards, Amelia Anne Blandford
1831-1892 . . . . .DLB-174

Edwards, Edward 1812-1886 . . . . DLB-184

Edwards, James [publishing house]. DLB-154

Edwards, Jonathan 1703-1758. . . . . DLB-24

Edwards, Jonathan, Jr. 1745-1801 . . . . DLB-37

Edwards, Junius 1929- DLB-33

Edwards, Matilda Barbara Betham-
1836-1919 . . . . .DLB-174

Edwards, Richard 1524-1566 . . . . DLB-62

Edwards, Sarah Pierpont 1710-1758 . . . . . DLB-200

Effinger, George Alec 1947- DLB-8

Egerton, George 1859-1945 . . . . DLB-135

Eggleston, Edward 1837-1902. . . . . DLB-12

Eggleston, Wilfred 1901-1986 . . . . DLB-92

Eglītis, Anšlavs 1906-1993 . . . . DLB-220

Ehrenstein, Albert 1886-1950 . . . . DLB-81

Ehrhart, W. D. 1948- DS-9

Ehrlich, Gretel 1946- DLB-212

Eich, Günter 1907-1972. . . . . DLB-69, 124

Eichendorff, Joseph Freiherr von
1788-1857 . . . . DLB-90

Eifukumon'in 1271-1342. . . . . DLB-203

1873 Publishers' Catalogues DLB-49

Eighteenth-Century Aesthetic Theories . . . DLB-31

Eighteenth-Century Philosophical
Background DLB-31

Eigner, Larry 1926-1996 . . . . DLB-5, 193

Eikon Basilike 1649. . . . . DLB-151

Eilhart von Oberge
circa 1140-circa 1195 . . . . DLB-148

Einhard circa 770-840 . . . . DLB-148

Eiseley, Loren 1907-1977 . . . . .DS-17

Eisenreich, Herbert 1925-1986 . . . . DLB-85

Eisner, Kurt 1867-1919 . . . . DLB-66

Eklund, Gordon 1945- Y-83

Ekwensi, Cyprian 1921- DLB-117

Eld, George [publishing house]. DLB-170

Elder, Lonne III 1931- DLB-7, 38, 44

Elder, Paul, and Company DLB-49

The Electronic Text Center and the Electronic
Archive of Early American Fiction at the University of Virginia Library Y-98

Elements of Rhetoric (1828; revised, 1846),
by Richard Whately [excerpt] DLB-57

Eliade, Mircea 1907-1986 . . . . DLB-220

Elie, Robert 1915-1973 . . . . DLB-88

Elin Pelin 1877-1949 . . . . DLB-147

Eliot, George 1819-1880 . . . . DLB-21, 35, 55

Eliot, John 1604-1690 . . . . DLB-24

Eliot, T. S. 1888-1965. . . . . .DLB-7, 10, 45, 63

Eliot's Court Press DLB-170

Elizabeth I 1533-1603. . . . . DLB-136

Elizabeth of Nassau-Saarbrücken
after 1393-1456 . . . . .DLB-179

Elizondo, Salvador 1932- DLB-145

Elizondo, Sergio 1930- DLB-82

Elkin, Stanley 1930-1995 . . . .DLB-2, 28, 218; Y-80

Elles, Dora Amy (see Wentworth, Patricia)

Ellet, Elizabeth F. 1818?-1877 . . . . DLB-30

Elliot, Ebenezer 1781-1849 . . . . DLB-96, 190

Elliot, Frances Minto (Dickinson)
1820-1898 . . . . DLB-166

Elliott, Charlotte 1789-1871 . . . . DLB-199

Elliott, George 1923- DLB-68

Elliott, Janice 1931- DLB-14

Elliott, Sarah Barnwell 1848-1928 . . . . . . DLB-221

Elliott, William 1788-1863 . . . . DLB-3

Elliott, Thomes and Talbot DLB-49

Ellis, Alice Thomas (Anna Margaret Haycraft)
1932- DLB-194

Ellis, Edward S. 1840-1916. . . . . DLB-42

Ellis, Frederick Staridge
[publishing house] DLB-106

The George H. Ellis Company. DLB-49

Ellis, Havelock 1859-1939 . . . . DLB-190

Ellison, Harlan 1934- DLB-8

Ellison, Ralph Waldo
1914-1994 . . . . DLB-2, 76; Y-94

Ellmann, Richard 1918-1987 . . . . . .DLB-103; Y-87

Ellroy, James 1948- DLB-226

The Elmer Holmes Bobst Awards in Arts
and Letters . . . . : . . Y-87

Elyot, Thomas 1490?-1546 . . . . DLB-136

Emanuel, James Andrew 1921- DLB-41

Emecheta, Buchi 1944- DLB-117

The Emergence of Black Women Writers DS-8

Emerson, Ralph Waldo
1803-1882 . . . . .DLB-1, 59, 73, 183, 223

Emerson, William 1769-1811 . . . . DLB-37

Emerson, William 1923-1997 . . . . Y-97

Emin, Fedor Aleksandrovich
circa 1735-1770 . . . . DLB-150

Empedocles fifth century B.C. DLB-176

Empson, William 1906-1984 . . . . DLB-20

Enchi Fumiko 1905-1986 . . . . DLB-182

Encounter with the West DLB-180

The End of English Stage Censorship,
1945-1968 . . . . DLB-13

Ende, Michael 1929-1995. . . . . DLB-75

Endō Shūsaku 1923-1996. . . . . DLB-182

Engel, Marian 1933-1985 . . . . DLB-53

Engels, Friedrich 1820-1895 . . . . DLB-129

Engle, Paul 1908- DLB-48

English, Thomas Dunn 1819-1902. . . . . . DLB-202

English Composition and Rhetoric (1866),
by Alexander Bain [excerpt]. DLB-57

The English Language: 410 to 1500. . . . . DLB-146

The English Renaissance of Art (1908),
  by Oscar Wilde DLB-35

Ennius 239 B.C.-169 B.C. DLB-211

Enright, D. J. 1920- DLB-27

Enright, Elizabeth 1909-1968. . . . . .DLB-22

L'Envoi (1882), by Oscar Wilde DLB-35

Epic and Beast Epic DLB-208

Epictetus circa 55-circa 125-130 . . . . .DLB-176

Epicurus 342/341 B.C.-271/270 B.C.
  . . . . .DLB-176

Epps, Bernard 1936- DLB-53

Epstein, Julius 1909- and
  Epstein, Philip 1909-1952 . . . . .DLB-26

Equiano, Olaudah circa 1745-1797 . . . . . DLB-37, 50

Eragny Press DLB-112

Erasmus, Desiderius 1467-1536 . . . . .DLB-136

Erba, Luciano 1922- DLB-128

Erdrich, Louise 1954- DLB-152, 175, 206

Erichsen-Brown, Gwethalyn Graham
  (see Graham, Gwethalyn)

Eriugena, John Scottus circa 810-877 . . . . .DLB-115

Ernest Hemingway: A Centennial
  Celebration Y-99

The Ernest Hemingway Collection at the
  John F. Kennedy Library. Y-99

Ernest Hemingway's Reaction to James Gould
  Cozzens Y-98

Ernest Hemingway's Toronto Journalism
  Revisited: With Three Previously
  Unrecorded Stories Y-92

Ernst, Paul 1866-1933 . . . . .DLB-66, 118

Ershov, Petr Pavlovich 1815-1869. . . . . . .DLB-205

Erskine, Albert 1911-1993 . . . . Y-93

Erskine, John 1879-1951 . . . . .DLB-9, 102

Erskine, Mrs. Steuart ?-1948 . . . . .DLB-195

Ervine, St. John Greer 1883-1971 . . . . . . .DLB-10

Eschenburg, Johann Joachim
  1743-1820 . . . . .DLB-97

Escoto, Julio 1944- DLB-145

Esdaile, Arundell
  1880-1956 . . . . .DLB-201

Eshleman, Clayton 1935- DLB-5

Espriu, Salvador 1913-1985 . . . . .DLB-134

Ess Ess Publishing Company. DLB-49

Essay on Chatterton (1842), by
  Robert Browning. DLB-32

Essex House Press DLB-112

Essop, Ahmed 1931- DLB-225

Estes, Eleanor 1906-1988 . . . . .DLB-22

Eszterhas, Joe 1944- DLB-185

Estes and Lauriat DLB-49

Estleman, Loren D. 1952- DLB-226

Etherege, George 1636-circa 1692 . . . . . . .DLB-80

Ethridge, Mark, Sr. 1896-1981 . . . . .DLB-127

Ets, Marie Hall 1893- DLB-22

Etter, David 1928- DLB-105

Ettner, Johann Christoph 1654-1724 . . . . .DLB-168

Eudora Welty: Eye of the Storyteller Y-87

Eudora Welty Newsletter Y-99

Eudora Welty's Ninetieth Birthday Y-99

Eugene O'Neill Memorial Theater
  Center DLB-7

Eugene O'Neill's Letters: A Review Y-88

Eupolemius flourished circa 1095 . . . . . . .DLB-148

Euripides circa 484 B.C.-407/406 B.C.
  . . . . .DLB-176

Evans, Caradoc 1878-1945. . . . . .DLB-162

Evans, Charles 1850-1935 . . . . .DLB-187

Evans, Donald 1884-1921 . . . . .DLB-54

Evans, George Henry 1805-1856. . . . . . . .DLB-43

Evans, Hubert 1892-1986 . . . . .DLB-92

Evans, Mari 1923- DLB-41

Evans, Mary Ann (see Eliot, George)

Evans, Nathaniel 1742-1767 . . . . .DLB-31

Evans, Sebastian 1830-1909. . . . . .DLB-35

Evans, M., and Company DLB-46

Everett, Alexander Hill 1790-1847 . . . . . . .DLB-59

Everett, Edward 1794-1865 . . . . .DLB-1, 59

Everson, R. G. 1903- DLB-88

Everson, William 1912-1994 . . . . . .DLB-5, 16, 212

Every Man His Own Poet; or, The
  Inspired Singer's Recipe Book (1877),
  by W. H. Mallock DLB-35

Ewart, Gavin 1916-1995 . . . . .DLB-40

Ewing, Juliana Horatia 1841-1885 . . . .DLB-21, 163

The Examiner 1808-1881 . . . . .DLB-110

Exley, Frederick 1929-1992 . . . . . . .DLB-143; Y-81

Experiment in the Novel (1929),
  by John D. Beresford DLB-36

von Eyb, Albrecht 1420-1475. . . . . DLB-179

"Eyes Across Centuries: Contemporary
  Poetry and 'That Vision Thing,'"
  by Philip Dacey DLB-105

Eyre and Spottiswoode DLB-106

Ezzo ?-after 1065 . . . . .DLB-148

F

"F. Scott Fitzgerald: St. Paul's Native Son
  and Distinguished American Writer":
  University of Minnesota Conference,
  29-31 October 1982 . . . . Y-82

Faber, Frederick William 1814-1863 . . . . . .DLB-32

Faber and Faber Limited DLB-112

Faccio, Rena (see Aleramo, Sibilla)

Fagundo, Ana María 1938- DLB-134

Fair, Ronald L. 1932- DLB-33

Fairfax, Beatrice (see Manning, Marie)

Fairlie, Gerard 1899-1983 . . . . .DLB-77

Fallada, Hans 1893-1947 . . . . .DLB-56

Falsifying Hemingway Y-96

Fancher, Betsy 1928- Y-83

Fane, Violet 1843-1905 . . . . .DLB-35

Fanfrolico Press .DLB-112

Fanning, Katherine 1927 . . . . .DLB-127

Fanshawe, Sir Richard 1608-1666 . . . . . . .DLB-126

Fantasy Press Publishers DLB-46

Fante, John 1909-1983 . . . . DLB-130; Y-83

Al-Farabi circa 870-950. . . . . .DLB-115

Farah, Nuruddin 1945- DLB-125

Farber, Norma 1909-1984 . . . . .DLB-61

Farigoule, Louis (see Romains, Jules)

Farjeon, Eleanor 1881-1965 . . . . .DLB-160

Farley, Walter 1920-1989 . . . . .DLB-22

Farmborough, Florence 1887-1978 . . . . . . .DLB-204

Farmer, Penelope 1939- DLB-161

Farmer, Philip José 1918- DLB-8

Farquhar, George circa 1677-1707 . . . . . . .DLB-84

Farquharson, Martha (see Finley, Martha)

Farrar, Frederic William 1831-1903. . . . . .DLB-163

Farrar and Rinehart DLB-46

Farrar, Straus and Giroux DLB-46

Farrell, James T. 1904-1979 . . . .DLB-4, 9, 86; DS-2

Farrell, J. G. 1935-1979 . . . . .DLB-14

Fast, Howard 1914- DLB-9

Faulks, Sebastian 1953- DLB-207

Faulkner and Yoknapatawpha Conference,
  Oxford, Mississippi Y-97

"Faulkner 100—Celebrating the Work," University of
  South Carolina, Columbia Y-97

Faulkner, William 1897-1962
  . . . . DLB-9, 11, 44, 102; DS-2; Y-86

Faulkner, George [publishing house] DLB-154

Fauset, Jessie Redmon 1882-1961 . . . . .DLB-51

Faust, Irvin 1924- DLB-2, 28, 218; Y-80

Fawcett, Edgar 1847-1904 . . . . .DLB-202

Fawcett, Millicent Garrett 1847-1929 . . . . .DLB-190

Fawcett Books DLB-46

Fay, Theodore Sedgwick 1807-1898 . . . . .DLB-202

Fearing, Kenneth 1902-1961 . . . . .DLB-9

Federal Writers' Project DLB-46

Federman, Raymond 1928- Y-80

Feiffer, Jules 1929- DLB-7, 44

Feinberg, Charles E. 1899-1988 . . . .DLB-187; Y-88

Feind, Barthold 1678-1721 . . . . .DLB-168

Feinstein, Elaine 1930- DLB-14, 40

Feiss, Paul Louis 1875-1952 . . . . .DLB-187

Feldman, Irving 1928- DLB-169

Felipe, Léon 1884-1968 . . . . .DLB-108

Fell, Frederick, Publishers DLB-46

Fellowship of Southern Writers Y-98

Felltham, Owen 1602?-1668 . . . . . . .DLB-126, 151

Fels, Ludwig 1946- DLB-75

Felton, Cornelius Conway 1807-1862 . . . . . .DLB-1

Fenn, Harry 1837-1911 . . . . .DLB-188

Fennario, David 1947- DLB-60

Fenno, Jenny 1765?-1803 . . . . .DLB-200

Fenno, John 1751-1798. . . . . .DLB-43

Fenno, R. F., and Company. DLB-49

Fenoglio, Beppe 1922-1963 . . . . .DLB-177

Fenton, Geoffrey 1539?-1608. . . . . .DLB-136

Fenton, James 1949- DLB-40

Ferber, Edna 1885-1968 . . . . DLB-9, 28, 86

Ferdinand, Vallery III (see Salaam, Kalamu ya)

Ferguson, Sir Samuel 1810-1886 . . . . DLB-32

Ferguson, William Scott 1875-1954 . . . . . DLB-47

Fergusson, Robert 1750-1774 . . . . DLB-109

Ferland, Albert 1872-1943 . . . . DLB-92

Ferlinghetti, Lawrence 1919- DLB-5, 16

Fermor, Patrick Leigh 1915- DLB-204

Fern, Fanny (see Parton, Sara Payson Willis)

Ferrars, Elizabeth 1907- DLB-87

Ferré, Rosario 1942- DLB-145

Ferret, E., and Company DLB-49

Ferrier, Susan 1782-1854 . . . . DLB-116

Ferril, Thomas Hornsby 1896-1988 . . . . . DLB-206

Ferrini, Vincent 1913- DLB-48

Ferron, Jacques 1921-1985 . . . . DLB-60

Ferron, Madeleine 1922- DLB-53

Ferrucci, Franco 1936- DLB-196

Fetridge and Company DLB-49

Feuchtersleben, Ernst Freiherr von
1806-1849 . . . . DLB-133

Feuchtwanger, Lion 1884-1958 . . . . DLB-66

Feuerbach, Ludwig 1804-1872 . . . . DLB-133

Feuillet, Octave 1821-1890 . . . . DLB-192

Feydeau, Georges 1862-1921 . . . . DLB-192

Fichte, Johann Gottlieb 1762-1814 . . . . . . DLB-90

Ficke, Arthur Davison 1883-1945 . . . . DLB-54

Fiction Best-Sellers, 1910-1945 . . . . DLB-9

Fiction into Film, 1928-1975: A List of Movies
Based on the Works of Authors in
British Novelists, 1930-1959 . . . . DLB-15

Fiedler, Leslie A. 1917- DLB-28, 67

Field, Edward 1924- DLB-105

Field, Eugene
1850-1895 . . . . DLB-23, 42, 140; DS-13

Field, John 1545?-1588 . . . . DLB-167

Field, Marshall, III 1893-1956 . . . . DLB-127

Field, Marshall, IV 1916-1965 . . . . DLB-127

Field, Marshall, V 1941- DLB-127

Field, Nathan 1587-1619 or 1620 . . . . DLB-58

Field, Rachel 1894-1942 . . . . DLB-9, 22

A Field Guide to Recent Schools of American
Poetry Y-86

Fielding, Henry 1707-1754 . . . . DLB-39, 84, 101

Fielding, Sarah 1710-1768 . . . . DLB-39

Fields, Annie Adams 1834-1915 . . . . DLB-221

Fields, James Thomas 1817-1881 . . . . DLB-1

Fields, Julia 1938- DLB-41

Fields, W. C. 1880-1946 . . . . DLB-44

Fields, Osgood and Company DLB-49

Fifty Penguin Years Y-85

Figes, Eva 1932- DLB-14

Figuera, Angela 1902-1984 . . . . DLB-108

Filmer, Sir Robert 1586-1653 . . . . DLB-151

Filson, John circa 1753-1788 . . . . DLB-37

Finch, Anne, Countess of Winchilsea
1661-1720 . . . . DLB-95

Finch, Robert 1900- DLB-88

"Finding, Losing, Reclaiming: A Note on My
Poems," by Robert Phillips DLB-105

Findley, Timothy 1930- DLB-53

Finlay, Ian Hamilton 1925- DLB-40

Finley, Martha 1828-1909 . . . . DLB-42

Finn, Elizabeth Anne (McCaul)
1825-1921 . . . . DLB-166

Finney, Jack 1911-1995 . . . . DLB-8

Finney, Walter Braden (see Finney, Jack)

Firbank, Ronald 1886-1926 . . . . DLB-36

Fire at Thomas Wolfe Memorial Y-98

Firmin, Giles 1615-1697 . . . . DLB-24

Fischart, Johann
1546 or 1547-1590 or 1591 . . . . DLB-179

First Edition Library/Collectors'
Reprints, Inc. Y-91

First International F. Scott Fitzgerald
Conference Y-92

First Strauss "Livings" Awarded to Cynthia
Ozick and Raymond Carver
An Interview with Cynthia Ozick
An Interview with Raymond
Carver Y-83

Fischer, Karoline Auguste Fernandine
1764-1842 . . . . DLB-94

Fish, Stanley 1938- DLB-67

Fishacre, Richard 1205-1248 . . . . DLB-115

Fisher, Clay (see Allen, Henry W.)

Fisher, Dorothy Canfield
1879-1958 . . . . DLB-9, 102

Fisher, Leonard Everett 1924- DLB-61

Fisher, Roy 1930- DLB-40

Fisher, Rudolph 1897-1934 . . . . DLB-51, 102

Fisher, Steve 1913-1980 . . . . DLB-226

Fisher, Sydney George 1856-1927 . . . . DLB-47

Fisher, Vardis 1895-1968 . . . . DLB-9, 206

Fiske, John 1608-1677 . . . . DLB-24

Fiske, John 1842-1901 . . . . DLB-47, 64

Fitch, Thomas circa 1700-1774 . . . . DLB-31

Fitch, William Clyde 1865-1909 . . . . DLB-7

FitzGerald, Edward 1809-1883 . . . . DLB-32

Fitzgerald, F. Scott 1896-1940
. . . . DLB-4, 9, 86, 219; Y-81; DS-1, 15, 16

F. Scott Fitzgerald Centenary Celebrations Y-96

F. Scott Fitzgerald Inducted into the American
Poets' Corner at St. John the Divine;
Ezra Pound Banned Y-99

Fitzgerald, Penelope 1916- DLB-14, 194

Fitzgerald, Robert 1910-1985 . . . . Y-80

Fitzgerald, Thomas 1819-1891 . . . . DLB-23

Fitzgerald, Zelda Sayre 1900-1948 . . . . Y-84

Fitzhugh, Louise 1928-1974 . . . . DLB-52

Fitzhugh, William circa 1651-1701 . . . . . . DLB-24

Flagg, James Montgomery 1877-1960 . . . . DLB-188

Flanagan, Thomas 1923- Y-80

Flanner, Hildegarde 1899-1987 . . . . DLB-48

Flanner, Janet 1892-1978 . . . . DLB-4

Flaubert, Gustave 1821-1880 . . . . DLB-119

Flavin, Martin 1883-1967 . . . . DLB-9

Fleck, Konrad (flourished circa 1220)
. . . . DLB-138

Flecker, James Elroy 1884-1915 . . . . . . DLB-10, 19

Fleeson, Doris 1901-1970 . . . . DLB-29

Fleißer, Marieluise 1901-1974 . . . . . . DLB-56, 124

Fleming, Ian 1908-1964 . . . . DLB-87, 201

Fleming, Paul 1609-1640 . . . . DLB-164

Fleming, Peter 1907-1971 . . . . DLB-195

The Fleshly School of Poetry and Other
Phenomena of the Day (1872), by Robert
Buchanan DLB-35

The Fleshly School of Poetry: Mr. D. G.
Rossetti (1871), by Thomas Maitland
(Robert Buchanan) DLB-35

Fletcher, Giles, the Elder 1546-1611 . . . . . DLB-136

Fletcher, Giles, the Younger
1585 or 1586-1623 . . . . DLB-121

Fletcher, J. S. 1863-1935 . . . . DLB-70

Fletcher, John (see Beaumont, Francis)

Fletcher, John Gould 1886-1950 . . . . . . DLB-4, 45

Fletcher, Phineas 1582-1650 . . . . DLB-121

Flieg, Helmut (see Heym, Stefan)

Flint, F. S. 1885-1960 . . . . DLB-19

Flint, Timothy 1780-1840 . . . . DLB-73, 186

Flores-Williams, Jason 1969- DLB-209

Florio, John 1553?-1625 . . . . DLB-172

Fo, Dario 1926- Y-97

Foix, J. V. 1893-1987 . . . . DLB-134

Foley, Martha (see Burnett, Whit, and
Martha Foley)

Folger, Henry Clay 1857-1930 . . . . DLB-140

Folio Society DLB-112

Follen, Eliza Lee (Cabot) 1787-1860 . . . . . . DLB-1

Follett, Ken 1949- DLB-87; Y-81

Follett Publishing Company DLB-46

Folsom, John West [publishing house] DLB-49

Folz, Hans
between 1435 and 1440-1513 . . . . DLB-179

Fontane, Theodor 1819-1898 . . . . DLB-129

Fontes, Montserrat 1940- DLB-209

Fonvisin, Denis Ivanovich
1744 or 1745-1792 . . . . DLB-150

Foote, Horton 1916- DLB-26

Foote, Mary Hallock
1847-1938 . . . . DLB-186, 188, 202, 221

Foote, Samuel 1721-1777 . . . . DLB-89

Foote, Shelby 1916- DLB-2, 17

Forbes, Calvin 1945- DLB-41

Forbes, Ester 1891-1967 . . . . DLB-22

Forbes, Rosita 1893?-1967 . . . . DLB-195

Forbes and Company DLB-49

Force, Peter 1790-1868 . . . . DLB-30

Forché, Carolyn 1950- DLB-5, 193

Ford, Charles Henri 1913- DLB-4, 48

Ford, Corey 1902-1969 . . . . .DLB-11

Ford, Ford Madox 1873-1939 . . . .DLB-34, 98, 162

Ford, Jesse Hill 1928-1996 . . . . .DLB-6

Ford, John 1586-? .DLB-58

Ford, R. A. D. 1915- DLB-88

Ford, Worthington C. 1858-1941 . . . . .DLB-47

Ford, J. B., and Company DLB-49

Fords, Howard, and Hulbert DLB-49

Foreman, Carl 1914-1984 . . . . .DLB-26

Forester, C. S. 1899-1966 . . . . .DLB-191

Forester, Frank (see Herbert, Henry William)

"Foreword to *Ludwig of Baviria*," by
    Robert Peters DLB-105

Forman, Harry Buxton 1842-1917 . . . . . . .DLB-184

Fornés, María Irene 1930- DLB-7

Forrest, Leon 1937-1997 . . . . .DLB-33

Forster, E. M. 1879-1970
    . . . . DLB-34, 98, 162, 178, 195; DS-10

Forster, Georg 1754-1794 . . . . .DLB-94

Forster, John 1812-1876 . . . . .DLB-144

Forster, Margaret 1938- DLB-155

Forsyth, Frederick 1938- DLB-87

Forten, Charlotte L. 1837-1914 . . . . .DLB-50

Fortini, Franco 1917- DLB-128

Fortune, T. Thomas 1856-1928 . . . . .DLB-23

Fosdick, Charles Austin 1842-1915 . . . . . .DLB-42

Foster, Genevieve 1893-1979 . . . . .DLB-61

Foster, Hannah Webster
    1758-1840 . . . . DLB-37, 200

Foster, John 1648-1681 . . . . .DLB-24

Foster, Michael 1904-1956 . . . . .DLB-9

Foster, Myles Birket 1825-1899 . . . . .DLB-184

Foulis, Robert and Andrew / R. and A.
    [publishing house] DLB-154

Fouqué, Caroline de la Motte
    1774-1831 . . . . .DLB-90

Fouqué, Friedrich de la Motte
    1777-1843 . . . . .DLB-90

Four Essays on the Beat Generation,
    by John Clellon Holmes DLB-16

Four Seas Company DLB-46

Four Winds Press .DLB-46

Fournier, Henri Alban (see Alain-Fournier)

Fowler and Wells Company DLB-49

Fowles, John 1926- DLB-14, 139, 207

Fox, John, Jr. 1862 or 1863-1919 . . . .DLB-9; DS-13

Fox, Paula 1923- DLB-52

Fox, Richard Kyle 1846-1922 . . . . .DLB-79

Fox, William Price 1926- DLB-2; Y-81

Fox, Richard K. [publishing house] DLB-49

Foxe, John 1517-1587 . . . . .DLB-132

Fraenkel, Michael 1896-1957 . . . . .DLB-4

France, Anatole 1844-1924 . . . . .DLB-123

France, Richard 1938- DLB-7

Francis, Convers 1795-1863 . . . . .DLB-1

Francis, Dick 1920- DLB-87

Francis, Sir Frank 1901-1988 . . . . .DLB-201

Francis, Jeffrey, Lord 1773-1850 . . . . .DLB-107

Francis, C. S. [publishing house] DLB-49

François 1863-1910 . . . . .DLB-92

François, Louise von 1817-1893 . . . . .DLB-129

Franck, Sebastian 1499-1542 . . . . .DLB-179

Francke, Kuno 1855-1930 . . . . .DLB-71

Frank, Bruno 1887-1945 . . . . .DLB-118

Frank, Leonhard 1882-1961 . . . . . . .DLB-56, 118

Frank, Melvin (see Panama, Norman)

Frank, Waldo 1889-1967 . . . . .DLB-9, 63

Franken, Rose 1895?-1988 . . . . Y-84

Franklin, Benjamin
    1706-1790 . . . . DLB-24, 43, 73, 183

Franklin, James 1697-1735 . . . . .DLB-43

Franklin Library .DLB-46

Frantz, Ralph Jules 1902-1979 . . . . .DLB-4

Franzos, Karl Emil 1848-1904 . . . . .DLB-129

Fraser, G. S. 1915-1980 . . . . .DLB-27

Fraser, Kathleen 1935- DLB-169

Frattini, Alberto 1922- DLB-128

Frau Ava ?-1127 .DLB-148

Frayn, Michael 1933- DLB-13, 14, 194

Frederic, Harold
    1856-1898 . . . . .DLB-12, 23; DS-13

Freeling, Nicolas 1927- DLB-87

Freeman, Douglas Southall
    1886-1953 . . . . DLB-17; DS-17

Freeman, Legh Richmond 1842-1915 . . . .DLB-23

Freeman, Mary E. Wilkins
    1852-1930 . . . . .DLB-12, 78, 221

Freeman, R. Austin 1862-1943 . . . . .DLB-70

Freidank circa 1170-circa 1233 . . . . .DLB-138

Freiligrath, Ferdinand 1810-1876 . . . . . . .DLB-133

Frémont, John Charles 1813-1890 . . . . . .DLB-186

Frémont, John Charles 1813-1890 and
    Frémont, Jessie Benton 1834-1902 . . .DLB-183

French, Alice 1850-1934 . . . . .DLB-74; DS-13

French Arthurian Literature DLB-208

French, David 1939- DLB-53

French, Evangeline 1869-1960 . . . . .DLB-195

French, Francesca 1871-1960 . . . . .DLB-195

French, James [publishing house] DLB-49

French, Samuel [publishing house] DLB-49

Samuel French, Limited DLB-106

Freneau, Philip 1752-1832 . . . . DLB-37, 43

Freni, Melo 1934- DLB-128

Freshfield, Douglas W. 1845-1934 . . . . . .DLB-174

Freytag, Gustav 1816-1895 . . . . .DLB-129

Fried, Erich 1921-1988 . . . . .DLB-85

Friedman, Bruce Jay 1930- DLB-2, 28

Friedrich von Hausen circa 1171-1190 . . . .DLB-138

Friel, Brian 1929- DLB-13

Friend, Krebs 1895?-1967? DLB-4

Fries, Fritz Rudolf 1935- DLB-75

Fringe and Alternative Theater in
    Great Britain DLB-13

Frisch, Max 1911-1991 . . . . .DLB-69, 124

Frischlin, Nicodemus 1547-1590 . . . . . . .DLB-179

Frischmuth, Barbara 1941- DLB-85

Fritz, Jean 1915- DLB-52

Froissart, Jean circa 1337-circa 1404 . . . . .DLB-208

Fromentin, Eugene 1820-1876 . . . . .DLB-123

From *The Gay Science*, by E. S. Dallas DLB-21

Frontinus circa A.D. 35-A.D. 103/104 . . . .DLB-211

Frost, A. B. 1851-1928 . . . . .DLB-188; DS-13

Frost, Robert 1874-1963 . . . . .DLB-54; DS-7

Frothingham, Octavius Brooks
    1822-1895 . . . . .DLB-1

Froude, James Anthony
    1818-1894 . . . . DLB-18, 57, 144

Fruitlands 1843-1844 . . . . .DLB-223

Fry, Christopher 1907- DLB-13

Fry, Roger 1866-1934 . . . . DS-10

Fry, Stephen 1957- DLB-207

Frye, Northrop 1912-1991 . . . . DLB-67, 68

Fuchs, Daniel 1909-1993 . . . . .DLB-9, 26, 28; Y-93

Fuentes, Carlos 1928- DLB-113

Fuertes, Gloria 1918- DLB-108

Fugard, Athol 1932- DLB-225

The Fugitives and the Agrarians:
    The First Exhibition Y-85

Fujiwara no Shunzei 1114-1204 . . . . .DLB-203

Fujiwara no Tameaki 1230s?-1290s? DLB-203

Fujiwara no Tameie 1198-1275 . . . . .DLB-203

Fujiwara no Teika 1162-1241 . . . . .DLB-203

Fulbecke, William 1560-1603? DLB-172

Fuller, Charles H., Jr. 1939- DLB-38

Fuller, Henry Blake 1857-1929 . . . . .DLB-12

Fuller, John 1937- DLB-40

Fuller, Margaret (see Fuller, Sarah Margaret,
    Marchesa D'Ossoli)

Fuller, Roy 1912-1991 . . . . .DLB-15, 20

Fuller, Samuel 1912- DLB-26

Fuller, Sarah Margaret, Marchesa
    D'Ossoli 1810-1850 . . . DLB-1, 59, 73, 183, 223

Fuller, Thomas 1608-1661 . . . . .DLB-151

Fullerton, Hugh 1873-1945 . . . . .DLB-171

Fulton, Alice 1952- DLB-193

Fulton, Len 1934- Y-86

Fulton, Robin 1937- DLB-40

Furbank, P. N. 1920- DLB-155

Furman, Laura 1945- Y-86

Furness, Horace Howard 1833-1912 . . . . .DLB-64

Furness, William Henry 1802-1896 . . . . . . .DLB-1

Furnivall, Frederick James 1825-1910 . . . .DLB-184

Furthman, Jules 1888-1966 . . . . .DLB-26

Furui Yoshikichi 1937- DLB-182

Fushimi, Emperor 1265-1317 . . . . .DLB-203

Futabatei, Shimei (Hasegawa Tatsunosuke)
    1864-1909 . . . . .DLB-180

The Future of the Novel (1899), by
  Henry James. DLB-18

Fyleman, Rose 1877-1957 . . . . DLB-160

G

The G. Ross Roy Scottish Poetry
  Collection at the University of
  South Carolina. Y-89

Gadda, Carlo Emilio 1893-1973 . . . . .DLB-177

Gaddis, William 1922-1998 . . . . .DLB-2, Y-99

Gág, Wanda 1893-1946 . . . . DLB-22

Gagarin, Ivan Sergeevich 1814-1882 . . . . DLB-198

Gagnon, Madeleine 1938- DLB-60

Gaine, Hugh 1726-1807 . . . . DLB-43

Gaine, Hugh [publishing house] DLB-49

Gaines, Ernest J. 1933- DLB-2, 33, 152; Y-80

Gaiser, Gerd 1908-1976 . . . . DLB-69

Galarza, Ernesto 1905-1984 . . . . DLB-122

Galaxy Science Fiction Novels DLB-46

Gale, Zona 1874-1938. . . . . DLB-9, 78

Galen of Pergamon 129-after 210 . . . . . . .DLB-176

Gales, Winifred Marshall 1761-1839 . . . . DLB-200

Gall, Louise von 1815-1855 . . . . DLB-133

Gallagher, Tess 1943- DLB-120, 212

Gallagher, Wes 1911- DLB-127

Gallagher, William Davis 1808-1894 . . . . . DLB-73

Gallant, Mavis 1922- DLB-53

Gallegos, María Magdalena 1935- DLB-209

Gallico, Paul 1897-1976. . . . . .DLB-9, 171

Galloway, Grace Growden 1727-1782. . . . DLB-200

Gallup, Donald 1913- DLB-187

Galsworthy, John
  1867-1933. . . . . . . .DLB-10, 34, 98, 162; DS-16

Galt, John 1779-1839. . . . . DLB-99, 116

Galton, Sir Francis 1822-1911. . . . . DLB-166

Galvin, Brendan 1938- DLB-5

Gambit DLB-46

Gamboa, Reymundo 1948- DLB-122

Gammer Gurton's Needle. DLB-62

Gan, Elena Andreevna (Zeneida R-va)
  1814-1842. . . . . DLB-198

Gannett, Frank E. 1876-1957 . . . . DLB-29

Gaos, Vicente 1919-1980 . . . . DLB-134

García, Andrew 1854?-1943. . . . . DLB-209

García, Lionel G. 1935- DLB-82

García, Richard 1941- DLB-209

García-Camarillo, Cecilio 1943- DLB-209

García Lorca, Federico 1898-1936 . . . . . . DLB-108

García Márquez, Gabriel 1928- . . .DLB-113; Y-82

Gardam, Jane 1928- DLB-14, 161

Garden, Alexander circa 1685-1756 . . . . . . DLB-31

Gardiner, Margaret Power Farmer (see
  Blessington, Marguerite, Countess of)

Gardner, John 1933-1982 . . . . DLB-2; Y-82

Garfield, Leon 1921-1996. . . . . DLB-161

Garis, Howard R. 1873-1962 . . . . DLB-22

Garland, Hamlin
  1860-1940 . . . . .DLB-12, 71, 78, 186

Garneau, Francis-Xavier 1809-1866. . . . . . DLB-99

Garneau, Hector de Saint-Denys
  1912-1943 . . . . DLB-88

Garneau, Michel 1939- DLB-53

Garner, Alan 1934- DLB-161

Garner, Hugh 1913-1979 . . . . DLB-68

Garnett, David 1892-1981 . . . . DLB-34

Garnett, Eve 1900-1991 . . . . DLB-160

Garnett, Richard 1835-1906. . . . . DLB-184

Garrard, Lewis H. 1829-1887. . . . . DLB-186

Garraty, John A. 1920- DLB-17

Garrett, George
  1929- DLB-2, 5, 130, 152; Y-83

Garrett, John Work 1872-1942. . . . . DLB-187

Garrick, David 1717-1779 . . . . DLB-84, 213

Garrison, William Lloyd 1805-1879. . . . DLB-1, 43

Garro, Elena 1920-1998 . . . . DLB-145

Garth, Samuel 1661-1719 . . . . DLB-95

Garve, Andrew 1908- DLB-87

Gary, Romain 1914-1980. . . . . DLB-83

Gascoigne, George 1539?-1577. . . . . DLB-136

Gascoyne, David 1916- DLB-20

Gaskell, Elizabeth Cleghorn
  1810-1865 . . . . DLB-21, 144, 159

Gaspey, Thomas 1788-1871 . . . . DLB-116

Gass, William Howard 1924- DLB-2

Gates, Doris 1901- DLB-22

Gates, Henry Louis, Jr. 1950- DLB-67

Gates, Lewis E. 1860-1924 . . . . DLB-71

Gatto, Alfonso 1909-1976 . . . . DLB-114

Gault, William Campbell 1910-1995 . . . . DLB-226

Gaunt, Mary 1861-1942 . . . . .DLB-174

Gautier, Théophile 1811-1872 . . . . DLB-119

Gauvreau, Claude 1925-1971 . . . . DLB-88

The *Gawain*-Poet
  flourished circa 1350-1400. . . . . DLB-146

Gay, Ebenezer 1696-1787 . . . . DLB-24

Gay, John 1685-1732 . . . . DLB-84, 95

The *Gay Science* (1866), by E. S. Dallas
  [excerpt] DLB-21

Gayarré, Charles E. A. 1805-1895 . . . . . . DLB-30

Gaylord, Edward King 1873-1974 . . . . . . DLB-127

Gaylord, Edward Lewis 1919- DLB-127

Gaylord, Charles [publishing house] DLB-49

Geddes, Gary 1940- DLB-60

Geddes, Virgil 1897- DLB-4

Gedeon (Georgii Andreevich Krinovsky)
  circa 1730-1763. . . . . DLB-150

Gee, Maggie 1948- DLB-207

Geibel, Emanuel 1815-1884 . . . . DLB-129

Geiogamah, Hanay 1945- DLB-175

Geis, Bernard, Associates DLB-46

Geisel, Theodor Seuss 1904-1991. . . .DLB-61; Y-91

Gelb, Arthur 1924- DLB-103

Gelb, Barbara 1926- DLB-103

Gelber, Jack 1932- DLB-7

Gelinas, Gratien 1909- DLB-88

Gellert, Christian Füerchtegott
  1715-1769. . . . . DLB-97

Gellhorn, Martha 1908-1998 . . . . Y-82, Y-98

Gems, Pam 1925- DLB-13

A General Idea of the College of Mirania (1753),
  by William Smith [excerpts]. DLB-31

Genet, Jean 1910-1986 . . . . .DLB-72; Y-86

Genevoix, Maurice 1890-1980 . . . . DLB-65

Genovese, Eugene D. 1930- DLB-17

Gent, Peter 1942- Y-82

Geoffrey of Monmouth
  circa 1100-1155 . . . . DLB-146

George, Henry 1839-1897 . . . . DLB-23

George, Jean Craighead 1919- DLB-52

George, W. L. 1882-1926. . . . . .DLB-197

George III, King of Great Britain and Ireland
  1738-1820. DLB-213

George V. Higgins to Julian Symons Y-99

Georgslied 896? DLB-148

Gerber, Merrill Joan 1938- DLB-218

Gerhardie, William 1895-1977 . . . . DLB-36

Gerhardt, Paul 1607-1676. . . . . DLB-164

Gérin, Winifred 1901-1981 . . . . DLB-155

Gérin-Lajoie, Antoine 1824-1882 . . . . DLB-99

German Drama 800-1280. . . . . DLB-138

German Drama from Naturalism
  to Fascism: 1889-1933 . . . . DLB-118

German Literature and Culture from
  Charlemagne to the Early Courtly
  Period DLB-148

German Radio Play, The DLB-124

German Transformation from the Baroque
  to the Enlightenment, The. DLB-97

The Germanic Epic and Old English Heroic
  Poetry: *Widseth, Waldere,* and *The
  Fight at Finnsburg*. DLB-146

Germanophilism, by Hans Kohn DLB-66

Gernsback, Hugo 1884-1967 . . . . .DLB-8, 137

Gerould, Katharine Fullerton
  1879-1944. . . . . DLB-78

Gerrish, Samuel [publishing house] DLB-49

Gerrold, David 1944- DLB-8

The Ira Gershwin Centenary. Y-96

Gerson, Jean 1363-1429 . . . . DLB-208

Gersonides 1288-1344 . . . . DLB-115

Gerstäcker, Friedrich 1816-1872. . . . . . . DLB-129

Gerstenberg, Heinrich Wilhelm von
  1737-1823. . . . . DLB-97

Gervinus, Georg Gottfried
  1805-1871. DLB-133

Geßner, Salomon 1730-1788. . . . . DLB-97

Geston, Mark S. 1946- DLB-8

"Getting Started: Accepting the Regions You Own–
  or Which Own You," by
  Walter McDonald DLB-105

Al-Ghazali 1058-1111 . . . . DLB-115

Gibbings, Robert 1889-1958 . . . . .DLB-195

Gibbon, Edward 1737-1794 . . . . .DLB-104

Gibbon, John Murray 1875-1952 . . . . .DLB-92

Gibbon, Lewis Grassic (see Mitchell, James Leslie)

Gibbons, Floyd 1887-1939 . . . . .DLB-25

Gibbons, Reginald 1947- DLB-120

Gibbons, William ?-? DLB-73

Gibson, Charles Dana 1867-1944 . . . . DS-13

Gibson, Charles Dana
1867-1944 . . . . .DLB-188; DS-13

Gibson, Graeme 1934- DLB-53

Gibson, Margaret 1944- DLB-120

Gibson, Margaret Dunlop 1843-1920 . . . . DLB-174

Gibson, Wilfrid 1878-1962 . . . . .DLB-19

Gibson, William 1914- DLB-7

Gide, André 1869-1951 . . . . .DLB-65

Giguère, Diane 1937- DLB-53

Giguère, Roland 1929- DLB-60

Gil de Biedma, Jaime 1929-1990 . . . . .DLB-108

Gil-Albert, Juan 1906- DLB-134

Gilbert, Anthony 1899-1973 . . . . .DLB-77

Gilbert, Michael 1912- DLB-87

Gilbert, Sandra M. 1936- DLB-120

Gilbert, Sir Humphrey 1537-1583 . . . . . . .DLB-136

Gilchrist, Alexander 1828-1861 . . . . .DLB-144

Gilchrist, Ellen 1935- DLB-130

Gilder, Jeannette L. 1849-1916 . . . . .DLB-79

Gilder, Richard Watson 1844-1909 . . . .DLB-64, 79

Gildersleeve, Basil 1831-1924 . . . . .DLB-71

Giles, Henry 1809-1882 . . . . .DLB-64

Giles of Rome circa 1243-1316 . . . . .DLB-115

Gilfillan, George 1813-1878 . . . . .DLB-144

Gill, Eric 1882-1940 . . . . .DLB-98

Gill, Sarah Prince 1728-1771 . . . . .DLB-200

Gill, William F., Company DLB-49

Gillespie, A. Lincoln, Jr. 1895-1950 . . . . . . .DLB-4

Gilliam, Florence ?-? DLB-4

Gilliatt, Penelope 1932-1993 . . . . .DLB-14

Gillott, Jacky 1939-1980 . . . . .DLB-14

Gilman, Caroline H. 1794-1888 . . . . . . .DLB-3, 73

Gilman, Charlotte Perkins 1860-1935 . . . .DLB-221

Gilman, W. and J. [publishing house] DLB-49

Gilmer, Elizabeth Meriwether
1861-1951 . . . . .DLB-29

Gilmer, Francis Walker 1790-1826 . . . . . . .DLB-37

Gilroy, Frank D. 1925- DLB-7

Gimferrer, Pere (Pedro) 1945- DLB-134

Gingrich, Arnold 1903-1976 . . . . .DLB-137

Ginsberg, Allen 1926-1997 . . . . . . .DLB-5, 16, 169

Ginzburg, Natalia 1916-1991 . . . . .DLB-177

Ginzkey, Franz Karl 1871-1963 . . . . .DLB-81

Gioia, Dana 1950- DLB-120

Giono, Jean 1895-1970 . . . . .DLB-72

Giotti, Virgilio 1885-1957 . . . . .DLB-114

Giovanni, Nikki 1943- DLB-5, 41

Gipson, Lawrence Henry 1880-1971 . . . . .DLB-17

Girard, Rodolphe 1879-1956 . . . . .DLB-92

Giraudoux, Jean 1882-1944 . . . . .DLB-65

Gissing, George 1857-1903 . . . . .DLB-18, 135, 184

Giudici, Giovanni 1924- DLB-128

Giuliani, Alfredo 1924- DLB-128

Glackens, William J. 1870-1938 . . . . .DLB-188

Gladstone, William Ewart
1809-1898 . . . . DLB-57, 184

Glaeser, Ernst 1902-1963 . . . . .DLB-69

Glancy, Diane 1941- DLB-175

Glanville, Brian 1931- DLB-15, 139

Glapthorne, Henry 1610-1643? DLB-58

Glasgow, Ellen 1873-1945 . . . . .DLB-9, 12

Glasier, Katharine Bruce 1867-1950 . . . . . .DLB-190

Glaspell, Susan 1876-1948 . . . . .DLB-7, 9, 78

Glass, Montague 1877-1934 . . . . .DLB-11

The Glass Key and Other Dashiell Hammett
Mysteries Y-96

Glassco, John 1909-1981 . . . . .DLB-68

Glauser, Friedrich 1896-1938 . . . . .DLB-56

F. Gleason's Publishing Hall DLB-49

Gleim, Johann Wilhelm Ludwig
1719-1803 . . . . .DLB-97

Glendinning, Victoria 1937- DLB-155

Glinka, Fedor Nikolaevich
1786-1880 . . . . .DLB-205

Glover, Richard 1712-1785 . . . . .DLB-95

Glück, Louise 1943- DLB-5

Glyn, Elinor 1864-1943 . . . . .DLB-153

Gnedich, Nikolai Ivanovich
1784-1833 . . . . .DLB-205

Go-Toba 1180-1239 . . . . .DLB-203

Gobineau, Joseph-Arthur de
1816-1882 . . . . .DLB-123

Godbout, Jacques 1933- DLB-53

Goddard, Morrill 1865-1937 . . . . .DLB-25

Goddard, William 1740-1817 . . . . .DLB-43

Godden, Rumer 1907-1998 . . . . .DLB-161

Godey, Louis A. 1804-1878 . . . . .DLB-73

Godey and McMichael DLB-49

Godfrey, Dave 1938- DLB-60

Godfrey, Thomas 1736-1763 . . . . .DLB-31

Godine, David R., Publisher DLB-46

Godkin, E. L. 1831-1902 . . . . .DLB-79

Godolphin, Sidney 1610-1643 . . . . .DLB-126

Godwin, Gail 1937- DLB-6

Godwin, Mary Jane Clairmont
1766-1841 . . . . .DLB-163

Godwin, Parke 1816-1904 . . . . .DLB-3, 64

Godwin, William
1756-1836 . . . . . . .DLB-39, 104, 142, 158, 163

Godwin, M. J., and Company DLB-154

Goering, Reinhard 1887-1936 . . . . .DLB-118

Goes, Albrecht 1908- DLB-69

Goethe, Johann Wolfgang von
1749-1832 . . . . .DLB-94

Goetz, Curt 1888-1960 . . . . .DLB-124

Goffe, Thomas circa 1592-1629 . . . . .DLB-58

Goffstein, M. B. 1940- DLB-61

Gogarty, Oliver St. John 1878-1957 . . . .DLB-15, 19

Gogol, Nikolai Vasil'evich 1809-1852 . . . .DLB-198

Goines, Donald 1937-1974 . . . . .DLB-33

Gold, Herbert 1924- DLB-2; Y-81

Gold, Michael 1893-1967 . . . . .DLB-9, 28

Goldbarth, Albert 1948- DLB-120

Goldberg, Dick 1947- DLB-7

Golden Cockerel Press DLB-112

Golding, Arthur 1536-1606 . . . . .DLB-136

Golding, Louis 1895-1958 . . . . .DLB-195

Golding, William 1911-1993 . . . DLB-15, 100; Y-83

Goldman, Emma 1869-1940 . . . . .DLB-221

Goldman, William 1931- DLB-44

Goldring, Douglas 1887-1960 . . . . .DLB-197

Goldsmith, Oliver
1730?-1774 . . . . DLB-39, 89, 104, 109, 142

Goldsmith, Oliver 1794-1861 . . . . .DLB-99

Goldsmith Publishing Company DLB-46

Goldstein, Richard 1944- DLB-185

Gollancz, Sir Israel 1864-1930 . . . . .DLB-201

Gollancz, Victor, Limited DLB-112

Gombrowicz, Witold 1904-1969 . . . . .DLB-215

Gómez-Quiñones, Juan 1942- DLB-122

Gomme, Laurence James
[publishing house] DLB-46

Goncourt, Edmond de 1822-1896 . . . . . . .DLB-123

Goncourt, Jules de 1830-1870 . . . . .DLB-123

Gonzales, Rodolfo "Corky" 1928- DLB-122

Gonzales-Berry, Erlinda 1942- DLB-209

González, Angel 1925- DLB-108

Gonzalez, Genaro 1949- DLB-122

Gonzalez, Ray 1952- DLB-122

González de Mireles, Jovita
1899-1983 . . . . .DLB-122

González-T., César A. 1931- DLB-82

"The Good, The Not So Good," by
Stephen Dunn DLB-105

Goodbye, Gutenberg? A Lecture at
the New York Public Library,
18 April 1995 . . . . Y-95

Goodis, David 1917-1967 . . . . .DLB-226

Goodison, Lorna 1947- DLB-157

Goodman, Paul 1911-1972 . . . . .DLB-130

The Goodman Theatre DLB-7

Goodrich, Frances 1891-1984 and
Hackett, Albert 1900-1995 . . . . .DLB-26

Goodrich, Samuel Griswold
1793-1860 . . . . .DLB-1, 42, 73

Goodrich, S. G. [publishing house] DLB-49

Goodspeed, C. E., and Company DLB-49

Goodwin, Stephen 1943- Y-82

Googe, Barnabe 1540-1594 . . . . .DLB-132

Gookin, Daniel 1612-1687 . . . . .DLB-24

Gordimer, Nadine 1923- DLB-225; Y-91

Gordon, Caroline
1895-1981 ...... DLB-4, 9, 102; DS-17; Y-81

Gordon, Giles 1940- DLB-14, 139, 207

Gordon, Helen Cameron, Lady Russell
1867-1949 .... DLB-195

Gordon, Lyndall 1941- DLB-155

Gordon, Mary 1949- DLB-6; Y-81

Gordone, Charles 1925-1995 .... DLB-7

Gore, Catherine 1800-1861 .... DLB-116

Gores, Joe 1931- DLB-226

Gorey, Edward 1925- DLB-61

Gorgias of Leontini
circa 485 B.C.-376 B.C. DLB-176

Görres, Joseph 1776-1848 .... DLB-90

Gosse, Edmund 1849-1928 ...... DLB-57, 144, 184

Gosson, Stephen 1554-1624 .... DLB-172

Gotlieb, Phyllis 1926- DLB-88

Gottfried von Straßburg
died before 1230 .... DLB-138

Gotthelf, Jeremias 1797-1854 .... DLB-133

Gottschalk circa 804/808-869 .... DLB-148

Gottsched, Johann Christoph
1700-1766 .... DLB-97

Götz, Johann Nikolaus 1721-1781 .... DLB-97

Goudge, Elizabeth 1900-1984 .... DLB-191

Gould, Wallace 1882-1940 .... DLB-54

Govoni, Corrado 1884-1965 .... DLB-114

Gower, John circa 1330-1408 .... DLB-146

Goyen, William 1915-1983 ..... DLB-2, 218; Y-83

Goytisolo, José Augustín 1928- DLB-134

Gozzano, Guido 1883-1916 .... DLB-114

Grabbe, Christian Dietrich
1801-1836 .... DLB-133

Gracq, Julien 1910- DLB-83

Grady, Henry W. 1850-1889 .... DLB-23

Graf, Oskar Maria 1894-1967 .... DLB-56

Graf Rudolf between circa 1170
and circa 1185 .... DLB-148

Grafton, Richard [publishing house] DLB-170

Grafton, Sue 1940- DLB-226

Graham, George Rex 1813-1894 .... DLB-73

Graham, Gwethalyn 1913-1965 .... DLB-88

Graham, Jorie 1951- DLB-120

Graham, Katharine 1917- DLB-127

Graham, Lorenz 1902-1989 .... DLB-76

Graham, Philip 1915-1963 .... DLB-127

Graham, R. B. Cunninghame
1852-1936 .... DLB-98, 135, 174

Graham, Shirley 1896-1977 .... DLB-76

Graham, Stephen 1884-1975 .... DLB-195

Graham, W. S. 1918- DLB-20

Graham, William H. [publishing house] ... DLB-49

Graham, Winston 1910- DLB-77

Grahame, Kenneth
1859-1932 .... DLB-34, 141, 178

Grainger, Martin Allerdale 1874-1941 .... DLB-92

Gramatky, Hardie 1907-1979 .... DLB-22

Grand, Sarah 1854-1943 .... DLB-135, 197

Grandbois, Alain 1900-1975 .... DLB-92

Grandson, Oton de circa 1345-1397 ..... DLB-208

Grange, John circa 1556-? DLB-136

Granich, Irwin (see Gold, Michael)

Granovsky, Timofei Nikolaevich
1813-1855 .... DLB-198

Grant, Anne MacVicar 1755-1838 ..... DLB-200

Grant, Duncan 1885-1978 .... DS-10

Grant, George 1918-1988 .... DLB-88

Grant, George Monro 1835-1902 .... DLB-99

Grant, Harry J. 1881-1963 .... DLB-29

Grant, James Edward 1905-1966 .... DLB-26

Grass, Günter 1927- DLB-75, 124

Grasty, Charles H. 1863-1924 .... DLB-25

Grau, Shirley Ann 1929- DLB-2, 218

Graves, John 1920- Y-83

Graves, Richard 1715-1804 .... DLB-39

Graves, Robert 1895-1985
.... DLB-20, 100, 191; DS-18; Y-85

Gray, Alasdair 1934- DLB-194

Gray, Asa 1810-1888 .... DLB-1

Gray, David 1838-1861 .... DLB-32

Gray, Simon 1936- DLB-13

Gray, Thomas 1716-1771 .... DLB-109

Grayson, William J. 1788-1863 .... DLB-3, 64

The Great Bibliographers Series Y-93

The Great Modern Library Scam Y-98

The Great War and the Theater, 1914-1918
[Great Britain] DLB-10

The Great War Exhibition and Symposium at the
University of South Carolina Y-97

Grech, Nikolai Ivanovich 1787-1867 ..... DLB-198

Greeley, Horace 1811-1872 ...... DLB-3, 43, 189

Green, Adolph (see Comden, Betty)

Green, Anna Katharine
1846-1935 .... DLB-202, 221

Green, Duff 1791-1875 .... DLB-43

Green, Elizabeth Shippen 1871-1954 .... DLB-188

Green, Gerald 1922- DLB-28

Green, Henry 1905-1973 .... DLB-15

Green, Jonas 1712-1767 .... DLB-31

Green, Joseph 1706-1780 .... DLB-31

Green, Julien 1900-1998 .... DLB-4, 72

Green, Paul 1894-1981 .... DLB-7, 9; Y-81

Green, T. and S. [publishing house] DLB-49

Green, Thomas Hill 1836-1882 .... DLB-190

Green, Timothy [publishing house] DLB-49

Greenaway, Kate 1846-1901 .... DLB-141

Greenberg: Publisher DLB-46

Green Tiger Press DLB-46

Greene, Asa 1789-1838 .... DLB-11

Greene, Belle da Costa 1883-1950 ..... DLB-187

Greene, Benjamin H.
[publishing house] DLB-49

Greene, Graham 1904-1991 ....
DLB-13, 15, 77, 100, 162, 201, 204; Y-85, Y-91

Greene, Robert 1558-1592 .... DLB-62, 167

Greene Jr., Robert Bernard (Bob)
1947- DLB-185

Greenhow, Robert 1800-1854 .... DLB-30

Greenlee, William B. 1872-1953 .... DLB-187

Greenough, Horatio 1805-1852 .... DLB-1

Greenwell, Dora 1821-1882 .... DLB-35, 199

Greenwillow Books DLB-46

Greenwood, Grace (see Lippincott, Sara Jane Clarke)

Greenwood, Walter 1903-1974 ...... DLB-10, 191

Greer, Ben 1948- DLB-6

Greflinger, Georg 1620?-1677 .... DLB-164

Greg, W. R. 1809-1881 .... DLB-55

Greg, W. W. 1875-1959 .... DLB-201

Gregg, Josiah 1806-1850 .... DLB-183, 186

Gregg Press DLB-46

Gregory, Isabella Augusta
Persse, Lady 1852-1932 .... DLB-10

Gregory, Horace 1898-1982 .... DLB-48

Gregory of Rimini circa 1300-1358 ..... DLB-115

Gregynog Press DLB-112

Greiffenberg, Catharina Regina von
1633-1694 .... DLB-168

Grenfell, Wilfred Thomason
1865-1940 .... DLB-92

Gress, Elsa 1919-1988 .... DLB-214

Greve, Felix Paul (see Grove, Frederick Philip)

Greville, Fulke, First Lord Brooke
1554-1628 .... DLB-62, 172

Grey, Sir George, K.C.B. 1812-1898 .... DLB-184

Grey, Lady Jane 1537-1554 .... DLB-132

Grey Owl 1888-1938 .... DLB-92; DS-17

Grey, Zane 1872-1939 .... DLB-9, 212

Grey Walls Press DLB-112

Griboedov, Aleksandr Sergeevich
1795?-1829 .... DLB-205

Grier, Eldon 1917- DLB-88

Grieve, C. M. (see MacDiarmid, Hugh)

Griffin, Bartholomew flourished 1596 .... DLB-172

Griffin, Gerald 1803-1840 .... DLB-159

Griffith, Elizabeth 1727?-1793 .... DLB-39, 89

Griffith, George 1857-1906 .... DLB-178

Griffiths, Trevor 1935- DLB-13

Griffiths, Ralph [publishing house] DLB-154

Griggs, S. C., and Company DLB-49

Griggs, Sutton Elbert 1872-1930 .... DLB-50

Grignon, Claude-Henri 1894-1976 ...... DLB-68

Grigson, Geoffrey 1905- DLB-27

Grillparzer, Franz 1791-1872 .... DLB-133

Grimald, Nicholas
circa 1519-circa 1562 .... DLB-136

Grimké, Angelina Weld
1880-1958 .... DLB-50, 54

Grimm, Hans 1875-1959 .... DLB-66

Grimm, Jacob 1785-1863 .... DLB-90

Grimm, Wilhelm 1786-1859 . . . . .DLB-90

Grimmelshausen, Johann Jacob Christoffel von
    1621 or 1622-1676. . . . . .DLB-168

Grimshaw, Beatrice Ethel 1871-1953 . . . . . DLB-174

Grindal, Edmund 1519 or 1520-1583 . . . .DLB-132

Griswold, Rufus Wilmot 1815-1857 . . . .DLB-3, 59

Grosart, Alexander Balloch 1827-1899. . . .DLB-184

Gross, Milt 1895-1953 . . . . .DLB-11

Grosset and Dunlap. DLB-49

Grossman, Allen 1932- DLB-193

Grossman Publishers DLB-46

Grosseteste, Robert circa 1160-1253 . . . . .DLB-115

Grosvenor, Gilbert H. 1875-1966 . . . . .DLB-91

Groth, Klaus 1819-1899. . . . . .DLB-129

Groulx, Lionel 1878-1967 . . . . .DLB-68

Grove, Frederick Philip 1879-1949 . . . . . . .DLB-92

Grove Press DLB-46

Grubb, Davis 1919-1980 . . . . .DLB-6

Gruelle, Johnny 1880-1938 . . . . .DLB-22

von Grumbach, Argula
    1492-after 1563? DLB-179

Grymeston, Elizabeth
    before 1563-before 1604 . . . . .DLB-136

Gryphius, Andreas 1616-1664. . . . . .DLB-164

Gryphius, Christian 1649-1706 . . . . .DLB-168

Guare, John 1938- DLB-7

Guerra, Tonino 1920- DLB-128

Guest, Barbara 1920- DLB-5, 193

Guèvremont, Germaine 1893-1968 . . . . . .DLB-68

Guidacci, Margherita 1921-1992 . . . . . . .DLB-128

Guide to the Archives of Publishers, Journals,
    and Literary Agents in North American
    Libraries Y-93

Guillén, Jorge 1893-1984 . . . . .DLB-108

Guilloux, Louis 1899-1980 . . . . .DLB-72

Guilpin, Everard
    circa 1572-after 1608? DLB-136

Guiney, Louise Imogen 1861-1920 . . . . . . .DLB-54

Guiterman, Arthur 1871-1943 . . . . .DLB-11

Günderrode, Caroline von
    1780-1806 . . . . .DLB-90

Gundulić, Ivan 1589-1638 . . . . .DLB-147

Gunn, Bill 1934-1989. . . . . .DLB-38

Gunn, James E. 1923- DLB-8

Gunn, Neil M. 1891-1973 . . . . .DLB-15

Gunn, Thom 1929- DLB-27

Gunnars, Kristjana 1948- DLB-60

Günther, Johann Christian
    1695-1723 . . . . .DLB-168

Gurik, Robert 1932- DLB-60

Gustafson, Ralph 1909- DLB-88

Gütersloh, Albert Paris 1887-1973 . . . . . . .DLB-81

Guthrie, A. B., Jr. 1901-1991 . . . . .DLB-6, 212

Guthrie, Ramon 1896-1973 . . . . .DLB-4

The Guthrie Theater DLB-7

Guthrie, Thomas Anstey (see Anstey, FC)

Gutzkow, Karl 1811-1878 . . . . .DLB-133

Guy, Ray 1939- DLB-60

Guy, Rosa 1925- DLB-33

Guyot, Arnold 1807-1884 . . . . DS-13

Gwynne, Erskine 1898-1948 . . . . .DLB-4

Gyles, John 1680-1755 . . . . .DLB-99

Gysin, Brion 1916- DLB-16

H

H.D. (see Doolittle, Hilda)

Habington, William 1605-1654 . . . . .DLB-126

Hacker, Marilyn 1942- DLB-120

Hackett, Albert (see Goodrich, Frances)

Hacks, Peter 1928- DLB-124

Hadas, Rachel 1948- DLB-120

Hadden, Briton 1898-1929 . . . . .DLB-91

Hagedorn, Friedrich von 1708-1754. . . . . .DLB-168

Hagelstange, Rudolf 1912-1984. . . . . .DLB-69

Haggard, H. Rider
    1856-1925 . . . . .DLB-70, 156, 174, 178

Haggard, William 1907-1993 . . . . Y-93

Hahn-Hahn, Ida Gräfin von
    1805-1880 . . . . .DLB-133

Haig-Brown, Roderick 1908-1976 . . . . . . .DLB-88

Haight, Gordon S. 1901-1985 . . . . .DLB-103

Hailey, Arthur 1920- DLB-88; Y-82

Haines, John 1924- DLB-5, 212

Hake, Edward flourished 1566-1604 . . . . .DLB-136

Hake, Thomas Gordon 1809-1895 . . . . . . .DLB-32

Hakluyt, Richard 1552?-1616 . . . . .DLB-136

Halas, František 1901-1949 . . . . .DLB-215

Halbe, Max 1865-1944 . . . . .DLB-118

Haldone, Charlotte 1894-1969 . . . . .DLB-191

Haldane, J. B. S. 1892-1964 . . . . .DLB-160

Haldeman, Joe 1943- DLB-8

Haldeman-Julius Company DLB-46

Hale, E. J., and Son DLB-49

Hale, Edward Everett 1822-1909. . . . DLB-1, 42, 74

Hale, Janet Campbell 1946- DLB-175

Hale, Kathleen 1898- DLB-160

Hale, Leo Thomas (see Ebon)

Hale, Lucretia Peabody 1820-1900 . . . . . . .DLB-42

Hale, Nancy
    1908-1988 . . . . DLB-86; DS-17; Y-80, Y-88

Hale, Sarah Josepha (Buell)
    1788-1879 . . . . DLB-1, 42, 73

Hale, Susan 1833-1910 . . . . .DLB-221

Hales, John 1584-1656. . . . . .DLB-151

Halévy, Ludovic 1834-1908 . . . . .DLB-192

Haley, Alex 1921-1992 . . . . .DLB-38

Haliburton, Thomas Chandler
    1796-1865 . . . . .DLB-11, 99

Hall, Anna Maria 1800-1881 . . . . .DLB-159

Hall, Donald 1928- DLB-5

Hall, Edward 1497-1547. . . . . .DLB-132

Hall, James 1793-1868 . . . . DLB-73, 74

Hall, Joseph 1574-1656 . . . . DLB-121, 151

Hall, Radclyffe 1880-1943 . . . . .DLB-191

Hall, Sarah Ewing 1761-1830. . . . . .DLB-200

Hall, Samuel [publishing house]. DLB-49

Hallam, Arthur Henry 1811-1833 . . . . . . .DLB-32

Halleck, Fitz-Greene 1790-1867 . . . . .DLB-3

Haller, Albrecht von 1708-1777 . . . . .DLB-168

Halliday, Brett (see Dresser, Davis)

Halliwell-Phillipps, James Orchard
    1820-1889 . . . . .DLB-184

Hallmann, Johann Christian
    1640-1704 or 1716? DLB-168

Hallmark Editions DLB-46

Halper, Albert 1904-1984 . . . . .DLB-9

Halperin, John William 1941- DLB-111

Halstead, Murat 1829-1908 . . . . .DLB-23

Hamann, Johann Georg 1730-1788 . . . . . . .DLB-97

Hamburger, Michael 1924- DLB-27

Hamilton, Alexander 1712-1756. . . . . .DLB-31

Hamilton, Alexander 1755?-1804 . . . . .DLB-37

Hamilton, Cicely 1872-1952 . . . . DLB-10, 197

Hamilton, Edmond 1904-1977. . . . . .DLB-8

Hamilton, Elizabeth 1758-1816 . . . . . DLB-116, 158

Hamilton, Gail (see Corcoran, Barbara)

Hamilton, Gail (see Dodge, Mary Abigail)

Hamilton, Ian 1938- DLB-40, 155

Hamilton, Janet 1795-1873 . . . . .DLB-199

Hamilton, Mary Agnes 1884-1962 . . . . . .DLB-197

Hamilton, Patrick 1904-1962. . . . . . . DLB-10, 191

Hamilton, Virginia 1936- DLB-33, 52

Hamilton, Hamish, Limited. DLB-112

Hammett, Dashiell 1894-1961 . . . . .DLB-226; DS-6

Dashiell Hammett: An Appeal in *TAC* Y-91

Hammon, Jupiter 1711-died between
    1790 and 1806. . . . . .DLB-31, 50

Hammond, John ?-1663. . . . . .DLB-24

Hamner, Earl 1923- DLB-6

Hampson, John 1901-1955 . . . . .DLB-191

Hampton, Christopher 1946- DLB-13

Handel-Mazzetti, Enrica von 1871-1955 . . .DLB-81

Handke, Peter 1942- DLB-85, 124

Handlin, Oscar 1915- DLB-17

Hankin, St. John 1869-1909. . . . . .DLB-10

Hanley, Clifford 1922- DLB-14

Hanley, James 1901-1985 . . . . .DLB-191

Hannah, Barry 1942- DLB-6

Hannay, James 1827-1873 . . . . .DLB-21

Hansberry, Lorraine 1930-1965 . . . . . . .DLB-7, 38

Hansen, Martin A. 1909-1955 . . . . .DLB-214

Hansen, Thorkild 1927-1989 . . . . .DLB-214

Hanson, Elizabeth 1684-1737 . . . . .DLB-200

Hapgood, Norman 1868-1937 . . . . .DLB-91

Happel, Eberhard Werner 1647-1690 . . . .DLB-168

The Harbinger 1845-1849 . . . . .DLB-223

Harcourt Brace Jovanovich DLB-46

Hardenberg, Friedrich von (see Novalis)

Harding, Walter 1917- DLB-111

Hardwick, Elizabeth 1916- DLB-6

Hardy, Thomas 1840-1928 . . . . . DLB-18, 19, 135

Hare, Cyril 1900-1958 . . . . DLB-77

Hare, David 1947- DLB-13

Hargrove, Marion 1919- DLB-11

Häring, Georg Wilhelm Heinrich (see Alexis, Willibald)

Harington, Donald 1935- DLB-152

Harington, Sir John 1560-1612 . . . . DLB-136

Harjo, Joy 1951- DLB-120, 175

Harkness, Margaret (John Law) 1854-1923 . . . . DLB-197

Harley, Edward, second Earl of Oxford 1689-1741 . . . . DLB-213

Harley, Robert, first Earl of Oxford 1661-1724 . . . . DLB-213

Harlow, Robert 1923- DLB-60

Harman, Thomas flourished 1566-1573 . . . . DLB-136

Harness, Charles L. 1915- DLB-8

Harnett, Cynthia 1893-1981 . . . . DLB-161

Harper, Fletcher 1806-1877 . . . . DLB-79

Harper, Frances Ellen Watkins 1825-1911 . . . . DLB-50, 221

Harper, Michael S. 1938- DLB-41

Harper and Brothers DLB-49

Harraden, Beatrice 1864-1943 . . . . DLB-153

Harrap, George G., and Company Limited DLB-112

Harriot, Thomas 1560-1621 . . . . DLB-136

Harris, Benjamin ?-circa 1720 . . . . DLB-42, 43

Harris, Christie 1907- DLB-88

Harris, Frank 1856-1931 . . . . .DLB-156, 197

Harris, George Washington 1814-1869 . . . . DLB-3, 11

Harris, Joel Chandler 1848-1908 . . . . .DLB-11, 23, 42, 78, 91

Harris, Mark 1922- DLB-2; Y-80

Harris, Wilson 1921- DLB-117

Harrison, Mrs. Burton (see Harrison, Constance Cary)

Harrison, Charles Yale 1898-1954 . . . . DLB-68

Harrison, Constance Cary 1843-1920 . . . DLB-221

Harrison, Frederic 1831-1923 . . . . .DLB-57, 190

Harrison, Harry 1925- DLB-8

Harrison, Jim 1937- Y-82

Harrison, Mary St. Leger Kingsley (see Malet, Lucas)

Harrison, Paul Carter 1936- DLB-38

Harrison, Susan Frances 1859-1935 . . . . . . DLB-99

Harrison, Tony 1937- DLB-40

Harrison, William 1535-1593 . . . . DLB-136

Harrison, James P., Company DLB-49

Harrisse, Henry 1829-1910 . . . . DLB-47

The Harry Potter Phenomenon Y-99

Harryman, Carla 1952- DLB-193

Harsdörffer, Georg Philipp 1607-1658 . . . DLB-164

Harsent, David 1942- DLB-40

Hart, Albert Bushnell 1854-1943 . . . . DLB-17

Hart, Anne 1768-1834 . . . . DLB-200

Hart, Elizabeth 1771-1833 . . . . DLB-200

Hart, Julia Catherine 1796-1867 . . . . DLB-99

The Lorenz Hart Centenary Y-95

Hart, Moss 1904-1961 . . . . DLB-7

Hart, Oliver 1723-1795 . . . . DLB-31

Hart-Davis, Rupert, Limited DLB-112

Harte, Bret 1836-1902 . . . .DLB-12, 64, 74, 79, 186

Harte, Edward Holmead 1922- DLB-127

Harte, Houston Harriman 1927- DLB-127

Hartlaub, Felix 1913-1945 . . . . DLB-56

Hartlebon, Otto Erich 1864-1905 . . . . . . DLB-118

Hartley, L. P. 1895-1972 . . . . DLB-15, 139

Hartley, Marsden 1877-1943 . . . . DLB-54

Hartling, Peter 1933- DLB-75

Hartman, Geoffrey H. 1929- DLB-67

Hartmann, Sadakichi 1867-1944 . . . . DLB-54

Hartmann von Aue circa 1160-circa 1205 . . . . DLB-138

Harvey, Gabriel 1550?-1631 . . . . . . .DLB-167, 213

Harvey, Jean-Charles 1891-1967 . . . . DLB-88

Harvill Press Limited DLB-112

Harwood, Lee 1939- DLB-40

Harwood, Ronald 1934- DLB-13

Hašek, Jaroslav 1883-1923 . . . . DLB-215

Haskins, Charles Homer 1870-1937 . . . . . . DLB-47

Haslam, Gerald 1937- DLB-212

Hass, Robert 1941- DLB-105, 206

Hatar, Győző 1914- DLB-215

The Hatch-Billops Collection DLB-76

Hathaway, William 1944- DLB-120

Hauff, Wilhelm 1802-1827 . . . . DLB-90

A Haughty and Proud Generation (1922), by Ford Madox Hueffer DLB-36

Haugwitz, August Adolph von 1647-1706 . . . . DLB-168

Hauptmann, Carl 1858-1921 . . . . DLB-66, 118

Hauptmann, Gerhart 1862-1946 . . . . DLB-66, 118

Hauser, Marianne 1910- Y-83

Havergal, Frances Ridley 1836-1879 . . . . DLB-199

Hawes, Stephen 1475?-before 1529 . . . . . DLB-132

Hawker, Robert Stephen 1803-1875 . . . . . DLB-32

Hawkes, John 1925-1998 . . . .DLB-2, 7; Y-80, Y-98

Hawkesworth, John 1720-1773 . . . . DLB-142

Hawkins, Sir Anthony Hope (see Hope, Anthony)

Hawkins, Sir John 1719-1789 . . . . . . DLB-104, 142

Hawkins, Walter Everette 1883-? DLB-50

Hawthorne, Nathaniel 1804-1864 . . . . .DLB-1, 74, 183, 223

Hawthorne, Nathaniel 1804-1864 and Hawthorne, Sophia Peabody 1809-1871 . . . . DLB-183

Hay, John 1835-1905 . . . . .DLB-12, 47, 189

Hayashi, Fumiko 1903-1951 . . . . DLB-180

Haycox, Ernest 1899-1950 . . . . DLB-206

Haycraft, Anna Margaret (see Ellis, Alice Thomas)

Hayden, Robert 1913-1980 . . . . .DLB-5, 76

Haydon, Benjamin Robert 1786-1846 . . . . DLB-110

Hayes, John Michael 1919- DLB-26

Hayley, William 1745-1820 . . . . DLB-93, 142

Haym, Rudolf 1821-1901 . . . . DLB-129

Hayman, Robert 1575-1629 . . . . DLB-99

Hayman, Ronald 1932- DLB-155

Hayne, Paul Hamilton 1830-1886 . . .DLB-3, 64, 79

Hays, Mary 1760-1843 . . . . DLB-142, 158

Hayward, John 1905-1965 . . . . DLB-201

Haywood, Eliza 1693?-1756 . . . . DLB-39

Hazard, Willis P. [publishing house] DLB-49

Hazlitt, William 1778-1830 . . . . .DLB-110, 158

Hazzard, Shirley 1931- Y-82

Head, Bessie 1937-1986 . . . . .DLB-117, 225

Headley, Joel T. 1813-1897 . . DLB-30, 183; DS-13

Heaney, Seamus 1939- DLB-40; Y-95

Heard, Nathan C. 1936- DLB-33

Hearn, Lafcadio 1850-1904 . . . . . .DLB-12, 78, 189

Hearne, John 1926- DLB-117

Hearne, Samuel 1745-1792 . . . . DLB-99

Hearne, Thomas 1678?-1735 . . . . DLB-213

Hearst, William Randolph 1863-1951 . . . . DLB-25

Hearst, William Randolph, Jr. 1908-1993 .DLB-127

Heartman, Charles Frederick 1883-1953 .DLB-187

Heath, Catherine 1924- DLB-14

Heath, Roy A. K. 1926- DLB-117

Heath-Stubbs, John 1918- DLB-27

Heavysege, Charles 1816-1876 . . . . DLB-99

Hebbel, Friedrich 1813-1863 . . . . DLB-129

Hebel, Johann Peter 1760-1826 . . . . DLB-90

Heber, Richard 1774-1833 . . . . DLB-184

Hébert, Anne 1916- DLB-68

Hébert, Jacques 1923- DLB-53

Hecht, Anthony 1923- DLB-5, 169

Hecht, Ben 1894-1964 . . . . .DLB-7, 9, 25, 26, 28, 86

Hecker, Isaac Thomas 1819-1888 . . . . DLB-1

Hedge, Frederic Henry 1805-1890 . . . . . DLB-1, 59

Hefner, Hugh M. 1926- DLB-137

Hegel, Georg Wilhelm Friedrich 1770-1831 . . . . DLB-90

Heidish, Marcy 1947- Y-82

Heike monogatari DLB-203

Hein, Christoph 1944- DLB-124

Hein, Piet 1905-1996 . . . . DLB-214

Heine, Heinrich 1797-1856 . . . . DLB-90

Heinemann, Larry 1944- DS-9

Heinemann, William, Limited DLB-112

Heinesen, William 1900-1991 . . . . DLB-214

Heinlein, Robert A. 1907-1988 . . . . DLB-8

Heinrich Julius of Brunswick
    1564-1613 . . . . .DLB-164

Heinrich von dem Türlîn
    flourished circa 1230 . . . . .DLB-138

Heinrich von Melk
    flourished after 1160 . . . . .DLB-148

Heinrich von Veldeke
    circa 1145-circa 1190. . . . . .DLB-138

Heinrich, Willi 1920- DLB-75

Heinse, Wilhelm 1746-1803. . . . . .DLB-94

Heinz, W. C. 1915- DLB-171

Heiskell, John 1872-1972 . . . . .DLB-127

Heißenbüttel, Helmut 1921-1996. . . . . . . .DLB-75

Hejinian, Lyn 1941- DLB-165

Heliand circa 850 . . . . .DLB-148

Heller, Joseph 1923-1999 . . . DLB-2, 28; Y-80, Y-99

Heller, Michael 1937- DLB-165

Hellman, Lillian 1906-1984 . . . . DLB-7; Y-84

Hellwig, Johann 1609-1674 . . . . .DLB-164

Helprin, Mark 1947- Y-85

Helwig, David 1938- DLB-60

Hemans, Felicia 1793-1835. . . . . .DLB-96

The Hemingway Centenary Celebration at the
    JFK Library. Y-99

Hemingway, Ernest 1899-1961 . . . .
    DLB-4, 9, 102, 210; Y-81, Y-87, Y-99; DS-1,
    DS-15, DS-16

Hemingway in the JFK Y-99

Hemingway: Twenty-Five Years Later Y-85

Hémon, Louis 1880-1913 . . . . .DLB-92

Hempel, Amy 1951- DLB-218

Hemphill, Paul 1936- Y-87

Hénault, Gilles 1920- DLB-88

Henchman, Daniel 1689-1761 . . . . .DLB-24

Henderson, Alice Corbin 1881-1949 . . . . . .DLB-54

Henderson, Archibald 1877-1963. . . . . . . .DLB-103

Henderson, David 1942- DLB-41

Henderson, George Wylie 1904- DLB-51

Henderson, Zenna 1917-1983 . . . . .DLB-8

Henisch, Peter 1943- DLB-85

Henley, Beth 1952- Y-86

Henley, William Ernest 1849-1903 . . . . . . .DLB-19

Henningsen, Agnes 1868-1962 . . . . .DLB-214

Henniker, Florence 1855-1923. . . . . .DLB-135

Henry, Alexander 1739-1824. . . . . .DLB-99

Henry, Buck 1930- DLB-26

Henry VIII of England 1491-1547 . . . . . .DLB-132

Henry, Marguerite 1902-1997 . . . . .DLB-22

Henry, O. (see Porter, William Sydney)

Henry of Ghent
    circa 1217-1229 - 1293. . . . . .DLB-115

Henry, Robert Selph 1889-1970. . . . . . . .DLB-17

Henry, Will (see Allen, Henry W.)

Henryson, Robert
    1420s or 1430s-circa 1505. . . . . .DLB-146

Henschke, Alfred (see Klabund)

Hensley, Sophie Almon 1866-1946 . . . . . .DLB-99

Henson, Lance 1944- DLB-175

Henty, G. A. 1832?-1902. . . . . DLB-18, 141

Hentz, Caroline Lee 1800-1856. . . . . .DLB-3

Heraclitus flourished circa 500 B.C.
    . . . . DLB-176

Herbert, Agnes circa 1880-1960 . . . . DLB-174

Herbert, Alan Patrick 1890-1971 . . . . . DLB-10, 191

Herbert, Edward, Lord, of Cherbury
    1582-1648 . . . . .DLB-121, 151

Herbert, Frank 1920-1986 . . . . .DLB-8

Herbert, George 1593-1633. . . . . .DLB-126

Herbert, Henry William 1807-1858. . . . . DLB-3, 73

Herbert, John 1926- DLB-53

Herbert, Mary Sidney, Countess of Pembroke
    (see Sidney, Mary)

Herbst, Josephine 1892-1969 . . . . .DLB-9

Herburger, Gunter 1932- DLB-75, 124

Hercules, Frank E. M. 1917-1996. . . . . . . .DLB-33

Herder, Johann Gottfried 1744-1803 . . . . . .DLB-97

Herder, B., Book Company. DLB-49

Heredia, José-María de 1842-1905. . . . . . .DLB-217

Herford, Charles Harold 1853-1931 . . . . .DLB-149

Hergesheimer, Joseph 1880-1954. . . . . . DLB-9, 102

Heritage Press DLB-46

Hermann the Lame 1013-1054 . . . . .DLB-148

Hermes, Johann Timotheus
    1738-1821 . . . . .DLB-97

Hermlin, Stephan 1915-1997 . . . . .DLB-69

Hernández, Alfonso C. 1938- DLB-122

Hernández, Inés 1947- DLB-122

Hernández, Miguel 1910-1942. . . . . .DLB-134

Hernton, Calvin C. 1932- DLB-38

"The Hero as Man of Letters: Johnson,
    Rousseau, Burns" (1841), by Thomas
    Carlyle [excerpt] DLB-57

The Hero as Poet. Dante; Shakspeare (1841),
    by Thomas Carlyle DLB-32

Herodotus circa 484 B.C.-circa 420 B.C.
    . . . . DLB-176

Heron, Robert 1764-1807. . . . . .DLB-142

Herr, Michael 1940- DLB-185

Herrera, Juan Felipe 1948- DLB-122

Herrick, Robert 1591-1674 . . . . .DLB-126

Herrick, Robert 1868-1938 . . . . DLB-9, 12, 78

Herrick, William 1915- Y-83

Herrick, E. R., and Company DLB-49

Herrmann, John 1900-1959. . . . . .DLB-4

Hersey, John 1914-1993 . . . . .DLB-6, 185

Hertel, François 1905-1985 . . . . .DLB-68

Hervé-Bazin, Jean Pierre Marie (see Bazin, Hervé)

Hervey, John, Lord 1696-1743 . . . . .DLB-101

Herwig, Georg 1817-1875. . . . . .DLB-133

Herzog, Emile Salomon Wilhelm (see
    Maurois, André)

Hesiod eighth century B.C. DLB-176

Hesse, Hermann 1877-1962 . . . . .DLB-66

Hessus, Helius Eobanus 1488-1540. . . . . . DLB-179

Hewat, Alexander circa 1743-circa 1824 . . .DLB-30

Hewitt, John 1907- DLB-27

Hewlett, Maurice 1861-1923 . . . . .DLB-34, 156

Heyen, William 1940- DLB-5

Heyer, Georgette 1902-1974 . . . . DLB-77, 191

Heym, Stefan 1913- DLB-69

Heyse, Paul 1830-1914 . . . . .DLB-129

Heytesbury, William
    circa 1310-1372 or 1373. . . . . .DLB-115

Heyward, Dorothy 1890-1961. . . . . .DLB-7

Heyward, DuBose 1885-1940 . . . . DLB-7, 9, 45

Heywood, John 1497?-1580?. DLB-136

Heywood, Thomas
    1573 or 1574-1641 . . . . .DLB-62

Hibbs, Ben 1901-1975 . . . . .DLB-137

Hichens, Robert S. 1864-1950. . . . . .DLB-153

Hickey, Emily 1845-1924 . . . . .DLB-199

Hickman, William Albert 1877-1957 . . . . . .DLB-92

Hidalgo, José Luis 1919-1947 . . . . .DLB-108

Hiebert, Paul 1892-1987 . . . . .DLB-68

Hieng, Andrej 1925- DLB-181

Hierro, José 1922- DLB-108

Higgins, Aidan 1927- DLB-14

Higgins, Colin 1941-1988 . . . . .DLB-26

Higgins, George V.
    1939-1999 . . . . .DLB-2; Y-81, Y-98, Y-99

Higginson, Thomas Wentworth
    1823-1911 .DLB-1, 64

Highwater, Jamake 1942?- DLB-52; Y-85

Hijuelos, Oscar 1951- DLB-145

Hildegard von Bingen 1098-1179. . . . . . .DLB-148

Das Hildesbrandslied circa 820 . . . . .DLB-148

Hildesheimer, Wolfgang
    1916-1991 . . . . .DLB-69, 124

Hildreth, Richard 1807-1865 . . . . . . .DLB-1, 30, 59

Hill, Aaron 1685-1750 . . . . .DLB-84

Hill, Geoffrey 1932- DLB-40

Hill, "Sir" John 1714?-1775. . . . . .DLB-39

Hill, Leslie 1880-1960 . . . . .DLB-51

Hill, Susan 1942- DLB-14, 139

Hill, Walter 1942- DLB-44

Hill and Wang. DLB-46

Hill, George M., Company DLB-49

Hill, Lawrence, and Company,
    Publishers DLB-46

Hillberry, Conrad 1928- DLB-120

Hillerman, Tony 1925- DLB-206

Hilliard, Gray and Company DLB-49

Hills, Lee 1906- DLB-127

Hillyer, Robert 1895-1961. . . . . .DLB-54

Hilton, James 1900-1954 . . . . DLB-34, 77

Hilton, Walter died 1396. . . . . .DLB-146

Hilton and Company. DLB-49

Himes, Chester 1909-1984 . . . DLB-2, 76, 143, 226

Hindmarsh, Joseph [publishing house] . . . DLB-170

Hine, Daryl 1936- DLB-60

Hingley, Ronald 1920- DLB-155

Hinojosa-Smith, Rolando 1929- DLB-82

Hippel, Theodor Gottlieb von
1741-1796 . . . . DLB-97

Hippocrates of Cos flourished circa 425 B.C.
. . . . .DLB-176

Hirabayashi, Taiko 1905-1972 . . . . DLB-180

Hirsch, E. D., Jr. 1928- DLB-67

Hirsch, Edward 1950- DLB-120

The History of the Adventures of Joseph Andrews
(1742), by Henry Fielding [excerpt] . . . DLB-39

Hoagland, Edward 1932- DLB-6

Hoagland, Everett H., III 1942- DLB-41

Hoban, Russell 1925- DLB-52

Hobbes, Thomas 1588-1679 . . . . DLB-151

Hobby, Oveta 1905- DLB-127

Hobby, William 1878-1964 . . . . DLB-127

Hobsbaum, Philip 1932- DLB-40

Hobson, Laura Z. 1900- DLB-28

Hobson, Sarah 1947- DLB-204

Hoby, Thomas 1530-1566 . . . . DLB-132

Hoccleve, Thomas
circa 1368-circa 1437 . . . . DLB-146

Hochhuth, Rolf 1931- DLB-124

Hochman, Sandra 1936- DLB-5

Hocken, Thomas Morland
1836-1910 . . . . DLB-184

Hodder and Stoughton, Limited DLB-106

Hodgins, Jack 1938- DLB-60

Hodgman, Helen 1945- DLB-14

Hodgskin, Thomas 1787-1869 . . . . DLB-158

Hodgson, Ralph 1871-1962 . . . . DLB-19

Hodgson, William Hope
1877-1918 . . . . DLB-70, 153, 156, 178

Hoe, Robert III 1839-1909 . . . . DLB-187

Hoeg, Peter 1957- DLB-214

Højholt, Per 1928- DLB-214

Hoffenstein, Samuel 1890-1947 . . . . DLB-11

Hoffman, Charles Fenno 1806-1884 . . . . . DLB-3

Hoffman, Daniel 1923- DLB-5

Hoffmann, E. T. A. 1776-1822 . . . . DLB-90

Hoffman, Frank B. 1888-1958 . . . . DLB-188

Hoffmanswaldau, Christian Hoffman von
1616-1679 . . . . DLB-168

Hofmann, Michael 1957- DLB-40

Hofmannsthal, Hugo von
1874-1929 . . . . DLB-81, 118

Hofstadter, Richard 1916-1970 . . . . DLB-17

Hogan, Desmond 1950- DLB-14

Hogan, Linda 1947- DLB-175

Hogan and Thompson DLB-49

Hogarth Press DLB-112

Hogg, James 1770-1835 . . . . DLB-93, 116, 159

Hohberg, Wolfgang Helmhard Freiherr von
1612-1688 . . . . DLB-168

von Hohenheim, Philippus Aureolus
Theophrastus Bombastus (see Paracelsus)

Hohl, Ludwig 1904-1980 . . . . DLB-56

Holbrook, David 1923- DLB-14, 40

Holcroft, Thomas 1745-1809 . . . . DLB-39, 89, 158

Holden, Jonathan 1941- DLB-105

Holden, Molly 1927-1981 . . . . DLB-40

Hölderlin, Friedrich 1770-1843 . . . . DLB-90

Holiday House DLB-46

Holinshed, Raphael died 1580 . . . . DLB-167

Holland, J. G. 1819-1881 . . . . .DS-13

Holland, Norman N. 1927- DLB-67

Hollander, John 1929- DLB-5

Holley, Marietta 1836-1926 . . . . DLB-11

Hollinghurst, Alan 1954- DLB-207

Hollingsworth, Margaret 1940- DLB-60

Hollo, Anselm 1934- DLB-40

Holloway, Emory 1885-1977 . . . . DLB-103

Holloway, John 1920- DLB-27

Holloway House Publishing Company . . . DLB-46

Holme, Constance 1880-1955 . . . . DLB-34

Holmes, Abraham S. 1821?-1908 . . . . DLB-99

Holmes, John Clellon 1926-1988 . . . . DLB-16

Holmes, Mary Jane 1825-1907 . . . . . DLB-202, 221

Holmes, Oliver Wendell 1809-1894 . . . DLB-1, 189

Holmes, Richard 1945- DLB-155

Holmes, Thomas James 1874-1959 . . . . . . DLB-187

Holroyd, Michael 1935- DLB-155

Holst, Hermann E. von 1841-1904 . . . . . . DLB-47

Holt, John 1721-1784 . . . . DLB-43

Holt, Henry, and Company DLB-49

Holt, Rinehart and Winston DLB-46

Holtby, Winifred 1898-1935 . . . . DLB-191

Holthusen, Hans Egon 1913- DLB-69

Hölty, Ludwig Christoph Heinrich
1748-1776 . . . . DLB-94

Holz, Arno 1863-1929 . . . . DLB-118

Home, Henry, Lord Kames (see Kames, Henry
Home, Lord)

Home, John 1722-1808 . . . . DLB-84

Home, William Douglas 1912- DLB-13

Home Publishing Company DLB-49

Homer circa eighth-seventh centuries B.C.
. . . . .DLB-176

Homer, Winslow 1836-1910 . . . . DLB-188

Homes, Geoffrey (see Mainwaring, Daniel)

Honan, Park 1928- DLB-111

Hone, William 1780-1842 . . . . .DLB-110, 158

Hongo, Garrett Kaoru 1951- DLB-120

Honig, Edwin 1919- DLB-5

Hood, Hugh 1928- DLB-53

Hood, Thomas 1799-1845 . . . . DLB-96

Hook, Theodore 1788-1841 . . . . DLB-116

Hooker, Jeremy 1941- DLB-40

Hooker, Richard 1554-1600 . . . . DLB-132

Hooker, Thomas 1586-1647 . . . . DLB-24

Hooper, Johnson Jones 1815-1862 . . . . . DLB-3, 11

Hope, Anthony 1863-1933 . . . . DLB-153, 156

Hope, Christopher 1944- DLB-225

Hopkins, Ellice 1836-1904 . . . . DLB-190

Hopkins, Gerard Manley
1844-1889 . . . . .DLB-35, 57

Hopkins, John (see Sternhold, Thomas)

Hopkins, Lemuel 1750-1801 . . . . DLB-37

Hopkins, Pauline Elizabeth 1859-1930 . . . . DLB-50

Hopkins, Samuel 1721-1803 . . . . DLB-31

Hopkins, John H., and Son DLB-46

Hopkinson, Francis 1737-1791 . . . . DLB-31

Hoppin, Augustus 1828-1896 . . . . DLB-188

Hora, Josef 1891-1945 . . . . DLB-215

Horace 65 B.C.-8 B.C. DLB-211

Horgan, Paul 1903-1995 . . . . . .DLB-102, 212; Y-85

Horizon Press DLB-46

Hornby, C. H. St. John 1867-1946 . . . . . DLB-201

Hornby, Nick 1957- DLB-207

Horne, Frank 1899-1974 . . . . DLB-51

Horne, Richard Henry (Hengist)
1802 or 1803-1884 . . . . DLB-32

Hornung, E. W. 1866-1921 . . . . DLB-70

Horovitz, Israel 1939- DLB-7

Horton, George Moses 1797?-1883? DLB-50

Horváth, Ödön von 1901-1938 . . . . . DLB-85, 124

Horwood, Harold 1923- DLB-60

Hosford, E. and E. [publishing house] DLB-49

Hoskens, Jane Fenn 1693-1770? DLB-200

Hoskyns, John 1566-1638 . . . . DLB-121

Hosokawa Yūsai 1535-1610 . . . . DLB-203

Hostovský, Egon 1908-1973 . . . . DLB-215

Hotchkiss and Company DLB-49

Hough, Emerson 1857-1923 . . . . DLB-9, 212

Houghton Mifflin Company DLB-49

Houghton, Stanley 1881-1913 . . . . DLB-10

Household, Geoffrey 1900-1988 . . . . DLB-87

Housman, A. E. 1859-1936 . . . . DLB-19

Housman, Laurence 1865-1959 . . . . DLB-10

Houwald, Ernst von 1778-1845 . . . . DLB-90

Hovey, Richard 1864-1900 . . . . DLB-54

Howard, Donald R. 1927-1987 . . . . DLB-111

Howard, Maureen 1930- Y-83

Howard, Richard 1929- DLB-5

Howard, Roy W. 1883-1964 . . . . DLB-29

Howard, Sidney 1891-1939 . . . . .DLB-7, 26

Howard, Thomas, second Earl of Arundel
1585-1646 . . . . DLB-213

Howe, E. W. 1853-1937 . . . . DLB-12, 25

Howe, Henry 1816-1893 . . . . DLB-30

Howe, Irving 1920-1993 . . . . DLB-67

Howe, Joseph 1804-1873 . . . . DLB-99

Howe, Julia Ward 1819-1910 . . . . DLB-1, 189

Howe, Percival Presland 1886-1944 . . . . . DLB-149

Howe, Susan 1937- DLB-120

Howell, Clark, Sr. 1863-1936 . . . . DLB-25

Howell, Evan P. 1839-1905 . . . . .DLB-23

Howell, James 1594?-1666. . . . . .DLB-151

Howell, Warren Richardson
    1912-1984 . . . . .DLB-140

Howell, Soskin and Company DLB-46

Howells, William Dean
    1837-1920 . . . . DLB-12, 64, 74, 79, 189

Howitt, Mary 1799-1888 . . . . DLB-110, 199

Howitt, William 1792-1879 and
    Howitt, Mary 1799-1888. . . . . .DLB-110

Hoyem, Andrew 1935- DLB-5

Hoyers, Anna Ovena 1584-1655 . . . . .DLB-164

Hoyos, Angela de 1940- DLB-82

Hoyt, Palmer 1897-1979. . . . . .DLB-127

Hoyt, Henry [publishing house] DLB-49

Hrabanus Maurus 776?-856. . . . . .DLB-148

Hronský, Josef Cíger 1896-1960 . . . . .DLB-215

Hrotsvit of Gandersheim
    circa 935-circa 1000. . . . . .DLB-148

Hubbard, Elbert 1856-1915 . . . . .DLB-91

Hubbard, Kin 1868-1930. . . . . .DLB-11

Hubbard, William circa 1621-1704 . . . . . .DLB-24

Huber, Therese 1764-1829. . . . . .DLB-90

Huch, Friedrich 1873-1913. . . . . .DLB-66

Huch, Ricarda 1864-1947 . . . . .DLB-66

Huck at 100: How Old Is
    Huckleberry Finn? Y-85

Huddle, David 1942- DLB-130

Hudgins, Andrew 1951- DLB-120

Hudson, Henry Norman 1814-1886 . . . . . .DLB-64

Hudson, Stephen 1868?-1944 . . . . .DLB-197

Hudson, W. H. 1841-1922 . . . . . DLB-98, 153, 174

Hudson and Goodwin DLB-49

Huebsch, B. W. [publishing house] DLB-46

Hueffer, Oliver Madox 1876-1931. . . . . . .DLB-197

Hugh of St. Victor circa 1096-1141 . . . . . .DLB-208

Hughes, David 1930- DLB-14

Hughes, John 1677-1720. . . . . .DLB-84

Hughes, Langston
    1902-1967 . . . . DLB-4, 7, 48, 51, 86

Hughes, Richard 1900-1976. . . . . . . .DLB-15, 161

Hughes, Ted 1930-1998 . . . . .DLB-40, 161

Hughes, Thomas 1822-1896 . . . . . . .DLB-18, 163

Hugo, Richard 1923-1982 . . . . .DLB-5, 206

Hugo, Victor 1802-1885 . . . . . . DLB-119, 192, 217

Hugo Awards and Nebula Awards DLB-8

Hull, Richard 1896-1973 . . . . .DLB-77

Hulme, T. E. 1883-1917 . . . . .DLB-19

Hulton, Anne ?-1779? DLB-200

Humboldt, Alexander von 1769-1859 . . . . .DLB-90

Humboldt, Wilhelm von 1767-1835. . . . . . .DLB-90

Hume, David 1711-1776. . . . . .DLB-104

Hume, Fergus 1859-1932. . . . . .DLB-70

Hume, Sophia 1702-1774 . . . . .DLB-200

Humishuma (see Mourning Dove)

Hummer, T. R. 1950- DLB-120

Humorous Book Illustration DLB-11

Humphrey, Duke of Gloucester
    1391-1447 . . . . .DLB-213

Humphrey, William
    1924-1997 . . . . .DLB-6, 212

Humphreys, David 1752-1818. . . . . .DLB-37

Humphreys, Emyr 1919- DLB-15

Huncke, Herbert 1915-1996 . . . . .DLB-16

Huneker, James Gibbons 1857-1921 . . . . . .DLB-71

Hunold, Christian Friedrich
    1681-1721 . . . . .DLB-168

Hunt, Irene 1907- DLB-52

Hunt, Leigh 1784-1859 . . . . DLB-96, 110, 144

Hunt, Violet 1862-1942. . . . . DLB-162, 197

Hunt, William Gibbes 1791-1833 . . . . . . .DLB-73

Hunter, Evan 1926- Y-82

Hunter, Jim 1939- DLB-14

Hunter, Kristin 1931- DLB-33

Hunter, Mollie 1922- DLB-161

Hunter, N. C. 1908-1971 . . . . .DLB-10

Hunter-Duvar, John 1821-1899. . . . . .DLB-99

Huntington, Henry E. 1850-1927 . . . . . . .DLB-140

Huntington, Susan Mansfield
    1791-1823 . . . . .DLB-200

Hurd and Houghton DLB-49

Hurst, Fannie 1889-1968 . . . . .DLB-86

Hurst and Blackett. DLB-106

Hurst and Company DLB-49

Hurston, Zora Neale
    1901?-1960 . . . . .DLB-51, 86

Husson, Jules-François-Félix (see Champfleury)

Huston, John 1906-1987 . . . . .DLB-26

Hutcheson, Francis 1694-1746. . . . . .DLB-31

Hutchinson, R. C. 1907-1975. . . . . .DLB-191

Hutchinson, Thomas 1711-1780 . . . . . .DLB-30, 31

Hutchinson and Company
    (Publishers) Limited DLB-112

von Hutton, Ulrich 1488-1523 . . . . .DLB-179

Hutton, Richard Holt 1826-1897. . . . . . . .DLB-57

Huxley, Aldous
    1894-1963 . . . . DLB-36, 100, 162, 195

Huxley, Elspeth Josceline
    1907-1997 . . . . DLB-77, 204

Huxley, T. H. 1825-1895 . . . . .DLB-57

Huyghue, Douglas Smith 1816-1891. . . . . .DLB-99

Huysmans, Joris-Karl 1848-1907 . . . . .DLB-123

Hwang, David Henry 1957- DLB-212

Hyde, Donald 1909-1966 and
    Hyde, Mary 1912- DLB-187

Hyman, Trina Schart 1939- DLB-61

I

Iavorsky, Stefan 1658-1722 . . . . .DLB-150

Iazykov, Nikolai Mikhailovich
    1803-1846 . . . . .DLB-205

Ibáñez, Armando P. 1949- DLB-209

Ibn Bajja circa 1077-1138 . . . . .DLB-115

Ibn Gabirol, Solomon
    circa 1021-circa 1058. . . . . .DLB-115

Ibuse, Masuji 1898-1993 . . . . .DLB-180

Ichijō Kanera (see Ichijō Kaneyoshi)

Ichijō Kaneyoshi (Ichijō Kanera)
    1402-1481 . . . . .DLB-203

The Iconography of Science-Fiction Art DLB-8

Iffland, August Wilhelm 1759-1814. . . . . . .DLB-94

Ignatow, David 1914-1997. . . . . .DLB-5

Ike, Chukwuemeka 1931- DLB-157

Ikkyū Sōjun 1394-1481 . . . . .DLB-203

Iles, Francis (see Berkeley, Anthony)

The Illustration of Early German
    Literary Manuscripts,
    circa 1150-circa 1300. . . . . .DLB-148

Illyés, Gyula 1902-1983 . . . . .DLB-215

"Images and 'Images,'" by
    Charles Simic DLB-105

Imbs, Bravig 1904-1946. . . . . .DLB-4

Imbuga, Francis D. 1947- DLB-157

Immermann, Karl 1796-1840. . . . . .DLB-133

Impressions of William Faulkner. Y-97

Inchbald, Elizabeth 1753-1821 . . . . . . .DLB-39, 89

Inge, William 1913-1973 . . . . .DLB-7

Ingelow, Jean 1820-1897 . . . . .DLB-35, 163

Ingersoll, Ralph 1900-1985 . . . . .DLB-127

The Ingersoll Prizes. Y-84

Ingoldsby, Thomas (see Barham, Richard Harris)

Ingraham, Joseph Holt 1809-1860. . . . . . . .DLB-3

Inman, John 1805-1850 . . . . .DLB-73

Innerhofer, Franz 1944- DLB-85

Innis, Harold Adams 1894-1952 . . . . .DLB-88

Innis, Mary Quayle 1899-1972 . . . . .DLB-88

Inō Sōgi 1421-1502 . . . . .DLB-203

Inoue Yasushi 1907-1991 . . . . .DLB-181

International Publishers Company DLB-46

Interviews:

    Anastas, Benjamin Y-98

    Bank, Melissa Y-98

    Burnshaw, Stanley Y-97

    Carpenter, Humphrey Y-99

    Ellroy, James. Y-91

    Greenfield, George. Y-91

    Higgins, George V. Y-98

    Hoban, Russell. Y-90

    Holroyd, Michael. Y-99

    Jenks, Tom. Y-86

    Mailer, Norman Y-97

    McCormack, Thomas Y-98

    O'Connor, Patrick Y-99

    Plimpton, George. Y-99

    Prescott, Peter S. Y-86

    Rabe, David Y-91

    Schroeder, Patricia Y-99

"Into the Mirror," by Peter Cooley DLB-105

Introduction to Paul Laurence Dunbar,
Lyrics of Lowly Life (1896),
by William Dean Howells DLB-50

Introductory Essay: *Letters of Percy Bysshe Shelley* (1852), by Robert Browning . . . DLB-32

Introductory Letters from the Second Edition
of *Pamela* (1741), by Samuel
Richardson. DLB-39

Irving, John 1942- DLB-6; Y-82

Irving, Washington 1783-1859
. . . . DLB-3, 11, 30, 59, 73, 74, 183, 186

Irwin, Grace 1907- DLB-68

Irwin, Will 1873-1948. . . . . DLB-25

Isherwood, Christopher
1904-1986 . . . . .DLB-15, 195; Y-86

Ishiguro, Kazuo 1954- DLB-194

Ishikawa Jun 1899-1987 . . . . DLB-182

The Island Trees Case: A Symposium on
School Library Censorship
An Interview with Judith Krug
An Interview with Phyllis Schlafly
An Interview with Edward B. Jenkinson
An Interview with Lamarr Mooneyham
An Interview with Harriet Bernstein Y-82

Islas, Arturo 1938-1991 . . . . DLB-122

Ivanišević, Drago 1907-1981. . . . . DLB-181

Ivers, M. J., and Company DLB-49

Iwaniuk, Wacław 1915- DLB-215

Iwano, Hōmei 1873-1920 . . . . DLB-180

Iwaszkiewicz, Jarosław 1894-1980. . . . . . DLB-215

Iyayi, Festus 1947- DLB-157

Izumi, Kyōka 1873-1939. . . . . DLB-180

J

Jackmon, Marvin E. (see Marvin X)

Jacks, L. P. 1860-1955 . . . . DLB-135

Jackson, Angela 1951- DLB-41

Jackson, Helen Hunt
1830-1885 . . . . .DLB-42, 47, 186, 189

Jackson, Holbrook 1874-1948. . . . . DLB-98

Jackson, Laura Riding 1901-1991. . . . . . . DLB-48

Jackson, Shirley 1919-1965. . . . . DLB-6

Jacob, Naomi 1884?-1964. . . . . DLB-191

Jacob, Piers Anthony Dillingham
(see Anthony, Piers)

Jacobi, Friedrich Heinrich 1743-1819 . . . . . DLB-94

Jacobi, Johann Georg 1740-1841. . . . . DLB-97

Jacobs, Joseph 1854-1916 . . . . DLB-141

Jacobs, W. W. 1863-1943. . . . . DLB-135

Jacobs, George W., and Company DLB-49

Jacobsen, Jørgen-Frantz 1900-1938 . . . . . DLB-214

Jacobson, Dan 1929- DLB-14, 207, 225

Jacobson, Howard 1942- DLB-207

Jacques de Vitry
circa 1160/1170-1240 . . . . DLB-208

Jæger, Frank 1926-1977. . . . . DLB-214

Jaggard, William [publishing house]. DLB-170

Jahier, Piero 1884-1966. . . . . DLB-114

Jahnn, Hans Henny 1894-1959 . . . . . DLB-56, 124

Jakes, John 1932- Y-83

James, Alice 1848-1892. . . . . DLB-221

James, C. L. R. 1901-1989 . . . . DLB-125

James Dickey Tributes Y-97

James, George P. R. 1801-1860 . . . . DLB-116

James Gould Cozzens—A View from Afar Y-97

James Gould Cozzens Case Re-opened Y-97

James Gould Cozzens: How to Read Him Y-97

James, Henry
1843-1916 . . . . . . .DLB-12, 71, 74, 189; DS-13

James, John circa 1633-1729 . . . . DLB-24

James Jones Papers in the Handy Writers' Colony
Collection at the University of Illinois at
Springfield Y-98

The James Jones Society. Y-92

James Laughlin Tributes. Y-97

James, M. R. 1862-1936 . . . . DLB-156, 201

James, Naomi 1949- DLB-204

James, P. D. 1920- DLB-87; DS-17

James, Thomas 1572?-1629 . . . . DLB-213

James, Will 1892-1942 . . . . .DS-16

James Joyce Centenary: Dublin, 1982 . . . . Y-82

James Joyce Conference Y-85

James VI of Scotland, I of England
1566-1625 . . . . .DLB-151, 172

James, U. P. [publishing house] DLB-49

Jameson, Anna 1794-1860 . . . . DLB-99, 166

Jameson, Fredric 1934- DLB-67

Jameson, J. Franklin 1859-1937 . . . . DLB-17

Jameson, Storm 1891-1986. . . . . DLB-36

Jančar, Drago 1948- DLB-181

Janés, Clara 1940- DLB-134

Janevski, Slavko 1920- DLB-181

Janvier, Thomas 1849-1913 . . . . DLB-202

Jaramillo, Cleofas M. 1878-1956. . . . . . . DLB-122

Jarman, Mark 1952- DLB-120

Jarrell, Randall 1914-1965 . . . . DLB-48, 52

Jarrold and Sons DLB-106

Jarry, Alfred 1873-1907. . . . . DLB-192

Jarves, James Jackson 1818-1888 . . . . . . DLB-189

Jasmin, Claude 1930- DLB-60

Jaunsudrabiņš, Jānis 1877-1962. . . . . DLB-220

Jay, John 1745-1829 . . . . DLB-31

Jean de Garlande (see John of Garland)

Jefferies, Richard 1848-1887 . . . . DLB-98, 141

Jeffers, Lance 1919-1985. . . . . DLB-41

Jeffers, Robinson 1887-1962 . . . . DLB-45, 212

Jefferson, Thomas 1743-1826 . . . . DLB-31, 183

Jégé 1866-1940 . . . . DLB-215

Jelinek, Elfriede 1946- DLB-85

Jellicoe, Ann 1927- DLB-13

Jenkins, Elizabeth 1905- DLB-155

Jenkins, Robin 1912- DLB-14

Jenkins, William Fitzgerald (see Leinster, Murray)

Jenkins, Herbert, Limited DLB-112

Jennings, Elizabeth 1926- DLB-27

Jens, Walter 1923- DLB-69

Jensen, Johannes V. 1873-1950. . . . . DLB-214

Jensen, Merrill 1905-1980. . . . . .DLB-17

Jensen, Thit 1876-1957 . . . . DLB-214

Jephson, Robert 1736-1803. . . . . DLB-89

Jerome, Jerome K. 1859-1927. . . . .DLB-10, 34, 135

Jerome, Judson 1927-1991 . . . . DLB-105

Jerrold, Douglas 1803-1857 . . . . DLB-158, 159

Jesse, F. Tennyson 1888-1958 . . . . DLB-77

Jewett, Sarah Orne 1849-1909 . . . .DLB-12, 74, 221

Jewett, John P., and Company DLB-49

The Jewish Publication Society. DLB-49

Jewitt, John Rodgers 1783-1821 . . . . DLB-99

Jewsbury, Geraldine 1812-1880 . . . . DLB-21

Jewsbury, Maria Jane 1800-1833 . . . . DLB-199

Jhabvala, Ruth Prawer 1927- DLB-139, 194

Jiménez, Juan Ramón 1881-1958 . . . . DLB-134

Joans, Ted 1928- DLB-16, 41

Jōha 1525-1602. DLB-203

Johannis de Garlandia (see John of Garland)

John, Eugenie (see Marlitt, E.)

John of Dumbleton
circa 1310-circa 1349 . . . . DLB-115

John of Garland (Jean de Garlande, Johannis de
Garlandia) circa 1195-circa 1272 . . . . DLB-208

John Edward Bruce: Three Documents . . . DLB-50

John Hawkes: A Tribute Y-98

John O'Hara's Pottsville Journalism. Y-88

John Steinbeck Research Center. Y-85

John Updike on the Internet. Y-97

John Webster: The Melbourne
Manuscript. Y-86

Johns, Captain W. E. 1893-1968 . . . . DLB-160

Johnson, Mrs. A. E. ca. 1858-1922. . . . . . DLB-221

Johnson, Amelia (see Johnson, Mrs. A. E.)

Johnson, B. S. 1933-1973 . . . . DLB-14, 40

Johnson, Charles 1679-1748 . . . . DLB-84

Johnson, Charles R. 1948- DLB-33

Johnson, Charles S. 1893-1956. . . . . . DLB-51, 91

Johnson, Denis 1949- DLB-120

Johnson, Diane 1934- Y-80

Johnson, Dorothy M. 1905–1984. . . . . . . DLB-206

Johnson, Edgar 1901-1995 . . . . DLB-103

Johnson, Edward 1598-1672. . . . . DLB-24

Johnson E. Pauline (Tekahionwake)
1861-1913 .DLB-175

Johnson, Fenton 1888-1958 . . . . DLB-45, 50

Johnson, Georgia Douglas 1886-1966 . . . . DLB-51

Johnson, Gerald W. 1890-1980 . . . . DLB-29

Johnson, Helene 1907-1995 . . . . DLB-51

Johnson, James Weldon 1871-1938 . . . . . . DLB-51

Johnson, John H. 1918- DLB-137

Johnson, Linton Kwesi 1952- DLB-157

Johnson, Lionel 1867-1902 . . . . DLB-19

Johnson, Nunnally 1897-1977 . . . . .DLB-26

Johnson, Owen 1878-1952 . . . . Y-87

Johnson, Pamela Hansford 1912- DLB-15

Johnson, Pauline 1861-1913 . . . . .DLB-92

Johnson, Ronald 1935-1998 . . . . .DLB-169

Johnson, Samuel 1696-1772 . . . . .DLB-24

Johnson, Samuel
1709-1784 . . . . DLB-39, 95, 104, 142, 213

Johnson, Samuel 1822-1882 . . . . .DLB-1

Johnson, Susanna 1730-1810 . . . . .DLB-200

Johnson, Uwe 1934-1984 . . . . .DLB-75

Johnson, Benjamin [publishing house] DLB-49

Johnson, Benjamin, Jacob, and
Robert [publishing house] DLB-49

Johnson, Jacob, and Company DLB-49

Johnson, Joseph [publishing house] DLB-154

Johnston, Annie Fellows 1863-1931 . . . . . .DLB-42

Johnston, David Claypole 1798?-1865 . . . .DLB-188

Johnston, Basil H. 1929- DLB-60

Johnston, Denis 1901-1984 . . . . .DLB-10

Johnston, Ellen 1835-1873 . . . . .DLB-199

Johnston, George 1913- DLB-88

Johnston, Sir Harry 1858-1927 . . . . DLB-174

Johnston, Jennifer 1930- DLB-14

Johnston, Mary 1870-1936 . . . . .DLB-9

Johnston, Richard Malcolm 1822-1898 . . . .DLB-74

Johnstone, Charles 1719?-1800? DLB-39

Johst, Hanns 1890-1978 . . . . .DLB-124

Jolas, Eugene 1894-1952 . . . . .DLB-4, 45

Jones, Alice C. 1853-1933 . . . . .DLB-92

Jones, Charles C., Jr. 1831-1893 . . . . .DLB-30

Jones, D. G. 1929- DLB-53

Jones, David 1895-1974 . . . . DLB-20, 100

Jones, Diana Wynne 1934- DLB-161

Jones, Ebenezer 1820-1860 . . . . .DLB-32

Jones, Ernest 1819-1868 . . . . .DLB-32

Jones, Gayl 1949- DLB-33

Jones, George 1800-1870 . . . . .DLB-183

Jones, Glyn 1905- DLB-15

Jones, Gwyn 1907- DLB-15, 139

Jones, Henry Arthur 1851-1929 . . . . .DLB-10

Jones, Hugh circa 1692-1760 . . . . .DLB-24

Jones, James 1921-1977 . . . . DLB-2, 143; DS-17

Jones, Jenkin Lloyd 1911- DLB-127

Jones, John Beauchamp 1810-1866 . . . . . .DLB-202

Jones, LeRoi (see Baraka, Amiri)

Jones, Lewis 1897-1939 . . . . .DLB-15

Jones, Madison 1925- DLB-152

Jones, Major Joseph (see Thompson, William
Tappan)

Jones, Preston 1936-1979 . . . . .DLB-7

Jones, Rodney 1950- DLB-120

Jones, Sir William 1746-1794 . . . . .DLB-109

Jones, William Alfred 1817-1900 . . . . .DLB-59

Jones's Publishing House DLB-49

Jong, Erica 1942- DLB-2, 5, 28, 152

Jonke, Gert F. 1946- DLB-85

Jonson, Ben 1572?-1637 . . . . .DLB-62, 121

Jordan, June 1936- DLB-38

Joseph and George Y-99

Joseph, Jenny 1932- DLB-40

Joseph, Michael, Limited DLB-112

Josephson, Matthew 1899-1978 . . . . .DLB-4

Josephus, Flavius 37-100 . . . . .DLB-176

Josiah Allen's Wife (see Holley, Marietta)

Josipovici, Gabriel 1940- DLB-14

Josselyn, John ?-1675 . . . . .DLB-24

Joudry, Patricia 1921- DLB-88

Jovine, Giuseppe 1922- DLB-128

Joyaux, Philippe (see Sollers, Philippe)

Joyce, Adrien (see Eastman, Carol)

A Joyce (Con)Text: Danis Rose and the Remaking of
Ulysses Y-97

Joyce, James 1882-1941 . . . . . . DLB-10, 19, 36, 162

Jozsef, Attila 1905-1937 . . . . .DLB-215

Judd, Sylvester 1813-1853 . . . . .DLB-1

Judd, Orange, Publishing Company DLB-49

Judith circa 930 . . . . .DLB-146

Julian of Norwich 1342-circa 1420 . . . . . .DLB-1146

Julian Symons at Eighty Y-92

Julius Caesar 100 B.C.-44 B.C. DLB-211

June, Jennie (see Croly, Jane Cunningham)

Jung, Franz 1888-1963 . . . . .DLB-118

Jünger, Ernst 1895- DLB-56

Der jüngere Titurel circa 1275 . . . . .DLB-138

Jung-Stilling, Johann Heinrich
1740-1817 . . . . .DLB-94

Justice, Donald 1925- Y-83

Juvenal circa A.D. 60-circa A.D. 130 . . . . .DLB-211

The Juvenile Library (see Godwin, M. J., and
Company)

K

Kacew, Romain (see Gary, Romain)

Kafka, Franz 1883-1924 . . . . .DLB-81

Kahn, Roger 1927- DLB-171

Kaikō Takeshi 1939-1989 . . . . .DLB-182

Kaiser, Georg 1878-1945 . . . . .DLB-124

Kaiserchronik circca 1147 . . . . .DLB-148

Kaleb, Vjekoslav 1905- DLB-181

Kalechofsky, Roberta 1931- DLB-28

Kaler, James Otis 1848-1912 . . . . .DLB-12

Kames, Henry Home, Lord
1696-1782 . . . . .DLB-31, 104

Kamo no Chōmei (Kamo no Nagaakira)
1153 or 1155-1216 . . . . .DLB-203

Kamo no Nagaakira (see Kamo no Chōmei)

Kampmann, Christian 1939-1988 . . . . . . .DLB-214

Kandel, Lenore 1932- DLB-16

Kanin, Garson 1912-1999 . . . . .DLB-7

Kant, Hermann 1926- DLB-75

Kant, Immanuel 1724-1804 . . . . .DLB-94

Kantemir, Antiokh Dmitrievich
1708-1744 . . . . .DLB-150

Kantor, MacKinlay 1904-1977 . . . . .DLB-9, 102

Kanze Kōjirō Nobumitsu 1435-1516 . . . . .DLB-203

Kanze Motokiyo (see Zeimi)

Kaplan, Fred 1937- DLB-111

Kaplan, Johanna 1942- DLB-28

Kaplan, Justin 1925- DLB-111

Kapnist, Vasilii Vasilevich 1758?-1823 . . .DLB-150

Karadžić, Vuk Stefanović 1787-1864 . . . . . .DLB-147

Karamzin, Nikolai Mikhailovich
1766-1826 . . . . .DLB-150

Karinthy, Frigyes 1887-1938 . . . . .DLB-215

Karsch, Anna Louisa 1722-1791 . . . . .DLB-97

Kasack, Hermann 1896-1966 . . . . .DLB-69

Kasai, Zenzō 1887-1927 . . . . .DLB-180

Kaschnitz, Marie Luise 1901-1974 . . . . . . .DLB-69

Kassák, Lajos 1887-1967 . . . . .DLB-215

Kaštelan, Jure 1919-1990 . . . . .DLB-147

Kästner, Erich 1899-1974 . . . . .DLB-56

Katenin, Pavel Aleksandrovich
1792-1853 . . . . .DLB-205

Kattan, Naim 1928- DLB-53

Katz, Steve 1935- Y-83

Kauffman, Janet 1945- DLB-218; Y-86

Kauffmann, Samuel 1898-1971 . . . . .DLB-127

Kaufman, Bob 1925- DLB-16, 41

Kaufman, George S. 1889-1961 . . . . .DLB-7

Kavanagh, P. J. 1931- DLB-40

Kavanagh, Patrick 1904-1967 . . . . . . .DLB-15, 20

Kawabata, Yasunari 1899-1972 . . . . .DLB-180

Kaye-Smith, Sheila 1887-1956 . . . . .DLB-36

Kazin, Alfred 1915-1998 . . . . .DLB-67

Keane, John B. 1928- DLB-13

Keary, Annie 1825-1879 . . . . .DLB-163

Keating, H. R. F. 1926- DLB-87

Keats, Ezra Jack 1916-1983 . . . . .DLB-61

Keats, John 1795-1821 . . . . DLB-96, 110

Keble, John 1792-1866 . . . . .DLB-32, 55

Keeble, John 1944- Y-83

Keeffe, Barrie 1945- DLB-13

Keeley, James 1867-1934 . . . . .DLB-25

W. B. Keen, Cooke and Company DLB-49

Keillor, Garrison 1942- Y-87

Keith, Marian 1874?-1961 . . . . .DLB-92

Keller, Gary D. 1943- DLB-82

Keller, Gottfried 1819-1890 . . . . .DLB-129

Kelley, Edith Summers 1884-1956 . . . . .DLB-9

Kelley, Emma Dunham ?-? DLB-221

Kelley, William Melvin 1937- DLB-33

Kellogg, Ansel Nash 1832-1886 . . . . .DLB-23

Kellogg, Steven 1941- DLB-61

Kelly, George 1887-1974 . . . . .DLB-7

Kelly, Hugh 1739-1777 . . . . .DLB-89

Kelly, Robert 1935- DLB-5, 130, 165

Kelly, Piet and Company DLB-49

Kelman, James 1946- DLB-194

Kelmscott Press.................... DLB-112

Kemble, E. W. 1861-1933 .... DLB-188

Kemble, Fanny 1809-1893 .... DLB-32

Kemelman, Harry 1908- DLB-28

Kempe, Margery circa 1373-1438...... DLB-146

Kempner, Friederike 1836-1904 .... DLB-129

Kempowski, Walter 1929- DLB-75

Kendall, Claude [publishing company].... DLB-46

Kendell, George 1809-1867 .... DLB-43

Kenedy, P. J., and Sons............. DLB-49

Kenkō circa 1283-circa 1352.......... DLB-203

Kennan, George 1845-1924 .... DLB-189

Kennedy, Adrienne 1931- DLB-38

Kennedy, John Pendleton 1795-1870 ...... DLB-3

Kennedy, Leo 1907- DLB-88

Kennedy, Margaret 1896-1967 .... DLB-36

Kennedy, Patrick 1801-1873 .... DLB-159

Kennedy, Richard S. 1920- DLB-111

Kennedy, William 1928- DLB-143; Y-85

Kennedy, X. J. 1929- DLB-5

Kennelly, Brendan 1936- DLB-40

Kenner, Hugh 1923- DLB-67

Kennerley, Mitchell [publishing house] ... DLB-46

Kenneth Dale McCormick Tributes........ Y-97

Kenny, Maurice 1929- DLB-175

Kent, Frank R. 1877-1958............. DLB-29

Kenyon, Jane 1947-1995 .... DLB-120

Keough, Hugh Edmund 1864-1912 ..... DLB-171

Keppler and Schwartzmann DLB-49

Ker, John, third Duke of Roxburghe
1740-1804.................... DLB-213

Ker, N. R. 1908-1982 .... DLB-201

Kerlan, Irvin 1912-1963 .... DLB-187

Kern, Jerome 1885-1945............. DLB-187

Kerner, Justinus 1776-1862 .... DLB-90

Kerouac, Jack 1922-1969 .... DLB-2, 16; DS-3

The Jack Kerouac Revival Y-95

Kerouac, Jan 1952-1996 .... DLB-16

Kerr, Orpheus C. (see Newell, Robert Henry)

Kerr, Charles H., and Company DLB-49

Kesey, Ken 1935- DLB-2, 16, 206

Kessel, Joseph 1898-1979 .... DLB-72

Kessel, Martin 1901- DLB-56

Kesten, Hermann 1900- DLB-56

Keun, Irmgard 1905-1982 .... DLB-69

Key and Biddle...................... DLB-49

Keynes, Sir Geoffrey 1887-1982 .... DLB-201

Keynes, John Maynard 1883-1946........DS-10

Keyserling, Eduard von 1855-1918 ...... DLB-66

Khan, Ismith 1925- DLB-125

Khaytov, Nikolay 1919- DLB-181

Khemnitser, Ivan Ivanovich
1745-1784 .... DLB-150

Kheraskov, Mikhail Matveevich
1733-1807..................... DLB-150

Khomiakov, Aleksei Stepanovich
1804-1860 .... DLB-205

Khristov, Boris 1945- DLB-181

Khvostov, Dmitrii Ivanovich
1757-1835 .... DLB-150

Kidd, Adam 1802?-1831.............. DLB-99

Kidd, William [publishing house]...... DLB-106

Kidder, Tracy 1945- DLB-185

Kiely, Benedict 1919- DLB-15

Kieran, John 1892-1981 ....DLB-171

Kiggins and Kellogg DLB-49

Kiley, Jed 1889-1962.................. DLB-4

Kilgore, Bernard 1908-1967 .... DLB-127

Killens, John Oliver 1916- DLB-33

Killigrew, Anne 1660-1685........... DLB-131

Killigrew, Thomas 1612-1683 .... DLB-58

Kilmer, Joyce 1886-1918............. DLB-45

Kilwardby, Robert circa 1215-1279 ..... DLB-115

Kimball, Richard Burleigh 1816-1892 ... DLB-202

Kincaid, Jamaica 1949- DLB-157

King, Charles 1844-1933 .... DLB-186

King, Clarence 1842-1901 .... DLB-12

King, Florence 1936 .... Y-85

King, Francis 1923- DLB-15, 139

King, Grace 1852-1932..............DLB-12, 78

King, Harriet Hamilton 1840-1920...... DLB-199

King, Henry 1592-1669 .... DLB-126

King, Stephen 1947- DLB-143; Y-80

King, Thomas 1943- DLB-175

King, Woodie, Jr. 1937- DLB-38

King, Solomon [publishing house] DLB-49

Kinglake, Alexander William
1809-1891 .... DLB-55, 166

Kingsley, Charles
1819-1875........DLB-21, 32, 163, 178, 190

Kingsley, Mary Henrietta 1862-1900 .....DLB-174

Kingsley, Henry 1830-1876 .... DLB-21

Kingsley, Sidney 1906- DLB-7

Kingsmill, Hugh 1889-1949 .... DLB-149

Kingsolver, Barbara 1955- DLB-206

Kingston, Maxine Hong
1940- DLB-173, 212; Y-80

Kingston, William Henry Giles
1814-1880 .... DLB-163

Kinnan, Mary Lewis 1763-1848 .... DLB-200

Kinnell, Galway 1927- DLB-5; Y-87

Kinsella, Thomas 1928- DLB-27

Kipling, Rudyard
1865-1936 ....DLB-19, 34, 141, 156

Kipphardt, Heinar 1922-1982.......... DLB-124

Kirby, William 1817-1906............ DLB-99

Kircher, Athanasius 1602-1680........ DLB-164

Kireevsky, Ivan Vasil'evich
1806-1856 .... DLB-198

Kireevsky, Petr Vasil'evich
1808-1856 .... DLB-205

Kirk, Hans 1898-1962 .... DLB-214

Kirk, John Foster 1824-1904........... DLB-79

Kirkconnell, Watson 1895-1977........ DLB-68

Kirkland, Caroline M.
1801-1864 ....DLB-3, 73, 74; DS-13

Kirkland, Joseph 1830-1893 .... DLB-12

Kirkman, Francis [publishing house] DLB-170

Kirkpatrick, Clayton 1915- DLB-127

Kirkup, James 1918- DLB-27

Kirouac, Conrad (see Marie-Victorin, Frère)

Kirsch, Sarah 1935- DLB-75

Kirst, Hans Hellmut 1914-1989 .... DLB-69

Kiš, Danilo 1935-1989 .... DLB-181

Kita Morio 1927- DLB-182

Kitcat, Mabel Greenhow 1859-1922..... DLB-135

Kitchin, C. H. B. 1895-1967........... DLB-77

Kittredge, William 1932- DLB-212

Kiukhel'beker, Vil'gel'm Karlovich
1797-1846 .... DLB-205

Kizer, Carolyn 1925- DLB-5, 169

Klabund 1890-1928 .... DLB-66

Klaj, Johann 1616-1656 .... DLB-164

Klappert, Peter 1942- DLB-5

Klass, Philip (see Tenn, William)

Klein, A. M. 1909-1972 .... DLB-68

Kleist, Ewald von 1715-1759 .... DLB-97

Kleist, Heinrich von 1777-1811......... DLB-90

Klinger, Friedrich Maximilian
1752-1831 .... DLB-94

Klopstock, Friedrich Gottlieb
1724-1803.................... DLB-97

Klopstock, Meta 1728-1758............ DLB-97

Kluge, Alexander 1932- DLB-75

Knapp, Joseph Palmer 1864-1951........ DLB-91

Knapp, Samuel Lorenzo 1783-1838 ...... DLB-59

Knapton, J. J. and P.
[publishing house] DLB-154

Kniazhnin, Iakov Borisovich
1740-1791 .... DLB-150

Knickerbocker, Diedrich (see Irving, Washington)

Knigge, Adolph Franz Friedrich Ludwig,
Freiherr von 1752-1796 .... DLB-94

Knight, Damon 1922- DLB-8

Knight, Etheridge 1931-1992 .... DLB-41

Knight, John S. 1894-1981 .... DLB-29

Knight, Sarah Kemble 1666-1727 .... DLB-24, 200

Knight, Charles, and Company DLB-106

Knight-Bruce, G. W. H. 1852-1896......DLB-174

Knister, Raymond 1899-1932........... DLB-68

Knoblock, Edward 1874-1945 .... DLB-10

Knopf, Alfred A. 1892-1984................Y-84

Knopf, Alfred A. [publishing house]...... DLB-46

Knorr von Rosenroth, Christian
1636-1689 . . . . .DLB-168

"Knots into Webs: Some Autobiographical
Sources," by Dabney Stuart DLB-105

Knowles, John 1926- DLB-6

Knox, Frank 1874-1944 . . . . .DLB-29

Knox, John circa 1514-1572 . . . . .DLB-132

Knox, John Armoy 1850-1906 . . . . .DLB-23

Knox, Ronald Arbuthnott 1888-1957 . . . . .DLB-77

Knox, Thomas Wallace 1835-1896 . . . . . .DLB-189

Kobayashi, Takiji 1903-1933 . . . . .DLB-180

Kober, Arthur 1900-1975 . . . . .DLB-11

Kocbek, Edvard 1904-1981 . . . . .DLB-147

Koch, Howard 1902- DLB-26

Koch, Kenneth 1925- DLB-5

Kōda, Rohan 1867-1947 . . . . .DLB-180

Koenigsberg, Moses 1879-1945 . . . . .DLB-25

Koeppen, Wolfgang 1906-1996 . . . . .DLB-69

Koertge, Ronald 1940- DLB-105

Koestler, Arthur 1905-1983 . . . . Y-83

Kohn, John S. Van E. 1906-1976 and
Papantonio, Michael 1907-1978 . . . . . .DLB-187

Kokoschka, Oskar 1886-1980 . . . . .DLB-124

Kolb, Annette 1870-1967 . . . . .DLB-66

Kolbenheyer, Erwin Guido
1878-1962 . . . . .DLB-66, 124

Kolleritsch, Alfred 1931- DLB-85

Kolodny, Annette 1941- DLB-67

Kol'tsov, Aleksei Vasil'evich
1809-1842 . . . . .DLB-205

Komarov, Matvei circa 1730-1812 . . . . . .DLB-150

Komroff, Manuel 1890-1974 . . . . .DLB-4

Komunyakaa, Yusef 1947- DLB-120

Koneski, Blaže 1921-1993 . . . . .DLB-181

Konigsburg, E. L. 1930- DLB-52

Konparu Zenchiku 1405-1468? DLB-203

Konrad von Würzburg
circa 1230-1287 . . . . .DLB-138

Konstantinov, Aleko 1863-1897 . . . . .DLB-147

Kooser, Ted 1939- DLB-105

Kopit, Arthur 1937- DLB-7

Kops, Bernard 1926?- DLB-13

Kornbluth, C. M. 1923-1958 . . . . .DLB-8

Körner, Theodor 1791-1813 . . . . .DLB-90

Kornfeld, Paul 1889-1942 . . . . .DLB-118

Kosinski, Jerzy 1933-1991 . . . . DLB-2; Y-82

Kosmač, Ciril 1910-1980 . . . . .DLB-181

Kosovel, Srečko 1904-1926 . . . . .DLB-147

Kostrov, Ermil Ivanovich 1755-1796 . . . . .DLB-150

Kotzebue, August von 1761-1819 . . . . . . .DLB-94

Kotzwinkle, William 1938- DLB-173

Kovačić, Ante 1854-1889 . . . . .DLB-147

Kovič, Kajetan 1931- DLB-181

Kozlov, Ivan Ivanovich 1779-1840 . . . . . .DLB-205

Kraf, Elaine 1946- Y-81

Kramer, Jane 1938- DLB-185

Kramer, Mark 1944- DLB-185

Kranjčević, Silvije Strahimir
1865-1908 . . . . .DLB-147

Krasko, Ivan 1876-1958 . . . . .DLB-215

Krasna, Norman 1909-1984 . . . . .DLB-26

Kraus, Hans Peter 1907-1988 . . . . .DLB-187

Kraus, Karl 1874-1936 . . . . .DLB-118

Krauss, Ruth 1911-1993 . . . . .DLB-52

Kreisel, Henry 1922- DLB-88

Kreuder, Ernst 1903-1972 . . . . .DLB-69

Krėvė-Mickevičius, Vincas 1882-1954 . . . .DLB-220

Kreymborg, Alfred 1883-1966 . . . . .DLB-4, 54

Krieger, Murray 1923- DLB-67

Krim, Seymour 1922-1989 . . . . .DLB-16

Kristensen, Tom 1893-1974 . . . . .DLB-214

Krleža, Miroslav 1893-1981 . . . . .DLB-147

Krock, Arthur 1886-1974 . . . . .DLB-29

Kroetsch, Robert 1927- DLB-53

Krúdy, Gyula 1878-1933 . . . . .DLB-215

Krutch, Joseph Wood 1893-1970 . . . . .DLB-63, 206

Krylov, Ivan Andreevich 1769-1844 . . . . .DLB-150

Kubin, Alfred 1877-1959 . . . . .DLB-81

Kubrick, Stanley 1928-1999 . . . . .DLB-26

Kudrun circa 1230-1240 . . . . .DLB-138

Kuffstein, Hans Ludwig von
1582-1656 . . . . .DLB-164

Kuhlmann, Quirinus 1651-1689 . . . . .DLB-168

Kuhnau, Johann 1660-1722 . . . . .DLB-168

Kukol'nik, Nestor Vasil'evich
1809-1868 . . . . .DLB-205

Kukučín, Martin 1860-1928 . . . . .DLB-215

Kumin, Maxine 1925- DLB-5

Kuncewicz, Maria 1895-1989 . . . . .DLB-215

Kunene, Mazisi 1930- DLB-117

Kunikida, Doppo 1869-1908 . . . . .DLB-180

Kunitz, Stanley 1905- DLB-48

Kunjufu, Johari M. (see Amini, Johari M.)

Kunnert, Gunter 1929- DLB-75

Kunze, Reiner 1933- DLB-75

Kupferberg, Tuli 1923- DLB-16

Kurahashi Yumiko 1935- DLB-182

Kureishi, Hanif 1954- DLB-194

Kürnberger, Ferdinand 1821-1879 . . . . . .DLB-129

Kurz, Isolde 1853-1944 . . . . .DLB-66

Kusenberg, Kurt 1904-1983 . . . . .DLB-69

Kuttner, Henry 1915-1958 . . . . .DLB-8

Kyd, Thomas 1558-1594 . . . . .DLB-62

Kyffin, Maurice circa 1560?-1598 . . . . . . .DLB-136

Kyger, Joanne 1934- DLB-16

Kyne, Peter B. 1880-1957 . . . . .DLB-78

Kyōgoku Tamekane 1254-1332 . . . . .DLB-203

L

L. E. L. (see Landon, Letitia Elizabeth)

Laberge, Albert 1871-1960 . . . . .DLB-68

Laberge, Marie 1950- DLB-60

Labiche, Eugène 1815-1888 . . . . .DLB-192

Labrunie, Gerard (see Nerval, Gerard de)

La Capria, Raffaele 1922- DLB-196

Lacombe, Patrice (see Trullier-Lacombe,
Joseph Patrice)

Lacretelle, Jacques de 1888-1985 . . . . .DLB-65

Lacy, Ed 1911-1968 . . . . .DLB-226

Lacy, Sam 1903- DLB-171

Ladd, Joseph Brown 1764-1786 . . . . .DLB-37

La Farge, Oliver 1901-1963 . . . . .DLB-9

Lafferty, R. A. 1914- DLB-8

La Flesche, Francis 1857-1932 . . . . .DLB-175

Laforge, Jules 1860-1887 . . . . .DLB-217

Lagorio, Gina 1922- DLB-196

La Guma, Alex 1925-1985 . . . . DLB-117, 225

Lahaise, Guillaume (see Delahaye, Guy)

Lahontan, Louis-Armand de Lom d'Arce,
Baron de 1666-1715? DLB-99

Laing, Kojo 1946- DLB-157

Laird, Carobeth 1895- Y-82

Laird and Lee DLB-49

Lalić, Ivan V. 1931-1996 . . . . .DLB-181

Lalić, Mihailo 1914-1992 . . . . .DLB-181

Lalonde, Michèle 1937- DLB-60

Lamantia, Philip 1927- DLB-16

Lamartine, Alphonse de 1790-1869 . . . . . .DLB-217

Lamb, Charles 1775-1834 . . . . . . DLB-93, 107, 163

Lamb, Lady Caroline 1785-1828 . . . . .DLB-116

Lamb, Mary 1764-1874 . . . . .DLB-163

Lambert, Betty 1933-1983 . . . . .DLB-60

Lamming, George 1927- DLB-125

L'Amour, Louis 1908-1988 . . . . . . DLB-206; Y-80

Lampman, Archibald 1861-1899 . . . . .DLB-92

Lamson, Wolffe and Company DLB-49

Lancer Books DLB-46

Landesman, Jay 1919- and
Landesman, Fran 1927- DLB-16

Landolfi, Tommaso 1908-1979 . . . . .DLB-177

Landon, Letitia Elizabeth 1802-1838 . . . . . .DLB-96

Landor, Walter Savage 1775-1864 . . . . DLB-93, 107

Landry, Napoléon-P. 1884-1956 . . . . .DLB-92

Lane, Charles 1800-1870 . . . . .DLB-1, 223

Lane, Laurence W. 1890-1967 . . . . .DLB-91

Lane, M. Travis 1934- DLB-60

Lane, Patrick 1939- DLB-53

Lane, Pinkie Gordon 1923- DLB-41

Lane, John, Company DLB-49

Laney, Al 1896-1988 . . . . DLB-4, 171

Lang, Andrew 1844-1912 . . . . . DLB-98, 141, 184

Langevin, André 1927- DLB-60

Langgässer, Elisabeth 1899-1950 . . . . .DLB-69

Langhorne, John 1735-1779 . . . . .DLB-109

Langland, William
circa 1330-circa 1400 . . . . .DLB-146

Langton, Anna 1804-1893 . . . . DLB-99

Lanham, Edwin 1904-1979. . . . . DLB-4

Lanier, Sidney 1842-1881. . . . . . . DLB-64; DS-13

Lanyer, Aemilia 1569-1645. . . . . DLB-121

Lapointe, Gatien 1931-1983 . . . . DLB-88

Lapointe, Paul-Marie 1929- DLB-88

Lardner, John 1912-1960 . . . . .DLB-171

Lardner, Ring
1885-1933 . . . . . . .DLB-11, 25, 86, 171; DS-16

Lardner, Ring, Jr. 1915- DLB-26

Lardner 100: Ring Lardner
Centennial Symposium Y-85

Larkin, Philip 1922-1985 . . . . DLB-27

La Roche, Sophie von 1730-1807 . . . . DLB-94

La Rocque, Gilbert 1943-1984 . . . . DLB-60

Larcom, Lucy 1824-1893 . . . . DLB-221

Laroque de Roquebrune, Robert (see Roquebrune,
Robert de)

Larrick, Nancy 1910- DLB-61

Larsen, Nella 1893-1964. . . . . DLB-51

La Sale, Antoine de
circa 1386-1460/1467 . . . . DLB-208

Lasker-Schüler, Else 1869-1945 . . . . . DLB-66, 124

Lasnier, Rina 1915- DLB-88

Lassalle, Ferdinand 1825-1864 . . . . DLB-129

Latham, Robert 1912-1995. . . . . DLB-201

Lathrop, Dorothy P. 1891-1980 . . . . DLB-22

Lathrop, George Parsons 1851-1898 . . . . . DLB-71

Lathrop, John, Jr. 1772-1820. . . . . DLB-37

Latimer, Hugh 1492?-1555. . . . . DLB-136

Latimore, Jewel Christine McLawler (see Amini,
Johari M.)

Latymer, William 1498-1583 . . . . DLB-132

Laube, Heinrich 1806-1884 . . . . DLB-133

Laud, William 1573-1645 . . . . DLB-213

Laughlin, James 1914-1997 . . . . DLB-48

Laumer, Keith 1925- DLB-8

Lauremberg, Johann 1590-1658 . . . . DLB-164

Laurence, Margaret 1926-1987. . . . . DLB-53

Laurentius von Schnüffis 1633-1702. . . . . DLB-168

Laurents, Arthur 1918- DLB-26

Laurie, Annie (see Black, Winifred)

Laut, Agnes Christiana 1871-1936 . . . . . . DLB-92

Lauterbach, Ann 1942- DLB-193

Lautreamont, Isidore Lucien Ducasse, Comte de
1846-1870. DLB-217

Lavater, Johann Kaspar 1741-1801. . . . . . DLB-97

Lavin, Mary 1912-1996 . . . . DLB-15

Law, John (see Harkness, Margaret)

Lawes, Henry 1596-1662 . . . . DLB-126

Lawless, Anthony (see MacDonald, Philip)

Lawrence, D. H.
1885-1930 . . . . . .DLB-10, 19, 36, 98, 162, 195

Lawrence, David 1888-1973 . . . . DLB-29

Lawrence, Seymour 1926-1994 . . . . Y-94

Lawrence, T. E. 1888-1935 . . . . DLB-195

Lawson, George 1598-1678 . . . . DLB-213

Lawson, John ?-1711. . . . . DLB-24

Lawson, Robert 1892-1957. . . . . DLB-22

Lawson, Victor F. 1850-1925 . . . . DLB-25

Layard, Sir Austen Henry
1817-1894. . . . . DLB-166

Layton, Irving 1912- DLB-88

LaZamon flourished circa 1200 . . . . DLB-146

Lazarević, Laza K. 1851-1890. . . . . DLB-147

Lazarus, George 1904-1997 . . . . DLB-201

Lazhechnikov, Ivan Ivanovich
1792-1869. . . . . DLB-198

Lea, Henry Charles 1825-1909 . . . . DLB-47

Lea, Sydney 1942- DLB-120

Lea, Tom 1907- DLB-6

Leacock, John 1729-1802 . . . . DLB-31

Leacock, Stephen 1869-1944 . . . . DLB-92

Lead, Jane Ward 1623-1704 . . . . DLB-131

Leadenhall Press. DLB-106

Leapor, Mary 1722-1746. . . . . DLB-109

Lear, Edward 1812-1888 . . . . . . DLB-32, 163, 166

Leary, Timothy 1920-1996. . . . . DLB-16

Leary, W. A., and Company DLB-49

Léautaud, Paul 1872-1956 . . . . DLB-65

Leavitt, David 1961- DLB-130

Leavitt and Allen DLB-49

Le Blond, Mrs. Aubrey 1861-1934. . . . . . .DLB-174

le Carré, John 1931- DLB-87

Lécavelé, Roland (see Dorgeles, Roland)

Lechlitner, Ruth 1901- DLB-48

Leclerc, Félix 1914- DLB-60

Le Clézio, J. M. G. 1940- DLB-83

Lectures on Rhetoric and Belles Lettres (1783),
by Hugh Blair [excerpts] DLB-31

Leder, Rudolf (see Hermlin, Stephan)

Lederer, Charles 1910-1976 . . . . DLB-26

Ledwidge, Francis 1887-1917 . . . . DLB-20

Lee, Dennis 1939- DLB-53

Lee, Don L. (see Madhubuti, Haki R.)

Lee, George W. 1894-1976. . . . . DLB-51

Lee, Harper 1926- DLB-6

Lee, Harriet (1757-1851) and
Lee, Sophia (1750-1824). DLB-39

Lee, Laurie 1914-1997 . . . . DLB-27

Lee, Li-Young 1957- DLB-165

Lee, Manfred B. (see Dannay, Frederic, and
Manfred B. Lee)

Lee, Nathaniel circa 1645 - 1692 . . . . DLB-80

Lee, Sir Sidney 1859-1926 . . . . DLB-149, 184

Lee, Sir Sidney, "Principles of Biography," in
Elizabethan and Other Essays. DLB-149

Lee, Vernon
1856-1935 . . . . . . .DLB-57, 153, 156, 174, 178

Lee and Shepard. DLB-49

Le Fanu, Joseph Sheridan
1814-1873 . . . . .DLB-21, 70, 159, 178

Leffland, Ella 1931- Y-84

le Fort, Gertrud von 1876-1971. . . . . DLB-66

Le Gallienne, Richard 1866-1947 . . . . DLB-4

Legaré, Hugh Swinton 1797-1843. . . .DLB-3, 59, 73

Legaré, James M. 1823-1859 . . . . DLB-3

The Legends of the Saints and a Medieval
Christian Worldview. DLB-148

Léger, Antoine-J. 1880-1950. . . . . DLB-88

Le Guin, Ursula K. 1929- DLB-8, 52

Lehman, Ernest 1920- DLB-44

Lehmann, John 1907- DLB-27, 100

Lehmann, Rosamond 1901-1990 . . . . DLB-15

Lehmann, Wilhelm 1882-1968. . . . . DLB-56

Lehmann, John, Limited. DLB-112

Leiber, Fritz 1910-1992. . . . . DLB-8

Leibniz, Gottfried Wilhelm 1646-1716 . . . DLB-168

Leicester University Press DLB-112

Leigh, W. R. 1866-1955 . . . . DLB-188

Leinster, Murray 1896-1975 . . . . DLB-8

Leisewitz, Johann Anton 1752-1806 . . . . . . DLB-94

Leitch, Maurice 1933- DLB-14

Leithauser, Brad 1943- DLB-120

Leland, Charles G. 1824-1903 . . . . DLB-11

Leland, John 1503?-1552 . . . . DLB-136

Lemay, Pamphile 1837-1918. . . . . DLB-99

Lemelin, Roger 1919- DLB-88

Lemercier, Louis-Jean-Népomucène
1771-1840. DLB-192

Lemon, Mark 1809-1870 . . . . DLB-163

Le Moine, James MacPherson
1825-1912 . . . . DLB-99

Le Moyne, Jean 1913- DLB-88

Lemperly, Paul 1858-1939 . . . . .DLB-187

L'Engle, Madeleine 1918- DLB-52

Lennart, Isobel 1915-1971 . . . . DLB-44

Lennox, Charlotte
1729 or 1730-1804 . . . . DLB-39

Lenox, James 1800-1880. . . . . DLB-140

Lenski, Lois 1893-1974. . . . . DLB-22

Lenz, Hermann 1913-1998 . . . . DLB-69

Lenz, J. M. R. 1751-1792. . . . . DLB-94

Lenz, Siegfried 1926- DLB-75

Leonard, Elmore 1925- DLB-173, 226

Leonard, Hugh 1926- DLB-13

Leonard, William Ellery 1876-1944 . . . . . . DLB-54

Leonowens, Anna 1834-1914 . . . . DLB-99, 166

LePan, Douglas 1914- DLB-88

Leprohon, Rosanna Eleanor 1829-1879 . . . DLB-99

Le Queux, William 1864-1927 . . . . DLB-70

Lermontov, Mikhail Iur'evich
1814-1841 . . . . DLB-205

Lerner, Max 1902-1992 . . . . DLB-29

Lernet-Holenia, Alexander 1897-1976. . . . . DLB-85

Le Rossignol, James 1866-1969 . . . . DLB-92

Lescarbot, Marc circa 1570-1642 . . . . DLB-99

LeSeur, William Dawson 1840-1917 . . . . . DLB-92

LeSieg, Theo. (see Geisel, Theodor Seuss)

Leslie, Doris before 1902-1982 . . . . .DLB-191

Leslie, Eliza 1787-1858 . . . . .DLB-202

Leslie, Frank 1821-1880. . . . . .DLB-43, 79

Leslie, Frank, Publishing House DLB-49

Leśmian, Bolesław 1878-1937 . . . . .DLB-215

Lesperance, John 1835?-1891 . . . . .DLB-99

Lessing, Bruno 1870-1940 . . . . .DLB-28

Lessing, Doris 1919- DLB-15, 139; Y-85

Lessing, Gotthold Ephraim
1729-1781 .DLB-97

Lettau, Reinhard 1929- DLB-75

Letter from Japan. Y-94, Y-98

Letter from London. Y-96

Letter to [Samuel] Richardson on *Clarissa*
(1748), by Henry Fielding DLB-39

A Letter to the Editor of *The Irish Times* Y-97

Lever, Charles 1806-1872 . . . . .DLB-21

Leverson, Ada 1862-1933 . . . . .DLB-153

Levertov, Denise 1923-1997 . . . . .DLB-5, 165

Levi, Peter 1931- DLB-40

Levi, Primo 1919-1987. . . . . .DLB-177

Levien, Sonya 1888-1960. . . . . .DLB-44

Levin, Meyer 1905-1981 . . . . DLB-9, 28; Y-81

Levine, Norman 1923- DLB-88

Levine, Philip 1928- DLB-5

Levis, Larry 1946- DLB-120

Levy, Amy 1861-1889. . . . . .DLB-156

Levy, Benn Wolfe 1900-1973 . . . . . .DLB-13; Y-81

Lewald, Fanny 1811-1889 . . . . .DLB-129

Lewes, George Henry 1817-1878 . . . . .DLB-55, 144

Lewis, Agnes Smith 1843-1926 . . . . .DLB-174

Lewis, Alfred H. 1857-1914 . . . . .DLB-25, 186

Lewis, Alun 1915-1944 . . . . .DLB-20, 162

The Lewis Carroll Centenary Y-98

Lewis, C. Day (see Day Lewis, C.)

Lewis, C. S. 1898-1963 . . . . . . .DLB-15, 100, 160

Lewis, Charles B. 1842-1924. . . . . .DLB-11

Lewis, Henry Clay 1825-1850. . . . . .DLB-3

Lewis, Janet 1899-1999 . . . . Y-87

Lewis, Matthew Gregory
1775-1818 . . . . DLB-39, 158, 178

Lewis, Meriwether 1774-1809 and
Clark, William 1770-1838 . . . . . .DLB-183, 186

Lewis, Norman 1908- DLB-204

Lewis, R. W. B. 1917- DLB-111

Lewis, Richard circa 1700-1734 . . . . .DLB-24

Lewis, Sinclair 1885-1951 . . . . . .DLB-9, 102; DS-1

Lewis, Wilmarth Sheldon 1895-1979. . . .DLB-140

Lewis, Wyndham 1882-1957. . . . . .DLB-15

Lewisohn, Ludwig 1882-1955 . . DLB-4, 9, 28, 102

Leyendecker, J. C. 1874-1951 . . . . .DLB-188

Lezama Lima, José 1910-1976 . . . . .DLB-113

The Library of America. DLB-46

Libbey, Laura Jean 1862-1924. . . . . .DLB-221

The Licensing Act of 1737 . . . . .DLB-84

Lichfield, Leonard I [publishing house] . . . DLB-170

Lichtenberg, Georg Christoph
1742-1799 . . . . .DLB-94

The Liddle Collection Y-97

Lieb, Fred 1888-1980. . . . . .DLB-171

Liebling, A. J. 1904-1963 . . . . DLB-4, 171

Lieutenant Murray (see Ballou, Maturin Murray)

The Life of James Dickey: A Lecture to the Friends
of the Emory Libraries, by Henry Hart . . Y-98

Lighthall, William Douw 1857-1954 . . . . . .DLB-92

Lilar, Françoise (see Mallet-Joris, Françoise)

Lili'uokalani, Queen 1838-1917. . . . . . . .DLB-221

Lillo, George 1691-1739. . . . . .DLB-84

Lilly, J. K., Jr. 1893-1966 . . . . .DLB-140

Lilly, Wait and Company DLB-49

Lily, William circa 1468-1522 . . . . .DLB-132

Limited Editions Club DLB-46

Limón, Graciela 1938- DLB-209

Lincoln and Edmands DLB-49

Lindesay, Ethel Forence (see Richardson, Henry Handel)

Lindsay, Alexander William, Twenty-fifth Earl
of Crawford 1812-1880. . . . . .DLB-184

Lindsay, Sir David
circa 1485-1555. . . . . .DLB-132

Lindsay, Jack 1900- Y-84

Lindsay, Lady (Caroline Blanche Elizabeth Fitzroy
Lindsay) 1844-1912. . . . . .DLB-199

Lindsay, Vachel 1879-1931 . . . . .DLB-54

Linebarger, Paul Myron Anthony (see Smith,
Cordwainer)

Link, Arthur S. 1920-1998. . . . . .DLB-17

Linn, John Blair 1777-1804. . . . . .DLB-37

Lins, Osman 1924-1978 . . . . .DLB-145

Linton, Eliza Lynn 1822-1898. . . . . .DLB-18

Linton, William James 1812-1897 . . . . . . .DLB-32

Lintot, Barnaby Bernard
[publishing house] DLB-170

Lion Books DLB-46

Lionni, Leo 1910-1999. . . . . .DLB-61

Lippard, George 1822-1854. . . . . .DLB-202

Lippincott, Sara Jane Clarke
1823-1904 . . . . .DLB-43

Lippincott, J. B., Company DLB-49

Lippmann, Walter 1889-1974 . . . . .DLB-29

Lipton, Lawrence 1898-1975 . . . . .DLB-16

Liscow, Christian Ludwig 1701-1760. . . . . .DLB-97

Lish, Gordon 1934- DLB-130

Lisle, Charles-Marie-René Leconte de
1818-1894 .DLB-217

Lispector, Clarice 1925-1977 . . . . .DLB-113

A Literary Archaeologist Digs On: A Brief
Interview with Michael Reynolds by
Michael Rogers Y-99

The Literary Chronicle and Weekly Review
1819-1828. . . . . .DLB-110

Literary Documents: William Faulkner
and the People-to-People Program Y-86

Literary Documents II: *Library Journal*
Statements and Questionnaires from
First Novelists Y-87

Literary Effects of World War II
[British novel] DLB-15

Literary Prizes [British] DLB-15

Literary Research Archives: The Humanities
Research Center, University of
Texas Y-82

Literary Research Archives II: Berg
Collection of English and American
Literature of the New York Public
Library Y-83

Literary Research Archives III:
The Lilly Library Y-84

Literary Research Archives IV:
The John Carter Brown Library. Y-85

Literary Research Archives V:
Kent State Special Collections Y-86

Literary Research Archives VI: The Modern
Literary Manuscripts Collection in the
Special Collections of the Washington
University Libraries Y-87

Literary Research Archives VII:
The University of Virginia
Libraries Y-91

Literary Research Archives VIII:
The Henry E. Huntington
Library Y-92

Literary Research Archives IX:
Special Collections at Boston University. . Y-99

The Literary Scene and Situation and . . . Who
(Besides Oprah) Really Runs American
Literature?. Y-99

Literary Societies Y-98, Y-99

"Literary Style" (1857), by William
Forsyth [excerpt] DLB-57

Literatura Chicanesca: The View From
Without. DLB-82

Literature at Nurse, or Circulating Morals (1885),
by George Moore DLB-18

Littell, Eliakim 1797-1870 . . . . .DLB-79

Littell, Robert S. 1831-1896. . . . . .DLB-79

Little, Brown and Company DLB-49

Little Magazines and Newspapers DS-15

The Little Review 1914-1929 . . . . DS-15

Littlewood, Joan 1914- DLB-13

Lively, Penelope 1933- DLB-14, 161, 207

Liverpool University Press DLB-112

The Lives of the Poets. DLB-142

Livesay, Dorothy 1909- DLB-68

Livesay, Florence Randal 1874-1953 . . . . . .DLB-92

"Living in Ruin," by Gerald Stern. DLB-105

Livings, Henry 1929-1998. . . . . .DLB-13

Livingston, Anne Howe 1763-1841 . . . DLB-37, 200

Livingston, Myra Cohn 1926-1996. . . . . . .DLB-61

Livingston, William 1723-1790 . . . . .DLB-31

Livingstone, David 1813-1873 . . . . .DLB-166

Livingstone, Douglas 1932-1996. . . . . . .DLB-225

Livy 59 B.C.-A.D. 17 . . . . .DLB-211

Liyong, Taban lo (see Taban lo Liyong)

Lizárraga, Sylvia S. 1925- DLB-82

Llewellyn, Richard 1906-1983 . . . . DLB-15

Lloyd, Edward [publishing house] DLB-106

Lobel, Arnold 1933- DLB-61

Lochridge, Betsy Hopkins (see Fancher, Betsy)

Locke, David Ross 1833-1888 . . . . DLB-11, 23

Locke, John 1632-1704 . . . . DLB-31, 101, 213

Locke, Richard Adams 1800-1871 . . . . DLB-43

Locker-Lampson, Frederick
1821-1895 . . . . DLB-35, 184

Lockhart, John Gibson
1794-1854 . . . . DLB-110, 116 144

Lockridge, Ross, Jr. 1914-1948 . . . . .DLB-143; Y-80

Locrine and Selimus DLB-62

Lodge, David 1935- DLB-14, 194

Lodge, George Cabot 1873-1909 . . . . DLB-54

Lodge, Henry Cabot 1850-1924 . . . . DLB-47

Lodge, Thomas 1558-1625 . . . . .DLB-172

Loeb, Harold 1891-1974 . . . . DLB-4

Loeb, William 1905-1981 . . . . DLB-127

Lofting, Hugh 1886-1947 . . . . DLB-160

Logan, Deborah Norris 1761-1839 . . . . . . DLB-200

Logan, James 1674-1751 . . . . DLB-24, 140

Logan, John 1923- DLB-5

Logan, Martha Daniell 1704?-1779 . . . . . DLB-200

Logan, William 1950- DLB-120

Logau, Friedrich von 1605-1655 . . . . DLB-164

Logue, Christopher 1926- DLB-27

Lohenstein, Daniel Casper von
1635-1683 . . . . DLB-168

Lomonosov, Mikhail Vasil'evich
1711-1765 . . . . DLB-150

London, Jack 1876-1916 . . . . . . .DLB-8, 12, 78, 212

The London Magazine 1820-1829 . . . . DLB-110

Long, Haniel 1888-1956 . . . . DLB-45

Long, Ray 1878-1935 . . . . DLB-137

Long, H., and Brother DLB-49

Longfellow, Henry Wadsworth
1807-1882 . . . . DLB-1, 59

Longfellow, Samuel
1819-1892 . . . . DLB-1

Longford, Elizabeth 1906- DLB-155

Longinus circa first century DLB-176

Longley, Michael 1939- DLB-40

Longman, T. [publishing house] DLB-154

Longmans, Green and Company DLB-49

Longmore, George 1793?-1867 . . . . DLB-99

Longstreet, Augustus Baldwin
1790-1870 . . . . .DLB-3, 11, 74

Longworth, D. [publishing house] DLB-49

Lonsdale, Frederick 1881-1954 . . . . DLB-10

A Look at the Contemporary Black Theatre
Movement DLB-38

Loos, Anita 1893-1981 . . . . .DLB-11, 26; Y-81

Lopate, Phillip 1943- Y-80

López, Diana (see Isabella, Ríos)

López, Josefina 1969- DLB-209

Loranger, Jean-Aubert 1896-1942 . . . . DLB-92

Lorca, Federico García 1898-1936 . . . . . . DLB-108

Lord, John Keast 1818-1872 . . . . DLB-99

The Lord Chamberlain's Office and Stage
Censorship in England DLB-10

Lorde, Audre 1934-1992 . . . . DLB-41

Lorimer, George Horace 1867-1939 . . . . . DLB-91

Loring, A. K. [publishing house] DLB-49

Loring and Mussey DLB-46

Lorris, Guillaume de (see *Roman de la Rose*)

Lossing, Benson J. 1813-1891 . . . . DLB-30

Lothar, Ernst 1890-1974 . . . . DLB-81

Lothrop, Harriet M. 1844-1924 . . . . DLB-42

Lothrop, D., and Company DLB-49

Loti, Pierre 1850-1923 . . . . DLB-123

Lotichius Secundus, Petrus
1528-1560 .DLB-179

Lott, Emeline ?-? DLB-166

The Lounger, no. 20 (1785), by Henry
Mackenzie DLB-39

Louisiana State University Press Y-97

Lounsbury, Thomas R. 1838-1915 . . . . . . DLB-71

Louÿs, Pierre 1870-1925 . . . . DLB-123

Lovelace, Earl 1935- DLB-125

Lovelace, Richard 1618-1657 . . . . DLB-131

Lovell, Coryell and Company DLB-49

Lovell, John W., Company DLB-49

Lover, Samuel 1797-1868 . . . . DLB-159, 190

Lovesey, Peter 1936- DLB-87

Lovinescu, Eugen 1881-1943 . . . . DLB-220

Lovingood, Sut
(see Harris, George Washington)

Low, Samuel 1765-? DLB-37

Lowell, Amy 1874-1925 . . . . DLB-54, 140

Lowell, James Russell
1819-1891 . . . . .DLB-1, 11, 64, 79, 189

Lowell, Robert 1917-1977 . . . . DLB-5, 169

Lowenfels, Walter 1897-1976 . . . . DLB-4

Lowndes, Marie Belloc 1868-1947 . . . . DLB-70

Lowndes, William Thomas 1798-1843 . . . DLB-184

Lownes, Humphrey [publishing house] . . .DLB-170

Lowry, Lois 1937- DLB-52

Lowry, Malcolm 1909-1957 . . . . DLB-15

Lowther, Pat 1935-1975 . . . . DLB-53

Loy, Mina 1882-1966 . . . . DLB-4, 54

Lozeau, Albert 1878-1924 . . . . DLB-92

Lubbock, Percy 1879-1965 . . . . DLB-149

Lucan A.D. 39-A.D. 65 . . . . DLB-211

Lucas, E. V. 1868-1938 . . . . DLB-98, 149, 153

Lucas, Fielding, Jr. [publishing house] DLB-49

Luce, Henry R. 1898-1967 . . . . DLB-91

Luce, John W., and Company DLB-46

Lucian circa 120-180 . . . . .DLB-176

Lucie-Smith, Edward 1933- DLB-40

Lucilius circa 180 B.C.-102/101 B.C. DLB-211

Lucini, Gian Pietro 1867-1914 . . . . DLB-114

Lucretius circa 94 B.C.-circa 49 B.C. DLB-211

Luder, Peter circa 1415-1472 . . . . .DLB-179

Ludlum, Robert 1927- Y-82

Ludus de Antichristo circa 1160 . . . . DLB-148

Ludvigson, Susan 1942- DLB-120

Ludwig, Jack 1922- DLB-60

Ludwig, Otto 1813-1865 . . . . DLB-129

Ludwigslied 881 or 882 . . . . DLB-148

Luera, Yolanda 1953- DLB-122

Luft, Lya 1938- DLB-145

Lugansky, Kazak Vladimir (see
Dal', Vladimir Ivanovich)

Lukács, György 1885-1971 . . . . DLB-215

Luke, Peter 1919- DLB-13

Lummis, Charles F. 1859-1928 . . . . DLB-186

Lupton, F. M., Company DLB-49

Lupus of Ferrières circa 805-circa 862 . . . DLB-148

Lurie, Alison 1926- DLB-2

Luther, Martin 1483-1546 . . . . .DLB-179

Luzi, Mario 1914- DLB-128

L'vov, Nikolai Aleksandrovich
1751-1803 . . . . DLB-150

Lyall, Gavin 1932- DLB-87

Lydgate, John circa 1370-1450 . . . . DLB-146

Lyly, John circa 1554-1606 . . . . .DLB-62, 167

Lynch, Patricia 1898-1972 . . . . DLB-160

Lynch, Richard flourished 1596-1601 . . . .DLB-172

Lynd, Robert 1879-1949 . . . . DLB-98

Lyon, Matthew 1749-1822 . . . . DLB-43

Lysias circa 459 B.C.-circa 380 B.C. DLB-176

Lytle, Andrew 1902-1995 . . . . .DLB-6; Y-95

Lytton, Edward (see Bulwer-Lytton, Edward)

Lytton, Edward Robert Bulwer 1831-1891 . . .DLB-32

M

Maass, Joachim 1901-1972 . . . . DLB-69

Mabie, Hamilton Wright 1845-1916 . . . . . DLB-71

Mac A'Ghobhainn, Iain (see Smith, Iain Crichton)

MacArthur, Charles 1895-1956 . . . . .DLB-7, 25, 44

Macaulay, Catherine 1731-1791 . . . . DLB-104

Macaulay, David 1945- DLB-61

Macaulay, Rose 1881-1958 . . . . DLB-36

Macaulay, Thomas Babington
1800-1859 . . . . DLB-32, 55

Macaulay Company DLB-46

MacBeth, George 1932- DLB-40

Macbeth, Madge 1880-1965 . . . . DLB-92

MacCaig, Norman 1910-1996 . . . . DLB-27

MacDiarmid, Hugh 1892-1978 . . . . DLB-20

MacDonald, Cynthia 1928- DLB-105

MacDonald, George 1824-1905 . . . . DLB-18, 163, 178

MacDonald, John D. 1916-1986 . . . . . .DLB-8; Y-86

MacDonald, Philip 1899?-1980 . . . . DLB-77

Macdonald, Ross (see Millar, Kenneth)

MacDonald, Wilson 1880-1967 . . . . DLB-92

Macdonald and Company
(Publishers) DLB-112

MacEwen, Gwendolyn 1941- DLB-53

Macfadden, Bernarr 1868-1955 . . . . . . .DLB-25, 91

MacGregor, John 1825-1892 . . . . .DLB-166

MacGregor, Mary Esther (see Keith, Marian)

Machado, Antonio 1875-1939 . . . . .DLB-108

Machado, Manuel 1874-1947 . . . . .DLB-108

Machar, Agnes Maule 1837-1927 . . . . .DLB-92

Machaut, Guillaume de
circa 1300-1377 . . . . .DLB-208

Machen, Arthur Llewelyn Jones
1863-1947 . . . . DLB-36, 156, 178

MacInnes, Colin 1914-1976 . . . . .DLB-14

MacInnes, Helen 1907-1985 . . . . .DLB-87

Mačiulis, Jonas (see Maironis, Jonas)

Mack, Maynard 1909- DLB-111

Mackall, Leonard L. 1879-1937 . . . . .DLB-140

MacKaye, Percy 1875-1956 . . . . .DLB-54

Macken, Walter 1915-1967 . . . . .DLB-13

Mackenzie, Alexander 1763-1820 . . . . .DLB-99

Mackenzie, Alexander Slidell
1803-1848 . . . . .DLB-183

Mackenzie, Compton 1883-1972 . . . . .DLB-34, 100

Mackenzie, Henry 1745-1831 . . . . .DLB-39

Mackenzie, William 1758-1828 . . . . .DLB-187

Mackey, Nathaniel 1947- DLB-169

Mackey, William Wellington
1937- DLB-38

Mackintosh, Elizabeth (see Tey, Josephine)

Mackintosh, Sir James 1765-1832 . . . . . . .DLB-158

Maclaren, Ian (see Watson, John)

Macklin, Charles 1699-1797 . . . . .DLB-89

MacLean, Katherine Anne 1925- DLB-8

Maclean, Norman 1902-1990 . . . . .DLB-206

MacLeish, Archibald
1892-1982 . . . . DLB-4, 7, 45; Y-82

MacLennan, Hugh 1907-1990 . . . . .DLB-68

Macleod, Fiona (see Sharp, William)

MacLeod, Alistair 1936- DLB-60

Macleod, Norman 1906-1985 . . . . .DLB-4

Mac Low, Jackson 1922- DLB-193

Macmillan and Company DLB-106

The Macmillan Company DLB-49

Macmillan's English Men of Letters,
First Series (1878-1892) DLB-144

MacNamara, Brinsley 1890-1963 . . . . .DLB-10

MacNeice, Louis 1907-1963 . . . . .DLB-10, 20

MacPhail, Andrew 1864-1938 . . . . .DLB-92

Macpherson, James 1736-1796 . . . . .DLB-109

Macpherson, Jay 1931- DLB-53

Macpherson, Jeanie 1884-1946 . . . . .DLB-44

Macrae Smith Company DLB-46

Macrone, John [publishing house] DLB-106

MacShane, Frank 1927-1999 . . . . .DLB-111

Macy-Masius DLB-46

Madden, David 1933- DLB-6

Madden, Sir Frederic 1801-1873 . . . . . . .DLB-184

Maddow, Ben 1909-1992 . . . . .DLB-44

Maddux, Rachel 1912-1983 . . . . Y-93

Madgett, Naomi Long 1923- DLB-76

Madhubuti, Haki R. 1942- DLB-5, 41; DS-8

Madison, James 1751-1836 . . . . .DLB-37

Madsen, Svend Åge 1939- DLB-214

Maeterlinck, Maurice 1862-1949 . . . . . . .DLB-192

Magee, David 1905-1977 . . . . .DLB-187

Maginn, William 1794-1842 . . . . . . .DLB-110, 159

Mahan, Alfred Thayer 1840-1914 . . . . . . .DLB-47

Maheux-Forcier, Louise 1929- DLB-60

Mafūz, Najīb 1911- Y-88

Mahin, John Lee 1902-1984 . . . . .DLB-44

Mahon, Derek 1941- DLB-40

Maikov, Vasilii Ivanovich
1728-1778 . . . . .DLB-150

Mailer, Norman 1923-
. . . . DLB-2, 16, 28, 185; Y-80, Y-83; DS-3

Maillart, Ella 1903-1997 . . . . .DLB-195

Maillet, Adrienne 1885-1963 . . . . .DLB-68

Maillet, Antonine 1929- DLB-60

Maillu, David G. 1939- DLB-157

Maimonides, Moses 1138-1204 . . . . .DLB-115

Main Selections of the Book-of-the-Month
Club, 1926-1945 . . . . .DLB-9

Main Trends in Twentieth-Century Book
Clubs DLB-46

Mainwaring, Daniel 1902-1977 . . . . .DLB-44

Mair, Charles 1838-1927 . . . . .DLB-99

Maironis, Jonas 1862-1932 . . . . .DLB-220

Mais, Roger 1905-1955 . . . . .DLB-125

Major, Andre 1942- DLB-60

Major, Charles 1856-1913 . . . . .DLB-202

Major, Clarence 1936- DLB-33

Major, Kevin 1949- DLB-60

Major Books DLB-46

Makemie, Francis circa 1658-1708 . . . . . . .DLB-24

The Making of Americans Contract Y-98

The Making of a People, by
J. M. Ritchie DLB-66

Maksimović, Desanka 1898-1993 . . . . . . .DLB-147

Malamud, Bernard
1914-1986 . . . . . . DLB-2, 28, 152; Y-80, Y-86

Malerba, Luigi 1927- DLB-196

Malet, Lucas 1852-1931 . . . . .DLB-153

Mallarmé, Stéphane 1842-1898 . . . . .DLB-217

Malleson, Lucy Beatrice (see Gilbert, Anthony)

Mallet-Joris, Françoise 1930- DLB-83

Mallock, W. H. 1849-1923 . . . . .DLB-18, 57

Malone, Dumas 1892-1986 . . . . .DLB-17

Malone, Edmond 1741-1812 . . . . .DLB-142

Malory, Sir Thomas
circa 1400-1410 - 1471 . . . . .DLB-146

Malraux, André 1901-1976 . . . . .DLB-72

Malthus, Thomas Robert
1766-1834 . . . . DLB-107, 158

Maltz, Albert 1908-1985 . . . . .DLB-102

Malzberg, Barry N. 1939- DLB-8

Mamet, David 1947- DLB-7

Manaka, Matsemela 1956- DLB-157

Manchester University Press DLB-112

Mandel, Eli 1922- DLB-53

Mandeville, Bernard 1670-1733 . . . . .DLB-101

Mandeville, Sir John
mid fourteenth century DLB-146

Mandiargues, André Pieyre de 1909- . . .DLB-83

Manfred, Frederick 1912-1994 . . . . . . .DLB-6, 212

Manfredi, Gianfranco 1948- DLB-196

Mangan, Sherry 1904-1961 . . . . .DLB-4

Manganelli, Giorgio 1922-1990 . . . . .DLB-196

Manilius fl. first century A.D. DLB-211

Mankiewicz, Herman 1897-1953 . . . . .DLB-26

Mankiewicz, Joseph L. 1909-1993 . . . . . . .DLB-44

Mankowitz, Wolf 1924-1998 . . . . .DLB-15

Manley, Delarivière 1672?-1724 . . . . . .DLB-39, 80

Mann, Abby 1927- DLB-44

Mann, Charles 1929-1998 . . . . Y-98

Mann, Heinrich 1871-1950 . . . . .DLB-66, 118

Mann, Horace 1796-1859 . . . . .DLB-1

Mann, Klaus 1906-1949 . . . . .DLB-56

Mann, Thomas 1875-1955 . . . . .DLB-66

Mann, William D'Alton 1839-1920 . . . . . .DLB-137

Mannin, Ethel 1900-1984 . . . . .DLB-191, 195

Manning, Marie 1873?-1945 . . . . .DLB-29

Manning and Loring DLB-49

Mannyng, Robert
flourished 1303-1338 . . . . .DLB-146

Mano, D. Keith 1942- DLB-6

Manor Books DLB-46

Mansfield, Katherine 1888-1923 . . . . .DLB-162

Manuel, Niklaus circa 1484-1530 . . . . . . .DLB-179

Manzini, Gianna 1896-1974 . . . . .DLB-177

Mapanje, Jack 1944- DLB-157

Maraini, Dacia 1936- DLB-196

March, William 1893-1954 . . . . .DLB-9, 86

Marchand, Leslie A. 1900-1999 . . . . .DLB-103

Marchant, Bessie 1862-1941 . . . . .DLB-160

Marchessault, Jovette 1938- DLB-60

Marcus, Frank 1928- DLB-13

Marden, Orison Swett 1850-1924 . . . . . . .DLB-137

Marechera, Dambudzo 1952-1987 . . . . . .DLB-157

Marek, Richard, Books DLB-46

Mares, E. A. 1938- DLB-122

Mariani, Paul 1940- DLB-111

Marie de France flourished 1160-1178 . . . .DLB-208

Marie-Victorin, Frère 1885-1944 . . . . .DLB-92

Marin, Biagio 1891-1985 . . . . .DLB-128

Marincović, Ranko 1913- DLB-147

Marinetti, Filippo Tommaso 1876-1944 . . . . DLB-114

Marion, Frances 1886-1973 . . . . DLB-44

Marius, Richard C. 1933-1999 . . . . Y-85

The Mark Taper Forum DLB-7

Mark Twain on Perpetual Copyright Y-92

Markfield, Wallace 1926- DLB-2, 28

Markham, Edwin 1852-1940 . . . . . . DLB-54, 186

Markle, Fletcher 1921-1991 . . . . . . DLB-68; Y-91

Marlatt, Daphne 1942- DLB-60

Marlitt, E. 1825-1887 . . . . DLB-129

Marlowe, Christopher 1564-1593 . . . . DLB-62

Marlyn, John 1912- DLB-88

Marmion, Shakerley 1603-1639 . . . . DLB-58

Der Marner before 1230-circa 1287 . . . . . DLB-138

Marnham, Patrick 1943- DLB-204

The Marprelate Tracts 1588-1589 . . . . . . DLB-132

Marquand, John P. 1893-1960 . . . . . . DLB-9, 102

Marqués, René 1919-1979 . . . . DLB-113

Marquis, Don 1878-1937 . . . . DLB-11, 25

Marriott, Anne 1913- DLB-68

Marryat, Frederick 1792-1848 . . . . . . DLB-21, 163

Marsh, George Perkins 1801-1882 . . . . . DLB-1, 64

Marsh, James 1794-1842 . . . . DLB-1, 59

Marsh, Capen, Lyon and Webb DLB-49

Marsh, Narcissus 1638-1713 . . . . DLB-213

Marsh, Ngaio 1899-1982 . . . . DLB-77

Marshall, Edison 1894-1967 . . . . DLB-102

Marshall, Edward 1932- DLB-16

Marshall, Emma 1828-1899 . . . . DLB-163

Marshall, James 1942-1992 . . . . DLB-61

Marshall, Joyce 1913- DLB-88

Marshall, Paule 1929- DLB-33, 157

Marshall, Tom 1938- DLB-60

Marsilius of Padua circa 1275-circa 1342 . . . . DLB-115

Mars-Jones, Adam 1954- DLB-207

Marson, Una 1905-1965 . . . . DLB-157

Marston, John 1576-1634 . . . . DLB-58, 172

Marston, Philip Bourke 1850-1887 . . . . . DLB-35

Martens, Kurt 1870-1945 . . . . DLB-66

Martial circa A.D. 40-circa A.D. 103 . . . . DLB-211

Martien, William S. [publishing house] . . . DLB-49

Martin, Abe (see Hubbard, Kin)

Martin, Charles 1942- DLB-120

Martin, Claire 1914- DLB-60

Martin, Jay 1935- DLB-111

Martin, Johann (see Laurentius von Schnüffis)

Martin, Thomas 1696-1771 . . . . DLB-213

Martin, Violet Florence (see Ross, Martin)

Martin du Gard, Roger 1881-1958 . . . . . DLB-65

Martineau, Harriet 1802-1876 . . . . DLB-21, 55, 159, 163, 166, 190

Martínez, Demetria 1960- DLB-209

Martínez, Eliud 1935- DLB-122

Martínez, Max 1943- DLB-82

Martínez, Rubén 1962- DLB-209

Martyn, Edward 1859-1923 . . . . DLB-10

Martone, Michael 1955- DLB-218

Marvell, Andrew 1621-1678 . . . . DLB-131

Marvin X 1944- DLB-38

Marx, Karl 1818-1883 . . . . DLB-129

Marzials, Theo 1850-1920 . . . . DLB-35

Masefield, John 1878-1967 . . . . DLB-10, 19, 153, 160

Mason, A. E. W. 1865-1948 . . . . DLB-70

Mason, Bobbie Ann 1940- DLB-173; Y-87

Mason, William 1725-1797 . . . . DLB-142

Mason Brothers DLB-49

Massey, Gerald 1828-1907 . . . . DLB-32

Massey, Linton R. 1900-1974 . . . . DLB-187

Massinger, Philip 1583-1640 . . . . DLB-58

Masson, David 1822-1907 . . . . DLB-144

Masters, Edgar Lee 1868-1950 . . . . DLB-54

Mastronardi, Lucio 1930-1979 . . . . DLB-177

Matevski, Mateja 1929- DLB-181

Mather, Cotton 1663-1728 . . . . . DLB-24, 30, 140

Mather, Increase 1639-1723 . . . . DLB-24

Mather, Richard 1596-1669 . . . . DLB-24

Matheson, Richard 1926- DLB-8, 44

Matheus, John F. 1887- DLB-51

Matthew of Vendôme circa 1130-circa 1200 . . . . DLB-208

Mathews, Cornelius 1817?-1889 . . . . . DLB-3, 64

Mathews, John Joseph 1894-1979 . . . . . . DLB-175

Mathews, Elkin [publishing house] DLB-112

Mathias, Roland 1915- DLB-27

Mathis, June 1892-1927 . . . . DLB-44

Mathis, Sharon Bell 1937- DLB-33

Matković, Marijan 1915-1985 . . . . DLB-181

Matoš, Antun Gustav 1873-1914 . . . . . . DLB-147

Matsumoto Seichō 1909-1992 . . . . DLB-182

The Matter of England 1240-1400 . . . . . DLB-146

The Matter of Rome early twelfth to late fifteenth century DLB-146

Matthews, Brander 1852-1929 . . . . DLB-71, 78; DS-13

Matthews, Jack 1925- DLB-6

Matthews, Victoria Earle 1861-1907 . . . . DLB-221

Matthews, William 1942-1997 . . . . DLB-5

Matthiessen, F. O. 1902-1950 . . . . DLB-63

Maturin, Charles Robert 1780-1824 . . . . DLB-178

Matthiessen, Peter 1927- DLB-6, 173

Maugham, W. Somerset 1874-1965 . . . . . DLB-10, 36, 77, 100, 162, 195

Maupassant, Guy de 1850-1893 . . . . . . DLB-123

Mauriac, Claude 1914-1996 . . . . DLB-83

Mauriac, François 1885-1970 . . . . DLB-65

Maurice, Frederick Denison 1805-1872 . . . . DLB-55

Maurois, André 1885-1967 . . . . DLB-65

Maury, James 1718-1769 . . . . DLB-31

Mavor, Elizabeth 1927- DLB-14

Mavor, Osborne Henry (see Bridie, James)

Maxwell, Gavin 1914-1969 . . . . DLB-204

Maxwell, William 1908- DLB-218; Y-80

Maxwell, H. [publishing house] DLB-49

Maxwell, John [publishing house] DLB-106

May, Elaine 1932- DLB-44

May, Karl 1842-1912 . . . . DLB-129

May, Thomas 1595 or 1596-1650 . . . . . . DLB-58

Mayer, Bernadette 1945- DLB-165

Mayer, Mercer 1943- DLB-61

Mayer, O. B. 1818-1891 . . . . DLB-3

Mayes, Herbert R. 1900-1987 . . . . DLB-137

Mayes, Wendell 1919-1992 . . . . DLB-26

Mayfield, Julian 1928-1984 . . . . . . DLB-33; Y-84

Mayhew, Henry 1812-1887 . . . . . DLB-18, 55, 190

Mayhew, Jonathan 1720-1766 . . . . DLB-31

Mayne, Ethel Colburn 1865-1941 . . . . . DLB-197

Mayne, Jasper 1604-1672 . . . . DLB-126

Mayne, Seymour 1944- DLB-60

Mayor, Flora Macdonald 1872-1932 . . . . DLB-36

Mayröcker, Friederike 1924- DLB-85

Mazrui, Ali A. 1933- DLB-125

Mažuranić, Ivan 1814-1890 . . . . DLB-147

Mazursky, Paul 1930- DLB-44

McAlmon, Robert 1896-1956 . . . . DLB-4, 45; DS-15

McArthur, Peter 1866-1924 . . . . DLB-92

McBride, Robert M., and Company DLB-46

McCabe, Patrick 1955- DLB-194

McCaffrey, Anne 1926- DLB-8

McCarthy, Cormac 1933- DLB-6, 143

McCarthy, Mary 1912-1989 . . . . . . DLB-2; Y-81

McCay, Winsor 1871-1934 . . . . DLB-22

McClane, Albert Jules 1922-1991 . . . . . DLB-171

McClatchy, C. K. 1858-1936 . . . . DLB-25

McClellan, George Marion 1860-1934 . . . . DLB-50

McCloskey, Robert 1914- DLB-22

McClung, Nellie Letitia 1873-1951 . . . . . DLB-92

McClure, Joanna 1930- DLB-16

McClure, Michael 1932- DLB-16

McClure, Phillips and Company DLB-46

McClure, S. S. 1857-1949 . . . . DLB-91

McClurg, A. C., and Company DLB-49

McCluskey, John A., Jr. 1944- DLB-33

McCollum, Michael A. 1946 . . . . Y-87

McConnell, William C. 1917- DLB-88

McCord, David 1897-1997 . . . . DLB-61

McCorkle, Jill 1958- Y-87

McCorkle, Samuel Eusebius 1746-1811 . . . . DLB-37

McCormick, Anne O'Hare 1880-1954 . . . . DLB-29

McCormick, Robert R. 1880-1955 . . . . . DLB-29

McCourt, Edward 1907-1972 . . . . DLB-88

McCoy, Horace 1897-1955 . . . . .DLB-9

McCrae, John 1872-1918 . . . . .DLB-92

McCullagh, Joseph B. 1842-1896. . . . . . . .DLB-23

McCullers, Carson 1917-1967 . . . . . . DLB-2, 7, 173

McCulloch, Thomas 1776-1843 . . . . .DLB-99

McDonald, Forrest 1927- DLB-17

McDonald, Walter 1934- DLB-105, DS-9

McDougall, Colin 1917-1984 . . . . .DLB-68

McDowell, Obolensky DLB-46

McEwan, Ian 1948- DLB-14, 194

McFadden, David 1940- DLB-60

McFall, Frances Elizabeth Clarke
(see Grand, Sarah)

McFarlane, Leslie 1902-1977 . . . . .DLB-88

McFee, William 1881-1966 . . . . .DLB-153

McGahern, John 1934- DLB-14

McGee, Thomas D'Arcy 1825-1868 . . . . . .DLB-99

McGeehan, W. O. 1879-1933 . . . . DLB-25, 171

McGill, Ralph 1898-1969. . . . . .DLB-29

McGinley, Phyllis 1905-1978 . . . . .DLB-11, 48

McGinniss, Joe 1942- DLB-185

McGirt, James E. 1874-1930 . . . . .DLB-50

McGlashan and Gill. DLB-106

McGough, Roger 1937- DLB-40

McGraw-Hill DLB-46

McGuane, Thomas 1939- DLB-2, 212; Y-80

McGuckian, Medbh 1950- DLB-40

McGuffey, William Holmes 1800-1873 . . . .DLB-42

McHenry, James 1785-1845. . . . . .DLB-202

McIlvanney, William 1936- DLB-14, 207

McIlwraith, Jean Newton 1859-1938 . . . . . .DLB-92

McIntyre, James 1827-1906 . . . . .DLB-99

McIntyre, O. O. 1884-1938 . . . . .DLB-25

McKay, Claude 1889-1948 . . . . DLB-4, 45, 51, 117

The David McKay Company DLB-49

McKean, William V. 1820-1903 . . . . .DLB-23

McKenna, Stephen 1888-1967 . . . . .DLB-197

The McKenzie Trust Y-96

McKerrow, R. B. 1872-1940 . . . . .DLB-201

McKinley, Robin 1952- DLB-52

McLachlan, Alexander 1818-1896. . . . . . . .DLB-99

McLaren, Floris Clark 1904-1978 . . . . . . .DLB-68

McLaverty, Michael 1907- DLB-15

McLean, John R. 1848-1916 . . . . .DLB-23

McLean, William L. 1852-1931. . . . . .DLB-25

McLennan, William 1856-1904 . . . . .DLB-92

McLoughlin Brothers. DLB-49

McLuhan, Marshall 1911-1980 . . . . .DLB-88

McMaster, John Bach 1852-1932. . . . . . . .DLB-47

McMurtry, Larry
1936- DLB-2, 143; Y-80, Y-87

McNally, Terrence 1939- DLB-7

McNeil, Florence 1937- DLB-60

McNeile, Herman Cyril 1888-1937 . . . . . . .DLB-77

McNickle, D'Arcy 1904-1977. . . . . . . DLB-175, 212

McPhee, John 1931- DLB-185

McPherson, James Alan 1943- DLB-38

McPherson, Sandra 1943- Y-86

McWhirter, George 1939- DLB-60

McWilliams, Carey 1905-1980 . . . . .DLB-137

Mda, Zakes 1948- DLB-225

Mead, L. T. 1844-1914 . . . . .DLB-141

Mead, Matthew 1924- DLB-40

Mead, Taylor ?- DLB-16

Meany, Tom 1903-1964 . . . . .DLB-171

Mechthild von Magdeburg
circa 1207-circa 1282 . . . . .DLB-138

Medieval French Drama DLB-208

Medieval Travel Diaries DLB-203

Medill, Joseph 1823-1899 . . . . .DLB-43

Medoff, Mark 1940- DLB-7

Meek, Alexander Beaufort 1814-1865 . . . . . .DLB-3

Meeke, Mary ?-1816? DLB-116

Meinke, Peter 1932- DLB-5

Mejia Vallejo, Manuel 1923- DLB-113

Melanchthon, Philipp 1497-1560 . . . . .DLB-179

Melançon, Robert 1947- DLB-60

Mell, Max 1882-1971 . . . . .DLB-81, 124

Mellow, James R. 1926-1997 . . . . .DLB-111

Meltzer, David 1937- DLB-16

Meltzer, Milton 1915- DLB-61

Melville, Elizabeth, Lady Culross
circa 1585-1640 . . . . DLB-172

Melville, Herman 1819-1891 . . . . DLB-3, 74

Memoirs of Life and Literature (1920),
by W. H. Mallock [excerpt] DLB-57

Mena, María Cristina 1893-1965. . . .DLB-209, 221

Menander 342-341 B.C.-circa 292-291 B.C.
. . . . DLB-176

Menantes (see Hunold, Christian Friedrich)

Mencke, Johann Burckhard
1674-1732 . . . . .DLB-168

Mencken, H. L.
1880-1956 . . . . DLB-11, 29, 63, 137, 222

Mencken and Nietzsche: An Unpublished
Excerpt from H. L. Mencken's *My Life
as Author and Editor* Y-93

Mendelssohn, Moses 1729-1786. . . . . .DLB-97

Mendes, Catulle 1841-1909 . . . . .DLB-217

Méndez M., Miguel 1930- DLB-82

Mens Rea (or Something) Y-97

The Mercantile Library of New York Y-96

Mercer, Cecil William (see Yates, Dornford)

Mercer, David 1928-1980 . . . . .DLB-13

Mercer, John 1704-1768 . . . . .DLB-31

Meredith, George
1828-1909 . . . . DLB-18, 35, 57, 159

Meredith, Louisa Anne 1812-1895 . . . . . .DLB-166

Meredith, Owen (see Lytton, Edward Robert
Bulwer)

Meredith, William 1919- DLB-5

Mergerle, Johann Ulrich
(see Abraham ä Sancta Clara)

Mérimée, Prosper 1803-1870 . . . . . . .DLB-119, 192

Merivale, John Herman 1779-1844 . . . . . . .DLB-96

Meriwether, Louise 1923- DLB-33

Merlin Press. DLB-112

Merriam, Eve 1916-1992 . . . . .DLB-61

The Merriam Company DLB-49

Merrill, James 1926-1995 . . . . . . DLB-5, 165; Y-85

Merrill and Baker DLB-49

The Mershon Company DLB-49

Merton, Thomas 1915-1968 . . . . DLB-48; Y-81

Merwin, W. S. 1927- DLB-5, 169

Messner, Julian [publishing house] DLB-46

Metcalf, J. [publishing house]. DLB-49

Metcalf, John 1938- DLB-60

The Methodist Book Concern. DLB-49

Methuen and Company. DLB-112

Meun, Jean de (see *Roman de la Rose*)

Mew, Charlotte 1869-1928 . . . . DLB-19, 135

Mewshaw, Michael 1943- Y-80

Meyer, Conrad Ferdinand 1825-1898 . . . .DLB-129

Meyer, E. Y. 1946- DLB-75

Meyer, Eugene 1875-1959 . . . . .DLB-29

Meyer, Michael 1921- DLB-155

Meyers, Jeffrey 1939- DLB-111

Meynell, Alice 1847-1922 . . . . DLB-19, 98

Meynell, Viola 1885-1956 . . . . .DLB-153

Meyrink, Gustav 1868-1932 . . . . .DLB-81

Mézières, Philipe de circa 1327-1405 . . . . .DLB-208

Michael, Ib 1945- DLB-214

Michael M. Rea and the Rea Award for the
Short Story Y-97

Michaëlis, Karen 1872-1950. . . . . .DLB-214

Michaels, Leonard 1933- DLB-130

Micheaux, Oscar 1884-1951 . . . . .DLB-50

Michel of Northgate, Dan
circa 1265-circa 1340. . . . . .DLB-146

Micheline, Jack 1929-1998. . . . . .DLB-16

Michener, James A. 1907?-1997. . . . . .DLB-6

Micklejohn, George
circa 1717-1818 . . . . .DLB-31

Middle English Literature:
An Introduction DLB-146

The Middle English Lyric DLB-146

Middle Hill Press. DLB-106

Middleton, Christopher 1926- DLB-40

Middleton, Richard 1882-1911 . . . . .DLB-156

Middleton, Stanley 1919- DLB-14

Middleton, Thomas 1580-1627 . . . . .DLB-58

Miegel, Agnes 1879-1964. . . . . .DLB-56

Mieželaitis, Eduardas 1919-1997 . . . . . . .DLB-220

Mihailović, Dragoslav 1930- DLB-181

Mihalić, Slavko 1928- DLB-181

Miles, Josephine 1911-1985 . . . . .DLB-48

Miliković, Branko 1934-1961 . . . . .DLB-181

Milius, John 1944- DLB-44

Mill, James 1773-1836 . . . . DLB-107, 158

Mill, John Stuart 1806-1873 . . . . DLB-55, 190

Millar, Kenneth
1915-1983 . . . . DLB-2, 226; Y-83; DS-6

Millar, Andrew [publishing house] DLB-154

Millay, Edna St. Vincent 1892-1950 . . . . . DLB-45

Millen, Sarah Gertrude 1888-1968 . . . . . . DLB-225

Miller, Arthur 1915- DLB-7

Miller, Caroline 1903-1992 . . . . DLB-9

Miller, Eugene Ethelbert 1950- DLB-41

Miller, Heather Ross 1939- DLB-120

Miller, Henry 1891-1980 . . . . DLB-4, 9; Y-80

Miller, Hugh 1802-1856 . . . . DLB-190

Miller, J. Hillis 1928- DLB-67

Miller, James [publishing house] DLB-49

Miller, Jason 1939- DLB-7

Miller, Joaquin 1839-1913 . . . . DLB-186

Miller, May 1899- DLB-41

Miller, Paul 1906-1991 . . . . DLB-127

Miller, Perry 1905-1963 . . . . DLB-17, 63

Miller, Sue 1943- DLB-143

Miller, Vassar 1924-1998 . . . . DLB-105

Miller, Walter M., Jr. 1923- DLB-8

Miller, Webb 1892-1940 . . . . DLB-29

Millhauser, Steven 1943- DLB-2

Millican, Arthenia J. Bates 1920- DLB-38

Mills and Boon DLB-112

Milman, Henry Hart 1796-1868 . . . . DLB-96

Milne, A. A. 1882-1956 . . . . . DLB-10, 77, 100, 160

Milner, Ron 1938- DLB-38

Milner, William [publishing house] DLB-106

Milnes, Richard Monckton (Lord Houghton)
1809-1885 . . . . DLB-32, 184

Milton, John 1608-1674 . . . . DLB-131, 151

Miłosz, Czesław 1911- DLB-215

Minakami Tsutomu 1919- DLB-182

Minamoto no Sanetomo 1192-1219 . . . . . DLB-203

The Minerva Press DLB-154

Minnesang circa 1150-1280 . . . . DLB-138

Minns, Susan 1839-1938 . . . . DLB-140

Minor Illustrators, 1880-1914 . . . . DLB-141

Minor Poets of the Earlier Seventeenth
Century DLB-121

Minton, Balch and Company DLB-46

Mirbeau, Octave 1848-1917 . . . . DLB-123, 192

Mirk, John died after 1414? DLB-146

Miron, Gaston 1928- DLB-60

A Mirror for Magistrates DLB-167

Mishima Yukio 1925-1970 . . . . DLB-182

Mitchel, Jonathan 1624-1668 . . . . DLB-24

Mitchell, Adrian 1932- DLB-40

Mitchell, Donald Grant
1822-1908 . . . . DLB-1; DS-13

Mitchell, Gladys 1901-1983 . . . . DLB-77

Mitchell, James Leslie 1901-1935 . . . . DLB-15

Mitchell, John (see Slater, Patrick)

Mitchell, John Ames 1845-1918 . . . . DLB-79

Mitchell, Joseph 1908-1996 . . . . DLB-185; Y-96

Mitchell, Julian 1935- DLB-14

Mitchell, Ken 1940- DLB-60

Mitchell, Langdon 1862-1935 . . . . DLB-7

Mitchell, Loften 1919- DLB-38

Mitchell, Margaret 1900-1949 . . . . DLB-9

Mitchell, S. Weir 1829-1914 . . . . DLB-202

Mitchell, W. O. 1914- DLB-88

Mitchison, Naomi Margaret (Haldane)
1897-1999 . . . . DLB-160, 191

Mitford, Mary Russell 1787-1855 . . . . DLB-110, 116

Mitford, Nancy 1904-1973 . . . . DLB-191

Mittelholzer, Edgar 1909-1965 . . . . DLB-117

Mitterer, Erika 1906- DLB-85

Mitterer, Felix 1948- DLB-124

Mitternacht, Johann Sebastian
1613-1679 . . . . DLB-168

Miyamoto, Yuriko 1899-1951 . . . . DLB-180

Mizener, Arthur 1907-1988 . . . . DLB-103

Mo, Timothy 1950- DLB-194

Modern Age Books DLB-46

"Modern English Prose" (1876),
by George Saintsbury DLB-57

The Modern Language Association of America
Celebrates Its Centennial Y-84

The Modern Library DLB-46

"Modern Novelists – Great and Small" (1855), by
Margaret Oliphant DLB-21

"Modern Style" (1857), by Cockburn
Thomson [excerpt] DLB-57

The Modernists (1932),
by Joseph Warren Beach DLB-36

Modiano, Patrick 1945- DLB-83

Moffat, Yard and Company DLB-46

Moffet, Thomas 1553-1604 . . . . DLB-136

Mohr, Nicholasa 1938- DLB-145

Moix, Ana María 1947- DLB-134

Molesworth, Louisa 1839-1921 . . . . DLB-135

Möllhausen, Balduin 1825-1905 . . . . DLB-129

Molnár, Ferenc 1878-1952 . . . . DLB-215

Momaday, N. Scott 1934- DLB-143, 175

Monkhouse, Allan 1858-1936 . . . . DLB-10

Monro, Harold 1879-1932 . . . . DLB-19

Monroe, Harriet 1860-1936 . . . . DLB-54, 91

Monsarrat, Nicholas 1910-1979 . . . . DLB-15

Montagu, Lady Mary Wortley
1689-1762 . . . . DLB-95, 101

Montague, C. E. 1867-1928 . . . . DLB-197

Montague, John 1929- DLB-40

Montale, Eugenio 1896-1981 . . . . DLB-114

Montalvo, José 1946-1994 . . . . DLB-209

Monterroso, Augusto 1921- DLB-145

Montesquiou, Robert de 1855-1921 . . . . . DLB-217

Montgomerie, Alexander
circa 1550?-1598 . . . . DLB-167

Montgomery, James 1771-1854 . . . . . DLB-93, 158

Montgomery, John 1919- DLB-16

Montgomery, Lucy Maud
1874-1942 . . . . DLB-92; DS-14

Montgomery, Marion 1925- DLB-6

Montgomery, Robert Bruce (see Crispin, Edmund)

Montherlant, Henry de 1896-1972 . . . . . . DLB-72

The Monthly Review 1749-1844 . . . . DLB-110

Montigny, Louvigny de 1876-1955 . . . . . . DLB-92

Montoya, José 1932- DLB-122

Moodie, John Wedderburn Dunbar
1797-1869 . . . . DLB-99

Moodie, Susanna 1803-1885 . . . . DLB-99

Moody, Joshua circa 1633-1697 . . . . DLB-24

Moody, William Vaughn 1869-1910 . . . . DLB-7, 54

Moorcock, Michael 1939- DLB-14

Moore, Catherine L. 1911- DLB-8

Moore, Clement Clarke 1779-1863 . . . . DLB-42

Moore, Dora Mavor 1888-1979 . . . . DLB-92

Moore, George 1852-1933 . . . . DLB-10, 18, 57, 135

Moore, Marianne 1887-1972 . . . . . . DLB-45; DS-7

Moore, Mavor 1919- DLB-88

Moore, Richard 1927- DLB-105

Moore, T. Sturge 1870-1944 . . . . DLB-19

Moore, Thomas 1779-1852 . . . . DLB-96, 144

Moore, Ward 1903-1978 . . . . DLB-8

Moore, Wilstach, Keys and Company DLB-49

Moorehead, Alan 1901-1983 . . . . DLB-204

Moorhouse, Geoffrey 1931- DLB-204

The Moorland-Spingarn Research
Center DLB-76

Moorman, Mary C. 1905-1994 . . . . DLB-155

Mora, Pat 1942- DLB-209

Moraga, Cherríe 1952- DLB-82

Morales, Alejandro 1944- DLB-82

Morales, Mario Roberto 1947- DLB-145

Morales, Rafael 1919- DLB-108

Morality Plays: *Mankind* circa 1450-1500 and
Everyman circa 1500 . . . . DLB-146

Morante, Elsa 1912-1985 . . . . DLB-177

Morata, Olympia Fulvia 1526-1555 . . . . . DLB-179

Moravia, Alberto 1907-1990 . . . . DLB-177

Mordaunt, Elinor 1872-1942 . . . . DLB-174

More, Hannah
1745-1833 . . . . DLB-107, 109, 116, 158

More, Henry 1614-1687 . . . . DLB-126

More, Sir Thomas
1477 or 1478-1535 . . . . DLB-136

Moreno, Dorinda 1939- DLB-122

Morency, Pierre 1942- DLB-60

Moretti, Marino 1885-1979 . . . . DLB-114

Morgan, Berry 1919- DLB-6

Morgan, Charles 1894-1958 . . . . DLB-34, 100

Morgan, Edmund S. 1916- DLB-17

Morgan, Edwin 1920- DLB-27

Morgan, John Pierpont 1837-1913 . . . . . DLB-140

Morgan, John Pierpont, Jr. 1867-1943 . . . . DLB-140

Morgan, Robert 1944- DLB-120

Morgan, Sydney Owenson, Lady
1776?-1859. . . . . .DLB-116, 158

Morgner, Irmtraud 1933- DLB-75

Morhof, Daniel Georg 1639-1691 . . . . . . .DLB-164

Mori, Ōgai 1862-1922 . . . . .DLB-180

Morier, James Justinian
1782 or 1783?-1849 . . . . .DLB-116

Mörike, Eduard 1804-1875 . . . . .DLB-133

Morin, Paul 1889-1963 . . . . .DLB-92

Morison, Richard 1514?-1556 . . . . .DLB-136

Morison, Samuel Eliot 1887-1976. . . . . . . .DLB-17

Morison, Stanley 1889-1967 . . . . .DLB-201

Moritz, Karl Philipp 1756-1793 . . . . .DLB-94

Moriz von Craûn circa 1220-1230 . . . . .DLB-138

Morley, Christopher 1890-1957. . . . . .DLB-9

Morley, John 1838-1923 . . . . DLB-57, 144, 190

Morris, George Pope 1802-1864 . . . . .DLB-73

Morris, James Humphrey (see Morris, Jan)

Morris, Jan 1926- DLB-204

Morris, Lewis 1833-1907 . . . . .DLB-35

Morris, Margaret 1737-1816. . . . . .DLB-200

Morris, Richard B. 1904-1989 . . . . .DLB-17

Morris, William
1834-1896 . . . . . .DLB-18, 35, 57, 156, 178, 184

Morris, Willie 1934-1999. . . . . Y-80

Morris, Wright
1910-1998 . . . . DLB-2, 206, 218; Y-81

Morrison, Arthur 1863-1945 . . . . DLB-70, 135, 197

Morrison, Charles Clayton 1874-1966. . . . .DLB-91

Morrison, Toni
1931- DLB-6, 33, 143; Y-81, Y-93

Morrow, William, and Company DLB-46

Morse, James Herbert 1841-1923 . . . . .DLB-71

Morse, Jedidiah 1761-1826. . . . . .DLB-37

Morse, John T., Jr. 1840-1937 . . . . .DLB-47

Morselli, Guido 1912-1973. . . . . .DLB-177

Mortimer, Favell Lee 1802-1878 . . . . .DLB-163

Mortimer, John 1923- DLB-13

Morton, Carlos 1942- DLB-122

Morton, H. V. 1892-1979 . . . . .DLB-195

Morton, John P., and Company DLB-49

Morton, Nathaniel 1613-1685 . . . . .DLB-24

Morton, Sarah Wentworth 1759-1846. . . . . .DLB-37

Morton, Thomas circa 1579-circa 1647 . . . .DLB-24

Moscherosch, Johann Michael
1601-1669 . . . . .DLB-164

Moseley, Humphrey
[publishing house] DLB-170

Möser, Justus 1720-1794. . . . . .DLB-97

Mosley, Nicholas 1923- DLB-14, 207

Moss, Arthur 1889-1969 . . . . .DLB-4

Moss, Howard 1922-1987 . . . . .DLB-5

Moss, Thylias 1954- DLB-120

The Most Powerful Book Review in America
[*New York Times Book Review*] Y-82

Motion, Andrew 1952- DLB-40

Motley, John Lothrop 1814-1877. . . . DLB-1, 30, 59

Motley, Willard 1909-1965 . . . . DLB-76, 143

Motte, Benjamin Jr. [publishing house] . . .DLB-154

Motteux, Peter Anthony 1663-1718. . . . . . .DLB-80

Mottram, R. H. 1883-1971. . . . . .DLB-36

Mouré, Erin 1955- DLB-60

Mourning Dove (Humishuma) between
1882 and 1888?-1936 . . . . DLB-175, 221

Movies from Books, 1920-1974 . . . . .DLB-9

Mowat, Farley 1921- DLB-68

Mowbray, A. R., and Company,
Limited DLB-106

Mowrer, Edgar Ansel 1892-1977 . . . . .DLB-29

Mowrer, Paul Scott 1887-1971 . . . . .DLB-29

Moxon, Edward [publishing house]. DLB-106

Moxon, Joseph [publishing house]. DLB-170

Móricz, Zsigmond 1879-1942 . . . . .DLB-215

Mphahlele, Es'kia (Ezekiel) 1919- DLB-125

Mtshali, Oswald Mbuyiseni 1940- DLB-125

Mucedorus. .DLB-62

Mudford, William 1782-1848 . . . . .DLB-159

Mueller, Lisel 1924- DLB-105

Muhajir, El (see Marvin X)

Muhajir, Nazzam Al Fitnah (see Marvin X)

Mühlbach, Luise 1814-1873. . . . . .DLB-133

Muir, Edwin 1887-1959 . . . . DLB-20, 100, 191

Muir, Helen 1937- DLB-14

Muir, John 1838-1914 . . . . .DLB-186

Muir, Percy 1894-1979. . . . . .DLB-201

Mujū Ichien 1226-1312 . . . . .DLB-203

Mukherjee, Bharati 1940- DLB-60, 218

Mulcaster, Richard
1531 or 1532-1611 . . . . .DLB-167

Muldoon, Paul 1951- DLB-40

Müller, Friedrich (see Müller, Maler)

Müller, Heiner 1929-1995 . . . . .DLB-124

Müller, Maler 1749-1825 . . . . .DLB-94

Muller, Marcia 1944- DLB-226

Müller, Wilhelm 1794-1827 . . . . .DLB-90

Mumford, Lewis 1895-1990 . . . . .DLB-63

Munby, A. N. L. 1913-1974. . . . . .DLB-201

Munby, Arthur Joseph 1828-1910. . . . . . . .DLB-35

Munday, Anthony 1560-1633 . . . . . . DLB-62, 172

Mundt, Clara (see Mühlbach, Luise)

Mundt, Theodore 1808-1861 . . . . .DLB-133

Munford, Robert circa 1737-1783. . . . . . . .DLB-31

Mungoshi, Charles 1947- DLB-157

Munk, Kaj 1898-1944 . . . . .DLB-214

Munonye, John 1929- DLB-117

Munro, Alice 1931- DLB-53

Munro, H. H. 1870-1916. . . . . .DLB-34, 162

Munro, Neil 1864-1930 . . . . .DLB-156

Munro, George [publishing house] DLB-49

Munro, Norman L. [publishing house] DLB-49

Munroe, James, and Company DLB-49

Munroe, Kirk 1850-1930. . . . . .DLB-42

Munroe and Francis. DLB-49

Munsell, Joel [publishing house] DLB-49

Munsey, Frank A. 1854-1925 . . . . .DLB-25, 91

Munsey, Frank A., and Company. DLB-49

Murakami Haruki 1949- DLB-182

Murav'ev, Mikhail Nikitich
1757-1807. . . . . .DLB-150

Murdoch, Iris 1919-1999. . . . . .DLB-14, 194

Murdoch, Rupert 1931- DLB-127

Murfree, Mary N. 1850-1922 . . . . .DLB-12, 74

Murger, Henry 1822-1861. . . . . .DLB-119

Murger, Louis-Henri (see Murger, Henry)

Murner, Thomas 1475-1537 . . . . .DLB-179

Muro, Amado 1915-1971. . . . . .DLB-82

Murphy, Arthur 1727-1805 . . . . .DLB-89, 142

Murphy, Beatrice M. 1908- DLB-76

Murphy, Dervla 1931- DLB-204

Murphy, Emily 1868-1933 . . . . .DLB-99

Murphy, John H., III 1916- DLB-127

Murphy, John, and Company DLB-49

Murphy, Richard 1927-1993 . . . . .DLB-40

Murray, Albert L. 1916- DLB-38

Murray, Gilbert 1866-1957 . . . . .DLB-10

Murray, Judith Sargent 1751-1820. . . . DLB-37, 200

Murray, Pauli 1910-1985. . . . . .DLB-41

Murray, John [publishing house] DLB-154

Murry, John Middleton 1889-1957 . . . . . .DLB-149

Musäus, Johann Karl August 1735-1787 . . .DLB-97

Muschg, Adolf 1934- DLB-75

The Music of *Minnesang*. DLB-138

Musil, Robert 1880-1942. . . . . .DLB-81, 124

Muspilli circa 790-circa 850. . . . . .DLB-148

Musset, Alfred de 1810-1857 . . . . . . .DLB-192, 217

Mussey, Benjamin B., and Company DLB-49

Mutafchieva, Vera 1929- DLB-181

Mwangi, Meja 1948- DLB-125

Myers, Frederic W. H. 1843-1901. . . . . . .DLB-190

Myers, Gustavus 1872-1942 . . . . .DLB-47

Myers, L. H. 1881-1944 . . . . .DLB-15

Myers, Walter Dean 1937- DLB-33

Mykolaitis-Putinas, Vincas 1893-1967. . . .DLB-220

Myles, Eileen 1949- DLB-193

N

Na Prous Boneta circa 1296-1328 . . . . . . .DLB-208

Nabl, Franz 1883-1974. . . . . .DLB-81

Nabokov, Vladimir
1899-1977 . . . . DLB-2; Y-80, Y-91; DS-3

Nabokov Festival at Cornell Y-83

The Vladimir Nabokov Archive
in the Berg Collection Y-91

Nádaši, Ladislav (see Jégé)

Naden, Constance 1858-1889 . . . . .DLB-199

Nadezhdin, Nikolai Ivanovich 1804-1856 . . . . DLB-198

Naevius circa 265 B.C.-201 B.C. DLB-211

Nafis and Cornish. DLB-49

Nagai, Kafū 1879-1959 . . . . DLB-180

Naipaul, Shiva 1945-1985 . . . . DLB-157; Y-85

Naipaul, V. S. 1932- . . . DLB-125, 204, 207; Y-85

Nakagami Kenji 1946-1992 . . . . DLB-182

Nakano-in Masatada no Musume (see Nijō, Lady)

Nałkowska, Zofia 1884-1954 . . . . DLB-215

Nancrede, Joseph [publishing house] DLB-49

Naranjo, Carmen 1930- DLB-145

Narezhny, Vasilii Trofimovich 1780-1825 . . . . DLB-198

Narrache, Jean 1893-1970 . . . . DLB-92

Nasby, Petroleum Vesuvius (see Locke, David Ross)

Nash, Ogden 1902-1971 . . . . DLB-11

Nash, Eveleigh [publishing house] DLB-112

Nashe, Thomas 1567-1601? DLB-167

Nast, Conde 1873-1942 . . . . DLB-91

Nast, Thomas 1840-1902 . . . . DLB-188

Nastasijević, Momčilo 1894-1938 . . . . DLB-147

Nathan, George Jean 1882-1958 . . . . DLB-137

Nathan, Robert 1894-1985 . . . . DLB-9

The National Jewish Book Awards Y-85

The National Theatre and the Royal Shakespeare Company: The National Companies. DLB-13

Natsume, Sōseki 1867-1916 . . . . DLB-180

Naughton, Bill 1910- DLB-13

Navarro, Joe 1953- DLB-209

Naylor, Gloria 1950- DLB-173

Nazor, Vladimir 1876-1949 . . . . DLB-147

Ndebele, Njabulo 1948- DLB-157

Neagoe, Peter 1881-1960 . . . . DLB-4

Neal, John 1793-1876 . . . . DLB-1, 59

Neal, Joseph C. 1807-1847 . . . . DLB-11

Neal, Larry 1937-1981 . . . . DLB-38

The Neale Publishing Company DLB-49

Nebel, Frederick 1903-1967 . . . . DLB-226

Neely, F. Tennyson [publishing house]. . . . DLB-49

Negoiţescu, Ion 1921-1993 . . . . DLB-220

Negri, Ada 1870-1945 . . . . DLB-114

"The Negro as a Writer," by G. M. McClellan DLB-50

"Negro Poets and Their Poetry," by Wallace Thurman DLB-50

Neidhart von Reuental circa 1185-circa 1240 . . . . DLB-138

Neihardt, John G. 1881-1973 . . . . DLB-9, 54

Neledinsky-Meletsky, Iurii Aleksandrovich 1752-1828. DLB-150

Nelligan, Emile 1879-1941 . . . . DLB-92

Nelson, Alice Moore Dunbar 1875-1935 . . DLB-50

Nelson, Thomas, and Sons [U.S.] DLB-49

Nelson, Thomas, and Sons [U.K.] DLB-106

Nelson, William 1908-1978. . . . . DLB-103

Nelson, William Rockhill 1841-1915 . . . . . DLB-23

Nemerov, Howard 1920-1991 . . . . .DLB-5, 6; Y-83

Nepos circa 100 B.C.-post 27 B.C. DLB-211

Nèris, Salomėja 1904-1945 . . . . DLB-220

Nerval, Gerard de 1808-1855 . . . . DLB-217

Nesbit, E. 1858-1924 . . . . .DLB-141, 153, 178

Ness, Evaline 1911-1986. . . . . DLB-61

Nestroy, Johann 1801-1862 . . . . DLB-133

Neukirch, Benjamin 1655-1729. . . . . DLB-168

Neugeboren, Jay 1938- DLB-28

Neumann, Alfred 1895-1952 . . . . DLB-56

Neumann, Ferenc (see Molnár, Ferenc)

Neumark, Georg 1621-1681. . . . . DLB-164

Neumeister, Erdmann 1671-1756 . . . . DLB-168

Nevins, Allan 1890-1971. . . . . .DLB-17; DS-17

Nevinson, Henry Woodd 1856-1941 . . . . DLB-135

The New American Library DLB-46

New Approaches to Biography: Challenges from Critical Theory, USC Conference on Literary Studies, 1990. . . . . Y-90

New Directions Publishing Corporation DLB-46

A New Edition of *Huck Finn* Y-85

New Forces at Work in the American Theatre: 1915-1925 . . . . DLB-7

New Literary Periodicals: A Report for 1987 . . . . Y-87

New Literary Periodicals: A Report for 1988 . . . . Y-88

New Literary Periodicals: A Report for 1989 . . . . Y-89

New Literary Periodicals: A Report for 1990 . . . . Y-90

New Literary Periodicals: A Report for 1991 . . . . Y-91

New Literary Periodicals: A Report for 1992 . . . . Y-92

New Literary Periodicals: A Report for 1993 . . . . Y-93

The New Monthly Magazine 1814-1884 . . . . DLB-110

The New Ulysses Y-84

The New Variorum Shakespeare Y-85

A New Voice: The Center for the Book's First Five Years Y-83

The New Wave [Science Fiction] DLB-8

New York City Bookshops in the 1930s and 1940s: The Recollections of Walter Goldwater. . . Y-93

Newbery, John [publishing house] DLB-154

Newbolt, Henry 1862-1938 . . . . DLB-19

Newbound, Bernard Slade (see Slade, Bernard)

Newby, Eric 1919- DLB-204

Newby, P. H. 1918- DLB-15

Newby, Thomas Cautley [publishing house] DLB-106

Newcomb, Charles King 1820-1894. . . DLB-1, 223

Newell, Peter 1862-1924. . . . . DLB-42

Newell, Robert Henry 1836-1901. . . . . . . DLB-11

Newhouse, Samuel I. 1895-1979 . . . . DLB-127

Newman, Cecil Earl 1903-1976 . . . . .DLB-127

Newman, David (see Benton, Robert)

Newman, Frances 1883-1928 . . . . Y-80

Newman, Francis William 1805-1897. . . . DLB-190

Newman, John Henry 1801-1890 . . . . DLB-18, 32, 55

Newman, Mark [publishing house] DLB-49

Newnes, George, Limited. DLB-112

Newsome, Effie Lee 1885-1979. . . . . DLB-76

Newspaper Syndication of American Humor DLB-11

Newton, A. Edward 1864-1940 . . . . DLB-140

Nexø, Martin Andersen 1869-1954 . . . . . DLB-214

Nezval, Vítěslav 1900-1958 . . . . DLB-215

Németh, László 1901-1975 . . . . DLB-215

Ngugi wa Thiong'o 1938- DLB-125

Niatum, Duane 1938- DLB-175

The *Nibelungenlied* and the *Klage* circa 1200. . . . . DLB-138

Nichol, B. P. 1944- DLB-53

Nicholas of Cusa 1401-1464. . . . . DLB-115

Nichols, Beverly 1898-1983 . . . . DLB-191

Nichols, Dudley 1895-1960 . . . . DLB-26

Nichols, Grace 1950- DLB-157

Nichols, John 1940- Y-82

Nichols, Mary Sargeant (Neal) Gove 1810-1884 . . . . DLB-1

Nichols, Peter 1927- DLB-13

Nichols, Roy F. 1896-1973 . . . . .DLB-17

Nichols, Ruth 1948- DLB-60

Nicholson, Edward Williams Byron 1849-1912 . . . . DLB-184

Nicholson, Norman 1914- DLB-27

Nicholson, William 1872-1949 . . . . DLB-141

Ní Chuilleanáin, Eiléan 1942- DLB-40

Nicol, Eric 1919- DLB-68

Nicolai, Friedrich 1733-1811. . . . . DLB-97

Nicolas de Clamanges circa 1363-1437. . . DLB-208

Nicolay, John G. 1832-1901 and Hay, John 1838-1905. . . . . DLB-47

Nicolson, Harold 1886-1968 . . . . . . .DLB-100, 149

Nicolson, Nigel 1917- DLB-155

Niebuhr, Reinhold 1892-1971. . . . . .DLB-17; DS-17

Niedecker, Lorine 1903-1970 . . . . DLB-48

Nieman, Lucius W. 1857-1935 . . . . DLB-25

Nietzsche, Friedrich 1844-1900. . . . . DLB-129

Nievo, Stanislao 1928- DLB-196

Niggli, Josefina 1910- Y-80

Nightingale, Florence 1820-1910 . . . . DLB-166

Nijō, Lady (Nakano-in Masatada no Musume) 1258-after 1306 . . . . DLB-203

Nijō, Yoshimoto 1320-1388 . . . . DLB-203

Nikolev, Nikolai Petrovich 1758-1815. . . . . DLB-150

Niles, Hezekiah 1777-1839 . . . . DLB-43

Nims, John Frederick 1913-1999 . . . . DLB-5

Nin, Anaïs 1903-1977 . . . . DLB-2, 4, 152

1985: The Year of the Mystery:
A Symposium Y-85

The 1997 Booker Prize Y-97

The 1998 Booker Prize Y-98

Niño, Raúl 1961- DLB-209

Nissenson, Hugh 1933- DLB-28

Niven, Frederick John 1878-1944. . . . . DLB-92

Niven, Larry 1938- DLB-8

Nixon, Howard M. 1909-1983 . . . . DLB-201

Nizan, Paul 1905-1940. . . . . DLB-72

Njegoš, Petar II Petrović 1813-1851 . . . . . DLB-147

Nkosi, Lewis 1936- DLB-157

"The No Self, the Little Self, and the Poets,"
by Richard Moore. DLB-105

Nobel Peace Prize

The 1986 Nobel Peace Prize: Elie Wiesel Y-86

The Nobel Prize and Literary Politics Y-86

Nobel Prize in Literature

The 1982 Nobel Prize in Literature:
Gabriel García Márquez Y-82

The 1983 Nobel Prize in Literature:
William Golding Y-83

The 1984 Nobel Prize in Literature:
Jaroslav Seifert. Y-84

The 1985 Nobel Prize in Literature:
Claude Simon Y-85

The 1986 Nobel Prize in Literature:
Wole Soyinka Y-86

The 1987 Nobel Prize in Literature:
Joseph Brodsky Y-87

The 1988 Nobel Prize in Literature:
Najīb Mahfūz Y-88

The 1989 Nobel Prize in Literature:
Camilo José Cela. Y-89

The 1990 Nobel Prize in Literature:
Octavio Paz Y-90

The 1991 Nobel Prize in Literature:
Nadine Gordimer Y-91

The 1992 Nobel Prize in Literature:
Derek Walcott. Y-92

The 1993 Nobel Prize in Literature:
Toni Morrison Y-93

The 1994 Nobel Prize in Literature:
Kenzaburō Ōe Y-94

The 1995 Nobel Prize in Literature:
Seamus Heaney. Y-95

The 1996 Nobel Prize in Literature:
Wisława Szymborsha Y-96

The 1997 Nobel Prize in Literature:
Dario Fo Y-97

The 1998 Nobel Prize in Literature:
José Saramago Y-98

The 1999 Nobel Prize in Literature:
Günter Grass. Y-99

Nodier, Charles 1780-1844 . . . . DLB-119

Noel, Roden 1834-1894. . . . . DLB-35

Nogami, Yaeko 1885-1985. . . . . DLB-180

Nogo, Rajko Petrov 1945- DLB-181

Nolan, William F. 1928- DLB-8

Noland, C. F. M. 1810?-1858. . . . . DLB-11

Noma Hiroshi 1915-1991 . . . . DLB-182

Nonesuch Press DLB-112

Noonan, Robert Phillipe
(see Tressell, Robert)

Noonday Press. DLB-46

Noone, John 1936- DLB-14

Nora, Eugenio de 1923- DLB-134

Nordbrandt, Henrik 1945- DLB-214

Nordhoff, Charles 1887-1947. . . . . DLB-9

Norman, Charles 1904-1996 . . . . DLB-111

Norman, Marsha 1947- Y-84

Norris, Charles G. 1881-1945 . . . . DLB-9

Norris, Frank 1870-1902 . . . . DLB-12, 71, 186

Norris, Leslie 1921- DLB-27

Norse, Harold 1916- DLB-16

Norte, Marisela 1955- DLB-209

North, Marianne 1830-1890 . . . . DLB-174

North Point Press DLB-46

Nortje, Arthur 1942-1970. . . . . DLB-125

Norton, Alice Mary (see Norton, Andre)

Norton, Andre 1912- DLB-8, 52

Norton, Andrews 1786-1853 . . . . DLB-1

Norton, Caroline 1808-1877 . . . . DLB-21, 159, 199

Norton, Charles Eliot 1827-1908 . . . . . . DLB-1, 64

Norton, John 1606-1663 . . . . DLB-24

Norton, Mary 1903-1992. . . . . DLB-160

Norton, Thomas (see Sackville, Thomas)

Norton, W. W., and Company DLB-46

Norwood, Robert 1874-1932 . . . . DLB-92

Nosaka Akiyuki 1930- DLB-182

Nossack, Hans Erich 1901-1977 . . . . DLB-69

Not Immediately Discernible . . . but Eventually
Quite Clear: The *First Light* and *Final Years*
of Hemingway's Centenary Y-99

A Note on Technique (1926), by
Elizabeth A. Drew [excerpts]. DLB-36

Notker Balbulus circa 840-912. . . . . DLB-148

Notker III of Saint Gall
circa 950-1022 . . . . DLB-148

Notker von Zweifalten ?-1095 . . . . DLB-148

Nourse, Alan E. 1928- DLB-8

Novak, Slobodan 1924- DLB-181

Novak, Vjenceslav 1859-1905 . . . . DLB-147

Novalis 1772-1801 . . . . DLB-90

Novaro, Mario 1868-1944. . . . . DLB-114

Novás Calvo, Lino 1903-1983. . . . . DLB-145

"The Novel in [Robert Browning's] 'The Ring
and the Book'" (1912), by
Henry James DLB-32

The Novel of Impressionism,
by Jethro Bithell DLB-66

Novel-Reading: *The Works of Charles Dickens,
The Works of W. Makepeace Thackeray*
(1879), by Anthony Trollope DLB-21

Novels for Grown-Ups Y-97

The Novels of Dorothy Richardson (1918),
by May Sinclair DLB-36

Novels with a Purpose (1864), by
Justin M'Carthy DLB-21

Noventa, Giacomo 1898-1960. . . . . DLB-114

Novikov, Nikolai Ivanovich
1744-1818 . . . . DLB-150

Novomeský, Laco 1904-1976. . . . . DLB-215

Nowlan, Alden 1933-1983. . . . . DLB-53

Noyes, Alfred 1880-1958. . . . . DLB-20

Noyes, Crosby S. 1825-1908 . . . . DLB-23

Noyes, Nicholas 1647-1717. . . . . DLB-24

Noyes, Theodore W. 1858-1946. . . . . DLB-29

N-Town Plays circa 1468 to early
sixteenth century DLB-146

Nugent, Frank 1908-1965 . . . . DLB-44

Nugent, Richard Bruce 1906- DLB-151

Nušić, Branislav 1864-1938 . . . . DLB-147

Nutt, David [publishing house] DLB-106

Nwapa, Flora 1931-1993 . . . . DLB-125

Nye, Bill 1850-1896. . . . . DLB-186

Nye, Edgar Wilson (Bill)
1850-1896 . . . . DLB-11, 23

Nye, Naomi Shihab 1952- DLB-120

Nye, Robert 1939- DLB-14

Nyka-Niliūnas, Alfonsas 1919- DLB-220

O

Oakes, Urian circa 1631-1681 . . . . DLB-24

Oakley, Violet 1874-1961 . . . . DLB-188

Oates, Joyce Carol 1938- . . . DLB-2, 5, 130; Y-81

Ōba Minako 1930- DLB-182

Ober, Frederick Albion 1849-1913 . . . . . . DLB-189

Ober, William 1920-1993 . . . . Y-93

Oberholtzer, Ellis Paxson 1868-1936. . . . . DLB-47

Obradović, Dositej 1740?-1811 . . . . DLB-147

O'Brien, Edna 1932- DLB-14

O'Brien, Fitz-James 1828-1862. . . . . DLB-74

O'Brien, Kate 1897-1974 . . . . DLB-15

O'Brien, Tim 1946- DLB-152; Y-80; DS-9

O'Casey, Sean 1880-1964 . . . . DLB-10

Occom, Samson 1723-1792 . . . . DLB-175

Ochs, Adolph S. 1858-1935 . . . . DLB-25

Ochs-Oakes, George Washington
1861-1931 . . . . DLB-137

O'Connor, Flannery
1925-1964 . . . . DLB-2, 152; Y-80; DS-12

O'Connor, Frank 1903-1966 . . . . DLB-162

Octopus Publishing Group DLB-112

Oda Sakunosuke 1913-1947 . . . . DLB-182

Odell, Jonathan 1737-1818 . . . . DLB-31, 99

O'Dell, Scott 1903-1989. . . . . DLB-52

Odets, Clifford 1906-1963 . . . . DLB-7, 26

Odhams Press Limited DLB-112

Odoevsky, Aleksandr Ivanovich
1802-1839 . . . . DLB-205

Odoevsky, Vladimir Fedorovich
1804 or 1803-1869 . . . . DLB-198

O'Donnell, Peter 1920- DLB-87

O'Donovan, Michael (see O'Connor, Frank)

Ōe Kenzaburō 1935- DLB-182; Y-94

O'Faolain, Julia 1932- DLB-14

O'Faolain, Sean 1900- DLB-15, 162

Off Broadway and Off-Off Broadway DLB-7

Off-Loop Theatres DLB-7

Offord, Carl Ruthven 1910- DLB-76

O'Flaherty, Liam 1896-1984....DLB-36, 162; Y-84

Ogilvie, J. S., and Company DLB-49

Ogilvy, Eliza 1822-1912 .... DLB-199

Ogot, Grace 1930- DLB-125

O'Grady, Desmond 1935- DLB-40

Ogunyemi, Wale 1939- DLB-157

O'Hagan, Howard 1902-1982 .... DLB-68

O'Hara, Frank 1926-1966....... DLB-5, 16, 193

O'Hara, John 1905-1970........ DLB-9, 86; DS-2

O'Hegarty, P. S. 1879-1955 .... DLB-201

Okara, Gabriel 1921- DLB-125

O'Keeffe, John 1747-1833 .... DLB-89

Okes, Nicholas [publishing house] DLB-170

Okigbo, Christopher 1930-1967........ DLB-125

Okot p'Bitek 1931-1982 .... DLB-125

Okpewho, Isidore 1941- DLB-157

Okri, Ben 1959- DLB-157

Olaudah Equiano and Unfinished Journeys:
    The Slave-Narrative Tradition and
    Twentieth-Century Continuities, by
    Paul Edwards and Pauline T.
    Wangman DLB-117

Old English Literature:
    An Introduction DLB-146

Old English Riddles
    eighth to tenth centuries.......... DLB-146

Old Franklin Publishing House DLB-49

Old German Genesis and Old German Exodus
    circa 1050-circa 1130 .... DLB-148

Old High German Charms and
    Blessings..................... DLB-148

The Old High German Isidor
    circa 790-800 .... DLB-148

The Old Manse DLB-223

Older, Fremont 1856-1935........... DLB-25

Oldham, John 1653-1683 .... DLB-131

Oldman, C. B. 1894-1969............. DLB-201

Olds, Sharon 1942- DLB-120

Olearius, Adam 1599-1671 .... DLB-164

Oliphant, Laurence 1829?-1888 ..... DLB-18, 166

Oliphant, Margaret 1828-1897 ...... DLB-18, 190

Oliver, Chad 1928- DLB-8

Oliver, Mary 1935- DLB-5, 193

Ollier, Claude 1922- DLB-83

Olsen, Tillie
    1912 or 1913- DLB-28, 206; Y-80

Olson, Charles 1910-1970....... DLB-5, 16, 193

Olson, Elder 1909- DLB-48, 63

Omotoso, Kole 1943- DLB-125

"On Art in Fiction "(1838),
    by Edward Bulwer................ DLB-21

On Learning to Write.................... Y-88

On Some of the Characteristics of Modern
    Poetry and On the Lyrical Poems of
    Alfred Tennyson (1831), by Arthur
    Henry Hallam DLB-32

"On Style in English Prose" (1898), by
    Frederic Harrison................. DLB-57

"On Style in Literature: Its Technical
    Elements" (1885), by Robert Louis
    Stevenson DLB-57

"On the Writing of Essays" (1862),
    by Alexander Smith DLB-57

Ondaatje, Michael 1943- DLB-60

O'Neill, Eugene 1888-1953.............. DLB-7

Onetti, Juan Carlos 1909-1994........ DLB-113

Onions, George Oliver 1872-1961 ...... DLB-153

Onofri, Arturo 1885-1928 .... DLB-114

Opie, Amelia 1769-1853 .... DLB-116, 159

Opitz, Martin 1597-1639.............. DLB-164

Oppen, George 1908-1984 .... DLB-5, 165

Oppenheim, E. Phillips 1866-1946....... DLB-70

Oppenheim, James 1882-1932 .... DLB-28

Oppenheimer, Joel 1930-1988 .... DLB-5, 193

Optic, Oliver (see Adams, William Taylor)

Oral History: B. W. Huebsch............. Y-99

Oral History Interview with Donald S.
    Klopfer.......................... Y-97

Orczy, Emma, Baroness 1865-1947 ..... DLB-70

Origo, Iris 1902-1988 .... DLB-155

Orlovitz, Gil 1918-1973 .... DLB-2, 5

Orlovsky, Peter 1933- DLB-16

Ormond, John 1923- DLB-27

Ornitz, Samuel 1890-1957 .... DLB-28, 44

O'Rourke, P. J. 1947- DLB-185

Orten, Jiří 1919-1941 .... DLB-215

Ortese, Anna Maria 1914- DLB-177

Ortiz, Simon J. 1941- DLB-120, 175

Ortnit and Wolfdietrich circa 1225-1250.... DLB-138

Orton, Joe 1933-1967 .... DLB-13

Orwell, George 1903-1950 ...... DLB-15, 98, 195

The Orwell Year....................... Y-84

Ory, Carlos Edmundo de 1923- DLB-134

Osbey, Brenda Marie 1957- DLB-120

Osbon, B. S. 1827-1912................ DLB-43

Osborn, Sarah 1714-1796 .... DLB-200

Osborne, John 1929-1994.............. DLB-13

Osgood, Herbert L. 1855-1918......... DLB-47

Osgood, James R., and Company DLB-49

Osgood, McIlvaine and Company DLB-112

O'Shaughnessy, Arthur 1844-1881....... DLB-35

O'Shea, Patrick [publishing house]....... DLB-49

Osipov, Nikolai Petrovich 1751-1799 .... DLB-150

Oskison, John Milton 1879-1947 ....DLB-175

Osler, Sir William 1849-1919 .... DLB-184

Osofisan, Femi 1946- DLB-125

Ostenso, Martha 1900-1963 .... DLB-92

Ostriker, Alicia 1937- DLB-120

Osundare, Niyi 1947- DLB-157

Oswald, Eleazer 1755-1795 .... DLB-43

Oswald von Wolkenstein
    1376 or 1377-1445 ....DLB-179

Otero, Blas de 1916-1979 .... DLB-134

Otero, Miguel Antonio 1859-1944 ...... DLB-82

Otero, Nina 1881-1965............... DLB-209

Otero Silva, Miguel 1908-1985........ DLB-145

Otfried von Weißenburg
    circa 800-circa 875? DLB-148

Otis, James (see Kaler, James Otis)

Otis, James, Jr. 1725-1783 .... DLB-31

Otis, Broaders and Company........... DLB-49

Ottaway, James 1911- DLB-127

Ottendorfer, Oswald 1826-1900........ DLB-23

Ottieri, Ottiero 1924- DLB-177

Otto-Peters, Louise 1819-1895 .... DLB-129

Otway, Thomas 1652-1685 .... DLB-80

Ouellette, Fernand 1930- DLB-60

Ouida 1839-1908 .... DLB-18, 156

Outing Publishing Company DLB-46

Outlaw Days, by Joyce Johnson........ DLB-16

Overbury, Sir Thomas
    circa 1581-1613 .... DLB-151

The Overlook Press DLB-46

Overview of U.S. Book Publishing,
    1910-1945 .... DLB-9

Ovid 43 B.C.-A.D. 17............... DLB-211

Owen, Guy 1925- DLB-5

Owen, John 1564-1622............... DLB-121

Owen, John [publishing house]......... DLB-49

Owen, Robert 1771-1858 ....DLB-107, 158

Owen, Wilfred 1893-1918 .... DLB-20; DS-18

Owen, Peter, Limited DLB-112

The Owl and the Nightingale
    circa 1189-1199 .... DLB-146

Owsley, Frank L. 1890-1956 ....DLB-17

Oxford, Seventeenth Earl of, Edward de Vere
    1550-1604 ....DLB-172

Ozerov, Vladislav Aleksandrovich
    1769-1816.................... DLB-150

Ozick, Cynthia 1928- DLB-28, 152; Y-82

P

Pace, Richard 1482?-1536 .... DLB-167

Pacey, Desmond 1917-1975 .... DLB-88

Pack, Robert 1929- DLB-5

Packaging Papa: The Garden of Eden Y-86

Padell Publishing Company DLB-46

Padgett, Ron 1942- DLB-5

Padilla, Ernesto Chávez 1944- DLB-122

Page, L. C., and Company............. DLB-49

Page, P. K. 1916- DLB-68

Page, Thomas Nelson
    1853-1922 ....DLB-12, 78; DS-13

Page, Walter Hines 1855-1918........DLB-71, 91

Paget, Francis Edward 1806-1882 ...... DLB-163

Paget, Violet (see Lee, Vernon)

Pagliarani, Elio 1927- DLB-128

Pain, Barry 1864-1928 . . . . DLB-135, 197

Pain, Philip ?-circa 1666 . . . . .DLB-24

Paine, Robert Treat, Jr. 1773-1811 . . . . . . .DLB-37

Paine, Thomas 1737-1809 . . . . DLB-31, 43, 73, 158

Painter, George D. 1914- DLB-155

Painter, William 1540?-1594 . . . . .DLB-136

Palazzeschi, Aldo 1885-1974 . . . . .DLB-114

Paley, Grace 1922- DLB-28, 218

Palfrey, John Gorham 1796-1881 . . . . . . .DLB-1, 30

Palgrave, Francis Turner 1824-1897 . . . . . .DLB-35

Palmer, Joe H. 1904-1952 . . . . .DLB-171

Palmer, Michael 1943- DLB-169

Paltock, Robert 1697-1767 . . . . .DLB-39

Paludan, Jacob 1896-1975 . . . . .DLB-214

Pan Books Limited DLB-112

Panama, Norman 1914- and
    Frank, Melvin 1913-1988 . . . . .DLB-26

Panaev, Ivan Ivanovich 1812-1862 . . . . . .DLB-198

Pancake, Breece D'J 1952-1979 . . . . .DLB-130

Panduro, Leif 1923-1977 . . . . .DLB-214

Panero, Leopoldo 1909-1962 . . . . .DLB-108

Pangborn, Edgar 1909-1976 . . . . .DLB-8

"Panic Among the Philistines": A Postscript,
    An Interview with Bryan Griffin Y-81

Panizzi, Sir Anthony 1797-1879 . . . . .DLB-184

Panneton, Philippe (see Ringuet)

Panshin, Alexei 1940- DLB-8

Pansy (see Alden, Isabella)

Pantheon Books DLB-46

Papadat-Bengescu, Hortensia
    1876-1955 . . . . .DLB-220

Papantonio, Michael (see Kohn, John S. Van E.)

Paperback Library .DLB-46

Paperback Science Fiction DLB-8

Paquet, Alfons 1881-1944 . . . . .DLB-66

Paracelsus 1493-1541 . . . . .DLB-179

Paradis, Suzanne 1936- DLB-53

Pardoe, Julia 1804-1862 . . . . .DLB-166

Paredes, Américo 1915-1999 . . . . .DLB-209

Pareja Diezcanseco, Alfredo
    1908-1993 . . . . .DLB-145

Parents' Magazine Press DLB-46

Parise, Goffredo 1929-1986 . . . . .DLB-177

Parisian Theater, Fall 1984: Toward
    A New Baroque Y-85

Parizeau, Alice 1930- DLB-60

Parke, John 1754-1789 . . . . .DLB-31

Parker, Dorothy 1893-1967 . . . . . . .DLB-11, 45, 86

Parker, Gilbert 1860-1932 . . . . .DLB-99

Parker, James 1714-1770 . . . . .DLB-43

Parker, Matthew 1504-1575 . . . . .DLB-213

Parker, Theodore 1810-1860 . . . . .DLB-1

Parker, William Riley 1906-1968 . . . . . . .DLB-103

Parker, J. H. [publishing house] DLB-106

Parker, John [publishing house] DLB-106

Parkman, Francis, Jr.
    1823-1893 . . . . DLB-1, 30, 183, 186

Parks, Gordon 1912- DLB-33

Parks, William 1698-1750 . . . . .DLB-43

Parks, William [publishing house] DLB-49

Parley, Peter (see Goodrich, Samuel Griswold)

Parmenides late sixth-fifth century B.C.
    . . . . .DLB-176

Parnell, Thomas 1679-1718 . . . . .DLB-95

Parnicki, Teodor 1908-1988 . . . . .DLB-215

Parr, Catherine 1513?-1548 . . . . .DLB-136

Parrington, Vernon L. 1871-1929 . . . . . DLB-17, 63

Parrish, Maxfield 1870-1966 . . . . .DLB-188

Parronchi, Alessandro 1914- DLB-128

Partridge, S. W., and Company DLB-106

Parton, James 1822-1891 . . . . .DLB-30

Parton, Sara Payson Willis
    1811-1872 . . . . .DLB-43, 74

Parun, Vesna 1922- DLB-181

Pasinetti, Pier Maria 1913- DLB-177

Pasolini, Pier Paolo 1922- DLB-128, 177

Pastan, Linda 1932- DLB-5

Paston, George (Emily Morse Symonds)
    1860-1936 . . . . DLB-149, 197

The Paston Letters 1422-1509 . . . . .DLB-146

Pastorius, Francis Daniel
    1651-circa 1720 . . . . .DLB-24

Patchen, Kenneth 1911-1972 . . . . .DLB-16, 48

Pater, Walter 1839-1894 . . . . DLB-57, 156

Paterson, Katherine 1932- DLB-52

Patmore, Coventry 1823-1896 . . . . . . .DLB-35, 98

Paton, Alan 1903-1988 . . . . DS-17

Paton, Joseph Noel 1821-1901 . . . . .DLB-35

Paton Walsh, Jill 1937- DLB-161

Patrick, Edwin Hill ("Ted") 1901-1964 . . .DLB-137

Patrick, John 1906-1995 . . . . .DLB-7

Pattee, Fred Lewis 1863-1950 . . . . .DLB-71

Pattern and Paradigm: History as
    Design, by Judith Ryan DLB-75

Patterson, Alicia 1906-1963 . . . . .DLB-127

Patterson, Eleanor Medill 1881-1948 . . . . .DLB-29

Patterson, Eugene 1923- DLB-127

Patterson, Joseph Medill 1879-1946 . . . . . .DLB-29

Pattillo, Henry 1726-1801 . . . . .DLB-37

Paul, Elliot 1891-1958 . . . . .DLB-4

Paul, Jean (see Richter, Johann Paul Friedrich)

Paul, Kegan, Trench, Trubner and Company
    Limited DLB-106

Paul, Peter, Book Company DLB-49

Paul, Stanley, and Company Limited DLB-112

Paulding, James Kirke 1778-1860 . . . .DLB-3, 59, 74

Paulin, Tom 1949- DLB-40

Pauper, Peter, Press DLB-46

Pavese, Cesare 1908-1950 . . . . DLB-128, 177

Pavlova, Karolina Karlovna
    1807-1893 . . . . .DLB-205

Pavić, Milorad 1929- DLB-181

Pavlov, Konstantin 1933- DLB-181

Pavlov, Nikolai Filippovich 1803-1864 . . . . .DLB-198

Pavlova, Karolina Karlovna 1807-1893 . . . .DLB-205

Pavlović, Miodrag 1928- DLB-181

Paxton, John 1911-1985 . . . . .DLB-44

Payn, James 1830-1898 . . . . .DLB-18

Payne, John 1842-1916 . . . . .DLB-35

Payne, John Howard 1791-1852 . . . . .DLB-37

Payson and Clarke DLB-46

Paz, Octavio 1914-1998 . . . . .Y-90, Y-98

Pazzi, Roberto 1946- DLB-196

Peabody, Elizabeth Palmer 1804-1894 . .DLB-1, 223

Peabody, Elizabeth Palmer
    [publishing house] DLB-49

Peabody, Oliver William Bourn
    1799-1848 . . . . .DLB-59

Peace, Roger 1899-1968 . . . . .DLB-127

Peacham, Henry 1578-1644? DLB-151

Peacham, Henry, the Elder 1547-1634 . . . .DLB-172

Peachtree Publishers, Limited DLB-46

Peacock, Molly 1947- DLB-120

Peacock, Thomas Love 1785-1866 . . .DLB-96, 116

Pead, Deuel ?-1727 . . . . .DLB-24

Peake, Mervyn 1911-1968 . . . . .DLB-15, 160

Peale, Rembrandt 1778-1860 . . . . .DLB-183

Pear Tree Press .DLB-112

Pearce, Philippa 1920- DLB-161

Pearson, H. B. [publishing house] DLB-49

Pearson, Hesketh 1887-1964 . . . . .DLB-149

Peck, George W. 1840-1916 . . . . .DLB-23, 42

Peck, H. C., and Theo. Bliss
    [publishing house] DLB-49

Peck, Harry Thurston 1856-1914 . . . . .DLB-71, 91

Peele, George 1556-1596 . . . . .DLB-62, 167

Pegler, Westbrook 1894-1969 . . . . .DLB-171

Pekić, Borislav 1930-1992 . . . . .DLB-181

Pellegrini and Cudahy DLB-46

Pelletier, Aimé (see Vac, Bertrand)

Pemberton, Sir Max 1863-1950 . . . . .DLB-70

de la Peña, Terri 1947- DLB-209

Penfield, Edward 1866-1925 . . . . .DLB-188

Penguin Books [U.S.] DLB-46

Penguin Books [U.K.] DLB-112

Penn Publishing Company DLB-49

Penn, William 1644-1718 . . . . .DLB-24

Penna, Sandro 1906-1977 . . . . .DLB-114

Pennell, Joseph 1857-1926 . . . . .DLB-188

Penner, Jonathan 1940- Y-83

Pennington, Lee 1939- Y-82

Pepys, Samuel 1633-1703 . . . . .DLB-101, 213

Percy, Thomas 1729-1811 . . . . .DLB-104

Percy, Walker 1916-1990 . . . . DLB-2; Y-80, Y-90

Percy, William 1575-1648 . . . . .DLB-172

Perec, Georges 1936-1982 . . . . .DLB-83

Perelman, Bob 1947- DLB-193

Perelman, S. J. 1904-1979 . . . . DLB-11, 44

Perez, Raymundo "Tigre" 1946- DLB-122

Peri Rossi, Cristina 1941- DLB-145

Periodicals of the Beat Generation DLB-16

Perkins, Eugene 1932- DLB-41

Perkoff, Stuart Z. 1930-1974 . . . . DLB-16

Perley, Moses Henry 1804-1862 . . . . DLB-99

Permabooks DLB-46

Perovsky, Aleksei Alekseevich (Antonii Pogorel'sky)
    1787-1836 . . . . DLB-198

Perrin, Alice 1867-1934 . . . . DLB-156

Perry, Bliss 1860-1954 . . . . DLB-71

Perry, Eleanor 1915-1981 . . . . DLB-44

Perry, Matthew 1794-1858 . . . . DLB-183

Perry, Sampson 1747-1823 . . . . DLB-158

Persius A.D. 34-A.D. 62 . . . . DLB-211

"Personal Style" (1890), by John Addington
    Symonds DLB-57

Perutz, Leo 1882-1957 . . . . DLB-81

Pesetsky, Bette 1932- DLB-130

Pestalozzi, Johann Heinrich 1746-1827 . . . . DLB-94

Peter, Laurence J. 1919-1990 . . . . DLB-53

Peter of Spain circa 1205-1277 . . . . DLB-115

Peterkin, Julia 1880-1961 . . . . DLB-9

Peters, Lenrie 1932- DLB-117

Peters, Robert 1924- DLB-105

Petersham, Maud 1889-1971 and
    Petersham, Miska 1888-1960 . . . . DLB-22

Peterson, Charles Jacobs 1819-1887 . . . . . . DLB-79

Peterson, Len 1917- DLB-88

Peterson, Levi S. 1933- DLB-206

Peterson, Louis 1922-1998 . . . . DLB-76

Peterson, T. B., and Brothers DLB-49

Petitclair, Pierre 1813-1860 . . . . DLB-99

Petrescu, Camil 1894-1957 . . . . DLB-220

Petronius circa A.D. 20-A.D. 66 . . . . DLB-211

Petrov, Aleksandar 1938- DLB-181

Petrov, Gavriil 1730-1801 . . . . DLB-150

Petrov, Vasilii Petrovich 1736-1799 . . . . DLB-150

Petrov, Valeri 1920- DLB-181

Petrović, Rastko 1898-1949 . . . . DLB-147

Petruslied circa 854? DLB-148

Petry, Ann 1908-1997 . . . . DLB-76

Pettie, George circa 1548-1589 . . . . DLB-136

Peyton, K. M. 1929- DLB-161

Pfaffe Konrad flourished circa 1172 . . . . DLB-148

Pfaffe Lamprecht flourished circa 1150 . . DLB-148

Pfeiffer, Emily 1827-1890 . . . . DLB-199

Pforzheimer, Carl H. 1879-1957 . . . . DLB-140

Phaedrus circa 18 B.C.-circa A.D. 50 . . . . DLB-211

Phaer, Thomas 1510?-1560 . . . . DLB-167

Phaidon Press Limited DLB-112

Pharr, Robert Deane 1916-1992 . . . . DLB-33

Phelps, Elizabeth Stuart 1815-1852 . . . . . . DLB-202

Phelps, Elizabeth Stuart 1844-1911 . . . DLB-74, 221

Philander von der Linde
    (see Mencke, Johann Burckhard)

Philby, H. St. John B. 1885-1960 . . . . DLB-195

Philip, Marlene Nourbese 1947- DLB-157

Philippe, Charles-Louis 1874-1909 . . . . . . DLB-65

Philips, John 1676-1708 . . . . DLB-95

Philips, Katherine 1632-1664 . . . . DLB-131

Phillipps, Sir Thomas 1792-1872 . . . . DLB-184

Phillips, Caryl 1958- DLB-157

Phillips, David Graham 1867-1911 . . . . . DLB-9, 12

Phillips, Jayne Anne 1952- Y-80

Phillips, Robert 1938- DLB-105

Phillips, Stephen 1864-1915 . . . . DLB-10

Phillips, Ulrich B. 1877-1934 . . . . DLB-17

Phillips, Willard 1784-1873 . . . . DLB-59

Phillips, William 1907- DLB-137

Phillips, Sampson and Company DLB-49

Phillpotts, Adelaide Eden (Adelaide Ross)
    1896-1993 . . . . DLB-191

Phillpotts, Eden
    1862-1960 . . . . DLB-10, 70, 135, 153

Philo circa 20-15 B.C.-circa A.D. 50
    . . . . DLB-176

Philosophical Library DLB-46

"The Philosophy of Style" (1852), by
    Herbert Spencer DLB-57

Phinney, Elihu [publishing house] DLB-49

Phoenix, John (see Derby, George Horatio)

PHYLON (Fourth Quarter, 1950),
    The Negro in Literature:
    The Current Scene DLB-76

Physiologus circa 1070-circa 1150 . . . . DLB-148

Piccolo, Lucio 1903-1969 . . . . DLB-114

Pickard, Tom 1946- DLB-40

Pickering, William [publishing house] . . . DLB-106

Pickthall, Marjorie 1883-1922 . . . . DLB-92

Pictorial Printing Company DLB-49

Piercy, Marge 1936- DLB-120

Pierro, Albino 1916- DLB-128

Pignotti, Lamberto 1926- DLB-128

Pike, Albert 1809-1891 . . . . DLB-74

Pike, Zebulon Montgomery
    1779-1813 . . . . DLB-183

Pillat, Ion 1891-1945 . . . . DLB-220

Pilon, Jean-Guy 1930- DLB-60

Pinckney, Eliza Lucas 1722-1793 . . . . DLB-200

Pinckney, Josephine 1895-1957 . . . . DLB-6

Pindar circa 518 B.C.-circa 438 B.C.
    . . . . DLB-176

Pindar, Peter (see Wolcot, John)

Pineda, Cecile 1942- DLB-209

Pinero, Arthur Wing 1855-1934 . . . . DLB-10

Pinget, Robert 1919-1997 . . . . DLB-83

Pinnacle Books DLB-46

Piñon, Nélida 1935- DLB-145

Pinsky, Robert 1940- Y-82

Pinter, Harold 1930- DLB-13

Piontek, Heinz 1925- DLB-75

Piozzi, Hester Lynch [Thrale]
    1741-1821 . . . . DLB-104, 142

Piper, H. Beam 1904-1964 . . . . DLB-8

Piper, Watty DLB-22

Pirckheimer, Caritas 1467-1532 . . . . DLB-179

Pirckheimer, Willibald 1470-1530 . . . . . . DLB-179

Pisar, Samuel 1929- Y-83

Pitkin, Timothy 1766-1847 . . . . DLB-30

The Pitt Poetry Series: Poetry Publishing
    Today Y-85

Pitter, Ruth 1897- DLB-20

Pix, Mary 1666-1709 . . . . DLB-80

Pixerécourt, René Charles Guilbert de
    1773-1844 . . . . DLB-192

Plaatje, Sol T. 1876-1932 . . . . DLB-125, 225

The Place of Realism in Fiction (1895), by
    George Gissing DLB-18

Plante, David 1940- Y-83

Platen, August von 1796-1835 . . . . DLB-90

Plath, Sylvia 1932-1963 . . . . DLB-5, 6, 152

Plato circa 428 B.C.-348-347 B.C.
    . . . . DLB-176

Platon 1737-1812 . . . . DLB-150

Platt and Munk Company DLB-46

Plautus circa 254 B.C.-184 B.C. DLB-211

Playboy Press DLB-46

Playford, John [publishing house] DLB-170

Plays, Playwrights, and Playgoers DLB-84

Playwrights and Professors, by
    Tom Stoppard DLB-13

Playwrights on the Theater DLB-80

Der Pleier flourished circa 1250 . . . . DLB-138

Plenzdorf, Ulrich 1934- DLB-75

Plessen, Elizabeth 1944- DLB-75

Pletnev, Petr Aleksandrovich
    1792-1865 . . . . DLB-205

Pliekšāne, Elza Rozenberga (see Aspazija)

Pliekšāns, Jānis (see Rainis, Jānis)

Plievier, Theodor 1892-1955 . . . . DLB-69

Plimpton, George 1927- DLB-185

Pliny the Elder A.D. 23/24-A.D. 79 . . . . . DLB-211

Pliny the Younger
    circa A.D. 61-A.D. 112 . . . . DLB-211

Plomer, William
    1903-1973 . . . . DLB-20, 162, 191, 225

Plotinus 204-270 . . . . DLB-176

Plume, Thomas 1630-1704 . . . . DLB-213

Plumly, Stanley 1939- DLB-5, 193

Plumpp, Sterling D. 1940- DLB-41

Plunkett, James 1920- DLB-14

Plutarch circa 46-circa 120 . . . . DLB-176

Plymell, Charles 1935- DLB-16

Pocket Books DLB-46

Poe, Edgar Allan 1809-1849 . . . . . DLB-3, 59, 73, 74

Poe, James 1921-1980 . . . . DLB-44

The Poet Laureate of the United States Statements from Former Consultants in Poetry Y-86

"The Poet's Kaleidoscope: The Element of Surprise in the Making of the Poem," by Madeline DeFrees DLB-105

"The Poetry File," by Edward Field DLB-105

Pogodin, Mikhail Petrovich 1800-1875 . . . . DLB-198

Pogorel'sky, Antonii (see Perovsky, Aleksei Alekseevich)

Pohl, Frederik 1919- DLB-8

Poirier, Louis (see Gracq, Julien)

Polanyi, Michael 1891-1976 . . . . DLB-100

Poláček, Karel 1892-1945 . . . . DLB-215

Pole, Reginald 1500-1558 . . . . DLB-132

Polevoi, Nikolai Alekseevich 1796-1846 . . . . DLB-198

Polezhaev, Aleksandr Ivanovich 1804-1838 . . . . DLB-205

Poliakoff, Stephen 1952- DLB-13

Polidori, John William 1795-1821 . . . . . . DLB-116

Polite, Carlene Hatcher 1932- DLB-33

Pollard, Alfred W. 1859-1944 . . . . DLB-201

Pollard, Edward A. 1832-1872 . . . . DLB-30

Pollard, Graham 1903-1976 . . . . DLB-201

Pollard, Percival 1869-1911 . . . . DLB-71

Pollard and Moss DLB-49

Pollock, Sharon 1936- DLB-60

Polonsky, Abraham 1910-1999 . . . . DLB-26

Polotsky, Simeon 1629-1680 . . . . DLB-150

Polybius circa 200 B.C.-118 B.C. DLB-176

Pomilio, Mario 1921-1990 . . . . DLB-177

Ponce, Mary Helen 1938- DLB-122

Ponce-Montoya, Juanita 1949- DLB-122

Ponet, John 1516?-1556 . . . . DLB-132

Poniatowski, Elena 1933- DLB-113

Ponsard, François 1814-1867 . . . . DLB-192

Ponsonby, William [publishing house] . . . DLB-170

Pontiggia, Giuseppe 1934- DLB-196

Pony Stories DLB-160

Poole, Ernest 1880-1950 . . . . DLB-9

Poole, Sophia 1804-1891 . . . . DLB-166

Poore, Benjamin Perley 1820-1887 . . . . . . DLB-23

Popa, Vasko 1922-1991 . . . . DLB-181

Pope, Abbie Hanscom 1858-1894 . . . . . . DLB-140

Pope, Alexander 1688-1744 . . . . . DLB-95, 101, 213

Popov, Mikhail Ivanovich 1742-circa 1790 . . . . DLB-150

Popović, Aleksandar 1929-1996 . . . . DLB-181

Popular Library DLB-46

Porete, Marguerite ?-1310 . . . . DLB-208

Porlock, Martin (see MacDonald, Philip)

Porpoise Press DLB-112

Porta, Antonio 1935-1989 . . . . DLB-128

Porter, Anna Maria 1780-1832 . . . . . DLB-116, 159

Porter, David 1780-1843 . . . . DLB-183

Porter, Eleanor H. 1868-1920 . . . . DLB-9

Porter, Gene Stratton (see Stratton-Porter, Gene)

Porter, Henry ?-? DLB-62

Porter, Jane 1776-1850 . . . . DLB-116, 159

Porter, Katherine Anne 1890-1980 . . . . . . DLB-4, 9, 102; Y-80; DS-12

Porter, Peter 1929- DLB-40

Porter, William Sydney 1862-1910 . . . . DLB-12, 78, 79

Porter, William T. 1809-1858 . . . . DLB-3, 43

Porter and Coates DLB-49

Portillo Trambley, Estela 1927-1998 . . . . DLB-209

Portis, Charles 1933- DLB-6

Posey, Alexander 1873-1908 . . . . DLB-175

Postans, Marianne circa 1810-1865 . . . . . DLB-166

Postl, Carl (see Sealsfield, Carl)

Poston, Ted 1906-1974 . . . . DLB-51

Postscript to [the Third Edition of] *Clarissa* (1751), by Samuel Richardson DLB-39

Potok, Chaim 1929- DLB-28, 152; Y-84

Potter, Beatrix 1866-1943 . . . . DLB-141

Potter, David M. 1910-1971 . . . . DLB-17

Potter, John E., and Company DLB-49

Pottle, Frederick A. 1897-1987 . . . . . DLB-103; Y-87

Poulin, Jacques 1937- DLB-60

Pound, Ezra 1885-1972 . . . . . DLB-4, 45, 63; DS-15

Povich, Shirley 1905- DLB-171

Powell, Anthony 1905- DLB-15

Powell, John Wesley 1834-1902 . . . . DLB-186

Powers, J. F. 1917-1999 . . . . DLB-130

Pownall, David 1938- DLB-14

Powys, John Cowper 1872-1963 . . . . DLB-15

Powys, Llewelyn 1884-1939 . . . . DLB-98

Powys, T. F. 1875-1953 . . . . DLB-36, 162

Poynter, Nelson 1903-1978 . . . . DLB-127

The Practice of Biography: An Interview with Stanley Weintraub Y-82

The Practice of Biography II: An Interview with B. L. Reid Y-83

The Practice of Biography III: An Interview with Humphrey Carpenter Y-84

The Practice of Biography IV: An Interview with William Manchester Y-85

The Practice of Biography V: An Interview with Justin Kaplan Y-86

The Practice of Biography VI: An Interview with David Herbert Donald Y-87

The Practice of Biography VII: An Interview with John Caldwell Guilds Y-92

The Practice of Biography VIII: An Interview with Joan Mellen Y-94

The Practice of Biography IX: An Interview with Michael Reynolds Y-95

Prados, Emilio 1899-1962 . . . . DLB-134

Praed, Winthrop Mackworth 1802-1839 . . . . DLB-96

Praeger Publishers DLB-46

Praetorius, Johannes 1630-1680 . . . . DLB-168

Pratolini, Vasco 1913-1991 . . . . DLB-177

Pratt, E. J. 1882-1964 . . . . DLB-92

Pratt, Samuel Jackson 1749-1814 . . . . DLB-39

Preciado Martin, Patricia 1939- DLB-209

Preface to *Alwyn* (1780), by Thomas Holcroft DLB-39

Preface to *Colonel Jack* (1722), by Daniel Defoe DLB-39

Preface to *Evelina* (1778), by Fanny Burney DLB-39

Preface to *Ferdinand Count Fathom* (1753), by Tobias Smollett DLB-39

Preface to *Incognita* (1692), by William Congreve DLB-39

Preface to *Joseph Andrews* (1742), by Henry Fielding DLB-39

Preface to *Moll Flanders* (1722), by Daniel Defoe DLB-39

Preface to *Poems* (1853), by Matthew Arnold DLB-32

Preface to *Robinson Crusoe* (1719), by Daniel Defoe DLB-39

Preface to *Roderick Random* (1748), by Tobias Smollett DLB-39

Preface to *Roxana* (1724), by Daniel Defoe DLB-39

Preface to *St. Leon* (1799), by William Godwin DLB-39

Preface to Sarah Fielding's *Familiar Letters* (1747), by Henry Fielding [excerpt] DLB-39

Preface to Sarah Fielding's *The Adventures of David Simple* (1744), by Henry Fielding DLB-39

Preface to *The Cry* (1754), by Sarah Fielding DLB-39

Preface to *The Delicate Distress* (1769), by Elizabeth Griffin DLB-39

Preface to *The Disguis'd Prince* (1733), by Eliza Haywood [excerpt] DLB-39

Preface to *The Farther Adventures of Robinson Crusoe* (1719), by Daniel Defoe DLB-39

Preface to the First Edition of *Pamela* (1740), by Samuel Richardson DLB-39

Preface to the First Edition of *The Castle of Otranto* (1764), by Horace Walpole DLB-39

Preface to *The History of Romances* (1715), by Pierre Daniel Huet [excerpts] DLB-39

Preface to *The Life of Charlotta du Pont* (1723), by Penelope Aubin DLB-39

Preface to *The Old English Baron* (1778), by Clara Reeve DLB-39

Preface to the Second Edition of *The Castle of Otranto* (1765), by Horace Walpole DLB-39

Preface to *The Secret History, of Queen Zarah, and the Zarazians* (1705), by Delariviere Manley DLB-39

Preface to the Third Edition of *Clarissa* (1751), by Samuel Richardson [excerpt] DLB-39

Preface to *The Works of Mrs. Davys* (1725), by Mary Davys DLB-39

Preface to Volume 1 of *Clarissa* (1747), by Samuel Richardson DLB-39

Preface to Volume 3 of *Clarissa* (1748), by Samuel Richardson DLB-39

Préfontaine, Yves 1937- DLB-53

Prelutsky, Jack 1940- DLB-61

Premisses, by Michael Hamburger DLB-66

Prentice, George D. 1802-1870 . . . . DLB-43

Prentice-Hall DLB-46

Prescott, Orville 1906-1996 . . . . Y-96

Prescott, William Hickling
1796-1859 . . . . DLB-1, 30, 59

The Present State of the English Novel (1892),
by George Saintsbury DLB-18

Prešeren, Francn 1800-1849 . . . . DLB-147

Preston, May Wilson 1873-1949 . . . . DLB-188

Preston, Thomas 1537-1598 . . . . DLB-62

Price, Reynolds 1933- DLB-2, 218

Price, Richard 1723-1791 . . . . DLB-158

Price, Richard 1949- Y-81

Priest, Christopher 1943- DLB-14, 207

Priestley, J. B. 1894-1984
. . . . DLB-10, 34, 77, 100, 139; Y-84

Primary Bibliography: A Retrospective Y-95

Prime, Benjamin Young 1733-1791 . . . . DLB-31

Primrose, Diana floruit circa 1630 . . . . . . DLB-126

Prince, F. T. 1912- DLB-20

Prince, Thomas 1687-1758 . . . . DLB-24, 140

The Principles of Success in Literature (1865), by
George Henry Lewes [excerpt] DLB-57

Pringle, Thomas 1789-1834 . . . . DLB-225

Printz, Wolfgang Casper 1641-1717 . . . . . DLB-168

Prior, Matthew 1664-1721 . . . . DLB-95

Prisco, Michele 1920- DLB-177

Pritchard, William H. 1932- DLB-111

Pritchett, V. S. 1900-1997 . . . . DLB-15, 139

Probyn, May 1856 or 1857-1909 . . . . DLB-199

Procter, Adelaide Anne 1825-1864 . . . DLB-32, 199

Procter, Bryan Waller 1787-1874 . . . . DLB-96, 144

Proctor, Robert 1868-1903 . . . . DLB-184

*Producing Dear Bunny, Dear Volodya: The Friendship
and the Feud* Y-97

The Profession of Authorship:
Scribblers for Bread Y-89

The Progress of Romance (1785), by Clara Reeve
[excerpt] DLB-39

Prokopovich, Feofan 1681?-1736 . . . . DLB-150

Prokosch, Frederic 1906-1989 . . . . DLB-48

The Proletarian Novel DLB-9

Pronzini, Bill 1943- DLB-226

Propertius circa 50 B.C.-post 16 B.C. DLB-211

Propper, Dan 1937- DLB-16

The Prospect of Peace (1778),
by Joel Barlow DLB-37

Protagoras circa 490 B.C.-420 B.C.
. . . . .DLB-176

Proud, Robert 1728-1813 . . . . DLB-30

Proust, Marcel 1871-1922 . . . . DLB-65

Prynne, J. H. 1936- DLB-40

Przybyszewski, Stanislaw 1868-1927 . . . . . DLB-66

Pseudo-Dionysius the Areopagite floruit
circa 500 . . . . DLB-115

Public Domain and the Violation of Texts Y-97

The Public Lending Right in America
Statement by Sen. Charles McC.
Mathias, Jr. PLR and the Meaning
of Literary Property Statements on
PLR by American Writers Y-83

The Public Lending Right in the United Kingdom
Public Lending Right: The First Year in the
United Kingdom Y-83

The Publication of English
Renaissance Plays DLB-62

Publications and Social Movements
[Transcendentalism] DLB-1

Publishers and Agents: The Columbia
Connection Y-87

A Publisher's Archives: G. P. Putnam Y-92

Publishing Fiction at LSU Press Y-87

The Publishing Industry in 1998:
Sturm-und-drang.com Y-98

The Publishing Industry in 1999 . . . . Y-99

Pückler-Muskau, Hermann von
1785-1871 . . . . .DLB-133

Pufendorf, Samuel von 1632-1694 . . . . . DLB-168

Pugh, Edwin William 1874-1930 . . . . DLB-135

Pugin, A. Welby 1812-1852 . . . . DLB-55

Puig, Manuel 1932-1990 . . . . DLB-113

Pulitzer, Joseph 1847-1911 . . . . DLB-23

Pulitzer, Joseph, Jr. 1885-1955 . . . . DLB-29

Pulitzer Prizes for the Novel, 1917-1945 . . . . DLB-9

Pulliam, Eugene 1889-1975 . . . . DLB-127

Purchas, Samuel 1577?-1626 . . . . DLB-151

Purdy, Al 1918- DLB-88

Purdy, James 1923- DLB-2, 218

Purdy, Ken W. 1913-1972 . . . . DLB-137

Pusey, Edward Bouverie
1800-1882 . . . . DLB-55

Pushkin, Aleksandr Sergeevich
1799-1837 . . . . DLB-205

Pushkin, Vasilii L'vovich
1766-1830 . . . . DLB-205

Putnam, George Palmer 1814-1872 . . . . DLB-3, 79

Putnam, Samuel 1892-1950 . . . . DLB-4

G. P. Putnam's Sons [U.S.] DLB-49

G. P. Putnam's Sons [U.K.] DLB-106

Puzo, Mario 1920-1999 . . . . DLB-6

Pyle, Ernie 1900-1945 . . . . DLB-29

Pyle, Howard 1853-1911 . . . . DLB-42, 188; DS-13

Pym, Barbara 1913-1980 . . . . . .DLB-14, 207; Y-87

Pynchon, Thomas 1937- DLB-2, 173

Pyramid Books DLB-46

Pyrnelle, Louise-Clarke 1850-1907 . . . . . . DLB-42

Pythagoras circa 570 B.C.-? DLB-176

Q

Quad, M. (see Lewis, Charles B.)

Quaritch, Bernard 1819-1899 . . . . DLB-184

Quarles, Francis 1592-1644 . . . . DLB-126

The Quarterly Review 1809-1967 . . . . . . DLB-110

Quasimodo, Salvatore 1901-1968 . . . . DLB-114

Queen, Ellery (see Dannay, Frederic, and
Manfred B. Lee)

The Queen City Publishing House DLB-49

Queneau, Raymond 1903-1976 . . . . DLB-72

Quennell, Sir Peter 1905-1993 . . . . . DLB-155, 195

Quesnel, Joseph 1746-1809 . . . . DLB-99

The Question of American Copyright
in the Nineteenth Century Headnote
Preface, by George Haven Putnam
The Evolution of Copyright, by
Brander Matthews
Summary of Copyright Legislation in
the United States, by R. R. Bowker
Analysis oæ the Provisions of the
Copyright Law of 1891, by
George Haven Putnam
The Contest for International Copyright,
by George Haven Putnam
Cheap Books and Good Books,
by Brander Matthews DLB-49

Quiller-Couch, Sir Arthur Thomas
1863-1944 . . . . .DLB-135, 153, 190

Quin, Ann 1936-1973 . . . . DLB-14

Quincy, Samuel, of Georgia ?-? DLB-31

Quincy, Samuel, of Massachusetts
1734-1789 . . . . DLB-31

Quinn, Anthony 1915- DLB-122

Quinn, John 1870-1924 . . . . .DLB-187

Quiñónez, Naomi 1951- DLB-209

Quintana, Leroy V. 1944- DLB-82

Quintana, Miguel de 1671-1748
A Forerunner of Chicano
Literature DLB-122

Quintillian circa A.D. 40-circa A.D. 96 . . . DLB-211

Quist, Harlin, Books DLB-46

Quoirez, Françoise (see Sagan, Françoise)

R

R-va, Zeneida (see Gan, Elena Andreevna)

Raabe, Wilhelm 1831-1910 . . . . DLB-129

Raban, Jonathan 1942- DLB-204

Rabe, David 1940- DLB-7

Raboni, Giovanni 1932- DLB-128

Rachilde 1860-1953 . . . . DLB-123, 192

Racin, Kočo 1908-1943 . . . . .DLB-147

Rackham, Arthur 1867-1939 . . . . DLB-141

Radauskas, Henrikas 1910-1970 . . . . DLB-220

Radcliffe, Ann 1764-1823 . . . . .DLB-39, 178

Raddall, Thomas 1903- DLB-68

Radichkov, Yordan 1929- DLB-181

Radiguet, Raymond 1903-1923 . . . . DLB-65

Radishchev, Aleksandr Nikolaevich
1749-1802 . . . . DLB-150

Radnóti, Miklós 1909-1944 . . . . DLB-215

Radványi, Netty Reiling (see Seghers, Anna)

Rahv, Philip 1908-1973 . . . . .DLB-137

Raich, Semen Egorovich 1792-1855 . . . . . DLB-205

Raičković, Stevan 1928- DLB-181

Raimund, Ferdinand Jakob 1790-1836.....DLB-90

Raine, Craig 1944- DLB-40

Raine, Kathleen 1908- DLB-20

Rainis, Jānis 1865-1929 ....DLB-220

Rainolde, Richard
    circa 1530-1606..................DLB-136

Rakić, Milan 1876-1938..............DLB-147

Rakosi, Carl 1903- DLB-193

Ralegh, Sir Walter 1554?-1618 ....DLB-172

Ralin, Radoy 1923- DLB-181

Ralph, Julian 1853-1903...............DLB-23

Ralph Waldo Emerson in 1982...........Y-82

Ramat, Silvio 1939- DLB-128

Rambler, no. 4 (1750), by Samuel Johnson
    [excerpt]........................DLB-39

Ramée, Marie Louise de la (see Ouida)

Ramírez, Sergío 1942- DLB-145

Ramke, Bin 1947- DLB-120

Ramler, Karl Wilhelm 1725-1798........DLB-97

Ramon Ribeyro, Julio 1929- DLB-145

Ramos, Manuel 1948- DLB-209

Ramous, Mario 1924- DLB-128

Rampersad, Arnold 1941- DLB-111

Ramsay, Allan 1684 or 1685-1758.......DLB-95

Ramsay, David 1749-1815..............DLB-30

Ramsay, Martha Laurens 1759-1811.....DLB-200

Ranck, Katherine Quintana 1942- DLB-122

Rand, Avery and Company.............DLB-49

Rand McNally and Company..........DLB-49

Randall, David Anton 1905-1975.......DLB-140

Randall, Dudley 1914- DLB-41

Randall, Henry S. 1811-1876...........DLB-30

Randall, James G. 1881-1953...........DLB-17

The Randall Jarrell Symposium: A Small
    Collection of Randall Jarrells
    Excerpts From Papers Delivered at
    the Randall Jarrel Symposium......Y-86

Randolph, A. Philip 1889-1979 ....DLB-91

Randolph, Anson D. F.
    [publishing house] DLB-49

Randolph, Thomas 1605-1635 ......DLB-58, 126

Random House DLB-46

Ranlet, Henry [publishing house] DLB-49

Ransom, Harry 1908-1976.............DLB-187

Ransom, John Crowe 1888-1974.....DLB-45, 63

Ransome, Arthur 1884-1967 ....DLB-160

Raphael, Frederic 1931- DLB-14

Raphaelson, Samson 1896-1983 ....DLB-44

Rashi circa 1040-1105 ....DLB-208

Raskin, Ellen 1928-1984 ....DLB-52

Rastell, John 1475?-1536 .... DLB-136, 170

Rattigan, Terence 1911-1977 ....DLB-13

Rawlings, Marjorie Kinnan
    1896-1953 ....DLB-9, 22, 102; DS-17

Rawlinson, Richard 1690-1755 ....DLB-213

Rawlinson, Thomas 1681-1725 ....DLB-213

Raworth, Tom 1938- DLB-40

Ray, David 1932- DLB-5

Ray, Gordon Norton 1915-1986 .... DLB-103, 140

Ray, Henrietta Cordelia 1849-1916......DLB-50

Raymond, Ernest 1888-1974 ....DLB-191

Raymond, Henry J. 1820-1869 .... DLB-43, 79

Raymond Chandler Centenary Tributes
    from Michael Avallone, James Elroy, Joe Gores,
    and William F. Nolan Y-88

Reach, Angus 1821-1856..............DLB-70

Read, Herbert 1893-1968 ....DLB-20, 149

Read, Herbert, "The Practice of Biography," in *The
    English Sense of Humour and Other
    Essays*.........................DLB-149

Read, Martha Meredith...............DLB-200

Read, Opie 1852-1939................DLB-23

Read, Piers Paul 1941- DLB-14

Reade, Charles 1814-1884..............DLB-21

Reader's Digest Condensed Books DLB-46

Readers Ulysses Symposium Y-97

Reading, Peter 1946- DLB-40

Reading Series in New York City Y-96

The Reality of One Woman's Dream:
    The de Grummond Children's
    Literature Collection................Y-99

Reaney, James 1926- DLB-68

Rebhun, Paul 1500?-1546 ....DLB-179

Rèbora, Clemente 1885-1957..........DLB-114

Rebreanu, Liviu 1885-1944 ....DLB-220

Rechy, John 1934- DLB-122; Y-82

The Recovery of Literature: Criticism in the 1990s:
    A Symposium Y-91

Redding, J. Saunders 1906-1988 ...... DLB-63, 76

Redfield, J. S. [publishing house] DLB-49

Redgrove, Peter 1932- DLB-40

Redmon, Anne 1943- Y-86

Redmond, Eugene B. 1937- DLB-41

Redpath, James [publishing house] DLB-49

Reed, Henry 1808-1854................DLB-59

Reed, Henry 1914- DLB-27

Reed, Ishmael 1938- DLB-2, 5, 33, 169; DS-8

Reed, Rex 1938- DLB-185

Reed, Sampson 1800-1880..............DLB-1

Reed, Talbot Baines 1852-1893........DLB-141

Reedy, William Marion 1862-1920.......DLB-91

Reese, Lizette Woodworth 1856-1935.....DLB-54

Reese, Thomas 1742-1796..............DLB-37

Reeve, Clara 1729-1807................DLB-39

Reeves, James 1909-1978..............DLB-161

Reeves, John 1926- DLB-88

"Reflections: After a Tornado,"
    by Judson Jerome DLB-105

Regnery, Henry, Company.............DLB-46

Rehberg, Hans 1901-1963 ....DLB-124

Rehfisch, Hans José 1891-1960 ....DLB-124

Reich, Ebbe Kløvedal 1940- DLB-214

Reid, Alastair 1926- DLB-27

Reid, B. L. 1918-1990 ....DLB-111

Reid, Christopher 1949- DLB-40

Reid, Forrest 1875-1947 ....DLB-153

Reid, Helen Rogers 1882-1970 ....DLB-29

Reid, James ?-?........................DLB-31

Reid, Mayne 1818-1883...........DLB-21, 163

Reid, Thomas 1710-1796 ....DLB-31

Reid, V. S. (Vic) 1913-1987 ....DLB-125

Reid, Whitelaw 1837-1912.............DLB-23

Reilly and Lee Publishing Company......DLB-46

Reimann, Brigitte 1933-1973 ....DLB-75

Reinmar der Alte
    circa 1165-circa 1205..............DLB-138

Reinmar von Zweter
    circa 1200-circa 1250..............DLB-138

Reisch, Walter 1903-1983 ....DLB-44

Reizei Family DLB-203

Remarks at the Opening of "The Biographical
    Part of Literature" Exhibition, by
    William R. Cagle Y-98

Remarque, Erich Maria 1898-1970 ....DLB-56

"Re-meeting of Old Friends": The Jack
    Kerouac Conference Y-82

Reminiscences, by Charles Scribner Jr...... DS-17

Remington, Frederic
    1861-1909 .... DLB-12, 186, 188

Renaud, Jacques 1943- DLB-60

Renault, Mary 1905-1983 .... Y-83

Rendell, Ruth 1930- DLB-87

Rensselaer, Maria van Cortlandt van
    1645-1689 ....DLB-200

Repplier, Agnes 1855-1950............DLB-221

Representative Men and Women: A Historical
    Perspective on the British Novel,
    1930-1960.......................DLB-15

(Re-)Publishing Orwell Y-86

Research in the American Antiquarian Book
    Trade Y-97

Responses to Ken Auletta Y-97

Rettenbacher, Simon 1634-1706 ....DLB-168

Reuchlin, Johannes 1455-1522..........DLB-179

Reuter, Christian 1665-after 1712 ....DLB-168

Reuter, Fritz 1810-1874...............DLB-129

Reuter, Gabriele 1859-1941.............DLB-66

Revell, Fleming H., Company..........DLB-49

Reventlow, Franziska Gräfin zu
    1871-1918 ....DLB-66

Review of Reviews Office DLB-112

Review of [Samuel Richardson's] *Clarissa* (1748), by
    Henry Fielding DLB-39

The Revolt (1937), by Mary Colum
    [excerpts].......................DLB-36

Rexroth, Kenneth
    1905-1982 .... DLB-16, 48, 165, 212; Y-82

Rey, H. A. 1898-1977 ....DLB-22

Reynal and Hitchcock DLB-46

Reynolds, G. W. M. 1814-1879.........DLB-21

Reynolds, John Hamilton 1794-1852.....DLB-96

Reynolds, Mack 1917- DLB-8

Reynolds, Sir Joshua 1723-1792 . . . . DLB-104

Reznikoff, Charles 1894-1976. . . . . DLB-28, 45

"Rhetoric" (1828; revised, 1859), by
    Thomas de Quincey [excerpt] DLB-57

Rhett, Robert Barnwell 1800-1876 . . . . . . DLB-43

Rhode, John 1884-1964 . . . . DLB-77

Rhodes, James Ford 1848-1927. . . . . DLB-47

Rhodes, Richard 1937- DLB-185

Rhys, Jean 1890-1979 . . . . DLB-36, 117, 162

Ricardo, David 1772-1823 . . . . .DLB-107, 158

Ricardou, Jean 1932- DLB-83

Rice, Elmer 1892-1967 . . . . DLB-4, 7

Rice, Grantland 1880-1954. . . . . .DLB-29, 171

Rich, Adrienne 1929- DLB-5, 67

Richard de Fournival
    1201-1259 or 1260. . . . . DLB-208

Richards, David Adams 1950- DLB-53

Richards, George circa 1760-1814 . . . . DLB-37

Richards, I. A. 1893-1979 . . . . DLB-27

Richards, Laura E. 1850-1943 . . . . DLB-42

Richards, William Carey 1818-1892 . . . . . DLB-73

Richards, Grant [publishing house] DLB-112

Richardson, Charles F. 1851-1913 . . . . DLB-71

Richardson, Dorothy M. 1873-1957 . . . . . DLB-36

Richardson, Henry Handel (Ethel Florence
    Lindesay) 1870-1946 . . . . DLB-197

Richardson, Jack 1935- DLB-7

Richardson, John 1796-1852. . . . . DLB-99

Richardson, Samuel 1689-1761 . . . . . . DLB-39, 154

Richardson, Willis 1889-1977 . . . . DLB-51

Riche, Barnabe 1542-1617 . . . . DLB-136

Richepin, Jean 1849-1926 . . . . DLB-192

Richler, Mordecai 1931- DLB-53

Richter, Conrad 1890-1968 . . . . DLB-9, 212

Richter, Hans Werner 1908- DLB-69

Richter, Johann Paul Friedrich
    1763-1825. . . . . DLB-94

Rickerby, Joseph [publishing house]. DLB-106

Rickword, Edgell 1898-1982 . . . . DLB-20

Riddell, Charlotte 1832-1906 . . . . DLB-156

Riddell, John (see Ford, Corey)

Ridge, John Rollin 1827-1867 . . . . .DLB-175

Ridge, Lola 1873-1941 . . . . DLB-54

Ridge, William Pett 1859-1930. . . . . DLB-135

Riding, Laura (see Jackson, Laura Riding)

Ridler, Anne 1912- DLB-27

Ridruego, Dionisio 1912-1975 . . . . DLB-108

Riel, Louis 1844-1885. . . . . DLB-99

Riemer, Johannes 1648-1714. . . . . DLB-168

Rifbjerg, Klaus 1931- DLB-214

Riffaterre, Michael 1924- DLB-67

Riggs, Lynn 1899-1954. . . . . .DLB-175

Riis, Jacob 1849-1914 . . . . DLB-23

Riker, John C. [publishing house]. DLB-49

Riley, James 1777-1840 . . . . DLB-183

Riley, John 1938-1978. . . . . DLB-40

Rilke, Rainer Maria 1875-1926. . . . . DLB-81

Rimanelli, Giose 1926- DLB-177

Rimbaud, Jean-Nicolas-Arthur
    1854-1891 . . . . DLB-217

Rinehart and Company DLB-46

Ringuet 1895-1960 . . . . DLB-68

Ringwood, Gwen Pharis 1910-1984 . . . . . DLB-88

Rinser, Luise 1911- DLB-69

Ríos, Alberto 1952- DLB-122

Ríos, Isabella 1948- DLB-82

Ripley, Arthur 1895-1961. . . . . DLB-44

Ripley, George 1802-1880 . . . . DLB-1, 64, 73

The Rising Glory of America:
    Three Poems DLB-37

The Rising Glory of America: Written in 1771
    (1786), by Hugh Henry Brackenridge and
    Philip Freneau DLB-37

Riskin, Robert 1897-1955 . . . . DLB-26

Risse, Heinz 1898- DLB-69

Rist, Johann 1607-1667 . . . . DLB-164

Ristikivi, Karl 1912-1977 . . . . DLB-220

Ritchie, Anna Mowatt 1819-1870 . . . . DLB-3

Ritchie, Anne Thackeray 1837-1919. . . . . . DLB-18

Ritchie, Thomas 1778-1854 . . . . DLB-43

Rites of Passage [on William Saroyan] Y-83

The Ritz Paris Hemingway Award. Y-85

Rivard, Adjutor 1868-1945. . . . . DLB-92

Rive, Richard 1931-1989 . . . . DLB-125, 225

Rivera, Marina 1942- DLB-122

Rivera, Tomás 1935-1984 . . . . DLB-82

Rivers, Conrad Kent 1933-1968. . . . . DLB-41

Riverside Press DLB-49

Rivington, James circa 1724-1802. . . . . . . DLB-43

Rivington, Charles [publishing house] . . . DLB-154

Rivkin, Allen 1903-1990. . . . . DLB-26

Roa Bastos, Augusto 1917- DLB-113

Robbe-Grillet, Alain 1922- DLB-83

Robbins, Tom 1936- Y-80

Robert Pinsky Reappointed Poet Laureate. . . . Y-98

Roberts, Charles G. D. 1860-1943 . . . . . . DLB-92

Roberts, Dorothy 1906-1993 . . . . DLB-88

Roberts, Elizabeth Madox
    1881-1941 . . . . DLB-9, 54, 102

Roberts, Kenneth 1885-1957 . . . . DLB-9

Roberts, William 1767-1849 . . . . DLB-142

Roberts Brothers. DLB-49

Roberts, James [publishing house] DLB-154

Robertson, A. M., and Company. DLB-49

Robertson, William 1721-1793 . . . . DLB-104

Robins, Elizabeth 1862-1952 . . . . DLB-197

Robinson, Casey 1903-1979 . . . . DLB-44

Robinson, Edwin Arlington 1869-1935 . . . DLB-54

Robinson, Henry Crabb 1775-1867 . . . . . .DLB-107

Robinson, James Harvey 1863-1936 . . . . . DLB-47

Robinson, Lennox 1886-1958 . . . . DLB-10

Robinson, Mabel Louise 1874-1962 . . . . . DLB-22

Robinson, Marilynne 1943- DLB-206

Robinson, Mary 1758-1800 . . . . DLB-158

Robinson, Richard circa 1545-1607 . . . . . DLB-167

Robinson, Therese 1797-1870 . . . . DLB-59, 133

Robison, Mary 1949- DLB-130

Roblès, Emmanuel 1914-1995 . . . . DLB-83

Roccatagliata Ceccardi, Ceccardo
    1871-1919. . . . . DLB-114

Rochester, John Wilmot, Earl of
    1647-1680 . . . . DLB-131

Rock, Howard 1911-1976. . . . . .DLB-127

Rockwell, Norman Perceval
    1894-1978. . . . . DLB-188

Rodgers, Carolyn M. 1945- DLB-41

Rodgers, W. R. 1909-1969. . . . . DLB-20

Rodríguez, Claudio 1934-1999. . . . . DLB-134

Rodríguez, Joe D. 1943- DLB-209

Rodríguez, Luis J. 1954- DLB-209

Rodriguez, Richard 1944- DLB-82

Rodríguez Julia, Edgardo 1946- DLB-145

Roe, E. P. 1838-1888 . . . . DLB-202

Roethke, Theodore 1908-1963 . . . . . . DLB-5, 206

Rogers, Jane 1952- DLB-194

Rogers, Pattiann 1940- DLB-105

Rogers, Samuel 1763-1855 . . . . DLB-93

Rogers, Will 1879-1935 . . . . DLB-11

Rohmer, Sax 1883-1959 . . . . DLB-70

Roiphe, Anne 1935- Y-80

Rojas, Arnold R. 1896-1988. . . . . DLB-82

Rolfe, Frederick William
    1860-1913 . . . . DLB-34, 156

Rolland, Romain 1866-1944. . . . . DLB-65

Rolle, Richard circa 1290-1300 - 1340 . . . DLB-146

Rölvaag, O. E. 1876-1931. . . . . DLB-9, 212

Romains, Jules 1885-1972. . . . . DLB-65

Roman, A., and Company DLB-49

Roman de la Rose: Guillaume de Lorris
    1200 to 1205-circa 1230, Jean de Meun
    1235-1240-circa 1305 . . . . DLB-208

Romano, Lalla 1906- DLB-177

Romano, Octavio 1923- DLB-122

Romero, Leo 1950- DLB-122

Romero, Lin 1947- DLB-122

Romero, Orlando 1945- DLB-82

Rook, Clarence 1863-1915. . . . . DLB-135

Roosevelt, Theodore 1858-1919. . . . . .DLB-47, 186

Root, Waverley 1903-1982 . . . . DLB-4

Root, William Pitt 1941- DLB-120

Roquebrune, Robert de 1889-1978. . . . . . DLB-68

Rosa, João Guimarães 1908-1967 . . . . . . DLB-113

Rosales, Luis 1910-1992 . . . . DLB-134

Roscoe, William 1753-1831 . . . . DLB-163

Rose, Reginald 1920- DLB-26

Rose, Wendy 1948- DLB-175

Rosegger, Peter 1843-1918. . . . . DLB-129

Rosei, Peter 1946- DLB-85

Rosen, Norma 1925- DLB-28

Rosenbach, A. S. W. 1876-1952........DLB-140

Rosenbaum, Ron 1946- DLB-185

Rosenberg, Isaac 1890-1918........DLB-20, 216

Rosenfeld, Isaac 1918-1956 ....DLB-28

Rosenthal, M. L. 1917-1996.............DLB-5

Rosenwald, Lessing J. 1891-1979........DLB-187

Ross, Alexander 1591-1654 ....DLB-151

Ross, Harold 1892-1951 ....DLB-137

Ross, Leonard Q. (see Rosten, Leo)

Ross, Lillian 1927- DLB-185

Ross, Martin 1862-1915..............DLB-135

Ross, Sinclair 1908- DLB-88

Ross, W. W. E. 1894-1966 ....DLB-88

Rosselli, Amelia 1930-1996 ....DLB-128

Rossen, Robert 1908-1966............DLB-26

Rossetti, Christina Georgina
    1830-1894 ....DLB-35, 163

Rossetti, Dante Gabriel 1828-1882 ......DLB-35

Rossner, Judith 1935- DLB-6

Rostand, Edmond 1868-1918 ....DLB-192

Rosten, Leo 1908-1997 ....DLB-11

Rostenberg, Leona 1908- DLB-140

Rostopchina, Evdokiia Petrovna
    1811-1858 ....DLB-205

Rostovsky, Dimitrii 1651-1709 ....DLB-150

Rota, Bertram 1903-1966............DLB-201

Bertram Rota and His Bookshop..........Y-91

Roth, Gerhard 1942- DLB-85, 124

Roth, Henry 1906?-1995 ....DLB-28

Roth, Joseph 1894-1939...............DLB-85

Roth, Philip 1933- DLB-2, 28, 173; Y-82

Rothenberg, Jerome 1931- DLB-5, 193

Rothschild Family DLB-184

Rotimi, Ola 1938- DLB-125

Routhier, Adolphe-Basile 1839-1920 .....DLB-99

Routier, Simone 1901-1987 ....DLB-88

Routledge, George, and Sons..........DLB-106

Roversi, Roberto 1923- DLB-128

Rowe, Elizabeth Singer 1674-1737 .....DLB-39, 95

Rowe, Nicholas 1674-1718.............DLB-84

Rowlands, Samuel circa 1570-1630 ......DLB-121

Rowlandson, Mary
    circa 1637-circa 1711 ....DLB-24, 200

Rowley, William circa 1585-1626 ....DLB-58

Rowse, A. L. 1903-1997..............DLB-155

Rowson, Susanna Haswell
    circa 1762-1824 ....DLB-37, 200

Roy, Camille 1870-1943...............DLB-92

Roy, Gabrielle 1909-1983 ....DLB-68

Roy, Jules 1907- DLB-83

The Royal Court Theatre and the English
    Stage Company..................DLB-13

The Royal Court Theatre and the New
    Drama.......................DLB-10

The Royal Shakespeare Company
    at the Swan Y-88

Royall, Anne 1769-1854...............DLB-43

The Roycroft Printing Shop DLB-49

Royde-Smith, Naomi 1875-1964 ....DLB-191

Royster, Vermont 1914- DLB-127

Royston, Richard [publishing house].....DLB-170

Ruark, Gibbons 1941- DLB-120

Ruban, Vasilii Grigorevich 1742-1795 ....DLB-150

Rubens, Bernice 1928- DLB-14, 207

Rudd and Carleton DLB-49

Rudkin, David 1936- DLB-13

Rudolf von Ems
    circa 1200-circa 1254............DLB-138

Ruffin, Josephine St. Pierre
    1842-1924 ....DLB-79

Ruganda, John 1941- DLB-157

Ruggles, Henry Joseph 1813-1906........DLB-64

Ruiz de Burton, María Amparo
    1832-1895 ....DLB-209, 221

Rukeyser, Muriel 1913-1980 ....DLB-48

Rule, Jane 1931- DLB-60

Rulfo, Juan 1918-1986...............DLB-113

Rumaker, Michael 1932- DLB-16

Rumens, Carol 1944- DLB-40

Runyon, Damon 1880-1946 ..... DLB-11, 86, 171

Ruodlieb circa 1050-1075............DLB-148

Rush, Benjamin 1746-1813 ....DLB-37

Rush, Rebecca 1779-?................DLB-200

Rushdie, Salman 1947- DLB-194

Rusk, Ralph L. 1888-1962 ....DLB-103

Ruskin, John 1819-1900........DLB-55, 163, 190

Russ, Joanna 1937- DLB-8

Russell, B. B., and Company...........DLB-49

Russell, Benjamin 1761-1845 ....DLB-43

Russell, Bertrand 1872-1970...........DLB-100

Russell, Charles Edward 1860-1941 ......DLB-25

Russell, Charles M. 1864-1926 ....DLB-188

Russell, Countess Mary Annette Beauchamp
    (see Arnim, Elizabeth von)

Russell, George William (see AE)

Russell, R. H., and Son DLB-49

Rutebeuf flourished 1249-1277 ....DLB-208

Rutherford, Mark 1831-1913............DLB-18

Ruxton, George Frederick 1821-1848 ....DLB-186

Ryan, Michael 1946- Y-82

Ryan, Oscar 1904- DLB-68

Ryga, George 1932- DLB-60

Rylands, Enriqueta Augustina Tennant
    1843-1908 ....DLB-184

Rylands, John 1801-1888.............DLB-184

Ryleev, Kondratii Fedorovich
    1795-1826 ....DLB-205

Rymer, Thomas 1643?-1713 ....DLB-101

Ryskind, Morrie 1895-1985.............DLB-26

Rzhevsky, Aleksei Andreevich
    1737-1804.....................DLB-150

S

The Saalfield Publishing Company DLB-46

Saba, Umberto 1883-1957 ....DLB-114

Sábato, Ernesto 1911- DLB-145

Saberhagen, Fred 1930- DLB-8

Sabin, Joseph 1821-1881 ....DLB-187

Sacer, Gottfried Wilhelm 1635-1699.....DLB-168

Sachs, Hans 1494-1576 ....DLB-179

Sack, John 1930- DLB-185

Sackler, Howard 1929-1982 ....DLB-7

Sackville, Thomas 1536-1608 ....DLB-132

Sackville, Thomas 1536-1608
    and Norton, Thomas
    1532-1584 ....DLB-62

Sackville-West, Edward 1901-1965 ......DLB-191

Sackville-West, V. 1892-1962 ....DLB-34, 195

Sadlier, D. and J., and Company........DLB-49

Sadlier, Mary Anne 1820-1903 ....DLB-99

Sadoff, Ira 1945- DLB-120

Sadoveanu, Mihail 1880-1961 ....DLB-220

Sáenz, Benjamin Alire 1954- DLB-209

Saenz, Jaime 1921-1986 ....DLB-145

Saffin, John circa 1626-1710...........DLB-24

Sagan, Françoise 1935- DLB-83

Sage, Robert 1899-1962...............DLB-4

Sagel, Jim 1947- DLB-82

Sagendorph, Robb Hansell 1900-1970....DLB-137

Sahagún, Carlos 1938- DLB-108

Sahkomaapii, Piitai (see Highwater, Jamake)

Sahl, Hans 1902- DLB-69

Said, Edward W. 1935- DLB-67

Saigyō 1118-1190...................DLB-203

Saiko, George 1892-1962.............DLB-85

St. Dominic's Press DLB-112

Saint-Exupéry, Antoine de 1900-1944.....DLB-72

St. John, J. Allen 1872-1957 ....DLB-188

St. Johns, Adela Rogers 1894-1988 ....DLB-29

The St. John's College Robert Graves Trust.. Y-96

St. Martin's Press...................DLB-46

St. Omer, Garth 1931- DLB-117

Saint Pierre, Michel de 1916-1987 ....DLB-83

Sainte-Beuve, Charles-Augustin
    1804-1869......................DLB-217

Saints' Lives......................DLB-208

Saintsbury, George 1845-1933....... DLB-57, 149

Saiokuken Sōchō 1448-1532 ....DLB-203

Saki (see Munro, H. H.)

Salaam, Kalamu ya 1947- DLB-38

Šalamun, Tomaž 1941- DLB-181

Salas, Floyd 1931- DLB-82

Sálaz-Marquez, Rubén 1935- DLB-122

Salemson, Harold J. 1910-1988 ....DLB-4

Salinas, Luis Omar 1937- DLB-82

Salinas, Pedro 1891-1951.............DLB-134

Salinger, J. D. 1919- DLB-2, 102, 173

Salkey, Andrew 1928- DLB-125

Sallust circa 86 B.C.-35 B.C........... DLB-211

Salt, Waldo 1914- DLB-44

Salter, James 1925- DLB-130

Salter, Mary Jo 1954- DLB-120

Saltus, Edgar 1855-1921 .... DLB-202

Salustri, Carlo Alberto (see Trilussa)

Salverson, Laura Goodman 1890-1970.... DLB-92

Samain, Albert 1858-1900............ DLB-217

Sampson, Richard Henry (see Hull, Richard)

Samuels, Ernest 1903-1996........... DLB-111

Sanborn, Franklin Benjamin 1831-1917 DLB-1, 223

Sánchez, Luis Rafael 1936- DLB-145

Sánchez, Philomeno "Phil" 1917- DLB-122

Sánchez, Ricardo 1941-1995........... DLB-82

Sánchez, Saúl 1943- DLB-209

Sanchez, Sonia 1934- DLB-41; DS-8

Sand, George 1804-1876......... DLB-119, 192

Sandburg, Carl 1878-1967 ....DLB-17, 54

Sanders, Ed 1939- DLB-16

Sandoz, Mari 1896-1966 .... DLB-9, 212

Sandwell, B. K. 1876-1954 .... DLB-92

Sandy, Stephen 1934- DLB-165

Sandys, George 1578-1644 .... DLB-24, 121

Sangster, Charles 1822-1893 .... DLB-99

Sanguineti, Edoardo 1930- DLB-128

Sanjōnishi Sanetaka 1455-1537........ DLB-203

Sansay, Leonora ?-after 1823 .... DLB-200

Sansom, William 1912-1976 .... DLB-139

Santayana, George
  1863-1952 .... DLB-54, 71; DS-13

Santiago, Danny 1911-1988 .... DLB-122

Santmyer, Helen Hooven 1895-1986 ....Y-84

Sanvitale, Francesca 1928- DLB-196

Sapidus, Joannes 1490-1561 ....DLB-179

Sapir, Edward 1884-1939 .... DLB-92

Sapper (see McNeile, Herman Cyril)

Sappho circa 620 B.C.-circa 550 B.C.
  ....DLB-176

Saramago, José 1922- Y-98

Sardou, Victorien 1831-1908 .... DLB-192

Sarduy, Severo 1937- DLB-113

Sargent, Pamela 1948- DLB-8

Saro-Wiwa, Ken 1941- DLB-157

Saroyan, William 1908-1981 ...DLB-7, 9, 86; Y-81

Sarraute, Nathalie 1900-1999 .... DLB-83

Sarrazin, Albertine 1937-1967 .... DLB-83

Sarris, Greg 1952- DLB-175

Sarton, May 1912-1995 .... DLB-48; Y-81

Sartre, Jean-Paul 1905-1980 .... DLB-72

Sassoon, Siegfried
  1886-1967............. DLB-20, 191; DS-18

Sata, Ineko 1904- DLB-180

Saturday Review Press DLB-46

Saunders, James 1925- DLB-13

Saunders, John Monk 1897-1940 .... DLB-26

Saunders, Margaret Marshall
  1861-1947.................... DLB-92

Saunders and Otley DLB-106

Savage, James 1784-1873............. DLB-30

Savage, Marmion W. 1803?-1872....... DLB-21

Savage, Richard 1697?-1743 .... DLB-95

Savard, Félix-Antoine 1896-1982 .... DLB-68

Saville, (Leonard) Malcolm 1901-1982... DLB-160

Sawyer, Ruth 1880-1970.............. DLB-22

Sayers, Dorothy L.
  1893-1957............. DLB-10, 36, 77, 100

Sayle, Charles Edward 1864-1924 ...... DLB-184

Sayles, John Thomas 1950- DLB-44

Sbarbaro, Camillo 1888-1967 .... DLB-114

Scalapino, Leslie 1947- DLB-193

Scannell, Vernon 1922- DLB-27

Scarry, Richard 1919-1994 .... DLB-61

Schaefer, Jack 1907-1991.............. DLB-212

Schaeffer, Albrecht 1885-1950 .... DLB-66

Schaeffer, Susan Fromberg 1941- DLB-28

Schaff, Philip 1819-1893 ....DS-13

Schaper, Edzard 1908-1984 .... DLB-69

Scharf, J. Thomas 1843-1898 .... DLB-47

Schede, Paul Melissus 1539-1602 ....DLB-179

Scheffel, Joseph Viktor von 1826-1886... DLB-129

Scheffler, Johann 1624-1677 .... DLB-164

Schelling, Friedrich Wilhelm Joseph von
  1775-1854..................... DLB-90

Scherer, Wilhelm 1841-1886 .... DLB-129

Scherfig, Hans 1905-1979 .... DLB-214

Schickele, René 1883-1940 .... DLB-66

Schiff, Dorothy 1903-1989 .... DLB-127

Schiller, Friedrich 1759-1805............ DLB-94

Schirmer, David 1623-1687 .... DLB-164

Schlaf, Johannes 1862-1941 .... DLB-118

Schlegel, August Wilhelm 1767-1845 ..... DLB-94

Schlegel, Dorothea 1763-1839.......... DLB-90

Schlegel, Friedrich 1772-1829 .... DLB-90

Schleiermacher, Friedrich 1768-1834 ..... DLB-90

Schlesinger, Arthur M., Jr. 1917- DLB-17

Schlumberger, Jean 1877-1968 .... DLB-65

Schmid, Eduard Hermann Wilhelm (see
  Edschmid, Kasimir)

Schmidt, Arno 1914-1979 .... DLB-69

Schmidt, Johann Kaspar (see Stirner, Max)

Schmidt, Michael 1947- DLB-40

Schmidtbonn, Wilhelm August
  1876-1952..................... DLB-118

Schmitz, James H. 1911- DLB-8

Schnabel, Johann Gottfried
  1692-1760..................... DLB-168

Schnackenberg, Gjertrud 1953- DLB-120

Schnitzler, Arthur 1862-1931 .... DLB-81, 118

Schnurre, Wolfdietrich 1920-1989 .... DLB-69

Schocken Books DLB-46

Scholartis Press..................... DLB-112

Scholderer, Victor 1880-1971 .... DLB-201

The Schomburg Center for Research
  in Black Culture................. DLB-76

Schönbeck, Virgilio (see Giotti, Virgilio)

Schönherr, Karl 1867-1943 .... DLB-118

Schoolcraft, Jane Johnston 1800-1841.....DLB-175

School Stories, 1914-1960............. DLB-160

Schopenhauer, Arthur 1788-1860....... DLB-90

Schopenhauer, Johanna 1766-1838....... DLB-90

Schorer, Mark 1908-1977 .... DLB-103

Schottelius, Justus Georg 1612-1676..... DLB-164

Schouler, James 1839-1920............ DLB-47

Schrader, Paul 1946- DLB-44

Schreiner, Olive
  1855-1920 ....DLB-18, 156, 190, 225

Schroeder, Andreas 1946- DLB-53

Schubart, Christian Friedrich Daniel
  1739-1791..................... DLB-97

Schubert, Gotthilf Heinrich 1780-1860.... DLB-90

Schücking, Levin 1814-1883........... DLB-133

Schulberg, Budd 1914- DLB-6, 26, 28; Y-81

Schulte, F. J., and Company DLB-49

Schulz, Bruno 1892-1942 .... DLB-215

Schulze, Hans (see Praetorius, Johannes)

Schupp, Johann Balthasar 1610-1661 .... DLB-164

Schurz, Carl 1829-1906 .... DLB-23

Schuyler, George S. 1895-1977 ...... DLB-29, 51

Schuyler, James 1923-1991........... DLB-5, 169

Schwartz, Delmore 1913-1966 .... DLB-28, 48

Schwartz, Jonathan 1938- Y-82

Schwartz, Lynne Sharon 1939- DLB-218

Schwarz, Sibylle 1621-1638 .... DLB-164

Schwerner, Armand 1927-1999........ DLB-165

Schwob, Marcel 1867-1905 .... DLB-123

Sciascia, Leonardo 1921-1989 ....DLB-177

Science Fantasy...................... DLB-8

Science-Fiction Fandom and Conventions .. DLB-8

Science-Fiction Fanzines: The Time
  Binders....................... DLB-8

Science-Fiction Films.................. DLB-8

Science Fiction Writers of America and the
  Nebula Awards DLB-8

Scot, Reginald circa 1538-1599......... DLB-136

Scotellaro, Rocco 1923-1953 .... DLB-128

Scott, Dennis 1939-1991 .... DLB-125

Scott, Dixon 1881-1915 .... DLB-98

Scott, Duncan Campbell 1862-1947 ...... DLB-92

Scott, Evelyn 1893-1963............. DLB-9, 48

Scott, F. R. 1899-1985............... DLB-88

Scott, Frederick George 1861-1944....... DLB-92

Scott, Geoffrey 1884-1929 .... DLB-149

Scott, Harvey W. 1838-1910 .... DLB-23

Scott, Paul 1920-1978 ....DLB-14, 207

Scott, Sarah 1723-1795 .... DLB-39

Scott, Tom 1918- DLB-27

Scott, Sir Walter
   1771-1832 . . . . DLB-93, 107, 116, 144, 159

Scott, William Bell 1811-1890 . . . . .DLB-32

Scott, Walter, Publishing
   Company Limited DLB-112

Scott, William R. [publishing house] DLB-46

Scott-Heron, Gil 1949- DLB-41

Scribe, Eugene 1791-1861 . . . . .DLB-192

Scribner, Arthur Hawley 1859-1932 . . . . DS-13, 16

Scribner, Charles 1854-1930 . . . . DS-13, 16

Scribner, Charles, Jr. 1921-1995 . . . . Y-95

Charles Scribner's Sons DLB-49; DS-13, 16, 17

Scripps, E. W. 1854-1926 . . . . .DLB-25

Scudder, Horace Elisha 1838-1902 . . . . DLB-42, 71

Scudder, Vida Dutton 1861-1954 . . . . .DLB-71

Scupham, Peter 1933- DLB-40

Seabrook, William 1886-1945 . . . . .DLB-4

Seabury, Samuel 1729-1796 . . . . .DLB-31

Seacole, Mary Jane Grant 1805-1881 . . . . .DLB-166

The Seafarer circa 970 . . . . .DLB-146

Sealsfield, Charles (Carl Postl)
   1793-1864 . . . . .DLB-133, 186

Sears, Edward I. 1819?-1876 . . . . .DLB-79

Sears Publishing Company DLB-46

Seaton, George 1911-1979 . . . . .DLB-44

Seaton, William Winston 1785-1866 . . . . . .DLB-43

Scckcr, Martin, and Warburg Limited . . . .DLB 112

Secker, Martin [publishing house] DLB-112

Second-Generation Minor Poets of the
   Seventeenth Century DLB-126

Second International Hemingway Colloquium:
   Cuba Y-98

Sedgwick, Arthur George 1844-1915 . . . . . .DLB-64

Sedgwick, Catharine Maria
   1789-1867 . . . . DLB-1, 74, 183

Sedgwick, Ellery 1872-1930 . . . . .DLB-91

Sedley, Sir Charles 1639-1701 . . . . .DLB-131

Seeberg, Peter 1925-1999 . . . . .DLB-214

Seeger, Alan 1888-1916 . . . . .DLB-45

Seers, Eugene (see Dantin, Louis)

Segal, Erich 1937- Y-86

Šegedin, Petar 1909- DLB-181

Seghers, Anna 1900-1983 . . . . .DLB-69

Seid, Ruth (see Sinclair, Jo)

Seidel, Frederick Lewis 1936- Y-84

Seidel, Ina 1885-1974 . . . . .DLB-56

Seifert, Jaroslav 1901-1986 . . . . DLB-215; Y-84

Seigenthaler, John 1927- DLB-127

Seizin Press DLB-112

Séjour, Victor 1817-1874 . . . . .DLB-50

Séjour Marcou et Ferrand, Juan Victor
   (see Séjour, Victor)

Sekowski, Jósef-Julian, Baron Brambeus
   (see Senkovsky, Osip Ivanovich)

Selby, Bettina 1934- DLB-204

Selby, Hubert, Jr. 1928- DLB-2

Selden, George 1929-1989 . . . . .DLB-52

Selden, John 1584-1654 . . . . .DLB-213

Selected English-Language Little Magazines
   and Newspapers [France, 1920-1939] . . .DLB-4

Selected Humorous Magazines
   (1820-1950) DLB-11

Selected Science-Fiction Magazines and
   Anthologies DLB-8

Selenić, Slobodan 1933-1995 . . . . .DLB-181

Self, Edwin F. 1920- DLB-137

Self, Will 1961- DLB-207

Seligman, Edwin R. A. 1861-1939 . . . . . . .DLB-47

Selimović, Meša 1910-1982 . . . . .DLB-181

Selous, Frederick Courteney
   1851-1917 . . . . .DLB-174

Seltzer, Chester E. (see Muro, Amado)

Seltzer, Thomas [publishing house] DLB-46

Selvon, Sam 1923-1994 . . . . .DLB-125

Semmes, Raphael 1809-1877 . . . . .DLB-189

Senancour, Etienne de 1770-1846 . . . . . . .DLB-119

Sendak, Maurice 1928- DLB-61

Seneca the Elder
   circa 54 B.C.-circa A.D. 40 . . . . .DLB-211

Seneca the Younger
   circa 1 B.C.-A.D. 65 . . . . .DLB-211

Senécal, Eva 1905- DLB-92

Sengstacke, John 1912- DLB-127

Senior, Olive 1941- DLB-157

Senkovsky, Osip Ivanovich (Józef-Julian Sekowski,
   Baron Brambeus) 1800-1858 . . . . .DLB-198

Šenoa, August 1838-1881 . . . . .DLB-147

"Sensation Novels" (1863), by
   H. L. Manse .DLB-21

Sepamla, Sipho 1932- DLB-157, 225

Seredy, Kate 1899-1975 . . . . .DLB-22

Sereni, Vittorio 1913-1983 . . . . .DLB-128

Seres, William [publishing house] DLB-170

Serling, Rod 1924-1975 . . . . .DLB-26

Serote, Mongane Wally 1944- DLB-125, 225

Serraillier, Ian 1912-1994 . . . . .DLB-161

Serrano, Nina 1934- DLB-122

Service, Robert 1874-1958 . . . . .DLB-92

Sessler, Charles 1854-1935 . . . . .DLB-187

Seth, Vikram 1952- DLB-120

Seton, Elizabeth Ann 1774-1821 . . . . .DLB-200

Seton, Ernest Thompson
   1860-1942 . . . . .DLB-92; DS-13

Setouchi Harumi 1922- DLB-182

Settle, Mary Lee 1918- DLB-6

Seume, Johann Gottfried 1763-1810 . . . . . .DLB-94

Seuse, Heinrich 1295?-1366 . . . . .DLB-179

Seuss, Dr. (see Geisel, Theodor Seuss)

The Seventy-fifth Anniversary of the Armistice: The
   Wilfred Owen Centenary and the Great War
   Exhibit at the University of Virginia Y-93

Severin, Timothy 1940- DLB-204

Sewall, Joseph 1688-1769 . . . . .DLB-24

Sewall, Richard B. 1908- DLB-111

Sewell, Anna 1820-1878 . . . . .DLB-163

Sewell, Samuel 1652-1730 . . . . .DLB-24

Sex, Class, Politics, and Religion [in the
   British Novel, 1930-1959] DLB-15

Sexton, Anne 1928-1974 . . . . .DLB-5, 169

Seymour-Smith, Martin 1928-1998 . . . . . .DLB-155

Sgorlon, Carlo 1930- DLB-196

Shaara, Michael 1929-1988 . . . . Y-83

Shadwell, Thomas 1641?-1692 . . . . .DLB-80

Shaffer, Anthony 1926- DLB-13

Shaffer, Peter 1926- DLB-13

Shaftesbury, Anthony Ashley Cooper,
   Third Earl of 1671-1713 . . . . .DLB-101

Shairp, Mordaunt 1887-1939 . . . . .DLB-10

Shakespeare, William 1564-1616 . . . . .DLB-62, 172

The Shakespeare Globe Trust Y-93

Shakespeare Head Press DLB-112

Shakhovskoi, Aleksandr Aleksandrovich
   1777-1846 . . . . .DLB-150

Shange, Ntozake 1948- DLB-38

Shapiro, Karl 1913- DLB-48

Sharon Publications DLB-46

Sharp, Margery 1905-1991 . . . . .DLB-161

Sharp, William 1855-1905 . . . . .DLB-156

Sharpe, Tom 1928- DLB-14

Shaw, Albert 1857-1947 . . . . .DLB-91

Shaw, George Bernard
   1856-1950 . . . . DLB-10, 57, 190

Shaw, Henry Wheeler 1818-1885 . . . . .DLB-11

Shaw, Joseph T. 1874-1952 . . . . .DLB-137

Shaw, Irwin 1913-1984 . . . . DLB-6, 102; Y-84

Shaw, Robert 1927-1978 . . . . .DLB-13, 14

Shaw, Robert B. 1947- DLB-120

Shawn, William 1907-1992 . . . . .DLB-137

Shay, Frank [publishing house] DLB-46

Shea, John Gilmary 1824-1892 . . . . .DLB-30

Sheaffer, Louis 1912-1993 . . . . .DLB-103

Shearing, Joseph 1886-1952 . . . . .DLB-70

Shebbeare, John 1709-1788 . . . . .DLB-39

Sheckley, Robert 1928- DLB-8

Shedd, William G. T. 1820-1894 . . . . .DLB-64

Sheed, Wilfred 1930- DLB-6

Sheed and Ward [U.S.] DLB-46

Sheed and Ward Limited [U.K.] DLB-112

Sheldon, Alice B. (see Tiptree, James, Jr.)

Sheldon, Edward 1886-1946 . . . . .DLB-7

Sheldon and Company DLB-49

Shelley, Mary Wollstonecraft
   1797-1851 . . . . DLB-110, 116, 159, 178

Shelley, Percy Bysshe
   1792-1822 . . . . DLB-96, 110, 158

Shelnutt, Eve 1941- DLB-130

Shenstone, William 1714-1763 . . . . .DLB-95

Shepard, Ernest Howard 1879-1976 . . . . . .DLB-160

Shepard, Sam 1943- DLB-7, 212

Shepard, Thomas I, 1604 or 1605-1649 . . .DLB-24

Shepard, Thomas II, 1635-1677 . . . . DLB-24

Shepard, Clark and Brown DLB-49

Shepherd, Luke
flourished 1547-1554 . . . . DLB-136

Sherburne, Edward 1616-1702 . . . . DLB-131

Sheridan, Frances 1724-1766. . . . . DLB-39, 84

Sheridan, Richard Brinsley 1751-1816 . . . . DLB-89

Sherman, Francis 1871-1926 . . . . DLB-92

Sherriff, R. C. 1896-1975 . . . . DLB-10, 191

Sherry, Norman 1935- DLB-155

Sherwood, Mary Martha 1775-1851 . . . . . DLB-163

Sherwood, Robert 1896-1955 . . . . .DLB-7, 26

Shevyrev, Stepan Petrovich
1806-1864 . . . . DLB-205

Shiel, M. P. 1865-1947 . . . . DLB-153

Shiels, George 1886-1949 . . . . DLB-10

Shiga, Naoya 1883-1971 . . . . DLB-180

Shiina Rinzō 1911-1973 . . . . DLB-182

Shikishi Naishinnō 1153?-1201 . . . . DLB-203

Shillaber, B.[enjamin] P.[enhallow]
1814-1890. DLB-1, 11

Shimao Toshio 1917-1986. . . . . DLB-182

Shimazaki, Tōson 1872-1943 . . . . DLB-180

Shine, Ted 1931- DLB-38

Shinkei 1406-1475. . . . . DLB-203

Ship, Reuben 1915-1975 . . . . DLB-88

Shirer, William L. 1904-1993 . . . . DLB-4

Shirinsky-Shikhmatov, Sergii Aleksandrovich
1783-1837 . . . . DLB-150

Shirley, James 1596-1666 . . . . DLB-58

Shishkov, Aleksandr Semenovich
1753-1841 . . . . DLB-150

Shockley, Ann Allen 1927- DLB-33

Shōno Junzō 1921- DLB-182

Shore, Arabella 1820?-1901 and
Shore, Louisa 1824-1895 . . . . DLB-199

Short, Peter [publishing house] DLB-170

Shorthouse, Joseph Henry 1834-1903 . . . . DLB-18

Shōtetsu 1381-1459. . . . . DLB-203

Showalter, Elaine 1941- DLB-67

Shulevitz, Uri 1935- DLB-61

Shulman, Max 1919-1988. . . . . DLB-11

Shute, Henry A. 1856-1943 . . . . DLB-9

Shuttle, Penelope 1947- DLB-14, 40

Sibbes, Richard 1577-1635 . . . . DLB-151

Siddal, Elizabeth Eleanor 1829-1862 . . . . DLB-199

Sidgwick, Ethel 1877-1970. . . . . DLB-197

Sidgwick and Jackson Limited DLB-112

Sidney, Margaret (see Lothrop, Harriet M.)

Sidney, Mary 1561-1621 . . . . DLB-167

Sidney, Sir Philip 1554-1586. . . . . DLB-167

Sidney's Press DLB-49

Siegfried Loraine Sassoon: A Centenary Essay
Tributes from Vivien F. Clarke and
Michael Thorpe Y-86

Sierra, Rubén 1946- DLB-122

Sierra Club Books. DLB-49

Siger of Brabant
circa 1240-circa 1284 . . . . DLB-115

Sigourney, Lydia Howard (Huntley)
1791-1865. . . . . .DLB-1, 42, 73, 183

Silkin, Jon 1930- DLB-27

Silko, Leslie Marmon 1948- DLB-143, 175

Silliman, Benjamin 1779-1864 . . . . DLB-183

Silliman, Ron 1946- DLB-169

Silliphant, Stirling 1918- DLB-26

Sillitoe, Alan 1928- DLB-14, 139

Silman, Roberta 1934- DLB-28

Silva, Beverly 1930- DLB-122

Silverberg, Robert 1935- DLB-8

Silverman, Kenneth 1936- DLB-111

Simak, Clifford D. 1904-1988. . . . . DLB-8

Simcoe, Elizabeth 1762-1850. . . . . DLB-99

Simcox, Edith Jemima 1844-1901. . . . . . . DLB-190

Simcox, George Augustus 1841-1905 . . . . . DLB-35

Sime, Jessie Georgina 1868-1958 . . . . DLB-92

Simenon, Georges 1903-1989 . . . . . .DLB-72; Y-89

Simic, Charles 1938- DLB-105

Simmel, Johannes Mario 1924- DLB-69

Simmes, Valentine [publishing house] DLB-170

Simmons, Ernest J. 1903-1972 . . . . DLB-103

Simmons, Herbert Alfred 1930- DLB-33

Simmons, James 1933- DLB-40

Simms, William Gilmore
1806-1870. . . . . .DLB-3, 30, 59, 73

Simms and M'Intyre. DLB-106

Simon, Claude 1913- DLB-83; Y-85

Simon, Neil 1927- DLB-7

Simon and Schuster DLB-46

Simons, Katherine Drayton Mayrant
1890-1969 . . . . .Y-83

Simović, Ljubomir 1935- DLB-181

Simpkin and Marshall
[publishing house] DLB-154

Simpson, Helen 1897-1940 . . . . DLB-77

Simpson, Louis 1923- DLB-5

Simpson, N. F. 1919- DLB-13

Sims, George 1923- DLB-87; Y-99

Sims, George Robert
1847-1922. . . . . .DLB-35, 70, 135

Sinán, Rogelio 1904- DLB-145

Sinclair, Andrew 1935- DLB-14

Sinclair, Bertrand William 1881-1972. . . . . DLB-92

Sinclair, Catherine 1800-1864. . . . . DLB-163

Sinclair, Jo 1913-1995 . . . . DLB-28

Sinclair Lewis Centennial Conference Y-85

Sinclair, Lister 1921- DLB-88

Sinclair, May 1863-1946. . . . . DLB-36, 135

Sinclair, Upton 1878-1968 . . . . DLB-9

Sinclair, Upton [publishing house] DLB-46

Singer, Isaac Bashevis
1904-1991 . . . . .DLB-6, 28, 52; Y-91

Singer, Mark 1950- DLB-185

Singmaster, Elsie 1879-1958 . . . . DLB-9

Sinisgalli, Leonardo 1908-1981. . . . . DLB-114

Siodmak, Curt 1902- DLB-44

Siringo, Charles A. 1855-1928 . . . . DLB-186

Sissman, L. E. 1928-1976 . . . . DLB-5

Sisson, C. H. 1914- DLB-27

Sitwell, Edith 1887-1964 . . . . DLB-20

Sitwell, Osbert 1892-1969. . . . . .DLB-100, 195

Skalbe, Kārlis 1879-1945. . . . . DLB-220

Skármeta, Antonio 1940- DLB-145

Skeat, Walter W. 1835-1912 . . . . DLB-184

Skeffington, William
[publishing house] DLB-106

Skelton, John 1463-1529. . . . . DLB-136

Skelton, Robin 1925- DLB-27, 53

Škėma, Antanas 1910-1961 . . . . DLB-220

Skinner, Constance Lindsay
1877-1939 . . . . DLB-92

Skinner, John Stuart 1788-1851 . . . . DLB-73

Skipsey, Joseph 1832-1903 . . . . DLB-35

Skou-Hansen, Tage 1925- DLB-214

Slade, Bernard 1930- DLB-53

Slamnig, Ivan 1930- DLB-181

Slančeková, Božena (see Timrava)

Slater, Patrick 1880-1951 . . . . DLB-68

Slaveykov, Pencho 1866-1912 . . . . .DLB-147

Slaviček, Milivoj 1929- DLB-181

Slavitt, David 1935- DLB-5, 6

Sleigh, Burrows Willcocks Arthur
1821-1869 . . . . DLB-99

A Slender Thread of Hope: The Kennedy
Center Black Theatre Project. DLB-38

Slesinger, Tess 1905-1945 . . . . DLB-102

Slick, Sam (see Haliburton, Thomas Chandler)

Sloan, John 1871-1951 . . . . DLB-188

Sloane, William, Associates DLB-46

Small, Maynard and Company DLB-49

Small Presses in Great Britain and Ireland,
1960-1985 . . . . DLB-40

Small Presses I: Jargon Society Y-84

Small Presses II: The Spirit That Moves
Us Press Y-85

Small Presses III: Pushcart Press Y-87

Smart, Christopher 1722-1771 . . . . DLB-109

Smart, David A. 1892-1957 . . . . .DLB-137

Smart, Elizabeth 1913-1986 . . . . DLB-88

Smedley, Menella Bute 1820?-1877 . . . . . DLB-199

Smellie, William [publishing house] DLB-154

Smiles, Samuel 1812-1904 . . . . DLB-55

Smith, A. J. M. 1902-1980 . . . . DLB-88

Smith, Adam 1723-1790 . . . . DLB-104

Smith, Adam (George Jerome Waldo Goodman)
1930- DLB-185

Smith, Alexander 1829-1867 . . . . DLB-32, 55

Smith, Amanda 1837-1915 . . . . DLB-221

Smith, Betty 1896-1972. . . . . .Y-82

Smith, Carol Sturm 1938- Y-81

Smith, Charles Henry 1826-1903 . . . . . . .DLB-11

Smith, Charlotte 1749-1806 . . . . .DLB-39, 109

Smith, Chet 1899-1973. . . . . .DLB-171

Smith, Cordwainer 1913-1966. . . . . .DLB-8

Smith, Dave 1942- DLB-5

Smith, Dodie 1896- DLB-10

Smith, Doris Buchanan 1934- DLB-52

Smith, E. E. 1890-1965 . . . . .DLB-8

Smith, Elihu Hubbard 1771-1798 . . . . .DLB-37

Smith, Elizabeth Oakes (Prince)
    1806-1893 . . . . .DLB-1

Smith, Eunice 1757-1823 . . . . .DLB-200

Smith, F. Hopkinson 1838-1915. . . . . DS-13

Smith, George D. 1870-1920 . . . . .DLB-140

Smith, George O. 1911-1981 . . . . .DLB-8

Smith, Goldwin 1823-1910 . . . . .DLB-99

Smith, H. Allen 1907-1976 . . . . .DLB-11, 29

Smith, Harry B. 1860-1936 . . . . .DLB-187

Smith, Hazel Brannon 1914- DLB-127

Smith, Henry circa 1560-circa 1591. . . . . .DLB-136

Smith, Horatio (Horace) 1779-1849 . . . . . .DLB-116

Smith, Horatio (Horace) 1779-1849 and
    James Smith 1775-1839 . . . . .DLB-96

Smith, Iain Crichton 1928- DLB-40, 139

Smith, J. Allen 1860-1924 . . . . .DLB-47

Smith, Jessie Willcox 1863-1935 . . . . . . .DLB-188

Smith, John 1580-1631. . . . . .DLB-24, 30

Smith, Josiah 1704-1781 . . . . .DLB-24

Smith, Ken 1938- DLB-40

Smith, Lee 1944- DLB-143; Y-83

Smith, Logan Pearsall 1865-1946. . . . . . . .DLB-98

Smith, Mark 1935- Y-82

Smith, Michael 1698-circa 1771 . . . . .DLB-31

Smith, Pauline 1882-1959 . . . . .DLB-225

Smith, Red 1905-1982 . . . . DLB-29, 171

Smith, Roswell 1829-1892 . . . . .DLB-79

Smith, Samuel Harrison 1772-1845 . . . . . . .DLB-43

Smith, Samuel Stanhope 1751-1819 . . . . . . .DLB-37

Smith, Sarah (see Stretton, Hesba)

Smith, Sarah Pogson 1774-1870 . . . . .DLB-200

Smith, Seba 1792-1868. . . . . .DLB-1, 11

Smith, Sir Thomas 1513-1577 . . . . .DLB-132

Smith, Stevie 1902-1971 . . . . .DLB-20

Smith, Sydney 1771-1845. . . . . .DLB-107

Smith, Sydney Goodsir 1915-1975 . . . . . . .DLB-27

Smith, Wendell 1914-1972. . . . . .DLB-171

Smith, William flourished 1595-1597. . . . .DLB-136

Smith, William 1727-1803 . . . . .DLB-31

Smith, William 1728-1793 . . . . .DLB-30

Smith, William Gardner 1927-1974 . . . . . . .DLB-76

Smith, William Henry 1808-1872 . . . . . . .DLB-159

Smith, William Jay 1918- DLB-5

Smith, Elder and Company DLB-154

Smith, Harrison, and Robert Haas
    [publishing house] DLB-46

Smith, J. Stilman, and Company DLB-49

Smith, W. B., and Company DLB-49

Smith, W. H., and Son DLB-106

Smithers, Leonard [publishing house] DLB-112

Smollett, Tobias 1721-1771 . . . . .DLB-39, 104

Smythe, Francis Sydney 1900-1949 . . . . .DLB-195

Snelling, William Joseph 1804-1848 . . . . .DLB-202

Snellings, Rolland (see Touré, Askia Muhammad)

Snodgrass, W. D. 1926- DLB-5

Snow, C. P. 1905-1980 . . . . DLB-15, 77; DS-17

Snyder, Gary 1930- DLB-5, 16, 165, 212

Sobiloff, Hy 1912-1970. . . . . .DLB-48

The Society for Textual Scholarship and
    TEXT Y-87

The Society for the History of Authorship, Reading
    and Publishing. Y-92

Sønderby, Knud 1909-1966. . . . . .DLB-214

Sørensen, Villy 1929- DLB-214

Soffici, Ardengo 1879-1964 . . . . .DLB-114

Sofola, 'Zulu 1938- DLB-157

Solano, Solita 1888-1975 . . . . .DLB-4

Soldati, Mario 1906-1999. . . . . .DLB-177

Šoljan, Antun 1932-1993 . . . . .DLB-181

Sollers, Philippe 1936- DLB-83

Sollogub, Vladimir Aleksandrovich
    1813-1882 . . . . .DLB-198

Solmi, Sergio 1899-1981 . . . . .DLB-114

Solomon, Carl 1928- DLB-16

Solway, David 1941- DLB-53

Solzhenitsyn and America Y-85

Somerville, Edith Œnone 1858-1949 . . . . .DLB-135

Somov, Orest Mikhailovich
    1793-1833 . . . . .DLB-198

Song, Cathy 1955- DLB-169

Sono Ayako 1931- DLB-182

Sontag, Susan 1933- DLB-2, 67

Sophocles 497/496 B.C.-406/405 B.C.
    . . . . .DLB-176

Šopov, Aco 1923-1982. . . . . .DLB-181

Sorensen, Virginia 1912-1991 . . . . .DLB-206

Sorge, Reinhard Johannes 1892-1916 . . . .DLB-118

Sorrentino, Gilbert 1929- DLB-5, 173; Y-80

Sotheby, James 1682-1742 . . . . .DLB-213

Sotheby, John 1740-1807 . . . . .DLB-213

Sotheby, Samuel 1771-1842 . . . . .DLB-213

Sotheby, Samuel Leigh 1805-1861. . . . . . .DLB-213

Sotheby, William 1757-1833. . . . . . . .DLB-93, 213

Soto, Gary 1952- DLB-82

Sources for the Study of Tudor and Stuart
    Drama. DLB-62

Souster, Raymond 1921- DLB-88

The *South English Legendary* circa thirteenth-fifteenth
    centuries. DLB-146

Southerland, Ellease 1943- DLB-33

Southern Illinois University Press Y-95

Southern, Terry 1924-1995 . . . . .DLB-2

Southern Writers Between the Wars. DLB-9

Southerne, Thomas 1659-1746 . . . . .DLB-80

Southey, Caroline Anne Bowles
    1786-1854 . . . . .DLB-116

Southey, Robert 1774-1843 . . . . . DLB-93, 107, 142

Southwell, Robert 1561?-1595. . . . . .DLB-167

Sowande, Bode 1948- DLB-157

Sowle, Tace [publishing house] DLB-170

Soyfer, Jura 1912-1939 . . . . .DLB-124

Soyinka, Wole 1934- DLB-125; Y-86, Y-87

Spacks, Barry 1931- DLB-105

Spalding, Frances 1950- DLB-155

Spark, Muriel 1918- DLB-15, 139

Sparke, Michael [publishing house] DLB-170

Sparks, Jared 1789-1866. . . . . .DLB-1, 30

Sparshott, Francis 1926- DLB-60

Späth, Gerold 1939- DLB-75

Spatola, Adriano 1941-1988. . . . . .DLB-128

Spaziani, Maria Luisa 1924- DLB-128

Special Collections at the University of Colorado
    at Boulder Y-98

The Spectator 1828- DLB-110

Spedding, James 1808-1881 . . . . .DLB-144

Spee von Langenfeld, Friedrich
    1591-1635 . . . . .DLB-164

Speght, Rachel 1597-after 1630 . . . . .DLB-126

Speke, John Hanning 1827-1864 . . . . .DLB-166

Spellman, A. B. 1935- DLB-41

Spence, Thomas 1750-1814 . . . . .DLB-158

Spencer, Anne 1882-1975. . . . . .DLB-51, 54

Spencer, Charles, third Earl of Sunderland
    1674-1722 . . . . .DLB-213

Spencer, Elizabeth 1921- DLB-6, 218

Spencer, George John, Second Earl Spencer
    1758-1834 . . . . .DLB-184

Spencer, Herbert 1820-1903 . . . . .DLB-57

Spencer, Scott 1945- Y-86

Spender, J. A. 1862-1942 . . . . .DLB-98

Spender, Stephen 1909-1995 . . . . .DLB-20

Spener, Philipp Jakob 1635-1705 . . . . . . .DLB-164

Spenser, Edmund circa 1552-1599. . . . . . .DLB-167

Sperr, Martin 1944- DLB-124

Spicer, Jack 1925-1965. . . . . .DLB-5, 16, 193

Spielberg, Peter 1929- Y-81

Spielhagen, Friedrich 1829-1911 . . . . . . .DLB-129

"Spielmannsepen"
    (circa 1152-circa 1500) DLB-148

Spier, Peter 1927- DLB-61

Spillane, Mickey 1918- DLB-226

Spinrad, Norman 1940- DLB-8

Spires, Elizabeth 1952- DLB-120

Spitteler, Carl 1845-1924 . . . . .DLB-129

Spivak, Lawrence E. 1900- DLB-137

Spofford, Harriet Prescott
    1835-1921 . . . . .DLB-74, 221

Spring, Howard 1889-1965 . . . . DLB-191

Squier, E. G. 1821-1888 . . . . DLB-189

Squibob (see Derby, George Horatio)

Stacpoole, H. de Vere 1863-1951 . . . . . . DLB-153

Staël, Germaine de 1766-1817 . . . . . DLB-119, 192

Staël-Holstein, Anne-Louise Germaine de
(see Staël, Germaine de)

Stafford, Jean 1915-1979 . . . . DLB-2, 173

Stafford, William 1914-1993 . . . . DLB-5, 206

Stage Censorship: "The Rejected Statement"
(1911), by Bernard Shaw [excerpts] . . . DLB-10

Stallings, Laurence 1894-1968 . . . . DLB-7, 44

Stallworthy, Jon 1935- DLB-40

Stampp, Kenneth M. 1912- DLB-17

Stanev, Emiliyan 1907-1979 . . . . DLB-181

Stanford, Ann 1916- DLB-5

Stangerup, Henrik 1937-1998 . . . . DLB-214

Stankevich, Nikolai Vladimirovich
1813-1840 . . . . DLB-198

Stanković, Borisav ("Bora")
1876-1927 . . . . DLB-147

Stanley, Henry M. 1841-1904 . . . . DLB-189; DS-13

Stanley, Thomas 1625-1678 . . . . DLB-131

Stannard, Martin 1947- DLB-155

Stansby, William [publishing house] DLB-170

Stanton, Elizabeth Cady 1815-1902 . . . . . . DLB-79

Stanton, Frank L. 1857-1927 . . . . DLB-25

Stanton, Maura 1946- DLB-120

Stapledon, Olaf 1886-1950 . . . . DLB-15

Star Spangled Banner Office DLB-49

Stark, Freya 1893-1993 . . . . DLB-195

Starkey, Thomas circa 1499-1538 . . . . . . DLB-132

Starkie, Walter 1894-1976 . . . . DLB-195

Starkweather, David 1935- DLB-7

Starrett, Vincent 1886-1974 . . . . DLB-187

Statements on the Art of Poetry DLB-54

The State of Publishing Y-97

Stationers' Company of London, The DLB-170

Statius circa A.D. 45-A.D. 96 . . . . DLB-211

Stead, Robert J. C. 1880-1959 . . . . DLB-92

Steadman, Mark 1930- DLB-6

The Stealthy School of Criticism (1871), by
Dante Gabriel Rossetti DLB-35

Stearns, Harold E. 1891-1943 . . . . DLB-4

Stedman, Edmund Clarence 1833-1908 . . . DLB-64

Steegmuller, Francis 1906-1994 . . . . DLB-111

Steel, Flora Annie 1847-1929 . . . . . . DLB-153, 156

Steele, Max 1922- Y-80

Steele, Richard 1672-1729 . . . . DLB-84, 101

Steele, Timothy 1948- DLB-120

Steele, Wilbur Daniel 1886-1970 . . . . DLB-86

Steere, Richard circa 1643-1721 . . . . DLB-24

Stefanovski, Goran 1952- DLB-181

Stegner, Wallace 1909-1993 . . . . DLB-9, 206; Y-93

Stehr, Hermann 1864-1940 . . . . DLB-66

Steig, William 1907- DLB-61

Stein, Gertrude
1874-1946 . . . . DLB-4, 54, 86; DS-15

Stein, Leo 1872-1947 . . . . DLB-4

Stein and Day Publishers DLB-46

Steinbeck, John 1902-1968 . . . . DLB-7, 9, 212; DS-2

Steiner, George 1929- DLB-67

Steinhoewel, Heinrich 1411/1412-1479 . . . . DLB-179

Steloff, Ida Frances 1887-1989 . . . . DLB-187

Stendhal 1783-1842 . . . . DLB-119

Stephen Crane: A Revaluation Virginia
Tech Conference, 1989 . . . . Y-89

Stephen, Leslie 1832-1904 . . . . . . DLB-57, 144, 190

Stephen Vincent Benét Centenary Y-97

Stephens, Alexander H. 1812-1883 . . . . . . DLB-47

Stephens, Alice Barber 1858-1932 . . . . . . DLB-188

Stephens, Ann 1810-1886 . . . . DLB-3, 73

Stephens, Charles Asbury 1844?-1931 . . . . DLB-42

Stephens, James 1882?-1950 . . . . . DLB-19, 153, 162

Stephens, John Lloyd 1805-1852 . . . . DLB-183

Sterling, George 1869-1926 . . . . DLB-54

Sterling, James 1701-1763 . . . . DLB-24

Sterling, John 1806-1844 . . . . DLB-116

Stern, Gerald 1925- DLB-105

Stern, Gladys B. 1890-1973 . . . . DLB-197

Stern, Madeleine B. 1912- DLB-111, 140

Stern, Richard 1928- DLB-218; Y-87

Stern, Stewart 1922- DLB-26

Sterne, Laurence 1713-1768 . . . . DLB-39

Sternheim, Carl 1878-1942 . . . . DLB-56, 118

Sternhold, Thomas ?-1549 and
John Hopkins ?-1570 . . . . DLB-132

Steuart, David 1747-1824 . . . . DLB-213

Stevens, Henry 1819-1886 . . . . DLB-140

Stevens, Wallace 1879-1955 . . . . DLB-54

Stevenson, Anne 1933- DLB-40

Stevenson, D. E. 1892-1973 . . . . DLB-191

Stevenson, Lionel 1902-1973 . . . . DLB-155

Stevenson, Robert Louis 1850-1894
. . . . DLB-18, 57, 141, 156, 174; DS-13

Stewart, Donald Ogden
1894-1980 . . . . DLB-4, 11, 26

Stewart, Dugald 1753-1828 . . . . DLB-31

Stewart, George, Jr. 1848-1906 . . . . DLB-99

Stewart, George R. 1895-1980 . . . . DLB-8

Stewart and Kidd Company DLB-46

Stewart, Randall 1896-1964 . . . . DLB-103

Stickney, Trumbull 1874-1904 . . . . DLB-54

Stieler, Caspar 1632-1707 . . . . DLB-164

Stifter, Adalbert 1805-1868 . . . . DLB-133

Stiles, Ezra 1727-1795 . . . . DLB-31

Still, James 1906- DLB-9

Stirner, Max 1806-1856 . . . . DLB-129

Stith, William 1707-1755 . . . . DLB-31

Stock, Elliot [publishing house] DLB-106

Stockton, Frank R.
1834-1902 . . . . DLB-42, 74; DS-13

Stoddard, Ashbel [publishing house] DLB-49

Stoddard, Charles Warren
1843-1909 . . . . DLB-186

Stoddard, Elizabeth 1823-1902 . . . . DLB-202

Stoddard, Richard Henry
1825-1903 . . . . DLB-3, 64; DS-13

Stoddard, Solomon 1643-1729 . . . . DLB-24

Stoker, Bram 1847-1912 . . . . DLB-36, 70, 178

Stokes, Frederick A., Company DLB-49

Stokes, Thomas L. 1898-1958 . . . . DLB-29

Stokesbury, Leon 1945- DLB-120

Stolberg, Christian Graf zu 1748-1821 . . . . DLB-94

Stolberg, Friedrich Leopold Graf zu
1750-1819 . . . . DLB-94

Stone, Herbert S., and Company DLB-49

Stone, Lucy 1818-1893 . . . . DLB-79

Stone, Melville 1848-1929 . . . . DLB-25

Stone, Robert 1937- DLB-152

Stone, Ruth 1915- DLB-105

Stone, Samuel 1602-1663 . . . . DLB-24

Stone, William Leete 1792-1844 . . . . DLB-202

Stone and Kimball DLB-49

Stoppard, Tom 1937- DLB-13; Y-85

Storey, Anthony 1928- DLB-14

Storey, David 1933- DLB-13, 14, 207

Storm, Theodor 1817-1888 . . . . DLB-129

Story, Thomas circa 1670-1742 . . . . DLB-31

Story, William Wetmore 1819-1895 . . . . . . DLB-1

Storytelling: A Contemporary Renaissance . . . Y-84

Stoughton, William 1631-1701 . . . . DLB-24

Stow, John 1525-1605 . . . . DLB-132

Stowe, Harriet Beecher
1811-1896 . . . . DLB-1, 12, 42, 74, 189

Stowe, Leland 1899- DLB-29

Stoyanov, Dimitr Ivanov (see Elin Pelin)

Strabo 64 or 63 B.C.-circa A.D. 25
. . . . DLB-176

Strachey, Lytton
1880-1932 . . . . DLB-149; DS-10

Strachey, Lytton, Preface to Eminent
Victorians DLB-149

Strahan and Company DLB-106

Strahan, William [publishing house] DLB-154

Strand, Mark 1934- DLB-5

The Strasbourg Oaths 842 . . . . DLB-148

Stratemeyer, Edward 1862-1930 . . . . DLB-42

Strati, Saverio 1924- DLB-177

Stratton and Barnard DLB-49

Stratton-Porter, Gene
1863-1924 . . . . DLB-221; DS-14

Straub, Peter 1943- Y-84

Strauß, Botho 1944- DLB-124

Strauß, David Friedrich 1808-1874 . . . . . . DLB-133

The Strawberry Hill Press DLB-154

Streatfeild, Noel 1895-1986 . . . . DLB-160

Street, Cecil John Charles (see Rhode, John)

Street, G. S. 1867-1936 . . . . DLB-135

Street and Smith. DLB-49

Streeter, Edward 1891-1976. . . . . .DLB-11

Streeter, Thomas Winthrop
    1883-1965 . . . . .DLB-140

Stretton, Hesba 1832-1911. . . . . .DLB-163, 190

Stribling, T. S. 1881-1965 . . . . .DLB-9

Der Stricker circa 1190-circa 1250 . . . . . .DLB-138

Strickland, Samuel 1804-1867 . . . . .DLB-99

Stringer and Townsend DLB-49

Stringer, Arthur 1874-1950 . . . . .DLB-92

Strittmatter, Erwin 1912- DLB-69

Strniša, Gregor 1930-1987 . . . . .DLB-181

Strode, William 1630-1645 . . . . .DLB-126

Strong, L. A. G. 1896-1958 . . . . .DLB-191

Strother, David Hunter 1816-1888 . . . . . . .DLB-3

Strouse, Jean 1945- DLB-111

Stuart, Dabney 1937- DLB-105

Stuart, Jesse 1906-1984 . . . . . DLB-9, 48, 102; Y-84

Stuart, Ruth McEnery 1849?-1917. . . . . .DLB-202

Stuart, Lyle [publishing house]. DLB-46

Stubbs, Harry Clement (see Clement, Hal)

Stubenberg, Johann Wilhelm von
    1619-1663 . . . . .DLB-164

Studio. DLB-112

The Study of Poetry (1880), by
    Matthew Arnold DLB-35

Sturgeon, Theodore 1918-1985 . . . . . .DLB-8; Y-85

Sturges, Preston 1898-1959 . . . . .DLB-26

"Style" (1840; revised, 1859), by
    Thomas de Quincey [excerpt] DLB-57

"Style" (1888), by Walter Pater DLB-57

Style (1897), by Walter Raleigh
    [excerpt]. DLB-57

"Style" (1877), by T. H. Wright
    [excerpt]. DLB-57

"Le Style c'est l'homme" (1892), by
    W. H. Mallock DLB-57

Styron, William 1925- DLB-2, 143; Y-80

Suárez, Mario 1925- DLB-82

Such, Peter 1939- DLB-60

Suckling, Sir John 1609-1641?. DLB-58, 126

Suckow, Ruth 1892-1960. . . . . .DLB-9, 102

Sudermann, Hermann 1857-1928 . . . . . . .DLB-118

Sue, Eugène 1804-1857 . . . . .DLB-119

Sue, Marie-Joseph (see Sue, Eugène)

Suetonius circa A.D. 69-post A.D. 122 . . .DLB-211

Suggs, Simon (see Hooper, Johnson Jones)

Sui Sin Far (see Eaton, Edith Maude)

Suits, Gustav 1883-1956 . . . . .DLB-220

Sukenick, Ronald 1932- DLB-173; Y-81

Suknaski, Andrew 1942- DLB-53

Sullivan, Alan 1868-1947 . . . . .DLB-92

Sullivan, C. Gardner 1886-1965 . . . . .DLB-26

Sullivan, Frank 1892-1976 . . . . .DLB-11

Sulte, Benjamin 1841-1923 . . . . .DLB-99

Sulzberger, Arthur Hays 1891-1968 . . . . .DLB-127

Sulzberger, Arthur Ochs 1926- DLB-127

Sulzer, Johann Georg 1720-1779 . . . . .DLB-97

Sumarokov, Aleksandr Petrovich
    1717-1777 . . . . .DLB-150

Summers, Hollis 1916- DLB-6

A Summing Up at Century's End Y-99

Sumner, Henry A. [publishing house] DLB-49

Surtees, Robert Smith 1803-1864. . . . . . . .DLB-21

Surveys: Japanese Literature,
    1987-1995 . . . . .DLB-182

A Survey of Poetry Anthologies,
    1879-1960 . . . . .DLB-54

Sutherland, Efua Theodora
    1924-1996 . . . . .DLB-117

Sutherland, John 1919-1956. . . . . .DLB-68

Sutro, Alfred 1863-1933. . . . . .DLB-10

Svendsen, Hanne Marie 1933- DLB-214

Swados, Harvey 1920-1972 . . . . .DLB-2

Swain, Charles 1801-1874 . . . . .DLB-32

Swallow Press DLB-46

Swan Sonnenschein Limited DLB-106

Swanberg, W. A. 1907- DLB-103

Swenson, May 1919-1989 . . . . .DLB-5

Swerling, Jo 1897- DLB-44

Swift, Graham 1949- DLB-194

Swift, Jonathan 1667-1745 . . . . . . DLB-39, 95, 101

Swinburne, A. C.
    1837-1909 .DLB-35, 57

Swineshead, Richard
    floruit circa 1350 . . . . .DLB-115

Swinnerton, Frank 1884-1982 . . . . .DLB-34

Swisshelm, Jane Grey 1815-1884. . . . . . . .DLB-43

Swope, Herbert Bayard
    1882-1958 . . . . .DLB-25

Swords, T. and J., and Company DLB-49

Swords, Thomas 1763-1843 and
    Swords, James ?-1844 . . . . .DLB-73

Sykes, Ella C. ?-1939 . . . . .DLB-174

Sylvester, Josuah
    1562 or 1563 - 1618 . . . . .DLB-121

Symonds, Emily Morse (see Paston, George)

Symonds, John Addington
    1840-1893 . . . . DLB-57, 144

Symons, A. J. A. 1900-1941. . . . . .DLB-149

Symons, Arthur 1865-1945 . . . . . . DLB-19, 57, 149

Symons, Julian
    1912-1994 . . . . DLB-87, 155; Y-92

Symons, Scott 1933- DLB-53

A Symposium on The Columbia History of
    the Novel Y-92

Synge, John Millington 1871-1909 . . . . .DLB-10, 19

Synge Summer School: J. M. Synge and the
    Irish Theater, Rathdrum, County Wiclow,
    Ireland. Y-93

Syrett, Netta 1865-1943 . . . . .DLB-135, 197

Szabó, Lőrinc 1900-1957 . . . . .DLB-215

Szabó, Magda 1917- DLB-215

Szymborska, Wisława 1923- Y-96

T

Taban lo Liyong 1939?- DLB-125

Tabucchi, Antonio 1943- DLB-196

Taché, Joseph-Charles 1820-1894 . . . . .DLB-99

Tachihara Masaaki 1926-1980 . . . . .DLB-182

Tacitus circa A.D. 55-circa A.D. 117 . . . . .DLB-211

Tadijanović, Dragutin 1905- DLB-181

Tafdrup, Pia 1952- DLB-214

Tafolla, Carmen 1951- DLB-82

Taggard, Genevieve 1894-1948. . . . . .DLB-45

Taggart, John 1942- DLB-193

Tagger, Theodor (see Bruckner, Ferdinand)

Taiheiki late fourteenth century DLB-203

Tait, J. Selwin, and Sons DLB-49

Tait's Edinburgh Magazine 1832-1861. . . . . .DLB-110

The Takarazaka Revue Company Y-91

Talander (see Bohse, August)

Talese, Gay 1932- DLB-185

Talev, Dimitr 1898-1966 . . . . .DLB-181

Taliaferro, H. E. 1811-1875 . . . . .DLB-202

Tallent, Elizabeth 1954- DLB-130

TallMountain, Mary 1918-1994 . . . . .DLB-193

Talvj 1797-1870 . . . . .DLB-59, 133

Tamási, Áron 1897-1966 . . . . .DLB-215

Tammsaare, A. H.
    1878-1940 . . . . .DLB-220

Tan, Amy 1952- DLB-173

Tanner, Thomas
    1673/1674-1735 . . . . .DLB-213

Tanizaki, Jun'ichirō 1886-1965 . . . . .DLB-180

Tapahonso, Luci 1953- DLB-175

Taradash, Daniel 1913- DLB-44

Tarbell, Ida M. 1857-1944 . . . . .DLB-47

Tardivel, Jules-Paul 1851-1905 . . . . .DLB-99

Targan, Barry 1932- DLB-130

Tarkington, Booth 1869-1946 . . . . . . .DLB-9, 102

Tashlin, Frank 1913-1972 . . . . .DLB-44

Tate, Allen 1899-1979 . . . . . . DLB-4, 45, 63; DS-17

Tate, James 1943- DLB-5, 169

Tate, Nahum circa 1652-1715 . . . . .DLB-80

Tatian circa 830 .DLB-148

Taufer, Veno 1933- DLB-181

Tauler, Johannes circa 1300-1361 . . . . . . .DLB-179

Tavčar, Ivan 1851-1923. . . . . .DLB-147

Taylor, Ann 1782-1866 . . . . .DLB-163

Taylor, Bayard 1825-1878 . . . . .DLB-3, 189

Taylor, Bert Leston 1866-1921 . . . . .DLB-25

Taylor, Charles H. 1846-1921. . . . . .DLB-25

Taylor, Edward circa 1642-1729 . . . . .DLB-24

Taylor, Elizabeth 1912-1975 . . . . .DLB-139

Taylor, Henry 1942- DLB-5

Taylor, Sir Henry 1800-1886 . . . . .DLB-32

Taylor, Jane 1783-1824 . . . . .DLB-163

Taylor, Jeremy circa 1613-1667. . . . . . . .DLB-151

Taylor, John 1577 or 1578 - 1653 . . . . DLB-121

Taylor, Mildred D. ?- DLB-52

Taylor, Peter
1917-1994 . . . . DLB-218; Y-81, Y-94

Taylor, Susie King 1848-1912 . . . . DLB-221

Taylor, William, and Company DLB-49

Taylor-Made Shakespeare? Or Is "Shall I Die?" the
Long-Lost Text of Bottom's Dream? Y-85

Teasdale, Sara 1884-1933 . . . . DLB-45

The Tea-Table (1725), by Eliza Haywood
[excerpt] DLB-39

Telles, Lygia Fagundes 1924- DLB-113

Temple, Sir William 1628-1699 . . . . DLB-101

Tenn, William 1919- DLB-8

Tennant, Emma 1937- DLB-14

Tenney, Tabitha Gilman
1762-1837 . . . . DLB-37, 200

Tennyson, Alfred 1809-1892 . . . . DLB-32

Tennyson, Frederick 1807-1898 . . . . DLB-32

Tenorio, Arthur 1924- DLB-209

Tepliakov, Viktor Grigor'evich
1804-1842 . . . . DLB-205

Terence
circa 184 B.C.-159 B.C. or after DLB-211

Terhune, Albert Payson 1872-1942 . . . . DLB-9

Terhune, Mary Virginia
1830-1922 . . . . DS-13, DS-16

Terry, Megan 1932- DLB-7

Terson, Peter 1932- DLB-13

Tesich, Steve 1943-1996 . . . . Y-83

Tessa, Delio 1886-1939 . . . . DLB-114

Testori, Giovanni
1923-1993 . . . . DLB-128, 177

Tey, Josephine 1896?-1952 . . . . DLB-77

Thacher, James 1754-1844 . . . . DLB-37

Thackeray, William Makepeace
1811-1863 . . . . DLB-21, 55, 159, 163

Thames and Hudson Limited DLB-112

Thanet, Octave (see French, Alice)

Thatcher, John Boyd
1847-1909 . . . . DLB-187

Thayer, Caroline Matilda Warren
1785-1844 . . . . DLB-200

The Theater in Shakespeare's Time DLB-62

The Theatre Guild DLB-7

Thegan and the Astronomer
flourished circa 850 . . . . DLB-148

Thelwall, John 1764-1834 . . . . DLB-93, 158

Theocritus circa 300 B.C.-260 B.C.
. . . . DLB-176

Theodorescu, Ion N. (see Arghezi, Tudor)

Theodulf circa 760-circa 821 . . . . DLB-148

Theophrastus circa 371 B.C.-287 B.C.
. . . . DLB-176

Theriault, Yves 1915-1983 . . . . DLB-88

Thério, Adrien 1925- DLB-53

Theroux, Paul 1941- DLB-2, 218

Thesiger, Wilfred 1910- DLB-204

They All Came to Paris DS-16

Thibaudeau, Colleen 1925- DLB-88

Thielen, Benedict 1903-1965 . . . . DLB-102

Thiong'o Ngugi wa (see Ngugi wa Thiong'o)

Third-Generation Minor Poets of the
Seventeenth Century DLB-131

This Quarter 1925-1927, 1929-1932 . . . . DS-15

Thoma, Ludwig 1867-1921 . . . . DLB-66

Thoma, Richard 1902- DLB-4

Thomas, Audrey 1935- DLB-60

Thomas, D. M. 1935- DLB-40, 207

Thomas, Dylan 1914-1953 . . . . . . DLB-13, 20, 139

Thomas, Edward
1878-1917 . . . . DLB-19, 98, 156, 216

Thomas, Frederick William
1806-1866 . . . . DLB-202

Thomas, Gwyn 1913-1981 . . . . DLB-15

Thomas, Isaiah 1750-1831 . . . . DLB-43, 73, 187

Thomas, Isaiah [publishing house] DLB-49

Thomas, Johann 1624-1679 . . . . DLB-168

Thomas, John 1900-1932 . . . . DLB-4

Thomas, Joyce Carol 1938- DLB-33

Thomas, Lorenzo 1944- DLB-41

Thomas, R. S. 1915- DLB-27

The Thomas Wolfe Collection at the University of
North Carolina at Chapel Hill Y-97

The Thomas Wolfe Society Y-97

Thomasîn von Zerclære
circa 1186-circa 1259 . . . . DLB-138

Thomasius, Christian 1655-1728 . . . . DLB-168

Thompson, David 1770-1857 . . . . DLB-99

Thompson, Daniel Pierce 1795-1868 . . . . DLB-202

Thompson, Dorothy 1893-1961 . . . . DLB-29

Thompson, Francis 1859-1907 . . . . DLB-19

Thompson, George Selden (see Selden, George)

Thompson, Henry Yates 1838-1928 . . . . DLB-184

Thompson, Hunter S. 1939- DLB-185

Thompson, Jim 1906-1977 . . . . DLB-226

Thompson, John 1938-1976 . . . . DLB-60

Thompson, John R. 1823-1873 . . . . DLB-3, 73

Thompson, Lawrance 1906-1973 . . . . DLB-103

Thompson, Maurice 1844-1901 . . . . . . DLB-71, 74

Thompson, Ruth Plumly 1891-1976 . . . . . DLB-22

Thompson, Thomas Phillips 1843-1933 . . . DLB-99

Thompson, William 1775-1833 . . . . DLB-158

Thompson, William Tappan
1812-1882 . . . . DLB-3, 11

Thomson, Edward William 1849-1924 . . . DLB-92

Thomson, James 1700-1748 . . . . DLB-95

Thomson, James 1834-1882 . . . . DLB-35

Thomson, Joseph 1858-1895 . . . . DLB-174

Thomson, Mortimer 1831-1875 . . . . DLB-11

Thoreau, Henry David 1817-1862 DLB-1, 183, 223

The Thoreauvian Pilgrimage: The Structure of an
American Cult DLB-223

Thornton Wilder Centenary at Yale Y-97

Thorpe, Thomas Bangs 1815-1878 . . . . . DLB-3, 11

Thorup, Kirsten 1942- DLB-214

Thoughts on Poetry and Its Varieties (1833),
by John Stuart Mill DLB-32

Thrale, Hester Lynch (see Piozzi, Hester
Lynch [Thrale])

Thubron, Colin 1939- DLB-204

Thucydides circa 455 B.C.-circa 395 B.C.
. . . . DLB-176

Thulstrup, Thure de 1848-1930 . . . . DLB-188

Thümmel, Moritz August von
1738-1817 . . . . DLB-97

Thurber, James 1894-1961 . . . . . DLB-4, 11, 22, 102

Thurman, Wallace 1902-1934 . . . . DLB-51

Thwaite, Anthony 1930- DLB-40

Thwaites, Reuben Gold 1853-1913 . . . . . . DLB-47

Tibullus circa 54 B.C.-circa 19 B.C. DLB-211

Ticknor, George 1791-1871 . . . . . . DLB-1, 59, 140

Ticknor and Fields DLB-49

Ticknor and Fields (revived) DLB-46

Tieck, Ludwig 1773-1853 . . . . DLB-90

Tietjens, Eunice 1884-1944 . . . . DLB-54

Tilney, Edmund circa 1536-1610 . . . . DLB-136

Tilt, Charles [publishing house] DLB-106

Tilton, J. E., and Company DLB-49

Time and Western Man (1927), by Wyndham
Lewis [excerpts] DLB-36

Time-Life Books DLB-46

Times Books DLB-46

Timothy, Peter circa 1725-1782 . . . . DLB-43

Timrava 1867-1951 . . . . DLB-215

Timrod, Henry 1828-1867 . . . . DLB-3

Tindal, Henrietta 1818?-1879 . . . . DLB-199

Tinker, Chauncey Brewster
1876-1963 . . . . DLB-140

Tinsley Brothers DLB-106

Tiptree, James, Jr. 1915-1987 . . . . DLB-8

Tišma, Aleksandar 1924- DLB-181

Titus, Edward William
1870-1952 . . . . DLB-4; DS-15

Tiutchev, Fedor Ivanovich
1803-1873 . . . . DLB-205

Tlali, Miriam 1933- DLB-157, 225

Todd, Barbara Euphan 1890-1976 . . . . . . DLB-160

Tofte, Robert
1561 or 1562-1619 or 1620 . . . . DLB-172

Toklas, Alice B. 1877-1967 . . . . DLB-4

Tokuda, Shūsei 1872-1943 . . . . DLB-180

Tolkien, J. R. R. 1892-1973 . . . . DLB-15, 160

Toller, Ernst 1893-1939 . . . . DLB-124

Tollet, Elizabeth 1694-1754 . . . . DLB-95

Tolson, Melvin B. 1898-1966 . . . . DLB-48, 76

Tom Jones (1749), by Henry Fielding
[excerpt] DLB-39

Tomalin, Claire 1933- DLB-155

Tomasi di Lampedusa,
Giuseppe 1896-1957 . . . . DLB-177

Tomlinson, Charles 1927- DLB-40

Tomlinson, H. M. 1873-1958
..........................DLB-36, 100, 195

Tompkins, Abel [publishing house].......DLB-49

Tompson, Benjamin 1642-1714.........DLB-24

Ton'a 1289-1372.....................DLB-203

Tondelli, Pier Vittorio 1955-1991.......DLB-196

Tonks, Rosemary 1932-..........DLB-14, 207

Tonna, Charlotte Elizabeth
1790-1846.......................DLB-163

Tonson, Jacob the Elder
[publishing house]................DLB-170

Toole, John Kennedy 1937-1969...........Y-81

Toomer, Jean 1894-1967............DLB-45, 51

Tor Books..........................DLB-46

Torberg, Friedrich 1908-1979..........DLB-85

Torrence, Ridgely 1874-1950...........DLB-54

Torres-Metzger, Joseph V. 1933-......DLB-122

Toth, Susan Allen 1940-...............Y-86

Tottell, Richard [publishing house]......DLB-170

Tough-Guy Literature..................DLB-9

Touré, Askia Muhammad 1938-......DLB-41

Tourgée, Albion W. 1838-1905.........DLB-79

Tourneur, Cyril circa 1580-1626........DLB-58

Tournier, Michel 1924-...............DLB-83

Tousey, Frank [publishing house].......DLB-49

Tower Publications....................DLB-46

Towne, Benjamin circa 1740-1793.......DLB-43

Towne, Robert 1936-.................DLB-44

The Townely Plays fifteenth and sixteenth
centuries.......................DLB-146

Townshend, Aurelian
by 1583 - circa 1651..............DLB-121

Toy, Barbara 1908-.................DLB-204

Tracy, Honor 1913-.................DLB-15

Traherne, Thomas 1637?-1674.........DLB-131

Traill, Catharine Parr 1802-1899........DLB-99

Train, Arthur 1875-1945.........DLB-86; DS-16

The Transatlantic Publishing Company ...DLB-49

The Transatlantic Review 1924-1925.........DS-15

The Transcendental Club 1836-1840....DLB-223

Transcendentalism....................DLB-223

Transcendentalists, American............DS-5

A Transit of Poets and Others: American
Biography in 1982..................Y-82

transition 1927-1938....................DS-15

Translators of the Twelfth Century:
Literary Issues Raised and Impact
Created.......................DLB-115

Travel Writing, 1837-1875.............DLB-166

Travel Writing, 1876-1909............DLB-174

Traven, B. 1882? or 1890?-1969?......DLB-9, 56

Travers, Ben 1886-1980.............DLB-10

Travers, P. L. (Pamela Lyndon)
1899-1996.....................DLB-160

Trediakovsky, Vasilii Kirillovich
1703-1769.......................DLB-150

Treece, Henry 1911-1966.............DLB-160

Trejo, Ernesto 1950-..............DLB-122

Trelawny, Edward John
1792-1881..............DLB-110, 116, 144

Tremain, Rose 1943-...............DLB-14

Tremblay, Michel 1942-............DLB-60

Trends in Twentieth-Century
Mass Market Publishing............DLB-46

Trent, William P. 1862-1939............DLB-47

Trescot, William Henry 1822-1898.......DLB-30

Tressell, Robert (Robert Phillipe Noonan)
1870-1911.....................DLB-197

Trevelyan, Sir George Otto
1838-1928.....................DLB-144

Trevisa, John circa 1342-circa 1402.....DLB-146

Trevor, William 1928-.........DLB-14, 139

Trierer Floyris circa 1170-1180..........DLB-138

Trillin, Calvin 1935-...............DLB-185

Trilling, Lionel 1905-1975..........DLB-28, 63

Trilussa 1871-1950..................DLB-114

Trimmer, Sarah 1741-1810...........DLB-158

Triolet, Elsa 1896-1970................DLB-72

Tripp, John 1927-..................DLB-40

Trocchi, Alexander 1925-...........DLB-15

Troisi, Dante 1920-1989..............DLB-196

Trollope, Anthony 1815-1882.... DLB-21, 57, 159

Trollope, Frances 1779-1863........DLB-21, 166

Trollope, Joanna 1943-.............DLB-207

Troop, Elizabeth 1931-..............DLB-14

Trotter, Catharine 1679-1749...........DLB-84

Trotti, Lamar 1898-1952...............DLB-44

Trottier, Pierre 1925-...............DLB-60

Troubadours, *Trobairitz,* and
Trouvères.....................DLB-208

Troupe, Quincy Thomas, Jr. 1943-.....DLB-41

Trow, John F., and Company..........DLB-49

Trowbridge, John Townsend
1827-1916.....................DLB-202

Truillier-Lacombe, Joseph-Patrice
1807-1863.......................DLB-99

Trumbo, Dalton 1905-1976............DLB-26

Trumbull, Benjamin 1735-1820..........DLB-30

Trumbull, John 1750-1831..............DLB-31

Trumbull, John 1756-1843............DLB-183

Tscherning, Andreas 1611-1659........DLB-164

T. S. Eliot Centennial...................Y-88

Tsubouchi, Shōyō 1859-1935..........DLB-180

Tucholsky, Kurt 1890-1935............DLB-56

Tucker, Charlotte Maria
1821-1893..................DLB-163, 190

Tucker, George 1775-1861...........DLB-3, 30

Tucker, Nathaniel Beverley 1784-1851.....DLB-3

Tucker, St. George 1752-1827..........DLB-37

Tuckerman, Henry Theodore
1813-1871.......................DLB-64

Tumas, Juozas (see Vaižgantas)

Tunis, John R. 1889-1975.........DLB-22, 171

Tunstall, Cuthbert 1474-1559.........DLB-132

Tuohy, Frank 1925-............DLB-14, 139

Tupper, Martin F. 1810-1889...........DLB-32

Turbyfill, Mark 1896-...............DLB-45

Turco, Lewis 1934-...................Y-84

Turgenev, Aleksandr Ivanovich
1784-1845.....................DLB-198

Turnball, Alexander H.
1868-1918.....................DLB-184

Turnbull, Andrew 1921-1970..........DLB-103

Turnbull, Gael 1928-...............DLB-40

Turner, Arlin 1909-1980..............DLB-103

Turner, Charles (Tennyson)
1808-1879.......................DLB-32

Turner, Frederick 1943-.............DLB-40

Turner, Frederick Jackson
1861-1932.................. DLB-17, 186

Turner, Joseph Addison 1826-1868.......DLB-79

Turpin, Waters Edward 1910-1968.......DLB-51

Turrini, Peter 1944-...............DLB-124

Tutuola, Amos 1920-1997............DLB-125

Twain, Mark (see Clemens, Samuel Langhorne)

Tweedie, Ethel Brilliana
circa 1860-1940..................DLB-174

The 'Twenties and Berlin,
by Alex Natan....................DLB-66

Twysden, Sir Roger 1597-1672.........DLB-213

Tyler, Anne 1941-.........DLB-6, 143; Y-82

Tyler, Mary Palmer 1775-1866........DLB-200

Tyler, Moses Coit 1835-1900........DLB-47, 64

Tyler, Royall 1757-1826...............DLB-37

Tylor, Edward Burnett 1832-1917........DLB-57

Tynan, Katharine 1861-1931..........DLB-153

Tyndale, William circa
1494-1536.....................DLB-132

U

Udall, Nicholas 1504-1556.............DLB-62

Ugrêsić, Dubravka 1949-............DLB-181

Uhland, Ludwig 1787-1862.............DLB-90

Uhse, Bodo 1904-1963................DLB-69

Ujević, Augustin ("Tin") 1891-1955.....DLB-147

Ulenhart, Niclas flourished circa 1600....DLB-164

Ulibarrí, Sabine R. 1919-............DLB-82

Ulica, Jorge 1870-1926................DLB-82

Ulivi, Ferruccio 1912-...............DLB-196

Ulizio, B. George 1889-1969..........DLB-140

Ulrich von Liechtenstein
circa 1200-circa 1275..............DLB-138

Ulrich von Zatzikhoven
before 1194-after 1214............DLB-138

Ulysses, Reader's Edition.................Y-97

Unamuno, Miguel de 1864-1936........DLB-108

Under, Marie 1883-1980..............DLB-220

Under the Microscope (1872), by
A. C. Swinburne.................DLB-35

Unger, Friederike Helene 1741-1813......DLB-94

Ungaretti, Giuseppe 1888-1970........DLB-114

United States Book Company DLB-49

Universal Publishing and Distributing
    Corporation DLB-46

The University of Iowa Writers' Workshop
    Golden Jubilee Y-86

The University of South Carolina Press Y-94

University of Wales Press DLB-112

University Press of Kansas Y-98

University Press of Mississippi Y-99

"The Unknown Public" (1858), by
    Wilkie Collins [excerpt] DLB-57

Uno, Chiyo 1897-1996 . . . . DLB-180

Unruh, Fritz von 1885-1970 . . . . DLB-56, 118

Unspeakable Practices II: The Festival of Vanguard
    Narrative at Brown University Y-93

Unsworth, Barry 1930- DLB-194

The Unterberg Poetry Center of the
    92nd Street Y Y-98

Unwin, T. Fisher [publishing house] DLB-106

Upchurch, Boyd B. (see Boyd, John)

Updike, John 1932-
    . . . . DLB-2, 5, 143, 218; Y-80, Y-82; DS-3

Upīts, Andrejs 1877-1970 . . . . DLB-220

Upton, Bertha 1849-1912 . . . . DLB-141

Upton, Charles 1948- DLB-16

Upton, Florence K. 1873-1922 . . . . DLB-141

Upward, Allen 1863-1926 . . . . DLB-36

Urban, Milo 1904-1982 . . . . DLB-215

Urista, Alberto Baltazar (see Alurista)

Urrea, Luis Alberto 1955- DLB-209

Urzidil, Johannes 1896-1976 . . . . DLB-85

Urquhart, Fred 1912- DLB-139

The Uses of Facsimile Y-90

Usk, Thomas died 1388 . . . . DLB-146

Uslar Pietri, Arturo 1906- DLB-113

Ussher, James 1581-1656 . . . . DLB-213

Ustinov, Peter 1921- DLB-13

Uttley, Alison 1884-1976 . . . . DLB-160

Uz, Johann Peter 1720-1796 . . . . DLB-97

V

Vac, Bertrand 1914- DLB-88

Vaičiulaitis, Antanas 1906-1992 . . . . DLB-220

Vail, Laurence 1891-1968 . . . . DLB-4

Vailland, Roger 1907-1965 . . . . DLB-83

Vajda, Ernest 1887-1954 . . . . DLB-44

Vaižgantas 1869-1933 . . . . DLB-220

Valdés, Gina 1943- DLB-122

Valdez, Luis Miguel 1940- DLB-122

Valduga, Patrizia 1953- DLB-128

Valente, José Angel 1929- DLB-108

Valenzuela, Luisa 1938- DLB-113

Valeri, Diego 1887-1976 . . . . DLB-128

Valerius Flaccus fl. circa A.D. 92 . . . . DLB-211

Valerius Maximus fl. circa A.D. 31 . . . . . DLB-211

Valesio, Paolo 1939- DLB-196

Valgardson, W. D. 1939- DLB-60

Valle, Víctor Manuel 1950- DLB-122

Valle-Inclán, Ramón del 1866-1936 . . . . . DLB-134

Vallejo, Armando 1949- DLB-122

Vallès, Jules 1832-1885 . . . . DLB-123

Vallette, Marguerite Eymery (see Rachilde)

Valverde, José María 1926-1996 . . . . DLB-108

Van Allsburg, Chris 1949- DLB-61

Van Anda, Carr 1864-1945 . . . . DLB-25

van der Post, Laurens 1906-1996 . . . . . . DLB-204

Van Dine, S. S. (see Wright, Williard Huntington)

Van Doren, Mark 1894-1972 . . . . DLB-45

van Druten, John 1901-1957 . . . . DLB-10

Van Duyn, Mona 1921- DLB-5

Van Dyke, Henry 1852-1933 . . . . . DLB-71; DS-13

Van Dyke, John C. 1856-1932 . . . . DLB-186

Van Dyke, Henry 1928- DLB-33

van Gulik, Robert Hans 1910-1967 . . . . DS-17

van Itallie, Jean-Claude 1936- DLB-7

Van Loan, Charles E. 1876-1919 . . . . DLB-171

Van Rensselaer, Mariana Griswold
    1851-1934 . . . . DLB-47

Van Rensselaer, Mrs. Schuyler (see Van
    Rensselaer, Mariana Griswold)

Van Vechten, Carl 1880-1964 . . . . DLB-4, 9

van Vogt, A. E. 1912- DLB-8

Vanbrugh, Sir John 1664-1726 . . . . DLB-80

Vance, Jack 1916?- DLB-8

Vančura, Vladislav 1891-1942 . . . . DLB-215

Vane, Sutton 1888-1963 . . . . DLB-10

Vanguard Press DLB-46

Vann, Robert L. 1879-1940 . . . . DLB-29

Vargas, Llosa, Mario 1936- DLB-145

Varley, John 1947- Y-81

Varnhagen von Ense, Karl August
    1785-1858 . . . . DLB-90

Varro 116 B.C.-27 B.C. DLB-211

Vasiliu, George (see Bacovia, George)

Vásquez, Richard 1928- DLB-209

Varnhagen von Ense, Rahel
    1771-1833 . . . . DLB-90

Vásquez Montalbán, Manuel
    1939- DLB-134

Vassa, Gustavus (see Equiano, Olaudah)

Vassalli, Sebastiano 1941- DLB-128, 196

Vaughan, Henry 1621-1695 . . . . DLB-131

Vaughn, Robert 1592?-1667 . . . . DLB-213

Vaughan, Thomas 1621-1666 . . . . DLB-131

Vaux, Thomas, Lord 1509-1556 . . . . DLB-132

Vazov, Ivan 1850-1921 . . . . DLB-147

Véa Jr., Alfredo 1950- DLB-209

Vega, Janine Pommy 1942- DLB-16

Veiller, Anthony 1903-1965 . . . . DLB-44

Velásquez-Trevino, Gloria 1949- DLB-122

Veley, Margaret 1843-1887 . . . . DLB-199

Velleius Paterculus
    circa 20 B.C.-circa A.D. 30 . . . . DLB-211

Veloz Maggiolo, Marcio 1936- DLB-145

Vel'tman Aleksandr Fomich
    1800-1870 . . . . DLB-198

Venegas, Daniel ?-? DLB-82

Venevitinov, Dmitrii Vladimirovich
    1805-1827 . . . . DLB-205

Vergil, Polydore circa 1470-1555 . . . . DLB-132

Veríssimo, Erico 1905-1975 . . . . DLB-145

Verlaine, Paul 1844-1896 . . . . .DLB-217

Verne, Jules 1828-1905 . . . . DLB-123

Verplanck, Gulian C. 1786-1870 . . . . DLB-59

Very, Jones 1813-1880 . . . . DLB-1

Vian, Boris 1920-1959 . . . . DLB-72

Viazemsky, Petr Andreevich 1792-1878 . . DLB-205

Vickers, Roy 1888?-1965 . . . . DLB-77

Vickery, Sukey 1779-1821 . . . . DLB-200

Victoria 1819-1901 . . . . DLB-55

Victoria Press DLB-106

Vidal, Gore 1925- DLB-6, 152

Viebig, Clara 1860-1952 . . . . DLB-66

Viereck, George Sylvester 1884-1962 . . . . . DLB-54

Viereck, Peter 1916- DLB-5

Viets, Roger 1738-1811 . . . . DLB-99

Viewpoint: Politics and Performance, by
    David Edgar DLB-13

Vigil-Piñon, Evangelina 1949- DLB-122

Vigneault, Gilles 1928- DLB-60

Vigny, Alfred de 1797-1863 . . . .DLB-119, 192, 217

Vigolo, Giorgio 1894-1983 . . . . DLB-114

The Viking Press DLB-46

Vilde, Eduard 1865-1933 . . . . DLB-220

Villanueva, Alma Luz 1944- DLB-122

Villanueva, Tino 1941- DLB-82

Villard, Henry 1835-1900 . . . . DLB-23

Villard, Oswald Garrison 1872-1949 . . DLB-25, 91

Villarreal, Edit 1944- DLB-209

Villarreal, José Antonio 1924- DLB-82

Villaseñor, Victor 1940- DLB-209

Villegas de Magnón, Leonor
    1876-1955 . . . . DLB-122

Villehardouin, Geoffroi de
    circa 1150-1215 . . . . DLB-208

Villemaire, Yolande 1949- DLB-60

Villena, Luis Antonio de 1951- DLB-134

Villiers de l'Isle-Adam, Jean-Marie
    Mathias Philippe-Auguste, Comte de
    1838-1889 . . . . DLB-123, 192

Villiers, George, Second Duke
    of Buckingham 1628-1687 . . . . DLB-80

Villon, François 1431-circa 1463? DLB-208

Vine Press DLB-112

Viorst, Judith ?- DLB-52

Vipont, Elfrida (Elfrida Vipont Foulds,
    Charles Vipont) 1902-1992 . . . . DLB-160

Viramontes, Helena María 1954- DLB-122

Virgil 70 B.C.-19 B.C. DLB-211

Vischer, Friedrich Theodor
   1807-1887 . . . . .DLB-133

Vitruvius circa 85 B.C.-circa 15 B.C.. . . . .DLB-211

Vitry, Philippe de 1291-1361 . . . . .DLB-208

Vivanco, Luis Felipe 1907-1975 . . . . .DLB-108

Viviani, Cesare 1947- DLB-128

Vivien, Renée 1877-1909 . . . . .DLB-217

Vizenor, Gerald 1934- DLB-175

Vizetelly and Company DLB-106

Voaden, Herman 1903- DLB-88

Voigt, Ellen Bryant 1943- DLB-120

Vojnović, Ivo 1857-1929 . . . . .DLB-147

Volkoff, Vladimir 1932- DLB-83

Volland, P. F., Company DLB-46

Vollbehr, Otto H. F. 1872?-
   1945 or 1946. . . . . .DLB-187

Volponi, Paolo 1924- DLB-177

von der Grün, Max 1926- DLB-75

Vonnegut, Kurt
   1922- DLB-2, 8, 152; Y-80; DS-3

Voranc, Prežihov 1893-1950 . . . . .DLB-147

Voß, Johann Heinrich 1751-1826 . . . . . . .DLB-90

Voynich, E. L. 1864-1960 . . . . .DLB-197

Vroman, Mary Elizabeth
   circa 1924-1967 . . . . .DLB-33

W

Wace, Robert ("Maistre")
   circa 1100-circa 1175 . . . . .DLB-146

Wackenroder, Wilhelm Heinrich
   1773-1798. . . . . .DLB-90

Wackernagel, Wilhelm 1806-1869 . . . . . .DLB-133

Waddington, Miriam 1917- DLB-68

Wade, Henry 1887-1969 . . . . .DLB-77

Wagenknecht, Edward 1900- DLB-103

Wagner, Heinrich Leopold 1747-1779 . . . . .DLB-94

Wagner, Henry R. 1862-1957 . . . . .DLB-140

Wagner, Richard 1813-1883 . . . . .DLB-129

Wagoner, David 1926- DLB-5

Wah, Fred 1939- DLB-60

Waiblinger, Wilhelm 1804-1830 . . . . .DLB-90

Wain, John 1925-1994. . . . . . DLB-15, 27, 139, 155

Wainwright, Jeffrey 1944- DLB-40

Waite, Peirce and Company DLB-49

Wakeman, Stephen H. 1859-1924 . . . . . . .DLB-187

Wakoski, Diane 1937- DLB-5

Walahfrid Strabo circa 808-849 . . . . .DLB-148

Walck, Henry Z. .DLB-46

Walcott, Derek 1930- DLB-117; Y-81, Y-92

Waldegrave, Robert [publishing house]. . .DLB-170

Waldman, Anne 1945- DLB-16

Waldrop, Rosmarie 1935- DLB-169

Walker, Alice 1900-1982 . . . . .DLB-201

Walker, Alice 1944- DLB-6, 33, 143

Walker, George F. 1947- DLB-60

Walker, Joseph A. 1935- DLB-38

Walker, Margaret 1915- DLB-76, 152

Walker, Ted 1934- DLB-40

Walker and Company DLB-49

Walker, Evans and Cogswell
   Company DLB-49

Walker, John Brisben 1847-1931 . . . . .DLB-79

Wallace, Alfred Russel 1823-1913 . . . . . . .DLB-190

Wallace, Dewitt 1889-1981 and
   Lila Acheson Wallace
   1889-1984 . . . . .DLB-137

Wallace, Edgar 1875-1932 . . . . .DLB-70

Wallace, Lew 1827-1905 . . . . .DLB-202

Wallace, Lila Acheson (see Wallace, Dewitt,
   and Lila Acheson Wallace)

Wallant, Edward Lewis
   1926-1962 . . . . .DLB-2, 28, 143

Waller, Edmund 1606-1687 . . . . .DLB-126

Walpole, Horace 1717-1797 . . . . .DLB-39, 104, 213

Walpole, Hugh 1884-1941. . . . . .DLB-34

Walrond, Eric 1898-1966 . . . . .DLB-51

Walser, Martin 1927- DLB-75, 124

Walser, Robert 1878-1956 . . . . .DLB-66

Walsh, Ernest 1895-1926. . . . . .DLB-4, 45

Walsh, Robert 1784-1859 . . . . .DLB-59

Walters, Henry 1848-1931 . . . . .DLB-140

Waltharius circa 825 . . . . .DLB-148

Walther von der Vogelweide
   circa 1170-circa 1230 . . . . .DLB-138

Walton, Izaak 1593-1683 . . . . .DLB-151, 213

Wambaugh, Joseph 1937- DLB-6; Y-83

Waniek, Marilyn Nelson 1946- DLB-120

Wanley, Humphrey 1672-1726 . . . . .DLB-213

Warburton, William 1698-1779 . . . . .DLB-104

Ward, Aileen 1919- DLB-111

Ward, Artemus (see Browne, Charles Farrar)

Ward, Arthur Henry Sarsfield
   (see Rohmer, Sax)

Ward, Douglas Turner 1930- DLB-7, 38

Ward, Lynd 1905-1985 . . . . .DLB-22

Ward, Lock and Company DLB-106

Ward, Mrs. Humphry 1851-1920 . . . . . . .DLB-18

Ward, Nathaniel circa 1578-1652 . . . . . . .DLB-24

Ward, Theodore 1902-1983 . . . . .DLB-76

Wardle, Ralph 1909-1988 . . . . .DLB-103

Ware, William 1797-1852 . . . . .DLB-1

Warne, Frederick, and Company [U.S.] . . .DLB-49

Warne, Frederick, and
   Company [U.K.] DLB-106

Warner, Anne 1869-1913 . . . . .DLB-202

Warner, Charles Dudley 1829-1900 . . . . . .DLB-64

Warner, Marina 1946- DLB-194

Warner, Rex 1905- DLB-15

Warner, Susan Bogert 1819-1885 . . . . . .DLB-3, 42

Warner, Sylvia Townsend
   1893-1978 . . . . .DLB-34, 139

Warner, William 1558-1609 . . . . .DLB-172

Warner Books DLB-46

Warr, Bertram 1917-1943 . . . . .DLB-88

Warren, John Byrne Leicester
   (see De Tabley, Lord)

Warren, Lella 1899-1982. . . . . Y-83

Warren, Mercy Otis 1728-1814 . . . . .DLB-31, 200

Warren, Robert Penn
   1905-1989 . . . . DLB-2, 48, 152; Y-80, Y-89

Warren, Samuel 1807-1877 . . . . .DLB-190

Die Wartburgkrieg
   circa 1230-circa 1280. . . . . .DLB-138

Warton, Joseph 1722-1800. . . . . . . .DLB-104, 109

Warton, Thomas 1728-1790 . . . . . . .DLB-104, 109

Washington, George 1732-1799 . . . . .DLB-31

Wassermann, Jakob 1873-1934 . . . . .DLB-66

Wasson, David Atwood 1823-1887 . . . .DLB-1, 223

Watanna, Onoto (see Eaton, Winnifred)

Waterhouse, Keith 1929- DLB-13, 15

Waterman, Andrew 1940- DLB-40

Waters, Frank 1902-1995 . . . . .DLB-212; Y-86

Waters, Michael 1949- DLB-120

Watkins, Tobias 1780-1855 . . . . .DLB-73

Watkins, Vernon 1906-1967 . . . . .DLB-20

Watmough, David 1926- DLB-53

Watson, James Wreford (see Wreford, James)

Watson, John 1850-1907 . . . . .DLB-156

Watson, Sheila 1909- DLB-60

Watson, Thomas 1545?-1592 . . . . .DLB-132

Watson, Wilfred 1911- DLB-60

Watt, W. J., and Company DLB-46

Watten, Barrett 1948- DLB-193

Watterson, Henry 1840-1921 . . . . .DLB-25

Watts, Alan 1915-1973. . . . . .DLB-16

Watts, Franklin [publishing house] DLB-46

Watts, Isaac 1674-1748. . . . . .DLB-95

Wand, Alfred Rudolph 1828-1891 . . . . . .DLB-188

Waugh, Alec 1898-1981 . . . . .DLB-191

Waugh, Auberon 1939- DLB-14, 194

Waugh, Evelyn 1903-1966 . . . . .DLB-15, 162, 195

Way and Williams. DLB-49

Wayman, Tom 1945- DLB-53

Weatherly, Tom 1942- DLB-41

Weaver, Gordon 1937- DLB-130

Weaver, Robert 1921- DLB-88

Webb, Beatrice 1858-1943 and
   Webb, Sidney 1859-1947 . . . . .DLB-190

Webb, Frank J. ?-? DLB-50

Webb, James Watson 1802-1884. . . . . . . .DLB-43

Webb, Mary 1881-1927 . . . . .DLB-34

Webb, Phyllis 1927- DLB-53

Webb, Walter Prescott 1888-1963. . . . . . .DLB-17

Webbe, William ?-1591 . . . . .DLB-132

Webber, Charles Wilkins 1819-1856? DLB-202

Webster, Augusta 1837-1894 . . . . .DLB-35

Webster, Charles L., and Company DLB-49

Webster, John
  1579 or 1580-1634? DLB-58

Webster, Noah 1758-1843 . . . DLB-1, 37, 42, 43, 73

Weckherlin, Georg Rodolf 1584-1653 . . . DLB-164

Wedekind, Frank 1864-1918 . . . . DLB-118

Weeks, Edward Augustus, Jr.
  1898-1989 . . . . DLB-137

Weeks, Stephen B. 1865-1918 . . . . DLB-187

Weems, Mason Locke
  1759-1825 . . . . DLB-30, 37, 42

Weerth, Georg 1822-1856 . . . . DLB-129

Weidenfeld and Nicolson DLB-112

Weidman, Jerome 1913-1998 . . . . DLB-28

Weigl, Bruce 1949- DLB-120

Weinbaum, Stanley Grauman
  1902-1935 . . . . DLB-8

Weintraub, Stanley 1929- DLB-111

Weise, Christian 1642-1708 . . . . DLB-168

Weisenborn, Gunther 1902-1969 . . . . DLB-69, 124

Weiß, Ernst 1882-1940 . . . . DLB-81

Weiss, John 1818-1879 . . . . DLB-1

Weiss, Peter 1916-1982 . . . . DLB-69, 124

Weiss, Theodore 1916- DLB-5

Weisse, Christian Felix 1726-1804 . . . . DLB-97

Weitling, Wilhelm 1808-1871 . . . . DLB-129

Welch, James 1940- DLB-175

Welch, Lew 1926-1971? DLB-16

Weldon, Fay 1931- DLB-14, 194

Wellek, René 1903-1995 . . . . DLB-63

Wells, Carolyn 1862-1942 . . . . DLB-11

Wells, Charles Jeremiah
  circa 1800-1879 . . . . DLB-32

Wells, Gabriel 1862-1946 . . . . DLB-140

Wells, H. G. 1866-1946 . . . . . DLB-34, 70, 156, 178

Wells, Helena 1758?-1824 . . . . DLB-200

Wells, Robert 1947- DLB-40

Wells-Barnett, Ida B. 1862-1931 . . . . . DLB-23, 221

Welty, Eudora
  1909- DLB-2, 102, 143; Y-87; DS-12

Wendell, Barrett 1855-1921 . . . . DLB-71

Wentworth, Patricia 1878-1961 . . . . DLB-77

Werder, Diederich von dem
  1584-1657 . . . . DLB-164

Werfel, Franz 1890-1945 . . . . DLB-81, 124

The Werner Company DLB-49

Werner, Zacharias 1768-1823 . . . . DLB-94

Wersba, Barbara 1932- DLB-52

Wescott, Glenway 1901- DLB-4, 9, 102

We See the Editor at Work Y-97

Wesker, Arnold 1932- DLB-13

Wesley, Charles 1707-1788 . . . . DLB-95

Wesley, John 1703-1791 . . . . DLB-104

Wesley, Richard 1945- DLB-38

Wessels, A., and Company DLB-46

Wessobrunner Gebet circa 787-815 . . . . DLB-148

West, Anthony 1914-1988 . . . . DLB-15

West, Dorothy 1907-1998 . . . . DLB-76

West, Jessamyn 1902-1984 . . . . .DLB-6; Y-84

West, Mae 1892-1980 . . . . DLB-44

West, Nathanael 1903-1940 . . . . DLB-4, 9, 28

West, Paul 1930- DLB-14

West, Rebecca 1892-1983 . . . . .DLB-36; Y-83

West, Richard 1941- DLB-185

Westcott, Edward Noyes 1846-1898 . . . . DLB-202

West and Johnson DLB-49

The Western Messenger 1835-1841 . . . . DLB-223

Western Publishing Company DLB-46

Western Writers of America Y-99

The Westminster Review 1824-1914 . . . . DLB-110

Weston, Elizabeth Jane
  circa 1582-1612 . . . . .DLB-172

Wetherald, Agnes Ethelwyn 1857-1940 . . . DLB-99

Wetherell, Elizabeth (see Warner, Susan Bogert)

Wetzel, Friedrich Gottlob 1779-1819 . . . . . DLB-90

Weyman, Stanley J. 1855-1928 . . . . DLB-141, 156

Wezel, Johann Karl 1747-1819 . . . . DLB-94

Whalen, Philip 1923- DLB-16

Whalley, George 1915-1983 . . . . DLB-88

Wharton, Edith
  1862-1937 . . . . . . .DLB-4, 9, 12, 78, 189; DS-13

Wharton, William 1920s?- Y-80

"What You Lose on the Swings You Make Up
  on the Merry-Go-Round" Y-99

Whately, Mary Louisa 1824-1889 . . . . . . DLB-166

Whately, Richard 1787-1863 . . . . DLB-190

What's Really Wrong With Bestseller Lists . . . Y-84

Wheatley, Dennis Yates 1897-1977 . . . . DLB-77

Wheatley, Phillis circa 1754-1784 . . . . . DLB-31, 50

Wheeler, Anna Doyle 1785-1848? DLB-158

Wheeler, Charles Stearns 1816-1843 . . DLB-1, 223

Wheeler, Monroe 1900-1988 . . . . DLB-4

Wheelock, John Hall 1886-1978 . . . . DLB-45

Wheelwright, John circa 1592-1679 . . . . . . DLB-24

Wheelwright, J. B. 1897-1940 . . . . DLB-45

Whetstone, Colonel Pete (see Noland, C. F. M.)

Whetstone, George 1550-1587 . . . . DLB-136

Whicher, Stephen E. 1915-1961 . . . . DLB-111

Whipple, Edwin Percy 1819-1886 . . . . . DLB-1, 64

Whitaker, Alexander 1585-1617 . . . . DLB-24

Whitaker, Daniel K. 1801-1881 . . . . DLB-73

Whitcher, Frances Miriam
  1812-1852 . . . . DLB-11, 202

White, Andrew 1579-1656 . . . . DLB-24

White, Andrew Dickson 1832-1918 . . . . . . DLB-47

White, E. B. 1899-1985 . . . . DLB-11, 22

White, Edgar B. 1947- DLB-38

White, Ethel Lina 1887-1944 . . . . DLB-77

White, Henry Kirke 1785-1806 . . . . DLB-96

White, Horace 1834-1916 . . . . DLB-23

White, Phyllis Dorothy James (see James, P. D.)

White, Richard Grant 1821-1885 . . . . DLB-64

White, T. H. 1906-1964 . . . . DLB-160

White, Walter 1893-1955 . . . . DLB-51

White, William, and Company DLB-49

White, William Allen 1868-1944 . . . . . DLB-9, 25

White, William Anthony Parker
  (see Boucher, Anthony)

White, William Hale (see Rutherford, Mark)

Whitechurch, Victor L. 1868-1933 . . . . . . DLB-70

Whitehead, Alfred North 1861-1947 . . . . DLB-100

Whitehead, James 1936- Y-81

Whitehead, William 1715-1785 . . . . . DLB-84, 109

Whitfield, James Monroe 1822-1871 . . . . . DLB-50

Whitfield, Raoul 1898-1945 . . . . DLB-226

Whitgift, John circa 1533-1604 . . . . DLB-132

Whiting, John 1917-1963 . . . . DLB-13

Whiting, Samuel 1597-1679 . . . . DLB-24

Whitlock, Brand 1869-1934 . . . . DLB-12

Whitman, Albert, and Company DLB-46

Whitman, Albery Allson 1851-1901 . . . . . . DLB-50

Whitman, Alden 1913-1990 . . . . Y-91

Whitman, Sarah Helen (Power)
  1803-1878 . . . . DLB-1

Whitman, Walt 1819-1892 . . . . DLB-3, 64, 224

Whitman Publishing Company DLB-46

Whitney, Geoffrey
  1548 or 1552?-1601 . . . . DLB-136

Whitney, Isabella
  flourished 1566-1573 . . . . DLB-136

Whitney, John Hay 1904-1982 . . . . .DLB-127

Whittemore, Reed 1919-1995 . . . . DLB-5

Whittier, John Greenleaf 1807-1892 . . . . . . DLB-1

Whittlesey House DLB-46

Who Runs American Literature? Y-94

Whose *Ulysses?* The Function of
  Editing Y-97

Wicomb, Zoë 1948- DLB-225

Wideman, John Edgar 1941- DLB-33, 143

Widener, Harry Elkins 1885-1912 . . . . . . DLB-140

Wiebe, Rudy 1934- DLB-60

Wiechert, Ernst 1887-1950 . . . . DLB-56

Wied, Martina 1882-1957 . . . . DLB-85

Wiehe, Evelyn May Clowes (see Mordaunt,
  Elinor)

Wieland, Christoph Martin
  1733-1813 . . . . DLB-97

Wienbarg, Ludolf 1802-1872 . . . . DLB-133

Wieners, John 1934- DLB-16

Wier, Ester 1910- DLB-52

Wiesel, Elie 1928- DLB-83; Y-86, Y-87

Wiggin, Kate Douglas 1856-1923 . . . . DLB-42

Wigglesworth, Michael 1631-1705 . . . . DLB-24

Wilberforce, William 1759-1833 . . . . DLB-158

Wilbrandt, Adolf 1837-1911 . . . . DLB-129

Wilbur, Richard 1921- DLB-5, 169

Wild, Peter 1940- DLB-5

Wilde, Lady Jane Francesca Elgee
  1821?-1896 . . . . DLB-199

Wilde, Oscar 1854-1900
.... DLB-10, 19, 34, 57, 141, 156, 190

Wilde, Richard Henry 1789-1847 ...... DLB-3, 59

Wilde, W. A., Company DLB-49

Wilder, Billy 1906- DLB-26

Wilder, Laura Ingalls 1867-1957 .... DLB-22

Wilder, Thornton 1897-1975 .... DLB-4, 7, 9

Wildgans, Anton 1881-1932 .... DLB-118

Wiley, Bell Irvin 1906-1980. .... DLB-17

Wiley, John, and Sons DLB-49

Wilhelm, Kate 1928- DLB-8

Wilkes, Charles 1798-1877. .... DLB-183

Wilkes, George 1817-1885 .... DLB-79

Wilkinson, Anne 1910-1961 .... DLB-88

Wilkinson, Eliza Yonge
1757-circa 1813 .... DLB-200

Wilkinson, Sylvia 1940- Y-86

Wilkinson, William Cleaver
1833-1920 .... DLB-71

Willard, Barbara 1909-1994 .... DLB-161

Willard, Frances E. 1839-1898. .... DLB-221

Willard, L. [publishing house] DLB-49

Willard, Nancy 1936- DLB-5, 52

Willard, Samuel 1640-1707 .... DLB-24

Willeford, Charles 1919-1988 .... DLB-226

William of Auvergne 1190-1249 .... DLB-115

William of Conches
circa 1090-circa 1154. .... DLB-115

William of Ockham
circa 1285-1347 .... DLB-115

William of Sherwood
1200/1205 - 1266/1271 .... DLB-115

The William Chavrat American Fiction
Collection at the Ohio State University
Libraries Y-92

William Faulkner Centenary Y-97

Williams, A., and Company DLB-49

Williams, Ben Ames 1889-1953. .... DLB-102

Williams, C. K. 1936- DLB-5

Williams, Chancellor 1905- DLB-76

Williams, Charles 1886-1945. ..... DLB-100, 153

Williams, Denis 1923-1998 .... DLB-117

Williams, Emlyn 1905- DLB-10, 77

Williams, Garth 1912-1996 .... DLB-22

Williams, George Washington
1849-1891 .... DLB-47

Williams, Heathcote 1941- DLB-13

Williams, Helen Maria 1761-1827 .... DLB-158

Williams, Hugo 1942- DLB-40

Williams, Isaac 1802-1865 .... DLB-32

Williams, Joan 1928- DLB-6

Williams, John A. 1925- DLB-2, 33

Williams, John E. 1922-1994 .... DLB-6

Williams, Jonathan 1929- DLB-5

Williams, Miller 1930- DLB-105

Williams, Raymond 1921- DLB-14

Williams, Roger circa 1603-1683. .... DLB-24

Williams, Rowland 1817-1870 .... DLB-184

Williams, Samm-Art 1946- DLB-38

Williams, Sherley Anne 1944-1999 ...... DLB-41

Williams, T. Harry 1909-1979. .... DLB-17

Williams, Tennessee
1911-1983 .... DLB-7; Y-83; DS-4

Williams, Terry Tempest 1955- DLB-206

Williams, Ursula Moray 1911- DLB-160

Williams, Valentine 1883-1946 .... DLB-77

Williams, William Appleman 1921- DLB-17

Williams, William Carlos
1883-1963 .... DLB-4, 16, 54, 86

Williams, Wirt 1921- DLB-6

Williams Brothers DLB-49

Williamson, Henry 1895-1977. .... DLB-191

Williamson, Jack 1908- DLB-8

Willingham, Calder Baynard, Jr.
1922-1995 .... DLB-2, 44

Williram of Ebersberg
circa 1020-1085. .... DLB-148

Willis, Nathaniel Parker
1806-1867 ..... DLB-3, 59, 73, 74, 183; DS-13

Willkomm, Ernst 1810-1886 .... DLB-133

Willumsen, Dorrit 1940- DLB-214

Wilmer, Clive 1945- DLB-40

Wilson, A. N. 1950- DLB-14, 155, 194

Wilson, Angus 1913-1991 ...... DLB-15, 139, 155

Wilson, Arthur 1595-1652. .... DLB-58

Wilson, Augusta Jane Evans
1835-1909 .... DLB-42

Wilson, Colin 1931- DLB-14, 194

Wilson, Edmund 1895-1972 .... DLB-63

Wilson, Ethel 1888-1980 .... DLB-68

Wilson, F. P. 1889-1963. .... DLB-201

Wilson, Harriet E. Adams
1828?-1863? DLB-50

Wilson, Harry Leon 1867-1939. .... DLB-9

Wilson, John 1588-1667 .... DLB-24

Wilson, John 1785-1854. .... DLB-110

Wilson, John Dover 1881-1969. .... DLB-201

Wilson, Lanford 1937- DLB-7

Wilson, Margaret 1882-1973 .... DLB-9

Wilson, Michael 1914-1978 .... DLB-44

Wilson, Mona 1872-1954. .... DLB-149

Wilson, Robley 1930- DLB-218

Wilson, Romer 1891-1930. .... DLB-191

Wilson, Thomas 1523 or
1524-1581 .... DLB-132

Wilson, Woodrow 1856-1924. .... DLB-47

Wilson, Effingham [publishing house]. ... DLB-154

Wimsatt, William K., Jr. 1907-1975 ...... DLB-63

Winchell, Walter 1897-1972. .... DLB-29

Winchester, J. [publishing house]. DLB-49

Winckelmann, Johann Joachim
1717-1768 .... DLB-97

Winckler, Paul 1630-1686 .... DLB-164

Wind, Herbert Warren 1916- DLB-171

Windet, John [publishing house] DLB-170

Windham, Donald 1920- DLB-6

Wing, Donald Goddard 1904-1972 ...... DLB-187

Wing, John M. 1844-1917 .... DLB-187

Wingate, Allan [publishing house]. DLB-112

Winnemucca, Sarah 1844-1921. .... DLB-175

Winnifrith, Tom 1938- DLB-155

Winning an Edgar. Y-98

Winsloe, Christa 1888-1944 .... DLB-124

Winslow, Anna Green 1759-1780 .... DLB-200

Winsor, Justin 1831-1897 .... DLB-47

John C. Winston Company. DLB-49

Winters, Yvor 1900-1968 .... DLB-48

Winterson, Jeanette 1959- DLB-207

Winthrop, John 1588-1649 .... DLB-24, 30

Winthrop, John, Jr. 1606-1676. .... DLB-24

Winthrop, Margaret Tyndal
1591-1647 .... DLB-200

Winthrop, Theodore 1828-1861 .... DLB-202

Wirt, William 1772-1834 .... DLB-37

Wise, John 1652-1725 .... DLB-24

Wise, Thomas James 1859-1937 .... DLB-184

Wiseman, Adele 1928- DLB-88

Wishart and Company DLB-112

Wister, Owen 1860-1938. .... DLB-9, 78, 186

Wister, Sarah 1761-1804 .... DLB-200

Wither, George 1588-1667 .... DLB-121

Witherspoon, John 1723-1794 .... DLB-31

Withrow, William Henry
1839-1908 .... DLB-99

Witkacy (see Witkiewicz, Stanisław Ignacy)

Witkiewicz, Stanisław Ignacy
1885-1939 .... DLB-215

Wittig, Monique 1935- DLB-83

Wodehouse, P. G. 1881-1975 .... DLB-34, 162

Wohmann, Gabriele 1932- DLB-75

Woiwode, Larry 1941- DLB-6

Wolcot, John 1738-1819 .... DLB-109

Wolcott, Roger 1679-1767 .... DLB-24

Wolf, Christa 1929- DLB-75

Wolf, Friedrich 1888-1953. .... DLB-124

Wolfe, Gene 1931- DLB-8

Wolfe, John [publishing house] DLB-170

Wolfe, Reyner (Reginald)
[publishing house] DLB-170

Wolfe, Thomas
1900-1938 .... DLB-9, 102; Y-85; DS-2, DS-16

Wolfe, Tom 1931- DLB-152, 185

Wolfenstein, Martha 1869-1906 .... DLB-221

Wolff, Helen 1906-1994 .... Y-94

Wolff, Tobias 1945- DLB-130

Wolfram von Eschenbach
circa 1170-after 1220 .... DLB-138

Wolfram von Eschenbach's *Parzival*:
Prologue and Book 3 .... DLB-138

Wollstonecraft, Mary
1759-1797 . . . . DLB-39, 104, 158

Wolker, Jiří 1900-1924 . . . . DLB-215

Wondratschek, Wolf 1943- DLB-75

Wood, Anthony à 1632-1695 . . . . DLB-213

Wood, Benjamin 1820-1900 . . . . DLB-23

Wood, Charles 1932- DLB-13

Wood, Mrs. Henry 1814-1887 . . . . DLB-18

Wood, Joanna E. 1867-1927 . . . . DLB-92

Wood, Sally Sayward Barrell Keating
1759-1855 . . . . DLB-200

Wood, Samuel [publishing house] DLB-49

Wood, William ?-? DLB-24

Woodberry, George Edward
1855-1930 . . . . .DLB-71, 103

Woodbridge, Benjamin 1622-1684 . . . . . . DLB-24

Woodcock, George 1912-1995 . . . . DLB-88

Woodhull, Victoria C. 1838-1927 . . . . DLB-79

Woodmason, Charles circa 1720-? DLB-31

Woodress, Jr., James Leslie 1916- DLB-111

Woodson, Carter G. 1875-1950 . . . . DLB-17

Woodward, C. Vann 1908-1999 . . . . DLB-17

Woodward, Stanley 1895-1965 . . . . .DLB-171

Wooler, Thomas 1785 or 1786-1853 . . . . DLB-158

Woolf, David (see Maddow, Ben)

Woolf, Leonard 1880-1969 . . . . . DLB-100; DS-10

Woolf, Virginia
1882-1941 . . . . .DLB-36, 100, 162; DS-10

Woolf, Virginia, "The New Biography,"
New York Herald Tribune, 30 October 1927
. . . . DLB-149

Woollcott, Alexander 1887-1943 . . . . DLB-29

Woolman, John 1720-1772 . . . . DLB-31

Woolner, Thomas 1825-1892 . . . . DLB-35

Woolrich, Cornell 1903-1968 . . . . DLB-226

Woolsey, Sarah Chauncy 1835-1905 . . . . . DLB-42

Woolson, Constance Fenimore
1840-1894 . . . . .DLB-12, 74, 189, 221

Worcester, Joseph Emerson 1784-1865 . . . . DLB-1

Worde, Wynkyn de [publishing house] . . .DLB-170

Wordsworth, Christopher 1807-1885 . . . . DLB-166

Wordsworth, Dorothy 1771-1855 . . . . DLB-107

Wordsworth, Elizabeth 1840-1932 . . . . DLB-98

Wordsworth, William 1770-1850 . . . . DLB-93, 107

Workman, Fanny Bullock 1859-1925 . . . . DLB-189

The Works of the Rev. John Witherspoon
(1800-1801) [excerpts] DLB-31

A World Chronology of Important Science
Fiction Works (1818-1979) DLB-8

World Publishing Company DLB-46

World War II Writers Symposium at the University
of South Carolina, 12–14 April 1995 . . . . . Y-95

Worthington, R., and Company DLB-49

Wotton, Sir Henry
1568-1639 . . . . DLB-121

Wouk, Herman 1915- Y-82

Wreford, James 1915- DLB-88

Wren, Sir Christopher
1632-1723 . . . . DLB-213

Wren, Percival Christopher
1885-1941 . . . . DLB-153

Wrenn, John Henry 1841-1911 . . . . DLB-140

Wright, C. D. 1949- DLB-120

Wright, Charles 1935- DLB-165; Y-82

Wright, Charles Stevenson 1932- DLB-33

Wright, Frances 1795-1852 . . . . DLB-73

Wright, Harold Bell 1872-1944 . . . . DLB-9

Wright, James 1927-1980 . . . . DLB-5, 169

Wright, Jay 1935- DLB-41

Wright, Louis B. 1899-1984 . . . . DLB-17

Wright, Richard 1908-1960 . . . .DLB-76, 102; DS-2

Wright, Richard B. 1937- DLB-53

Wright, Sarah Elizabeth 1928- DLB-33

Wright, Willard Huntington ("S. S. Van Dine")
1888-1939 . . . . DS-16

Writers and Politics: 1871-1918,
by Ronald Gray DLB-66

Writers and their Copyright Holders:
the WATCH Project Y-94

Writers' Forum Y-85

Writing for the Theatre,
by Harold Pinter DLB-13

Wroth, Lady Mary 1587-1653 . . . . DLB-121

Wroth, Lawrence C. 1884-1970 . . . . DLB-187

Wurlitzer, Rudolph 1937- DLB-173

Wyatt, Sir Thomas
circa 1503-1542 . . . . DLB-132

Wycherley, William
1641-1715 . . . . DLB-80

Wyclif, John
circa 1335-31 December 1384 . . . . . . DLB-146

Wyeth, N. C. 1882-1945 . . . . DLB-188; DS-16

Wylie, Elinor 1885-1928 . . . . DLB-9, 45

Wylie, Philip 1902-1971 . . . . DLB-9

Wyllie, John Cook
1908-1968 . . . . DLB-140

Wyman, Lillie Buffum Chace
1847-1929 . . . . DLB-202

Wynne-Tyson, Esmé 1898-1972 . . . . DLB-191

X

Xenophon circa 430 B.C.-circa 356 B.C. .DLB-176

Y

Yasuoka Shōtarō 1920- DLB-182

Yates, Dornford
1885-1960 . . . . .DLB-77, 153

Yates, J. Michael 1938- DLB-60

Yates, Richard 1926-1992 . . . . .DLB-2; Y-81, Y-92

Yavorov, Peyo 1878-1914 . . . . DLB-147

The Year in Book Publishing Y-86

The Year in Book Reviewing and the Literary
Situation Y-98

The Year in British Drama Y-99

The Year in British Fiction Y-99

The Year in Children's
Books Y-92–Y-96, Y-98, Y-99

The Year in Children's Literature Y-97

The Year in Drama Y-82-Y-85, Y-87–Y-96

The Year in Fiction. . . Y-84–Y-86, Y-89, Y-94–Y-99

The Year in Fiction: A Biased View Y-83

The Year in Literary Biography Y-83–Y-98

The Year in Literary Theory Y-92–Y-93

The Year in London Theatre Y-92

The Year in the Novel Y-87, Y-88, Y-90–Y-93

The Year in Poetry Y-83–Y-92, Y-94–Y-99

The Year in Short Stories Y-87

The Year in the Short Story Y-88, Y-90–Y-93

The Year in Texas Literature Y-98

The Year's Work in American Poetry Y-82

The Year's Work in Fiction: A Survey Y-82

Yearsley, Ann 1753-1806 . . . . DLB-109

Yeats, William Butler
1865-1939 . . . . .DLB-10, 19, 98, 156

Yep, Laurence 1948- DLB-52

Yerby, Frank 1916-1991 . . . . DLB-76

Yezierska, Anzia 1880-1970 . . . . DLB-28, 221

Yolen, Jane 1939- DLB-52

Yonge, Charlotte Mary 1823-1901 . . . DLB-18, 163

The York Cycle circa 1376-circa 1569 . . . DLB-146

A Yorkshire Tragedy DLB-58

Yoseloff, Thomas [publishing house] DLB-46

Young, Al 1939- DLB-33

Young, Arthur 1741-1820 . . . . DLB-158

Young, Dick 1917 or 1918 - 1987 . . . . . . .DLB-171

Young, Edward 1683-1765 . . . . DLB-95

Young, Francis Brett 1884-1954 . . . . DLB-191

Young, Gavin 1928- DLB-204

Young, Stark 1881-1963 . . . . . . .DLB-9, 102; DS-16

Young, Waldeman 1880-1938 . . . . DLB-26

Young, William [publishing house] DLB-49

Young Bear, Ray A. 1950- DLB-175

Yourcenar, Marguerite 1903-1987 . . .DLB-72; Y-88

"You've Never Had It So Good," Gusted by
"Winds of Change": British Fiction in the
1950s, 1960s, and After DLB-14

Yovkov, Yordan 1880-1937 . . . . .DLB-147

Z

Zachariä, Friedrich Wilhelm 1726-1777 . . . DLB-97

Zagoskin, Mikhail Nikolaevich
1789-1852 . . . . DLB-198

Zajc, Dane 1929- DLB-181

Zamora, Bernice 1938- DLB-82

Zand, Herbert 1923-1970 . . . . DLB-85

Zangwill, Israel 1864-1926 . . . . . .DLB-10, 135, 197

Zanzotto, Andrea 1921- DLB-128

Zapata Olivella, Manuel 1920- DLB-113

Zebra Books DLB-46

Zebrowski, George 1945- DLB-8

Zech, Paul 1881-1946 . . . . DLB-56

Zeimi (Kanze Motokiyo) 1363-1443 . . . . . DLB-203

Zepheria DLB-172

Zeidner, Lisa 1955- DLB-120

Zelazny, Roger 1937-1995 . . . . DLB-8

Zenger, John Peter 1697-1746 . . . . . . DLB-24, 43

Zesen, Philipp von 1619-1689 . . . . DLB-164

Zhukovsky, Vasilii Andreevich
1783-1852 . . . . DLB-205

Zieber, G. B., and Company DLB-49

Zieroth, Dale 1946- DLB-60

Zigler und Kliphausen, Heinrich Anshelm von 1663-1697 ....DLB-168

Zimmer, Paul 1934- DLB-5

Zinberg, Len (see Lacy, Ed)

Zingref, Julius Wilhelm 1591-1635 ......DLB-164

Zindel, Paul 1936- DLB-7, 52

Zinnes, Harriet 1919- DLB-193

Zinzendorf, Nikolaus Ludwig von 1700-1760.....................DLB-168

Zitkala-Ša 1876-1938 ....DLB-175

Zīverts, Mārtiņš 1903-1990 ....DLB-220

Zola, Emile 1840-1902...............DLB-123

Zolla, Elémire 1926- DLB-196

Zolotow, Charlotte 1915- DLB-52

Zschokke, Heinrich 1771-1848...........DLB-94

Zubly, John Joachim 1724-1781 ....DLB-31

Zu-Bolton II, Ahmos 1936- DLB-41

Zuckmayer, Carl 1896-1977 ....DLB-56, 124

Zukofsky, Louis 1904-1978 ....DLB-5, 165

Zupan, Vitomil 1914-1987.............DLB-181

Župančič, Oton 1878-1949.............DLB-147

zur Mühlen, Hermynia 1883-1951 ....DLB-56

Zweig, Arnold 1887-1968...............DLB-66

Zweig, Stefan 1881-1942 ....DLB-81, 118

Cumulative Index

ISBN 0-7876-3135-3

90000

9 780787 631352